MOON HANDBOOKS

# CALIFORNIA

LIZ HAMILL SCOTT

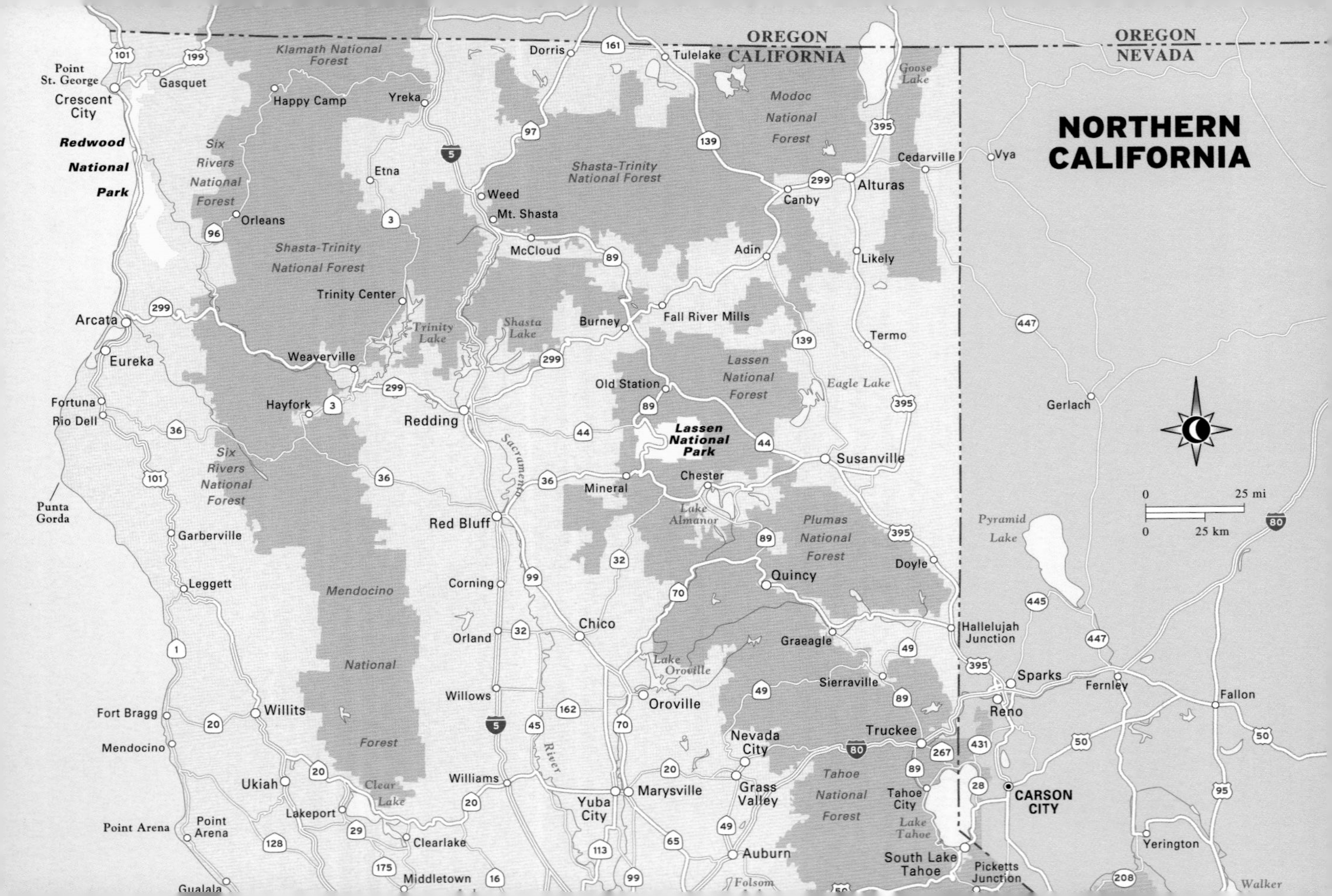
NORTHERN CALIFORNIA
OREGON
CALIFORNIA
OREGON
NEVADA
0 25 mi
0 25 km
Point St. George
Crescent City
Gasquet
Redwood National Park
Klamath National Forest
Happy Camp
Yreka
Dorris
Tulelake
Goose Lake
Modoc National Forest
Cedarville
Vya
Alturas
Canby
Six Rivers National Forest
Orleans
Etna
Weed
Mt. Shasta
McCloud
Shasta-Trinity National Forest
Adin
Likely
Trinity Center
Trinity Lake
Shasta Lake
Burney
Fall River Mills
Termo
Arcata
Eureka
Weaverville
Hayfork
Redding
Old Station
Lassen National Forest
Eagle Lake
Gerlach
Fortuna
Rio Dell
Lassen National Park
Susanville
Punta Gorda
Sacramento
Chester
Mineral
Red Bluff
Lake Almanor
Plumas National Forest
Pyramid Lake
Garberville
Doyle
Quincy
Leggett
Corning
Mendocino National Forest
Chico
Orland
Hallelujah Junction
Graeagle
Lake Oroville
Sparks
Fernley
Fallon
Sierraville
Reno
Willows
Oroville
Fort Bragg
Willits
Nevada City
Truckee
Mendocino
River
Tahoe National Forest
Ukiah
Williams
Clear Lake
Marysville
Grass Valley
Tahoe City
CARSON CITY
Yuba City
Lake Tahoe
Lakeport
Point Arena
Clearlake
Auburn
South Lake Tahoe
Yerington
Pickets Junction
Middletown
Folsom
Walker
Gualala
101
199
97
5
161
139
395
299
3
96
89
299
139
447
44
36
36
101
36
89
32
395
99
70
445
447
1
32
49
395
20
162
45
70
49
89
80
267
431
50
50
20
20
28
95
29
20
49
128
65
113
175
16
99
208
80

CALIFORNIA REGIONS
North Coast
Lake Tahoe and the Northern Sierra
Wine Country
San Francisco and the Bay Area
Sacramento and Gold Country
Yosemite
Central Coast
The Deserts
Los Angeles and Orange County
San Diego
PACIFIC OCEAN
NEVADA
CALIFORNIA
SACRAMENTO
San Francisco
Oakland
San Jose
Calistoga
Santa Rosa
Bodega Bay
Sonoma
Napa
Davis
Vacaville
Fairfield
Point Reyes National Seashore
Point Reyes
San Rafael
Rio Vista
Concord
Walnut Creek
Lodi
Stockton
Tracy
Livermore
Pleasanton
Half Moon Bay
Pigeon Point
Santa Cruz
Watsonville
Morgan Hill
Gilroy
Hollister
Monterey
Carmel
Salinas
Point Sur
Big Sur
King City
Los Padres National Forest
Cambria
Morro Bay
San Luis Obispo
Paso Robles
Jackson
San Andreas
Angels Camp
Sonora
Groveland
Modesto
Turlock
Merced
San Luis Reservoir
Los Banos
Chowchilla
Madera
San Joaquin River
Fresno
Selma
Kingsburg
Hanford
Lemoore
Coalinga
Avenal
Kettleman City
Cholame
Wasco
Delano
Buttonwillow
Bakersfield
Los Padres NF
Eldorado National Forest
Stanislaus National Forest
Dardanelle
Bridgeport
Yosemite National Park
Yosemite Village
Mariposa
Oakhurst
Millerton Lake
Mono Lake
Benton
Hawthorne
Mammoth Lakes
Bishop
Sierra National Forest
Pine Flat Reservoir
Kings Canyon National Park
Sequoia National Park
Sequoia National Forest
Visalia
Tulare
Porterville
© AVALON TRAVEL

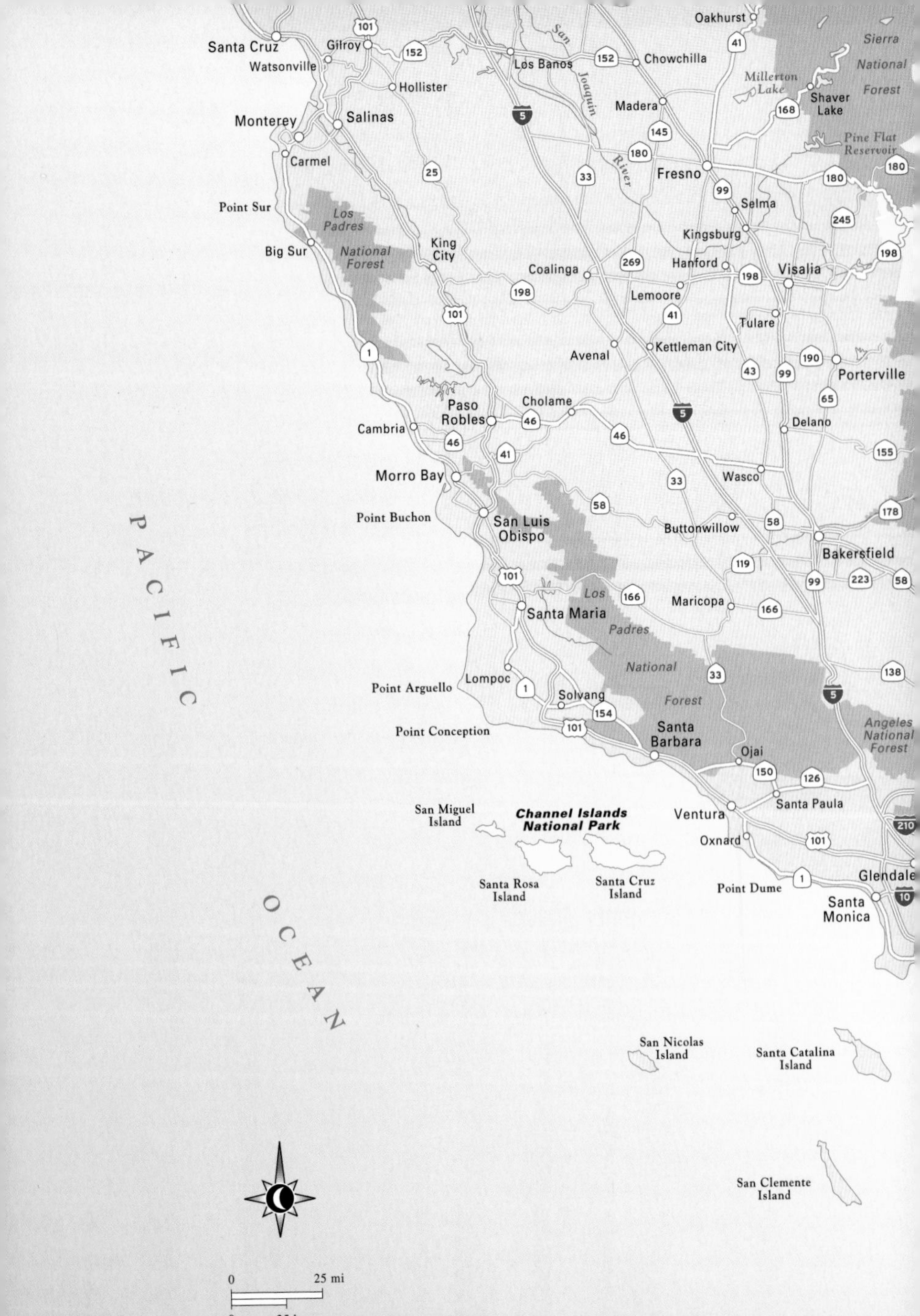

Santa Cruz
Gilroy
Watsonville
Hollister
Monterey
Salinas
Carmel
Point Sur
Los Padres National Forest
Big Sur
King City
Los Banos
San Joaquin River
Chowchilla
Madera
Oakhurst
Millerton Lake
Shaver Lake
Sierra National Forest
Pine Flat Reservoir
Fresno
Selma
Kingsburg
Hanford
Visalia
Coalinga
Lemoore
Tulare
Avenal
Kettleman City
Porterville
Cholame
Paso Robles
Cambria
Delano
Morro Bay
Wasco
Point Buchon
San Luis Obispo
Buttonwillow
Bakersfield
Los Padres National Forest
Santa Maria
Maricopa
Lompoc
Point Arguello
Solvang
Point Conception
Santa Barbara
Ojai
Angeles National Forest
Santa Paula
Ventura
Oxnard
San Miguel Island
Channel Islands National Park
Santa Rosa Island
Santa Cruz Island
Point Dume
Glendale
Santa Monica
PACIFIC OCEAN
San Nicolas Island
Santa Catalina Island
San Clemente Island
101
152
5
145
180
33
25
99
245
198
269
41
1
190
43
65
46
155
178
58
119
223
166
138
154
150
126
210
10
0
25 mi
0
25 km

SOUTHERN CALIFORNIA
Bishop
Kings Canyon National Park
Big Pine
Independence
Death Valley National Park
Sequoia National Park
Lone Pine
Owens Lake
Beatty
Death Valley
Death Valley Junction
Olancha
Sequoia National Forest
Ridgecrest
Isabella Lake
NEVADA
CALIFORNIA
Las Vegas
Lake Mead
Lake Mead National Recreation Area
NEVADA
ARIZONA
Lake Mojave
Kingman
Mojave
Baker
Mojave National Preserve
Barstow
Lancaster
Palmdale
Ludlow
Needles
Colorado River
Amboy
Angeles National Forest
Los Angeles
San Bernardino
San Bernardino
Riverside
Long Beach
Santa Ana
Cleveland National Forest
San Juan Capistrano
Palm Springs
National Forest
Indio
Joshua Tree National Park
Lake Havasu
Blythe
Oceanside
Escondido
Borrego Springs
Anza-Borrego Desert State Park
Salton Sea
Julian
Cleveland National Forest
La Jolla
San Diego
Brawley
El Centro
ARIZONA
USA
MEXICO
Tijuana
MEXICALI
Yuma
395
6
168
266
375
95
93
15
190
178
127
14
58
247
40
138
18
2
38
60
57
91
10
215
405
1
74
111
62
72
79
371
5
86
78
67
S2
94
805
8
98

# Contents

# Discover California

Diverse, wacky, and unforgettable, California is larger than life. The boisterous cities seem bigger, redwood forests and snow-capped mountains loom taller, and sandy coastlines stretch longer than anywhere else.

If you love the outdoors, remote backpacking spots, and extreme sports, you could spend a month exploring California and never once enter the city limits of San Francisco or Los Angeles. If high art, nightlife, and gourmet restaurants top your list, you can stay entirely inside those cities, soaking in their infinitely variable culture. Hot-spot clubbing, award-winning plays, experimental art exhibits and splashy gallery openings, and some of the best cuisine in the country often coexist within the same six-block street.

There's no one true way to describe California, just as there's no one true way to experience it. Southern California isn't all surfers and movie stars, while Northern California is more than just expensive real estate and radical politics. Tiny coastal towns, sweeping farmlands, and forested mountain ranges all defy stereotypes – from oases of swimming pools in the desert to remote wineries nestled within rural mountains.

The pace of life is as diverse as everything else in the state. Fast moving and fast living are hallmarks of the Los Angeles basin, yet the quiet frenzy of the San Francisco Bay Area sometimes seems just

as fast. Outside the major urban areas, the hectic speed diminishes. The Central Valley supports a huge agricultural industry, and a growing movement towards sustainability helps bring an older rhythm – that of small-time farming – to California. California's numerous wine regions invite visitors to relax and slow that pace even further. Beyond the farms and vineyards, an even more venerable and variable pace emerges – that of nature. The gushing waterfalls of Yosemite, towering redwoods of Humboldt, bone-dry deserts of Death Valley, delicate native wildflowers along the coast, even the imperceptible crawl and occasional sudden jolt of the land itself all make up the unique rhythm of California.

To best discover what California has to offer, choose something that you want to fall in love with and pursue it here – whether your passion is organic wine, Gold Country ghost towns, Hollywood movie stars, or just lying on the beach. No matter who you are or what you're into, you can make this place your own.

# Planning Your Trip

## ▶ WHERE TO GO

### San Francisco and the Bay Area

The weather, the politics, the technology, the food—San Francisco is world famous. Come dine on cutting-edge cuisine, tour the museums, smell the roses in Golden Gate Park, and stroll the waterfront at Fisherman's Wharf and Pier 39. Excursions around the Bay Area include the unspoiled wilderness of the North Bay, the radical yet cultural East Bay, the elephant seals of Coastside, and the latest technology in Silicon Valley.

### Wine Country

California rivals France in both quantity and quality of wine production. The heart and soul of California's collection of vineyards are the Napa and Sonoma Valleys. Locals and travelers alike crowd Highway 29 and the Silverado Trail every weekend to swirl and sip top Napa vintages. Sonoma is more spread out; tasters take their time journeying from Carneros up to the appellations of the Russian River Valley.

### North Coast

Many locals run north to spend weekends meditating on the wild waters of the North Coast. Mendocino welcomes all with its plethora of B&Bs, fine art galleries, small wineries, and rugged rocky beaches. Farther north, the town of Eureka celebrates history while offering all the conveniences of the modern age. In between, the groves of the Redwood National and State Parks create a unique landscape.

### Lake Tahoe and the Northern Sierra

Mountains dot California, but three draw

Wine Country vineyards

towering redwoods

Sacramento's Capitol Building

Chinatown

outdoor sporting enthusiasts the world over. Lake Tahoe offers fabulous skiing and snowboarding, while the lake beckons wakeboarders in the summertime. Mount Shasta challenges mountaineers, and surrounding Shasta Lake offers beautiful wilderness. Mount Lassen is one of only two active volcanoes on the continent, and the main road tours past the devastation caused by a 20th-century eruption.

## Sacramento and Gold Country

California's capital, Sacramento is the river town that served as a transport and communication center for the sprawling gold fields of the Sierra foothills. View the Capitol Building and enjoy the history of the state through Sutter's Fort. Gold Country's tiny towns—once booming mining communities—keep the Gold Rush history alive through restored mines and cavern tours, while the Central Valley shelters a thriving agricultural community.

## Yosemite

The work of Ansel Adams and John Muir have helped make Yosemite National Park a worldwide icon. Thousands crowd into Yosemite Valley to view the much-photographed Half Dome, Yosemite Falls, and El Capitan. On the other side of the Sierras, Mono Lake, Mammoth Lakes, and the Sequoia and Kings Canyon National Parks provide a wealth of recreation and wilderness to explore.

## Central Coast

Some of the most beautiful coastal country in all of California sits right in the middle of the state. Cruise the boardwalk in Santa Cruz, ogle sea anemones in Monterey's world-class aquarium, or camp and hike in the unspoiled

## IF YOU HAVE...

- **A weekend:** Visit San Francisco or Los Angeles.
- **One week:** From San Francisco, add the Wine Country; from Los Angeles, add Palm Springs.
- **Two weeks:** Add the Central Coast, Tahoe, and Yosemite.
- **A month:** Add the North Coast, Gold Country, San Diego, and the Deserts.

Fox Bar at Borrego Ranch, Anza-Borrego Desert

Death Valley's lowest point

wilderness of Big Sur. San Simeon offers the grandiose home of Hearst Castle, or go wine tasting in Paso Robles. Farther south, shop and sunbathe in Santa Barbara.

### Los Angeles and Orange County

For an iconic visit to California, you can't beat a trip to Los Angeles. From the glitz and glamour of Hollywood and Beverly Hills to the camp and kitsch of Santa Monica, L.A. is all California, all the time. Families come from all over to visit Disneyland, while sun and surf worshippers ply the waves or lie on the sands of Long Beach.

### The Deserts

A different kind of beauty makes the deserts of California legendary and popular attractions. Palm Springs takes the cake as the biggest and coolest desert city. Joshua Tree—named for its funky namesake plant—straddles two major desert ecosystems. Death Valley boasts the lowest and hottest spot in the Western Hemisphere. Far south, Anza-Borrego is California's biggest state park and one of its most intriguing regions.

### San Diego

For the sun-drenched California beach experience portrayed in endless films, venture south to San Diego. Balboa Park's world-renowned San Diego Zoo lures millions of visitors annually, while across the bay Coronado's famed "Hotel Del" is a vibrant centerpiece. Gorgeous beaches stretch north up to Encinitas, La Jolla, and Del Mar, begging for surfers, swimmers, strollers, and sunbathers to ply their sands.

## ▸ WHEN TO GO

California's best feature is its all-season appeal. Whenever you come, you'll get a great experience highlighting some of the best aspects of the state. In winter, take advantage of the mild temperatures to visit the southern part of the state and the deserts. Spring sees the desert wildflowers begin to bloom, and warming temperatures in April and May also make for a beautiful time to travel along the southern coast.

Summer brings the most visitors to California, whether to sweat through the crowds at Disneyland or take in the natural wonders of Yosemite. Sunshine even visits the North Coast, making walks on the near-deserted beaches alluring. In fall, the San Francisco Bay Area turns on the charm, with less fog and warm air making both indoor and outdoor activities attractive, while the Wine Country's grape harvest brings out tons of visitors to enjoy the festivities.

# BEFORE YOU GO

California boasts plenty of major airports, train stations, and interstate highways. The easiest places to fly into are the Los Angeles and San Francisco metro areas, though the suburban airports offer a minimum of hassle compared to the major city hub airports.

If you're planning to leave the confines of L.A. or S.F., get a car. Really. Public transit can get you to and from a number of cities, but you'll miss anything outside of the urban reaches of the state—which would be a shame, because the wilderness, beaches, and parks are more than worth your time. Expect to pay to park in the cities.

Coming to California from abroad? You'll need your passport and possibly a visa.

Unless you're visiting the deserts in the heat of summer, bring layered clothing. Coastal fog socks in many of the beaches and seaside cities for much of the summer, especially in Northern California, making the air damp and chilly. But no matter what, bring (and use!) sunscreen; that cold fog doesn't stop the rays from burning unwary beachcombers.

Make reservations and buy tickets in advance, especially if you're visiting a region during its high season or on a holiday weekend. For Disneyland, you'll save money buying online in advance. For The French Laundry, it's the only way to get in the door. It's also a good idea to make early reservations at popular hotels and inns—for example, Yosemite's Ahwahnee books up fast in the summertime!

San Francisco's iconic streetcars

# Explore California

## THE BEST OF CALIFORNIA

### Day 1

Fly into Los Angeles and rent a car. Cruise along Wilshire Boulevard, one of the most famous streets in California, heading from coastal Santa Monica, past the downtown L.A. business district, through Korea Town, into Beverly Hills, down the Miracle Mile, and on to inland Los Angeles. Stop by LACMA and the La Brea Tar Pits along the way before checking in to your hotel.

### Day 2

Go to Disneyland! If this is your first trip to California, get the Park Hopper pass and spend some time in California Adventure. You'll get a light and fluffy overview of many of the Golden State's star regions and attractions.

### Day 3

Head three hours east on I-10 to taste the sands of California's vast arid deserts in bright, fun-loving Palm Springs. Hike out to a native palm oasis in one of the Indian Canyons, visit a date farm, or play a round of golf. In the evening, dine at Pomme Frites, then head to Mixie's Boy Bar to dance and drink into the night.

### Day 4

No visit would be complete without Yosemite National Park. Hop back on I-5 and take U.S. 99 to the south entrance and drive up to the world-famous Yosemite Valley. Board the valley shuttle to avoid the bumper-to-bumper traffic. Take the short hike to Bridalveil Fall or tackle a tougher climb to Upper Yosemite Fall. Then take Tioga Pass Road (summer only) to Tuolumne Meadows, leaving behind the crowds as you enjoy the alpine meadows and lakes. Reserve in advance to spend the night at one of the High Sierra camps.

### Day 5

Continue east on Tioga Pass to U.S. 395, turning north to Mono Lake. Spend half a day exploring the silent, eerie Tufa Preserve and swimming in this controversial body of salty water. Drive about 20 miles north on U.S. 395 to Highway 270 to the slowly decaying ghost town of Bodie—a hard-bitten mining town that once rivaled Tombstone with its one-a-day murder rate. Return south to the tiny town of Lee Vining for a casual dinner and crash in one of the rustic lodges.

### Day 6

Head north on U.S. 395 to join in the fun and adventure at Lake Tahoe. In the winter, stay

crystal-clear Lake Tahoe

Fisherman's Wharf

Carmel Mission

at Squaw Valley, Alpine Meadows, or one of a dozen other alpine ski resorts. In summer, dive into the pristine waters of Lake Tahoe. At night, the casinos on the Nevada side heat up with high-end nightclubs and always-busy gambling floors.

## Day 7

Drive west on I-80 to visit California's legendary Wine Country. New to wine tasting? Start at the Culinary Institute of America, a chef training center with cooking classes and a restaurant in St. Helena. Next, go wine tasting at any of the stellar vineyards lining the Silverado Trail. End your day by dressing to the nines to dine out at Bouchon, or head farther north to dive feet-first into a Calistoga mud bath.

## Day 8

Take Highway 121 west to U.S. 101 to explore San Francisco's North Bay. Visit Muir Woods and walk the main trail among the redwoods before stopping off for lunch at the Pelican Inn. Finish with a winding coastal tour through the Marin Headlands before crossing the Golden Gate Bridge to spend the night in "the City."

## Day 9

You're probably staying downtown, so take a stroll along the Embarcadero and check out Fisherman's Wharf. Grab a casual meal at Fog City Diner then take Fell Street to Golden Gate Park to wander around the Japanese Tea Garden or just people-watch. For dinner, dine upscale at Hayes Valley's Jardinière, then round out your evening with some live music—perhaps the San Francisco Symphony or Biscuits and Blues.

## Day 10

The most beautiful way to head back south is along coastal route Highway 1. Stop in Monterey to watch the sea otters at the Monterey Bay Aquarium before heading to beautiful Carmel. Stop for lunch and stroll the zillions of art galleries downtown. Get back on Highway 1 to cruise the stunning Big Sur Coast Highway. Spend the night at one of the many Big Sur campgrounds (advance reservations recommended) or rustic cabins.

## Day 11

Traveling farther south, take a break from the beaches by taking Route 46 east to experience the inland valleys of Paso Robles. This off-the-beaten-path agricultural region is rising in prominence as a producer of fine wines to rival Napa itself. A cute downtown area gets lively with local college students, but the wine roads seem pleasantly crowd-free and the tasting experience at wineries like Midlife Crisis and Hunt Cellars feels friendly and personal. From Paso, it's an easy drive down Highway 1 to have dinner and spend the night in coastside Cambria.

# A GOLDEN STATE HISTORY

The modern history of the state of California began in 1849 when gold was discovered by accident at Sutter's Mill. But the best place for you to begin your exploration of California's history as written by the miners, laborers, owners, Native Americans, and Chinese immigrants is in the capital city of Sacramento. Tour the **Capitol Building** for a general overview of California's political history, then visit the **Railroad Museum** to learn how the Transcontinental Railroad affected the culture and economy of the state. Finally, take a taste of pioneer life at **Sutter Fort State Historic Park,** sipping from the well of living history programs that run here almost every weekend.

Drive east from Sacramento out on I-80, then take the cutoff to Nevada City and Grass Valley. Here you'll pick up Highway 49, which threads down the middle of the most prosperous and prolific gold-mining regions of California. These towns comprise the northern edge of **Gold Country,** though intrepid gold-seekers dug mines in almost every part of the state. The **Empire Mine State Historic Park** shows off two distinct faces of mining: the huge mansion "cottage" and manicured acres of lawn belonging to the owner, and the equally huge and utterly dangerous machines, timbers, and shafts the miners shot down each day. The galleries of the museum showcase California's innovations in hard rock mining.

The town of **Placerville** was once nicknamed Old Hangtown because criminals were brought from miles around to be executed at the hanging tree. While the site of the tree now shelters a bar, a monument to capital punishment remains. Just outside of town, **Apple Hill** pays homage to the rich agricultural and vinous history of Gold Country – after all, the miners had to eat and drink when they weren't working!

The site of **Sutter's Mill** is worth a quick stop, with its reconstructed mill apparatus and authentic stores and cabins set back from the river. Farther south, museums and historical sites become thick along the roads. **Indian Grinding Rock State Historic Park** recognizes the life and times of the indigenous tribes that inhabited the Sierra Foothills for centuries before the gold drew wealth-hunters from around the globe. **Mercer Caverns** gives visitors a glimpse of the geological history of the Foothills, including the aragonite formations that delighted the world at the Paris 1900 World's Fair. **Moaning Cavern** remains a monument to human enthusiasm and stupidity – an attempt to widen the mouth to accommodate more paying tourists destroyed the characteristic moaning sound that gave the cavern its name. Finally, **Columbia State Historic Park** attempts to re-create the real life of average citizens in a 19th-century mining town. Shop in a dry-goods store, have a meal and a beer in a saloon, or take a horse-drawn carriage ride up and down the main street

the main shaft, Empire Mine State Historic Park

the Neptune Pool at Hearst Castle

Pacific Park at night, Santa Monica

### Day 12

A few miles north of Cambria, Hearst Castle draws visitors for tours through the fantastic property. Walk through bedrooms filled with ancient European art in the Guest Houses, picture partying in the grand rooms with their antique furniture, or imagine taking a dip in a swimming pool clad entirely in precious marble. For a more history-oriented experience, take a nighttime tour, when volunteers dress in vintage 1930s party clothing and you're treated as an invited guest to the Castle. Fill out your day with a beachcombing expedition to Cambria's Moonstone Beach before dining in the quaint downtown.

### Day 13

Time to head back to Los Angeles. A great way to spend your final day in California is to stroll the chaotic Venice Boardwalk, then compare it to a quiet walk along the Canals. Dine on Washington Street, then head up to Santa Monica for some kitschy fun on the Pier and a final shopping trip on the Third Street Promenade.

### Day 14

Have breakfast at Cora's in Santa Monica and take a final walk on the beach before heading to Long Beach Airport or LAX for your flight home.

## SURF, SUN, AND STARS

Many visitors to the Golden State come seeking an iconic surf, sun, and stars experience. Southern California offers all three in spades—from Disneyland to the deserts.

### Family Fun

Southern California is a great place to bring kids of all ages for a family vacation. Naturally, just about everyone will want to go to Disneyland. Teens often prefer to bounce over to California Adventure for the roller coasters and thrill rides. Considering buying two- or three-day passes, and spend the whole weekend getting Disneyfied to the max. Cap a long day of fun with dinner and a show at Medieval Times or Pirate's Dinner Adventure.

Continue your theme park adventure by checking out other Southern California amusement parks, such as Knott's Berry Farm in nearby Buena Park. Cool off on the waterslides at Knott's Soak City or head for the stars at Universal Studios Hollywood for movie-centric attractions and tours. The La Brea Tar Pits remain a kids' favorite, with bubbling stinky water and a huge collection of bones.

Equally fun and slightly less commercial

boulders at Joshua Tree National Park

entertainment abounds in San Diego. Spend a half-day in SeaWorld taking in killer whale shows and riding the coasters. Stroll the meandering paths at the San Diego Zoo in Balboa Park, where you'll meet lions, elephants, pandas, meerkats, and hundreds of exotic animals. To watch animals live and play in more natural environments, head to North County's Wild Animal Park.

Kids and adults alike love the wide, flat beaches of Southern California. Park your towel at Ocean Beach, Coronado, Zuma Beach, or Malibu Lagoon State Beach. Many hotels keep a store of loaner beach chairs and sand and surf toys that are perfect for a day spent lounging out on the sand. Got older kids? Sign 'em up for surfing lessons! San Diego, coastal Orange County, and even Santa Barbara have surf schools that offer everything from two-hour lessons up to multi-day kids' surf camps.

## Desert Rats

Some people's idea of the perfect vacation includes dust, rocks, scorpions, and spiky shrubs. In Southern California, that means desert. March is usually the best time to catch the wildflowers blooming (check the wildflower reports on your favorite desert's website).

Start out in the south at Anza-Borrego Desert State Park. Hike, bike, or off-road in the biggest state park in California. You can even camp wherever you want to in this lovely southern desert. The wildflowers bloom earlier here than at any other California desert—sometimes even in February.

Next, drive north up to Joshua Tree National Monument for nature both accessible and extreme. Day-trippers from nearby Palm Springs tend to stick to the roads and the short hikes to native palm oases; rock climbers will camp for days while scaling the thousands of big rocks. Expect the wildflowers earliest in the less-traveled southern end of Joshua Tree, with later blooms in the popular northern sections.

Farther north is Death Valley National Park. California's most famous desert sits lower than any other land in the Western Hemisphere. Sticking to the road gets you to

## EAT, DRINK, CALIFORNIA

Fine wine and haute cuisine are California's two great tastes that taste best together. And the winemakers and chefs of the state capitalize on the sublime amalgam, creating unusual combinations to tempt oenophiles to nibble and foodies to sip.

Naturally, Napa leads the way. **Domaine Chandon's** estate includes four-star restaurant Etoile, where the wine list is all in-house vintages and the chefs design unique delicacies specifically to pair with the winery's bubblies and stills. In neighboring Sonoma, **J Winery** leads a new trend, bringing small bites of top cuisine right into the tasting room. Tasters pay a higher fee, but they get their money's worth as wait staff bring out plates of tiny but tasty dishes that pair with each taste of J's wine, giving the wine a needed boost.

In the San Francisco Bay Area, fine wines and cutting-edge cuisine practically litter the ground. One forward-thinking Santa Cruz chef decided that instead of bringing fine wines and great produce out of the fields and into a restaurant, he'd bring the tables, kitchen, and chef out of the restaurant and into the fields. Thus began **Outstanding in the Field,** a series of haute cuisine dinners featuring local wineries and food producers, set out where the food really comes from.

The masters of the food and wine festival reside up the coast in Mendocino and the Anderson Valley. Each January, the week-long **Crab and Wine Festival** brings hundreds of visitors from the Bay Area and beyond up to the chilly and stunning North Coast to taste the best of two worlds – land and sea. Winemakers and top chefs throughout this region pull out all the stops to pair the finest local varietals to the indigenous Dungeness crabs as the crabbing season reaches its peak. Dress up for fine winemakers dinners, pull on your parka to go out crab fishing, then come in and take a cooking class to learn how to cook up your catch to best pair it with your favorite wine.

Santa Barbara has yet to come into its own as a wine region, but at least one local restaurant, **Bouchon,** is trying to help. Bouchon's wine list offers almost exclusively local wines – *really* local wines. Bouchon sticks to wines from the Santa Ynez Valley and other nearby appellations, occasionally straying as far north as Paso Robles but no farther. The wait staff love their homegrown Rhone varietals and will happily tell you not only which wines will fit your meal, but which vineyards to visit on the following day.

The new "red gold" – Italian varietals and Zinfandel wines – has brought a bigger economy and more tourism to Gold Country. Yet the Sierra Foothills have long been a fertile agricultural region, with apples as the star crop. Today, visitors to **Apple Hill** just past Placerville can gorge on apples, wines, and even apple wines at the more than two dozen orchards and 12 or so wineries. It's not often that wine tasters get the chance to seek out the perfect vintage to pair with apple pie, but here it's as easy as....

many of the gorgeous sights in the parched valley. But head off-road, or hike out away from the highway, to listen to the quietest landscape anywhere in the state.

### Seeing Stars

Have you come to California in the hopes of seeing a movie star—or at least some great movie history? Los Angeles can certainly hook you up. Start your quest in Hollywood. Catch a premiere at Grauman's Chinese Theater and stroll along the Hollywood Walk of Fame. If you love rock stars too, grab tickets for a show at the Roxy or the Whisky A Go-Go along Sunset Strip.

Head out of Hollywood to take a spin up into the hills along Mulholland Drive, where several A-listers are known to live. You'll probably have a better shot at actually seeing a star if you stroll down to Rodeo Drive and peer at the racks in Dior or Michael Kors.

Combine beachcombing with star-searching by taking a trip down the magnificent coastline, where many celebrities live—or at least hang out during downtime. Walk the beachside promenade of Venice Beach and see a few former homes of mega-stars. Or drive north along Highway 1 through legendary Malibu for a tour of the garages and back gates of favorite celebrities.

To vacation like the stars, head out into the desert to Palm Springs. Stay in the very rooms the film crew inhabited at A Place in the Sun, play golf on a championship course at Trilogy, or even pay homage to lost lights in the celebrity cemeteries.

## ROAD TRIPPING THE PACIFIC COAST

Looking for the ultimate California road trip? The best and consistently prettiest drive in California runs up the craggy curving coastline on the Pacific Coast Highway. The Pacific Coast Highway starts in San Juan Capistrano as the PCH and terminates in Leggett as Highway 1. This route is sometimes a highway, sometimes a city street, and often a twisty slow road. Wherever you are, it shows off the edge of California as it meets the Pacific Ocean.

Pacific Coast Highway

### Day 1

Book your car rental and fly into either the San Diego or Long Beach Airport. From San Diego, you'll head north along I-5 until meeting the Pacific Coast Highway in San Juan Capistrano; from Long Beach, the PCH starts 40 miles south at Dana Point. Enjoy the drive in either direction, and consider a quick detour inland to see some California history at Mission San Juan Capistrano. At the end of a day of touring, the resorts of Huntington Beach await.

### Day 2

Begin your day with a morning tour of the famously haunted *Queen Mary* in Long Beach. Then spend the afternoon meandering up the PCH, through the L.A. beach towns of Manhattan, Hermosa, and Redondo

Venice Boardwalk architecture

Pebble Beach, Carmel

Beach. Stop in Venice for tour of the Venice Boardwalk, finishing up with dinner at one of Washington Street's amazing restaurants.

## Day 3

From Venice, the PCH makes a big bend at Santa Monica; as you pass through the 22-mile long town of Malibu you'll be driving straight west. Stop at Malibu Lagoon State Beach to frolic in the surf or watch the surfers at Malibu Pier. The road again turns north and takes you through the center of Oxnard in a sometimes-confusing series of jogs out to Harbor Boulevard. At Pierpont Bay just before Ventura, Highway 101 merges with Harbor Boulevard to again become the PCH. Turn off the car and take a break in the southern-facing city of Santa Barbara.

## Day 4

Spend the day in Santa Barbara. Play a game of beach volleyball, take a swim in the ocean, go shopping, or enjoy the Spanish Colonial history in and around the Mission Santa Barbara. Have dinner at The Endless Summer, and cap the evening with a moonlit walk on the beach.

## Day 5

Get back on Highway 101, which becomes the historic Mission road, El Camino Real, north of Santa Barbara. You'll leave the coastline until Gaviota State Park (maybe stop for a picnic and a quick hike) before turning left away from El Camino Real and onto the next iteration of the PCH: the Cabrillo Highway. Things get a bit complicated as you drive through the middle of downtown Lompoc to pick up Highway 1 again. Highway 1 and Highway 135 merge briefly, then there's not much to see until Highway 1 joins Highway 101 again just south of Pismo Beach. From Pismo, take the slower but more scenic Los Osos Valley Road and rejoin the PCH to spend the night in Cambria.

## Day 6

Stop for breakfast downtown before heading north to San Simeon for a tour of famous Hearst Castle. Spend the night in one of the many abodes lining Moonstone Beach.

## Day 7

Heading north, Highway 1 stops diverging for a while, clinging tenaciously to the coastline. Stop at Piedras Blancas to see the elephant seals in winter, or head directly into Big Sur. Make reservations to camp at Julia Pfeiffer Burns State Park or splurge on a room at Ventana Inn. Take an easy walk out to the famous McWay Falls waterfall that drops onto a cove beach. Do some more serious woodsy hiking in Pfeiffer Big Sur State Park, then clean up for a top-end meal at Cielo at the Ventana. If you're still awake after midnight, take a dip in the cliff-top hot tubs at Esalen.

## Day 8

Breakast at Deetjen's before continuing through the north end of Big Sur. Be sure to stop at the many pullouts to photograph the unbelievably beautiful rugged coastal panorama. Stop for a hike at Point Lobos before returning to civilization in Carmel. The 17-Mile Drive makes a great detour off the highway. Visit the hallowed greens and fairways of Pebble Beach, go wine tasting in nearby Carmel Valley, or take in a show at one of the local live theaters. After dinner, spend the night in Monterey.

the Golden Gate Bridge shrouded in fog

## Day 9

Get an early start to hit the Monterey Bay Aquarium before the crowds and stroll Cannery Row. Back on the road, lush, fertile farmland surrounds Highway 1 on either side up to Santa Cruz, a funky, liberal town—even for California. Kids love taking a break to ride the roller coasters and play the games at the Santa Cruz Beach Boardwalk. Farther up the coast, stop at Davenport to watch the parasurfers, then continue on up to Half Moon Bay to stay at one of the charming B&Bs.

## Day 10

Be sure Devil's Slide is open before taking Highway 1 from Half Moon Bay up into San Francisco. Here, Highway 1 is also called 19th Avenue, and takes you across the Golden Gate Bridge in about 30 minutes. But Skyline Boulevard (Rte. 35) makes a prettier drive, letting you see Ocean Beach and some of the city's most stunning mansions. At the Golden Gate Bridge, Highway 1 and U.S. 101 merge before taking you into Marin, where plenty of restaurants and hotels welcome weary travelers.

## Day 11

From Marin, Highway 1 hugs the rough, rocky coastline as towns become scarce and the scenery amazing. Wend your way through Muir Beach, past Stinson Beach, through Point Reyes, along Tomales Bay, and up to Bodega Bay. Lunch at Hog Island Oyster Company and continue north to Fort Ross for some largely overlooked history of the California coast. Spend the night at Sea Ranch, or push on to the B&Bs and inns that dot the roadside up into Mendocino and Fort Bragg.

## Day 12

Continuing north, you'll see fewer cars on the road. Highway 1 turns inland at Leggett and terminates at U.S. 101, skirting the wilderness area known as the Lost Coast. To get the best possible view of this remote and beautiful region without actually backpacking the Lost Coast Trail, take slow and twisting Mattole Road through the wilderness to the Victorian town of Ferndale and stay at a B&B.

## Day 13

Take U.S. 101, now called the Redwood Highway, north to slow down and spend some time in the fabulous Redwood National and State Parks. Patrick's Point State Park boasts a re-created Native American village, while farther north Prairie Creek Redwoods State Park offers lovely, shady day hikes through the trees and down to the beaches. Or, head south on the Redwood Highway to visit the Avenue of the Giants in Humboldt Redwoods State Park. Camp in the park or treat yourself to a night at the Benbow Inn and dine in the excellent restaurant.

### Day 14

It's a 3–4-hour drive south on U.S. 101 to San Francisco for your flight home. Stay on Highway 1 (19th Ave.) for a last glimpse of the coast from the Cliff House for lunch before continuing to SFO.

## PLAYGROUNDS FOR YOUR INNER CHILD

Northern California has some of the best playgrounds for grownups in the world. Kids can come and play too—in fact, kids enjoy watching their parents and other adults cutting loose and having a seriously great time. Whatever your age, Northern California's vast attractions will bring out your sense of wonder and adventure.

### Arts and Crafts

The Northern California art scene is the stuff of story and song—literally—and San Francisco's performing arts are the best in the state. Get tickets to the San Francisco Opera, Ballet, or Symphony for stellar productions. Check out one of the cool blues clubs, like the Boom Boom Room, or head down to the Castro to take in a gay-themed play at Theatre Rhino. For visual and cultural arts, the galleries at the de Young, Legion of Honor, and the Asian Art Museum don't disappoint.

Still hungry for art? Drive up the coast to Mendocino, a longtime artists' colony, where shops and studios sell the work of both locals and artists from around the world.

Legion of Honor, San Francisco

### Extreme Sports

Is your inner child a thrill-seeking teenager? The opportunities for life- and limb-risking fun in California's northern mountains are nearly limitless. Tahoe offers wild, winter sports where you can snowboard a double-black diamond slope at Squaw Valley. Farther north, hike or rock-climb to the summit of Mount Shasta, an enormous dormant volcano. Those who prefer their volcanoes active can hike across the warm rocks of Mount Lassen.

The Gold Country offers more than just mining history. Explore the region from the water by signing up for a whitewater rafting trip on the South and Middle Fork American Rivers. For bigger waves, head south to Half Moon Bay to surf the giant breaks at Mavericks. Or get lost on the Lost Coast by hiking the Lost Coast Trail. Prepare for three days of backpacking along gorgeous but rugged beaches.

### Wet and Dirty

Even if you don't feel like dangling off a sheer

cliff face or plummeting down a waterfall, Northern California has endless interactive attractions that let your inner child touch and taste or get wet, slimy, and dirty while experiencing the Golden State. In San Francisco, hit the Exploratorium, and buy the extra ticket to take the tour of this legendary science museum's Tactile Dome. Head south to Silicon Valley to run around the Tech Museum of Innovation, touching the interactive displays about medical technology, computers, biology, chemistry, and physics.

Head north into Gold Country and scrabble through the old, rusted mining equipment in the abundant mining parks, touch the partially restored locomotives at Railtown 1897, or go underground at Mercer or Black Chasm Caverns. Another grubby caving experience awaits at Lake Shasta Caverns. Once there, you might as well dive into the Shasta Lake, or rent a boat for some wakeboarding or ski tubing. To the northwest, book a deep-sea fishing trip on the *Tally Ho II* in fish-centric Crescent City. Driving back south, get covered in sawdust at the Blue Ox Millworks in Eureka. Finally, stop in Fort Bragg to comb Glass Beach and take home sea-worn chunks of glass thrown into the city landfill many decades ago.

## A PLETHORA OF PARKS

California boasts some of the most beautiful parks in the world. They're everywhere and they come in all sizes, from tiny city and county greenscapes on up to multi-thousand-acre wilderness wonderlands.

If you visit only one park in California, make it **Yosemite National Park.** The endless parade of sights, the sounds of forest life, the clean smell of fresh air, and the feel of the wind combine to create an iconic California park experience. A very different but equally astonishing landscape greets you at **Death Valley,** another of California's massive national parks. You could easily spend a week at either of these parks and not see all there is or hike even half the trails.

viewing Yosemite

**Anza-Borrego Desert State Park** is the biggest state park in the California system. Come spend a spring weekend here to see some of the most beautiful desert wildflowers around. At the other end of the state – and the other end of the climate spectrum – the **Redwood National and State Parks** are actually half a dozen semi-separate entities clustered together and managed cooperatively. Camp in coastal redwood groves, hike fern-strewn trails down to the cool coast, and educate yourself about California's natural and human history. Speaking of history, California's many state historic parks are gems too often overlooked. Fort Ross, Railtown 1889, Bodie, and even all of Old Town San Diego make history far more fun than any book ever could.

The park with the most natural drama in the state must be **Mount Lassen** – one of only two active volcanoes in the contiguous 48 states and one of the most remote parks in the state. On the other hand, **Griffith Park** in Los Angeles has all the comforts of a big city, with swimming pools, sports courts, museums, and even an observatory. Yet it's got a lovely greenbelt and hiking trails, reminders that even Los Angeles treasures its parks.

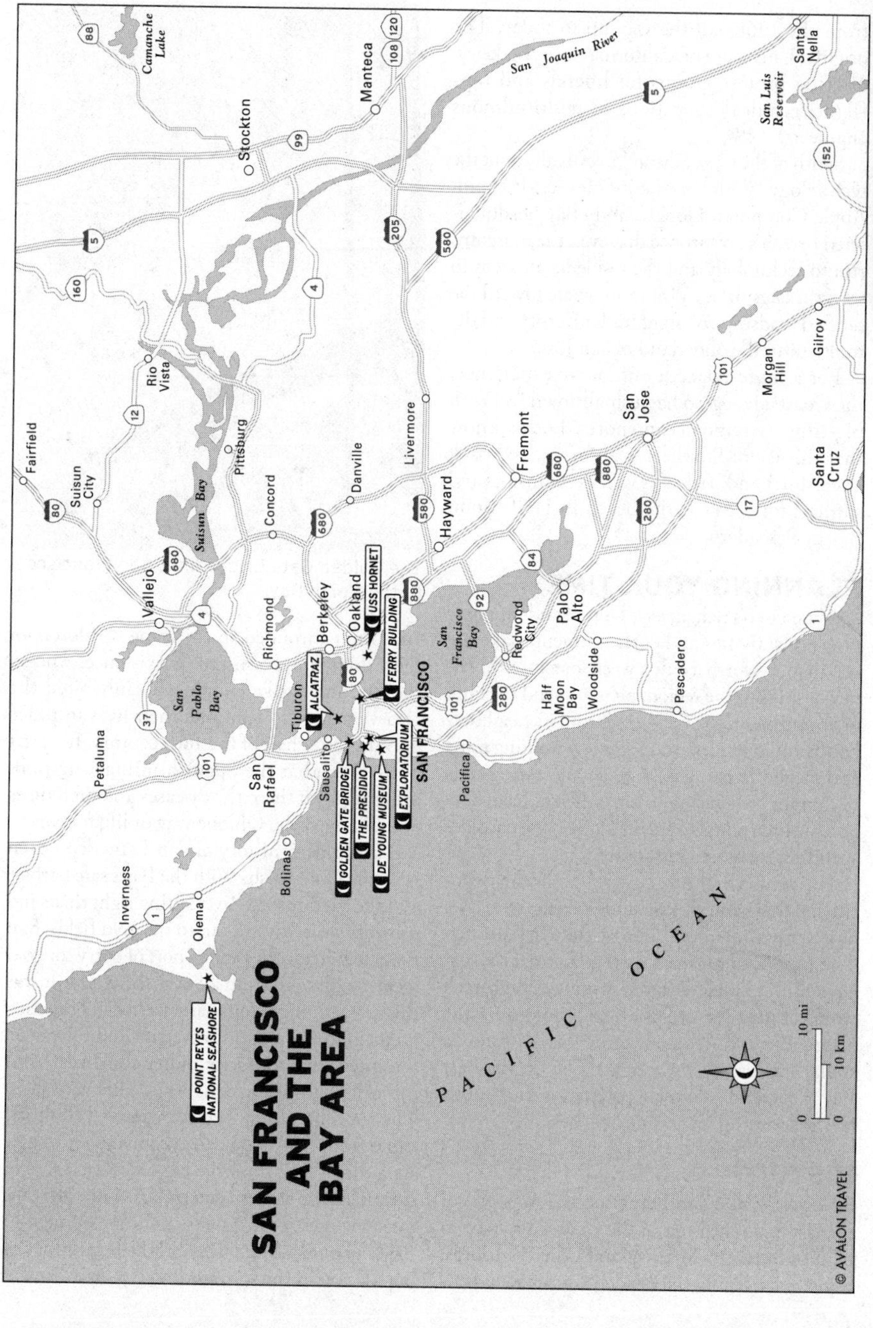
SAN FRANCISCO AND THE BAY AREA
POINT REYES NATIONAL SEASHORE
GOLDEN GATE BRIDGE
THE PRESIDIO
DE YOUNG MUSEUM
EXPLORATORIUM
ALCATRAZ
FERRY BUILDING
USS HORNET
SAN FRANCISCO
PACIFIC OCEAN
San Pablo Bay
Suisun Bay
San Francisco Bay
San Joaquin River
Camanche Lake
San Luis Reservoir
Inverness
Olema
Bolinas
Petaluma
San Rafael
Sausalito
Tiburon
Richmond
Berkeley
Oakland
Vallejo
Fairfield
Suisun City
Rio Vista
Pittsburg
Concord
Danville
Livermore
Hayward
Fremont
San Jose
Morgan Hill
Gilroy
Santa Cruz
Palo Alto
Redwood City
Half Moon Bay
Woodside
Pescadero
Pacifica
Stockton
Manteca
Santa Nella
10 mi
10 km
0
© AVALON TRAVEL

from the 1960s all the way up to today. The original University of California sits in Berkeley, offering protest groups for liberals and top-flight technical educations to multitudinous engineers.

South of the City, Silicon Valley is all about the technology. With the likes of Hewlett-Packard, Apple Computer, Google, and eBay headquartered here, it's no surprise that even the museums run to technology and the residents all seem to own the latest iPod. Visitors gravitate toward the rarified landscape of Stanford University and the multicultural wonderland of San Jose.

For a more relaxed, outdoorsy experience, the Coastside region has a small-town feel with big-time extreme ocean sports. Locals know that this is not Southern California, and pack sweatshirts and parkas as well as swimsuits and sunhats for a day at the beach in Half Moon Bay or Pescadero.

ROBERT HOLMES / CALTOUR

The Golden Gate Bridge links San Francisco to the North Bay.

## PLANNING YOUR TIME

San Francisco's rich, diverse culture and immense range of activities and entertainment make it a destination worth a day, a week, or a month. For new visitors to the region, plan to spend the bulk of your time in the City, exploring its neighborhoods and museums, taking a few walking tours and maybe catching a cable car, and eating at its restaurants whenever possible. If you have only two or three hours to spend in the City, consider spending them in a restaurant.

For return visitors, as well as more adventurous first-timers, consider taking at least a day or two (or more) out of the City proper. The Bay Area grew up as rich as the city that gave it life. Spend a day visiting the high-tech world of the Silicon Valley, stopping to try the affordable and delicious ethnic food. Enjoy a stellar meal and a view of activism in the East Bay. Or spend a whole weekend on the beautiful, welcoming Coastside beaches.

## HISTORY

Amazingly, the San Francisco Bay was one of the last major features of the California coast to be discovered by Spanish and other European explorers. Because the Golden Gate is so narrow and often shrouded in thick fog, explorers in their ships simply missed its existence. And so the Ohlone native people who inhabited the area were able to continue their lives in peace into the latter half of the 18th century. It wasn't until 1776 that the Spanish military arrived, bringing with them the diseases and prejudices that changed the Ohlone way of life forever.

The modern history of San Francisco began with the Gold Rush. With the Bay's safe harbor, and the Sacramento River sitting right there and providing easy transit out to the gold fields, San Francisco made the perfect port of entry for gold seekers sailing in from all over the world. It was this mass immigration that started San Francisco on its journey of ethnic diversity and tolerance. (Granted, this tolerance didn't come easy, and minorities fight for equality to this very day.) The funding of the Transcontinental Railroad came from San Francisco tycoons eager to create a direct link from the big cities back east to their lucrative western enterprises. The 19th century saw incredible growth and development in the City of San Francisco and the beginnings of population in the surrounding Bay Area.

© LANCE SCOTT

The Bay Bridge connects San Francisco to the East Bay.

San Francisco had a strong identity as a military town in the middle of the 20th century. Tens of thousands of troops shipped out of the Presidio and Angel Island to the Pacific theater in World War II. It was only in the 1980s and 1990s that the military presence at Alameda and the Presidio declined and eventually ceased altogether.

In the late 1960s, San Francisco became a haven for flower children, anti-war activists, and civil rights leaders working to usher a new era of peace and tolerance to the United States. One lasting result of the City's tolerance of the hippies was its rise as a great place to live gay. Unlike much of the rest of the country, San Francisco's citizens have allowed and even encouraged the gay culture in their town, inviting queer folk by the thousands to live in a place that acccepted them. Sadly, the large concentration of gay men in San Francisco led to the City becoming an early epicenter of the AIDS epidemic. AIDS activism followed soon afterward, and today the gay community spearheads organizations that educate and inform the public about HIV/AIDS.

Down south, Stanford University and its associated research organizations spent the 1960s and 1970s quietly working on a crazy new idea. They had the bizarre notion that if they used telephone lines and special equipment, they could get one computer to talk to another computer all the way across the country at MIT. And so the Internet was born. The 1980s in the formerly pastoral Santa Clara Valley saw the rise of Apple and the personal computer and the coining of the nickname "Silicon Valley." The 1990s hosted the dot-com boom, with money being thrown around like confetti and jobs for everyone who wanted them. In the 21st century, the dot-com bust leveled out an industry that had gone completely out of its mind. Despite the bust, the whole of the Bay Area was changed forever, and technology remains an integral part of a region that's almost always the first to adopt the latest new high-tech gadgets.

Today, technology, tolerance, and innovation continue to inform the unique culture that permeates the San Francisco Bay Area.

# Sights

## UNION SQUARE AND NOB HILL

Wealth and style mark these areas near the center of San Francisco. Known for their lavish shopping areas, cable cars, and mansions, Union Square and Nob Hill draw both local and visiting crowds all year long. Sadly, the stunning 19th-century mansions built by the robber barons on Nob Hill are almost all gone—shaken then burned in the 1906 earthquake and fire. But the area still exudes a certain elegance; restaurants are particularly good on Nob Hill.

If you shop in only one part of San Francisco, make it Union Square. Even if you don't like chain stores, you can just climb up to the top

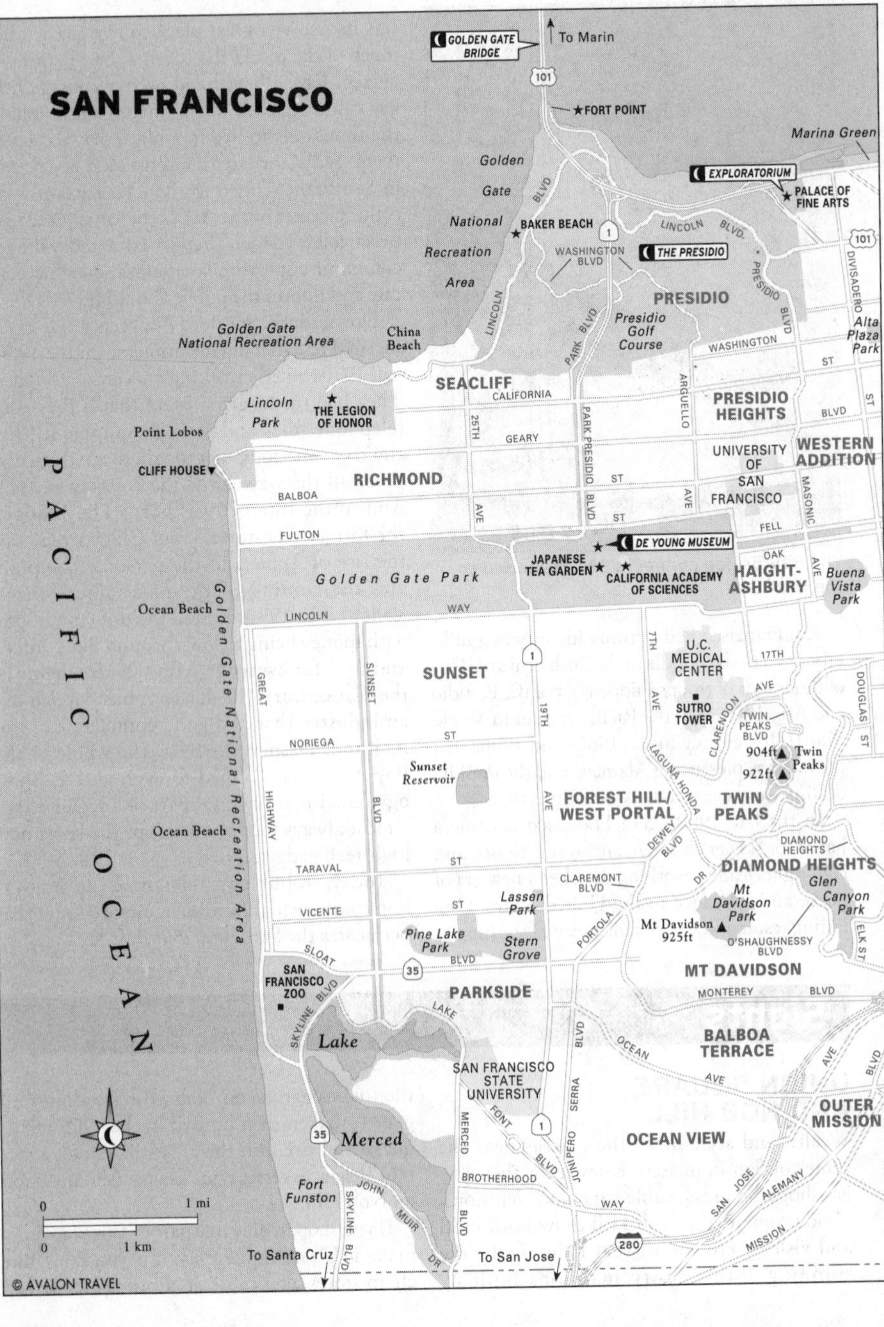
SAN FRANCISCO
GOLDEN GATE BRIDGE
To Marin
101
FORT POINT
Marina Green
Golden Gate National Recreation Area
EXPLORATORIUM
PALACE OF FINE ARTS
BAKER BEACH
LINCOLN BLVD
THE PRESIDIO
WASHINGTON BLVD
PRESIDIO
PRESIDIO BLVD
DIVISADERO
Alta Plaza Park
Presidio Golf Course
PARK BLVD
WASHINGTON
Golden Gate National Recreation Area
China Beach
SEACLIFF
CALIFORNIA
ARGUELLO
PRESIDIO HEIGHTS
Lincoln Park
THE LEGION OF HONOR
Point Lobos
25TH AVE
GEARY
PARK PRESIDIO BLVD
UNIVERSITY OF SAN FRANCISCO
WESTERN ADDITION
CLIFF HOUSE
RICHMOND
BALBOA
FULTON
MASONIC
FELL
DE YOUNG MUSEUM
JAPANESE TEA GARDEN
CALIFORNIA ACADEMY OF SCIENCES
OAK
HAIGHT-ASHBURY
Buena Vista Park
Golden Gate Park
PACIFIC OCEAN
Ocean Beach
LINCOLN WAY
7TH AVE
U.C. MEDICAL CENTER
17TH
SUNSET
GREAT HIGHWAY
SUNSET BLVD
19TH AVE
SUTRO TOWER
CLARENDON AVE
TWIN PEAKS BLVD
DOUGLAS ST
NORIEGA ST
904ft
922ft
Twin Peaks
Sunset Reservoir
LAGUNA HONDA
FOREST HILL/ WEST PORTAL
TWIN PEAKS
Golden Gate National Recreation Area
Ocean Beach
DEWEY BLVD
DIAMOND HEIGHTS
TARAVAL ST
CLAREMONT BLVD
DIAMOND HEIGHTS
Glen Canyon Park
Mt Davidson Park
VICENTE ST
Lassen Park
Mt Davidson 925ft
PORTOLA DR
Pine Lake Park
Stern Grove
O'SHAUGHNESSY BLVD
ELK ST
SLOAT BLVD
35
SAN FRANCISCO ZOO
PARKSIDE
MT DAVIDSON
MONTEREY BLVD
SKYLINE BLVD
LAKE
Lake Merced
OCEAN AVE
BALBOA TERRACE
SAN FRANCISCO STATE UNIVERSITY
FONT BLVD
MERCED
SERRA BLVD
JUNIPERO
OUTER MISSION
OCEAN VIEW
Fort Funston
JOHN MUIR DR
BROTHERHOOD WAY
SAN JOSE
ALEMANY
MISSION
280
0 1 mi
0 1 km
To Santa Cruz
To San Jose
© AVALON TRAVEL

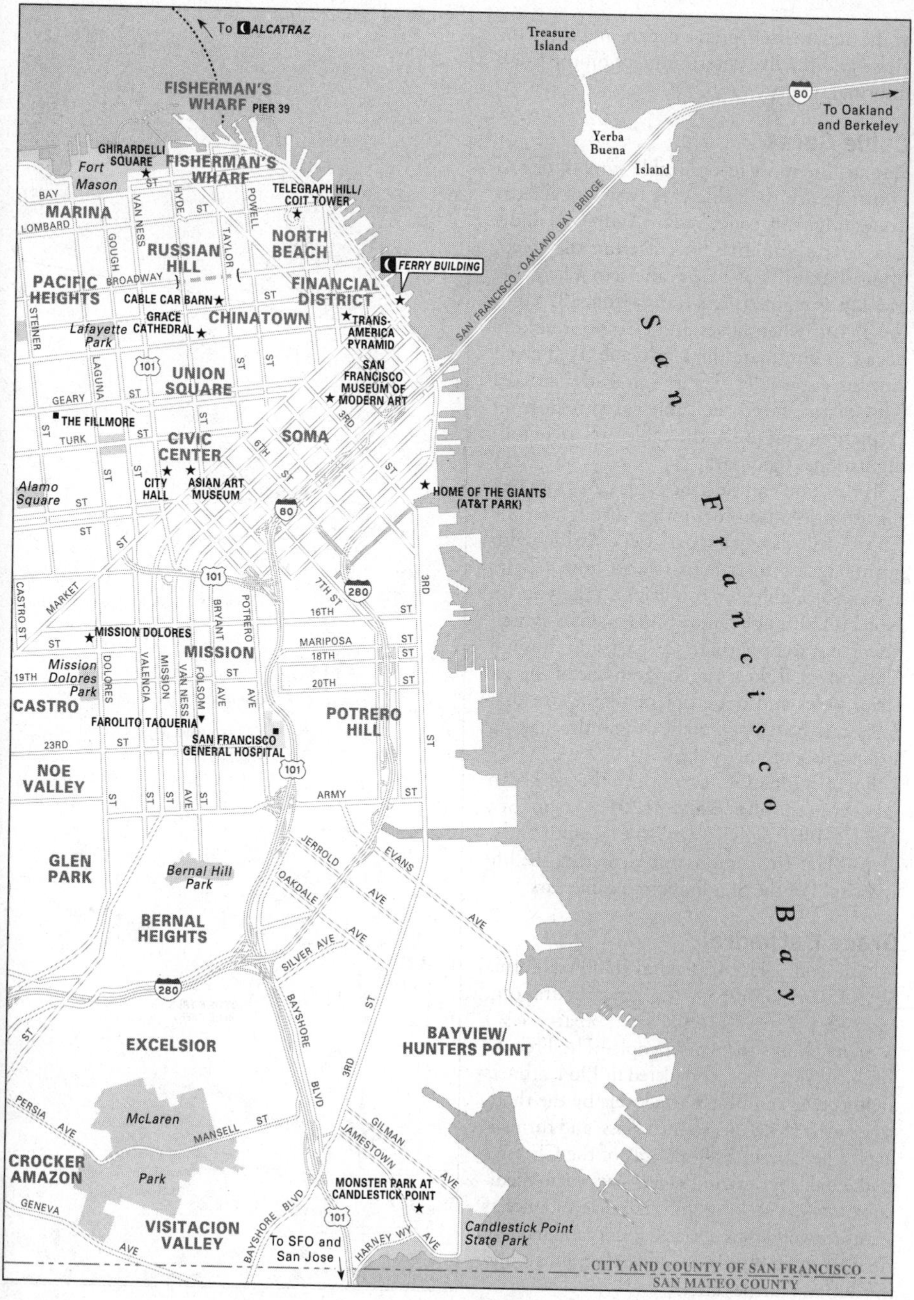

To ALCATRAZ
Treasure Island
To Oakland and Berkeley
Yerba Buena Island
SAN FRANCISCO - OAKLAND BAY BRIDGE
FISHERMAN'S WHARF
PIER 39
GHIRARDELLI SQUARE
Fort Mason
MARINA
TELEGRAPH HILL/ COIT TOWER
NORTH BEACH
RUSSIAN HILL
FERRY BUILDING
PACIFIC HEIGHTS
FINANCIAL DISTRICT
CABLE CAR BARN
CHINATOWN
GRACE CATHEDRAL
Lafayette Park
TRANS-AMERICA PYRAMID
UNION SQUARE
SAN FRANCISCO MUSEUM OF MODERN ART
THE FILLMORE
CIVIC CENTER
SOMA
CITY HALL
ASIAN ART MUSEUM
Alamo Square
HOME OF THE GIANTS (AT&T PARK)
San Francisco Bay
MISSION DOLORES
MISSION
Mission Dolores Park
CASTRO
FAROLITO TAQUERIA
SAN FRANCISCO GENERAL HOSPITAL
POTRERO HILL
NOE VALLEY
GLEN PARK
Bernal Hill Park
BERNAL HEIGHTS
EXCELSIOR
BAYVIEW/ HUNTERS POINT
McLaren Park
CROCKER AMAZON
MONSTER PARK AT CANDLESTICK POINT
VISITACION VALLEY
To SFO and San Jose
Candlestick Point State Park
CITY AND COUNTY OF SAN FRANCISCO
SAN MATEO COUNTY

of the Square itself, grab a bench, and enjoy the views and the live entertainment on the small informal stage.

## Cable Cars

Perhaps the most recognizable symbol of San Francisco are the cable cars (www.sfcablecar.com), originally conceived by Andrew Hallidie as a safer alternative for traveling the steep, often slick hills of San Francisco. The cable cars ran as regular mass transit from 1873 into the 1940s, when buses and electric streetcars began to dominate the landscape. Dedicated citizens, especially "Cable Car Lady" Friedel Klussmann, saved the cable car system from extinction, and today the cable cars are a rolling national landmark.

Today, you can ride the cable cars from one tourist destination to another throughout the City. A full day "passport" ticket (which also grants access to streetcars and buses) costs about $9. Cable car routes can take you up Nob Hill, through Union Square, down Powell Street, out to Fisherman's Wharf, and through Chinatown. Take a seat, or grab one of the exterior poles and hang on! Just be aware that cable cars have open-air seating only, making a ride chilly on foggy days.

For aficionados, a ride on the cars can take you to **The Barn** (1201 Mason St., 415/474-1887, daily 10 A.M.–6 P.M., until 5 P.M. Oct.–Mar., free), a museum depicting the life and times of the San Francisco cable cars.

## Grace Cathedral

A local icon, Grace Cathedral (1100 California St., 415/749-6300, www.gracecathedral.org, Mon.–Fri. 7 A.M.–6 P.M., Sat. 7 A.M.–7 P.M.) is many things to many people. The French-Gothic-style edifice, completed in 1964, attracts architecture and beaux-arts lovers by the thousands with its facade, stained glass, and furnishings. The labyrinths—replicas of the Chartres Cathedral labyrinth in France—appeal to meditative walkers seeking spiritual solace. Concerts featuring world music, sacred music, and modern classical ensembles draw audiences from around the Bay and farther afield.

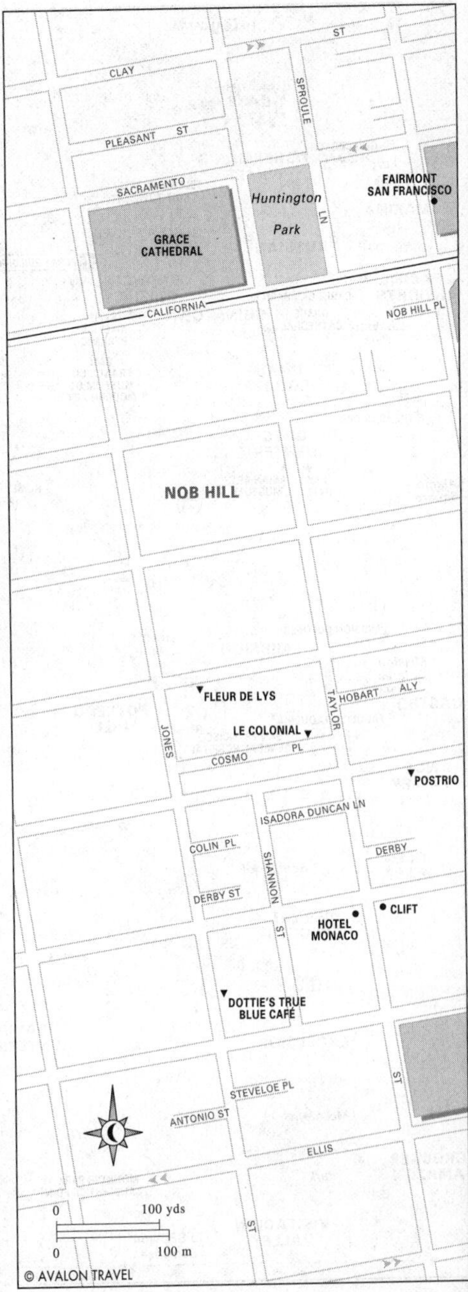

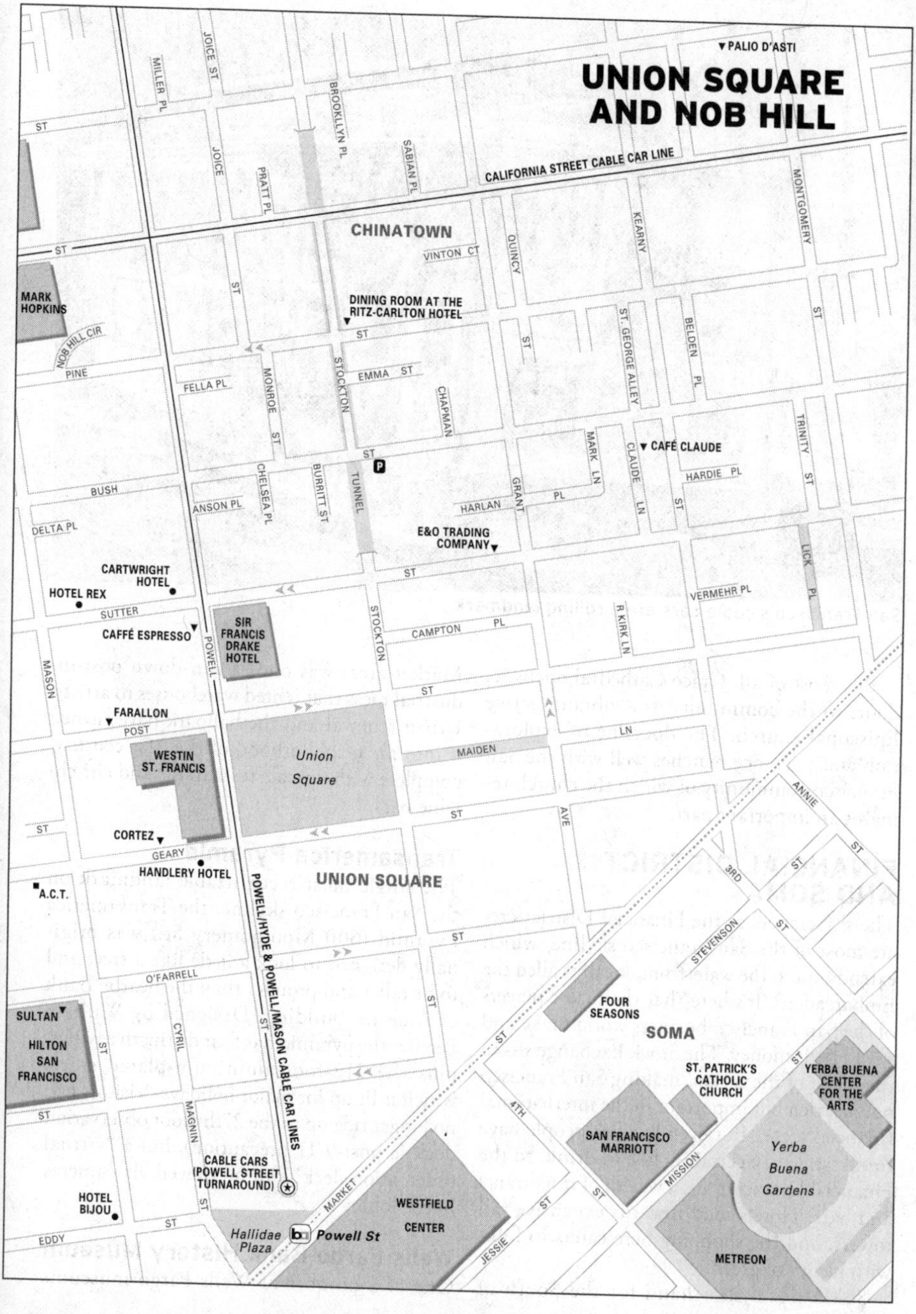
UNION SQUARE AND NOB HILL
PALIO D'ASTI
CALIFORNIA STREET CABLE CAR LINE
CHINATOWN
JOICE ST
MILLER PL
BROOKLYN PL
SABIAN PL
JOICE
PRATT PL
MONTGOMERY
KEARNY
QUINCY
VINTON CT
DINING ROOM AT THE RITZ-CARLTON HOTEL
MARK HOPKINS
NOB HILL CIR
PINE
ST
EMMA ST
STOCKTON
CHAPMAN
ST. GEORGE ALLEY
BELDEN PL
FELLA PL
MONROE ST
MARK LN
CLAUDE LN
CAFÉ CLAUDE
TRINITY ST
HARDIE PL
BUSH
CHELSEA PL
BURRITT ST
TUNNEL
GRANT
HARLAN PL
ANSON PL
DELTA PL
E&O TRADING COMPANY
LICK PL
CARTWRIGHT HOTEL
HOTEL REX
VERMEHR PL
SUTTER
CAFFÉ ESPRESSO
SIR FRANCIS DRAKE HOTEL
CAMPTON PL
R KIRK LN
MASON
POWELL
FARALLON
POST
WESTIN ST. FRANCIS
Union Square
MAIDEN LN
ANNIE ST
AVE
CORTEZ
GEARY
HANDLERY HOTEL
A.C.T.
UNION SQUARE
3RD ST
STEVENSON ST
POWELL/HYDE & POWELL/MASON CABLE CAR LINES
O'FARRELL
FOUR SEASONS
SULTAN
HILTON SAN FRANCISCO
CYRIL
SOMA
ST. PATRICK'S CATHOLIC CHURCH
YERBA BUENA CENTER FOR THE ARTS
4TH ST
MAGNIN
SAN FRANCISCO MARRIOTT
MISSION
Yerba Buena Gardens
CABLE CARS (POWELL STREET TURNAROUND)
HOTEL BIJOU
MARKET
WESTFIELD CENTER
EDDY
Hallidae Plaza
Powell St
JESSIE
METREON

ROBERT HOLMES / CALTOUR

San Francisco's cable cars are a rolling landmark.

But most of all, Grace Cathedral opens its doors to the community as a vibrant, active Episcopal church. The doctrine of exploration and tolerance matches well with the San Francisco community of which the church remains an important part.

## FINANCIAL DISTRICT AND SOMA

The skyscrapers of the Financial District create most of the San Francisco skyline, which extends out to the waterfront, locally called the Embarcadero. It's here that the major players of the San Francisco business world make and spend their money. The Stock Exchange sits in the midst of the action, making San Francisco not just rich but important in the international financial scene. But even businesspeople have to eat, and they certainly like to drink, so the Financial District offers a wealth of restaurants and bars. Hotels tend towards expensive tall towers, and the shopping here caters to folks with plenty of green.

SoMa (local shorthand for the South of Market area) was once a run-down post-industrial mess that rented warehouses to artists. Urban renewal and the ballpark have turned it into *the* neighborhood of the 21st century, complete with upscale restaurants and chi-chi wine bars.

### Transamerica Pyramid

The single most recognizable landmark on the San Francisco skyline, the Transamerica Pyramid (600 Montgomery St.) was originally designed to look a little like a tree, and to be taller and prouder than the nearby Bank of America building. Designed by William Pereira, the pyramid has four distinctive wings, plus the 212-foot aluminum-plated spire, which is lit up for major holidays. Visitors can no longer ride up to the 27th-floor observation deck (a post-9/11 precaution), but a "virtual observation deck" can be viewed via cameras in the lobby.

### Wells Fargo Bank History Museum

One of a number of Wells Fargo museums

© LANCE SCOTT

the Transamerica Pyramid

in California and the West, the Wells Fargo Bank History Museum (420 Montgomery St., 415/396-2619, www.wellsfargohistory.com, Mon.–Fri. 9 A.M.–5 P.M., free) in San Francisco boasts the distinction of sitting on the land of the original Wells Fargo office, opened in 1852. Here you'll see an 1860s Concord stagecoach, gold dust and ore from the Gold Rush era, and an exhibit called "Wells Fargo C.S.I. Officers in Pursuit." Enjoy the history of the stagecoach line that became one of the country's most powerful banks.

### Ferry Building

In 1898, the City of San Francisco created a wonderful new Ferry Building to facilitate commuting from the East Bay. But the rise of the automobile after World War II rendered the gorgeous construction obsolete, and its aesthetic ornamentation was covered over and filled in. But then the roads jammed up and ferry service began again, and the 1989 earthquake led to the removal of the Embarcadero Eyesore (an elevated freeway). Restored to

## QUAKING AND SHAKING

The single most famous event ever to occur in San Francisco happened at 5:12 A.M. on Wednesday, April 18, 1906, when the ground beneath the City jolted violently as the result of a magnitude 7.8 earthquake. Buildings shook and tumbled and a great crack opened along the San Andreas Fault. Gas and water mains ruptured all over the City, and even as the trembling earth settled down, fires broke out. It was the fires that caused the widespread devastation of San Francisco – with the water mains broken, firemen couldn't adequately fight the conflagrations that engulfed whole neighborhoods. Neither rich nor poor residents were spared as the mansions on Nob Hill and the slums of Chinatown felt equal destruction and desolation.

Despite $235-400 million in damage (well over $5 billion in today's dollars), the City persevered. Rebuilding quickly (and with a shocking lack of concern for earthquake safety in construction), San Francisco was back on its feet by the time the 1915 World Exposition rolled around.

Then, in 1989, right in the middle of a San Francisco-Oakland World Series game, another major earthquake struck the Bay Area. Known as the Loma Prieta Quake (the epicenter was down by Loma Prieta near Santa Cruz), this quake registered 6.9 on the Richter scale and was not nearly as destructive as the 1906 monster. Still, a section of the arterial Bay Bridge collapsed, as did part of an Oakland freeway. The disused Embarcadero freeway was badly damaged (and later torn down). Much of downtown Santa Cruz was destroyed, and the quake affected the lives of almost all Bay Area residents – but again rebuilding started almost before the ground stopped quivering.

Today, it's hard to find evidence of the Loma Prieta quake anywhere in the Bay Area. Meanwhile, earthquakes continue to remake the land, reminding us that the only constant here is change.

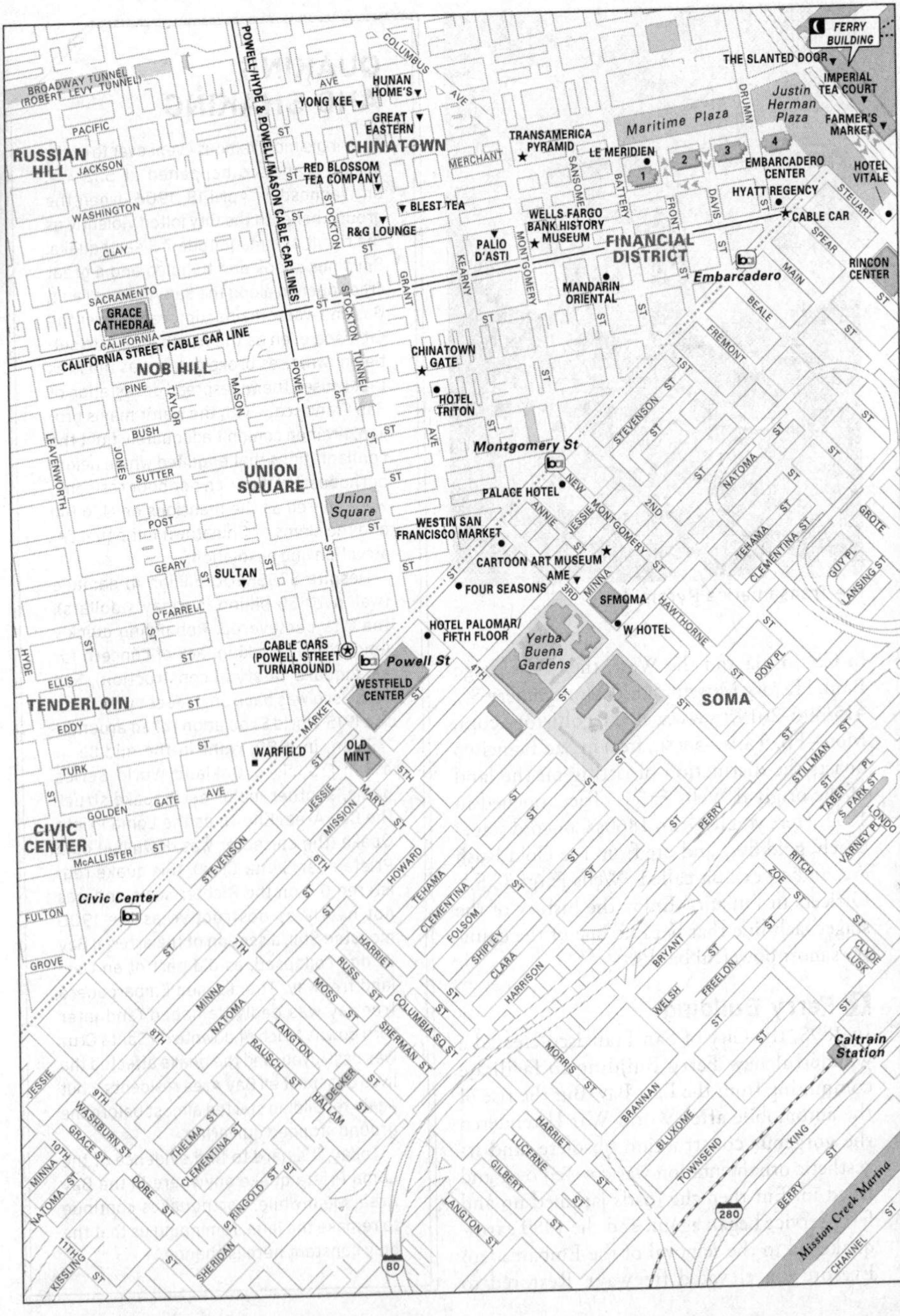
FERRY BUILDING
THE SLANTED DOOR
IMPERIAL TEA COURT
Justin Herman Plaza
FARMER'S MARKET
Maritime Plaza
DRUMM
HOTEL VITALE
EMBARCADERO CENTER
HYATT REGENCY
CABLE CAR
STEUART
SPEAR
RINCON CENTER
MAIN
BEALE
FREMONT
Embarcadero
FINANCIAL DISTRICT
MANDARIN ORIENTAL
LE MERIDIEN
TRANSAMERICA PYRAMID
WELLS FARGO BANK HISTORY MUSEUM
PALIO D'ASTI
MERCHANT
BATTERY
SANSOME
MONTGOMERY
FRONT
DAVIS
KEARNY
GRANT
STOCKTON
CHINATOWN
HUNAN HOME'S
YONG KEE
GREAT EASTERN
RED BLOSSOM TEA COMPANY
BLEST TEA
R&G LOUNGE
COLUMBUS AVE
POWELL/HYDE & POWELL/MASON CABLE CAR LINES
BROADWAY TUNNEL (ROBERT LEVY TUNNEL)
PACIFIC
JACKSON
WASHINGTON
CLAY
SACRAMENTO
CALIFORNIA
RUSSIAN HILL
GRACE CATHEDRAL
CALIFORNIA STREET CABLE CAR LINE
NOB HILL
PINE
BUSH
SUTTER
POST
GEARY
O'FARRELL
ELLIS
EDDY
TURK
GOLDEN GATE AVE
McALLISTER
FULTON
GROVE
LEAVENWORTH
JONES
TAYLOR
MASON
POWELL
HYDE
STOCKTON TUNNEL
CHINATOWN GATE
HOTEL TRITON
Montgomery St
UNION SQUARE
Union Square
PALACE HOTEL
WESTIN SAN FRANCISCO MARKET
CARTOON ART MUSEUM
AME
FOUR SEASONS
SFMOMA
W HOTEL
HOTEL PALOMAR/ FIFTH FLOOR
Yerba Buena Gardens
SULTAN
CABLE CARS (POWELL STREET TURNAROUND)
Powell St
WESTFIELD CENTER
OLD MINT
WARFIELD
TENDERLOIN
CIVIC CENTER
Civic Center
MARKET
NEW MONTGOMERY
ANNIE
JESSIE
MINNA
NATOMA
TEHAMA
CLEMENTINA ST
HOWARD
FOLSOM
HARRISON
BRYANT
BRANNAN
TOWNSEND
KING
BERRY
CHANNEL
1ST
2ND
3RD
4TH
5TH
6TH
7TH
8TH
9TH
10TH
11TH
STEVENSON
MISSION
MARY
HAWTHORNE
GROTE
GUY PL
LANSING ST
DOW PL
SOMA
STILLMAN
TABER PL
S. PARK ST
LONDON
VARNEY PL
PERRY
RITCH
ZOE
CLYDE
LUSK
WELSH
FREELON
MORRIS
BLUXOME
HARRIET
LUCERNE
GILBERT
LANGTON
SHIPLEY
CLARA
RUSS
MOSS
RAUSCH
COLUMBIA SQ ST
SHERMAN ST
DECKER
HALLAM
THELMA ST
WASHBURN ST
GRACE ST
DORE
RINGOLD ST
SHERIDAN
KISSLING
Caltrain Station
Mission Creek Marina
280
80

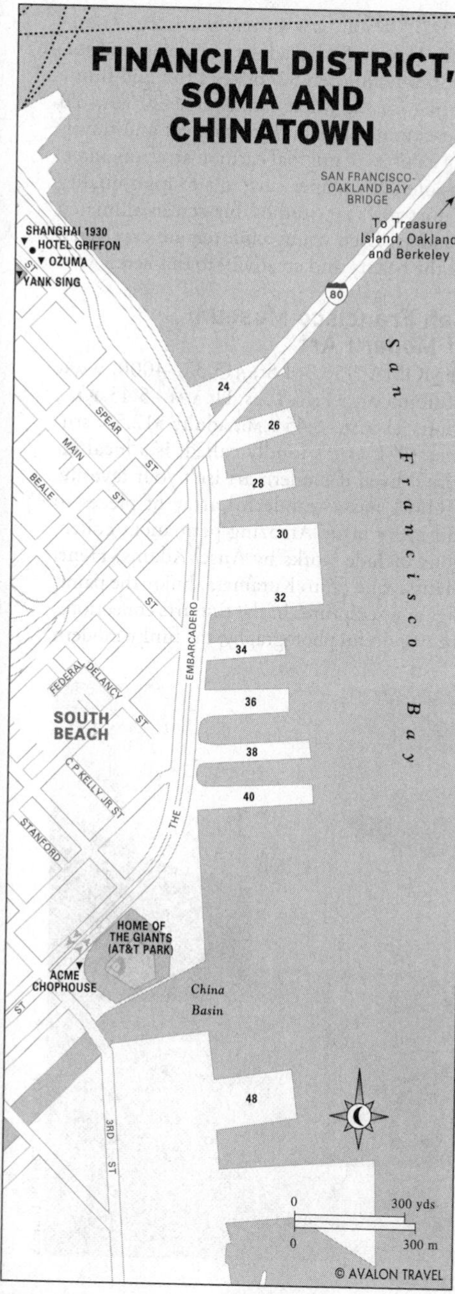

**the Ferry Building clock tower**

glory in the 1990s, the San Francisco Ferry Building (1 Ferry Bldg, 415/693-0966, www.ferrybuildingmarketplace.com, Mon.–Fri. 10 A.M.–6 P.M., Sat. 9 A.M.–6 P.M., Sun. 11 A.M.–5 P.M., check with businesses for individual hours) stands at the end of the Financial District at the edge of the water. You can get a brief lesson in the history of the edifice just inside the main lobby, where photos and interpretive plaques describe the life of the Ferry Building.

Inside the handsome structure, it's all about the food. The famous **Farmers Market** draws crowds each Tuesday and Saturday. Accompanying the fresh produce, the permanent shops provide top-tier artisan food and drink, from wine to cheese to high-end kitchenware. Local favorites Cowgirl Creamery and Acme Bread Company maintain storefronts here. For immediate gratification, a few incongruous quick-and-easy restaurants offer reasonable eats.

Perhaps surprisingly, out on the water side of the Ferry Building, you can actually catch a ferry. Boats come in from Larkspur, Sausalito, Tiburon, Vallejo, and Alameda each day. Check with the Blue and Gold Fleet (www.blueandgoldfleet.com), Golden Gate Ferry (www.goldengateferry.org), and Bay Link Ferries (www.baylinkferry.com) for information about service, times, and fares.

## AT&T Park

The name changes every few years, but the place remains the same. AT&T Park (24 Willie Mays Plaza, 415/972-2000, http://sfgiants.com) is home to the San Francisco Giants, endless special events, several great restaurants, and arguably California's best garlic fries. From the ballpark, you can look right out onto the Bay. During baseball games, a motley collection of boats float beside the stadium, hoping that an out-of-the-park fly ball will come sailing their way.

## Cartoon Art Museum

The Cartoon Art Museum (655 Mission St., 415/227-8666, www.cartoonart.org, Tues.–Sun. 11 A.M.–5 P.M., adults $6, seniors and students $4, children $2) offers a fun and funny outing for the whole family. The 20-year-old museum displays both permanent and traveling exhibits of original cartoon art, from international newspaper cartoons to high-quality comics to Pixar Studios' big-screen animated wonders. Even young children are captivated by the beauty and creativity found here.

## San Francisco Museum of Modern Art

SFMOMA (151 3rd St, 415/357-4000, www.sfmoma.org, Fri.–Tues 11 A.M.–5:45 P.M., Thurs 11 A.M.–8:45 P.M., adults $12.50, students $7), as it's fondly called, is a local favorite. Even if modern art isn't your favorite, MOMA has a wonderful array of pieces to suit every taste. Amazing permanent collections include works by Ansel Adams, Henri Matisse, and Shiro Kuramata. Enjoy the paintings and sculptures in the fine arts collections, the wonderful photography, the funky modern

ROBERT HOLMES / CALTOUR

San Francisco Museum of Modern Art (SFMOMA)

furniture, and some truly bizarre installation art. MOMA brings in a number of special exhibitions each year, featuring the works of the hottest current artists and retrospectives of post-1900 legendary figures.

## CHINATOWN

The massive Chinese migration to California began almost as soon as the news of easy gold in the mountain streams made it to East Asia. And despite rampant prejudice and increasingly desperate attempts on the part of "good" Americans to rid their pristine country of these immigrants, the Chinese not only stayed, they persevered and eventually prospered. Many never made it to the gold fields, preferring instead to remain in bustling San Francisco to open shops and begin the business of commerce in their new home. They were basically segregated to a small area beneath Nob Hill, where they created a motley collection of wooden shacks that served as homes, restaurants, shops, and more. This neighborhood quickly became known as Chinatown. Chinatown, along with much of San Francisco, was destroyed in the 1906 earthquake and fire. Despite xenophobic attempts to relocate Chinatown as far away from downtown San Francisco as possible (back to China was a suggestion), the Chinese prevailed and the neighborhood was rebuilt where it originally stood.

Today, visitors see the post-1906 tourist-friendly Chinatown that was built after the quake. Beautiful Asian architecture mixes with the more pedestrian blocky city buildings to create a unique skyscape. Small alleyways wend between the broad touristy avenues, creating an atmosphere that speaks of the secrecy and much closed culture of the Chinese in San Francisco.

### Chinatown Gate

Visible from the streets leading into Union Square, the Chinatown Gate (Grant Ave. at Bush St.) perches at the southern "entrance" to the famous Chinatown neighborhood. The gate, built in 1970, is a relatively recent addition to this history-filled neighborhood. The design features Chinese dragons, pagodas, and other charming details. The inscription reads "All under heaven is for the good of the people," originally said by Dr. Sun Yat-sen. Its gaudy colorful splendor draws droves of tourists with cameras each day. On weekends it can be tough to find a quick moment to get your own picture taken at the gate!

© LANCE SCOTT

carved dogs guard the Chinatown Gate

Chinatown truly is a sight in and of itself. Visitors stroll the streets, exploring the tiny alleys and peeking into the temples, admiring the wonderful Asian architecture on occasionally unlikely buildings. Among the best known of these is the **Bank of America Building** (555 California St.)—an impressive edifice with a Chinese tiled roof and 60 dragon medallions decorating the facade. The **Bank of Canton** (743 Washington St.) is even more traditional in its look. The ultra-Chinese style of this small beautiful building that acted as the Chinatown Telephone Exchange came to be just after the 1906, when the Great Earthquake demolished the original structure. The Bank purchased the bereft building in 1960 and rehabilitated it. The **Sing Chong Building** (Grant Ave. at California St.) was another 1906 quick-rebuild, the reconstruction beginning shortly after the ground stopped shuddering and the smoke cleared.

The **Golden Gate Fortune Cookie Company** (56 Ross Alley, 415/781-3956, daily 8 A.M.–8 P.M.) makes for a great stop, especially if you've brought the kids along. Heck, even if you're alone, the delicious aromas wafting from the building as you pass the alley on Jackson Street may draw you inside. Expect to have a tray of sample cookies pressed upon you as soon as you enter. Inside the factory, you'll see the cookies being folded into their traditional shapes by workers, but the best part of coming to the factory is checking out all the different types of fortune cookies therein. Yes, there are lots of kinds you'll never see on the tablecloth at a restaurant: chocolate and strawberry flavors, funky shapes, various sizes, and who can leave out the cookies with the X-rated fortunes.

© LANCE SCOTT

Asian architecture mixes with city buildings to create a unique skyscape.

Perfect to bring home and share with friends! Bags of cookies cost only $3–4, making them attractive souvenirs to pick up, though with their lovely scent, they might not make it all the way home with you!

## NORTH BEACH AND FISHERMAN'S WHARF

The Fisherman's Wharf and North Beach areas are an odd amalgam of old-school residential neighborhood and total tourist mecca. North Beach has long served as the Italian district of San Francisco and the restaurants in the area bear this out. Fisherman's Wharf was the spot where 19th-century Italians came to work; they were a big part of the fishing fleet that provided San Francisco with its legendary supply of fresh seafood.

Today, Fisherman's Wharf is *the* spot where tourists to San Francisco come to visit and snap photos. If you're not into crowds, avoid the area in the summertime. For visitors who can hack a ton of other people, some of the best views of the air show during Fleet Week and the fireworks on the Fourth of July can be found down on the Wharf.

### Alcatraz

Going to Alcatraz (www.nps.gov/alcatraz), one of the most famous landmarks in the City, feels a bit like going to purgatory; this military fortress turned maximum-security prison, nicknamed "The Rock," has little of warmth or welcome on its craggy forbidding shores. The fortress became a prison in the 19th century while it still belonged to the military, which used it to house Civil War prisoners. The isolation of the island in the Bay, the frigid waters, and the nasty currents surrounding Alcatraz made it a perfect spot to keep prisoners contained with little hope of escape and near-certain death if the attempt was ever made. In 1934, after the military closed down their prison and handed over the island to the Department of Justice, construction began to turn Alcatraz into a new style of prison ready to house a new style of prisoner: Depression-era gangsters. A few of the honored guests of

ROBERT HOLMES / CALTOUR

Alcatraz, also known as "The Rock"

this maximum-security penitentiary were Al Capone, George "Machine Gun" Kelly, and Robert Stroud ("the Birdman of Alcatraz"). The prison closed in 1963, and in both 1964 and 1969, occupations were staged by Indians of All Tribes, an exercise that led to the privilege of self-determination for North America's original inhabitants.

Today, Alcatraz acts primarily as a tourist attraction for visitors to San Francisco. **Alcatraz Cruises** (415/981-7625, www.alcatrazcruises.com, 9 A.M.–3:55 P.M., 6:15 and 6:50 P.M., adults $24.50–31.50, children $15.25–18.75) offers ferry rides out to Alcatraz and tours of the island and the prison. Tours depart daily from Pier 33. It's a good idea to buy tickets at least a week in advance, especially if you'll be in town in the summertime and want to visit Alcatraz on a weekend. Tours often sell out, especially evening tours. Be carefully after dark; the prison and the island are both said to be haunted!

## Fisherman's Wharf

Welcome to the tourist mecca of San Francisco! Just don't go looking for an actual wharf or single pier when you come to visit Fisherman's Wharf. In fact, the Fisherman's Wharf (Beach St. from Powell St. to Van Ness, backs onto Bay St., reachable by Muni F line, www.fishermanswharf.org) area sprawls along the waterfront and inland several blocks, creating a large tourist neighborhood. The Wharf—as it's called by locals, who avoid the area at all costs—features all crowds, all the time. Be prepared to push through a sea of humanity to see sights, buy souvenirs, and eat seafood. Fisherman's Wharf includes many of the sights that tourists come to San Francisco to see: Pier 39, Ghirardelli Square, and of course **The Wax Museum of Fisherman's Wharf** (145 Jefferson St., 800/653-9592, www.waxmuseum.com, adults $12.95, juniors $9.95, children $6.95), the presence of which tells most serious travelers all they need to know about the Wharf.

## Pier 39

One of the most-visited spots in San Francisco, Pier 39 hosts a wealth of restaurants and shops. If you've come down to the pier to see the sea life, start with the unusual **Aquarium of the Bay** (888/732-3483, www.aquariumofthebay.com, 9 A.M.–8 P.M. daily in summer, call for winter hours, $13.95 adults, $7 seniors, $7 children). This 300-foot clear-walled tunnel lets visitors see thousands of species native to the San Francisco Bay, including sharks, rays, and plenty of fish. For a special treat, take the

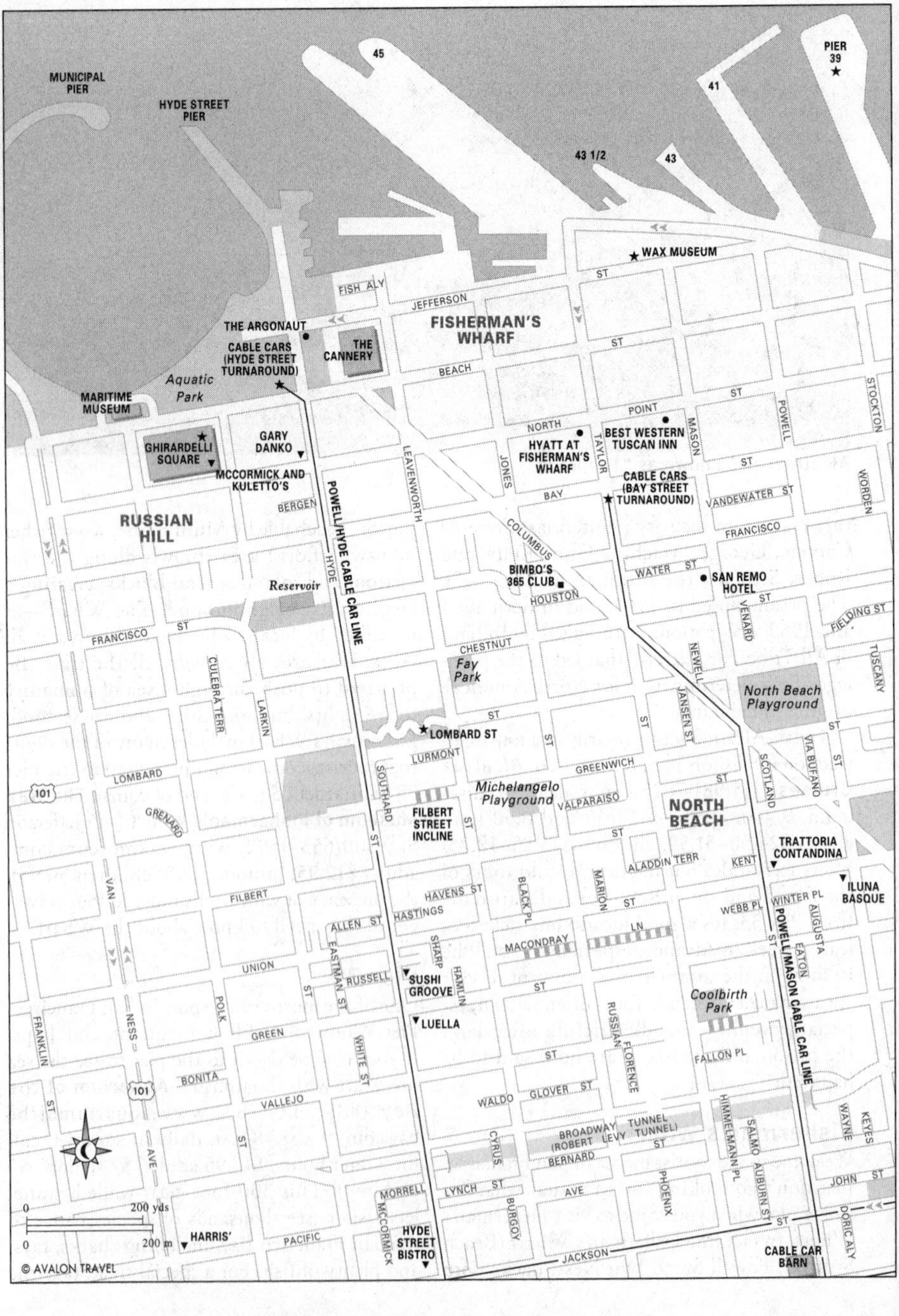
MUNICIPAL PIER
HYDE STREET PIER
45
41
PIER 39
43 1/2
43
WAX MUSEUM
FISH ALY
JEFFERSON ST
FISHERMAN'S WHARF
THE ARGONAUT
CABLE CARS (HYDE STREET TURNAROUND)
THE CANNERY
BEACH ST
Aquatic Park
MARITIME MUSEUM
GHIRARDELLI SQUARE
GARY DANKO
MCCORMICK AND KULETTO'S
POINT
NORTH
HYATT AT FISHERMAN'S WHARF
BEST WESTERN TUSCAN INN
CABLE CARS (BAY STREET TURNAROUND)
BAY ST
VANDEWATER ST
FRANCISCO
WATER ST
SAN REMO HOTEL
BIMBO'S 365 CLUB
HOUSTON
COLUMBUS
RUSSIAN HILL
BERGEN
Reservoir
POWELL/HYDE CABLE CAR LINE
FRANCISCO ST
CHESTNUT
Fay Park
FIELDING ST
North Beach Playground
LOMBARD ST
LURMONT
GREENWICH
Michelangelo Playground
VALPARAISO
FILBERT STREET INCLINE
NORTH BEACH
TRATTORIA CONTANDINA
ILUNA BASQUE
ALADDIN TERR
KENT
HAVENS ST
HASTINGS
ALLEN ST
WINTER PL
WEBB PL
MACONDRAY LN
SUSHI GROOVE
LUELLA
RUSSELL
Coolbirth Park
FALLON PL
POWELL/MASON CABLE CAR LINE
LOMBARD
GRENARD
FILBERT
UNION
GREEN
BONITA
VALLEJO
WALDO
GLOVER ST
BROADWAY TUNNEL (ROBERT LEVY TUNNEL)
BERNARD
MORRELL
LYNCH ST
JOHN ST
PACIFIC
HARRIS'
HYDE STREET BISTRO
JACKSON
CABLE CAR BARN
LEAVENWORTH
JONES
TAYLOR
MASON
POWELL
STOCKTON
WORDEN
TUSCANY
VIA BUFANO
SCOTLAND
JANSEN ST
NEWELL
VENARD
AUGUSTA
EATON
CULEBRA TERR
LARKIN
SOUTHARD
HYDE ST
EASTMAN ST
WHITE ST
SHARP
HAMLIN
BLACK PL
MARION
RUSSIAN
FLORENCE
HIMMELMANN PL
SALMO
AUBURN ST
WAYNE
KEYES
DORIC ALY
CYRUS
BURGOY
PHOENIX
MCCORMICK
POLK
VAN NESS AVE
FRANKLIN ST
101
0 200 yds
0 200 m
© AVALON TRAVEL

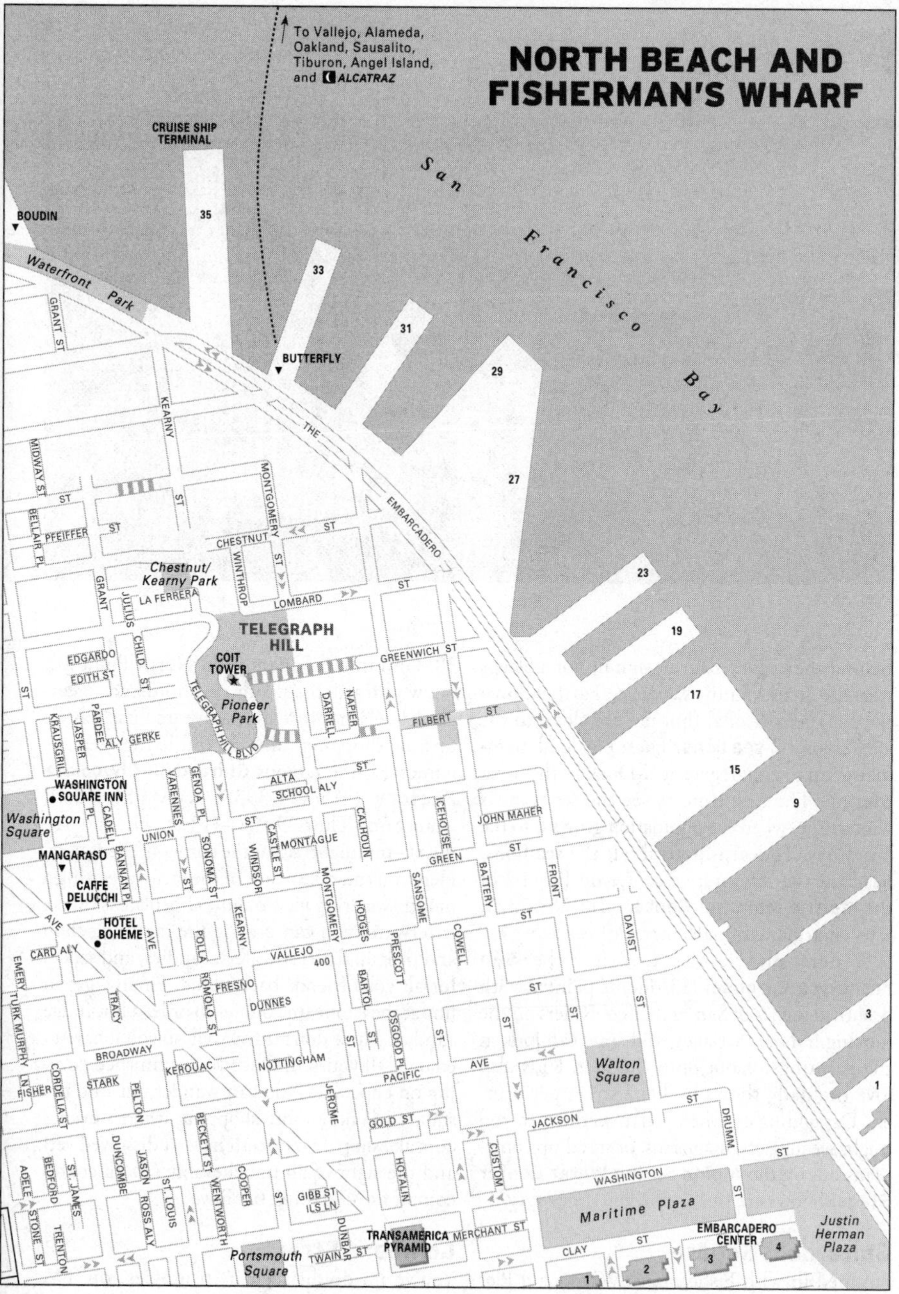
NORTH BEACH AND FISHERMAN'S WHARF
To Vallejo, Alameda, Oakland, Sausalito, Tiburon, Angel Island, and ALCATRAZ
San Francisco Bay
CRUISE SHIP TERMINAL
BOUDIN
BUTTERFLY
Waterfront Park
THE EMBARCADERO
35
33
31
29
27
23
19
17
15
9
3
1
GRANT ST
KEARNY ST
MIDWAY ST
BELLAIR PL
PFEIFFER ST
MONTGOMERY ST
CHESTNUT ST
Chestnut/Kearny Park
LA FERRERA
WINTHROP
LOMBARD ST
JULIUS
CHILD ST
TELEGRAPH HILL
COIT TOWER
GREENWICH ST
EDGARDO
EDITH ST
Pioneer Park
TELEGRAPH HILL BLVD
DARRELL
NAPIER
FILBERT ST
KRAUSGRILL
JASPER
PARDEE ALY
GERKE
WASHINGTON SQUARE INN
Washington Square
VARENNES
GENOA PL
ALTA ST
SCHOOL ALY
CALHOUN
ICEHOUSE
JOHN MAHER
CADELL PL
UNION ST
SONOMA ST
CASTLE ST
MONTAGUE
WINDSOR
MANGARASO
BANNAN PL
GREEN ST
SANSOME
BATTERY
FRONT
CAFFE DELUCCHI
HOTEL BOHÉME
COLUMBUS AVE
KEARNY
POLLA
HODGES
PRESCOTT
COWELL
DAVIST
VALLEJO ST
400
CARD ALY
EMERY
TURK MURPHY LN
TRACY
ROMOLO ST
FRESNO
DUNNES
BARTOL
OSGOOD PL
BROADWAY
KEROUAC
NOTTINGHAM
PACIFIC AVE
Walton Square
FISHER
CORDELIA ST
STARK
PELTON
JEROME
GOLD ST
JACKSON ST
DRUMM
DUNCOMBE
BEDFORD
ST. JAMES
JASON
ROSS ALY
ST. LOUIS
BECKETT ST
WENTWORTH
COOPER
HOTALING
CUSTOM
WASHINGTON ST
GIBB ST
ILS LN
Maritime Plaza
ADELE
STONE ST
TRENTON
TRANSAMERICA PYRAMID
MERCHANT ST
EMBARCADERO CENTER
Justin Herman Plaza
Portsmouth Square
TWAIN ST
DUNBAR
CLAY ST
1
2
3
4

© LANCE SCOTT

Pier 39

Behind the Scenes Tour or sign up for a Sleeps with the Sharks family sleepover. Farther down the pier, get personal (but not *too* close) to the local colony of **sea lions.** These big, loud mammals tend to congregate at K-Dock in the West Marina. The best time to see the sea lions is wintertime, when the population grows into the hundreds. To learn more about the sea lions, head for the interpretive center on Level 2 of the **Marine Mammal Center** (415/289-7325, www.marinemammalcenter.org).

A perennial family favorite, the **San Francisco Carousel** ($3/ride) is painted with beautiful scenes of San Francisco. Riders on the moving horses, carriages, and seats can look at the paintings or out onto the Pier. Kids also love the daily shows by local street performers. Depending on when you're on the Pier, you might see jugglers, magicians, or stand-up comedians out on the **Alpine Spring Water Center Stage.** Shows are free, and show times vary.

## Ghirardelli Square

Jammed in with Fisherman's Wharf and Pier 39, Ghirardelli Square (900 North Point St., www.ghirardellisq.com, pronounced "geer-ah-del-ee") has recently reinvented itself as an upscale shopping, dining, and living area. Its namesake, the famous **Ghirardelli Chocolate Factory** (415/474-3938, www.ghirardelli.com, Sun.–Thurs. 9 A.M.–11 P.M., Fri. and Sat. 9 A.M.–midnight) sits at the corner of the square. Here you can take a tour of the factory, getting a mouth-watering view of how chocolate is made. Afterward, you can browse the rambling shop and pick up truffles, wafers, candies, and sauces for all your friends back home. Finally, get in line at the ice cream counter to order a hot-fudge sundae. These don't travel well, so you'll have to enjoy it all yourself. Once you've finished gorging on chocolate, you can wander out into the square to enjoy more shopping (there's even a cupcake shop if your teeth haven't dissolved yet) and the sight of an unbelievably swank condo complex overlooking the Bay.

## Lombard Street

You've no doubt seen it in movies, on TV,

and on postcards: Lombard Street, otherwise known as "the crookedest street in the world." The truth is, Lombard Street is a major artery running through San Francisco. So, why bother braving the bumper-to-bumper cars navigating its zigzag turns? For one, you can't beat the view from the top. With its 27-percent grade, Lombard Street offers unobstructed vistas of San Francisco Bay, Alcatraz Island, Fisherman's Wharf, Coit Tower, and the city.

The part that visitors flock to spans only a block, from Hyde Street at the top to Leavenworth Street at the bottom. Lombard was originally created to keep people from rolling uncontrolled down the treacherously steep grade. Brave travelers can walk up and down the sides of the brick-paved street, enjoying the hydrangeas and Victorian mansions that line the roadway. For convenience during the peak summer months, take a cable car directly to the top of Lombard Street and walk down the non-curvy stairs on either side.

### Coit Tower

It's big, it's phallic, and it may or may not have been designed to look like a fire hose nozzle or a power station. But since 1933, Coit Tower (1 Telegraph Hill Blvd., 415/362-0808, daily 10 A.M.–7 P.M., call for tour times) has beautified the City just as benefactor Lillie Hitchcock Coit intended when she willed San Francisco one-third of her monumental estate. Inside, murals depicting city life and works of the 1930s cover the walls. From the top of the tower on a clear day, you can see the whole of the City and the Bay. Part of what makes Coit Tower special is the walks up to it. Rather than contributing to acute congestion in the area, consider taking public transit to the area and walking up the Filbert Steps to the tower. It's steep, but there's no other way to see the lovely little cottages and gardens that mark the path up from the streets to the top of Telegraph Hill.

## MARINA AND PACIFIC HEIGHTS

The Marina and Pacific Heights shelter some of the amazing amount of money that flows in the City by the Bay. The Marina is one of the San Francisco neighborhoods constructed on landfill (sand dredged up from the bottom of the ocean and piled in what was once a marsh). It was badly damaged in the 1989 Loma Prieta earthquake, but you won't see any of that damage today. Instead, you'll find a wealthy neighborhood, a couple of yacht harbors, and lots of good museums, dining, and shopping.

### Palace of Fine Arts

The Palace of Fine Arts (Bay and Lyon Sts., 415/567-6642, www.nps.gov) was originally meant to be nothing but a temporary structure—part of the Panama Pacific Exposition in 1915. But the lovely structure won the hearts of San Franciscans, and a fund was started to preserve the Palace beyond the Exposition. Through the first half of the 20th century efforts could not keep it from crumbling, but in the 1960s and '70s, serious rebuilding work took place, and today the Palace of Fine Arts stands proud and strong and beautiful. It houses the Palace of Fine Arts Theater, which hosts events nearly every day, from beauty pageants to conferences on the future of artificial intelligence. It also houses the Exploratorium.

### ☾ Exploratorium

Kids around the Bay Area have loved the Exploratorium (3601 Lyon St., www.exploratorium.edu, Tues.–Sun. 10 A.M.–5 P.M. plus some Mon. holidays, adults $14, youth and students $11, children $9) for decades. This innovative museum makes science the funnest thing ever for kids of all ages—though adults are welcome to join in on the interactive exhibits too! Here you can learn about everything from frogs to the physics of baseball, sound to seismology; the Exploratorium seeks to be true to its name and encourage exploration into all aspects of science. For an utterly unusual experience, pay an extra $3 and walk bravely (and blindly) into the Tactile Dome, a lightless space where you can "see" your way only by reaching out and touching the environment around you.

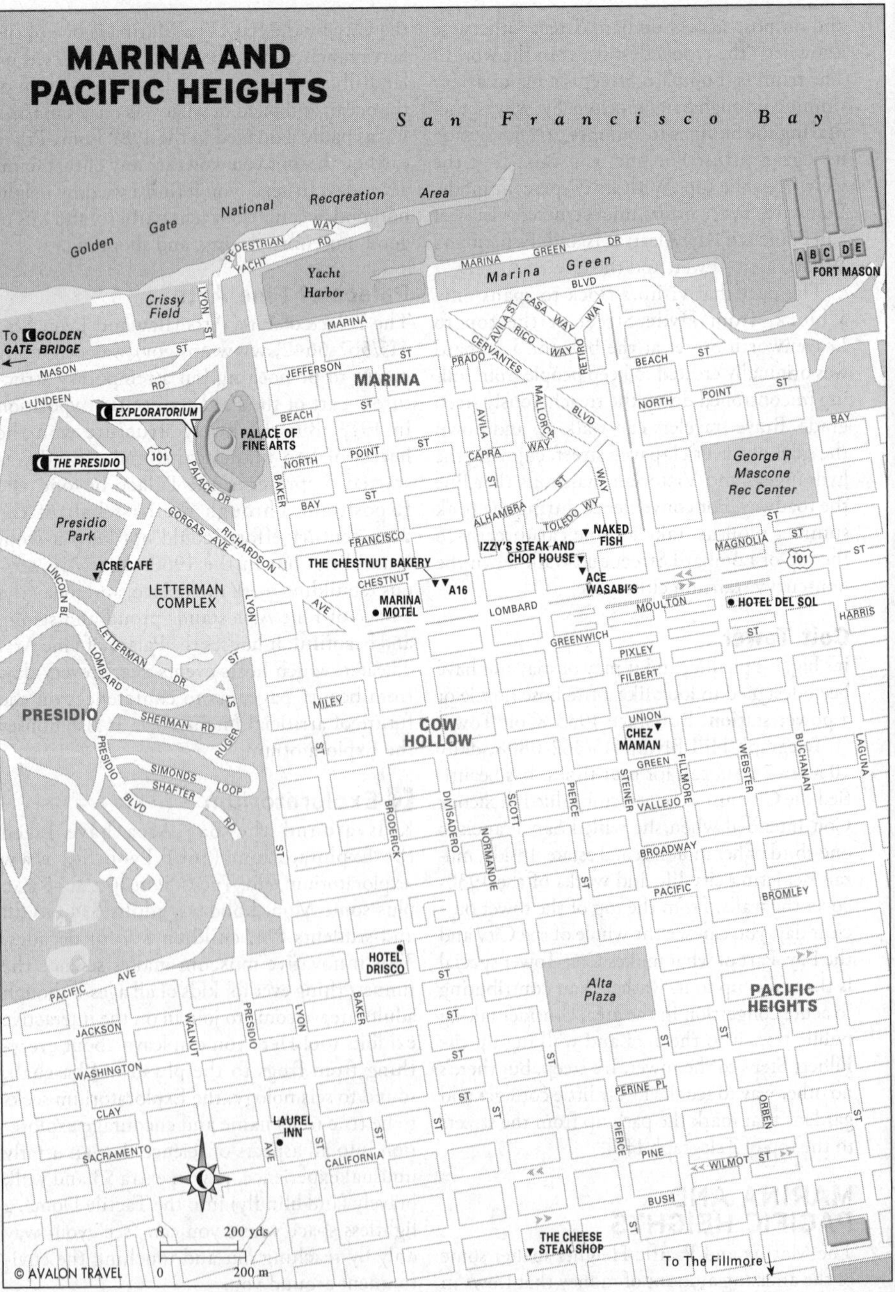
MARINA AND PACIFIC HEIGHTS
San Francisco Bay
Golden Gate National Recqreation Area
Yacht Harbor
Marina Green
Crissy Field
FORT MASON
A B C D E
To GOLDEN GATE BRIDGE
EXPLORATORIUM
THE PRESIDIO
PALACE OF FINE ARTS
MARINA
Presidio Park
ACRE CAFÉ
LETTERMAN COMPLEX
PRESIDIO
THE CHESTNUT BAKERY
A16
MARINA MOTEL
IZZY'S STEAK AND CHOP HOUSE
NAKED FISH
ACE WASABI'S
HOTEL DEL SOL
George R Mascone Rec Center
COW HOLLOW
CHEZ MAMAN
HOTEL DRISCO
Alta Plaza
PACIFIC HEIGHTS
LAUREL INN
THE CHEESE STEAK SHOP
To The Fillmore
0 200 yds
0 200 m
© AVALON TRAVEL

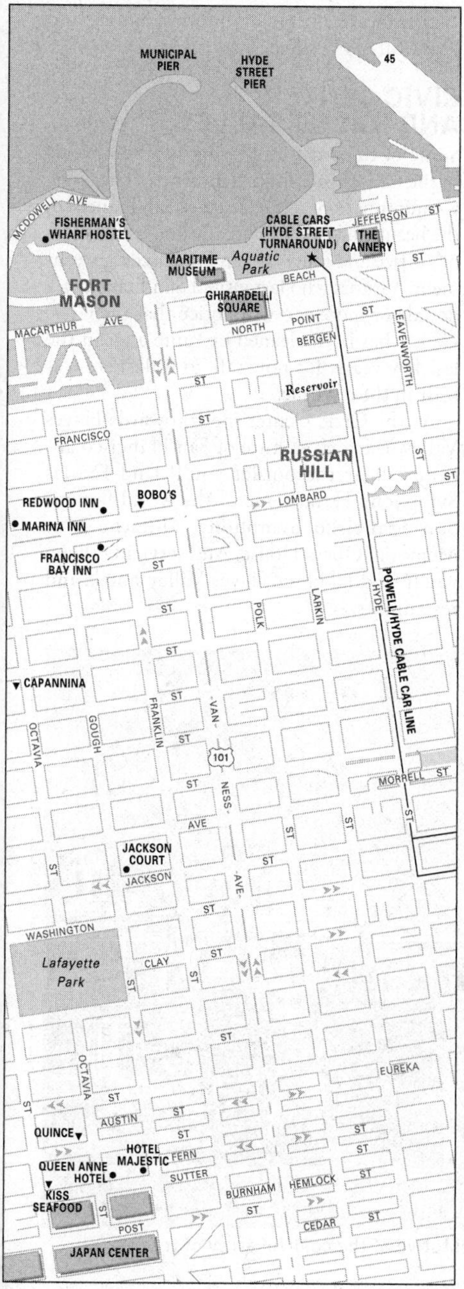


## Fort Mason

Once the Port of Embarkation from which the United States waged World War II in the Pacific, Fort Mason Center (Buchanan St. and Marina Blvd., www.fortmason.org) now acts as home to numerous nonprofit, multicultural, and artistic organizations. Where soldiers and guns departed to fight the Japanese, now visitors find dance performances, independent theatrical productions, art galleries, and the annual **San Francisco Blues Festival** (www.sfblues.com). At any time of year, a number of great shows go on in the renovated historic white and red buildings of the complex; check the online calendar to see what's coming up during your visit.

## The Presidio

It seems strange to think of progressive, peace-loving San Francisco as a town with tremendous military history. Yet the City's warlike past is nowhere more evident than at the Presidio (foot of Lombard St., www.nps.gov/prsf). This sweeping stretch of land running along the San Francisco Headlands down to the Golden Gate has been a military installation since 1776, when the Spanish created their El Presidio del San Francisco fort on the site. In 1846, the United States army took the site (peacefully) and in 1848 the American Presidio military installation formally opened for business. It was finally abandoned by the military and became a national park in 1994. The Presidio had a role in every Pacific-touching war from the Civil War through Desert Storm.

To orient yourself among the more than 800 buildings that make up the Presidio, start at the **visitors center** at the Officers' Club, Building 50 (Moraga Ave. near Arguello Blvd., 415/561-4323, daily 9 A.M.–5 P.M.). As you explore the huge park, you can visit pioneering aviation area **Crissy Field,** Civil War–era fortifications at **Fort Point,** and the **Letterman Digital Arts Center** (Chesnut and Lyon Sts., www.lucasfilm.com) built on the site of the Letterman Army Hospital, which served as a top-notch care facility for returning wounded and ailing soldiers over more than a century's worth of wars.

### Golden Gate Bridge

People come from the world over to see and walk the Golden Gate Bridge (Hwy. 101/Hwy.1 at Lincoln Blvd., http://goldengatebridge.org, $6 toll for cars). A marvel of human engineering constructed in 1936 and 1937, the suspension bridge spans the narrow "gate" from which the Pacific Ocean enters the San Francisco Bay. On a clear day, walkers can see the whole Bay from the east sidewalk, then turn around to see the Pacific Ocean spreading out on the other. The bridge itself is not golden, but a rich orange color called "international orange" that shines like gold when the sun sets behind it on a clear evening. But newcomers to the City beware—not all days and precious few evenings at the bridge are clear. One of the most beautiful sights in San Francisco is the fog blowing in over the Golden Gate late in the afternoon. Unfortunately, once the fog stops blowing and settles in, the bridge is cold, damp, and viewless. So plan to come early in the morning, or pick the springtime or the fall for your best chance of a clear sight of this most famous and beautiful of manmade structures.

## CIVIC CENTER AND HAYES VALLEY

Some of the most interesting neighborhoods in the City cluster toward its center. The Civic Center functions as the heart of San Francisco; the beautiful building actually houses the mayor's office and much of San Francisco's government. Visitors who last visited San Francisco a decade or more ago will notice that the Civic Center has been cleaned up quite a lot in the last few years. It's now safe to walk here—at least in the daytime.

As the Civic Center melts towards Hayes Valley, the high culture of San Francisco appears. Near the border you'll find Davies Symphony Hall, home of the world-famous San Francisco Symphony, and the War Memorial Opera House. And servicing these, you'll find fabulous Hayes Valley hotels and restaurants.

SAN FRANCISCO CONVENTION & VISITORS BUREAU PHOTO BY PHILLIP H. COBLENTZ

**The beautiful row of "painted ladies" is representative of the colorful array of traditional Victorian houses in San Francisco.**

### City Hall

Look at San Francisco's City Hall (1 Dr. Carleton B. Goodlett Pl., www.sfgov.org, Mon.–Fri. 8 A.M.–8 P.M.) and you'll think you've somehow been transported to Europe. The stately building with the gilded dome is the pride of the City, and houses much of its government. Enjoy walking through the park-like square in front of City Hall (though this area can get a bit sketchy after dark). The inside has been extensively renovated after being damaged in the Loma Prieta earthquake in 1989. You'll find a combination of historical grandeur and modern accessibility and convenience as you tour the Arthur Brown Jr.–designed edifice.

### Alamo Square

Possibly the most photographed neighborhood in San Francisco, Alamo Square (Hayes and Steiner Sts.) is home to the "painted ladies" on "postcard row." These are a row of stately Victorian mansions, all immaculately maintained, that appear in images of the City. Stroll in Alamo Square's green park and enjoy the serenity of this charming residential neighborhood.

## MISSION AND CASTRO

Perhaps the most famous, or infamous, neighborhoods in the City are the Mission district and the Castro district. The Castro is the heart of Gay San Francisco, complete with leather shops, bars, and all sorts of fun festivals. It's become pretty touristy, but you can still find the occasional jewel here. Just don't expect the Halloween party you've heard about—the City law has cracked down and Halloween has become sedate in this party-happy neighborhood.

With its mix of Latino immigrants, working artists, and SUV-driving professionals, the Mission is a neighborhood bursting at the seams with idiosyncratic energy. Changing from block to block, the zone manages to be blue-collar, edgy, and gentrified all at once. The heart of the neighborhood is still very much Latin American, with delicious burritos and *pupusas* around every corner. It's a haven for ethnic restaurants and real bargains in thrift shops, as well as the hippest (and most self-conscious) clubs in the City.

### Mission Dolores

Mission Dolores (3321 16th St., 415/621-8203, www.missiondolores.org, daily May–Oct. 9 A.M.–4:30 P.M., Nov.–Apr. 9 A.M.–4 P.M.), formally named Mission San Francisco des Asis, was founded in 1776. Today, the Mission is the oldest intact building in the City, survivor of the 1906 earthquake and fire, the 1989 Loma Prieta quake, and more than 200 years of use. You can attend Catholic services here each Sunday. Or you can visit the Old Mission Museum and the Basilica, which houses artifacts from the Native Americans and Spanish of the 18th century. The beauty and grandeur of the Mission recall the heyday of the Spanish empire in California, so important to the history of the state as it is today.

## GOLDEN GATE PARK AND THE HAIGHT

Perhaps the most spectacular "sight" in Golden Gate Park is, well, Golden Gate Park (main entrance at Stanyan St. at Fell St., McLaren Lodge Visitor Center at JFK Dr., 415/831-2700, www.golden-gate-park.com). Acres of land roll from forest to desert to formal garden to museum to buffalo pasture. Enjoy a free concert in the summertime, or a walk under the trademark fog in the summertime.

Haight-Ashbury (locally known as "the Haight") is best known for the wave of counterculture energy that broke here in the 1960s. The area became a magnet for drifters, dropouts, and visionaries who preached (and practiced) a heady blend of peace, love, and psychedelic drugs. If the door to the promised new consciousness never swung fully open, it nevertheless remains ajar here today, where head shops and tie-dye emporiums hold their own amid an influx of upscale boutiques.

### de Young Museum

Haven't been to the City in a while? Then take some time out to visit the completely rebuilt de Young Museum (50 Hagiwara Tea Garden

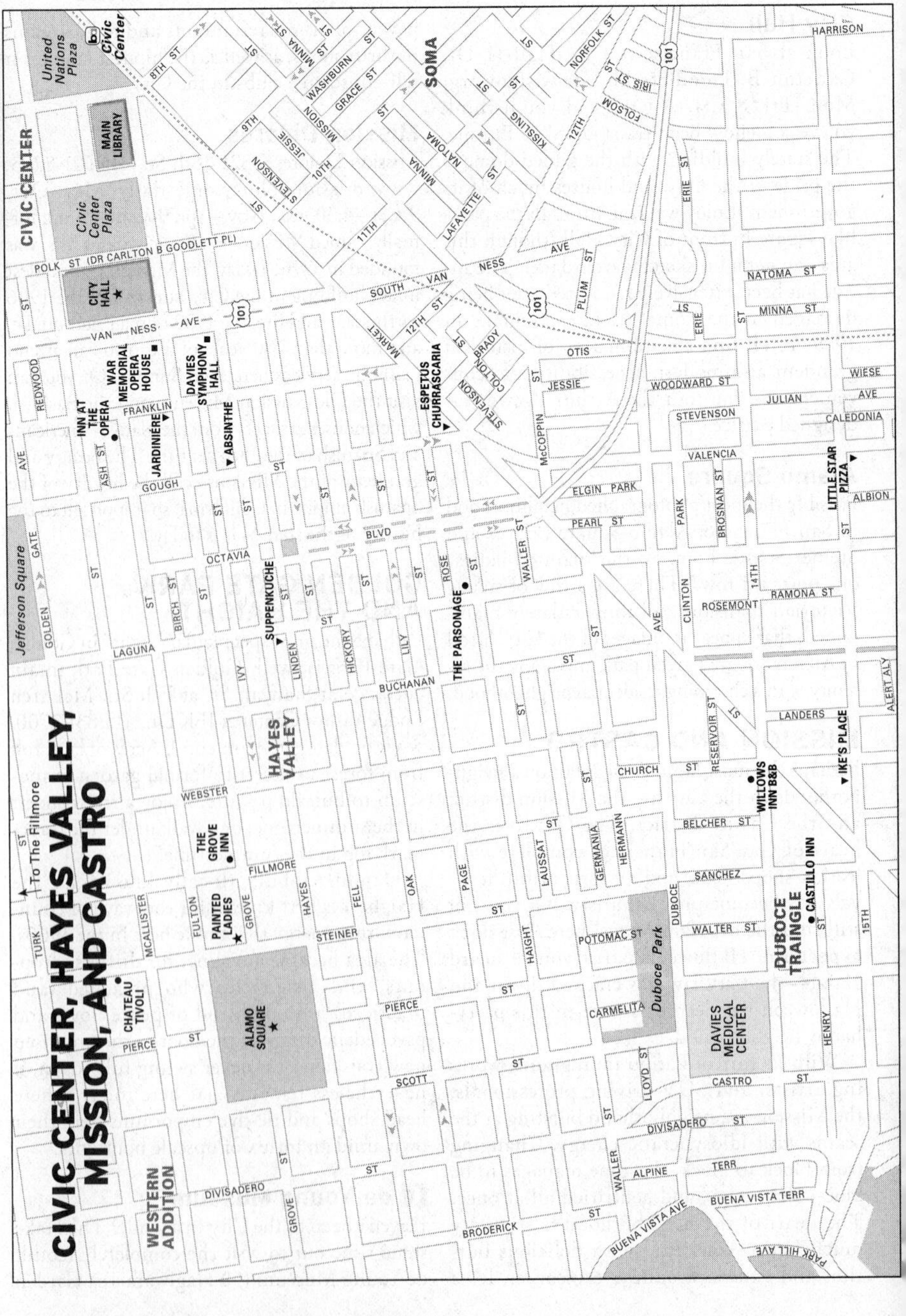
CIVIC CENTER, HAYES VALLEY, MISSION, AND CASTRO
To The Fillmore
CIVIC CENTER
United Nations Plaza
Civic Center
MAIN LIBRARY
Civic Center Plaza
CITY HALL
POLK ST (DR CARLTON B GOODLETT PL)
VAN NESS AVE
SOUTH VAN NESS AVE
WAR MEMORIAL OPERA HOUSE
DAVIES SYMPHONY HALL
INN AT THE OPERA
JARDINIERE
ABSINTHE
ESPETUS CHURRASCARIA
SOMA
SUPPENKUCHE
THE PARSONAGE
HAYES VALLEY
THE GROVE INN
PAINTED LADIES
CHATEAU TIVOLI
ALAMO SQUARE
WESTERN ADDITION
Jefferson Square
Duboce Park
DUBOCE TRAINGLE
DAVIES MEDICAL CENTER
WILLOWS INN B&B
CASTILLO INN
IKE'S PLACE
LITTLE STAR PIZZA
MARKET ST
MISSION
HAYES
FELL
OAK
PAGE
HAIGHT
GOUGH
OCTAVIA BLVD
LAGUNA
BUCHANAN
WEBSTER
FILLMORE
STEINER
PIERCE
SCOTT
DIVISADERO
BRODERICK
GROVE
FULTON
MCALLISTER
TURK
GOLDEN GATE AVE
REDWOOD
FRANKLIN
ASH ST
IVY
LINDEN
HICKORY
LILY
ROSE
BIRCH
WALLER
LAUSSAT
GERMANIA
HERMANN
POTOMAC ST
CARMELITA
LLOYD ST
ALPINE TERR
BUENA VISTA TERR
BUENA VISTA AVE
PARK HILL AVE
CHURCH
SANCHEZ
BELCHER ST
WALTER ST
DUBOCE
CASTRO
HENRY
15TH
14TH
LANDERS
ALERT ALY
RESERVOIR ST
ROSEMONT
RAMONA ST
CLINTON PARK
BROSNAN ST
ELGIN PARK
PEARL ST
McCOPPIN
VALENCIA
ALBION
STEVENSON
JULIAN AVE
CALEDONIA
WIESE
WOODWARD ST
OTIS
JESSIE
BRADY
COLTON
12TH ST
11TH
10TH
9TH
8TH ST
LAFAYETTE
NATOMA
MINNA
KISSLING
12TH
FOLSOM
IRIS ST
NORFOLK ST
HARRISON
PLUM ST
ERIE ST
WASHBURN
GRACE ST
MINNA ST
101

MISSION
16th St
24th St
MISSION DOLORES
INN ON CASTRO
RANDALL MUSEUM
DELFINA
ANCHOR OYSTER BAR
CASTRO
NOE VALLEY
Dolores Park
TREAT
FOLSOM
SHOTWELL
SOUTH VAN NESS AVE
CAPP
MISSION ST
SAN CARLOS ST
LEXINGTON ST
VALENCIA ST
GUERRERO ST
DOLORES ST
CHURCH ST
SANCHEZ ST
NOE ST
CASTRO ST
DIAMOND ST
DOUGLASS ST
HOFF ST
RONDEL PL
CLARION ALY
SYCAMORE ST
ALBION ST
CAMP ST
DEARBORN
BIRD ST
LAPIDGE ST
LINDA ST
OAKWOOD ST
CUMBERLAND ST
DOLORES TERR
DORLAND ST
ABBEY ST
CHULA LN
16TH ST
17TH ST
18TH ST
19TH ST
20TH ST
21ST ST
22ND ST
23RD ST
24TH ST
25TH ST
LIBERTY ST
HILL ST
ALVARADO ST
AMES ST
QUANE ST
FAIR OAKS ST
SAN JOSE AVE
ELIZABETH ST
BARTLETT ST
LUCKY ST
CYPRESS ST
LILAC ST
OSAGE ALY
ORANGE ALY
POPLAR ST
MERSEY ST
CHATTANOOGA ST
SEVERN ST
NELLIE ST
VICKSBURG ST
BLANCHE ST
RAYBURN ST
JERSEY ST
HANCOCK ST
FORD ST
PROSPER ST
POND ST
HARTFORD ST
COLLINGWOOD ST
EUREKA ST
MARKET ST
BEAVER ST
FLINT ST
STATES ST
MUSEUM WAY
ENTERPRISE ST
300 yds
300 m
0
0
© AVALON TRAVEL

Dr., 415/750-3600, www.famsf.org/deyoung, Tues.–Sun. 9:30 A.M.–5:15 P.M., Fri. until 8:45 P.M., adults $10, children $6) in Golden Gate Park. Everything from the striking exterior, to the art collections and exhibitions, to the 360-degree panoramic view of San Francisco from the top of the tower have been renewed, reborn, replaced, or newly re-created. The reason for the recent renewal was the 1989 earthquake, which damaged the original de Young beyond simple repair. The renovation took more than 10 years, and the results are a smashing success. For a special treat, brave the lines and grab a meal at the museum's café.

The collections at the de Young include works of varying media: painting, sculpture, textiles, ceramics, and more modern graphic designs and "contemporary crafts." Some collections focus on artists from the United States, while many others contain art from around the world. The exhibitions that come through the de Young range from the William Morris Art

Nouveau art from Britain to the exquisite glass of the Chihuly collection. There's something for just about everyone here—even classic art purists who eschew SFMOMA will find a gallery to love inside the de Young.

## Japanese Tea Garden

The Japanese Tea Garden (Golden Gate Park, summer daily 8:30 A.M.–6 P.M., winter daily 8:30 A.M.–5 P.M.) is a haven of peace and tranquility that's a local favorite within the park. The planting and design of the garden began in 1894 for the California Exposition. Today the flourishing garden displays a wealth of beautiful flora, including stunning examples of rare Chinese and Japanese plants, some quite old. As you stroll along the paths, you'll come upon sculpture, bridges, ponds, and even traditional *tsukubai* (a tea ceremony sink). If that's your taste, you can visit the tea house, the brilliant pagoda and temple, and the gift shop as well.

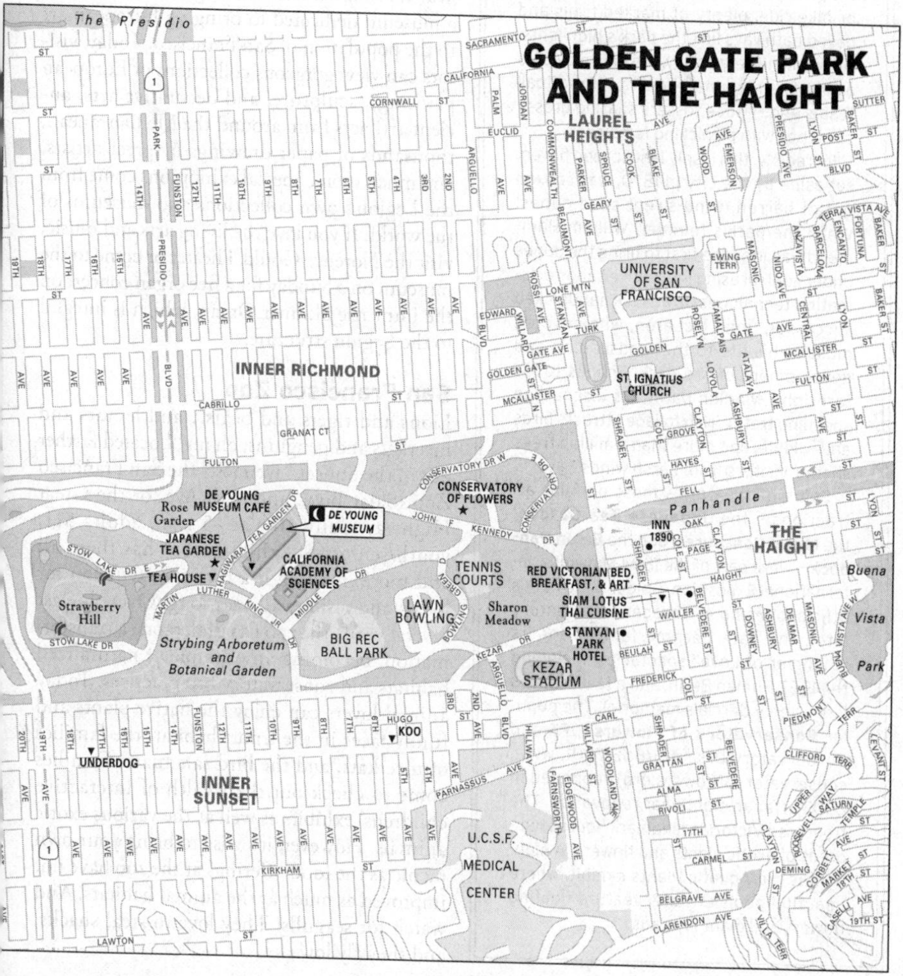

## GREENING THE CITY

Encompassing more than 1,000 acres of meadows, lakes, forests, and exotic gardens, Golden Gate Park provides plenty of refreshing green space and amusements for the urban dwellers and visitors it serves. Extending from Haight-Ashbury for more than three miles to the Pacific Ocean, the park makes a great spot for a long walk or bike ride; plenty of marked trails and paved pathways link the park's highlights. On weekends especially, the entire place is a hub of recreational pursuits, with softball teams and Frisbee tossers sharing grassy stretches with picnicking families.

Incredibly, this lushly landscaped haven, set aside by the city in 1870, was coaxed out of barren, wind-swept sand dunes. While the park's founder, William Hammond Hall, was the first to bring the dunes under control using innovative sand-reclamation techniques, it was his handpicked successor, John McLaren, who devoted most of his life to the landscaping and development of the park. Thanks to his foresight, winding pathways discourage speeding traffic, rich foliage attracts birds and wildlife, and more than a million trees shelter visitors from harsh winds.

Some of the park's most popular attractions – the **Japanese Tea Garden,** the **Music Concourse,** and the **Bison Paddock** – were part of the 1894 Midwinter International Exposition, Golden Gate Park's official opening extravaganza. A century later, the park became famous for its "Summer of Love" spectacles, including the 1967 Human Be-In, and a few decades later, Jerry Garcia's memorial. The popular **Conservatory of Flowers** (JFK and Conservatory Drs., 415/666-7001, www.conservatoryofflowers.org) reopened in 2003 after an eight-year renovation. The treasured Victorian landmark houses hundreds of exotic plants and flowers. A highlight is the Aquatic Plants exhibit, where beautiful pools of water feature floating flowers and giant lily pads.

### The Legion of Honor

A beautiful museum in a town filled with beauty, The Legion of Honor (near 34th Ave. and Clement St., 415/750-3600, www.famsf.org/legion, Tues.–Sun. 9:30 A.M.–5:15 P.M., adults $10, seniors $7, youth $6) sits on its lonely promontory in Lincoln Park, overlooking the Golden Gate. A gift to the City from philanthropist Alma Spreckels in 1924, this French beaux arts–style building was built to honor the memory of California soldiers who died in World War I. From the first, the Legion of Honor was a museum dedicated to bringing European art to the population of San Francisco. Today, visitors can view gorgeous collections of European paintings, sculpture, and decorative arts, ancient artifacts from around the Mediterranean, thousands of paper drawings by great artists, and much more. Special exhibitions come from the Legion's own collections and museums of the world. If you love the living arts and music, visit the Florence Gould Theater or come to the museum on a Sunday for a free organ concert on the immense Skinner Organ, which is integral to the Legion structure.

### San Francisco Zoo

Lions and tigers and bears...and lemurs and meerkats and penguins, oh my! Located farther out in the Sunset "avenues," the San Francisco Zoo (Sloat Blvd. and 47th Ave. or the Great Highway, daily 10 A.M.–5 P.M., adults $11, youth/seniors $8, children $5) has them all and more, making it a favorite excursion for locals and visitors all year long. Over the last several years, the zoo has undergone a transformation, becoming an example of naturalized habitats and conservatory zoo practices. Today animal-lovers can enjoy the native plants and funny faces in the lemur habitat, the families of meerkats, and the bird sanctuary. Families come to check out the wealth of interactive childrens' exhibits as well as the various exotic animals. However, it's wise to bring your own picnic as the food offerings at the zoo have not improved as much as the animal habitats. And watch for seagulls! They love to steal snacks, and they fly low.

# Entertainment and Events



## NIGHTLIFE

### Bars

#### UNION SQUARE AND NOB HILL

These ritzy areas are better known for their shopping than their nightlife, but a few bars hang in there, plying weary shoppers with good drinks. Most tend toward the upscale. Some inhabit upper floors of the major hotels, like the **Tonga Room and Hurricane Bar** (950 Mason St., 415/772-5278, www.fairmont.com, Sun.–Thurs. 5 P.M.–11:45 P.M., Fri.–Sat. 5 P.M.–12:45 A.M.), where an over-the-top tiki theme adds a whimsical touch to the stately Fairmont Hotel on Nob Hill. Enjoy the tropical atmosphere with a fruity rum drink topped with a classic paper umbrella.

Just outside the Union Square area in the sketchy Tenderloin neighborhood, lucky brave souls find a gem. **Café Royale** (800 Post St., 415/441-4099, www.caferoyale-sf.com, Sun.–Thurs. 4 P.M.–midnight, Fri.–Sat. 4 P.M.–2 A.M.) isn't a typical watering hole by any city's standards, but its intense focus on art fits in perfectly with the endlessly eclectic ethos of San Francisco. Local artists exhibit their work in the Café Royale on a monthly basis, and plenty of live performers grace the space. Live music tends toward the folksy and indie unplugged. In amongst the artwork some liquor lurks—think trendy sake and soju cocktails, good glasses of wine, and imported beers. The menu includes French sandwiches, gourmet salads, and small plates.

Part live music venue, part elegant bar, **Top of the Mark** (InterContinental Mark Hopkins, 999 California St., 415/616-6916, www.topofthemark.com, Sun.–Thurs. 5 P.M.–midnight, Fri.–Sat 4 P.M.–1 A.M.) has something for every discerning taste in nighttime entertainment. Since World War II, the views and drinks in this wonderful lounge at the top of the InterContinental Mark Hopkins hotel have drawn visitors from around the world. The lounge doubles as a restaurant that serves breakfast and lunch, but the best time for cocktails is of course at night. That's when live bands play almost every night of the week. Dress code is business casual or better, and is enforced, so leave the jeans in your room. Have a top-shelf martini and let your toes tap along!

A classic American bar and restaurant, **Lefty O'Doul's** (333 Geary St., 415/982-8900, www.leftyodouls.biz, daily 7 A.M.–2 A.M.) offers one of the biggest selections of liquor in the Union Square area, along with plenty of on-tap beers and inexpensive Woodbridge wines. Stop in and enjoy a pint, and maybe a good American meal while you're at it.

Do you love the color red? Then the best place in the City to grab a drink is no doubt **The Red Room** (827 Sutter St., 415/346-7666, Mon.–Sat 5 P.M.–2 A.M., Sun. 7 P.M.–2 A.M.). The decor can best be described as *red,* right down to the speaker system. The crowd tends toward the young and single, and they type to enjoy a mellower vibe than what's found in some of the louder local clubs. The small room fills up quickly, so come early if you want to grab a seat and stay a while.

#### FINANCIAL DISTRICT AND SOMA

All those high-powered, business suit–clad executive types working in the Financial District need places to drink too. One of these is the **Royal Exchange** (301 Sacramento St., 415/956-1710, www.royalexchange.com, Mon.–Fri. 11 A.M.–11 P.M.). This classic pub-style bar has a green-painted exterior, big windows overlooking the street, and a long narrow barroom. The Royal Exchange serves a full lunch and dinner menu, a small wine list, and a full complement of top-shelf spirits. But most of all, the Exchange serves beer. With 73 taps pouring out 32 different types of beer, the hardest problem will be choosing one. This businessman's watering hole is open to the public on weekdays only—on weekends they host private parties only.

Looking for something a bit more chic in an upscale downtown bar? Order your favorite top-shelf vodka at **Voda** (56 Belden Pl., 415/677-9242, www.vodasf.com, Mon.–Fri. 4:30 P.M.–2 A.M., Sat.–Sun. 7 P.M.–2 A.M.). Tucked away in one of the City's many little alleys, Voda brings a taste of the luxury vodka lounge to the Financial District. Inside, the decor runs to stark white walls and bright red banquettes and settees, lit with blue to complete the ultra-modern streamlined effect. Any vodka lover will be amazed by the fabulous list of popular and arcane vodkas from around the world—and a few from right nearby. (Hangar One comes from Alameda across the Bay, and Skyy originates right here in San Francisco.) A true drinking establishment, Voda doesn't offer a dinner menu—just a few light snacks. Voda attracts two distinct crowds: the after-work crowd in the early evening and young urban partiers later at night. DJs start spinning late, and a dance floor offers space to sweat out the vodka to make room for more.

**The Cosmopolitan Café** (121 Spear St., Ste. B8, 415/543-4001, www.thecosmopolitancafe.com, Mon.–Sat. 6 P.M.–2 A.M.) offers the best of both worlds: a bar and piano lounge serving top-shelf liquors and reasonably priced well drinks, and a large dining room serving an ever-changing California cuisine menu. You're more than welcome to enjoy drinks only at the bar, or make a reservation for a complete upscale dinner in the restaurant. If you're lucky, you might even get some live entertainment from a local musician plying the lounge piano.

In recently urban-renewed South of Market (SoMa to the locals), upscale wine bars are all the rage. Among the trendiest you'll find **District** (216 Townsend, 415/896-2120, www.districtsf.com, Mon.–Sat. 5 P.M.–2 A.M.). A perfect example of its kind, District features bare-brick walls, simple wooden furniture, and a big U-shaped bar at the center of the room with wine glasses hanging above it. While you can get a cocktail or even a beer here, the point of coming to District is to sip the finest wines from California, Europe, and beyond. With more than 30 wines available by the glass each night, it's easy to find a favorite, or enjoy a "flight" of three similar wines to compare. While you can't quite get a full dinner at District, you will find a lovely lounge menu filled with small portions of delicacies to enhance your tasting experience (and perhaps soak up some of the alcohol).

## CHINATOWN

Nightlife in Chinatown runs to dark, quiet dive bars filled with locals. Perhaps the perfect Chinatown dive, **Li Po Lounge** (916 Grant Ave., 415/982-0072, daily 2 P.M.–2 A.M., cash only) has an appropriately dark and slightly spooky atmosphere that recalls the opium dens of another century. Cheap drinks and Chinese dice games attract locals, and it's definitely helpful to speak Cantonese. But even an English-speaking out-of-town visitor can get a good cheap (and strong!) mai-tai or a beer here. The hanging lantern and Buddha statue behind the bar complete the picture.

**Red's Place** (672 Jackson St., 415/956-4490, cash only) is the oldest bar in Chinatown. It's a classic dive filled with hard-drinking, hard-smoking, hard-gambling locals, but visitors can come for an inexpensive, quiet drink and a taste of the "real" Chinatown most tourists never see. Another great local hangout worth checking out is the **Buddha Cocktail Lounge** (901 Grant Ave., 415/362-1792, daily 1 P.M.–2 A.M.).

## NORTH BEACH AND FISHERMAN'S WHARF

For a good time down on the Wharf, you can choose from a number of popular bars. **Rosewood** (732 Broadway, 415/951-4886, www.rosewoodbar.com, Mon.–Sat. 5 P.M.–2 A.M.) glows with namesake wood paneling and soft lighting. Join the young, hip, urban crowd and sip a specialty cocktail, or quaff a draft beer inside the bar or out on the bamboo-strewn patio. A popular hangout, Rosewood can get crowded (and service can get spotty) on weekends.

One of the oldest and most celebrated bars in the City, **Tosca** (242 Columbus Ave.,

415/986-9651, Tues.–Sat. 5 P.M.–2 A.M., Sun. 5 P.M.–midnight) loves its unpretentious yet glam 1940s style. Hunter S. Thompson once tended bar here when the owner was out at the dentist. The jukebox plays grand opera to the patrons clustered in the big red booths. Locals love the lack of trendiness, the classic cocktails, and the occasional star sightings.

Dress up a little for a night out at **15 Romolo** (15 Romolo Pl., 415/398-1359, daily 5:30 P.M.–2 A.M.). You'll have to hike up the steep little alley (Fresno Street crosses Romolo, which can be a little hard to find) to this hotel bar, but once you're there you'll love the fab cosmos, edgy jukebox music, and often-mellow crowd. The bar is smallish and can get crowded on the weekends, so come on a weeknight if you prefer a quiet drink.

If you prefer pool and a plasma big-screen showing sports, head for **Gino & Carlo** (548 Green St., 415/421-0896, daily 6 A.M.–2 A.M.), an Italian sports bar in the heart of North Beach. Buy a huge beer or moderate cocktail, yell at the football and baseball games, and enjoy being part of the local crowd.

## MARINA AND PACIFIC HEIGHTS

Marina and Pacific Heights denizens enjoy a good glass of vino, and the wine bars in the area cater to local tastes. The **Bacchus Wine Bar** (1954 Hyde St., 415/928-2633, nightly 5:30 P.M.–2 A.M.) is a tiny local watering hole that offers an array of wines, sake cocktails, and even delivered-to-your-table sushi from nearby Sushi Groove. DJs sometimes spin on Thursday and Friday nights. For a high-end wine experience, visit **Nectar Wine Lounge** (3330 Steiner St., 415/345-1377, www.nectarwinelounge.com, Mon.–Thurs. 5 P.M.–10:30 P.M., Fri.–Sat. 5 P.M.–midnight, Sun. 3 P.M.–10 P.M.). Choose from an ever-changing menu of 50 wines by the glass, or order one of the 800-plus bottles on the list. An intricate menu of small plates complements the day's featured wine selections.

If you love Old World style and New World wines, stop in for a glass at **Ottimista Enoteca** (1838 Union St., 415/674-8400, www.ottimistasf.com, Tues.–Thurs. 2 P.M.–11 P.M., Fri. noon–2 A.M., Sat. 11 A.M.–2 A.M., Sun. 11 A.M.–10 P.M.). This Italian wine bar showcases its heritage with a list of the best wines in Italy (including artisan Tuscan wines) mixed with great vintages from elsewhere in Europe, California, and the New World. Don't be shy—this wine bar seeks to take the pretension out of wine, creating a welcoming atmosphere for anyone who wants to sip. Small plates made with fresh local ingredients complement the wine selection

Another favorite bar is the **City Tavern** (3200 Fillmore St., 415/567-0918, Mon.–Fri. 3 P.M.–2 A.M., Sat.–Sun. 10 A.M.–2 A.M.). Here you'll get a mix of sports, drinks, and good company. Good solid American food comes at reasonable prices. Weekend brunch features an array of tasty classics as well as some health-conscious fare. The full bar pours an array of beers, wines, liquors, and cocktails.

All that's really left of the original Matrix is the ground you stand on, but the **MatrixFillmore** (3138 Fillmore St., 415/563-4180, Mon.–Thurs. 8 P.M.–2 A.M., Fri.–Sun. 6 P.M.–2 A.M.) does claim huge mid-20th-century musical fame. The Matrix, then a live music venue, was opened by Marty Balin so his freshly named band, Jefferson Airplane, would have a place to play. Subsequent acts included The Grateful Dead, Janis Joplin, and The Doors. Today, the MatrixFillmore's Lincoln-log fireplace and top-shelf cocktails appeal to the quiet drinking crowd on weeknights and the bridge-and-tunnel–heavy singles scene on the weekends. DJs spin techno most nights, though you can catch an occasional live act here too. There's valet parking at the Balboa Café down the street.

## CIVIC CENTER AND HAYES VALLEY

Hayes Valley bleeds into Lower Haight (Haight St. btw. Dividadero and Octavia) and supplies most of the neighborhood bars. For proof that the independent spirit of the Haight lives on in spite of encroaching commercialism, stop in and have a drink at the **Noc Noc** (557 Haight St., 415/861-5811, www.nocnocs.com, nightly 5 P.M.–2 A.M.). The whole small bar is alive with modern art, and there's no mass-produced American beer on the menu. Enjoy imported and microbrews on tap, California wine, and even premium sake. DJs spin every night of the week. Do take care when you walk from public transit to the bar—the Lower Haight area can be sketchy at night, especially if you're a woman walking alone.

**Mad Dog in the Fog** (530 Haight St., 415/626-7279, nightly 5 P.M.–2 A.M.) feels as much like an English (or Irish, depending on whom you talk to) pub as you can find on the left coast of America. You'll meet rowdy expat Londoners and authentic Haight weirdos here when you in come for a pint of Guinness. You can watch a game of *real* football on the televisions, or enjoy the DJs on weekends.

In this part of the City, you can find just about any style of bar you want. If the young punk scene is what you crave, go to **Molotov's** (582 Haight St., 415/558-8019, Mon.–Fri. 4 P.M.–2 A.M., Sat.–Sun. noon–2 A.M.). Cement and stainless steel provide the perfect backdrop for the tattooed and pierced clientele. The jukebox is hand-stocked with classic and unusual punk music. Strong drinks served in the big bar room please the crowd, which can get rowdy on weekends.

The bar scene heads upscale with **Cav** (1666 Market St., 415/437-1770, www.cavwinebar.com, Mon.–Thurs. 5:30 P.M.–11 P.M., Fri.–Sat 5:30 P.M.–midnight). This wine bar offers a wide array of still, sparkling, and dessert wines by the glass and by the bottle as well as in tasting flights for those who prefer variety. The small plates menu pairs perfectly with the wines.

A classy Hayes Valley lounge, **Jade** (650 Gough St., 415/869-1900, www.jadebar.com, Tues.–Sat. 5 P.M.–2 A.M., Sun. 8 P.M.–2 A.M.) specializes in signature cocktails and top-quality wines and beers.

If what you really want is a dive bar, **Place Pigalle** (520 Hayes St., 415/552-2671) is the place for you. This hidden gem in Hayes Valley offers beer and wine only, a pool table, lots of sofas for lounging, and an uncrowded genuinely laid-back vibe on weeknights and even sometimes on weekends. The too-cool-for-school hipster vibe somehow missed this place, which manages to maintain its friendly neighborhood feel.

## MISSION AND CASTRO

These neighborhoods seem to hold a whole city's worth of bars. The Mission, despite a recent upswing in its economy, still has plenty of no-frills bars, many with a Latino theme. And of course, men seeking men flock to the Castro's endless array of gay bars. (But if you're a lesbian, the Mission might be a better bet.)

For folks who believe that "bar" means "live music," there's **Blondie's Bar and No Grill** (540 Valencia St., 415/864-2419, www.blondiesbar.com, Mon.–Thurs. 4 P.M.–2 A.M., Fri.–Sun. 2 P.M.–2 A.M.). Specializing in Latin, jazz, and funk, Blondie's has all sorts of acts playing throughout the week. A dance floor complements the bar's musical nature, but it's the martinis that make Blondie's special. A second bar operates in the lounge on weekend evenings. Blondie's is known to locals as something of a tourist trap and haven for the bridge-and-tunnel crowd, but that doesn't stop it from being lots of fun.

**Dalva** (3121 16th St., 415/252-7740, daily 4 P.M.–2 A.M.) is a small but sophisticated oasis in an ocean of overcrowded Mission hipster hangouts. You'll find dramatic high ceilings, modern paintings, and a jukebox stuffed with indie rock and electronica.

You'll have no trouble finding a gay bar in the Castro. One of the best is called simply **The Bar on Castro** (456 Castro St., 415/626-7220, www.thebarsf.com, Mon.–Fri. 4 P.M.–2 A.M., San.–Sun. 2 P.M.–2 A.M.). Just look for the red neon Bar sign set in steel out front. Inside, expect to find the fabulous red decor known as "retro-glam," delicious top-shelf cocktails, and thrumming beats spun by popular DJs almost every night of the week. Check the website for a list of weekly events and pick your favorite night to show up and party. Believe it or not, the Bar even has a ladies' night! Unlike many Castro establishments, the Bar caters to pretty much everybody: gay men, gay women, and gay-friendly straight folks. You'll find a coat check and adequate restroom facilities here, and the strength of the drinks will make you want to take off your jacket and stay awhile.

### GOLDEN GATE PARK AND THE HAIGHT

Haight Street crowds head out in droves to the **Alembic** (1725 Haight St., 415/666-0822, www.alembicbar.com, Mon.–Thurs. 5 P.M.–2 A.M., Fri.–Sun. noon–2 A.M.) for artisan cocktails laced with American spirits. On par with the whiskey and bourbon menu is the cuisine: Wash down truffle mac-and-cheese with a Sazerac.

The restored **Beach Chalet Brewery** (1000 Great Hwy., 415/386-8439, Sun.–Thurs. 9 A.M.–10 P.M., Fri.–Sat. until 11 P.M.) is now an attractive brewpub and restaurant. Directly across from Ocean Beach, you can sip a pale ale while watching the sunset. Check out the historic murals downstairs.

In the neighboring Sunset district, bars profligate along 9th and Irving, a quick jaunt from the park. The **Blackthorne Tavern** (834 Irving St., 415/564-6627, www.blackthornsf.com, Mon.–Thurs. 4 P.M.–2 A.M., Fri.–Sat 3 P.M.–midnight, Sun. 12:30 P.M.–2 A.M.) is an honest-to-goodness Irish tavern owned by genuine Irish immigrants. You can get a pint of Guinness here, play a game of pool or darts, and get to know a mostly local crowd. This neighborhood tavern has a small, funkily shaped bar and a big open seating area that invites folks in and makes them feel at home. Lots of evening activities find their way to the Blackthorne—you might stop in and find trivia night, a live football game, a karaoke setup, or a live band. Join in the fun with the usually manageable crowds to get the best laidback local-style experience.

Another Inner Sunset watering hole, the **Mucky Duck** (1315 9th Ave., 415/661-4340, www.muckyduckpub.com, daily 11 A.M.–2 A.M.) offers fun, beer, and a really silly name. This low-key bar, often described as a dive, serves Pabst Blue Ribbon *and* Guinness on tap. It also serves up decorative bras on the ceiling and a "boobie memory" game along the back wall (not kidding). A mixed, mainly local crowd includes kids in their twenties and folks in their forties.

## Clubs

Some folks are surprised at the smallish list of San Francisco clubs. The truth is, San Francisco just isn't a see-and-be-seen, hip-new-club-every-week kind of town. In the City, you'll find gay clubs, vintage dance clubs, goth clubs, and the occasional underground Burner rave mixed in with the more standard dance floor and DJ fare.

If you're up for a full night of club-hopping and don't want to deal with transit headaches, several bus services can ferry your party from club to club. Many of these offer VIP entrance to clubs, and will stop wherever you want to go. **Think Escape** (800/823-7249, www.thinkescape.com, $30/person minimum) has buses and limos with drivers and guides to get you to the hottest spots with ease.

### UNION SQUARE AND NOB HILL

Defying San Francisco expectation, **Ruby Skye** (420 Mason St., 415/693-0777, www.rubyskye.com, Thurs.–Sat. 9 P.M.–4 A.M., cover $15–20) books top DJs and occasional live acts into a big, crowded dance club. The building, built in 1890, was originally once the Stage Door Theatre, but it's been redone to create dance floors, bars, DJ booths, and VIP spaces. Crowds can get big on the weekends, and the patrons tend to be young and pretty and looking for action. The sound system rocks (so conversation isn't happening) and the drinks tend towards pricey vodka and Red Bull.

For a chic, New York–style club experience, check out **Vessel** (85 Campton Place, 414/433-8585, www.vesselsf.com, Wed.–Thurs. 5 P.M.–midnight, Fri. 5 P.M.–2 A.M., Sat. 9 P.M.–2 A.M., cover up to $20). With old-school bottle service at some tables (and they'll save your bottle for you if you don't finish it), Vessel caters to a wealthier crowd that likes postmodern decor, top-shelf liquors, and a bit of dancing to round out the evening. Dress up if you plan to get in.

Down the brightly lit staircase in the aptly-named **The Cellar** (685 Sutter St., 415/441-5678, www.cellarsf.com, Mon.–Fri. 9 P.M.–2 A.M., Sat. 9 P.M.–2 A.M., cover varies), you'll find a combo bar-and-club. Two dance floors share the space with pool tables favored by the after-work happy hour crowd. (Beers are $1 during weekday happy hour.) With regular themes like '80s night, this red-and-blue plush velvet club often attracts a slightly older crowd, and there's often no cover before 10 or 11 P.M. An online guest list, reserved tables, and bottle and cocktail service are available through the website. The Cellar's a favorite with many local urbanites.

**Harry Denton's Starlight Room** (450 Powell St., 21st Floor, 415/395-8595, www.harrydenton.com, opens nightly at 6 P.M., cover up to $15) brings the flamboyant side of San Francisco downtown. Enjoy a cocktail

## FESTIVALS AND EVENTS

No town does a festival, holiday, or parade like San Francisco. If you're in town for a big event, prepare to check your inhibitions at the airport. Nudity, sex displays, and oddity abound. Even the "tame" festivals include things like fireworks and skeletons.

### GAY PRIDE

Pride parades and events celebrating queer life have sprung up all over the country, spreading joy and love across the land. But the granddaddy of all Pride events still reigns in San Francisco. San Francisco Lesbian Gay Bisexual Pride (Market St., 415/864-3733, www.sfpride.org) officially lasts for a weekend – the last weekend of June of each year. But in truth, the fun and festivities surrounding Pride go on for weeks. The rainbow flags go up all over the City at the beginning of June, and the excitement slowly builds, culminating in the fabulous parade and festival. Everyone is welcome to join the wall-to-wall crowds out in the streets to stroll the vendor booths and pack in to see the Dykes on Bikes and cadres of magnificent drag queens.

### BAY TO BREAKERS

Are those naked people you see trotting through the fog? Yes! But why? It must be Bay to Breakers (www.ingbaytobreakers.com)! On the third Sunday of May every year since 1912, San Franciscans have gotten up early to get to the starting line of the legendary 12K race. But Bay to Breakers is like no other race in the world. Sure, there are plenty of serious runners who enter the race to win it or to challenge themselves and their abilities. And then there are the other racers...San Franciscans and visitors who turn out by the thousands wearing astonishing outfits, pulling carts and wagons, and stripping down to the buff as they make their way along the course without any care for their pace. A huge audience packs the racecourse, eager to see costumes and conveyances that may well be recycled for Pride the following month. If you want to participate in B2B, check the website for all the details you'll need. Specatators can also scope out the course location and best spots to find a place to watch.

### CHINESE NEW YEAR

When Chinese immigrants began pouring into San Francisco in the 19th century, they brought their culture with them. One of the most important (and most fun) traditions the Chinese gave us is the Southwest Chinese New Year Festival and Parade (www.chineseparade.com, $30 parade bleacher seating). Cast off the weariness and bad luck of the old year, and come party with the dragons to celebrate the new! Chinese New Year is a major cultural event in San Francisco – schoolchildren of all races are taught the significance of the dancing dragons and the little red envelopes. The parade, with its costumed fan dancers and stunning handmade multicolored dragon's heads, is one of the most beautiful in the world. It's got more history than almost any other California celebration; the parades and festival events began in the 1860s, helping to bring a few days of joy to a Chinese population feeling the hardships of a life thousands of miles from home. Today, crowds in the tens of thousands join to help bring in the new year towards the end of January or the beginning of February each annum (on the Western calendar).

in the early evening or a nightcap and a bite of dessert after the theater later on in this true old-school nightclub. Dress in your best to match with the glitzy red-and-gold decor and mirrors. On Sundays, come during the afternoon to whoop it up at Sunday's a Drag shows (noon and 2:30 P.M. every Sun.). Management recommends making reservations.

Small, crowded, and hip, the **Element Lounge** (1028 Geary St., 415/440-1125, www.elementlounge.com, Wed.–Thurs. 9 P.M.–2 A.M., Sat.–Sun. 9 P.M.–3 A.M., cover $10) is a favorite for birthday and bachelorette parties. Put your name on the online guest list for a lower cover charge, and stick by the fans on the dance floor to stay cool.

SAN FRANCISCO CONVENTION & VISITORS BUREAU PHOTO BY GARRETT CULHANE

Chinatown dragon parade

## DIA DE LOS MUERTOS

On the other end of the thematic spectrum, the Hispanic community turns out into the so-often marched upon San Francisco streets each autumn to celebrate their ancestors. The dead ones, that is. The Dia de los Muertos and Festival of Altars procession takes place as close as possible to All Saint's Day (also Halloween, Samhain, and other cultures' harvest festivals) in the Mission District. Walkers are encouraged to bring flowers, candles, and special items to create altars in honor of their deceased loved ones, and artists create beautiful murals and signs to celebrate those who have come and gone. You'll note a distinct theme to the artwork: skulls and bones, mostly, though roses also tend to twine through the scenes. Unlike a funeral, Dia de los Muertos truly is a celebration, so expect music and dancing and a genuine sense of joy in the lives of the dead, rather than somber mourning.

## FOLSOM STREET FAIR

Celebrating the uninhibited side of San Francisco each year, the Folsom Street Fair (www.folsomstreetfair.com) brings sex out of the bedroom and into the street. Literally. This fair pays homage to the best perversions and fetishes of consenting adults. You can watch a live BDSM show, shop for sex toys, get something pierced, or just listen to the top alternative bands rocking out on the main stage. The fair takes place at the end of September each year on Folsom Street between 7th and 12th Streets. To say too much more about this major leather event would do damage to the rating of this book; check the fair's website, or better still, head on down to find out what's really going on.

## FINANCIAL DISTRICT AND SOMA

**111 Minna Street Gallery** (111 Minna St., 415/974-1719, www.111minnagallery.com, Tues. noon–10 P.M., Wed. noon–11 P.M., Thurs.–Fri. noon–2 A.M., Sat. 5 P.M.–2 A.M., cover $5) really is an art gallery. But it's also one of the hottest dance clubs in SoMa. Artophiles who come to 111 Minna to enjoy the changing exhibitions of new art in peace and quiet do so during the daytime (up until 5 P.M.). After 5 P.M., gallery transforms into a nightclub, opening up the full bar and bringing in DJs who spin late into the weekend nights. While it sounds pretentious, really the mix of modern art and lots of liquor feels just right. Check the website for special events, including '80s dance parties and art show openings.

On the other end of the spectrum, you've got **House of Shields** (39 New Montgomery St, 415/975-8651, www.houseofshields.com, Mon.–Fri. 2 P.M.–2 A.M., Sat. 7 P.M.–2 A.M.). This club has a 100 -year history in the City. The original incarnation opened in 1908, the bar became an illegal speakeasy during Prohibition (it's even got an under-street tunnel to the neighboring Sheraton hotel), the whole thing closed down for years, and now it has reopened as a live jazz and underground party venue. During happy hour, expect a huge crowd of local working stiffs, which thins out after about 8 P.M. or so. Check the website for dance parties and live music during your stay. And when you visit, take a moment to look up at the ceiling.

It's dark, it's dank, and it's very, very goth. Okay, so the **Cat Club** (1190 Folsom St., 415/703-8964, www.catclubsf.com, Tues. and Thurs.–Sat. 9 P.M.–3 A.M., cover varies) does get pretty energetic on '80s dance party and "hot pants" (lesbian) nights. But it's still a great place to go after you've donned your best down-rent black attire and painted your face deathly pale, especially on goth/industrial/electronica nights. In fact, there's no dress code at the Cat Club (unlike many local night spots), which makes it great for travelers who live in their jeans. You'll find a friendly crowd, decent bartenders, mediocre cocktails, and easy access to smoking areas. Each of the two rooms here has its own DJ, which somehow works perfectly even though they're only a wall apart from each other. Check the website to find the right party night for you, and expect the crowd to heat up after 11 P.M.

And of course, there's the **DNA Lounge** (375 11th St., 415/626-1409, www.dnalounge.com, Thurs. 9:30 P.M.–3 A.M., Fri.–Sat. 9:30 P.M.–4 A.M.). Looking for *the* DJs and dance parties? You'll find them here. With Bootie twice a month, '80s parties, lots of sex-themed (both gay and straight) parties and shows, and even live music, the DNA Lounge has been one of the City's perpetual hot night spots for decades. (It's even got its own entry in Wikipedia.) It's also one of the few clubs that's open till 4 A.M. on weekends.

## NORTH BEACH AND FISHERMAN'S WHARF

The North Beach neighborhood has long been San Francisco's best-known red-light district. To this day, Broadway Avenue is lined with the neon signs of strip clubs and adult stores, all promising grown-up good times. Do be aware that cover charges at most of the strip clubs tend to be on the high side, and lone women should approach this area with extreme caution after dark.

If you're just looking for a good time at a PG-rated (okay, maybe R-rated if you get lucky) dance club, check out the **Bamboo Hut** (479 Broadway, 415/989-8555, www.maximumproductions.com, Mon.–Fri. 5 P.M.–2 A.M., Sat.–Sun. 7 P.M.–2 A.M.). It's part tacky tiki bar, part impromptu dance club, with a cheerful vibe and friendly scene that can be hard to come by in this part of town. You'll see the tiki god, the bamboo decor, and the fun umbrella-clad fruity rum drinks. The house specialty is the Flaming Volcano Bowl—yes, it's really on fire, and it's probably a good idea to share one with a friend. DJs spin on weekends at the Bamboo Hut; they might not be the hippest in town, but regulars have a great time dancing anyhow.

The reality is that the clubs people come to

North Beach to visit are the strip clubs. One of these is **Broadway Showgirls** (412 Broadway, 415/391-2800, www.showgirlssf.com, nightly 6 P.M.–2 A.M., cover $20). This club aspires to elegance, and actually manages to pull it off better than many. After paying your cover (check the website for no-cover days and hours), you'll be ushered into a plush red main room, rife with smaller VIP rooms and of course the multi-level main stage at one end of the room. Upstairs, you'll find the Sizzle Lounge (a small dance club-like space with more VIP rooms and its own full-service restaurant). Lots of solo straight women and couples frequent Showgirls, and are made welcome (though most must pay the cover). Because Showgirls has a full bar, the dancers don't get completely nude (in California it's one or the other, but not both, by law).

### MARINA AND PACIFIC HEIGHTS

Clubs in the Marina are all about the trendy and the spendy. Among these, you can check out **Gravity** (3251 Scott St., 415/776-1928, www.gravityroomsf.com). Sure it's crowded, parking is awful, it's sometimes tough to get in, and the drinks can sometimes be weak. But DJs do spin decent hip-hop and pop, and plenty of young singles crowd in every weekend.

The **Hi-Fi Lounge** (2125 Lombard St., 415/345-8663, www.maximumproductions.com, Wed.–Sat. 8 P.M.–2 A.M., Fri. 5 P.M.–2 A.M.) personifies the fun that can be had in smaller San Francisco venues. This one-floor wonder with a tiny dance floor gets incredibly crowded. Yet even the locals have a good time when they come out to the Hi-Fi. The decor is funky and fun, and the patrons are young and affluent. Most visitors find the staff friendly and the bartenders attentive. It being the Marina, come early to get decent parking and to avoid the cover charge.

### CIVIC CENTER AND HAYES VALLEY

Not your slick, shiny nightclub, the **Rickshaw Stop** (155 Fell St., 415/861-2011, www.rickshawstop.com, Wed.–Thurs. 5 P.M.–midnight, Fri.–Sat. 5 P.M.–2 A.M.) in the Hayes Valley neighborhood next door to the Civic Center welcomes one and all with a cavernous lower bar/room/stage area/dance floor, and a quirky balcony area complete with comfy old sofas. Up-and-coming live acts play here, DJs spin, and special events and parties add to the action most every week. Have a drink, enjoy the music, grab a small bite if you're hungry, and get comfortable! You'll feel almost as though you're in a friendly neighborhood coffee shop (albeit a really big one) than some fancy nightspot.

True adult entertainment lovers know that the most famous gentlemen's club in the City is **Mitchell Brothers O'Farrell Theatre** (895 O'Farrell St., 415/776-6686, www.ofarrell.com, Mon.–Thurs. 11:30 A.M.–1:30 A.M., Fri.–Sat. 11:30 A.M.–2:30 A.M., Sun. 5:30 P.M.–1:30 A.M., cover $20 before 6 P.M., $40 after 6 P.M.). The O'Farrell started out as a adult movie house in 1969, featuring its own productions on the silver screen. Live shows began in 1976, though films still run in the CineStage room to this day. Today, patrons can choose between five different show rooms, plus VIP booths. Unlike many City strip clubs, Mitchell Brothersoffers full nudity and features live shows. Many of the performers and dancers are major adult film stars who perform limited engagements at the O'Farrell. The catch? No liquor. Of course that means that 18–20 year old patrons are welcome to join in the fun....

The **Crazy Horse Gentlemen's Club** (980 Market St., 415/771-6259, Mon.–Wed. noon–2 A.M., Thurs.–Sat. noon–3 A.M., Sun. 6 P.M.–2 A.M., 18 and older) is another favorite. Much smaller than the O'Farrell, with one main movie-theater-style room containing a single stage, the Crazy Horse offers a more (ahem) intimate adult experience. There's also the semi-private "couch room" and of course a few private VIP spaces. A few adult film stars do guest shows at this all-nude, liquor-free club. Expect to see more true pole dancing than at the O'Farrell.

### MISSION AND CASTRO

The Mission and the Castro are *the* clubbing

districts in San Francisco, and as the urban renewal continues, SoMa is making its own play to create a hot nightlife rep. Naturally the biggest concentration of gay clubs sits in the Castro.

Looking for something a little different in the Mission? Check out **Levende Lounge** (1710 Mission St., 415/864-5585, www.levendesf.com, Wed.–Fri. 5 P.M.–2 A.M., Sat. 6 P.M.–2 A.M., Sun. 11 A.M.–4 P.M.). This new-school establishment fuses two of the coolest things in San Francisco; a high-end restaurant and top-shelf cocktail bar come together to bring you in early and keep you in late. The short but luscious world cuisine–inspired menu is served until 11 P.M. most nights, while the cocktail and wine bar stays open late. Margaritas are the house specialty, but don't overlook the other mixed drinks and the wine selection. Or if you're hung over on a Sunday morning and in need of replenishment, Levende can hook you up with some hearty made-to-order brunch fare.

Fans of the hipster lounge scene flock to the **Fluid Ultra Lounge** (662 Mission St., 415/615-6888, www.fluidsf.com, Thurs.–Sat. 9 P.M.–2 A.M., cover varies). The second you walk in, you'll probably feel you're not chic enough for this David Oldroyd–designed post-modern wonderland. Gleaming metal meets fascinating floral-esque accessories in a series of rooms that boast really uncomfortable white chairs. If you're not up for lots of young and *ultra* cool clubsters, you may find the decor the best part of Fluid. You can definitely dance on an interestingly lit floor, though it can be tough to pry a drink out of the bartenders at times. Come early or get your name on the guest list (you can sign up online) to avoid the hefty cover charge.

Looking for a stylin' gay bar-turned-club, Castro style? Head for **Badlands** (4121 18th St., 415/626-9320, www.sfbadlands.com, daily 2 P.M.–2 A.M.). This Castro icon was once an old-school bar with pool tables on the floor and license plates on the walls. Now you'll find an always-crowded dance floor, au courant peppy pop music, ever-changing video screens, and plenty of gay men out for a good time. Are you a straight woman who loves the energy and lack of sleaze at gay clubs? You're welcome to get your groove on at Badlands! Any number of local straight ladies count themselves among the regulars at this friendly establishment, which attracts a youngish but mixed-age crowd. Do be aware that Badlands gets incredibly crowded, complete with a hot and packed dance floor, especially on weekend nights. There's a coat check on the bottom level.

#### GOLDEN GATE PARK AND THE HAIGHT

In the infamous Haight, the club scene is actually an eclectic mix of everything from trendy to retro. **Milk** (1840 Haight St., 415/387-6455, www.milksf.com, nightly 7 P.M.–2 A.M., cover varies) counts itself among the trendy. It's tiny. It's often empty on weekdays and packed solid on weekends. The music ranges from reggae to hip hop to '80s tunes depending on the night and the DJ. Don't expect much of a tourist crowd here; Milk attracts more locals than out-of-towners, but if that's what you're looking for in your visit to the City, a night of Milk might be just what the doctor ordered.

### Live Music

#### ROCK AND POP

Opened in the late 1960s, **The Fillmore** (1805 Geary Blvd., 415/346-6000, www.thefillmore.com) ignited the careers of legendary bands such as Santana and The Grateful Dead. This popular venue now hosts everything from concerts to theme parties.

Started by rock veteran Boz Scaggs in 1988, **Slim's** (333 11th St., 415/255-0333, www.slims-sf.com) showcases everything from the Subhumans to Billy Bob Thornton. Dinner tickets are the only way to score an actual seat.

The **Warfield** (982 Market St., 415/567-2060) is one of the older rock venues in the City. It started out as a vaudeville palace in the early 1900s, booking major jazz acts as well as variety shows. The Warfield's configuration is that of a traditional theater, with a raised stage, an open orchestra section below it, and two balconies rising up and facing the stage. There's limited table seating on the lowest level (mostly by reservation), reserved seats in the balconies, and open standing in the orchestra below the stage. The Warfield books all sorts of acts, from Bill Maher to alternative rock; the likes of Evanescence, Weezer, and Death Cab for Cutie have played the Warfield. The downsides of hitting the shows at the Warfield include the somewhat shabby details of the interior, which is minor. The bigger problem is the total lack of parking—you'll need to hunt for a spot at one of the local public parking structures, and you'll pay for the privilege.

Given the dense crowd of tourists in the Fisherman's Wharf area, it's no surprise that a few bars and clubs offer live music to entertain the masses and keep them buying drinks late into the evening. Despite its locale, **Bimbo's 365 Club** (1025 Columbus Ave., 415/474-0365, www.bimbos365club.com, tickets $15–35, cash-only bar) retains its reputation as a favorite venue for locals. Opened in 1931 by an Italian immigrant looking to create a fun and fabulous club to help San Francisco residents take their minds off the gloom of the Depression. The club moved to the Columbus Avenue location in 1951, and became a favorite of San Francisco legend Herb Caen as well as many other local socialites. Today, major accessible acts such as Chris Isaak and the Brian Setzer Orchestra play Bimbo's. You might even luck out and catch Robin Williams working up new stand-up material here. The club itself, with its shabby chic interior and atmosphere, remains a beloved elder statesman with a heavy local following.

The **Gold Dust Lounge** (247 Powell St., 415/397-1695, daily 7 A.M.–2 A.M.) hosts country, pop, and R&B bands most every night of the week. You can also get a decent drink, and enjoy the slightly bizarre red and gold decor of this San Francisco landmark.

### BLUES AND JAZZ

The neighborhood surrounding Union Square is one of the most fertile areas in San Francisco for live music. Whether you're into blues or rock, or even country, you'll find a spot to have a drink and listen to some wonderful live tunes.

**Biscuits and Blues** (401 Mason St., 415/292-2583, www.biscuitsandblues.com, Tues.–Thurs., Sun. 6 P.M.–midnight, Fri.–Sat 3:30 P.M.–12:30 A.M.) is a local musicians' favorite. Just around the corner from the big live drama theaters, this house dedicates itself to jazz and blues. Headliners at Biscuits and Blues can range from Joe Louis Walker to Jimmy Thackery to Jim Kimo. One of the best things about this club is that you can in fact get biscuits as well as blues. Dinner is served nightly, and features a surprisingly varied and upscale menu combining California cuisine with the mystical flavors of New Orleans. Yum! So when you plan for your night of blues, consider showing up early to enjoy a jam session and a meal, then stay on for the main acts and headliners (and of course cocktails).

At the **Boom Boom Room** (1601 Fillmore St., 415/673-8000, www.boomboomblues.com, Tues.–Sat. 4 P.M.–2 A.M., Sun. 2 P.M.–1 A.M.), you'll find the latest in a legacy of live blues, boogie, groove, soul, and funk music.

**The Saloon** (1232 Grant Ave., 415/989-7666) fills the role of the live-music dive in North Beach. Don't expect much in the way of decor or chic amenities, and do expect the clientele to more closely resemble the denizens of Mos Eisley Space Port than the hip clubs of the Mission or the wine bars of SoMa. So what kind of music goes up at a low-rent live-music bar in North Beach? The blues, of course. So grab a pint of beer and sit back to enjoy the show (half of which is put on by the patrons).

## Comedy

San Francisco's oldest comedy club, the **Punch Line** (444 Battery St., 415/397-7573, www.punchlinecomedyclub.com) is an elegant and intimate venue that earned its top-notch reputation with stellar headliners such as Robin Williams, Ellen DeGeneres, and Dave Chappelle. An on-site bar keeps the audience primed.

**Cobb's Comedy Club** (915 Columbus Ave.,

415/928-4320, www.cobbscomedy.com) has played host to star comedians such as Jerry Seinfeld, Sarah Silverman, and Margaret Cho since 1982. The 425-seat venue offers a full dinner menu and a bar to slake your thirst.

## THE ARTS

### Theater

#### UNION SQUARE AND NOB HILL

Just up from Union Square, on Geary Street, the traditional San Francisco theater district continues to entertain crowds almost every day of the week. The old Geary Theater is now the permanent home of **A.C.T.** (415 Geary St., 415/749-2228, www.act-sf.org, shows Tues.–Sun., $17–82). A.C.T. puts on a season filled with big-name, big-budget productions. Each season sees an array of high-production-value musicals such as *Urinetown,* American classics by the likes of Sam Shepard and Somerset Maugham, and intriguing new works; you might even get to see a world premiere here. Don't expect to find street parking on Geary. Discount parking is available at the Mason-O'Farrell garage around the corner with a ticket stub from A.C.T. Tickets can be reasonably priced, especially on weeknights, but do be aware that the 2nd Balcony seats are truly high altitude—expect to look nearly straight down to the stage, and take care if you're prone to vertigo.

The **Curran Theater** (445 Geary St., 415/551-2000, www.curran-theater.com, $105–250), right next door to the A.C.T., has a state-of-the-art stage on which to put up classic, high-budget musicals. Audiences have watched *Les Miserables, Phantom of the Opera,* and *High School Musical* from the plush red velvet seats. Expect to pay a premium for tickets to these musicals, which can sometimes run at the Curran for months or even years. Check the schedule for current shows, and please leave children under five years old at home—they won't be permitted in the Curran.

#### NORTH BEACH AND FISHERMAN'S WHARF

There's one live show that's always different, yet it's been running continuously for three and a half decades. This musical revue is crazy and wacky and offbeat and pretty much defines live theater in San Francisco. It's **Beach Blanket Babylon** (678 Green St., 415/421-4222, www.beachblanketbabylon.com, shows Wed.–Sun., $25–78). Even if you saw *Beach Blanket Babylon* 10 years ago, you should come see it again; because it mocks current pop culture, the show evolves almost continually to take advantage of tabloid treasures. While minors are welcome at the Sunday matinees, evening shows can get pretty racy (and liquor is involved) so these are restricted to attendees 21 and over.

The hats. Oh, the hats. You'll never forget the hats.

#### MARINA AND PACIFIC HEIGHTS

Beyond the bright lights of Geary and Market Streets lie any number of tiny up-and-coming (or down-and-going, depending) theaters, many of which produce new plays by local playwrights. One of the best known of the "small" theaters, the **Magic Theatre** (Fort Mason Center, Bldg. D, 415/441-8822, www.magictheatre.org, $25–75) produced Sam Shepard's new works back before he was anyone special. They're still committed to new works, so when you go to a show at the Magic you're taking a chance or having an adventure, depending on how you look at it. For some of the cheapest seats in the City, show up at the box office on a Wednesday for same-day, cash-only, sliding scale $5–25 tickets to the current show.

At the **Palace of Fine Arts Theatre** (3301 Lyon St., 415/567-6642, www.palaceoffinearts.org, $25–100) you'll find accessible avant-garde performing arts pieces, live music performance, dance recitals, and the occasional children's musical recital or black-and-white film.

#### CIVIC CENTER AND HAYES VALLEY

Down on Market Street, the **Orpheum Theater** (1192 Market St., 415/551-2000, www.shnsf.com, $91–214) runs touring productions of popular Broadway musicals.

#### MISSION AND CASTRO

Take care getting to **Theatre Rhinoceros** (2926 16th St., 415/552-4140, www.therhino.org, $15–25), as it's in a less-than-ritzy part of town. But it's worth it. The Rhino puts on a wonderfully entertaining set of gay and lesbian plays, and has recently been branching out to explore the whole spectrum of human sexuality, especially as it's expressed in anything-goes (even conservative Republicans!) San Francisco.

Focusing on short works by new writers, **Three Wise Monkeys** (415/776-7427, www.threewisemonkeys.org, $19–22) productions usually run at the **Eureka Theater** (215 Jackson St.). Each year TWM hosts the Bay One Acts (BOAs) as well as the Short Leaps Festival, where all plays read are 10 minutes or less. Another favorite is the **EXIT Theatre** (156 Eddy St., 415/931-1094, www.sffringe.org), where you'll see plenty of unusual experimental plays, many by local playwrights. The EXIT also participates in the annual San Francisco Fringe Festival.

### Classical Music and Opera

Right around the Civic Center, music takes a turn for the upscale. This is the neighborhood where the ultra-rich (and not so much) classics lovers come to enjoy a night out. Acoustically renovated in 1992, **Davies Symphony Hall** (201 Van Ness Ave., 415/864-6000, www.sfsymphony.org) is home to Michael Tilson Thomas' San Francisco Symphony. Loyal patrons flock for performances that range from the classic to the avant-garde.

The **War Memorial Opera House** (301 Van Ness Ave., 415/621-6600, www.sfwmpac.org), a beaux arts–style building designed by Coit Tower and City Hall architect Arthur Brown, Jr., houses the San Francisco Opera and San Francisco Ballet. Tours are available Mondays 10 A.M.–2 P.M.

## Shopping

#### UNION SQUARE AND NOB HILL

For the biggest variety of chain and department stores, plus a few select designer boutiques, locals and tourists alike flock to Union Square (btwn. Geary St., Stockton St., Post St., and Powell St.). The shopping area includes more than just the square proper. More designer and brand-name stores cluster for several blocks in all directions.

### Clothing

The wealthy and stylish of San Francisco shop Union Square for the premier designers who maintain shops here. If you feel you can afford to breathe the rarified air, go in to **Dior** (216 Stockton St., 415/544-0394, Mon.–Sat. 10 A.M.–6 P.M., Sun. noon–5 P.M.) and the others of his ilk who sell their multi-thousand dollar blouses and dresses here. On the other end of the style spectrum, and far more accessible to the masses, you'll find **Niketown** (278 Post St., 415/392-6453, Mon.–Sat. 10 A.M.–8 P.M., Sun. 11 A.M.–7 P.M.). Got shoes?

### Department Stores

Several big, high-end department stores call Union Square home. **Macy's** (170 O'Farrell St., 415/397-3333, Mon.–Wed. 10 A.M.–8 P.M., Thurs.–Sat. 10 A.M.–9 P.M., Sun. 11 A.M.–7 P.M.) has two immense locations, one for women's clothing and another for the men's store and housewares. **Neiman Marcus** (150 Stockton St., 415/362-3900, www.neimanmarcus.com, Mon.–Wed. and Fri.–Sat 10 A.M.–7 P.M., Thurs. 10 A.M.–8 P.M., Sun. noon–6 P.M.) is a favorite among high-budget shoppers and PETA fur protesters, while **Saks Fifth Avenue** (384 Post St., 415/986-4758, Mon.–Wed. and Fri.–Sat. 10 A.M.–7 P.M., Thurs 10 A.M.–8 P.M., Sun. 11 A.M.–6 P.M.) adds a touch of New York style to funky-but-wealthy San Francisco.

© LANCE SCOTT

shopping in Union Square

### Health and Beauty

Another thing the elite of the City do down at Union Square is attend to their hair, faces, nails, and general beauty. One of the most rarified salons in Union Square is the **Elizabeth Arden Red Door** (126 Post St., #4, 415/989-4888, Mon.–Wed. and Sat. 9 A.M.–7 P.M., Thurs.–Fri. 9 A.M.–8 P.M., Sun. 10 A.M.–6 P.M.). You'll definitely need an appointment to get a trim or a color touch-up here.

## FINANCIAL DISTRICT AND SOMA

Is there anyplace in San Francisco where you *can't* shop? Even the Financial District has plenty of retail opportunities. Antique, art, and design lovers come down to **Jackson Square** (Jackson and Montgomery Sts., 415/398-8115) for the plethora of high-end shops and galleries. Don't expect to find much in the way of cheap tchotchkes here—the objets d'art and interior accessories here find places in the exquisite homes of the wealthy buyers who can afford such luxuries. But as always, it's free to look, to imagine, and to dream.

### Art and Design

**Kathleen Taylor - The Lotus Collection** (445 Jackson St., 415/398-8115, www.ktaylor-lotus.com, Mon.–Fri. 10 A.M.–5 P.M., Sat. 11 A.M.–4 P.M.) specializes in antique textiles from around the world. Whether you fancy a medieval tapestry for your wall or an ancient Asian table runner, this is the place to find it. A more classic but intensely high-end and well-known gallery sells works of fine art to the cream of West Coast society. The **Montgomery Gallery** (406 Jackson St., 415/788-8300, www.montgomerygallery.com, Tues.–Fri. 10 A.M.–5:30 P.M., Sat. 11 A.M.–5 P.M.) seems like a museum, displaying works of the Old Masters as well as the top tier of more modern artists.

The modern design shops, while still catering to the high end, offer more items within the reach of normal folks. **Area** (540 Jackson St., 415/989-2732, www.areasanfrancisco.com, Tues.–Fri. 11 A.M.–6 P.M., Sat. 10 A.M.–6 P.M.) is one of these, offering both indoor and outdoor decorative items of the very latest styles. While much of their stock is pricey, some of the smaller items such as planters and knickknacks, cost under $100.

## NORTH BEACH AND CHINATOWN

Shopping in Chinatown isn't really about seeking out a specific store. Instead, visitors stroll Grant Street, browsing in the dozens of similar souvenir shops, marveling at the strange herbal medicines in the windows of the apothecaries, and contemplating cups of tea from the scattered tea shops. For a sense (and a scent) of the more authentic side of Chinatown, head off the main drag to Stockton Street and seek out the local food markets.

### Books and Music

The North Beach district is filled with fun, beauty, and great Italian restaurants and cafés. The Italian district also boasts some of the hippest shops in all the City, so it's a great place for shoppers who eschew chains to seek out thrift shops and funky independents. One of the most famous independent bookshops in a city famous for its literary bent is **City Lights** (261 Columbus Ave., 415/362-8193, www.citylights.com, daily 10 A.M.–midnight). It opened in 1953 as an all-paperback bookstore with a decidedly Beat aesthetic, focused on selling modern literary fiction and progressive political tomes. As the Beats flocked to San Francisco and to City Lights, the shop put on another hat—that of publisher. Allen Ginsberg's *Howl* was published by the erstwhile independent, which never looked back. Today they're still selling and publishing the best of cutting-edge fiction and non-fiction. The store still sits in its original location on the point of Columbus Avenue, though it's expanded somewhat since the '50s. Expect to find your favorite genre paperbacks along with the latest intriguing new works. The nonfiction selections can really make you take a step back and think about your world in a new way, which is just what the founders of City Lights wanted.

Finally, to top of the ultimate hip North Beach shopping trip, stop in at **101 Music** (1414 Grant Ave., 415/382-6369). This independent shop is short on copies of the latest pop CDs and long on vintage vinyl and secondhand instruments and musical equipment. Expect to see turntables, keyboards, and all sorts of fun arcane stuff as soon as you walk in the door. The vinyl collection hides downstairs. The organization of the records and CDs could be better, but isn't browsing for treasure in the bins part of the fun at such a shop? Customer service, much of it provided by the owner, keeps locals coming back.

### Clothing

For hip dressers who prefer classic style to the latest stuff fresh out of the sweatshops, **Old Vogue** (1412 Grant Ave., 415/392-1522, Mon.–Tues. and Thurs. 11 A.M.–6 P.M., Wed. 11 A.M.–8 P.M., Fri.–Sat. 11 A.M.–10 P.M., Sun. noon–6 P.M.) is the perfect North Beach destination. Stop in at the funky little storefront and plan to spend a little while browsing through the racks of vintage apparel: one floor dedicated to comfy old jeans and pants, the other to coats, blouses, dresses, and accessories. Old Vogue can provide you with just the perfect hat to top off your favorite clubbing outfit.

## MARINA AND PACIFIC HEIGHTS

Pacific Heights and its neighbor Presidio Heights, two quiet residential areas, are connected by Sacramento Street. Sacramento is home to interior design and clothing boutiques that display high-end wares that appeal to the well-heeled residents of this area. With 12 blocks' worth of shops, galleries, salons, and eateries, the main trouble folks have is getting through all of it in one shopping session.

### Clothing

You'll have plenty of high-end boutiques to choose from. For the latest outfits, try **Bettina** (3615 Sacramento St., 415/563-8002, www.bettinasf.com, Mon.–Fri. 11 A.M.–7 P.M., Sat. 11 A.M.–6:30 P.M., Sun. noon–5 P.M.). If you prefer fashions from earlier decades, browse through **GoodByes Consignment Shop** (3483 Sacramento St., 415/674-0151, www.goodbyessf.com, Mon.–Wed. and Fri.–Sat. 10 A.M.–6 P.M., Thurs. 10 A.M.–8 P.M., Sun. 11 A.M.–5 P.M.). GoodByes also has a men's store just across the street at 3464 Sacramento.

### Unique

It takes a ritzy San Francisco neighborhood to support a six-day-a-week orchid store. **Beautiful Orchids** (3319 Sacramento St., 415/567-2443, www.beautifulorchids.com, Mon.–Fri. 10 A.M.–9 P.M., Sat. 10 A.M.–5 P.M.) specializes in rarified live orchid plants. Every color of the rainbow, amazing shapes, and waterfall figures spill from elegant planters. Expect to pay a premium for these rare hand-tended flowers, and to spend even more to ship them home. You can also find elegant home accessories here, most picked to complement the orchids rather than the other way around.

## CIVIC CENTER AND HAYES VALLEY

In the Hayes Valley neighborhood adjacent to the Civic Center, shopping goes uptown, but the unique scent of counterculture creativity makes it in somehow. This is a fun neighborhood to get your stroll on, checking out the art galleries and peeking in to the boutiques for clothing and upscale housewares, then stopping at one of the lovely cafés for a restorative bite to eat.

### Art

The **Tinhorn Press/Gallery** (511 Laguna St., 415/621-1292) is at once a gallery and an artists' workshop. All the works you'll see are rendered on that most common of media: paper. The owners and resident artists can often be found working on their stone lithography and intaglio works. They display their own creations as well as works on paper by select other artists.

### Clothing

**Ver Unica** (437-B Hayes St., 415/431-0688, www.ver-unica.com)is a vintage boutique that attracts locals and celebrities alike with high-quality men's and women's clothing and accessories dating from the 1920s to the 1980s, as well as a small selection of new apparel by up-and-coming designers.

Fake fur–covered lights and orange walls contribute to the funky decor at **Stitch Lounge** (182 Gough St., 415/431-3739, www.stitchlounge.com). The sewing collective sells moderately priced T-shirts, bags, skirts, and dresses.

## MISSION AND CASTRO

In the 21st century, the closest you can come to the old-school Haight Street shopping experience is in the Mission. The big shopping street with the coolest stuff is definitely Valencia Street, which has all the best thrift shops and funky stuff.

On Castro Street, shopping is sexy. Whether you want toys or leather, fetish or lace, or just a pair of fabulous spike-heeled boots, you can find it in one of the racy shops found in the City's notoriously "everything goes" district.

### Books

There's a **Books Inc.** (2275 Market St., 415/864-6777, www.booksinc.net, daily 10 A.M.–11 P.M.) in the Castro. This small independent Bay Area bookseller's chain hosts numerous author events and stocks plenty of local authors. You can also find your favorite paperbacks here. At this location, the managers stock lots of great gay literature (fiction and nonfiction) in keeping with the neighborhood. You're welcome to stay as long as you like, browsing through the books here. (I love the Books Inc. chain and wrote much of this guidebook in the café at the Mountain View location.)

### Clothing

One of the local favorite vintage/secondhand clothing stores in the Mission is **Schauplatz** (791 Valencia St., 415/864-5665, daily 1–6 P.M., closed Tues.). It might be a bit more expensive than your average Goodwill, but you'll be wowed by the fabulous and unusual apparel at this unique vintage shop. Surf the racks for everything from 1940s dresses to vintage sunglasses.

Need shoes? One of the few honest-to-goodness local, family-owned shoe stores, **De La Sole** (4126 18th St., 415/255-3140, www.delasole.com, daily 11 A.M.–7 P.M.) in the Castro proffers both men's and women's foot fashions. You'll find the shop friendly to all shoppers, even those who come in often if you know what I mean. The shoes shine with the latest fashions, from sneakers to formals. Even the shop's interior carries on the theme of fun, fashinable modernity, making visitors feel hip just by walking in the door.

### Unique

**Five and Diamond** (510 Valencia St., 415/255-9747, www.fiveanddiamond.com) can bring you every aspect of the stereotypical San Francisco experience all in one storefront. Inside this unique space, you'll find off-the-wall art, unusual clothing, and downright scary jewelry. Those who make an appointment in advance can also get a tattoo here, or purchase some keen body jewelry. A trip inside

Five and Diamond can be an exciting adventure for the bold, but might be a bit much for the faint of heart. Decide for yourself whether you dare to take the plunge.

**Rock Hard** (518 Castro St., 415/437-2430) is one of the neighborhood's favorite "adult stores." This store sells large selection of large, uhm, products at prices lower than many similar shops in the City. Expect to find dildos, vibrators, lubricants, S&M toys, porn DVDs, and much, much more. Though it's in the Castro and it's primarily known as a gay men's shop, women are welcome and can certainly find their share of fun. Call for store hours, or just drop by since Rock Hard is likely to be open late.

## GOLDEN GATE PARK AND THE HAIGHT

The Haight-Ashbury shopping district isn't what it used to be, but if you're willing to poke around a bit, you can still find a few bargains in the remaining thrift shops.

### Books and Music

Music has always been a part of the Haight. To this very day, you'll find ill-bathed folks pounding out rhythms on *doumbeks* and congas on the sidewalks. The ever-changing face of commerce has made the old favorite all-local, all-handmade **Sol Drums** (3275 San Bruno Ave., 415/468-4700, www.soldrums.com) part of the megalithic Drum Workshop. But the legendary **Haight-Ashbury Music Center** (1540 Haight St., 415/863-7327, www.haight-ashbury-music.com, call for hours) remains. Come in and check out one of the best collections of musical instruments and gear anywhere on the West Coast.

Located in an old bowling alley, **Amoeba** (1855 Haight St., 415/831-1200, www.amoeba.com, Mon.–Sat. 10:30 A.M.–10 P.M., Sun. 11 A.M.–9 P.M.) is a larger-than-life record store that promotes every type of music imaginable. Amoeba's staff, many of whom are musicians themselves, are among the most knowledgeable in the business.

The award-winning **Booksmith** (1644 Haight St., 415/863-8688, www.booksmith.com, Mon.–Sat. 10 A.M.–10 P.M., Sun. 10 A.M.–8 P.M.) bookstore boasts a helpful and informed staff, a fabulous magazine collection, and Northern California's preeminent calendar of readings by internationally renowned authors.

### Clothing

If it's used clothing you're after, try the legendary **Aardvark's Odd Ark** (1501 Haight St., 415/621-3141, Mon.–Fri. 11 A.M.–7 P.M., Sat.–Sun. 11 A.M.–8 P.M.), known to its friends as Aardvark. Join the countless bargain shoppers who prowl the racks for fabulous forgotten garments. Just don't expect to pay $0.25 for that great 1930s bias-cut dress or $0.50 for a cast-off Dior blouse; the merchants in the Haight are experienced used clothiers who know what the good stuff is worth.

### Unique

Get yourself a new tattoo, a split tongue, or a Prince Albert down at **Mom's Body Shop**

SAN FRANCISCO CONVENTION & VISITORS BUREAU PHOTO BY JACK HOLLINGSWORTH

Unique shops line Haight Street.

(1408 Haight St., 415/864-6667, www.momsbodyshop.com, opens daily at noon).

One relic of the 1960s counterculture still thrives on the Haight: smoke shops. All pipes, water pipes, and other paraphernalia are *strictly for use in smoking legal tobacco,* you understand. Be sure not to mention anything else inside these shops, for legal reasons. Shops like **Ashbury Tobacco Center** (1524 Haight St., 415/552-5556) also sell clothing and accessories made from the much-maligned hemp plant, stickers and T-shirts bearing pretty green leafy designs, cigarette lighters, and other such trinkets. You know why you're in the Haight, so go on in and look at all the pretty swirling colors!

# Sports and Recreation

## PARKS

**Crissy Field** (603 Mason St. at Halleck St., 415/561-7690, www.crissyfield.org, daily 9 A.M.–5 P.M.), in the Golden Gate National Recreation Area, is a park with a mission. In partnership with the National Park Service, ecology programs are the centerpiece of the Center. Check the website for a list of classes, seminars, and fun hands-on activities for kids of all ages. Many of these include walks out into the marsh beyond the center and the landscape of the Presidio and beyond.

Many people who like to hike, like to do it in some semblance of solitude. That can be tough to come by in the ever-crowded Golden Gate Park and Presidio. **McLaren Park** (Persia Ave. at Naples St., 415/239-7735, www.jennalex.com/projects/fomp/homepage/index.html) is something of a hidden gem in the busy City—an uncrowded park with miles of hiking trails, dozens of picnic tables, athletic fields, an indoor pool, and even a nine-hole golf course. You can enjoy a set of tennis, swim some laps, or play a quick round. But most of all, you can walk. Seven miles' worth of trails are asphalt paved, and plenty of undeveloped trails wend off into the brush and trees all around. If you've got the stamina, you can circle the whole park just by following its trails. Feel free to bring your canine companion with you to this dog-friendly park. On the other hand, take care walking here if you're a woman alone. McLaren Park is generally quite safe in the daylight hours. But at night it becomes much less safe, so plan to finish up your hiking, picnicking, and playing by sunset.

## BEACHES

San Francisco boasts of being a city that has everything, and it certainly comes close. This massive urban wonderland even claims several genuine sand beaches within its city limits. No doubt the biggest and most famous of these is **Ocean Beach** (The Great Highway, parking at Sloat, Golden Gate Park, and the Cliff House). This five-mile stretch of sand forms the breakwater for the Pacific Ocean along the whole west side of the City. Because it's so large, you're likely to find a spot sit down and maybe even a parking place somewhere on Ocean Beach, except perhaps on that rarest of occasions in San Francisco: a sunny, warm day. Locals love Ocean Beach, but there's plenty of room for visitors too. Just please, we're begging you, *don't* go out for a nice ocean swim at Ocean Beach. Extremely dangerous rip currents kill at least one person every single year.

The **Aquatic Park** (Beach St. and Hyde St.) beach sits right in the middle of Touristville, San Francisco (Fisherman's Wharf, that is). Of course this makes Aquatic Park incredibly convenient for visitors who want to grab a picnic on the Wharf to enjoy down on the beach. To be honest, the coolest part of Aquatic Park is its history rather than its current presence. The park was built in the late 1930s as a bathhouse catering to wealthy San Franciscans, and today one of the main attractions of Aquatic Park remains swimming: triathletes and hard-core swimmers brave the frigid waters to swim for miles in the protected cove. More sedate visitors prefer to find a seat and enjoy a cup of coffee, a newspaper, and some people-watching.

**Baker Beach** (Golden Gate Point and the Presidio) is best known for its scenery. And that doesn't just mean the lovely views of the Golden Gate Bridge from a new angle (from the west and below). Baker is San Francisco's own clothing-optional (that is, nude) beach. But don't worry, plenty of the denizens of Baker Beach wear clothes while flying kites, playing volleyball and Frisbee, and even just strolling the beach. Baker Beach was the original home of the Burning Man festival, before it moved out to the Black Rock Desert of Nevada. Because Baker is much smaller than Ocean Beach, it gets crowded in the summertime. Whether you choose to sunbathe nude or not, don't try to swim here. So close to the gate, the currents at Baker get seriously strong and dangerous. Stay safe by staying on land.

## HIKING

Yes, you can go for a hike inside the city of San Francisco. Most of the parks in the City offer hiking trails to suit various tastes and ability levels. The City also boasts some longer and more interesting trails that present serious hikers with a real challenge.

For an easy nature walk in the Presidio, try the **Lobos Creek Trail** (Lincoln St. at Bowley St., daily dawn–dusk, 0.6 mi, easy). Less than a mile long, this flat boardwalk trail is wheelchair-accessible and shows off the beginning successes of the ecological restoration of the Presidio. You'll get to see restored sand dunes and native vegetation, which has attracted butterflies and other insects, which in turn bring the birds to the trail area. While it's still in the City, this trail gives walkers a glimpse of what the Presidio might have been like 500 years ago, before the encroachment of the European military.

The closest thing to a true serene backwoods hike in San Francisco can probably be found at **Mount Davidson** (Dalewood St., West Portal, daily 6 A.M.–10 P.M., 0.5 mi, easy). Park in the adjacent West Portal residential area and wander through the gate and into the woods, or something like them. Take the main fire road straight up the gentle slope to the top of the mountain, then find the smaller track off to the left that leads to the famous "cross at the top of the mountain." To extend your stay in this pleasant place, either walk down the other side of the mountain, or head back to find the smaller branch trails that lead off into the trees.

For a stouter and better-known walk, take the trail at **Glen Canyon** (Bosworth St., 1 mi, moderate). Feel free to bring your canine companion on this trail through a lovely little unlikely urban canyon. It only takes about a half an hour to explore Islais Creek, the non-native eucalyptus and blackberry, and the attractive if non-spectacular views. Take care to avoid the prolific poison oak that spreads throughout the canyon.

The **California Coastal Trail** (Golden Gate National Recreation Area, 10.5 miles, difficult) runs right through the city of San Francisco on its way down the state. Originating beneath the Golden Gate Bridge, the Coastal Trail meanders all the way down the west side of the City. It passes by many major monuments and parks, so you can take a break from hiking to visit Fort Point, the Palace of the Legion of Honor, and the site of the Sutro Baths. You'll get to walk right along the famous beaches of San Francisco as well, from Baker Beach to China Beach and on down to Ocean Beach, which comprises five miles of the Coastal Trail. You can keep on walking all the way down to Fort Funston, and the San Francisco portion of the trail terminates at Philip Burton Memorial State Beach. You can enter the trail from just about any place, and exit wherever feels convenient. Just be sure you've got a current trail map to be sure you're aware of any partial trail closures.

## BIKING

In other places, bicycling is a sport or a mode of transportation. In San Francisco, bicycling is a religion. (The concept of mountain biking

## TWIN PEAKS

Twin Peaks rises up from the center of San Francisco, and is the second-highest point in the City. Twin Peaks divides the City between north and south, catching the fog bank that rolls in from the Golden Gate and providing a habitat for lots of wild birds and insects, including the endangered Mission Blue Butterfly.

While you barely need to get out of your car to enjoy the stunning 360-degree views of the City from the peaks, the best way to enjoy the view is to take a hike. If you want to scale the less traveled South Peak, start at the pullout on the road below the parking lot. You'll climb a steep set of stairs up to the top of the South Peak in less than 0.2 mile. Stop and marvel at man's industry: the communications tower that's the massive eyesore just over the peak. Carefully cross the road to access the red-rock stairway up to the North Peak. It's only a 0.25 mile, but as with the South Peak, those stairs seem to go straight up! It's worth it when you look out across the Golden Gate to Mount Tamalpais in the north and Mount Diablo in the east.

If it's the view you're seeking rather than the wildlife and exercise, head to Twin Peaks only on a sunny day. If the fog is in, as so often happens in the summertime, you'll have trouble seeing five feet in front of you. Oh, and don't expect a verdant paradise up there – the grass doesn't stay green long in the spring, so most visitors get to see the dried-out brush that characterizes much of the Bay Area in the summertime and fall.

To get there, drive west up Market Street (eventually turning into Portola Dr.), and turn right onto Twin Peaks Boulevard and past the parade of tour buses to the parking lot past the north peak. Parking is free and Twin Peaks is open year-round.

originated in the City.) As a newcomer to biking in the City, it's wise to start off gently, perhaps with a guided tour that avoids the dangerous traffic areas. The fabulously named **Blazing Saddles** (2715 Hyde St., 415/202-8888, www.blazingsaddles.com) rents bikes and offers guided bicycling tours all over the Bay Area. If you prefer the safety of a group, take the daily guided tour (10 A.M., 3 hours, reservations required) through San Francisco and across the Golden Gate Bridge into Marin. You'll return to the City by ferry. Blazing Saddles can also supply intrepid cyclists with bike maps of the City and the greater Bay Area. For a sedate introductory ride, you can take the popular self-guided tour of the waterfront. With five Blazing Saddles locations, most set into the touristy Fisherman's Wharf area, it's easy to find yourself a cruiser and head out for a spin.

Not a serious cyclist? Or are you a serious cyclist who's new to the City? Take the easy and flat nine-mile ride across the **Golden Gate Bridge** and back. This is a great way to see the Bridge and the Bay for the first time, and it takes only an hour or two to complete. Another option is to ride across the Bridge and into the town of Sausalito (8 miles) or **Tiburon** (16 miles), enjoy an afternoon and dinner in Marin, then ride the ferry back into the City. (Bikes are allowed onboard.)

If you've got a bit more time and leg strength, consider a scenic ride on the paved paths of **Golden Gate Park and the Presidio** (20 miles, 2–4 hours without stops). A bike makes a perfect mode of transportation from which to explore the various museums and attractions of these two large parks, and you can spend all day and never have to worry about finding parking spaces.

Looking for some great urban mountain biking? Miles of unpaved roads and trails right inside the city limits are open to bikers, and provide technically challenging rides for adventurous bikers willing to get away from the tourist realms and take a risk or two. Check out the website for **San Francisco Mountain Biking** (www.sfmtb.com) for information about trails, roads, routes, and regulations.

## GOLF

A number of golf courses hide in the parks of San Francisco. The premier golf course in the City, the **Presidio Golf Course** (Arguello St., 50 yards from Arguello Gates, 415/561-4653, www.presidiogolf.com) was once reserved for the exclusive use of military officers, government officials, and visiting dignitaries. Since 1995, its 18-hole, par 72 course, driving range, practice putting greens, and clubhouse have been available to the public. Reserve your tee time by phone or online. Lessons are available, offered by the Arnold Palmer Golf Academy (the Arnold Palmer Management Company operates the course).

**Lincoln Park Golf Course** (34th Ave. and Clement St., 415/750-4653) is an 80-year-old, public 18-hole, par 68 course in the Outer Richmond district. It hosts the annual San Francisco City Golf Championships. Another 18-hole municipal golf courses is the **Harding Park Golf Course** (Skyline Blvd. at Harding Rd., 415/664-4690).

Nine-hole courses with challenging golf and great views include the **Golden Gate Park Golf Course** (47th Ave. at Fulton St., www.goldengateparkgolf.com) and the **Gleneagles Golf Course** (2100 Sunnydale Ave., www.gleneaglesgolfsf.com).

For tee times at any municipal course, call 415/750-4653.

## KAYAKING

For the adventurous, kayaking on San Francisco Bay is a great way to experience the famous waterway on a personal level. **City Kayak** (415/357-1010, www.citykayak.com) has locations at both South Beach Harbor (Pier 40, Embarcadero at Townsend St.) and Fisherman's Wharf (Pier 39, slip A21). Beginners can take guided paddles along the shoreline, getting a new view on familiar sights. More advanced kayakers can take trips out to the Golden Gate and around Alcatraz Island. Rental equipment is available daily 10 A.M.–7 P.M. at the South Beach Harbor location.

SAN FRANCISCO CONVENTION & VISITORS BUREAU PHOTO BY MAMI MIYATA

Lincoln Park Golf Course, the first public golf course in San Francisco

### TRAMPOLINE

**Frequent Flyers** (Fisherman's Wharf, Pier 39, 415/981.6300, $10/session) offers a high-flying view of Pier 39, the marina, and the Bay. This bungee-cord secured trampoline experience lets bouncers safely jump 20 feet into the air, and try a few gymnastic tricks while they're up there. Kids must be at least 30 pounds to jump.

### SPECTATOR SPORTS

Big-league lovers will find fun in San Francisco and around the Bay Area. The City plays home to the NFL's **San Francisco 49ers** (www.sf49ers.com). The 49ers play at **Monster Park** (490 Jamestown Ave.) way out away from the center of the City on Candlestick Point. This doesn't seem to matter to "the Faithful," the loyal fans who've seen the team through their dismal beginnings, rejoiced in their domination of the NFL through the 1980s and 90s, and continued to cheer as the team "rebuilds" (that is, loses a lot) in the 21st century. Check the website for current single-ticket prices. And be sure to bring a coat to the games—the fog rolls in off the Bay and makes the park chilly and windy.

The MLB's **San Francisco Giants** (http://sanfrancisco.giants.mlb.com) play out the long summer baseball season at **AT&T Park** (24 Willie Mays Plaza, 3rd and King Sts.). Come out to enjoy the game, the food, and the views at San Francisco's still-shiny and new ballpark. Giants games take place on weekdays and weekends, both day and night. It's not hard to snag last-minute tickets to a regular season game. Oh, and be sure to check out the gourmet restaurants that ring the stadium; it wouldn't be San Francisco without top-tier cuisine to complement a midsummer ball game.

## Accommodations

San Francisco has plenty of accommodations to suit every taste and budget. The most expensive places tend to be in Union Square and SoMa.You'll find the most character in the smaller "boutique" hotels, but plenty of big chain hotels have at least one site here, if you prefer a known quantity.

Be aware that many hotels in San Francisco are entirely non-smoking. If you need a smoking room, you may have to hunt for one.

Parking is not included free with your hotel room, and can be excruciatingly expensive in the overnight garages. Check with your hotel to see if they have a "parking package" that takes care of this expense (and possibly offers valet service as well). Otherwise, if you don't plan to leave the City, consider saving a bundle by using public transit.

### UNION SQUARE AND NOB HILL

In and around Union Square and Nob Hill, you'll find about a zillion different hotels. As a rule, those closest to the top of the Hill or to Union Square proper are the most expensive. For a one- or two-block walk, you get more personality and genuine San Francisco experience for less money and less prestige. There's little cheap in these areas; hostels run down in the direction of the Tenderloin, where safety becomes an issue after dark.

#### Under $150

While the best bargains aren't in these neighborhoods, you can still find one or two budget-conscious lodgings in the Union Square and Nob Hill regions. The **Hotel Bijou** (111 Mason St., 800/771-1022, www.jdvhotels.com/bijou, $100–150) might be the most fun of the inexpensive lot. Whimsical decor mimics an old-fashioned movie theater, and in fact a tiny "movie house" downstairs runs free-to-patrons double features every night—with all movies shot in San Francisco. Guest rooms are small, clean, and nicely appointed.

## $150-250

**Hotel Rex** (562 Sutter St., 800/433-4434, www.jdvhotels.com/rex, $235–275) has a classic feel, evoking a hotel in San Francisco early in the 1900s. Guest rooms are comfortable and spacious, decorated with the work of local artists and artisans. The dimly lit lobby bar is famous in the City for its literary bent—you may find yourself embroiled in a fascinating conversation as you enjoy your evening glass of wine. Amenities include a small elevator (not all boutique hotels in SF have them), access to a nearby gym, and valet parking packages for an additional fee. The attached Café Andre serves dinner each night; ask at the desk about reservations.

It might look small compared to the mammoth hotels on Union Square, but **The Cartwright Hotel** (524 Sutter St., 415/421-2865, www.cartwrighthotel.com, $175–285) has plenty of room for budget-minded guests. Guest rooms are freshly redecorated with antiques, and the small lobby has a light, airy feel. Enjoy a complimentary continental breakfast, a wine reception each evening, and free Wi-Fi access. Only about two blocks from Union Square and half a block from the Powell cable car line, this boutique hotel is perfectly located for both business and pleasure travelers.

Just off Union Square, the **Handlery Hotel** (351 Geary St., 800/995-4874, www.handlery.com, $175–330) offers a wide variety of rooms for all different price ranges. Value rooms in the historical section of the hotel tend to be small, and the appointments a bit sterile, but the amenities are as good as those in the newer, pricier Club section of the complex. For a serious splurge, rent the Rooftop Garden Suite, complete with an outdoor patio overlooking the City. A heated outdoor pool is available to all, and the Daily Grill restaurant serves up large portions of standard California cuisine all day long.

Only half a block down from the square, the **Sir Francis Drake** (450 Powell St., 800/795-7129, www.sirfrancisdrake.com, $190–250) has its own history beginning in the late 1920s. Here at the Drake you'll find a bit less opulence in the lobby (compared to the St. Francis) and a bit more in the guest rooms. The Beefeater doorman (almost always available for a photo), the unique door overhang, and the red and gold interior all add to the character of this locals' and tourists' favorite.

## Over $250

The **Hotel Monaco** (501 Geary St., 415/292-0100, www.monaco-sf.com, $310–600) shows the vibrant side of San Francisco. Big guest rooms are whimsically decorated with bright colors, while baths are luxurious and feature cushy animal-print bathrobes. Friendly service comes from purple-velour coated staff, who know the hotel and the City and will cheerfully tell you all about both. Chair massage complements the free wine and cheese in the large, open guest lounge. Be sure to check out the Grand Café and the dining room as well. Because the Hotel Monaco is located a couple of blocks off the Union Square, you get more, and more fun, for your money.

A San Francisco legend, the **Clift** (495 Geary St., 415/775-4700, www.clifthotel.com, $350) has a lobby worth walking into, whether you're a guest of the hotel or not. The high-ceilinged, industrial gray space is devoted entirely to modern art. Yes, you really are supposed to sit on the antler sofa and the metal chairs, though most folks avoid the *seriously* oversized vintage seat. By contrast, the big Philippe Starke–designed guest rooms are almost Spartan in their simplicity, with colors meant to mimic the City skyline. Stop in for a drink at the Redwood Room, done in brown leather and popular with a younger crowd. For dinner, a branch of Jeffrey Chodorow's Asia de Cuba restaurant is located inside the hotel. The Clift is perfectly located for theatergoers, and the Square is an easy walk away.

The opulence of the lobby at the **Westin St. Francis** (335 Powell St., 415/397-7000, www.westinstfrancis.com, $390–490) matches its elegant address. With more than a century of history as San Francisco's great gathering spot, the St. Francis still garners great prestige.

Rooms are attractive but small. The price of admission pays mainly for the decadent fixtures of the common areas, the four eateries (including Michael Mina, the executive chef's signature restaurant), the state-of-the-art gym, top-quality meeting and banquet spaces, and the address on Union Square.

Certain names just mean luxury in the hotel world. The **Fairmont San Francisco** (950 Mason St., 415/772-5000, www.fairmont.com, $460) is among the best of these. With a rich history, above-and-beyond service, and spectacular views, the Fairmont makes any stay in the City memorable. Check online for package specials or to book a tee time or spa treatment, and note that some of the rooms in this rarified hostelry actually allow smoking.

Another Nob Hill contender with a top name, the **Ritz-Carlton** (600 Stockton St., 415/296-7465, www.ritzcarlton.com, $490) provides patrons with ultimate pampering. From the high-thread-count sheets to the five-star dining room to the full-service spa, guests at the Ritz all but drown in sumptuous amenities. Even the "standard" rooms are exceptional, but if you've got the bread, spring for the Club Floors, where they'll give you an iPod, a personal concierge, and possibly the kitchen sink if you ask for it.

## FINANCIAL DISTRICT AND SOMA

Top business execs make it their, well . . . business to stay near the towering offices of the Financial District, down by the water on the Embarcadero, or in SoMa. Thus, most of the lodgings in these areas cater to the expense account set.

### $150-250

An unlikely hotel in the midst of the stuffy suit-clad Financial District, the ☾ **Hotel Triton** (342 Grant Ave., 800/800-1299, www.hoteltriton.com, $170–400) welcomes guests with whimsical decor and an ecological theme. Jerry Garcia and Carlos Santana both decorated guest rooms here, and the environmentally friendly practices developed at the Triton are being adopted by sister hotels all over the world. You'll find the rooms tiny but comfortable, and well stocked with eco-friendly amenities and bath products. The flat-panel televisions offer a 24-hour yoga channel, and complimentary yoga props can be delivered to your room upon request. For the most eco-zany experience at the Triton, book a Celebrity Eco-Suite. Or if you're traveling alone, consider reserving a Zen Den—specially designed for solo travelers and offering the finest Buddhist-inspired amenities. And don't forget to adopt a rubber ducky for the duration of your stay!

For something posh but not overwhelmingly huge, check out **Hotel Griffon** (155 Steuart St., 800/321-2201, www.hotelgriffon.com, $185–450). A boutique business hotel with a prime vacation locale, the Griffon offers business and leisure packages to suit all travelers' needs. They're a bit pricier, but the best guest rooms overlook the Bay, with views of the Bay Bridge and Treasure Island.

It may be part of a chain, but at the **Westin San Francisco Market** (50 Third St., 415/974-6400, www.westinsf.com, $182–600) you'll find plenty of San Francisco charm at your doorstep. Guests stay in pleasant rooms with pretty cityscapes at this large hotel (formerly known as The Argent). Amenities mimic the more expensive SoMa hotels, and seasonal special rates dip down into the genuinely affordable. The attached Ducca restaurant serves three meals each day, and the lounge is open until midnight for nightcaps.

### Over $250

**Le Meridien San Francisco** (333 Battery St., 415/296-2900, $350) stands tall in the Embarcadero Center, convenient to shopping, dining, and the streetcar and cable car lines to all the favorite downtown destinations. This expensive luxury hotel pampers guests with Frette sheets, plush robes, marble bathrooms, and stellar views. Expect nightly turndown service, free newspapers, and 24-hour room service.

The perennial business favorite, sitting right in the midst of the Embarcadero

Center, the **Hyatt Regency San Francisco** (5 Embarcadero Center, 415/788-1234, www.sanfranciscoregency.hyatt.com, $270–355) has it all. A great location across the street from the Ferry Building, more than 800 rooms for easy bookings anytime, fabulous views, and every amenity the business (or pleasure) traveler needs. Guests enjoy the comforts provided with the Hyatt name, a café and bar in-house, and convenient access to Muni, BART, and cable car lines.

**Hotel Vitale** (8 Mission St., 888/890-8688, www.hotelvitale.com, $300–800) professes to restore guests' vitality with its lovely guest rooms and exclusive spa, complete with rooftop hot soaking tubs and yoga studio. Many of the good-sized guest rooms also have private deep soaking tubs. If you happen to reside in the greater Bay Area (or you know someone who does), check out the deeply discounted "Sunday Locals Only" package.

The only problem with staying at the **Mandarin Oriental San Francisco** (222 Sansome St., 415/276-9888, www.mandarinoriental.com, $690) is that you may never leave your room. Redefining decadence, the Mandarin Oriental includes raised beds in all rooms so guests can enjoy the panoramic city and bay views while snuggling under the covers. In the swank corner rooms and suites, raised bathtubs let bathers enjoy stunning sights (such as the Transamerica Pyramid, Alcatraz, and the Golden Gate Bridge) from the warmth of the bubbly water. All rooms boast top amenities and Asian-inspired decor, and families are welcome. You can find the best room rates on the hotel's website (the prices will make a budget-minded traveler's eyes bleed), as well as various stay-and-play packages with an emphasis on golf and spa treatments.

The tall, proud **Four Seasons Hotel San Francisco** (757 Market St., 415/633-3000, www.fourseasons.com, $450) sits right on Market Street, convenient to SoMa, Union Square, and all of downtown San Francisco. Unlike many of the City's other luxury hotels, the Four Seasons interiors sparkle with ultramodern art and decor. Spacious guest rooms feature tasteful appointments, and many have picture windows with city and bay views. A large lobby, bar, and dining room provide guests with services day and night.

With specials occasionally ranging under the $250 mark, The **W San Francisco** (181 3rd St., 415/777-5300, www.starwoodhotels.com, $310) brings City luxury to an almost reasonable level. In the heart of SoMa, W guests can walk to the Yerba Buena Gardens or the SFMOMA. Inside the hotel, you'll enjoy spa pampering, fine dining, and rooms with a view. Check out the Internet packages, which cater to everyone from businesspeople to Pride-goers.

For a unique San Francisco hotel experience, book at room at the famous **Hotel Palomar** (12 Fourth St., 866/373-4941, www.hotelpalomar-sf.com, $260–575). You'll find every amenity imaginable, from extra-long beds for taller guests to in-room spa services to temporary pet goldfish. The overall decorative motif evokes M. C. Escher, and whimsical colorful touches accent each room. Be sure to book reservations for dinner at the award-winning Fifth Floor restaurant during your stay. Check the website for special deals, some quite reasonably priced, that focus on shopping and spa-style relaxation. You can even book a spa package with your dog!

The **Palace Hotel** (2 New Montgomery St., 415/512-1111, www.sfpalace.com, $300–575) enjoys its reputation as the grande dame of all San Francisco hotels. The original Palace was the dream of William Ralston, who bankrupted himself creating the immense hotel. The rich history of the Palace began when its doors opened in 1875. It was gutted by fires following the 1906 earthquake, rebuilt and reopened in 1909, and refurbished for the new millennium over the years 1989–1991. In 1919, President Woodrow Wilson negotiated terms of the Treaty of Versailles over lunch at the Garden Court. Today, guests take pleasure in beautiful bedrooms, exercise and relax in the full-service spa and fitness center, and dine in the Palace's three restaurants. If you're staying at the Palace, having a meal in the exquisite Garden Court dining room is a must, though you may forget to eat as you gaze upward at the stained-glass domed ceiling.

## NORTH BEACH AND FISHERMAN'S WHARF

Perhaps it's odd, but the tourist mecca of San Francisco is not its land of a zillion hotels. Most of the major hostelries sit down nearer to Union Square. But you can stay near the Wharf or in North Beach if you choose; you'll find plenty of chain motels here, plus a few select boutique hotels in all price ranges.

### Under $100

The **San Remo Hotel** (2237 Mason St., 415/776-8688, www.sanremohotel.com, $85–105) is one of the best bargains in the City. The old yellow blocky building has been around since just after the 1906 earthquake, offering inexpensive rooms to budget-minded travelers. One of the reasons for the rock-bottom pricing is the bathrooms—you don't get your own. Four shared baths with shower facilities located in the hallways are available to guests day and night. The rooms boast the simplest of furnishings and decorations, as well as clean white painted walls and ceiling. Some rooms have their own sinks, all have either double beds or two twin beds, and none have telephones or televisions—so this might not be the best choice of lodgings for large, media-addicted families. Couples on a romantic vacation can rent the Penthouse, a lovely room for two people with lots of windows and a rooftop terrace boasting views of North Beach and the Bay.

### $150-250

**Hotel Bohème** (444 Columbus Ave., 415/433-9111, www.hotelboheme.com, $200–225) offers comfort, history, and culture at a pleasantly low price for San Francisco. At the Bohème, a long history in the City meets a recent renovation to create an intriguing, comfortable lodging. Rooms are small but comfortable, Wi-Ri is free, and the spirit of the 1950s bohemian Beats lives on. Smallish, warmly, colored and gently lit rooms are particularly welcoming to solo travelers and couples, with their retro brass beds covered by postmodern geometric spreads. All rooms include private bathrooms, and the double-queen rooms can sleep up to four people for an additional charge.

The **Washington Square Inn** (1660 Stockton St., 415/981-4220, www.wsisf.com, $195–350) doesn't look like a typical California B&B. With its city-practical architecture and canopy out on the sidewalk, it's more of a small, elegant hotel. The Inn offers 16 rooms with queen or king beds, private bathrooms, elegant appointments, and fine linens. Some rooms have spa bathtubs, and others have views of Coit Tower and Grace Cathedral. Only the larger rooms and junior suites are spacious; the standard rooms are "cozy" in the European urban style. A few of the amenities include a generous continental breakfast brought to your room daily, afternoon tea, a flat-screen TV (all rooms), and free Wi-Fi. To stay at the Washington Square Inn is to get a true sense of the beauty and style of San Francisco.

### Over $250

For an ultra-luxurious stay in the City, save up for a room at **The Argonaut** (495 Jefferson St., 866/415-0704, www.argonauthotel.com, $350). With stunning bay views from its prime Fisherman's Wharf location, in-room spa services, and a yoga channel, The Argonaut is all San Francisco, all the time. Bold patterns in blues, golds, and black and white dominate guest room decor. Rooms range from cozy standards up to posh suites with separate bedrooms and whirlpool tubs. The hotel is located steps from the Maritime Museum and Ghirardelli Square.

It may be part of a chain, but the **Hyatt at Fisherman's Wharf** (555 North Point St., 415/563-1234, www.fishermanswharf.hyatt.com, $300) still merits a visit. The unusual-for-San Francisco brick facade hides an ultra-modern lobby and matching guest rooms. Though not too big, rooms are elegantly appointed with lots of decadent white linens. Many packages aim at both business travelers and visiting families. Perhaps the best of these is the "Summer

Parking Package," which includes overnight valet parking with the room rate.

Another great upscale hotel in the heart of San Francisco's visitors' district is the **Best Western Tuscan Inn** (425 North Point St., 415/561-1100, www.tuscaninn.com, $275–725). This luxurious Italian-inspired hotel offers great amenities and prime access to Fisherman's Wharf, Pier 39, Alcatraz, and all local shopping and dining. The attractive and very modern exterior gives way to earth tones and country-style charm in the common areas. The guest rooms boast bright colors and up-to-date furnishings—much fancier than you might be accustomed to from a Best Western. All rooms have private baths. They've also got Internet access, cable TV, and limo service to the Financial District three times daily. Check online for discount rates if you're coming during the middle of the week or booking more than two weeks in advance.

## MARINA AND PACIFIC HEIGHTS

These areas are close enough to Fisherman's Wharf to walk there for dinner, and the lodgings are far more affordable than downtown digs.

### Under $100

For an unexpected, bucolic park hostel within walking and biking distance to frenetic downtown San Francisco, stop for a night at the **Fisherman's Wharf Hostel** (Fort Mason Bldg. 240, 415/771-7277, www.sfhostels.com/fishermans-wharf, bed $26–30, private room $75–125). The hostel sits on Golden Gate National Recreation Area land, pleasantly far from the problems that plague other SF hostels. The best amenities (aside from the free linens, breakfast, and no curfews or chores) are the views of the Bay and Alcatraz, and the sweeping lawns and mature trees all around the hostel.

Few frills clutter the clean comfortable guest rooms at the **Redwood Inn** (1530 Lombard St., 800/221-6621, www.sfredwoodinn.com, $105–120). But if you need a reasonably priced motel room in ever-expensive San Francisco, this is a great place to grab one. From the location on Lombard, you can get to points of interest throughout the City.

### $100-150

The **Marina Inn** (3110 Octavia St., 800/274-1420, www.marinainn.com, $110–120), built in 1924, exudes old-fashioned San Francisco charm but boasts pleasant modern amenities. This small family-friendly hotel offers a continental breakfast, concierge services, and free Wi-Fi. The Inn is within walking distance of major City attractions, including Fisherman's Wharf, Ghirardelli Square, and the cable cars. And if you're feeling a bit scruffy and want to freshen up before your big night on the town, visit the Inn's attached barbershop or salon.

The rooms at the **Marina Motel** (2576 Lombard St., 800/346-6118, www.marinamotel.com, $147–200) may be small, but the motel is big on charm and character. At this friendly little motel, decorated in French-country style, you're welcome whether you smoke, have kids, or bring your dog. Just ask for the room type that best suits your needs when you make your reservations. Rooms are pleasantly priced for budget travelers, and several vacation packages offer deep discounts on tours, spa treatments, and outdoor adventures.

The stately **Queen Anne Hotel** (1590 Sutter St., 800/227-3970, www.queenanne.com, $109–259) brings the elegance of downtown San Francisco out to Pacific Heights. Sumptuous fabrics and rich colors spread through the guest rooms and common areas add to the feelings of decadence and luxury in this boutique hotel. Small, moderate rooms offer attractive accommodations on a budget, while superior rooms and suites take guests up the scale. Continental breakfast is included with each room, as are a number of high-end services such as courtesy car service and afternoon tea and sherry.

### $150-250

The **Francisco Bay Inn** (1501 Lombard St., 800/410-7007, www.franciscobayinn.com, $172–210) offers good motel lodgings at reasonable-for–San Francisco rates. The stellar location provides easy access to the Golden Gate Bridge, famously crooked Lombard Street, and Fisherman's Wharf. Best of all, the Francisco Bay offers free parking—a City rarity worth upwards of $50 per day.

Pack the car and bring the kids to the **Hotel del Sol** (3100 Webster St., 415/921-5520, www.thehoteldelsol.com, $230–275). This unique hotel-motel embraces its origins as a 1950s motor lodge, decorating the guest rooms in bright bold colors with whimsical accents, maintaining the heated courtyard pool, and offering the ever-popular free parking with rooms. Family suites and larger rooms have kitchenettes. The Marina locale offers trendy cafés, restaurants, bars, and shopping within walking distance, as well as access to major tourist attractions.

A cute small inn only a short walk from the Presidio, the **Laurel Inn** (444 Presidio Ave., 800/552-8735, www.jdvhotels.com/laurel_inn, $230–265) provides the perfect place for people with pets, or for travelers who want to stay a bit longer in the City. Many of the rooms have kitchenettes, and all are comfortable and modern. The G Bar lounge next door offers a nice place to stop and have a cocktail, and the exclusive boutiques of Pacific Heights beckon visitors looking for a way to part with their cash.

The exterior and interior amenities of the **Hotel Majestic** (1500 Sutter St., 415/441-1100, www.thehotelmajestic.org, $185–295) evoke the grandeur of early 20th-century San Francisco. The Edwardian-styled 1902 building now boasts antique furnishings and decorative items from England and France. Cozy guest rooms, junior suites, and one-bedroom suites are available. If you're in the City on business or just want to go shopping, take advantage of free car service to Union Square and the Financial District on weekday mornings. The Café Majestic serves breakfast and dinner, with a focus on local, healthful ingredients.

Another Pacific Heights jewel, the **Jackson Court** (2198 Jackson St., 415/929-7670, www.jacksoncourt.com, $210) presents a lovely brick facade out into the exclusive neighborhood. The 10-room inn offers comfortable, uniquely decorated queen-bed rooms and a luscious continental breakfast each morning.

### Over $250

Tucked in with the money-laden mansions of Pacific Heights, **Hotel Drisco** (2901 Pacific Ave., 800/634-7277, www.jdvhotels.com/drisco, $300–700) offers elegance to discerning visitors. Away from the frenzied pace and noise of downtown, at the Drisco you get quiet, comfy rooms with overstuffed furniture, breakfast with a latte (if you want it), and a glass of wine in the evening. Economy rooms have detached baths, and lavish suites have stellar views.

## CIVIC CENTER AND HAYES VALLEY

You'll find a few reasonably priced accommodations and classic inns in the Civic Center and Hayes Valley areas.

### $100–150

**The Grove Inn** (890 Grove St., 415/929-0780, www.grovinn.com, $138) offers simple, quiet rooms with double-paned windows and fluffy feather beds. Rooms are equipped with televisions and phones, and a continental breakfast is served every morning. You can walk from the Inn to "postcard row" (ask the innkeepers for directions), take a longer stroll down to the Civic Center, or take public transit or a cab to any of the City's attractions.

### $150–250

Located in Hayes Valley a few blocks from the Opera House, the **Inn at the Opera** (333 Fulton St., 800/325-2708, www.shellhospitality.com/hotels/inn_at_the_opera, $205) promises to have guests ready for a swanky night of San Francisco culture. In fact, overnight shoeshine and clothes-pressing services count among the inn's many amenities. French interior styling in the rooms and suites once impressed visiting opera stars and now welcomes guests from all over the world.

Take a step back into an older San Francisco

at the **Chateau Tivoli** (1057 Steiner St., 800/228-1647, www.chateautivoli.com, $150–340). The over-the-top colorful exterior matches perfectly with the American Renaissance interior decor. Each unique room and suite showcases an exquisite style evocative of the Victorian era. Most rooms have private baths, though the two least expensive share a bath. With a reasonable price tag even on the most opulent suites, this B&B is perfect for families (though there are no TVs in any room) and for longer stays. Try to get a room for a weekend so you can partake of the gourmet champagne brunch.

It might seem strange to stay at an inn called **The Parsonage** (198 Haight St., 888/763-7722, www.theparsonage.com, $180). But this classy Victorian bed-and-breakfast exemplifies the bygone elegance of the City in one of its most colorful neighborhoods. Rooms are decorated with antiques, and each bathroom has a stunning marble shower. Enjoy pampering, multi-course breakfasts, and brandy and chocolates when you come "home" each night.

## MISSION AND CASTRO

Accommodations in these neighborhoods are few and tend to run toward modest B&Bs.

### Under $100

For a sweet, affordable little Castro inn experience, try the **Castillo Inn** (48 Henry St., 800/865-5112, $95). With only four rooms and shared baths, you'll imagine you've found a family pension in Tuscany transported to San Francisco. In the midst of the Castro, you've got all sorts of queer-life entertainment options only a short stroll way.

### $100-150

For a romantic visit to the Castro with your partner, stay at the **Willows Inn Bed & Breakfast** (710 14th St., 800/431-0277, www.willowssf.com, $125–180). The Willows has European-style shared baths and comfortable guest rooms with private sinks and bent willow furnishings, and serves a yummy continental breakfast each morning. Catering to the queer community, the innkeepers at the Willows can help you with nightclubs, restaurants, and festivals in the City and local to the Castro. One of the best amenities is the friendship and camaraderie you'll find with the other guests and staff at this great Edwardian B&B.

At the **Inn on Castro** (321 Castro St., 415/861-0321, www.innoncastro.com, $120–220), you've got all kinds of choices. You can pick an economy room with a shared bath, a posh private suite, or a self-service apartment. Once ensconced, you can chill out on the cute patio, or go out into the Castro to take in the legendary entertainment and nightlife. The self-catering apartments can sleep up to four and have fully furnished and appointed kitchens and dining rooms. Amenities include cable LCD televisions, DVD players, and colorful modern art.

## GOLDEN GATE PARK AND THE HAIGHT

Accommodations around Golden Gate Park are surprisingly reasonable. Leaning towards Victorian and Edwardian inns, most lodgings sit in the mid-tier price range for well-above-average rooms and services. However, getting downtown from the quiet residential spots can be a trek; ask at your inn about car services, cabs, and the nearest bus lines.

### $100-150

The Summer of Love seems endless to guests at the **Red Victorian Bed, Breakfast, and Art** (1665 Haight St., 415/864-1978, www.redvic.com, $105–270). The Red Vic serves up peace, love, and literature along with breakfast, while community and color (but absolutely no TVs) decorate the guest rooms. Part of the economy of this B&B includes shared, named bathrooms for some rooms, though many rooms do have their own private baths. Enjoy the intellectual, peaceful conversations over breakfast, browse the Peace Arts Gift Shop, and if you can, get in a chat with owner Sami Sunchild.

A charming Victorian, the **Inn 1890** (1890 Page St., 415/386-0436, www.inn1890.com,

$115–195) embodies truth in advertising. The Queen Anne Victorian mansion was built in 1890, at 1890 Page Street. Budget travelers enjoy the smaller rooms with private baths and memory-foam mattresses, while those with a bit more money pick the larger rooms with the original wood fireplaces. Enjoy a continental breakfast each morning, and feel free to use the guest kitchen 24 hours a day.

Down in the residential Richmond district, the **Ocean Beach Bed & Breakfast** (611 42nd Ave., 415/668-0193, www.oceanbeachbb.com, $140–175) sits three blocks from the all-day attractions of Golden Gate Park. Book early, since this B&B has only two rooms: a queen room and a suite both decorated with country-style antiques and traditional quilts. With its family-style continental breakfast each morning and cookies and milk in the afternoons, this inn may be as close as you can come to living in San Francisco by the sea. To round out your stay, peruse the collection of movies set in San Francisco, books on local history, and menus for local restaurants.

### $150-250

The **Stanyan Park Hotel** (750 Stanyan St., 415/751-1000, www.stanyanpark.com, $170–400) graces the Upper Haight area across the street from Golden Gate Park. This renovated 1904–1905 building, listed on the National Register of Historic Places, shows off its Victorian heritage both inside and out. Rooms can be small, but are elegantly decorated, and a number of multi-room suites are available. For a special treat, ask for a room overlooking the park.

# Food

One of the main reasons people come from near and far to San Francisco is to eat. Some of the greatest culinary innovation in the world comes out of the kitchens in the City. The only real problem is how to choose which restaurant to eat dinner at tonight!

## UNION SQUARE AND NOB HILL

### American

Looking for a good old-fashioned American breakfast? Walk on down to **Dottie's True Blue Café** (522 Jones St., 415/885-2767, Wed.–Mon. 7:30 A.M.–3 P.M., $6–12). The menu is simple: classic egg dishes, light fruit plates, and an honest-to-goodness blue-plate special for breakfast, and salads, burgers, and sandwiches for lunch. The service is friendly and the portions are huge. So what's the catch? Everyone in San Francisco knows that there's a great breakfast to be had at Dottie's. Expect lines up to an hour long for a table at this locals' mecca, especially at breakfast on weekend mornings.

### Asian Fusion

It seemed unlikely that anything worthy could possibly replace Trader Vic's, but **Le Colonial** (20 Cosmo Pl., 415/931-3600, www.lecolonialsf.com, Sun.–Wed. 5:30 P.M.–10 P.M., Thurs.–Sat. 5:30–11 P.M., $25–40) does it. This Vietnamese-fusion hot spot takes pride in its tiki lounge, which features local DJs spinning Thursday–Saturday 4:30 P.M.–2 A.M. Cocktails are big and tropical, and pay proper homage to the building's illustrious former occupant. But don't skip the food; the lush French-Vietnamese fare comes family-style and blends flavors in a way that seems just perfect for San Francisco.

You'll find all of Southeast Asia in the food at **E&O Trading Company** (314 Sutter St., 415/693-0303, www.eotrading.com, lunch Mon.–Sat 11:30 A.M.–5 P.M., dinner Mon.–Thurs. 5–10 P.M., Fri.–Sat. 5–11 P.M., Sun. 5–9:30 P.M.). This fusion grill serves up Indian flatbreads with Vietnamese small plates mixed in with big grilled dishes. Enjoy the wine list and full bar, or consider ordering takeout. Reservations are recommended.

## California

A San Francisco legend, make reservations in advance if you want to dine at **Farallon** (450 Post St., 415/956-6969, www.farallonrestaurant.com, Mon.–Thurs. 5:30–10 P.M., Fri.–Sat. 5:30–11 P.M., Sun. 5–10 P.M., $30–55). Dark, cavelike rooms are decorated in an undersea theme—complete with the unique Jellyfish Bar. The cuisine, on the other hand, is out of this world. Chef Mark Franz has made Farallon a 10-year fad that just keeps gaining ground. The major culinary theme, seafood, dominates the pricey-but-worth-it menu. Desserts by award-winning pastry chef Emily Luchetti round out what many consider to be the perfect California meal.

Another local mainstay of San Francisco haute cuisine is Wolfgang Puck's **Postrio** (545 Post St., 415/776-7825, www.postrio.com, Sun.–Wed. 5:30–10 P.M., Thurs.–Sat. 5:30–10:30 P.M., $30–40). Here you'll find everything from Puck's famed pizzas to the best of rarified local, sustainable fare. The restaurant has three levels, all of which see their share of celebrities. Not surprisingly, reservations are highly recommended if you want to dine chez Puck.

Even with high name-brand and San Francisco–level expectations, the **Dining Room at the Ritz-Carlton** (600 Stockton St., 415/773-6168, www.ritzcarlton.com, Tues.–Thurs. 6 P.M.–9 P.M., Fri.–Sat. 5:30–9:30 P.M.) measures up. Consistently named a top national restaurant by major ratings organizations, the Dining Room serves up mouth-watering French-inspired California cuisine, including plenty of meat, seafood, and creative vegetarian options. You don't need to be a hotel guest to get a reservation here or to take advantage of the convenient valet parking.

## Chinese

It may not be in Chinatown, but the dim sum at **Yank Sing** (101 Spear St., 415/957-9300, www.yanksing.com, Mon.–Fri. 11 A.M.–3 P.M., Sat.–Sun. 10 A.M.–4 P.M.) is second to none. The family owns and operates both this restaurant and its sister on Stevenson Street, and now the third generation is training to take over. In addition to the traditional steamed pork buns, shrimp dumplings, egg custard tarts and such, the "Creative Collection" offers unique bites you won't find elsewhere in the City. Lunch only!

## French

The famed **Fleur de Lys** (777 Sutter St., 415/673-7779, www.fleurdelyssf.com, daily 5:30–10:30 P.M., prix fixe $70–92, reservations strongly recommended) is open again. The San Francisco institution burned nearly to the ground in 2001, and the rebuilding took over a year to complete. But now one of the longest running and finest dining establishments has had the time to re-establish itself, and chef Hubert Keller (Keller may be *the* best name in Bay Area dining, ever) continues to create delectable and inventive dishes. The dining room is magnificent, with its elaborate tented ceiling, lushly upholstered chairs, and perfect glass accent pieces. But the reason people flock to Fleur de Lys is and has always been the food. The absolutely cream-of-the-crop menu isn't really à la carte-instead, you're encouraged to peruse the items and create your own three-, four-, or five-course feast. Vegetarians aren't left out here, since Keller creates fish-only and vegetable-only with the same love he dedicates to his meats. You'll probably want wine with your meal, which means it's going to cost a bundle. But it's worth your money to save up and splurge at this world-famous spot.

Tucked away in a tiny alley that looks like it might have been transported from St. Michel in Paris, ☾ **Café Claude** (7 Claude Ln., 415/392-3505, www.cafeclaude.com, Mon.–Sat. 11:30 A.M.–10:30 P.M., Sun. 5:30–10:30 P.M., bar Mon.–Sat. until 2 A.M., $10–25) serves classic brasserie cuisine to French expatriates and Americans alike. Much French is spoken here, but the simple food tastes fantastic in any language. Café Claude is open from lunch all the way through dinner, serving an attractive post-lunch menu for weary shoppers looking for sustenance at 3 or 4 P.M. In the evening it can get crowded, but reservations aren't strictly necessary if you're willing to order a classic French cocktail or a glass of wine and enjoy the bustling atmosphere and live music (on weekends) for a few minutes.

### Mediterranean

**Cortez** (550 Geary Blvd., 415/292-6360, www.cortezrestaurant.com, nightly 5:30–10:30 P.M., $10–15/small plate) exemplifies what happens when nouveau cuisine goes *right.* The Mediterranean-inspired food is utterly delectable. Friendly servers know the menu and the wine list, and are happy to make recommendations. It's best to order two or three small plates per person, and it's also the most fun. The more people you bring, the more dishes you get to try! The desserts, created by a master pastry chef, are worth saving room for. The sugar and spice beignets (with a chocolate fondue for dipping) are a house favorite, but must be ordered in advance. Rservations are a good idea on weekend evenings, especially for theatergoers.

### Coffee

The best latte I have ever tasted came from **Caffé Espresso** (462 Powell St., 415/395-8585, www.caffeespresso.com, breakfast, lunch, and dinner daily). On the ground floor of the Sir Francis Drake Hotel, this coffee bar with its soft yellow walls and vintage Parisian framed prints feels like it belongs in Europe. Alcoholic coffee drinks are served at the bar, and off to one side you can get a sandwich, salad, or panini from the little deli counter. This is the perfect place to sit and rest your weary feet after a long day of shopping or sightseeing, and watch the cable cars roll past the window on Powell Street.

## FINANCIAL DISTRICT AND SOMA

### California

A locals' favorite, especially for weekend brunch, **Butterfly** (Pier 33, 415/864-8999, www.butterflysf.com, Mon.–Fri. 11:30 A.M.–3 P.M., 3:30–11 P.M., Sat.–Sun. 11 A.M.–3 P.M., 3:30–10 P.M., $16–30) attracts a young, hip crowd with its ultra-modern decor and cocktails for both lunch and dinner. You can sit at a window table enjoying the Asian-inspired California cuisine and watching the city-sized cruise ships dock next door. The brunch menu offers fun breakfast-type dishes. Butterfly can draw a crowd, so make reservations to get a seat at your favorite time. The bar is open until 2 A.M. nightly.

### Chinese

**Shanghai 1930** (133 Steuart St., 415/896-5600, www.shanghai1930.com, Mon.–Thurs. 11:30 A.M.–2 P.M., 5:30–10 P.M., Fri.–Sat. 11:30 A.M.–2 P.M., 5:30–11 P.M., $16–35) evokes the bygone elegance of Shanghai in the early 1900s. Classic American-Chinese restaurant styling meets San Francisco elegance in a dining room decorated with Asian antiques and Oriental rugs. Even if you're new to serious Chinese food, you'll enjoy the choice of dim sum baskets, upscale entrées, and tasty hot appetizers. The American twist comes in the evening, when local jazz combos play live music for diners six nights a week.

### French

There's no question that the **Fifth Floor** (12 Fourth St., 415/348-1555, www.fifthfloorrestaurant.com, Mon.–Sat. 5:30–10 P.M., $30–40) is one of the top French restaurants in San Francisco. Which is saying something. The restaurant sits on the fifth floor of the Hotel Palomar. It's got both a casual café and a full-scale formal dining room to serve as many diners as possible. The cuisine exemplifies the best of southern France—the chef specializes in Gascon food and loves to create dishes that show off his early life and training. An ultra-expensive dinner up on the Fifth Floor is the perfect excuse to dress to the nines. Don't worry, the dining room decor can take it.

For the lower end of the French cuisine spectrum, check out **Crepes A Go Go** (350 11th St, 415/503-1294, daily 11 A.M.–10 P.M., $3.50–6) in SoMa. Believe it or not, the tiny but clean premises, single guy working the crepes, and late-night hours (call to check what the *real* closing hours are) are all quite reminiscent of

Paris. Crepes A Go Go can make you up some quick and hearty nighttime sustenance or perhaps a fruity dessert. The house special is the turkey, egg, and cheese—a great way to fuel a full night of drinking and clubbing.

## Italian

**Palio d'Asti** (640 Sacramento St., 415/395-9800, www.paliodasti.com, lunch Mon.–Fri. 11:30 A.M.–2:30 P.M., dinner Mon.–Fri. 5:30–9 P.M., $15–33) is one of the City's elder statesmen. The restaurant has been around since just after the 1906 earthquake, and the decor in the dining areas recreates an era further gone in the Old Country. Try either lunch or dinner, and enjoy the classical Italian menu, which includes wood-fired handmade pizzas as well as homemade pastas and classic Italian entrées. If you're in the City in fall, be sure to stop in and sample the luscious, expensive, and exceedingly rare Piedmont white truffles.

## Japanese

In these neighborhoods, you'll find plenty of sushi restaurants to choose from, from the most ultra-casual walk-up lunch places to the fanciest fusion joints. **Ame** (689 Mission St., St. Regis Hotel, 415/284-4040, www.amerestaurant.com, daily 5:30–10 P.M., $34–42) is one of the latter. Appropriately situated in stylish SoMa, this upscale eatery serves a California-Japanese fusion style of seafood. Raw fish fanciers can start out with (or make a meal of) the offerings from the sashimi bar, while folks who prefer their food cooked will find a wealth of options in the appetizers and main courses. The attractively colored blocky dining room has a modern flair that's in keeping with the up-to-date cuisine coming out of the kitchen. You can either start out or round off your meal with a cocktail from the shiny black bar.

Forget your notions of the plain-Jane sushi bar; **Ozumo** (161 Steuart St., 415/882-1333, www.ozumo.com, lunch Mon.–Fri. 11:30 A.M.–2 P.M., dinner Sun.–Wed. 5:30–10 P.M., Thurs.–Sat. 5:30–11 P.M.) takes Japanese cuisine upscale, San Francisco style. Order some classic nigiri, a small-plate Izakaya pub dish, or a big chunk of meat off the traditional robata grill. The high-quality sake lines the shelves above the bar and along the walls. For non-imbibers, choose from a selection of premium teas. If you're a night owl, enjoy a late dinner on weekends and drinks in the lounge nightly.

## Steak

An old-school chop house seems like an unlikely venture for sustainable food junkie Traci Des Jardins. But the **Acme Chophouse** (24 Willie Mays Plaza, 415/644-0240, www.acmechophouse.com, lunch Tues.–Fri. 11 A.M.–2:30 P.M., dinner Tues.–Sat. 5:30–10 P.M., $23–47) proves that great food truly comes in all styles. The perfect place to enjoy an upscale meal before a ballgame, Acme serves locally ranched steaks, delicious fries, stylish salads, and yummy desserts. If you spring for the grass-fed beef, you're in for a special treat. Though the sauces that come with each steak are delicious in their own right, the grass-fed steaks are so juicy and flavorful you'll forget all about the sauce. With a big sweeping dining room and an open kitchen, Acme succeeds in creating a casual atmosphere apropos of the ballpark and welcoming to diners in jeans. Sure, you'll spend a pretty penny on your meal, but at least you'll feel comfy while you're eating it.

## Vietnamese

Probably the single most famous Asian restaurant in a city filled with eateries of all types is **The Slanted Door** (1 Ferry Plaza, #3, 415/861-8032, lunch daily 11 A.M.–2:30 P.M., tea daily 2:30–5:30 P.M., dinner Sun.–Thurs. 5:30–10 P.M., Fri.–Sat. 5:30–10:30 P.M.). If all you know of Vietnamese cuisine is rubbery summer rolls and tripe-and-tendon *pho,* you are in for some seriously tasty re-education. Owner Charles Phan, along with more than 20 family members and the rest of his staff, pride themselves on welcoming service and top-quality food. Organic, local ingredients get used in both traditional and innovative Vietnamese cuisine, creating a unique dining experience. Even experienced local foodies often remark that they've never had green papaya salad, glass noodles, or shaking beef like this before. The light afternoon tea menu can be the perfect pick-me-up for weary travelers who need some sustenance to get them through the long afternoon until dinner. (Vietnamese coffee: the ultimate Southeast Asian caffeine experience!)

### Bakeries and Delis

One of the Ferry Building mainstays, the **Acme Bread Company** (1 Ferry Plaza, #15, 415/288-2978, Mon.–Wed. and Fri. 6:20 A.M.–7:30 P.M., Thurs. 6:20 A.M.–8 P.M., Sat.–Sun. 8 A.M.–7 P.M.) remains true to its name. You can buy bread here, but not sandwiches, croissants, or frou-frou pastries. But the bread you'll get tastes better than just about anything west of Paris. The original bakery was the brainchild of Steve Sullivan, who began his baking career while working as a busboy at (where else?) Chez Panisse in Berkeley. To this day, all the bread that Acme sells is made with fresh organic ingredients in traditional style. Beware: The baguettes are traditionally French, so they start to go stale after only 4–6 hours. Eat fast!

### Coffee and Tea

For their daily caffeine, local workers rely on the usual Starbucks and Peet's shoved into every convenient small storefront. If it's tea you favor, try the **Imperial Tea Court** (1 Ferry Plaza, #27, 415/544-9830, www.imperialtea.com, Tues.–Fri. 10 A.M.–6 P.M., Sat. 8 A.M.–6 P.M., Sun. 11 A.M.–5 P.M.) at the Ferry Building. This intensely Chinese tea shop sells black teas in bulk, beautiful Asian tea ware, and of course serves hot tea at its six Chinese rosewood tables. If you want to get *into* the tea experience, consider signing up for a class with owner Ray Fong, who is a published author and tea consultant. You'll learn about the traditions of tea, from plant to cup, including the Chinese ceremonial modes of serving.

### Farmers Markets

While farmers markets litter the landscape in just about every California town, the **Ferry Plaza Farmer's Market** (1 Ferry Plaza, 415/291-3276, www.ferrybuildingmarketplace.com, Tues. 10 A.M.–2 P.M., Sat. 8 A.M.–2 P.M.) is special. At the granddaddy of Bay Area farmers markets, you'll find a wonderful array of produce, cooked foods, and even locally raised meats and locally caught seafood. Expect to see the freshest fruits and veggies from local growers, grass-fed beef from Marin, and seasonal seafood pulled from the Pacific beyond the Golden Gate. Granted, you'll pay for the privilege of purchasing from this market—if you're seeking bargain produce, you'll be better served at one of the weekly suburban farmers markets. But even locals flock downtown to the Ferry Building on Saturday mornings, especially in the summertime when the variety of California's agricultural bounty become staggering.

## CHINATOWN

### Chinese Banquets

The "banquet" style of Chinese restaurant may be a bit more familiar to American travelers. Banquet restaurants offer tasty meat, seafood, and veggie dishes, and rice, soups, and appetizers, all served family-style. Tables are often round, with a lazy Susan in the middle to facilitate the passing of communal serving bowls around the table. In the City, most banquet Chinese restaurants have at least a few dishes that will feel familiar to the American palate, and menus often have English translations.

The **R&G Lounge** (631 Kearny St., 415/982-7877, www.rnglounge.com, daily 11 A.M.–9:30 P.M., $12–40, reservations suggested) takes traditional Chinese-American cuisine to the next level. The menu is divided by colors that represent the five elements, according to Chinese tradition and folklore. In addition to old favorites like mu shu, chow mein, and lemon chicken, you'll find spicy Szechuan and Mongolian dishes and an array of house specialties. Salt-and-pepper Dungeness crab (served whole on a plate) acts as the R&G signature dish, though many of the other seafood dishes are just as special. Expect your seafood to be fresh, since it comes right out of the tank in the dining room. California cuisine mores have made their way into the R&G Lounge, in the form of some innovative dishes and haute cuisine presentations. This is a great place to enjoy Chinatown cuisine in an American-friendly setting.

Another great banquet house is the **Hunan Home's Restaurant** (622 Jackson St., 415/982-2844, http://hunanhome.ypguides.net, Mon.–Thurs. and Sun. 11:30 A.M.–9:30 P.M., Fri.–Sat. 11:30 A.M.–10 P.M., $20). This one's a bit more on the casual side, and it's even got another location in suburban Los Altos. You'll find classic items on the menu such as broccoli beef and kung pao chicken, but do take care if something you plan to order has a "spicy" notation next to it. At Hunan Home's (and in fact at most Bay Area Chinese restaurants), they mean *really* spicy.

## Dim Sum

The Chinese culinary tradition of dim sum is literally translated as "touch the heart" or "order to your heart's content" in Cantonese. In practical terms, it's a light meal—a lunch or an afternoon tea—composed of small bites of a wide range of dishes. Americans tend to eat dim sum at lunchtime, though it can just as easily be dinner or even Sunday brunch. In a proper dim sum restaurant, you do not order anything or see a menu. Instead, you sip your oolong and sit back as servers push loaded steam trays out of the kitchen, one after the other. Servers and trays make their way around the tables; you pick out what you'd like to try as it passes and enough of that dish for everyone at your table is placed before you.

One of the many great dim sum places in Chinatown is the **Great Eastern Restaurant** (649 Jackson St., 415/986-2500, daily 10 A.M.–midnight, $15–25). Ironically it's *not* a standard dim sum place—instead of the steam carts, you'll get a menu and a list. You must write down everything you want on your list and hand it to your waiter, and your choices will be brought out to you. (Family-style is undoubtedly the way to go here.) Reservations are strongly recommended for diners who don't want to wait 30–60 minutes or more for a table at Great Eastern. This restaurant jams up fast, right from the moment it opens, especially on weekends. The good news is that most of the folks crowding into Great Eastern are locals. You know what that means.

Another well-known dim sum spot, **Yong Kee** (732 Jackson St., 415/986-3759, Tues.–Sun. 7 A.M.–6 P.M., $10, cash only) offers a completely different dim sum experience. This Cantonese-only hole in the wall caters primarily to locals, but if you've ever had dim sum or even just Chinese steamed buns before, you'll want to try them here. They're famous for their enormous fresh-made chicken buns *(gai bow),* though you can also get a great pork bun here if that's your preference. (The Chinese women lined up at the take-out counter have come for the buns.) The rest of their dim sum nibbles are right tasty too. No reservations are necessary (or taken) here. Do be aware that Yong Kee isn't a good beginner's dim sum place unless you've got a Cantonese-speaking friend to guide you. But if you're a fan of the cuisine already, you'll love Yong Kee even if you can't understand the menu or the staff.

## Tea Shops

Official or not, there's no doubt that the world believes that tea is the national drink of China. While black tea (often oolong) is the staple in California Chinese restaurants, you'll find an astonishing variety of teas if you step into one of Chinatown's small tea shops. You can enjoy a hot cup of tea in these, and buy yourself a pound of loose-leaf to take home with you. Most tea shops also sell lovely imported teapots and other implements of proper tea-making.

At the **Red Blossom Tea Company** (831 Grant Ave., 415/395-0868, www.redblossomtea.com, Mon.–Sat. 10 A.M.–6:30 P.M., Sun. 10 A.M.–6 P.M., $10–20) you'll find top-quality teas of every type you can think of and probably some you've never heard of before. Red Blossom has been in business for more than 25 years importing the best teas available from all over Asia. For the tea-adventurous, the blossoming teas, specific varieties of oolong, and *pu-erh* teas make great souvenirs to bring home and share with friends. And if you fall in love, never fear; Red Blossom takes advantage of Bay Area technology to offer all their loose teas on the Internet. (Sadly, their website isn't scratch-and-sniff, or they'd probably run out.)

Another option is **Blest Tea** (752 Grant Ave., 415/951-8516, http://hk.myblog.yahoo.com/blesttea, tasting $3). This shop boasts of the healthful qualities of their many varieties of tea. You're welcome to taste what's available for a nominal fee, to be sure you're purchasing something you'll really enjoy. If you're lucky enough to visit when the owner is minding her store, ask lots of questions—she'll tell you everything you ever needed to know about tea. Be aware that the Blest website isn't particularly English-friendly.

## NORTH BEACH AND FISHERMAN'S WHARF

### California

San Francisco culinary celebrity Gary Danko has a number of restaurants around town, but perhaps the finest is the one that bears his name. **Gary Danko** (800 North Point St., 415/749-2060, www.garydanko.com, nightly 5:30–10 P.M., prix fixe $65–96) offers the best of Danko's California cuisine, from the signature horseradish-crusted salmon medallions to the array of delectable fowl dishes. The herbs and veggies come from Danko's own farm in Napa. Make reservations in advance to get a table, and consider dressing up a little for your sojourn in the elegant white-tablecloth dining room.

### European

Basque cuisine is all the rage these days, and you can experience it in San Francisco at **Iluna Basque** (701 Union St., 415/402-0011, www.ilunabasque.com, Sun.–Thurs. 5:30–11 P.M., Fri.–Sat. 5:30 P.M.–midnight, $9–15). Start your meal with tapas (which come from this region) so you can linger over drinks before indulging in a flavorful main course, and finishing up with a fruity Mediterranean dessert. In Basque country, dinner traditionally starts late and goes on for hours; to mimic this charming custom in the New World, Iluna Basque is open late, even on weeknights.

With a culinary style perhaps best described as European fusion, **Luella** (1896 Hyde St., 415/674-4343, www.luellasf.com, Mon.–Sat. 5:30–10 P.M., Sun. 5–9 P.M., $17–28) brings the flavors of Italy, France, and Spain to the City. The tasty original dishes, most with a distinctive splash of California style that complements the European roots, are best enjoyed with a glass of wine from the extensive wine bar. If you're out late or on the run, dinner is served at the wine bar, and a bar menu offers tasty treats after the dining room closes.

### French

The **Hyde Street Bistro** (1521 Hyde St., 415/292-4415, Wed.–Mon. 5:30–10:30 P.M., $20) definitely belongs in San Francisco, what with the cable car clanging by outside the front door and the fog blowing past overhead. But in romance and cuisine, it's all Parisian splendor. A prix-fixe menu offers economy, while the à la carte menu provides a variety of traditional French bistro fare, including snails, foie gras, and coq au vin. Perhaps best of all, the prices at the Hyde Street Bistro are affordable by the masses. This is a perfect place to bring a date for romantic night out, or to celebrate an anniversary.

### Italian

Some of the best Italian food in the City hides in family-owned North Beach restaurants. Poke around and find your favorite hole in the wall, or try a bigger, more upscale spot.

At busy **Caffe Delucchi** (500 Columbus Ave., 415/393-4515, www.caffedelucchi.com, Mon.–Wed, 11 A.M.–10 P.M., Thurs, 11 A.M.–11 P.M., Fri.–Sat, 8 A.M.–11 P.M., Sun. 8 A.M.–10 P.M., $12–20), down-home Italian cooking meets fresh San Francisco produce to create affordable, excellent cuisine. You can get hand-tossed pizzas, salads, and entrées for lunch and dinner, plus tasty traditional American breakfast fare with an Italian twist on the weekends. Drinks run to soju cocktails and artisan Italian and California wines.

**Trattoria Contadina** (1800 Mason St., 415/982-5728, Sun.–Thurs. 5:30–9:30 P.M., Fri.–Sat. 5:30–10:30 P.M., $15–23) presents mouthwatering Italian fare in a fun, eclectic dining room. Dozens of framed photos line the walls and fresh ingredients stock the kitchen in this San Francisco take on the classic Italian trattoria. Kids are welcome, and vegetarians will find good meatless choices on the menu.

### Japanese

Even in a town with hundreds of sushi bars, **Sushi Groove** (1916 Hyde St., 415/440-1905, www.sushigroove.com, Sun.–Thurs. 5:30–10 P.M., Fri.–Sat. 5:30–10:30 P.M., $15–23) stands out. With an immense sushi bar, friendly chefs, and innovative sushi that blends traditional Japanese fish with unusual California touches, the Groove finds favorites with locals and visitors alike. For a special treat, order one of the chef's choice specials.

### Seafood

Don't be shocked, but the major ingredient in the cuisine of an area called Fisherman's Wharf is...fish! It's tough to walk down the streets of the Wharf without tripping over at least three big shiny seafood restaurants. You can pick just about any of the big ones and come up with a decent (if touristy) meal. A good way to choose is to stroll past the front doors and take a look at the menus.

It's got the look of a big tourist trap, but at **McCormick and Kuleto's** (900 North Point St., 415/929-1730, www.mccormickand schmicks.com, Sun.–Thurs. 11:30 A.M.–10 P.M., Fri.–Sat. 11:30 A.M.–11 P.M., $18–25), the chefs know how to cook seafood to satisfy even the pickiest local foodie. In the grand dining room with slightly scary light fixtures and the stellar views out to the Bay, you'll find an array of fresh fish and a list of innovative preparations. For fresh fish beginners, McCormick does offer some classic fries and grills as well. Be aware that this is a seafood restaurant, so land-based entrées are minimal here. Enjoy the fine wine list, and save room for in-season dessert.

### South American

If you're looking for something different and special for dinner in North Beach, seek out **Mangarosa** (1548 Stockton St., 415/956-3211, www.mangarosasf.com, Tues.–Thurs. 6–11 P.M., Fri. 6 P.M.–midnight, Sat. 5 P.M.–midnight Sun. 5 P.M.–10 P.M., $16–30). The "pink mango" offers a scrumptious taste of sunny Brazil under the chill San Francisco fog. The Italian neighborhood influence touches the South American cuisine here, and the dining room is open late for visitors who prefer to eat like Europeans.

### Steak

A New York stage actress wanted a classic steakhouse in San Francisco, and so **Harris'** (2100 Van Ness Ave., 415/673-1888, www.harris restaurant.com, Mon.–Thurs. 5:30–9:30 P.M., Fri. 5:30–10:30 P.M., Sat.–Sun. 5–10 P.M., $25–40) came to be. The fare runs to traditional steaks and prime rib, with a bit of upscale with a Kobe rib-eye steak and a surf-and-turf featuring a whole Maine lobster. Music lovers can catch live jazz in the lounge on weekends.

### Bakeries and Delis

Serving some of the most famous sourdough in the City, the **Boudin** (Pier 39, Space 5-Q, 415/421-0185, www.boudinbakery.com, $6–8) is a Pier 39 institution. Grab a loaf of bread to take with you, or order in one of the Boudin classics. Nothing draws tourists like the fragrant clam chowder in a bread bowl, but if you prefer you can try another soup, a signature sandwich, or even a fresh salad. For a more upscale dining experience with the same great breads, try **Bistro Boudin** (160 Jefferson St., 415/351-5561, Mon.–Fri. 11:30 A.M.–9:30 P.M., Sat.–Sun. 11 A.M.–9:30 P.M. $19–39).

## MARINA AND PACIFIC HEIGHTS

### French

Classic **Chez Maman** (2223 Union St., 415/771-7771, www.chezmamansf.com, daily 11:30 A.M.–11 P.M., $9–18) has not succumbed to modern food fancification. A host of simple lunch and dinner dishes add a distinct California flair to the classic French bistro fare. You can get a crepe or a quesadilla, a burger or a croque monsieur. Enjoy the tasty, inexpensive dishes in the soft pastel dining room that evokes the south of France. And if you're looking for good food outside the Marina, Chez Maman has another location in Potrero Hill.

For the finest European cuisine, make a reservation at **Quince** (1701 Octavia St., 415/775-8500, www.quincerestaurant.com, Mon.–Wed. and Sun. 5:30–10 P.M. Fri.–Sat. 5:30–10:30 P.M., $27–39) in Pacific Heights. Chef/owner Michael Tusk blends French and Italian culinary aesthetics to create his own unique style of cuisine. It's best to arrive at Quince hungry; the menu is divided into four different courses, or you can try the six-course tasting menu. And once you've gotten a look at the dishes, almost all made with the finest local and sustainable ingredients, you'll want to try at least one from every course!

## Italian

The name **A 16** (2355 Chestnut St., 415/771-2216, www.a16sf.com, lunch Wed.–Fri. 11:30 A.M.–2:30 P.M., dinner Sun.–Thurs. 5–10 P.M., Fri.–Sat. 5–11 P.M., $8–20) refers to the major road cutting through the Campania region of southern Italy. But at A 16 in San Francisco, you'll find fabulous southern Italian food rather than traffic. Handmade artisan pizzas, pastas, and entrées tempt the palate with a wealth of hearty flavors. Pasta dishes come in two sizes—a great thing for those with smaller appetites. Also in the proper Old Country tradition, a wonderful wine list has been built to complement the food.

For a southern Italian meal with a soft touch, **Capannina** (1809 Union St., 415/409-8001, Mon.–Thurs. 4:30–10:30 P.M., Fri.–Sun. 4:30–11 P.M., $17–23) is the place to dine. Soft green walls with marble and glass accents provide a sense of peace. The menu features classic Italian styling with an emphasis on the fruits of the sea. Many of the ingredients are imported directly from Italy, enhancing the authenticity of each dish.

## Japanese

For a super-hip San Francisco sushi experience, strut on down to **Ace Wasabi's** (3339 Steiner St., 415/567-4903, www.acewasabisushi.com, Mon.–Thurs. 5:30–10:30 P.M., Fri.–Sat. 5:30–11 P.M., Sun. 5–10 P.M., $6–13 per item). Advertising "rock 'n' roll sushi" and created with the atmosphere of an Izakaya (a sort of Japanese bar and grill), Ace Wasabi's appeals to a young, fun crowd. Be aware that the party can get loud on weekends.

On the other hand, the **Naked Fish** (2084 Chestnut St., 415/771-1168, www.nakedfishsf.com, Mon.–Thurs. 5:30–10 P.M., Fri.–Sat. 5:30–11 P.M., Sun. 5:30–9:30 P.M., $5–12 per item) proffers an upscale Japanese dining experience. In a fine dining room, taste the sushi, robata grill skewers, Hawaiian-style tapas, and spicy appetizers. Don't skip the sake—Naked Fish has a stellar menu of premium sakes, including unfiltered and high-quality bottles rarely found outside of Japan. Consider taking a date here for dinner to start an elegant night on the town.

If you're in Pacific Heights, give **Kiss Seafood** (1700 Laguna St., 415/474-2866, Tues.–Sat. 5:30–9:30 P.M., $30–50) a try. This tiny restaurant (12 seats total) boasts some of the freshest fish in town—no mean feat in San Francisco. The single chef prepares all the fish himself, possibly due to the tiny size of the place. Obviously, reservations are a good idea. When it comes to the menu, anything seafood is recommended, but if you're up for sashimi you'll be in raw-fish heaven. Round off your meal with a glass of chilled premium sake.

## Steak

The Marina is a great place to find a big thick steak. One famed San Francisco steakhouse, **Bobo's** (1450 Lombard St., 415/441-8880, www.boboquivaris.com, nightly 5–11 P.M., $25–40) prides itself on its dry-aged beef and fresh seafood. In season, enjoy whole Dungeness crab. But most of all, enjoy "The

Steak," thickly cut and simply prepared to enhance the flavor of the beef.

Another great house of beef is **Izzy's Steak and Chop House** (3345 Steiner St., 415/563-0487, www.izzyssteaksandchops.com, Mon.–Thurs. 5:30–10 P.M., Fri.–Sat. 5:30–10:30 P.M., Sun. 5–10 P.M., $17–26). Here you'll find an array of tasty steak preparations, seafood, and select non-steak entrées. Be sure to save room for one of Izzy's classic desserts! Izzy's has two out-of-the-City locations, in Corte Madera and San Carlos (convenient to the airport).

### Bakeries and Delis

Just looking for a quick snack to tide you over? Drop in at **The Chestnut Bakery** (2359 Chestnut St., 415/567-6777, www.chestnutbakery.com, Mon. 7 A.M.–noon, Tues.–Sat. 7 A.M.–6 P.M., Sun. 8 A.M.–5 P.M.). This smallish, family-owned storefront opened in 2002 and quickly drew a devoted local following. Only a block and a half from Lombard Street, it's also a perfect spot for weary tourists to take the weight off their feet and enjoy a cookie, pastry, or one of the bakery's famous cupcakes. If you come in the morning, you'll find scones, croissants, and other favorite breakfast pastries. Do be aware that this is a favorite spot for locals, which means that some items sell out during each day. Come early or call ahead if you've got a specific goodie in mind that you just can't live without.

## CIVIC CENTER AND HAYES VALLEY

### Brazilian

Some diners prefer a little South American flare with their steak dinner. **Espetus Churrascaria** (1686 Market St., 415/552-8792, www.espetus.com, lunch Mon.–Thurs. 11 A.M.–3 P.M., Fri. 11:30 A.M.–3 P.M., and Sat.–Sun. noon–3 P.M., dinner Mon.–Thurs. 5–10 P.M., Fri.–Sat. 5–11 P.M., Sun. 4–9 P.M., $30–80) can give you all the fire you want and more. Most of all, Espetus will give you meat. Lots of meat, both in quantity and variety. As much meat as you can handle, and more, until you wave a little flag of surrender to get the servers to stop bringing around the hot carts of meat carved to order. You'll pay handsomely for the delectable privilege of stuffing yourself at Espetus, but if you love meat, it will be worth every penny.

### French

☾ **Jardinière** (300 Grove St., 415/861-5555, www.jardiniere.com, nightly 5–10:30 P.M., later on performance nights, $20–60) was the first restaurant opened by local celebrity chef Traci Des Jardins. The bar and dining room blend into one another, and feature stunning art deco decor (the light fixtures are particularly fabulous if you're into that sort of thing). The ever-changing menu is a masterpiece of French-California cuisine. Des Jardins has long supported the sustainable restauranting movement, and she creates her enticing dishes with a wealth of local, organic ingredients. And her staff, even the bussers and dishwashers, are paid above industry standard wages and are given English classes that help them to move into higher-paying positions. Eating at Jardinière is not only a treat for your senses, it is a way to support the best of trends in San Francisco restaurants.

Be sure to make reservations if you're trying to catch dinner before a show. If you're dining before a performance, be sure to let your server know, and prompt service will be forthcoming. Or if you can wait until after the symphony or opera for dinner, Jardinière takes late-night diners on a first-come, first-served basis, so hit the exits at a run to get a good table.

**Absinthe** (398 Hayes St., 415/551-1590, www.absinthe.com, Tues.–Fri. 11:30 A.M.–12 A.M., Sat. 11 A.M.–12 A.M., Sun. 11 A.M.–10 P.M., $23–28) takes its name from the notorious "green fairy" drink made of liquor and wormwood. The U.S. ban on absinthe was lifted in 2007 and Absinthe indeed does now serve absinthe—including St. George Spirits Absinthe Verte, the first domestically produced absinthe since Prohibition, made locally in Alameda by St. George Spirits.

It also serves upscale French bistro fare, including what may be the best French fries in the

City. The French theme carries on into the decor as well—expect the look of a Parisian brasserie or perhaps a café in Nice, with retro-modern furniture and classic prints on the walls. The bar is open until 2 P.M., so if you want drinks or dessert after your show at the Opera or Davies Hall, just walk around the corner.

### German

In a city full of ethnic food, it can be tough to find German food. **Suppenkuche** (525 Laguna St., 415/252-9289, www.suppenkuche.com, nightly 5–10 P.M., Sun. 10 A.M.–2:30 P.M., $8–18.50) brings a taste of Bavaria to the Bay Area. The beer list makes a great place to start, since you can enjoy a wealth of classic German brews on tap and in bottles, plus a few Belgians thrown in for variety. On the dinner menu, expect to find German classics from various regions of the Old Country, with a focus on Bavarian cuisine. Spätzle, pork, sausage...you name it, they've got it, and it will harden your arteries right on up. Eat and enjoy!

### Indian

You can find amazing East Indian cuisine within the city limits, including at **Sultan** (340 O'Farrell St., 415/775-1709, daily 11:30 A.M.–2:30 P.M., 5–10 P.M., $15–20). The simplicity of the red-walled dining room makes it all the easier to concentrate on the cuisine. The chicken masala and garlic naan are local favorites, and the lunch buffet costs about $12.95 for all-you-can-eat delicious food. Just be aware that if you're not familiar with spicy cuisines, you'll want to ask for "not spicy" versions of most dishes. On the other hand, if you're into the high spice, you'll find Sultan perfect.

## MISSION AND CASTRO

### Mexican

Much of the rich heritage of the Mission district is Hispanic, thus leading to the Mission's being *the place* to find a good taco or burrito. The **Farolito Taqueria** (2950 24th St., 415/641-0758, Sun.–Thurs. 10 A.M.–12:45 A.M., Fri.–Sat. 10 A.M.–2:45 A.M., $10) has found favor with the ultra-picky locals who have dozens of taqueria options within a few blocks. It seems that every regular has a different favorite: the burritos, the enchiladas, the quesadillas...whatever your pleasure, you'll find a tasty version of it at Farolito. A totally casual spot, you'll order at the counter and sit at picnic-style tables to chow down on the properly greasy Mexican fare. Do be aware that if you come late at night, you'll encounter some of the less savory residents of the Mission. (Don't confuse this Farolito with the taqueria by the same name on Mission St.)

### Italian

Sometimes, even the most dedicated culinary explorer needs a break from the endless fancy food of San Francisco. When the time is right for a plain ol' pizza, head for **Little Star Pizza** (400 Valencia St., 415/551-7827, www.littlestarpizza.com, Tues.–Thurs., Sun. 5–10 P.M. Fri.–Sat. 5–11 P.M., $10–15). A jewel of the Mission district, this pizzeria specializes in Chicago-style deep-dish pies, but also serves thin-crust pizzas for devotees of the New York style. Once you've found the all-black building and taken a seat inside the casual eatery, grab a beer or a cocktail from the bar if you have to wait for a table. Pick one of Little Star's specialty pizzas, or create your own variation from the toppings they offer. Can't get enough of Little Star? They've got a second restaurant in the Western Addition at 846 Divisadero Street (415/441-1118).

On the other end of the Italian spectrum, you'll find **Delfina** (3621 18th St., 415/552-4055, www.delfinasf.com, Mon.–Thurs. and Sun. 5:30–10 P.M., Fri.–Sat, 5:30–11 P.M., $18–26). Delfina takes Italian cuisine and gives it a hearty California twist. From the antipasti to the entrées, all the dishes speak of local farms and ranches, fresh seasonal produce, and the best Italian-American taste that money can buy. With both a charming warm indoor dining room and an outdoor garden patio, there's plenty of seating at this lovely restaurant. As for the service? The wait staff at Delfina have actually won awards.

### Seafood

For great seafood in a lower-key atmosphere, locals eschew the tourist traps on the Wharf and head for the **Anchor Oyster Bar** (579 Castro St., 415/431-3990, Mon.–Fri. 11:30 A.M.–10 P.M., Sat. noon–10 P.M., Sun. 4–9:30 P.M., $15–30) in the Castro. Yes, it's got a raw bar that features oysters—enough different varieties, but not so many as to be overwhelming or pretentious. The dining room serves all sorts of seafood, including local favorite Dungeness crab. Service is friendly as befits a neighborhood spot, and the odd overlooking of the place by the restaurant-hungry media means that it sees fewer ridiculous crowds than other places. This doesn't diminish its quality, and it makes for a great spot to get a delicious meal before heading out to the local clubs for a late night out.

### Bakeries and Delis

Need to grab a quick sandwich before heading off on another San Francisco adventure? Get it at **Ike's Place** (3506 16th St., 415/553-6888, Mon. noon–4:30 P.M., Tues.–Thurs., Sat.–Sun. 11 A.M.–4:30 P.M., Fri. 11 A.M.–8 P.M., $10). An independent deli, Ike's serves big hearty homemade sandwiches that will fuel up even the most energetic travelers. The place really is owned by a man named Ike, who operates the deli with his mother. So if you prefer to patronize local family-owned businesses, Ike's is the perfect place to buy your daily carry-away lunch.

## GOLDEN GATE PARK AND THE HAIGHT

### American

Sometimes even the most dedicated of healthy eaters find themselves craving pizza, TV dinners, even (oh, the horror) hot dogs. If you happen to find yourself suffering with such a craving while touring the Sunset, **Underdog** (1634 Irving St., 415/665-8881, www.myspace.com/underdogorganic, daily 11:30 A.M.–9 P.M., $4) can hook you up. This genuine hot-dog stand sells organic sausages, from full-fledged brats to grass-fed beef dogs to vegetarian and even vegan sausages. Everything else is organic too-the rolls, the condiments, the side salads, and the sodas. Even the packaging and disposable items are made with recycled and biodegradable materials. So grab yourself a dog—guilt free! Be prepared to carry it with you or eat standing up, since seating at this tiny eatery is severely limited.

For visitors from parts east who long for a taste of home, **The Cheese Steak Shop** (1716 Divisadero St., 415/346-3712, www.cheesesteakshop.com, Mon. and Sat. 10 A.M.–9 P.M., Tues.–Thurs. 9 A.M.–9 P.M., Fri. 9 A.M.–10 P.M., Sun. 11 A.M.–8 P.M., $10) provides a welcome respite from the endless California cuisine. Heck, even locals can't live on bean sprouts all the time. This smallish franchise serves up hearty cheesesteak sandwiches, Philadelphia style, to order. You can even get a Tastykake, a goodie you won't find many other places in California.

### Cafés

The Sunset lends itself to a proliferation of cafes. Among the best of these is the **de Young Museum Café** (50 Hagiwara Tea Garden Dr., 415/750-2614, Tues.–Thurs. and Sat.–Sun. 9:30 A.M.–4 P.M., Fri. 9:30 A.M.–8:30 P.M., $10–20). Situated inside the museum on the ground floor, with a generous dining room plus outdoor terrace seating, the Café was created with the same care that went into the de Young's galleries. From the day it opened, the focus has been on local, sustainable food that's often organic but always affordable. Service is cafeteria-style, but the salads and sandwiches in the boxes are made fresh several times each day on the premises. Perhaps most surprising of all is the cheeseburger—you wouldn't think that one of the best cheeseburgers in the City is made at a museum café, but it is. Just be sure to get lunch early, or pick an off hour to eat; the lines at lunchtime can extend for what feels like miles.

Visitors to the Presidio can enjoy a quick bite or a leisurely lunch at the **Acre Café** (1013 Torney Ave., 415/561-2273, Mon.–Fri. 7:30 A.M.–3 P.M., $10). This simple café serves up fresh food for almost (but not quite) reasonable prices. Open for both breakfast and lunch, it's also a good spot to grab a cup of coffee to enjoy with a morning walk along the paths of the Presidio. Just keep in mind that this is a walk-up style café, so don't expect much by way of customer service.

### California

One of the most famous restaurant locations on the San Francisco coast is the Cliff House. It's been through a number of different restaurants over the decades. Currently, the high-end eatery inhabiting the famed facade is **Sutro's** (1090 Point Lobos, 415/386-3330, www.cliffhouse.com, daily lunch 11:30 A.M.–3:30 P.M., dinner 5–9:30 P.M., $18–36). The appetizers and entrées here run to seafood in somewhat snooty preparations. Though the cuisine is expensive and fancy, in all honesty it's not the best in the City. What *is* amazing are the views from the floor-to-ceiling windows of Sutro's out over the vast expanse of the Pacific Ocean. These views make Sutro's a perfect spot to enjoy a romantic dinner while watching the sun set into the sea.

### Japanese

Sushi restaurants are immensely popular in these residential neighborhoods. **Koo** (408 Irving St., 415/731-7077, www.sushikoo.com, Tues.–Thurs. 5:30–10:30 P.M., Fri.–Sat. 5:30–11 P.M., Sun. 5–10 P.M., $30–50) is a favorite in the Sunset. While sushi purists are happy with the selection of nigiri and sashimi, lovers of fusion and experimentation love the small plates and unusual rolls the chef/owner creates to delight his diners. Complementing the Japanese cuisine is a small but scrumptious list of premium sakes. Only the cheap stuff is served hot, as high-quality sake is always chilled.

### Thai

Dining in the Haight? If the touristy cafés don't appeal to you, check out the flavorful dishes at **Siam Lotus Thai Cuisine** (1705 Haight St., 415/933-8031, daily 11 A.M.–10 P.M., $7–13). You'll find a rainbow of curries, pad thai, and all sorts of meat, poultry, and vegetarian dishes in the Thai style. Look to the lunch specials for bargains, and to the Thai iced tea for a lunchtime pick-me-up. Locals enjoy the casually romantic ambiance at Siam Lotus, and visitors will make special trips down to the Haight just to dine here.

### Coffee and Tea

One of the prettiest spots in Golden Gate Park is the Japanese Tea Garden. And within the garden, you'll find the famous **Tea House** (Tea Garden Dr. and Martin Luther King Jr. Dr, 415/752-1171, daily 10 A.M. to 4:30 P.M., $10–20), where you can purchase a cup of hot tea to take with you on a soothing walk through the beautiful and inspiring garden.

# Information and Services

## INFORMATION

### Tourist Information

The main San Francisco **Visitor Information Center** (900 Market St., 415/3911-2000, www.onlyinsanfrancisco.com, Mon.–Fri. 9 A.M.–5 P.M., Sat.–Sun. 9 A.M.–3 P.M., closed Sun. Nov.–Apr.) can help you even before you arrive. See the website for information about attractions and hotels, and to order a visitors' kit. Once you're in town, you can get a "San Francisco Book" at the Market Street location, as well as the usual brochures and a few useful coupons.

English not your first language? You'll find materials at the Visitor Information Center in 12 different languages, as well as multilingual staff.

### Media and Communications

The major daily newspaper in San Francisco is the ***San Francisco Chronicle*** (www.sfgate.com). With an appropriately liberal slant on the national political news, a free website, and separate food and wine sections, it's the right paper for its city.

San Francisco also has about a zillion alternative

papers, free at newsstands all over town. The ***San Francisco Bay Guardian*** (www.sfbg.com) is one of the best known and best reputed of these. The alternative rags often have the best up-to-date entertainment information available, so if you're looking for nighttime fun, be sure to pick one up while you're out and about.

Need the **Internet?** You got it! This is San Francisco, after all. Most hotels have Internet access of some kind, the jillion Starbucks locations (sometimes two in the same block) often have Wi-Fi for a fee, and plenty of other restaurants and cafés also make it easy to get online. You can even try war-hacking if you're brave enough.

## SERVICES

### Banks and Post Offices

Just about every **bank** on earth seems to have a branch in San Francisco. **ATMs** abound, especially in well-traveled areas like Fisherman's Wharf and Union Square. Ask at your hotel or restaurant for the location of the nearest branch or ATM.

Post offices and mailing centers are common in San Francisco; again, ask your concierge or desk clerk for the facility nearest to your hotel. The **main post office** (1300 Evans Ave., 415/550-5501) boasts of its short lines and friendly(!) employees.

### Luggage and Laundry

If your hotel doesn't have valet service, you can take your dirty linen down to a coin laundry. As with most cities, take care—especially if you're a woman alone. Don't go after dark if you can help it, and bring a buddy if possible. My favorite laundry sits in Hayes Valley. It's the **Don't Call It Frisco Laundromat** (609 Hayes St., 415/626-1835, daily until 9 P.M.). It's clean and it's in a good, centrally located neighborhood, and the name says it all.

If you want to store your bags for a short time to make exploring easier, you can do so through the **Airport Travel Agency** (650/877-0422, daily 7 A.M.–11 P.M., no reservations necessary) on the Departures/Ticketing Level of the International Terminal at SFO, near Gates G91–G102. Fees vary by size of object stored, from $3 for a purse to $6–10 for a suitcase, up to $15 for surfboards or bicycles. All rates are for 24 hours storage.

### Medical Services

The **San Francisco Police Department** (766 Vallejo St., 415/315-2400) is headquartered in Chinatown, on Vallejo Street between Powell and Stockton.

San Francisco boasts a large number of full-service hospitals. The **UCSF Medical Center** (1600 Divisadero, 415/567-6600) is world renowned for its research and advances in cancer treatments and other important medical breakthroughs. People come from all over the world to be treated here. The main hospital sits at the corner of Divisadero and Geary, a mile or three west of Union Square. Right downtown, **St. Francis Memorial Hospital** (900 Hyde St., 415/353-6000, www.saintfrancismemorial.org) at the corner of Hyde and Bush has an emergency department.

# Getting There and Around

## GETTING THERE

### Air

The **San Francisco International Airport** (800/435-9736, www.flysfo.com) doesn't sit within the City of San Francisco. SFO is actually about 13 miles south in the town of Milbrae, right on the Bay. You can easily get a taxi or other ground transportation into the heart of the City from the airport. Both CalTrain and BART are accessible from SFO, and Some San Francisco hotels offer complimentary shuttles from the airport as well. You can also rent a car here.

As one of the 30 busiest airports in the world, SFO has long check-in and security lines much of the time, and dreadful overcrowding

## WALKING TOURS

The best way to see San Francisco is to get out and take a walk. You can find dozens of companies offering walking tours of different parts of the City. Here are a few of the best and most interesting:

One of the most popular walking tour companies in the city is **Foot** (800/979-3370, www.foottours.com, $30-45/person). Foot was founded by stand up comedian Robert Mac, and hires comics to act as guides for their many different tours around San Francisco. If you're a brand-new visitor to the City, pick the two-hour *San Francisco in a Nutshell* tour for a funny look at the basics of San Francisco landmarks and history, or the three-hour *Whole Shebang*, a comprehensive if speedy look at Chinatown, Nob Hill, and North Beach. For visitors who are back for the second or third time, check out the more in-depth neighborhood tours that take in Chinatown, the Castro, or the Haight. You can even hit *Nude, Lewd, and Crude*, a look at the rise of 18-and-up entertainment in North Beach. Tour departure points vary, so check the website for more information about your specific tour and about packages of more than one tour in a day or two.

San Francisco is famous for its incredibly steep hills. Logic suggests that residents would build stairways to make getting to their homes and businesses easier. And so it went. Today, some of the best and most beautiful walks in the City run up and down these stairways. A great guide to these walks is ***Stairway Walks in San Francisco*** (http://wildernesspress.com/book148.htm); with this book, you can plan routes through beautiful residential neighborhoods filled with lush gardens and attractive vintage homes. At the tops of the hills you'll be rewarded for your efforts with amazing views out over the City – one of the big reasons residents are willing to deal with all those steps and slopes. Just be aware that you'll need to be in reasonably good shape to tackle the stair walks.

For an inside look at the culinary delights of Chinatown, sign up for a spot on **I Can't Believe I Ate My Way Through Chinatown** (212/209-3370, www.wokwiz.com, $80/person). This three-hour bonanza will take you first

on major travel holidays. On a normal day, plan to arrive at the airport about two hours before your domestic flight, or three hours before an international flight.

### Train

Amtrak does not run directly into San Francisco. You can ride into San Jose, Oakland, or Emeryville, then take a connecting bus into the City. See the *San Jose* section of this chapter for more information about Amtrak service into the Bay Area.

### Bus

**Greyhound** (www.greyhound.com) offers bus service to San Francisco from all over the country. Buses usually come in to the **Transbay Terminal** (435 Mission St., 415/495-1569, station open 5:30 A.M.–1 A.M., ticket window open 5:30 A.M.–midnight).

### Car

Certainly you can drive into San Francisco. All major highways funnel onto the City. The Bay Bridge links I-80 from the east and the Golden Gate connects Highway 1 from the north. From the south, U.S. 101 and I-280 snake up the Peninsula and into the City. Be sure to get a detailed map and good directions to drive into San Francisco—the freeway interchanges, especially surrounding the east side of the Bay Bridge, can be confusing.

## GETTING AROUND

### Car

A car of your own is not necessarily a boon in San Francisco. The hills are daunting, traffic is excruciating, and parking prices are absurd. If you plan to spend all of your time in the City, consider dispensing with a car and using cabs and public transit options.

for a classic Chinese breakfast, then out into the streets of Chinatown for a narrated tour around Chinatown's food markets, apothecaries, and tea shops. You'll finish up with lunch at one of Chef Shirley's favorite hole-in-the-wall dim sum places. For folks who just want the tour and lunch, or the tour alone, check out the standard Wok Wiz Daily Tour ($40/person with lunch, $30/person tour only).

To check out another side of Chinatown, take the **Chinatown Ghost Tour** (877/887-3373, www.sfchinatownghosttours.com, Fri.-Sat. 7:30 P.M., adults $24, children $16, tour lasts 1.5 hours). It's hard to find a neighborhood with a richer history rife with ghost stories than San Francisco's Chinatown. The whole thing burned down more than a century ago, and it was rebuilt in exactly the same spot, complete with countless narrow alleyways. This tour will take you into these alleys after the sun sets, when the spirits are said to appear on the streets. You'll start out at Kan's Restaurant (708 Grant Ave.) and follow your loquacious guide along the avenues and side streets of Chinatown. As you stroll, your guide will tell you the stories of the neighborhood spirits, spooks, and ancestors. The curious get to learn about the deities worshipped by devout Chinese to this day, along with the folklore that permeates what was until recently a closed and secretive culture. This information delights all walkers, whether or not they actually get to see one of the legendary spirits.

Can't get enough of the spooky side of San Francisco? Check out a walking tour that's a favorite even with the locals: the **San Francisco Vampire Tour** (866/424-8836, www.sfvampiretour.com, Fri.-Sat. 8 P.M., adults $20, children $15). You'll take a two-hour walk around some of the City sites rich with history, and learn both about that history and some charming stories about the vampires' role in the creation and culture of the City. Guide Mina Harker is something of a vamp herself – at least she dresses the part. In fact, goth dress is encouraged for participants in the tour, so break out your black lace, your top hat, and your white makeup and become part of the show! This walking tour sticks mostly to the sights and famous hotels of Nob Hill.

Driving in San Francisco can be even more confusing. Like most major metropolitan centers, one-way streets, alleys, streetcars, taxis, bicycles, and pedestrians all provide impediments to navigation. Touring around the City to see the sights means traffic jams filled with workers on weekdays and tourists on weekends. It means negotiating the legendary steep hills without crashing into the cars behind and in front of you. And after all that, you come to the worst part....

To call parking in San Francisco a nightmare is to insult nightmares. Every available scrap of land that can be built on has been built on, with little left over to create parking for the zillions of cars that pass through on a daily basis. Parking a car in San Francisco can easily cost $50 per day or more. Street parking spots are as rare as unicorns, and often require permits (which visitors as a rule cannot obtain,

© LANCE SCOTT

Scooters are popular with City residents.

unless they're friends of Danielle Steel). Lots and garages fill up quickly, especially during special events.

If you can avoid it, don't bring a car into the City. Start your journey here and rent a car when you're ready to leave San Francisco, or turn your rental in early if the City is your last stop.

But if you absolutely must have your car with you, try to get a room at a hotel with a parking lot and either free parking or a parking package for the length of your stay.

All the major car rental agencies have a presence at SFO. In addition, if you're staying at a big hotel, check at the desk to see if they offer a car rental service. Rates tend to run $90–160 per day (including most taxes and fees), with discounts for full-week and longer rentals.

## Muni

The local opinion of the Muni (www.sfmta.com, adults $1.50 basic, $7 special event) light rail system isn't printable in guidebooks. The truth is, Muni can get you where you want to go in San Francisco, so long as time isn't a concern. A variety of lines snake through the City—those that go down to Fisherman's Wharf use vintage streetcars to heighten the fun for the tourists. See the website for a route map, ticket information, and (ha, ha, ha) schedules.

To buy tickets, use one of the vending machines that sit near some stops. Muni ticket machines sit outside of the CalTrain station. See the website for more information about purchasing tickets.

Muni also runs the bus lines, which require the same fares and can be slightly more reliable than the trains and go all over the City. Muni's website can get you to information about bus routes, schedules, and fares.

## BART

Bay Area Rapid Transit, or BART (www.bart.gov, fares vary $3–10/one-way) to locals, is the Bay Area's late-coming answer to major metropolitan underground railways like Chicago's L-train and New York's subway system. Sadly, there's only one arterial line

© LANCE SCOTT

The N Judah Muni line runs from Ocean Beach to downtown San Francisco.

through the City. However, service directly from San Francisco International Airport into the City now runs daily, as does service to Oakland International Airport, the cities of Oakland and Berkeley, plus many other East Bay destinations. BART connects to the CalTrain system and SFO in Milbrae. See the website for route maps, schedules (BART usually runs on time), and fare information.

To buy tickets, use the vending machines found in every BART station. If you plan to ride more than once, you can "add money" to a single ticket. Then keep that ticket and reuse it for each ride.

### CalTrain

This traditional commuter rail line runs along the Peninsula into Silicon Valley, from San Francisco to San Jose with limited continuing service to Gilroy. CalTrain (www.caltrain.com, fares vary $2.25–11/one-way) "Baby Bullet" trains can get you from San Jose to San Francisco in under an hour during commuter hours. Extra trains are often added for San Francisco Giants, San Francisco 49ers, and San Jose Sharks games.

You must purchase a ticket in advance at the vending machines in all stations, or get your 10-ride card stamped before you board a train. The San Francisco main CalTrain station sits at the corner of 4th Street and King Street, within walking distance of AT&T Park and Moscone Center.

### Taxis

You'll find plenty of taxis scooting around all the major tourist areas of the City. Feel free to wave one down or ask your hotel to call you a cab. If you need to call a cab yourself, try **City Wide Dispatch** (415/920-0700).

# North Bay

## MARIN HEADLANDS

Over the Golden Gate Bridge and through the Rainbow Tunnels, to Marin County we go! The Marin Headlands begins at the north side of the Golden Gate and encompass a wide swath of virgin wilderness, former military land, and an historic lighthouse.

### Visitors Center

A great place to start your exploration of the Marin Headlands is at the visitors center (Field Rd. and Bunker Rd., 415/331-1540, daily 9:30 A.M.–4:30 P.M.), located in the old chapel on Fort Barry. The rangers here can give you the current lowdown on the best trails, beaches, and campgrounds in the Headlands.

**Point Bonita Lighthouse** (415/331-1540, www.nps.gov/goga/pobo.htm, Sat.–Mon. 12:30 P.M.–3:30 P.M.) has been protecting the Headlands for over 150 years. It remains an active light station to this day. You need some dedication to visit Point Bonita, since it's only open a few days each week and there's no direct access by car. A half-mile trail with steep sections leads from the trailhead on Field Road. Along the way, you'll pass through a handmade tunnel chiseled from the hard rock by the original builders of the lighthouse, then over the bridge that leads to the building proper. Point Bonita was the third lighthouse built on the West Coast and is now the last manned lighthouse in California. Today, the squat hexagonal building shelters automatic lights, horns, and signals. For a special treat, call the lighthouse to book a spot on a romantic full-moon tour.

### Muir Beach

Few coves on the California coast can boast as much beauty as Muir Beach (just south of the town of Muir Beach, www.nps.gov/goga, daily sunrise–sunset). From the overlook above Highway 1 to the edge of the ocean beyond the dunes, Muir Beach is a haven for both wildlife and beachcombers. In the wintertime, beachgoers bundle up against the chill and walk the

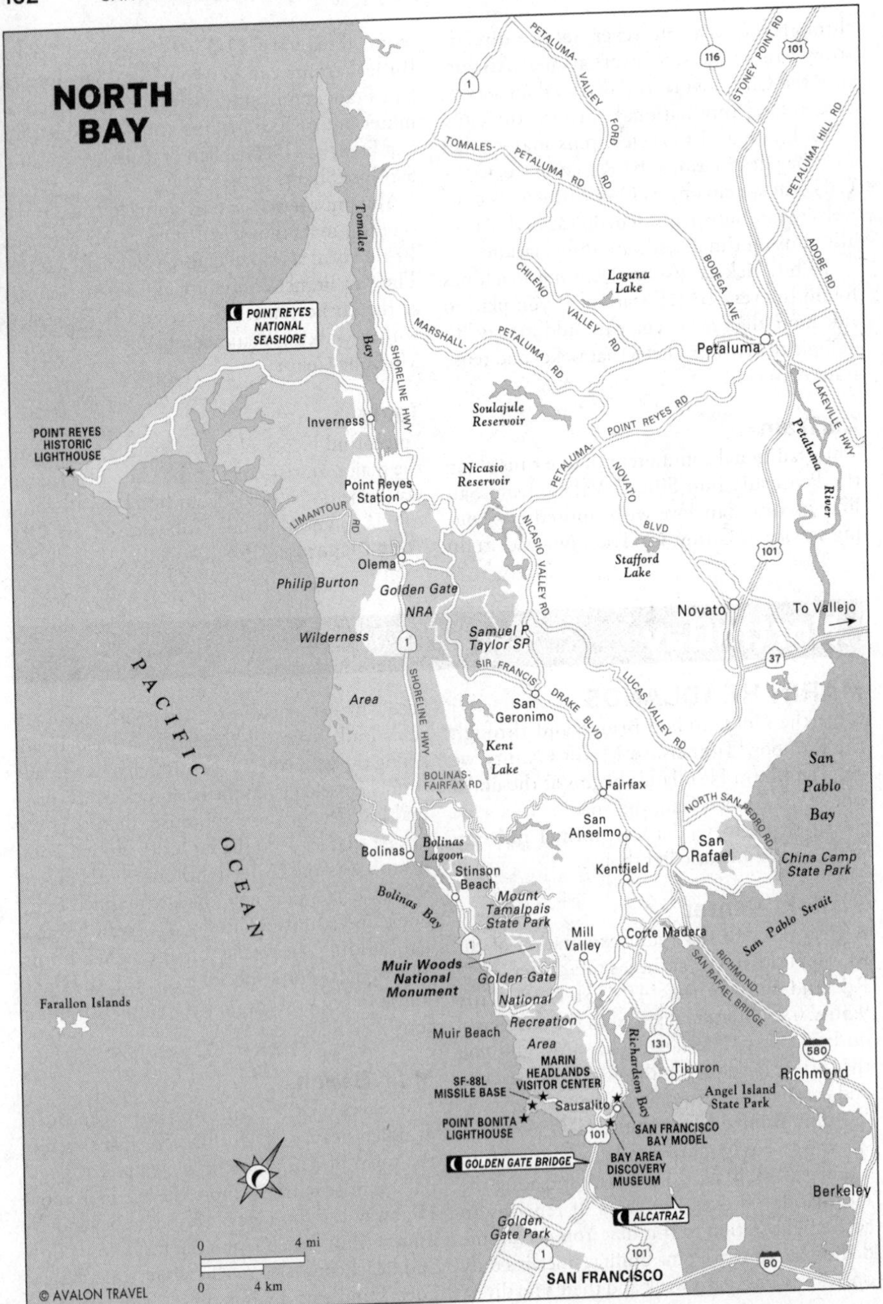
NORTH BAY
POINT REYES NATIONAL SEASHORE
POINT REYES HISTORIC LIGHTHOUSE
Tomales Bay
Inverness
Point Reyes Station
LIMANTOUR RD
Olema
Philip Burton Wilderness Area
Golden Gate NRA
PACIFIC OCEAN
SHORELINE HWY
PETALUMA-VALLEY FORD RD
TOMALES-PETALUMA RD
STONEY POINT RD
PETALUMA HILL RD
ADOBE RD
BODEGA AVE
CHILENO VALLEY RD
MARSHALL-PETALUMA RD
Laguna Lake
Petaluma
LAKEVILLE HWY
Petaluma River
Soulajule Reservoir
POINT REYES RD
PETALUMA-
NOVATO BLVD
Nicasio Reservoir
NICASIO VALLEY RD
Stafford Lake
Novato
To Vallejo
Samuel P Taylor SP
SIR FRANCIS DRAKE BLVD
LUCAS VALLEY RD
San Geronimo
Kent Lake
BOLINAS-FAIRFAX RD
Fairfax
San Anselmo
San Rafael
NORTH SAN PEDRO RD
San Pablo Bay
China Camp State Park
Kentfield
Bolinas
Bolinas Lagoon
Stinson Beach
Bolinas Bay
Mount Tamalpais State Park
Mill Valley
Corte Madera
San Pablo Strait
RICHMOND-SAN RAFAEL BRIDGE
Muir Woods National Monument
Golden Gate National Recreation Area
Farallon Islands
Muir Beach
Richardson Bay
Tiburon
Richmond
MARIN HEADLANDS VISITOR CENTER
SF-88L MISSILE BASE
Sausalito
Angel Island State Park
POINT BONITA LIGHTHOUSE
SAN FRANCISCO BAY MODEL
GOLDEN GATE BRIDGE
BAY AREA DISCOVERY MUSEUM
Berkeley
ALCATRAZ
Golden Gate Park
SAN FRANCISCO
1
116
101
37
131
580
80
0 4 mi
0 4 km
© AVALON TRAVEL

sands of the cove or along the many trails that spread out from the beach. If you're lucky, you might find a Monterey pine tree filled with sleepy monarch butterflies, here to overwinter before making their long migration back north in the spring. Springtime brings rare rays of sunshine to Muir Cove, and as the air grows (a little bit) warmer in summer, the north end of the cove attracts another breed of beach life: nudists. If the clothing-optional California lifestyle makes you uncomfortable, stick to the south side, the brackish Redwood Creek lagoon, and the wind-swept picnic grounds.

### SF-88L Missile Base

Military history buffs jump at the chance to tour a restored Cold War-era Nike missile base. The lyrically named SF-88L (Field Rd. past the Headlands visitors center, 415/331-1453, www.nps.gov/goga/nike-missile-site.htm, Wed.–Fri. 12:30 P.M.–3:30 P.M. and 1st Sat. each month, fees) is the only such restored Nike base in the United States. Volunteers continue the restoration and lead tours every half-hour at the base, which is overseen by the Golden Gate National Recreation Area. On the tour, you'll get to see the fueling area, the testing and assembly building, and even take a ride on the missile elevator down into the pits that once stored missiles created to defend the United States from the Soviet Union. Because restoration work continues endlessly, the tour changes as new areas become available to visitors.

### Hiking

Folks come from all over the world to hike the trails that thread through the Marin Headlands. The landscape is some of the most beautiful in the state. One of the most popular (and crowded, especially on summer weekends) places to start is the **Tennessee Valley Trailhead** (end of Tennessee Valley Rd., portable toilets, no water). A wealth of trails spring from this major trailhead. A quicker hike from the trailhead can take you out to the **Haypress Campground** (about 1.5 mi, moderate), which has picnic tables and pretty views. For a nice long hike, take the **Old Springs Trail** (2 mi) down to the **Wolf Ridge Trail** (0.7 mi) heading west, then across to the **Valley Trail** (2 mi) back north to the trailhead.

The **Rodeo Beach Trailhead** (end of Bunker Rd., running water, flush toilets, paved parking lot) offers access to Point Bonita, loop and one-way trails, and of course Rodeo Beach. An easy spot to get to, Rodeo Beach draws many tourists on summer weekends—expect not to be alone on the beach or the trails, or even in the water. Locals come out to surf at Rodeo when the break is going, while beachcombers watch from the shore. An easy walk from this trailhead is the **Lagoon Trail** (0.5 mi, easy), which gives bird-watchers an eagle's-eye view of the egrets, pelicans, and other seabirds that call the shelter of the Rodeo lagoon home. For a longer hike, you can take the **Miwok Trail** (1.8 mi) north, catch the **Wolf Ridge Trail** (2.3 mi) heading west, then pick up the **California Coastal Trail** (approx. 2 mi) heading back south past the Marine Mammal Center toward the road and the parking lots.

Naturally, hardcore hikers doing a serious

© LANCE SCOTT

the Marin coastline

survey of the **California Coastal Trail** can get in a good chunk of it here at the Headlands. Head north from Rodeo Beach and meander through the hills, then down closer to the beach past Tennessee Valley at Pirate's Cove. This chunk of the trail terminates at Muir Beach.

For more information about hiking and biking trails, visit the Golden Gate National Recreation Area online at www.nps.gov/goga.

## Biking

If you prefer two wheels to two feet, you'll find the road and trail biking in the Marin Headlands both plentiful and spectacular. From the Tennessee Valley Trailhead, you'll find plenty of multi-use trails designated for bikers as well as hikers. The **Valley Trail** (4 mi round-trip) takes you down the Tennessee Valley and all the way out to Tennessee Beach. A longer ride runs up the **Miwok Trail** (2 mi) northward. Turn southwest onto the **Coyote Ridge Trail** (0.9 mi), then catch the **Coastal Fire Road** (2 mi) the rest of the way west to Muir Beach. Another fun ride leads from just off U.S. 101 at the Rodeo Avenue exit. Park your car on the side of Rodeo Avenue, then bike down the **Bobcat Trail** (2.5 mi) straight through the Headlands to the **Miwok Trail** for just 0.5 mile, and you'll find yourself out at Rodeo Beach.

Need to rent a bike for your travels? In San Francisco, **Bike and Roll** (899 Columbus Ave., 415/771-8735, www.bikerental.com, daily 8 A.M.–10 P.M. in summer, until 6 P.M. in winter) offers off-road biking tours of the Marin Headlands, plus bike rentals that let you go wherever the spirit moves you.

## Accommodations

Lodging options are fairly limited in the Marin Headlands. Options run toward hostels and campgrounds, along with one lonely posh inn. Many luxury-minded travelers choose to stay in Tiburon or Sausalito, while budget-motel seekers head for San Rafael. While camping might sound appealing, it requires some planning. It can be foggy, cold, and windy in July and August (or any other month) in Marin. So bring your warm camping gear if you plan to seek out one of the precious few campsites in the Marin Headlands.

The most popular and biggest campground in the region is **Kirby Cove** (877/444-6777, www.recreation.gov, reservations required). Secluded and shaded campsites provide a beautiful respite from the busy world. Do make your reservations well in advance for summer weekends, since this popular campground fills up fast.

The **Bicentennial Campground** (Battery Wallace parking lot, 415/331-1540) boasts a whopping three campsites, each easily accessible from the parking lot. Each site can accommodate two people maximum, and there's no water or fires allowed on-site. A nearby picnic area has barbecue grills that campers can use to cook themselves a nice hot dinner. On the opposite end of the accessibility spectrum, you'll find the **Hawk Campground** (415/331-1540). The three-site (four people per) campground sits a two-mile hike up from the Tennessee Valley trailhead. Your reward for the work of packing in all your gear and water is a near-solitary camping experience that lets you kick back and get to know the wilderness surrounding you. Amenities include chemical toilets, but no water or fires.

Travelers who want budget accommodations indoors often choose the **Marin Headlands Hostel** (Fort Barry Bldg. 941, 415/331-2777, www.norcalhostels.org/marin, $22 dorm bed, $60 private room). You'll find full kitchen facilities, Internet access, laundry rooms, and a rec room—all the amenities you'd expect from a high-end U.S. hotel. Surprisingly cozy and romantic, the hostel is sheltered in the turn of the (last) century buildings of Fort Barry, creating a unique atmosphere. And of course, with the Headlands right outside your door and 24-hour access to all registered guests, no visitor lacks in activities or exploration opportunities here.

One fine Marin lodging rests inside **The Pelican Inn** (10 Pacific Way, Muir Beach, 415/383-6000, www.pelicaninn.com, $215). Inside the Tudor structure, the guest room decor continues the historic ambiance, with big beam construction, canopy beds, and historic portrait prints. The seven mostly small rooms each come with private bathrooms and a full English-style breakfast, but no televisions or telephones. The Pelican Inn is a perfect spot to unplug, disconnect, and truly get away from it all.

### Food

Few restaurants grace the wilderness and abandoned forts of the Marin Headlands. Never fear: The fine dining and fast food of Sausalito and Tiburon are a short drive away. You can also pick up supplies for camping or hostel cooking in either of these towns.

In addition to quaint bedchambers, you can get hearty food at **The Pelican Inn** (daily lunch 11:30 A.M.–3 P.M., dinner 5:30–9 P.M., $15–30). Dark wood and a long trestle table give the proper Old English feeling to the dimly lit dining room. The cuisine brings home the flavors of Merry Old England, with dishes like beef wellington and shepherd's pie, and sherry trifle and bread pudding for dessert. Though breakfast is served only to overnight guests, lunch and dinner are open to anyone who passes by. True fans of the Isles will round off their meal with a pint of stout.

## SAUSALITO AND TIBURON

Once a plain-Jane fishing town, Tiburon now supports some of the most expensive waterfront real estate in the world. The small downtown area that backs onto the marina is popular with the young and affluent crowd as well as the longtime yacht owners.

The affluent town of Sausalito wraps around the north end of the San Francisco Bay. The main drag runs along the shore, and the concrete boardwalk is perfect for strolling and biking. A former industrial fishing town, Sausalito still has a few old cannery buildings and plenty of docks, most now lined with pleasure boats.

### Angel Island State Park

Angel Island has a long history, beginning with regular visits (though no permanent

© LANCE SCOTT

downtown Tiburon

settlements) by the Coastal Miwok tribe. The Northern U.S. army created a fort on the island in anticipation of Confederate sea attacks from the Pacific. Though those attacks never came, the army maintained a base. Today, many 19th-century army buildings remain. You can see them on the tram tour ($13.50, 1 hour), walking, or on a docent-led segway tour ($65 per person). Later, the Army built a Nike missile base on the island to protect strategically important San Francisco from possible Soviet attacks. The missile base is not open to the public, but can be seen from roads and trails.

Not all the history of Angel Island brings pride to the state of California. The West Coast's answer to Ellis Island in the early 20th century, Angel Island served as an immigration station for incoming ships, and a concentration camp for the flood of Chinese attempting to escape the collapse of their homeland. While Europeans were waved through with little more than a head-lice check, the Chinese were herded into barracks while government officials scrutinized their papers. After months and sometimes years of waiting, many were shipped back to China. Today, poetry lines the walls of the barracks, expressing the despair of the immigrants who had hoped for a better life and found little more than prison. Docent-led tours show this poetry and the buildings of the camps.

Angel Island is a major destination for hikers both casual and serious. The island-wide park offers kayaking, swimming, hiking, and road and mountain biking. Trails of varying difficulty levels crisscross the island, creating fun for hikers and bikers alike. Adventurous trekkers can scale Mount Livermore via either the **North Ridge Trail** or the **Sunset Trail.** Each runs about 4.5 miles round-trip for a moderate, reasonably steep hike. But stopping at the top for a rest and some of the gorgeous Bay views hardly feels like a chore or a defeat. For the best experience, make a loop of your trip, taking one trail up and the other one back down the mountain. If you're up for a long paved-road hike, take the **Perimeter Road** (5 mi, moderate) all the way around the island.

© LANCE SCOTT

barracks at Angel Island State Park

Angel Island is located in the middle of San Franicsco Bay. To get there, you must either boat yourself in or take one of the ferries that services the island. The harbor at Tiburon is the easiest place from which to access Angel Island State Park (415/435-1915, www.parks.ca.gov, daily 8 A.M.–sunset, prices vary by ferry company). The private **Angel Island-Tiburon Ferry** (21 Main St., Tiburon, 415/435-2131, www.angelislandferry.com, $13.50 adults, $11.50 children, $1 bikes, no advance ticket sales) can get you out to the island in about 10 minutes and runs several times a day. You can also explore the **Blue and Gold Fleet** (415/703-8200, www.blueandgoldfleet.com), which runs out to Angel Island from Oakland/Alameda and San Francisco.

Ferries have plenty of room for you to bring your own bike, or you can rent one at the main visitors' area for $10 per hour or $35 per day. Grab a map from the gift shop. Not all trails are open to bikes, but those that are include the easy five-mile, paved Perimeter Road around the island, which is perfect for newcomers.

## Bay Area Discovery Museum

The Bay Area Discovery Museum (557 McReynolds Rd., Sausalito, 415/339-3900, www.baykidsmuseum.org, Tues.–Fri. 9 A.M.–4 P.M., Sat.–Sun. 10 A.M.–5 P.M., $10 adults, $8 children) offers kids of all ages a chance to explore the world they live in. The focus definitely rests on the younger set here; most of the permanent exhibits are geared toward small children, with lots of interactive components and places to play. Kids can check out easy-to-understand displays that describe the natural world, plus lots of Bay Area–specific exhibits. The Discovery Museum also boasts a theater and a café.

## San Francisco Bay Model

One of the odder attractions you'll find in the North Bay is the an Francisco Bay Model (2100 Bridgeway, Sausalito, 415/332-3871, www.spn.usace.army.mil/bmvc, summer Tues.–Fri. 9 A.M.–4 P.M., Sat.–Sun. 10 P.M.–5 P.M., call for hours in fall, winter, and spring). Here you can see a scale model of the way the Bay works, complete with currents and tides. Why would you want to see this? Scientist and engineering types love to see how the waters of the bay really move and work. For the rest of us…aw heck, why not?

## Accommodations

Sausalito and Tiburon together make up some of the swankest, most expensive real estate in the United States. If you're staying as a guest, you'll absorb a little bit of that expense, but a few bargains hide here and there.

### SAUSALITO

The **The Gables Inn** (62 Princess St., Sausalito, 415/289-1100, www.gablesinnsausalito.com, $200) inn was opened in 1869 and is the oldest B&B in the area. Each of the nine rooms is appointed in tasteful earth tones, with white linens and bountiful bathrooms. Though this inn honors its long history, it has also kept up with the times, adding cable televisions and Internet access. Genial innkeepers serve a buffet breakfast (available for a couple of hours) each morning and host a wine and cheese soiree each evening.

With a checkered history dating back to 1915, the **Hotel Sausalito** (16 El Portal, Sausalito, 888/442-0700, www.hotelsausalito.com, $178–325) may once have been a speakeasy, a bordello, and a home for the writers and artists of the beat generation. Today, this tiny boutique hotel, with its yellow walls and locally built furnishings, evokes the Mediterranean coast. Sink into your cozy room after a day spent walking or biking along the water and a scrumptious dinner out.

Then there's the **Casa Madrona Hotel and Spa** (801 Bridgeway, Sausalito, 800/288-0502, www.casamadrona.com, $325–575). This sprawling collection of structures, built up the side of Sausalito's hill over the course of 100 years, houses contemporary luxury hotel rooms and suites that satisfy even the pickiest celebrity guest. Poggio, the on-site restaurant, serves award-winning Italian food, and the full service spa pampers guests with a full menu of body and salon treatments. If you're treating yourself to a room at Casa Madrona, be sure to ask for one with a view overlooking the Bay or the harbor!

For a taste of the life of the richest residents of the area, stay at Sausalito's **Inn Above Tide** (30 El Portal, Sausalito, 800/893-8433, www.innabovetide.com, $350). Billed as the only hotel in the Bay Area that's actually *on* the Bay, the inn sits over the edge of the water looking out over the San Francisco skyline. Most rooms have private decks that let guests take advantage of the sublime views (well, except when it's foggy). Inside the rooms, the appointments look like something you'd find in an upscale home rather than a hotel. Guests love the rooms with oversized bathtubs set by windows to take advantage of the Bay views. From the hotel, you can walk downtown to enjoy the shops, spas, and restaurants of Sausalito.

### TIBURON

The lovely **Waters Edge Hotel** (25 Main St., Tiburon, 415/789-5999, www.marinhotels.com, $310–350) is a boutique lodging that lives up to its name, backing on to the marina and docks. You can stumble right out of your room, onto the dock, and over to the Angel Island ferry. Inside, you'll love the featherbeds, cushy robes, and breakfast delivered to your room each morning. Also wonderfully close to the water and attractions of downtown Tiburon, the **Lodge at Tiburon** (1651 Tiburon Blvd., Tiburon, 415/435-3133, www.thelodgeattiburon.com, $285–500) offers the comforts and conveniences of a larger hotel while providing the personal attention and atmosphere of a boutique inn. All the guest rooms are soothing and pretty, but for a special treat book a Spa Room with a huge raised whirlpool tub set in an alcove overlooking the water. Have dinner or a drink at the attached Three Degrees Restaurant and Bar in the evening, or take a walk downtown to look into the shops.

## Food

### SAUSALITO

If you're jonesing for some Chinese food, go to **Tommy's Wok Chinese Cuisine** (3001 Bridgeway, Sausalito, 415/332-5818, http://tommyswok.com, Mon.–Thurs. 11:30 A.M.–9:30, Fri.–Sat. 11:30 A.M.–10 P.M., Sun. 4–9:30 P.M., $10–20). Unlike a typical Chinese restaurant, Tommy's has gotten into the swing of California cuisine fashions. This includes organic free-range chicken, organic tofu, and a heavy emphasis on fresh vegetables—even in the meat dishes. Don't expect to find too many of your sweet syrupy favorites here. Instead, take a chance on some tasty broccoli or asparagus.

It's hard to get away from the sea when you're visiting Sausalito. So it's logical that many visitors find themselves wanting a seafood meal to accompany their experience. **Fish** (350 Harbor Dr., Sausalito, 415/331-3474, www.331fish.com, daily 11:30 A.M.–4:30 P.M., 5:30–8:30 P.M., $10–25) can hook you up with some of the best sustainable seafood in the North Bay. No farmed salmon, overfished swordfish, or other more-harm-than-good seafood makes its way into the kitchen. Fresh wild fish prepared perfectly using a California-style mix of ethnic cooking techniques results in amazing dishes you can't find anywhere else, not even in the Bay Area.

### TIBURON

With its marina ferrying folks to Angel Island and the City, expect many tourist-friendly restaurants in downtown Tiburon. For a surprisingly good Italian meal, head for **Servino** (9 Main St., Tiburon, 415/435-2676, www.bestservino.com, $13–25) on the waterfront. A huge outdoor patio offers diners stunning views of the Bay, Angel Island, and the San Francisco cityscape. It can get chilly in the evening, though, so if you hate the cold, get a table inside instead. Service is as warm and friendly as the classic Italian cuisine. A full bar caters to locals and visitors alike. The menu runs to hearty, somewhat Americanized Italian dishes. You can eat yourself senseless by trying all the courses, or choose just an entrée or a "primi" to keep your meal a bit lighter. The full bar makes a great place to sit should you need to

© LANCE SCOTT

**The outdoor patio at Servino offers diners stunning views.**

wait for a table, and Servino's hosts live music on Thursday and Friday nights.

**Rooney's** (38 Main St., Tiburon, 415/435-1911, lunch Mon.–Thurs. 11:30 A.M.–3:30 P.M., Fri.–Sun. 11:30 A.M.–4 P.M., dinner Wed.–Thurs. and Sun. 5:30–9 P.M., Fri.–Sat. 5:30–9:30 P.M.) is a local favorite, serving French bistro fare in a semi-casual, semi-subterranean dining room. While the food is universally admired at Rooney's, unfortunately it seems that good service is a privilege reserved exclusively for locals. Don't expect much in the way of promptness or friendliness here. Though the overgrown outdoor patio is pretty, it can attract flies and other unwelcome visitors to your table. Reservations are recommended, especially for weekend dinners.

## Practicalities

Sausalito lies just over the Golden Gate Bridge from San Francisco and is easily accessible on side roads on a bicycle or on U.S. 101 in a car. Once you're in town, navigating in a car can be a challenge, as the narrow oceanfront main road gets super-crowded on weekends. If you can, park your car and walk around town, both for your own comfort and to do your part to minimize traffic congestion. Street parking is mostly by meter.

Tiburon lies a few exits farther up U.S. 101. It's a bit easier to drive around and find parking here. To park your car still costs a pretty penny, but it's worth it to explore Main Street on foot.

Internet access is widely available in both Sausalito and Tiburon. Your hotel may have wireless, and if you ask locally you'll be able to locate the nearest Internet café. The Sausalito post office sits at 150 Harbor Drive. In Tiburon, you'll find one at 6 Beach Road. Looking for a newspaper? For something even more local than the *Chronicle,* pick up a copy of the *Marin Independent Journal* (www.marinij.com).

## MUIR WOODS

The **Muir Woods National Monument** (Panoramic Hwy. off Hwy. 1, 415/388-2596, www.visitmuirwoods.com, www.nps.gov/goga, daily 8 A.M.–sunset, $5) comprises acres of staggeringly beautiful redwood forest nestled in Marin. If you're visiting on a holiday or a summer weekend, get to the Muir Woods parking areas early—they fill up and afternoon hopefuls often cannot find a spot. Lit signs on U.S. 101 will alert you to parking status at the main parking lot. To avoid all the traffic hassle, check the NPS website for information about the Muir Woods Shuttle.

### Visitors Center

The Muir Woods Visitors Center (1 Muir Woods Rd., follow the signs from the Stinson Beach exit off Hwy. 1) abut the main parking area and marked the entrance to Muir Woods. In addition to the ranger station, where you can get maps, information, and advice about hiking, you'll also find a few amenities. The visitors center includes a bookstore and a café where you can purchase souvenirs and sustenance. If you're new to Muir Woods, the visitors center is a great place to begin your exploration.

### Hiking

The first hike you should take if you're a first-time visitor is the **Main Trail Loop** (1 mi, easy). Leading right from the visitors center on an easy and flat walk through the beautiful Muir Woods, this trail has its own leaflet (pick one up at the visitors center) and numbers along the trail to help describe the forest-dwellers that visitors can see. You'll cross from one side to the other of the Redwood Creek on cute pedestrian bridges. This trail is wheelchair- and stroller-accessible.

The **Fern Creek Trail** (3 mi, moderate) follows—you guessed it—Fern Creek down into the depths of the redwood forest. Along the way you'll see the much-lauded Kent Tree, a 220-foot Douglas fir. (William Kent donated the whole of Muir Woods to the government for a park, and all he got was this lousy fir tree.) At the Alice Eastwood Camp, you can get a nice drink of water, use the restrooms, and even have a picnic in this developed area. You'll follow the old railroad grade back to your starting place.

The **Ocean View Trail** (5.2 mi, difficult) is a bit of a misnomer—you can't see too much of the ocean from this trail anymore. Once upon a time, a big fire cleared the view to the Pacific from this path, but the trees have since grown back and blocked the view again. But if you take Ocean View out to the Redwood Trail, you'll get one or two quick peaks of the ocean before you reach the Tourist Club for a rest and some pretty views. At the Tourist Club, ignore the sign pointing back to Muir Woods and instead take the much safer Sun Trail back to catch the Dipsea Trail which leads you into central Muir Woods.

Muir Woods boasts many lovely trails that crisscross the gorgeous redwood forests. Check the websites for more trails and loop hikes.

## MOUNT TAMALPAIS

If you want to see the whole Bay Area in a single day, go to **Mount Tamalpais State Park** (801 Panoramic Hwy., Mill Valley, www.parks.ca.gov). Always called Mount Tam by locals, this park boasts views of all nine counties of the greater San Francisco Bay Area—from Mount. St. Helena in Napa down to San Jose and across to Mount Diablo and the East Bay. The Pacific Ocean peeks from around the corner of the western Peninsula, and on a clear day you can just make out the foothills of the Sierra Nevada mountains to the east. Ample parking, interpretive walks, and friendly rangers make a visit to Mount Tam a hit even for less outdoorsy travelers.

Once upon a time, well-heeled visitors could take a scenic train ride up to and across Mount Tam. Today, you'll probably want to drive up to one of the parking lots from which you can explore the trails. Take Highway 1 to the Stinson Beach exit, then follow the (fairly good) signs up the mountain.

### Hiking

Up on Mount Tam, you can try anything from a leisurely 30-minute interpretive stroll up to a strenuous hike up and down one of the many deep ravines. Mount Tam's hiking areas divide into three major sections: the East Peak, the Pantoll area, and the Rock Springs area. Each of these regions offers a number of beautiful trails, so you'll want to grab a map from the visitors center or online to get a sense of the mountain and its hikes.

At the top of the paved road up to the East Peak, you'll find a small visitors center that's open on weekends. The clearing also shelters a small refreshment stand that's open on weekends in the winter and daily in the summer. The charming interpretive **Verna Dunshee Trail** offers a short, mostly flat walk along a wheelchair-accessible trail. The views are fabulous, and you can get a leaflet at the visitors center that describes many of the things you'll see along the trail. For something with a little more vertical challenge to it, head for the Pantoll Station and take the **Old Stage Road.** For a shorter loop (about 2 mi, moderate), turn off onto **Easy Grade,** and then take the **Old Mine Trail** back. If you're looking for a longer hike, start out the same, but instead of cutting back quickly, take Easy Grade to **Rock Springs Trail,** then on to **Nora,** and finally return on **Matt Davis** for a total of five miles. This way you also get to take a peak at the Rock Spring part of the mountain.

Looking for a guided hike to help you to better understand the landscape you're seeing? The Mount Tamalpais Interpretive Association (www.mttam.net) offers a full schedule of guided hikes. Choose anything from a sedate, flat nature walk to a strenuous steep trek, all with an experienced guide who'll enrich your experience tremendously. Check the website for a schedule of upcoming guided hikes.

### Biking

To bike up to the peak of Mount Tam is a watermark of local bicyclists' strength and endurance. Rather than driving up to the East Peak or the Mountain Home Inn, sturdy cyclists pedal up the paved road to the East Peak. It's a long, hard ride, but for an experienced cyclist the challenge and the views make it more than worthwhile. And then comes the fun part—whizzing back down the twisting roads at (safe) high speeds! Just take care, since this road is open to cars, many of which may not realize that bikers frequent the area.

On the other hand, mountain bikers carry their machines up the mountain on racks, then take them up and down Mount Tam's extensive network of fire roads (open to hikers, bikers, and horseback riders). Check the park map to find a great loop!

## STINSON BEACH

The primary attraction at Stinson Beach is the tiny town's namesake: a broad, sandy stretch of coastline that's unusually (for Northern California) congenial to visitors. Though it's as plagued by fog as anywhere else in the Bay Area, on rare clear days Stinson Beach is the favorite destination for San Franciscans seeking some surf and sunshine.

Beachcombers can tread the sands of the beach while sunbathers plant themselves and their towels and beach chairs and catch the all-too-rare rays. Out in the water, surfers brave the chill of the Pacific to surf and kayak-surf the waves that roll in to pound the beaches. A plethora of local surf shops can hook you up with rental equipment if you didn't bring your own.

### Accommodations

Given its status as a beach resort town, you will find a few inns and motels in which you can stay the night. The **Sandpiper Inn** (1 Marine Way, 415/868-1632, www.sandpiperstinsonbeach.com, $120–170) is one such spot. With six rooms and four cabins, you can choose between motel-style accommodations with comfortable queen beds, private bathrooms, and gas fireplaces. The four individual redwood cabins offer additional privacy, bed space for families, and full kitchens.

Another nice spot is the **Stinson Beach Motel** (3416 Shoreline Hwy. 1, 415/868-1712, www.stinsonbeachmotel.com, $150). It features eight "vintage" beach bungalow-style rooms sleeping two to four guests apiece. Some rooms have substantial kitchenettes; all have private baths, garden views, televisions, and blue decor. The motel is a great spot to bring the family for a (possibly chilly) beach vacation.

### Food

A few smallish restaurants dot the town of

Stinson Beach, most of which serve seafood. Among the best is the **Sand Dollar Restaurant** (3458 Hwy. 1, 415/868-0434, www.stinsonbeachrestaurant.com, daily lunch and dinner, $15–30). This so-called fish joint actually serves more land-based dishes than seafood, but perhaps the fact that the dining room is constructed out of three old barges makes up the differences. In addition to lunch and dinner, the Sand Dollar serves a popular Sunday brunch.

### Practicalities

So what's the catch to this idyllic recreation spot? As with so many other things in and near metropolitan California areas, it's the traffic. You'll learn quickly what the problem is if you try to drive into Stinson Beach on a sunny summer weekend day. With only one lane each way, and a couple of intersections with stop signs, backups that stretch for miles are all too common. Your best bet is to drive in on a weekday, or in the evening when everyone else is leaving the beach.

The nearest major medical services lie 20 miles south in San Francisco.

Out on Stinson Beach, if you possibly can, turn off your cell phone and put away your laptop. But if you can't possibly manage to disconnect, you will find limited Internet service around town. Cell phones will probably function here, though you might lose signal on Highway 1 in the more rural coastal reaches.

## POINT REYES NATIONAL SEASHORE

A haven for hippies and a mecca for wilderness buffs, the Point Reyes area boasts acres of unspoiled forest and beach country in the grandest Northern California tradition. Expect cool weather even in the summer, but enjoy the lustrous green foliage and spectacular scenery that result. Point Reyes National Seashore (Bear Valley Rd., 415/464-5100, www.nps.gov/pore, open daily dawn–midnight), the gem of the North Bay, stretches for miles between Tomales Bay and the Pacific, north from Stinson Beach to the tip of the land at the end of the bay. Dedicated hikers can trek from the bay to the ocean, or the beach to land's end. The protected lands shelter a range of wildlife. In the marshes and lagoons, a wide variety of birds—including three different species of pelican—make their nests. The pine forests shade shy deer and bigger elk. The land not protected often shelters and feeds some of the luckiest livestock in the country: the grass-fed cows and sheep of the local sustainable ranches.

The Point Reyes area includes the tiny towns of Olema, Point Reyes Station, and Inverness.

### Visitors Centers

The **Bear Valley Visitors Center** (Bear Valley Rd., 415/464-5100, Mon.–Fri. 9 A.M.–5 P.M., Sat.–Sun. 8 A.M.–5 P.M.) acts as the central visitors center for Point Reyes National Seashore. In addition to the maps, fliers, and interpretive exhibits, you can watch a short video introducing you to the Point Reyes region. You can also talk to the rangers, either just to ask advice or to obtain beach fire permits and boat-in backcountry camping permits.

Two other visitors centers sit at different spots in the vast acreage of Point Reyes. The **Ken Patrick Visitor Center** (Drake's Beach, 415/669-1250, Sat.–Sun. 10 A.M.–5 P.M.) sits right on the beach in a decidedly appropriate structure. Its small museum focuses on the maritime history of the region, and it acts as the hosting area for the annual Sand Sculpture event held on the beach. The **Drake Beach Café** (hours and days of operation vary by season, call 415/669-1297) serves delicious food with an appropriate focus on the local, organic, and sustainable.

Finally, the **Historic Lighthouse and Visitors Center** (415/669-1534, Thurs.–Mon. 10 A.M.–4:30 P.M.) is the most difficult of the three to access. You must walk about a half a mile up a steep hill from the parking lot to get to this visitors center. On the other hand, you'll find the bonus of the lighthouse right at your feet once you arrive.

### Point Reyes Historic Lighthouse

The jagged rocky shores of Point Reyes make

## GRAZING POINT REYES

The Point Reyes food obsession encompasses far more than just restaurants. Local producers take enormous pride in their work, and offer it for sale retail to local cooks and visitors alike. Stopping at one or two local food markets or shops is essential to complete a true Point Reyes experience.

Several oyster farms make their home in Tomales Bay, providing their wares to fine restaurants locally and across the state. The **Hog Island Oyster Co.** (20215 Hwy. 1, 415/663-9218, www.hogislandoysters.com, daily 9 A.M.–5 P.M.) is open rain or shine and offers a picnic ground with barbecue grills. (Reservations are required for picnic tables on weekends in summer.) Far from a chi-chi tourist trap, Hog Island doesn't pretend to be anything other than a working oyster farm. You can buy the goods from a walk-up shack in the midst of warehouses, working buildings, and oyster tanks. If you prefer them raw and completely fresh, a shucker in orange hip-waders stands ready to pry open your jewels then and there. Lemon wedges and a bottle of hot sauce sit carelessly on a folding table that serves as the oyster bar. To take your oysters home, request them packed in ice for a small additional charge.

© LANCE SCOTT

Hog Island Oyster Co., Point Reyes

If you prefer land mammals to shellfish, Point Reyes is like a dream. Both beef and dairy cattle are grazed all over the place – even on legacy leased parkland. At the **Marin Sun Farms Butcher Shop** (10905 Hwy. 1, Point Reyes Station, 415/663-8997, www.marinsunfarms.com) you can pick up possibly the best cut of beef you'll ever eat. All Marin Sun Farms cattle are 100 percent grass-fed and humanely (even lovingly) treated. The result is beef that melts like butter and barely requires a knife to cut. Marin Sun also cuts and sells pork, lamb, goat, chicken, and eggs in season; the butcher will be happy to explain meat seasons to you, as well as give you a life history of the meat you're purchasing.

Point Reyes cheeses have become a national phenomenon in top-tier restaurants. To get some of the world's best cheese right from the source, visit the **Cowgirl Creamery** (80 Fourth St., Point Reyes Station, 415/663-9335, www.cowgirlcreamery.com, Wed.–Sun. 10 A.M.–6 P.M.) in Point Reyes Station. It's taken only a little over 10 years for this woman-owned farmhouse cheese factory to become a heavyweight in the artisan cheese world. Though Cowgirl distributes over 200 artisan cheeses from around the world, they deliberately keep their in-house production small – only seven kinds of cheese come from their factory in Point Reyes. They purchase their milk and cream locally, from the nearby Straus Family Creamery. Want to go behind the scenes of this unusual cheesemaking haven? Make a reservation for the weekly tour on Friday at 11:30 A.M.

Finally, for the best fruits and veggies the region has to offer, hit one of the weekly local farmers markets. Point Reyes Station holds its market at **Toby's** (11250 Hwy. 1, 415/663-1223, www.tobysfeedbarn.com) on Saturdays 9 A.M.–1 P.M. You can also pick up botanical bath products, locally grown and spun wool, and handmade jewelry and crafts.

great sightseeing but incredibly dangerous marine navigation. In 1870, the first lighthouse was constructed on the Headlands. Its first-order Fresnel lens threw out light far enough for ships to see and avoid the treacherous granite cliffs. Yet the danger remained, and soon after a life-saving station was constructed alongside the light station. It wasn't until the 20th century, when a ship-to-shore radio station and newer life-saving station were put in place, that the Point Reyes shore became truly safer for ships.

The Historic Lighthouse (415/669-1534, www.nps.gov/pore, Thurs.–Mon. 10 A.M.–4:30 P.M., light room Thurs.–Mon. 2:30–4 P.M.) still stands today. It sits down on the point past the visitors center—specifically, down 300 sometimes-treacherous, cold, and windblown stairs. (The stairs often close to visitors during bad weather for safety reasons.) But the reward can be worth it. The Fresnel lens and original workings all remain in place, and the adjacent equipment building contains foghorns, air compressors, and other implements of safety from decades gone by. Check the website for information about twice-monthly special events during which the light is lit.

## Hiking and Biking

One of the main reasons people make the trip out to Point Reyes is to explore its beautiful scenery up close. Hikers fan out on the trails winding through the national seashore and surrounding state parks. Bicyclists, sometimes in big packs, ply the many small roads.

Many hiking trails, biking trails, and smallish roads run around the northern reaches of Point Reyes. To see the famed Tule elk, take the **Tomales Point Trail** (foot of Pierce Point Rd., 6 miles round-trip, difficult) right through the midst of the Tule Elk Reserve. For hikers who feel still feel energetic, 1.7 miles of additional unmaintained trail run all the way out to the tip of Tomales Point.

For a much quicker little walk from the same trailhead, stroll down to **McClures Beach** (0.8 miles round-trip, easy).

If you're staying at the local hostel, you can roll out of your bunk and onto the **Coastal Trail** (5-mile loop, moderate). This biking/hiking path takes you right to Limantour Beach. Bring a picnic or some toys and take a break on the sands. For a nice walk back along a different route, walk the Fire Lane for a mile, then take the Laguna Trail back to the hostel. (The Fire Lane and the Laguna Trail are *not* bike-accessible.)

Down in the south reaches of the park, the hikes get much longer. From the Bear Valley Visitors Center trailhead, you can hike the aptly named **Rift Zone Trail** (8.5 miles round-trip, difficult). For beach lovers, the Palomarin trailhead at the foot of Mesa Road opens onto the **Coastal Trail,** which can be as short or as long as you please. This is a great multi-day hike for backpackers, since both Wildcat Camp and Coastal Camp offer respite for weary travelers. Day hikers with good legs and lungs can stick with a 10-mile round-trip out past Bass Lake, Pelican Lake, and Crystal Lake, winding up at Alamere Falls.

For a stout mountain bike ride, take the **Bolinas Ridge Trail** (11 miles one-way, moderate), which is open to both bikers and hikers and offers stunning views down toward Tomales Bay. Trailheads sit on Sir Francis Drake Road at the north end and at the foot of Bolinas-Fairfax Road on the south side. An easier trail, more suitable for families, runs west down to **Marshall Beach** on Tomales Bay.

As for road biking, most all the paved roads in Point Reyes are open to both bicycles and cars. Ask for information about this year's hot biking spots and any trail closures at one of the local bike shops. **Cycle Analysis Point Reyes** (Hwy. 1 next to the Bovine Bakery, 415/663-9164, www.cyclepointreyes.com, Fri.–Sun. 10 A.M.–5 P.M. or by appointment) rents mountain bikes, tandem road bikes, and child trailers.

## Accommodations

Unless you're camping, budget-friendly accommodations are thin in the Point Reyes area, with its local reputation as a playground for Bay Area rich folks. Prepare to spend a bundle

© LANCE SCOTT

Biking trails lead down to Tomales Bay.

on that quaint B&B, so choose carefully to make sure you find the perfect inn for your tastes. If you prefer indoor accommodations to the camping options in the national seashore and state parks, exclusive inns and boutique hotels proliferate in the small towns that dot the Point Reyes region.

#### OLEMA

The **Point Reyes Seashore Lodge** (10021 Hwy. 1, Olema, 415/663-9000, www.pointreyesseashorelodge.com, $150–330) offers both budget and luxury in its 23 rooms. Attractive florals mix with clean white walls and attractive wooden accents. All rooms have private baths, some have whirlpool tubs, and a couple of special suites sit away from the main lodge for extra privacy and special amenities. Outside, guests can enjoy the attractive gardens with winding brick pathways that roll out to Olema Creek. The Farm House Restaurant, Bar, and Deli adjoin the hotel, providing plenty of food and drink options for all visitors of the tiny town of Olema.

#### POINT REYES STATION

In Point Reyes Station, you can find a room and tasty board for a reasonable price in **One Mesa Bed & Breakfast** (1 Mesa Rd., Pt. Reyes Station, 415/663-8866, www.onemesa.com, $132–210). All three rooms have private baths, down comforters and featherbeds, and free all-day and all-night coffee service. Each is decorated with a different style—most have fireplaces, some have soaking tubs, and all have televisions and VCRs. Guests can make use of the inn's hot tub and enjoy a self-service breakfast on weekdays and a basket of goodies delivered right to your door on weekends.

#### INVERNESS

For the flush, Point Reyes boasts an array of accommodations in the over-$250-plus range. One of the most original, the **Blackthorne Inn** (266 Vallejo Ave., Inverness, 415/663-8621, www.blackthorneinn.com, $215–360) perches on a hillside to the west of Tomales Bay in Inverness Park. This fascinating treehouse–meets–medieval castle was designed by its owner, who was not an architect by trade. Each guest room takes one floor of the central tower. All are spacious and pretty, with cute electric fireplaces that work as well as the heaters to warm the often-chilly rooms. A hot tub welcomes all guests until 10 P.M., when it becomes private to the top floor. While all baths are private, not all connect directly to the bedrooms. The tempting breakfast buffet changes daily, and provides hearty enough fare to sustain hikers bound for the wilds of the many parks.

## Food

Dining in Point Reyes tends toward down-home country-style fare or upscale California cuisine. Few chain restaurants clutter the area. Most food comes from local, sustainable sources, a huge source of pride to the whole area.

### OLEMA

If you're seeking rarified organic California cuisine, head for the tiny town of Olema and get a meal in the dining room at the **Olema Inn** (10,000 Sir Francis Drake Blvd., 415/663-9559, www.theolemainn.com, lunch Sat.–Sun., dinner Wed.–Mon., closed Tues., $30–34). Here you'll find cuisine after Alice Waters' own heart—the freshest of local, organic fare presented with elegance and grace. Most shellfish comes from Tomales Bay, the beef from local ranches, and the produce from local farms. Relaxed, formal-yet-friendly service complements the fabulous food and local-heavy wine list. Be sure to save room for dessert!

### POINT REYES STATION

Much of the expensive organic meat and produce that's raised in Point Reyes goes down to San Francisco for consumption in $200-a-plate restaurants. By comparison, **Rosie's Cowboy Cookhouse** (11285 Hwy. 1, Pt. Reyes Station, 415/663-8868, Wed.–Mon. 11:30 A.M.–8 P.M., $10–20) serves fairly plain Mexican and Tex-Mex food. You can get tacos, quesadillas, and tamales or ribs and mac 'n' cheese as you prefer. Right on the main drag and definitely catering to the tourist trade, Rosie's has a colorful family-friendly dining room and a fun ambiance. Most folks prefer Rosie's for lunch, though it's open for dinner as well.

Need a drink? Right off Highway 1 along Tomales Bay sits the unassuming **Point Reyes Vineyard** (12700 Hwy. 1, Pt. Reyes Station, 415/663-1011, www.ptreyesvineyardinn.com/winery.htm, Sat.–Sun. 11 A.M.–5 P.M. and by appointment). Hinting at the glory of the California wine country without the crowds and pretensions, this small winery pours some surprisingly tasty vintages. Staff can tell you about the wines as well as direct you to their favorite local restaurants and recreation spots.

### INVERNESS

Of all the strange things, **Vladimir's Czechoslovakian Restaurant** (12785 Sir Francis Drake Blvd., Inverness, 415/669-1021, Tues.–Sun. 11 A.M.–2 P.M. and 5–10 P.M., $30–50) is a favorite of both locals and visitors. Enter the cool old dining room, complete with stuffed deer heads on the walls, and take a seat. The Vladimir who owns the restaurant can be rude one minute, and then hand you the best pint of beer you ever drank the next. Vlad's wife runs the kitchen, and you'll get to choose from an array of serious Czech food: borscht, rabbit, duck, and all manner of things that might seem heavy or strange to the American palate. But they're delicious.

One caution: Vladimir's is *very* serious about its no-children policy. If you bring your baby, toddler, or small child, you will be turned away at the door. The bright side? Vladimir's thus makes a perfect retreat for romantic couples looking for an escape the kids for a short time.

A great, convenient coffee stop is the **Busy Bee Bakery** (12301 Sir Francis Drake Blvd., Inverness, 415/663-9496, Mon. and Thurs.–Fri. 7:30 A.M.–4 P.M., Sat.–Sun. 8 A.M.–5 P.M.). This owner-run shop offers good espresso drinks, delectable homemade (right there in the back of the shop) pastries, and some lovely photo prints done by the owner. It's worth the time to take a table and sample a slice of whatever fresh baked goodie is on the counter!

### Practicalities

Getting to Point Reyes can be quite a drive for newcomers. Though it's only an hour or so north of San Francisco, Highway 1 isn't exactly a superhighway through the wilds of Marin. Expect twists, turns, and generally slow going as you approach Point Reyes.

Once you're in the Point Reyes region, Sir Francis Drake Highway and all the other paved roads are open to bicyclists, and motorcyclists ply the fabulous twisties, so keep an eye out when you're driving from place to place. The good news is that parking is almost always free and easy in the towns and parks of Point Reyes.

As for services, there's not much out in the wilderness of Point Reyes. You can get gas in Point Reyes Station and at the Olema Ranch Campground only (no gas in Inverness), so plan carefully. You'll find mini-marts with the gas stations, but no big-box supermarkets or department stores anywhere in the region. If you need to stock up, Petaluma is the nearest major town.

Cell phones *do not work* across the majority of the Point Reyes National Seashore and adjoining parklands. Check with your inn or hotel for information about Internet access. You'll find a **post office** (11260 Hwy. 1, Point Reyes Station, 415/663-1305) in the town of Point Reyes Station.

The closest hospital to Point Reyes is **Novato Community Hospital** (180 Rowland Way, Novato, 415/209-1300, www.novatocommunity.sutterhealth.org).

# East Bay

## BERKELEY

There's no place on earth quite like Berkeley (except maybe Santa Cruz). While the Haight in San Francisco nurtured the creative side of the 1960s flower children, Berkeley brought out their fire. The town has long been known for its radical, liberal, progressive activism. No matter what you're doing, someone, somewhere in Berkeley is probably protesting against it right now. The youthful urban culture tends to revolve around the University of California. Yet well-heeled foodies also flock to town to sample some of the finest cuisine on earth, served only a block or two from the homeless people panhandling at the BART station.

### University of California Berkeley

Berkeley is a college town, and fittingly the University of California (www.berkeley.edu) offers the most interesting places to go and things to see. If your visit to the area includes your teenagers, think about taking a free guided campus tour (510/642-3175, www.berkeley.edu/visitors/free_tours.html, Mon.–Sat. 10 A.M., Sun. 1 P.M.) to acquaint them (and yourself) with the UC and all it has to offer. To get a great view of the campus from above, take an elevator ride up the **Campanile** (Mon.–Fri. 10 A.M.–4 P.M., Sat. 10 A.M.–5 P.M., Sun. 10 A.M.–1:30 P.M., 3–5 P.M., adults $2, seniors $1), formally called Sather Tower. If you prefer to wander around campus on your own, discovering the halls where students live and learn, the stadium (perhaps you'll even see a protester up a tree!), and architectural details such as Sather Gate. Or stop in at the **Lawrence Hall of Science** (Centennial Drive, 510/642-5132, www.lawrencehallofscience.org, daily 10 A.M.–5 P.M., adults $10, seniors/students $8, children $5.50) for a look at the latest exhibits and interactive displays.

Also on campus you'll find the **University of California Botanical Garden** (foot of Centennial Dr., 510/643-2755, http://botanicalgarden.berkeley.edu, adults $7, seniors $5, children $2, daily 9 A.M.–5 P.M.), an immense space with an astounding array of wild plants from around the world. Botany buffs love to spend hours in this place, studying and examining plants outdoors, in the greenhouses, and in the "arid house" (a habitat for plants requiring extremely dry, hot conditions). Others just come to

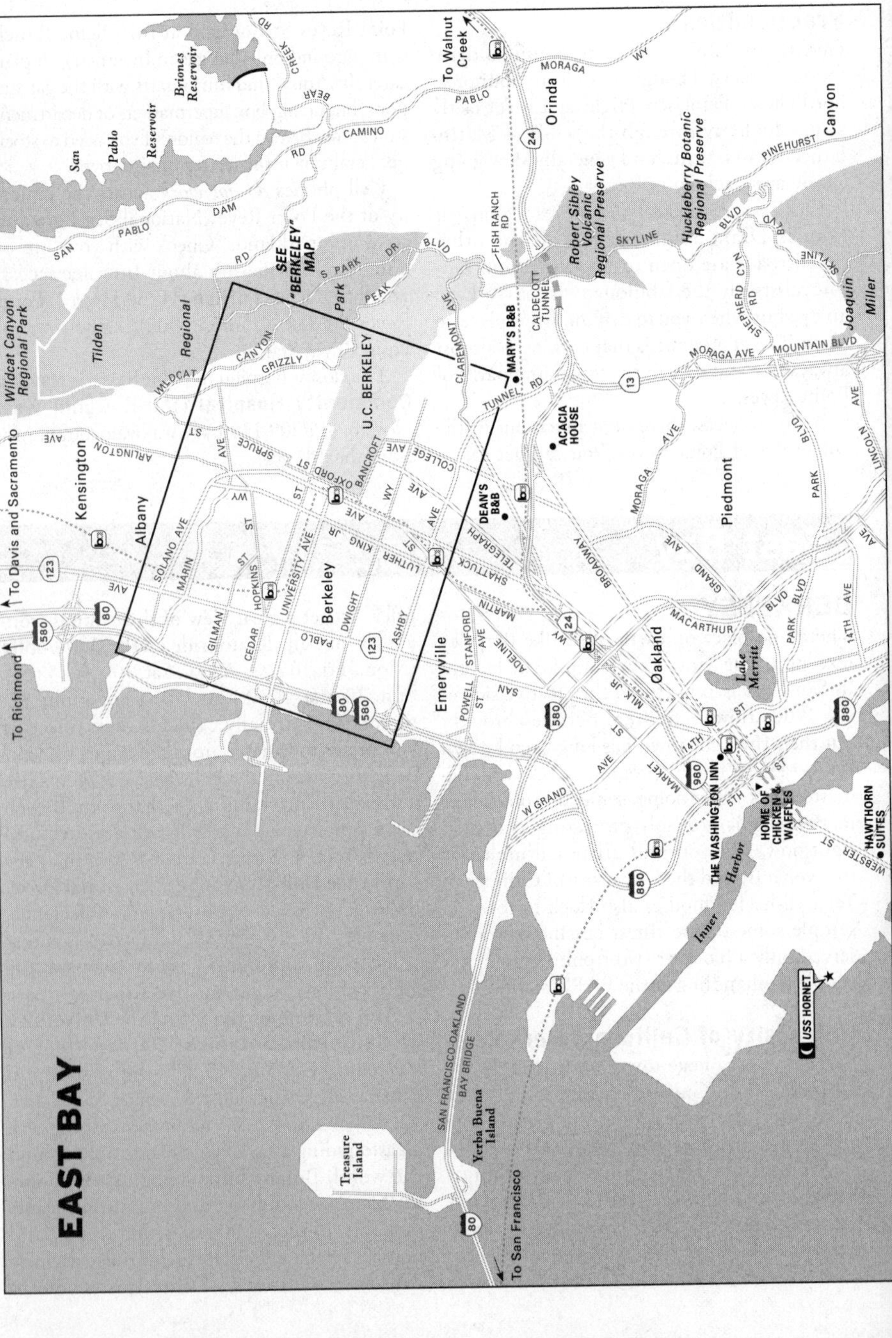
EAST BAY
To Richmond
To Davis and Sacramento
To Walnut Creek
To San Francisco
SEE "BERKELEY" MAP
Wildcat Canyon Regional Park
Tilden Regional Park
San Pablo Reservoir
Briones Reservoir
Kensington
Albany
Berkeley
U.C. BERKELEY
Emeryville
Oakland
Piedmont
Orinda
Robert Sibley Volcanic Regional Preserve
Huckleberry Botanic Regional Preserve
Joaquin Miller
Canyon
Lake Merritt
Inner Harbor
Treasure Island
Yerba Buena Island
SAN FRANCISCO-OAKLAND BAY BRIDGE
CALDECOTT TUNNEL
MARY'S B&B
ACACIA HOUSE
DEAN'S B&B
THE WASHINGTON INN
HOME OF CHICKEN & WAFFLES
HAWTHORN SUITES
USS HORNET
SAN PABLO DAM RD
BEAR CREEK RD
CAMINO PABLO
MORAGA WY
FISH RANCH RD
SKYLINE BLVD
PINEHURST
SHEPHERD CYN RD
MORAGA AVE
MOUNTAIN BLVD
WILDCAT CANYON
GRIZZLY PEAK BLVD
S PARK DR
CLAREMONT AVE
TUNNEL RD
ARLINGTON AVE
SPRUCE ST
OXFORD ST
BANCROFT WY
COLLEGE AVE
TELEGRAPH AVE
SHATTUCK AVE
MARTIN LUTHER KING JR WY
SOLANO AVE
MARIN AVE
HOPKINS ST
UNIVERSITY AVE
DWIGHT WY
GILMAN ST
CEDAR ST
SAN PABLO AVE
ASHBY AVE
STANFORD AVE
POWELL ST
ADELINE ST
SAN PABLO AVE
BROADWAY
GRAND AVE
MACARTHUR BLVD
PARK BLVD
14TH AVE
LINCOLN AVE
W GRAND AVE
MARKET ST
MLK JR WY
14TH ST
5TH ST
WEBSTER ST
80
580
880
980
24
13
123

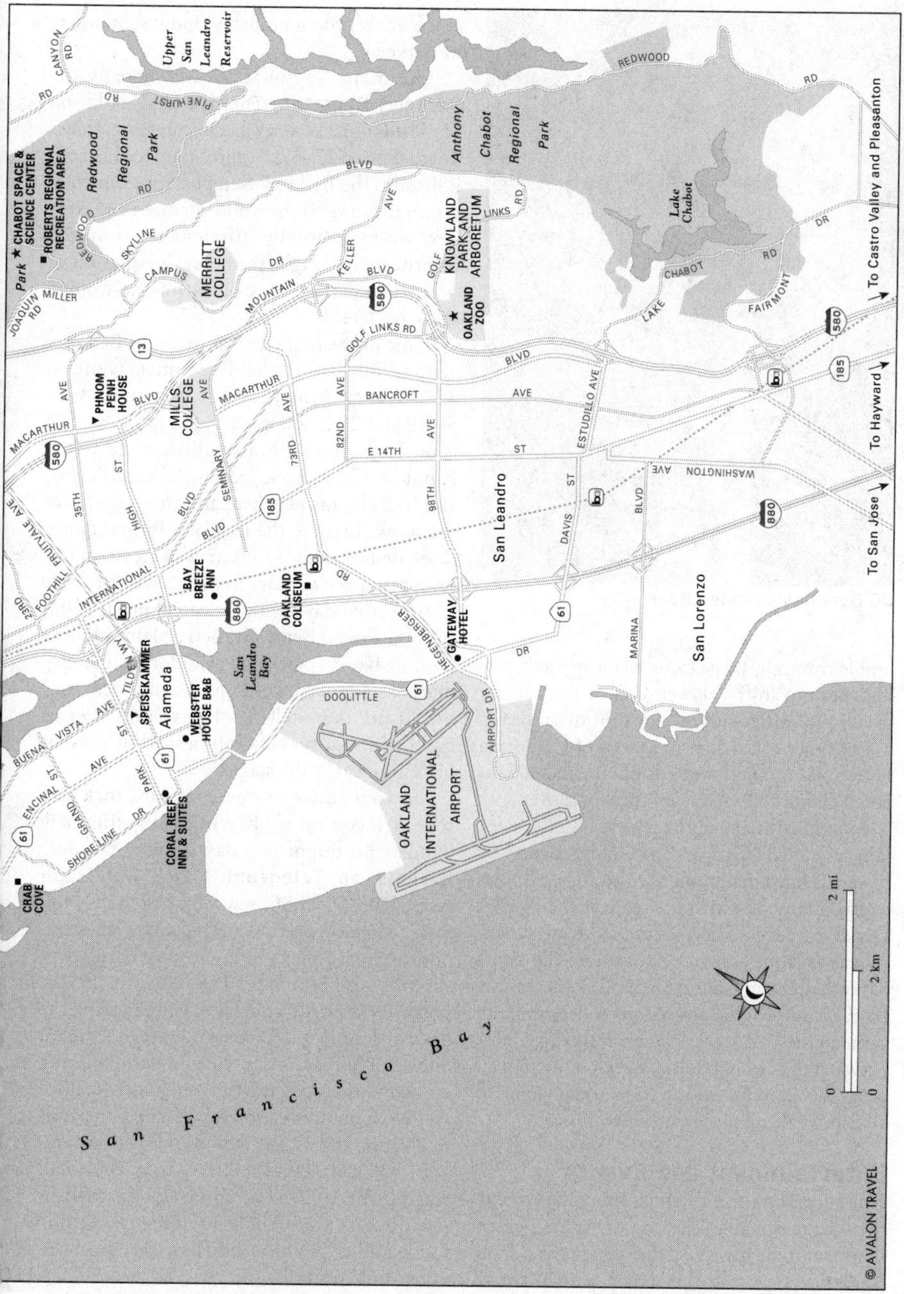
Upper San Leandro Reservoir
Redwood Regional Park
Anthony Chabot Regional Park
Lake Chabot
CHABOT SPACE & SCIENCE CENTER
ROBERTS REGIONAL RECREATION AREA
MERRITT COLLEGE
KNOWLAND PARK AND ARBORETUM
OAKLAND ZOO
MILLS COLLEGE
PHNOM PENH HOUSE
BAY BREEZE INN
OAKLAND COLISEUM
GATEWAY HOTEL
SPEISEKAMMER
WEBSTER HOUSE B&B
CORAL REEF INN & SUITES
CRAB COVE
Alameda
San Leandro Bay
San Leandro
San Lorenzo
OAKLAND INTERNATIONAL AIRPORT
San Francisco Bay
To Castro Valley and Pleasanton
To Hayward
To San Jose
2 mi
2 km
© AVALON TRAVEL

ROBERT HOLMES / CALTOUR

UC Berkeley's Golden Bear

amble through the peaceful plantings and perhaps stop to sniff a flower or two. You can see over 1,000 different kinds of sunflower, nearly 2,500 types of cactus, thousands of California native plants, and hundreds of rare and endangered plants collected from the world over.

Like most major universities, UC Berkeley (always called "Cal" or "the Golden Bears" by its sports fans) maintains a wide range of sports teams, many of which compete at the NCAA Division 1 level. The Cal football team's quality varies from year to year, as does the men's basketball team. Cal's main rival sits across the Bay at Stanford; the one serious college football game in the Bay Area each year is the Big Game between the two schools. Check out http://calbears.cstv.com for information about games of all kinds taking place during your visit.

## Entertainment and Events

Not surprising for a happenin' college town, there's a reasonable selection of evening entertainment to be had. Whether you prefer a show (theatrical or musical), a dance, a drink, or all of the above, you'll probably find it somewhere in Berkeley.

The major regional theater here is the **Berkeley Repertory Theatre** (2025 Addison St., 510/647-2949, www.berkeleyrep.org, shows Tues.–Sun., $27–69). Appropriate to the town it lives in, the Berkeley Rep puts up a bunch of unusual shows, from world premieres of edgy new works to totally different takes on old favorites. You might see a new adaptation of *Figaro* or a performance of the hit one-woman show *No Child*.

Some of the best entertainment in Berkeley echoes out from the live music venues. The **Starry Plough** (3101 Shattuck Ave., 510/841-0282, www.starryploughpub.com) is an Irish pub with a smallish stage setup. Fabulous Celtic rock groups, folk musicians, and indie bands play here almost every day of the week. Despite the lack of a formal dance floor, dedicated fans find ways to create an impromptu space to move to their favorite bands. Each Wednesday night, instead of music you'll find the famed Berkeley Poetry Slam—there's nothing like it anywhere in California. Hungry music and spoken word lovers can order a full meal from the kitchen, while the thirsty can quaff a pint or two of Guinness while they sit back and watch the stage.

Do your tastes run more toward rock and roll? Are you up for hearing struggling new bands who might one day become famous? **Blake's on Telegraph** (2367 Telegraph Ave., 510/848-0886, www.blakesontelegraph.com, Mon.–Fri. 11:30 A.M.–2 A.M., Sat.–Sun. noon–2 A.M.) plays home to any number of such bands. From the 1960s to the 1990s, Blake's was a dedicated blues club, hosting the likes of John Lee Hooker and Gregg Allman. Since 1993, Blake's has gone modern, offering up shows by top-tier bands such as Metallica and No Doubt. It's also given chances to bands like Train and Cake, who didn't yet have recording contracts when they took the small stage in Berkeley. The three-floor establishment boasts a full kitchen serving classic pub food, and a bar on each floor serving beer, wine, and cocktails.

In Berkeley, the big name acts come to the **Greek Theater** (Gayley Rd., 510/642-9988, www.ticketmaster.com/venue/229421). This outdoor amphitheater constructed in the classic Greek style sits on the UC Berkeley campus. Expect to see top-tier performers playing the Greek; you can check out artists like Steely Dan, R.E.M., and Death Cab for Cutie here. See the Ticketmaster website for a list of shows coming to the Greek

For a slightly less formal night out, Berkeley has any number of bars and clubs that offer DJs, dancing, or just a quiet drink. **The Shattuck Down Low Lounge** (2284 Shattuck Ave., 510/548-1159, www.shattuckdownlow.com, Tues.–Sat. 8 P.M.–2 A.M., Sun. 9 P.M.–2 A.M.) is a big dance club that often has live musical acts playing to get the audience up and moving. The bar serves up cocktails and wine and beer, and there's plenty of room to sit when you're tired and have a drink or two.

**The Albatross Pub** (1822 San Pablo Ave., 510/843-2473, www.albatrosspub.com, Sun.–Tues. 6 P.M.–2 A.M., Wed.–Sat. 4:30 P.M.–2 A.M.) might be Berkeley's favorite down-home drinking establishment. With six dart lanes, board games, Chicago deep-dish feta and spinach pizza for snacks, and a full bar, the

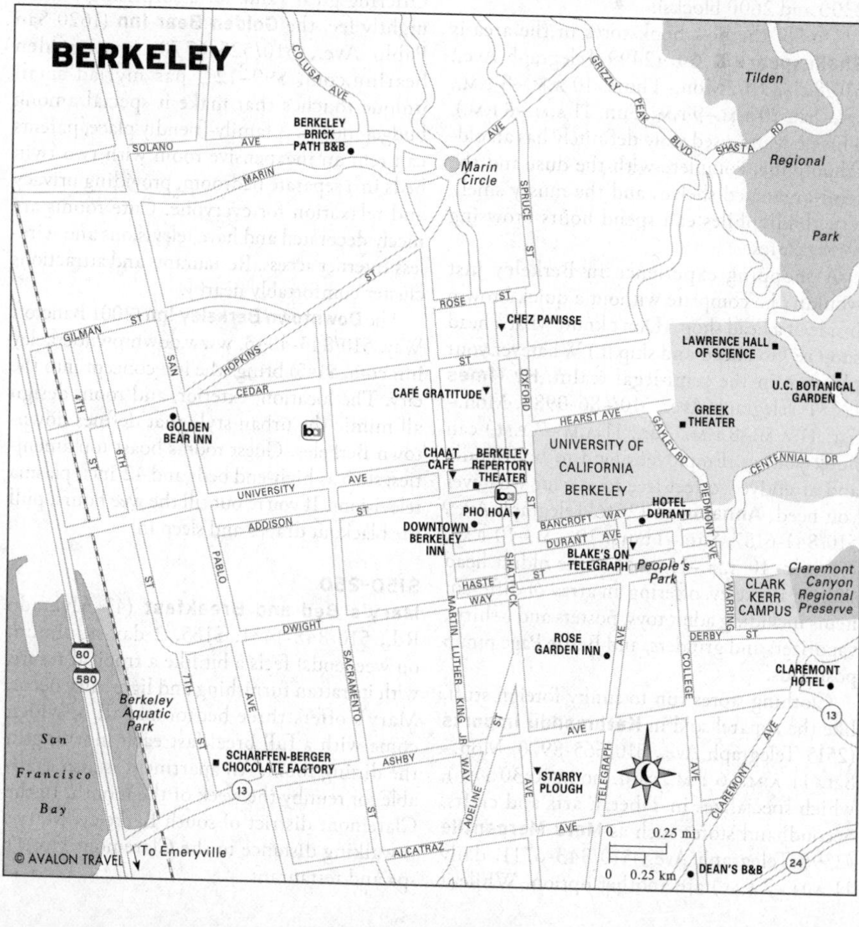

Albatross has all you need for a totally laid-back night out. If you're not a lover of Guinness, you can order a fabulous hot Irish coffee—*the perfect* drink for those foggy Bay Area nights. Perhaps best of all, the relaxed crowd at the Albatross makes it easy to make new friends and really get into the local scene.

## Shopping

Berkeley's citizens grow fierce at the very thought of big chain stores invading their precious downtown area. A few have succeeded, but you'll still find a variety of funky independent shops on **Telegraph Avenue** (btwn. the 2300 and 2600 blocks).

One of the best bookstores in the area is **Shakespeare & Co.** (2499 Telegraph Ave., 510/841-8916, Mon.–Thurs. 10 A.M.–8 P.M., Fri.–Sat. 10 A.M.–9 P.M., Sun. 11 A.M.–8 P.M.). This new-and-used store definitely has an old-school vibe, complete with the dust and the semi-organized shelves and the musty smell. True bibliophiles can spend hours browsing for treasures.

A shopping experience in Berkeley just wouldn't be complete without a quick browse inside of a head shop. (Don't know what a head shop is? Go ahead and skip it.) Whatever your pleasure in the semi-legal realm, **Hi Times** (2374 Telegraph Ave., 510/486-0988, Mon.–Sat. 11 A.M.–8 P.M., Sun. 11 A.M.–7 P.M.) can hook you up. Employees tend to be friendly and attentive, so feel free to ask for whatever you need. **Annapurna** (2416 Telegraph Ave., 510/841-6187, Sun.–Thurs. 10 A.M.–10 P.M., Fri.–Sat. 10 A.M.–11 P.M.) is the oldest head shop in Berkeley, offering an array of different items including adult toys, posters and t-shirts, vaporizers and grinders, and Bettie Page pinup postcards.

Clothing stores run to funky foreign stuff, like the apparel sold in **Kathmandu Imports** (2515 Telegraph Ave., 510/665-8970, Mon.–Sat. 11 A.M.–6 P.M., Sun. noon–6:30 P.M.), which specializes in Tibetan arts and crafts. Secondhand stores such as **Mars Mercantile** (2398 Telegraph Ave., 510/843-6711, daily 11 A.M.–7 P.M.) are another option. While it bills itself as a "vintage store," the selection actually feels more like a downscale thrift shop. The provocative window displays lure shoppers inside, where a few solid basic items can be had for a reasonable price.

## Accommodations

When you look for a place to stay in Berkeley, check both the hotel and the neighborhood. Plenty of unique B&Bs offer rooms in Berkeley, and adequate motel rooms make it easy for family and friends to visit students.

### $100-150

Offering great value for a surprisingly small nightly fee, the **Golden Bear Inn** (1620 San Pablo Ave., 510/525-6770, www.goldenbearinn.com, $99–121) has myriad small unique touches that make it special among budget motels. A family-friendly place, parents can rent an inexpensive room with two twin beds in a separate bedroom, providing privacy and relaxation for everyone. Cute rooms are nicely decorated and have televisions and wireless Internet access. Restaurants and attractions cluster comfortably nearby.

The **Downtown Berkeley Inn** (2001 Bancroft Way, 510/843-4043, www.downtownberkeleyinn.com, $145) brings the inn concept into the city. The location, exterior, and room design all mimic the urban style that defines downtown Berkeley. Guest rooms boast top amenities, such as high-end beds and 42-inch plasma televisions. If you're out till the wee hours, pull the blackout drapes and sleep in!

### $150-250

**Mary's Bed and Breakfast** (47 Alvarado Rd., 510/848-1431, $165, 2-day minimum on weekends) feels a bit like a tropical resort, with its rattan furnishing and light, airy decor. Mary's offers three bedrooms, all of which come with a full breakfast each morning in the dining room. An apartment is also available for rent by the week or the month. In the Claremont district of south Berkeley, Mary's is walking distance to the Claremont Hotel's spa and restaurant.

The **Rose Garden Inn** (2740 Telegraph Ave., 510/549-2145, www.rosegardeninn.com, $170–260, 2-night minimum over Sat. nights) is a large rambling structure with 40 guest rooms and gorgeous rose bushes (don't worry—the bushes are not in the rooms). If you come in the spring, take the time to stroll in the lush gardens and smell the pungent jasmine. Rooms are decorated in floral themes, many with light wood, white wicker, and other cute garden cottage-style touches. All rooms have private baths and televisions, and a hearty buffet breakfast is included.

Book a room at the **Berkeley Brick Path Bed & Breakfast** (1805 Marin Ave., 510/524-4277, www.thebrickpath.com, $170–210). The garden is the pride of this inn, and you can stroll down the namesake brick path among the lush greenery and gorgeous flowers, take a seat out on the patio to enjoy your breakfast, or sip an afternoon glass of wine in the gazebo. (For a complete list of the plants in the garden, complete with identifying photos and descriptions, see the inn's website.) Each of the three guest rooms has a unique style: one with a brick fireplace, one with a huge whirlpool tub, and the East-West cottage with a full kitchen and private entrance.

The **Hotel Durant** (2600 Durant St., 510/845-8981, www.hoteldurant.com, $176–215) has it all: location, location, views, and location. If you can, get a room on the upper floors to take in a view of Oakland, San Francisco, or the Bay. From the lobby, you can walk to the University, Telegraph Avenue, and the Elmwood shopping district.

Got plenty of budget for your Berkeley lodgings? Then stay at the famous **Claremont Resort and Spa** (41 Tunnel Rd., 510/843-3000, www.claremontresort.com, $210–350). Since 1915, the Claremont has catered to rich and famous East Bay visitors. No two of the 279 elegantly furnished rooms look quite the same, so you'll get a unique accommodation experience even in this large resort hotel. The rooms may be plush, but the real focus at the Claremont is fitness and pampering. A full-fledged health club, complete with yoga, Pilates, and spinning classes takes up part of the huge complex. And the full-service spa, which offers all the current popular body treatments plus aesthetic services, finds favor with visitors and locals alike.

## Food

Even if you can't stomach the politics of Berkeley, try the food. Berkeley is home to Alice Waters, grandmother of the organic and sustainable restaurant movement, and amazing restaurants fall thick on the ground here.

### CASUAL DINING

Only in Berkeley could any traveler expect to find a multitude of all-organic, all-raw food restaurants. Of them all, **Café Gratitude** (1730 Shattuck Ave., 415/824-4652, www.cafegratitude.com, $7–12) might be the hippiest eatery in all of hippiedom. Not only is all the food as natural as it's possible to get, each dish is named as an affirmation. Instead of ordering a kale, beet, and celery juice, you'll ask for an "I am Worthy," or instead of a pesto pizza, order an "I am Sensational." Really. All dishes are 100 percent vegetarian, many are vegan, and most are a bit strange even for the expanded palates of the average Bay Area diner. But the chefs do work good and hard to spin the fresh ingredients into tasty dishes. So if you're willing to brave the kale, tofu, and sprouted everything, give it a shot! (Maybe even a wheatgrass shot.) You might like it.

Sometimes, a weary traveler just needs a bowl of soup on the cheap. In Berkeley (and at any number of other towns around the Bay Area), your best choice is **Pho Hoa** (2272 Shattuck Ave., 510/540-9228, www.phohoa.com). Yes, it's a chain—there's even a location in Saigon. But for the classic Vietnamese rice noodle soup called *pho,* Pho Hoa provides some of the best big bowls of soup around. The dining rooms are clean if a bit sterile and cafeteria-like. Newcomers to the world of *pho* can choose a bowl of chicken, steak, or seafood soup, while the more adventurous (and familiar with Southeast Asian cuisine) might choose some fatty flank, tendon, or even tripe. If you've got

## A TASTE OF THE EAST BAY

Food and drink rule Berkeley. For the best of the food, visit the **Scharffen Berger** (914 Heinz Ave., 510/981-4066, www.artisanconfection.com, Mon.-Sat. 10 A.M.-6 P.M., Sun. 10 A.M.-5 P.M., tours free) chocolate factory. Scharffen Berger prides itself on a wonderful array of artisanal chocolate products. Daily tours take visitors through the factory and provide a history of both chocolate itself and the chocolate-making company.

Grab a glass of a different kind of wine at **Taraka Sake USA** (708 Addison Ave., 510/540-8250, daily noon-6 P.M.). Here you can take a tour of an authentic sake factory, which ends with a complimentary sake sampling in the tasting room. Sakes made here tend toward the inexpensive types served warm here in America; the factory also produces mirin and plum wine. For true sake connoisseurs, you can buy premium sakes imported from Japan at the factory.

If your idea of a good time is a good stiff drink, you'll love a visit to one of the local area alcohol producers. Have a sip (or more) of fine California wine at either **Lost Canyon Winery** (2102 Dennison, Ste. A, Oakland, 510/534-9314, www.lostcanyonwinery.com, Fri.-Sun. 1-6 P.M., complimentary tastings) or **Rosenblum Cellars** (2900 Main St., Ste. 1100, Alameda, 510/865-7007, www.rosenblumcellars.com, daily 11 A.M.-6 P.M.). Lost Canyon specializes in Pinot Noir and Syrah, while you'll find a wide array of reds, whites, and dessert wines at Rosenblum.

For the stronger stuff, head down to **Hangar One Vodka** (2601 Monarch St., Alameda Point, 800/782-8145, www.hangarone.com, Wed.-Sat. noon-7 P.M., Sun. noon-6 P.M.) tasting room. Look out over the view of the San Francisco Bay as you sip the vodkas named for the building in which they are created.

a huge appetite, go for a large bowl; a big appetite, go for a small bowl; a normal appetite, split a large with a friend! Top it off with an iced milk coffee for the ultimate pick-me-up. All for well under $10 per person.

Another downscale but well worth the time ethnic enclave, the **Chaat Café** (1902 University Ave., 510/845-1431, www.chaatcafes.com) offers spicy Indian cuisine for the right prices. This Bay Area local chain serves chaat (small plates and appetizers), of course. You can also get a meaty curry, a tandoori dish, stuffed naan, and more. (Though you'll find a few vegetarian specialties on the menu, this particular Indian place sticks more to the northern meat-eating tradition.)

### FINE DINING

The very, very best of these, and Alice Waters' baby, is **Chez Panisse** (1517 Shattuck Ave., restaurant 510/548-5525, café 510/548-5049, www.chezpanisse.com, restaurant prix fixe $55–85, café $19–24). If you plan to dine in the restaurant at Chez Panisse, you need to make your reservations early and possibly plan your entire trip to Berkeley around the date on which you get a table. You can make a dinner reservation up to one month in advance. (No, we're not kidding. You should try to get a reservation at French Laundry if you think this is ridiculous.) The desk takes phone calls 9 A.M.–9:30 P.M. Monday–Saturday. You'll get the chance to enjoy some of the best cuisine that's ever graced a plate in Berkeley or anywhere else on earth. Waters and her successors create French-California dishes at the bleeding edge of current trends—Waters sets trends, she doesn't follow them.

Upstairs, the café offers food that's a bit more casual but just as good as the rarified dining room downstairs. It's much easier to get a reservation in the bustling, energetic café than it is the restaurant, and the casual atmosphere is less intimidating for diners who are new to all this California haute cuisine excess.

## Information and Services

Newcomers to Berkeley can start at the

**Visitor Information Center** (2015 Center St., 510/549-7040, www.berkeleycvb.com, Mon.–Fri. 9 A.M.–5 P.M.). If you prefer to read about your destination in its local rags, you'll certainly be able to find some free newspapers on the street corners of Berkeley. The ***Berkeley Daily News*** is published (surprise!) every day. The ***Berkeley Daily Planet*** comes out twice a week. Check the *Daily Planet* for live entertainment listings and reviews.

As a major metropolitan city, you'll find most all the services you need in Berkeley. ATMs for most major banks appear on Shattuck and Telegraph Avenues, and close by all the major tourist areas. Just take care using them, especially after dark. You can find **post offices** at 1521 Shattuck Avenue and 2111 San Pablo Avenue.

For medical assistance, the **Alta Bates Summit Medical Center** (2001 Dwight Way, 510/204-4444) has a 24-hour emergency room.

### Getting There and Around

The closest airport to Berkeley is Oakland International (see the *Oakland and Alameda* section). From the Oakland airport, rent a car, catch a cab, or take BART to the Colesium/Airport stop and then catch the AirBART shuttle to the terminals. If you're flying into San Francisco, you can take BART across the Bay to Berkeley.

As a matter of fact, **BART** (www.bart.gov) is a major form of transit in and around Berkeley. The Downtown Berkeley station underneath Shattuck Avenue is a major structure, with six exits that can create confusion for unfamiliar riders. Other stops include North Berkeley, Ashby, and Rockridge. See BART's website for schedules and tickets.

Berkeley sits to the north of Oakland and Alameda along the east side of the San Francisco Bay. If you're driving into Berkeley, take the Bay Bridge from San Francisco, then turn north onto Highway 580/80. Major roads in town include San Pablo, Ashby, Shattuck, Telegraph, and University.

Parking in Berkeley can be a bona fide nightmare. The town can be actively hostile to the notion of new parking lots and structures. Expect to pay for the privilege of parking here, and to walk a few blocks to your destination. If you're visiting Berkeley for the day or in for an evening show, consider taking BART in and out of the town to avoid the parking hassle.

## OAKLAND AND ALAMEDA

The view across the Bay from San Francisco includes both Oakland and Alameda. Oakland is the biggest city in the East Bay. Though Oakland's reputation hasn't always been perfect (and visitors should probably stay in the popular tourist areas), today a great deal of downtown urban renewal has made it a visitor-friendly place with plenty of attractions, accommodations, and good food.

Long ago, Alameda grew up around its Naval base, providing a residential community for sailors, their families, and support businesses. The base closed in the 1990s, but the quiet, pleasant community remains.

### USS *Hornet*

Military historians, ghost hunters, and swing dancers meet aboard the USS *Hornet* museum (Ferry Point, Alameda, 510/521-8448, www.uss-hornet.org, daily 10 A.M.–4 P.M., adults $14, students/seniors/military $12, children $6) moored at the former naval base in Alameda. Small by comparison to modern aircraft carriers, the *Hornet* doesn't seem so small when you stand on the hangar deck staring at the half-dozen planes and helicopters displayed as part of the museum. Several open decks reveal to curious crawlers what cramped, steel-clad life was like aboard the Constitution-class carriers. (Bring a map; it's easy to get lost in the maze-like lower decks.) Claustrophobic visitors can spend their time up on the flight deck or touring "the island," imagining what it must have been like to experience the stress and action of one plane launching off the carrier every 45 seconds, all day long.

The *Hornet* is reputed to be one of the most haunted structures in the Bay Area, with the ghosts of sailors who lost their lives on duty floating through their favorite spots onboard ship. Most ghost activity seems to occur at night, and overnight visits and flashlight tours are available (check the website for dates and times). Finally, the *Hornet* acts as a local dance hall and event center for Alameda, hosting swing dance soirees and holiday parties on a regular basis.

## Chabot Space and Science Center

One of the most spectacular sights in the East Bay, Chabot Space and Science Center (10000 Skyline Blvd., Oakland, 510/336-7300, www.chabotspace.org, Wed.–Thurs. 10 A.M.–5 P.M., Fri.–Sat. 10 A.M.–10 P.M., Sun. 11 A.M.–5 P.M., adults $13, seniors/students $10, youth $9) makes science and space super cool. Set up in the Oakland Hills, the Chabot complex includes observatories, the planetarium, the museum, and the Megadome theater, all available to the public. (Most Bay Area observatory telescopes are private.) Unlike the other area science museums that focus most on life on earth, Chabot focuses on the life *of* earth and of the universe. You and your family can create your own solar system in an interactive exhibit, "ride" a space shuttle in the Megadome, and check out Saturn's rings through the telescopes. If your visit runs long, grab a bite to eat and a cup of coffee at the on-site Celestial Café.

## Oakland Zoo and Crab Cove

Do you love animals? You can visit all different kinds in the East Bay. For a day with creatures of the land, go to the Oakland Zoo (9777 Golf Links Rd., Oakland, 510/632-9525, www.oaklandzoo.org, daily 10 A.M.–4 P.M., adults $9.50, seniors/youth $6). Here you'll discover an array of amphibians, mammals, reptiles, and birds, plus children's rides. Or if you prefer sea life, head for the Crab Cove Visitor's Center (1252 McKay Ave., Alameda, 510/521-6887, www.ebparks.org, Wed.–Sun. 10 A.M.–4:30 P.M., parking $5) in Alameda. Find out what the Bay looks like from the fish's perspective, say hello to the world under the sea, or take a peek at the exhibit on local Alameda history.

## Entertainment and Events

Ballroom dancers from all around the Bay gather in Oakland on a regular basis to attend the famous **Ye Gaskell Occasional Dance Society** ball (1547 Lakeside Dr., www.gaskellball.com). This fabulous fancy-dress event encourages everybody to dress in their finest (from whatever era from 1800 through today, but Victorian is encouraged) to create a picture of beauty swirling around the dance floor. You don't need to be an accomplished dancer to enjoy Gaskell's. Dance classes are offered during the afternoon before the ball, and a quick brush-up takes place before the official opening dance—always the Viennese waltz. Oakland's Scottish Rite Temple provides the perfect backdrop for the silk dresses, swirling hoopskirts, and handsome tuxedos of the dancers. Even if you don't dance much, come to admire the beautiful costumes and skillful regulars.

If you prefer a more modern beat to dance to, you can find some good live music and dancing in Oakland. Perhaps the best-known venue is, of all things, a sushi bar called **Yoshi's** (510 Embarcadero Way, Oakland, 510/238-9200, www.yoshis.com, lunch Tues.–Fri. 11:30 A.M.–2 P.M., dinner Mon.–Wed. 5:30–9 P.M., Thurs. 5:30–10 P.M., Fri.–Sat. 5:30–10:30 P.M., Sun. 5–9 P.M., shows 8 P.M. and 10 P.M.). With the restaurant in one room and the legendary jazz club right next door at Yoshi's on Jack London Square, it's possible to enjoy the sushi without attending the concert, or vice versa. The restaurant has recently been revitalized; a new chef brought in to create an up-to-date menu of raw and cooked Japanese cuisine with just enough California flair to make it different. If you're a dinner patron, it's a *very* good idea to make reservations for the show and get your seat tag on a chair before you sit down for your meal. You might see Otis Taylor or Kurt Elling in the club at Yoshi's. Any jazz fan who's come to the Bay Area owes it to herself to check the calendar on the website and see who's playing while she's in town.

Or perhaps you'd prefer DJs and cocktails. **Luka's Taproom & Lounge** (2221 Broadway,

510/451-4667, www.lukasoakland.com, Mon.–Wed 11:30 A.M.–midnight, Thurs.–Fri. 11:30 A.M.–2 A.M., Sat. 5:30 P.M.–2 A.M., Sun. 11 A.M.–midnight) can give you all that, and a Sunday hangover brunch as a bonus. What spends the day and early evening as a restaurant becomes a lounge and dance club with full bar after the sun sets. With a separate room for the DJs and dancing, and another space that serves as a full-on pool room with 45-playing jukebox, plus the Taproom with its brasserie-style food and 16 beers on tap, almost everyone can find something to enjoy at Luka's.

## Shopping

**Jack London Square** (www.jacklondonsquare.com) is a great place to go if you're new to shopping in Oakland. Down on Oakland's surprisingly pretty waterfront, the Square is a bustling crowd of tourists and locals come to eat, shop, or catch a movie. The shops here tend toward the big chains.

For more local, specialized shops with a neighborhood feel, head to **Rockridge** (bwtn. Alcatraz Ave. and 51st St.) or **Piedmont.** In Rockridge, foodies will want to explore epicurian Market Hall (5655 College Ave.), while bookworms get their fix at well-regarded and independent Diesel Bookstore (5433 College Ave., 510/653-9965). At the foot of the Oakland Hills, the Piedmont district's main draw is the delightfully retro Fenton's Creamery (4226 Piedmont Ave., 510/658-7000) which has been serving scoops since 1894. A local theater, antique shops, and several restaurants line the easily walkable neighborhood.

## Sports and Recreation

The jewel of Oakland's renewed downtown culture is **Lake Merritt and Lakeside Park** (650 Bellevue Ave., 510/238-7275). Here you can take a walk around the lake, play a few holes of golf, rent a kayak for a peaceful paddle, or even get in a set of tennis. For families, Children's Fairyland provides hours of entertainment and diversion.

Recreation buffs can peruse **California Canoe and Kayak** (409 Water St., 510/893-7833, www.calkayak.com, daily 10 A.M.–6 P.M.). CCK carries not only kayaks and equipment, but a wide selection of outdoor fashions for both men and women.

If you'd rather watch than play, Oakland is home to several professional sports teams of varying reputations and records. The best consistent players are the MLB **Oakland A's** (510/762-2277, http://oakland.athletics.mlb.com). Part of the American League, the A's have seen their ups and downs, but they almost always put on a good show for their fans. The NBA's **Golden State Warriors** (510/625-8497, www.nba.com/warriors) court action can be fun to watch, particularly if you're rooting for the away team.

The most notorious team in pro football, the **Oakland Raiders** (510/625-8497, www.raiders.com) call the East Bay home again after a stint in Los Angeles. The fact that they haven't been getting their game on too well in recent years has not lessened the devotion of Bay Area fans to their beloved Raiders. If you get tickets to a game, be aware that the gangster reputation is not for nothing—the home side of the stadium can get rowdy and rough.

All three teams play at the **Oracle Arena and McAfee Coliseum** (7000 Coliseum Way, Oakland, 510/569-2121, www.coliseum.com), a complex with both a covered basketball arena and an open-air stadium that hosts both the A's and the Raiders. Though the vast majority of event and game-goers are perfectly safe, the Coliseum isn't in the best neighborhood, so pay attention as you walk out to your car.

## Accommodations

In addition to the many chain motels in Oakland and Alameda, a number of independent inns and hotels offer a more unique East Bay experience.

### $100-150

In Oakland, try the **Bay Breeze Inn** (4919 Coliseum Way, Oakland, 510/536-5972, www.baybreezeinnoakland.com, $95–150). With all the amenities of a higher-priced chain motel, the Bay Breeze offers both comfort and convenience. Located just down the street from the Coliseum and only a few miles from the Oakland Airport, this is the perfect place to stay if you're into football, baseball, basketball, concerts, or other live events. Do be aware that the Coliseum area can be sketchy after dark, so take care if you're walking alone. Or across the street from the Oakland Airport, stay at the **Gateway Hotel** (10 Hegenberger Rd., Oakland, 510/635-1892, www.gatewayhotel resort.com, $77–99). In addition to the usual motel amenities, enjoy the ultra-comfy Sleep Number bed and the on-site restaurant and bar, or take a dip in the pool.

At the **Acacia House** (Acacia Ave., Oakland, 510/601-9837, www.acaciahousebb.com, $140–195, 2-night minimum), you'll find a lovely three-room suite with soaring windows overlooking the Oakland Hills, native trees, and the upscale Rockridge neighborhood. A stay at the Acacia House feels more like visiting a friend's home than checking into an anonymous motel. Walk to the Rockridge BART station to explore the area, or sit in the garden, sipping a drink from the wet bar and relaxing. But book early during high season! Another unique lodging, **Dean's Bed & Breakfast** (480 Pedestrian Way, Oakland, 510/652-5024, $140) is also in the heart of charming Rockridge. It's actually a cottage stocked with fresh food and coffee, making each guest's stay completely private. You'll enjoy the heated pool and Japanese garden in summertime, as well as the sights and attractions of Oakland and nearby Berkeley.

Stay right on the waters of Alameda at the **Coral Reef Inn & Suites** (400 Park St., Alameda, 800/533-2330, www.coralreefinn .com, $95–115). This down-to-earth motel has large rooms, all with kitchenettes and small dining tables—perfect for a longer stay in the area.

If you've got a bigger budget, grab a nice room at an upscale inn. The oldest home in Alameda is **Webster House B&B** (1238 Versailles Ave., 510/523-9697, http://webster-house2.home.comcast.net/~websterhouse2/, $105–195). Set back from the street in an older residential neighborhood, trees shade the whole Gothic Revival house (one grows right up through the deck). Guests lounge on the deck sipping tea each afternoon. Breakfast is made to order. Each of the four guest rooms is uniquely decorated, and one has a view of the waterfall in the yard.

### $150-250

**The Washington Inn** (495 10th St., Oakland, 510/452-1776, www.thewashingtoninn.com, $165–190) brings a hint of European elegance to Oakland. Guest rooms are done in clean lines, simple furnishings, and bright whites linens with touches of brilliant color. This inn prides itself on pampering its guests, so be sure to take advantage of the extras. And make a dinner reservation at TWIST, the hotel's wonderful white-tablecloth California-Italian restaurant. The inn's location in the heart of downtown makes it perfect for business and pleasure travelers alike.

If you prefer to stay in Alameda, the **Hawthorn Suites** (1628 Webster St., Alameda, 510/522-1000, www.oaklandhs.com, $132–165) has all the appointments and amenities of a good motel, plus big, extra-nicely decorated guest rooms. Sure, it's a chain, but it's one of the nicer ones and it's conveniently located in downtown Alameda, only a short drive from the USS *Hornet* museum.

## Food

### CASUAL DINING

The **Home of Chicken and Waffles** (444 Embarcadero West, 510/836-4446, www.hcw chickenandwaffles.com, Sun.–Thurs. 8 A.M.–midnight, Fri.–Sat. 8 A.M.–4 A.M., $7–14) serves up good ol' Southern comfort food late into the night. Specialties of the house include the gooey mac 'n' cheese, true Southern sides (lots of grits), and of course chicken and waffles—served together, if you please. This definitely isn't the best spot for low-carb dieters to slake their appetites! But if you don't count calories and you need some late-night grub (or breakfast, or lunch, or dinner), HCW can hook you up. Note that after 11:30 P.M., you must prepay for your meal.

Some travelers take the opportunity to try

just about every type of world cuisine that's available in the Bay Area. At **Phnom Penh House** (3912 MacArthur Blvd., 510/482-8989, Mon.–Thurs. 11 A.M.–9:15 P.M., Fri.–Sat. 11 A.M.–9:45 P.M., $7–14), you can give Cambodian food a whirl. You'll find the dishes similar to Thai cooking, with some different spice combinations. At Phnom Penh, the fish, the soup, and the green papaya salad all draw rave reviews from frequent diners. Rumor has it that the curries are worth trying as well.

If you're out on the island of Alameda and you're looking for a tasty meal, consider sampling the German food at **Speisekammer** (2424 Lincoln Ave., 510/522-1300, www.speisekammer.com, lunch Fri.–Sun. noon–3 P.M., dinner Tues.–Wed. 5–9 P.M., Thurs.–Sat. 5–10 P.M., Sun. 4–9 P.M., $15–24). This Old World eatery specializes in sausages, marinated meat, red cabbage, and sauerkraut. And, of course, beer. Check the website for information about the beer drinking contests. Just to make your dining experience that much more fun, Speisekammer hosts live entertainment every Thursday, Friday, and Saturday night—mostly jazz combos, but you might find a country band or even a local musicians showcase to enjoy with your wiener schnitzel.

### FINE DINING

For a delicious upscale meal on Jack London Square, try **Soizic** (300 Broadway, 510/251-8100, www.soizicbistro.com, lunch Tues.–Fri. 11:30 A.M.–2 P.M., dinner Tues.–Thurs. 5:30–9 P.M., Fri.–Sat. 5:30–10 P.M., $16–24). You'll need to round the corner onto Third Street to find the front door. This charming spot offers French-Californian cuisine served on sparkling white tablecloths and attractive modern dinnerware. The elegant dining room with its classic tables and banquets has seen the patronage of California governors and other local celebrities. On the menu, you'll find fish, vegetarian fare, and tender meats prepared with an eye to French traditional cuisine and current California sensibilities.

## Information and Services

Its proximity to San Francisco can make it easy to forget that Oakland is a major city in its own right. You can start at the **Oakland Convention and Visitors Bureau** (463 11th St., Oakland, 510/839-9000, www.oaklandcvb.com) to get good advice, maps, restaurant recommendations, and traffic tips.

You'll find plenty of banks and ATM machines scattered around Oakland; it's a good idea to stick to the ATM machines in well-lit, touristy areas rather than picking a random spot off the freeway at midnight. The same goes for gas stations and mini-marts.

Oakland boasts many **post offices.** One near Lake Merritt sits at 1955 Broadway. Internet access should be little trouble in a city filled with Starbucks outlets and connected hotels.

For medical attention, you can head out to the **Alameda Hospital** (2070 Clinton Ave., 510/522-3700, www.alamedahospital.org), which has a 24-hour emergency room. In Oakland, **Alta Bates** has a summit campus (350 Hawthorne Ave., 510/655-4000).

## Getting There and Around

The truth is, if you can fly into and out of the **Oakland International Airport** (www.flyoakland.com) rather than SFO, you should do so. As one of the satellite airports, it sees less traffic than San Francisco, and it's easier to get into and out of with shorter security lines.

Bay Area Rapid Transit, or **BART** (www.bart.gov) is a good means of public transportation for visitors to Oakland. It can take you up to Berkeley, across the Bay into San Francisco or down onto the Peninsula, and all over the East Bay. BART can be a little bit intimidating for lone females after dark, but it's reasonably safe these days.

Bus service in Oakland and Alameda is run by **AC Transit** (www.actransit.org, adults $1.75, children/seniors $0.85, Transbay adults $3.50, children/seniors $1.70). Check the website for route maps and schedules for local East Bay bus service.

The major freeways surrounding Oakland and Alameda are, to put it politely, a mess. Try to avoid driving I-880, I-580, or I-680 during either the morning or evening rush hour periods (8 A.M.–10 A.M. and 4–7 P.M.). And if you should find yourself on the interchange referred to on local traffic reports as the MacArthur Maze…er, good luck. Don't feel bad if you get lost and need to get off a freeway and circle back; it happens. No lane instructions are listed here for the Maze because they'd probably be wrong by the time this book is published.

Getting out to Alameda can be a bit less than straightforward, as it's not totally obvious that the city of Alameda sits out on an island in the Bay. You'll need to take one of the bridges or the "tube" accessible from I-880 to get onto the island. Find a good map or get directions in advance to avoid getting lost in what can be a confusing area for newcomers.

Parking in Oakland and Alameda is easier than in San Francisco, most of the time. Street parking can be extremely difficult to come by; it's best to follow the signs to the parking garages surrounding Jack London Square and other major attractions and areas.

# Silicon Valley

Here began the Information Age, and here much of the new technology that still astounds the world gets developed every day. What was once a fertile valley filled with orchards is now an endless procession of cities that shelter the major players of the high-tech world. No less than Apple Computer, Hewlett-Packard, and Intel, among many others, maintain their headquarters here.

Because of the huge number of good tech jobs here, people of all ethnicities and from countries around the world call the Silicon Valley home. The cultural diversity makes it a fascinating place to live and visit, with food and entertainment from all around the planet represented.

## SAN JOSE

Sprawled across the south end of Silicon Valley, San Jose proudly claims the honor of "biggest city in the Bay Area." It is the beating heart of the Valley's high-tech industry, and eBay, Intel, Adobe, IBM, and many more call San Jose home. Long considered a cultural wasteland, San Jose has worked in the last decade to change its image, supporting local art and attracting high-end restaurants. If you want to get a sense of how Silicon Valley residents really live, spend a few days in San Jose.

### Tech Museum of Innovation

The appropriately situated Tech Museum of Innovation (201 S. Market St., 408/294-8324, www.thetech.org, Mon.–Wed. 9 A.M.–5 P.M., Thurs.–Sun. 9 A.M.–8 P.M., $8) brings technology of all kinds to kids, families, and science lovers. The interactive displays at The Tech invite touching, letting children explore and learn about medical technology, computers, biology, chemistry, physics, and more using all their senses. The IMAX theater shows films dedicated to science, learning, technology, and adventure. The standard museum ticket price includes an IMAX show, and the long daily hours allow both early birds and night owls to get their learning on at The Tech.

### Winchester Mystery House

For good old-fashioned, cheesy haunted house fun, stop in at the Winchester Mystery House (525 S. Winchester Blvd., 408/247-2101, www.winchestermysteryhouse.com, daily 9 A.M.–5 P.M., adults $26, children $20). A San Jose attraction that pre-dates the rise of Silicon Valley, the huge bizarre mansion was built by famous wacko Sarah Winchester. Kids love the doors that open onto brick walls, stairwells that go nowhere, and oddly shaped rooms, while adults enjoy the story of Sarah and the antiques displayed in many of the rooms. Sarah married into the gun-making Winchesters, and became disturbed later in life by the destruction and death wrought

ROBERT HOLMES / CALTOUR

Winchester Mystery House

by her husband's products. She designed the house to both facilitate communication with the spirits of the dead, and to confound them and keep herself safe. Whether or not ghosts still haunt the mansion is a matter of debate and of faith—visit and make up your own mind. For an extra-spooky experience, take a Friday the 13th or Halloween flashlight tour (book early, as these tours fill up fast).

## Rosicrucian Egyptian Museum

Perhaps more genuinely creepy than the Winchester Mystery House, the Rosicrucian Egyptian Museum (1342 Naglee Ave., 408/947-3636, Mon.–Fri. 10 A.M.–5 P.M., Sat.–Sun. 11 A.M.–6 P.M., adults $9, seniors/students $7, children $5) has been a part of San Jose culture for almost a century. First opened by the Rosicrucian Order AMORC in 1928, the museum has a wonderful collection of ancient Egyptian artifacts, including several mummies—partly unwrapped, a rarity today. Local children and adults love the Rosicrucian's jewels, tomb artifacts, tools, and textiles. In addition, the complex includes a planetarium (shows Mon.–Fri. 2 P.M., Sat.–Sun. 2 and 3:30 P.M.). Planetarium shows are free with admission to the museum.

## Entertainment and Events

San Jose is definitely blessed with all sorts of entertainment. Cultural travelers can get seats to **Ballet San Jose** (408/288-2800, www.balletsanjose.org, $25–82) at the Center for the Performing Arts (255 S. Almaden Blvd.) or to **Opera San Jose** (408/437-4950, www.operasj.org) at the California Theatre (345 S. First St.).

Live theater options also abound in downtown San Jose. The big pro company is the **San Jose Repertory Theatre** (101 Paseo de San Antonio, 408/367-7255, www.sjrep.com, $30–60), locally known as the Rep. They've rebuilt their theater space and made over their company in an attempt to lure in a younger audience with edgy new works. It's only been partly successful—the audience still leans toward their canes, and the shows sometimes get so close to the edge that they fall off into the abyss of bad theater. Still, it can be fun to see the action in the gorgeous newer space. On the other hand, **City Lights Theatre** (529 S. Second St., 408/295-4200, www.cltc.org, $25–40) just down the block from the Rep, has a tiny, black-box-style theater and little money to spend on fancy lobby light fixtures. But the shows, mostly acted by up-and-coming local performers, never fail to entertain. Their take on everything from *Lysistrata* to *The Waiting Room* is fresh and original, providing a perfect local theater experience with a definite Silicon Valley flavor.

The clubs in San Jose certainly are suburban, but the lack of self-conscious hipness can make a night out at **Agenda Lounge** (399 S. First St., 408/287-3991, www.agendalounge.com, Wed.–Sat. 5:30 P.M.–2 A.M., Sun. 9 P.M.–2 A.M.) or the **Voodoo Lounge** (14 S. Second St., 408/286-8636, www.voodooloungesj.com) more relaxed than a trek up to the City.

Live comedy is another popular Silicon

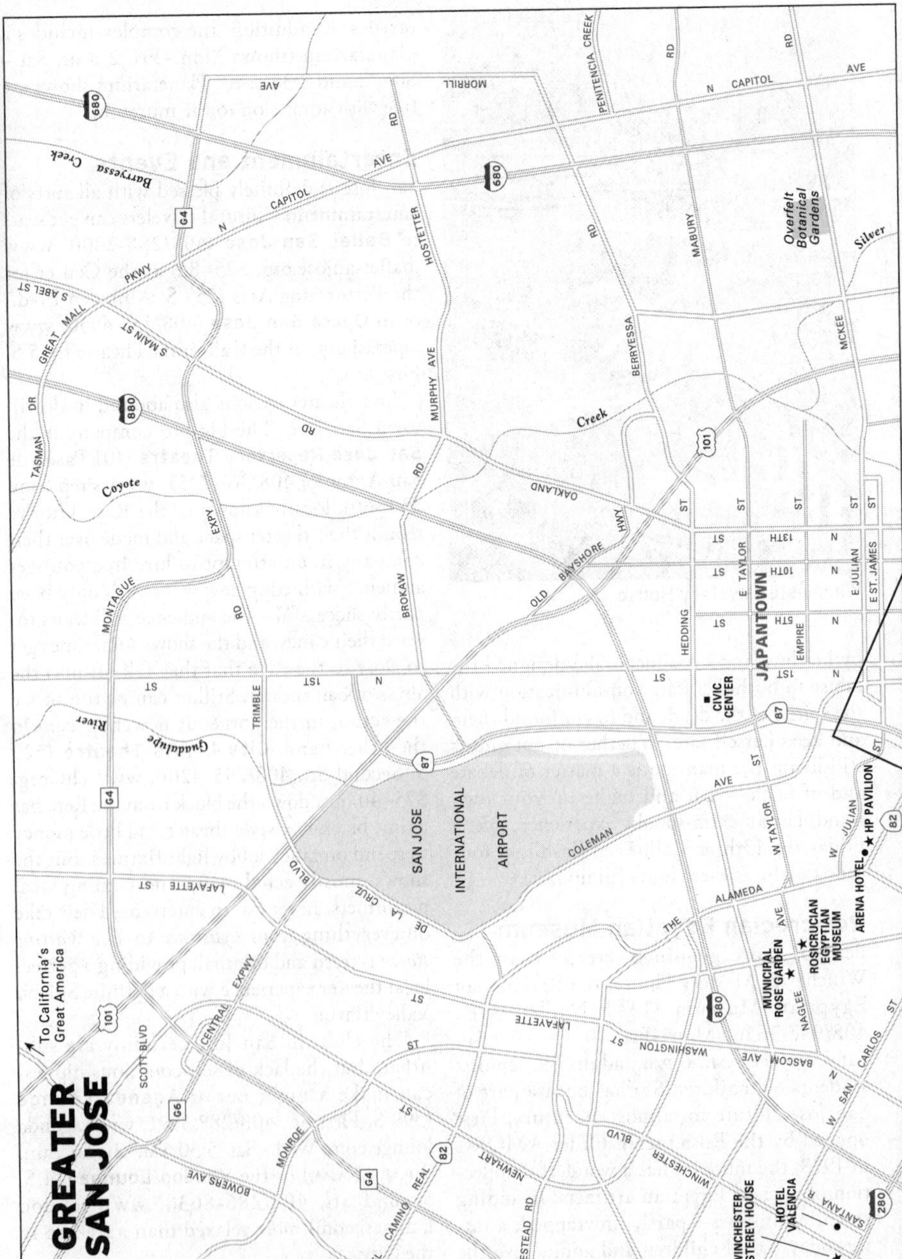
GREATER SAN JOSE
To California's Great America
SAN JOSE INTERNATIONAL AIRPORT
JAPANTOWN
CIVIC CENTER
Overfelt Botanical Gardens
MUNICIPAL ROSE GARDEN
ROSICRUCIAN EGYPTIAN MUSEUM
ARENA HOTEL
HP PAVILION
WINCHESTER MYSTEREY HOUSE
HOTEL VALENCIA
Coyote Creek
Guadalupe River
Barryessa Creek
Silver
Penitencia Creek
N CAPITOL AVE
MORRILL AVE
HOSTETTER RD
MURPHY AVE
BERRYESSA RD
MABURY RD
MCKEE
OAKLAND RD
OLD BAYSHORE HWY
BROKAW RD
N 1ST ST
TRIMBLE RD
MONTAGUE EXPY
TASMAN DR
GREAT MALL PKWY
S ABEL ST
S MAIN ST
HEDDING ST
E TAYLOR ST
E JULIAN ST
E ST. JAMES
EMPIRE
5TH ST
10TH ST
13TH ST
COLEMAN AVE
W TAYLOR ST
W JULIAN ST
THE ALAMEDA
NAGLEE AVE
DE LA CRUZ BLVD
LAFAYETTE ST
CENTRAL EXPWY
SCOTT BLVD
BOWERS AVE
MONROE ST
EL CAMINO REAL
HOMESTEAD RD
NEWHART
WINCHESTER BLVD
WASHINGTON ST
BASCOM AVE
N SAN CARLOS ST
W SAN
SANTANA R
880
680
101
87
82
280
G4
G6

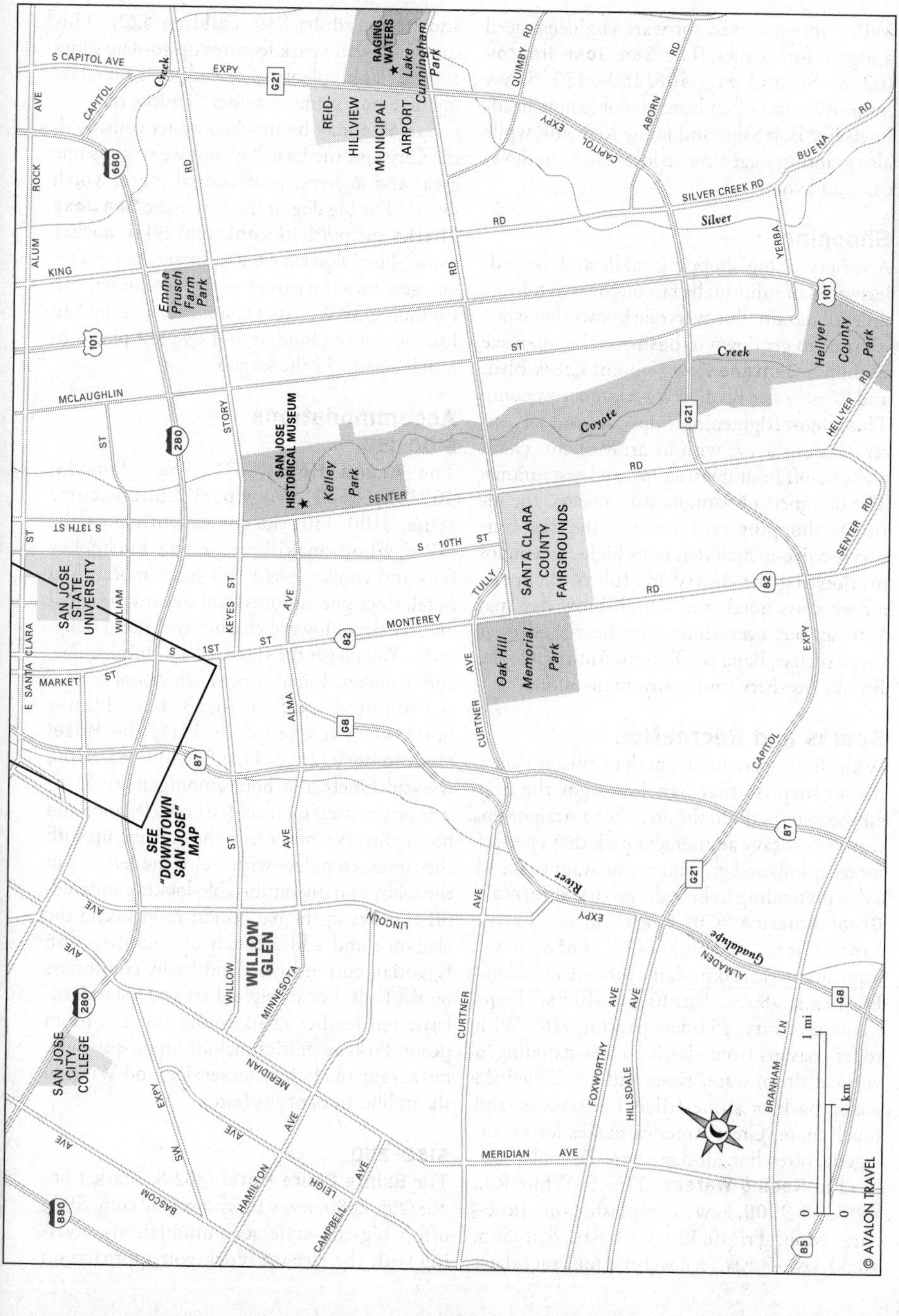
S CAPITOL AVE
EXPY
G21
RAGING WATERS
Lake Cunningham Park
REID-HILLVIEW MUNICIPAL AIRPORT
QUIMBY RD
ABORN RD
CAPITOL EXPY
BUENA RD
SILVER CREEK RD
Silver
Creek
CAPITOL
AVE
680
ROCK
ALUM
KING
RD
Emma Prusch Farm Park
101
YERBA
Hellyer County Park
HELLYER RD
ST
MCLAUGHLIN
STORY
280
SAN JOSE HISTORICAL MUSEUM
Kelley Park
SENTER
Coyote
RD
SANTA CLARA COUNTY FAIRGROUNDS
SENTER RD
S 13TH ST
S 10TH ST
SAN JOSE STATE UNIVERSITY
WILLIAM
KEYES ST
TULLY
82
MONTEREY
E SANTA CLARA
S 1ST
MARKET ST
Oak Hill Memorial Park
CURTNER AVE
ALMA AVE
G8
87
SEE "DOWNTOWN SAN JOSE" MAP
River
Guadalupe
ALMADEN EXPY
LINCOLN
WILLOW GLEN
MINNESOTA
MERIDIAN AVE
FOXWORTHY AVE
HILLSDALE AVE
BRANHAM LN
SAN JOSE CITY COLLEGE
EXPY
HAMILTON AVE
BASCOM
CAMPBELL AVE
LEIGH
880
85
0 1 mi
0 1 km
© AVALON TRAVEL

Valley option—even software engineers need a giggle sometimes! The **San Jose Improv** (62 S. Second St., 408/280-7475, www.improv2.com) often hosts major-league headliners like Bob Saget and Jamie Kennedy, while also granting stage time to local talent in showcases and contests.

## Shopping

A variety of big shopping malls and an endless series of mini-malls fan out over San Jose's miles of terrain. But everyone knows that when it's time to get down to business, the top place to shop is **Santana Row** (Stevens Creek Blvd. and Winchester Blvd., www.santanarow.com). This almost frighteningly upscale outdoor center dazzles the eye with its array of chic chain and one-off boutiques, shops, and restaurants. The designers of Santana Row created the ultimate shopping experience of the 21st century—a live-in mall that rents high-end condos overlooking the courtyards full of shoppers, a high-class hotel, and a high-brow day spa. You can buy everything your heart desires at shops such as Bang & Olufsen, Anthropologie, Brooks Brothers, and many, many more.

## Sports and Recreation

With all the space in the south of Silicon Valley, it's no surprise that San Jose's got the best amusement parks in the area. For a straight-up, thrill-ride-heavy amusement park that's perfect for older kids and grownups who want to spend a day pretending to be kids, go to **California's Great America** (4701 Great America Pkwy., Santa Clara, 408/988-1776 x8858, www.cagreatamerica.com, daily June–Aug., Sun.–Fri. 10 A.M.–8 P.M., Sat. 10 A.M.–10 P.M., hours sometimes vary, $54/day, parking $10). With roller coasters from classic to legs-dangling, a vertical drop, water rides and a full-fledged water park, a slime-filled kid's zone, and much more, Great America makes for an energetic, often hot, all-day romp. To cool down, head to **Raging Waters** (2333 S. White Rd., 408/238-9900, www.rwsplash.com, June–Aug., Mon.–Fri. 10:30 A.M.–6 P.M., Sat.–Sun. 10:30 A.M.–7 P.M., see website for exact dates and times, adults $30, children $22). This sprawling water park features up-to-date slides and rides, plus plenty of serene pools for relaxing on a hot, sunny summer San Jose day.

San Jose may be mocked by its cousins in the City and the East Bay, but we've got some great and *different* professional sports worth seeing. The big dog in the area is the **San Jose Sharks** (http://sharks.nhl.com) NHL hockey team. They don't have a Cup yet, but everyone gets into the games at the downtown HP Pavilion (525 W. Santa Clara St.), making San Jose one of the loudest and liveliest places to watch a game in the league.

## Accommodations

### $100-150

The **Arena Hotel** (817 The Alameda, 408/294-6500, www.pacifichotels.com/arena, $100–150) sits conveniently near the HP Pavilion, making it perfect for hockey fans and concert-goers. It's more motel than hotel, since guest rooms tend toward the small and the decor toward chain-motel floral ticky-tacky. You do get the standard TV, mini-fridge, coffee maker, and a surprise whirlpool tub.

Promoted as San Jose's first luxury hotel when it opened in 1911, the **Hotel Montgomery** (211 S. First St., 408/282-8800, www.jdvhotels.com/hotels/montgomery, $145) still prides itself on its old-school elegance and hospitality. But never fear, they've kept up with the times, complete with weird modern art in the lobby and uncomfortable-looking squared-off couches in the bar. Guest rooms echo the elegance and add a touch of comfort, with Egyptian cotton linens and cushy comforters on the beds. Local original art and a standard-issue red leather chair round out the room decor. Posh amenities include an on-site gym, restaurant and bar, room service, and Wi-Fi in the public areas of the hotel.

### $150-250

The **Sainte Claire Hotel** (302 S. Market St., 408/295-2000, www.thesainteclaire.com, $155) offers big-city-style accommodations, starting with the elegant block you approach on

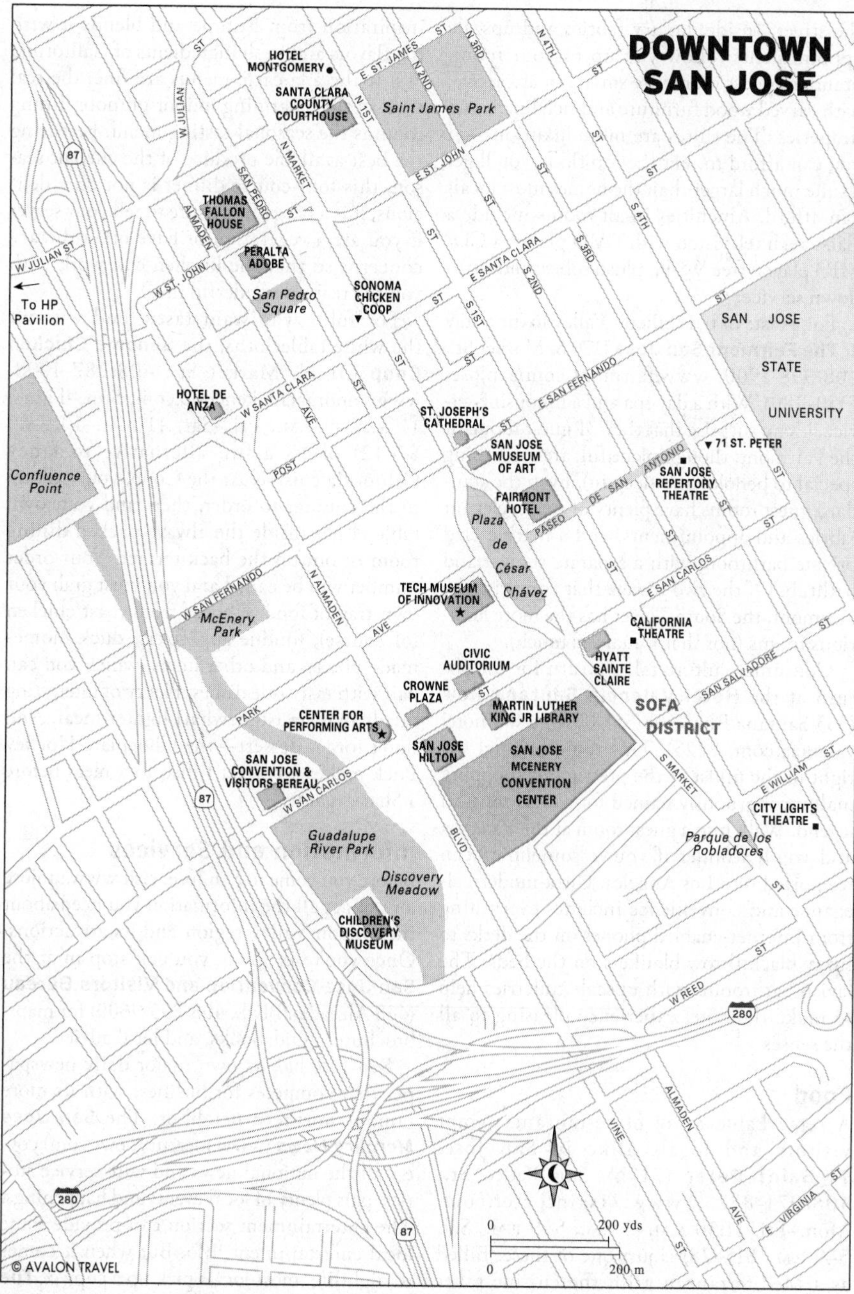
DOWNTOWN SAN JOSE
HOTEL MONTGOMERY
SANTA CLARA COUNTY COURTHOUSE
Saint James Park
THOMAS FALLON HOUSE
PERALTA ADOBE
SONOMA CHICKEN COOP
San Pedro Square
To HP Pavilion
HOTEL DE ANZA
Confluence Point
ST. JOSEPH'S CATHEDRAL
SAN JOSE MUSEUM OF ART
FAIRMONT HOTEL
Plaza de César Chávez
SAN JOSE STATE UNIVERSITY
71 ST. PETER
SAN JOSE REPERTORY THEATRE
TECH MUSEUM OF INNOVATION
McEnery Park
CALIFORNIA THEATRE
HYATT SAINTE CLAIRE
CIVIC AUDITORIUM
CROWNE PLAZA
MARTIN LUTHER KING JR LIBRARY
SOFA DISTRICT
CENTER FOR PERFORMING ARTS
SAN JOSE HILTON
SAN JOSE MCENERY CONVENTION CENTER
SAN JOSE CONVENTION & VISITORS BEREAU
Guadalupe River Park
Discovery Meadow
CHILDREN'S DISCOVERY MUSEUM
CITY LIGHTS THEATRE
Parque de los Pobladores
W JULIAN ST
W ST. JOHN
W SANTA CLARA
W SAN FERNANDO
W SAN CARLOS
E ST. JAMES
E ST. JOHN
E SANTA CLARA
E SAN FERNANDO
E SAN CARLOS
SAN SALVADORE
E WILLIAM
W REED
E VIRGINIA
PASEO DE SAN ANTONIO
N 1ST
N 2ND
N 3RD
N 4TH
S 1ST
S 2ND
S 3RD
S 4TH
N MARKET
S MARKET
SAN PEDRO
ALMADEN
N ALMADEN
PARK AVE
POST
BLVD
VINE
87
280
0 200 yds
0 200 m
© AVALON TRAVEL

the street. Inside, luxury fabrics and upscale appointments follow you up to your room. Standard guest rooms are small but attractive, with carved wood furniture and rich linens and draperies. The suites are more luxurious—if you can afford to rent the top floor, you'll get a suite much larger than the homes most locals can afford. Amenities in all rooms include a flat-screen television with DVD player, a CD/MP3 player, free Wi-Fi, plush robes, and turndown service.

For a taste of true Silicon Valley luxury, stay at **The Fairmont San Jose** (170 S. Market St., 408/998-1900, www.fairmont.com/sanjose, $150–180). With a day spa and a limousine service, it's no surprise that the 731 guest rooms at the Fairmont, though plentiful, are something special to behold (and sleep in). Even the standard guest rooms have plenty of space, elegant fabrics and appointments, and a marble-clad private bathroom with a separate shower and bathtub. Of the two towers that comprise the Fairmont, the South Tower has the more luxurious rooms (not that it matters much).

Consumer culture takes a turn for the absurd at the **Hotel Valencia Santana Row** (355 Santana Row, 408/551-0010, www.hotelvalencia.com, $225). This top-tier hotel sits right in the midst of the prestigious shopping mall incongruously named for a local musical legend. Walk into a guest room at the Valencia and you'll wonder if you've somehow been teleported into Los Angeles. Ultra-modern elegance and convenience includes everything from Internet-enabled phones on the desks to fuzzy black throw blankets on the beds. The lavish bathrooms with upscale toiletries help to make the hotel experience pleasing to all the senses.

## Food

A remarkable array of restaurants tempt visitors and locals alike in San Jose. **71 Saint Peter** (71 N. San Pedro St., 408/971-8523, www.71saintpeter.com, Mon.–Fri. 11:30 A.M.–2 P.M., 5–9 P.M., Sat. 5–9 P.M., $15–28) is just one of these. Billed as a Mediterranean grill, the cuisine takes inspiration from Europe and blends it with the flavors and fresh ingredients of California. While the à la carte menus are fine, the real treat in this charming indoor-outdoor dining room is the seasonal tasting menu. Featuring the best available produce of the current season, this four-course dinner is not only delicious, it is a bargain. Be sure to tell your server if you are a vegetarian or have other dietary concerns so that the kitchen can work with you to create a wonderful meal.

For folks who want tasty food without the white tablecloths, the **Sonoma Chicken Coop** (31 N. Market St., 408/287-4098, www.sonomachickencoop.com, Sun.–Thurs. 11 A.M.–9 P.M., Fri.–Sat. 11 A.M.–10 P.M., $7–12) offers a fun alternative to fancy California cuisine. At the Coop, you walk up to the counter to order, then find your own table either inside the always-packed dining room or out on the back terrace. Your order number will be called and you must grab your own tray of food. Choose from roast chicken (of course), fondue appetizers, duck, homemade pizzas, and other items, which you can pair with tasty side dishes. Plenty of interesting salads make a (somewhat) lighter meal. And don't forget dessert—the Chocolate Hockey Puck makes a perfect finish to a meal before a Sharks game.

## Information and Services

Before you come to San Jose, visit www.sanjose.org to get all the information you need about the Silicon Valley region and its attractions. Once you're in town, you can stop in at the **San Jose Convention and Visitors Bureau** (408 Almaden Blvd., 408/295-9600) for maps, brochures, guidebooks, and local advice.

San Jose has its own major daily newspaper that competes for business with its more famous northern neighbor. The ***San Jose Mercury News*** (www.mercurynews.com) covers all the national news and wire service stories, plus plenty of local events and happenings. The entertainment section can provide some local entertainment info. But when it comes to nightlife, most locals pick up a copy of ***The***

**Wave** (www.thewavemag.com), a free rag that proclaims itself the hippest of the Silicon Valley entertainment publications.

San Jose has plenty of **post offices** available for your use; downtown, you can find one at 200 South Third Street.

Here in the heart of Silicon Valley, it's tough to find a patch of air that doesn't have some Wi-Fi flowing through it. Do expect to pay for Internet access at Starbucks and some of the luxury hotels. If that's not to your taste, war-hacking is practically an art form here. (But you didn't hear that from us!)

For medical attention, **Good Samaritan Hospital** (2425 Samaritan Dr., 408/559-2552, www.goodsamsj.org) has 24-hour emergency services.

### Getting There and Around

Travelers heading straight for the Silicon Valley should skip SFO and fly into **Mineta San Jose International Airport** (1667–2077 Airport Blvd., 408/501-0979, www.sjc.org) if at all possible. This suburban commercial airport has shorter lines, less parking and traffic congestion, and is convenient to downtown San Jose.

**Amtrak** (www.amtrak.com) trains come into San Jose, and you can catch either the Coast Starlight or the Capitol Express at the **San Jose-Diridon Station** (65 Cahill St.). See the Amtrak website for information about scheduling and fares.

The San Jose-Diridon station is also a hub for **CalTrain** (www.caltrain.com, fares $3–11), a commuter train that runs from Gilroy up to San Francisco. If you'd like to spend a day or even two up in the City but base yourself in Silicon Valley, taking CalTrain is an excellent way to go.

At Diridon, you can even catch the **VTA Light Rail** (www.vta.org, fares $2–4), a streetcar network that services San Jose and some of Silicon Valley up as far as Mountain View.

The VTA also operates Silicon Valley **buses** (same fares as light rail), which can get you almost anywhere you need to go if you're willing to be patient enough.

As with most of the Bay Area, it's best to avoid all of San Jose's major freeways 7–9:30 A.M., and again at 7:30 P.M. Arterial U.S. 101 is a dank, dirty stretch of road that's convenient to much of the Peninsula. I-280 is much prettier and less convenient, and definitely the easiest (but not the shortest) car route up to San Francisco. Highway 17 is the fast, treacherous route over the hill to the coast and Santa Cruz; it turns into I-880 in the midst of San Jose and runs past the foot of the Bay and then up the east side of the water all the way to Oakland. Highway 87, sometimes called the Guadalupe Parkway, can provide convenient access to downtown San Jose and the airport.

Parking in San Jose isn't anywhere near as bad as in San Francisco, but you should still be prepared to pay a premium for event parking and closed lots at the fancier hotels.

## PALO ALTO

In a region filled with commuter towns and ever-evolving industry, the city of Palo Alto sits like an elder statesman among adolescents. This older town owes much of its prosperity to neighboring Stanford University, which was founded by Leland and Jane Stanford in memory of their deceased son.

### Stanford University

The major sight in Palo Alto is of course Stanford University (at the end of University Ave., Stanford, 650/723-2560, www.stanford.edu). Stanford is one of the top universities in the world, and less than a tenth of the high school students who apply each year are accepted. The visitors center sits inside **Memorial Hall** (Memorial Auditorium, across the street from Hoover Tower, www.stanford.edu/dept/visitorinfo, Mon.–Fri. 8 A.M.–5 P.M., Sat.–Sun. 9 A.M.–5 P.M.) and can help you with campus maps and tours. Definitely download or procure a map of campus before getting started on your explorations, as Stanford is infamously hard for newcomers to navigate.

For a taste of the beauty that surrounds students on a daily basis, begin your tour with **The Quad** (Oval at University Ave.) and

**Memorial Church** (Main Quad, you can't miss it). Located at the center of campus, these architectural gems are still in active use. Classes are held in the quad every day, and services take place in the church each Sunday.

Almost next door to the Quad lies **Cantor Art Center** (Lomita Dr. and Museum Way, 650/723-4177, www.museum.stanford.edu, Wed.–Sun. 11 A.M.–5 P.M., Thurs. until 8 P.M.). This free art museum features both permanent collections of classic paintings and sculpture donated by the Cantors and other philanthropists, as well as traveling exhibitions. On the other side of the Quad, down Palm Drive towards town, the **Rodin Sculpture Garden** (Lomita Dr. and Museum Way, daily 24 hours) finds favor with students who visit at night. The sculptures in the garden were cast in France from Rodin's originals and include the surprisingly petit-in-person *Thinker* and the *Gates of Hell.*

Perhaps the single most visited spot on the Stanford Campus is **Hoover Tower** (daily 10 A.M.–4:30 P.M.), the tall tower that's visible from as much as 30 miles away and from incoming airplanes. For great views of the Bay Area, head on up to the observation platform and take a look around.

Farther toward the edges of campus lurk two more treasures. **The Dish** (http://dish.stanford.edu) perches high on the Stanford hills, visible from Palm Drive and many other spots on the Peninsula. Along Junipero Serra Drive/Campus Drive East, several trails run up the hillside to the Dish. Once up the hill, you can hike back down-the observatory and radio telescope are not open to visitors. Built by the Stanford Research Institute in 1966 to study Earth's atmosphere and later used to communicate with spacecraft and satellites, the Dish rarely sees any action these days. But "hiking the Dish" along the many pedestrian trails is a time-honored Stanford tradition.

The second monument to science stretches for a full mile across Stanford land into the hills, though the building stays level. **Stanford Linear Accelerator Center** (2575 Sand Hill Rd,, Menlo Park, 650/926-2204, www.slac.stanford.edu), or SLAC to its friends, is one of only a few research facilities of its kind in the world. Here atoms are launched at one end of the building and reach high speeds before smashing into a barrier at the other end. Stanford researchers study the smashed pieces, increasing the body of knowledge about the subatomic world.

Due to a massive construction project and shift in research focus, tours were suspended at the time this book was written. Call SLAC for current information about public tour hours and prices.

## Entertainment and Events

Palo Alto, with Stanford's help, enjoys a vibrant entertainment scene. **Stanford Lively Arts** (650/725-2787, http://livelyarts.stanford.edu, prices and locations vary by show) puts on an array of concerts and live staged entertainments each season. Expect to see several jazz ensembles each year, some world music, definitely a world premiere or two, and perhaps an unusual dance piece.

In town, the small **Dragon Theatre** (535 Alma St., 650/493-2006, www.dragonproductions.net) puts up both well-known plays and premieres by local playwrights. You might see *Rough Crossing* by Tom Stoppard or *The Underpants* by Steve Martin go up at the Dragon. The acting pool is deep, since nearby Foothill College has an award-winning theater conservatory program that turns out excellent actors, directors, and stagehands.

Many students and long-time residents of Palo Alto enjoy seeing classic black-and-white movies back up on the big screen where they belong. Old-school movie house **The Stanford Theatre** (221 University Ave., 650/324-3700, www.stanfordtheatre.org) has red plush velvet seats, beautifully painted walls and ceiling, and a year-round schedule of fabulous old films. You might see a beloved Audrey Hepburn film or a run of Bogey's classics, since the Stanford Theatre often hosts festivals to highlight a specific star or genre.

## Shopping

For a downtown boutique shopping experience in Palo Alto, head for **University Avenue** and its surrounding neighborhood. Here you'll find restaurants, salons, and both chain and independent shops and boutiques. The best art supply store in the whole of the Silicon Valley is **University Arts** (267 Hamilton St., 650/328-5000, www.universityart.com, Mon.–Sat. 9:30 A.M.–5:30 P.M., Thurs. until 7 P.M., Sun. noon–4 P.M.). Even out-of-town artists make it a point to come down to check out the vast shelves filled with the finest brushes, colors, and raw materials. Sadly, the once-fabulous, aging, and elegant Varsity Theater now houses a **Borders** (456 University Ave., 650/326-3670, www.bordersstores.com, Mon.–Thurs. 9 A.M.–11 P.M., Fri.–Sat. 9 A.M.–noon, Sun. 9 A.M.–10 P.M.). It's got everything most Borders bookstores have, plus a decent collection of Palo Alto and California local literature.

An independent jeweler with three locations in the Bay Area (and that's all), **Gleim the Jeweler** (322 University Ave., 650/323-1331, www.gleimjewelers.com) offers a wonderful range of upscale jewelry targeting the many wealthy residents of Palo Alto and the surrounding towns. Specialties of the house include diamonds, designers, and estate jewels. At Gleim, you'll find shiny baubles that don't exist anywhere else.

Gleim also has a storefront in the major area mall: the stunningly landscaped, open-air **Stanford Shopping Center** (Sand Hill Rd. and El Camino Real, www.stanfordshop.com, Mon.–Fri. 10 A.M.–9 P.M., Sat. 10 A.M.–7 P.M., Sun. 11 A.M.–6 P.M.). Here you'll find the upscale boutiques and top-tier department stores befitting the affluence of the area. Big stores include Bloomingdales, Nordstrom, Macy's, and Neiman Marcus. Smaller shops range from designer boutiques such as Ann Taylor and to more affordable chain retailers like Banana Republic. A few truly special specialty stores, such as L'Occitane and Smith & Hawken, also cluster in the large complex.

## Sports and Recreation

Stanford enjoys a reputation for athletics almost as great as its rep for academics, which makes it a great spot to enjoy some spectator sports. While the high-profile men's football and basketball teams tend to toil, the so-called lesser sports and women's teams excel. The women's basketball program is legendary, as is the men's baseball team. The golf team boasts Tiger Woods as an alumnus, and more than a few Olympians have swum in the pools and run on the tracks. For a good match, meet, or game, check the year's schedule at www.stanford.edu/home/athletics.

After a long day of exploring the Stanford campus, hiking the Dish, and touring SLAC, an hour or two in a gorgeous tiled hot tub followed by a luxurious spa treatment makes the perfect end to the day. **Watercourse Way** (165 Channing Ave., 650/462-2000, www.watercourseway.com, Sun.–Thurs. 8 A.M.–11:30 P.M., Fri.–Sat. 8 A.M.–12:30 A.M., tubs $18–28/person/hour) enjoys the title of the Silicon Valley's premier day spa. Former 49er (and Raider) Jerry Rice has been seen there on occasion. Even without the celebrity endorsement, this spa stands out in its amazing tiled tub rooms, range of treatments, and array of top-tier products. Each rentable hot tub room boasts unique and serene decor. The spa treatments are reasonably priced (relatively), and the pampering is second to none.

## Accommodations

Lodgings near Palo Alto on the cheap can be had in the serene farm setting of **Hidden Villa Hostel** (26870 Moody Rd., Lost Altos Hills, 650/949-8648, www.hiddenvilla.org/hostel.php, Sept.–May only, members $21, nonmembers $24). A sustainably constructed main hostel building and a private cabin that's perfect for families and romantic honeymooners, the Hidden Villa hostel also has access to beautiful wilderness hiking trails, the surrounding organic farm, and the small wealthy town of Los Altos Hills. Hidden Villa is the oldest operating youth hostel in the United States, and it's incredibly popular. The newer buildings are more unique and attractive than those of most hostels, and were created to showcase features such as the radiant floor heating and bale wall construction. Reservations are required on weekends, and are a good idea even on weekdays.

Down on El Camino, south of Stanford but near enough to visit, **Dinah's Garden Hotel** (4261 El Camino Real, 800/227-8220, www.dinahshotel.com, $140–825) doesn't quite feel like a chain, despite its location and basic shape. The cute koi ponds and gardens mix with the bright floral interior decor to create a working, if kitschy, tropical paradise theme. The basic rooms tend toward the size and shape of an average motel, but the high-priced suites are something to behold. Attached to the hotel you'll find both a casual poolside grill and an upscale restaurant, a branch of the legendary **Trader Vic's.** If you're staying at Dinah's, you can enjoy as many mai tais and scorpion bowls as you please—you've only got to stumble a few yards to your room.

The **Creekside Inn** (3400 El Camino Real, 650/493-2411, www.creekside-inn.com, $145–260) provides garden accommodations set back a bit from the noisy road. The guest rooms have a touch more class than many motels in the same price range, with stylish fabrics and up-to-date amenities. This larger boutique hotel has more than 100 rooms, an outdoor heated pool, and an exercise room. All rooms have free Wi-Fi, fully stocked private bathrooms, refrigerators, coffee makers, in-room safes, and comfy bathrobes. You can get a package deal that includes breakfast with your room.

Much closer to the Stanford campus, the **Stanford Terrace Inn** (531 Stanford Ave., 650/857-0333, www.stanfordterraceinn.com, $220–360) provides appropriate luxury to parents who are spending a sweet mint to send their kids to a top private university. With all the correct pretensions of a Bay Area business, the Terrace rents "green" rooms with all hypoallergenic and sustainable furnishings, linens, and toiletries, plus filtered water and air. All the rooms, even the standards, are huge and come with attractive furnishings and luxury amenities. If you know what a T-1 line is, you'll be thrilled to know you've got access to one inside your room. The lovely indoor-outdoor restaurant is popular with the locals on holiday weekends.

## Food

The denizens of Palo Alto, especially those who live near the university and downtown (sometimes called the Faculty Ghetto by locals who can't afford the area), like their food. They like it ethnic sometimes, expensive sometimes, but always delicious.

An historic favorite often associated with Stanford is **Sundance the Steakhouse** (1921 El Camino Real, 650/321-6798, http://sundancethesteakhouse.com, lunch Mon.–Fri. 11:30 A.M.–2 P.M., dinner Mon.–Thurs. 5–10 P.M., Fri.–Sat. 5–10:30 P.M., Sun. 5–9 P.M., $19–36). This place reeks of "old boys' club" from the moment you walk in the door. Dimly lit even for a restaurant, Sundance's interior features dark wood, dark booths, black-and-white prints, and antique sporting equipment. The food tends toward—you guessed it—steak. You can order a big cut of beef complete with traditional sides, or opt for a more interesting California-style seafood preparation. The salads and starters are tempting, but if you want to save room for dessert you might need to split an entrée with a dinner companion.

For something a little bit different and a whole lot more reasonably priced, pack in with the locals at **Zao Noodles** (261 University Ave., 650/328-1988, www.zaonoodle.com, $10–15). This pan-Asian noodle house shows off its popularity with bright colors and close-packed tables. Zao serves spicy, reasonably healthy noodle and rice bowls containing all manner of ingredients, plus curries, pad Thai, summer rolls, and more. You can choose from vegetarian, seafood, or meat dishes here. Be sure to pay attention to the little chile pepper markers—when Zao claims a dish is spicy, they mean it! Despite the number of folks who come to Zao, especially on weekend nights, the service is consistently fast and the servers do an amazing job of navigating the warren of tables.

Though it's not as near to the sea as some other parts of the Bay Area, Palo Alto is home to one of the most venerable seafood institutions: **Scott's Seafood Grill & Bar** (855 El Camino Real, #1, 650/323-1555, www

.scottsseafood.com, Mon. 7 A.M.–9 P.M., Tues.–Fri. 7 A.M.–9:30 P.M., Sat. 9 A.M.–9:30 P.M., Sun. 9 A.M.–9 P.M., $18–30). Scott's sits right across the street from Stanford Stadium in one of the last surviving "Town and Country Villages" in the Silicon Valley. This elegant white-tablecloth restaurant has a large window-lined dining room, and a bar on the other side. While you can wear casual clothes to Scott's, a dinner here is also a great excuse to dress up a bit. At breakfast and lunch, Scott's caters to the business set—many power lunches take place over salmon and sole here. The seafood at Scott's runs to a good variety of fish done up in fine preparations, often with exotic sauces. The wine list is worth perusing, with its fine California vintages and European wines.

Even the ultra-multicultural and sometimes snooty town of Palo Alto has its local favorite down-home diner. The **Palo Alto Creamery** (566 Emerson St., 650/323-3131, www.paloaltocreamery.com, Mon.–Fri. noon–9 P.M., Sat. 9 A.M.–midnight, Sun. 8 A.M.–10 P.M., $8–15) has all the old kitschy decor to make diners believe that they've really entered some sort of time warp and a genuine 1950s soda shop. Red vinyl, shiny chrome, a black-and-white checked floor, a long counter, and funky booths help complete the total picture. The food runs to burgers, sandwiches, and American classic entrées. But what you really come to the creamery for is the house-made ice cream. Whether you order an extra-thick shake with your burger or wait for a sundae for dessert, don't skip this all-important Creamery staple. Just be aware that the Creamery gets crowded, especially on weekends. Locals know it's open pretty late and can often fill the place to the brim for an after-show meal.

### Practicalities

Palo Alto is equidistant between the **Mineta San Jose International Airport** (1667–2077 Airport Blvd., 408/501-0979, www.sjc.org) and the **San Francisco International Airport** (800/435-9736, www.flysfo.com). **CalTrain** (www.caltrain.com, fares $3–11) can get you there as well. The commuter train runs from Gilroy to San Francisco, with a hub in San Jose. That same hub serves access to the **VTA Light Rail** (www.vta.org, fares $2–4), servicing San Jose up to Mountain View.

Palo Alto is easily accessed via U.S. 101 and I-280.

# Coastside

The region known to locals as Coastside encompasses the San Mateo Coast area from Pacifica down to Año Nuevo State Reserve and on towards Santa Cruz. Many Bay Area locals escape to Coastside for weekend vacations, enjoying the small-town atmosphere in Half Moon Bay and Pescadero along with the unspoiled beauty of the dozens of miles of undeveloped coastline. Peak seasons for major attractions on Coastside are October (pumpkin season) and winter (elephant seals return to Año Nuevo).

## HALF MOON BAY

To this day, the coastal city of Half Moon Bay retains its character as an ag town. The locals all know each other, and a spirit of community and cooperation pervades. Locally grown crops include pumpkins, strawberries, artichokes, and stinky-at-harvest-time brussels sprouts. Small family farms grow many other vegetables and fruits as well. Half Moon Bay enjoys a beautiful natural setting, and earns significant income from tourism, especially during the world-famous Pumpkin Festival each October.

### Beaches

The beaches of Half Moon Bay draw visitors from over the hill and farther afield all year long. As with most of the northern Pacific, summer can be a chilly, foggy time on the beaches here. For the best beach weather, plan your Half Moon Bay trip for September or October. **Half Moon Bay State Beach** (www.parks.ca.gov) actually encompasses three discrete beaches stretching four miles down the coast, each with its own access point and parking lot. **Francis Beach** (95 Kelly Ave.) has the most developed amenities, including a good-sized campground with grassy areas to pitch tents and enjoy picnics, a visitors center, and indoor hot showers. **Venice Beach** (Venice Blvd. off Hwy. 1) offers outdoor showers and flush toilets. **Dunes Beach** (Young Ave. off Hwy. 1) is the southernmost major beach in the chain, and the least developed. The whole beach complex has wireless Internet access, but use care bringing sensitive electronic devices onto a sandy, salty, windy beach!

Perhaps the most famous beach in the area is **Mavericks** (Pillar Point Marsh parking lot, past Pillar Point Harbor). Named for the unpredictable immense waves that pile up to crash into this beach, Mavericks holds a legendary place in the California surfing world. Each winter during storm season, the Mavericks Surf Contest (http://mavericks-surf.com) happens here. *Novice surfers beware!* Mavericks is not a beginner's break, especially in winter. The giant breakers can be deadly. If you aren't positive you're up to the challenge, don't paddle out.

Just north of Half Moon Bay, **Montara State Beach** (2nd St,. Montara, www.parks.ca.gov) appeals to tidepoolers and surf fishermen as much as to picnickers and beachcombers. Bring your dogs for a wonderful walk on this windy, sandy, life-filled beach.

## Entertainment and Events

The biggest annual event in this small agricultural town is the **Half Moon Bay Art & Pumpkin Festival** (www.miramarevents.com/pumpkinfest). Every October, nearly a quarter of a million people trek to Half Moon Bay to pay homage to the big orange squash. The festival includes live music, food, artists' booths, contests, kids' activities, an adults lounge area, and a parade. Perhaps the best-publicized event is the pumpkin weigh-off, which takes place before the festivities begin. Farmers bring their tremendous squash in on flatbed trucks from all over the country to determine which is the biggest of all. The winner gets paid per pound, a significant prize when the biggest pumpkins weigh over 1,000 pounds!

## Sports and Recreation

For a sedate ocean adventure, take a winter whale-watching cruise or a shallow-water fishing trip on board the ***Queen of Hearts*** (Pillar Point Harbor, 510/581-2628, www.fishingboat.com, adults $69, children $50, tackle rental $8–12, 1-day license $13, reservations highly recommended). Whale watching trips run January through April and cost a bit less than fishing trips on the *Queen of Hearts.* Deep-sea fishing makes for a more energetic day out on the Pacific, though Dramamine is often recommended.

You can fish for albacore tuna, rockfish, or salmon (if the season isn't cancelled) with **Huck Finn Sportfishing** (Pillar Point Harbor, 650/726-7133, www.huckfinnsportfishing.com, tackle $5–14, 1-day license $12). This major outfitter offers eight boats for a wide variety of trips. Call for trip rates.

One of the coolest ways to see the coast is from the deck of a sea kayak. It's good to be healthy and fit, but Many kayak tours with the **Half Moon Bay Kayaking Company** (2 Johnson Pier, 650/773-6101, www.hmbkayak.com) require no previous kayaking experience. For an easy first paddle, try the Pillar Point tour, the full-moon tour, or the sunset paddle. If you're looking for a wilder ride, sign up for a kayak surfing class—you'll learn how to catch waves safely in specially designed kayaks. Or if you're serious about learning to sea kayak, HMB Kayak also offers beginner through advanced classes in closed-deck kayaks.

Some visitors see the wide cool beaches of Half Moon Bay and dream of watching the sun go down over the ocean from the back of a horse. **Sea Horse and Friendly Acres Ranches** (1828 N. Hwy. 1, 650/726-9903, www.horserentals.com/seahorse.html, daily from 8 A.M., $40/hour) offers one-hour,

90-minute, and two-hour guided tours that take you along the cliffs and down onto the sands at Half Moon Bay's state beaches. Children over the age of five are welcome, as are riders of all ability levels. The horses here are sedate rental nags who know the routes in their sleep, allowing their riders to sit back and enjoy the stunning views and the company of their fellow riders. Don't expect much from the guides; they generally speak little English and simply ride along to be sure you stay safely on the horse trails.

After a long day paddling a sea kayak or reeling up rock cod, a nice massage or facial might sound just perfect. The **Primrose Day Spa** (630 Purissima St., 650/726-1244, http://primrosespa.com, daily by appointment) nods to its locale by offering pumpkin enzyme facials and body wrap treatments. You can choose any style of massage, classic facials and spa treatments, or an aesthetic treatment at Primrose.

## Accommodations

Half Moon Bay offers several lovely bed-and-breakfasts and one luxury resort hotel. That resort is the **Ritz-Carlton Half Moon Bay** (1 Miramontes Point Rd., 650/712-7000, www.ritzcarlton.com, $550). Looming large over the Pacific, the hotel resembles a cliff-side medieval castle. Inside, guests enjoy the finest of modern amenities. The Ritz-Carlton has a top-tier restaurant (Navio), a world-class day spa, and posh guest rooms that really are worth the price. If you can, get a room facing the ocean. While you're there, enjoy free access to the spa's bathing rooms, an outdoor hot tub overlooking the ocean, tennis courts, and basketball court. The golfing at the Ritz is second to none in the Bay Area. And of course, the service will make you feel like royalty.

For a more personal lodging experience, try one of the local inns. The **Old Thyme Inn** (779 Main St., 650/726-1616, www.oldthymeinn.com, $195–375) is located right downtown, next door to the Cetrella Bistro. Playing on the inn's name, each uniquely decorated room has its own garden theme. Rooms are comfortable, with luxurious amenities. Downstairs, guests can enjoy the common sitting rooms and the gorgeous garden (yes, they do grow thyme). Each morning the owners serve up a sumptuous breakfast using fresh ingredients.

In the neighboring community of Montara, the **Goose and Turrets** (835 George St., Montara, 650/728-5451, http://goose.montara.com, $160–210) is a locals' getaway favorite. The rambling old building that houses the inn has had an exciting life—ask the friendly and knowledgeable owners about its story. Decor here runs to the eclectic, and folks who find the usual flowery B&Bs a bit cloying will love the Goose and Turrets. The Clipper Room is perfect for aviation buffs, and guests who like their space will love the sweeping expanse of hardwood floor in the Hummingbird Room. The food and accommodations here keep an eye towards ecologically friendly choices, and the owners are active in local park and community environmental organizations.

## Food

The quality of food in Half Moon Bay is superb. Chefs are drawn to the array of produce fresh from the local fields, and to the idyllic Coastside setting. **Cetrella** (845 Main St., 650/726-4090, www.cetrella.com, Sun. and Tues.–Thurs. 5:30–9:30 P.M., Fri.–Sat. 5:30–10 P.M., $18–35) bills itself as a Mediterranean bistro. In truth, the menu includes a range of Mediterranean-themed California cuisine, and the big-beam construction looks like something out of the redwood forests up north. The chef uses local, often organic ingredients to create stunning fare that varies by season. Look for Dungeness crab in wintertime and artichokes in the spring.

**Pasta Moon** (315 Main St., 650/726-5125, www.pastamoon.com, lunch Mon.–Fri. 11:30 A.M.–2:30 P.M., Sat.–Sun. noon–3 P.M., dinner Sun.–Thurs. 5:30–9:30 P.M., Fri.–Sat. 5:30–10 P.M., $14–34) manages to be both casual and upscale all at once. The restaurant serves updated Italian cuisine with an emphasis on fresh, light dishes. The rustic dining room, with a view of the woods and creek, completes the experience.

## THE BLUE LADY

With all its history, it's easy to get lost in the ghost stories that haunt the San Francisco. Yet two of the most famous Bay Area hauntings aren't anywhere close to Chinatown or Nob Hill. Instead, strange stories and creepy occurrences perch nearer to the perilous cliffs of the Pacific Coast, and lurk in the Santa Cruz Mountain forests.

Just north of Half Moon Bay, the **Moss Beach Distillery** (see *Food* in the *Half Moon Bay* section) has been featured on *Unsolved Mysteries* and written up in countless publications. Not for its food, but for its famous ghost: the Blue Lady. Rumor has it that a beautiful young woman walked the cliffs of Moss Beach from her home to the coastside speakeasy (now the Distillery) to meet her lover, a handsome piano player who worked in the bar. The Lady, whose name has never been discovered, perished one night on the cliffs under suspicious circumstances. Some say that her lover had left her, and she threw herself down onto the rocks out of grief; others claim that her seafaring husband came home, discovered his wife's infidelity, and shoved her to eternity. However it happened, in the middle of the 20th century, odd things started occurring at the Distillery. A storage room with only one door and a barred-over window became stuck from the inside. Eventually, several men bashed it open, only to discover several heavy cases of spirits that had been shoved up against the door to keep it closed. But by whom? No one was in the room, and no one could have gotten out. Many years and a major reconstruction later (the building sits on a slowly eroding cliff that will eventually lie beneath the ocean), an accountant was working late one night in the restaurant's offices. She was startled to hear her printer turn itself on...startled because she was in another office using a different computer and was alone in the building. Upon examination, the printer yielded a single piece of paper with a tiny heart printed on it. The accountant believes this means the ghost likes her.

Today, the Distillery is a favorite with ghost-hunting groups, who often come to spend the night in an old building that gets decidedly creepy after the lights go out. Restaurant patrons rarely have ghostly experiences, unless you count those created by the owner for the entertainment of his customers.

As many people come to the **Moss Beach Distillery** (140 Beach Way, Moss Beach, 650/728-5595, www.mossbeachdistillery.com, brunch 11 A.M.–2 P.M., dinner daily $15–30) for the ghost stories (see *The Blue Lady* sidebar) as for the hearty food and terrific ocean views. The Distillery operated as a speakeasy in the 1930s, with the basement rooms in the cliffside building storing cases of illegal alcohol.

The restaurant offers something of a cross between traditional American food and California cuisine. Portions tend to be large, and service is friendly if occasionally slow during peak crowd times. Folks who want to soak up the old-school speakeasy atmosphere like to sit in the bar, while visitors who want to stare out over the ocean prefer the terrace.

When all you need is a quick bite or a casual lunch, the **Moonside Bakery & Cafe** (604 Main St., 650/726-9070, www.moonsidebakery.com, daily 7 A.M.–5 P.M.) can fix you up. Stop in the morning for breakfast pastries and espresso. In the afternoon and evening, expect sandwiches and hand-fired pizzas.

### Practicalities

The best way to get to Half Moon Bay is to drive. Half Moon Bay sits on Highway 1 about 45 minutes south of San Francisco. Drivers can take the Great Highway down to Highway 35 (aka Skyline Blvd.) in Pacifica and catch Highway 1 from there.

An alternate route is to take I-280 from either the north or the south, then turn onto CA-92 west. This two-lane state highway goes over the Santa Cruz Mountains that separate the Valley from the coast. Because it's the major truck route over the hill, it can get jammed up even on weekdays, but it's worst on sunny summer weekends when everyone on the Peninsula wants to hit the beach.

Parking in downtown Half Moon Bay is usually a fairly easy proposition. Except, of course, if you're in town for the Pumpkin Festival, when parking is a nightmare of epic proportions; your best bet is to already be staying in town with your car safely stowed in a hotel parking lot before the festival.

The two local Coastside publications are the ***Half Moon Bay Review*** (www.hmbreview.com) and ***CoastViews Magazine*** (www.coastviewsmag.com). The *Review,* published weekly, provides the best information about live local entertainment. *CoastViews* comes out monthly and is free around the Coastside region. It's got more in-depth coverage of the region's attractions, restaurants, and farms.

The nearest major trauma centers are in San Francisco, Santa Cruz, and on the Peninsula, and helicopter transport may be involved. For less-serious health services, you can visit the **Coastside Family Medical Clinic** (225 S. Hwy. 1, Half Moon Bay, 650/712-7330, www.coastsidedocs.org, Mon.–Fri. 8 A.M.–5 P.M.).

Cell phones work fine in the town of Half Moon Bay, but coverage can be spotty up in the hills above town and out on the undeveloped coastline and beaches along Highway 1. For Internet access, head downtown to the local cafés or ask at your inn or hotel, since most offer some form of Wi-Fi or wired access.

## PESCADERO

One of the last true small towns in the Bay Area, Pescadero is a tiny dot on the coastline, south of Half Moon Bay and well north of Santa Cruz. With one main street, one side street, and several smallish farms, in Pescadero pretty much everyone knows everyone else, and there's a strong sense of community. Despite its tiny size, many Bay Area denizens find reasons to visit Pescadero, including twisty roads that challenge motorcyclists and bicyclists, fresh produce, and, of course, the legendary Duarte's Tavern.

### Año Nuevo State Reserve

The best sights in Pescadero are outside. Año Nuevo State Reserve (Hwy. 1 south of Pescadero, look for signs, 650/879-2025, www.parks.ca.gov, daily 8 A.M.–sunset, $8/car) is world-famous as the winter home and breeding ground of the once-endangered elephant seals. The reserve also shelters Pomponio Native American remains and extensive dune and marshland. The beaches and wilderness are open all year. The elephant seals start showing up in late November and stay to breed, birth pups, and loll on the beach until early March. Visitors are not allowed down to the elephant seal habitats on their own and must sign up for a guided walking tour. Once you see two giant males crashing into one another in a fight for dominance, you won't want to get too close! Book your tour at least a day or two in advance since the seals are popular with both locals and travelers.

### Pescadero Marsh Natural Preserve

Bird-lovers flock to Pescadero Marsh Natural Preserve (www.parks.ca.gov), located on Highway 1 right across the freeway from Pescadero State Beach. This protected wetland is home to a variety of avian species, including blue herons, great and snowy egrets, and northern harriers. For the best birding, visit the marsh in late fall or early springtime, when migration is in full swing.

### Pigeon Point Lighthouse

South of Pescadero proper sits Pigeon Point Lighthouse (210 Pigeon Point Rd. at Hwy. 1, 650/879-2120, www.parks.ca.gov, daily 8 A.M.–sunset). First lit in 1872, Pigeon Point is one of the most photographed lighthouses in the United States. Sadly, visitors find the lighthouse itself in a state of some disrepair, and recent earthquakes have made climbing to the top unsafe. Yet the monument stands, its hostel still shelters travelers, and visitors still marvel at the incomparable views from the point. Winter guests can see migrating whales from the rocks beyond the tower.

ROBERT HOLMES / CALTOUR

Pigeon Point Lighthouse

## Beaches

**Pescadero State Beach** (Hwy. 1 just north of Pescadero Rd., 650/879-2170, www.parks.ca.gov, daily 8 A.M.–sunset, $8 parking, no fires) is the closest beach to the town of Pescadero. Though it's a great spot to walk in the sand and stare out into the Pacific, near-constant winds make it less than ideal for picnics or sunbathing. It does have some facilities, including public bathrooms.

North of Pescadero, at the intersection of Highway 84 and Highway 1, **San Gregorio State Beach** (650/879-2170, www.parks.ca.gov, daily 8 A.M.–sunset, $8/car) stretches farther than it seems. Once you're walking toward the ocean, the small-seeming cove stretches out beyond the cliffs that bound it to create a long stretch of beach perfect for contemplative strolling. San Gregorio is a local favorite in the summer, despite the regular appearance of thick, chilly fog over the sand. Brave beachgoers can even swim and bodysurf here, though doing so without a wetsuit gets swimmers cold fast. Picnic tables and bathrooms cluster near the parking lot, though picnicking can be hampered by wind.

## Accommodations

Pescadero has a small but surprisingly good array of lodging options. If budget is a factor, try the **Pigeon Point Hostel** (210 Pigeon Point Rd. at Hwy. 1, 650/879-0633, http://norcal-hostels.org/pigeon, dorm bed $20–24, private room $55–100). This HI hostel has simple but comfortable accommodations, both private and dorm-style. And the locale can't be beat! Amenities include three kitchens, free Wi-Fi, and beach access. But the best amenity of all is the cliff-top hot tub, which makes the hostel more than special.

Another option in the **Costanoa Lodge and Campground** (2001 Rossi Rd. at Hwy. 1, 650/879-1100, www.costanoa.com, camping $55/night, lodge and cabin rooms $143–400). At this eco-lodge you can do anything from pitch a tent in the campground to rent a whirlpool suite in the lodge. Other lodging options include log-style cabins with shared baths, small tent cabins with shared baths, and private rooms. Costanoa's many nature programs seek to educate visitors about the ecology of the San Mateo coast and the preservation efforts underway. A small general store offers s'mores makings and souvenirs. You'll pay for the privilege of staying at Costanoa, but the location is beautiful and the eco-chic atmosphere is all the rage these days.

For a little more luxury, the **Pescadero Creek Inn Bed & Breakfast** (393 Stage Rd., 888/307-1898, www.pescaderocreekinn.com, $209–264) sits conveniently in downtown Pescadero, an easy walk from Duarte's, the grocery stores, the local cemetery, and the creek. While the house isn't completely soundproof, the rooms are high ceilinged and prettily appointed. The owners serve up a delectable breakfast each morning, plus wine and cheese in the afternoon. If you ask nicely, you might get a bottle of the house vintage, handmade by the owner.

If you want something unique, Pescadero has lodgings available year-round. The **Pescadero Creekside Barn** (248 Stage Rd., 650/879-0868, www.pescaderolodging.com, call for rates) nestles in the loft of an old barn downtown. This studio-apartment style space sleeps two, has a TV with DVD player, a kitchen, and a clawfoot tub. The seclusion and charm make the space perfect for a romantic getaway or solitary weekend retreat.

## Food

The one true restaurant in Pescadero is **Duarte's Tavern** (202 Stage Rd., 650/879-0464, www.duartestavern.com, daily 7 A.M.–9 P.M., $10–20). The rambling building features sloping floors and age-darkened wooden walls. The food is excellent, the service friendly, and the coffee plentiful. Almost everybody in the Bay Area comes to Duarte's eventually—whether it's for a bowl of artichoke soup, some great local fish, a slice of olallieberry pie, or just a drink at the dimly lit, often-crowded bar.

To enjoy the best of Coastside food, hit a local farm or two and put together your own picnic lunch (or dinner). **Harley Farms** (205 North St., 650/879-0480, www.harleyfarms.com, call for tour information) boasts of being the last working dairy on the San Mateo coast. Their goat cheese is locally famous, sold at high-end grocery stores and offered in restaurants around the Bay Area. Look for the small wheels with colorful edible flower petals pressed into pretty patterns—a Harley Farms trademark. You can even assist in the cheese-making process, taking a tour that teaches you how to milk a goat, then create fresh artisan cheese.

For scrumptious homemade bread and pastries, stop in at **Arcangeli Grocery** (287 Stage Rd., 650/879-0147, www.normsmarket.com/store) across the street from Duarte's. All breads are homemade and delicious, and the pastries (especially the raspberry twists) are to die for. The store also carries many grocery staples and plenty of cold drinks and California wines.

## Practicalities

Pescadero Road lies 17 miles south of Half Moon Bay on Highway 1 at Pescadero State Beach. Watch for signs, and turn east, away from the ocean onto Pescadero Road. Town lies a few miles east of the ocean in a tiny valley. When you come to the stop sign (it's the only one in town), you've hit the town center. Turn left onto Stage Road to find most of the rest of Pescadero.

Parking is free and generally easy to find on Stage Road or in the Duarte's parking lot. On weekends, you might need to park down the road a ways and walk a block or two.

Pescadero maintains two local-style markets and a gas station with a mini-mart. That's pretty much it for services.

Cell phone coverage is spotty in Pescadero, and Internet service somewhat rare. Don't expect to be completely connected while you're visiting this tiny rural town.

# WINE COUNTRY

Entering California's Wine Country is an unmistakable experience. From the crest of the last hill, sunlight paints golden streaks on endless rows of grapevines that stretch out in every direction for as far as the eye can see. Trellises run along both sides of every road, tempting visitors to question the unplucked weeds beneath the vines, the rose bushes capping each row, and the strange still fans standing guard high above. A heady aroma of earth and grapes permeates the area. Welcome to the Napa and Sonoma Valleys.

The area's beautiful grapevines are renown worldwide for producing top-quality vintages and economical varietal table wines. But foodies also know the area as a center for stellar cuisine. Yountville, a tiny upscale town in the middle of the Napa Valley, is the favorite haven of celebrity chef Thomas Keller. The food served at his French Laundry restaurant is legendary (as is its price). Keller's influence helped to usher in a culinary renaissance, and today the lush flavors of local, sustainable produce are available throughout the region.

The Sonoma Valley has long played second fiddle to Napa in terms of viticultural prestige, but the wines coming out of the area are second to none. The Russian River Valley wineries are often friendlier and less crowded than their Napa counterparts, while the wineries in the southern Carneros region are few and far between. Each offers visitors a more personal experience than Napa and the chance to sample unique and amazing varietals. Sonoma County's craggy coastline and natural beauty provide great recreation opportunities for visitors more fond of the outdoors than grapes.

© LANCE SCOTT

## HIGHLIGHTS

**Domaine Chandon:** This Yountville winery offers a gorgeous setting whereby to sample their premier champagne. Their wine and champagne-making tour is one of the best in Napa (page 152).

**Grgich Hills:** Home of the California Chardonnay that won the Paris Tasting of 1976, Grgich Hills uses a biodynamic farming process to produce exquisite wines (page 153).

**Culinary Institute of America:** The ancient grey stonework and quietly forested surroundings of the CIA belie the bevy of culinary activity inside. Stop by for cooking classes and demonstrations, to peruse the museum, or to indulge in a meal at the exemplary restaurant or café (page 160).

**A. Rafanelli:** The best Sonoma reds are produced at this small, unpretentious, and appointment-only winery. Be sure to pick up one of their stunning Cabs (page 178).

**Mission San Francisco Solano de Sonoma:** Sonoma is home to the last California Mission and the centerpiece of Sonoma State Historic Park (page 192).

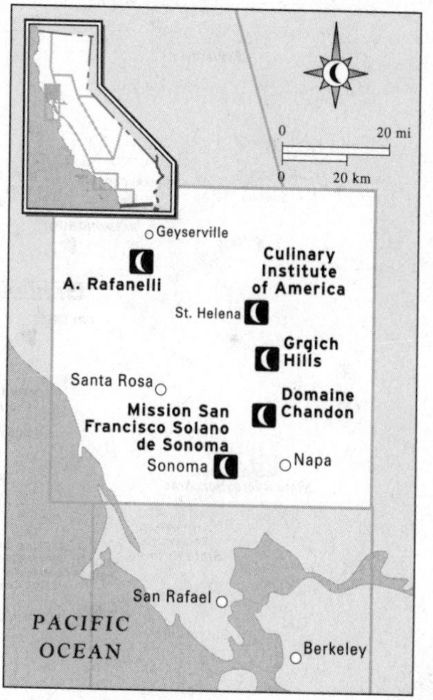


LOOK FOR [icon] TO FIND RECOMMENDED SIGHTS, ACTIVITIES, DINING, AND LODGING.



## PLANNING YOUR TIME

If you're coming to Wine Country for the first time, you'll probably spend most of your visit paying homage to the grape. After all, Napa and Sonoma form the beating heart of California's great Wine Country. Literally hundreds of wineries cluster within the relatively small valleys of Napa and the Russian River, while other wineries call the regions of Carneros and outer Sonoma home. Most visitors plan a weekend in Napa, with weekend trips back to explore the outer valleys. If you come during the summer or fall seasons, you'll find a crush in almost every tasting room in the valley; even the smaller boutique labels do big business during the six-month high season (May–Oct.).

To make the most of your trip, do a little advance research. Plan out which wineries are must-sees, and which routes you'll take. Be aware that Highway 29 (which runs through the heart of Napa Valley) gets jammed up around St. Helena and can be very slow on weekends. U.S. 101 slows through Santa Rosa during the weekday rush hour commutes. Check to see whether any events are going on during your stay as they can increase crowds both at the wineries and on the roads. If you're

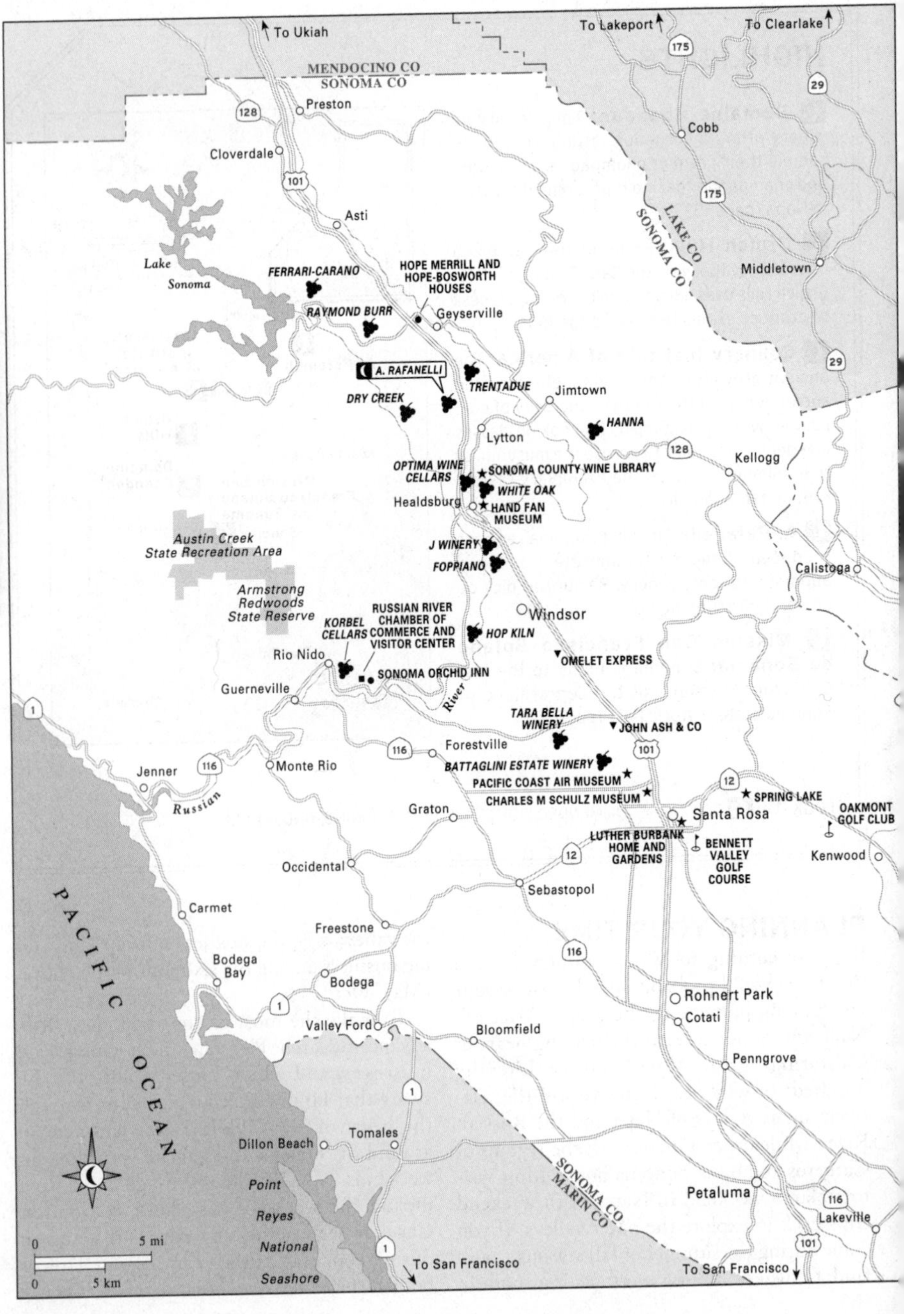
To Ukiah
To Lakeport
To Clearlake
MENDOCINO CO
SONOMA CO
Preston
Cloverdale
Cobb
LAKE CO
SONOMA CO
Asti
Middletown
Lake Sonoma
FERRARI-CARANO
HOPE MERRILL AND HOPE-BOSWORTH HOUSES
RAYMOND BURR
Geyserville
A. RAFANELLI
TRENTADUE
Jimtown
DRY CREEK
HANNA
Lytton
Kellogg
OPTIMA WINE CELLARS
SONOMA COUNTY WINE LIBRARY
WHITE OAK
Healdsburg
HAND FAN MUSEUM
Austin Creek State Recreation Area
J WINERY
FOPPIANO
Calistoga
Armstrong Redwoods State Reserve
Windsor
RUSSIAN RIVER CHAMBER OF COMMERCE AND VISITOR CENTER
KORBEL CELLARS
HOP KILN
OMELET EXPRESS
Rio Nido
SONOMA ORCHID INN
Guerneville
River
TARA BELLA WINERY
JOHN ASH & CO
Forestville
Jenner
Monte Rio
BATTAGLINI ESTATE WINERY
PACIFIC COAST AIR MUSEUM
SPRING LAKE
OAKMONT GOLF CLUB
Russian
CHARLES M SCHULZ MUSEUM
Graton
Santa Rosa
LUTHER BURBANK HOME AND GARDENS
BENNETT VALLEY GOLF COURSE
Kenwood
Occidental
Sebastopol
PACIFIC OCEAN
Carmet
Freestone
Bodega Bay
Bodega
Rohnert Park
Cotati
Valley Ford
Bloomfield
Penngrove
Dillon Beach
Tomales
SONOMA CO
MARIN CO
Petaluma
Point Reyes National Seashore
Lakeville
0
5 mi
0
5 km
To San Francisco
To San Francisco

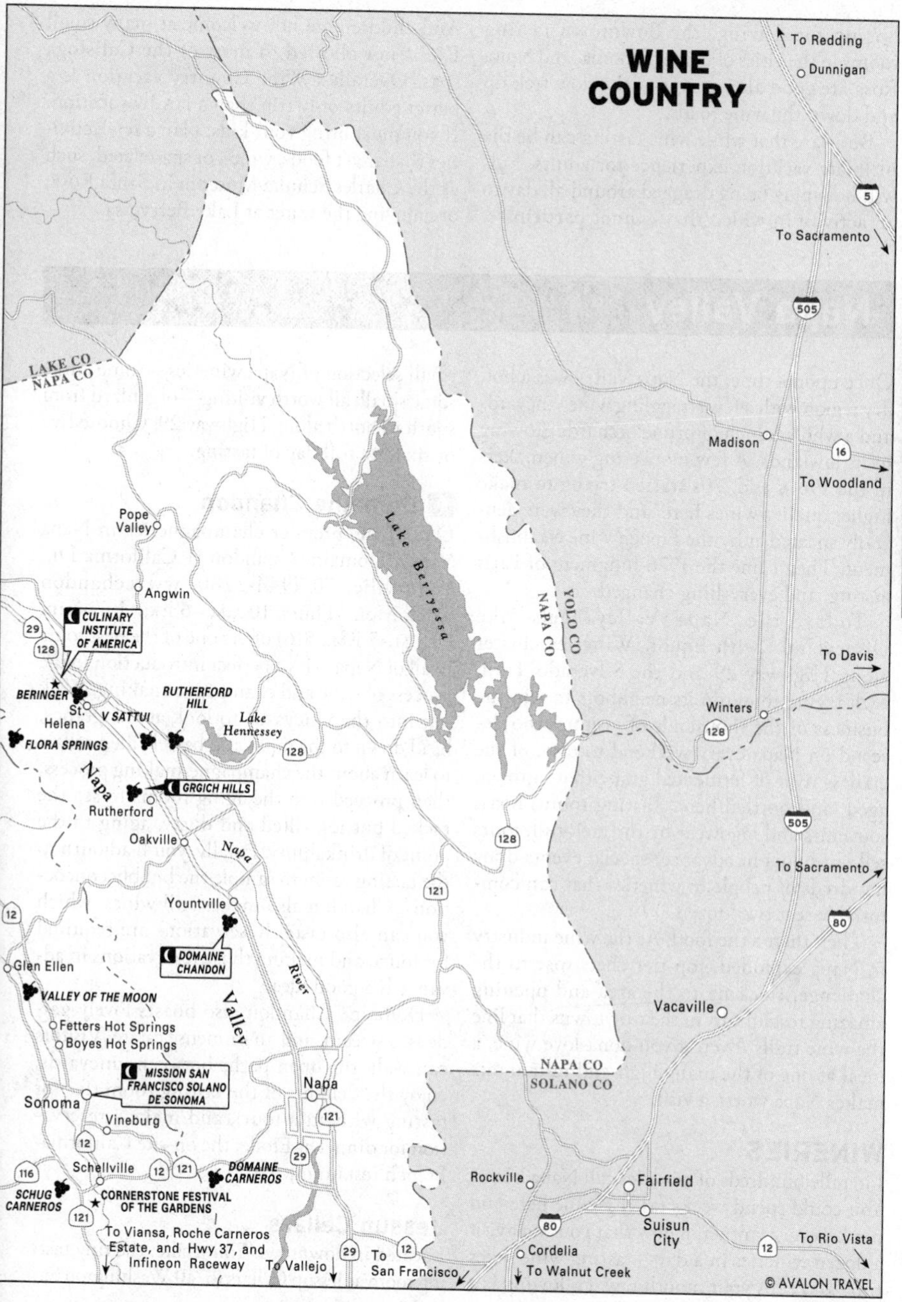
WINE COUNTRY
To Redding
Dunnigan
5
To Sacramento
505
LAKE CO
NAPA CO
Madison
16
To Woodland
Pope Valley
Lake Berryessa
Angwin
YOLO CO
NAPA CO
29
128
CULINARY INSTITUTE OF AMERICA
To Davis
BERINGER
St. Helena
RUTHERFORD HILL
V SATTUI
Lake Hennessey
Winters
FLORA SPRINGS
128
128
Napa
GRGICH HILLS
Rutherford
505
Oakville
Napa
128
To Sacramento
Yountville
121
12
80
DOMAINE CHANDON
Glen Ellen
River
VALLEY OF THE MOON
Valley
Vacaville
Fetters Hot Springs
Boyes Hot Springs
MISSION SAN FRANCISCO SOLANO DE SONOMA
NAPA CO
SOLANO CO
Napa
Sonoma
121
Vineburg
12
29
116
Schellville
12
121
DOMAINE CARNEROS
Rockville
Fairfield
SCHUG CARNEROS
CORNERSTONE FESTIVAL OF THE GARDENS
121
80
Suisun City
To Viansa, Roche Carneros Estate, and Hwy 37, and Infineon Raceway
29
12
To Rio Vista
To Vallejo
To San Francisco
Cordelia
To Walnut Creek
12
© AVALON TRAVEL

not up for driving, the downtown tasting rooms in the cities of Napa, Sonoma, and Santa Rosa are good alternatives to the slow trek up and down the wine roads.

Be aware that while wine tasting can be the ultimate vacation experience for adults, kids will not enjoy being dragged around all day to an activity in which they cannot participate. And children are not welcome at many small B&Bs nor allowed in most of the Calistoga spas. Overall, a Wine Country vacation is a better adults-only trip than a family vacation. If you must bring your kids, plan a few activities that aren't food-, wine-, or spa-related, such as the Charles Schultz Museum in Santa Rosa, or enjoying the water at Lake Berryessa.



# Napa Valley

Once upon a time, the Napa Valley was a hot, dry region with a few straggling wine vineyards and a whole bunch of prune orchards growing in its lowlands. A few pioneering winemakers in the 1960s and '70s started trying to make higher quality wines here, and they were generally sneered at by the French wine establishment. Then came the 1976 Judgment of Paris tasting, and everything changed.

Today, the Napa Valley feels like Disneyland...with liquor. Wineries cluster along Highway 29 and the Silverado Trail, each trying to outdo its neighbors to win the business of the thousands of visitors who descend on Napa every weekend to taste of the endless river of fermented grape that's grown, aged, and bottled here. Tasting rooms boast souvenirs and logowear by the rack-full, tours sell out hours in advance, special events draw hundreds of people to wineries that can comfortable seat two-dozen.

Then there's the food. As the wine industry in Napa exploded, top-tier chefs rose to the challenge, flocking to the area and opening amazing restaurants in the tiny towns that line the wine trails. Even if you don't love wine, a meal at one of the many high-end restaurants makes Napa worth a visit.

## WINERIES

Literally hundreds of wineries call Napa home. You could spend weeks tasting wine here and not hit every vintner. Know that you can't visit a dozen wineries in a day—tasting wine takes time and rubs your mouth raw. Following is a small selection of Napa wineries—some large, some small, all worth visiting—organized from south to north along Highway 29. Choose five or six for a full day of tasting.

### ☾ Domaine Chandon

One of the premier champagneries in Napa Valley, Domaine Chandon (1 California Dr., Yountville, 707/944-2280, www.chandon.com, Mon.–Thurs. 10 A.M.–6 P.M., Fri.–Sun. 10 A.M.–7 P.M., $16) offers one of the best tours in all of Napa—it's a perfect introduction to the process of wine and champagne-making. Walk out into the vineyards to look at the grapes, head down to the tank- and barrel-filled cellars to learn about the champagne-making process, then proceed into the aging rooms to see the racked bottles, tilted and dusty, aging to the point of drinkability. Finally, you'll adjourn to the tasting room to sample the bubbly concoctions. Chandon also makes still wines, which you can also taste. Reservations are required for tours, and making those reservations in advance is a good idea.

Domaine Chandon also boasts lovely gardens, a stream, and an immense estate. Visitors can walk the open paths between vineyards, enjoy the delights of the tasting room (fee for tasting without a tour), and make a reservation for dinner at Étoile, the on-site California-French restaurant.

### Jessup Cellars

Located in downtown Yountville, the tiny tasting room at Jessup Cellars (6740 Washington St.,

Wine Country is filled with scenic drives.

Yountville, 707/944-8523, www.jessupcellars.com, daily 10 A.M.–6 P.M.) offers tastes of incredible boutique red wines you'll have a hard time finding anyplace else. You'll get no tours here, no picnic grounds or fancy gardens. But you'll find lush, rich Zinfandels and deep, smoky Cabernets that are more than worth the sometimes-steep price tag. The tasting room boasts a cute little bar, a few shelves with items for purchase, and staff that love their jobs. If you chat them up, you may find yourself tasting rare Jessup vintages that are not on the usual list.

### Grgich Hills

The tasting room at Grgich Hills Winery (1829 St. Helena Hwy., Rutherford, 800/532-3057, www.grgich.com, daily 9:30 A.M.–4:30 P.M., $10) isn't housed in the most elaborate building. The gardens aren't showy, and the working vineyards run right up to the back of the winemaking facility. Active aging barrels crowd the main building and narrow the path to the tasting room's restrooms. If you're looking for a showy Napa Valley "experience," this might not be the best place for you.

What you *will* find at Grgich are some of the best wines in the valley, an entirely biodynamic winemaking operation, and the rich history of fine wine from California taking its rightful place alongside and even ahead of the great French vintages. Mike Grgich took his California Chardonnay to the Paris Tasting of 1976 and entered it in the White Burgundy blind-tasting competition. It won. The French winemakers were incensed at the result and demanded that the contest be re-run. Grgich's Chardonnay won again. (That same year, Robert Mondavi's Cabernet Sauvignon also took top honors in its category at the same contest.) The quality of California wines could no longer be ignored by even the snottiest of French wine connoisseurs.

Today, you'll learn about this history when visiting Grgich Hills. You'll also see plenty of information about biodynamic farming, a process that takes organic to the next level, using all-natural processes and including phenomenon such as the phases of the moon in the growing and harvesting cycles of the vineyards. All Grgich wines are biodynamically grown and made. Their best wine might be the descendants of Mike's legendary Chardonnay—arguable the best Chardonnay made in Napa or anywhere else in California. But don't ignore the reds; Grgich offers some lovely Zinfandels and Cabernets. And the Violetta, a dessert wine named for Mike's daughter, is a special treat that's only made in years when the grape conditions are perfect. None of the Grgich wines are cheap, and there's a fee for tasting, but it's more than worth it when you sip these rare, exquisite elixirs.

### Opus One

Yup, that huge thing on the rise that looks like a missile silo really is a winery. Opus One (7900 Hwy. 29, Oakville, 707/948-2426, www.opusonewinery.com, daily 10 A.M.–4 P.M.) boasts a reputation as one of the most prestigious, and definitely one of the most expensive vintners in Napa. The echoing halls inside the facility add to the grandeur of the place, as does the price of a tasting ($25 for a three-ounce pour of a

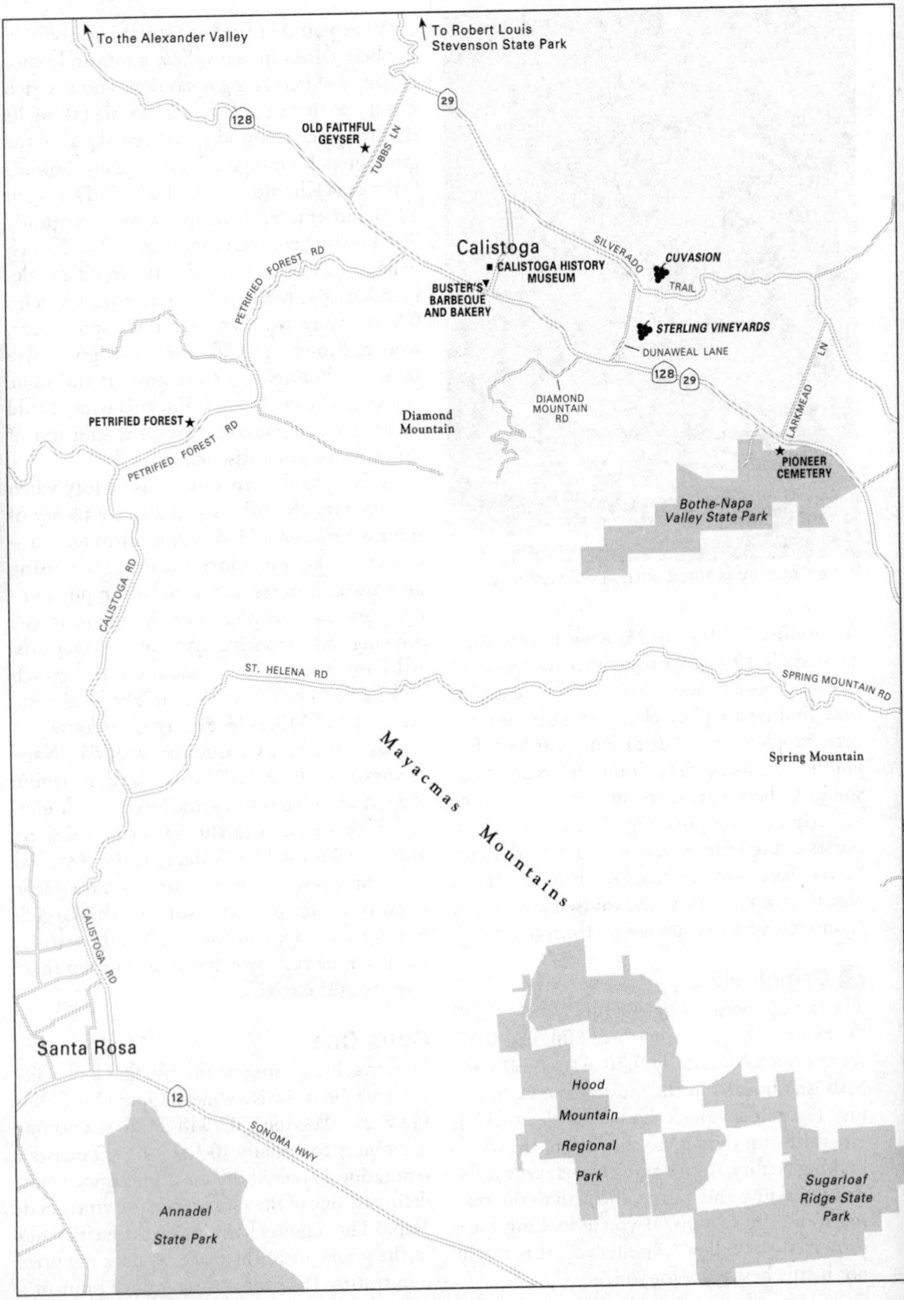

To the Alexander Valley
To Robert Louis Stevenson State Park
128
29
OLD FAITHFUL GEYSER
TUBBS LN
Calistoga
CALISTOGA HISTORY MUSEUM
BUSTER'S BARBEQUE AND BAKERY
SILVERADO TRAIL
CUVASION
STERLING VINEYARDS
DUNAWEAL LANE
PETRIFIED FOREST RD
DIAMOND MOUNTAIN RD
LARKMEAD LN
PETRIFIED FOREST
Diamond Mountain
PIONEER CEMETERY
Bothe-Napa Valley State Park
CALISTOGA RD
ST. HELENA RD
SPRING MOUNTAIN RD
Mayacmas Mountains
Spring Mountain
Santa Rosa
12
SONOMA HWY
Hood Mountain Regional Park
Sugarloaf Ridge State Park
Annadel State Park

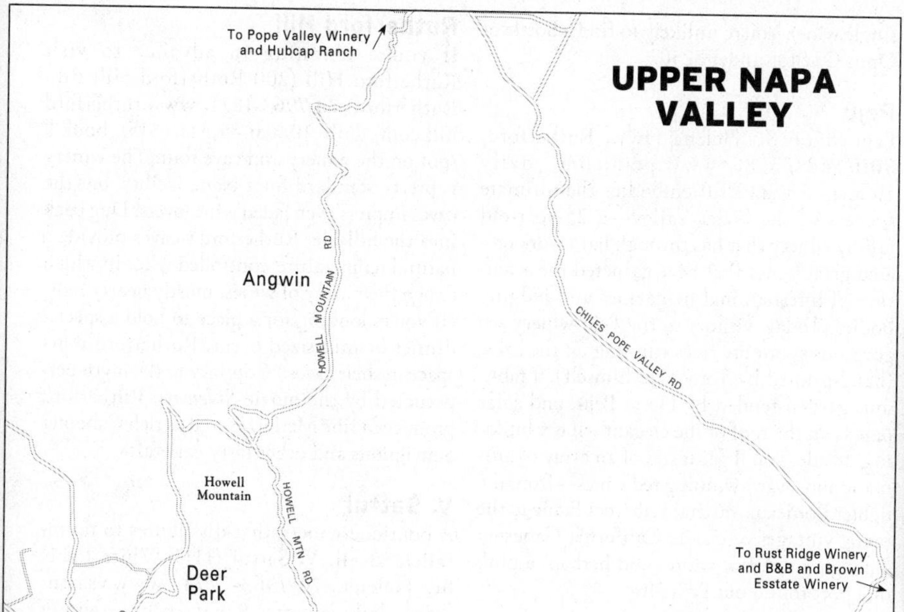
UPPER NAPA VALLEY
To Pope Valley Winery and Hubcap Ranch
Angwin
HOWELL MOUNTAIN RD
CHILES POPE VALLEY RD
Howell Mountain
HOWELL MTN RD
Deer Park
To Rust Ridge Winery and B&B and Brown Esstate Winery
LODI LN
DEER PARK RD
BERINGER VINEYARD
CULINARY INSTITUTE OF AMERICA
MAIN ST
St. Helena
SILVERADO TRAIL
RUTHERFORD HILL
To Kuleto Estate Winery
FLORA SPRINGS
V SATTUI
ZINFANDEL LN
Lake
Hennessey
SAGE CANYON RD
128
CONN CREEK RD
GRGICH HILLS
BEAULIEU VINEYARD
RUTHERFORD RD
Rutherford
RUBICON
29
PEJU
ST. HELENA HWY
OAKVILLE CROSS RD
OPUS ONE
0
2 mi
0
2 km
Oakville
© AVALON TRAVEL

single wine). You're unlikely to find a bottle of Opus One for under $250.

### Peju

Peju (8466 St. Helena Hwy., Rutherford, 800/446-7358, www.peju.com, daily 10 A.M.–6 P.M., $10) embodies the ultimate success of the Napa Valley—a 25-year-old family winery that has through hard work created great wines that have garnered the attention of international magazines and judging bodies. Today, visitors to the Peju winery see gorgeous sycamore trees running up the drive (hand-pruned by Tony Peju himself), a fabulous garden tended by Herta Peju, and solar panels on the roof of the elegant winery building. Inside, you'll get tastes of an array of aromatic and award-winning red wines—from the lighter Bordeaux-varietal Cabernet Franc to the many vintages of classic California Cabernet Sauvignons. A few whites and perhaps a pink or a port round out Peju's list.



### Rubicon

As many movie buffs as wine lovers come to the grand tasting room and museum at Rubicon (1991 St. Helena Hwy., Rutherford, 707/968-1100, www.rubiconestate.com, daily 10 A.M.–5 P.M.), formerly Niebaum-Coppola. This estate winery, a pet project of Francis Ford Coppola himself, also houses a small but delightful museum showcasing famed Coppola movies. You'll see memorabilia from the *Godfather* series and other films, period costumes, some of Coppola's awards, and a few documents that film buffs find fascinating. Over in the large, elegant tasting room, you'll find a generous bar area with plenty of staff to help you navigate the Rubicon wine list. Despite the famous name, this isn't just another star-owned vanity winery; the winemakers take their job seriously and the results can be spectacular. Rubicon offers a wide range of varietals, including a few whites. But the specialty of the house is the selection of big, heavy, serious reds that run like blood from the bottle into your glass. Appropriate, don't you think?

### Rutherford Hill

If you're planning in advance to visit Rutherford Hill (200 Rutherford Hill Rd., Rutherford, 707/963-1871, www.rutherfordhill.com, daily 10 A.M.–5 P.M., $15), book a spot on the winery and cave tour. The winery is pretty standard for a Napa facility, but the caves impress even jaded wine lovers. Dug back into the hillside, Rutherford's caves provide a natural temperature-controlled space in which to age their array of wines, mostly hearty reds. (If you're looking for a place to hold a special dinner or mid-sized event, Rutherford rents space in their caves.) Contrary to the myth perpetuated by the movie *Sideways,* Rutherford produces a fine Merlot, as well as rich Cabernet Sauvignons and other tasty varietals.

### V. Sattui

A boutique winery that distributes to no retailers at all, V. Sattui (1111 White Lane, St. Helena, 707/963-7774, www.vsattui.com, daily summer 9 A.M.–6 P.M., winter 9 A.M.–5 P.M., $5–15) won the "Best Winery" award at the California State Fair in both 2006 and 2007—a mighty feat in a state filled with excellent vintners. Sattui produces a wide selection of varietals—everything from light-bodied whites to full-flavored Cabernet Sauvignons. The dessert Madeira is particularly fine—if it's not on the tasting menu, ask your pourer at the bar if they've got a bottle open and you might just get lucky.

The big tasting room on Highway 29 boasts three big bar areas, endless stacks and cases of wine out and ready for purchase, a separate register, and a full deli. The gardens surrounding the facility include a number of picnic tables and Sattui is a popular lunchtime stop for all-day tasters. But beware: All the recent good press makes even the big Sattui tasting room fill up on in-season weekends.

### Flora Springs

This winery straddles the line between boutique and big-deal Napa player. You'll find Flora Springs (677 S. St. Helena Hwy., St. Helena, 707/967-8032, www.floraspprings.com,

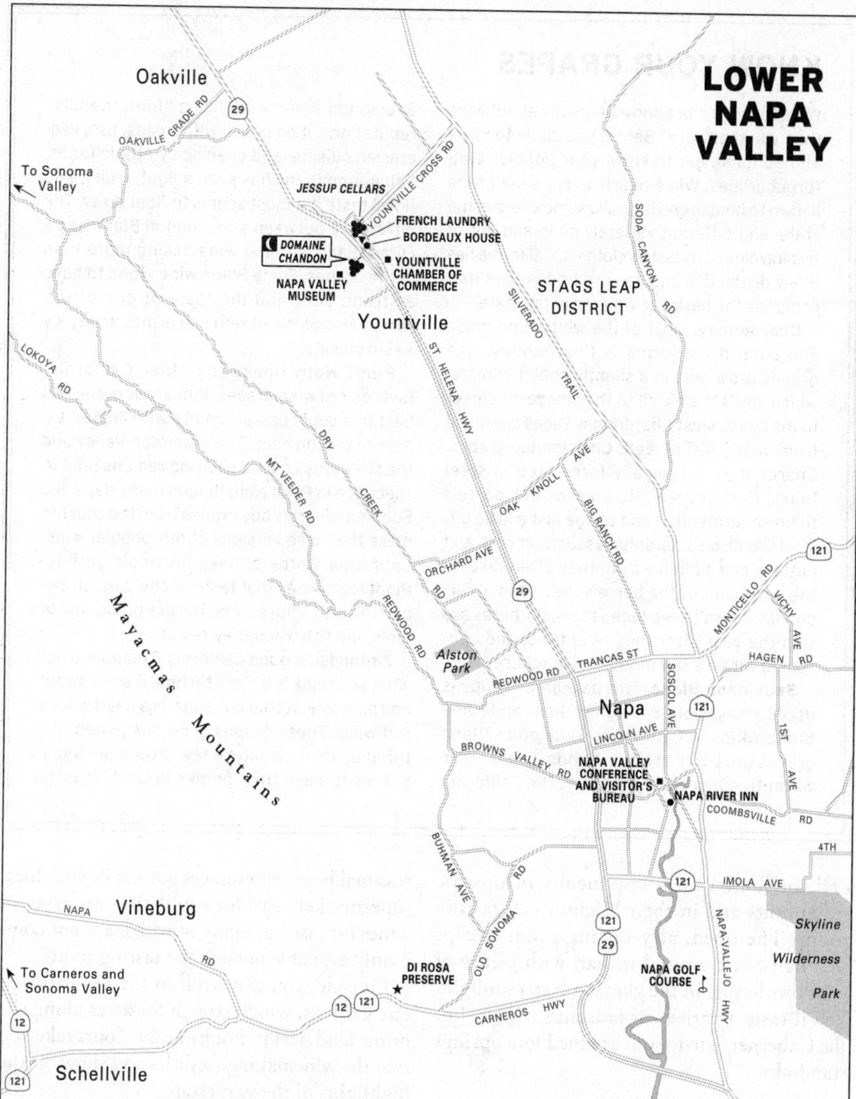
LOWER NAPA VALLEY
Oakville
OAKVILLE GRADE RD
29
To Sonoma Valley
YOUNTVILLE CROSS RD
JESSUP CELLARS
FRENCH LAUNDRY
BORDEAUX HOUSE
DOMAINE CHANDON
YOUNTVILLE CHAMBER OF COMMERCE
NAPA VALLEY MUSEUM
Yountville
STAGS LEAP DISTRICT
SODA CANYON RD
SILVERADO TRAIL
LOKOYA RD
ST HELENA HWY
DRY CREEK RD
MT VEEDER RD
OAK KNOLL AVE
BIG RANCH RD
ORCHARD AVE
REDWOOD RD
121
MONTICELLO RD
VICHY AVE
Mayacmas Mountains
Alston Park
TRANCAS ST
HAGEN RD
SOSCOL AVE
Napa
1ST AVE
LINCOLN AVE
BROWNS VALLEY RD
NAPA VALLEY CONFERENCE AND VISITOR'S BUREAU
NAPA RIVER INN
COOMBSVILLE RD
4TH
BUHMAN AVE
OLD SONOMA RD
IMOLA AVE
Skyline Wilderness Park
NAPA-VALLEJO HWY
Vineburg
NAPA RD
To Carneros and Sonoma Valley
DI ROSA PRESERVE
12
NAPA GOLF COURSE
CARNEROS HWY
Schellville
Napa River
0 2 mi
0 2 km
© AVALON TRAVEL
To Vallejo

## KNOW YOUR GRAPES

Want to seem more knowledgeable about wine than you really are? Before you come to Napa and Sonoma, get to know your popular California grapes. While nearly every wine grape known to humankind is grown somewhere in the state, and different varietals go in and out of fashion almost as fast as clothing, California has a few distinctive and easy to find grapes that comprise the basics of vintning in the state.

**Chardonnay.** Most of the white wine made and sold in California is Chardonnay. The grapes grow best in a slightly cooler climate, which lends them well to the vineyards closer to the coast. Most Chardonnay wines are made from nearly 100 percent Chardonnay grapes. Chardonnay is typically fermented in steel tanks, then poured into steel or oak barrels to finish fermenting and to age just a little bit. Most California Chardonnays taste smooth and buttery and a bit like fruit; they often take on the oak flavor of the barrels they sit in. Chardonnay doesn't keep (age), so most Chards are sold the year after they're bottled, and consumed within a few months of purchase.

**Sauvignon Blanc.** This pale green grape is used to make both Sauvignon Blanc and Fumé Blanc wines in California. Sauvignon Blanc grapes grow well in Napa, Sonoma, and other warm-to-hot parts of the state. The California Sauvignon Blanc wine has a "food friendly" reputation – it goes well with salads, fish, vegetarian cuisine, and even spicy ethnic foods. Sauvignon Blanc has such a light, fruity, and floral taste it almost seems to float away. The difference between a Sauvignon Blanc and a Fumé Blanc is in the winemaking more than in the grapes. Fumé Blanc wines tend to have a strong odor and the taste of grapefruit. Fumes also pair well with fish dishes and spicy Asian cuisine.

**Pinot Noir.** Unlike the other California-favored red wine grapes, Pinot Noir grapes do best in a cool coastal climate with limited exposure to high heat. The Anderson Valley and the Monterey coastal growing regions tend to specialize in Pinot Noir, though many Napa and Sonoma wineries buy grapes from the coast to make their own versions of this popular wine. California vintners make up single-varietal Pinot Noir wines that taste of cherries, strawberries, and smoke when they're great, and of mold and fish when they're not.

**Zinfandel.** A good California Zinfandel is not what you think is it. For starters, it's not sweet and pale pink. A true Zinfandel is a hearty deep red wine. These grapes grow best when tortured by their climate; a few grow near Napa, but most make their homes in Gold Country



call for hours) on a few menus in upscale restaurants and in their Highway 29 tasting room. The open, airy tasting room sweeps in a half-circle around its bar, with plenty of windows letting in the glowing Napa sunlight. You'll taste a variety of reds and whites, but the Cabernet Sauvignons are the Flora Springs standouts.

### Beringer Vineyards

You may recognize the Beringer name, since this winery sells large quantities of inexpensive wines across the country. The palatial stone estate buildings of Beringer Vineyard (2000 Main St., St. Helena, 707/967-4412, www.beringer.com, daily 10 A.M.–5 P.M., $10–25) belie the reasonably priced vintages you see in your local supermarket. Inside, you'll find an array of wines for tasting, many of which are not commonly available outside the tasting room.

Outside, you can stroll in the beautiful estate gardens, which stretch for acres along the prime land next to Highway 29. Tours take you into the winemaking facilities and show off the highlights of the vast estate.

### Sterling Vineyards

Sterling Vineyards (1111 Dunaweal Ln., Calistoga, 800/726-6136, www.sterlingvineyards.com, daily 10:30 A.M.–4:30 P.M., $20) is more appealing for folks who are touring Wine Country for the first time to see the sights than

wine grapes

and the inland Central Coast. Zinfandel was one of the first types of grape introduced in California, and a few lucky vineyards have "Old Vines," Zinfandel vines that have been producing grapes for nearly 100 years. A great Zinfandel wine boasts the flavors and smells of blackberry jam and the dusky hues of venous blood. Zinfandel often tastes wonderful all by itself, but it's also good with beef, buffalo, and even venison.

**Cabernet Sauvignon.** If you spend any length of time in Napa or Sonoma, you'll hear the phrase "Cab is King." This always means Cabernet Sauvignon, a grape from the Bordeaux region of France that creates a deep, dark, strong red wine. The grapes that get intense summer heat make the best wine, which makes them a perfect fit in the scorching Napa Valley. In France, Cabernet Sauvignon grapes mix with several other varieties to create the famed Bordeaux Blends. In California, especially in Napa, winemakers use Cabernet Sauvignon on its own to brew some of the most intense single-grape wine in the world. A good dry Cab might taste of leather, tobacco, and Bing cherries. Harsh tannins can create a sandpapery feeling in the mouth and an unpleasant tree-bark flavor, making Cabernet Sauvignon difficult for newcomers to the wine world to enjoy. Cabs age well, often hitting their peak of flavor and smoothness over a decade after bottling. (By then, the tannins have mellowed and the wine tastes less like chewing on an oak branch.)



for serious wine aficionados. The jewel of the new "Disneyland with wine" culture of Napa, Sterling features a gondola ride and an enforced "tasting tour" through their estate rather than a traditional tasting room experience. It's expensive, and the lines can get long on in-season weekends.

To be fair, once you've stood in line and bought your tickets, the gondola ride up the mountain to the estate shows off Napa Valley at its best. Take advantage of the time to admire the stellar views of forested hills and endless vineyard lands. Once up at the estate, you'll be led around by signs to each tasting glass of wine. Frankly, the wine isn't worth the effort or the high per-bottle price tag. But the estate has some charm, and the views off the deck match those from the gondola.

## Cuvaison

This small winery harkens back to the Napa of decades past. The intimate tasting room at Cuvaison (4550 Silverado Trail N., Calistoga, 707/942-6266, www.cuvaison.com, Apr.–Nov. daily 10 A.M.–5 P.M., Dec.–Mar. Sun.–Thurs. 11 A.M.–4 P.M., Fri.–Sat. 10 A.M.–5 P.M., $10–$15) doesn't hold busloads of tourists and the bar might show a few scars, but the tasting room staff know quite a bit about the wine they're pouring and they want to tell you all about it. The quaint building sits on the slope of the mountains bordering Napa Valley and

© LANCE SCOTT

Cuvaison on the Silverado Trail



shelters several friendly cats. A picnic area invites a longer stop to enjoy the vineyard views with your lunch and a nice bottle of Cuvaison Chardonnay, or just to relax and sip one of their light, tasty reds.

## SIGHTS

Believe it or not, there are a few things worth seeing in Napa outside of the wineries. Granted, the major industry pervades even the museums here, but the arts and parks of Napa can make a wonderful break from tasting wine, or a whole-day adventure if vino isn't your thing.

### COPIA

If you're a novice in the world of fine food and wine, or if you're an expert, it's more than worth your time to stop at COPIA: The American Center for Wine, Food, & the Arts (500 1st St., Napa, 707/259-1600, www.copia.org, daily 10 A.M.–6 P.M., free). This center seeks to educate and enlighten all visitors on the subjects of both food and wine. After purchasing admission tickets, begin your visit downstairs where you'll be treated to a taste of the day's wine. Beyond the tasting, you'll find an interactive interpretive exhibit on wine. This is the perfect place for wine newbies to learn enough to get comfortable in even the snootiest Napa Valley tasting rooms. Next, you can purchase a card and use it to learn about wine tasting in the best way—by doing it.

Note: At the time of publication, COPIA closed suddenly with future plans to be announced. Please call to confirm before planning a trip.

### Culinary Institute of America

The premier institute for professional chef training in America has only two campuses: one in upstate New York and one right here in the Napa Valley. The Culinary Institute of America at Greystone (2555 Main St., St. Helena, 707/967-1010, www.ciachef.edu/restaurants/wsgr, Sun.–Thurs. 11:30 A.M.–9 P.M., Fri.–Sat. 11:30 A.M.–10 P.M.) has it all: a restaurant, a café, a gourmet shop, one-day cooking classes and demos, a food history museum, and a stunning set of campus buildings set into the forests and vineyards near the town of St. Helena right on Highway 29. If Napa is the perfect place to introduce newcomers to the world of high-end food and wine, Greystone takes it to the intermediate and advanced levels. No matter who you are, you'll love the De Baun Café and the Spice Islands Marketplace, and you'll want to make a reservation in the Wine Spectator Greystone Restaurant. But if you're a for-real foodie or cork dork, consider signing up in advance to attend a cooking demo or even a seminar at this haven for haute cuisine. And be sure to take a few minutes to wander the charming grounds and marvel at the imposing structures of the campus—made from (of course) gray stonework.

### Napa Valley Museum

The small Napa Valley Museum (55 Presidents Circle, Yountville, 707/944-0500, www.napavalleymuseum.org, Wed.–Mon. 10 A.M.–5 P.M., $4.50) sits tucked away behind Domaine Chandon on the other side of Highway 29 in Yountville. Here you'll find perhaps the most complete description of the winemaking process available in all of Wine Country. The main feature of the downstairs gallery is a big, high-tech, multimedia display that categorizes each step and month in the life of a wine (and a winemaker). If you're interested in learning the details of the grape, plan on spending at least half an hour reading the left-hand wall. Next, you can test what you've learned with a variety of interactive "quizzes" on winemaking, and finally you can examine information about how different types of wine taste and how to eat and drink them. A tiny exhibit tells the history of Napa Valley, from the earliest pioneers through the current wine boom. The upstairs gallery provides space for rotating exhibitions; you're likely to find the work of local artists or art depicting food and wine.

### Skyline Wilderness Park

Once you're on the trails of Skyline Wilderness Park (2201 Imola Ave., Napa, 707/252-0481, www.skylinepark.org, daily sunrise–sunset), you may forget you're even in the Wine Country. Up at this park, no vineyards encroach on the natural chaparral landscape of Napa's high country. This park includes the Martha Walker Garden—a botanical garden planted with California and Napa native plants in honor of a legendary figure in the local horticultural community. The rest of this 850-acre park is given over to multiple community uses. You'll find halls suitable for events, campgrounds, hiking trails, horse and bike paths, a disc golf course, and more. Be aware that it gets *hot* here in the summertime, and not all the campgrounds and trails offer adequate shade to cool visitors off. Even so, the natural beauty of this protected wilderness makes Skyline Park a favorite with both locals and travelers to the Wine Country area.

### Old Faithful Geyser

No, that's not a typo, and you haven't accidentally turned east into Yellowstone. The Napa Valley has its own Old Faithful Geyser (1299 Tubbs Ln., Calistoga, 707/942-6463, www.oldfaithfulgeyser.com, $8 adults). Unlike its more famous counterpart, this geothermal geyser was manmade. In the 19th and early 20th centuries, more than 100 wells were drilled into the geothermal springs of the Calistoga area, and many of these created geysers. Old

© LIZ SCOTT

Old Faithful gets ready . . .

© LIZ HAMILL SCOTT

Old Faithful erupts.

Faithful is one of the few that wasn't eventually capped off, and it's the only one that erupts with clockwork regularity. When you visit the geyser, expect no more than a 40-minute wait to see it erupt 60 or more feet into the air. A grassy area surrounds the geyser, with benches and chairs scattered about to allow visitors an easy wait for the show. A bamboo garden surrounds the grassy spot (bamboo is one of the few plants that can tolerate the hot mineral water of this area). Also at Old Faithful you'll find an incongruous but cute petting zoo that shelters several "fainting goats," plus a few sheep and llamas. A coin-op feeder lets visitors feed and pet the animals—a perfect means of inspiring patience in children who may grow tired of waiting for the geyser to erupt. Note that the pool the geyser erupts from, as well as the geyser itself, spew *very hot water.* It's not safe to wade in the water, nor to stand too close when the geyser goes off. Watch small children when you visit.

© LIZ HAMILL SCOTT

Petrified Forest

## Petrified Forest

The petrified trees of the Petrified Forest (4100 Petrified Forest Rd., Calistoga, 707/942-6667, www.petrifiedforest.org, daily 9 A.M.–5 P.M., summer until 7 P.M., adults $6, seniors/juniors $5, children $3) no longer stand—technically this is an archaeological dig that uncovered a forest that existed more than three million years ago. A volcano that no longer exists erupted, blowing over the trees and covering them with ash. Over hundreds of thousands of years, the minerals in that ash traded places with the contents of the cells that made up the wood of the trees, "petrifying" them. Now these long-dead trees are made of stone. When you visit the forest, you'll see plenty of live, upright trees. Follow your trail map along a 0.5-mile loop to visit the various excavated petrified trees and chunks of trees. You can touch some of the chunks of petrified wood, but most of the large fallen stone trees enjoy the protection of fences to preserve their pristine state. You'll get to see one rare petrified pine tree, and a number of petrified Coast Redwoods, almost all of which have names. A fun note: All the trees fell in the same direction (and still face that way), showing us which way the blast came when the volcano blew up. Inside the visitors center and gift shop, you'll find lots of rocks and minerals, books on geology, plus a few rare shards of the petrified trees from this very forest.

## Calistoga History Museum

The Calistoga History Museum (1311 Washington St., Calistoga, 707/942-5911, www.sharpsteen-museum.org, daily 11 A.M.–4 P.M.) is also known as the Sharpsteen Museum after its founder Ben Sharpsteen. Sharpsteen, an Academy Award–winning animator for Disney, had a passion for dioramas. It was through his desire (and money) that the immense, exquisitely detailed dioramas depicting the 1860s Calistoga hot springs resort and life in 19th-century Calistoga were built. The other major player in the museum, Sam Brannan, was the first pioneer to Calistoga to build a hot springs resort using the geothermal springs in the area. At the museum, you'll learn of Brannan's success and subsequent ruin in the resort business, as well as his unsuccessful attempt to convert the Napa Valley to Mormonism. Other museum exhibits highlight daily life in 19th-century Napa, complete with artifacts and a nod to the Wappo Native American tribe who were the first residents of this area.

### di Rosa Preserve

At the unique di Rosa Preserve (5200 Hwy. 21, Napa, 707/226-5991, ext. 25, www.dirosapreserve.org, Tues.–Fri. 9:30 A.M.–3 P.M., Sat. tours 10 A.M.–noon, $10–$15), you'll see the cutting edge of modern California art. With 217 acres at its disposal, the di Rosa Preserve has ample room for its three galleries, outdoor sculpture meadow, and on-site lake. Take in the festival of color and creativity in the galleries and sculpture garden, or wander the undeveloped portion of the preserve to soak in the colors and shapes nature chose for this area.

### Pioneer Cemetery

Looking for your Napa ancestors? Just like prowling through historic graveyards? Stop at the Napa Valley Pioneer Cemetery (Bothe-Napa Valley State Park, 3801 St. Helena Hwy. N., Calistoga, www.parks.ca.gov). Here you'll find the graves of many of Napa's earliest settlers and some of the more prominent early families. The cemetery seems to undergo regular maintenance since paths between plots are kept clear and walkable. But many of the graves are overgrown with vines—some even have full-sized oak trees growing through them. The whole area is covered by a dense canopy of forest foliage, making it a pleasantly cool place to visit on hot summer days. You can explore up the hillside, where the paths get more overgrown and some of the tombstones are still old wooden planks, their lettering worn away. If you're interested in genealogy, start at the front entrance of the cemetery, where a map and alphabetical survey of the cemetery are posted. One warning about visiting this cemetery: No, not ghosts—lack of parking. There's enough room at the front for one small car. Otherwise, you'll need to park elsewhere and

© LIZ HAMILL SCOTT

Napa Valley Pioneer Cemetery

walk carefully along and across Highway 29 to the gate.

## ENTERTAINMENT AND EVENTS

A visit to Napa Valley is all about wine, but there are also plenty of events to suit every taste and desire. (But the focus of many of the festivals and festivities is, of course, wine and food.)

### Bars and Clubs

Feeding the needs of the cocktail dress and suit-and-tie crowd, **Étoile Lounge** (1 California Dr., Yountville, www.chandon.com) at Domaine Chandon offers drinks, dancing, and DJs most nights of the week. Sip Chandon's lovely bubbly as you enjoy the scene in this elegant wine bar. Snack food is served in the lounge if you need a nibble (though you won't if you started your evening in the Étoile restaurant).

### Theater

More than 50 years ago, the **Lincoln Theatre** (100 California Dr., Yountville, 707/944-1300, www.lincolntheatre.org) ran its first show at the Veterans Home in Yountville. Today, a packed year-round season brings top-end live entertainment of all kinds to the Wine Country. You can get tickets to touring Broadway shows, locally produced plays, stand-up comedy, dance productions, music nights, and more. Many of the productions at the Lincoln welcome family audiences. Though this large theater seats hundreds, purchase tickets in advance if you can—especially for one-night-only special performances or if you'll be in the area only over one weekend. Ticket prices range $10–125, depending on the seats and the show. The theater recommends arriving half an hour in advance of show time, to ensure that you've got time to park your car, walk from the parking lot, and find your seat before the curtain goes up.



### Festivals and Events

By far, the biggest thing that happens in Napa every year is the grape harvest, sometimes called "Crush" because the grapes get crushed as part of the first stage of winemaking. During September and October (dates can vary depending on the weather conditions and growing season), events spring up all over Napa Valley. Many wineries host gala festivals for their wine club members, but you must be part of the club to join in the fun. On the other hand, the **Napa Harvest Festival** (www.copia.org/content/harvest) takes place towards the end of the season (late October); it's open to all and is one of the best celebrations in Wine Country. The Kiwanis Club of Napa also puts on a **Napa Valley Harvest Festival** (800/550-6260, www.napakiwanis.com) in Yountville at the Lincoln Theatre, featuring fine wines, great food, live music, and local art.

If you prefer smaller crowds but bigger fun, consider coming to Napa in February or March to enjoy the events of the **Napa Valley Mustard Festival** (www.mustardfestival.org). Each year in the not-so-dead of winter, wild mustard plants bloom brilliant yellow throughout the vineyards of Napa. (Mustard acts as a cover crop, protecting and nurturing the soil in which the precious grape vines grow.) Festival attendees can check the festival website and choose the opening gala, closing gala, or any of the grand events that happen on the weekends in between. Restaurants and wineries open their doors for special dinners and tasting events. Do be aware that February and March are the rainy season in Napa, so the weather for this festival isn't always the best.

Another fun festival that takes advantage of the off-season, the **Festival of Trees** (707/226-6872, ext. 24) has opened the holiday season in Wine Country for the last 15 years. Put on by the Napa Valley Symphony League, this festival focuses on music as well as food and wine. Make your reservations early (starting in October) to attend the three days' worth of events that make up this festival.

## SPORTS AND RECREATION

### Spas

Rivaling the wineries for popularity in the Napa Valley, the Calistoga hot springs spas have been drawing visitors for over 150 years. Underneath Calistoga, early pioneers to the area found a geothermal spring. It wasn't long before that spring was channeled into pools, and thus the Calistoga spas began. Now, almost a dozen spas compete for the business of locals and tourists alike, offering an array of standard spa services, plus the famous Calistoga mud and mineral baths.

The award-winning **Calistoga Oasis Spa** (1300 Washington St., 707/942-2122) offers a complete range of day-spa treatments and services. Their signature service, the mud bath, includes time in a tub full of Calistoga mud followed by a soak in a local mineral water bubble bath and finishing with a few minutes wrapped in cotton blankets in a peaceful dark room. Each private treatment room is set up for two people. Throughout your treatment, an attendant will see to your every wish, providing cold cucumber water to drink and wrapping chilled towels around the your neck to create a wonderful juxtaposition of hot bath and cool head. For a special treat, add a massage to the end of your mud bath for a full-fledged pampering session. At the Oasis, the therapists have training in an array of techniques, including reiki energy work. Or pick an herbal facial using your favorite scents to complete your perfect day.

For an old-school Calistoga spa experience, head down the main drag to **Dr. Wilkinson's Hot Springs Resort** (1507 Lincoln Ave., 707/942-4102, www.drwilkinson.com, daily 8:30 A.M.–5:30 P.M.). Tucked into a charmingly run-down 1950s motel building, this spa was opened by "Doc" Wilkinson in 1952. Doc's proprietary blend of Calistoga mineral water and volcanic ash, Canadian peat, and lavender is still the gold standard for the Calistoga mud bath today. "The Works" includes the mud bath (complete with a soothing mud masque for your face), mineral bath, and finishing blanket wrap. And of course you can also get or add a facial and a massage to your treatment. The men's and women's spa areas are separated at Dr. Wilkinsons. If you're a guest of the hotel, be sure to take a swim or a soak in one of the three mineral water pools (there are two outdoor pools and one huge spa inside).

At the **Calistoga Hot Springs Spa** (1006 Washington St., 707/942-6269, www.calistogaspa.com, Tue.–Thurs. 8:30 A.M.–4:30 P.M., Fri.–Mon. 8:30 A.M.–9 P.M.), indulge in a mud bath, mineral bath, or all the usual spa treatments. Also available to the public and guaranteed with a spa reservation is access to Calistoga Hot Springs' four outdoor mineral pools. The lap pool is the coolest at 80°, and set up for serious swimmers. The 90° wading pool with fountains offers fun and health benefits for the whole family. Another large soaking pool is set to 100° and meant primarily for adults. Finally, the 104° enormous octagonal jetted spa sits under a gazebo—the perfect location to relax and enjoy the serenity of spa country.

Two other lovely Calistoga spas, both of which offer full mud and mineral baths as well as spa services are **Golden Haven** (1713 Lake St., 707/942-8000, www.goldenhaven.com, daily 8 A.M.–11 P.M.) and **Indian Springs** (1712 Lincoln Ave., 707/942-4913, www.indianspringscalistoga.com, daily 9 A.M.–8 P.M.). The **Lincoln Avenue Spa** (1339 Lincoln Ave., 707/942-2950, www.lincolnavenuespa.com) does not have mud bath facilities, offers a wider array of spa and esthetic treatments.

## Hot Air Ballooning

Another near-unique Wine Country experience is rising into the morning sun over the valley in a brightly colored hot air balloon. Be sure to make your reservations in advance as trips can fill up quickly, especially during the high season (which extends well into fall in Napa). You must be an early riser, since most balloon trips depart shortly after dawn. You'll float serenely over the vineyards of Napa Valley on your trip, before a gentle descent into a predetermined spot.

**Calistoga Balloons** (888/995-7700, www.calistogaballoons.com) is the only company offering regular flights in the north end of Napa Valley, so they've got the lock on some of the prettiest scenery around. In addition to the vineyards, wineries, spas, and charming town of Calistoga, you'll get to see Mount St. Helena and the lush forests of the hills surrounding this lovely area.

© LANCE SCOTT

ballooning over Wine Country

On the other end of Napa, **Balloons Above the Valley** (800/464-6824, www.balloonrides.com) offers the full package—from lodging packages that include transportation to the launch site to included-with-every-ride champagne brunch after you touch down. Be sure to bring your camera to capture those otherwise-impossible shots of the vineyards and wineries from above!

## Golf

Since you're already in the land of upscale entertainment options, it seems only natural to enjoy a round of golf during your Wine Country vacation. At the par 72 **Napa Golf Course** (2295 Streblow Dr., Napa, 707/255-4333, www.playnapa.com, $33–43), golfers of all levels—even beginners—can enjoy a full 18 holes. More experienced players will enjoy (or curse!) the plethora of water and full-sized trees on this course, known locally as a bargain. Another charming, inexpensive course up north in the Valley is the **Mt. St. Helena Golf Course** (Napa County Fairgrounds, 707/942-9966, www.napacountyfairgrounds.com/golf.htm, $18 weekdays, $24 weekends). This 9-hole, par 36 course offers a perfect spot to take your younger or less experienced golfing buddies. It's flat and straight, with easier lines than some other courses. On the other hand, all those trees along the fairways and the small greens make it interesting for intermediate-level players.

## Bicycling

Biking is a popular way to see the vineyards, forests, and wineries of Napa. You'll get out away from the highways and the endless traffic of the wine roads on two wheels under your own power. If you don't know the area, the best way to bike the area is to take a tour. **Napa Valley Bike Tours** (6488 Washington St, Yountville, 800/707-2453, www.napavalleybiketours.com) offers standard and custom tours all over the area, from central Napa to Calistoga. You'll get a first-year, brand-name bike, a map, a helmet, and an orientation before beginning your trek. Then you'll be off on your chosen tours: a pedal through the vineyards, a half-day tour or a full-day tour including both wine tasting and meals, or a multi-sport "adventure package" that includes kayaking, a balloon ride, or a horseback ride.

If you prefer to go off on your own rather than follow a guide, you can also rent a bike from Napa Valley Bike Tours. Or you can select from a more diverse fleet at the **Calistoga Bikeshop** (1318 Lincoln Ave., Calistoga, 707/942-9687, http://calistogabikeshop.com). With cruisers and touring bikes, mountain and road bikes, tandems and trailers, this shop has whatever you need to suit your travel plans. Ask at the shop for directions and maps for whatever kind of ride you want to take, from a simple couple of hours puttering through the vineyards up to the most challenging mountain bike tracks in the area.

## Horseback Riding

If you don't want to use your own legs to get around Napa Valley, consider borrowing the four strong legs of a horse. Take a break from the endless vineyards and explore some of Napa's most beautiful parks with the **Triple Creek Horse Outfit** (707/933-1600, www.triplecreekhorseoutfit.com). Choose from Jack London State Historic Park, Sugarloaf Ridge State Park, or Bothe-Napa Valley State Park in Calistoga. Rides run 1–3 hours and cover a variety of terrain. Explore both the natural beauty and the historic significance of these parts of Napa. Whether you're an experienced rider or this is your first time on a horse, Triple Creek will find the right horse for you. Check with the ranch for limitation on rider age, fitness, and weight.

## Boating and Fishing

Tired of the often dry land of Napa in the summertime? Get out into the water! If you like your water running, take a cruise on the Napa River with **Napa River Adventures** (Kennedy Park Boat Dock, 707/224-9080, www.napariveradventures.com). Float along the river in a lovely small covered motor launch in cushy seats, enjoying the view out the massive wraparound windows. Bring along a picnic and a bottle of wine to make the most of your pleasure cruising experience. The trip takes you right into the heart of downtown Napa and back to the dock.

If you're looking for a lake vacation adjacent to Wine Country, drive a few miles out to **Lake Berryessa** (Berryessa-Knoxville Rd.). On this largish lake, you can power boat, Jet Ski, kayak, canoe, and fish—or just sunbathe on the shore and splash about in the shallows with your family. If you've got your own boat, you can launch it at one of the marinas or the **Capell Cove Boat Ramp** (Knoxville Rd.). Or you can rent from one of the lakeside resorts. The **Lake Berryessa Marina Resort** (5800 Knoxville Rd., Napa, 707/966-4204, www.lakeberryessaboats.com) offers all kinds of boats, from patio cruisers to high-end ski tow boats to personal watercraft to kayaks. Make reservations well in advance to get the boat you want! You can also rent water skis, wakeboards, and ski tubes.

Lake Berryessa also boasts some of the best fishing in California. You can fish for cold- and warm-water fish, including bass, rainbow trout, and kokanee salmon. Rent a boat from one of the resorts, launch your own, or enjoy some relaxed fishing from the shore. The resorts can sell California fishing licenses and bait, and advise you about the season's hottest fishing holes.

## ACCOMMODATIONS

### Napa

Within the town limits of Napa, you'll find clean, comfy rooms at prices that let you splurge on the food and wine.

#### $100-150

The **Chateau Hotel** (4195 Solano Ave., 707/253-9300, www.thechateauhotel.com, $100) actually has a pleasantly unpretentious motel feel. The guest rooms are reasonably sized with colorful decor, carpet, and linens. Some rooms offer larger baths or sink areas where you can really spread out if you're staying several days. Choose from an array of room arrangements, including two-bed rooms that work well for families or couples traveling together who want to save money on lodgings. The Chateau Hotel even has some smoking-allowed rooms—a diminishing rarity in California. At only two stories, it's easy to get to whatever room you've rented, even if it's been a long day wine tasting. The pool and spa beckon guests morning, noon, and night, and both remain heated even in winter.

#### $150-250

At the **Chablis Inn** (3360 Solano Ave., 800/443-3490, www.chablisinn.com, $175), the guest rooms include all the usual amenities: wet bar with mini fridge, in-room coffee maker, TVs with cable, and more. Rooms are simply decorated, but the beds are comfortable, the carpets are dark (perfect for drinking just a little bit of red wine in the rooms!), and the address is central to both the attractions of downtown Napa and the famous Highway 29 wine road.

The pretty, unassuming **Wine Valley Lodge** (200 S. Coombs St., 800/696-7911, www.winevalleylodge.com, $175) welcomes guests with its red brick and adobe tiled exterior. Inside, guests enjoy the serene rooms with unobtrusive art, pale yellow walls, and soothing pastel comforters. The rooms are nicely sized, and you can get your choice of king bed, two doubles, or a suite depending on the needs of your party. The Wine Valley Lodge also boasts a significant past; in the late 1950s and early '60s, several movies were filmed in Napa. Various A-list stars, including Rock Hudson, Jean Simmons, and even Elvis himself stayed at the lodge during filming. If you're a movie buff, ask for the Elvis suite!

The **Napa River Inn** (500 Main St., 877/251-8500, www.napariverinn.com, $225) has one of the best locations in Napa. It sits inside the historic Napa Mill, so you can practically fall out of your hotel room and hit the General Store (and restaurant), several galleries, the candy store, and at least one other restaurant on the way down. You're also located steps from the center of Napa's bustling downtown, and if you're lucky your room might afford you a view of the Napa River. Inside, this luxury hotel is crammed with high-end antiques and reproductions in the common area. Best of all, you can choose from three styles of interior decor: Historic Victorian rooms come with canopy beds, floral prints, cushy chairs, and slipper tubs; the Nautical rooms (many of which face the river) look like the inside of a yacht, with wood paneling, porthole-style mirrors, and rope-styled accents; the Wine Country rooms echo the natural wealth of the Napa Valley with floral linens, marble bathrooms, and oak moldings.

For a different style of historic lodging experience, stay at the **Napa Inn** (1137 Warren St., 800/435-1144, http://napainn.com, $175), which inhabits two Victorian houses, both painted blue, in the historic downtown Napa area. You can walk from either to downtown shops and restaurants, and take very short drives to the Wine Train depot.

As B&Bs go, the Napa Inn is a big one, with more than 10 rooms and suites. If you plan to travel with your pet, talk to the inn well in advance to get one of their two pet-friendly rooms. Elegant fabrics and lush modern textures moderate the florals and carved wood of the Victorian era. The nicest rooms have corner whirlpool tubs and king-sized beds. Breakfast at the Napa Inn is an event, with multiple courses served by candlelight. For the ultimate in pampering, book a spa treatment in the privacy of your room.

#### OVER $250

The king of Napa lodging is the **Silverado** (1600 Atlas Peak Rd., 707/257-0200, www.silveradoresort.com, $275). Your resort experience begins as you drive up and catch your first sight of the stately white colonial main building. You'll find the finest in modern amenities and decorations in your suite (all rooms at the Silverado are full suites with kitchens and dining rooms), from the high-thread-count linens to the complimentary Wi-Fi to the private patio or deck overlooking the grounds. Pale colors with eye-popping jewel-toned accents speak of the best current designers. Outside your room, there's so much to do at the Silverado that you'll find it hard to pry yourself off the grounds to go wine-tasting. Choose from the immense spa with full fitness and salon services, the two 18-hole golf courses, the two restaurants, the 17 tennis courts, the 10 pools, and—believe it or not—more.

### Yountville

If you've come to Napa Valley to dine at the French Laundry or immerse yourself in the food scene, you'll want to stay in Yountville if you can. Several inns sit within stumbling distance of the French Laundry, which is convenient for gourmands who want to experience a range of wines with their unearthly meal.

#### $100–150

A French-styled inn, the **Maison Fleurie** (6529 Yount St., 800/788-0369, www.foursisters.com, $140) offers the best of small inn style for a more reasonable nightly rate. On Yount Street, the Maison Fleurie has a perfect location for walking to Bouchon, the Bouchon Bakery, and the many other amazing restaurants, boutiques, and tasting rooms in town. The 13 rooms in this "house of flowers" have an attractive but not overwhelming floral decorative theme. The more economical rooms, described as "cozy," are small but attractive. If you've got the budget to splurge, opt for a room in the Bakery Building, where you'll get a fireplace, jetted spa tub, and king bed. All guests enjoy a full breakfast each morning, afternoon wine reception, fresh cookies, and complimentary access to the inn's bikes.

#### OVER $250

The **Bordeaux House** (6600 Washington St., 707/944-2855, www.bordeauxhouse.com, $325) has it all: a beautiful brick facade (an unusual sight this close to the fault lines!), lovely French country interior design, and a location that's literally three doors down from the French Laundry. It's not cheap, but the amenities in each individually decorated room make you feel as though you're staying in a quaint country inn in the south of France. Throughout your stay, take a stroll through the inn's gardens, enjoy a splash in the outdoor spa, and partake of the better-than-continental breakfast down in the common area each morning. Perhaps best of all, the location on Washington Street makes a walk through the best of downtown Yountville an easy prospect from the inn.

The **Napa Valley Lodge** (2230 Madison St., 888/455-2468, www.napavalleylodge.com, $285), a stunning Mediterranean-style hotel with stucco walls and red-tiled roofs, loves the sunshine and warmth of the Napa Valley summer. Guests are steeped in the luxury that the Wine Country in general, and Yountville in particular, is known for. Book a spa treatment either in your guestroom or out beside the heated pool. Start each day off right with the complimentary champagne buffet breakfast, or order from the California cuisine room service menu. And finish off each night in the luxury of your room—be it a Parkside Terrace room with a king bed topped with a European-style duvet, a Vineyard Courtyard Terrace room with its own patio and sweeping views of the surrounding vineyards, or a luxurious King Suite with a fireplace, two-person soaking tub, and the ubiquitous valley vineyard views.

At **The Cottages of Napa Valley** (1012 Darms Ln., two miles south of Yountville, 707/252-7810, www.napacottages.com, $460), you'll pay a princely sum to gain a home away from home in the heart of Wine Country. Each cottage has its own king bed, private garden, outdoor fireplace, and kitchenette. Every morning the quiet staff drops off a basket of fresh pastries from Bouchon Bakery and a pot of great coffee for breakfast to greet you whenever you feel like waking up. Simple yet luxurious country-cottage furnishings feel welcoming and homey, and the staff can help you plan and execute the ultimate Wine Country vacation—whatever that means to you.

## St. Helena

The charming small village of St. Helena sits right on Highway 29, and its stop signs and traffic signals are often the cause of the endless weekend Wine Country traffic jams. But if you're staying here, you can avoid the worst of the traffic and enjoy the wooded central Napa Valley area.

### $150-250

At the **Zinfandel Bed & Breakfast** (800 Zinfandel Ln., 700/963-3512, www.zinfandelinn.com, $175), you'll find yourself inside a 1980s reproduction of a Shakespearean castle. Lavish stonework coats the outside of this unique structure. Inside, you'll stay in one of three exquisitely decorated suite-like rooms. Each guest room boasts a unique design, complete with antique bedsteads and dressers, featherbeds, fireplaces, and tiled whirlpool tubs. All guests enjoy the full breakfast every morning of their stay, plus the rich amenities suitable to a Wine Country inn.

A less imposing structure, **The Ink House** (1575 St. Helena Highway at Whitehall Lane, 707/963-3890, www.inkhouse.com, $185) prides itself in its more casual elegance. A pretty yellow facade looks almost like a wedding cake. Inside, the breakfast room inhabits the first floor, all the guest rooms live on the second floor, and the small third floor solarium is open as a parlor to all guests. Enjoy the many amenities of the Ink House, from the full gourmet breakfast and afternoon wine social to the complimentary nightcaps and loaner bicycles. The lounge areas include a pool table and a TV with a VCR (plus a VHS library). Your room will be individually decorated, but every one of the rooms has a view of the surrounding forest and vineyards. Furnishings tend toward American and European antiques, and all beds are queen-sized.

## Calistoga

A plethora of places to stay cluster at the north end of Napa Valley. Here's where you'll find most of the hotel-and-spa combos, plus plenty of mineral water pools and hot tubs for your pleasure.

### $100-150

On the other hand, the **Calistoga Inn** (1259 Lincoln Ave., 707/942-4101, www.calistogainn.com,

$90–140) gives guests an old-school hotel experience, complete with shared bathrooms and showers. The inn, in continuous operation for over 100 years, offers a continental breakfast each morning, an English pub downstairs that serves lunch and dinner, and perhaps the best bargain rooms in the whole of Napa Valley. Each of the 18 guest rooms provides a small, cozy haven with a queen bed, simple furnishings, and a view of the town. Be sure to make reservations in advance—at these prices, rooms go quickly especially in summer and fall! And be aware that the pub downstairs has live music acts four nights a week, so the party can get loud (and fun!) on weekends.



### $150-250

The **Roman Spa Hot Springs Resort** (1300 Washington St., 707/942-4441, www.romanspahotsprings.com, $150–310 in high season) in the heart of downtown Calistoga has it all. Three mineral water pools, each set at a different temperature (no children under four are allowed in any pool, and the 105° spa is adults-only) plus saunas inspire guests to relax and refresh themselves with daily soaks and swims. Guest rooms run the range from inexpensive motel-style rooms with floral comforters to whirlpool rooms that include your own private two-person mineral bath, to kitchen suites (pots, pans, and dishes provided) that beckon families or groups who plan to stay a while. The Roman Spa connects to the Calistoga Oasis, which offers an array of spa treatments, including the famous mud baths.

If you're looking for a more traditional B&B experience, you can't miss **The Pink Mansion** (1415 Foothill Blvd., 800/238/7465, www.pinkmansion.com, $165–345). Literally. The 1875 mansion is painted bright, unmistakable pink from stem to stern, making it a local landmark. Each lush room features a unique theme suitable to romance and wine. The more economical rooms have queen beds and pretty antique furnishings; the larger suites are spacious enough to dwarf their king-sized beds, and you'll also find fireplaces, whirlpool tubs, and top-tier amenities. You'll also get the use of the heated indoor pool and spa, a full breakfast each morning, and use of the various TVs and VCRs (plus movie library) secreted around the house.

Want to combine all the elements of a Wine Country vacation into one inclusive spot? Visit the **Silver Rose Resort Winery** (351 Rosedale Rd., 800/995-9381, www.silverrose.com, $175–325). Choose your favorite of the 20 individually styled rooms, each with its own theme and country-elegant appointments. Your queen or king bed will invite you to a comfortable night's sleep each evening. The Silver Rose has its own winery, where you can taste and tour. Or spend a few hours in the spa, getting a massage-and-mud-bath combo. If you prefer to get active on your vacation, check out the tennis courts, swimming pool (shaped like a wine bottle), putting green, or hiking and biking roads and trails. Whatever your dream for your trip in the Napa Valley, the Silver Rose can probably accommodate you.

Another fabulous spa and hotel is the **Mount View Hotel and Spa** (1457 Lincoln Ave., 800/816-6877, www.mountviewhotel.com, $175–375). Perfectly located on Calistoga's main drag, the Mount View offers more than 30 posh rooms in which to break for the night between wine tasting adventures and pampered spa days. You'll find rooms, suites, and cottages decorated with tasteful 19th- century antiques and soothing colors inspired by the vines and vintages of the local area. Rooms have either a queen or twin beds or a king bed, all softened with featherbeds and down comforters. The spa offers facials, body wraps, steam showers, and scrubs. Enjoy the outdoor pool and spa at your leisure.

## FOOD

The restaurants of Napa glean almost as much fame as the wine. Some of the best food in California, and possibly the world, clusters near the vineyards of the Napa Valley. You'll find everything from kickin' barbecue to the hautest of haute French cuisine, all with an unforgettable California touch. And of course, most of it goes perfectly with wine!

## Yountville

The tiny town of Yountville boasts perhaps the biggest reputation for culinary excellence in California—a big deal when you consider the offerings of San Francisco and Los Angeles! The reason for this reputation starts and finishes with Thomas Keller's indisputably amazing **French Laundry** (6640 Washington St., 707/944-2380, www.frenchlaundry.com, daily 5:30–9 P.M., Fri.–Sun. 11 A.M.–1 P.M., reservation only, $240). Once you've gotten that all-important reservation, the fun begins! From the moment you walk in the door of the rambling Victorian, you're treated like royalty. You'll be led to your seat in one of the small dining rooms by one of the many, many pristine black-and-white clad staff. Even if you're new to this level of dining (and most of us are), you'll be made to feel more than welcome here. The menu, which changes often, offers two

### RESERVATIONS FOR FRENCH LAUNDRY

Most people familiar with the world of high-end food know that the best restaurant in all of California, and possibly all of the United States, is the **French Laundry.** Thomas Keller's culinary haven in tiny Yountville was the only restaurant in the greater Bay Area to earn the hallowed three-star rating from the Michelin Guide in 2007. The restaurant sits inside a charming vintage house; its kitchen garden grows right across the street where anyone can walk down the rows of vegetables and herbs.

Sounds like foodie paradise, right? There's just one problem: getting a table.

The difficulty in getting reservations to the French Laundry is almost as legendary as the French Laundry itself. Rather than expecting to dine at the French Laundry during a planned trip to the Wine Country, savvy travelers expect to plan their whole trip around whatever French Laundry reservation they manage to get.

The bare facts: The French Laundry takes reservations two months in advance. *Precisely* two months. The restaurant accepts reservations by phone, online, and via local concierges. Reservations are accepted for parties of two, four, or six. No more and no less. Diners can choose between lunch and dinner seatings that offer the same menu. It's easier to get a table for lunch than it is for dinner. Lunch or dinner takes two and a half to four hours to consume. Budget $500 *per person* for your meal if you plan to drink wine, and $300-350 if you don't.

The French Laundry starts taking **phone reservations** at 9 A.M. daily. Between 8:30 and 8:45 A.M., program their number on your speed-dial and begin calling. Continue calling again and again until you get an answer. If you get a continuous busy signal past 11 A.M., you'll probably need to try again the next day. And maybe the day after that.

Making **reservations online** works much the same way as on the phone, only it's harder. The French Laundry offers only one table (for lunch) online per day. Go online at OpenTable (www.opentable.com) at about 8:30 A.M. and start trying to snag that table. If you're still trying at 9:30 A.M., it's probably already gone.

Hands down the low-stress way to get a coveted French Laundry table is to hire a concierge to do it for you. The French Laundry lets concierges walk downtown to the restaurant each day to put in bookings for their clients. Call or email a concierge and expect to pay a nominal fee ($20-30), but if you can afford to dine at the French Laundry, that's pocket change. Give your new best friend a range of dates and times that will suit you, and he or she will do their best to accommodate your request. Do not expect get your first choice of times; flexible diners will find themselves with a remarkably trouble-free reservation experience.

So is it *really* worth all this rigmarole just to get into one lousy restaurant, then pay a sizeable part of a month's salary for a single meal? Yes.

From the gracious welcome at the door to the stunning service throughout the meal to the food that can be found nowhere else, dining at the French Laundry is worth both the hassle and the price tag. I speak from experience and am dying to go back!

main selections: the regular nine-course tasting menu and the vegetarian nine-course tasting menu. You'll have a few either/or choices as you run down each list—usually you'll see two options for the fish course and two options for the entrée. The wait staff can help you identify anything you don't recognize, or if you're having a crisis of decision-making. The sommelier is at your beck and call to assist you with a wine list that weighs several pounds.

Then the meal begins. From the first, waiters and footmen ply you with extras—an amuse-bouche here, an extra middle course there… and if you mention that someone else has something on their plate that you'd like to try, it appears in front of you as if by magic. Finally, the desserts come. And come. And come. After the fourth separate dessert course, you may want to ask for a white flag with which to signal your surrender. All together, a meal at the French Laundry can run up to 13 courses and take four hours to eat. Afterward, you might not eat normally for a couple of days, and you'll have spent a good chunk of rent money on a single meal, but it will seem worth it.



Another high-end restaurant in Yountville, **Étoile** (1 California Dr., 707/204-7529, www.chandon.com, Mon.–Thurs. 11:30 A.M.–2:30 P.M., 6–9:30 P.M., $32–41) sits inside the tasting facility at the prestigious Domaine Chandon champagnery. Lovely white tablecloths sparkle in the sunlight and overlook Chandon's lush green gardens. The menu at Étoile is inventive even for Napa, and each dish is prepared to utter perfection. Order the chef's tasting menu with wine pairings to sample Chandon's wine list at its best and enjoy the delectable cuisine as it was intended to be eaten.

If you can't quite manage the French Laundry, try Thomas Keller's other Yountville option: **Bouchon** (6534 Washington St., 707/944-8037, www.bouchonbistro.com, daily 11:30 A.M.–12:30 A.M., $24–34). Reservations are still strongly recommended, but you can get one a week in advance. Bouchon's atmosphere and food scream Parisian bistro. Order traditional favorites such as the croque monsieur or steak frites, or opt for a California-influenced specialty salad or entrée made with local, sustainable ingredients.

If you're just looking for a breakfast pastry or a sandwich, walk from Bouchon to the **Bouchon Bakery** (6528 Washington St., 707/944-2253, www.bouchonbakery.com, daily 7 A.M.–7 P.M.) next door. This ultra-high-end bakery supplies both Bouchon and the French Laundry with pastries and breads, as well as operating a retail storefront. Locals and visitors flock to the bakery at breakfast and lunchtime, so expect a line.

## Rutherford

The historic **Auberge du Soleil** (180 Rutherford Hill Rd., 800/348-5406, www.aubergedusoleil.com, daily 7 A.M.–11 A.M., 11:30 A.M.–2:30 P.M., 5:30–9:30 P.M., tasting menu $98) has an inn where you can stay the night, but some visitors come to the Auberge just for the food. The charming Mediterranean-style dining room has drawn visitors from all over the world for decades. Sunny yellow tablecloths, a central fireplace, exposed wooden beams, and wall-to-wall picture windows welcome diners to the restaurant. Executive Chef Robert Curry, a legend of the Napa Valley culinary scene, uses the finest local ingredients to create his own take on Mediterranean/California cuisine. Choose one item from each course list on the short but exquisite tasting menu to create a four-course dinner. If you ask, they can also serve you è la carte items from any of the courses. After all that rich food and fine wine, you might find yourself at the inn's desk, begging to be allowed to stay the night within staggering distance of the restaurant.

Another long-standing Wine Country favorite is the **Rutherford Grill** (1180 Rutherford Rd., 707/963-1792, www.hillstone.com, $10–30), which is more casual than many of its Napa Valley brethren. Some of the best seats in the house cluster outside the dining room on the wide porch; Covered by a collection of umbrellas, guests enjoy the pretty gardens while they wait for their classic grill fare—cheeseburgers, salads (with grilled items), bangers and mash, and a whole array of grilled meats—as well as an extensive and impressive wine list. Perhaps the best news of all?You can escape from the Rutherford Grill for well under $100 per person.

### St. Helena

A highlight of the St. Helena dining scene is the **Wine Spectator Greystone Restaurant** (2555 Main St., 707/967-1010, http://ciachef.edu, Sun.–Thurs. 11:30 A.M.–9 P.M., Fri.–Sat. 11:30 A.M.–10 P.M., $21–34), better known to its friends as "the restaurant at the CIA." Here the world's top aspiring chefs practice their craft. It's easier to get a reservation here than in Thomas Keller's hallowed halls; with several big dining rooms, the CIA can seat large numbers every night. And the ever-changing menu highlights the best of each season. If you get the right table, you can watch your food being prepared in the open kitchen. The wine list highlights the best of Napa Valley's vintages, and the student chefs plan menus with an eye to wine pairings.

### Calistoga

Small, homey Calistoga offers a pleasing combination of high-end California cuisine and simpler yet still delicious fare. If you need a break from rich, expensive food, a great place to stop for a meal sits right at the corner of Lincoln and Highway 29. **Buster's Barbecue and Bakery** (1207 Foothill Blvd., 707/942-5605, $4–10) brings unpretentious barbecue to Wine Country. At this walk-up eatery, you may find lines at lunch and dinner time—mostly locals looking for a good, quick meal. The simple fare includes huge hot dogs, homemade barbecued tri-tip sandwiches, barbecued pork, and chicken. You'll also have your pick of traditional sides (baked beans, slaw, potato salad, cornbread, and such) and Southern-style baked goods. The sweet potato pie is a reputed local favorite. Portions are huge, the quality rocks even for Wine Country food, and when they say that the "hot" barbecue sauce is serious, they really mean it.

## INFORMATION AND SERVICES

### Tourist Information

If you hit only one visitors center during your whole stay in California, make it one of the ones in the Napa Valley. Why? For the complimentary wine tasting passes. Tastings in the Napa region grow ever more expensive—you can easily spend $20–30 per person, per winery these days. But if you ask at the visitors centers, you can easily get up to six free passes for two tasters. That means you'll save $100–180 based on just 15 minutes chatting with a friendly local who can also direct you to the locals' favorite wineries, restaurants, and attractions, which tend to be cheaper and better than those that spend bucketloads of money on advertising.

The **Napa Valley Conference and Visitors Bureau** (1310 Napa Town Center, 707/226-7459, www.napavalley.org, daily 9 A.M.–5 P.M.), right in the middle of downtown Napa, is one good place to start; another is the **Yountville Chamber of Commerce** (6484 Washington St., 707/944-0904, http://yountville.com, daily 10 A.M.–5 P.M.), located right in the midst of the downtown main drag.

### Media and Communications

A plethora of publications offer all the information you could ever use to tour Wine Country. Most of the free magazines, which can be overwhelming in number when you see them in the racks, are available in hotels, inns, visitors centers, wineries, restaurants—wherever you look, really. For current events, ***Wine Country This Week*** (www.winecountrythisweek.com) has the best up-to-date information.

If it's the local news you're seeking, you can find it in the daily ***Napa Valley Register*** (www.napanews.com).

You will find a **post office** in most of the Napa Valley municipalities. In downtown Napa, one post office sits at 1351 Second Street (707/255-0621).

### Medical Services

For medical treatment (including alcohol

poisoning), the **Queen of the Valley** (1000 Trancas St., Napa. 707/257-4038, www.thequeen.org) has both a 24-hour emergency room/trauma center, and a by-appointment urgent care clinic.

## GETTING THERE AND AROUND

### Car

Think you're going to enjoy a lovely weekend wine tasting tour at the height of harvest season, bopping quickly from winery to winery without a care in the world? Think again. Many thousands of visitors from the Bay Area and all over the world will be plying the same two major Napa Valley wine routes. **Highway 29** runs through the center of the valley and becomes something akin to a 20-mile parking lot on weekend afternoons. It can take a ridiculous amount of time to get just from one winery to the next. **The Silverado Trail** isn't much better.



To get the best experience with the least traffic headaches, make a few adjustments to your plans:

1. Take your tasting tour on Monday, Tuesday, or Wednesday. These are the least popular days with the Bay Area weekend hordes.
2. Get going early. If you can stomach wine with breakfast, start your tour at 9–10 A.M., right when the tasting rooms start to open. If you can finish up with the wineries by noon or 1 P.M., you might be able to grab lunch in Calistoga and then go for a mud bath or a walk in the woods while everyone else is sitting in gridlock.
3. Consider postponing your Wine Country trip until the rainy season (Nov.–Feb.). This is the least popular season in Napa, since the grape vines are hibernating and the dank weather doesn't show off the valley to its most scenic advantage. But the wines still taste fabulous, and you'll avoid the worst car traffic and crowding in the tasting rooms. Heck, you might even get a chance to *talk* to your pourer about the vintages you're tasting!

Before beginning your trip, be sure to bring a map with you when you drive to Napa; it's not the most straightforward trip from the Bay Area or points east. From San Francisco, take the Golden Gate Bridge north across the Bay to U.S. 101. From there, pick up Highway 37 in Novato (you'll see signs on U.S. 101 directing you to Napa), which takes you right into the city of Napa. If you're staying in Calistoga or someplace farther north, continue on U.S. 101 all the way to Highway 128, which will take you straight into Calistoga.

If you're driving down to Napa from Sonoma, U.S. 101 to Highway 128 is your best option. This route also works if you're coming from the North Coast.

Driving from the East Bay? Take I-80 and turn off at Highway 37; you'll see the Six Flags amusement park at this freeway interchange. Highway 37 will take you all the way to Napa. This route also works for travelers coming from Lake Tahoe or the Sacramento/Gold Country area.

### Bus

The **VINE** bus (800/696-6443, www.nctpa.net/vine.cfm, Mon.–Fri. 5:20 A.M.–9:25 P.M., Sat. 6:30 A.M.–8:40 P.M., Sun. 8:30 A.M.–7 P.M., adults $1.25–2.75, youth $1–2) provides public transportation to the Napa Valley. Check the website for routes, stations, and fares. You can pay cash when you get on the bus, but you must have exact change.

### Wine Tours

A popular and wonderful way to tour the Napa Valley wineries is *not* to drive yourself. If you hire a limo or join up with a tour, no one in your party must abstain as the designated driver, and everyone has a better time because no one's worried about traffic. You'll find plenty of tour operators and limo companies in the area happy to take your reservations. Calling at least a few days in advance is recommended, or even earlier during late summer and fall. Expect to spend $100–300 on your tour or limo service, depending on the size of your party and the level of service and tour customizing you want.

**Napa Valley Wine Country Tours** (707/226-3333, www.winecountrylimos.com, $79/person, 11 A.M.–5 P.M.) runs a luxury van to some of the most prestigious wineries, plus a few great boutiques you might not be familiar with. With a flexible schedule and a 13-passenger limit, this tour makes a great choice for more serious cork dorks as well as Wine Country newcomers. A picnic lunch is included in this six-hour tour, though you're expected to pay your own tasting fees.

If you're in Napa with a small party or just your sweetie, consider hiring **Elegant Tours** (707/312-1352, www.elegantwinetours.com). Stretch limos in several styles are available, but so are smaller, unobtrusive sedans that can take smaller parties on custom tours. They'll take you tasting, to dinner, and to the airport.

For visitors looking to meet new people on their travels, a seat on the bus with **California Wine Tours and Transportation** (800/294-6386, www.californiawinetours.com) might be the perfect choice. Leaving from either Napa or San Francisco, these large package tours offer a great overview of the biggest Napa wineries. You'll be seated in a comfortable bus for the duration of the trip, swapping tasting notes with your fellow travelers. Or if you prefer a smaller tour of the more intimate winemakers, consider hiring one of the company's smaller vehicles for your trip.

### Walking Tours

Many Napa Valley towns invite walking tours—a great way to learn about the areas you're visiting and work off some of the rich food and wine at the same time. In downtown Napa, there's a short but fascinating self-guided walking tour at the **Historic Napa Mill** (500 Main St.). You can stroll the outer perimeter and then the inner corridors of this 100-plus-year-old building created by some of Napa's founders. Maps are available in front of some of the shops to guide you and teach you about the origins of each storefront. Expect this tour to take 30–60 minutes, depending on whether you stop to shop.

Another great place to take a historical walk is **Yountville** (Washington and Yount Sts.). Stop in at the visitors center to get a Historical Walking Tour map, then take off to explore the history of the town that's turned into the culinary mecca of California. Along the two-mile loop you'll see parks, the local pioneer cemetery, original Victorian homes, century-old storefronts, wineries, and much more. If you do the full loop and stop to admire the various sights, this walk may take you as much as 2–3 hours.



# Russian River Valley

The Russian River Valley may be the prettiest part of Wine Country. The Russian River runs through it, providing ample water for forests and meadows, as well as wide, calm spots with sandy banks. Rafting, canoeing, and kayaking opportunities abound on the zippier stretches of the river, making this area as much of destination for outdoor enthusiasts as for cork dorks. If you are visiting for the vino, the area called the "Russian River Valley" actually encompasses several prestigious AVAs, including Dry Creek, the Alexander Valley, and of course the Russian River.

A little to the west of the area's concentrated wine region, you'll reach the river in Guerneville—a noted gay and lesbian resort destination. Even if you're straight (but not narrow) you'll love the kitschy downtown, clothing-optional resorts, and general sense of friendliness and fun that permeate this area.

## WINERIES

### Hanna

The first thing you'll notice when you drive up to Hanna (5353 Occidental Rd., Santa Rosa, 707/575-3371, www.hannawinery.com, daily 10 A.M.–4 P.M.) is the stunning view down the hillside into the Alexander Valley. The tasting room is surrounded by vineyards climbing up the hills and flowing downward to the foot of the valley. The tasting room has plenty of windows and a broad wraparound porch to help you take in the vistas. But don't neglect the wines! Hanna offers a large list, plus a reserve tasting of their finest vintages. In addition to the inevitable Cabernet Sauvignons and Chardonnays, you might find some unusual varieties such as Malbec—ask nicely and you might even sneak a taste!

### Battaglini Estate Winery

Many large Russian River wineries make a wine out of every varietal under the hot Sonoma sun, but Battaglini Estate Winery (2948 Piner Rd., Santa Rosa, 707/578-4091, www.battaglini wines.com) has chosen instead to specialize. Inside the cute wood-paneled tasting room with the homey cluttered bar, you'll find only Zinfandels, Chardonnays, and Petit Sirahs. However, the expression of each of these grapes approaches perfection. You'll also see a few unusual manifestations, such as a late-harvest dessert Chardonnay. For the most fun you can have during the crowded harvest season, join Battaglini in the fall for a "Stomp" event, during which you'll literally take off your shoes and dive into a bucket of grapes.



### Tara Bella Winery

You must call ahead to arrange a private appointment if you want to visit the tiny, exclusive Tara Bella Winery (3701 Viking Rd., Santa Rosa, 707/544-9049, www.tarabellawinery.com). Tara Bella represents the ultimate in intimate family-owned wineries; the husband and wife team, Tara and Rich, tend their own vineyard, press their own grapes by hand, and make their own wine. From their eight-acre Russian River vineyard, they create *one* Cabernet Sauvignon each year. And each November, they release a new vintage to the public (most of which is snapped up by their wine club, though you can purchase a bottle if you taste at the winery). A visit to Tara Bella is a visit to the roots of California wine-family-owned and handcrafted, with a flavor all its own.

### Korbel Cellars

Champagne grapes like cooler climates, so it makes sense that Korbel Cellars (13250 River Rd., Guerneville, 707/824-7000, www.korbel .com, 9 A.M.–4:30 P.M., until 5 P.M. May–Oct., first three tastes free), the leading producer of California champagnes, maintains a winery and tasting room on the Sonoma coast. The large, lush estate welcomes visitors with elaborate landscaping and attractive buildings, including a small area serving as a visitors center. Tours of the estate are offered several times daily for a fee. Inside the tasting room, visitors get to sample far more than the ubiquitous Korbel Brut that appears each New Year's. Korbel makes and sells a wide variety of high-end champagnes, plus a few boutique still wines and a line of brandies. You can't taste the brandy (that's a different and harder-to-obtain liquor license), but you can purchase it from the winery store. The facility also has a full-service gourmet deli and picnic grounds for tasters who want to stop for lunch.

### Hop Kiln

Bringing truth in advertising to Sonoma, Hop Kiln (6050 Westside Rd., Healdsburg, 707/433-6491, www.hopkilnwinery.com, daily 10 A.M.–5 P.M.) winery is housed in an old hop kiln. Earlier in its history, the Russian River Valley grew more beer-making ingredients than grapes, and this distinctively shaped hop kiln dried the valley's crop each year. Today, you'll find an extensive wine tasting bar and gift shop inside the main kiln.

### J Winery

Unlike many wineries that cling to Old World traditions, J Winery (11447 Old Redwood Hwy., Healdsburg, 888/594-6326, www.jwine .com, Thurs.–Tues. 11 A.M.–4 P.M., $10–55) loves the cutting edge of the California wine scene. J specializes in sparkling wines, California style. Their tasting room is a triumph of modern design, and their tasting experience gives visitors a taste of the best that Wine Country has to offer. Instead of the standard tasting bar and pouring staff, J has tables and wait staff. And instead of just the standard one-ounce pour of a bunch of wines, you'll be served the wines with specially paired small

© LIZ HAMILL SCOTT

Hop Kiln winery, Russian River Valley

bites of high-end California cuisine prepared in J's own kitchens by their own team of gourmet chefs. You'll get the chance to taste J's sparkly vintages as they are meant to be enjoyed—with an array of (often spicy!) foods.

## Foppiano

One of the oldest wineries in the Russian River Valley, Foppiano (12707 Old Redwood Hwy., Healdsburg, 707/433-7272, www.foppiano.com) dates from 1896. Today Foppiano is still making a small list of premium red wines. Their signature wine is a legendary Petit Sirah, unusual for the area. They've also got a great Sangiovese, a Zin, a Cab, and a Merlot under the Foppiano label. A second label, Riverside, encompasses a few tasty but exceedingly inexpensive varietals that let drinkers on a budget enjoy Foppiano wines. Inside the farmhouse-style tasting room, enjoy sips of the various vintages. But also be sure to ask for Susan's recipes; the hospitality director and fourth-generation member of the Foppiano family creates and adapts dishes to match the family wines.

## Optima Wine Cellars

Mike Duffy started making homemade wine with his dad when he was less than 10 years old. He got his degree in winemaking (enology) from the prestigious UC Davis program, and from there on it was only a matter of time before he opened his own winery. Today, Optima Wine Cellars (498 "C" Moore Ln., Healdsburg, 707/431-8222, www.optimawinery.com, by appointment only) makes a small list of premium wines from single appellations within the Russian River Valley wine area. These include Cabernet Sauvignon, Zinfandel, and Chardonnay. They also produce a luscious Zinfandel port—perfect for dessert, or at the end of a long day of wine tasting.

## Dry Creek Vineyard

It seems odd that a winery named Dry Creek should have sailboats on all its labels, but that's the signature icon on each bottle produced by Dry Creek Vineyard (3770 Lambert Bridge Rd., Healdsburg, 800/864-9463, www.drycreekvineyard.com, daily 10:30 A.M.–4:30 P.M.,

$5–15). This mid-sized winery focuses much effort within its own appellation (Dry Creek, of course), producing many single-vineyard wines from grapes grown within a few miles of the estate. Other wines include grapes from the Russian River Valley appellation. Dry Creek prides itself on both its classic California varietals such as Chardonnay, Cabernet, and Merlot, and on occasionally hopping out of that box and producing something unusual, like a Musque, a Chenin Blanc, or a Sauternes-style dessert wine. Try as many as you can when you enter the ivy-covered tasting room, styled after a French chateau.



### A. Rafanelli

Tasting at A. Rafanelli (4685 W. Dry Creek Rd., Healdsburg, 707/433-1385, www.arafanelliwinery.com) feels just about as different from the standard big-business high-end wineries of Wine Country as it's possible to get. You can't just walk in to A. Rafanelli, since they offer tastings by appointment only. There's no marble-covered bar, no chic tasting room. Instead, you'll walk into the barrel room of the working winery and stand in the oak-and-grape-scented air on the concrete floor. The owner-winemaker will hand out glasses to your group, and you begin to taste some of the best red wines produced anywhere in Sonoma County. In a region where the phrase "Cab is king" comes up at almost every winery, Rafanelli's Cabernet Sauvignons are still special. If you can't taste at Rafanelli, look for their Zins and Cabs at local Sonoma restaurants, to whom they sell the bulk of their wholesale wines.

### Trentadue

As you walk up to the magnificent Italianate tasting room at Trentadue (19170 Geyserville Ave., Geyserville, 707/433-3104, www.trentadue.com, daily 10 A.M.–5 P.M., $5), the first thing you'll notice are the gardens sweeping out toward the vineyards. Many of Trentadue's vintages get made from estate-grown grapes, and the gorgeous grounds surrounding the winery get used for weddings and events almost every weekend. Inside the tall, narrow tasting room you'll find European-style decor, the usual gifts (including bottled water and nonalcoholic drinks), and a sometimes-too-small-for-the-crowd tasting bar. Trentadue offers a wide variety of still wines and a couple of sparklers. But the stars of Trentadue's show are unquestionably the ports. Trentadue makes an array of different styles and flavors of the famed fortified dessert wines. Any chocolate lover will need to take home a bottle of their Chocolate Amore. Trentadue offers a "port club" that sends members several bottles of different ports each year.

### White Oak

At White Oak (7505 Hwy. 128, Healdsburg, 707/433-8429, www.whiteoakwinery.com, daily 10 A.M.–5 P.M.), you'll find a wonderful combination of whimsy and wine. This Spanish mission–inspired winery complex is surrounded by green gardens dotted with fun sculptures. Beyond the gardens, estate vineyards grow grapes for Old Vine Zinfandels and other fine wines. Go inside to taste some of those wines—the tasting list is small but prestigious. While white wine drinkers enjoy the Sauvignon Blanc and Chardonnay, big reds are the specialty of the house. Cabernet Sauvignon and Zinfandel lovers flock to White Oak for the fabulous regular releases and occasional special library selections. Tours at White Oak give participants a special look at wine tasting, describing and illustrating the various components that make up a wine's fragrance.

### Ferrari-Carano

One of the best large wineries in Dry Creek Valley, Ferrari-Carano (8761 Dry Creek Rd., Healdsburg, 707/433-6700, www.ferrari-carano.com, daily 10 A.M.–5 P.M., $5–35) provides great standard and reserve wines in an upscale tasting room and winery facility. Upstairs you'll get to taste from Ferrari-Carano's large menu of large-production, moderately priced whites and reds. Downstairs, enjoy the elegant lounge area, which includes comfortable seating and a video describing the F-C winemaking process, from grape to glass. Look down into one of the major barrel storage areas, where F-C's wines age right before your eyes. And finally, open the glass doors and enter the reserve tasting room, where for an additional fee you can taste the best of F-C's vintages—smaller runs that are mostly bold, assertive reds. Back upstairs you can also browse the larger-than-average gift shop for gourmet edible goodies, wine and kitchen gadgets, and Ferrari-Carano logowear.

### Raymond Burr

As well as portraying detective Perry Mason on the famous 1980s TV series, Raymond Burr had a second life as a wine connoisseur and orchid lover. He, along with his partner Robert Benevides, combined these loves to create the Raymond Burr Vineyards (8339 West Dry Creek Rd., 888/900-0024, www.raymondburrvineyards.com, daily 11 A.M.–5 P.M. by appointment only). You'll drive up a bumpy driveway past the greenhouse to reach the parking lot. Wine seekers then enter the tiny (by Wine Country standards) tasting room to sip a few of the Burr label vintages. Frankly, most of the wines are tasty but not amazing compared to some other Sonoma products. But the staff and the winery's cats are fun and friendly, the views from the tasting room porch out over the valley are stunning, and the tiny bar and small-town experience are reminiscent of an early time in the Wine Country.

Flower lovers must come on specific days or make an appointment in advance to take a tour of the greenhouses. Burr and Benevides have bred more than a thousand new orchid varieties, and you'll get to see many of them here on the estate.

## SIGHTS

There's lots to do in the Russian River Valley besides taste wine—especially in and around Santa Rosa. Spend a day exploring an array of museums the likes of which you won't find elsewhere in the state.

### Charles M. Schulz Museum

Charles Schulz drew the world-famous Peanuts comic strip for almost 50 years, and from 1958 until his death in 2000, he lived in Sonoma County. In honor of Schulz and the Peanuts gang, the Charles M. Schulz Museum and Research Center (2301 Hardies Ln., Santa Rosa, 707/579-4452, www.schulzmuseum.org, Mon. and Wed.–Fri. 11 A.M.–5 P.M., Sat.–Sun. 10 A.M.–5 P.M., adults $8, seniors/children $5) opened in 2002. Inside the 27,000-square-foot building, which somehow manages to look like it comes from a four-inch comic strip, you'll find an incredible wealth of multimedia art, original drawings, and changing exhibitions based on the works of Charles Schulz. No matter how many times you visit, you're likely to see something new in the ever-changing exhibits. Plenty of permanent collections provide stability and a base for the museum's theme. The museum owns most of the original Peanuts strips, a large collection of Schulz's personal possessions, and an astonishing array of tribute artwork (from everyone from other comic strip artists to urban installation designers the world over). Outside the building, the grounds include attractive gardens, the Snoopy Labyrinth, and even the infamous Kite-Eating Tree.

Schulz's influence is felt outside the museum property as well. Across the street you can skate at Snoopy's Home Ice. (Schulz was an avid hockey player for most of his life.) And throughout downtown Santa Rosa, especially in Historic Railroad Square, you'll see colorful sculptures depicting favorite members of the Peanuts gang brightening the streets, making people smile.

### Pacific Coast Air Museum

Even if you're not an aviation buff, the Pacific Coast Air Museum (2230 Becker Blvd., Santa Rosa, 707/575-7900, http://pacificcoastairmuseum.org, Tues., Thurs., Sat.–Sun. 10 A.M.–4 P.M.) is worth a stop. Through interpretive and photographic exhibits, learn about the history of aviation in America. Spend some time studying the cutaways and bits and pieces to enhance your understanding of the mechanics of powered flights. And finally, fantasize about flying the fine examples of F-series

WINE COUNTRY

fighters and many other military and civilian aircraft on display. Many of the planes here are examples of modern war machines—such as those you'd see on the deck of an aircraft carrier in the Persian Gulf today. Or if you prefer to see civilian craft, check out the funky little Pitts aerobatic plane, the sort of thing you'll see doing impossible-looking tricks during the museum's annual **Wings over Wine Country** air show, held each August.



### Luther Burbank Home and Gardens

If you love plants and gardening, don't miss the Luther Burbank Home and Gardens (Sonoma and Santa Rosa Aves., Santa Rosa, 707/524-5445, www.lutherburbank.org, gardens 8 A.M.–dusk year-round, tours Apr.–Oct. Tues.–Sun. 10 A.M.–4 P.M., fee). Luther Burbank personally created (using hybridization techniques) some of the most popular plants growing in California gardens and landscapes today. You don't have to go to his gardens to see examples of his famous Shasta Daisy—an incredibly hardy pure-white daisy hybrid that now covers vast areas throughout the state. But you will see them in the Luther Burbank gardens within the more than acre's worth of horticulture ranging from medicinal herbs through showy roses. Check the website for a list of what's in bloom during your visit, as something will be showing off its finest flowers every month of the year!

### Sonoma County Wine Library

If you're a serious student of wine, don't miss out on the Sonoma County Wine Library (Piper and Center Sts. at the Healdsburg Regional Library, Healdsburg, 707/433-3772, www.sonomalibrary.org/wine). This public library extension contains a collection of over 5,000 books on wine, subscriptions to more than 80 wine periodicals, photos, prints, wine labels, and an online resource for wine lovers at http://winefiles.org. Among the 1,000 or so rare wine books, you'll find treatises on the history, business, and art of wine from back as far as 1512. The library is a perfect place for wine drinkers who want to take their habit or hobby to the next level.

### Hand Fan Museum

Yes, you really can visit a museum dedicated exclusively to the display and description of hand fans. The tiny Hand Fan Museum of Healdsburg (327A Healdsburg Ave. at the Healdsburg Hotel, 707/431-2500, www.handfanmuseum.com, Wed.–Sun. 11 A.M.–4 P.M.) seeks to tell the cultural histories of Europe, America, and Asia through the creation, decoration, and use of fans. It doesn't take long to view and enjoy both the permanent collection and seasonal exhibits at this fun little museum. You might be surprised to discover the level of artistry put into some of the fans here, be they paper or lace, antique or modern. And you'll learn a little bit about how fans were and are used in various societies (the 17th–19th-century courting practices and sexual invitations in some European countries included intricate movements of a lady's fan, directed at the gentleman of the hour).

## ENTERTAINMENT AND EVENTS

### Bars and Clubs

One way to taste wines from a wider variety of vineyards is to stop into a wine bar. **Willi's Wine Bar** (4404 Old Redwood Hwy., Santa Rosa, 707/526-3096, www.williswinebar.net, Wed.–Thurs. 11:30 A.M.–9:30 P.M., Fri.–Sat. 11:30 A.M.–10 P.M., Sun.–Mon. 5–9:30 P.M.) offers flights of small pours and bottles of high-end vintages from Sonoma, Napa, and around the world. To go with their wines, this upscale establishment offers cheese plates, charcuterie plates, and small plates of haute cuisine. Your server should be able to advise you as to which plates pair best with which wines. For a more casual wine bar atmosphere, drop in at **The Wine Shop** (331 Healdsburg Ave., Healdsburg, 707/433-0433).

Want to find a bar that *doesn't* pander to the ubiquitous wine trade? Check out the **Sonoma Brewing Company** (725 Fourth St., Santa Rosa, 707/545-2237, www.russianriverbrewing

.com, Sun.–Thurs. 11 A.M.–midnight, Fri.–Sat. 11 A.M.–1 A.M.), which both makes and serves lots and lots of beer. And what goes better with beer than pizza? The food menu leans heavily on pizza and calzones to satisfy folks who build up their appetites by trying the various (strong!) local brews. The brew pub also acts as a venue for local and regional blues, funk, and jazz bands—Saturday, Sunday, and Wednesday nights feature live music.

Guerneville wouldn't be a proper gay resort town without at least a couple of good gay bars creating a proper nightlife for visitors and locals alike. The most visible and funky looking (from the outside) of these is the **Rainbow Cattle Company** (16220 Main St., Guerneville, 707/869-0206, www.queersteer.com). Mixing the vibes of a down-home country saloon with happenin' San Francisco nightspot, the Rainbow serves up cold drinks and hot men with equal abandon. Think cocktails in Mason jars, wood paneling, and leather nights. And yet this is just the kind of queer bar where you can bring your mom or your straight-but-not-narrow friends, and they'll have just as much fun as you do.

Both the ladies and the dudes, and even the straights, come out to dance and party at **Liquid Sky** (16225 Main St., Guerneville, 707/869-9910). Right across the street from the Rainbow, Liquid Sky lures DJs up from the Bay Area to spin for the dancing, groping crowds that populate the floor. Call or drop by to get the low-down on parties going on when you're in town.

## Live Music

Live music venues are few and far between in the Russian River region. But for big shows, you can get tickets for the **Wells Fargo Center for the Arts** (50 Mark West Springs Rd., Santa Rosa, 707/546-3600, http://wellsfargocenterarts.org, ticket prices vary by show). This full-sized theater hosts any number of national acts each year (plus the occasional play or headlining comic). You might see Melissa Etheridge, the Beach Boys, or Donna Summer at this Santa Rosa concert hall.

## Theater

Wine makes many people think of high art and high culture. Accordingly, Sonoma County supports a number of theater groups that put up everything from funky black-box originals to big-budget Broadway musicals. The **Sonoma County Repertory Theater** (104 N. Main St., Sebastopol, 707/823-0177, http://the-rep.com, adults $23, children/seniors $18) sits in Sebastopol, producing a mix of beloved classics like *Taming of the Shrew* and *A Christmas Carol,* plus a generous helping of newer works such as *Rabbit Hole.* While the weekend prices are reasonable, the Sonoma Rep also has "Pay What You Can" Thursdays; you walk up to the door on Thursday evening, and if tickets are left for the show, you can get in for whatever price you deem to be reasonable.

The **Raven Players** (115 North St., Healdsburg, 707/433-6335, www.ravenplayers.org, adults $18–25, seniors/students $15) ply their art in the boutique town of Healdsburg. This ambitious company stages five plays per year—primarily award-winning and established works, such as Arthur Miller's *After the Fall* and Christopher Durang's *Beyond Therapy.* For their last show each season, the Ravens produce a big, dramatic musical; the last two were *Evita* and *Miss Saigon.*

## Festivals and Events

One of the biggest annual events in this agricultural region is the **Sonoma County Fair** (1350 Bennett Valley Rd., Santa Rosa, 707/545-4200, www.sonomacountyfair.com), held over two weeks at the end of July. Even the biggest Sonoma wineries prize the awards they win at their local county fair, and you'll see fair ribbons displayed proudly in many a Russian River tasting room. If you're lucky enough to be able to attend, you'll find far more than just wine—live entertainment acts, family shows, and an amazing array of contests and exhibitions featuring the work of folks from all over the Sonoma region. Live horse racing and an adjacent golf course round out the many attractions.

On the other hand, the **Harvest Fair** (1350

Bennett Valley Rd., Santa Rosa, www.sonomacountyfair.com, Oct.), also held on the Sonoma County Fairgrounds in Santa Rosa, focuses almost exclusively on competition between wineries and farmers in Sonoma County. All the growers and vintners gather their finest produce and pit it against their local competitors' items.

## SPORTS AND RECREATION

### Hot Air Ballooning



Just as in Napa, one of the popular ways to get a great view of the Russian River Valley is from the basket of a hot air balloon. Granted, you and your hangover must fall out of bed *before* dawn for this particular treat—so you might want to make this a first-day adventure before you start wine tasting. **Above the Wine Country** (meeting site at Kal's Kaffe Mocha, 397 Aviation Blvd., Santa Rosa, 707/538-7359, www.balloontours.com, adults $225, children $195, flights daily) can get you up in the air to start the day high above Wine Country. This big company maintains a whole fleet of balloons, which can carry 2–16 passengers. Expect your total experience time to be 3–4 hours, with 1–1.5 hours in the air.

### Hiking

The Russian River Valley offers a wide variety of hiking trails suited to everyone from sedate walkers to brawny backpackers. Many of these lie away from central Wine Country, out in the mountains near the river itself and Guerneville. One of the best of these spots is undoubtedly **Armstrong Redwoods** (17000 Armstrong Woods Rd., Guerneville, 707/869-2015, ww.parks.ca.gov, daily 8 A.M.–sunset, $6). It's an easy, five-minute drive from Guerneville on one mostly straight road. This little redwoods park often gets overlooked, which makes it a little bit less crowded than some of the most popular North Coast and Sierra redwood forests. But you can still get a fabulous hike in here—either a short stroll in the shade of the trees or a multi-day backcountry adventure. The easiest walk ever to a big tree is the 0.1-mile stagger from the visitors center to the tallest tree in the park, named the **Parson Jones Tree.** If you saunter another half-mile, you'll reach the **Armstrong Tree,** which grows next to the Armstrong Pack Station—your first stop if you're doing the heavy-duty hiking thing. From the Pack Station, another quarter-mile of moderate hiking gets you to the **Icicle Tree.** If you want more advice on the trails here, stop in and talk to the rangers at the visitors center; they're both knowledgeable and helpful, and love to share information about their park.

Bored with redwoods and yearning for a different landscape? Right next to Armstrong sits the **Austin Creek State Recreation Area** (17000 Armstrong Woods Rd., Guerneville, 707/869-2015, www.parks.ca.gov. 8 A.M.–sunset, $6 per vehicle) It's rough going (2.5 miles of steep, narrow, treacherous dirt road) to get to the main entrance and parking area. No vehicles over 20 feet long and no trailers of any kind are permitted. But once you're in, some great—and very difficult—hiking awaits you. The eponymous **Austin Creek Trail** (4.7 miles one-way) takes you down from the hot meadows into the cool forest fed by Austin Creek. To avoid monotony on this challenging route, create a loop by taking the turn onto the **Gilliam Creek Trail** (4 miles one-way). This way you get to see another of the park's cute little creeks as you walk back to your starting point.

### Biking

Bicycling is a popular way of exploring Wine Country, and Sonoma is a major bicyclists' mecca, boasting some of the finest road biking anywhere in the world. Out in the Russian River Valley, you can find easy tours, more strenuous trail rides, and even some mountain biking possibilities.

Newcomers to bike touring in the area can choose from several reputable touring companies that can get them up on the saddle and pointed in the right direction. **Wine Country Bikes** (61 Front St., Healdsburg, 866/922-4537, www.winecountrybikes.com, $129/person) sits right on the square in downtown Healdsburg. Its Classic Wine Tour starts at 10 A.M. and runs until 3:30 P.M. During your leisurely pedal through the Dry Creek region, you'll get to stop and taste wine, take walks in vineyards, and learn more about the history of wine in this small, proud appellation. A gourmet picnic lunch is included with your bike tour. From there, the tours get longer and/or more luxurious—check the website for information about multi-day bike tour packages that include accommodations. For independent souls who prefer to carve their own routes, Wine Country Bikes also rents road bikes, tandem bikes, and hybrids that you can also take out on moderate park trails that permit biking.

To become a part of the larger bicycling culture in the area, consider participating in the annual **Harvest Century Bicycle Tour** (www.healdsburg.com/chamber/bike_tour, July). This event requires some degree of physical fitness, since riders must register to ride 23-, 37-, or 60-mile routes. The roads are moderate, however; while you'll find some inclines, experienced cyclists won't be tortured so much as to preclude enjoying the rest of the day with great food, wine, and the companionship of plenty of like-minded souls.

### Water Sports

Between the various creeks, Spring Lake, Lake Sonoma, and the Russian River, it's no wonder that many people view the Russian River Valley as a recreation destination as much as a wine region.

Guerneville and its surrounding forest land act as the center for fun on the river. **Russian River Adventures** (www.rradventures.info) offers guided paddles down a secluded section of the river in stable, sturdy inflatable canoes. Dogs, children, and even infants are welcomed by Russian River Adventures. The trip usually lasts 4–5 hours, with little white water and lots of serene shaded pools.

Fly-fishers can cast their lines out into the Russian River, hunting for some seriously enormous trout. A couple of recommended spots include the Wohler Bridge (9765 Wohler Rd., Forestville) and Steelhead Beach (9000 River Rd., Forestville).

At the north end of the valley, **Lake Sonoma** (3333 Skaggs Springs Rd., Geyserville, 707/433-2200, www.parks.sonoma.net/laktrls.html) sprawls in a series of skinny fingers, holding water for both recreation and more practical uses. A public boat launch at Warm Springs Bridge lets you launch your own ski or fishing boats for a $3 fee. A marina (Stewart's Point Rd.) offers boat rentals (plus slip rentals) for guests who don't have their own. Bass anglers school at the Warm Springs Creek and Dry Creek fingers of the lake, where trees shade the water and create a hospitable home for bass, perch, catfish, and sunfish.

A smaller but also less crowded lake, **Spring Lake** (391 Violetti Dr., Santa Rosa, www.sonoma-county.org/parks/pk_slake.htm, parking $6) has a bit more in the way of quiet and solitude than its bigger brethren. Anglers can launch electric-motor boats (but not gas-powered boats) into Spring Lake anglers out to stalk the wily largemouth bass. Lifeguards watch over a cordoned swimming lagoon that's perfect for kids, and the nearby concession stand rents paddle boats and canoe-like craft during the summertime.

## ACCOMMODATIONS

It's easy to find a place to stay in the Russian River Valley. Even the smaller towns perched along the state roads host any number of inns and cabins. For a more elegant hostelry, plan to stay in one of the luxury hotels or resorts in Santa Rosa or Healdsburg.

### Santa Rosa

In the big city of Santa Rosa, you'll find all the familiar chain motels you can imagine. You'll also see a few charming inns and upper-tier hotels that show off the unique aspects of the city that divides the Bay Area from true Northern California.

The **Sandman Motel** (3421 Cleveland Ave., 707/544-8570, www.sonoma.com/lodging/sandman, $90–135) offers clean, comfortable motel rooms for pleasantly reasonable prices. The guest rooms are decorated in a standard motel style, with dark carpets and floral bedspreads. Amenities include a big heated swimming pool, outdoor whirlpool tub (heated year-round), coffee and continental breakfast in the lobby each morning, and in-room refrigerators and satellite TVs. The Sandman is a great place to bring the family.

At the corner of Historic Railroad Square, **Hotel la Rose** (308 Wilson St., 800/527-6738, www.hotellarose.com, $110–300) exemplifies the luxury hotel concept as it has evolved over 100 years. The stone-clad main building rises high over Railroad Square, with more rooms available in the more modern carriage house just across the street. Because Hotel la Rose has only 47 guest rooms, you'll see an attention to detail and level of service that's missing in the larger motels and hotels in the area. The carriage house offers modern decor and amenities, and each large room and suite feels light and bright. In the Main Building, you'll find an older style of elegance, with antique furniture and floral wallpaper appealing to guests who want a taste of what the hotel might have been like back in 1907. A quick trip downstairs takes you to the breakfast room, where you'll get your complimentary continental breakfast each morning, and across to Josef's—one of the finest restaurants in the city.

At the north end of Santa Rosa, convenient to the major Russian River wine roads, you can stay at the lovely upscale **Vintners Inn** (4350 Barnes Rd., 800/421-2584, http://vintnersinn.com, $225–500). The low, attractive red-tiled-roof buildings that comprise the inn and the fabulous John Ash & Co. restaurant sit adjacent to a large stretch of vineyard. Every room has a king-sized bed, fluffy down bedding, and patio or balcony overlooking a cute gardenlike courtyard. Many rooms boast fireplaces and spa tubs, and all feature luxurious appointments. Your stay includes a full breakfast each morning, plus access to the inn's outdoor whirlpool tub and the common den with fireplace. The only downside to the Vintners Inn is its regrettable proximity to a local power station, so just try to look in the other direction when you're admiring the view.

## Sebastopol

In Sebastopol, the best place to stay is the expensive but lovely **Avalon, a Luxury Bed and Breakfast** (11910 Graton Rd., 707/824-0880, www.avalonluxuryinn.com, $375). With only three rooms, the Avalon offers the ultimate in private and romantic accommodations. All rooms have king beds, a hot tub or access to the garden hot tub, a fireplace, air conditioning, and many luxurious amenities. Because Avalon was purpose-built as a B&B, each room is actually a suite, with plenty of space to spread out and enjoy a longer stay. At breakfast time, you'll be served an organic feast, with produce purchased from a local CSA and a loving attention to the details of preparation.

## Guerneville

Because it's the major resort town for lovers of Russian River recreation, you'll find a couple dozen B&Bs and cabin resorts in town. Many of these spots are gay-friendly, some with clothing-optional hot tubs and such.

The **Sonoma Orchid Inn** (12850 River Rd., 888/877-4466, www.sonomaorchidinn.com, $165–270, pets welcome) experience is made by its amazing owners. They've created beautiful guest rooms with elegant linens and furniture, plus just enough tchotchkes to keep things interesting. The best (and spendiest) rooms have satellite TVs with TiVo as well as DVD players and VCRs, and microwaves and small refrigerators. On the economy end of the spectrum, rooms are tiny but cute, with private baths and pretty decorations. But best of all, the owners of the Orchid will offer to help you with absolutely everything you need. They not only recommend restaurants and spas, they'll make reservations for you. They've got opinions about the local wineries, hikes, river spots, and just about everything else in the region. The Orchid makes a perfect inn for visitors who've never been to the area before—they're dog friendly, clothing-mandatory, and welcoming to travelers of all persuasions.

On the gay resort end of the spectrum, there's the **Russian River Resort** (16390 Fourth St., 707/869-0691, www.russianriverresort.com,

$110–220, two-night minimum May–Oct.). This absolutely adults-only resort offers economical but comfortable accommodations, a popular pool, a hot tub, and a near-endless stream of entertainment and events on-site and in town. An equal opportunity resort, both gay men and lesbians (and a few liberal straights) stay here regularly. Granted, many of the pool parties tend toward the masculine, but there's plenty of fun for anybody's who's interested in finding it here. The RRR isn't clothing optional, because it's got two restaurants and a bar on-site. It is dog-friendly, though it's got a no-dogs-on-holiday-weekends policy.

### Healdsburg

Travelers planning to stay a night in Healdsburg had best get their credit cards ready. None of the boutique inns and hotels in this utterly yuppified town come cheap. But if you pick a room at the **Honor Mansion** (14891 Grove St., 707/433-4277, www.honormansion.com, $245–660), you probably won't feel like all that cash went to waste. Each of the 13 rooms and suites has been furnished and decorated with exquisite attention to even the smallest details. Whatever room you choose, you'll be overwhelmed with luxury, and want to spend all day every day in the soft cocoon of your oversized elegant feather bed. All rooms have private baths (at these prices, they'd better!) stocked with high-end toiletries, TVs, CD players, bathrobes, phones, air conditioning, turn-down service, and more. Naturally, all rooms come with a full gourmet breakfast each morning. The Honor Mansion also has a lap pool, tennis court, croquet lawn, bocce pit, and outdoor professional massage service.

Set on the central town plaza, the **Hotel Healdsburg** (25 Matheson St., 707/431-2800, www.hotelhealdsburg.com, $290–870) is a local icon. The 55-room boutique hotel offers the most posh amenities, including Frette towels and linens, TVs with DVD players, soaking tubs and walk-in showers, and beautiful decor. Your guest room will great you with shining wood floors and furniture, Tibetan throw rugs, and spotless white down comforters. All rooms include free Wi-Fi and a gourmet breakfast, among other amenities, and guests can enjoy the outdoor pool, fitness center, and full-service day spa.

**Raford House Bed and Breakfast Inn** (10630 Wohler Rd., 800/887-9503, www.rafordhouse.com, $165–260) offers Healdsburg-level luxury at slightly less stratospheric prices than its nearby competitors. Each of the six rooms has a queen bed, air conditioning, a CD player, and a private bath. Some have fireplaces, oversized showers, and other luxury amenities. All rooms have been decorated with an attractive minimalist-Victorian style that feels historic but doesn't overwhelm a modern guest. Every morning, the Raford serves up a hearty country breakfast—the perfect start to a day of wine tasting.

### Geyserville

In tiny Geyserville, the B&Bs to visit are the ☾ **Hope-Merrill and Hope-Bosworth Houses** (21238 and 21253 Geyserville Ave., 800/825-4233, www.hope-inns.com, $165–310). This Victorian charmer, which does in fact include two separate historic houses across the street from one another, harkens to classic B&Bs on the East Coast. The owners come from Back East, and they've brought their traditions and aesthetics with them out to the Alexander Valley. If loud floral wallpaper covering every surface of your bedroom causes nightmares and hallucinations, this might not be the inn for you. But true aficionados of the Victorian style will love the flowers, lace, frills, and geegaws. Amenities include a pool and two hot tubs, plenty of common space in both houses, Friday evening wine tastings out in the yard, and an enormous, homemade, multi-course breakfast each morning. At breakfast, the owners preside over the tables, offering touring advice to guests. Each room has its own private bath—most in the same room, and one or two lying just across the room. The most comfortable rooms with the good mattresses tend to be the spendier rooms—if you're in a less-expensive room, you may find yourself with less-than-plush pillows. But overall, the Hope Houses make for a great base from which to explore the Alexander, Dry Creek, and Russian River Valley wineries.

## FOOD

### Santa Rosa

**John Ash & Co.** (4350 Barnes Rd., 707/527-7687, www.vintnersinn.com, $30–50) stands out as one of the best high-end California cuisine restaurants in the Russian River region. This large dining room is part of the Vintners Inn, and the only unappetizing thing about it is its location across the street from a power plant. Try not to think about it as you step in to the elegant dining room done up in the Mediterranean style. The food runs to pure California cuisine in the Wine Country style, with lots of local and sustainable produce prepared to show off its natural flavors. The menu runs fairly short, making it easy to choose from each of the three courses (often highlighting seafood, beef, lamb, and seasonal specialties). And of course, the wine list at John Ash & Co. is something special. They've got some amazing local vintages that are tough to find anywhere outside of the Russian River Valley. Be sure to ask your server for assistance with the wine list—it's worth it to get the lowdown on the best wines they've got in your price range.

**Josef's** (308 Wilson St., 707/571-8664, www.josefsrestaurant.com, lunch Tues.–Fri., dinner daily, $20–32), a quiet little restaurant inside the historic Hotel la Rose, offers fine French food in a romantic setting. The low-key decor belies the elegance of the cuisine served here. The menu offers a mix of truly classic French dishes, such as mussels, sole amandine, and beef bourguignon, and interesting California twists like Asian- and Middle Eastern–spiced dishes. While the wine list has lots of great local selections, it includes fine vintages from around the world as well. Open for lunch during the week and serving breakfast to hotel guests only, Josef's offers opportunities to enjoy fine meals in smaller portions and at smaller prices.

Need something a bit more casual? Get in line for breakfast (or brunch, or lunch) at the **Omelet Express** (112 Fourth St., 707/525-1690, www.omelette.com, Mon.–Fri. 6:30 A.M.–3 P.M., Sat.–Sun. 7 A.M.–4 P.M.). Owned by local character Don Taylor, who might even be acting as host at the front door on weekends, this spot is definitely ruled by locals. Don calls many of his customers by their first names, but he also welcomes newcomers with enthusiasm. After a stint waiting on line (it seems like all of Santa Rosa makes it down here for weekend brunch), you'll get seated in one of the ultra-casual dining rooms decorated with the front ends of classic cars of a certain stripe. The menu runs to—surprise—lots and lots of omelets. Dishes are huge, and come with a side of toast made with honest-to-goodness homemade bread, so consider splitting with a friend. For a tremendous and delicious breakfast to start your day, you really can't do better than Omelet Express, especially for the moderate prices charged here.

### Sebastopol

A great break from the endless fancy food is to find yourself a nice ethnic restaurant. In Sebastopol, one of the best of these is the **Himalayan Tandoori and Curry House** (969 Gravenstein Hwy. S., 707/829-2679, $10–16), which serves up Indian food in the Himalayan style. You'll find both vegetable curries and meat tandoori here, both properly spicy, as well as fresh naan, spicy rice pudding, and all sorts of Eastern treats. You'll even get a break from the endless river of wine, since there's plenty of beer on the drinks menu.

### Guerneville

At **Charizma Wine Lounge & Deli** (16337 Main St., 707/869-0909, www.charizmawinelounge.com, Mon.–Tues. 11:30 A.M.–9 P.M., Wed 11:30 A.M.–4 P.M., Thurs. 11:30 A.M.–10 P.M., Fri.–Sat. 10 A.M.–10 P.M., Sun. 10 A.M.–9 P.M., $10–19), you can get a cheeseburger with your 2001 Cabernet. Milkshakes are also a specialty of this fun, casual spot. Wine geeks can sip wine and nibble brie on comfortable sofas, or belly up to the redwood bar. Culinary enthusiasts might even find a cooking class held on the premises!

A focal point of downtown Guerneville, **Main Street Station** (16280 Main St., 707/869-0501, www.mainststation.com, daily) offers a big menu filled with homey, casual grub. The Station's mainstay is its handmade pizzas; you can grab a quick slice for lunch, or bring friends and order a whole pie for dinner. In the evenings, locals and visitors come down to munch sandwiches and pizza, drink beer, and listen to live entertainment on the small stage. Though live folk, jazz, blues, and even comedy happen every single night, this tiny venue gets crowded when a popular act comes to town. Consider making reservations in advance to assure yourself of a seat.

### Healdsburg

In a sea of self-conscious, chi-chi restaurants cluttering Healdsburg, the **Healdsburg Charcuterie & Cafe** (335 Healdsburg Ave., 707/431-7213, Mon.–Thurs. 11 A.M.–3 P.M., 5:30–9 P.M., Fri.–Sat. noon–3:30 P.M., 5:30–9:30 P.M., Sun. noon–3:30 P.M., 5–9 P.M., $13.50–21.50) makes diners feel at home. With a cute but not annoying pig theme, local art on the walls, and a softly romantic atmosphere, the Charcuterie makes a great option for a romantic but not overwhelming dinner out. The house-cured pork tenderloin sandwich is the house specialty, but vegetarians certainly can find a tasty and well-prepared meal here. The Charcuterie pours some lovely local vintages and offers wine flights.

The most famous restaurant in Healdsburg is probably the **Dry Creek Kitchen** (317 Healdsburg Ave., 707/431-0330, www.charliepalmer.com/dry_creek/home.html, Fri.–Sun. 11:30 A.M.–2:30 P.M., Sun.–Thurs. 5:30–9:30 P.M., Fri.–Sat. 5:30–10 P.M., $26–38). This chic Charlie Palmer dining room takes the concept of California cuisine to the next level. Expect to see foam, froth, jus, and coulis splattered across the menu, which can range from upscale-but-recognizable to totally bizarre. The Dry Creek Kitchen serves brunch and lunch on the weekends, offering its own unique take on eggs Benedict, sliders, and other standards. This is a great place to check out some Dry Creek appellation vintages.

### Geyserville

*The* restaurant offering in Geyserville is **Taverna Santi** (21047 Geyserville Ave., 707/857-1790, www.tavernasanti.com, daily 11:30 A.M.–2 P.M., Mon.–Sat. 5:30–9 P.M., Sun. 5–9 P.M., $18–35). This elegant Italian eatery allows only the teensiest of California twists to interfere with its cuisine. Even truly Italian staples that rarely make American menus (such as tripe) can be found here. Santi cures many of its own sausages and meat products, and makes much of its own pasta. For a serious Italian feast, order a full four-course meal with one item from each menu category. Lighter eaters might enjoy a "first course" dish of pasta as their entrée. Service at Santi can be spotty (but not awful), though the dimly lit, softly colored dining room makes it easier to pay attention to your sweetie across the table and forget for a few minutes that your appetizers are overdue.

## INFORMATION AND SERVICES

In the Russian River region, you'll find a number of different Visitors Centers, though not necessarily in the spots you'd expect. Yes, there's a California Welcome Center in Santa Rosa, but frankly it's not the best source of local Russian River wine country information. A better spot, though it's off the beaten wine paths, is the **Russian River Chamber of Commerce and Visitor Center** (16209 First St., Guerneville, 707/869-9000, http://russianriver.com) in downtown Guerneville. Here you'll find local staff who can give you serious local recommendations not only for wineries, but for river recreation, restaurants, and other less-traveled local attractions.

The serious local daily newspaper is the ***Santa Rosa Press Democrat*** (www.pressdemocrat.com). Check the Living and Entertainment sections for tourist information. You can also check out the many wine country guides that proliferate in the tasting rooms, motels, and inns of the Russian River region.

As a major city, Santa Rosa has plenty of available medical services. If you need help, try to get to **Santa Rosa Memorial Hospital** (1165 Montgomery Ave., 707/546-3210, www.santarosamemorial.org), which includes an emergency room.

## GETTING THERE AND AROUND

To reach the Russian River Valley, take Highway 101 from the north or south right into the midst of the Valley. Highway 101 runs through Santa Rosa, Windsor, Healdsburg, and Geyserville, making access to the restaurants, inns, and shopping easy enough—in theory.

So what's the problem? In a misguided (and failed) attempt to discourage traffic in the area, Sonoma has refused for years to widen Highway 101 in key areas through the Russian River Valley. The too-narrow highway leads to traffic slowdowns at commute hours and massive jams when accidents happen. Expect slow traffic through and south of Santa Rosa most of the time.

The good news is that you leave Highway 101 to get to the Russian River wineries. To get to Guerneville, your best route is State Highway 116. In that direction less traffic and pretty forests make for a more serene on-the-road experience.

For wine and kitsch, you can take a horse-drawn carriage tour of the Sonoma Valley, stopping to taste wine along the way. The **Flying Horse Carriage Company** (707/849-8989, www.flyinghorse.org, $145) will take you off the paved roads and out into the vineyards of the Alexander Valley region. Here you'll get to see the wine grapes growing right in front of you as you slow down to really enjoy the sights and scenery of the Wine Country. Enjoy a picnic lunch (complete with dessert) in between stops at various tasting rooms to sample the local wines. Your tour starts at 12:30 P.M. and lasts four hours. This is an especially romantic pick for couples celebrating an anniversary or birthday.

# Sonoma and Carneros

The Sonoma and Carneros wine regions lie in the southeast part of Sonoma County. The scenery here features oak forests and vineyard-covered open spaces. The last California mission in the great chain and the terminus of El Camino Real sits in the small city of Sonoma, which includes the famed Sonoma Mission Inn. Wineries cluster here, though not as many as in the Russian River Valley; the tasting rooms still see plenty of traffic, but the crowding can be less vicious than in the ultra-popular Napa and Dry Creek Valleys.

## WINERIES

The Carneros region might be described as the "lost" area of Wine Country. Though the wines are spectacular, the wineries are a bit more spread out than in the Napa and Russian River Valleys, and fewer visitors cram into the tasting rooms every weekend. And yet some prestigious California names make their homes here, and some small boutique vintners quietly produce amazing varietals you won't find anywhere outside their tasting rooms. If you come to Carneros on a weekday, you might be the only person in a few of the tasting rooms, able to chat in depth with the staff about each wine you taste!

### Schug Carneros Estate

You might recognize the labels at the Schug Carneros Estate (602 Bonneau Rd., Sonoma, 800/966-9365, www.schugwinery.com, daily 10 A.M.–5 P.M., $5–10). One of the Carneros region's elder statesmen, Walter Schug has made wine that's set the tone for California vintages for many years. The estate itself is worth a visit; the Tudor-esque barn sits in the

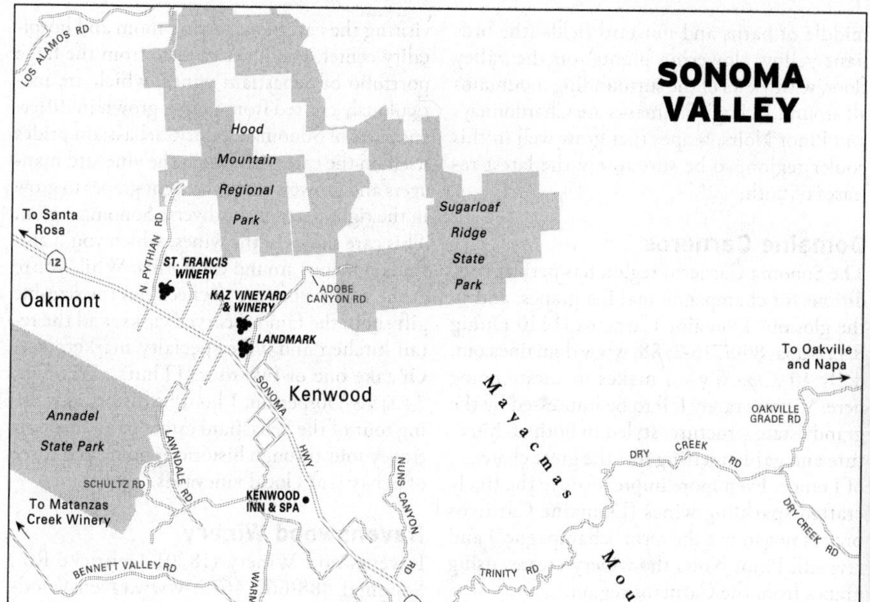



WINE COUNTRY

middle of barns and mustard fields (the brilliant yellow flowering plants) on the valley floor, with views of the surrounding mountains all around. Schug's hallmarks are Chardonnays and Pinot Noirs, grapes that grow well in this cooler region, so be sure to try the latest releases of both.

### Domaine Carneros

The Sonoma Carneros region has perfect conditions for champagne-making grapes, and so the glorious Domaine Carneros (1240 Duhig Rd., Napa, 800/716-2788, www.domaine.com, daily 10 A.M.–6 P.M.) makes its estate home here. Visitors rarely fail to be impressed by the grand estate structure, styled in both architecture and garden setting like the great chateaux of France. Even more impressive are the finely crafted sparkling wines (Domaine Carneros prefers not to use the term "champagne") and few still Pinot Noirs the winery creates using grapes from the Carneros region.



### Charles Creek Vineyard

Conveniently located on the square in downtown Sonoma, the tasting room at Charles Creek Vineyard (483 First St. W., Sonoma, 707/996-6622, www.charlescreek.com) beckons visitors with a giant cork cow standing proudly in the middle of its floor. This only-in-Wine-Country objet d'art was won at a charity auction, and now entices people to wander into the tasting room to take a closer look. Once inside, it's worth your time to taste the wines, too. This smaller production winemaker purchases grapes from Napa and Sonoma to create boutique Chardonnays, Merlots, and Cabernet Sauvignons. The winemaker takes care to produce vintages that are easy to drink, especially with food.

### Sebastiani Vineyards and Winery

The Sebastiani family has owned and operated Sebastiani Vineyards and Winery (389 Fourth St. E., Sonoma, 707/933-3230, www.sebastiani.com, daily 10 A.M.–5 P.M.) since 1904, making it the winery in longest continuous operation in Sonoma County. When visiting the cavernous tasting room and hospitality center, you'll get to taste from the huge portfolio of Sebastiani wines, which are meticulously crafted from grapes grown in different parts of Sonoma County. Sebastiani prides itself on the care with which the vineyard managers and growers select the right grapes to grow in the right parts of the diverse Sonoma region. This care shows in the wines, which you'll also find on menus around California. While you're at the winery, be sure to check out the sizeable gift shop, the famous carved casks, and the retail kitchen and wine specialty marketplace. Or take one of two tours (Thurs., Fri., Sat., 2 P.M., $7.50/person, 1 hour): a historical walking tour of the Sebastiani estate or an open-air trolley tour through historic Sonoma and three of Sebastiani's local vineyards.

### Ravenswood Winery

Ravenswood Winery (18701 Gehricke Rd., Sonoma, 888/669-4679, www.ravenswood-wine.com, daily 10 A.M.–4:30 P.M., $15) prides itself on making "no wimpy wines." Though the company is now owned by a large conglomerate, Ravenswood wines are still overseen by the original winemaker, Joel Peterson, who began making California Zinfandel in 1976. To this day, Zinfandel remains the signature varietal under the Ravenswood label. Many of the prized Zins come from individual vineyards in Sonoma County, while others are blends of grapes purchased from growers throughout California. When you come to taste, you won't find a stereotypical winery. Unlike many Napa and Sonoma wineries, Ravenswood sponsors a racecar, hosts a bevy of summer barbecues (yep, you can drink Zin with ribs!), and strives to make tasters of all types feel at home in the winery. Tours and barrel tastings teach newcomers the process of winemaking, while "blend your own" seminars beckon to serious winos. Perhaps best of all, Ravenswood wines are easy on the pocketbook, ranging $13–50 per bottle.

### St. Francis Winery

It is believed that the Franciscan order of monks

brought wine production to California. In their honor, the St. Francis Winery (100 Pythian Rd. at Hwy. 12, Santa Rosa, 888/675-9463, www.stfranciswine.com, daily 10 A.M.–5 P.M., $10–30) sells thick, rich wines that appeal to red lovers. The estate is built in the light adobe-style with red roof of the California missions, complete with square bell tower. Inside, visitors drink classic Sonoma Chardonnays and an array of yummy reds that show off the lush flavors of Sonoma grapes in both single varietals and blends.

## Valley of the Moon

At Valley of the Moon (777 Madrone Rd., Glen Ellen, 707/939-4510, www.valleyofthemoon winery.com, daily 10 A.M.–4:30 P.M., $2), 150 years of history juxtaposes with the highest winemaking technology California has to offer. Since the Civil War era, this Sonoma institution has passed through many hands and produced hundreds of wines. The circa-1860s stone buildings house late-model stainless steel fermentation tanks as well as classic oak barrels. In the tasting room, you'll find a small list of boutique wines, from an unusual Sangiovese rosé to a classic California Cabernet. Valley of the Moon takes pride in its awards, and you'll find that almost every wine you taste has its own list of medals. Check the website for a list of upcoming wine events that show off this great Sonoma landmark at its best.

## Mayo Family Winery

The Mayo Family Winery (13101 Arnold Dr. at Hwy. 12, Glen Ellen, 707/938-9401, www.mayofamilywinery.com, daily 10:30 A.M.–6:30 P.M.) breaks from the Chard-Cab-Merlot juggernaut of Sonoma, producing an array of interesting Italian varietals. Here you might taste your first smoky rich Carignane or Barbera, enjoy a fruity white Viognier, or savor the Chianti-based Sangiovese. The Mayo Family boasts a big presence in the region, with an at-the-winery tasting room, a small storefront tasting room in downtown Sonoma (on Sonoma Plaza), and the prized reserve tasting room up north in Kenwood (9200 Sonoma Hwy., Thurs.–Mon. 10:30 A.M.–6:30 P.M., reservations recommended, fee). At the reserve tasting room, your experience includes seven tasting pours of Mayo's very best wines, each paired with a small bite of gourmet California cuisine created by on-site chefs. Bon appetit!

## Landmark

It seems appropriate that Landmark (101 Adobe Canyon Rd., Kenwood, 707/833-0053, www.landmarkwine.com, 10 A.M.–4:30 P.M. daily) provides wine to the entire United States. Owned and operated by the descendents of John Deere, Landmark seeks to continue the agricultural traditions of America while producing top 21st-century wines. In the tasting room, you'll find premium Chardonnays and Pinot Noirs—wines that grow best in the cooler region of Sonoma. Outside the tasting room, you can walk in some of the most spectacular gardens in a region noted for its landscaping. If you're visiting in the summer, take a horse-drawn wagon ride through the vineyards. Or bring a picnic and enjoy a game of bocce ball (a popular local pastime) on the grassy court surrounded by flowers and fountains and grapes. And if you find that Landmark is the place for you, arrange in advance to stay in either the guest suite or the cottage on the estate grounds.

## Kaz Vineyard and Winery

At the other end of the spectrum from the multi-thousand barrel-making big boys of Wine Country, there's Kaz (233 Adobe Canyon Rd., Kenwood, 877/833-2536, www.kazwinery.com, Fri.–Mon. 11 A.M.–5 P.M.). This tiny winery is a family affair from start to finish—in the vineyards, the winery, and the tasting room. Inside Kaz, you'll find a broad array of ultra-small-production wines—sometimes only one barrel of a particular wine gets made. Reds are the Kaz specialty, including a number of blends and unusual varietals you just don't see at other Sonoma wineries. (Think Mouvedre, Grenache, and Barbera-Tannat blend.) Kaz also makes several unique ports—even whites and rosés! Inside the simple brown barn that's been made over into a tasting room, you'll get 6–9 tastes for $5, and if you're lucky, Kaz himself will be pouring and commenting on his wines.

## SIGHTS

### Mission San Francisco Solano de Sonoma

Mission San Francisco Solano de Sonoma (114 E. Spain St., Sonoma, 707/938-9560, www.parks.ca.gov, daily 10 A.M.–5 P.M.), or the Sonoma Mission to its friends, is the northernmost of the California Missions. It sits at the corner of the historic Plaza in downtown Sonoma—a low, surprisingly unpretentious block of buildings without much in the way of decoration or crowds. The last Mission (established in 1823) and one of the first restored as a historic landmark (finished in 1926), the Sonoma Mission isn't the prettiest or most elaborate of the California Mission chain. But visitors can see museum-style exhibits depicting the life of the later Missionaries and Native Americans who lived here, and a unique series of watercolor paintings depicting all the California Missions. Outdoors, guests can rest on benches by the fountain, observe a moment of silence at the Native American mortuary monument, or check out the cactus "wall" that's been living on the property since the Mission days.

### Bear Flag Monument

It's a little-known fact that California's state flag—the Bear Flag depicting a now-extinct California grizzly bear—first came to be in the tiny rural Mission town of Sonoma. To commemorate this historic beginning, the Bear Flag Monument (Sonoma Plaza at E. Spain St. and 1st St. E.) was erected. Visit the Monument as you stroll the Plaza or explore the various sites that comprise the Sonoma State Historic Park.

### Cornerstone Gardens

For a break from all the history of Sonoma's main attractions, take a walk in the ultra-modern gardens of Cornerstone Place (23570 Hwy. 121, Sonoma, 707/933-3010, www.cornerstonegardens.com, 9 A.M.–5 P.M.). This unique

© LIZ HAMILL SCOTT

Mission San Francisco Solano de Sonoma

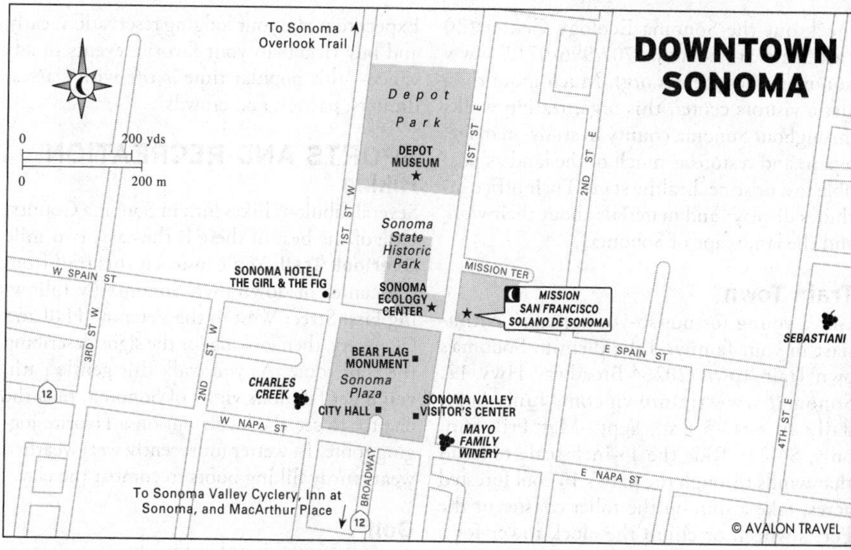


installation combines an art gallery with the work of the foremost landscape and garden designers in the world. Stroll these unusual gardens, which range from traditional plantings to post-modern multi-media installations. Finish up your excursion with a crawl through the boutiques, upscale foodie shops, and wine bars that have recently sprung up around the gardens. Daily wine tastings and various snacks and non-alcoholic drinks provide welcome refreshment, especially on hot Sonoma summer afternoons.

## Depot Park Museum

For a glimpse into the history of the ground you're treading, visit the Depot Park Museum (270 First St. West, Sonoma, 707/938-1762, www.vom.com/depot, Wed.–Sun. 1–4:30 P.M., free). The museum hosts a small set of exhibits inside a reproduction of the historic Northwestern Pacific railroad depot, hence the name. Inside are reconstructions of the active depot in the Rand Room, a showcase of the Bear Flag Rebellion, and the life of the native Miwok people. Depot Park makes a great half-hour break from the endless wine tastings and spa treatments of Sonoma.

## Jack London Historic State Park

Literary travelers come to Sonoma not just for the fine food and abundant wine, but for the chance to visit Jack London Historic State Park (2400 London Ranch Rd., Glen Ellen, 707/938-5216, www.parks.ca.gov). Famed author Jack London did in fact live and write in the midst of rural Sonoma at the beginning of the 20th century. On weekends, docents offer tours of the park, which include talks on the life and history of Mr. London. Explore the surviving buildings on London's prized Beauty Ranch or hike up Sonoma Mountain and check out the (artificial) Lake and Bath House. The pretty stone "House of Happy Walls," the creation of Jack London's wife, houses a small museum (daily 10 A.M.–5 P.M.). Though there's no camping at Jack London State Park, you can bring a picnic to enjoy on the attractive grounds.

## Sonoma Ecology Center

Many Sonoma wineries boast of being organic, biodynamic, or sustainable, and of the unique characteristics of the environment in their tiny pockets of Sonoma. To get deeper into the character and issues of Sonoma's landscape, check out the Sonoma Ecology Center (20 East Spain St., Sonoma, 707/996-0712, www.sonomaecologycenter.org). Much more than just a visitors center, this organization works throughout Sonoma county to study, manage, repair, and restore as much of the land as possible to a pristine, healthy state. Their office includes displays and materials about their work and the landscape of Sonoma.

### Train Town

Got a young (or not-so-young) train enthusiast in your family? Take them to Sonoma's own Train Town (20264 Broadway, Hwy. 12, Sonoma, www.traintown.com, June–Sept. daily 10 A.M.–5 P.M., Sept.–May Fri.–Sun. only, $4.25). Ride the 15-inch scale railroad that winds through the park's 10 cool forested acres, take a spin on the roller coaster or the Ferris wheel, or climb the clock tower for a magnificent view of the park and beyond.



## ENTERTAINMENT AND EVENTS

For a fun evening of drinking and live entertainment, head on down to **Murphy's Irish Pub** (464 1st St. E., 707/935-0660, www.sonomapub.com) on Sonoma Plaza. Grab an imported Irish pint or a glass of local wine, some barbecued oysters or a fine-dining entrée, and sit back to enjoy an evening of live music, literary entertainment, or perhaps a lively trivia game. Unlike many pubs and wine bars in Wine Country, Murphy's welcomes kids in its dining room, so feel free to bring the whole family for a meal and a good time.

Vineyards and olive groves have been associated with one another for thousands of years. Celebrating the symbiosis of these two historic staple crops is the **Sonoma Valley Olive Festival** (www.sonomavalley.com, Dec.–Feb.). Sonoma hosts a variety of annual events that highlight the growth, curing, pressing, and many uses of the noble olive. Check the online calendar for a list of olive-curing classes, olive-themed winemaker's dinners, and other celebrations. The "hot" olive weekend each year is the festival finale on President's Day weekend. Expect to make your lodging reservations early and buy tickets to your favorite events in advance—this popular time is rife with classes, dinners, parties, and crowds.

## SPORTS AND RECREATION

### Hiking

Several fabulous hikes lurk in Sonoma County. One of the best of these is the easy, two-mile **Overlook Trail.** You can reach this trail from the center of downtown Sonoma by following First Street West to the Veteran's Hall and Cemetery, then looking for the signs describing the trail route. As you walk this gentle path, you'll get fabulous views of Sonoma, plus the chance to see the locals out on a favorite jogging route. In wetter (or recently wet) weather, wear sturdy hiking boots to combat the clay.

### Golf

On the few acres of land in the Carneros region where vines don't grow, you can find a few great golf courses to help you pass the time. Between Kenwood and Santa Rosa, check out the **Bennett Valley Golf Club** (3300 Yulupa Ave., Santa Rosa, 707/528-3673, www.bvgolf.org, $26–47). This 18-hole medium-length par 72 course provides challenging play for beginners and intermediates, and some fun for advanced golfers too.

Practically next door, play a round at one of two 18-hole courses at the **Oakmont Golf Club** (7025 Oakmont Dr., Santa Rosa, 707/539-0415, www.oakmontgc.com, $32–64). The Oakmont East course offers executive-length, par 63 play—perfect for a shorter or slightly easier game. Oakmont West is a little bit bigger and more challenging, coming in at regulation length and par 72.

If you're lucky enough to be staying at the Sonoma Mission Inn, you can access the **Sonoma Golf Club** (17700 Arnold Dr., Sonoma, 707/939-4100, www.sonomagolfclub.com). This private 18-hole, par 72 course offers tee times only to guests of Sonoma Mission Inn or its spa. On the other hand, the public **Los Arroyos Golf Club** (5000 Stage Gulch Rd., 707/938-8835) is open to all comers. Great for newer players, Los Arroyos offers nine holes, par 29, and good fun for golfers.

## Horseback Riding

With its vineyards, open spaces, and state parks, the Sonoma Carneros region begs to be explored on horseback in homage to its pioneering history. The **Triple Creek Horse Outfit** (707/887-8700, www.triplecreekhorseoutfit.com, $60) offers guided rides at Jack London State Historic Park and Sugarloaf Ridge State Park. These rides, which can last from an hour up to half a day, take you beyond what you can see from the windows of your car. A ride through Jack London Park takes you through the writer's life in Sonoma and the literary history of the region. Up on Sugarloaf in the Mayacamas Mountains, you'll ride along the ridge and get glimpses of both the Sonoma and Napa Valleys. Or if you prefer, you can enjoy the forests and wildlife of Sugarloaf by moonlight on a two-hour full-moon ride.

## Motor Sports

Not every inch of ground in Sonoma County grows grapevines or houses inns and restaurants. One huge plot of invaluable dirt has long been given over to the **Infineon Raceway** (29355 Arnold Dr., Sonoma, 800/870-7223, www.infineonraceway.com). This massive motor sports complex hosts almost every sort of vehicular race there is. With several NASCAR events each year, various AMA motorcycle races, an Indy car race, and of course an NHRA drag race, Infineon sees more action than many of the country's most popular racetracks. It has events scheduled literally 340 days per year, though many of these run to local track days and small-time club races. Ticket prices vary hugely, so check the website to learn the cost of your favorite event.

## Spas

The most famous spa in the area is the **Fairmont Sonoma Mission Inn & Spa** (100 Boyes Blvd., 707/938-9000, www.fairmont.com/sonoma, Sun.–Thurs. 8 A.M.–7 P.M. Fri.–Sat. 8 A.M.–9 P.M.). Its eminence literally springs from beneath the rocks on which it stands. A natural mineral hot spring lies beneath the Sonoma Mission Inn, lending its warm water to the indoor and outdoor pools and whirlpools

### INFINEON RACEWAY POST-RACE TRAFFIC

Don't give a darn about auto or bike racing? Think you can safely ignore Infineon's schedule during your travels in Sonoma? Not if you're wise in the ways of event traffic. The turnoff to Infineon Raceway lies roughly at the intersection of Highways 37 and 121. These charming and scenic two-lane roads are great for motoring and sightseeing – unless, of course, you're stuck in bumper-to-bumper race traffic. The absolute worst time to try to drive either of these roads (particularly Hwy. 37 out of Sonoma) is when a major race event has finished. The wretched traffic jams, which truly are more stop than go, can last for hours as people try to exit the racetrack into the unprotected intersection. In the summer, the sweltering heat causes both engines and tempers to overheat, to no good end.

So what can you do?

- Check the race schedule (www.infineonraceway.com), and avoid the roads in question for at least four hours after the scheduled or estimated end of a big race.
- Plot another route to your next destination, or stick around in Sonoma until well after the traffic is likely to have unsnarled. (Give it about six hours post-race.)
- Escape via Highway 12 east to Napa or north to Santa Rosa. From Santa Rosa, catch Highway 101 south to the Bay Area or north toward the Russian River. If heading to Napa, pick up Highway 37 at a less crowded spot and then follow it south to Highway 80. Highway 80 will either take you south to the East Bay or east into Sacramento and beyond.

that create the center of the Spa's signature Bathing Ritual. Whether you choose a relaxing massage or a challenging yoga class, be sure to arrive at least an hour early to allow time for each step of the Ritual, which will relax and focus you for your next treatment or activity. The Spa offers an almost bewildering variety of massages, scrubs, wraps, facials, and even more rarified treatments designed to pamper even the most discerning spa-goers.

A snack bar in the spa feeds the body, and the spa's facilities are surrounded by the Inn and gourmet restaurant, both of which draw visitors from around the world all on their own.

You can also get pampered for the day in downtown Sonoma at the **Sonoma Spa on the Plaza** (457 First St. W., 707/939/8770, www.sonomaspaontheplaza.com). This luxury day spa, sitting steps from the pretty shops and wine bars of Sonoma Plaza, offers a complete range of massage options and facials. Their signature treatments—several different flavors of mud and cream masks—include a relaxing period in an aromatherapy sauna and an exfoliating scrub. For the ultimate downtown spa experience, pick a multiple-treatment package. If you're on a honeymoon or anniversary trip, go for the couples' massages or therapies, which you'll get together in a private room.

If you're looking for a lift to your face, visit **The Pampered Pout** (678 Broadway, 707/938-9396, www.thepamperedpout.com). Here you'll choose from among a dozen different 30–90-minute facials to beautify your skin. Esthetician and owner Bridgene Raftery can do anything from a classic European pampering facial to a series of microdermabrasion treatments to makeup lessons for teenagers. Specialty facials for teens and men, plus eyebrow designs, round out a complete menu of face-perfect services.

## ACCOMMODATIONS

### Sonoma

For a charming room at a reasonable price within the town limits of Sonoma, stay in the **Sonoma Creek Inn** (239 Boyes Blvd., 888/712-1289, www.sonomacreekinn.com, $90–160). The whimsical, colorful decor and unique art pieces brighten each guest room and each guest's stay. Amenities include cable TV, free wireless Internet access, a refrigerator, and private garden patios. Located a few minutes away from downtown Sonoma and convenient to the Carneros wineries, the Sonoma Creek Inn is perfect for travelers who want to spend their money on the wine and dining of the region rather than their motel room.

Right on Sonoma Plaza in the heart of Sonoma, **Les Petites Maisons** (1190 E. Napa St., 800/291-8962, www.lespetitesmaisons.com, $130–325) offers four cute cottages for a homey stay in the Wine Country. Each cottage has its own style, but all have the warm colors and comfy furniture evoke the relaxation needed for a perfect vacation. All the cottages have fully equipped kitchens (one with kitchenette) that let you visit the fabulous Sonoma farmers markets and cook your own fresh food. Or you can eat at the girl and the fig or one of the other wonderful restaurants on the Plaza.

In 1850, one of the first Spanish settlers to the Sonoma area built a home for his family on the town square. For almost the last 100 years, the **Swiss Hotel** (18 W. Spain St., 707/938-2884, www.swisshotelsonoma.com, $110–250) has offered a bed and a meal to travelers from near and far. With a renovation in the 1990s, the guest rooms have plenty of modern amenities, while the outside of the building and the public spaces retain the historic feel of the original adobe building. You'll find your room light, bright, and airy with fresh paint and pretty floral comforters. Downstairs, take a meal at the restaurant or have a drink at the historic bar—or both! Step outside to take a walk around the historic Plaza.

### Glen Ellen and Kenwood

With its wraparound porches and lush gardens, the **Beltane Ranch** (11775 Hwy. 12, Glen Ellen, 707/996-6501, www.beltaneranch.com, $150–220) looks like it belongs outside of Savannah, Georgia rather than Sonoma, California. But this Valley of the Moon charmer sits right in the middle of Wine Country, offering five guest rooms and a detached cottage to wine lovers from around the world. After a good night's sleep in the pristine country-style rooms, guests enjoy a sumptuous breakfast in the dining room or on the porch overlooking the gardens and vineyards beyond.

For a fabulous wine-and-spa retreat away from anything resembling a city, stay at the **Kenwood Inn & Spa** (10400 Hwy. 12, Kenwood, 707/833-1293, www.kenwoodinn.com, $250–400, no children under 18, no pets). This Tuscan-style villa has 29 posh guest rooms, a world-renowned spa, and a rustic-elegant Italian restaurant on site. The only problem with the Kenwood Inn is that you may have trouble prying yourself away long enough to go wine tasting. Expect to pay premium room prices during the summer and fall high season.

Got lots of money to blow on one of the best-reviewed inns in all of Wine Country? Blow it at the **Gaige House Inn** (13540 Arnold Dr., Glen Ellen, 800/935-0237, www.gaige.com, $700), where comfort and luxury have been built into the design of guest rooms and common spaces, and special attention paid to every detail. Each of the 23 guest rooms and suites resembles an interior design magazine spread; suites have bathrooms the size of bedrooms and their own tiny garden spaces. Be aware that breakfast and spa treatments cost extra.

## FOOD

### Sonoma

A favorite with the local-sustainable-organic food crowd, **the girl and the fig** (110 West Spain St., Sonoma, 707/938-3634, www.thegirlandthefig.com, daily 11:30 A.M.–10 P.M., $20) sits right on Sonoma Plaza. The menu changes often to take advantage of the finest local seasonal ingredients, or for a special treat, order one of the amazing cheese plates. If you love the sauces and jams here, look for *the girl and the fig* products both on-site and at wineries and high-end food shops throughout Wine Country.

Another California cuisine hot spot with a beautiful outdoor patio and a seasonal local-focused menu is the **Harvest Moon Café** (487 First St. West, Sonoma, 707/933-8160, www.harvestmoonsonoma.com, Sun.–Thurs. 5:30–9 P.M., Fri.–Sat. 5:30–9:30 P.M., $17–25). The menu of this charmingly casual restaurant changes daily to take advantage of the best ingredients available.

If you just need a cup of coffee and maybe a quick pastry, stop in at the **Barking Dog Coffee Roasters** (201 W. Napa St., Sonoma, 707/996-7446, www.barkingdogcoffee.com, Mon.–Fri. 6 A.M.–8 P.M., Sat.–Sun. 7 A.M.–8 P.M.). Barking Dog is the spot where the locals go to get their morning mochas. Sip a latte or indulge in a scoop of Caffe Classico gelato, take a seat on a comfy old couch, and maybe even enjoy some live music.

### Glen Ellen and Kenwood

At the **Glen Ellen Inn Restaurant** (13670 Arnold Dr., Glen Ellen, 707/996-6409, www.glenelleninn.com, Fri.–Tues. 11:30 A.M.–9 P.M., $20), haute California cuisine meets small town kitsch. You'll find this self-described oyster grill and martini bar's dining room inside a cute low building in the tiny hamlet of Glen Ellen. In addition to the seafood-heavy gourmet menu, the Glen Ellen Inn boasts a full bar and a wine list worthy of its location.

Despite its Hispanic name, the cuisine at **Dóce Lunas** (8910 Sonoma Hwy., Kenwood, 707/833-4000, www.docelunasrestaurant.com, Wed.–Sat. 11:30 A.M.–2:30 P.M. and 5–8:30 P.M., Sun. 10 A.M.–2:30 P.M. and 5–8:30 P.M., $17–20) has a distinct Wine Country flare. Downstairs, enjoy a delectable meal in a country-style dining room. Upstairs, take a ramble through the Dóce Lunas antique store, which sells country-style kitsch and collectibles.

## INFORMATION AND SERVICES

Before you begin your Sonoma and Carneros wine tasting adventure, stop in at the **Sonoma Valley Visitors Center** (453 First St. East, Sonoma, 866/996-1090, www.sonomavalley.com, Mon.–Sat. 9 A.M.–5 P.M., Sun. 10 A.M.–5 P.M.). Ask the volunteers for advice on which wineries to hit, and be sure to pick up some complimentary tasting passes.

One of the local papers in the Sonoma Valley is the ***Sonoma Index-Tribune*** (www.sonomanews.com). Turn to the *Do* and *Shop* sections for visitor information.

For medical attention in Sonoma, head for the **Sonoma Valley Hospital** (347 Andrieux St., Sonoma, 707/935-5000, www.svh.com), which has a full-service emergency room.

## GETTING THERE AND AROUND

The town of Sonoma lies over the mountains west of the Napa Valley. The main route through the Valley is Highway 12, also called the Sonoma Highway. From Napa, drive south on Highway 29, turning west onto Highway 12/121. Turn north on Highway 12 to reach downtown Sonoma.

If driving from the Bay Area, take Highway 101 north, take Highway 37 northeast. It becomes Highway 121, then Highway 116 as it winds into the city of Sonoma. If you're driving south on U.S. 101, you can turn off onto Highway 12 south in Santa Rosa and take a scenic journey down into the Sonoma-Carneros wine region.

Parking in downtown Sonoma is easy in the off season and tougher in the high season (summer and fall). Expect to hunt hard for a spot during any local events, and prepare to walk several blocks. Most wineries provide ample free parking on their grounds.

For your public transit needs, use the buses run by **Sonoma County Transit** (707/576-7433, www.sctransit.com, $1.15–3.10). Several routes service the Sonoma Valley on both weekdays and weekends. You can use SCT to get from Sonoma Valley to Santa Rosa, Guerneville, and other spots in the Russian River Valley as well.

It's fitting that in Wine Country, a place at the bleeding edge of sustainable agriculture in a state known for its eco-mindedness, you can take a vineyard tour on a Segway. **Sonoma Segway** (524 Broadway, 707/938-2080, www.sonomasegway.com, $99/tour, $40/hour rental) offers a 2.5-hour tour that includes a visit to a local winery, a stop at a local food-based business, and a full-fledged visit to historic Sonoma. You'll start off with a lesson on the Segway, and when you finish you'll get a complimentary bottle of wine (if you're of age, of course). If you'd prefer to traverse the Sonoma streets and paths on your own, rent a Segway—for just two hours or up to a month at a time.

# NORTH COAST

The rugged north coast of California is a spectacular place. Its wild beauty is in many places unspoiled, and almost desolate. This is not the California coast of surfer movies, though hardy souls do ride the chilly Pacific waves all the way up to Crescent City. Cliffs are forbidding, beaches are rocky and windswept, and the surf thunders in with formidable authority.

The North Coast also means redwood country. South of the pretty college town of Eureka, the famously immense California redwood trees loom along the highway. Redwood National Park and the Humboldt Redwoods State Park boast some of the biggest, oldest trees on the continent.

Wending back toward the edge of the ocean to the south, nature-lovers traverse the 80-mile, highway-free Lost Coast. Accessed by steep, narrow roads and bereft of amenities, the scenic California Coastal Trail runs for 64 miles over mountains and across beaches. Finally, for the best mix of natural and cultural California, Mendocino County and the Sonoma coast offer lovely beaches and forests, top-notch cuisine, and a friendly, uncrowded wine region.

## PLANNING YOUR TIME

The outdoors is the primary attraction here, though Eureka offers some indoor attractions as well. Driving is the way to get from place to place, unless you're a hardcore backpacker. Plan some time on the beaches (in nice warm clothes) and some time in the forest as well. Hiking is the one don't-miss activity. Close second is some time fishing or whale-watching out on the cold, majestic café.

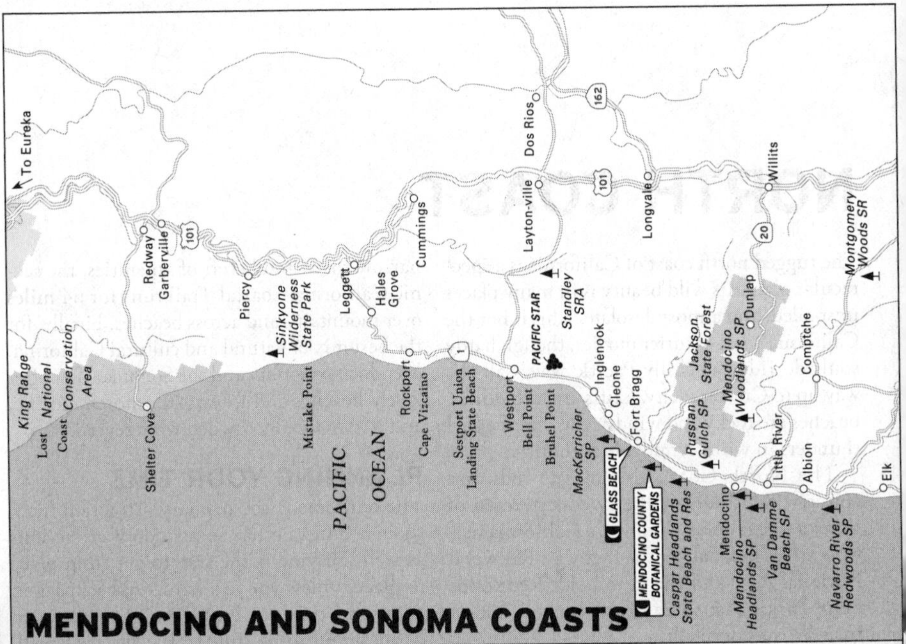
MENDOCINO AND SONOMA COASTS
To Eureka
King Range National Conservation Area
Lost Coast
Shelter Cove
Redway
Garberville
101
Piercy
Sinkyone Wilderness State Park
Mistake Point
PACIFIC OCEAN
Leggett
Hales Grove
Cummings
Rockport
Cape Vizcaino
1
Sestport Union Landing State Beach
Westport
Bell Point
Bruhel Point
PACIFIC STAR
Standley SRA
Layton-ville
Dos Rios
162
Longvale
Willits
20
Inglenook
Cleone
MacKerricher SP
GLASS BEACH
Fort Bragg
MENDOCINO COUNTY BOTANICAL GARDENS
Caspar Headlands State Beach and Res
Russian Gulch SP
Jackson State Forest
Dunlap
Mendocino Woodlands SP
Mendocino
Mendocino Headlands SP
Little River
Van Damme Beach SP
Comptche
Albion
Navarro River Redwoods SP
Elk
Montgomery Woods SR

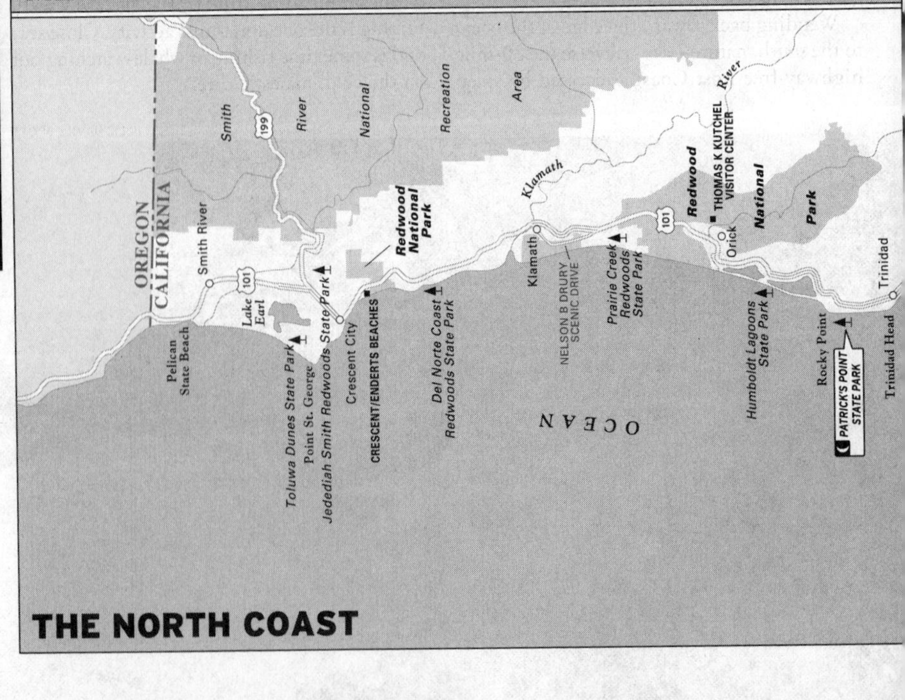
THE NORTH COAST
OREGON
CALIFORNIA
Pelican State Beach
Smith River
101
Lake Earl
Toluwa Dunes State Park
Point St. George
Jedediah Smith Redwoods State Park
Crescent City
CRESCENT/ENDERTS BEACHES
Redwood National Park
199
Smith River National Recreation Area
Del Norte Coast Redwoods State Park
OCEAN
Klamath
Klamath River
NELSON B DRURY SCENIC DRIVE
Prairie Creek Redwoods State Park
THOMAS K KUTCHEL VISITOR CENTER
Redwood National Park
Orick
Humboldt Lagoons State Park
Rocky Point
PATRICK'S POINT STATE PARK
Trinidad
Trinidad Head

NORTH COAST

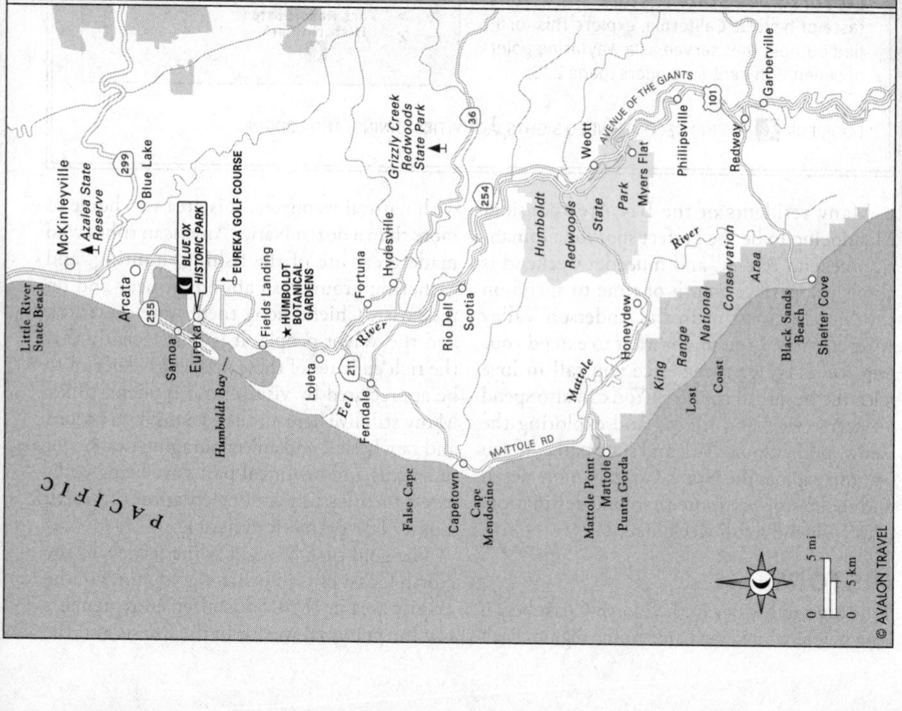
PACIFIC
Little River State Beach
McKinleyville
Azalea State Reserve
Blue Lake
299
Arcata
255
Samoa
Eureka
Humboldt Bay
BLUE OX HISTORIC PARK
EUREKA GOLF COURSE
HUMBOLDT BOTANICAL GARDENS
Fields Landing
Loleta
Fortuna
Hydesville
Grizzly Creek Redwoods State Park
36
Rio Dell
Scotia
Eel River
211
Ferndale
False Cape
Capetown
Cape Mendocino
MATTOLE RD
Mattole Point
Mattole
Punta Gorda
Mattole
Honeydew
254
Humboldt Redwoods State Park
Weott
Myers Flat
AVENUE OF THE GIANTS
Phillipsville
101
Redway
Garberville
River
King Range National Conservation Area
Lost Coast
Black Sands Beach
Shelter Cove
0 5 mi
0 5 km
© AVALON TRAVEL

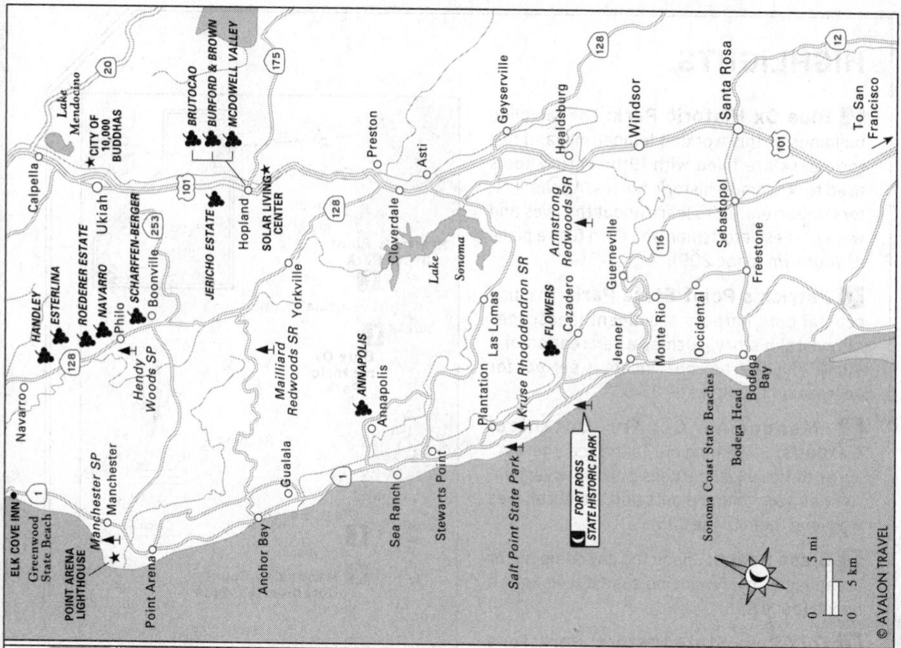
Point Arena
POINT ARENA LIGHTHOUSE
Greenwood State Beach
ELK COVE INN
Manchester SP
Manchester
1
Navarro
128
HANDLEY
ESTERLINA
ROEDERER ESTATE
NAVARRO
SCHARFFEN-BERGER
Philo
Hendy Woods SP
Boonville
253
Calpella
Lake Mendocino
20
CITY OF 10,000 BUDDHAS
Ukiah
101
BRUTOCAO
BURFORD & BROWN
MCDOWELL VALLEY
JERICHO ESTATE
Hopland
SOLAR LIVING CENTER
175
Anchor Bay
Gualala
Mailliard Redwoods SR
Yorkville
ANNAPOLIS
Annapolis
Sea Ranch
Stewarts Point
Preston
Cloverdale
Asti
Lake Sonoma
Geyserville
Salt Point State Park
Plantation
Kruse Rhododendron SR
Las Lomas
FLOWERS
Cazadero
FORT ROSS STATE HISTORIC PARK
Armstrong Redwoods SR
Healdsburg
Jenner
Guerneville
Monte Rio
Sonoma Coast State Beaches
Occidental
116
Windsor
Bodega Head
Bodega Bay
Freestone
Sebastopol
Santa Rosa
12
To San Francisco
0 5 mi
0 5 km
© AVALON TRAVEL

## HIGHLIGHTS

**Blue Ox Historic Park:** The rambling buildings of this working lumber mill and historic park are filled with 19th-century tools used to customize historic homes. A school offers opportunities to learn about the lives and work of these craftsmen and even turn a piece of your own (page 209).

**Patrick's Point State Park:** This tiny coastal park harbors prominent landscapes of coastal history, such as a re-creation of a Yurok Village. The cool climate is perfect for year-round hiking (page 224).

**Mendocino County Botanical Gardens:** Stretching out to the sea, these 47 acres of botanical gardens portray a vast variety of flowers and plants and the butterflies who love them (page 235).

**Glass Beach:** Spend the day combing for "sea glass" on Mendocino's most well-known beach (page 236).

**Fort Ross State Historic Park:** For a taste of historic California, explore this fortified outpost that served as a wayfaring point between 19th-century traders (page 236).

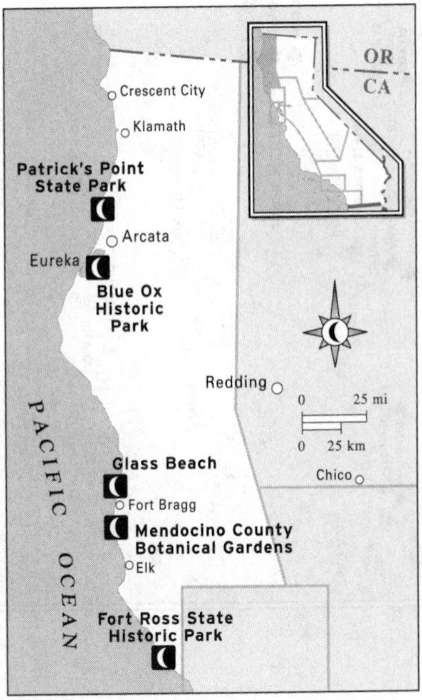


LOOK FOR ☾ TO FIND RECOMMENDED SIGHTS, ACTIVITIES, DINING, AND LODGING.

Many residents of the Bay Area consider Mendocino to be the perfect spot for a romantic weekend retreat, and indeed a weekend is about the perfect length of time to spend on the Mendo Coast or in the Anderson Valley wine country. (You might want to extend your trip for a day or three once you fall in love with the beautiful country.) You can also spend an active weekend hiking and exploring the Redwood National Park and state parks. If you want to explore the North Coast in more depth and make stops in more than one destination, plan to spend a full week here.

## HISTORY

True human history in the North Coast began long before white men came to the region. Rich with natural resources, this area was home to more than a dozen Native American tribes who made great use of the fishing, hunting, and gathering grounds so abundant near and on the coast. Chief among them were the Yurok and the Wiyot people. It is only recently that the rich cultures of these people have begun to be appreciated by visitors and residents alike. Many still live here on the various reservations and rancherias, and an encouraging number of museums and historical parks are being dedicated to the study and celebration of North Coast Native American heritage.

The gold rush brought white settlers to the North Coast of California—gold mines in the Trinity area in 1850. Soon after, entrepreneurs saw the potential wealth in the forests and the sea and began creating the now legendary lumber and fishing industries. The principal city of Eureka was founded in 1850, and the prosperity of the times is still visible in the elaborate Victorian shops and homes built along Humboldt Bay. Inland, a variety of Europeans emigrated to the rich farmland. Dairy cattle flourished, and so communities grew to support the ranchers.

In 1964, a tsunami from Alaska mangled Crescent City, but largely spared Eureka, Mendocino, and points south. The later 1960s brought a flood of a different kind—hippies and artists—to Mendocino. These rare creatures and their works can still be viewed in the area today, though the rise of the area as a tourist destination makes it more difficult for younger artists to find affordable living here.

## Crescent City

The northernmost city on the coast of California perches on the bay whose shape gave the town its name. Cool and windswept, Crescent City is a perfect place to put on a parka, stuff your hands deep in your pockets, and take a long contemplative walk along a wide, beautiful beach. Serious deep-sea fishing lovers will find fishing to their hearts content, and lovely and uncrowded redwood forests beckon hikers.

In 1964, much of Crescent City was destroyed in a tsunami caused by an Alaskan earthquake. The damage, estimated at $7–15 million, plus those who died and were injured in the disaster, amounts to the most severe tsunami damage ever recorded on the West Coast of the United States. More than 40 years have passed, but the ripples of the event still shudder through the small community. Look to the tops of phone poles to see old tsunami warning sirens, now rusted with disuse, but not yet removed.

the beach at Crescent City

## SIGHTS

### Point St. George

The wild, lonely, beautiful Point St. George (end of Washington Blvd.) epitomizes the glory of the North Coast of California. Walk out onto the cliffs to take in the deep blue sea, wild salt-and-flower scented air, and craggy cliffs and beaches here. On a clear day, you can see all the way to Oregon. Short (but steep) trails lead across wild beach prairie land and down to broad, flat, nearly deserted beaches. In spring and summer, wildflowers bloom across the cliffs and swallows nest in the cluster of buildings on the point. On rare and special clear days, you can almost make out the St. George Reef Lighthouse sitting lonely on its perch far out in the Pacific. Helicopter trips (707/464-8299) to this lighthouse are available from October 16 to June 1 each year.

### Battery Point Lighthouse Park

West of the middle of downtown Crescent City you'll find the Battery Point Lighthouse Park (at foot of A St., 707/464-3089, open Apr.–Oct. daily 10 A.M.–4 P.M. tides permitting) past the visitors center. Plan carefully and pick up a recent schedule, since the lighthouse is not always accessible to tourists. At high tide, the causeway that connects the city to the lighthouse is under water. But if you catch the tide at low or medium, you'll get an unadvertised treat as you walk to and fro: tidepools. The Battery Point tidepools are rife with life, from sea stars and sea anemones to worm colonies and barnacle clusters. Small fish are trapped by the receding tides, and hunt for food in the pools until the waters rise again. Up in the lighthouse, built in 1856, a tiny bookstore features local- and lighthouse-themed books and souvenirs. The guided tour takes visitors through the lighthouse, which is set up as a museum, though it is also a working private light station.

### Ocean World

Are the kids bored with all the gorgeous

© LIZ HAMILL SCOTT

Battery Point Lighthouse, Crescent City

scenery? A great family respite is Ocean World (304 Hwy. 101 S., 707/464-4900, www.oceanworldonline.com, 8 A.M.–8 P.M. daily, $9.95 adults, $5.95 kids). Tours of the small sea park depart about every 15 minutes, and last about 40 minutes. Featured attractions are the shark petting tank, the half-million gallon aquarium, and the sea lion show. After the tour, take a stroll through the immense souvenir shop, which sells gifts of all sizes, shapes, and descriptions, many with nautical themes.

### Del Norte County Historical Society Museum

The Del Norte County Historical Society Museum (577 H St., 707/464-3922, open May–Sept. Mon.–Sat. 10 A.M.–4 P.M.) provides an educational respite from the chilly sea breezes. The Historical Society maintains this small museum featuring the local history of both the Native Americans who once inhabited Del Norte County and the encroaching white settlers. Featured exhibits include the wreck of the *Brother Jonathan* at Point St. George, the story of the 1964 tsunami, and artifacts of the local Yurok and Tolowa tribes.

## ENTERTAINMENT AND EVENTS

### Bars and Clubs

If you're looking for a varied and rockin' night life, Crescent City is not your town. But a few options exist for insomniacs. Most of the hot action after 9 P.M. takes place at the **Elk Valley Casino** (2500 Howland Hill Rd., 888/574-2744, open 24 hrs) at the eastern edge of town. The Elk Valley is a bit more upscale than other local Native American casinos, with genuine aluminum-siding walls, poker and blackjack tables, a VIP card room, and a small non-smoking slots area.

The **Tsunami Lanes Bowling Center** (760 L St., 707/464-4323, Mon.–Thurs. 11 A.M.–11:30 P.M., Fri.–Sat. 11 A.M.–midnight, Sun. 11 A.M.–10 P.M., $2 games before 6 P.M., $3 after 6 P.M.) is a straight-up bowling alley, serving beer and greasy fries to all comers late into the night. For a more active evening, take a wheeled spin around the polished floor at the **Rollercade** (421 Hwy. 101 N., 707/465-0412, call for hours and rates).

A more civilized evening is available at performances of the **Lighthouse Repertory Theater** (707/465-3740). The **Del Norte Association for Cultural Awareness** (P.O. Box 1480, 707/464-1336) hosts several live musical acts and other entertainments each year. Check this year's schedule for upcoming shows, all of which take place at the Crescent Elk Auditorium (994 G St.). If all else fails, you can take in a first-run movie at the **Crescent City Cinemas** (375 M St., 707/465-4567).

### Festivals and Events

A must for serious birders, the **Aleutian Goose Festival** (www.aleutiangoosefestival.org) takes place each spring when the once endangered but now plentiful geese come to Crescent City during their annual migration. The highlight of the festival is the dawn viewing of tens of thousands of Aleutian geese rising all at once from their island sleeping grounds to come ashore to feed. Almost 100 other events highlight area avian diversity, natural education and appreciation, and celebration of the indigenous peoples of Del Norte County. This festival is sponsored by and centered in the Crescent City Cultural Center (1001 Front St.).

For almost 50 years, the Yurok tribe has held a festival to honor a creature most precious to them: the mighty salmon. The **Klamath Salmon Festival** (www.yuroktribe.org) takes place in August of each year and includes a parade, live music, games, and of course salmon dinners served all day.

## SPORTS AND RECREATION

### Beaches

The sands of Crescent City are a beachcomber's paradise. Wide, flat, sandy expanses invite strolling, running, and just sitting to contemplate the endless crashing Pacific. **South**

**Beach** is located, as advertised, at the south end of town. Long, wide, and flat, it's perfect for a romantic stroll, so long as you're bundled up. The adventurous and chill-resistant can try surfing and boogey-boarding here. Farther south, **Crescent** and **Enderts Beaches** (Enderts Rd.) offer picnic spots, tidepools, and acres of sand to walk and play on. The sand is dark colored, soft, and perfect for families. The trails down to the beach are steep and rocky, so take care getting to the beaches. Hikers enjoy the trails that lead away from the beach and into the national forest.

It might look tempting on the rare sunny days, but swimming from the beaches of Crescent City is not for the faint of heart or body. The water is icy cold, the shores are rocky, and as elsewhere in Northern California, undertow and rip currents can be dangerous. No lifeguards patrol these beaches, so you and your family are on your own.

## Bird-Watching

Birders flock to Crescent City since the diverse climates and habitats nourish a huge variety of avian residents. The parks and preserves have become destinations for enthusiasts looking for "lifers" hard to find anyplace else. Right in town, check out **Battery Point Lighthouse Park** and **Point St. George.** For a rare view of an Aleutian goose or a peregrine falcon, journey to **Tolowa Dunes State Park** (1375 Elk Valley Rd., 707/464-6101 x5151, www.parks.ca.gov) specifically the shores of Lake Earl and Kellog Beach. South of town, **Enderts Beach** is home to another large bird habitat.

## Surfing

For surfers and bodysurfers willing to don heavy wetsuits and brave the cold North Coast waters, some great waves are there for the catching. It may not be paradise, but **South Beach** is a longboarder's mecca. Longboard legend Greg Noll hosts an annual longboard contest here, and his son's **Noll Surf & Skate** (275 L St., Crescent City, 707/465-4400, www.noll.net) perches on the nearby wharf. The beach at **Point St. George** isn't always reliable, but in the right conditions it's got a rideable break.

## Fishing and Whale-Watching

Anglers can choose between excellent deep-sea fishing and exciting river trips. The Pacific yields ling cod, snapper, and salmon, while the rivers are famous for Chinook (king) salmon, steelhead, and cutthroat trout. Mammal-loving travelers can choose whale-watching over fishing. The ***Tally Ho II*** (1685 Del Mar Rd. at the harbor, 707/464-1236) is available for a variety of deep-sea fishing trips, whale-watching, and a combination of the two.

River fishers have a wealth of guides to choose from. **Ken Cunningham Guide Service** (10515 Salmina Rd., Kelseyville, 707/928-4762) and **North Coast Fishing Adventures** (1657 Childrens Ave., McKinleyville, 707/839-8127) cover the Klamath and Smith Rivers as well as smaller waterways.

## Hiking

The redwood forests that nearly meet wide sandy beaches make the Crescent City area a fabulous place to hike. The hikes at **Point St. George** aren't strenuous, and give hikers stunning views of the coastline and surrounding landscape. **Tolowa Dunes State Park** (1375 Elk Valley Rd., 707/464-6101 x5151, www.parks.ca.gov), north of Point St. George, offers miles of trails winding through forests, across beaches, and meandering along the shores of Lake Earl.

## Horseback Riding

The rugged land surrounding Crescent City looks even prettier from the back of a horse. Casual riders can rent horses from **Fort Dicks Stable** (2002 Moorehead Rd., 707/487-3014). A great place to ride is **Tolowa Dunes State Park** (1375 Elk Valley Rd., 707/464-6101 x5151, www.parks.ca.gov), which maintains 20 miles of trails accessible to horses. Serious equestrians with their own mounts can ride in to a campsite with corrals at the north end of the park off Lower Lake Road.

## ACCOMMODATIONS

Accommodations in Crescent City are affordable even during high season (midsummer) and can be surprisingly comfortable.

### Under $100

The aptly named **Curly Redwood Lodge** (701 Hwy. 101 S., 707/464-1655, www.curlyredwoodlodge.com, $64–89) is constructed of a single rare curly redwood tree. You'll get to see the lovely color and grain of the tree in your large, simply decorated room. A 1950s feel pervades this friendly, unpretentious motel that's located right on the freeway conveniently near some of the area's best restaurants.

Few frills decorate the family-owned **Pacific Inn** (220 M. St., 707/464-9553, $60) but the rooms are clean, inexpensive, and comfortable. Located right downtown, access to restaurants, museums, and points of interest is easy.

### $100–150

The **Lighthouse Inn** (681 Hwy. 101 S., 877/464-9035, www.lighthouse101.com, $99–119) brings more than a touch of class to this fisherman's town. An elegant, eclectic lobby filled with dolphins and dollhouses welcomes guests, and the enthusiastic staff can help with restaurants recommendations and sights. Stylish appointments and bold colors grace each room. Corner suites with oversized whirlpool tubs make a perfect romantic couples' retreat at a reasonable nightly rate, while standard double rooms are downright cheap given their comfort.

The **Anchor Beach Inn** (880 Hwy. 101 S., 800/837-4116, www.anchorbeachinn.com) at the south end of town offers great access to South Beach, the harbor, and several good seafood restaurants. The ocean views require guests to overlook (literally) a wide swath of asphalt RV park, but the in-room decor is attractive, the rooms are clean and well maintained, and there's free Wi-Fi.

For a more personal, intimate experience, try the **Castle Island Getaway** (1830 Murphy Ave., 707/465-5102, www.castleislandgetaway.com, $85–125). Offering lodgings to only one party of up to four people at a time, the innkeepers take special care of guests here. You'll get to choose your breakfast from a menu of options, and it will be served at your convenience. Light, bright, private rooms and a short walk to Pebble Beach (no, not that one!) make for a delightful romantic getaway.

### Over $150

Perhaps the best lodging location in town is the **Cottage By the Sea** (205 S. A St., 707/464-9068). Downtown and right on the coast, both the honeymoon cottage and the house rooms overlook the Battery Point Lighthouse. A nontraditional B&B, the owner stocks the fridge with food you can cook yourself, or the owner will cook breakfast upon request. Special rates are available for stays of at least three days.

## FOOD

Unsurprisingly, standard fare in Crescent City runs toward seafood, but family restaurants and even one or two ethnic eateries also offer tasty fare.

### American

The **Apple Peddler** (308 Hwy. 101 S., 707/464-5630, $8–18) is a 24-hour family restaurant with an extensive, classic American menu and great local dessert specials like summertime blackberry cobbler. Right next door to Ocean World, it's the perfect place to take the weary family for a hearty lunch or a mid-afternoon slice of pie. The service can be spotty, and the place can get crowded on summer weekends, but it's still the favored diner in the area.

### Seafood

Much of the fish is fresh and locally caught, so dig in! The **Beachcomber** (1400 Hwy. 101 S., 707/464-2205, $10–18) is the only beachfront restaurant in town, sitting in the middle of South Beach. The glass-front dining room is the perfect place to view the sun setting over the crescent-shaped bay while dining on delectable parmesan halibut or smoky pit-barbecued beef. Extra-friendly service makes even the first-time visitor feel like a local. Be aware that weekend evenings can be crowded.

**Northwood's Restaurant** (675 Hwy. 101 S., 707/465-5656, $8–20) prides itself on serving the freshest fish available, and in Crescent City that can mean the fillet you're eating for dinner was caught that very morning by a local fisherman. The varied menu also includes imported exotic fish, plus a number of land-based entrées to appeal to every palate. Northwood's is open for breakfast, lunch, and dinner.

**The Fisherman's Restaurant** (700 Hwy. 101 S., 707/465-3474) is a great place to walk into wearing jeans and sandy sneakers to grab a bite of great fresh fish. A local favorite is the **Harbor View Grotto** (150 Starfish Way, 707/464-3815, $6–20). While the steaks and sides are good, it's the seafood that stands out here and Clam chowder, shrimp appetizers, and fish are all favorites here.



### Coffee

The **Java Hut** (437 Hwy. 101 N., 707/465-4439, daily 5 A.M.–10 P.M., $5) is a drive-thru and walk-up coffee stand that serves a wide array of fancy coffee drinks, including some alcoholic treats. (Yes, at the drive-thru!) Beware of long lines of locals during morning hours. Downtown, check out **Coffee Corner** (530 L St., 707/464-9255, daily 5 A.M.–3 P.M.). Excellent pastries and sandwiches make this local shop stand out.

### Markets

Small, family-owned, award-winning **Rumiano Cheese Co.** (451 Hwy. 101 N., 707/465-2873, www.rumianocheese.com, call for hours) has been part of Crescent City since 1921. Come to the tasting room for the cheese, stay for, well, more cheese. The dry Jack cheese is a particular favorite, though lots of varieties are available.

Like most California towns, Crescent City runs a **farmers market** (451 Hwy. 101 N. at the Del Norte County Fairgrounds, 707/464-7441, June–Sept. on Sat.). While the harvest season is more restricted here than in points south, veggie lovers can still choose from an array of fresh local produce all summer long.

## INFORMATION AND SERVICES

The Crescent City **visitors center** (Mar.–Oct. daily 9 A.M.–5 P.M., Nov.–Feb. 9 A.M.–4 P.M.) is located at the Chamber of Commerce at 1001 Front Street. Here you'll find young but knowledgeable staffers who can advise you on "secret" local sights as well as the bigger tourist attractions advertised in the myriad brochures lining the walls.

***The Daily Triplicate,*** the local newspaper of Crescent City, is published Tuesday through Saturday. At the visitors center and many local businesses, you can pick up a Del Norte County Map and a copy of *101 Things to Do in Del Norte County and Southern Oregon*.

## GETTING THERE AND AROUND

### Air

**Jack McNamara Field** (5 miles northwest) serves as Crescent City's only airport. Commuter flights are available on several airlines from major airports in California and Oregon. Major Internet ticketing sights cover CEC.

### Bus

**Redwood Coast Transit (RCT)** (707/464-6400, $1 adults, $0.50 seniors/disabled, $10 punch passes) handles bus travel in and around Crescent City. Four in-town routes and a coastal bus from Smith River down to Arcata provide ample public-transit options for travelers without cars. Pick up a schedule at the visitors center (1001 Front St.) or local stores for current fares and times.

### Car

The main routes in and out of town are U.S. 101 and Highway 199. Though both are well maintained, they can get twisty in spots so take care, especially at night. Traffic isn't a big issue in Crescent City, and parking is free and easy to come by throughout town.

# Eureka

The town of Eureka began as a seaward access point to the remote gold mines of the Trinity area. Almost immediately, settlers realized the worth of the redwood trees surrounding them and started building the logging industry. In the late 19th century, men got rich here, and built a wealth of lovely Victorian homes and downtown commercial buildings. Today, lumber is still a major industry in Eureka. But tourism is another draw, with people coming to enjoy the waterfront wharf, the charming downtown shopping area, and the Victorian lumber-baron history that pervades the town. Active outdoors lovers can fish, whale-watch, and hike, while history buffs can explore museums, Victorian mansions, and even a working historic millworks.

## SIGHTS

### Blue Ox Historic Park

Even in a town that thrives on the history of man using wood, the Blue Ox Millworks and Historic Park (1 X St., 800/248-4259, www.blueoxmill.com, tours Mon.–Fri. 9 A.M.–5 P.M., Sat. 9 A.M.–4 P.M., adults $7.50, children $3.50) is unique. Blue Ox is at once a working lumber mill, upscale wood and cabinetry shop, ceramics studio, blacksmith forge, old-fashioned print shop, shipbuilding yard, school, and historic park. Owner Eric Hollenbeck

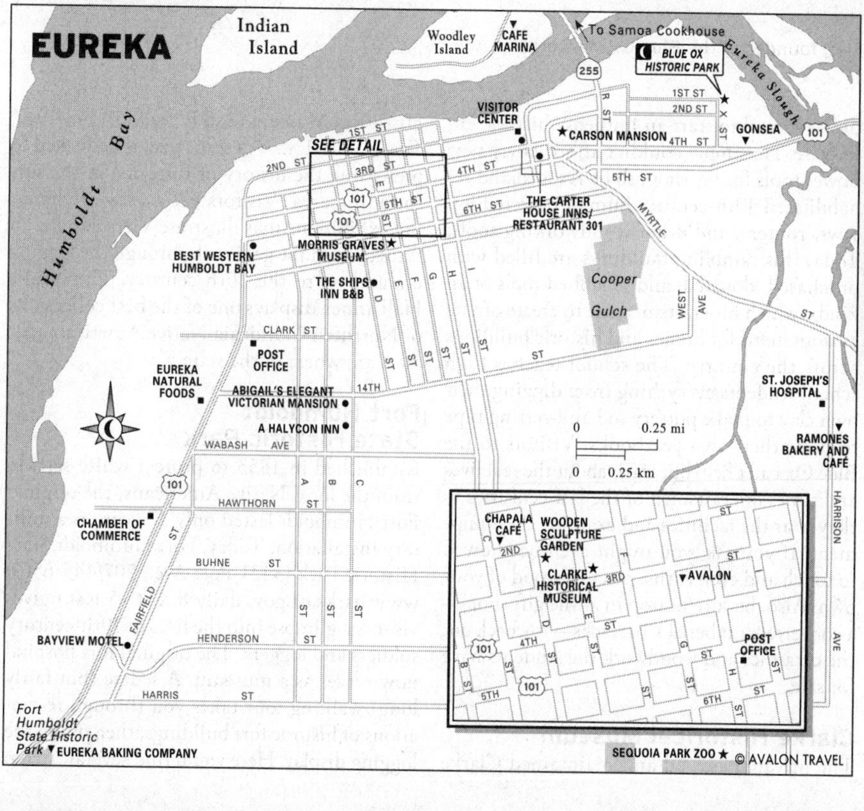

Eric, founder of the Blue Ox Millworks



didn't intend to start an immense historic enterprise. He simply couldn't afford fancy new power tools for his shop, so he rescued and rehabilitated 19th-century human-powered jigsaws, routers, and other woodworking tools. Today, his rambling buildings are filled with purchased, donated, and rehabbed tools of all kinds, which his craftsmen use to create ornate custom items for homes and historic buildings across the country. The school teaches high school students everything from digging their own clay to make pottery to hand-setting type to print their own yearbooks. Visitors to the Blue Ox can't help but learn about the real lives and times of craftsmen of the last centuries as they tour the facilities and examine the equipment. If you ask, you might even be allowed to touch and even turn a piece of wood of your own. Also, be sure to stop in at the gift shop—a converted lumberjack barracks—to check out the ceramics and woodwork the students have for sale.

## Clarke Historical Museum

The privately owned and maintained Clarke Historical Museum (240 E. St., 707/443-1947, Tues.–Sat. 11 A.M.–4 P.M., free) is dedicated to preserving the history of Eureka and the surrounding area. Visitors get a view of changing exhibitions that illustrate Victorian life in Eureka from the gold rush through the logging era and on to the 20th century. The Nealis Hall annex displays one of the best collections of Northern California Native American artifacts anywhere in the state.

## Fort Humboldt State Historic Park

Established in 1853 to protect white settlers from the local Native Americans, the original Fort Humboldt lasted only 17 years as a military installation. Today, Fort Humboldt State Historic Park (3431 Fort Ave., 707/445-6567, www.parks.ca.gov, daily 8 A.M.–5 P.M.) gives visitors a glimpse into the lives of 19th-century soldiers and loggers. The original fort hospital now serves as a museum. A sedate (but fairly long) walking tour takes you through re-creations of historic fort buildings, then out to the logging display. Here you'll find several "steam donkeys," a piece of equipment that revolutionized the logging industry as well as examples of the type and size of redwood trees loggers were cutting and removing from 19th-century forests. Finally, you can spend a few minutes enjoying the tranquil historic garden, where master gardeners maintain the type of garden fort residents kept a century and a half ago.

### Sequoia Park Zoo

The Sequoia Park Zoo (3414 W St., 707/442-6552, summer Tues.–Sun. 10 A.M.–7 P.M., winter Tues.–Sun. 10 A.M.–5 P.M., free) might seem small, but its mission is a big one. This zoo seeks not only to entertain visitors, but to preserve local species and educate the public about their needs. The Secrets of the Forest exhibit re-creates the ecology of the Northern California forest while letting children of all ages see the inner workings of the various species that live there. Be sure to say hi to Bill the Chimpanzee while you're there!

### Wooden Sculpture Garden

Conveniently located right downtown in the shopping district, Romano Gabriel's Wooden Sculpture Garden (315 Second St.) sits behind a glass wall for all to see. Gabriel created the bright, colorful artworks over many years and placed them in his front yard. Each piece has its own meaning; many are political.

### Humboldt Botanical Gardens

Brand new in 2008, the Humboldt Botanical Gardens (south of Eureka near College of the Redwoods, 707/442-6634, www.hbgf.org) are the product of years of work by staff and volunteers to create gardens that celebrate the ecosystems of Humboldt County.

## ENTERTAINMENT AND EVENTS

### Bars and Clubs

The biggest, most popular restaurant and bar in Eureka is definitely the **Lost Coast Brewery** (617 Fourth St., 707/445-4480, www.lostcoast.com, daily 11 A.M.–1 A.M.). The tall-for-its-street cream-and-green building perches off by itself on the main drag, easy even for casual drivers passing through town. The Brewery draws crowds, especially on the weekends. One thing that makes it special is that the Brewery makes all the beers you can get on tap at the bar, all of which are award winners in various microbrew competitions and the California State Fair. Come to eat tasty brew-pub style food and drink one or more of the delicious beers.

For a good solid dive bar experience on the North Coast, complete with occasional live music, spend an evening at **The Shanty** (213 Third St., 707/444-2053). You'll find all the proper dive bar accoutrements—older locals, loud young drinkers, vintage arcade games, funky decor (including light-up penguins), and plenty of cheap booze. On the rare warm evenings in summer, you can lounge outside on the patio for a smoke. Be sure to stop in for a pre-dinner drink during happy hour, when the prices are rock bottom and some of the beers and liquors are top shelf.

Even in far-out Eureka, you're still in California. So if you're looking for a gay bar, head on down to the aptly named **Auntie Mo's Lounge** (535 Fifth St., 707/442-0772, http://auntymoslounge.com, Mon.–Fri. 4 P.M.–close, Sat.–Sun. 6 P.M.–close). This newish venue hosts plenty of live music, drag and theme events, and of course nightly drinks and fun in downtown Eureka. Folks of all orientations are welcome here, so long as they get into the fun and fabulous spirit of the lounge.

### Theater

Don't confuse Eureka's **North Coast Repertory Theater** (300 Fifth St., 707/442-6278, www.ncrt.org, cash only) with the San Diego theater company of the same name. Here in Eureka, the company performs a mix of musicals, comedies, and the occasional Shakespeare or heavy-duty drama. Many performances benefit local charities.

### Festivals and Events

Eureka hosts a number of great festivals and events each year. The most unusual of these is the **Kinetic Sculpture Race** (www.kinetickingdom.com), which runs from Arcata down to Main Street in Ferndale each year on Memorial Day Weekend. Even if creating your own colorful, ridiculous human-powered locomotive sculpture isn't your thing, it's worth taking a spot along the racecourse to see what the artists have come up with this year. Be prepared for dinosaurs, donkeys, dung beetles, and other sublimely silly things not often seen outside of the Nevada playa. The sculptures cross pavement, sand, water, and mud over the course of the three-day race. While nowadays other towns have their own kinetic sculpture races (and yes, there's one at Burning Man), the North Coast is the origin of the event, and remains the grand championship of them all. For a great view, try to get a spot to watch Dead Man's Drop or the Water Entry.

Music lovers flock to Eureka each year for any one of a number of big music festivals. **Blues by the Bay** (www.bluesbythebay.org) is one of the largest. Held at Halvorsen Park right on Humboldt Bay, the two-day summer festival features many of the finest blues musicians alive playing in a spectacular setting. Accompanying the wailing blues are art, food, and microbrew booths. Another big event is the **Redwood Coast Jazz Festival** (www.redwoodjazz.org). For four days in mid-spring, music lovers can enjoy every style of jazz imaginable, from Dixieland to zydeco to big band. Dance contests and side events such as silent movie screenings are crowd favorites.



## SHOPPING

### Antiques

Even the cosmopolitan antique dealers of San Francisco and Los Angeles respect the Eureka antique scene, which is the largest California antiques market north of the Bay Area. In Old Town, seekers find lumber baron–era and Victorian antiques, from tiny porcelain figurines to huge pieces of furniture. **Vintage Home Antiques** (531 Third St., 707/443-1323, Tues.–Sat. noon–5:30 P.M.) specializes in vintage linens and laundry products. **Heritage Antique & Coins** (505 H St., 707/444-2908, Mon.–Sat. 10 A.M.–5 P.M.) is a coin shop that also carries jewelry and Native American artifacts. Music lovers must visit the **Antique Annex** (208 F St., 707/443-9113, Mon.–Sat. 11 A.M.–5 P.M.) to peruse the collection of vintage vinyl and antique sheet music. Generalists will love rooting through the huge **Antiques and Goodies** (1128 Third St., 707/442-0445, Mon.–Sat. 10 A.M.–5 P.M.) and **Old Town Antiques** (318 F St., 707/442-3235, daily 10:30 A.M.–5:30 P.M.).

### Books

For an afternoon of shopping in Eureka, head down toward the water to Second Street. Most of the buildings here are historic, and you might find an unassuming brass plaque describing the famous brothel that once inhabited what is now a toy store. Literature lovers have a nice selection of independent bookstores. **Eureka Books** (426 Second St., 707/444-9593, www.eurekabooksellers.com, Mon.–Sat. 10 A.M.–6 P.M., Sun. noon–5 P.M.) has a big, airy room in which to browse the selection of new and used books. **Booklegger** (402 Second St., 707/445-1344), just down the street, is a small but well-organized used bookshop that has a specialty in antique books.

### Clothing

Ladies have an array of clothing boutiques to choose from. As advertised, **Cotton Works** (420 Second St., 707/268-0895) sells stylish clothing made from cotton. Attractive undergarments are sold at the aptly named **Bliss** (527 Second St., 707/445-1733, Tues.–Sat. 10 A.M.–6 P.M.).

### Galleries

Galleries and gift shops abound, highlighting all aspects of California culture. The **Shorelines Gallery** (434 Second St., 707/443-7272, www.shorelinesgalleryeureka.com, hours vary) specializes in fun, sea-themed art and jewelry. Prices here start out quite reasonable—handmade jewelry starts at $10—and run up to five figures for the whimsical glass octopus coffee table. Native American art, including blankets, pottery, clothing, and jewelry is sold at **Indian-West Emporium** (326 Second St., 707/442-3042). Catering to a more modern California sensibility, the **Art of Wine Gallery and Tasting Room** (308 Second St., 707/268-0626, www.humboldtartofwine.com, Tues.–Fri. noon–6 P.M., Sat. noon–9 P.M.) offers photographs, mixed-media artwork, glass, and of course wines. **Many Hands Gallery** (438 Second St., 707/445-4700, www.manyhandsgallery.net) contains eclectic, hippie-style gifts and art items, including pleasantly inexpensive tea towels, potholders, note cards, candles, pottery, and drums.

## SPORTS AND RECREATION

### Fishing

Eureka is a serious fishing destination. Oodles of both ocean and river fishing opportunities abound all over this region, and several fishing tournaments are held each year. As everywhere else in California, you must have a valid state fishing license to fish in either the ocean or the rivers surrounding Eureka. Be sure to check with your charter service or guide to be sure they provide a day license with your trip. If they don't, you may have to provide your own.

For deep-sea fishing, **Celtic Charter Service** (Woodley Island Marina, Dock D, 707/442-7115) has daily trips leave at 6:30 A.M. each morning. They rent tackle and sell day licenses as well. **Full Throttle Sportfishing** (Woodley Island Marina, 707/498-7473, http://fullthrottlesportfishing.com) supplies all needed tackle and can take you out to fish for salmon, rockfish, tuna, or halibut. Trips last all day and most leave at 6:30 A.M. If you're launching your own boat, public launches are the **Samoa Boat Ramp** (New Navy Base Rd., 707/445-7651, daily 5 A.M.–midnight) and the **Fields Landing Boat Ramp** (Railroad Ave., 707/445-7651).

Eureka also has good spots for pier fishing. In town, try the K Street Pier, the pier at the east end of Commercial Street, or the per at the foot of Del Norte Street. Farther north, the north jetty (Hwy. 255 across the Samoa Bridge) also has a public pier open to fishing.

If an exciting fight with a steelhead trout is more your game, ample opportunities exist on the Klamath and Trinity Rivers. For a guided trip, check out **Jet Stream Guide Service** (707/826-2926).

### Kayaking and Rafting

The water is cold, but getting out on it in a kayak can be exhilarating. If you're new to the sport or just want a guided trip of the area, guided paddles, lessons, rentals, and kayak fishing trips are available through **Humboats Kayak Adventures** (Woodley Island Marina, 707/443-5157, www.humboats.com). Guides lead a huge variety of tours, from serene paddles in the harbor suitable for children or dogs to 30-plus-mile trips designed for experienced kayakers.

River rafters and kayakers have great opportunities for rapid fun on the Klamath and Trinity Rivers. **Bigfoot Rafting Company** (Willow Creek, 530/629-2263, www.bigfootrafting.com, $35–85) leads half-, full-, and multi-day trips of both these rivers as well as the Cal-Salmon and the Smith. Experts can take inflatable kayaks down the Class IV rapids, and newcomers can find a gentle paddle with just enough white water to make things interesting.

### Bird-Watching

The national, state, and county parks lacing through the Eureka area create ideal bird-watching conditions. Hundreds of species live here, and more migrate through seasonally (thespring and fall migrations are the best times to bird-watch around Eureka). Especially good spots for birding include the **Arcata Marsh and Wildlife Sanctuary** (foot of I St., Arcata, 707/826-2359, www.cityofarcata.com), the **Humboldt Bay National Wildlife Refuge** (1020 Ranch Rd., Loleta, 707/733-5406, www.fws.gov/humboldtbay) and the **Headwaters Forest Reserve** (707/825-2300, www.blm.gov/ca).

### Hiking and Biking

In addition to the vast trail systems in the state

and national parks, the city of Eureka maintains a number of multi-use (biking and hiking) trails. Most familiar is the Old Town Boardwalk, part of the **Waterfront Trail** which includes other disconnected sections along Humboldt Bay. **Sequoia Park Trail** begins at the Sequoia Park zoo and wends through redwood forests, past a duck pond, and through a meadow. This trail is paved and friendly to strollers and wheelchairs. The unpaved **Elk River Trail** (foot of Hilfiker Lane) stretches for a mile through wild meadows along the coast. **Cooper Gulch Trail** is more a sedate stroll than a strenuous hike, circling the Cooper Gulch park playing fields.

### Golf

With a surprisingly mild climate (it's not warm, but it doesn't snow much either), Eureka golf courses stay open all year long. Try the **Eureka Golf Course** (4750 Fairway Dr., 707/443-4808, public, 18-hole, par 70) or make the short drive north through Arcata to McKinleyville to visit the **Beau Pre Golf Course** (1777 Norton Rd., 707/839-2342, public, 18-hole, par 71).



### Casino Gambling

Just north of Eureka and Arcata, the **Blue Lake Casino** (777 Casino Way, Blue Lake, 877/252-2946, www.bluelakecasino.com) boasts the best gaming on the North Coast. In addition to its 700 slot machines, Blue Lake Casino has 16 card tables with a variety of games, plus bingo. For non-gamblers, the casino also features two restaurants, a lounge with live music and an open dance floor, and a large-act entertainment venue.

## ACCOMMODATIONS

With such a wealth of Victorian homes, Eureka is a natural location for classic bed-and-breakfast accommodations. Chain motels are also available in abundance, many of them quite cheap. But for a real taste of the town, try one of the many charming inns.

### $100-150

**A Halcyon Inn** (1420 C St., 888/882-1310, www.halcyoninn.com, $115–165) welcomes guests to a small Victorian house and a friendly, intimate Eureka experience. The brown-shingled exterior and verdant well-kept lawns give way to a gracious home. Only three guest rooms guarantee a quiet and uncrowded experience. Each room has its own four-poster bed and collection of antique furniture, floral bedspreads, and private bathroom. In the morning, come to the cozy dining room to enjoy a breakfast both sumptuous and health-conscious. Then wander out into the small but pretty gardens with summer flowers blooming and tables and chairs set up to encourage reading, card games, or just lounging with an extra cup of coffee or glass of wine.

**The Ship's Inn B&B** (821 D St., 877/443-7583, www.shipsinn.net, $130–175) is a newer B&B in an older, recently restored Victorian home on the east side of town. Few rooms and a friendly innkeeper make a stay at this inn delightfully like staying in a friend's grand home. Breakfast is particularly good here, and the small garden is the perfect place to sit out in the afternoon reading a good book. Each of the four rooms has its own decoration and theme; the Captain's Quarters take the inn's name to heart with a blue and gold nautical design, while the other rooms tend more toward classic Victorian florals. Unlike many B&Bs, you'll find televisions in every room, along with fireplaces, plush robes, and private bathrooms.

If B&Bs just aren't your style, get a room at the **Bayview Motel** (2844 Fairfield St., 866/725-6813, www.bayviewmotel.com, $100–175). This hilltop motel has lovely views of Humboldt Bay from many rooms and from the grounds. Rooms are spacious, and decorated in slightly more elegant colors and fabrics than the average chain motel room. You'll find wonderful whirlpool suites, free Wi-Fi, cable TV, wet bars, and coffee makers. If you're traveling with your family, you can rent a double-suite—two rooms with an adjoining door and separate bathrooms. Though not right in the midst of downtown Eureka, it's an easy drive from the Bayview for dinner, shopping, and strolling by the harbor.

## $150-250

For the most Victorian experience you can have, book a room at **Abigail's Elegant Victorian Mansion** (1406 C St., 707/444-3144, www.eureka-california.com, $180–300). Originally built by one of the founders of Eureka, the inn has retained many of the large home's original fixtures. The owners took pains to learn the history of the house and town, and has added appropriate decor to create a truly Victorian mansion, right down to the vintage books in the elegant library. Anyone with an interest in Victoriana need only ask for a tour, and the owners will gladly give an hour or more of his time to describe the artifacts in each room. Each of the three rooms comes with its own story and astonishing collection of antiques. All rooms have private baths, though the bathroom might be just across the hall. While you're not encouraged to bring small children to this romantic inn, families and groups traveling together can request combined rooms with additional beds. Come morning, all guests adjourn to the dining room for a sumptuous breakfast.

The **Carter House Inns** (301 L St., 800/404-1390, www.carterhouse.com, $200–335) encompass two inns and two smaller cottage, the larger mansions easily seen on either side of the street in the heart of downtown Eureka. The unusual smaller butter-yellow mansion is not the true Victorian dwelling it seems, but instead is a reproduction built in the 1980s. The rooms in each building are elegantly appointed, the dark wooden furniture evocative of the Victorian era while the minimum of floral geegaws caters to modern sensibilities. Standard rooms are small and stylish with particularly attractive baths. Larger suites are decorated with antiques and some have gorgeous soaking tubs set into windowed alcoves. Between the two buildings, the large inn offers nearly 30 rooms. Enjoy a truly magnificent dinner at the attached Restaurant 301, book an in-room massage, or even go for a wine-tasting package that delves into the Carter House's remarkable cellars.

Abigail's Elegant Victorian Mansion

# FOOD

## American

The **Samoa Cookhouse** (511 Vance Rd., Samoa, 707/442-1659, www.samoacookhouse.net, breakfast, lunch, and dinner daily) is an historic Eureka institution. Red-checked tablecloths cover long rough tables to re-create a logging-camp dining hall atmosphere. Meals are served family-style from huge serving platters. Diners sit on benches and pass the hearty fare down in turn. Think big hunks of roast beef, mountains of mashed potatoes, and piles of cooked vegetables. This is the place to bring your biggest appetite! After dinner, browse the small Historic Logging Museum and gift shop.

## California

**Restaurant 301 at the Carter House Inns** (301 L St., 800/404-1390, www.carterhouse.com, $18–29) seems like a top-shelf San Francisco or Los Angeles eatery lost on the distant North Coast. But in truth, the local ingredients and award-winning wine list are right at home in downtown Eureka. The chef creates an ever-changing menu of delectable delicacies, with tasting menus that give diners the best chance to experience this great restaurant. You'll find everything from exotic duck dishes to simple local seafood preparations to items out of the restaurant's own on-site kitchen garden on the succession of plates served at a relaxed pace. For a special treat, try the wine flights suggested with the menus.



Another high-end Eureka restaurant that impresses even the snootiest Bay Area–trained palates is **Avalon** (601 Third St., 707/445-0500, www.geocities.com/avaloneureka, Tues.–Sat. from 4:30 P.M., $20–28). This restaurant speaks to the hearts of eco-conscious carnivores, with sustainably-sourced steaks, mixed grills, and game meats prominent on the menu.

## Chinese

Looking for classic Chinese food in Eureka? Try **Gonsea** (2335 Fourth St., 707/444-8899). You'll find a fairly typical style of Americanized Chinese food here, complete with Hunan, Szechuan, and Mandarin dishes. (You might find it a bit unvaried if you're from a major metropolitan area.) Whether you come for lunch or dinner, the best way to order is family style so that you can try a variety of foods. Do be aware that portions are huge, so order lightly unless you've got a place to stash and chill the leftovers.

## Mexican

Some of the best Mexican food in Eureka can be had at **Chapala Café** (201 Second St., 707/443-9514, www.chapalacafe.com, daily 11 A.M.–9 P.M.). The large menu offers many Mexican classics, all available in both meat and vegetarian versions. The atmosphere at Chapala is friendly and festive, and you can't miss the gorgeous and colorful mural or the live entertainment on weekend evenings. Whether you order a classic taco-enchilada combination or one of the house-made slow-cooked chilis, be sure to get yourself a margarita to go with it. Kids and alcohol-free diners may prefer the imported Mexican Jarritos sodas. Chapala prides itself on its fast and excellent service, actually promising a free meal should your food not arrive in a timely fashion. The fish tacos are highly recommended.

## Seafood

**Café Marina** (601 Startare Dr., Woodley Island, 707/443-2233, www.samoacookhouse.net/cafe-marina.html, open daily) provides the right California coastal dining experience. Located on Woodley Island overlooking the harbor, diners can sit outdoors on rare sunny days and watch the sea lions lazing about between the docks as the fishing boats come and go. The seafood is good here, and the menu also includes an array of burgers and sandwiches, plus a few entrées at dinnertime. Portions are large and preparations are basic but tasty. The service is decent and the prices are reasonable, but the main reason to come out to the Café Marina is the location.

## Bakeries

**Ramone's Bakery and Café** (2223 Harrison Ave., 707/442-1336, http://ramonesbakery.com) is a genuine local North Coast chain.

All locations (including 209 E St. and 430 N. St. in Eureka, one in Arcata and one in McKinleyville) all sell fresh, made-from-scratch baked goodies and candies. Come in the morning to enjoy a fresh cup of coffee roasted in-house and a danish or a scone, indulge in an afternoon pastry, or even get a whole tart or cake to save for evening dessert. You can even buy a loaf of fresh-baked bread to take out for an afternoon picnic.

## INFORMATION AND SERVICES

The Eureka-Arcata corridor forms the urban center of the far-north coast of California. If you need urban services, you'll probably find them here.

### Tourist Information

Eureka's **visitors center** (1034 Second St., 707/443-5097, http://redwoods.info, Mon.–Fri. 9 A.M.–5 P.M.) covers the whole Redwood Coast region. Check out the website before you visit to get the scoop on lodgings and create an itinerary, then come into the office to grab a map and get recommendations for local restaurants.

### Media and Communications

The local daily paper is the ***Times-Standard*** (www.times-standard.com). It covers both national and wire news, as well as local news and events for the whole North Coast region. Check the entertainment section for the latest hot spots and live events during your stay.

There's also plenty of Internet access in and around Eureka. Your inn or motel may have Wi-Fi for free or for a fee, and Internet cafés abound.

### Banks and Post Office

As the big urban area on the North Coast, Eureka (and Arcata) has the major services travelers sometimes need. You'll find branches of most major banks, complete with ATMs, plus more ATMs at supermarkets, pharmacies, and other businesses.

Naturally, you'll find post offices in Eureka (337 W. Clark St. and 514 H St.) that can help you with any letters or packages.

### Medical Services

If you need medical assistance, Eureka has a full service hospital with both an emergency room and urgent care center (for less serious emergencies). For immediate health care needs, **St. Joseph Hospital** (2700 Dolbeer St., Eureka, 707/445-8121, www.stjosepheureka.org) can take care of you.

## GETTING THERE AND AROUND

### Car

Eureka lies right along U.S. 101, easily accessed by car from either the north or the south. If you're driving from the Bay Area, expect to spend six or so hours on the road. From Crescent City, Eureka is less than an hour without stops.

In Eureka, you'll need to drive if you're not staying downtown and if you want to head out to Woodley Island. You can easily traverse the Second Street shops and restaurants on foot. Parking downtown is by meter or is free on the streets, and not too difficult except on holiday or event weekends.

### Bus

Bus service in and around Eureka is operated by the Humboldt Transit Authority (www.hta.org, adults $1.30, children/seniors $1). The HTA's Eureka Transit System (ETS) runs within town limits, and the Redwood Transit System (RTS, adults $2, children/seniors $1.75) can take you up and down the coast, from Eureka up toward Crescent City or down to Ferndale, and out east to Willow Creek. Check the website for route maps and up-to-date schedules.

### Air

Eureka has a small commercial airport, **Arcata/Eureka Airport** (http://co.humboldt.ca.us/aviation) that serves the North Coast region. You can fly in and out on either Horizon Air (a division of Alaska), Delta, or United Airlines. Expect such flights to be expensive but convenient.

# Redwood National and State Parks

From Crescent City to the edge of Humboldt County run an interlocking series of national and state parks that feature the majestic Sequoia—redwood trees that can grow hundreds of feet high and live to be hundreds of years old. Though each park listed here has its own unique character and offerings, their proximity enables the park service (and the folks who paint the highway signs) to refer to them all as one: Redwood National and State Parks. The lone exception is Humboldt Redwoods State Park, which is farther south and treated separately from the other North Coast parks.

## Practicalities

Visitors centers abound in these parks. The largest is the **Thomas K. Kutchel Visitors Center** (U.S. 101 at Orick, watch for signs, 707/465-7765, Mar.–Oct. daily 9 A.M.–5 P.M., Nov.–Feb. daily 9 A.M.–4 P.M.) situated on Redwood National Park land on the coast. Here friendly and knowledgeable rangers can assist you with maps, directions, and recommendations for the best and least crowded trails and beaches throughout the park system. More detailed information is available at the **Prairie Creek Visitors Center** (Newton B. Drury Scenic Pkwy., 707/465-7354, Mar.–Oct. daily 9 A.M.–5 P.M., Nov.–Feb. daily Wed.–Sun. 9 A.M.–5 P.M.), **Jedediah Smith Visitors Center** (U.S. 101, 707/465-2144, May 20–Sept. 30 daily 9 A.M.–5 P.M., winter Fri.–Sun. 10 A.M.–6 P.M.) in the parks, and the **Hiochi Information Center** (Hwy. 199, 707/458-3209, June–Sept. daily 9 A.M.–5 P.M.) and the **Crescent City Information Center** (1001 Front St., Mar.–Oct. daily 9 A.M.–5 P.M., Nov.–Feb. 9 A.M.–4 P.M.) located in their respective towns.

© LIZ HAMILL SCOTT

coast redwoods

Most of the major park areas can be accessed via U.S. 101 and Highway 199. Follow the signs to the smaller roads that take you farther from civilization. To get to the redwood parks from the south, simply drive up U.S. 101 or the much slower but much prettier Highway 1. The two roads become one at the tiny town of Leggett north of Fort Bragg, then proceed north into the trees. Public transit options run to the Redwood County Transit bus system (707/464-6400), which runs daily from Smith River to Arcata.

Folks camping in the Redwood National and State Parks usually pack in their own food and cook at their campsites. To restock, you can drive into Crescent City to find a market or Eureka for a true supermarket.

## JEDEDIAH SMITH REDWOODS STATE PARK

The northernmost of the parks, Jed Smith (U.S. 199, nine miles east of Crescent City, 707/458-3018, www.parks.ca.gov) as it's known to locals, sits north of Crescent City along the Smith River, right next door to the immense Smith River National Recreation Area (Hwy.

199 west of Hiouchi). The State Park visitors center sits on the east side of the park, doubling as the Hiouchi Information Center.

## Sights

The best redwood grove in all the old growth of Jed Smith is **Stout Memorial Grove.** This bunch of coastal redwood trees are, as advertised, stout—though the grove was named for a Mr. Frank Stout, not for the size of the trees. These old giants make humans feel small as they wander in the grove. These are some of the biggest and oldest trees on the North Coast, somehow spared the loggers' saws. Another great thing about this grove is the lack of tourists, since its far-north latitude makes it harder to reach than some of the other big redwood groves in California.

## Hiking

The trails running through the trees make for wonderful summer hiking that's cool and shady. Many trails run along the river and the creeks, offering a variety of ecosystems and plenty of lush scenery to enjoy. Just be sure that wherever you hike, you stay on the established trails. Wandering into the forest, you can stomp on the delicate and shallow redwood root systems, unintentionally damaging the very trees you're here to visit.

The **Simpson Reed Trail** (1 mile, easy) takes you right from U.S. 199 (six miles east of Crescent City) down to the banks of the Smith River.

To get a good view of the Smith River, hike the **Hiouchi Trail** (2 miles, intermediate). From the visitors center and campgrounds, cross the Summer Footbridge then follow the river north. The Hiouchi Trail then meets the Hatton Loop Trail and takes you off away from the river and into the forest.

### SAVE THE REDWOODS

The stereotype of a tree-hugging conservationist usually brings to mind dirty, long-haired college students living on tarp-covered platforms and tying themselves to trees. Many visitors (and heck, residents) of California might imagine that it was a bunch of dreadlocked hippies and starving artists that saved the huge swaths of redwoods lining the North Coast region.

Nothing could be further from the truth. The California redwoods were saved by some very rich people.

Powerful rich white men poured their power, political connections, and, in some cases, millions of their own dollars into a group called the **Save the Redwoods League** (www.savetheredwoods.org). The three founders were a U.C. professor named John Merriam, and fellow conservationists Madison Grant and Henry F. Osborn. After surveying the destruction of the forests surrounding brand-new Highway 101 in 1917, the three men decided that something had to be done. And thus the League was born.

For 90 years, the Save the Redwoods League has aggressively pursued the conservation of redwood forests in California. Using high-level political connections, the League has successfully lobbied the U.S. government to create the Redwood National Park and to expand the territory protected by Sequoia National Park. They're also major players at the state level, creating and expanding state parks all over the landscape.

So how did they get hold of all those groves? They bought them. Large donations plus the resources of League members have given the League the ability to buy thousands of acres of redwood forest, then donate them to various parks. They're still doing it to this very day, and in the 21st century the League has made several major purchases to expand Sequoia National Park, Redwood National Park, and several state parks.

Got some spare change in your ashtray? You can donate to Save the Redwoods and help the group preserve and expand California's fabulous redwoods. Donate your life savings, and they might even name a grove after you! (No promises though.)

If you're looking for a longer and more aggressive trek, try the **Mill Creek Trail** (7.5 miles round-trip, difficult). A good place to start is at the Summer Footbridge. The trail then follows the creek down to the unpaved Howland Hill Road.

If it's redwoods you're looking for, take the **Boy Scout Tree Trail** (5.2 miles, difficult). It's a bit more of a trek out to the trailhead along an unpaved road, but rumor has it that's part of the beauty of this hike.

### Fishing

With the Smith River and numerous feeder and offshoot creeks running right through Jed Smith, it's not surprising that fishing is one of the most popular activities here. Chilly winter fishing draws a surprising number of anglers out to vie for king salmon up to 30 pounds and 20-pound steelhead.Seasons for both these fish run from October through February. In the summertime, cast out into the river to catch cutthroat trout.

### Boating and Swimming

You'll find two boat launches in the park: one at Society Hole and one adjacent to the Summer Footbridge that's open in the wintertime only.

Down by the River Beach Trail, you'll find **River Beach** (immediately west of the visitors center), a popular spot for swimming in the river. Swimming is allowed throughout the park, but please be very careful! Rivers and creeks move unpredictably, and you might not notice deep holes until you're upon them. Enjoy the cool water, but keep a close eye on your kids and loved ones to ensure that a good and safe time is had by all.

### Camping

The **Jedediah Smith campground** (Hwy. 199, Hiouchi, 800/444-7275, www.reserveamerica.com) clusters near the river, with most sites near the River Beach Trail (immediately west of the visitors center). There are 106 RV and tent sites for $15–20 per night, depending on the season (hike-in primitive sites are $3). Facilities include plenty of restrooms, fire pits, and coin-op showers. Reservations are advised in advance, especially for summer and holiday weekends.

### Information and Services

Jed Smith has a **visitors center** (U.S. 199, 1 mile west of Hiouchi) where you can get park information and purchase souvenirs and books. Ask for a schedule of nature programs and guided hikes.

## DEL NORTE COAST REDWOODS STATE PARK

South of Crescent City and Jedediah Smith State Park, Del Norte Coast Redwoods State Park (U.S. 101, accessible via Mill Creek Rd., 707/465-2146, www.parks.ca.gov) encompasses a variety of ecosystems, from eight miles of wild coastline to second-growth redwood forest to virgin old-growth forests. One of the largest in this system of parks, Del Norte is a great place to "get lost" in the backcountry with just your backpack and fishing rod ready to camp and ply the waters of the meandering branches of Mill Creek.

### Hiking

Guided tours, nature trails, and wheelchair-accessible trails and campgrounds are all amenities here. Dress in layers to hike at Del Norte, as it can get down into the 40s even in the summertime.

### Camping

The **Mill Creek** campground (Hwy. 101, 7 miles south of Crescent City, 800/444-7275, www.reserveamerica.com, May 1–Sept. 30, $12–20) sits in an attractive setting along its namesake creek. There are 145 sites for RVs and tents and facilities include restrooms and fire pits. Feel free to bring your camper to the Mill Creek campground; it's got spots for RVs and a dump station on-site. Call in advance to reserve a spot and to be sure that your camper does not exceed the park's length limit.

### Information and Services

Del Norte State Park has no visitors center. Minimal restroom facilities are available at the campgrounds, and the park has an RV dump station but no RV hookups.

## PRAIRIE CREEK REDWOODS STATE PARK

At the junction of the south end of the Nelson B. Drury Scenic Drive and U.S. 101, Prairie Creek Redwoods State Park (25 miles south of Crescent City on Nelson B. Drury Dr., 707/465-7347, www.parks.ca.gov) boasts large campgrounds and shady hiking trails through redwoods. Just beyond the entrance, the visitors center includes a small interpretive museum describing the history of the California redwood forests. A tiny bookshop adjoins the museum, well stocked with books describing the history, nature, and culture of the area. Many ranger-led programs originate at the visitors center.

### Sights

One of the cool things that make a drive to Prairie Creek worth the effort is the herd of **Roosevelt elk** that live there. The big guys with their huge racks hang out at—where else?—the Elk Prairie. This stretch of open grassland lies right along the highway. The best way to find the viewing platform is to watch for the road signs pointing you to the turnoff. The best times to see the elk out grazing in the field are early morning and around sunset. Please stay in the viewing area and let the elk enjoy their meals in peace.

A gorgeous scenic cutoffs through the redwoods, the **Nelson B. Drury Scenic Drive** (about 5 miles south of Klamath, cuts off U.S. 101) features old-growth trees lining the roads, a close-up view of the redwood forest ecosystem, and a grove or trailhead about every hundred yards or so. A great place to turn off is at the **Big Tree Wayside.** The namesake tree is only a short walk from the parking area, and several trails radiate from the little grove.

### Hiking

Perhaps the single most famous hiking trail

NORTH COAST

© LANCE SCOTT

Yurok home, Prairie Creek Redwoods State Park

along the redwood coast is **Fern Canyon** (2 miles of U.S. 101 on Davidson Rd. to Gold Bluffs Beach). This hike takes you through a narrow canyon carved by Home Creek. Ferns, mosses, and other water-loving plants grow thick up the sides of the canyon, creating a beautiful vertical carpet of green that made the perfect setting for Steven Spielberg's *Jurassic Park 2* and *The Return of the Jedi*.

A longer and tougher loop can take you from the visitors center on a more serious foot tour of the park. Start out on the **James Irvine Trail,** but don't follow it all the way to the coast. Instead, make a right onto the **Clintonia** and cut across to **Miner's Ridge.** The hike runs a total of about six miles.

If you're working on the **California Coastal Trail,** you can do a leg here at Prairie Creek. The Coastal Trail runs along the northern coast of this park. Another way to get to the campground is via the **Ossagon Creek Trail** (2 miles round-trip, north end of Newton B. Drury Dr., moderate). Though it's not too long, the steep grade makes it a tough haul in spots, but you'll get to see many lovely old-growth redwood trees along the way.



### Camping

The **Elk Prairie Campground** (Newton B. Drury Scenic Parkway, 800/444-7275, www.reserveamerica.com, $15–20) has 75 sites for tents or RVs and a full range of comfortable camping amenities. You can get a shower and purchase wood for your fire ring. Several campsites are wheelchair-accessible, so be sure to ask for one if needed when you reserve your site. A big campfire area sits to the north of the campground, an easy walk for campers interested in the evening programs put on by rangers and volunteers.

For a sand camping experience, head out to **Gold Bluffs Beach Campground** (Davidson Rd., 3 miles north of Orick, www.nps.gov/redw, no reservations, $14–15). There are 25–29 sites for tents or RVs. Amenities include flush toilets, water, solar showers, and wide ocean views. (The surf can be quite dangerous here, so be extremely careful if you choose to go into the water at all.)

### Information and Services

Stop in at the **visitors center** at the south end of the Nelson B. Drury Scenic Parkway. Enjoy the exhibits, chat with the rangers, or grab a field guide in the small bookstore. Campfire programs are held by rangers at the campfire area adjacent to the Elk Prairie Campground. Check with the visitors center for a schedule.

## REDWOOD NATIONAL PARK

The lands of Redwood National Park meander along the coast, abutting the various state parks that crowd to cover the bulk of California's northern redwood forests. The main bulk of Redwood National Park lies just south of Prairie Creek State Park along U.S. 101 to the north, meandering east away from the coast and the highway. In the south, driving access to the park runs along Bald Hills Road.

### Sights

Generations of kids have loved spotting the gigantic wooden Paul Bunyan and his blue ox Babe from U.S. 101. And the **Trees of Mystery** (15500 U.S. 101 N., 800/638-3389, www.treesofmystery.net, June–Aug. daily 8 A.M.–7 P.M., Sept.–May daily 9 A.M.–5 P.M., adults $13.50, children $6.50) doesn't disappoint as a great place to take a break from the road to let the family out for some good cheesy fun. Visitors can enjoy the original Mystery Hike as well as the Skytrail gondola ride through the old-growth redwoods and the palatial gift shop. Perhaps best of all, at the left end of the gift shop rests a little-known gem: the Native American museum. A large collection of artifacts from tribes across the country and native to the redwood forests grace several crowded galleries.

### Hiking

For an easy, fun little walk around the park, try the **Lady Bird Johnson Trail** (Bald Hills Rd., 1 mile, easy). This level loop can give you

© LIZ HAMILL SCOTT

Paul Bunyan and his blue ox, Babe, at the Trees of Mystery

a lovely view of the redwood and fir forest that informs this region. Another easy-access and pretty trail goes out to **Trillium Falls** (Davidson Rd. at Elk Meadow). In truth, you're likely to see more elk than trillium flowers, and find the redwood trees more exciting that the small waterfall. But it's still an attractive trail, best in the spring when the falls flow at their peak.

The **Lost Man Creek Trail** (1 mile off U.S. 101, east of Elk Meadow, 0.5 mile, easy–difficult) has it all. The first half-mile is perfect for wheelchair-users and families with small children. But as the trail rolls along, the grades get steeper and more challenging. You can spend all day trekking from the picnic grounds by the creek around and down to Bald Hills Road almost to the Redwood Creek Overlook.

Another fabulous long hike is the **Redwood Creek Trail** (Bald Hills Road spur off U.S. 101, difficult). This trail follows Redwood Creek all the way down to the **Tall Trees Grove.** If you've got someone willing to act as a shuttle, you can pick up the **Tall Trees Trail** and walk it to the **Dolason Prairie Trail,** which will take you back out to Bald Hills Road. For visitors who'd prefer to spend two days out on the trail, you can stop at either **Elam Camp** or **44 Camp**, both hike-in, primitive campgrounds.

## Accommodations

The **Redwood Hostel** (14480 U.S. 101 at Wilson Creek Rd., Klamath, 707/482-8265, www.norcalhostels.org/redwoods, $21–52) has fabulous views, abundant charm, and worthwhile amenities. South of Eureka along U.S. 101, the Redwood Hostel has ready access to parks, beaches, and trails. On the outside, you'll see an old green building that's obviously been around for a while. Inside, you'll find the casual clutter that defines most hostel common areas. Linens are included with the bunk rates, dorm rooms are small and have pretty wooden bunk beds, and private family rooms are available. Kitchen and laundry facilities are well lit and spacious. The cheerful young owners can help with transportation, food, and the nearest great hiking spots.

## Information and Services

If you're new to the Redwood National and State Parks region, the **Thomas H. Kuchel**

## WOODSY TOURIST TRAPS

As you wend your way up U.S. 101 through the verdant forests filled with rare trees, you'll become aware of something besides parks and trails luring visitors to pull over and rest awhile. You'll know them by the collections of tacky chainsaw carvings, the kitschy hand-painted signs, and the cheap, shiny toys out front. Whether you've found a Redwood Sculpture Emporium, a Drive-Thru Tree, or a Mystery Spot, hang on to your wallet when you stop at one of the infamous redwood coast tourist traps.

The granddaddy of all tourist traps – it's even an example of the concept in Wikipedia – is the **Trees of Mystery** (see *Sights*). Trees of Mystery has it all: tacky wood sculptures, a "mystery" visual-trickery trail, and a gondola ride. But most of all, it's got a gift shop the size of a supermarket selling some of the tackiest souvenirs you can possibly imagine and perhaps a few that will make you shriek softly with horror. Imagine a cheap build-a-bear machine sitting next to a display of varnished redwood slices painted with images of Jesus and the Virgin Mary.

The various Drive-Thru Trees are usually privately owned tourist traps, and you'll pay $10-20 to drive a tiny one-way street through a large mutilated tree. Why would anyone do this? Well, the novelty of finding trees big enough to create drive-thru tunnels catches the attention of many out-of-state visitors. And families on long road trips often shell out for the drive-thru trees to sidetrack their utterly bored kids for just five more minutes.

Finally, you can't miss the roadside redwood sculpture stands, even if you try. They dot the sides of the highway, selling the tackiest in wooden animals lovingly sculpted by chainsaw artists. You'll also find T-shirts, coffee mugs, shot glasses, and dozens of other tacky souvenirs. Little animal figurines made out of petrified moose and elk turds are a particular favorite with the children.



**Visitors Center** (U.S. 101, west of Orick, 707/465-7765, Mar.–Oct. daily 9 A.M.–5 P.M., Nov.–Feb. daily 9 A.M.–4 P.M.) is your main stop. This big center includes a ranger station, clean restrooms, and a path right out to the shore. You can get maps, advice, permits for backcountry camping, and books here. Picnic tables perch here, or you can walk just a short way up to Redwood Creek.

## PATRICK'S POINT STATE PARK

Patrick's Point State Park (U.S. 101, 25 miles north of Eureka, 707/677-3570, www.parks.ca.gov) is a rambling coastal park replete with campgrounds, trails, beaches, landmarks, and history. It's not the biggest of the many parks along the North Coast, but it might be the best. The climate remains cool year-round, making it perfect for hiking and exploring, if not for ocean swimming. Because Patrick's Point is tiny in comparison to the other parks, it's easy to get around by requesting a map at the gate and by following the signs along the tiny and often nameless park roads.

### Sights

Prominent among the landmarks is park namesake **Patrick's Point,** which offers panoramic Pacific views and can be reached by a brief hike from a convenient parking lot. Another popular spot is **Wedding Rock,** adjacent to Patrick's Point in a picturesque cove. People truly do hike the narrow trail out to the rock to get married and you might even see a bride and groom stumbling along holding hands on their way back from their ceremony.

Perhaps the most fascinating area in all of the park is **Sumeg Village.** This re-creation of a native Yurok village is based on an actual archaeological find that lies east of the "new" village. Visitors can crawl through the perfectly round hobbit-like hole-doors into semi-subterranean homes, meeting places, and storage buildings. Or check out the native plant garden, a collection of local plants the Yurok people used for food, basketry, and medicine. Today, the local Yurok people use Sumeg Village as a gathering place for education and celebrations, and request that visitors tread lightly and do not disturb this tranquil area.

### Hiking

Only six miles of trails thread their way through Patrick's Point. Choose from the **Rim Trail,** which will take you along the cliffs for a view of the sea and if you're lucky a view of migrating whales. On the other hand, tree-lovers might prefer the **Octopus Tree Trail,** which shows its walkers a great view of an old-growth Sitka spruce grove.

### Beaches

For those who want to dip a toe in the ocean rather than just gaze at it from afar, Patrick's Point encompasses a number of accessible beaches. The steep trail leading down to **Agate Beach** deters few visitors. This wide stretch of coarse sand bordered by cliffs shot through with shining quartz veins is perfect for lounging, playing, and beachcombing. The semi-precious stones for which it is named really do cluster here. The best time to find good agates is in the winter, after a storm.

### Camping

The campgrounds at Patrick's Point meanders through the park. It can be difficult to determine the difference between **Agate Beach, Abalone,** and **Penn Creek,** so be sure to get good directions from the rangers when you arrive. Most campsites are pleasantly shaded by the groves of trees; all include a picnic table, a propane stove, and a food storage cupboard. You'll find running water and restrooms nearby, plus showers.

### Information and Services

Patrick's Point does not have a visitors center. You can get a map and information at the entry gate, and information about nature walks and campfire programs is posted on the bulletin board. The nearest one sits to the north at Thomas H. Kuchel Visitors Center (U.S. 101, west of Orick, 707/465-7765).



# The Lost Coast

So how did this stretch of California become Lost? In the state that made the personal automobile a necessity, the area known as the Lost Coast is not accessible by any state or Interstate highway. In fact, much of the Lost Coast hasn't got so much as a gravel lane nearby. Many native Californians have never been anywhere near this region; others heft their backpacks and spend weeks hiking the Sinkyone and King's Mountain Range backcountry wilderness. A precious few towns service the general area, providing food, lodging, and lots of local history.

## FERNDALE

Ferndale was built in the 19th century by Scandinavian immigrants who came to California to farm. Dairy pastures and farmland still surround the town today, and many of the "happy cows" in California munch grass near Ferndale. In town, little has changed since the immigrants constructed their fanciful gingerbread Victorian homes and shops.

### Sights

The main "sight" in Ferndale is the town itself, since the whole thing is a designated historical landmark. Ferndale is all Victorian, all the time—just ask about the building you're in and you'll be told all about its specific architectural style, its construction date, and its original occupants. Even the public restrooms in Ferndale are housed in a small Victorianesque structure, surrounded by Main Street's shops, galleries, inns, and restaurants—all set into scrupulously maintained and restored late 19th-century

Lost Coast beaches



buildings. Architecture buffs can spend hours just strolling through downtown.

Inside the historic facades, two fascinating little museums open their doors to anyone who cares to come inside. The **Ferndale History Museum** (Shaw and Third Sts., 707/786-4466, June–Sept. Tues.–Sat. 11 A.M.–4 P.M., Sun. 1–4 P.M., $1) is a block off Main Street and tells the story of the town. Life-sized dioramas depict period life in a Victorian home, and an array of antique artifacts brings history to life. Downstairs, the implements of rural coast history vividly display the reality that farmers and craftspeople faced in the pre-industrial era. On the other hand, the **Kinetic Sculpture Museum** (580 Main St., 707/786-9259, Mon.–Sat. 10 A.M.–5 P.M., Sun. noon–4 P.M.) salutes wacky modernity in all its colorful, weird glory. As the endpoint of the region's annual Kinetic Sculpture Race, Ferndale has the honor of housing a number of the kinetic sculptures. No docents interpret the art displayed here, so visitors must make what they can of the duckies, froggies, aeroplanes, and bicycles.

To cruise further back into the town's history, consider wandering out into the **Ferndale Cemetery** on Ocean Street. Well-tended tombstones and mausoleums wend up the hillside that back the town. Genealogists will love reading the scrupulously maintained epitaphs that tell the human history of the region.

## Entertainment and Events

Expectedly, Ferndale is a quiet town where the sidewalks roll up early. But for visitors who like to be out and about after 6 P.M., a few fun options await. Locals collect in the bar at **Curley's Bar and Grill** (400 Ocean Ave., 707/786-9696, Mon.–Sat. 11:30 A.M.–9 P.M., Sun. 8 A.M.–9 P.M.), sipping the dangerously delicious signature cocktails and enjoying local live music several nights each week. The **Ferndale Repertory Theater** (447 Main St., 707/786-5483, www.ferndale-rep.org, $12–15) puts on a number of shows each year. Most are wholesome and well suited for the whole family, and many are put on by local kids and teens, but be sure to check what's on when you're in town. Also check the schedule for special events and performances. Late into the night, you can fill the slots at the **Bear River Casino** (11 Bear Paws Way, 707/733-9644, www.bearrivercasino.com).

Ferndale hosts the **Humboldt County Fair** (1250 Fifth St., www.humboldtcountyfair.org) each August. For 10 days, people from all around the county come to celebrate at the down-home fair, complete with livestock exhibits and horse racing, competitions, a carnival, musical entertainment each night, and a variety of shows for kids and adults on the fairground stages. If you're in the area, come join the fun!

## Shopping

A tour of Ferndale's Main Street shops makes for an idyllic morning stroll. The Victorian storefronts house antique stores, jewelry shops, clothing boutiques, and art galleries. Ferndale is also a surprisingly great place to buy a hat.

The **Golden Gait Mercantile** (421 Main St., 707/786-4891) has it all: antiques, candies, gourmet foodstuffs, clothing, hats, souvenirs, and more. Antiques and collectible tend to be small and reasonably priced. By comparison, **Silva's Fine Jewelry** (400 Ocean Ave., 707/786-4425, www.silvasjewelry.com), on the bottom floor of the Victorian Inn, is not a place for the faint of wallet. But the jewels, both contemporary and antique, are classically gorgeous. Another jewel is the **Blacksmith Shop** (455 Main St.707/786-4216, www.ferndaleblacksmith.com), which displays a striking array of useful art made by top blacksmiths and glass blowers around the country. Few art galleries can compare to the unique array of jewelry, furniture, kitchen implements, fireplace tools, and metal things defying common description. A gentler warmth comes from the **Golden Bee** (441–451 Main St.), a purveyor of fine products made with honey and beeswax. The candles, soaps, and much more make the whole store smell delicious.

## Accommodations

In Ferndale, lodgings run to (of course) Victorian-style inns, mostly bed-and-breakfasts. Guests of the **Shaw House B&B** (703 Main St., 800/557-7429, www.shawhouse.com, $125–275) must walk a block or two to get to the heart of downtown Ferndale. But the reward for staying outside of the town center is a spacious garden well worth a stroll of its own. In the heat of the afternoon, huge shade trees and perfectly positioned garden benches make a lovely spot to sit and read a book, hold a quiet conversation, or just enjoy the serene beauty of garden and town. A lush morning breakfast fortifies shoppers ready to walk up and down Main Street, as well as adventurers preparing to head out to the deserted beaches of the Lost Coast or the trails into the nearby redwood forests.

The **Victorian Inn** (400 Ocean Ave., 888/589-1808, $100–400) is an imposing structure at the corner of Main Street, which also houses Curley's Bar and Grill and Silva's Jewelry. The inn includes 13 rooms, all uniquely decorated with antique furnishings, luxurious linens, and pretty knickknacks. Package deals are available, including a rare chance to spend the night in the famous (private and inaccessible) Carson House in Eureka.

**Hotel Ivanhoe** (315 Main St., 707/786-9000, www.ivanhoe-hotel.com, $95–145) is cattie-corner across from the Victorian Inn. (Nothing in Ferndale is far from anything else in Ferndale.) In a town full of history, the Ivanhoe is the oldest hostelry still standing in town. Plaques on the outside of the building describe its rich legacy. Fully refurbished in the 1990s, the four guest rooms are done in rich colors that revive the western-Victorian atmosphere of the original hotel.

Two other great B&Bs in Ferndale are the award-winning **Collingwood Inn B&B** (831 Main St., 800/469-1632, www.collingwoodinn.com, $125–215), with uniquely decorated rooms, and the **Gingerbread Mansion Inn** (400 Berding St., 800/952-4136, www.gingerbread-mansion.com, $135–340), with lush antiques, luxurious linens, and turn-down service.

If bric-a-brac and scented soaps make your skin itch, an inexpensive not-an-inn accommodation option in Ferndale is the **Redwood Suites** (332 Ocean Ave., 707/786-5000, www.redwoodsuites.com, $75–105). Only a block off Main Street, the Fern Motel's rooms are simple yet comfortable. Family suites with full kitchens are available, and the price is right.

## Food

**Curley's Grill** (400 Ocean Ave. 707/786-9696, Mon.–Sat 11:30 A.M.–9 P.M., Sun. 8 A.M.–9 P.M. $13–30) is part of the Victorian Inn complex. Here California cuisine meets good old-fashioned bar-and-grill-style food. Salads are delicious, and so are the heartier entrées. Signature cocktails are big and potent, served in both the bar and the dining room. The dining room is a high-ceilinged, dimly lit barn of a place that somehow manages to be charming. Service is warm and timely, and both couples and family groups are welcome.

The restaurant at the **Hotel Ivanhoe** (315 Main St., 707/786-9000, www.ivanhoe-hotel.com) is a favorite for folks as far away as Eureka. It's all about the hearty homemade Italian dishes and friendly personal service. A more casual Italian dining experience can be had down the street at the **Ferndale Pizza Co.** (607 Main St., 707/786-4345, Tues.–Thurs. 11:30 A.M.–9:30 P.M., Fri.–Sat. 11:30 A.M.–10 P.M., Sun. noon–9:30 P.M.).

The **Candy Stick Fountain and Grill** (361 Main St., 707/786-9373) harkens back not to the 19th century, but to the 1950s. Come sit on a shining red vinyl bench at a big booth table, or on a matching stool at the old-fashioned counter. Enjoy retro-style soda fountain fare like burgers, fries, and ice cream treats. If your accommodations don't furnish breakfast, stop in at local favorite **Poppa Joe's** (409 Main St., 707/786-4180). The interior is dim and narrow, but the breakfast and lunch fare is yummy.

If you need to grab some grub and go, **Valley Grocery** (339 Main St., 707/786-9515) stocks staples and also maintains a deli; it's a perfect last stop on the way out to a beach picnic. Don't forget to stop at the heavenly candy store **Sweetness and Light** (554 Main St., 707/786-4403, www.sweetnessandlight.com, Mon.–Sat. 10 A.M.–5 P.M., Sun. 11 A.M.–5 P.M.).

## Practicalities

Ferndale's paper, the ***Ferndale Enterprise,*** is published weekly and also puts out a souvenir edition aimed at tourists once a year. Many inns and shops carry the souvenir edition, which is free, all year long.

If you need medical care, the **Humboldt Medical Group** (528 Washington St. 707/786-4028) can assist you. The **post office** is at 536 Main Street.

Ferndale, like much of the Lost Coast, is not directly accessible from the freeway. Leave U.S. 101 at Fernbridge and follow CA-211 right into town. Mattole Road leads out of town south toward the Sinkyone Wilderness area, while Centerville Road heads out to the beach. Walking provides the best views and feel of the town itself.

# MATTOLE TO SHELTER COVE

This is the true "Lost Coast," the remote rugged coastline accessible by few roads and no highways at all. Even GPS navigators lose connectivity out here, so bring an old-fashioned map if you plan to explore the unspoiled wilderness from Mattole to Shelter Cove. The reason to make the arduous trek out to the Lost Coast is to hike the miles of wilderness trails.

## Sights

One of the few drivable routes to view the Lost Coast is via **Mattole Road.** This narrow, mostly paved two-lane road affords views of remote ranchland, unspoiled forests, and a few short miles of barely accessible cliffs and beaches. In good weather, the vista points from Mattole Road are spectacular. This road also acts as the connecting access to the even smaller tracks out to the trails and campgrounds of the Sinkyone Wilderness.

**Big Black Sands Beach** is one of the most beautiful and accessible features of the Lost Coast. Just north of the town of Shelter Cove, you can enjoy a walk with your family along the dark sands of the wide beach. This beach also serves as the south end of the Lost Coast Trail.

At **Mal Coombs Park** in Shelter Cove, the tower of the **Cape Mendocino Lighthouse** now rests quiet and dark. It began its life on Cape Mendocino—a 400-foot cliff that marks the westernmost point of California—in 1868. In 1951 the tower was abandoned in favor of a light on a pole, and in 1998 the tower was moved to Shelter Cove, becoming a museum in 2000. The original first-order Fresnel lens is now on display in nearby Ferndale.

## Hiking and Backpacking

Easier day hikes include the long walk across **Big Black Sands Beach** to either Horse Creek or Gitchell Creek. Even kids can make these easy, pretty walks. **Mattole Beach** is another spot with a broad sandy beach that's perfect for an easy, contemplative stroll of any length you choose. The **Chemise Mountain Trail,** only 1.5 miles long, gives hikers beautiful views of beaches and mountains from the top of Chemise Mountain. For guided day hikes, contact the **Sanctuary Forest** (hike@sanctuaryforest.org) organization for their summer schedule of interpretive hikes.

Serious Lost Coasters bring their backpacks and spend days on the trail, enjoying the serenity of a place where few others come to disturb them. The ultimate Lost Coast experience, **Lost Coast Trail** (trailheads at Usal Campground, Big Black Sands Beach, Mattole Beach) takes about three days to traverse. Plenty of drinking water is a must, as is a current tide table since the beach areas of the trail dwindle and in some spots disappear at high tide. Campsites, many with restroom facilities (and small usage fees), cluster along the trail, making it easy for backpackers to rest when they need to. Be sure to pick up your backcountry permit at one of the ranger stations (Usal and Mattole have them), and apply for fire permits if you need them.

For another great hike, take the **King Crest Trail,** a mountain hike from the southern Saddle Mountain Trailhead to stunning King Peak and on to the North Slide Peak Trailhead. A good solid one-day round-trip (about 10 miles) can be done from either trailhead. An arduous but gorgeous loop trail, the eight-mile Hidden Valley–Chinquapin–Lost Coast Loop Trail can be done all in one day or in two with a stop at water-accessible Nick's Camp. **Buck Creek Trail** includes an infamous grade, descending more than 3,000 feet down an old logging road to the beach. The many other trails include **Rattlesnake Ridge, Kinsey Ridge, Spanish Ridge,** and **Lightning.**

## Surfing

**Big Flat** is a legendary surf spot about eight miles north of Shelter Cove. While the hike in is challenging, hardcore surfers will find it worth the effort. Other surf breaks along the Lost Coast are **Deadman's, No Pass,** and **Gale Point.**

## Fishing and Whale-Watching

The Lost Coast is a natural fishing haven. The harbor at Shelter Cove offers charter services for ocean fishing. **Salmon King Charters** (707/986-7521, www.innofthelostcoast.com) can accommodate up to six people for salmon (of course), rockfish, and other local delicacies—they'll even clean and fillet your catch for you. Another reputable charter service is **Shelter Cove Sport Fishing** (707/923-1668, www.codking.com). This company offers trips to hunt halibut, albacore, and salmon, as well as whale-watching trips.

If shellfish is your favorite, come to the Shelter Cove area in the springtime to enjoy the Northern California abalone season. Ask locally for this year's best diving spots.

## Camping

For many, staying on the Lost Coast means camping on the trails. Dozens of campgrounds welcome tired trekkers in need of respite. Some of the larger BLM camping areas (www.blm.gov/ca, no reservations) in the King Range include **Wailaki** (Chemise Mountain Rd., $8), **Nadelos** (Chemise Mountain Rd., $8), **Tolkan** (King Peak Rd., $8), **Horse Mountain** (King Peak Rd., $5), and **Mattole Campground** (end of Lighthouse

Rd., $8). Sites are semi- or fully developed with restrooms, grills, fire rings, picnic tables, bear boxes, and on-site water. Trailers and RVs up to 20 feet are allowed at these sites, though it's wise to check road conditions beforehand.

In Sinkyone Wilderness State Park (707/986-7711, www.parks.ca.gov), you can stay at **Usal Beach, Needle Rock,** or the **Sinkyone Wilderness Campground.** Sites are first come, first served.

## Accommodations

Shelter Cove offers several nice motels for folks who aren't up for roughing it in the wilderness overnight. At the **Shelter Cove Beachcomber Inn** (412 Machi Rd., 800/718-4789, $65–105), each room has its own character along with views of the coast or the woods. The inn is an easy stroll to the airstrip and downtown. **The Tides Inn of Shelter Cove** (59 Surf Point, 888/998-4337, www.sheltercovetidesinn.com, $95) has standard rooms and luxurious suites with fireplaces and full kitchens. Most rooms face the sea, which is only steps from the inn. The Tides Inn is centrally located within walking distance of the airstrip, local shops, and restaurants.

The **Inn of the Lost Coast** (205 Wave Dr., 888/570-9676, www.innofthelostcoast.com, $150) boasts an array of rooms and suites to suit even luxurious tastes. Rooms are large and airy, with stellar views. Ask about discounts for AOPA, AAA, and package deals with Salmon King Charters. The **Cliff House at Shelter Cove** (141 Wave Dr., 707/986-7344, www.cliffhousesheltercove.com, $150–170) perches atop the bluffs overlooking the black sand beaches. Only two suites are available; each has a full kitchen, living room, bedroom, gas fireplace, and satellite TV. These suites are a perfect spot from which to enjoy a romantic vacation or family getaway.

## Food

Most Lost Coast dining options cluster in Shelter Cove. For a delicious seafood meal, visit the glass-fronted A-frame **Chart Room** (210 Wave Dr., 707/986-9696, www.chartroom.cc, Sat.–Wed. 5–9 P.M.). In addition to seafood, the Chart Room serves hearty meat and pasta dishes, as well as vegetarian fare, sandwiches, and soups. Be sure to check out the nautical and aeronautical gift shop while you're there. At the **Cove Restaurant** (10 Seal Ct., 707/986-1197, www.shelltercoverestaurant.com, Thurs.–Sun. 5–9 P.M., Sun. 11:30 A.M.–3:30 P.M., $13–30), a solid hearty American menu, heavy on the seafood, looks perfect after a hard day of hiking, fishing, and beachcombing. A slice of pizza or a whole pie are on the menu for lunch or dinner at **Costa Cucina** (707/986-7672, Tues.–Sun. 11:30 A.M.–1:30 P.M., 4:30–8 P.M.).

For a quick bite of lunch or the ingredients for a trailside picnic, stop by the Campground Deli (492 Machi Rd., 707/986-7474). And if what you need is a hot cup of coffee or tea before an active day, buy it at **Cape Mendocino Tea** (1176 Lower Pacific Dr., 707/986-1138, Sat.–Mon. 11 A.M.–4 P.M., $7–21) or **Angel of the Sea Coffeehouse** (205 Wave Dr., 707/986-7888, Thurs.–Mon. 7:30 A.M.–noon).

## Practicalities

The **Sinkyone Wilderness State Park Visitors Center** (Usal Rd., 707/986-7711, www.parks.ca.gov) is the largest information center in the area. Mattole Campground and several of the other large campgrounds have information posted at the parking areas. Emergency services are coordinated through the Shelter Cove Fire Department (9126 Shelter Cove Rd., Whitethorn, 707/986-7507, www.sheltercove-ca.gov).

If you have access to a small airplane, consider flying in to the Shelter Cove Airport. If not, you can drive to the coast via Highway 1 or U.S. 101. Contact the State Parks department for maps and information about the trailheads in the Sinkyone and King's Range wilderness areas.

If you're up for a one-way journey through the Lost Coast Wilderness, look into a shuttle from one trailhead back to your car. **Lost Coast Trail Transport Service** (707/986-9909, www.lostcoasttrail.com) offers rides from the Shelter Cove Black Sands Beach to Usal Beach, Mattole Beach, and many other points along the trail.

## HUMBOLDT REDWOODS STATE PARK

Surprisingly, the largest stand of unlogged redwood trees anywhere in the world isn't on the coast and it isn't in the Sierras. It's right here in Humboldt, bisected by U.S. 101. Come to this park to hike beneath 300-plus-foot old-growth trees that began their lives centuries before Europeans knew California existed. The visitors center for the park rests along the Avenue of the Giants (CA-254), between the towns of Weott and Myers Flat. Start here if you're new to the region or need hiking or camping information. You can also enjoy the theater, interpretive museum, and gift shop here.

While it's more than worth the time to spend a weekend in the Humboldt Redwoods, you can also spend as little as an hour or two here. A drive through the Avenue of the Giants with a stop at the visitors center and a quick nature walk or picnic can give you a quick taste of this lovely south end of the coastal redwood region.

### Sights

The most famous stretch of redwood trees in the state, the **Avenue of the Giants** (look for signs on U.S. 101 to turnoffs, www.avenueofthegiants.net) parallels U.S. 101 and the Eel River between Fortuna and Garberville. Visitors come from all over the world to drive this stretch of road and gawk in wonder at the sky-high old-growth redwoods that line the pavement. Campgrounds and hiking trails sprout among the trees off the road. The Avenue's highest traffic time is July and August, when you can expect a bumper-to-bumper, stop-and-go traffic jam for almost the whole of the 31-mile stretch of road. If crowds aren't your thing, try visiting in the spring or fall, or even braving the rains of winter to gain a more secluded redwood experience.

### Hiking

With all that fabulous forest, it's hard to resist parking the car and getting out to enjoy the world of the big trees up close and personal. A great place to start is (duh!) Humboldt Redwoods State Park (707/946-2409, www.parks.ca.gov, day-use fee $6). Many visitors start with the **Founders Grove Nature Loop Trail** (0.5 mile, easy), located at mile marker 20.5 on the Avenue of the Giants. This flat nature trail gives sedate walkers a taste of the big old-growth trees in the park. Sadly, the one-time tallest tree in the world (the Dyerville Giant) fell. Now visitors can see it decomposing on the forest floor—a natural end to such a tree that feeds the newer life of the forest.

Right at the visitors center, you can enjoy the **Gould Grove Nature Trail** (0.5 mile, easy)—a wheelchair-accessible interpretive nature walk that includes signs describing the denizens of the forest.

If you're looking for a longer walk in the woods, try out the lovely **River Trail** (Mattole Rd., 1.1 miles west of Ave. of the Giants, 7 miles round-trip, moderate). It follows the South Fork Eel River, allowing access to yet another ecosystem. Check with the visitors center to be sure that the "summer bridges" are installed before trying to hike this trail.

Hardcore hikers who want to spend all day testing their legs can also find the fun at Humboldt Redwoods. Start at the **Grasshopper Multiuse Trail Head** (Mattole Rd., 5.1 miles west of Ave. of the Giants) to access the newer **Johnson Camp Trail** (10.5 miles round-trip, difficult) that takes you to the abandoned cabins of railroad tie makers. Or pick another fork from the same trailhead to climb more than 3,000 feet to **Grasshopper Peak** (13.5 miles, difficult). From the Peak, you can see for 100 miles in any direction, overlooking the whole of the park and beyond.

### Biking and Horseback Riding

Don't want to hoof it in the woods? You can bring your street bike up to the park and ply either the Avenue of the Giants or Mattole Road. A number of the trails throughout Humboldt Redwoods State Park are designated as multi-use, which means that mountain bikers can make the rigorous climbs and then rip their way back down.

Equestrians can also make use of the

multi-use trails, and the Cuneo Creek Horse Camp provides a place for riders who want to spend more than just a day exploring the thousands of acres of forest and meadowland.

## Swimming and Kayaking

The Eel River's forks meander through the Humboldt Redwoods, creating lots of great opportunities for cooling off on hot summer days. Check with the visitors center for this year's best swimming holes, though you can reliably find good spots at Eagle Point (near Hidden Valley Campground), Gould Bar, and Garden Club of America Grove. In addition to all the usual precautions you must take for unprotected river swimming, you must take care in the months of August and September. A poisonous (if ingested) blue-green algae can bloom late in the summer, making swimming in certain parts of the river hazardous.

In the springtime when the river flows high, kayakers and canoeists bring their craft out to launch into the Eel. Just call ahead to get river conditions before you strap your boat to the top of your car, as the flow can be unpredictable even in spring.

## HUMBOLDT'S TOP CASH CROP

Some people might not think first of pretty trees or cool coastlines when hearing the words "Humboldt County." Instead, many folks of a certain persuasion think of a lesser-seen plant that grows well in the damp temperate climate here. To be honest: Humboldt's (sub) culture is all about the pot.

Indeed, the climate, soil, and altitude of Humboldt County, as well as conditions in neighboring Mendocino and Trinity, are great for marijuana farming. And the dense forests make good cover for marijuana gardens in danger of discovery by DEA and CAMP helicopters. Better botanical knowledge of marijuana plants has led to a much bigger kick than pot smokers got back in the 1960s and '70s. Much of that knowledge has been gleaned right here in the redwoods as the counterculture hippies and artists of previous decades fled the increasingly hostile and overcrowded neighborhoods of San Francisco and Los Angeles to enjoy a "simpler" life on the land. That simplicity included green smoke as soon as the hippies arrived and growers have been making a living on the North Coast ever since. What was once a backyard-of-the-commune industry for the hippies has become a big business. Most of the pot smoked in the United States (and perhaps the world) comes from California.

The presence of Mexican drug cartels in the Humboldt redwoods is hotly debated these days. Whether you believe they're there or not, it's a good bet that if you stumble upon a remote pot garden, you should leave – quickly and quietly. It's a known fact that some major gardens, which can be worth billions of dollars on the open market, are guarded by big men with big guns who will shoot anyone trying to steal from their crop. South Humboldt County is rife with large farms, and even the locals recommend that hikers avoid trekking anywhere other than maintained, in-park trails to stay safe.

The state legalized medical marijuana by popular vote more than a decade ago, creating a pitched battle with the Feds over pot clubs and medical growers. CAMP, a state agency, leaves known medical marijuana growers alone.

Despite the roughly $4 billion per year the U.S. government spends on "marijuana suppression" these days, usage rates remain the same as they were during the Summer of Love.

Certainly marijuana plays a role in the lifestyle of many Humboldt residents. Most of the larger towns support at least one head shop, and local glassblowers can make a living creating and selling pipes that are works of art. The presence of Humboldt State University helps to bring in the next generation of pot smokers, and the local smokin' surf-and-arts crowd has been entrenched for decades. Several publications dealing with cannabis culture originate here, and the issue of marijuana never leaves the city and county governments.

## Entertainment and Events

The Humboldt Redwoods State Park area is quiet in general, but a few events draw visitors and locals alike. The **Humboldt Redwoods Marathon** (www.redwoodsmarathon.org), fondly known to participants as the Redwood Run, takes place each fall. Runners of all ability levels can participate; events include a full marathon, half-marathon, and 5K run.

## Accommodations

Few lodging options are really close to Humboldt Redwoods State Park other than the campgrounds in the park itself. For car and RV campers, you'll find plenty of options, including **Burlington Campground** adjacent to the visitors center, **Albee Creek** (Mattole Rd., 5 miles west of Ave. of the Giants), and the large and ever-popular **Hidden Springs Campground** (5 miles south of the visitors center, Ave. of the Giants). Minimalist campers will enjoy seclusion of the hike-in trail camps at **Johnson** and **Grasshopper Peak.** Reservations are strongly recommended for campsites, as this region is quite popular with weekend campers.

Folks on moderate budgets can find accommodations in nearby Garberville. Several small motels offer reasonable rooms, and many have outdoor pools where weary guests can cool off during the heat of summer. The best of these is the **Best Western Humboldt House Inn** (701 Redwood Dr., 707/923-2771, book.bestwestern.com, $143–165). Rooms are clean and comfortable, the pool is sparkling and cool, and the location is convenient to restaurants and shops in Garberville. You'll get the usual comforts of the Best Western chain. Most rooms have two queen beds, making this motel perfect for families and couples traveling together on a budget.

*The* place to stay in the Humboldt Redwoods area is the **Benbow Inn** (445 Lake Benbow Dr., 800/355-3301, www.benbowinn.com, $195–660). A swank resort backing onto Lake Benbow, this inn has it all: a gourmet restaurant, an 18-hole golf course, and a woodsy atmosphere that blends perfectly with the idyllic redwood forest surrounding it. Rooms glow with polished dark woods and jewel-toned carpets and decor. Wide king and comfy queen beds beckon to guests tired after a long day of hiking in the redwoods or golfing beside the inn.

## Food

The restaurant at the **Benbow Inn** (445 Lake Benbow Dr., 800/355-3301, www.benbowinn.com, dinner 6–9 P.M.) matches the lodgings for superiority in the area. It serves upscale California cuisine and features an extensive wine list with many regional wineries represented. The white-tablecloth dining room is exquisite, and the expansive outdoor patio overlooking the water is the perfect place to sit as the temperature cool on a summer evening. The only downside to this usually terrific restaurant is that service can lag on weekday nights when the dining room isn't full.

For travelers who can't spend a month's grocery money on one meal, Garberville proper has several modest eateries that appeal to weary travelers and families with kids. Drive or stroll down Redwood Drive and take your pick of a variety of restaurants. One of these is the **Woodrose Café** (911 Redwood Dr., 707/923-3191, www.woodrosecafe.com). You can get a traditional American-style breakfast and lunch at this small independent eatery, though it won't come cheap. The touristy nature of the locale has driven up the prices, but the food is usually palatable and the service acceptable.

Calling **Sicilito's** (445 Conger St., 707/923-2814, www.asis.com/sicilitos) "world cuisine" might be pushing it, especially when you see the funky signs out front advertising pizza and Mexican food. But the pizzas and taco salads are tasty (if unusual) and the beer and wine selection helps make diners happy with their choices. The small dining room's walls are crowded with American memorabilia, and the establishment sometimes gets filled with biker types making their way up U.S. 101.

Need a lift? You won't find too many Starbucks around here, so enjoy a taste of locally owned java instead. Grab a cup of coffee at **Signature Coffee** (3455 Redwood Dr., Redway, 707/923-2661).

### Practicalities

A few tiny towns dot the Humboldt Redwoods region, but they can be short on services such as gas stations. Top off in Fortuna or Willits if you can. There is a 76 station in Garberville, well off the highway at 790 Redwood Drive.

There's a supermarket, **Ray's Food Place** (875 Redwood Dr., 707/923-2279), in Garberville. You can also find ATMs and even some Internet service in town. The easiest post office to access is at 3400 Redwood Drive in Redway.

The nearest hospital with an emergency room is **Redwood Memorial Hospital** (3300 Renner Dr., Fortuna, 707/725-3361).

The best way to get to Humboldt Redwoods State Park from either the north or the south is via U.S. 101. You can also approach the center of the park from Mattole Road if you've been traversing the Lost Coast. Road signs direct visitors to the Avenue of the Giants. Bicycles are not permitted on U.S. 101, but you can ride the Avenue and Mattole Road.

# Mendocino and Sonoma Coasts



The coastline stretching from Sonoma County through Mendocino is the most popular retreat on the North Coast for locals. Weekends see Bay Area residents flock north to their favorite hideaways to enjoy the windswept beaches, secret coves, and luscious cuisine. This area has something for everyone, from dedicated deep-sea sport fishermen to wine aficionados to luxury spa lovers. Art is especially prominent in the culture here; from the 1960s onward, aspiring artists have found supportive communities, sales opportunities, and homes in Mendocino County. A wealth of galleries display their beautiful, often unusual work.

## WINERIES

The Pacific coastline is not an ideal climate for most wine grapes, thus you won't find dozens of wineries hugging the shore, even in famous Sonoma County. However, a few wineries persevere, growing grapes more suited to the cooler temperatures and using the salt air to create unique flavors in their wines.

### Pacific Star Winery

The only winery on the Mendocino Coast, Pacific Star Winery (33000 N. Hwy. 1, 707/964-1155, www.pacificstarwinery.com, daily 11 A.M.–5 P.M., tasting free) prides itself on using its unique location to create unique wines. Barrels of wine are left out in the salt air to age, incorporating a hint of the Pacific into each vintage. Friendly tasting room staffers will tell you how much they like their bosses, the winemaker, and which of the winery cats most likes to be picked up. Wines are tasty and reasonably priced, and the picnic grounds sit on a bluff overlooking the ocean.

### Annapolis Winery

A small winery up in the hills near Sonoma, Annapolis Winery (26055 Soda Springs Rd., Annapolis, 707/886-5460, www.annapoliswinery.com, daily noon–5 P.M.) sits just east of Sea Ranch. At this little family-owned winery, you'll find a pleasant coastal hill climate and a small list of classic California wines. You can taste sauvignon blanc, chardonnay, zinfandel, and cabernet here, all under the funky rooster-emblazoned label. Take a glass outside to enjoy the views from the estate vineyards out over the forested mountains.

### Flowers Vineyard

So what kind of grapes could possibly grow in the chilly, drippy air of the northern California coast? Pinot noir and chardonnay grapes not only survive in such a climate, they thrive in the cool moist conditions. Flowers Vineyard (28500 Seaview Rd., Cazadero, 707/847-3661, www.flowerswinery.com) makes the most of its locale by specializing in these varietals. In fact, that's all you'll find when you come to taste at Flowers, except for one annual red blend. To fill their list, Flowers creates single-vineyard estate vintages, selecting from their favorite blocks of grapes.

### Gourmet au Bay

Gourmet au Bay (913 Hwy. 1, Bodega Bay, 707/875-9875, www.gourmetaubay.com, Thurs.–Tues. 11 A.M.–7 P.M.) isn't a winery; it's a shop and tasting bar in the coastside town of Bodega Bay. The good news is that you get to taste wines from a variety of different vintners, some major players in the Napa wine scene, some from wineries so small that they don't have tasting rooms of their own. You might even get to taste the odd French or Australian varietal when you "wine surf," tasting three wines poured and laid out on a miniature "surfboard" for you to carry out to the deck to admire the view. Inside, you can sip as you peruse the gift shop, which includes some local artisanal foods plus plenty of handmade ceramics and pottery and an array of toys for wine lovers.

## SIGHTS

The shores of Mendocino are clustered with state beaches and picturesque secluded coves. While many of the major tourist attractions are well worth a visit, as a traveler along this stretch of coastline, seek out that perfect spot of sand and make it your own.

### Skunk Train

One of the famed attractions to Mendocino County, the Skunk Train (depot at foot of Laurel St., Fort Bragg, 800/866-1690, www.skunktrain.com, office daily 8 A.M.–8 P.M.) is perfect for rail buffs and traveling families alike. The restored steam locomotives pull trains from the coast of Fort Bragg through the redwood forest to the town of Willits and back. The adventure lets everyone see the true majesty of the redwoods, while giving a hint about life in Northern California before the state highways. The gaily painted trains appeal to children, and the historic aspects and scenery call to adults. You can board in either Fort Bragg or Willits, making a round-trip to return to your lodgings for the night. Check the website for special rides featuring the food of local chefs, the wines of local vintners, and even locally brewed beers.

### Point Arena Lighthouse

Though its magnificent Fresnel lens no longer turns through the night, the Point Arena Lighthouse (45500 Lighthouse Rd., Point Arena, 877/725-4448, www.pointarenalighthouse.com, daily summer 10 A.M.–3:30 P.M., winter 10 A.M.–3:30 P.M., $5 adults, $1 children) remains a Coast Guard light and fog station. But what makes this unusually-shaped beacon special is its history. When the 1906 Earthquake hit San Francisco, it jolted the land all the way up the coast, severely damaging the Point Arena Lighthouse. When the structure was rebuilt two years later, engineers devised the above-ground foundation that gives the lighthouse both its distinctive shape and additional structural stability.

Visitors can enjoy an the Lighthouse's extensive interpretive museum housed in the fog station beyond the gift shop. Docent-led tours up to the top of the lighthouse are well worth the trip, both for the views from the top of the lighthouse and for the fascinating story of its destruction and rebirth through the earthquake as told by the knowledgeable staff. Tour groups also have the opportunity to climb right up to the Fresnel lens, taking a rare close look at an astonishing invention that reflected pre-electric light far enough out to sea to protect passing ships.

### Mendocino County Botanical Gardens

No tiny space carved out to nurture a few precious plants, the Mendocino County Botanical Gardens (18220 N. Hwy. 1, 707/964-4352, www.gardenbythesea.org, Mar.–Oct. daily 9 A.M.–5 P.M., Nov.–Feb. daily 9 A.M.–4 P.M., $10 adult, $7.50 senior, $4 youth) is a vast expanse of land bearing an astonishing variety of vegetation. Stretching 47 acres down to the sea, these gardens offer literally miles of walking and hiking through careful plantings and wild landscapes. The gardens' map is also a seasonal guide, useful for folks who aren't sure whether it's rhododendron season, or whether the dahlia garden might be in bloom. Butterflies flutter and bees buzz, and good labels teach novice botany enthusiasts the names of the plants they see.

### Glass Beach

The most famous beach in the Mendo area, Glass Beach (Elm St. and Glass Beach Dr., Fort Bragg) is *not* a miracle of nature. The dubious origin of this fascinating beach strewn with "sea glass" was the Fort Bragg city dump. As the ocean rose over the landfill, the heavy glass that had been dumped there stayed put. Years of pounding in the surf polished and smoothed the broken edges, and now the surf returns our human refuse to the shore.

Beachcombers can collect smooth, coated shards of glass in hues of green, blue, brown, and clear. The trail down to Glass Beach is steep and treacherous, so don't wear sandals! Good walking or hiking shoes and attention to safety are a must.

### Fort Ross State Historic Park

In the 19th century, Russians came to the wilds of Alaska and paired with the native Alaskans to ply the fur trade, killing seals, otters, and sea lions as well as land mammals for their pelts. The enterprise required sea travel, as the hunters chased the animals all the way to California. Eventually, a group of fur hunters and traders came ashore on what is now the Sonoma coast to create a wayfaring point for their brethren. This fortified outpost became known as Fort Ross (19005 Coast Hwy. 1, Jenner, 707/847-3286, www.parks.ca.gov, hours vary), named for the "Ross-ians" who built it.

Today, visitors can walk into the reconstructed fort buildings and see how the settlers lived. (U.S. 101 was originally built right through the middle of the fort area, but it was moved to make way for the historic park.) The only original building still standing is the captain's quarters—a large, luxurious house for the era and situation. The other buildings, including the large bunkhouse, the chapel, and

ROBERT HOLMES / CALTOUR

Fort Ross State Historic Park

the two cannon-filled blockhouses, were rebuilt using much of the original lumber used by the Russians. Be aware that a serious visit of the whole fort and the beach beyond is a level but long walk; wear comfortable shoes and consider bringing a bottle of water.

### Salt Point State Park

Stretching for miles along the Sonoma coastline, Salt Point State Park (25050 Hwy. 1, 707/847-3221, www.parks.ca.gov, visitors center open Sat.–Sun. 10 A.M.–3 P.M., day use $6) provides easy access from U.S. 101 to over a dozen sandy state beaches. You don't have to visit the visitors center to enjoy this park and its many beaches—just follow the signs along the highway to the turnoffs and parking lots. If you're looking to scuba or free dive, head for **Gerstle Cove,** accessible from the visitors center just south of Salt Point proper. The cove was designated as one of California's first underwater parks, and divers who can deal with the chilly water have a wonderful time exploring the diverse undersea wildlife here. For a more genteel experience at Salt Point State Park, head east off the freeway to the **Krause Rhododendron State Reserve.** Here you can meander along the China Gulf Trail in the springtime, admiring the profusion of pink rhododendron flowers blooming beneath the second-growth redwood forest. If you prefer a picnic, you'll find tables at many of the beaches—just be aware that the North Coast can be quite windy in the summertime. Campers throng to Salt Point in the summertime, and a number of campgrounds serve both tent campers and RVs stretch along the shore. Check the park website for campsite reservation information.

## Kelley House Museum

The mission of the lovely, stately Kelley House Museum (45007 Albion St., Mendocino Village, 707/937-5791, www.mendocinohistory.org, summer Thurs.–Tues. 11 A.M.–3 P.M., winter Fri.–Mon. 11 A.M.–3 P.M., admission free, tours $10) is to preserve the history of Mendocino for future generations. The newer addition to the historic home houses the village archives, which include thousands of photos. In the museum proper, antique furniture and fixtures grace the rooms. A rotating collection of Victorian clothing is displayed, as are photos and documents that tell the story of historic Mendocino. To help tell that story, knowledgeable docents hang out in the house. Ask about the town's water-rights issues for a great lesson in the untold history of the Mendo Coast. For a special treat, come on a weekend and ask about a tour of the nearby Presbyterian Church.

## Triangle Tattoo Museum

Warning: This is not your grandmother's art museum, so enter at your own risk. For more than 20 years, the Triangle Tattoo Museum (356B N. Main St., Fort Bragg, 707/964-8814, www.triangletattoo.com, from noon) has displayed the implements of tattooing and photos of their results. To enter, walk up a flight of narrow stairs and stare at the walls completely covered with photos of tattoos. All kinds are represented, from tribal to carnival to prison.

NORTH COAST

© LANCE SCOTT

Kelley House Museum

In glass cases upstairs, all types of tattooing apparatus, some antique and many tribal, stare out as if to dare passersby to allow them out onto live human skin. More photos grace the walls of the warren of small rooms in a never-ending collage. The street-side rooms comprise the working tattoo parlor, and you can find intrepid artists and their canvases working late into the evenings. If you're brave enough, talk to an artist about scheduling an appointment.

## ENTERTAINMENT AND EVENTS

### Bars and Clubs

Not too many happening nightclubs make their homes on the Mendocino coast. If you're looking for a local-style night out, get tickets to one of the live theater performances, find a winemaker's dinner or bundle up for a moonlit stroll on the coast. But if all you need is a pint of beer or a good stiff drink (or maybe a hot toddy after that beach stroll), the towns along the coastline have a number of pubs, breweries, and bars that open their doors into the night. The **North Coast Brewing Company** (455 N. Main St., Fort Bragg, 707/964-2739, www.northcoastbrewing.com, daily from noon) opened in 1988, aiming at the then-nascent artisanal beer market. Come in, grab a classic brewpub meal, then check out the latest beers. Whether you choose an Acme, a Red Seal Ale, or an Old Rasputin (yes, really), you'll definitely enjoy.



For a place to hunker down over a pint in Mendocino proper, saunter on over to **Patterson's Pub** (10485 Lansing St., Mendocino Village, 707/937-4782, www.pattersonspub.com). This traditional Irish-style pub sits in the former rectory of a 19th-century Catholic church. It nods to the 21st century with six plasma TVs that screen the current games. You can order a blessedly simple and filling meal either at the tables or the bar here. You'll find a dozen beers on tap, a full-fledged wine list, and hard liquors imported from around the world.

So where do the locals go for a drink in tourist-heavy Mendocino? That would be **Dick's Place** (45080 Main St., 707/937-5643, daily until 2 A.M.), sometimes called Richard's by the Sea. It's easy to find, just next to the Hotel with the only neon sign on Main Street. (It's a martini glass). The vintage-y decor pales next to the colorful array of resident drinkers perched around the bar at Dick's.

For nightlife lovers who don't need copious liquor to lubricate a good time, **Headlands Coffee House** (120 Laurel St., Fort Bragg, 707/964-1987, www.headlandscoffeehouse.com, Sun.–Thurs. 7 A.M.–10 P.M., Fri.–Sat. 7 A.M.–11 P.M.) makes a perfect destination. The pale blue walls and woven French-style chairs make this a light and bright place to grab coffee and a sandwich during the day. The coffee house really heats up with live entertainment every single night—usually a local jazz group. Order a cuppa, sit back, and enjoy a chill-out evening filled with music and conversation.

### Theater

The **Mendocino Theater Company** (707/937-4477, www.mendocinotheatre.org, $10–25, shows Thurs.–Sat. 8 P.M., Sun. 2 P.M., $15–20) offers a genuine small community theater experience. All plays are put up in the 81-seat Helen Schonei Theater (45200 Little Lake St., Mendocino), which definitely makes for an intimate night of live drama or comedy. The small, weathered old building exudes just the right kind of charm to draw lovers of quirky community theater inside its door. But this little theater company has big goals, and they show mostly newer works by playwrights who take on some of the toughest issues that resonate with modern audiences. You might see *Gross Indecency* or *Rabbit Hole* or another thought-provoking contemporary work here. Do keep in mind that this is a community theater company; don't expect Broadway quality, but do expect lots of fun and surprises.

The **Gloriana Opera Company** (210 N. Corry St., Fort Bragg, 707/964-7469, www.gloriana.org) focuses more on musicals than true operas, but their shows still delight young and old theatergoers alike. Gloriana seeks to bring music and theater to young people—accordingly, they produce major musicals that appeal to kids, such as *The Aristocats.* On the other hand, *Into the Woods* appeals mostly to kids who are past their second decade. Local performers star in the two major shows and numerous one-off performances that Gloriana puts up each year.

### Cinema

If you prefer your entertainment on a screen but still like a little atmosphere, take in a show at the **Arena Theater** (210 Main St., Point Arena, 707/882-3456, www.mendocino.com). This one-time vaudeville theater was also a "movie palace" of the old school when it opened in 1928. In the 1990s, the old theater got a restorative facelift that returned it to its art deco glory. Today, you can see all kinds of films at the Arena, from recent box office toppers to new documentaries to fun independent films. If the cinema isn't playing, you might find a live musical or theatrical show.

### Festivals and Events

Perhaps nowhere in California are festivals so much a part of life as in Mendocino. It's difficult to find a weekend in the region without something going on. Whether you prefer wine, art, music, or wildlife, you'll find a celebration of it somewhere on Mendo's packed festival and events calendar.

Art is a big deal in Mendocino. Accordingly, the area hosts any number of art events each year. **Art in the Gardens** (www.gardenbythesea.com, $20 at the door) takes place at the Mendocino County Botanical Gardens, for which it is an annual fundraiser. Each August, the gardens are decked out with the finest local artwork, food, and wine. Music entertains the crowds who come to eat, drink, view, and purchase art.

For folks whose tastes run more toward the musical arts, the annual **Whale and Jazz Festival** (www.mendocino.com) takes place all around Mendocino in April of each year. Some of the nation's finest jazz performers play in a variety of venues, while the whales put on their own show out in the Pacific. Point Arena Lighthouse offers whale-watching from the shore each day, and the wineries and restaurants of the region provide refreshment and relaxation every evening of the festival weekend.

In July, musicians of all types descend on the temporarily warmish coast for the **Mendocino Music Festival** (www.mendocino.com). For two weeks, live performances dot the landscape. Take your family to a children's matinee or your sweetie to a dance. Enjoy the soft relaxation of a chamber music performance or the lively beats of the famed big band concert, an annual fixture of the festival.

If restaurants are the heart of the Mendocino food scene, festivals are its soul. **Taste of Mendocino** (www.mendocino.com/mendocino-crab-wine-days-festival.html), also sometimes known as the Mendocino Crab and Wine Days, takes place from November through March each year. The Dungeness crab season, the wild mushroom season, and wine releases converge to create a fabulous time to visit the blustery Mendo Coast. Just about every restaurant in the area, plus all the wineries of Hopland and the Anderson Valley, gets in on the action for the weekends of the festival run. Check the website for the year's plethora of wine dinners, mushroom-hunting seminars, crab feeds, and special events. Take a cooking class put on by a local celebrity chef, deepen your knowledge of local wine varietals, or even head out onto the ocean to learn how the crab fishermen do their jobs.

## SHOPPING

On the coast, the best place to browse is **Mendocino Village.** Not only are the galleries and boutiques welcoming and fun, the whole downtown area is beautiful. It seems that every shop in the Main Street area has its own garden, and each fills with a riotous cascade of flowers in the summertime. Even if you hate to shop, make the trip down to the village just to (literally) smell the roses.

### Books

On the other end of the spectrum, pick up a new-to-you tome to read in your cushy bed at the **Main Street Book Shop** (990 Main

St., 707/937-1537). Next door to the funky Sweetwater, this used bookshop harkens back to Mendocino's days as an art colony. The books are vaguely organized into sections—the fiction and nonfiction at least seem separated on the cluttered tables and overstuffed shelves. It's easy to spend an hour in here, hunting bargains or for your next throwaway thriller.

### Galleries

**Panache** (45110 Main St. and 10400 Kasten St., Mendocino Village, 707/937-0947, www.thepanachegallery.com) displays and sells beautiful works of art in all sorts of media. You'll find paintings and jewelry, sculpture and art glass. Much of the artistic focus reminds viewers of the sea crashing just outside the large multi-room gallery. The wooden furniture and boxes are a special treat—handmade treasures using rare woods combined and then sanded and polished to silk-smooth finishes.

Even folks who find most art galleries pretentious can find the fun at the **Leedy Art Gallery** (45000 Main St., Mendocino Village, 707/937-1354, www.leedyart.com). Billed as "Art That Makes You Laugh," the pastel originals and reproductions in this smallish gallery really are that funny. You'll find the lawyer series, the golf series, and many other vividly colorful paintings that depict the human condition and American life just a little bit too well. If you're really lucky, you might find artist Jeff Leedy in the gallery when you visit. Laugh a bit and he'll gladly tell you all about the picture you're looking at and take you for a tour of the gallery.

### Gift and Home

The lavish B&Bs of Mendocino get many guests thinking about upgrading their home boudoirs. Knowing this, the **Golden Goose** (45094 Main St., 707/937-4655) offers all the linens and accessories that a (wealthy) shopper might need to create a soft and luxurious bed and bath all her own. The shopkeepers encourage you to pet the Egyptian cotton sheets and towels, sniff the sachets and soaps, and try on the thick spa-style robes. You'll find yourself longing for (and perhaps purchasing) a Mendocino inn sleep experience for every day of the week.

## SPORTS AND RECREATION

Resist the urge to spend all your time in Mendocino inside your inn, shopping at the galleries, and eating endless plates of fine food. Spend at least a few hours outdoors in the verdant wilderness and on the wild seashore that so beautifully define this region.

### Fishing and Whale-Watching

The Mendocino coast is an ideal location to watch whales dance, or try to land the big one (salmon, halibut, rockcod, or tuna). During Dungeness season, you can even go out on a crab boat, learn to set pots, and catch your own crab feed's worth of the delectable delicacy.

Many charters leave out of Noyo Harbor in Fort Bragg. The ***Trek II*** (Noyo Harbor, 707/964-4550, www.anchorcharterboats.com) offers five-hour fishing trips and two-hour whale-watching cruises. Aboard the ***Rumblefish*** (Noyo Harbor, 707/964-3000, www.fortbraggfishing.com), you can watch a demonstration of crab fishing or spot for whales in the winter from the comfort of the heated cabin, or fish for various deep-sea dwellers in the summer (and year-round for cod). The crew can even clean and vacuum-pack your catch on the dock before you leave.

### Canoeing and Kayaking

Kayak and canoe trips are a popular summertime activity on the Mendo coast. To explore the more sedate waters of the Big River estuary, consider renting an outrigger or even a sailing canoe from **Catch a Canoe & Bicycles Too!** (Hwy. 1 and Comptche Ukiah Rd., 707/937-0273, www.stanfordinn.com) at the Stanford Inn. For an adventurous day on the ocean, consider taking a sea cave tour by kayak. **Lost Coast Kayaking** (707/964-7480, www.lostcoastkayaking.com) launches three two-hour tours each day from Van Damme State Park. Because these tours use sit-on-top kayaks, no previous experience is necessary.

### Hiking and Biking

A wealth of smaller state parks makes hiking and biking on the Mendocino coast a pleasure. At **Van Damme State Park** (Hwy. 1, 3 miles south of Mendocino Village, 707/937-5804, www.parks.ca.gov), take a walk to the park's centerpiece: the wheelchair-accessible **Pygmy Forest** (0.25 mile, easy) loop trail. Here you'll see a true biological rarity: mature yet tiny cypress and pine trees perpetually stunted by a unique combination of always-wet ground and poor soil nutrient conditions. You can get to the Pygmy Forest from the **Fern Canyon Trail** (6 miles one-way, difficult), or drive Airport

## SWEATPANTS, PARKAS, AND NORTH COAST BEACHES

The Hollywood view of California beaches includes long, flat stretches of sugary white sand drenched in warm sunshine, populated by beautiful blondes in teeny bikinis and studly surfer boys riding the moderate waves.

Nothing could be further from the reality of the Northern California coast. Make no mistake – you'll find an overwhelming number of gorgeous beaches in the north, but it's a different kind of beauty. Craggy cliffs rise up to tower over narrow, rocky sand spits teeming with tidepools and backing into ever-changing sea caves. Wide swaths of beach become covered with driftwood, semiprecious minerals, and even fossils. Nonetheless, hardy beachgoers bring out their folding chairs, umbrellas, coolers, wetsuits, and surfboards to these beaches to enjoy a day on the sand and surf. If you aim to become one of these, here are some tips for equipment and preparation for your North Coast beach trip:

- **Dress in layers.** North Coast beach temperatures can hover in the 50s even in the middle of summer. Wear a sweatshirt and warm pants over shorts and T-shirt and wear that over your swimsuit.
- **Prepare for dampness.** Fog and drizzle often coalesce right on the coastline, even when it's sunny and hot only a few miles inland. Bring a hat and possibly a parka.
- **Bring appropriate footwear.** Most North Coast beaches are *not* barefoot friendly. Exploration of rocky beaches and tidepools demand either specialized shoes or good, broken-in hiking boots. Jellyfish sometimes wash ashore on California's northern beaches, making bare feet or even beach sandals a painful idea. And on fire-legal beaches, some folks just cover over an abandoned fire with a little sand, making for hot footing for the next beachcomber to walk by. Even if you choose to go on a barefoot walk on the sand, carry a pair of closed-toed shoes with you, just in case the going gets tough farther down the beach.
- **Going swimming or surfing?** That water is cold. Wear a wetsuit and booties if you don't want to experience hypothermia and possibly even the hospitality of the California Coast Guard rescue teams.
- **Learn about fire restrictions.** Fires are illegal on many California beaches. Check restrictions on the beach you are visiting before lighting up a nice big driftwood bonfire to keep warm.
- **Wear sunscreen!** Even if a layer of fog covers the sun, you are still at risk of a nasty sunburn. (California natives call it a "cloud tan.")
- **Prepare your kids.** Bring plenty of beach toys and talk up tidepool walks, but *do not* promise the little ones a swim in the ocean. The reality is that is may be too cold or just generally unsafe to swim.

Road to the trail parking lot (opposite the county airport) directly to the loop.

Perhaps the most popular hiking trails in coastal Mendocino wind through **Russian Gulch State Park** (Hwy. 1, 2 miles north of Mendocino Village, 707/937-5804, www.parks.ca.gov). Russian Gulch has its own **Fern Canyon Trail** (3 miles round-trip), winding into the second-growth redwood forest filled with lush green ferns. At the four-way junction, turn left to hike another 0.75 mile to the ever-popular waterfall. Be aware that you're likely to be part of a crowd visiting the falls on summer weekends. To the right at the four-way junction, you can take a three-mile loop (bringing your total hike to six miles) that brings you to the top of the small attractive waterfall. If you prefer the shore to the forest, hike west rather than east to take in the lovely wild headlands and see blowholes, grasses, and even trawlers out seeking the day's fresh catch.

Just north of Fort Bragg, tiny **MacKerricher State Park** (Hwy. 1, 3 miles north of Fort Bragg, 707/964-9112, www.parks.ca.gov) boasts cute Cleone Lake and miles of sand dunes and shoreline. *The* hike to take here is the **Ten Mile Beach Trail** (14 miles round-trip, moderate), starting at the Beachcomber Motel at the north end of Fort Bragg and running up an ironic seven miles to the Ten Mile River. Most of this path is fairly level and paved. It's an easy walk you can take at your own pace and turn around whenever you feel comfortable. Don't want to walk? Street bikes and inline skates are allowed on this trail.



### Horseback Riding

What better way to enjoy the rugged cliffs, windy beaches, and quiet forests of Mendocino than on the back of a horse? **Ricochet Ridge Ranch** (24201 N. U.S. 101, 707/964-7669, www.horse-vacation.com) has short trail rides departing four times a day, morning and afternoon. They also offer longer beach and trail rides, sunset beach rides, and full-fledged riding vacations by reservation. **Ross Ranch** (707/877-1834, www.rossranch.biz) provides horses and guides *by reservation only* for private treks at the south end of the county. Ross's horses are well cared-for and will please even the most discerning advanced rider.

### Diving

The best abalone in the region usually clusters in the waters of **Van Damme State Park** (Hwy. 1, 3 miles south of Mendocino Village, www.parks.ca.gov), which also makes a good entry point for shore divers. Another is **The Blowhole** (at the end of Main St., Mendocino Village), a favorite summer lounging spot for locals. In the water, you'll find tons of abalone and their empty shells, colorful tiny nudibranches, and, occasionally, overly friendly seals. The kelp beds just off the shore attract divers who don't fear cold water and want to check out the complex ecosystem.

Check with the park service or online for the abalone season opening and closing dates, limits, licensing information, and the best spots to dive each year.

### Spas

Relaxation is key to any Mendo coast vacation. A variety of spas can help out with this goal. The **Sweetwater** day spa (44840 Main St., Mendocino Village, 800/300-4140, www.sweetwaterspa.com) rents indoor hot tubs by the hour and offers a range of massage services at reasonable rates. The rustic buildings and garden setting complete the experience. In Fort Bragg, the **Bamboo Garden Spa** (303-C N. Main St., 707/962-9396, www.bamboogardenspa.com) pampers its guests with a wide array of massage, skin, and beauty treatments. Two-person hot tubs can be rented for $45 per hour.

Would you prefer a massage in the luxury of your own accommodations? In Mendocino, you can do that too. Call **The Body Works** (707/877-3430, www.massagetime.biz, $85/hour) for an appointment for a foot rub, herbal facial, full-body massage, or all of the above.

## ACCOMMODATIONS

Wherever you choose to stay in the Mendocino coast region, be aware that with the dozens of festivals all year long and the proximity to the

Bay Area, the most popular inns fill up fast on many weekends throughout the year. Fall and winter can be high season, with the Crab Festival, the Mushroom Festival, and the various harvest and post-harvest wine celebrations. The moral of all this: If you want to stay someplace specific on the Mendocino coast, book your room early—at least a month ahead of time for weekdays and six months or more in advance for major festival weekends.

So what's up with the range of room rates? The truth of it is that you'll only get the cheap end of the spectrum on unpopular weeknights. If you're visiting for a weekend—or worse, during a festival—expect to pay the premium room rates.

## $100-150

You'll find the bulk of less-expensive lodgings in and around Fort Bragg. The **Beachcomber Motel** (1111 N. Main St., Fort Bragg, 707/964-2402, $132–300, pets allowed) is clean and decent, boasting many rooms with an ocean view. Amenities are minimal but acceptable—about what you'd find at a low-end chain motel. Expect shampoo and soap in your tiny bathroom, but little else. Guest rooms are big enough to satisfy, though some visitors find them a bit dark and sparsely furnished; certainly the decor is nothing to write home about. Thin walls and shared patios make noise a problem, especially if a biker group is sharing the motel with you. At the north end of town, the Beachcomber isn't too convenient to downtown Fort Bragg, but it's a short drive to restaurants and services. What makes the Beachcomber worthwhile, besides its lower-than-a-B&B prices, is its location. It sits right on the beach so ground-floor guests can walk right out of their back doors, across the busy pedestrian and bike path, and onto the sand.

If the crowds in Mendocino Village and Fort Bragg aren't your style and you prefer a more secluded getaway, the **Elk Cove Inn** (6300 S. Hwy. 1, 800/275-2967, www.elkcoveinn.com, $135–395) is the perfect spot. This inn's unpretentious exterior barely hints at the luxurious room appointments inside. Choose from an antique-furnished room in the historic main building or a posh spa cabin overlooking the lawn. The attached day spa pampers guests with organic products and treatments especially designed for couples. Best of all, the tiny restaurant holds a secret: a chef worthy of the top San Francisco dining scene. The innovative dinner menu impresses even jaded big-city foodies, and a sumptuous breakfast is included with a stay at the inn. To work off all that rich cuisine, take a hike down to Elk Cove—the not-quite-private-but-close-enough secluded beach cove that foots the inn and lends it a spectacular view.

Fun and funky, the **Sweetwater Inn and Spa** (44840 Main St., Mendocino Village, 800/300-4140, www.sweetwaterspa.com, $125–300) harkens back to the days when Mendocino was a starving artists' colony rather than a yuppie weekend retreat. A redwood water tower was converted into a guest room, joined by a motley connection of detached cottages that guarantee guests great privacy. Every room and cottage has its own style—you'll find a spiral staircase in the water tower, a two-person tub set in a windowed alcove in the Zen Room, and fireplaces in many of the cottages. The eclectic decor makes each room unique, and many return guests request their favorite room again and again. Thick gardens surround the building complex, and a path leads back to the Garden Spa. The location, just past downtown on Main Street in Mendocino Village, is perfect for dining, shopping, and art walks.

## $150-250

The **Little River Inn** (7901 N. Hwy. 1, Little River, 888/466-5683, www.littleriverinn.com, $143–400) appeals to a more active coastal vacationer, boasting a 9-hole golf course and two lighted tennis courts. All of the recreation areas overlook the Pacific, crashing into the shore just across the highway from the inn. The sprawling white Victorian house and barns hide the sprawl of this inn, which also has a great restaurant and a charming sea-themed bar. The inn can cater to all sorts of travelers, from families looking for the privacy of a detached cottage to luxury-loving travelers to pet

© LANCE SCOTT

Sweetwater Inn and Spa



lovers who've brought their furry friends with them. Special guest room treats can include a fireplace, a spa, and a view of the ocean. Want to relax even further? Make a reservation for a massage or a manicure at the in-house Third Court Salon and Day Spa.

If you've got money to spare, the place to stay is **MacCallum House** (45020 Albion St., 800/609-0492, www.maccallumhouse.com, \$150–395). With several properties in addition to the main hotel in Mendocino Village, MacCallum is the king of luxury on the Mendo coast. Choose from private cottages with hot tubs, suites with jetted baths, and regular rooms with opulent antique appointments. The woodwork gleams and the service pleases here. Note that a two-night minimum is required on weekends, and a three-night minimum goes into effect for most holidays.

The **Stanford Inn** (Comptche Ukiah Rd., about 0.5 mile past the Hwy. 1 intersection, 800/331-8884, www.stanfordinn.com, \$225–500) is one of the largest accommodations in the Mendocino area. This resort hotel sits up away from the beaches, surrounded by redwood forest. Gardens surround the resort (in fact there's a nursery on the property), perfect for an after-dinner stroll. The location is convenient to hiking and only a short drive down to Mendocino Village and the coastline. Guest room have beautiful honey wood-paneled walls, pretty furniture, and puffy down comforters. You'll get the feel of an upscale forest lodge, whether you choose a basic Big River Room or one of the many varieties of suites. If you're traveling with a larger group, consider one of the elegant two-bedroom suites. (Be aware that here "executive suite" means "junior suite.") All rooms include breakfast at Ravens, a wood-burning fireplace, a TV with DVD player, a stereo, and Internet access.

One of the few true inns in Fort Bragg, the **Grey Whale Inn** (615 N. Main St., Fort Bragg, 800/382-7244, www.greywhaleinn.com, \$165–215) was once a community hospital. The blocky Craftsman-era building was erected by the Union Lumber Company in 1915. Today, 13 spacious, simply appointed guest rooms welcome travelers. Whether you get a view of the water or a more pedestrian city view, you'll get a lovely individually decorated room with a private bath and queen or king bed, perhaps covered by an old-fashioned quilt. The inn prides itself on simplicity and friendliness, and its perfect location in the heart of downtown Fort Bragg makes visitors feel right at home walking to dinner or the beach.

The **Auberge Mendocino** (8200 N. Hwy. 101, Little River, 800/347-9252, www.aubergemendocino.com, $160–325) is an elegant Victorian with a sweeping common area and four generous guest rooms. The lovely room appointments mix antiques and modern items, and the beds are supremely comfortable. You'll feel relaxed and at home with the designer-style fabrics, original artwork, and real plants and flowers. Be prepared for a huge breakfast in the morning, and if you can snag a slice of the owner's pear bread, take it—in fact, take two! A pretty garden leads out to a path that in turn picks up a trail right out to the ocean. On a nice summer day, you can walk from the inn to the secluded beach with a picnic lunch and enjoy yourself without ever getting in your car.

© LANCE SCOTT

breakfast, Auberge Mendocino

## Over $250

Making a refreshing change of pace from the endless North Coast Victorian inns, **Stevenswood Spa Resort** (8211 N. Hwy. 1, Little River, 800/421-2810, www.stevenswood.com, $166–1,000) offers contemporary lodgings in a contemporary lodge. The emphasis here lies in relaxation and pampering. Two restaurants and a day spa help towards this end, as do the convenient beaches and forestlands of Van Damme State Park, which surrounds the resort on three sides. When you book your room, also be sure to book one of the outdoor in-ground hot tubs at the spa for a relaxing evening with your sweetie. After your tub appointment, your ultra-luxurious room with its bright white linens, memory foam mattress, sparkling picture windows, modern furniture, and peaceful appointments will seem the perfect haven in which to snuggle down and sleep.

# FOOD

Mendocino prides itself on leading the California art scene, and the art of food is no exception. Some of the best cuisine in the state hides in small restaurants on the Mendo coast. It's hard to catch it all, so just try to hit as many different dining spots as you can.

## American

Visitors and locals alike can find themselves growing weary of the endless parade of haute cuisine served on the Mendocino coast. For a more down-to-earth meal, try the **Mendocino Café** (10451 Lansing St., Mendocino Village, 707/937-6141, lunch daily from 11 A.M., dinner daily from 5 P.M., $12–26) for a bowl of soup, salad, or filling sandwich. Granted, this is simpler food California-style; the lunch menu's focal point is its burrito bar, while Asian flavors populate the salad menu. At dinnertime, you'll find things like Thai burritos and barbecued ribs on offer. The café has a small kid's menu, a wine list, and a beer list. The café sits right in the midst of the gardens of downtown Mendocino Village—yes, that's a giant American flag with Rosie the Riveter on the side of the older building.

### California

It's strange that one of the best restaurants in an area known for its haute California cuisine is an open, airy bistro. **Mendo Bistro** (301 N. Main St., Fort Bragg, 707/964-4974, www.mendobistro.com, nightly 5–9 P.M., $10–28) wins with an unusual menu, dedication to local ingredients, and just plain great food. An unusual and fun culinary option is to create your own entrée from a pick-it-yourself menu of meats and vegetables you can mix and match with different sauces and cooking methods. In season be sure to try the award winning crab cakes. The restaurant sits upstairs on the balcony of the historical multi-use building, and no walls block your view of the other upstairs shops or the entrance below. The whole bistro feels completely open and airy, with a casual atmosphere that makes diners in jeans feel just as comfortable as those in dress clothes. If you're lucky, you might catch a glimpse of local celebrity chef-owner Nicholas Petti—he's the one in the chef's whites, funky cap, pirate's beard, and gold hoop earring.



### French

**Café Beaujolais** (961 Ukiah St., Mendocino Village, 707/937-5614, www.cafebeaujolais.com, lunch Wed.–Sun. 11:30 A.M.–2:30 P.M., dinner nightly from 5:30 P.M., $24–42) is a stand-out French-California restaurant in an area dense with great upscale cuisine. This charming out-of-the-way spot sits a few blocks away from the center of downtown Mendocino Village in a creeper-covered older home. Despite the white tablecloths and fancy crystal, the atmosphere here is casual at lunchtime and gets only a little bit more formal at the dinner hour. In step with California trends for sustainability, the giant salads and delectable entrées are made with organic produce, humanely raised meats, and locally caught seafood. Beware: The portions can be enormous, but you can get half-sized portions just by asking. Having trouble deciding what to order? Ask the wait staff, who are friendly, helpful, and quite knowledgeable about the menu and wine list, and the attractions of the local area, for that matter. Online reservations are available directly from the restaurant's website.

### Mexican

Perched improbably beside the entrance of MacKerricher State Park, the reputed best margaritas in all of Mendocino county are blended at the **Purple Rose Mexican Restaurant** (24300 N. Hwy. 1, Fort Bragg, 707/964-6507). While many locals find the food only average, it's said that if you just have a 'rita or two beforehand, you won't care too much about the cuisine.

### Seafood

Along the coast and with the small fishing and crabbing fleet of Fort Bragg's Noyo Harbor, it's natural that lots of seafood restaurants cluster nearby. For the most authentic, fresh, and simple fish preparations, head down to the harbor to any one of the several ultra-casual restaurants and fish markets. This harbor deals in salmon, mussels, and, of course, Dungeness crab, all in their seasons. You can try the regrettably named **Nemo's Fish Market & Grill** (32410 N. Harbor Dr., Fort Bragg, 707/964-1600) or the ratty-looking but tasty **Carine's Fish Grotto** (32430 N. Harbor Dr., 707/964-2429)—try the clam chowder! Another option is **Sharon's by the Sea** (32096 N. Harbor Dr., Fort Bragg, 707/962-0680, www.sharonsbythesea.com, daily 11:30 A.M.–3 P.M., 5 P.M.–close, $16–26), which boasts expensive prices, good service, and fabulous views.

### Vegetarian

Vegetarians and omnivores alike rave about **Ravens** (0.5 mile past Hwy. 1 on Comptche Ukiah Rd, 800/331-8884, www.stanfordinn

.com/ravens.html, breakfast daily from 7:30 A.M., dinner daily from 5:30 P.M., $17–25) at the Stanford Inn. Inside the lodge-style building surrounded by lush organic gardens, you'll find a big open dining room. Many of the vegetarian and vegan dishes served here use produce from the inn's own organic farm; otherwise, Ravens purchases from local organic and sustainable farmers whenever possible. At breakfast, enjoy delectable vegetarian (or vegan with tofu) scrambles, omelets, and Florentines, complete with homemade breads and English muffins. At dinnertime, try one of the unique salads or a seasonal vegetarian entrée. Even the wine list reflects the restaurant's commitment to its cause—most vintages come from organic, biodynamic, and sustainable-practice wineries. (Luckily for wine lovers, some of the best and most prestigious wineries in California use such practices.)

### Bakery and Dessert

Despite the often drizzly overcast weather, denizens and visitors to the Mendocino Coast crave ice cream in the summertime. **Cowlick's Ice Cream** (250 N. Main St., Fort Bragg, 707/962-9271, www.cowlicksicecream.com) serves delectable handmade ice creams in a variety of flavors. Yes, they really do serve mushroom ice cream during the famous fall Mendo mushroom season. You can get the perennial favorite flavors, such as vanilla, chocolate, coffee, and strawberry. If you're lucky, you might also find your favorite sometime-specialty flavor (banana daiquiri, cinnamon, green tea) on tap when you visit. If you're not in downtown Fort Bragg, you can also find this ultra-local family-owned chain at the Mendocino Botanical Gardens, Frankie's Ice Cream Parlor in Mendocino Village, and on the Skunk Train.

An unusual but tasty place to grab a latte and a pastry is the **Mendocino Cookie Company** (301 N. Main St, Fort Bragg, 707/964-0282, www.mendocinocookies.com). Their house special is obvious and baked on-site, making the storefront smell heavenly each morning. They prepare more than a dozen types of cookies, plus scones and croissants and other breakfast pastries. You'll usually find a line out the door of the tiny spot (which sits in the same building as the Mendo Bistro) as locals favor the coffee and espresso drinks. Most of the cookies lean heavily on the chocolate, but the cinnamon-sugar and ginger spice varieties are the bomb.

### Farmers Markets

Local, sustainable produce is a staple of Mendocino County food culture. On the coast, you can choose between three weekly farmers markets, open May through October. **Fort Bragg** hosts a market at Laurel and Franklin Streets 3:30–6 P.M. on Wednesdays. **Mendocino's** market appears on Fridays noon–2 P.M. at the corner of Howard and Main Streets. And farther south, the **Gualala** market opens 10 A.M.–12:30 P.M. on Saturdays at the Gualala Community Center.

## INFORMATION AND SERVICES



As a major tourist destination, the Mendocino coast region offers more services than you might expect for a string of small towns on a craggy stretch of coast. For the most urban atmosphere, complete with supermarkets and big-box stores, head for Fort Bragg.

The **Mendocino Coast Chamber of Commerce and Visitors Center** in Fort Bragg (332 N. Main St., 707/961-6300, www.mendocinocoast.com) gets travelers the maps, brochures, and information they need to have a great time in Mendocino County.

The major daily newspapers you might find in Mendocino are the ***San Francisco Chronicle*** and the ***Santa Rosa Press Democrat.*** In the visitors center and many of the inns and businesses, you'll find a wealth of tourist and travel publications. Both Mendocino Village (10500 Ford St.) and Fort Bragg (1605 Reilly St.) have **post offices,** as do Little River (7748 N. Hwy. 1) and Albion (3350 Albion Ridge Rd.).

The **Mendocino Coast District Hospital** (700 River Dr. at Cypress St., Fort Bragg, 707/961-4652, www.mcdh.org) has the closest full-service emergency room.

## GETTING THERE AND AROUND

### Car

Most folks travel around the Mendocino coast by automobile. Highway 1 is the main drag all the way from Elk up through Mendocino to Fort Bragg and beyond. If you're in Mendocino Village on a festival weekend, expect to have trouble finding parking downtown. Be prepared to pay premium event and lot fees, or to walk a good distance into the downtown area.

Coming up to Mendo from the Bay Area or from the northern reaches of California? The "short way" takes you up U.S. 101, then across the mountains to the coast via one of the passes. CA-20 takes you from Willits to Fort Bragg in the north, which is the shortest route from U.S. 101 to Highway 1. The longer route, CA-128, runs from Cloverdale to a spot south of Albion on the coast. Beware, especially if you're traveling at night, that these pass roads are narrow and twisty. Slow down and take your time getting through to be safe. All together, it takes about 2.5 hours to get from the City up to Mendo.

The longer but undeniably more beautiful way to get to Mendocino is to jump on Highway 1 just past the Golden Gate (or at any point north of Mendo). Expect to spend several hours traversing the cliffs and beaches, taking time to stop and take photos if you've gotten lucky enough to pick a sunny day.

### Air

The nearest major airports to Mendocino are San Francisco and Oakland International. You can also fly in to the **Sonoma County Airport** (2290 Airport Blvd., Santa Rosa, 707/565-7243, www.sonomacountyairport.org) on Horizon Air from Los Angeles, Seattle, Portland, or Las Vegas.

### Bus

The **Mendocino Transit Authority** (800/696-4682, www.4mta.org) runs bus service throughout the county. Ukiah acts as the hub for the MTA, but you can catch buses in Mendocino Village and Fort Bragg as well.



# Mendocino Wine Region

Mendocino's interior valley might not be quite so glamorous as the coast, but it is home to history, art, and liquor. The Anderson Valley is the apex of Mendocino's wine region, though the tiny town of Hopland also boasts its share of tasting rooms. Ukiah, the county seat, is home to a number of microbreweries and a thriving agricultural industry. The apples from the Anderson Valley and the pears from Ukiah are some of the best fruit in the state. Up in determinedly funky Willits, a late 1960s art vibe thrives in the 21st century.

Unlike the chilly, windy coast, the interior valleys of Mendocino get *hot* in the summertime. Bring shorts, a swimsuit, and an air-conditioned car if you plan to visit in the months from June to September.

## WINERIES

The two best areas in which to taste wine in Mendocino County are the Anderson Valley and the miniscule town of Hopland. You can cover either one thoroughly in half a day, or do both in one long day.

### Anderson Valley

The Anderson Valley wine trail, also known as CA-128, begins in Boonville and continues northwest toward the coast. Watch for wild turkeys and flocks of quail scuttling in the vineyards. The largest of these is **Navarro** (5601

Hwy. 128, 707/895-3686, www.navarrowine.com, daily 10 A.M.–5 P.M.). A broad-ranging winery with a large estate vineyard and event center, Navarro offers a range of tasty wines as well as some interesting specialty products such as verjuice. Another big name in the Anderson Valley, **Scharffenberger Cellars** (8501 Hwy. 128, 707/895-2957, www.scharffenbergercellars.com, daily 11 A.M.–5 P.M., tasting $3) makes chocolate in Berkeley and wine in Mendocino. While the wine isn't much to write home about, the tasting room is elegant and unusually child-friendly.

Small boutique wineries cluster in the Anderson Valley, enjoying an area less crowded than Napa or Sonoma. Any of these are worth a visit to seek out gem wines that aren't available in shops. **Handley Cellars** (3151 Hwy. 128, 707/895-3876, www.handleycellars.com, daily 10 A.M.–5 P.M., until 6 P.M. May.–Oct.) offers a complimentary tasting of hand-crafted wines you probably won't see in your local grocery store. The intriguing Handley tasting room features folk art from around the world for show and sale. Books on wine are sold too, especially those that focus on women making and drinking wine. **Esterlina** (1200 Holmes Ranch Rd., 707/895-2920, www.esterlinavineyards.com, tastings by appointment only) boasts the best view in the valley—come close to sunset if you can. Beyond the spectacular vineyard vistas, Esterlina tastes a unique selection of sparkling and still wines that make it well worth the trip to the top of its hill.

In a valley full of great wineries, **Roederer Estate** (4501 Hwy. 128, 707/895-2288, www.roedererestate.com, daily 11 A.M.–5 P.M., tasting fee) sparkles. The California sparkling wines they create are some of the best you'll taste. The large tasting room features a bar with sweeping views of the estate vineyards and huge cases filled with Roederer's well-deserved awards. Pourers are knowledgeable here, and you'll get to taste from magnum bottles—a rarity in any winery. Be sure to ask for a taste of Roederer's rarely seen still wines—you might find something wonderful.

For visitors who prefer a cold beer to a glass of wine, **Anderson Valley Brewing Company** (17700 Hwy. 253, 707/895-2337, www.avbc.com, Sat.–Mon. 11 A.M.–6 P.M., Thurs. 1–6 P.M., Fri. 11 A.M.–7 P.M., with longer hours in summer) serves up an array of microbrews

## BOONTLING: THE NORTH COAST DIALECT

Take your oddly broken English, throw in some old Scottish and Irish, add a pinch of Spanish and a dash of Pomo, then season with real names and allusions to taste. Speak among friends and family in an isolated community for a dozen years or more. The results: Boontling.

Boontling is a unique and almost dead language developed by the denizens of the then-remote town of Boonville in the Anderson Valley late in the 19th century. The beginnings of Boontling are obscured by time since all the originators of the language are "piked for dusties – that is, in the cemetery. And many Boonters – speakers of Boontling – are intensely protective of the local lingo. But in the 1960s, Professor Charles C. Adams of Cal State Chico came to town to study the language. He gradually gained the trust of the locals, and was able to write a doctoral thesis eventually published as a book, *Boontling: An American Lingo.* The book documents the history and acts as a dictionary for the more than 1,000 Boontling terms on record.

So if you find yourself in the Horn of Zeese (a café named for the Boontling term for "cup of coffee") and hear older folks speaking a language like none you've ever heard, you might just be listening to a rare and endangered conversation in Boontling.

NORTH COAST

that changes each year and each season. The warehouse-sized beer hall has a bar, a number of tables, and a good-sized gift shop. A beer garden out back is comfortable in spring and fall, and a disc golf course out back is popular with tourists and locals alike.

### Hopland

To get to the best wineries in Hopland, you never need to leave U.S. 101. The highway runs right through the center of town, and almost all the tasting rooms sit right against it. The star of this mini-region is **Brutocao Cellars** (13500 S. U.S. 101, 800/433-3689, www.brutocaocellars.com). Their vineyards crowd the land surrounding the town, and they took over the old high school to create their tasting room and restaurant complex. The wide, stone-tiled tasting room houses exceptional wines poured by knowledgeable staff. A sizeable gift shop offers gourmet goodies under the Brutacao label.

Can't get enough of Brutocao? They've got another tasting room out in the Anderson Valley (7000 Hwy. 128).

For folks who love wine but hate crowds, the tiny wineries and tasting rooms in Hopland are the perfect place to relax, enjoy sipping each vintage, and really chat with the pourer who just might be the winemaker and owner too. **Burford & Brown** (13265 S. U.S. 101, Ste. 5, 707/744-8781, www.burfordandbrown.com) is one of these. Step into the narrow tasting room to get the real story of each wine poured. Right next door, **Graziano** (13251 S. U.S. 101, 707/744-8466, www.grazianofamilyofwines.com, daily 10 A.M.–5 P.M.) provides another great small winery experience. Across the street, **McDowell Valley Vineyards** (13380 S. U.S. 101, 707/744-8911, www.mcdowellsyrah.com, Mon.–Fri. 11 A.M.–5 P.M., Sat.–Sun. 10 A.M.–5 P.M., free) inhabits a weathered old general store, complete with a central counter that's now the wine bar. Check out the cool kitchen kitsch as you enjoy your tasting.

Driving north out of town, the highway passes through acres of vineyards spreading out toward the forest in all directions. Many of these grapes belong to **Jeriko** (12141 Hewlitt and Sturtevant Rd., 707/744-1140, www.jeriko.us, Apr.–Dec. daily 10 A.M.–5 P.M., Jan.–Mar. daily 11 A.M.–4 P.M.). Visitors drive right between the chardonnay and the cabernet to get to the immense Napa-style tasting room. A glass wall exposes the barrel room with aging wines stacked high, tempting tasters to learn their secrets.

## SIGHTS

### City of 10,000 Buddhas

Treat respectfully when you visit the Sagely City of 10,000 Buddhas (4951 Bodhi Way, Ukiah, 707/462-0939, www.cttbusa.org). This active Buddhist college and monastery asks that guests wear modest clothing (try to avoid short shorts and short skirts, bare chests, and skimpy tank tops) and keep their voices down out of respect for the nuns and monks who make their lives here. Still, there's plenty for the spiritually curious to see here. The showpiece is the temple, which really does contain 10,000 golden Buddha statues. An extensive gift and book shop provides slightly silly souvenirs as well as serious scholarly text on Buddhism. For a treat, stop in for lunch at the vegan restaurant on the grounds, open to the public most afternoons.

### Solar Living Center

The Solar Living Center (13771 S. U.S. 101, Hopland, 707/744-2017, www.solarliving.org) successfully demonstrates what life might be like without petroleum. In Hopland, it's pretty darn good. The center presents a wide array of permaculture exhibits, from the organic garden to the solar-powered water system to the showpiece gift shop. The completely recycled bathrooms are worth a look even if you just went. If your vehicle happens to run on biodiesel, you can fill your tank here. For all travelers interested in ecological living, the center is a must-see.

### Grace Hudson Museum and Sun House

One of the few truly cultural offerings in Ukiah is the Grace Hudson Museum (431 S. Main St., Ukiah, 707/467-2836, www.gracehudsonmuseum.org, Wed.–Sat 10 A.M.–4:30 P.M.,

Sun. noon–4:30 P.M.). This small set of galleries focuses on the life and work of artist Grace Hudson and her husband Dr. John Hudson. The couple's life work revolved, among other things, around the history and culture of the Pomo and other Native Americans. The permanent collection of the museum includes many of Grace's paintings, a number of Pomo baskets, and the works of dozens of other California artists. For visitors whose imaginations are captured by the Hudsons' work, the museum offers docent-guided tours of the Sun House, which sits adjacent to the main museum building. This 1911 Craftsman-style house was in fact the eclectic and Bohemian Hudsons' home.

## ENTERTAINMENT AND EVENTS

### Bars and Clubs

While the daytime in Mendocino wine country is given over to the vino, the nightlife focuses around beer. Ukiah has a couple of top-notch brewpubs where you can a delicious pint of handcrafted brew.

The **Hopland Brew Pub** (13351 S. U.S. 101, Hopland, 707/744-1361, www.mendobrew.com, Wed.–Mon. noon–7 P.M.) serves some of the best local beer in the region. Mendocino Brewing Company produces one of California quaffers' favorite beers: Red Tail Ale. But don't stop at the Red Tail, and try some of the brewery's other great bird-named beers. Step inside the old red-brick square in downtown Hopland and you'll find a true traditional bar. It's dark, the wood is smooth and well worn, and regulars perch on barstools knocking back their favorite local brews.

For a later night out on the tiny town of Hopland, head for the bar downstairs in the **Hopland Inn** (13401 S. U.S. 101, Hopland, 800/266-1891, www.hoplandin.com, Sun.–Tues. and Thurs. 4–10 P.M., Fri.–Sat. 4–11 P.M., closed Wed., bar may be open later). Grab a barstool (if the locals don't have them all) and order a glass of local wine, a pint of local beer, or one of the wonderful single-malt scotches. On weekends, the restaurant often hosts local musical acts, livening up the night for restaurant and bar-goers alike.

The **Ukiah Brewing Company** (102 S. State St., Ukiah, 707/468-5898, www.ukiahbrewingco.com, Sun. 11:30 A.M.–9 P.M., Mon.–Thurs. 11:30 A.M.–11 P.M., Fri.–Sat. 11:30 P.M.–1 A.M.) offers good beer and good entertainment several nights each week. Settle in with a pilsner or an amber ale and enjoy the live music and other weekend evening entertainment. You might even get a chance to strut yourself at an open mic night.

### Festivals and Events

For the last 12 years, the Solar Living Center of Hopland has taken a weekend in August to put on "the greenest show on earth": **SolFest** (www.solfest.org). The hundreds of displays, demonstrations, and workshops go far beyond just solar power to teach and exemplify the ever-expanding world of permaculture and renewable energy. Keynote speakers each year include top names from the world of ecological activism and science. But it's not all serious business at SolFest; musicians perform on the main stage and the Saturday Night Moondance features entertainment and DJs for eco-lovers who love to dance deep into the night.

NORTH COAST

## SPORTS AND RECREATION

### Boating and Fishing

Even though a dry heat pervades inland Mendocino County in the summertime, a surprising range of water recreation is available. **Lake Mendocino** (www.lakemendocino.com) is an artificial lake along the Russian River that's held in place by Coyote Dam. It sits just off U.S. 101 north of Ukiah, allowing residents and visitors the chance to powerboat and water-ski, as well as canoe, kayak, and fish. Shockingly uncrowded even on the hottest summer afternoons, this locals' favorite is a great spot to cool off. You can even find a few beaches and lawns on which to spread out a blanket and lie down and shaded picnic tables where you can enjoy lunch.

You can access the lake from Lake Mendocino Drive, Calpella Drive, and a few other local roads off the freeway. Five marinas and two boat ramps sit along the shores of the lake, catering to boaters. A number of campgrounds also circle the lake—some are boat-in only.

### Hiking and Biking

The best hiking and biking trails in the area run in and around the Anderson Valley, where evergreen forests shade hikers from the worst of the summer heat. At **Hendy Redwoods State Park** (a half-mile south of CA-128 on Philo-Greenwood Rd., 707/895-3141, www.parks.ca.gov), you can hike to two old-growth redwood groves. For an easy shaded walk, visit the **Big Hendy** grove via its self-guided nature trail. This trail is wheelchair-accessible and perfect for folks looking for a sedate forest walk. Another fun little hike with some slope is the moderate **Hermit's Hut Trail**—yes, Hendy used to have its very own hermit. No one resides in the tree-stump hut anymore, though it remains a curiosity for hikers. Fit hikers who love longer treks can weave around the whole of the park; Big Hendy Loop connects to the Fire Road, which connects to the Hermit's Hut Trail, which intersects to the Azalea Loop and on down to the Little Hendy Loop for a complete survey of the park's best regions.



Another great place to take a nice, cool, shady hike is **Montgomery Woods State Nature Reserve** (Orr Springs Rd., 13 miles west of Ukiah, 707/937-5804, www.parks.ca.gov). This remote redwoods park is less crowded than its more accessible and popular brethren. The quintessential hike at Montgomery runs along **Montgomery Creek** (3 miles, moderate). Here you get a chance to see something special and unusual—both the Coastal and Giant Sequoia varieties of redwood tree growing in the same park. Montgomery's location and climate make it hospitable to both types of tree, which usually grow hundreds of miles apart.

### Spas

Wine and spas seem to go together naturally—perhaps it's the luxury factor. The most famous and historic spa in all of California sits tranquil and serene at the edge of Ukiah. Since its establishment in 1854, **Vichy Springs** (2605 Vichy Springs Rd., Ukiah, 707/462-9515, www.vichysprings.com, treatments $100–150 per hour, $40 non-resort all-day guest access to baths) has been patronized by Mark Twain, Jack London, Ulysses S. Grant, Teddy Roosevelt, and Jerry Brown. The hot springs, both mineral-heavy and naturally carbonated, closely resemble the world-famous waters of their namesake at Vichy in France. Spa-goers can view the source of the water bubbling out of the ground adjacent to the private bathhouses and the open-air hot pool. The water fills the baths, hot pool, and Olympic swimming pool. Day spa services include Swedish massage, hot stone massage, and facial-plus-massage treatments.

At the north end of the county in the artsy town of Willits, the **Baechtel Creek Day Spa** (101 Gregory Ln., Willits, 707/459-9063) offers a wide range of spa and aesthetic treatments. The serene woodsy retreat completes a relaxing day of pampering and beautifying. In the heart of downtown Ukiah, **Tranquility Day Spa** (203 S. State St., Ukiah, 707/463-2189, http://tranquilitydayspaukiah.com) caters to the hippie side of this culturally divided town. Swirling curtains match well with the sandalwood incense that pervades the big warehouse space. Tranquility has both salon and spa services—what's better than a new haircut *and* a relaxing massage?

## ACCOMMODATIONS

Accommodation options in and around the Anderson Valley vary widely. In the Valley proper you're more likely to find funky hotels and cabins, or forest-shaded campgrounds. Ukiah specializes in generic national chain motels from the modest to the mid-tier, and Hopland and Willits run to old-school independent hotels and motels.

### Camping

Stylish lodgings aren't thick on the ground in the Anderson Valley proper, but you can still find a pleasant place to stay near the wineries.

For wine and nature lovers on a budget, the campgrounds at **Indian Creek County Park** (Hwy. 128 at mile marker 23.48, 1 mile east of Philo, 707/463-4267, $10) and **Hendy Woods State Park** (8 miles northwest of Boonville, 0.5 mile south of Hwy. 128 on Philo-Greenwood Rd., 707/895-3141, www.parks.ca.gov, $20–25) provide woodsy, shady camp sites.

### Under $100

The **Anderson Valley Inn** (8480 Hwy. 128, Philo, 707/895-3325, www.avinn.com, $85–200), between Boonville and Philo, makes the perfect spot from which to divide your time between the Anderson Valley and the Mendocino coast. Eight small rooms are done up in bright colors and attractive appointments. Expect a small space with homey bedspreads that match the casual exterior of the small multi-building inn. A butterfly-filled garden invites guests to sit out on the porches reading the paper and sipping coffee. The two two-bedroom suites have full kitchens and are perfect for travelers looking to stay in the area a bit longer. The friendly owners welcome children and dogs (both must be attended at all times) and can be incredibly helpful with hints about how best to explore the region. This inn often books up fast on summer weekends, as it's one of the best value accommodations in the region. There's a two-night minimum on weekends May–October.

### $100–150

**The Hopland Inn** (13401 S. U.S. 101, 800/266-1890, www.hoplandinn.com, $120–150) was the original hostelry of Hopland. In 1890, William Wallace Thatcher strove to create an elegant hotel to rival those in San Francisco, so he built a large structure with more than 40 guest rooms, soaring ceilings, and elegant woodwork. Visitors today will find the creature comforts—such as air conditioning, huge bathrooms, and luxurious linens—updated to suit modern tastes. But the large rooms themselves remain as they were more than 100 years ago, with Victorian floral wallpaper and large antique furniture. Suites are also available. The bar and dining room welcome guests to enjoy a leisurely evening of drinking and dining, while the library filled with books to appeal to guests who prefer quiet literary contemplation. A complimentary buffet breakfast in the dining room each morning completes the inn experience.

In Ukiah, the plentiful lodging options run to standard chain motels. Out by the airport, the **Fairfield Inn** (1140 Airport Park Blvd., 707/463-3600, www.marriott.com, $115–165) is a comfortable choice. With an elegant lobby, indoor pool and spa, small exercise room, and generous complimentary continental breakfast, guests are comfortable and content in this motel. The guest rooms are about what you'd expect of a decent mid-priced chain: floral spreads, durable nondescript carpets, and comfortable and clean bathrooms. Next door, the **Hampton Inn** (1160 Airport Park Blvd., 707/462-6555, www.hamptoninnukiah.com) offers attractive rooms, an outdoor pool and spa, high-speed Internet access, and a buffet breakfast.

### $150–250

In the midst of Boonville, the quaint **Boonville Hotel** (14050 Hwy. 128, 707/895-2210, www.boonvillehotel.com, $140–310) pulls a switcheroo. The rough, weathered exterior belies the updated, comfortable guest rooms hiding inside this small-town hotel. Each of the 10 rooms is bright and airy, with light-colored, up-to-date furniture and an attractive collection of mismatched decorations. If you're traveling with children or pets, request one of the rooms that's set up to accommodate them. Downstairs, you'll find big, comfortable common areas and a huge garden suitable for strolling. Amenities include a book and gift shop, a good-sized bar, and a dining room. For a relaxing treat, book one of the rooms with a balcony—they come with a hammock set up and ready for napping.

## FOOD

### American

A locals' favorite, the **Maple Restaurant**

(295 S. State St., Ukiah, 707/462-5221, breakfast and lunch daily, $10) serves excellent and inexpensive breakfast and lunch fare. Excellent service complements good, uncomplicated American-style food. Shockingly good coffee makes a final charming touch to this lovely find.

The **Highpockety Ox** (14081 Hwy. 128, 707/895-2792, $10–20) touts itself a "civilized saloon." Indeed the atmosphere is about the best thing about this eatery. Meal prices are high and fare is basic, and clearly the dining room caters to the wine-tasting tourist crowd. But the bar is another high point. Most of the beer served at the Ox is locally brewed—just down the road at the Anderson Valley Brewing Company, in fact. Locals cluster at the bar and greet the bartender and wait staff as old friends, and visitors might even catch a syllable or two of Boontling.

## California

The tiny town of Hopland boasts few restaurants, but those available are worth the stop. The restaurant at the **Hopland Inn** (13401 S. U.S. 101, 800/266-1891, www.hoplandinn.com) serves dinner to inn guests and visitors alike. Locals prefer the big bar area, while diners are ushered in to the cavernous dining room or out to the pleasant two-level patio area. For late evening dining in the summertime, the patio is absolutely the place to be—the Inn hosts live musicians several times each week, and as the air cools into evening, the temperature becomes perfect. The menu is an innovative selection of California cuisine, and the wine list is a who's-who of local vintners. You might easily buy a bottle of something you tasted just across the street earlier in the afternoon.

Of the dining options in Ukiah, one of the very best is **Patrona** (130 W. Standley St., Ukiah, 707/462-9181, www.patronarestaurant.com, Tues.–Sat., 5:30–9 P.M., $15–30), where especially innovative California cuisine is served in a bistro-casual atmosphere by attentive servers. Portions are good-sized but not enormous, and the attention to detail from the kitchen is impressive. The wine list features all sorts of Mendocino County vintages, plus a good range of European wines. Most wines are available by the bottle only, but the servers will gladly cork an unfinished bottle for you and let you take it home to enjoy the following day.

## Italian

**The Crushed Grape** (13500 S. U.S. 101 Hopland, 707/744-2020, www.brutocaoschoolhouseplaza.com, Tues.–Sat. 11 A.M.–9 P.M., $10–20) is attached to the Brutocao tasting room. This elegant bistro features upscale Italian cuisine and house wines. The Lion Bistro is also part of the Brutocao complex, offering diners a more casual experience.

## Farmers Markets

A picnic makes a perfect lunch in the Anderson Valley, and farmers markets and farm stands can supply fresh local ingredients. The farmers market happens in Boonville on Saturday mornings 9 A.M.–1 P.M. It draws a crowd, so be prepared to hunt for parking. For fresh fruit and vegetables every day, try **Gowan's Oak Tree Farm Stand** (Hwy. 128, 2.5 miles north of Philo, daily 8:30 A.M.–5:30 P.M.). The stand belongs to the local farm of the same name, and sells only in-season local produce and homemade products made with the same fruits and veggies.

# INFORMATION AND SERVICES

If you need assistance with local lodgings, dining, or wine tasting, one place to find it is at the **Ukiah Chamber of Commerce** (200 S. School St. Ukiah, 707/462-4705, www.ukiahchamber.com). As the county seat, it offers plenty of information about both the city of Ukiah and the county of Mendocino.

For national news, most Mendocino residents read the ***San Francisco Chronicle.*** But if you want a paper with more local flavor, pick up a copy of the ***Ukiah Daily Journal*** (www.ukiahdailyjournal.com). This local daily paper can give the best in up-to-date entertainment and events throughout your visit.

The **Ukiah Valley Medical Center** (275 Hospital Dr., Ukiah, 707/462-3111, www.uvmc.org) has a 24-hour emergency room as part of its full service hospital, just in case.

As a good-sized city, Ukiah has branches of many major national banks. You'll find ATMs in many of the usual places: bank branches, supermarkets, pharmacies, and such. Internet access is available (often for a fee) at many of the chain motels and of course at the various Starbucks and other cafés.

You can find one or two ATMs in Hopland and more in Willits, which has a more modern big-box retail area at its south end. Check with your lodgings for Internet access, or stop by a café in Willits.

You can find **post offices** in Ukiah (224 N. Oak St.), Willits (315 S. Main St.), Hopland (13400 S. U.S. 101), and Boonville (14170 Hwy. 128).

## GETTING THERE AND AROUND

### Car

To get to the Mendocino wine country from either the south or the north in California, find U.S. 101. Drive until you get to Willits in the north or Hopland in the south, then stop.

The Anderson Valley wine road is CA-128, with most of the wineries clustering between Boonville and Philo. You can get to CA-128 from U.S. 101 either directly out of Hopland or from Ukiah on CA-253.

### Air

The closest major commercial airports to the Mendocino wine country are San Francisco and Oakland International. General aviation fliers can land at **Ukiah Municipal Airport** (1411 S. State St., Ukiah). From there, it's an easy trip to the heart of the local wine country.

### Bus

The **Mendocino Transit Authority** (800/696-4682, www.4mta.org) runs bus service throughout the county. Ukiah acts as the hub for the MTA, but you can catch buses in Mendocino Village and Fort Bragg as well.

### Tours

Many of the major wine country touring outfits that operate from San Francisco and the Napa Valley also offer trips in the Anderson Valley. Otherwise, try the folks at **Mendo Wine Tours** (888/805-8687, www.mendowinetours.com), a regional specialist offering a Lincoln Town Car for small groups and an SUV limo for groups of up to 10. Tours include a picnic lunch and expert knowledge of the region.

# LAKE TAHOE AND THE NORTHERN SIERRA

The mountains in the far north reaches of California are perhaps the most unspoiled areas in the state, protected by a wealth of national and state parks and forest lands. This region calls to all outdoor recreation enthusiasts—from downhill skiers to wakeboarders to serious hikers and backpackers.

Crystal-blue Lake Tahoe offers some of the best winter and summer outdoor recreation opportunities to be had statewide. Visitors who think that all of California consists of year-round warm, sunny beaches are often shocked to learn that Tahoe's ski resorts are some of the finest in the nation—second only to the Rockies for vertical drop, quality of snow, and number of resorts. In summer, wakeboarders, waterskiiers, and families all bring out their favorite toys to play in the pristine waters of the lake and to enjoy the stunning views of the wilderness areas that surround it.

Two mountains are notable as the most prominent features of this region: Shasta and Lassen. The snow-capped peak of Mount Shasta is a familiar picture-postcard sight, and is easily reached on I-5. Mount Shasta is quiet in contrast to Lassen—or at least it is for now. But Mount Shasta is not an extinct volcano; it is merely dormant and scientists are unsure as to when it will erupt again. South of Mount Shasta, its namesake Shasta Lake serves as a major resort area and boating vacation destination for Californians and visitors alike, with plentiful outdoor and indoor pursuits.

Mount Lassen, one of only two active volcanoes in the continental United States, is the more remote of the two and thus more of an

© PETTIT GILWEE / TOM ZIKAS

## HIGHLIGHTS

**The Village at Squaw Valley:** This adorable mountainside village, part of the Squaw Valley ski resort, is the perfect place to while away a winter day amid the numerous boutiques, galleries, restaurants, and entertainment (page 265).

**MacArthur-Burney Falls:** Touted as the "the most beautiful waterfall in California," these cascades run year-round and are accessible via a short, easy path (page 288).

**Lake Shasta Caverns:** A quick boat ride across Shasta Lake leads to these wonderful cathedral-like caverns, filled with natural limestone and marble stalactites, stalagmites, and new formations all their own (page 295).

**Loomis Museum and Manzanita Lake:** This interpretive museum offers a history of Lassen's volcanic eruptions through a series of stunning and informative pictorials (page 304).

**Bumpass Hell:** A two-mile hike leads through this hot bed of geothermal activity, including boiling mud pots, fumaroles, steaming springs, and pools of boiling, steaming water (page 305).

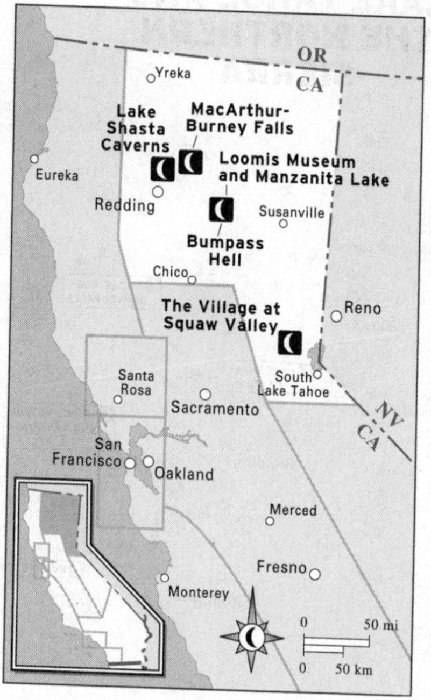


LOOK FOR TO FIND RECOMMENDED SIGHTS, ACTIVITIES, DINING, AND LODGING.

adventure to visit. Here, visitors are exposed to many unique volcanic features, including boiling mud pots, steam vents, and sulfur springs.

South of this mountain region, the city of Redding provides ready access and comparatively cosmopolitan entertainment before heading out to explore these vast outdoor pursuits.

## PLANNING YOUR TIME

Any of the major mountains make for a fabulous weekend getaway—particularly if you've got a three-day weekend to play with. Lake Tahoe has numerous recreation options and is usually accessible all year long. Many California residents take even longer trips to Tahoe; one or two week vacations to this area aren't uncommon because there's so much here to see and do. Mount Shasta and Mount Lassen are far more remote; it takes several hours driving from Tahoe (or most anywhere else in the state) to reach either of these peaks.

Mount Shasta offers fairly easy and reliable year-round access off I-5, plus both winter and summertime outdoor recreation. The weather on and near Shasta can get extreme; expect winter storms half the year and brutally high temperatures in the summer months. Check the weather reports so you pack the right clothes for your trip. If you're

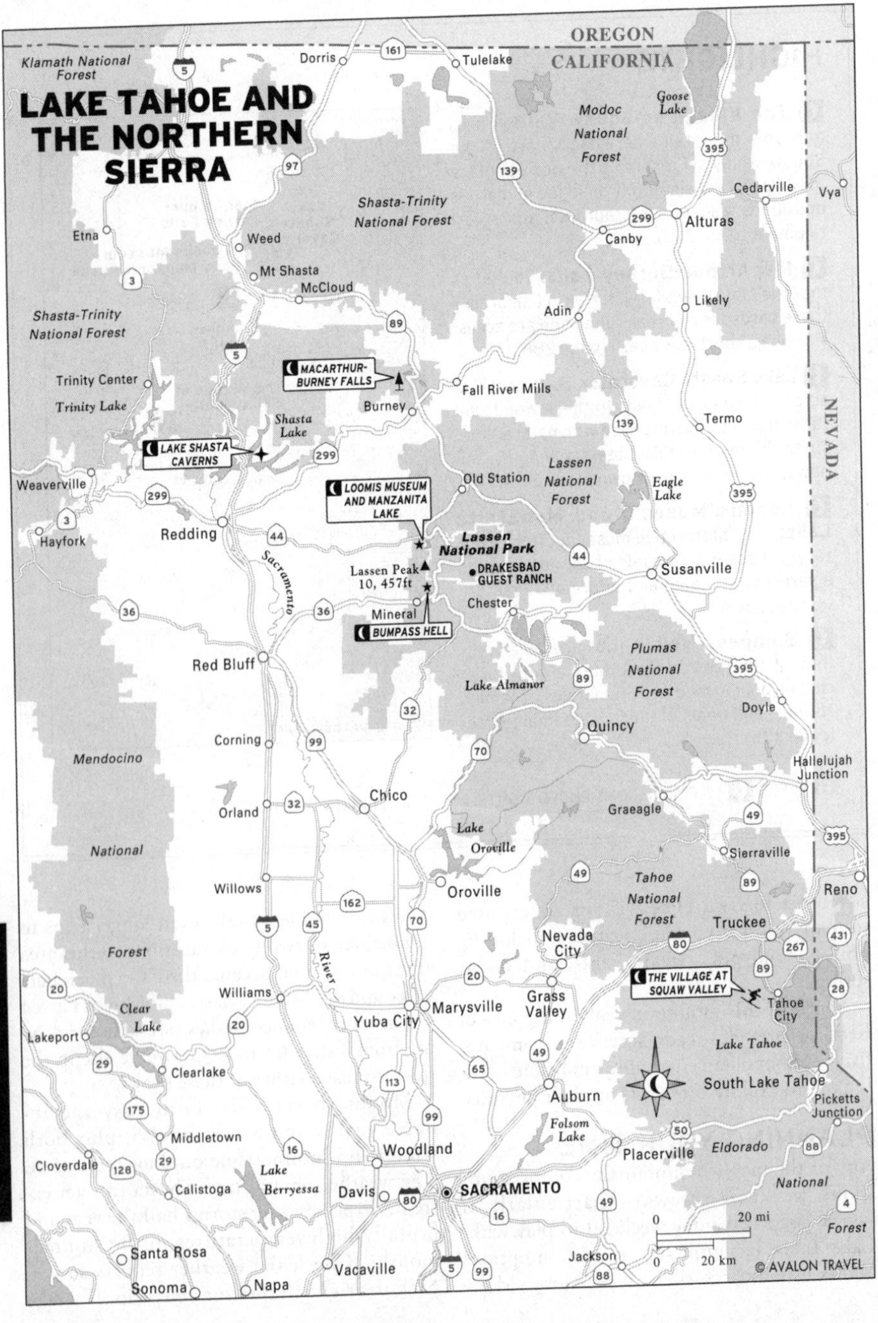
LAKE TAHOE AND THE NORTHERN SIERRA
OREGON
CALIFORNIA
NEVADA
Klamath National Forest
Dorris
Tulelake
Modoc National Forest
Goose Lake
Cedarville
Vya
Alturas
Canby
Shasta-Trinity National Forest
Etna
Weed
Mt Shasta
McCloud
Likely
Adin
Shasta-Trinity National Forest
MACARTHUR-BURNEY FALLS
Trinity Center
Trinity Lake
Fall River Mills
Burney
Termo
Shasta Lake
LAKE SHASTA CAVERNS
Lassen National Forest
Eagle Lake
Old Station
Weaverville
LOOMIS MUSEUM AND MANZANITA LAKE
Hayfork
Redding
Lassen National Park
Sacramento
DRAKESBAD GUEST RANCH
Susanville
Lassen Peak 10, 457ft
Chester
Mineral
BUMPASS HELL
Plumas National Forest
Red Bluff
Lake Almanor
Doyle
Quincy
Corning
Mendocino
Hallelujah Junction
Chico
Orland
Graeagle
Lake Oroville
National
Sierraville
Reno
Tahoe National Forest
Willows
Oroville
Truckee
Forest
Nevada City
River
THE VILLAGE AT SQUAW VALLEY
Williams
Grass Valley
Tahoe City
Clear Lake
Marysville
Yuba City
Lakeport
Lake Tahoe
Clearlake
Auburn
South Lake Tahoe
Picketts Junction
Folsom Lake
Middletown
Placerville
Eldorado
Woodland
Cloverdale
Lake Berryessa
National
Calistoga
Davis
SACRAMENTO
Forest
0
20 mi
20 km
Santa Rosa
Jackson
Vacaville
© AVALON TRAVEL
Sonoma
Napa
5
161
97
139
395
299
3
89
44
36
32
99
70
49
162
45
80
20
267
431
28
29
65
113
175
16
128
50
88
4

planning to climb high up the mountain, be aware that it's high enough to be create its own weather.

The best time to visit Mount Lassen, out in a remote eastern corner of the state where the weather gets serious, is the middle to end of summer. It can still be snowy on Lassen as late as June, so keep that in mind when you make your camping plans. During the winter the main road through the park closes, making your visit the region far less interesting.

Don't try to see all three mountains unless you've got a week or so to explore. If you do want to make a California mountains trip, start at Lake Tahoe and make your way up Highway 395 to Susanville and then across to Lassen. Hit Redding next, adding Shasta Lake and Mount Shasta.

# Lake Tahoe

Ask a California resident where to go for regular vacations or weekend getaways, and chances are high that at the answer will be 22-mile long Lake Tahoe. Tahoe's azure-blue waters and boulder-strewn shore draw visitors in summer while a plethora of snowy ski hills and forested wilderness draw winter sports enthusiasts.

Californians from the flatlands refer to Lake Tahoe as Tahoe. But the real locals get more specific—it's all about the North Shore versus the South Shore. Drive to the South Shore and you'll find a large town sprawling south along the huge lake, with glittering casinos just across (and I do mean *just* across) the state line. The South Shore offers great lakeshore parks with opportunities to access the water in the summertime.

The North Shore boasts the most downhill ski resorts, many of them clustered around the small, historic town of Truckee. It's possible

the shore of Lake Tahoe

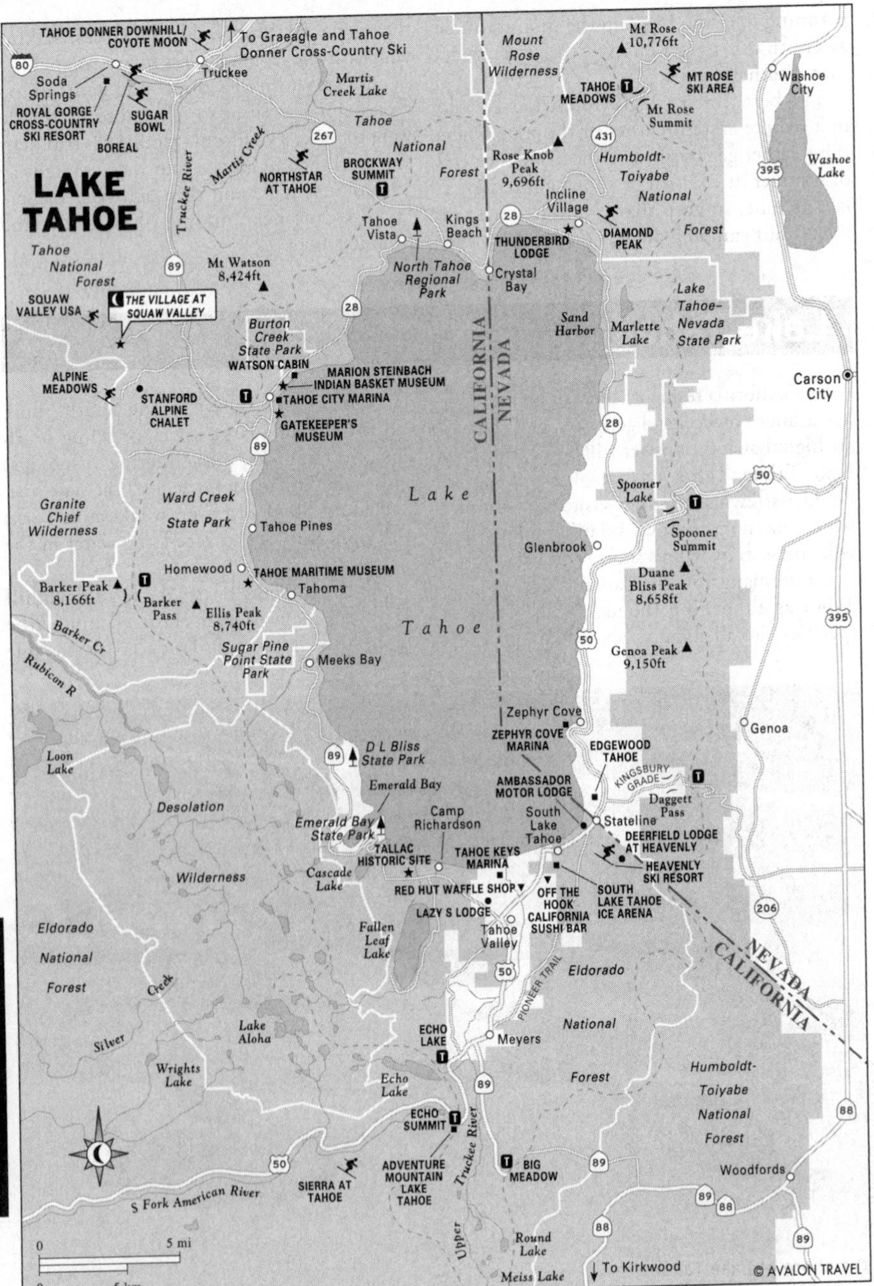
LAKE TAHOE
TAHOE DONNER DOWNHILL/ COYOTE MOON
To Graeagle and Tahoe Donner Cross-Country Ski
Soda Springs
Truckee
ROYAL GORGE CROSS-COUNTRY SKI RESORT
SUGAR BOWL
BOREAL
Martis Creek Lake
Tahoe National Forest
Martis Creek
Truckee River
NORTHSTAR AT TAHOE
BROCKWAY SUMMIT
Mount Rose Wilderness
Mt Rose 10,776ft
MT ROSE SKI AREA
TAHOE MEADOWS
Mt Rose Summit
Washoe City
Washoe Lake
Rose Knob Peak 9,696ft
Humboldt-Toiyabe National Forest
Incline Village
DIAMOND PEAK
THUNDERBIRD LODGE
Tahoe Vista
Kings Beach
North Tahoe Regional Park
Crystal Bay
Tahoe National Forest
Mt Watson 8,424ft
SQUAW VALLEY USA
THE VILLAGE AT SQUAW VALLEY
Burton Creek State Park
WATSON CABIN
MARION STEINBACH INDIAN BASKET MUSEUM
TAHOE CITY MARINA
GATEKEEPER'S MUSEUM
ALPINE MEADOWS
STANFORD ALPINE CHALET
Sand Harbor
Marlette Lake
Lake Tahoe-Nevada State Park
Carson City
CALIFORNIA
NEVADA
Granite Chief Wilderness
Ward Creek State Park
Tahoe Pines
Lake Tahoe
Spooner Lake
Spooner Summit
Glenbrook
Homewood
TAHOE MARITIME MUSEUM
Tahoma
Barker Peak 8,166ft
Barker Pass
Ellis Peak 8,740ft
Duane Bliss Peak 8,658ft
Barker Cr
Rubicon R
Sugar Pine Point State Park
Meeks Bay
Genoa Peak 9,150ft
Zephyr Cove
ZEPHYR COVE MARINA
Genoa
Loon Lake
D L Bliss State Park
Emerald Bay
EDGEWOOD TAHOE
KINGSBURY GRADE
Daggett Pass
AMBASSADOR MOTOR LODGE
Desolation Wilderness
Emerald Bay State Park
Camp Richardson
South Lake Tahoe
Stateline
DEERFIELD LODGE AT HEAVENLY
HEAVENLY SKI RESORT
TALLAC HISTORIC SITE
TAHOE KEYS MARINA
Cascade Lake
RED HUT WAFFLE SHOP
OFF THE HOOK CALIFORNIA SUSHI BAR
SOUTH LAKE TAHOE ICE ARENA
LAZY S LODGE
Tahoe Valley
Eldorado National Forest
Fallen Leaf Lake
PIONEER TRAIL
NEVADA
CALIFORNIA
Silver Creek
Lake Aloha
ECHO LAKE
Meyers
Humboldt-Toiyabe National Forest
Wrights Lake
Echo Lake
ECHO SUMMIT
Truckee River
ADVENTURE MOUNTAIN LAKE TAHOE
SIERRA AT TAHOE
BIG MEADOW
Woodfords
S Fork American River
Upper
Round Lake
Meiss Lake
To Kirkwood
0 5 mi
0 5 km
© AVALON TRAVEL
80
267
431
395
28
89
50
206
88

LAKE TAHOE

to drive all the way around the lake, stopping at both shores, state parks, and sights in both California and Nevada.

## SKI RESORTS

The number-one reason folks come to Tahoe is for the snow. Whether you're a skier or a snowboarder, into cross-country skiing or snowshoeing, or even just want to play in the snow with your kids, Tahoe's got a resort that's perfect for you.

### North Shore

Of the more than a dozen ski resorts surrounding Lake Tahoe, most of them sit on the North Shore. Tahoe regulars tend to divide into two camps: those faithful to Squaw Valley, and those in exclusive love with Alpine Meadows. Ne'er the two shall meet. (But skiing at any of the other resorts is acceptable.) Each resort has its own charms, strengths, and weaknesses. The best way to approach them is to try one or more and find your own favorites.

© LIZ HAMILL SCOTT

the mountain at Squaw Valley

#### SQUAW VALLEY

Squaw Valley (1960 Squaw Valley Rd., Olympic Valley, 530/583-6985, www.squaw.com, adults $55–73, youth $55, children under 12 $10) was the headquarters of alpine sports during the 1960 Winter Olympic Games. Today it is perhaps *the* most popular ski resort in California. The resort has every amenity you could possibly want and plenty of other activities, but skiing and boarding maintain their number-one precedence here. Squaw has a great ski school with plenty of fun on tap for new skiers and boarders of all ages, and a wide selection of fun intermediate slopes. Some of these, such as those serviced by the Squaw Creek, Red Dog, and Exhibition/Searchlight lifts are long—perfect for skiers who want to spend more time on the snow than on the lifts. But the jewels of Squaw are the many black diamond and double-black diamond slopes and the three terrain parks. Whether you prefer trees, moguls, narrow ridges, or wide open vertical bowls, you'll find your favorite at Squaw. The slopes off KT-22 are legendary with skiers around the world. If you want to try freestyle for the first time, head for Belmont Park. Hardcore freestylers go for The Ford Freestyle Park & Superpipe.

Squaw Valley offers night skiing free with a daytime lift ticket, or for a limited night-time-only fee. During the day, especially on weekends and holidays, expect long lines at the lifts, crowds in the (nice, big) locker rooms, and still more crowds at the (numerous) restaurants and cafés.

#### ALPINE MEADOWS

The other grand ski resort at Tahoe, Alpine Meadows (2600 Alpine Meadows Rd., Tahoe City, 530/583-4232, www.skialpine.com, mid-Nov.–mid-May, adults $44–63, youth $44–49, children 5–12 $10), sits just one ridge over from Squaw. This sprawling resort encompasses both sides of its two Sierra peaks: Scott and Ward. While Alpine has a ski school and a token small handful of green runs, it is not a beginner's resort. In fact, Alpine devotes considerable area to what it refers to as "Adventure Ski Zones."

These are large clusters of black diamond and double-black bowls and runs intended for expert skiers only. A dozen lifts service the mountains, including three high-speed chairs. An intermediate skier can have a great time at Alpine, especially coming off the Summit Six or the Roundhouse Chairs. Or try the south side—from Scott Peak off the Lakeview Chair, all runs are blues. If you're an expert, well, take just about any chair up the mountain and you'll find hair-raising excitement. The Scott Chair leads to a bunch of single blacks on the front of the mountain, as does the Summit Six Chair at the back of Ward Peak. Summit Six also services the famed Granite Chief area double-black slopes. Get to Art's Knob from Sherwood Express or possibly the Alpine Bowl Chair. Terrain parks aren't Alpine's long suit, but you can find three—not too creatively named Small, Medium, and Large—towards the bottom of the front side of the mountain.

## GETTING DISCOUNT LIFT TICKETS

The prices for skiing the famous mountains at Tahoe have garnered their own unique infamy. New skiers quickly learn that spending a day on the slopes of Squaw, Alpine, or Heavenly can cost almost as much as spending the night in the nearby hotels. So what's a budget-conscious boarder to do?

**Go coupon hunting.** Check the racks full of leaflets in Tahoe hotels, or go to the visitors centers. The advertisements for the various ski resorts often include discount coupons for lift tickets, or free rides on the resort ski shuttles. In supermarkets and pharmacies, look at the soda cans and popular snack products – some of these include a lift ticket coupon with proof-of-purchase. (This type of coupon gets popular every winter down on the flat land of Sacramento and the Bay Area.) Mine the Internet by entering "discount coupon [ResortName]" to find any online discounts or tips to find physical coupons.

**Ski in the afternoon.** If you're a casual skier who only needs a couple of hours on the slopes to feel satisfied, check with your favorite resort for its afternoon rates. Most resorts offer lower-priced lift tickets after 2 or 3 P.M.

**Ski a lot in one place.** Find your favorite resort and stick to it, taking advantage of the discounts built into two- and three-day (or more) lift passes.

### NORTHSTAR AT TAHOE

One of the best intermediate resorts in Tahoe, with over 60 percent blue slopes, is Northstar at Tahoe (100 Northstar Dr., Truckee, 800/466-6784, www.northstarattahoe.com, 8:30 A.M.–4 P.M., adults $60–75, youth $52–64, children $19–28). This smaller resort is often a bit less crowded than the big boys, and the slopes can be a bit friendlier here. At Northstar, even beginners can head way up the mountain on the fast Vista Express quad chair and still find green slopes heading gently all the way back to the Village. A "Slow Zone" creates a perfect spot for young children fresh out of ski school and wobbly adults who haven't spent their whole lives on the slopes. Intermediate runs crisscross the front of the mountain starting at the very peak off Comstock and running all the way down the mountain in what seems like every direction. The back side of the mountain, reachable via the Comstock Express quad chair and serviced by the Backside Express, is reserved for black diamond skiers, though adventurous intermediates can test their ski legs here. Freestylers will find the most terrain right off the Vista Express quad, though a couple of other small areas dot the mountain elsewhere.

### SUGAR BOWL

Another great mid-tier ski area is Sugar Bowl (629 Sugar Bowl Rd., Norden, 530/426-9000, www.sugarbowl.com, Nov.–May daily 9 A.M.–4 P.M., adults $60–70, youth 12–18 $50–60, children 6–12 $15). With lots of skiable snow spread across a wide area and plenty of vertical drop, Sugar Bowl can satisfy skiers and boarders of all ability levels. The mix of blue and black runs toward the top of the peaks offers intense variety, with a scattering of double-blacks out toward the edges and down the ridges. At the base near each lodge, green runs make it easy for younger and newer athletes to have a good time in the mountains. This resort offers two base lodges, one at Judah and the other at The Village. The Gondola takes visitors from a lower parking lot up to The Village.

#### BOREAL

If you can't afford nearly $75 per day to ski, consider one of the smaller resorts near Truckee. Boreal (19659 Boreal Ridge Rd., Soda Springs, 530/426-3666, www.rideboreal.com, Apr.–May daily 9 A.M.–9 P.M., Thanksgiving–Apr. daily, 9 A.M.–4 P.M., adults $44–47, youth $39, children 5–12 $12) feels low-rent compared to Squaw or Alpine, but many Californians found their snow legs at this resort. Boreal offers beginners' ski and snowboard lessons, and a kids' (and adults') ski racing school. From Claimjumper at the center of the resort all the way over to Cedar Ridge at the east edge of the resort, beginner skiers and boarders can have a great time on a number of runs and small bowls. The Accelerator chair serves Boreal's Superpipe and its night skiing area, while the 49er chair services the intermediate and advanced "Core," an area designed for boarders and freestylers. The small back-of-the-mountain offers fun for intermediate skiers who want to avoid the major boarding hot-doggers who favor the front of the mountain. Even on weekends, the lines at Boreal seem pleasingly short compared to the bigger resorts. While the services are minimal, you can get a hot meal, a cup of coffee, and a place to sit at the rather basic ski lodge at the bottom of the hill.

#### TAHOE DONNER DOWNHILL

Another great beginner hill is Tahoe Donner Downhill (11603 Slalom Way, Truckee, 530/587-9444, 9 A.M.–4 P.M., adults $25–35, children $10–15). With only four lifts (two of them conveyor belts) and 120 skiable acres, Donner seems miniscule. But it's a great spot to bring your family and get a feel for your board or your skis, take a lesson, and enjoy the California snow in the beautiful Tahoe forest.

### South Shore

#### HEAVENLY

On the less-skied South Shore, the queen bee of the few resorts is undoubtedly Heavenly (Wildwood and Saddle, South Lake Tahoe, 775/586-7000, www.skiheavenly.com, call for current hours and prices). Perhaps the most sprawling of any Tahoe ski resort, avid skiers can choose from four lodge/village access points up to the ski area: Heavenly Village and California Lodge down by the lake and in the South Shore downtown area, and Boulder Lodge and Stagecoach Lodge up inland. Zillions of runs snake down the mountainside, taking advantage of the more than 2,500 vertical feet of drop you'll enjoy at Heavenly. Beware: Even the lowland ski area near the California Lodge has mostly black diamond runs. Approach the Killbrew and Mott Canyons with prejudice—gates at the head of these runs underscore the fact that only expert skiers should even try to take them on. Frankly, Heavenly doesn't have tons of green runs, but most of the beginner areas is served by the Gondola and the Powderbowl Express Six Chair. Freestylers can find a number of terrain parks, none of which are named other than the traditional and uninspired Small, Medium and Large.

Heavenly enjoys its status as an intensely popular resort, so prepare to find parking a challenge at whatever lodge you choose. Crowding and lines at the lifts, especially those at the bottom of the mountain, can get bad on weekends and holidays. On the other hand, once you're out of your car and on the mountain you'll have access to nearly every service and amenity you need.

#### KIRKWOOD

The South Shore's mid-tier resort is Kirkwood

(1501 Kirkwood Meadows Dr. off Hwy. 88, 209/258-6000, www.kirkwood.com, lifts daily 9 A.M.–4 P.M.) offers dozens of downhill runs, plus everything from pipes to a cross-country space. Both the easiest runs and the children's ski school center are located around the Timber Creek Day Lodge. The Kirkwood Mountain Lodge lifts lead up to more intermediate and advanced runs; the back of the mountain is devoted to double-black-diamond runs. Kirkwood specializes in terrain parks for skiers and boarders, including a Cross Course, half-pipes, beginner terrain features, and areas with sound systems to complete the atmosphere. For a more sedate adventure, check out the snowshoe and cross-country park; you can rent equipment for both at the lodges.

You'll find plenty of sustenance in and around Kirkwood. Both lodges include restaurants and bars that serve lunch, dinner, and, in some cases, drinks to starving skiers and boarders. If you prefer to stay where you ski, look into Kirkwood's array of lodges and vacation rentals, most situated to make it easy to get to the slopes.

#### SIERRA-AT-TAHOE

For a smaller and less crowded South Shore ski experience, check out Sierra-at-Tahoe (1111 Sierra-at-Tahoe Rd., Twin Bridges, 530/659-7453, http://sierraattahoe.com, weekdays 9 A.M.–4 P.M., weekends 8:30 A.M.–4 P.M., adults $55–65, youth $45–55, children $14–16). Sierra-at-Tahoe offers plenty of long, sweeping advanced runs, as well as many fun intermediate tracks. The many beginners' green slopes run right down the middle of the mountain, all the way from the top. Take the Tahoe King or Grandview Express quad chairs or the Nob Hill double chair to the upper greens, or the Rock Garden or Easy Rider Express to stay lower on the mountain. It's all black diamonds on the east side of the big quads, and mostly blues with a few black diamonds for spice in the west, coming off the West Bowl Express quad or the Puma triple chair. A few more beginning and intermediate runs flow down the back of the mountain. For a nice, hot cup of coffee and a hearty meal, ski down either to the Base Lodge or the Baja Grill. Some skiers think Sierra-at-Tahoe is the best-kept secret in the area.

### Nevada Side

If you're staying over the state line in Incline Village or out in Reno, you can choose between two nearby ski resorts.

#### MT. ROSE

Mt. Rose (22222 Mt. Rose Hwy., Reno, NV, 800/754-7673, http://skirose.com, 9 A.M.–4 P.M., adults $48–62, youth $42, children 6–12 $17) has the most to choose from in terms of both variety and beginner routes. Lots of different ski school packages and private lesson options are offered for children as young as three on up to senior citizens who want to cut it up on a snowboard. You can even sign your kids up for ranger-guided exploration programs and ski or board camps where they'll have a great time, learn lots, and make ski buddies their own age.

Beware of the center of Mt. Rose, an area called Chutes with a morass of double-black runs with fun names like Detonater and Yellow Jacket. If you're on your own looking for the green runs, park at the Main Lodge and then take the Ponderosa or the Galena chairs up to beginner territory. For lots of great, long, intermediate tracks, start at Slide Lodge (the second access point for the Mt. Rose resort) and take the Blazing Zephyrs Six-Chair almost to the top of the mountain. You can grab a hot cocoa and a meal, or make a pit stop at either lodge.

#### DIAMOND PEAK

The smaller Diamond Peak (1210 Ski Way, Incline Village, NV, 775/832-1177, http://diamondpeak.com, 9 A.M.–4 P.M., adults $37–48, youth $29–38, children $14–18) is easy to access from the town of Incline Village. It has two—count them, two—green run at the bottom of the hill. Probably not the best place to bring young children or yourself if you're on your first ski trip. (You can go to ski school here for sure, but you won't find much in the way of route variety.) But if you're even an intermediate skier or boarder, be sure to take the Crystal Express quad up to the top of the peak. Stop for a moment and enjoy the amazing vistas down to Lake Tahoe before you take a wonderfully long run down the blue Crystal Ridge, continuing to enjoy the views, or cut in to one of the black chutes that branch off through the forest. You'll start your day down at the Base Lodge, where you can also eat, drink, make merry, or even stop in for a nondenominational prayer on Sunday mornings before you start skiing. In the middle of the day, the Snowflake Lodge on the ridge lets you spend all the time you like looking out onto the lake as you sip a drink or just sit with your feet up.

## SIGHTS

Most folks don't come to Tahoe to see its historic or cultural sights—which is a shame, really, because many of them are worth your time. Just be aware that sightseeing and museum-going in Tahoe are summertime activities. Most museums and cultural sights go to limited hours in the spring and fall, and close entirely in the wintertime. It's not that they're afraid of the weather, it's that the staff are all out skiing!

### The Village at Squaw Valley

You might think of The Village at Squaw Valley (1750 Village East Rd., Olympic Valley, 530/584-1000, www.thevillageatsquaw.com) as a ski area, but in truth it's an upscale small town designed to mimic a European Alpine village (but not quite succeeding). In fact, there's no need to ever hit a slope to enjoy the all The Village has to offer. You can spend hours just rambling around the colorfully painted clusters of buildings. Want to shop? Stroll the cute, exclusive boutiques and galleries, which are scattered throughout The Village. Souvenir seekers can go straight to **Squaw One Accessories** or the **Squaw Valley Clothing Company.** More than half a dozen restaurants, snack bars, and coffee shops offer everything from sushi to pizza to high-end wines. You can even stay at The Village if you've got enough cash.

The entertainment options are obvious; you can ski in the winter, hike in the summer, and take the **cable car** (adults $10–22, youth $10–17, child $5–6) up to **High Camp** (1960 Squaw Valley Rd., Olympic Valley, 800/403-0206, www.squaw.com). There you can ice skate, browse in the **Olympic Museum** (1960 Squaw Valley Rd., 800/403-0206, www.squaw.com/olympic-museum, admission free with cable car ride), or just stand outside and enjoy the tremendous views. Live music often makes its way up to the base of the mountain, as do other events that offer fun to adults and kids alike.

### Tahoe Maritime Museum

The Tahoe Maritime Museum (5205 W. Lake Blvd., Homewood, 530/525-9253, www.tahoemaritimemuseum.org, May 24–Sept. 30 daily 11 A.M.–5 P.M., Oct. 1–Dec. 20 daily 10 A.M.–5 P.M., adults $5, children free) seeks to illuminate the significant marine history of the large lake. On the West Shore of the lake, a shining new museum building was designed to resemble an old boathouse (a *big* old boathouse). It contains a fantastic collection of photos, artifacts, and a number of historic watercraft, some of which still run on the lake each summer. You'll learn about the "gentlemen's racing" history of the lake, the steam ferries that plied the waters, and the fishing that's been part of the lke's culture for over a century. The museum has the largest collection of outboard motors in the country, plus an exhibit on the history of water skis, from the days when they were handmade up to modern design and styling. You'll also find a children's area where younger visitors can enjoy interactive exhibits as they learn more about small and mid-sized boats, water skis, and more.

### Historical Society Museums

Serious museum buffs will be thrilled to learn that the Lake Tahoe Historical Society owns and operates three separate museums in and around Tahoe City. The **Gatekeeper's Museum** (130 West Lake Blvd., Tahoe City, 530/583-1762, www.northtahoemuseums.org, open year-round, schedule varies, adults $3, children $1) offers the most in-depth history of society around the lake. You'll find transcribed oral history, photos, artifacts, costumes, and more inside this funky local museum. If your tastes run more towards Native American artifacts, check out the **Marion Steinbach Indian Basket Museum** (130 West Lake Blvd., Tahoe City, 530/583-1762, www.northtahoe museums.org) at the same site as the Gatekeeper's Museum. Guess what its star collection consists of? In addition to a wonderful array of baskets exemplifying the work of tribes from across the country, you'll also see dolls, costumes, and many other artifacts displayed in attractive and unusual (for a museum) pine-and-glass cases that match the wooden floors of the attractive galleries.

Finally, you can visit an authentic early 20th-century log cabin: the **Watson Cabin** (560 North Lake Blvd., 530/583-8717, www.northtahoemuseums.org, Memorial Day–Labor Day, schedule varies) at Tahoe City. Unlike many historic California buildings, especially cabins, this one sits on its original building site. Inside, you'll find diorama-style displays of pioneer life in early modern Lake Tahoe.

## Tallac Historic Site

It sounds like something to do with Native American culture, but in fact the Tallac Historic Site (Hwy. 89, 3.1 miles north of Hwy. 50 intersection, South Lake Tahoe, 530/541-5227) pays homage to the lavish mansions built by white men in the early 20th century around Lake Tahoe. True, the centerpiece of the complex, the **Tallac Museum** (June 15–Labor Day, Tues.–Sun. 10 A.M.–4 P.M., free) in the Baldwin Estate, does include an exhibition focusing on the life and times of the local Washoe tribe. But most of this complex of 33 different buildings, including three major mansions, are all about wealth and privilege. In the Baldwin Estate, you'll find featured the importance of Lucky Baldwin and his family to the history of California. Walk the grounds of the Pope and Heller Estates, checking out the attractive gardens and many small cottages and outbuildings. If you make reservations in advance, you can take a tour of the interior of the **Pope Mansion** (Tues., Thurs., Fri. 1 P.M. and 2:30 P.M., $1.50). The Heller Estate has been set aside to showcase the arts and music of the Tahoe region. The smaller cabins spend each summer acting as galleries for photographers, fiber artists, and other local craftspeople. Check into children's workshops when you're in town. Out on the grounds, summer concerts rule the weekends, so you might hear jazz, bluegrass, or even classical music with the crystalline lake as your backdrop.

In addition to the history and grandeur, you'll find the Pope-Baldwin Recreation Area, a number of easy-to-walk nature trails, a picnic ground, and beach access with swimming permitted. It seems only proper, as these were beach resorts/retreats, after all!

## Thunderbird Lodge

The Nevada side of the lake boasts the Thunderbird Lodge (5000 Hwy. 28, Incline Village, NV, 775/832-8750, www.thunderbird lodge.org). Once again, if you're seeking Native Americana, you're in for a surprise. The Thunderbird Lodge was built in 1936 by a Tahoe resident locally called The Captain, who intended to create a luxury hotel and casino on his vast lakeside acreage. It was one of the last great posh residential mansions constructed alongside the lake. The property includes several outbuildings and a 600-foot underground tunnel from the mansion proper to the boathouse and card house.

When you visit the Thunderbird Lodge, you won't be able to drive to the property. Instead, park at the Crystal Bay Visitors Center in Incline Village and meet your tour guide and bus for the land tour (adults $39, children 6–11 $19). You'll be driven out to the lodge and take an hour-and-change walking tour through several of the buildings and the landscape. The tunnel is one of the tour highlights, especially for kids. Another highlight is the unbelievable 1930s-era mahogany yacht, *The Thunderbird,* which still floats in the boathouse.

If you're staying on the west side of the lake, you can book a boat tour (Tahoe Keys Marina, 775/588-1881, www.tahoeboatcruises.com/tbirdlodgetours.htm, adults $110, children 6–11 $55) on a historic wooden powerboat that will take you across the lake and along the eastern shore. The boat docks at the Thunderbird Lodge, and you'll take the walking tour from there. Snacks and a cold lunch spread are included with this tour package. Children under six years old are not permitted on any tour of the Thunderbird Lodge. Both tours operate in the summertime only.

## ENTERTAINMENT AND SHOPPING

### Bars and Clubs

With the youthful snowboarding crowd packing the Tahoe lodgings in the winter and the wakeboarders in the summertime, it's no surprise that some noticeable nightlife crops up around the lake. For the obvious reasons, the favorite clubs tend to be inside the Stateline casino resorts. Often you'll find that the hip dancing crew spills out of the clubs and onto the casino floor throughout the evening.

Many locals' favorite nightclub is **Vex at Harrah's** (15 Hwy. 50, Stateline, NV, 775/586-6705, Thurs.–Sat. 10 P.M.–close). This swank late-night watering hole features girls, girls, girls as the entertainment, the staff, and the clientele—every Friday night is "Ladies Night" (free cover for female guests). Whether the entertainment is a high-flying aerial act or just the Vex Girls dancing on the upper walkways, both locals and visitors alike have a great time here. You can shake it on the dance floor, sip a cocktail at the bar, or if you've got the money, get waited upon by the lovely cocktail staff in a posh VIP booth.

Even though **The Opal Ultra Lounge at MontBleu** (55 Hwy. 50, Stateline, NV, 775/586-2000, Wed.–Sun. 8 P.M.–close, cover varies) is technically in Nevada, you'll find a serious California-style fusion of cuisine and nightlife. The idea is for club-goers to start out with a nice sushi dinner, then move seamlessly into cocktails and the lounge scene. Each evening includes different featured entertainment—just don't mix up Wednesday night's lingerie party with Thursday's VIP professional mixer! Live drumming spices up Friday night, and "exotic" belly and fire dancers make Saturday intensely sexy.

### Comedy

If you crave more structure, more laughter, and less booty shorts in your evening's entertainment, get tickets to **The Improv at Harvey's** (15 Hwy. 50, Stateline, NV, 800/786-8208, www.harrahs.com, Sun. and Tues.–Fri. 9 P.M., Sat. 8 P.M. and 10 P.M., $25–30). Each night, an old-school Budd Friedman comic showcase goes up. You'll see national acts like Wendy Liebman and Dan Levy, as well as young up-and-coming comics who are building their careers. Once upon a time, Jay Leno, Jerry Seinfeld, Jim Carrey, and any number of famous comics whose names don't begin with "J" performed on this stage.

### Festivals and Events

Each year Lake Tahoe hosts a number of big festivals in both summer and wintertime, though undoubtedly summer is high festival season. One of the biggest of these is the **Lake Tahoe Music Festival** (www.tahoemusic.org). Players like Kenny Loggins and Big Bad Voodoo Daddy perform alongside symphony orchestras over a three-week stretch in late July and early August. Concerts are held at a number of venues—often ski resorts such as Homewood, Alpine Meadows, and Tahoe Donner. Check the festival website for this year's concert dates, times, venues, and ticket prices.

If you enjoy costumes and want to dive into the living history of the early 20th-century wealth and privilege that surrounded Lake Tahoe, hit the **Great Gatsby Festival** (http://tahoeheritage.org, Aug.) at the Tallac Historic Site. In the heat of August each year, actors and volunteers dress in period attire and stroll the grounds of the estates, mimicking 1920s vacationers. The most popular event of this two-day festival is the Gatsby Tea on Saturday afternoon. For $30, you'll enjoy a sumptuous afternoon high tea spiced up by entertainment that culminates in a vintage fashion show. On both days, additional entertainments, tours, and vendors selling early 1900s-styled items draw folks onto the estates.

California theater-lovers have been known to drive for hours to see the shows of the **Lake Tahoe Shakespeare Festival** (www.laketahoeshakespeare.com, July–Aug.). In 1995, a new stage facility was built at the classic **Sand Harbor State Park** beach location (three miles south of Incline Village on SR-28). Festival-goers can still flop onto a towel in the sand, but the play they'll watch will be a world-class Shakespearean production. (In truth, you'll be much comfier if you bring a low beach chair to sit in for the show.)

## SHOPPING

Lots of shopping opportunities cluster in South Lake Tahoe. If you're in need of basic necessities or discount factory outlet stores, head for the **Stores at the Y** (Intersection of Hwy. 89 and Hwy. 50, South Lake Tahoe, http://shopthe-y.com). For athletic equipment and apparel, check out **Adidas** (daily 10 A.M.–6 P.M.) and the **Great Outdoor Clothing Company** (daily 10 A.M.–6 P.M.). For après-ski apparel for the ladies, **Blue Willow** (daily 10 A.M.–6 P.M.) offers silky, sexy lingerie.

If it's ski equipment or apparel you need, the upscale **Shops at Heavenly Village** (1001 Heavenly Village Way) can hook you up. Guess what **Powder House Ski & Snowboard** (530/541-6422, www.tahoepowderhouse.com, Sat.–Thurs. 7 A.M.–10 P.M., Fri. 7 A.M.–midnight) sells? Granted, you'll pay a premium for equipment here. For the summertime sportsters, **Tahoe Boot 'n' Bike Works** (530/542-1388, www.tahoebootnbike.com) specializes in hiking and biking gear.

Snowboarders are one of the major communities served in Tahoe. And if you know snowboarding culture at all, you know what that means: head shops! Head shops are easy to find in South Lake strip malls. Redundantly named **Tahoe Hemp Company (THC)** (3117 Harrison Ave., South Lake Tahoe, 530/544-4367, http://lp8.tahoehemp.com, daily 10 A.M.–5 P.M.) sits next to Sprouts and Rude Brothers, selling all the usual pipes and glassware, stickers and T-shirts. You can also get yourself a stylin' hemp tuk and a couple of local alternative newspapers with semi-underground entertainment information.

## SPORTS AND RECREATION

### Skiing and Snowshoeing

There's far more land surrounding Tahoe that's available for cross-country skiing and snowshoeing than there is for downhill sports. In fact, Tahoe is something like heaven for strong-legged snow lovers of all types. It's hard to go more than five miles without tripping over a snowshoe trail or a cross-country track.

The granddaddy of Tahoe cross-country ski areas, the **Royal Gorge Cross Country Ski Resort** (Summit Station, Soda Springs, 800/500-3871, www.royalgorge.com, daily 9 A.M.–5 P.M., adults $15–29, youth 13–17 $15–16, children under 12 free) has a truly tremendous chunk of the Sierras within its boundaries. Striving to provide a luxurious ski experience comparable to what downhillers expect, the Royal Gorge offers lodgings, food, drink, a ski school, equipment rentals, equipment care facilities and services, and much more. Expect more than 185 miles of groomed trails, all with two stride tracks and a skate track to allow easy passing. Royal Gorge even offers four surface lifts for skiers who'd like to rest for a few minutes while getting from one area to another. Another option is to start out at the Soda Springs downhill ski resort gondola and spend the day exploring the Van Norden Track System, which connects down to the Summit Station.

The Royal Gorge Summit Station is the central Lodge for Royal Gorge. However, you'll also find four restaurants, two overnight lodges, and eight warming huts dotting the cross-country wonderland. Do be sure to grab a map before you head out for the day. Patches of mountains are off limits due to avalanche danger, and it's best to know where they are before you get deep into your cross-country ski adventure.

North Shore regulars say that **Tahoe Donner Cross Country** (15275 Alder Creek Rd., 530/587-9484, www.tdxc.com, adults $13–22, children under 12 free) offers some of the better cross-country skiing action in the area. It's true that Donner has a separate day lodge just for cross-country skiers, and another restaurant halfway up the mountain, the Euer Valley Cookhouse. It's also got almost 5,000 acres crisscrossed with trails ranging from easy greens all the way up through double-black diamonds. A cross-country ski school teaches newcomers to the sport and helps more experienced skiers expand their skills. This is more of a cross-country paradise than a big snowshoe area, and you'll find only two snowshoe-only trails at Donner.

If you're up for some cross-country skiing on the Nevada side of the lake, check out the **Spooner Lake** (Hwy. 28, 0.5 mile from Hwy. 50, 775/749-5349, www.spoonerlake.com, adults $10–21, teens $10, children under 12 free) cross-country and snowshoe resort. You can stride and glide by two small lakes in this region: Spooner and Marlette. Less experienced and more sedate skiers tend to stick to the well-groomed easy and moderate trails near Spooner Lake, Spooner Meadow, and the Lodge. The buns-and-thighs of steel crowd can head up North Canyone to Saints Rests beside Marlette Lake, or go all out and circle the aptly named Big Loop—a 21-mile advanced monster that will definitely give you a full day's workout. All cross-country ski trails at Spooner are snowshoe-accessible (be courteous by staying on the outside edges), and the resort maintains narrow marked snowshoe-only trails throughout the area. If you'd like to stay right at Spooner Lake, inquire about rental cabins, which are available year-round.

Many cross-country skiers and snowshoers eschew the groomed and crowded resorts for more virgin territory. At Tahoe, a number of cross-country trails that really do cross some country are maintained by the Forest Service. Some of these trails offer short, single-day excursions, while others go miles back into the ominously named Desolation Wilderness and appeal to hardcore ski-campers who want a multi-day adventure. Beginner explorers can have the safest fun at **Taylor Creek** (just north of Camp Richardson, Hwy. 89), an uncongested but reasonably populous area with many flat, marked trails to help newcomers get the feel for the forest. Lots of trails for skiers of all levels range out along the **South Shore** and the **West Shore** of Lake Tahoe. If you're planning to camp in Desolation Wilderness, the most popular trailhead first takes you past **Echo Lakes** (Hwy. 50 at Echo Lake Rd.) and then on into the backcountry along the Pacific Crest Trail.

A $5 Sno-Park parking pass is required for many forest ski trailheads, and can be purchased at places like Longs Drugs at the South Shore Y and the Chevron in Meyers. Folks planning overnight ski-camping trips must first get a wilderness permit from the El Dorado Information Center in Camino on Highway 50. While snow conditions are generally best in the mornings, nighttime "moonlight skiing" is allowed and even encouraged in some areas.

### Snowmobiling

There's enough room around Tahoe to create space to satisfy every different kind of snow activity—even snowmobiling. While you can't take your mad machine anywhere and everywhere, you'll find vast acreage at your disposal, whether you're a lifelong rider or want to go out for your very first guided tour. A number of companies offer snowmobile rentals, maps, groomed terrain, open fields, and guided tours of the winter scenery.

Operating out of the town of Meyers on the South Shore, **Lake Tahoe Adventures** (3071 Hwy. 50, Meyers, 530/577-2940, www.laketahoeadventures.com, Nov.–Apr. daily 9 A.M.–5 P.M.) specializes in group snowmobile tours on the Nevada side of the lake. A shuttle takes riders from the tour center up to the base camp in Hope Valley, where the fleet of Arctic Cat snowmobiles waits to ply the high-elevation backcountry Sierra terrain. First-time drivers and families with children should pick one of the more sedate trail tours or the snowmobile track, while expert snowmobile enthusiasts prefer the "Ultimate" off-trail tours that get deep into the backcountry and rougher riding. Children are welcome, but snowmobile drivers must be at least 15 years old. Reservations are required for all tours.

If you're up on the North Shore, check out **Lake Tahoe Snowmobile Tours, Inc.** (Hwy. 267, south of Northstar, 530/546-4280, www.laketahoesnowmobiling.com, daily, $90–250). Boasting a fleet of Sea-Doo snowmobiles and more than 20 years of guided touring experience, this outfit offers everything from 90-minute easy tours that give you gorgeous lake views (aptly named Lakeview Adventures) up through private three- and four-hour adventures geared toward expert riders up for tackling ungroomed backcountry terrain. You'll see sweeping North Shore views and drive through miles of unspoiled (if slightly singed) forest. Reservations are highly recommended, drivers must be 16 or older and have a valid driver's license, and no children under five may ride with this company for safety reasons.

Several snowmobiling outfits operate west of Truckee along the main roads—you'll see the tracks as you drive in and out of town. One company, **Cold Stream Adventures** (11760 Donner Pass Rd., Truckee, 530/582-9090, www.coldstreamadventures.com, daily, $130–155 for 2-hour tour), also offers tours into the mountains, promising climbs up to 2,000 feet above your starting point. These guided tours take routes through the forest that are private to this company—that is, you'll see forested landscapes available to you no other way. Make reservations, grab your sunglasses, and come on out!

Down south on the Nevada side, it's hard to miss the presence of the **Zephyr Cove Snowmobile Center** (760 Hwy. 50 at the Zephyr Cove Resort, 775/589-4906, www.laketahoesnowmobiles.com, $110–250). The free shuttle runs right along the freeway for all to see, and for all reserved riders to use at their convenience. A Lakeview or Sierra Summit tour on a new Sea Doo snowmobile will include breathtaking views, easy riding on groomed trails, and plenty of stops that let you take pictures. Advanced riders can work with the guides to create a challenging personal tour.

### Sledding and Snow Play

You don't need to be under the age of 12 to have a blast flying down a hill on a specially designed snow tube or saucer, or grabbing a handful of fresh powder and starting a roaring snowball fight. Any number of hills all around Tahoe become designated or impromptu play areas each season once the snow gets deep. A good way to find one near your accommodations is to ask a few locals; they'll be able to tell you which spots are the best for small children and which ones appeal more to big kids-at-heart. Many of the ski resorts, including Boreal and Donner, offer snow-play areas as well as their trademark steep ski slopes.

Just a couple of miles from Heavenly Valley in a cute residential area sits the **Tube & Saucer Hill at Hansen's Resort** (1360 Ski Run Blvd., 530/544-3361, daily 9 A.M.–5 P.M., $6/hour, $12 for 3 hours). One of the annual favorites, this hill offers more in the way of features than many impromptu play spots. Don't bother stacking a bunch of equipment in the car, since Hansen's requires that you use their saucers and tubes. With constructed runs, you'll definitely get some thrills as you slip down the hill through the scattered pine trees. The resort also makes a snack bar and a redwood hot tub available to fee-paying snow-lovers.

In the South Shore area past Meyers on Highway 50, **Adventure Mountain Lake Tahoe** (21220 Hwy. 50 at Echo Summit, 530/577-4352, www.adventuremountaintahoe.com, Dec.–Apr. daily 10 A.M.–5 P.M., $15/car) boasts the best groomed sledding area in all of Tahoe. With 40 acres of sled runs and play areas, plus restrooms and a concession stand that sells hot coffee and new sleds, Adventure Mountain works to make good on its promise. It's also got access to the Pacific Crest Trail and a few other cross-country skiing and snowshoeing trails for those who want a more quiet buy labor-intensive day in the snow. Feel free to bring your own sleds and tubes.

Up on the North Shore, the **North Tahoe Winter Adventures** (Donner Rd., Tahoe Vista, 530/546-0605, daily 9 A.M.–5 P.M., $5/all day) is part of the North Tahoe Regional Park. This fully developed seasonal recreation area includes warm restrooms, groomed hills, a snack bar, snowmobile tracks (plus on-site snowmobile rentals), and several miles of cross-country trails. Whatever kind of playing in the snow you want, you can do it here—and all within sight of the lovely north end of the lake.

## Sleigh and Sled Rides

Oh, what fun it is to ride in a one-horse open sleigh! No, really. You can take an old-school sleigh ride at several locations around Tahoe. Just over the state line, across the street from the Harrah's and MontBleu casinos, seek out **Sleigh Rides by the Borges Family** (50 Hwy. 50, Stateline, NV, 775/588-2953, www.sleighride.com, $20 adults, $10 children). These folks have been giving sleigh rides on the South Shore for more than 30 years. They've got five sleighs (seating 2–20 passengers) and some lovely blond Belgian draft horses. Each ride lasts 35 minutes and takes you through the woods to grandmother's spectacular lake view. Blankets to cuddle under are included with each ride, as are stories and songs, but you'll need to bring your own thermos of cocoa.

Over on the other side of the lake, you can catch a similar ride with **Wilderness Sleigh Rides at the Camp Richardson Corral** (530/541-3113, $25). Call ahead for reservations, and meet your horse and sleigh at the corner of Emerald Bay Road and Fallen Leaf Road on the west side of the lake.

If you prefer dogs to draft horses, make a journey with **Wilderness Adventures Dog Sled Tours** (530/550-8133, www.tahoedogsledtours.com, daily 10 A.M.–5 P.M., $95–110 passengers over 60 lbs., $45–55 passengers under 60 lbs.). Most tours last one hour, but if you're not afraid of cold and around on a weekday, you can sign up for a two-hour or more Wilderness Expedition that takes you 15–20 miles through the snows of the backcountry. Any time you want to sled, you can choose either Sugar Bowl (629 Sugar Bowl Rd., Norden) or the Resort at Squaw Creek (400 Squaw Creek Rd., Olympic Valley) as your starting point. Whichever you choose, you just won't be able to resist those adorable fuzzy Huskie faces!

## Ice Skating

Ice rinks proliferate all year, though wintertime is the most popular for visiting skaters.

It ain't cheap, but on a clear day skating at **High Camp at Squaw Valley** (1960 Squaw Valley Rd., Olympic Valley, 530/452-7246, www.squaw.com, adults $26, youth $22, children under 13 $14) can be a beautiful thing. You'll take the big cable car ride up to High Camp. At the Ice Pavilion, lace up your skates and enjoy the Olympic-sized rink with its panoramic views out over the Sierra forests and peaks.

At the South Shore, **Heavenly Gardens** (1021 Heavenly Village Way, South Lake Tahoe, 530/542-4230, www.theshopsatheavenly.com/skating, daily 10 A.M.–close) turns part of its landscape each year into a winter wonderland. This outdoor, winter-only rink appeals more to tourists and kids than serious skaters, but it definitely offers fun and a partylike atmosphere.

For more hardcore skaters and hockey players who want to indulge their obsession while vacationing in Tahoe, the **South Lake Tahoe Ice Arena** (1176 Rufus Allen Blvd., S. Lake Tahoe, 530/542-6262, www.recreationintahoe.com, adults $9, youth $8, children $6) can hook you up. This year-round ice center offers drop-in hockey, public skating hours, and even an "Adult Coffee Club" skating hour.

## Waterskiing and Wakeboarding

Once the summer sunshine has warmed the air—if not the waters of the lake—visitors' thoughts turn to those other kinds of skiing and boarding. The vast clear waters of Lake Tahoe are irresistible to water skiers, wakeboarders, Jet Skiers, and powerboaters. You've got miles of open water to cross, a number of docks and marinas, and a lovely coastline to explore. If you dive deeper than about a foot and a half, you'll find the water of Tahoe ice-cold (in the 40s) even in the height of summer. But that's no matter if you're sunning yourself on the bow of a speedboat or flying along behind the boat on a wakeboard.

Be aware that Tahoe takes the water quality of not only Lake Tahoe, but Falling Leaf, Echo, and the other small area lakes very, very seriously. Especially if you plan to bring your own powered watercraft, it's wise to familiarize yourself with the rules and restrictions governing all waterways in the Tahoe Basin. Check http://boattahoe.com/trparegs.htm for more information.

South Lake Tahoe's **Tahoe Keys Marina** (2435 Venice Dr., South Lake Tahoe, 530/541-2155, www.tahoemarina.com, powerboats $100–150/hr, $600–1,000/day) looms large as the only "inland" marina on the lake. This full-service marina sells gas, provides launch access, and rents slips, as well as offering boat rentals of all kinds and charter fishing trips. You can rent an array of ritzy Reinell powerboats, some of which seat up to 10 people and can work for either cruising, fishing, or skiing and wakeboarding. Yamaha personal watercraft come a bit cheaper and are all legal on prissy Lake Tahoe. For an extra fee, you'll get a pile of water toys, sets of water skis, or a high-class wakeboard. Just don't expect anything here to come cheap!

On the Nevada side, **Zephyr Cove Marina** (750 Hwy. 50, Zephyr Cove, NV, 775/589-4901, www.zephyrcove.com/marina/index.cfm, ski boats $150–175, WaveRunners $115–150) offers a full complement of services and watercraft rentals. For skiers and wakeboarders, Zephyr Cove has a small fleet of 22–24 foot Sea Ray open-bow ski boats, plus skis, boards, and toys. Personal watercraft riders can rent one of the marina's three-person WaveRunners. Truly adventurous visitors can also sign up for a parasailing session with the professional drivers from Zephyr Cove.

On the North Shore, **Tahoe City Marina** (700 N. Lake Blvd., Tahoe City, 530/583-1093, www.tahoecitymarina.com, ski boats $130–160/hr) has not only full marina facilities, but a shopping mall with a number of restaurants and boutiques. But if your main focus is out on the water rather than the shore, the marina can hook you up with one of three ski boats.

## Boating and Fishing

Among the most popular warm-weather activities on the waters of Lake Tahoe are fishing and pleasure boating. Many visitors also enjoy taking small human-powered watercraft out near the shore (or farther out for the stronger paddlers).

To rent a pontoon boat for a nice cruise around the lake, make a reservation at the Tahoe Keys Marina (see above) either with the **Tahoe Keys** rental company or with the **Ski Run** outfit. Each of these also offers a wide array of kayaks, canoes, and pedal boats. Ski Run even rents some truly weird apparatus, and for a small fee you can try an hour on a hydrobike or a water trike. Zephyr Cove also has a fleet of "beach craft" running to kayaks, canoes, pedal boats, and funky pedal kayaks.

Want to go fishing, but don't know where the good holes are or have tackle and the initiative to go out on your own? Several companies offer charter trips on Lake Tahoe for anglers looking to score Mackinaw lake trout, rainbow and brown trout, or kokanee salmon. Operating out of the **Ski Run Marina** (900 Ski Run Blvd.), **Tahoe Sport Fishing** (800/696-7797, www.tahoesportfishing.com, $85–135) offers half-day and full-day fishing trips tailored to suit all styles of lake fishing. Choose from among six fishing boats, all of which have heated cabins and modest bathroom facilities. Your trip will include all the trimmings: bait and tackle, cleaning and bagging services, cold beer and soda on board, and a choice of morning or afternoon half-day trips.

**Mickey's Big Mack Charters** (800/877-1462,

© PETTIT GILWEE / TOM ZIKAS

sailing on Lake Tahoe

www.mickeysbigmack.com, $65–85) operates out of the Sierra Boat Company in Carnelian Bay. The 43-foot fishing boat goes out twice daily, once for an early-morning trip and again for a late-afternoon cruise that includes spectacular sunset views. The cabin and restroom on board add to the comforts of your trip as you fish for Mackinaw, rainbows, and browns.

Down at Zephyr Cove, book a fishing trip with **O'Malley's Fishing Charters** (775/588-4102, $110). The cozy 22-foot boat guarantees an intimate angling experience. You can fish summer or winter with O'Malley's.

Do you prefer fly-fishing to lake fishing? With the proliferation of rivers and streams surrounding Lake Tahoe, it's easy to find a good place to cast. **Tahoe Fly Fishing Outfitters** (2705 Hwy. 50, South Lake Tahoe, 877/541-8208, http://tahoeflyfishing.com, $110–300) can take you on an expert guided fly-fishing or spin fishing trip on one of the smaller lakes, Walker Rivers, Carson Rivers, Truckee and Little Truckee Rivers, or the Pleasant Valley Fly Fishing Preserve.

## Hiking

In the summertime, many trails frequented by snowshoers and cross-country skiers turn into perfect paths for hiking. In fact, wonderful hikes abound all around the lake, up in the mountains, and out by the smaller alpine lakes surrounding Tahoe.

Along the South Shore, hikes range from easy walks along the shore at the Tallac Historic sight to hardcore treks up the **Mount Tallac Trail** (Hwy. 89 at Baldwin Beach, South Lake Tahoe, 10 miles round-trip, difficult). This long hike starts out easy, taking casual strollers past the Floating Island and Cathedral Lakes, then gets steeper and harsher as it ascends up the front face of the mountain. To access the trail, turn off the highway away from the beach toward the dirt road, which takes you to the trailhead parking lot. For a more moderate but equally beautiful hike, choose the **Echo Lakes Trail** (Johnson Pass Rd. at Lower Echo Lake, 5–12 miles, moderate to strenuous, wilderness permit may be required). You can pick your distance on this route, depending on how many small pristine alpine lakes you want to see. You'll start with a short walk to Upper Echo Lake, where you have an option to catch a water taxi rather than continuing on the trail along the lake. If you keep on going, you'll see Tamarack Lake, Lucille and Margery Lakes, Lake in the Woods, and maybe even Aloha.

Up North Shore way, the great hiking continues. For a quick easy walk, head up to the **State Lookout** (Forest Service Rd. 1601 at the iron pipe gate, 1 mile, easy). At the lookout, you'll find summer volunteers who can give you information about the region, including the short, self-guided nature trail that surrounds the lookout proper. For a heftier hike, try the **Marlette Lake Trail** (Spooner Lake Trailhead, 10 miles, moderate to difficult). The trailhead sits inside the Lake Tahoe Nevada State Park at the junction of Highways 50 and 28. You'll be charged a parking fee at the gate. The hike itself slopes uphill all the five miles up to the Marlette Dam. While you're free to enjoy the beauty and serenity of this manmade lake, no fishing is allowed because the lake serves as a fish hatchery.

Serious hikers challenge themselves with the **North** and **South Rim Trails** (www.tahoerimtrail.org, 40 miles total, difficult). These two trails put together encircle all of vast Lake Tahoe (minus a couple of spots where connectors have been proposed but not yet built). Check the map on the website for the various trailheads; about half a dozen fan out around the lake. To do the whole Rim Trail takes two or three days for a fit, experienced hiker who expects to camp along the way. Contact the visitors center for information about wilderness permits and backcountry camping along the Rim Trails. More casual day-hikers can pick one portion of the trail and tackle it, either doing a back-and-forth, or using some sort of shuttle service to get back home again at the end of the day.

## Biking

A great place to get out and walk or bike is summertime **Kirkwood** (1501 Kirkwood Meadows Dr. off Hwy. 88, Kirkwood, www.kirkwood.com, 209/258-7360). Without snow covering them, the slopes of the ski resort become great mountain biking tracks. For $30 (adult) or $15 (youth) per full day, you can take two different lifts up the mountain with your bike, then ride your way down. You can rent bikes from Kirkwood on the weekends, and hone your skills at the clinics held several times each season. The bike terrain opens for business in late June every year, and closes after Labor Day.

If you prefer your own two feet, take the lifts up (or don't, if you're strong and energetic), and hike down the multi-use trails to the lodge any day of the week during the summertime. Check the Kirkwood website for scheduled guided hikes and wildflower walks throughout the season.

## Horseback Riding

For travelers who prefer to explore the forests and trails on horseback, a few stables offer guided rides. On the west side of the South Shore, find the **Camp Richardson Corral** (Emerald Bay Rd. and Fallen Leaf Rd., 530/541-3113, $32–65). Choose between a one- or two-hour trail ride to explore the meadows and the forest, or a ride with a meal included. Camp Richardson offers an early morning ride that culminates in a hearty hot "cowboy-style" breakfast and an evening barbecued steak dinner ride. Riders must be at least six years old and weigh 225 pounds or less. Camp Richardson also offers horse boarding by the day, week, and month.

© PETTIT GILWEE / TOM ZIKAS

horseback riding

Over on the Nevada side, sign up for a ride with the **Zephyr Cove Resort Stables** (on Hwy. 50, 775/588-5664, http://zephyrcovestables.com, summer daily 9 A.M.–5 P.M., spring and fall daily 10 A.M.–4 P.M., $35/hour). Enjoy your lovely scenic trail rides, complete with panoramic views of the lake through the pine trees. Zephyr Cove also has "food rides" at breakfast, lunch, and dinnertime each day. Bring your appetite for these one-hour rides. (You'll need to make advanced arrangements if you're a vegetarian or have dietary restrictions.) As at most stables, restrictions include a

225-pound weight limit and a minimum rider age of seven.

Want to get out and see the Sierra Foothills and mountains from the back of a horse? Summertime at **Kirkwood** (1501 Kirkwood Meadows Dr. off Hwy. 88, Kirkwood, 209/258-4600, www.kirkwood.com, mid-June–Labor Day, $46) has what you need. Take a gorgeous guided trail ride out into the Mokelumne Wilderness. Pick a 1.5-hour or 2.5-hour ride, depending on your skill level and rear-end stamina. For kids who want to get more serious about their riding while on vacation, check out the children's Wrangler for a Day program. Kids spend most of the day caring for the horses with the experienced wranglers, plus they take a 90-minute ride through the forest.

## Golf

Amongst all the other summertime recreation available in and around Lake Tahoe, a number of golf courses offer surprisingly good games, plus a few unique lake and mountain views.

The championship George Fazio course at **Edgewood Tahoe** (180 Lake Pkwy., Stateline, NV, 775/588-3566, http://edgewoodtahoe.com, daily May.–Oct., $150–250) has been compared to the Pebble Beach Golf Links—and called *better.* Not everyone agrees with that bold statement, but the consensus is definitely that Edgewood is one of the top courses in the West, if not the nation. As you walk the course, you'll see views of the lake and mountains that are so wonderful that you may forget all about that pesky putting for a moment or two. Several holes sit right along the shores of Lake Tahoe—one of the bigger water hazards you'll find in California.

After your game, enjoy lunch and a stiff drink at the Brook's Golf Bar & Deck. You can call or go online to reserve a tee time ahead of time. Your rather hefty fee includes a golf cart, and you can rent clubs and hire a caddie as well.

On the other side of the lake, **Coyote Moon** (10685 Northwoods Blvd., Truckee, 530/587-0886, www.tahoemountainclub.com, $160) also imposes a hefty green fee, but according to expert golfers and writers, it's more than worth the money you'll lay down. Coyote Moon boasts fairways dotted with granite boulders and lined by dense natural forest. No, the builders didn't make it that way—instead, the designer created a layout that takes advantage of the natural features of this unique locale. While Coyote Moon tends to beckon more to advanced golfers, even beginners can play an enjoyable round here.

For golfers looking to play a few holes on the cheap, **Tahoe Paradise Golf Course** (530/577-2121, www.tahoeparadisegc.com, daily 6 A.M.–7 P.M., $20–60) offers a pleasant course as well as pleasantly small green fees. On the South Shore, in fact right off Highway 50, this convenient course has pretty mountain views and plenty of lovely pine trees—and 18 holes of moderate golf that provides a fun game for beginners and intermediate golfers. There's also a pro shop, practice area, and a modest snack bar that runs to hot dogs and beer.

## Spas

It's tough to go more than a block or two in South Lake Tahoe, Tahoe City, or even Truckee without tripping over some sort of day spa or massage parlor (the real kind, not the other kind). If you're staying at one of the big ski resorts or casinos, you're likely to find a spa attached to your accommodations, and perhaps even the option of in-room spa services. Campers and motel-goers can choose from the resort spas or pick out an independent provider for massages, facials, scrubs, and mani-pedis.

On the north side, one of the most popular day spas is the **Lighthouse Spa** (850 N. Lake Blvd. #20A, Tahoe City, 530/583-8100, www.lighthousespa.com, daily 9 A.M.–8 P.M.). Just look behind the Safeway (perhaps an unlikely spot for a spa). Inside, you can choose from Swedish, deep tissue, and hot stone massages, or get a special prenatal massage for your favorite expectant mom. Lighthouse also offers facials, body wraps, luxurious foot treatments, and aesthetic services including manicures, pedicures, and waxing. While they don't have the biggest spa menu ever, the services offered exemplify the heart of good California day spa care. Late appointments, up until 8 P.M., are available for those in desperate need of après-ski TLC.

Tired feet after a day of hiking, skiing, or snowshoeing? Walk them over to **Wish Hair & Skin Salon** (12030 Donner Pass Rd. Ste. 2, Truckee, 530/550-1319, www.wishsalon.com). You can also bring your tired hair, hands, face, and skin to this salon that doubles as a minimum-services day spa. Wish offers a full range of aesthetic services, including their signature four-hour mani-pedi with facial that creates a fabulous half-day of pampering. Book an appointment to get your hair done, your legs waxed, your face buffed and peeled, or even a full-body scrub. The website includes a full menu of services and prices, as well as an online appointment scheduler.

Among the wealth of day spas in South Lake Tahoe, **Shannon's Day Spa** (3600 Lake Tahoe Blvd., South Lake Tahoe, 530/542-4095, www.shannonsdayspa.com) stands out. You'll get plenty of personal attention here, plus a massage, facial, or luxurious body treatment that will leave you feeling refreshed and ready for another day out on the lake or up on the slopes. For the best experience at Shannon's, go for one of the packages that puts several treatments together for a full day of pleasure and well-being. Shannon's really is a spa, so don't expect to find waxing or nail services here.

So if you do want your nails done, head for **Tahoe Nail Spa** (2176 Lake Tahoe Blvd., #8, South Lake Tahoe, 530/541-1230). Be aware that it's a tough one to ferret out in the strip mall/plaza complex it's part of, but don't give up! The aestheticians at this small salon will give you great attention as they work on your feet and hands, clipping, buffing, and polishing to perfection.



### Casino Gambling

Think that casinos are disgusting smoke-filled holes sheltering nothing but lonely senior citizens pouring their Social Security into slot machines? Not in Tahoe! On the South Shore, just over the state line, the various casinos beckon to a young crowd looking for a lively, hip night out.

The gaming floor of the **MontBleu Casino** (55 Hwy. 50, Stateline, NV, 888/829-7630, www.montbleuresort.com) is great fun on weekend evenings, with its go-go dancers and youthful gamblers taking the free drinks as they hammer the slots and place bets on the tables. Since it (and all the other casinos listed here) are in Nevada, you'll find all the full-fledged table games of a Vegas casino: craps, roulette, blackjack, and Texas Hold 'Em, among others. "The Zone" contains the sports book and the poker room. And as with most casinos, the slots and video poker machines are everywhere. MontBleu's casino is better lit and less smoky than many, making it easy to stay and play late into the night. Or if you get tired of tossing your money away, wander around and you'll find a lingerie shop, an art gallery, and a hip nightclub.

Gambling fans should definitely bring their frequent-player cards to the casino floor at **Harrah's Lake Tahoe** (15 Hwy. 50, Stateline, NV, 800/427-7247, www.harrahs.com/). They've got all the Vegas gaming favorites, like classic craps, Rapid Roulette, and of course Keno pads and monitors scattered all over the place. The atmosphere is a bit more "classic casino" here, with fairly dim lights in the evenings and a warren of slot machines that make it easy to get lost and keep on spending money. Now that Harrah's has absorbed former neighbor Harvey's, it's got a solid lock on its block. Once you're done with gaming, check out the live entertainment or the locally popular nightclub.

## ACCOMMODATIONS

As a major vacation destination, you'll have no trouble finding a place to stay around Lake Tahoe. Some visitors camp around the lake, which can be beautiful in the summertime and frigid in winter, but most folks get rooms in the cute inns, historic hotels, budget motels, and upscale resorts that cluster in Tahoe's towns. Or they hook up with a rental agency and find a fully furnished vacation cabin or condo to call their own for the duration of their stay.

## North Shore

### $100-150

The **Truckee Hotel** (10007 Bridge St., 530/587-4444, www.truckeehotel.com, $55–187) offers a fabulous period ambiance for reasonable nightly rates. The hotel has been welcoming guests to the North Shore for more than 125 years. Rooms show their age with a gentle, shabby grace, and high ceilings, claw-foot tubs, and little Victorian touches delight visitors who appreciate a little history along with a comfortable bed. Part of the historic "charm" includes third- and fourth-floor rooms without an elevator on the premises, so prepare to climb and to haul luggage up narrow flights of stairs. One reason the rates are so reasonable here is that most of the 37 rooms have shared hall bathrooms. These are clean and comfortable, with either a shower or a bathtub and a lock for privacy. The few rooms with private baths are pricier. All rooms come with breakfast each morning. The Truckee Hotel building also shelters Moody's (the best restaurant in town) and sits only steps from historic downtown Truckee.

Be sure to listen to the friendly staff at the Truckee Hotel, especially when they tell you to move your car around to the back parking lot on winter evenings. If the police find your car blocking the snow-removal equipment in the dead of night, they will tow you without a second thought.

**Mother Nature's Inn** (551 N. Lake Blvd., Tahoe City, 800/558-4278, www.mothernaturesinn.com, $56–127) strives to bring a Tahoe camping experience inside, while still providing the creature comforts travelers expect in indoor accommodations. Guest rooms have a distinct theme based on a wild creature, and you can expect plenty of decorative tchotchkes in keeping with your room's animal totem. You'll also find lodge-style furnishings and linens arranged in cozy and somewhat cluttered arrangements. All rooms have private baths, refrigerators, and coffee makers. Pets are welcome for a small additional fee. The inn is only a few steps from the shores of the lake and the conveniences of downtown Tahoe City.

If you prefer to rent a condo with full kitchen facilities, especially for a longer stay, call the **Donner Lake Village Resort** (15695 Donner Pass Rd., #101, Truckee, 530/587-6081, www.donnerlakevillage.com, $140–170), situated right on the shores of Donner Lake. You can choose from regular motel rooms without kitchens, studio condos, and one- or two-bedroom condos. Inside your room, you'll find all the amenities of a nicer motel, including tea and coffee, private bathrooms, phones, and TVs with DVD players. But once you get a peek at the lake in summer or the mountains in winter, you won't want to stay inside for long. Donner Lake Village has its own marina with rental ski boats, fishing boats, and slips if you've brought your own watercraft. A bait and tackle shop across the street from the resort can hook you up with all the fishing equipment you need. And all the nearby North Shore ski resorts beckon in wintertime, an easy drive from your condo. After a long day out on the slopes, the fireplaces in the common rooms overlooking the lakes seem like the perfect location for a relaxing après-ski nightcap.

### $150-250

Devotees of Alpine Meadows vie for rooms at the exclusive and beautiful **Stanford Alpine Chalet** (1980 Chalet Rd., 530/583-1550, $220–270), situated right at the base of Alpine's mountain. With only 14 rooms, you'll feel like a rock star when you stay here. Guest rooms are done up in simple yet elegant style, with lots of real wood; all rooms have private baths and many have striking mountain views. Meals are served family or B&B style, at big communal tables. In the summertime, the chalet offers a heated swimming pool, sports courts, and horseshoe pit, while in the winter guests can enjoy a private ski shuttle and the warmth of a giant great room fireplace. The outdoor hot tub lures guests to its bubbling warmth year-round. Oh, and if you happen to be a Stanford grad, you can get a discount with your alumni membership number.

From the outside, the **Cedar House Sport Hotel** (10918 Brockway Rd., 866/582-5655, www.cedarhousesporthotel.com, $210–330) looks just like a lodge in a town called Truckee ought to look. Think all-exposed wood exterior, landscaped with live trees, fallen stumps, and a great big rusty steel girder. But don't let the rustic charm or the name fool you, since the guest room interiors are all about the luxury. All rooms boast ultra-modern decor that would look great even in San Francisco or Los Angeles, such as light wood platform beds, designer leather chairs and sofas, and shining stainless steel fixtures in the private bathrooms. Choose from comfortable rooms with queen or king beds, or fancy suites with flat-screen TVs and every possible amenity. So where does the "sport" part come in? The staff at Cedar House have the expertise to help you create your Tahoe dream expedition, and if you call in advance they'll be happy to put together guided hikes, bike rides, and rafting or kayaking trips.

For travelers who prefer an intimate inn to a big impersonal condo block, there's the **Donner Lake Inn** (10070 Gregory Pl., Truckee, 530/587-5574, www.donnerlakeinn.com, $176–200). This five-room and one-cabin B&B offers simple charm in pretty, rustic Truckee. Each guest room has its own simple, homelike decorating scheme, without too many flowers or Victorianoid geegaws. You'll find your own private bathroom with shower, a private entrance to your room, a queen bed, a TV set with DVD player, and free wireless Internet. Unlike many B&Bs, the Donner Lake Inn even has a "family" room with bunk beds to accommodate a couple with two children. Each morning, the friendly and hospitable owners serve up a delicious full breakfast down in the dining room. Just ask them, and they'll be happy to help you set up everything from ski days to in-room spa treatments.



For the ultimate convenience in ski vacations, you can get a condo at **The Village at Squaw Valley** (1750 Village East Rd., Olympic Valley, 866/818-6963, www.thevillageatsquaw.com, $260) and never leave the vicinity of the lifts. Elegant, modern condos can be anywhere from compact studios perfect for singles or couples up through three-bedroom home-away-from-homes that sleep up to eight people traveling together. The Village condos have full kitchens with all appliances, fully stocked with utensils, and you might even get granite countertops. Each condo also has a living room with TV, maybe even a fireplace, and a dining table at which to serve home-cooked meals. Of all the posh amenities in The Village condos, the skiers' favorite is almost always the heated tile floors in the private bathrooms and the kitchen.

## South Shore

Lots of chain motels cluster in the town of South Lake Tahoe, competing with the dozens of independent inns and lodges for the tourist trade. Despite the plethora of rooms available on the South Shore, it's still a good idea to make reservations well in advance for holiday weekends in both winter and summertime.

### UNDER $100

For inexpensive year-round rooms, check in to the **Ambassador Motor Lodge** (4310 Manzanita Ave, South Lake Tahoe, 530/544-6461, www.ambassadorcapritahoe.com, $72–100, children under 16 free with adult). With its private beach access and associated water recreation options, rates are a touch higher in the summer months and bargain basement in the wintertime. Guest rooms have that basic motel feel, but a few soft touches make them appear prettier than the average bargain chain room. Amenities are also reminiscent of low-end chain motels; you will find coffee and a coffee maker, a TV set, and a private bathroom, but little else in the way of extras. The good news is that the Ambassador is on the lake for summer visitors, and only a short walk to the Heavenly gondola for winter guests.

### $100–150

The small, rustic **Lazy S Lodge** (609 Emerald Bay Rd., South Lake Tahoe, 530/541-0230, www.lazyslodge.com, $105–140) has a great location away from the center of town, and some of the most reasonable room rates in the region. The 20 guest rooms all have microwaves, wet bars, TVs, phones, and private baths. You can choose from a studio room, with a nice bed, bath, and bar. Or choose a two-room cabin with sleeping room for several people, a kitchenette, and a nice warm fireplace that's perfect for chilly winter evenings. Facilities of this small lodge include a year-round hot tub, summer swimming pool, barbecue grills and outdoor picnic tables, and easy access to hiking and biking trails, warm lake swimming, and Heavenly ski resort.

Perhaps *the* most famous accommodation on Lake Tahoe is **Camp Richardson** (1900 Jameson Beach Rd., South Lake Tahoe, 800/544-1801, www.camprich.com, $145–275). Whether you just need a spot to pitch your own tent, or you want a luxurious private two-bedroom cabin to call your own, you can find the right space for you somewhere at Camp Richardson. Choose a room in the refurbished hotel or one of the many individual cabins, and you'll find rustic-style furnishings smoothed out by the luxurious fabrics and appointments. The hotel rooms are comfortable and quaint, with private baths and nice upscale amenities. Cabins offer full kitchens and linens, but no TVs or phones. (Note that all cabins are rented by the week in the summer months.) Outside your room, is a group recreation area, a beach, a marina, a restaurant, and the southern edge of the Tallac Historic Site, all on Camp Richardson's property.

For a condo on the South Shore, head on over to **The Lodge at Lake Tahoe** (3840 Pioneer Trail, South Lake Tahoe, 800/874-9900, www.lodgeatlaketahoe.com, $132–190). As Tahoe condo complexes go, it's not much to look at from the outside, and you might mistake it for a budget motel. But inside, the rooms have the elegant look of proper vacation condos, with colorful furnishings and tasteful prints on the walls. And the price is right for moderate budget travelers who want to save a few dollars by cooking for themselves. The smallest studios have only kitchenettes, but the larger condos offer fully equipped kitchens with utensils provided, as well as a nice table and chairs. Complex amenities include a summertime pool and spa, swing set, horseshoe pit, and outdoor barbecues near the pool area. Heavenly skiers will have easy access to the resort, and gamblers can get to the Stateline casinos in a few minutes.

### $150-250

**Spruce Grove Cabins** (3599–3605 Spruce Ave., South Lake Tahoe, 800/777-0914, www.sprucegrovetahoe.com, $165–330) boasts a gay-friendly, dog-friendly Tahoe vacation experience. With only seven cabins on the property, you're guaranteed peace and privacy throughout your stay. Choose from one-bedroom and two-bedroom cabins, all with full kitchens, dining rooms, and living rooms with pull-out sofas to accommodate extra guests. Each cabin has its own wilderness-based decoration theme, from Snowshoe to Steamboat to Washoe Native American. You'll get your own bathroom, plus proper accommodations for your favorite furry friend. As one of the closest resorts to the Heavenly ski resort (right at Ski Run Blvd.), Spruce Grove gets its heaviest traffic in the wintertime.

### OVER $250

Dedicated B&Bers enjoy the hospitality of the **Black Bear Inn** (1202 Ski Run Blvd., South Lake Tahoe, 877/232-7466, www.tahoeblackbear.com, $250–480). Located right on the road to Heavenly, you'll be thrilled when you spy the lovely large building with lodgepole and river-rock exterior accents. A giant fireplace dominates the great room, echoed by smaller but equally cozy river-rock fireplaces in the upstairs lodge guest rooms. Each unique room features a king-sized bed, posh private bathroom, free Wi-Fi, and an energy-building full breakfast. Appointments throughout the lodge rooms and cabins breathe luxury, from the cushy comforters to the rustic-elegant furniture. But the most beautiful spaces of all lie outside of the lodge and cabins, so be sure to take a few moments to stroll on the tree-lined paths and serene green lawns surrounding the inn.

Hardcore skiers who prefer to sleep as close to the slopes as possible book their rooms at the **Deerfield Lodge at Heavenly** (1200 Ski Run Blvd., 888/757-3337, www.tahoedeerfieldlodge.com, call for rates). This resort drips luxury, from the whirlpool tubs in every slate-and-granite bathroom to the stone fireplaces in the spacious living areas of each guest room. Contemporary furniture and striking black-and-white linens compliment the ultra-comfy beds, while TVs, DVD players, and wireless Internet access combine to create the perfect home away from home. A kitchenette makes it easy to make coffee for your morning enjoyment, while the aromatherapy bath products lure tired skiers and swimmers into their bathrooms to soak the evening away. A yummy buffet continental breakfast is served in the common areas, and drinks and snacks form a tasty après-ski happy hour for guests. Just be sure to bring your credit card to the Deerfield, since all this luxury doesn't come cheap.

## Nevada Side

The casino resorts are some of the spiffiest places to stay over on the Nevada side. In hopes of convincing you to come spend lots and lots of time gambling, they offer upscale, attractive hotel rooms, often at less-than-it-looks-like prices. You'll also find the occasional non-casino lakeshore resort that focuses more on the sports than the slots.

### $100-150

The most popular casino resort on the Nevada side, **Harrah's** (15 Hwy. 50, Stateline, NV, 800/417-7247, www.harrahs.com, $110) offers upscale accommodations, all the nightlife and entertainment you need, and easy access to Heavenly and the other South Shore ski resorts in the winter, and to the lakeshore in the summer. The high-rise hotel has more than 500 posh rooms; even the lowest-end rooms have ample space, a California king or two double beds (your choice), two bathrooms (his and hers), Wi-Fi, a TV with cable and premium movies (for a fee), mini-bar, and more. For (of course) more money, ask for a Premium Room that sits above the treeline to allow for excellent views of the lake and the mountains. Guest room decor is upscale and contemporary, with white linens and comforters, bright colorful accents, and sleek furnishings and wall art. With its variety of entertainment packages, Harrah's makes for a good location for both families and adults-only travelers. Be aware that rates vary hugely depending on the season, local events, and the weekday or weekend you plan to visit.

If you prefer the Nevada ski resorts, or you just want a change of scenery from Tahoe City or Truckee, try the **Inn at Incline** (1003 Tahoe Blvd., Incline Village, NV, 775/831-1052, $75–150). This budget inn offers 38 rooms in a mid-century-style modest motel. Guest rooms also feel reminiscent of a low-end motel, with older furniture and amenities. Notwithstanding the inn's age, the rooms are clean, and the private baths are adequate for their task. The amenities include an indoor pool and hot tub that are available year-round, TVs in all the rooms, and Wi-Fi in public areas.

### $150-250

**Club Tahoe** (914 Northwood Blvd., Incline Village, 775/831-5750, www.clubtahoe.com, $165–275) at Incline Village is a great place to rent a condo on the Nevada side of the lake. Each condo here is a three-story, two-bedroom townhome with a loft with twin beds that serves as the bonus "third floor." These condos are perfect for families, or for a group of couples traveling together on a budget. Certainly the decor isn't the most contemporary, and expect 1970s- or '80s-era sofas, bargain-basement wooden furniture, and old-style paneling on the walls. But the kitchens come fully stocked with appliances and utensils and a full-sized fridge, the mattresses are newer than the rest of the furnishings, and a second bathroom off the "guest" bedroom makes sharing the condo much easier. Exterior amenities include an outdoor pool and spa, tennis court, racquetball court, arcade, and full bar with pool table for adults looking to unwind in the evening.

### OVER $250

The **MontBleu Casino** (55 Hwy. 50, Stateline, NV, 888/829-7630, www.montbleuresort.com, $220–250) definitely shines when it comes to attractive hotel rooms with top amenities. Your tower room will include a comfortable bed, loud decor and fabrics, black-out curtains, room service, shiny clean private bathrooms, and all the conveniences you'd expect at an upper-tier chain. For extra luxury, try a Spa Room, which includes a pink marble bathroom, walk-in shower, and two-person hot tub in the bedroom. The one big downside in the MontBleu is the paper-thin room walls, so bring earplugs or expect to learn more than you ever wanted to know about your neighbors.

Perhaps the best-advertised Nevada-side non-casino resort is the **Zephyr Cove Resort** (750 Hwy. 50, Zephyr Cove, NV, 888/896-3830, www.zephyrcove.com, $220–375). This resort has it all: lakefront property, lodge rooms and individual cabins, its own full-service marina, a winter snowmobiling shuttle and park, restaurants, and evening entertainment options. Guests of Zephyr Cove can choose between a room inside the big lodge, or their own cabin down by the lake. The four lodge rooms all have private baths, attractive modern appointments and fabrics, TVs, microwaves, small fridges, and coffee makers. For a special treat, ask for the room with the spa tub. The 28 cabins run from cozy studios for couples to multi-story chalets that sleep up to 10 people. Though they look rustic and woodsy from the outside, indoors you'll find modern furniture, phones, TVs with cable and movie channels, and all the amenities you'd expect of a nice lakeside resort. Because Zephyr Cove bills itself as a rental resort rather than a full-scale hotel, maid service is provided only every other day inside the lodge, and every third day in the cabins. Zephyr Cove offers pet-friendly lodgings, but you'll need to let them know which furry friends you're bringing when you make your reservations.

# FOOD

## North Shore

### CAFE

To fuel up for a day out on the lake or in the mountains, head over to the **Fire Sign Café** (1785 W. Lake Blvd., 530/583-0871, daily 7 A.M.–3 P.M., $8–15). This breakfast-and-lunch spot, a favorite with locals, serves up an enormous menu of hearty fare. Choose from a whole-grain waffle with fruit to a kielbasa omelet, crepes to blueberry coffee cake. Expect a wait for a table on weekend mornings.

### CALIFORNIA

The best restaurant in Truckee, and possibly in all of the Tahoe region, is undoubtedly **Moody's** (10007 Bridge St., Truckee, 530/587-8688, www.moodysbistro.com, Mon.–Thurs. 11:30 A.M.–9:30 P.M., Fri. 11:30 A.M.–10 P.M., Sat. 11 A.M.–10 P.M., Sun. 11:30 A.M.–9:30 P.M., $22–30). This casual-elegant eatery with fresh herbs decorating its tables adjoins the historic Truckee Hotel, just off the main commercial drag in town. The warren of tiny rustic dining rooms show a few traditional French prints on the walls, plus a handwritten plug for the local CSA program. On weekends, strains of live jazz permeate from the lounge—just enough to be a charming background but not so loud as to forbid conversation. You'll definitely want to make reservations for weekend evenings since locals pack in here, making table space a premium. The reason everyone comes here isn't the lovely atmosphere—it's the food. Moody's puts together a menu that makes visiting chefs swoon with joy. Ingredients are seasonal, local, sustainable, and organic, while the preparations show off the chef's vivid imagination. You might find antelope on the menu, or local fish. For dessert, the cook-it-yourself s'mores brought to your table with a burner and skewers are the hands-down favorite. The alcoholic coffees are *not* old standards and are well worth your time; just imagine proper drinking chocolate laced with homemade peppermint schnapps! In the state that invented California cuisine, and that's filled to the brim with great upscale restaurants of all kinds, Moody's still manages to stand out and shine.

The combination of ethnic cuisines may seem catch-all and bizarre, but the taste tells the tale at **Wolfdale's** (640 N. Lake Blvd., Tahoe City, 530/583-5700, www.wolfdales.com, Wed.–Mon. 5–10 P.M., $15–25). Billing it as "cuisine unique," the Wolfdale serves dishes that fuse Western and Far Eastern foods to create tastes you can't find elsewhere. The small seasonal menu leans heavy on seafood, though you can also find some tasty beef and game meats at the right time of year. Lighter diners often prefer the homemade soups, salads, or unusual appetizers. Be sure to save room for the delicious desserts, most made in a light California style.

After a long day of skiing, the **Terrace Bar & Restaurant** (800/403-0206, www.squaw.com/terrace-bar-restaurant) at The Village at Squaw Valley can feed even the hungriest skiers. Non-skiers and casual visitors favor the Terrace because of its floor-to-ceiling windows offering fabulous views of the mountains. Everyone enjoys the casual California-style fare of mostly soups, salads, and sandwiches. If the Terrace isn't your preference, you can also try one of several other Squaw Valley eateries, including the **Wildflour Bakery & Café** (1960 Squaw Valley Rd., 530/583-1963, www.squaw.com/winter/wildflour/wf1.htm) and **Alexander's Café & Bar** (1960 Squaw Valley Rd., 530/581-7278, daily 5–9 P.M.).

### ITALIAN

**Zano's Pizza** (11401 Donner Pass Rd., 530/587-7411, www.zanos.net, daily 11:30 A.M.–2 P.M. and 4–9:30 P.M., Fri.–Sat. open until 10 P.M., $12–30) can hook you up with huge pizzas and tremendous salads in a big, casual dining room with the latest games playing on the TVs over the bar. A mural depicting the Italian countryside (complete with cows) graces the rear wall, and glass block semi-walls break up the sweeping dining space for a cozier feel. The full menu includes pastas and Italian entrées. At lunchtime, the hot, crisp paninis taste great. But it's the thin-crust pizzas that rule the house here, and you can pick one of Zano's interesting combinations or build your own from the list of fresh ingredients. Should the kids get bored, an arcade at the back can provide easy entertainment.



## South Shore

### BREAKFAST

For a classic American breakfast, it's tough to do better than the **Red Hut Waffle Shop** (2723 Lake Tahoe Blvd., South Lake Tahoe, 530/541-9024, $5–12, cash only). This down-home waffle spot serves classic crispy, thin waffles (if you're looking for huge, fat Belgian waffles, this isn't your place), plus biscuits and gravy, omelets, and plenty more. Locals recommend the waffle sandwich, which is a complete breakfast in a single dish. Expect to wait for a table or a seat at the counter on weekend mornings, as this spot gets popular with both visitors and residents.

### CAFÉ AND DELI

For an unusual combination of hardcore health food and budget dining, check out **Sprouts Cafe** (3123 Harrison Ave., South Lake Tahoe, 530/541-6969, daily 8 A.M.–9 P.M., $8–15) in town at South Lake Tahoe. This cute, casual walk-up eatery offers an array of ultra-healthy dishes make with all-fresh, mostly organic produce and ingredients. Despite the wheatgrass growing on purpose-built shelves and the giant juicer on the rear counter, Sprouts has a pleasantly surprising number of items that appeal to non-health-food nuts. Breakfast is served all day, and the lunch and dinner menus run on for pages. Choose from salads, burritos, rice bowls, and even tasty vegetarian and vegan desserts. If you're truly brave, start your day with the legendary Hot Shot. You'll take your order to one of the rough-hewn tables and spice it yourself from the array of condiments over to the side of the restaurant. From there, sit back and linger over your tasty guilt-free grub, herbal tea, or organic, fair-trade coffee.

**Rude Brothers Bagel & Coffee Haus** (3117 Harrison Ave., Ste. B, 530/541-8195) looks and feels just about right for an indie coffee shop and sandwich bar. It's got a big open room for hanging out, and a tasty array of lunch goodies on tap for hungry visitors. They've also got all the usual espresso drinks available at the counter. This is definitely a locals' hangout.

#### ITALIAN

If the crowds at Heavenly have got you longing for a more intimate evening, book one of the seven tables at **Café Fiore** (1169 Ski Run Blvd., #5, South Lake Tahoe, 530/541-2908, www.cafefiore.com, daily from 5:30 P.M., $17–35) for dinner. This tiny bistro serves upscale Italian fare with a fabulous wine list. The exterior charms with its alpine-chalet look, while the inside defines the concept of "romantic restaurant." Right on Ski Run Boulevard, Café Fiore is convenient to both the Heavenly ski resort and to the lakeshore resorts of South Lake Tahoe.

#### SEAFOOD

Serious sushi aficionados might be concerned about trying raw ocean fish way out east in Tahoe. But the **Off the Hook California Sushi Bar** (2660 Lake Tahoe Blvd., #E., 530/544-5599, www.offthehooksushi.com) offers good rolls and fresh nigiri for vaguely reasonable prices. Don't expect too much from some of the traditional Japanese dishes, and you'll have an enjoyable dining experience here.

### Nevada Side

The **Ciera Steakhouse at the MontBleu** (55 Hwy. 50, Stateline, NV, 800/648-3353, www.montbleuresort.com, Sun.–Thurs. 5:30–10 P.M., Fri.–Sat. 5:30–10:30 P.M., $20–35) provides precisely the experience diners expect from a mid-grade casino steakhouse. The dining room boasts blocky modern decor in soothing colors, an exposed wine cellar window, and big raised booths with plush red curtains that can be drawn to create a private dining experience. On the menu, you'll find plenty of steak and non-steak options, with preparations designed to appeal to visitors from across America. Sadly, the kitchen doesn't always get it quite right, and steaks tend to be overdone by California standards. But hang in there, since the coolest part of the Ciera dining experience comes in right at the end. Even if you don't usually do it, order coffee at the end of your meal. It comes with a fabulous tray of fixings, including delicious flavored whipped creams. And finally, you'll be presented with a complimentary dish of chocolate-covered strawberries resting atop a frothing container of dry ice. It's fabulous!

Sometimes, it's what a guidebook *doesn't* recommend that's most important. When you're driving up the backside of the lake in Nevada, the restaurant choices become thin for many miles. You may find yourself starving, and the only thing that you can find that's open is the **Café at the Biltmore Hotel and Casino.** You're better off scrounging from your leftover snacks. The only thing worse than the food here is the service. It's special to find a spot where the waiters actually hide from the customers. Granted, you can get coffee here, which might help you wake up enough to push on to Incline Village or even Tahoe City.

## INFORMATION AND SERVICES

### Tourist Information

The different regions around Lake Tahoe each have their own visitors centers. The **South Lake Tahoe Visitors Center** (Hwy. 50 at Tallack, 775/588-5900, www.bluelaketahoe.com) sits adjacent to the tiny Lake Tahoe Museum. It's got every brochure and leaflet you can possibly imagine, plus some good discount coupons. Sadly, the counter help tends towards younger folks who don't have as many decisive recommendations as might be helpful.

### Media and Communication

The Lake Tahoe region has its own daily newspaper, the ***Tahoe Daily Tribune*** (www.tahoedailytribune.com). Pick up a copy at any newsstand, or ask for it at your hotel.

Lots of Internet access graces the cities around Lake Tahoe, since most youthful snowboarders expect to be able to hit the Wi-Fi on their Blackberries. Ask at your hotel, or find one of the dozens of Internet cafés that clutter the landscape. Most of the casinos have access as well.

### Banks and Post Office

To get cash, you'll need to hit the ATMs in Truckee, Tahoe City, South Lake Tahoe, or Stateline. Naturally, all the casinos on the Nevada side proffer plenty of cash machines as well.

You can get to post offices easily in South Lake Tahoe (3180 Hwy. 50), Truckee (10050 Bridge St.), Tahoe City (7005 N. Lake Blvd., Tahoe Vista, 530/546-5600), and Stateline (223 Kingsbury Grade, 775/588-1943).

### Medical Services

Plenty of medical facilities open their doors to luckless skiers in the cities around Tahoe. The major ski resorts also tend to have high-tech and extremely functional medical facilities on-site. If you injure yourself on the slopes, your best bet is to let the ski patrol take care of you rather than trying to take care of yourself.

If you need medical attention off-slopes in the North Shore, the **Tahoe Forest Hospital** (10121 Pine Ave., Truckee, 530/587-6011, www.tfhd.com) in Truckee has a full-service emergency room and plenty of services. On the South Shore, you can go to **Barton Memorial Hospital** (2170 South Ave., South Lake Tahoe, 530/543-5605, www.bartonhealth.org).

## GETTING THERE AND AROUND

### Air

The closest commercial airport to Lake Tahoe sits in Reno. The **Reno International Airport** (2001 E. Plumb Ln., Reno, NV, 775/328-6870, www.renoairport.com) offers flights on many major airlines and a few smaller carriers. This airport is open year-round, but be sure to check your flights in advance in the wintertime since storms delay and sometimes cancel flights here. Once you're in Reno, it's easy to rent a car or a truck in the airport from any of the major agencies.



### Bus

You can't get to Tahoe by train, but **Amtrak** (1000 Emerald Bay Rd., 800/872-7245, www.amtrak.com) does run a bus service to South Lake Tahoe down at the South Y transit center.

### Car

The main roads to Lake Tahoe from points west (the Bay Area, Sacramento, Wine Country, the Central Coast) are I-80 and state Highway 50. I-80 takes you to the North Shore and Highway 50 to the South Shore. It takes about five hours to drive up to Lake Tahoe from the San Francisco Bay Area in good weather without traffic. From Sacramento, it's only about two hours. But don't expect good weather or light traffic if you're planning to drive up to Tahoe on a Friday in winter. Everybody else will be on the road with you, significantly slowing down the routes. Generally, Highway 50 runs a bit faster than I-80, but you'll want to check traffic reports before you hit the road to see which way will work best.

Visitors doing a full tour of the eastern California mountains starting in the Eastern Sierra will take state Highway 120 from Yosemite or Mammoth up to Tahoe. As always, check road conditions before attempting this route in winter. Storms may cause chain requirements or even wholesale road closures.

Carry chains that fit your vehicle in winter, unless you're driving a four-wheel drive *and* know how to navigate in snow. Chains are often required near and around Tahoe in winter. There are lots of spots to pull off and attach your chains on I-80 and Highway 50. You can also buy chains on the road, but the closer you get to Tahoe, the more expensive chains get.

In winter, even the highways can close during major storms. And the smaller roads surrounding the lake can shut down for weeks at a time. Again, traffic reports both on the radio and online can give you information about road closures and alternate routes. If you're planning a winter trip, be aware of the weather and plan for a certain amount of uncertainty.

### Ski Resort Shuttles

Parking at the ski resorts, especially on weekends, can be a serious hassle. A much better option, if you're staying in one of the towns, is the resort shuttles. Most of the major ski resorts maintain shuttles that bring skiers and their equipment up to the mountains in the morning and back down to their hotels in the late afternoon. You can usually find seasonal brochures for the shuttles in all the major hotels and resorts. If not, you can call or go online for the shuttles for Squaw Valley (www.squaw.com/getting-squaw), Heavenly (www.skiheavenly.com/mountain/services/shuttle_system), Alpine Meadows (www.skialpine.com/winter/plan/shuttle_schedule), and Kirkwood (www.kirkwood.com/winter/busshuttle.php), among others.

### Tours and Cruises

If exploring on your own isn't enough, or you're not comfortable driving your own boat and you really want to get out on the water, a number of cruises and tours are offered all around Lake Tahoe.

If you want to get out on the water in a bigger boat, book a cruise with **Lake Tahoe Cruises** (800/238-2463, http://laketahoecruises.com, http://zephyrcove.com, adults $40–70, children $20–40). Two honest-to-goodness paddlewheel riverboats make cruises on Lake Tahoe on a near-daily basis—even in the wintertime! In the south, the *Tahoe Queen* sails from Ski Run Marina and offers an array of cruises, several with meals, live music, and dancing. You can even take a ski shuttle-cruise that buses you up to Northstar in the morning, then takes you home across the breadth of the lake—an on-board après-ski party you'll enjoy whether you're up for dancing or just want a drink while sitting at one of the windows watching the water go by. The *MS Dixie II,* a rear paddlewheeler, was imported from the Mississippi River. It sails from the Zephyr Cove Marina, and you can choose from breakfast and brunch cruises, dinner and dancing cruises, and even on-the-water showings of the oh-so-appropriate musical *Show Boat.*

Another company that can take you to see the lovely Emerald Bay is **Bleu Wave** (866/413-0985, www.tahoebleuwave.com, adults $59–65, children $29.50), which operates from the **Round Hill Pine Beach & Marina** (325 Hwy. 50, Zephyr Cove, NV, 775/588-3055, www.rhpbeach.com) in Stateline. You'll see many of the most popular sights on the lake as you take a two-hour lunch cruise with an all-you-can-eat buffet and drinks included. For winter cruises, you'll enjoy the on-board fireplace and the spacious heated cabin. In the heat of summer, most folks prefer to sit outside in the fresh mountain air.

## Mount Shasta

Star of photo and video, and perhaps the most iconic single mountain peak in all California, is majestic Mount Shasta. Gorgeous views of the tremendous dormant volcano are available along more than a dozen miles on I-5. In the wintertime, snow covers much of the huge mountain, while in the summertime glaciers decorate only the upper reaches near the peak.

To truly appreciate Mount Shasta, either come and camp in the cool forest or get a room at one of the quaint inns or relaxing retreat centers in the tiny town that also goes by the name of Mount Shasta. Numerous small towns spread out away from the mountain in all directions, providing a few minutes of sightseeing or a spot to eat or lay your head.

Shasta makes for a great weekend trip all on its own, or it can be a fun overnight (or more) stop if you're making a trip up to the northern reaches of the California coast and want to loop back on a different set of roads.

### SIGHTS

Hands down, if you're going to Mount Shasta, the one sight you must see is...Mount Shasta. Not that it's easy to miss; the 14,000-foot-tall cluster of volcanic peaks creates a unique shape high on the skyline. Ample spots exist

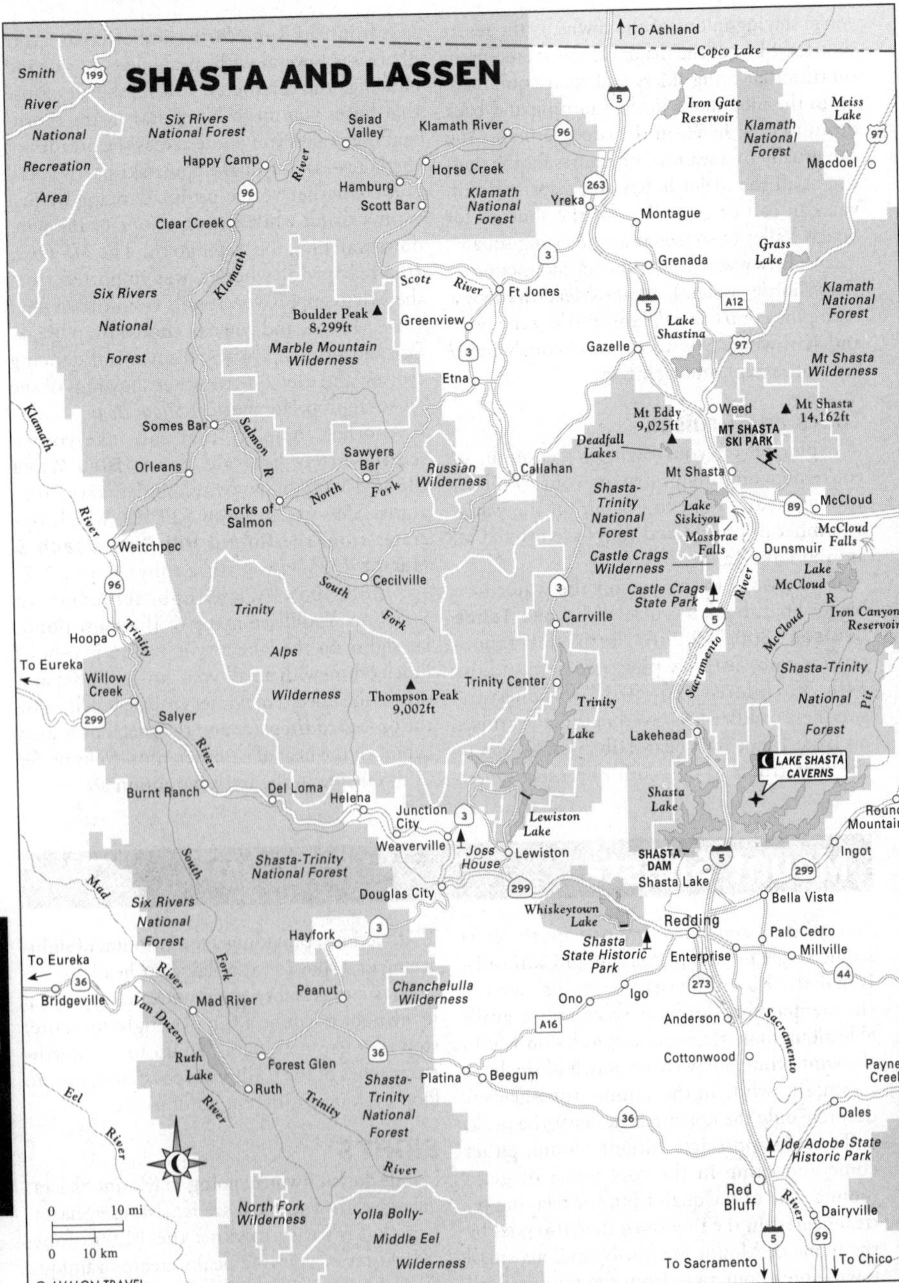
SHASTA AND LASSEN
To Ashland
Copco Lake
Iron Gate Reservoir
Meiss Lake
Klamath National Forest
Macdoel
Smith River National Recreation Area
Six Rivers National Forest
Seiad Valley
Klamath River
Happy Camp
River
Horse Creek
Hamburg
Scott Bar
Klamath National Forest
Yreka
Montague
Clear Creek
Klamath
Grenada
Grass Lake
Six Rivers National Forest
Scott River
Ft Jones
Klamath National Forest
Boulder Peak 8,299ft
Greenview
Lake Shastina
Marble Mountain Wilderness
Gazelle
Mt Shasta Wilderness
Etna
Klamath
Weed
Mt Shasta 14,162ft
Mt Eddy 9,025ft
Somes Bar
Salmon R
Deadfall Lakes
MT SHASTA SKI PARK
Orleans
Sawyers Bar
Russian Wilderness
Callahan
Mt Shasta
North Fork
Shasta-Trinity National Forest
McCloud
Forks of Salmon
Lake Siskiyou
River
Mossbrae Falls
McCloud Falls
Weitchpec
Castle Crags Wilderness
Dunsmuir
Cecilville
Lake McCloud
South Fork
Castle Crags State Park
River
Trinity
R
Iron Canyon Reservoir
Hoopa
Trinity
Carrville
McCloud
To Eureka
Alps
Sacramento
Shasta-Trinity
Willow Creek
Wilderness
Thompson Peak 9,002ft
Trinity Center
Trinity
National
Pit
Salyer
Lake
Lakehead
Forest
River
LAKE SHASTA CAVERNS
Burnt Ranch
Del Loma
Shasta Lake
Helena
Junction City
Lewiston Lake
Round Mountain
Weaverville
Joss House
Lewiston
SHASTA DAM
Ingot
South
Shasta-Trinity National Forest
Shasta Lake
Mad
Douglas City
Bella Vista
Six Rivers National Forest
Whiskeytown Lake
Redding
Hayfork
Palo Cedro
Shasta State Historic Park
Millville
To Eureka
Enterprise
River
Fork
Bridgeville
Peanut
Chanchelulla Wilderness
Igo
Van Duzen
Mad River
Ono
Anderson
Ruth Lake
Forest Glen
Sacramento
Cottonwood
River
Shasta-Trinity National Forest
Platina
Beegum
Payne's Creek
Eel
Ruth
Trinity
Dales
River
Ide Adobe State Historic Park
River
Red Bluff
River
North Fork Wilderness
Yolla Bolly-Middle Eel Wilderness
Dairyville
0 10 mi
0 10 km
To Sacramento
To Chico
© AVALON TRAVEL
199
96
263
5
3
A12
97
89
299
36
273
44
A16
99

LAKE TAHOE

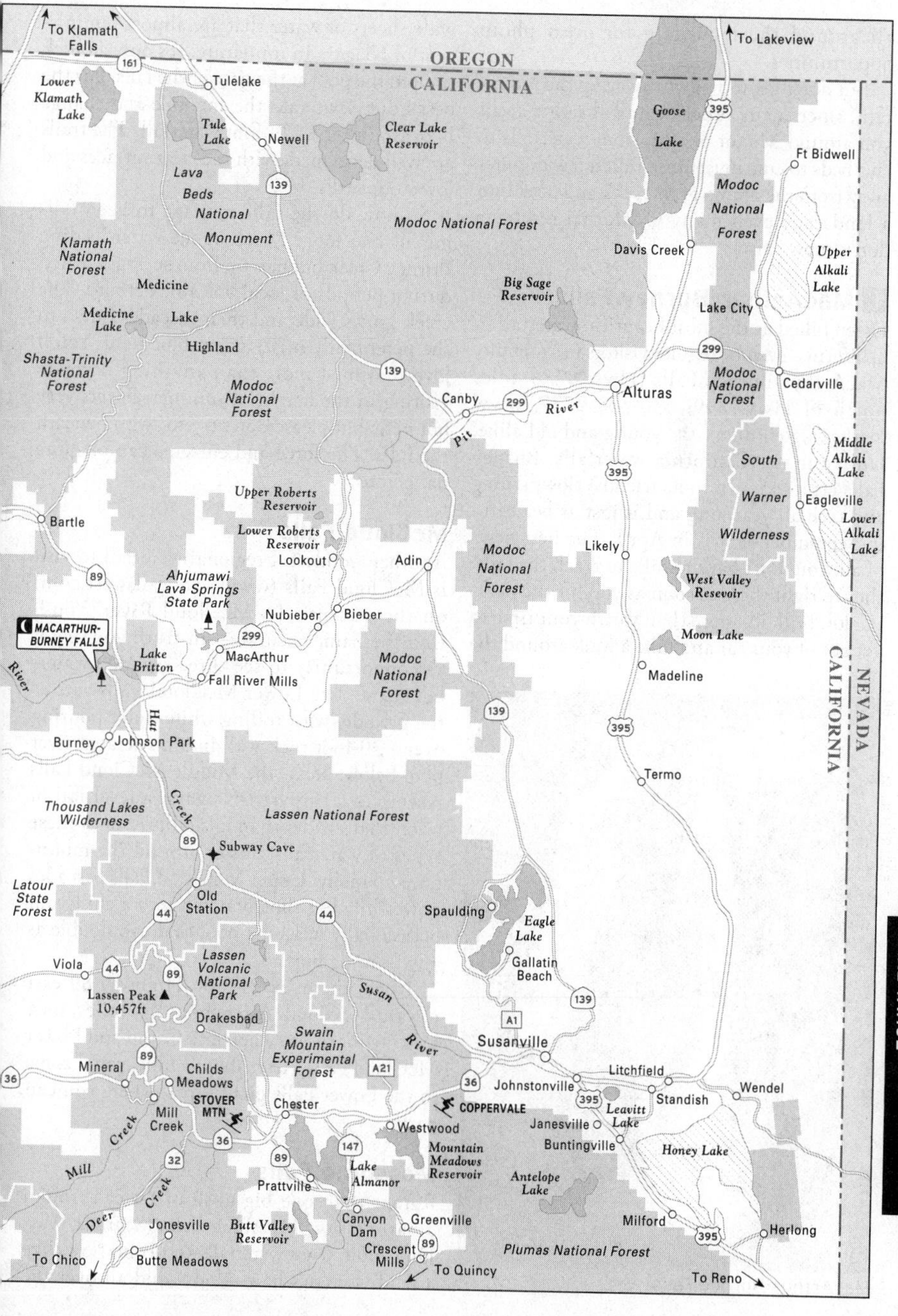
To Klamath Falls
161
OREGON
CALIFORNIA
To Lakeview
Lower Klamath Lake
Tulelake
Tule Lake
Newell
Clear Lake Reservoir
Goose Lake
395
Lava Beds National Monument
139
Ft Bidwell
Modoc National Forest
Klamath National Forest
Davis Creek
Upper Alkali Lake
Medicine Lake
Big Sage Reservoir
Lake City
Medicine Lake
Highland
299
Shasta-Trinity National Forest
Modoc National Forest
Canby
Pit River
Alturas
Cedarville
Middle Alkali Lake
South Warner Wilderness
Upper Roberts Reservoir
Eagleville
Bartle
Lower Roberts Reservoir
Lower Alkali Lake
Lookout
Adin
Likely
89
Ahjumawi Lava Springs State Park
West Valley Resevoir
Nubieber
Bieber
MACARTHUR-BURNEY FALLS
Moon Lake
MacArthur
Lake Britton
River
Fall River Mills
Madeline
NEVADA
CALIFORNIA
Hat Creek
Burney
Johnson Park
Termo
Thousand Lakes Wilderness
Lassen National Forest
Subway Cave
Latour State Forest
Old Station
44
Spaulding
Eagle Lake
Viola
Lassen Volcanic National Park
Gallatin Beach
Lassen Peak
10,457ft
Susan River
Drakesbad
A1
Swain Mountain Experimental Forest
Susanville
Mineral
Childs Meadows
A21
36
Johnstonville
Litchfield
Standish
Wendel
STOVER MTN
Chester
COPPERVALE
Leavitt Lake
Mill Creek
Westwood
Janesville
Buntingville
Honey Lake
147
Mountain Meadows Reservoir
32
Lake Almanor
Prattville
Antelope Lake
Deer Creek
Canyon Dam
Greenville
Milford
Jonesville
Butt Valley Reservoir
Herlong
Crescent Mills
Plumas National Forest
To Chico
Butte Meadows
To Quincy
To Reno

all around the mountain for great photo opportunities.

But don't get too blown away by the mountain, since many other beautiful sights await you around Mount Shasta, from waterfalls to lava beds to cute museums. Take a few minutes away from the drama of the peak and peek into a landscape even many California residents don't know exists.

## MacArthur-Burney Falls

Often billed as the most beautiful waterfall in California, even by regular visitors to Yosemite, MacArthur-Burney Falls (Hwy. 89, 6 miles north of Hwy. 299, 530/335-2777, www.parks.ca.gov) draws the young and old alike. Unlike many California waterfalls, Burney Falls (as it's known to its friends) flows strong and true all year long and is just as beautiful in September as it is in April. The best news of all, you don't have to hike to reach the falls; they're right there as soon as you hit the parking lot. Still, it's more than worth your time to get out of your car and take a walk around the wide sheets of water that are almost reminiscent of Niagara in miniature. It's only a quick walk to the pool at the base of the falls. For the best set of views, take the one-mile-and-change hike around the 129-foot waterfall. The trails are well developed, with nice flat surfaces and low stone walls.

So how do the falls manage to keep falling all year long? Much of the water feeding Burney Creek bubbles up from springs created during periods of local volcanic activity. The creek grows wide and then cascades down to the perennially misty green-blue pool. You'll love that mist more than anything if you're visiting in the height of summer. It gets very hot here, but please don't try to swim beneath the falls. The force and currents can be quite dangerous.

ROBERT HOLMES / CALTOUR

MacArthur-Burney Falls

## McCloud Falls

Another wonderful regional waterfall to visit is McCloud Falls (www.waterfallswest.com) on the—surprise!—McCloud River. You'll find the name accurate—in truth you've got the opportunity to see three separate waterfalls here. The Lower McCloud Falls acts as the prelude, with roiling white water pouring over a 30-foot rock wall into an aerated river pool below. Next, the Middle McCloud Falls resembles a tiny half-Niagara, a level fall of water that's wider than it is tall. (A lot of these types of waterfalls cluster around the mountains.) Finally, Upper McCloud Falls cascades powerfully but shortly down into a chilly but occasionally welcome pool that can double as a swimming hole.

To get there, exit I-5 on Highway 89 east toward McCloud. After about five miles, start looking for signs to Fowler's Camp and Lower McCloud Falls. After about a mile, you'll come to the Lower Falls picnic area, where you can park.

## Mossbrae Falls

Rather than one big gush of water through a narrow slot, Mossbrae Falls (Scarlett Way, Dunsmuir, www.waterfallswest.com) flows like a wild woman's hair—loose and all over the place. Just past the bridge and railroad tracks, these unique falls shower down into the deep blue-gray of the Sacramento River. The constant mists nourish an unbelievable cascade of greenery, from ferns to full-sized trees. You get to the beautiful and oddly pristine jungle by walking about 2.5 miles along the train tracks, then looking to the right just before you come to the railroad bridge.

### Lava Beds National Monument

Some of the best views of volcanic activity in extreme Northern California lie within Lava Beds National Monument (Hill Rd., www.nps.gov/labe, Memorial Day–Labor Day daily 8 A.M.–6 P.M., Labor Day–Memorial Day daily 8:30 A.M.–5 P.M.). Over hundreds of millennia, the Medicine Lake shield volcano has created an amazing landscape. In amongst the Modoc battle sites, campgrounds, and desert-like wilderness, you'll find numerous caves created by ancient lava tubes. Some of these have been developed with ladders and walkways, others remain in their original difficult-to-explore state. But they're worth your time and energy, even if you're not usually a spelunker. Not all of the lava tubes have remained empty for all these years; some have become home to whole ecosystems that thrive in the dark and the damp. Bring a flashlight, but be kind to the bats that dwell in these caves while you're checking out the ferns, mineral formations, and other unique features. Whether you've been into volcanoes in the past or not, the Lava Beds stand a good chance of winning you over.

## SPORTS AND RECREATION

The main reason folks come to the Mount Shasta region is to enjoy its outdoor wonders and challenges. Shasta offers nearly unlimited sporting opportunities year-round. Just be sure to prepare for whatever activities you plan to tackle and enjoy, as Shasta gets blisteringly hot in the summertime (well, except at the peak of the mountain) and frigid in the winter.

With all the climbing and skiing and hardcore hiking available on and around Mount Shasta, it's not surprising that you'll find a number of outdoor athletic stores in the town of the same name. **The Fifth Season** (300 N. Mt. Shasta Blvd., Mt. Shasta, 530/926-3606, www.thefifthseason.com, open daily) has not only mountain bikes, it's got ski and snowboard equipment and other recreation gear. Most of all, it's got all the mountain climbing equipment and advice you need to scale the peak of Mount Shasta. You can start at their website before you come, then go into their storefront in town to rent or purchase everything from boots to ice axes to crampons; before you start up the mountain, call 530/926-5555 for a recording that describes the current conditions approaching Mount Shasta's summit.

If it's ski and snowboard equipment, adjustment, rental, or repair you need, your best choice might be **The Sportsman's Den** (402 N. Mt. Shasta Blvd., Mt. Shasta, 530/926-2295, www.mtshastasports.com, daily 8 A.M.–6 P.M.). This shop specializes in fine-tuning high-end snowboards and fitting skis to a perfect T. In the summer, the Sportsman's Den offers fishing tackle and some sporting equipment.

### Hiking

The best way to see the Mount Shasta area is to get out of your car, onto your own two feet, and walk back into the wilderness. Some of the best hiking in all of California can be found on and around Mount Shasta. This beautiful region abounds with waterfalls, pine forests, rivers, streams, and fascinating geology. Informal camping and backpacking (wilderness permits required) can create a wonderful multi-day hiking trip. Day hikes offer everything from easy strolls great for kids and older travelers to strenuous miles that can take you up to minor mountain peaks for tremendous views of the whole southern Cascade mountain region.

The Shasta-Trinity National Recreation Area (www.fs.fed.us/r5/shastatrinity/recreation/nra/index.shtml#Recreation) encompasses quite a bit of land. Unlike many parks, the trailheads of Shasta-Trinity tend to be spread out. You'll need to do some highway driving between many of them.

### DAY HIKING

For an unlikely extension of a story that flowers way down on the Central Coast, take a walk along the **Ah-Di-Na Historic Trail** (0.25 mile, easy). Follow the signs from Squaw Valley Creek Road at the Reservoir to this odd little resort area along the McCloud River. The William Randolph Hearst family created a retreat here and you'll see photos of their property on the interpretive signs marking the short, flat trail. It's a bit of a drive out to Ah-Di-Na, and while you can take a passenger car, plan to traverse dirt roads and spend some time getting out there.

While the name of the **Sims Flat Historic Trail** (Sims Rd., south of the river, 1 mile, easy) refers to the name of the former logging town here, the trail itself is flat too. Sims Flat was once a bustling logging town, with the railroad running through it to carry products of the busy sawmill away to the big cities that needed fresh lumber. Nearly a century later, a few historic signs tell the story of this diverse ex-town. Another great thing about this walk are the up-close views of Mount Shasta, which looms over Sims Flat, offering many photo opportunities.

### BACKCOUNTRY HIKING

Way over on the other end of the hiking spectrum, heavy-duty hiking buffs seek out the **Sisson-Callahan National Recreation Trail** (North Shore Rd., 18 miles round-trip, difficult); just past Deer Creek Bridge, take the left fork and park off the road. Starting near Lake Siskyou, this trail gains almost a mile in elevation, peaking at over 8,000 feet at Deadfall Summit, then dropping 1,000 feet to Deadfall Lakes. Be sure to dress in layers, since you might start out in the intense summer heat of the lower elevations only to end up making snowballs up on the summit. Because it's long and steep and challenging, many hikers prefer to do this trail over more than one day. Any number of campsites lie along the North Fork of the Sacramento River and beyond, welcoming weary travelers with a spot to pitch a tent and enjoy a night's rest. In fact, the Sisson-Callahan links up with the Pacific Crest Trail down near Deadfall Lakes, letting backpackers keep on packin' if they choose to.

For a lovely long hike that takes you up to views of the whole of the Far North mountain region and into Oregon, trek up to **Mount Eddy** (Forest Service Rd. 17, 530/926-4511, 10 miles round-trip, difficult). You'll find a steep trail that takes you up to the 9,000-foot peak, where you can spin around and around, checking out various and sundry Cascade mountains: Shasta, Lassen, the Trinity Alps, and even Mount McLaughlin up in Oregon. The trail up from the Deadfall Lake trailhead is hot and dry, and you'll want to bring plenty of water as you'll find none here. You will find granite at the bottom of the mountain and green serpentine toward the top, lots of shade from the fir and pine trees proliferating on the mountainsides, and the clear waters of Deadfall Lake and Deadfall Creek on your way up to the lovely peak. (A number of hikers claim you can drink from the creek, but check with the rangers first and consider bringing purifiers if you plan to try this.) If you're not up for such a long day hike, consider an overnight camping trip; the lake makes a great informal primitive campground.

You know that cool brown-black cinder cone that sits close to the bottom of the mountain? Originally called Muir's Peak by humble naturalist John Muir, this "cinder cone" was created about 10,000 years ago during the same slow, thick magma eruption that created the Shastina crater. Believe it or not, you can scale the slick-looking sides of **Black Butte** (5 miles round-trip, difficult). It really is pretty slick. The trail ascends almost 1,900 feet in about 2.5 miles, with serious steep and rocky spots. In recent years, vegetation has started taking root in Black Butte, but the trail still offers precious little in the way of shade and no water at all. Bring plenty of water, and plan your hike for early morning if you're visiting in the summertime.

## Climbing

Climbers come from all over the world come

to tackle Shasta's majestic 14,162-foot peak. Be sure to pack your sturdiest hiking boots and your strongest leg muscles; less than one-third of the 15,000 intrepid mountaineers who try to conquer **Mount Shasta** (www.climbingmtshasta.org) each year actually make it to the top. If you're serious, you'll get plenty of help from the locals. Mountaineering and glacier classes are available, and several guides and outfitters can provide equipment and even lead you up the mountain. Take that help! You'll be required to negotiate Shasta's year-round icy glaciers, steep and rocky slopes, and extreme altitudes that thin the air to make the climb just that much tougher.

So what's the good news? There are more than a dozen routes you can take to ascend to the top. You can pick a quick, hardcore climb that takes you from the base camp up to the top in a single day, or choose a longer and more leisurely trail and spend two days making the trek, camping overnight in the ultimate California wilderness. The most popular route runs along Avalanche Gulch, and for the healthy and hearty, this can be the adventure of a lifetime. You'll see Mount Shasta up close in ways that most casual tourists could never even imagine. The peak climbing season is June through August.

If you are a casual tourist, exercise care accessing even the trailheads that lead to Shasta's peak. Some of the dirt roads around the base of the mountain require a four-wheel drive, and the weather conditions can severely impact the roads. To make this climb safely and successfully, you must be prepared, so check the web, talk to locals, and gather maps and equipment.

Nearby, the formation at **Castle Crags State Park** (on I-5, 6 miles south of Dunsmuir, 530/235-2684, www.parks.ca.gov) offers more than 40 established climbing routes, plus plenty of wide, open formations for explorers who prefer to climb where no one has climbed before. You'll get to tackle domes, spires, and walls of granite that reach 6,000 feet up toward the sky. The crags first thrusted upward, then broke off and were scrubbed by glaciers into the fascinating, climbable formations visible today. Some of the known favorite climbs at Castle Crags are the Cosmic Wall, Castle Dome East, and Six Toe Crack.

## Fishing

The rivers, streams, creeks, and lakes surrounding Mount Shasta make for some of the best freshwater fishing in all of California.

Fishing is permitted in Trinity Lake, Whiskeytown Lake, and most of the smaller lakes in the Shasta-Trinity National Recreation Area. You can bring your powered fishing boat to Trinity and Whiskeytown (be prepared to have it inspected for invasive mussels). Types of fish in these lakes include rainbow trout, German brown trout, kokanee salmon, and Mackinaw, among others. All you need is a California fishing license, tackle, and plenty of bait. Check with the bait and tackle shops in the area to learn what type of bait is working this season, and where the best spots are.

Almost all the major rivers and feeder streams running through the Mount Shasta region are open to fishing. You can tie your fly on and cast out into the McCloud River, the Sacramento River, the Trinity River, and many more. These rivers carry salmon, steelhead, and trout. If you want a guide to help you navigate these waters, contact one of the many services that can take you out to the perfect fishing holes. For fly-fishing, call **Jack Trout International Fly Fishing Guide Service** (530/926-4540, www.jacktrout.com). Jack's guides can both take you out to the rivers and help you improve your fly-casting technique. **Outdoor Adventures Sport Fishing** (800/670-4448, www.sacriverguide.com) not only takes trips out to the major NorCal rivers, it can guide you on a deep-water trip to Shasta Lake as well.

## Rafting and Kayaking

In the Cascades, the best whitewater rafting to be had is definitely on the **Trinity River.** And a good guide service to take you out onto the big white waters of this river is (naturally) **Trinity River Rafting** (800/307-4837, www.trinityriverrafting.com, $54–125). In addition to its flagship runs on the Trinity, this major rafting company runs on the Klamath, the Salmon, the Upper Fork Sacramento, and Canyon Creek. So depending on where you're staying and what level of rafting you're up to handling, you can choose your favorite river to paddle. Anywhere from half-day to three-day trips are available on various rivers, and you can choose from placid Class I and II float suitable for the whole family to an aggro Class IV–V run for fit, experienced rafters only. Trinity Rafting also rents small rafts and one- and two-person kayaks for paddlers who want to go off on their own.

Another major player in the northern mountains rafting scene is the **Bigfoot Rafting Company** (800/722-2223, www.bigfootrafting.com, $85). With day trips on the Trinity and Salmon, and multi-day rafting campouts on the Trinity and the Klamath, Bigfoot presents a depth of knowledge of the rivers it runs. Your guide will know a great deal about the history and natural surroundings of your chosen river, and as a bonus can cook you up fabulous meals on full-day and multi-day trips. Bigfoot also rents equipment.

New to river rafting? You probably won't meet at the rafting company's office. When you book your trip, you'll be given a spot to arrive at along your chosen river. The company will most likely also give you a list of items to bring with you, such as swimsuits, sweaters, specific shoes, waterproof cameras, and other such things. Be sure to ask questions when making your reservation.

## Skiing and Snowboarding

The snow pack on Mount Shasta each winter creates a haven for downhill skiers, cross-country skiers, snowboarders, and snowshoers. The place to go for all this is the **Mount Shasta Ski Park** (Ski Run Hwy., 530/926-8610, www.skipark.com, Dec.–Apr. Wed.–Sat. 9 A.M.–9 P.M., Sun.–Tues. 9 A.M.–4 P.M., lift tickets: adults $25–39, youth $15–20, children/seniors $5). This small but fun downhill park has 425 skiable acres, three chair lifts, and a tow rope. Nearly half the runs are open for night skiing, and the Marmot beginner area makes a perfect spot for beginners of all ages to gain their snow legs (at a fraction of the cost they'd pay in Tahoe). Half-day discount lift tickets and night-skiing-only lift tickets make skiing here even more attractive for snow-loving bargain hunters.

Cross-country lovers can also get their fix at the **Mt. Shasta Nordic Center** (Ski Park Hwy., 1 mile before downhill park, 530/926-2142, www.mtshastanordic.org, Dec.–Apr., free). With 15 miles of groomed trails, plus ample skiable backcountry, everyone from casual cross-country skiers and beginners to hardcore trail-breakers can have a good time here.

## Horseback Riding

The wilderness around and on Mount Shasta beckons to equestrians with a penchant for trail rides. Many of the hiking trails in the Shasta-Trinity wilderness and the surrounding regions also allow horseback riders. You can bring your own horse up to the majestic mountain region, or you can look to one of the local stable spread across the countryside.

**Shasta Cove Stables** (800/662-3529, www.visitsiskiyou.org/shastacovestables, $35/hour, $155/day) can take you on the ride of your dreams, whether that's a brief tour created by the stables or a multiday excursion into the back country planned by you and the stable together. Camps and lessons are available, focused on children.

Another outfit sits all the way up in Yreka is the **Rockin Maddy Ranch** (11921 Cram Gulch Rd., 530/340-2100, www.rockinmaddyranch.com, $45–175). Choose from the 90-minute Shasta View ride that features grand vistas of the mountain, or the 90-minute Shasta Lake ride. For a more intense experience, take a full-day ride through the mountains, including tracks along rivers, past waterfalls, and with time to stop to fish while you're out. Rockin Maddy allows smaller children to ride double on the same horse, and has a small herd of ponies for very small children. You can even book a hayride or a carriage ride.

## Mountain Biking

Some of the best and most unusual scenic mountain biking in all of California sits way up at **Lava Beds National Monument** (Hill Rd., www.nps.gov/labe, Memorial Day–Labor Day 8 A.M.–6 P.M., Labor Day–Memorial Day 8:30 A.M.–5 P.M.). You can bike on (relatively) recent lava flows, explore lava tubes, and check out the craters and calderas the volcano left behind. Or for an easier ride, explore the territory of the **Medicine Lake Highland** (530/233-5811, www.fs.fed.us/r5/modoc/recreation/mountain-biking.shtml) east of McCloud in the Modoc National Forest. This region contains Native American sacred sites, so please be respectful. Call the park for more information and the best spots to enter the mountain biking area.

# ACCOMMODATIONS

## Under $100

The cute **Dream Inn** (326 Chestnut St., 530/926-1536, www.dreaminnmtshastacity.com, $88–176) offers bed-and-breakfast accommodations right at the base of the magnificent mountain. The four small, inexpensive upstairs rooms have unique furnishings and shared hallway bathrooms. Downstairs, a bigger white antique bedroom has its own private bath and a view of Mount Eddy out of the lace-curtained window. Right next door, two large suites share space in a Spanish-adobe-style home; each has its own living space, bathroom, and truly homelike, cluttered decor. Rooms at the Dream Inn include a scrumptious full breakfast each morning.

The ultimate in clean, comfortable, and cheap lodgings at Shasta is the **Mount Shasta Ranch Bed and Breakfast** (1008 W. A. Barr Rd., 877/926-3870, www.stayinshasta.com, $66–130). The budget-friendly rooms in the Carriage House offer small spaces, queen beds, and shared bathrooms. The separate Cottage is the largest room in the house, with two bedrooms that can comfortably sleep up to six people. The four rooms in the Ranch House proper are spacious and comfortably furnished with a clutter of country-Victorian antiques and tchotckes, and each has its own big private bathroom. All rooms include a full country breakfast served just before 9 A.M. to get you up, moving, and fueled for a long day out in the Shasta wilderness.

## $100-150

To get a real sense of life in this remote region, book one of the rooms in the **Shasta MountInn Retreat & Spa** (203 Birch St., 530/926-1810, www.shastamountinn.com, $138–195). The big white farmhouse exterior fits perfectly into its semi-alpine setting, while the rooms ooze country charm and modern comforts. Each of the four rooms has its own private bath and high-end memory foam mattress, which tempts guests to loll about in bed all morning rather than heading downstairs for a healthy continental breakfast and a cup or two of organic coffee. The "spa" part comes in with on-site massage therapy services and a funky barrel-shaped redwood sauna. And if you're serious about taking a spiritual retreat into the local woods and waterways, your hosts can guide you to the sacred spots that dot this area, or you can strike out on your own to find your own holy places.

## $150-250

Perched between scenic Lake Siskyou and its own 18-hole golf course, the **Mount Shasta Resort** (1000 Siskyou Lake Blvd., 800/958-3363, www.mountshastaresort.com, $195) offers attractive lodgings and on-site sports to its guests. For a budget vacation, stay in one of the motel-style Woodland Rooms, each of which has a private bath with shower and two queen beds, making it perfect for families or couples traveling together. For a more private luxury experience, book one of the lovely individual chalets. Some of these sit right down by the lake, so you'll hardly ever want to leave your own front porch. Chalets can have private bathrooms, one or two bedrooms (sleeping up to six people), and full kitchens to make staying for a week or more a pleasure.

For more standard motel-style accommodations, check in to the **Mt. Shasta Inn and Suites** (710 S. Mt. Shasta Blvd., 530/918-9292, www.mtshastainn.com, $225–375). They're not unique, but the king, two-queen, and family suites here offer lots of space and the comfort of familiar surroundings. You'll get a standard-issue motel bathroom, a TV, a phone, and a good location central to town and close to both I-5 and Highway 89. An all-year outdoor hot tub welcomes weary sportsters after a long day out on the mountain or in the woods and lakes. The family suites are actually adjoining king and two-queen suites, offering sleeping spots for six people comfortably and two separate bathrooms.

# FOOD

## American

For diners, the best in the area is the local iteration of the **Black Bear Diner** (401 W. Lake St., Mount Shasta, 530/926-4669, www.blackbeardiner.com, $15–30).

## Asian Fusion

**KenZen Sushi Bar and Exotic Cuisine** (315 N. Mt. Shasta Blvd., 530/926-2345, www.kenzensushi.com/index.html, Tues.–Sat. 5–9:30 P.M., $8–20) can hook you up with some decent sushi and other Asian cuisine. Granted, if you've been eating in the Bay Area or Wine Country, the "exotic" items won't seem terribly uncommon to you. The menu features a pleasant array of Asian-themed soups and salads, a few steaks and grilled fish dishes, and a long (if fairly standard) sushi list. On the walls of this casual-elegant eatery you'll find the work of a number of local artists.

## Brewpub

For a yummy casual meal and a good beer, stroll on in to **Billy Goats Tavern** (107 Chestnut St., 530/926-0209, www.billygoatstavern.com, Tues.–Sat. 11:30 A.M.–10 P.M., $10–15). Here you'll find a great selection of imports and microbrews, plus a full menu of California-ized pub treats, including sandwiches, salads, and appetizers. This friendly spot welcomes locals and visitors alike, and you can wear your favorite jeans and battered T-shirt and feel right at home.

## Italian

If you're carbo-loading in preparation for climbing Mount Shasta, or carbo-loading to celebrate a successful climb, hike, swim, or ski, get a table at **Mike & Tony's Restaurant** (501 S. Mount Shasta Blvd., 530/926-4792, www.mikeandtonys.net, Mon. and Thurs. 5–9 P.M., Fri.–Sat. 5–10 P.M., Sun. 4–9 P.M., $13–22). This casual eatery serves up hearty Americanized Italian favorites, from big bowls of spaghetti to hefty broiled steaks. There are white cloths on the tables, so it's probably best to wear your clean T-shirt to this restaurant, but otherwise the atmosphere encourages family and friendliness and fun.

## Coffee and Groceries

Need a cup of coffee to get you going? Grab one at the **Seven Suns Coffee & Café** (1101 S. Mount Shasta Blvd., 530/918-9022, daily 8 A.M.–4 P.M., $10). This coffee house offers plenty of fair trade and organic coffees, plus tasty sandwiches and such for lunch.

To stock up on groceries for camping and picnics, stop by the **Berryvale Grocery** (305 S. Mount Shasta Blvd., 530/926-1576, www.berryvale.com, Mon.–Sat. 8:30 A.M.–7:30 P.M., Sun. 10 A.M.–6 P.M.). You can pick up high quality international foods here, grab a cup of coffee at the café, and then feast like a king back at your campsite.

# INFORMATION AND SERVICES

## Tourist Information

Need a leg up on your visit to Shasta? Start at the **Mount Shasta Visitors Bureau** (300 Pine St., Mt. Shasta, 800/926-4865, http://mtshastachamber.com). Here you can get information about hotels, restaurants, and local recreation.

On the other hand, if you need wilderness permits and trail advice, head for one of the local ranger stations. The **Mount Shasta Ranger Station** (204 W. Alma St., Mt. Shasta, 530/926-4511) can supply you with both wilderness and summit passes, plus park maps and information about current mountain conditions. Another station is the **Castle Crags**

**Ranger Station** (Castle Creek Rd. and Castle Crags State Park Rd., 530/235-2684).

### Media and Communications

Believe it or not, the Mount Shasta region has its own daily newspaper. In fact, the ***Siskyou Daily News*** (www.siskiyoudaily.com), published in Yreka, has been serving up current events to the mountain region for 150 years. Grab a copy and read up on the latest happenings around Mount Shasta and its surrounding towns and wilderness.

The Internet has made it even to the wilds of Mt. Shasta. Many of the quaint inns and small motels offer wi-fi in rooms or at least in common areas. You might also find access in local cafes.

### Banks and Post Office

The local **Mt. Shasta Post Office** (530/926-1343) is easy to access at 301 South Mount Shasta Boulevard.

Several banks have branches in Mount Shasta, and you'll have ample access to ATMs and possibly even the service of actual humans. Bank of America (100 Chestnut St., 800/346-7693) sits near many motels downtown. A branch of Washington Mutual (168 Morgan Way, 530/926-8910) graces the town of Mount Shasta.

### Medical Services

The town of Mount Shasta has a full-service hospital: **Mercy Medical Center Mt. Shasta** (914 Pine St., 530/926-6111) has a 24-hour emergency room and all the doctors you'll need.

## GETTING THERE AND AROUND

Mount Shasta is remote and to get here, you're going to need a car. The main road to Mount Shasta is I-5. This major thoroughfare can get you to the mountain from the north or from the south, and it's plowed constantly in winter to keep it open to trucking.

Parking in the town of Mount Shasta is usually easy—just beware of local events in town that might draw numerous visitors. The various parks and wilderness areas usually have parking lots, though some of the trailheads do not. In these cases, you can often park alongside the road, so long as you're not on a major highway.

## SHASTA LAKE

A good 45-minute drive down I-5 south from Mount Shasta, Shasta Lake sits shining and serene behind Shasta Dam. As you drive, you'll cross the lake twice. How is that possible? Rather than one big bowl, Shasta Lake is actually a series of fingers that connect at big, deep spots, then collect at the dam. Several of the fingers are actually incoming rivers that feed the reservoir. To create this mammoth spread-out lake, not one but *five* towns were drowned. The remains are still down there, most sunk so deep that even scuba divers cannot explore them.

Surrounding many fingers of the lake and some of the bigger pools are marinas, campgrounds, resorts, cabins, restaurants, and all the paraphernalia necessary for hundreds of people to enjoy lakeside vacations. Full powerboat access is permitted on Shasta Lake, and native Californians know that its size and variety of views make it a prime spot for weekend houseboating.

Not shockingly, most of the recreation at Shasta Lake centers around…the lake. Whether you want to paddle a kayak, tear it up on a wakeboard, or enjoy all the comforts of home on a houseboat, Shasta's got the water activities for you. Marinas dot the shores of the lake's fingers, offering boat rentals, gas, snacks, water, ice, and more. For those few folks who don't want to spend all day, every day on the water, hiking trails and four-wheel-drive roads thread through the forested wilderness areas surrounding the lake.

### Lake Shasta Caverns

Summer lake visitors can find themselves longing for cool air—hard to come by at Shasta in August! Perhaps the best natural air conditioning in the region can be had inside the Lake Shasta Caverns (20359 Shasta Caverns

Rd., 530/238-2341, www.lakeshastacaverns.com, year-round daily). Your tour begins across the lake from the caverns, at the Caverns Park and gift shop. During the summertime, tours leave every half-hour starting at 9 A.M. When your tour is called, you'll walk down to the boat launch and board a broad, flat-bottomed ferry with plenty of bench seats and a canopy. As you take the quick ride across a narrowish section of the lake, your driver will regale you with tales of the caverns. Pay attention; though there isn't a test, the tour is more fun if you know more about what you're looking at. At the dock (where boaters can meet their tour groups if they prefer), you'll get on a bus and take a staggeringly steep drive up 800 feet to the cavern entrance. The road permits some fabulous views out over the lake and all the way up to Mount Shasta.

Your cavern tour guide will meet you at the entrance, then lead you into a manmade tunnel. You'll head up a whole bunch of stairs and into the series of natural limestone and marble caverns. The guide will describe the amazing formations that spring from the walls, the ceiling, and even the floor. The guides have spent a lot of time in the caverns and have found shapes within the formations that they've named. The cathedral size of most of the cavern areas and the railed walkways help to remind visitors not to touch the delicate stalactites, drapes, pancakes, and ribbons of "cave bacon" that decorate each space. You're welcome to bring a camera to try to record the marvels you'll see here, but memories often provide better lighting.

Both kids and adults enjoy the tour of the Lake Shasta Caverns, but you'll want to keep an eye on younger children throughout the trip for their safety. No matter how hot it is outside, bring a jacket or sweater for your tour; the caverns remain a constant 50-something degrees all year long. While the tour isn't incredibly strenuous, you need to be able to walk and to climb over 100 stairs at a time.



## Shasta Dam

When you approach Shasta Dam (Shasta Dam Blvd., 530/275-4463) by water, it looks like, well, a big concrete dam. (Also, you're not allowed terribly close.) To learn what the pipes and structures actually *do,* you must get to the dam by car and take a tour of the facility. Even if hydro-engineering isn't your thing, it's worth your time to check out the dam, for the views of both lake and Mount Shasta if nothing else. But don't bother bringing a camera inside; for security reasons, no photography is allowed inside the dam. The tour lasts one hour and explains both the construction and the current function of the second-biggest dam in the United States.

## Shasta State Historic Park

Believe it or not, the Shasta region was once more populous than it is now;the area was once rich with 19th-century gold miners and all the folks providing goods and services to the miners. Today, the Shasta State Historic Park (Hwy. 299, 530/243-8194, www.parks.ca.gov, Wed.–Sun. 10 A.M.–5 P.M.) displays and honors that regional history. Two on-site museums, the **Litsch Store Museum** and the **Courthouse Museum,** allow history buffs to dig deeper into the life and times of early Shasta residents. See everything from an extensive collection of California landscape paintings to the original area gallows. Outdoors, you'll get the chance to wander through the remains of historic cottages and read the human history of Shasta through the grave markers in the cemeteries.

## Houseboating and Marinas

Most of the marinas inhabiting the Shasta Lake shores provide all the rentals and services you'll need while on the lake. If you've got a vacation rental or a campsite on or near the lake, you'll probably want to pick one of the marinas near your lodgings for convenience. (Shasta Lake really is that big and definitely that spread out.) But not all marinas offer public gas docks or public launch facilities, and one or two of them are primarily maintained for the owners of private slips. Just be sure that the marina nearest to home has everything you need—including a good reputation!

ROBERT HOLMES / CALTOUR

houseboating on Shasta Lake

**Note:** The marinas listed here offer a variety of amenities and services appropriate for a day on the lake. Folks staying up at the north end of the Sacramento River Arm of the lake might be tempted to rent from the wide selection of boats available at Antlers Marina and Resort. Resist that temptation if you're looking for a peaceful vacation without frustration, irritation, and angst. Unfortunately, Antlers is regarded by many respectable California publications as *the worst* marina anywhere on the lake and renters are advised to look elsewhere when possible.

### SUGARLOAF MARINA

Of the marinas on the Sacramento River Arm, **Sugarloaf Marina** (19761 Lakeshore Dr., Lakehead, 877/468-7326, www.houseboats.com, May–Oct.) offers the best customer service. Sugarloaf rents small aluminum fishing boats, personal watercraft, speedboats, patio boats with barbecue facilities, and a range of houseboats. It's easy to get to Sugarloaf from I-5, and the launch ramp is free to Sugarloaf guests (non-guests pay a launch fee). You can keep your own boat at Sugarloaf by renting a slip in one of the modern, wheelchair-accessible concrete docks. If you're houseboating, it's always best to bring your own supplies. But if you've forgotten anything, Sugarloaf offers a newly expanded convenience store that can provide paper towels and potato chips, live bait, an extra life jacket, cold beer, or whatever else you need. Out on the water, Sugarloaf sits away from the biggest boating areas on the lake, making it a little quieter and easier to get the hang of piloting your rental craft before you must contend with serious traffic. The one downside to Sugarloaf is its lack of a public fueling dock; you can get gas farther up the Sacramento Arm at Antlers if you're desperate.

### SHASTA MARINA RESORT

If your trip will focus on a visit to the Shasta Caverns, you'll find that one of the nearest marinas to the Cavern gift shop and loading dock is the Shasta Marina Resort (18390 O'Brien Inlet Rd., Lakehead, 800/959-3359, www.shastalake

.net). Easily accessed from I-5 towards the south end of the lake, this marina offers mid-sized houseboats and SeaSwirl BowRider ski boats with wakeboard towers. The marina facilities include a gas dock, convenience and souvenir store with ice and swimsuits (sold separately), and a boat launch (free with moorage or houseboat rental). This middle-of-the road rental spot definitely offers friendly service, so be sure to ask about good houseboating spots if you're new to Shasta Lake.

### PACKERS BAY MARINA

The Packers Bay Marina (16814 Packers Bay Rd., Lakehead, 800/331-3137, http://packersbay.com) is located in (surprise) Packers Bay, which sits a couple of miles west of I-5 near the big bridge. Getting to the marina from Redding is kind of tricky; you must get off I-5 at Shasta Caverns-O'Brien, then get *back on* going south to reach the Packers Bay Road exit. A small independent operator, this marina offers some of the rare, honest-to-goodness modest houseboats on Shasta Lake. These can sleep 10 people but are really comfortable for groups of 4–6 and are less expensive than the bigger models. Packers Bay Marina offers only houseboats, and fewer services than the larger places. But houseboat renters can expect more personal service, and nicer boats, here than at those big marinas. No pets are allowed on any boats.

## HOUSEBOATING ON SHASTA LAKE

The denizens of the Shasta Lake PR agencies have named the lake "the houseboating capital of the world." That bold statement may or may not be true, but Shasta Lake certainly is California's most popular houseboating lake. Most of the houseboats rented on Shasta Lake run in size from "silly" to "absurd" – it's quite difficult to find a houseboat that sleeps fewer than 10 people, and most sleep 14-18, with a few true leviathans that can hold more than 20 partying people. Granted, the beds aren't big and the private bedrooms few, so for true comfort, pile in no more than half to two-thirds the number of recommended overnight guests.

You can rent a houseboat at almost any marina on the lake. No special boating knowledge is required to rent a houseboat, though you may be required to provide a valid driver's license upon rental. The www.houseboats.com website makes it a little bit easier to shop for the houseboat rental of your dreams and it works with three of the lake's marinas: Jones Valley, Sugarloaf, and Lakeview. Whichever marina you rent from, expect to pay anywhere from $850 per weekend for a minimal smaller craft to $8,500 per weekend for a huge luxurious new boat. Weekly rates (which include one weekend) are often a bargain at double or less the cost of a single weekend.

Expect to find a fair amount of luxury; many Shasta houseboats come with upper-deck hot tubs, waterslides, barbecues, satellite TVs, and high-end entertainment systems. Your houseboat will also come with some necessities – most have fully equipped kitchens, basic cleaning supplies, and basic sanitary supplies (please read here: toilet paper). But you'll need to bring a bunch of your own stuff too, such as pillows, towels, sheets, paper towels, folding chairs, ski-quality life jackets, and first-aid kits. (And food and booze, of course.) See your renter for a full list of supplies they recommend bringing with you.

Piloting a mammoth houseboat on the waters of Shasta Lake is a bit like driving a big rental RV up I-5. Take it slow and careful, follow all the instructions you're given at your marina, and you'll do fine. Most Shasta houseboaters pull their craft into small inlets and moor them for the night. Your marina staff can advise you on how to safely maneuver your houseboat in toward shore in the evening and back out again the next morning.

Many Shasta houseboats have the equipment to tow smaller watercraft along behind them. If you choose, you can rent a ski boat, personal watercraft, or fishing boat and bring it along with you as you explore Shasta Lake.

**BRIDGE BAY MARINA**

You can see the Bridge Bay Marina (10300 Bridge Bay Rd., Redding, 800/752-9669, www.sevencrown.com/lakes/lake_shasta/bridge_bay/index.htm) from the big bridge on I-5. This huge marina is part of a full-scale resort that sees some of the biggest crowds on the lake. Bridge Bay Marina has a large rental fleet, which includes small-to-medium houseboats, closed-bow speedboats, personal watercraft, and patio boats. You can also moor your own boat in one of their many slips. From the water, this marina isn't too friendly to put into unless you're a customer, so if you need gas, ice, or snacks, you'll have to navigate carefully to avoid the renters-only area. But once you're in to the marina proper, you will find a fuel dock, a basic grocery store, a bait and tackle shop, and even a restaurant (Tail o' the Whale).

**JONES VALLEY MARINA**

One of the few year-round marinas on Shasta Lake, the Jones Valley Marina (22300 Jones Valley Marina Dr., Redding, 877/468-7326, www.houseboats.com) is situated on the secluded Pit River Arm, away from the higher traffic areas near the bridge but is still easily accessible from Redding and I-5. The McCloud Arm and the Squaw Creek Arm adjoin near this marina, which is one of the few that sells gas in this part of the lake. Jones Valley Marina is part of a larger resort, and includes a floating recreation area in addition to wheelchair-accessible docks and houseboats. Should you find yourself needing a three-deck houseboat with eight flat-screen TVs that sleeps 22 people, you can rent one at Jones Valley. They've also got a few more modest houseboats, plus the usual array of patio party boats and smaller craft, including a top-tier wakeboard-set speedboat.

## Waterskiing and Wakeboarding

The vast acreage and many distinct sections of Shasta Lake make it an ideal place to water-ski and wakeboard—even on crowded weekends, chances are good that you'll find someplace to ski. Just be sure to abide by the speed limit buoys surrounding the marinas and the "No Ski" buoys that warn of shallow water or other hazardous conditions.

If you've got your own tow boat, you can put it in at any number of public launches and rent a slip from one of the marinas. For renters, again, most of the marinas around the lake rent both speedboats and personal watercraft. You'll find a wide selection—everything from championship-quality late-model tow boats with towers for wakeboarders to older, open-bow speedboats that are perfect for cruising the lake with your family. Personal watercraft are mostly WaveRunners, with the occasional Sea-Doo for variety. (If you can get a Sea-Doo, do. They're better machines.) Prices run about $70–120 per hour, with good half-day, full-day, and full-week rates available at most marinas. Do be aware that no matter what marina you work with, these are high-performance rental boats, and problems sometimes crop up. The good news is that no matter where you rented, you can bring a busted boat into any nearby marina and they'll help take care of it for you.

Usually you'll need to rent your skis, boards, and other toys for a minimal extra fee. You can get double and slalom skis, wakeboards of different brands and sizes, purpose-built ski tubes, and even ridiculous "ski bananas" and other five- and six-seat towable toys that will definitely get you noticed all over the lake.

## Fishing and Patio Boating

If you just want to go out and putter on the lake for a day or host a sunset on-lake cocktail party, and all those beds and kitchens in the houseboats seem like overkill, what you want is a patio boat. These flat-bottomed, pontoon-style boats rent by the hour and by the day, and are much cheaper than the houseboats. Most come with plenty of seating and canopies for shade. Larger patio boats might have barbecues and storage chests as well. You're free to bring your own well-stocked coolers, fishing gear, stereo, and friends. Check with your favorite marina about renting one.

## Entertainment and Events

The main entertainment in the Shasta Lake area centers on the lake itself. The cool thing to do is to rent a patio boat or houseboat and throw your own party on the water. As with cars, it's necessary to designate a boat driver for your party to keep your friends and everyone else on the water safe.

The major annual festival at Shasta Lake each year is the **Shasta Damboree** (www.shastadamboree.com). Each May, a three-day weekend is devoted to family-friendly events that bring out the community and draw visitors to the region. The events feel typical of a good small-town celebration, with spaghetti feeds, pancake breakfasts, an arts-and-crafts area, and a parade and evening party with fireworks and live music. Check the website for dates and events for the coming year.

Some of the best drinking, pool playing, and occasional live music happens up on the northern Sacramento River Arm, just off the I-5 at **The Basshole** (20725 Lakeshore Dr., 530/238-2170, www.bassholebarandgrill.com, grill daily 11 A.M.–10 P.M., Tues. until 5 P.M., bar open until closing). Yeah, really, they went there. This bar, restaurant, pool hall, and bait shop comprise a single large hall for dining, drinking, and recreating, with the bait shop hiding in a tiny room just off the dining area. The food is nothing special—burgers and dogs and fairly tasty hot fries are the house specialties, though for dinner they do put out an array of slightly fancier entrées. Locals don't come here to eat, they come here for beer. Expect to find the occasional co-ed wet t-shirt contest and other such adult entertainment on summer weekend evenings.

Two other options are the **Wonderland Tavern** (15041 Wonderland Blvd., 530/275-2397) just off I-5 and the **Idle Hour Bar and Grill** (14961 Bear Mountain Rd., 530/275-0230), which sits south of the Silverthorn Resort, close to the intersection of Bear Mountain Road and Silverthorn Road.



## Accommodations

Many of the visitors who come to Shasta Lake rent houseboats or lakeside cabins in which to enjoy their vacation. (See *Houseboating and Marinas* for more information about these types of rentals.)

### $100–150

Because it's out in the woods a mile south of the lakeshore, the **Fawndale Lodge & RV Park** (15215 Fawndale Rd., 530/275-8000, www.fawndale.com, $80–130) offers comfy lodge rooms and cabins at bargain prices. Though you can't see the lake from the lodge, the surrounding forest has its own charm and the garden and pool offer plenty of beauty and comfort. All rooms include a fridge, microwave, and private bathrooms. Suites have full kitchens, bed space for six people, and (oh, true heaven!) air conditioning. The decor runs to rustic wood walls and furniture and simple amenities, and small TVs offer minimal entertainment and encouragement to get outside and play.

Tent campers and RV travelers are welcome at Fawndale; check the website or call for information about full-hookup RV spots and tent campsites, and make a reservation in advance to guarantee your spot.

Towards the north end of the lake, the **Shasta Lake Motel** (20714 Lakeshore Dr., Lakehead 530/238-2545, www.shastalakemotel.com, $83–150) is a favorite for regular visitors. For the small prices, you'll get some bigger lodge amenities, including air conditioning, cable TV, microwave, mini-fridge, and coffee maker. Each room glows softly with dark, honey-colored wood-paneled walls and furniture, and the decor runs to rustic prints and artifacts. One special amenity will thrill taller travelers; all the twin and double sized beds are "extra long," making them far more comfortable for folks over six feet tall. Outdoors, you can enjoy the motel pool, or take a quick walk down to the shores of the lake. The motel is only a few minutes off I-5, close enough for convenience but not so near that you'll be listening to the trucks all night.

The **Bridge Bay Resort** (10300 Bridge Bay Rd., 800/752-9669, www.sevencrown

.com/lakes/lake_shasta/bridge_bay/index.htm, $130–210) has one of the best locations of any resort on the lake, right where the big I-5 bridge crosses the lake. It's close to the center of the lake's arms, making it a perfect spot to launch a boat from the resort's full-service marina. Bridge Bay also includes a restaurant, a small grocery store, and a bait and tackle shop. The lodgings aren't terribly stylish, and the rooms are decorated in average budget-motel chic with colorful bedspreads, particle-board furniture, and generic prints on the walls. You'll definitely find a family-friendly vibe here—many of the guest rooms sleep 4–6 people, and some have full kitchens.

### $150-250

Some travelers simply cannot do without their creature comforts. For those, on Shasta Lake there's the **O'Brien Mountain Inn** (18026 O'Brien Inlet Rd., 530/238-8026, www.obrienmountaininn.com, $154–330). This casual-elegant bed-and-breakfast inn eschews the woodsy-lodge theme that most lodgings in the area use. Instead, the eight rooms and suites are painted in soft pastels with attractive matching furnishings and amenities. Some suites have kitchenettes, and some have fabulous whirlpool bathtubs, perfect for relaxing after a long day out playing on the lake! Breakfast includes fresh coffee and baked goodies delivered to the door of your room at 8 A.M., then a full meal is served in the dining room at 9 A.M. The only real downside of the O'Brien is its location. It's not right on the lakeshore, so the views and access won't be right there. But the drive to the lake is minimal, and Lake Shasta Caverns sits nearby.

### OVER $250

Well east of I-5 out on the tip of a small peninsula in the Pit River Arm, the **Silverthorn Resort** (16250 Silverthorn Rd., 530/275-1571, www.silverthornresort.com, $1,210–2,200 per week) definitely has the advantage of a location right on the water. The views from the common areas and guest cabins are phenomenal and the resort has its own full-service marina with houseboats for rent. Just don't expect to blow in and get a cabin for a single night in the midst of high season. At Silverthorne, cabins rent *only* by the week in summer and require a three-day minimum for the rest of the year. Each cabin sleeps 4–6 people, except for the large family cabin that can handle eight. Inside, you'll find the ubiquitous wood-paneled interior walls and simple but attractive lodge-style decor. All cabins include a full kitchen (thus making the by-the-week rental requirement a bit more attractive) with full-sized refrigerator, plus private bathrooms. Expect bedrooms to be small but cute, and the atmosphere to be woodsy and restful. Be sure to book your boat rentals with the marina at the same time you book your cabin to ensure that you get what you want, when you want it. A small grocery store and a "pizza pub" offer easy dining and shopping on-site for visitors who don't feel like driving far away for dinner.

## Food

The **Tail O' the Whale** (10300 Bridge Bay Rd., Redding, 800/752-9669, www.sevencrown.com/lakes/lake_shasta/bridge_bay/restaurants.htm) at the Bay Bridge Resort west of I-5 offers three meals daily in a casual dining room that's perfect for lakeside vacationers. The lengthy menu has plenty of American resort mid-scale favorites, with something to please almost everybody.

On the east side, the Silverthorn Resort boasts the only pizza along the lake at the **Silverthorn Pizza and Pub** (16250 Silverthorn Rd., Redding, www.silverthornresort.com/resort-svcs/pizza.html, Mon. 11 A.M.–10 P.M., Tues.–Wed. noon–10 P.M., Thurs. 11 A.M.–10 P.M., Fri.–Sat. 11 A.M.–1 A.M., Sun. 11 A.M.–9 P.M.). This ultra-casual eatery boasts ice-cold beer, piping hot pizzas, and other homey fare. A huge deck overlooking the lake lures folks out for cocktails, then bar games like pool and live music bring them back inside as night falls.

For supplies, Lakehead boasts the **Lakeshore Village Market** (20750 Lakeshore Dr., Lakehead, 530/238-8615) with plenty of food, plus basic camping, fishing, and outdoor recreation supplies for visitors staying at the north end of the lake.

A few miles north of the lake on I-5, where any hint of civilization disappears, you'll come upon the tiny "town" of Pollard Flat. This flat spot beside the road has one odd, rambling, blocky building, **The Restaurant at Pollard Flat** (24235 Eagles Roost Rd, Lakehead, 530/238-2534, $10), as well as a bar, mini-mart, and gas station. But what the restaurant at Pollard Flat has the most of is atmosphere. A few stools sit at a bar or counter (it's anyone's guess as to which it really is) just inside. Turn left and you'll be in the first of a warren of dark dining rooms, fitted out with ancient wooden tables and black vinyl booths. Just to sit down in this place and ask for a menu and a glass of water requires a degree of courage. To have a meal is the test of a genuine adventurer. A safer option might be the minimal packaged snacks and sodas sharing space with the bait and NRA stickers in the equally dim and creepy adjoining mini-mart.

## Information and Services

New to the Shasta Lake area? Stop in at the **Shasta Lake Visitor Information Center** (Holiday Rd., Mountain Gate, 530/275-1589, Memorial Day–Labor Day Wed.–Sun. 8 A.M.–4:30 P.M.). This small ranger station can provide you with information and local guidance, plus information on this year's hot fishing spots.

Believe it or not, Shasta Lake does boast its own tiny local paper: the ***Shasta Lake Bulletin*** (www.shastalake.ws). Check the "Visitor's Guide" section for basic traveler's information, and the "After Five Magazine" for local entertainment and event options.

Not all cell phone providers offer coverage out in the Shasta Lake region. If you plan to rely on your cell phone while you're here, check with your carrier before you arrive.

Some places do offer Internet access, but they can be few and far between. Certainly none of the houseboats offer DSL. Some of the lodges and inns offer Wi-Fi, but the nearest Starbucks is all the way down in Redding. Ask before you arrive to determine whether you'll have in-room Internet where you're staying, or check at www.shastalake.com/internet.

Another option is to leave the laptop and the Blackberry behind, unplug, and enjoy the beauty of the Shasta Lake region unspoiled by incessant beeping and buzzing and chirping.

There is a **post office** up at Lakehead (20856 Antlers Rd.), but the nearest major medical facilities are in Redding (see *Information and Services* in the *Redding* section for more information).

## Getting There and Around

The nearest full-service airport to Shasta Lakes is Redding Municipal. (See *Getting There* in the *Redding* section for more information). From there, you can rent a car at the airport to drive out to the lake.

Most folks come to Shasta Lake by car or RV via I-5, which runs right over the lake in two different places. Bridge Bay is one of the more popular (and populous) spots on the lake, due to its proximity and easy access to I-5. The Sacramento Arm to the north is also easily accessible from the freeway.

Shasta Lake is big and spread out. As big as it might look from the bridge, you're seeing only a small part of the lake. A network of smaller (but mostly paved) roads encircle most of the other arms of the lake, allowing access to the marinas and resorts and campgrounds.

Parking isn't generally a problem around Shasta Lake, except possibly on holiday weekends in the summertime. Parking at the resorts is usually free.

Many people bring their own boats to Shasta Lake rather than paying the high fees to rent from the marinas. Check the *Houseboating and Marinas* section of this chapter and local maps to find the public launch nearest to your accommodations. (Expect to pay a small launch-ing fee.) Before launching, your boat may be inspected both for proper state licensing and for pernicious mussels.

No special license is required to pilot a boat in California. All drivers of boats over 15 horsepower must be age 16 or over (that includes personal watercraft). Youth ages 12–15 can drive if directly supervised by an adult. All children under 12 must wear a life jacket at all times when on board a boat. Drunk boating laws are the same as drunk driving laws. The legal limit is BAC 0.08. Penalties for drunk boating can be severe. For more information about boating rules, visit www.co.shasta.ca.us/departments/sheriff/boatingsafety.htm.

## Lassen Volcanic National Park

Mount Lassen is an active volcano with a recorded history of eruptions, the last of which took place in 1914 and 1915. The mountain is a remote and beautiful sight, one that's only accessible to large numbers of visitors in the short summer months when the temperatures rise and the snow melts. A wonderful loop drive through Lassen Volcanic National Park (530/595-4444, open daily year-round, Headquarters Information Desk open Mon.–Fri. 8 A.M.–4:30 P.M.) takes you from the stark slopes and jagged brand-new rocks of the most recent eruption, around the back to an enormous ancient crater, the remains of a long-gone volcano as big or bigger than Mount Shasta.

Ample hiking trails, wonderful pristine ponds, and many campsites that let visitors settle in and really enjoy the amazing panoramas of Mount Lassen. Beyond the bounds of the state park, national forest lands allow for additional exploration. Do be aware that the "lower" elevations of Mount Lassen trails sit more than 7,000 feet above sea level. If you're planning serious hiking, come up a day early and camp on the mountain to acclimate to the elevation. The next day you'll be better able to take the longer and higher trails without succumbing to altitude sickness.

For true, unspoiled California wilderness, it's hard to beat the backcountry at Lassen. Even the most traveled roads and "front side" sights will seem empty to travelers who've visited Yosemite Valley or Lake Tahoe. *But* (you knew there had to be a catch to such an

ROBERT HOLMES / CALTOUR

Mount Lassen

amazing place), the only time to visit Lassen is the height of summer. Snow chokes the area from as early as October until as late as June, closing the main road through the park and making even the lower altitude campground snowy and cold. Most determined mountain-lovers pick August and early September as the best time to come to Lassen. On the other hand, active snow lovers will make the trek up the mountain in the wintertime to enjoy snowshoeing and cross-country skiing, or bring their sleds and their kids for a fun afternoon playing on the mountain slopes.

## SIGHTS

Lassen Volcanic National Park is one of the oldest national parks in the United States. It is also one of the most remote and primitive. On the other hand, a good (and paved) main road runs through the middle of the park, letting visitors enjoy many of the major attractions—including the park's active volcanic features.

The good news is that the rugged weather and isolated location mean that a visit to Lassen Volcanic National Park is a visit to an unspoiled wilderness area rather than an overdeveloped, Disney-fied amusement park with rocks. A good half of the park has only minimal dirt road access and offers its rugged beauty only to those travelers willing to hike for miles into the backcountry. Even the trails and campgrounds accessible by paved road maintain a kind of charm that's hard to find in the more popular California parks.



### Loomis Museum and Manzanita Lake

As you enter the northwest edge of the park on Highway 89, you'll almost immediately find the Loomis Museum (at the visitors center) and Manzanita Lake. Inside the museum, you've got a wonderful opportunity to learn about the known history of Mount Lassen, focusing heavily on the eruptions photographed by Mr. B. F. Loomis. Prints of those rare and stunning photos have been blown up and captioned to create these exhibits; the museum was named for the photographer, who later became a major player in the push to make Mount Lassen a national park. This interpretive museum offers a rare chance to see, through photos, the devastation and following stages of regrowth of the ecosystem of volcanic slopes.

### Chaos Jumbles

So this broken and decimated area is another spot that was overcome by the 1915 eruption of Mount Lassen, right? Nope! Lassen National Park is full of surprises, and the aptly named Chaos Jumbles is often the first that visitors stumble upon. Instead of volcanic activity, it was a massive avalanche that damaged this small part of the park about 300 years ago. The results seem quite similar to the regions that had the volcano erupt on them, with the devastation of the living ecosystem, the displacement of massive rocks, and the general disorder of the landscape. The avalanche that occurred here was so big, and came straight down so fast that it actually trapped a pocket of air underneath it, adding to the destruction. Now, visitors enjoy a wealth of new life, including a bigger-than-average variety of coniferous trees. The newness of the living landscape has allowed more competing types of plants to get a foothold here.

### Devastated Area

It seems like an odd name for a point of interest, but in fact the Devastated Area is one of the most fascinating geological and ecological sites anywhere in California. When Lassen blew its top in 1915 after nearly a year of sporadic eruptions, a tremendous part of the mountain and all the life on its slopes was destroyed. Boiling mud and exploding gases tore off the side of Lassen's mountain peak and killed all the vegetation in the area. A hail of lava rained down, creating brand-new rocks, from gravel to boulders, across the north side of the mountain.

Today visitors can easily see how a volcano's surface ecosystem recovers after an eruption. First, park at the Devastated Area lot and take the interpretive walk through a small part of the recently disrupted mountainside. You'll see everything from some of the world's youngest rocks to grasses and shrubs up through tall pine trees. Also be sure to check out the photos in the Loomis Museum that depict the area during and immediately after the eruption for a great comparison to the spot as it looks now.

The Devastated Area offers ample parking, and the interpretive walk is flat and wheelchair accessible. Please don't pick up any of the red and black volcanic rocks here; they are part of the redeveloping ecosystem and necessary to the area's recovery.

## Hot Rock

No, it's not hot anymore. But this huge boulder started out untouchable when the Loomises explored the eruption zone soon after the 1915 blast. Frankly, the site isn't all that amazing now, except when you think about that big rock remaining warm to the touch for months, so recently it was written about and even photographed. The Hot Rock turnout also offers more great views of the Devastated Area.

## Lassen Peak

It's not as tall as it used to be, but Lassen Peak still reaches over 10,000 feet up toward the sky. Even if you're not up to climbing it, it's worth stopping at the significant parking lot at the trailhead to crane your neck and enjoy the view. The craggy broken mountain peak is what's left after the most recent eruption—hence the lack of much in the way of vegetation. The elevation (more than 8,000 feet at the parking lot) makes the Lassen Peak trailhead cool even in the heat of summer when the temperatures only 1,000 feet below hit the 90s. You may need to break out a light windbreaker or sweatshirt if you plan to explore at length.

It's not marked on the park maps, but the Lassen Peak trailhead includes a huge parking lot and a spot to rest off the road. You'll find adequate chemical toilets and a trailer-housed concessionaire in this parking lot. Head into the store for souvenirs, that sweatshirt you forgot, or a snack. Minimal hot food (hot dogs, mostly) and plenty of drinks are available, and a few picnic tables outside the trailer make a decent spot for a picnic.

## Summit Lake

Lassen National Park is dotted all over with tiny lakes—most are more like ponds or even puddles than true lakes. One of the most popular and most easily accessible of these is Summit Lake, which sits right along the main road. The shining bright small lake attracts many campers to its two forest-shaded campgrounds. There's an easy walk around the lake that lets you see its waters and the plants that proliferate around it. Or find one of the small trails down to the edge of water and eke out a spot on the miniscule beach with all the other visitors who come to escape the blinding heat. You can swim and fish in Summit Lake, and even take rafts and canoes out to paddle around. (No powered boats are permitted on any lake at Lassen.)

## Bumpass Hell

The best and most varied area of volcanic geothermal activity on Lassen is at a location called Bumpass Hell (located six miles from the southwest entrance). The region was named for a Mr. Bumpass (no, really, this is the story) who, in his explorations, stepped through a thin crust over a boiling mud pot and severely burned his leg, ultimately losing the limb. In fact, the tale of the unfortunate Bumpass makes a good point for travelers visiting the mud pots and fumaroles here: *stay on the paths!* The dangers at Bumpass Hell are real, and if you step off the boardwalks or let your children run wild, you are risking serious injury and even death.

That said, a hike down to Bumpass Hell will prove fun enough to make the risks worthwhile. You'll need to walk about two miles from the parking lot and trailhead out to the good stuff—boiling mud pots, fumaroles, steaming springs, and pools of boiling, steaming water cluster here. Prepare for the strong smell of sulfur, more evidence that this volcano is anything but extinct. Boardwalks meander through the area, creating safe walking surfaces for all visitors.

The spacious parking lot also offers stunning views out east and south, giving you a hint at

ROBERT HOLMES / CALTOUR

Bumpass Hell

the scope of the ancient volcano that once stood here. Or if you need to, you can take advantage of the primitive but usable facilities.

## Sulphur Works

For visitors who can't quite manage the trek out to Bumpass Hell, the Sulphur Works offer a peak at the geothermal features of Lassen right on the main road. A boardwalk runs along the road and a parking area is nearby, allowing visitors to get out of their cars to examine the loud boiling mud pots and small steaming stream here. The mud pots both look and sound like a washing machine, sending up steam and occasional bursts of boiling water. Keep hold of your children!

As of the writing of this guide, the small loop trail and longer path out to Ridge Lake were closed. Check with the rangers on the status of these trails during your visit.

# SPORTS AND RECREATION

The reason to haul yourself and your family and your friends and your gear all the way out to Mount Lassen is to get out and experience this amazing scenic wilderness. Whether you prefer short nature walks or intense multi-day hikes, swimming in the little crystalline lakes or fishing for dinner in them, outdoor recreation calls to all Lassen visitors.

## Day Hiking

Most of the easy interpretive walks and short day hikes run out to the sights of Mount Lassen Volcanic Park. For hikers who want to get out away from the more touristy areas but still make it back to their cars before dark, moderate-to-difficult hiking trails offer adventure, challenge, and maybe even a touch of solitude.

The **Kings Creek Falls** (Road Marker 32, 3 miles round-trip, moderate) starts out easy. Your initial walk will be downhill to the falls. Be sure to stop to admire the small cascade and pool, perhaps sit down and have a drink and a snack to prepare for the 700-foot climb back up to the trailhead. This makes for a good hike for fitter day-hikers who've been on the mountain for a couple of hours.

It's the length of the trail that runs from **Summit Lake to Echo and Twin Lakes** (east side of Summit Lake, 8 miles round-trip, moderate to difficult) that makes it hard to do. But you can choose how many little lakes you really want to see as you run short on breath. Happily, the ascent over this long trail is only

500 feet total—a gentle slope in these mountainous reaches. If you just walk out to Echo Lake, you'll have a pleasant and sedate four-mile walk. It's another two miles to get out to Upper Twin Lake and back, and a final two miles to reach Lower Twin Lake. You might want to wear a swimsuit under your hiking clothes on hot summer days, and cool off in one of the lakes before trekking back to base.

One trail that does not offer much in the way of solitary communion with nature is the path up to **Lassen Peak** (difficult). A large parking lot with a gift/snack shop and chemical toilet facilities sits at the barren trailhead. In the parking area sit the cars of the many visitors who want to climb up to the highest point on Mount Lassen. It's not a pretty hike; the recent (by geologic standards) eruption and prevailing weather conditions leave this peak virtually bereft of plant life. Expect an utterly steep climb that winds up the barren peak to the sounds of gasping hikers and their screaming leg muscles. But at the top, the views will make you forget the torturous climb, if only for a few moments. Be sure to turn all the way around to get 360° views back down to the newest volcanic landscape, then across to the remains of the giant caldera of an extinct huge volcano, then out west toward Cascade Range neighbor Mount Shasta.

For a good, solid, all-day, steep hike, climb up **Brokeoff Mountain** (Road Marker 2, 7.5 miles round-trip, difficult). Brokeoff makes a good second or third day Lassen hike—with an unrelenting 2,600-foot ascent from an already mile-high starting point, thin air and altitude sickness can be a real concern for out-of-shape, unacclimated hikers. On the other hand, if you're ready for it, this can be one of the prettiest and most serene hikes in the populous section of the park. Enjoy the pretty mountain streams and stellar views out over the mountains and valleys of far-Northern California.

## Backcountry Hiking

Some of the most beautiful and interesting remote hiking in California can be found in Lassen's spreading expanse of backcountry. While you might not be the only backpacker out there, you'll definitely leave the crowds on the main road behind and find yourself with more trees, birds, and other mountain critters than people to talk to. You might even get lucky enough to have a pristine lake or mountain stream all to yourself.

Backcountry camping is permitted at Lassen, and several hike-in campgrounds offer some minimal facilities and a way to minimize your impact on the landscape. Check with the ranger station when you enter the park to obtain backcountry permits and get the season's scoop on trail and campground conditions. Be sure to bring your fishing gear! Tasty trout swim the lakes and streams of the remote Lassen wilderness, offering the chance at a fresh dinner or breakfast.

No major park in California would be complete without a hunk of the **Pacific Crest Trail** running through it. This high-altitude piece (17 miles, difficult) of the continent-spanning trail offers lots of challenge and solitude, and a fairly short window of months in which you can traverse this part of California. If you're doing the California leg of the Pacific Crest Trail, try to hit Lassen sometime between June and September, and be prepared for extreme weather conditions from blistering heat to snowstorms.

For a radical change of scenery, take the **Cinder Cone from Butte Lake** (west end of Butte Lake Campground, 4–5 miles, moderate). Be sure to wear your sturdiest ankle-covering hiking boots on this adventure, since the ground on the Cinder Cone is...well...cinders. Watch your footing so you don't slide down; even cold cinders can cut you up. The cone rises 800 feet over two miles; to lengthen the hike, walk down the south side of the cone. Geology and photography buffs particularly like this hike, which is accessible by dirt road and shows off some of the more interesting and less-seen volcanic history of Mount Lassen.

If you can't get enough of Lassen's geothermal features, enter the park from Warner Valley Road and take a hike to **Boiling Springs Lake** (Warner Campground Parking Lot, 3 miles, easy to moderate). You'll get to see bubbling mud pots and check out (from a safe distance) the waters of boiling springs. The walk out and back is reasonably short and non-strenuous. Just be *very* careful once you reach the geothermal area. Unlike Bumpass Hell, this region has no nice safe boardwalks encircling the mud pots and fumaroles. These features, along with the hot springs, can be extremely dangerous. This might not be a great hike for young, spirited children. But it's heaven for serious nature-lovers who want to see what volcanic geothermal features look like in their wild state. Needless to say, trying to swim in (sulfurous, acidic, 125°F) Boiling Springs Lake is a *very bad idea*.

Looking for a more serious backcountry trek that will take you more than a day? Check the park's website for maps, and feel free to call the park to get advice on route planning and necessary equipment before you come. Once you're in the park, the visitors centers can issue you a free wilderness permit for backcountry hiking and camping, and give you last-minute pointers and current trail information.

### Boating and Fishing

If you've got a canoe, a kayak, or a rowboat, bring it on up to Lassen in the summertime. Many of the small to midsized lakes on the mountain allow unpowered boating and fishing. While most of the lakes on the west side of the park near the road are too small to boat, out east Juniper, Snag, and Butte Lakes have plenty of space to row or paddle out and enjoy the serenity of water and earth. No boat rentals are available inside Lassen National Park.

Several varieties of trout inhabit the larger Lassen lakes. All you need is a pole, some bait, and a valid California fishing license. Manzanita Lake offers catch-and-release fishing only, but at all the other fishable lakes you're welcome to take a state limit of rainbows and browns. Fishing from several campgrounds makes it easy to enjoy the freshest dinner possible.



### Swimming

You're free to splash to your hearts content in Summit Lake, Manzanita Lake, King Creek, and almost all of the eastern backcountry lakes. Beware: These lakes can be icy cold! Summit Lake tends to get crowded with water-lovers on summer weekends.

## CAMPING

If you're planning to camp, please review the regulations and Leave No Trace guidelines at the Lassen camping website (www.lassen.volcanic.national-park.com/camping.htm) to help you get organized and pack for your trip.

### Paved Road Accessible Camping

Closest to the park entrance along Highway 89 you'll find the pleasant and serene **Manzanita Lake Campground** (179 sites, May–Sept., reservations recommended, $14). By far the largest campground in Lassen, Manzanita Lake has a full slate of amenities, including flush toilets, showers, potable running water, fire rings or pits, picnic tables in all campsites, and an RV dump station. Trailers and campers up to 35 feet are allowed at this campground.

Five miles south of Manzanita Lake, the more primitive and less expensive **Crags Campground** (45 sites, June–Sept., $8) offers a more out-in-the-woods style of camping. Crags does have potable running water and pit toilets, but no showers. Each site has its own table and fire pit.

Farther along Highway 89 at Summit Lake, the **Summit Lake North and South Campgrounds** (92 sites, June–Sept., $12–14) are among the most popular in the whole park, so reservations are recommended. Visitors can swim in Summit Lake, easily accessing its banks from campsites and paths. These two developed campgrounds have flush toilets, fire pits, and tables, but to be safe bring your own potable water, enough for the length of your trip for drinking and dishwashing. At 6,650 feet altitude, the Summit Lake campgrounds are among the highest in the park. Be sure to take it easy setting up camp on your first day so that you can get used to the thinner air.

### Dirt Road and Walk-In Camping

Out in the backcountry, well away from the main road, the **Butte Lake Campground** (turn off Hwy. 44 toward Butte Lake/Lassen, 42 sites, May–Sept., $10) shows off the beauty of Lassen to its best advantage. Despite its remote location at the northeast corner of the park, you'll find this to be a fairly well-developed campground, with pit toilets and running water. (Check with the park service to be sure water at this campground is drinkable.) Each site has a fire pit and table. Trailers and RVs up to 35 feet that can negotiate the road can camp at Butte Lake. To reach the campground, take Highway 44 up to the dirt road, then drive six miles to the campground. Reservations are recommended.

The **Juniper Lake Campground** (dirt road from Chester, 18 sites, June–Oct., $10) takes campers farther off the beaten path. Since the campground is located in the east side of the park, at the end of a rough dirt road, you'll do much better if you're a tent camper rather than an RVer or trailer-tower. This small campground beside beautiful Juniper Lake has pit toilets, fire pits, and tables, but the water here isn't drinkable. Either bring purifying agents or your own drinking water in containers. Because it sits at almost 7,000 feet, definitely take it easy during your first day at Juniper Lake. Reservations are recommended.

If you're bringing your horses on vacation with you, you can reserve a space at the Juniper Lake Corral ($4/animal).

**Warner Valley** (one mile off Warner Valley Rd., 18 sites, June–Oct., $12) lies along the south edge of the park. Another smaller gem of a semi-developed campground, Warner Valley has pit toilets and drinking water, as well as tables and fire pits at each site. No trailers, please! Though the dirt road is only a mile long, it's too rough for large campers and RVs to navigate.

## ACCOMMODATIONS

Indoor accommodations on Mount Lassen are few and far between. Most folks either camp or stay in Redding and day-trip up to the park. Expect little in the way of luxury or amenities if you do choose one of the indoor Lassen lodgings.

The one lonely non-camping lodging option in or even near Lassen National Park is the **Drakesbad Guest Ranch** (Warner Valley Rd., Chester, 530/529-1512, ext. 120, www.drakesbad.com, $155–179, summer only). This all-inclusive ranch includes three meals per day included with your room rate, though the national park fee is not included. The big brown barn of a lodge hints at the focus of this guest ranch—energetic exploration of the outdoors. The ranch maintains its own stable, making horseback riding all throughout Lassen Volcanic National Park an easy proposition. (Horseback rides cost extra.) You're also within easy reach of any number of trails, many of which are not accessible from the park's main paved roads. Bring your tackle along on a walk or a ride to take advantage of the fishing available in the local lakes and streams. Some anglers enjoy the guided fly-fishing program offered by the ranch, which teaches fly-fishing and practices catch-and-release sustainable fishing. (One-day California fishing licenses are available on-site.) The ranch even has a wonderful pool that's fed by the water from a local hot spring, making it healthful for soaking as well as for swimming laps.

A vacation at Drakesbad Guest Ranch is like few other retreats in all of California. The countryside really does have a wild feeling, with lots of backcountry riding and hiking trails and a general sense of solitude and serenity.

For inexpensive indoor lodgings that leave you free to explore on your own, check out **Lassen Mineral Lodge** (Hwy. 36E, Mineral, 530/595-4422, www.minerallodge.com, $72–85, open year-round) to the southwest of the park proper. The lodge offers small, cute, motel-style rooms with private baths and few frills. The lack of TVs and phones encourages visitors to get out and really visit Lassen National Park, just nine miles away, and its surrounding landscape. Hiking, fishing, and park exploration are favorite pastimes of guests here. The lodge does have its own casual family restaurant, which serves three meals each day to motel guests, campers, and passersby. A full bar satisfies the thirst of adult patrons well into the evening.

## FOOD

Mount Lassen boasts precious little in the way of dining options. If you're camping, shop in Redding and bring in *lots* of food. And don't expect to get to a restaurant during your stay unless you're willing to drive a good long ways. But the national park does allow a couple of vendors to sell a few basic food items in the park.

In the summertime, a trailer at the parking lot for the **Summit Trailhead** acts as a gift shop and small snack shack. You can get a hot dog or a basic sandwich, chips, drinks, a few packaged items, and very little else. But if you've been hiking and exploring for half the day, a nice dog and a soda will taste fabulous. This snack bar doesn't exactly have operating hours or a phone; it's open when it's open and it's not when it's not.

## INFORMATION AND SERVICES

The new **Kohm Yah-mah-nee Visitor Center** (Hwy. 89, year-round) is scheduled to open in fall 2008 at the south entrance station of the park. A ranger's station is located at the Highway 44/89 entrance. At each of these you can obtain wilderness permits for backcountry camping, any other necessary permits, and advice about where you can and should (and cannot and should not) hike, ride, swim, fish, and camp in Lassen.

Park rangers can provide first aid and help you get phone access to emergency services in Redding. If you're planning to hike seriously or camp, bring a well-stocked first-aid kit for minor injuries and illnesses.

## GETTING THERE AND AROUND

On Mount Lassen, winter begins in November and continues through May. Highway 89 through the park closes from about October to May, June, or July depending on the weather and snowfall in any given year. Highway 89 serves as the main road through the park, and the visitors center, campgrounds, trailheads, and lakes cluster along it. You can actually get a decent feel for Lassen just by taking a day trip along Highway 89.

On the northeast side of the park, Highway 44 brings in visitors from the remote town of Susanville; dirt roads lead from Highway 44 into the park.

South of Lassen, roads run out of the tiny town of Chester up to the park. The Warner Valley Road is paved, but other roads out of town to the park are good old-fashioned dirt.

However you get to Lassen, be sure to bring a good map and possibly a GPS device as well. (Garmin GPS does work even on the dirt roads of Mount Lassen. I got lost up there once and was glad to have mine!)

Note that there are no gas stations in the park. Gas up in Redding, Chester, or Susanville before driving up to Mount Lassen.

## REDDING

The good-sized city of Redding acts as a gateway town to the whole Shasta and Lassen region. Set right in the middle of the I-5 route, Redding has every major service you might need on your travels.

### Sundial Bridge

The best-known sight in the Redding region is undoubtedly the magnificent and unusual Sundial Bridge (daily 6 A.M.–midnight, free). Part of the Turtle Bay Exploration Park, the Sundial Bridge crosses the Sacramento River. It's a beautiful bit of architecture designated for pedestrians only, with a single large pylon structure anchoring the suspension cables that fan out over the bridge. Most folks get to the bridge from Turtle Bay and walk north across it. When you begin your stroll across the bridge, you'll see more of the unique design of the structure. You'll be walking on blocks of green glass, strips of granite, and ceramic tiles from Spain. The overall effect is breathtaking, and you'll probably stop a few times just to take in the details of the design.

On the other side of the bridge, you'll see how it got its name. The brilliant white pylon acts as a huge sundial; brass plaques embedded in the north side lawn act as timekeepers. You'll see that the bridge keeps pretty good time on sunny days; the shadow hits the 20-minute markers right about on time!

## Turtle Bay Exploration Park

Turtle Bay Exploration Park (840 Auditorium Dr., 800/887-8532, www.turtlebay.org) is also worth your time, though it (along with the rest of Redding) gets blisteringly hot in the summertime. To escape the heat, spend some quality time in the Turtle Bay Museum, with its air conditioning, art and nature displays, Native American exhibits, and traveling exhibits and shows. Turtle Bay gets great shows, like the Titanic history exhibit and Body Worlds 2. Much of the museum is geared for younger visitors, allowing kids to learn by listening, touching, and occasionally even smelling. Adults might be more fascinated by the information about California's water usage and management—one of the state's biggest ongoing natural, environmental, and political issues.

Outside of the museum, the Exploration Park includes the spacious **McConnell Arboretum and Gardens,** a 20-acre botanical garden that's perfect for spring and fall strolling, though it gets a bit hot in high summer. Beautiful plantings and areas include a children's garden, a medicinal garden, and two charming water features. Lots of butterflies are attracted to the flower plantings, so you'll get to see swallowtails, monarchs, and many other species. The arboretum is a 200-acre expanse of trees, and you can enjoy their shade as you explore the sustainable forest. The gardens have their own parking area on the west side, or you can reach them from the museum via the Sundial Bridge. Children enjoy the play areas and equipment in **Paul Bunyan's Forest Camp,** and one of the most interesting historical sites is the **Monolith**—a remnant of one of the plants that helped to build Shasta Dam.

## Entertainment and Events

To break the monotony of life along the I-5, the town of Redding hosts a number of monthly and annual events. The annual **Redding Rodeo** (715 Auditorium Dr., 530/241-8559, www.reddingrodeo.com, admission $11.50) acts as the annual star, with a weeks' worth of events each May. The rodeo itself runs from Thursday through Saturday and includes all the traditional riding, roping, and racing events. For a slightly more refined day out in Redding, come out to the **Beer and Wine Festival** (530/243-7773, www.vivadowntownredding.org/services.html, late Sept.) and **Blues by the River** (Lake Redding Park, www.shastablues.com, late Sept.)—two great festivals that are deliberately held together.

## Accommodations

If you're doing the long drive on I-5 and you need a place to lay your head for the night, Redding offers a wide array of clean and comfortable chain motels right off the freeway. If you're seeking a more quaint and unique inn experience, you can find that too in limited quantities. Folks who want to ply the waters of Shasta Lake but don't want the hassle of a rental cabin in the woods also often stay in Redding.

### UNDER $100

The **Motel 6 Redding South** (2385 Bechelli Ln., 530/221-0562, www.motel6.com, $55–75) is known to regular travelers as one of the best examples of a Motel 6 anywhere—it's definitely better than the other two in the Redding area. Sure, it's a Motel 6, so your room will be plain and you won't get a lot of frills or extras. What you will get is a clean bedroom with a clean bathroom and a comfortable bed for the night. Even the pool is clean and totally swimmable!

### $100-150

One tier up in the hierarchy of chain motels, the **Redding Travelodge** (540 N. Market St., 800/243-1106, www.reddingtravelodge.com, $94–115) offers a few more amenities for only a little more money. The pleasant light facade welcomes guests who need a comfortable bed in a clean room. Guest rooms have flowery comforters, dark carpets, white walls, and plenty of space. You can get queen or king beds and rooms with full refrigerators and partial kitchens. Free Wi-Fi graces the property—a rare amenity in the wilds of Northern California. You can take a dip in the outdoor pool in the summer months, or soak in the indoor whirlpool tub at any time of year.

If you're looking for something better than a corporate-issue motel room, book a room at the **Tiffany House B&B** (1510 Barbara Rd., 530/244-3225, www.tiffanyhousebb.com, $121–165). Sitting high on a hill in a quiet residential neighborhood, the Tiffany House shows off the best of Redding's views, accommodations, and people. Even if you're making your reservations on the spur of the moment, it's worth giving friendly owners Susan and Brady a call to see if any of the inn's four rooms are available. Each room has its own delightful decorations, including stunning handmade bedspreads created by Susan and members of her family. All the rooms offer charm and comfort, as well as views out over Redding and all the way out to Mount Lassen on a clear day. The spacious Cottage room has a huge spa tub, separate bathroom, private porch, and comfortable amenities. The common spaces of the inn include shady gardens and an outdoor pool, a music room, a parlor, and plenty of cozy nooks to sit and read a book. For great advice on the best sights, entertainment, and activities in town, be sure to ask Susan or Brady. Their suggestions, filled with civic pride, remind visitors that Redding can be much more than a waypoint on I-5, and for some it's a vacation destination in its own right.

Another lovely little inn is the **Bridge House Bed and Breakfast** (1455 Riverside Dr., 530/247-7177, www.reddingbridgehouse.com, $135–180). The distinctive steep-pitch-roofed yellow house sits along the Sacramento River just a block or two from historic downtown Redding. You can walk to some of the nicest restaurants and quirkiest shops on Market Street. Inside, you'll find a tranquil haven in one of four unique guest rooms. Each room is named after a bridge, and each is decorated with prints of its namesake, complementary colors, and attractive furniture. For folks who fear the plethora of flowers that often decorate B&B guest rooms, the Bridge House is a welcome surprise, with its quiet soothing solid colors and understated accessories. All rooms offer TVs, spa bathrobes, and lots of great amenities. The two largest rooms boast fancy "massage tubs" in the bathrooms. The Bridge House acts primarily as a romantic retreat for couples, so babies and small children are not always welcome.

## Food

After a day outdoors, sometimes you just need a big ol' steak. **Jack's Grill** (1743 California St., 530/241-9705, www.jacksgrillredding.com, Mon.–Sat. 5–11 P.M., $13–31) can hook you up. This locally owned favorite has been serving steaks for more than 70 years. Don't expect the ultra-high-end cuts and preparations of big-city steakhouses. Instead, look for tasty and less expensive steaks, ground steak, and skewers. All meals come with soup or salad and baked potato or fries. Jack's includes a full bar that serves beer, wine, and cocktails.

Want a hearty diner-style meal of noticeably higher quality than your average giant national chain beginning with D? Head straight for the **Black Bear Diner** (2605 Hilltop Dr., 530/221-7600, www.blackbeardiner.com, open daily). This NorCal chain began in the mountain reaches you're now visiting, offering classic American dishes made fresh with better ingredients than most similar restaurants. Today, they still do; travelers will go miles out of their way or wait an extra hour for lunch just to eat at Black Bear. Menus are printed in the style of a local newspaper. Choose from American breakfast classics, salads, sandwiches, chicken and meat entrées, fries and potatoes...the list goes on. Breakfast is served all day, as are the thick (and real) ice cream milkshakes—try the huckleberry flavor. Service is friendly, though the Redding Black Bear Diner can get incredibly crowded on weekends.

In the mood for a hearty Italian meal? **Gironda's Restaurant** (1100 Center St., 530/244-7663, www.girondas.com, Mon.–Thurs. 11 A.M.–9 P.M., Fri. 11 A.M.–10 P.M., Sat. 4:30–10 P.M., Sun. 4:30–9 P.M., $13–25) serves an array of raviolis, pastas, and big Italian-style entrées for lunch and dinner. Choose between dining in the casual-elegant white tablecloth dining room, or ordering take-out to enjoy elsewhere—even at your campsite.

If you're planning to camp on Lassen or Shasta, or houseboat on the lake, your cheapest options for groceries lay in Redding. The **Grocery Outlet** (2235 Churn Creek Rd., 530/221-4209, www.groceryoutlets.com, Mon.–Fri. 8 A.M.–9 P.M., Sat. 8 A.M.–8 P.M., Sun. 9 A.M.–7 P.M.) sits only a couple of blocks off I-5 for easy access for passers-through. The chain offers lots of prepared foods and frozen items at rock-bottom prices. For an array of slightly higher-end groceries, head for **Safeway** (2275 Pine St., 530/247-3030; 1070 E. Cypress Ave, 530/226-5871). With slightly higher prices comes the ultimate convenience: 24-hour shopping, which can be a lifesaver on road trips and camping expeditions.

## Information and Services

For visitors who intend to camp at Shasta Lake or Mount Lassen, Redding is the last outpost of serious civilization before the trek to the more remote reaches of the state. Especially if you're on your way out to Lassen, consider availing yourself of the shopping and services in Redding while you can.

If you're new to the Shasta and Lassen area, the **Redding Convention and Visitors Bureau** (777 Auditorium Dr., 530/225-4100, http://ci.redding.ca.us) is a good first stop. You'll find information and advice about the must-see sights, the best roads to travel, and good spots for impromptu meals.

The local daily newspaper of Redding is the ***Record Searchlight*** (www.redding.com). This paper covers national and local news, and devotes lots of space to local outdoor recreation. It's worth your while to grab at least one day's paper to find out what's happening while you're in the region.

In all the Shasta and Lassen region, the best place to find ATMs and even bank branches is Redding. A Bank of America (1300 Hilltop Dr., 530/246-5992, Mon.–Thurs. 9 A.M.–5 P.M., Fri. 9 A.M.–6 P.M.) and a Wells Fargo (830 E. Cypress Ave., 800/865-3997, Mon.–Fri. 9 A.M.–6 P.M., Sat. 9 A.M.–4 P.M.) sit right along I-5 for easy access. ATMs abound; you can find them in big grocery stores, pharmacies, and big-box department stores.

The **post office** in Redding sits at 2323 Churn Creek Road (530/223-7523).

Most of the chain motels in Redding offer Internet access (with or without a fee, depending on the motel). Redding also has a few Starbucks and other cafés with Internet access, and the occasional for-fee Wi-Fi network. Again, if you need to send urgent email from the Shasta-Lassen region, it's a good idea to get it done while you're in Redding.

Redding has the only major medical services available in the entire Shasta-Lassen region. **Mercy Medical Center Redding** (2175 Rosaline Ave., 530/225-6000, http://redding.mercy.org) has a 24-hour emergency room with a full-fledged trauma center for major medical problems.

## Getting There and Around

Most Californians get to Redding via I-5, whether they're coming from the north or the south. It's right on the freeway, with plenty of exits leading to the different parts of town. Watch for signs to take you where you need to go in town.

Redding also boasts a municipal airport with some commercial service. The **Redding Municipal Airport** (6751 Airport Rd., 530/224-4320, http://ci.redding.ca.us/transeng/airports/rma.htm) offers flights on Alaska-Horizon and United-Sky West airlines. Flying in and out of such a small airport ain't cheap, but you've got the advantage of far shorter ticketing and security lines.

Redding is an easy town to navigate, and parking tends to be a breeze (and free). You might have to hunt for a spot in historic downtown on summer weekends or during local events, but otherwise don't sweat it. Turtle Bay has two huge parking lots that make visiting a snap, and all the motels have private, ample lots.

# SACRAMENTO AND GOLD COUNTRY

The state capital of California, Sacramento, is a cosmopolitan city with a friendly vibe and a low-key, fun entertainment scene. The city of Sacramento grew along the Sacramento River during the Gold Rush era and provided a vital transit link between the mining country and the port of San Francisco. Today, politics is the new gold and it rules Sacramento with a constant presence—you might even spy the "Governator," Arnold Schwarzenegger, in his fleet of Hummers outside the historic Capitol building.

Most California mining history, however, rests outside the big city, in the small boom towns that sprang up throughout the 19th century near major mines. With the closing of the mines, these towns declined for decades, but were eventually rediscovered by tourists and travelers. A wealth of mining museums in the Gold Country region teaches guests about the backbreaking work of gold mining, while ghost stories entertain locals and visitors alike. For travelers who want less history and more action, this is also prime whitewater rafting and kayaking country.

While Sacramento pumps California's political heart, down south in the Central Valley lies its agricultural artery and the staple of the state's economy. The huge flat valley is where the majority of California's crops grow, as it offers a prime climate for a huge array of foods, especially citrus.

History buffs will enjoy visiting the Capitol Building and the historic sights around Old Sacramento, before taking a road trip through the various Gold Rush towns and mining

ROBERT HOLMES / CALTOUR

## HIGHLIGHTS

**Capitol Building:** Sacramento's iconic State Capitol building is the epicenter for the city's political history – past and present. Be sure to check out the museum's impressive collection of art and antiques (page 317).

**Old Sacramento:** Take a tour of Old Sacramento for a new sense of how the state capital of California grew up over its 150 year existence (page 317).

**Empire Mine State Historic Park:** The best example of Gold Country mining is this living history museum and park (page 333).

**Apple Hill:** East of Sacramento lies this 20-mile swath of grower heaven. The Apple Drive Scenic tour takes in dozens of orchards, vineyards, and pit stops for dining and relaxing along the way (page 335).

**Daffodil Hill:** This private ranch is carpeted in golden color every March, the rare time when visitors can explore the more than 300 species of daffodils on offer (page 336).

**Columbia State Historic Park:** A former Gold Rush town, Columbia is now a state park. The indoor-outdoor museum experience includes exhibits, shops, and even a saloon – all preserved in homage to the area's mining history (page 353).

LOOK FOR ☾ TO FIND RECOMMENDED SIGHTS, ACTIVITIES, DINING, AND LODGING.

museums along Highway 49. Outdoor lovers can start with a multi-day river rafting trip, then work their way north, hiking, kayaking, and spelunking as they go. Epicureans and wine lovers will find new delights along the farm trails of El Dorado County, through the Shenadoah Valley and Fair Play, and down to Fresno and the Citrus Belt. Whatever your pleasure, this diverse region of California has something for you.

## PLANNING YOUR TIME

Sacramento makes a nice day trip or weekend getaway from the Bay Area, or a fun one- or two-day start to a longer Gold Country and Sierra adventure. Winters are mild in Sacramento, while summers get blisteringly hot.

Gold Country is too big, physically, to take in all in one day, or even in one weekend. Highway 49 runs more than 100 miles through the precious-metal-bearing Sierra Foothills,

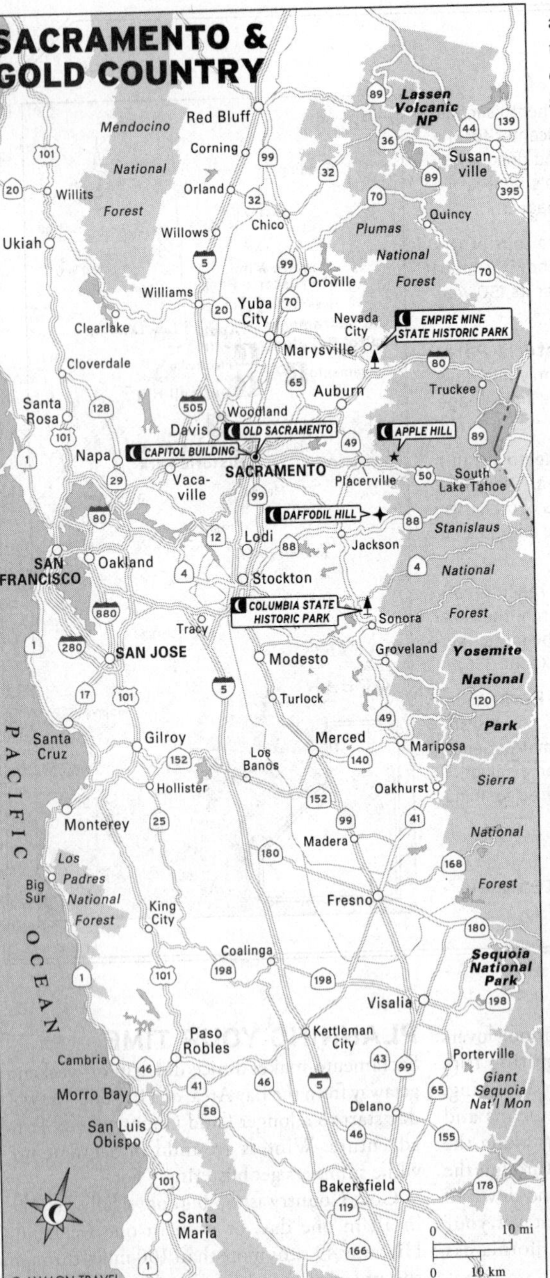


and it's impossible to resist side trips to smaller towns and specific caverns, mines, and museums along the way. If you've got one day, pick a specific Gold Country town as your destination, and one or two of the major parks and attractions nearby. In a weekend, you can get an overview of either northern or southern Gold Country, driving from town to town and making short stops along the way. With a whole week (or even five days) to play with, you can get serious about the region—tasting wine, sampling produce, spelunking, hiking, rafting, and catching up on your Gold Rush history.

Visiting season in Gold Country runs from late spring through late fall, when the weather is best. Winter brings snow to many of the Sierra Foothill towns, which draws skiers and other winter sports enthusiasts.

© LIZ HAMILL SCOTT

the State Capitol Building

# Sacramento

Many people outside the state don't realize that Sacramento is the state capitol of California. Despite the fact that hundreds of miles lay between this river town and Hollywood, many actors have made their homes here—the office of governor has belonged to the likes of B-movie actor Ronald Reagan and, more recently, big, buff Arnold Schwarzenegger. This surprisingly lovely town has lots to offer visitors, from whitewater rafting along the namesake river to one of the best jazz festivals in the state.

## SIGHTS

There's plenty to see in Sacramento, especially if you have an interest in the history of the state of California. From the State Capitol complex to the Railroad Museum, all aspects of California's growth from a (mostly) peaceful oasis for dozens of Native American tribes, through a Spanish colonial settlement, on to a land of opportunity for tremendous wealth in the gold mines, towards its modern persona as an agricultural, radical, fame-loving, innovative, expensive place to live, work, play, and visit.

### Capitol Building

The California State Capitol Building (10th and L Sts., 916/324-0333, http://capitolmuseum.ca.gov, daily 9 A.M.–5 P.M., free) displays a grandeur befitting the great state of California. On the ground floor, the museum's magnificent art collection includes California art and artifacts, oil portraits of the state's governors, two murals, and a collection of antiques. You can take in a free tour that highlights the Neoclassical architecture of the building, or learn about the most important legal decisions made in and for the state.

Once you've finished absorbing the history of California from inside the museum, go outside and take a stroll around the grounds. At the rear of the building you'll find an unusual treat, the **Arbor Tour.** An amazing array of trees from around the world are planted in the sweeping space, creating a garden that's perfect for exploring if you love botany, or just for finding a nice place to sit and relax in the shade.

### Governor's Mansion

Schoolchildren from all over the state journey to Sacramento to tour the Governor's Mansion (1526 H St., 916/323-3047, www.parks.ca.gov, daily 10 A.M.–5 P.M., adults $4, children $2). No, Arnold doesn't live here. In fact, the mansion served as the actual home of California governors for fewer than 100 years, 1903–1967. Governor Ronald Reagan and his wife Nancy were the last governing couple to live in the mansion—and they stayed only three months. Since then, the mansion has become an educational tool and a tourist attraction. To enter the Governor's Mansion, you must buy tickets and sign up for a guided tour, which happen frequently throughout the day. Guests get to see the ornate European interior decor, the evidence of different tastes and different generations, and the grandeur that has traditionally surrounded the governors of the great state of California.

### Old Sacramento

Sacramento became an important town as the Gold Rush progressed and supplies were sent up the Sacramento River from San Francisco. The most important part of the early town were the piers along the river, and that's where Old Sacramento (visitors center, 1002 Second St., 916/442-7644, daily 10 A.M.–5 P.M.) still sits today. The charming cobblestone streets and clattery wooden sidewalks pass old-time shops, restaurants, and attractions. You can take a carriage ride through the streets or walk the wharf and wander the decks of the Delta King. Check out the tiny **Wells Fargo Museum** (1000 Second St., 916/440-4263) and **Old Sacramento Schoolhouse Museum** (Front and L Sts., 916/483-8818, www.oldsacschoolhouse.org) or lighten your wallets in the

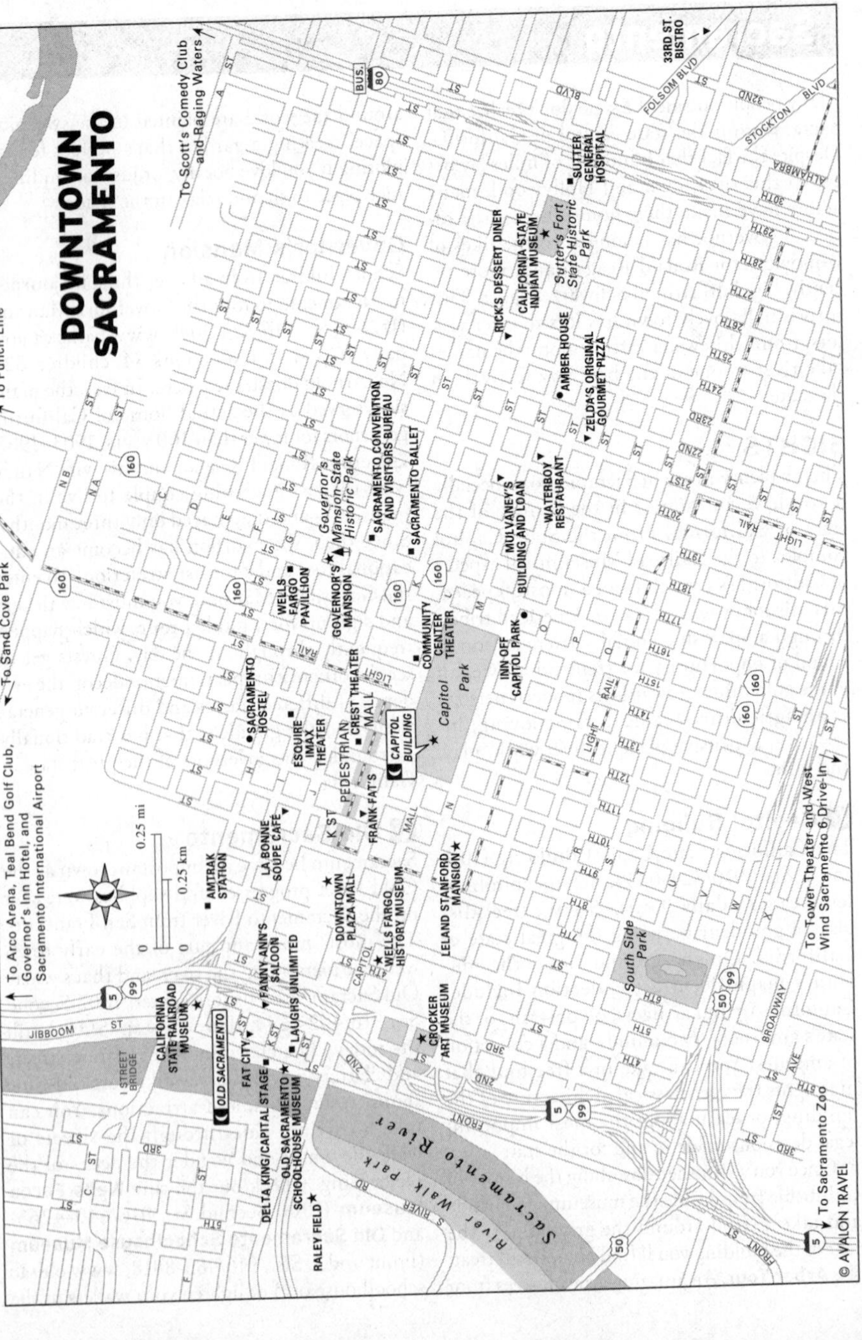
DOWNTOWN SACRAMENTO
To Punch Line
To Sand Cove Park
To Arco Arena, Teal Bend Golf Club, Governor's Inn Hotel, and Sacramento International Airport
To Scott's Comedy Club and Raging Waters
To Tower Theater and West Wind Sacramento 6 Drive-In
To Sacramento Zoo
33RD ST. BISTRO
0.25 mi
0.25 km
AMTRAK STATION
SACRAMENTO HOSTEL
ESQUIRE IMAX THEATER
CREST THEATER
PEDESTRIAN MALL
K ST
CAPITOL BUILDING
Capitol Park
COMMUNITY CENTER THEATER
GOVERNOR'S MANSION
Governor's Mansion State Historic Park
WELLS FARGO PAVILLION
SACRAMENTO CONVENTION AND VISITORS BUREAU
SACRAMENTO BALLET
LA BONNE SOUPE CAFÉ
FRANK FAT'S
DOWNTOWN PLAZA MALL
WELLS FARGO HISTORY MUSEUM
LELAND STANFORD MANSION
CROCKER ART MUSEUM
CALIFORNIA STATE RAILROAD MUSEUM
OLD SACRAMENTO
FANNY ANN'S SALOON
LAUGHS UNLIMITED
FAT CITY
DELTA KING/CAPITAL STAGE
OLD SACRAMENTO SCHOOLHOUSE MUSEUM
RALEY FIELD
I STREET BRIDGE
JIBBOOM ST
Sacramento River
River Walk Park
INN OFF CAPITOL PARK
MULVANEY'S BUILDING AND LOAN
WATERBOY RESTAURANT
RICK'S DESSERT DINER
CALIFORNIA STATE INDIAN MUSEUM
Sutter's Fort State Historic Park
SUTTER GENERAL HOSPITAL
AMBER HOUSE
ZELDA'S ORIGINAL GOURMET PIZZA
South Side Park
FOLSOM BLVD
STOCKTON BLVD
ALHAMBRA
BROADWAY
FRONT ST
LIGHT RAIL
© AVALON TRAVEL

shops and boutiques. Grab a bite at one of the many restaurants. To really get into the spirit of the location, look for the Old Sacramento Living History (916/445-3101, www.oslhp.net) activities that take place every month of the year. From May through October, join in on a Living History walk (May Sat.–Sun., June–Oct. Wed.–Sun.) with a costumed guide who'll tell you the story of this area from the point of view of a 19th-century resident. Enjoy the vintage-style clothes, the historic merchants, and the re-enactors engaging in period arts and crafts.

## California State Railroad Museum

If you've ever felt a lick of romance at the sight of a steam locomotive, or ever longed for an adventure on the rails, you've got to stop at the California State Railroad Museum (111 I St., 916/445-7387, www.parks.ca.gov, daily 10 A.M.–5 P.M., adults $8, children $3). Inside the mammoth museum buildings are artifacts and models that illustrate the building of the railroads to the West, especially the all-important Transcontinental Railroad. The main floor plays host to the museum's fabulous collection of rolling stock—locomotives, freight and passenger cars, and cabooses. It's strange to see mammoth locomotives standing still inside walls; these creations that made so much industry possible seem to belong outdoors. (And indeed, the museum occasionally lends its stock for photography and films.)

You can look in on the stylish appointments of the private rail cars of the rich and stand next to the immense wheels of mighty steam locomotives. Climb aboard the open cars and locomotives for a look inside the railroad that made the growth and expansion of California possible. Along the edges of the room, are memorabilia from the heyday of the railroads, from timetables to fine china. A gift shop offers souvenirs for visitors of all ages, including Thomas the Tank Engine toys for young kids, replica china for collectors, and thick tomes of railroad history for history buffs.

Cross the plaza to board the steam-powered **Excursion train** (916/445-6645, Apr.–Sept. Sat.–Sun. 11 A.M.–5 P.M., $8) for a 40-minute ride along the riverfront.

## Sutter Fort State Historic Park

For a visit into the history of the European settlement of California, come to Sutter Fort State Historic Park (2701 L St., 916/445-4422, www.parks.ca.gov, daily 10 A.M.–5 P.M.). Situated right in the middle of downtown Sacramento, the fort was originally the center of John Sutter's "New Helvetia" settlement. A tour of the park begins with the mazelike museum at the entrance. Inside the fort structure, the story of John Sutter is called out in photos, artifacts, and placards. After perusing the interpretive area, wander outside into the sunlight and enjoy the living history taking place all around you. Wander the inner walls of the fort to see how the early settlers lived—from dragging their luggage from the East to their bedrooms at the settlement. Denizens of the park, dressed in costumes of the 19th century, engage in the activities that filled the days of California's settlers. With their help, you can try your hand at making rope, baking bread, and doing all sorts of pioneer activities. Listen to the music of the era as you learn about the history of Sutter and his followers by living it for a few hours. Afterwards, stop at the gift shop, which evokes a small 1800s store, filled with historic costume patterns, books, and period toys.

## Leland Stanford Mansion

Railroad baron and Stanford University founder Leland Stanford and his family spent a number of years living in the capital city, close to Mr. Stanford's business interests, at what is now the Leland Stanford Mansion State Historic Park (800 N St., 916/324-0575, www.lelandstanfordmansion.org, fee for mansion tours). Some years after Leland Stanford's death, his wife Jane Stanford donated the family mansion to the Catholic Church for use as a children's home. It was eventually purchased by the state, and the current museum was constructed beginning in 1991. Your tour will begin in the visitors center, which sits next to the museum

Store outside the mansion proper. From there you'll journey inside the lavish main building, admiring the lovingly restored furnishings, carpets, walls, and antiques. Visitors get a hint of what it might have been like to live as one of the wealthiest men in the country in some of the most exciting years of California's history.

Mansion tours are wheelchair accessible, and assistive listening devices and other aids are available upon request. You must be part of a tour to explore the mansion; however, the visitors center, store, and parts of the gardens can be visited for free during open hours.

### Crocker Art Museum

For a detour from history into art, visit the Crocker Art Museum (216 O St., 916/808-1179, www.crockerartmuseum.org, Tues.–Sun. 10 A.M.–5 P.M., Thurs. until 9 P.M., adults $6, children $3). Ten centuries of fine arts are collected here, and traveling exhibitions visit on an ongoing basis. (Check the website for the latest and upcoming exhibitions.) The original gallery was donated to the city of Sacramento by the Crocker family—one of the Big Four railroad and industry barons who built California's infrastructure and made a fortune doing so. That fortune paid for the international art collection that Margaret Crocker donated to the public. Today, wander the galleries filled with paintings from Europe and Asia, ceramics from around the world, photography, drawing, and specifically California art. The galleries—housed inside Victorian mansions—are works of art themselves. Be sure to spend some time examining the floors, ceilings, and woodwork as you explore this wonderful world-class museum.

### Sacramento Zoo

Ready for a break from all those museums? Take a trip to visit the animals at the Sacramento Zoo (Sutterville Rd and Land Park Dr., 916/808-5888, http://saczoo.com, daily 9 A.M.–4 P.M., adults $9, children $6.50). A fabulous array of animals await you, including big kitties and other mammals, funky frogs and amphibians, big ol' snakes, a small-fish aquarium, and many more. Take cover from the summer heat under the shade of the century-old oak trees, as the critters enjoy their own custom-grown garden habitats. Check the website for a list of zoo activities each month, including educational talks, guided walks, special festivals, and other events—many of which center around fun and education for the younger set.

## ENTERTAINMENT AND EVENTS

### Live Music

For a night of impeccable classical music, buy tickets for a concert performed by the **Sacramento Philharmonic Orchestra** (916/264-5181, www.sacphil.org). The Philharmonic performs all over the greater Sacramento area, most often in the Community Center Theater (1301 L St.), the Mondavi Center at Davis (University of California Davis, 530/754-2787, www.mondaviarts.org), and the Magic Circle Roseville Theater (241 Vernon St., Roseville, 916/782-1777, www.mcircle.org). The comany plays a wide range of music, with something of a specialty in newer works by composers from around the world. You can also see occasional historic masterworks such as Berlioz's *Symphonie Fantastique*.

Each May, jazz lovers from all around the state flock to the capital for the **Sacramento Jazz Jubilee** (www.sacjazz.com). Over four days of Memorial Day Weekend, more than 100 jazz acts descend on Sacramento to perform in venues ranging from the lush Convention Center stage to the wooden planks of the Old Sacramento sidewalks. Check the website for a list of performers, which can include the top jazz musicians in the world today, with headliners like Kermit Ruffins and featured artists such as Joe Ascione, Harry Allen, and John Allred. Bands play every style of jazz imaginable—classic, zydeco, big band, western, skiffle, funk, and so much more. It seems amazing that a small city like Sacramento can handle so much raw talent, but it can—with the easy grace of a jazz riff. If you're already planning to come to Sacramento on Memorial

Day anyway, be sure to get tickets to shows in advance. If you've been looking for a reason to visit the state capital, this is one of the best Sacramento has to offer.

## Comedy

Need a laugh while you're in Sacto? You can find one at any of the city's three major comedy clubs. The **Punch Line** (2100 Arden Way, 916/925-5500), sister club to the San Francisco Punch Line, brings top national talent to the state capital. If you know you'll be coming in advance, buy tickets online. If not, calling ahead for reservations for popular comics is always your best bet for getting in. You might see the likes of Dana Carvey live and in person. Shows run nightly from Wednesday through Sunday every week, with hot local and up-and-coming national acts such as Gabriel Iglesias and Amy Schumer. All tickets are general admission, so you'll be able to find a seat at a table when the doors open. Come early for seats nearest the stage (not always recommended at a live comedy show).

Right in the midst of Old Sacramento, **Laughs Unlimited** (1207 Front St., 916/446-8128, www.laughsunlimited.com, shows Thurs.–Sun.) brings hilarity to the waterfront. With comics such as Todd Paul and Chris Titus doing multi-night engagements every week, and occasional shows by comedy legends like Jack Gallagher, Shawn Wayans, and Alonzo Bodden, you'll have a great time at this classic comedy venue. There's a two-drink minimum for all patrons, and a reasonable appetizer and dessert menu can slake appetites grown large from laughing.

For a more intimate evening of chuckles, head to **Scott's Comedy Club** (2600 Auburn Blvd., 916/267-0502), now located inside Zigato's Bar and Grille. Here you're less likely to see a mega-star, and more likely to laugh at the never-before-told jokes of someone who's currently on their way up the ladder of comedic fame. Heck—*you* can take the stage at Scott's on open mic nights. See the website for details on making your Scott's debut. Despite its size and local flair, it's still a good idea to call for reservations in advance for the bigger shows.

## Cinema

Sacramento is a great place to go to the movies. For a larger-than-life cinematic experience, get tickets for the **Esquire IMAX Theater** (1211 K St., 916/443-4629, www.imax.com/sacramento). The Esquire shows IMAX documentary films in traditional 2-D and mind-blowing 3-D. You can also see the occasional IMAX-remastered Hollywood blockbuster film here. Buy tickets online or at the box office.

On the other hand, if you're looking for a classic night out at the movies, drive in to the **West Wind Sacramento 6 Drive-In** (9616 Oates Dr., 916/363-6572, www.drive-ins.com/theater/catsacr, $4.25–6.50). This six-screen drive-in plays first- and second-run Hollywood films. You won't get a speaker for your car, instead you'll tune into a radio channel. Bring your own pillows and blankets and convertible for a truly luxurious movie experience. The old-school circular building at the center of the facility sells inexpensive movie concessions and includes a fun, cheap arcade. The restrooms are nothing to write home about, so go before you drive in if you can. But the overall fun and inexpensive prices make up for any run-down amenities.

For your indie and classic film pleasure, go down to the Capital area and hit **The Crest** (1013 K St., 916/442-7378, www.thecrest.com, $8.50). The interior of the theater is a show in itself—it was restored in the 1990s to the glitzy heights of its 1940s Art Deco glory. Be sure to look around at the walls and up at the glorious ceiling of the single screen's theater before the show starts. Check the website calendar for a list of what's playing while you're in town. In addition to films, The Crest occasionally puts up a live stand-up comedy show with a major star like Carrot Top or Sam Kinison. The Crest also hosts the Sacramento Symphony's community music series, such as "Mocha and Mozart" or "Jeans and Beer."

**The Tower** (2508 Land Park Dr., 916/442-4700, www.thetowertheatre.com,

$8.50–11) is a quirky, three-screen art house that shows popular, foreign, and independent films. It's not quite as grand as The Crest, but at the Tower you can enjoy an old-fashioned, elegant cinematic atmosphere and a first-run Hollywood flick all at the same time.

### Theater

In the tradition of historic Gold Country, live theater is an important part of the nightlife of Sacramento. In Old Sacramento, some of the best theater in the whole city happens on board the *Delta King.*

Performing aboard the *Delta King,* the **Capital Stage** (1000 Front St., 916/995-5464, http://capstage.org, $22–28) strives and succeeds at taking regional theater to the next level. This professional company has a small space to perform works by up-and-coming playwrights and classic, less-produced plays by heavy hitters like Sam Shepard. You'll feel like part of the action as you see great actors performing edgy "grown-up" shows. In fact, all the plays Capital Stage puts up are geared for the over-eighteen set, so they may include adult language and sexual situations. For a perfect night out on the town, have dinner on the *King* before the show.

Also on board the *Delta King,* **Suspects Murder Mystery Dinner Theater** (1000 Front St., 916/443-3600, $39.50) combines dinner and a fun show. As your dinner begins, gunshots ring out! You'll spend the rest of your meal laughing as you participate in an Agatha Christie–style murder mystery. You might find yourself a suspect, or possibly a victim. However the story plays out, you'll enjoy the comedy, the mystery, and the tasty food and drink at this fun, kitschy night of dinner theater.

If you just can't go more than a few days without a musical theater experience, get tickets for the latest show at **California Musical Theater** (916/557-1999, www.calmt.com, $15–70). CMT uses both the Wells Fargo Pavilion (1419 H St.) and the Community Center Theater (1301 L St.) for its productions. As advertised, the Broadway Series puts up iconic Broadway musicals—think *Phantom of the Opera* and *Mamma Mia.* On the other hand, the Music Circus shows off the classic musicals, from *Aida* to *Annie* to *The Best Little Whorehouse in Texas.* The high production values delight audiences at every show. Purchase single-show tickets online at the website, over the phone, or at the box office. You can also check out the seating charts for both theaters to pick out your perfect spot.

### Dance

Classical dance lovers can enjoy a night out at the **Sacramento Ballet** (1631 K St., 916/552-5800, www.sacballet.org, performances Thurs.–Sun., adults $25–55, children $12.50–32.50). For 50 years, this company has brought high-level dance spectacles to the capital; the Sacramento Ballet went fully professional in 1986. For the last 20 years, they've produced an array of famous ballets, including such classics as *Sleeping Beauty* and *The Nutcracker,* as well as any number of new and interpreted works—such as the world premiere of *A Woman's Journey: The Tamsen Donner Story* and *A Streetcar Named Desire.* You can purchase individual tickets directly from the box office, by phone, or online via the ballet's website. Most performances go up at the Sacramento Community Center theater—a large space with multiple tiers of seats. Check the website for special events while you're in town.

### Festivals and Events

Each year, the California State Fair takes place at the mammoth fairgrounds called the **California Exposition & State Fair Center** (1600 Exposition Blvd., 916/263-3000, www.calexpo.com), known to its friends as Cal Expo. The property is used all year long for every large-scale retail show imaginable, as well as shows and festivals that require plenty of exhibition space. The Quilt, Craft, and Sewing Festival comes here, as do RV shows, landscape shows, and boat shows. Year-round, horseracing fans can come to the Cal Expo Sports & Wagering Center at the Budweiser Grandstand to take a load off, enjoy a cold one, and place bets on their favorite ponies. Races play on the hundreds of flat-screen TVs set up all around the center. You've got access to free Wi-Fi at the Center as well.

The highlight of each year at Cal Expo is unquestionably the **California State Fair** (www.bigfun.org). The fair lasts for two weeks, usually at the end of August. During that period, nearly a million people pass through the gates of Cal Expo. They might come for the musical concerts performed by national acts, the horse races at the Budweiser Grandstand, the carnival, the exhibitions, or the contests. A major wine competition is held at the fair each year, and the biggest and most impressive wineries from around the state take it very seriously. If you want to taste the wines, along with top food, visit the SaveMart Supermarkets Wine Garden. A "Green Dreams" exposition shows off the best and brightest of ecologically friendly technology. For more classic fair fare, head for the concession stands at the Main Line or the Promenade. Everything from hot dogs on sticks to ice cream cones to Japanese food is served. Be sure to wear sunblock during the day and drink plenty of water any time you're there—it gets frighteningly hot in Sacto in August.

## SHOPPING

### Antiques

If you prefer the old to the new, come down to the **57th Street Antiques Mall** (875 57th St., 916/451-3110, www.57thstreetantiquemall.com, Tues.–Sun. 10 A.M.–5 P.M.). With more than 50 dealers selling here, you're likely to find whatever antique or collectible you're looking for. The Mall specializes in smaller items such as linens, jewelry, glass and china, and vintage clothing—perfect for non-local shoppers who'd like to pack their treasures into a suitcase. Inside the Mall, you'll find several unique antique shops with their own specialties. Discovery Antiques has furniture, Asian and French imported antiques, and a fine collection of estate jewelry. Seluka's features 20th-century vintage collectibles with a distinctive West Coast/California bent. If you prefer the excitement of buying your antiques in an auction setting, head for The Auction Block Company, which holds live auctions once or twice each month.

### Art Galleries

A plethora of galleries make Midtown home. Between H Street and Capitol Avenue you'll find any number of storefronts displaying works of local and worldwide artists working in all media. The best way to explore these is through **2nd Saturdays** (www.2nd-sat.com, 6–9 P.M., free), an art walk held the second Saturday of every month. Galleries stay open late and residents crowd the streets—usually Del Paso Boulevard or the Uptown Art District—filled with vendors, music, and food.

### Clothing

The revitalized Midtown "Grid" (www.midtowngrid.com) offers an array of boutiques, galleries, and shops that please shoppers. Fashionistas have a range of choices, from the sleek **Cuffs Urban Apparel** (2523 J St., 916/443-2881, www.myspace.com/cuffsurbanapparel) to the truth-in-advertising **Cotton Club** (2331 J St., 916/442-2990) and **Dara Denim** (2404 K St., 916/444-1188), each of which specializes in clothing made from its named material. Thrift and vintage hunters head for **French Cuff Consignment** (2419 J St., 916/442-3724, www.frenchcuffbtq.com).

### Department Stores

If you're looking for a standard urban-style shopping mall in Sacramento, go to the **Arden Fair** (1689 Arden Way, 916/920-1167, www.ardenfair.com, Mon.–Sat. 10 A.M.–9 P.M., Sun 10 A.M.–6 P.M.). It's perfectly placed near the junction of Highway 80 and Highway 50. In this typical American mall,—anchored by Sears, J.C. Penney's, Macy's, and Nordstrom—you'll find all your favorite midrange chain clothing stores, shoe stores, specialty shops, and a food court filled with junk food from around the world.

### Gift and Home

If you're looking for gifts to bring home to family and friends, check **Something Fabulous** (1927 L St., 916/442-0185, www.saccenter.org/something-fabulous) for unusual international art and home furnishings, and **Zanzibar Imports & Jewelry** (1731 L St., 916/443-2057, www.zanzibartribalart.com) for tribal art.

## SPORTS AND RECREATION

The Sacramento River and nearby delta are the center of recreation activities in Sacramento, but any number of other fun opportunities await adventurous visitors to this region.

### Swimming and Fishing

The heat of Sacto summers can make anyone want to go jump in the lake—or the river, as the case may be. All through Sacramento proper, you'll find parks along the river, offering a variety of boat launches, swimming holes, and fishing areas.

For a fun and refreshing day out on the banks of the Sacramento River, head for **Sand Cove Park** (2005 Garden Hwy., 916/264-5200). Walk from the parking lot down the trail to the sandy river beach, which makes for a perfect spot to swim or fish. The park also offers a grassy lawn area, shade trees, hiking trails, and a boat dock at the north end. (There's no launch here, however.) Bring a picnic and while away the day alternately swimming in the water, sunning yourself, and fishing for your dinner. The river shelters bass, sturgeon, and salmon; you'll need a California fishing license to fish here. Amenities at this municipal park are minimal—expect no food vendors and portable toilet facilities, so prepare accordingly.

One of the more famous Sacramento-area parks actually runs through the separate town of West Sacramento. **River Walk Park** (651 Second St., www.cityofwestsacramento.org) features a paved pathway that runs along the river. As you walk the path, read the interpretive plaques to learn about the flora and fauna that inhabit this part of the Sacramento River ecosystem. Bring a cooler and have a picnic at one of the various picnic areas along the path,

© LIZ HAMILL SCOTT

the Sacramento River

or bring your rod and tackle and walk out onto the fishing dock. A major boat dock lets private boaters moor at the park. River Walk Park also encourages visitors to jump out into the water for a refreshing swim in the river.

## Golf

You'll find more than a dozen golf courses in Sacramento and its surrounding lands and communities—not a surprise when you consider the relative density of politicians who live and work in town. With the endlessly mild weather of Sacramento winters and the heat of summer, it's always golf season in Sacto. Whatever skill level you play at, you can enjoy a round of golf while you're here. For information about public courses in the city proper, check the Capital City Golf website at www.capitalcitygolf.com. Perhaps you'll see Arnold himself as you tee off.

In town, perhaps the most beloved public course is the **Bing Maloney Golf Course** (6801 Freeport Blvd., 916/808-2283, www.bingmaloney.com, $9.50–40). Bing Maloney offers two courses: the historic 18-hole course that's been on the property since 1952, and the 20-year-old 9-hole executive course. The par-29, 9-hole executive course can be a genuine bargain on weekdays and is perfect for beginners to the game. Make your reservations for a tee time up to eight days in advance online or over the phone for either course. The par-72, 18-hole course has been described as "what you see is what you get"—a straightforward course that will challenge your game with sloping greens and huge heritage oak trees, but not frustrate you with gimmicks or unwelcome surprises. If you're interested in taking a lesson at Bing Maloney, check the website for information and call in advance for a reservation.

A newer course in town, the **Teal Bend Golf Club** (7200 Garden Hwy., 916/922-5209, www.tealbendgolf.com, $29–65) has been around for only 10 years. Conveniently located near the airport and the river, you can slip in a quick round of golf at Teal Bend no matter how little time you have in Sacto. As you walk and play, look out for the teal duck—the course's namesake—as well as deer, geese, and hawks, all of which make their home on the course. (You might want to watch your step in the rough, too.) This course, a locals' favorite, is famous for its many water features. Make your tee time reservations over the phone or online up to eight days in advance, or consider enrolling in one of the club's many annual tournaments. Check the website for Internet specials. After your game, relax at the Bar and Grille, enjoying a casual meal of a burger or a salad and a nice cold beer.

Just outside of town, still more golf courses invite politicians, pros, visitors, and amateurs alike. The **Empire Ranch Golf Club** (1620 E. Natoma, Folsom, 916/817-8100, www.empireranchgolfclub.com, $29–67) is the suburb of Folsom's first golf course, designed by Brad Bell (also the designer of the Teal Bend). The 18-hole course offers challenging play, especially on a windy day, and spectacular views out toward the Sierras. If you're just looking to hone your skills, Empire Ranch offers a full range of practice facilities—putting greens, chipping ranges, and a driving range. Check the website for special Internet prices.

## Spa

If you need to take a break, Sacramento has any number of spas to help you out. Midtown offers an especially dense spa concentration these days. **The Way Within Spa Retreat** (1722 J St., 916/446-4443) focuses its treatments on healing and retreat services for couples. Massages and foot treatments help weary travelers (and locals!) take a load off and get to feeling better. Baths, body scrubs, and steam treatments rejuvenate singles and couples. For a stretchy and wonderful California massage experience, book a Thai yoga massage.

## Yoga

Looking for some directed tranquility during your stay in Sacramento? Inside the 57th Street Antiques Mall, do a session of yoga at **The Yoga Solution** (887 57th St., Ste, B, 916/383-7933, www.theyogasolution.net). This studio offers classes each day, most in the Hatha and Iyengar schools.

## Amusement Parks

Kids and adults alike can use a refreshing play day to escape the summer's heat in Sacramento. A perfect place to get cool is **Raging Waters** (1600 Exposition Blvd., 916/924-3747, www.rwsac.com, $20–24). With rides like Shark Attack, Dragon's Den, and Honolulu Half-Pipe, thrill-seekers can get a full day of excitement here. For a more sedate day at the water park, ride a slow tube down the Calypso Cooler river, play in Hook's Lagoon, or catch a wave at Breakers Beach. At lunchtime, get a meal at the ample snack bar, or bring your own picnic to enjoy at the picnic tables or on the lawns. If you don't mind the heat and you're tired of the waterslides, play a game of pickup volleyball on one of the provided courts.

## Casino Gambling

Gamblers can take a spin through the slots and across the tables at the **Thunder Valley Casino** (1200 Athens Ave., Lincoln, 916/408-7777, www.thundervalleyresort.com, open daily), only a short drive from downtown Sacramento. You'll find more than 2,000 slot machines and nearly 100 table games here, along with a Vegas-style buffet and plenty of chain eateries. Be sure to stop for a drink at the Falls Bar for a drink, then head into the casino to play Ultimate Texas Hold 'Em, mini baccarat, or blackjack.

## Spectator Sports

Sacramento is the treasured home of many professional sports teams at all levels. It's easy to take in a game while you're visiting.

Basketball is a local favorite sport here. The NBA's **Sacramento Kings** (www.nba.com/kings, $10–165) play at the **Arco Arena** (1 Sports Pkwy.). A fast-paced basketball game can be a great way to unwind after a long day of historical sights and museums, so come on down and cheer for the purple and white! You can get tickets for cheap if you're willing to sit in the nosebleeds. Tickets are available online, or right at the arena box office. The arena has ample parking ($10).

If you prefer the ladies of the WNBA, Sacramento's got a great team in the **Sacramento Monarchs** (www.wnba.com/monarchs, $21–42). The Monarchs also call the Arco Arena home. Come and watch the most skilled women in basketball heat up the arena!

The hot, dry weather of the Sacto summer just begs for a baseball game. Take yourself out to one with the **Sacramento River Cats** (www.rivercats.com). The AAA (minor league) River Cats play **Raley Field** (400 Ball Park Dr., 916/376-4700, fee for parking), which appropriately sits right by the Sacramento River. At a River Cats game, you'll see serious baseball played by up-and-coming young men, many of whom have a serious eye on the majors. You can take a shuttle ($0.50) right to the field, buy a classic hot dog and a soda or a beer, sit back, and relax while the players do all the work. Ample pay parking is a short-to-medium walk from the stadium entrances.

# ACCOMMODATIONS

Sacramento tends to be a workman's town, with folks coming in for meetings and conventions and staying at big-box chain motels and hotels. As the city remakes its Old Town and Midtown areas, more unique lodgings will appear. For now, however, your best bet at a cheap-and-easy room are the various Holiday Inns, Quality Inns, and Sheratons.

## Under $100

For budget accommodations in Sacramento, you can't beat the **Sacramento Hostel** (900 H St., 916/443-1691, www.norcalhostels.org/sac, $23–50). The hostel sits inside a grand old Victorian home right downtwon. You'll love the parlor, drawing room, and recreation room—all with high ceilings and historic-style moldings. A full kitchen welcomes cooks with all the equipment needed to create tasty and inexpensive meals. On warm evenings, take your dinner out to the wraparound porch to enjoy the weather as the sun goes down. Guest rooms include both co-ed and single-sex dorms, plus a few private rooms for a higher price. Note that only one private room includes a private bath—all other hall baths are shared. The attractive wooden bunks do not include linens, so you'll need to bring your own sheets or sleeping bag. However, the hostel does have free DSL and Wi-Fi, laundry, on-site parking, and 24-hour guest access.

The **Governors Inn** (210 Richards Blvd., 916/448-7224, www.governorsinnhotel.com, $95–145) sits in near the Capitol in Sacramento. Walk from the Governors to the Capitol, or take a five-minute drive to Old Sacramento or Midtown. Your room, with classic motel styling, creates a perfect base for your stay. Whether you book a standard room or a two-room suite, you'll enjoy the understated elegance of this motel. Kids enjoy the outdoor pool in the hot summer months, and adults take advantage of the fitness center, free Wi-Fi, continental breakfast, and more. Check the website or ask at the desk for a plethora of recommendations for shopping, restaurants, golf courses, and sights to see throughout town.

## $100-150

At the **Inn off Capitol Park** (1530 N St., 916/447-8100, www.innoffcapitolpark.com, $117), you'll find attractive luxury at moderate prices. The inn sits within easy walking distance of the Capitol and the Sacramento Convention Center. The linens, wall art, and paint all match tastefully, and the furniture and lighting feel more like home than a motel. With an eye toward business and pleasure travelers, amenities include free Wi-Fi and voicemail, plus a continental breakfast and dinner recommendations. If you're planning a stay in Sacramento during any major events, book a room at the Inn early—with only 38 rooms, this friendly boutique hotel can fill up fast during conventions. The Inn Off Capitol Park is 100 percent non-smoking.

If you want to stay on a piece of history, book a stateroom on the ***Delta King*** (1000 Front St., 916/444-5464, www.deltaking.com, $119–149). An integral part of the Old Town neighborhood, the *Delta King* is at once a hotel, restaurant, theater, and gathering space. To stay on the *Delta King* means stepping back into

© LIZ HAMILL SCOTT

Book a stateroom on the *Delta King* and step back in time.

the Prohibition era, when the *King* plied the Sacramento River between Sacramento and San Francisco. Drinks, jazz, and dancing were the order of the evening then. Today you can stay in the very same staterooms, albeit refurbished to modern, elegant standards. Be aware that the less expensive staterooms can be quite small, as is common onboard ships. All rooms have their own private bathrooms, and for a slightly higher fee you can stay in a much larger and more luxurious stateroom or suite. High-rollers can take advantage of the Captain's Quarters—a palatial space with its own private observation deck. Multi-bed rooms are available for families, and couples can enjoy a Romance Package complete with champagne and a coupon for dinner at one of the *King's* two restaurants.

### $150-250

For a touch of luxury near the Capitol, stay at the **Inn and Spa at Parkside** (2116 Sixth St., 916/658-1818, www.innatparkside.com, $175–275). Each of the dozen rooms features unique decoration, with vibrant colors and sumptuous fabrics. Pick from rooms named Kiss, Passion, Refresh, and Extravagant. You'll feel as though you're in a cross between a small bed-and-breakfast and an elegant luxury hotel. Many rooms have spa tubs and showers, flat-screen TVs, balconies, fireplaces, and other great amenities. This inn is set up for romantic evenings for couples, so consider choosing a different lodging if you're traveling with children. To add extra pampering to your Sacramento stay, book a treatment at Spa Bloom—the attached luxury spa that offers beautifying facials (ask for microdermabrasion with any facial) and relaxing massages. Some rooms at the inn are set up for in-room massage; check when you book your reservations.

### Over $250

If you've got the money for luxury, the best B&B in Sacramento has long been the **Amber House** (1315 22nd St., 916/444-8085, www.amberhouse.com, $190–310). It's located in a quiet residential street in Midtown within walking distance of shopping, restaurants, and nightlife. Consisting of two separate houses, the Amber House prides itself on a level of service you'd find at the Ritz. The owner and innkeepers will see to your every need from the moment you enter the front door. Once inside, you'll find that no matter what room you've reserved, you'll be treated to the best. Every room at the inn has either a Jacuzzi or deep soaking bathtub, a super-comfortable bed, a subtly tucked-away TV, and top-end amenities.

The stellar comfort and service extends to the food as well. If you indicate you want them, fresh, warm chocolate chip cookies will be waiting for you when you come in from dinner in the evening. The next day, coffee (or your favorite morning beverage) is delivered to your door along with the morning paper. Breakfast, which can be served in the privacy of your room, in the formal dining room, or out in the shaded garden, is a multi-course masterpiece of fresh ingredients and original dishes. After one night and morning at the Amber House, you'll want to stay for weeks.

## FOOD

It might surprise new visitors to Sacramento to learn that the cuisine served in the smaller capital city can rival that of Los Angeles and even culinary heavyweight San Francisco. You'll find almost any kind of ethnic food you can imagine, upscale white-tablecloth bistros, and local favorite holes-in-the-wall with lines out the door. Whatever your tastes, you'll find dining in Sacto a welcome and tasty adventure.

### American

An outgrowth of the original Frank Fat's is Old Sacramento's **Fat City** (1001 Front St., 916/446-6768, www.fatsrestaurants.com/fatcity). Here, you'll imagine you've walked into an Old West saloon from the California gold mining heyday. Award-winning stained glass graces the windows, the lamps, and almost anything else they could affix it to. Dark furniture and linens complete the atmosphere in the high-ceiling dining room, which sits across the street from the *Delta King*. But it's the menu that makes Fat City stand out. A diverse selection of dishes appeals to any visitor's palate. You can get a plate of chow mein, an order of tacos, or an enormous gooey cheeseburger (the Bourbon Barbecue Burger is the best of these). At dinnertime, the entrées turn to American comfort food, including meat loaf, pot pie, and racks of ribs. Lighter eaters can get an entrée salad. Portions are enormous (perhaps appropriate given the restaurant's name), so consider splitting a meal with a friend. On weekend days, enjoy a mixed brunch menu that includes the best of the lunch menu, plus a number of Fat City breakfast specialties. Whenever you come in, you'll find the service friendly and helpful. Crowds can get heavy, especially during high tourist season, so you may have to wait a few minutes for a table. However, the large historic building accommodates plenty of diners, and the food is worth the wait.

Another good Old Sac burger joint is in **Fanny Ann's Saloon** (1023 Second St., 916/441-0505, www.fannyanns.com, $10–20). Enjoy classic American grub in an Old West setting.

## Asian

**Frank Fat's** (806 L St., 916/442-7092, www.fatsrestaurants.com, Mon.–Fri. 11 A.M.–10 P.M., Sat.–Sun. 5–10 P.M.) lives up to its reputation as a legendary Sacramento institution. The oldest restaurant in Sacramento was opened by Frank Fat in 1939. From the beginning, Fat's served authentic upscale Chinese food—which it still does today. Also from the beginning, the cream of capital city society came to eat at Fat's. On the menu, you'll find steaks to satisfy even the heartiest appetites, Chinese delicacies with and without meat or poultry, and more. Vegetarians can get a fabulous meal at Fat's, even as carnivores can sate their appetites. The hardest part is choosing just enough for your table without going totally overboard. The dimly lit, rich atmosphere invites romantic couples on a night out, and of course politicians looking for a quiet chat. Appropriately, Fat's sits near the Capitol complex.

For another side of Asian cuisine, have a tranquil Japanese meal at **Zen Sushi** (900 15th St., 916/446-9628, www.zen-sushi.com, Mon.–Thurs. 11:30 A.M.–2 P.M. and 5–9:30 P.M., Fri.–Sun. 11:30 A.M.–2 P.M. and 5–11 P.M., $5–15). This small, well-lit, casual sushi joint beckons visitors and locals with its wide array of house specialty rolls, fresh sashimi and nigiri, and plentiful vegetarian and cooked dishes. While Sacramento has no direct access to the sea, proximity to the San Francisco Bay Area guarantees the availability of the best fresh sushi-grade fish. Lunch and dinner combinations offer good value for plenty of food, plus lots of options for non-raw-fish eaters. But for the best Zen has to offer, look at the House Special Rolls list—that's where the good stuff hides. With your meal, quaff one of a variety of Japanese and American beers, a Japanese soda, or a glass of sweet fruity plum wine. Before you pick a time to eat, remember that Zen's downtown location makes it popular with the local business lunch crowd. Pick an off-time or the dinner hour for a smaller crowd.

## Cajun

**Hot & Spicy Café New Orleans** (117 J St., 916/443-5051, Sun.–Thurs. 11 A.M.–10 P.M., Fri.–Sat. 11 A.M.–11 P.M., $20) brings a taste of Louisiana to Sacto. With exposed brick and ductwork and bright, colorful tablecloths, the atmosphere at this eatery is friendly and fun. As for the food...When they say "Hot & Spicy," they mean it. For real. The Cajun foods—jambalaya, gumbo, and many other New Orleans favorites—are riddled with hot peppers and other spices. Be careful of what you order! To put out the fire, go downstairs for an after-dinner drink at the attached SpeakEasy bar.

## California

Calling the ☾ **33rd Street Bistro** (3301 Folsom Blvd., 916/455-2233, http://33rdstreetbistro.com, Sun.–Thurs. 8 A.M.–10 P.M., Fri.–Sat. 8 A.M.–11 P.M., $7–24) a "California cuisine" restaurant is somewhat misleading. In fact, the Bistro's menus are inspired by the foods of the Pacific Northwest—the training ground of executive chef Fred

Haines—and favorite dishes from around the country. The panini selection speaks to the Northwestern connection, while the salads offer original and delectable healthy fare. In fact, most of the food at the Bistro tends toward the current trend for local, health-conscious cuisine. The casual dining room features exposed brick, an open kitchen and pizza oven, and a fun party atmosphere. Feel free to wear your favorite jeans and t-shirt when you eat at this Sacto locals' favorite, which is open late-ish for dinner on weekends to accommodate people out for a night on the town.

**Mulvaney's Building & Loan** (1215 19th St., 916/441-6022, www.culinaryspecialists.com/mulvaneybl.htm) is a product of the Midtown renaissance. This upscale eatery showcases the best of California cuisine. It's not cheap, but for a romantic night out, the original dishes at Mulvaney's are more than worth it. The menu changes often to take advantage of local, seasonal produce. You can go for a standard appetizer-and-big-ol'-main dish, or order small plates to share around the table or to satisfy a smaller appetite. The wine list offers a reasonable number of tastings and interesting vintages, some of which you may never have seen before. (Try the Kung Fu Girl Riesling if it's available—how can you resist a good wine with a name like that!) Pick between a seat in the lively and loud dining room or a quieter table on the gardenlike back patio, which is a great choice most days of the year in Sacto. Wherever you sit, you'll enjoy friendly, attentive service with a smile and a good understanding of both menu and wine list.

## French

If you're looking for a tasty and inexpensive French lunch near the Capitol building, head for **La Bonne Soupe Café** (920 Eighth St., 916/492-9506, Mon.–Fri. 10:30 A.M.–2:30 P.M., $5–10). This is the kind of narrow-focus local favorite that visitors love to find. Beware, if you come right at noon, you'll likely spend some time standing in line with local businesspeople who come from miles around to have lunch here. La Bonne Soupe serves fresh hot soups and handmade sandwiches on crusty French breads. Soups range from classics such as French onion to tasty treats made with fresh, in-season produce. Sandwiches made with fresh ingredients are far superior to supermarket standards. Best of all, the lunch you get at La Bonne Soupe will make you feel great during and after you eat it, since the soups and sandwiches here burst with healthy nutrients. Be sure to say hi to the chef as you wait—he's often found lovingly preparing sandwiches behind the counter as the line snakes out the door. If you usually eat a smaller lunch, consider splitting an order of soup and one sandwich with a traveling companion—portions are pretty hefty.

For a fancier French restaurant experience, dine out at the **Waterboy Restaurant** (2000 Capitol Ave., 916/498-9891, www.waterboyrestaurant.com, Mon.–Fri. 11:30 A.M.–2:30 P.M., Sun.–Mon. 5–9 P.M., Tues.–Thurs. 5–9:30 P.M., Fri.–Sat. 5–10:30 P.M., $10–27). The light, bright dining room feels like something you'd walk into on the south coast of France. And in fact, the cuisine here takes much from the culinary traditions of Provence, as well as Tuscany and just a hint of California. If you've got a serious appetite, go for the full three courses: appetizer, first, and main. But if you've got a lighter appetite, the first course options can make adequate entrées and leave room for dessert. It's worth leaving room, since the dessert menu includes classical French favorites and interesting California innovations to tempt anyone with the slightest hint of a sweet tooth. Sit back in your white-and-black woven chair and finish off your meal with an espresso or a digestif to complete a near-perfect dining experience.

## Italian

**Zelda's Original Gourmet Pizza** (1415 21st St., 916/447-1400, www.zeldasgourmetpizza.com, Mon.–Thurs. 11:30 A.M.–10 P.M., Fri. 11:30 A.M.–11 P.M., Sat. 5–11 P.M. Sun. 5–9 P.M., $10–20) serves deep-dish Chicago-style pies that locals just can't resist—despite the fact that the grease off the pizza may well soak through the thick crust, then through the bottom of the box before you get it to your table. You won't find much to help your cholesterol level or waistline at Zelda's, but if you've been on the road a while feasting on an endless stream of leafy green California cuisine, a Zelda's pizza might just be the perfect answer to your craving. The handwritten menus add to the charm of the great service and the amazing pizzas.

### Bakeries and Cafés

Consider skipping dessert at whatever restaurant you dine in, just so you've got the appetite to hit ☾ **Rick's Dessert Diner** (2322 K St., 916/444-0969, http://ricksdessertdiner.com, Tues.–Thurs. 10 A.M.–midnight, Fri.–Sat. 10 A.M.–1 A.M., Sun. noon–11 P.M., Mon 10 A.M.–11 P.M.). This unique eatery delivers everything it promises—all desserts, all the time in a 1950s diner–style restaurant. Open late, Rick's finds favor with local teenagers as well as plenty of older patrons and there's often find a line out the door on weekends after 10 P.M. Rick's serves desserts and coffee only, so prepare to indulge yourself. The pies are nothing special, but the impossibly high layer cakes have wonderful flavor and texture in a wide variety of styles. An ice cream freezer makes pie and cake è la mode possible, as well as hot fudge sundaes and banana splits. You can take your choice out, or eat in the diner at one of the rather small booths clad in sparkling red vinyl upholstery.

## INFORMATION AND SERVICES

Sacramento offers all the services of a major metropolitan American city. You'll find hospitals, entertainment publications, an ATM on every corner, and Internet access all over the place. In fact, if you're out in Gold Country and need city-style services, Sacramento may be your closest destination.

### Tourist Information

Need help from local experts for your time in Sacto? Visit the **Sacramento Convention and Visitor's Bureau** (1608 I St., 916/808-7777, www.sacramentocvb.org, Mon.–Fri. 8 A.M.–5 P.M.). Call or check the website in advance for deals on hotels, advance reservations for attractions, and information about what's in and around the city. Or drop by the office while you're in town to get the locals' take on the best restaurants, the must-see museums, and more.

### Media and Communications

The major metropolitan daily paper for Sacto is the ***Sacramento Bee*** (www.sacbee.com). With the proximity to the hottest California politics, you'll find better-than-average coverage of local current events. You'll also get information you can use in the Food/Wine, Entertainment, and Outdoors sections.

All major banks are represented in Sacramento. You'll find ample ATMs and branches downtown near the capital and in Midtown. In Old Sacramento, you'll find the Wells Fargo Museum, plus Wells Fargo branches all over the city.

As a major metropolitan area, Sacramento has plenty of **post office** branches. On the grid, you can mail out from the Metro office at 801 I Street, Room 149. Just off I-80, the Broadway office sits on 2121 Broadway. In Old Sacramento, the post office shares space with the visitors center at 1303 J Street.

### Medical Services

Plenty of hospitals make Sacramento home, should you need medical services while you're in town. **Sutter General Hospital** (2801 L St., 916/454-2222, suttermedicalcenter.org) is located right downtown and has an emergency room. Another local emergency center is run by **UC Davis** on 10th Street between G and H Streets.

## GETTING THERE AND AROUND

As is the case in most major California cities, cars are the One True Way locals get around. You'll have the most flexibility to travel out to Gold Country if you've got access to a private car. But inside Sacramento, ample public transit makes getting around without your own wheels a viable option. Getting to and from Sacramento works fairly well via planes and trains.

## Air

Most major carriers fly into **Sacramento International Airport** (SMF, 6900 Airport Blvd., 916/929-5411, www.sacairports.org), which is your best bet for flying in to any location in and around Gold Country.

## Train

If you're coming into Sacramento from the San Francisco Bay Area, one of the best ways to do it is on the Capitol Corridor Amtrak train (www.amtrak.com). Serving the centrally located Amtrak station (401 I St.), this train runs from Sacramento to Oakland and down to San Jose and back several times each day. The trip lasts a little more than three hours. You can also get to or from Sacramento on the California Zephyr, which crosses the country, from Chicago to the Bay Area, or the Coast Starlight, which travels from Seattle all the way to Los Angeles. The San Joaquins runs right up the middle of California, from Sacramento to Bakersfield.

## Bus

Sacramento has a busy and reasonably extensive public transit system that includes both buses and a light rail train system: **Sacramento Regional Transit** (www.sacrt.com, single ride $2, day pass $5). Including the downtown trolley and the light rail lines, SACRT offers nearly 100 routes. Check the website for routes, schedules, and maps.

## Car

I-80 runs through Sacramento roughly east–west, and the Business 80 adjunct goes right into downtown by a slightly different route. I-5 splits the city on an east–west route. Highway 50 takes you east to Lake Tahoe, and Highway 99 runs south down to Los Angeles.

Parking in town can get difficult during major events, but otherwise spots aren't ridiculously hard to come by. Near the Capitol building, bring change to feed the meters. In Old Sacramento, spots right in the middle of the action can be at a premium during high season—you may have to walk a few blocks to get to Front Street. The theaters and arenas tend to have ample parking lots, though you'll pay at many of those. Most hotels offer on- or off-street parking free with your room.

## Tours

A number of tours can give you views high and low, distant and close, of Sacramento. Take a self-guided walking tour of Old Sacramento, or a fly-over of the whole city and delta region.

Enjoy sightseeing as you dine aboard the **Sacramento RiverTrain** (800/866-1690, www.sacramentorivertrain.com, $37–69). Outside the window or on the open-air observation deck, look down on the river and out at the stunning Fremont Trestle. Choose from a variety of rides, from a standard weekday lunch up to a fancy weekend Dinner Party, or even a re-enactment of the Great Train Robbery, complete with costumed robbers and a Western-style barbecue lunch. Most rides last 2–4 hours; check the website for departure times, ride lengths, and special event rides that happen several times each year.

To see all of Sacramento in only an hour, make a reservation with **Delta SeaPlane Tours** (Sacramento Executive Airport, 877/378-3597, http://deltaseaplanes.com, $250–600). You'll get a bird's-eye view of the Delta, the Sacramento River downtown area, and various Sacramento historic sights. If you're really into flying, consider extending your tour out to the Bay Area as well.

For an amphibious tour of the river and city sides of Sacramento, book a tour aboard the **Golden Dawn** (916/552-2933, www.sacramentoyachtcharters.com). This funky-looking trolley-boat takes its passengers to many of the major sights of downtown and Old Town Sacramento, then out onto the river for a view of the riverfront from the water. This tour lasts about an hour, and is a great way to see the major sights of Sacramento if you've only got one day in town.

If you're looking for a laugh with your

sidewalk tour, try one of the three **Hysterical Walks & Rides** (117 J St., 916/441-2527, www.hystericalwalks.com). The walking tours are evening affairs; the standard Hysterical tour leaves on Friday and Saturday evenings at 7 P.M. and lasts for one hour. Standup comedian-guides give you the story of Old Sacramento in the funniest way possible. At 8:30 P.M. on the same evenings, a costumed guide starts the Hysterical Walk of the Dead tour. On this hour-long walk through the back alleys of Old Sacramento, you'll alternately giggle and shiver as your guide relates all the best ghost stories from this historic area.

If you prefer a sleek, smooth ride to your own two feet, sign up for the daily Segway tour that takes you through Old Town, to the Capitol building and gardens, and past other historic Sacramento sights. Your standup comedian will share the history of the city as you glide across the sidewalks on your personal transport vehicle. This tour lasts 2.5 hours, and all riders must be at least 16 years old. Segway tours depart at 9:30 A.M. and 1:30 P.M. each day.

# Northern Gold Country

California's Gold Country is not a small area surrounding a single city. It's a great sprawling network of small towns and roads crisscrossing the Sierra Nevada foothills. (Technically, Sacramento can be considered part of Gold Country as well.) Here begins much of California's written history. It was the gold in these hills that drew immigrants from the East Coast and around the world to come and work the fields, build the railroads, and drag the wild California land into the modern era.

When visiting, it's easiest to traverse Gold Country from north to south. The northern Gold Country extends from Nevada City down to the famed Sutter Creek. The I-80 freeway can get you from Sacramento (or even the Bay Area) to the northern Gold Country town of Auburn. Here you can pick up Highway 49 North to Grass Valley and Nevada City. On Highway 49 South, head down to Placerville, Plymouth, Amador City, and finally to Sutter Creek. From here, small state highways and roads can take you east to Volcano, Pioneer, and other tiny dots on the map.

## SIGHTS

### Empire Mine State Historic Park

Arguably the best mining museum in Gold Country is the Empire Mine State Historic Park (10791 E. Empire St., Grass Valley, 530/273-8522, www.empiremine.org, May–Aug. daily 9 A.M.–6 P.M., Sept.–Apr. daily 10 A.M.–5 P.M., adults $3, children $1, tours $1.50 extra). Walking into the yard, you can see and feel the life of the 19th- and 20th-century miners who extracted tons of gold from the earth below your feet. Kids can run and

© LIZ HAMILL SCOTT

the main shaft at Empire Mine

shout in the yard, enjoying the open spaces and strange tools and machines. (Keep a close eye on children; the museum contains many obvious and hidden dangers.) Adults can enjoy the history of the place and imagine a hard-rock life in the mine, or a privileged existence up in the owner's cottage.

The mine yard holds a vast collection of tools and equipment used in the hard-rock mine shafts; the shop that kept the mine machinery functioning still works. If you come on the right day (weekends, usually), you might find a blacksmith working away inside. Duck inside for a glimpse of the main mineshaft itself. You can go a few feet down into the shaft, then look deep down and imagine what it was like to perch in a metal car and shoot down thousands of feet into the darkness. To get a real idea of the scale of the mine shafts and tunnels, go inside the museum. The showpiece of the collection is the scale model of the Empire Mine and the various nearby interconnected mines' tunnels. This model was top secret when it was first built—only the mine owner and select executives and guests could view it. Today, turn on the lights surrounding the mammoth glass case to highlight and hear the stories of the different parts of the overwhelmingly vast and complex underground maze.

For something completely different, leave the mine yard and take the path up the slight rise to the "cottage"—the mine owner's home. In stark contrast to the dust, rust, and timber of the yard, here you'll see acres of sweeping green lawn dotted with flowering shrubs and bisected with gently curving pathways.

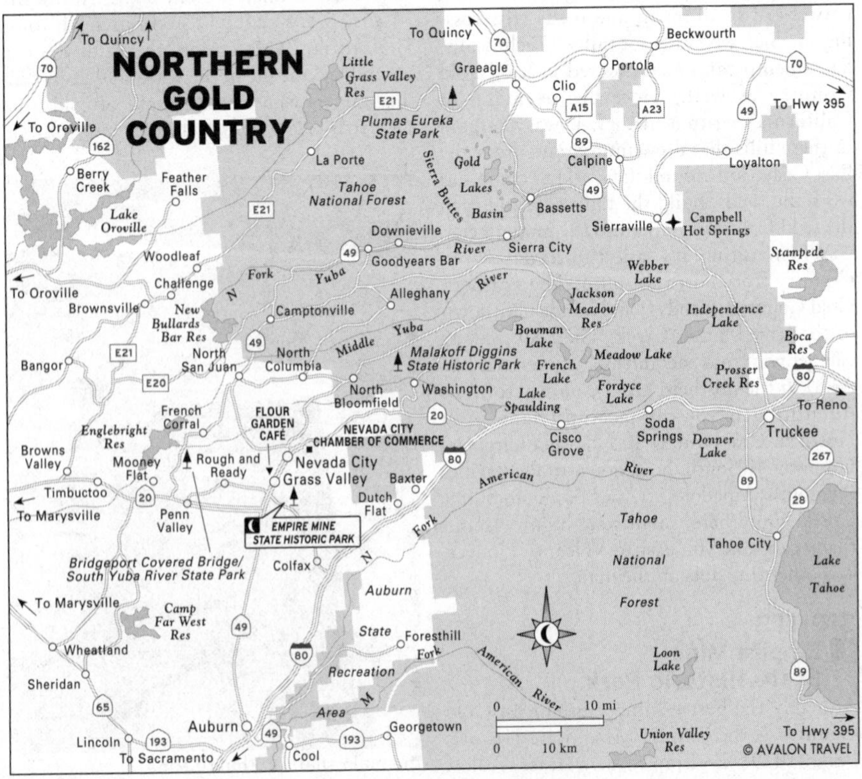

© LIZ HAMILL SCOTT

machinery in the mine yard, Empire Mine

The garden leads up to the mammoth brick mansion. Check the park schedule inside the museum for regular tours of the inside of the cottage and the surrounding gardens, as well as occasional living history events.

## Gold Bug Park

If you're traveling with your kids and want them to experience a gold mining museum, visit Hangtown's Gold Bug Park (Bedford Ave., Placerville, 530/642-5207, www.goldbugpark.org, Apr.–Oct. daily 10 A.M.–4 P.M., Nov.–Apr. daily Sat.–Sun. noon–4 P.M., adults $4, children $2, audio tour $1). This smaller mine, originally called the Hattie, dates from the 1850s. Today, the museum offers lessons in history, including tours of the mine, an interpretive museum, a gift shop, and more. For a small fee, you can pan for gold in a manufactured sluice. Many of the tour features and exhibits are designed for children, combining education and entertainment as kids don their hard hats, check out the mine shaft, and learn the function of a stamp mill.

## Apple Hill

Aptly named, Apple Hill (north of Hwy. 50, btwn. Placerville and Pollack Pines, 530/644-7692, www.applehill.com) produces many of the apples grown in California. Dozens of orchards cluster in the apple-friendly climate of this part of the Sierra Foothills. More recently, some of the orchards and vacant land have been converted to vineyards to help feed California's insatiable appetite for fine wines. For a scenic tour, download a map from the website or take Exit 48 or 54 from Highway 50 onto Apple Hill Scenic Drive. When you go out to Apple Hill, you'll drive charming country roads and pull up at the cute farm buildings that front the orchards filling out the landscape. At some orchards, you can pick your own apples in season. At others, you'll find a large shop stuffed with homemade pies frozen and ready to be baked, preserves, cookbooks, and every type of apple product you can imagine. Come in the middle of summer to enjoy the orchards' berry crops (raspberries, blackberries, blueberries), and later in the summer through the fall for the best of the dozens of varieties of apples grown in the region. Check the website for information about events and festivals that draw crowds out to Apple Hill to enjoy country fair–style activities, arts and craft shows, food and drink tastings, and more. The wineries get into the act as well, offering specials in their tasting rooms. If you have the slightest interest in California food and wine, you can't miss Apple Hill!

### Sutter Gold Mine

Though the stereotypical picture of a California miner is an old man panning for gold nuggets in a river, most of the gold found here was dug out of rock and quartz veins deep underground. The best way to really experience gold mining is to take a tour of the Sutter Gold Mine (Hwy. 49, Sutter Creek, 888/818-7462, www.caverntours.com). Even dedicated local cave experts love this tour, which takes you deep into the heart of a modern hard-rock gold mine. The Sutter Gold Mine was built in the 1980s, but only operated as a mine for 10 years before becoming a touring and park facility. It connects underground to historic mine shafts.

The Sutter Gold Mine experience includes plenty of kid and tourist-friendly activities, such as geode-breaking and panning for gemstones, but the real gem here is the rare chance to see the inside of a hard-rock mine. You'll take a brief safety course before heading down. Next, you'll don your required hard hat and jump into a specially designed vehicle that takes you deep into the mine shafts. Once down inside, a guide will explain the sights you're seeing on your hour-long tour. While it's best to be able to walk around to see everything, if you call ahead to make arrangements, Sutter Gold Mine's underground tunnels are accessible to visitors who need to sit through the tour. However, safety requirements make this underground adventure unsuitable for children under four.

### Amador Flower Farm

Ever wondered where pretty daylilies come from? Over 800 different kinds grow at the Amador Flower Farm (22001 Shenandoah School Rd., Plymouth, 209/245-6660, www.amadorflowerfarm.com, daily 9 A.M.–4 P.M.). Take a serene and colorful walk through the eight acres of farmland and four acres of demonstration gardens, enjoying the flowers and perennials. If you've got a picnic packed, enjoy it in the gardens shaded by heritage oak trees. In the gift shop, get a single lily for your sweetheart, or pick up a bundle of bulbs to take home and plant in your own garden.

### Black Chasm

If you're looking for a natural underground experience, take an easy one-hour tour of the Black Chasm Caverns (Volcano-Pioneer Rd., Volcano, 866/762-2837, www.caverntours.com, daily May–Oct. 9 A.M.–5 P.M., Nov.–Apr. 10 A.M.–4 P.M., adults $12.95, children $6.50). Though this tour isn't accessible to strollers or wheelchairs, walking-age kids enjoy the reasonably sedate stroll into the immense chasm filled with amazing calcite formations. In the Landmark Room, you'll get a chance to check out the rare helictite formations (a crystalline cave formation) that made Black Chasm famous. On your way out or as you wait for your tour, enjoy the new visitors center. Many guests enjoy the video that describes the use of the look and feeling of Black Chasm by the creators of *The Matrix* films. You can even see some of the immense stalagmite props made for the movies!

### Daffodil Hill

Spring is the time to visit the famed Daffodil Hill (Rams Horn Grade, Volcano, 209/296-7048, www.amadorcountychamber.com, daily late Mar.–mid-Apr., free). Perfect for travelers who love the greenery above ground as much as the minerals beneath it, Daffodil Hill explodes each March into a profusion of sunny yellow that lasts for about a month. Daffodil Hill is actually the private working ranch of the McLaughlin family, who have been planting daffodil bulbs on their property since they first acquired the land in 1887. Today, you'll see more than 300,000 flowers blooming, and more are planted each year. In addition to the more than 300 different species of daffodil, other bulb flowers and plants help create carpets of color across the meadows and hills. Even among the many fabulous landscapes and gardens of California, Daffodil Hill is special; out here, you can't help but feel the joy and promise of spring.

Daffodil Hill opens to the public *only* during daffodil season. Exact opening and closing dates vary each year. Call to get the latest information on this year's blooms.

### Small Museums

If you're a history buff with a few extra minutes on your hands, you can find a wealth of "15-minute museums" in northern Gold Country. In these tiny galleries, you can learn about little-explored aspects of California pioneer life. The **Shenandoah Valley Museum** (14430 Shenandoah Rd., Plymouth, 209/245-4456, www.sobonwine.com, free) describes the winemaking process that began in Gold Country almost as soon as the first miners arrived. It's part of the Sobon Estate—a winery that's been in continuous operation in the Shenandoah Valley since 1856.

Miners, their wives, and everybody else who came to live in the bustling boom towns of Gold Country needed supplies: food, cloth, tools, medicines, etc. In 19th-century California, many of those supplies were sold at the general store. The **Monteverde Store Museum** (11A Randolph St., Sutter Creek, 800/400-0305, www.suttercreek.org) sold staples to Sutter Creek residents for 75 years. After its last shopkeepers, Mary and Rose Monteverde, passed on, the city took over the building. The sisters had stipulated that it was to become a museum and so it is—a look into the hub of town life in the 19th century. Perhaps miners bought Sobon wines here 100 years ago?

## WINERIES

In the 21st century, the real gold in the Sierra Foothills flows from a bottle. The major tasting patch lies in the Shenandoah Valley, but you'll also find gems in the El Dorado, Amador, and Fair Play regions and appellations. Best of all, you'll find some fabulous wines, intriguing tasting rooms, and knowledgeable staff and winemakers in northern Gold Country—*without* the vast crowds you'll run into in Napa and Sonoma.

The truth is, there's been wine in them thar hills for almost 150 years. When European emigrants came to California to ply the gold fields, they found themselves longing for the wines they drank at home. The Italian miners who found no luck with gold began planting grapes, since the climate was similar to the Italian highlands. Vineyards grew around the mines, supplying wine to the hard-working miners and townsfolk of the Sierra Foothills. Then came the "noble experiment" that was Prohibition, and most of the Gold Country wineries ceased production. The vineyards languished for decades, until the growing California wine boom centering around Napa began spreading to other grape-growing regions of the state. By the 1990s, many of the wineries were back in business. Today, more than 100 wineries make their home in California's Gold Country.

### Apple Hill

The Apple Hill region grows more than just Fujis and Granny Smiths. This region, which runs just northeast of Placerville, also plays home to a number of vineyards that feed the local wineries.

#### BOEGER WINERY

Among the largest of the Apple Hill wineries is Boeger Winery (1709 Carson Rd., Placerville, 800/655-2634, www.boegerwinery.com, daily 10 A.M.–5 P.M., tasting free). Just outside of Placerville proper, visit the elegant new tasting room for a regular or reserve tasting of Boeger's best current release wines. Better yet, bring a lunch and have a picnic in the redwood grove or out by the cracked white facade of the historic wine cellar. Owner and vineyard manager Greg Boeger bought his vines to follow a family tradition; more than a century ago, his grandfather had a winery in the Napa Valley to serve the new residents of California during the Gold Rush. Today, Boeger's specialties tend to be big, hearty reds, though you can taste the occasional delicate white wine here too. Beware of crowds on Apple Hill event days!

### FENTON HERRIOTT VINEYARDS

At the opposite end of the spectrum, tiny Fenton Herriott Vineyards (120 Jacquier Ct., Placerville, 530/642-2021, www.fentonherriott.com) makes only a few hundred cases of wine each year. When you visit the little tasting room out off the main drag, you'll get to try a small variety of tasty and reasonably priced red wines you won't find in your local BevMo. The tasting staff knows lots about the wines they're pouring, and can tell you the story of each one. Fenton Herriott Vineyards gives you the perfect opportunity to see another side of the California wine scene: no huge souvenir shops, no fancy mostly-for-show estate, just good wine in small quantities made by folks who care more about grapes than anything else.

### PRIMUS VINEYARDS

Towards the east end of Apple Hill you'll find Primus Vineyards (2875 Larsen Dr., 530/647-9463, www.primuswinery.com, daily 11 A.M.–5 P.M.). The cute red barn shelters a surprisingly elegant tasting room, complete with a wooden tasting bar and shelving to hold bottles for sale. The elegance extends to the wines—all small-lot reds. Primus releases only about five wines each year. While you're sipping, be sure to check out the collection of antique wine tools—an unusual and extensive array. Finally, if you like laughter with your vino, check the winery website for information about Primus' regularly scheduled comedy nights.

### WOFFORD ACRES VINEYARDS

Wofford Acres Vineyards (1900 Hidden Valley Ln., Camino, 530/626-6858, Thurs.–Sun. 11 A.M.–5 P.M.), another red specialist, exemplifies the new era of small family wineries in California. Open for five years, Wofford Acres is owned and operated by the Wofford family, and you're likely to run into one or more Woffords when you visit the small tasting room. Look for low-priced but high-flavored red table wines, red varietals, and possibly even a yummy dessert port to finish off your tasting experience.

## Shenandoah Valley

The best known wine region in Gold Country is the Shenandoah Valley—and not just because this corner of Amador County takes its name from a famous part of the South. Dozens of wineries make their homes here, most using locally grown grapes that show off the best of what the Sierra Foothills can produce.

### STORY WINERY

Arguably the best of the small-to-medium Shenandoah wineries is Story Winery (10525 Bell Rd., Plymouth, 800/713-6390, www.zin.com, Mon.–Fri. noon–4 P.M., Sat.–Sun. 11 A.M.–5 P.M., tasting free). Here you can begin to taste the true history of Amador County wines. Some of the Story vineyards have lived nearly 100 years, and still produce grapes (albeit in tiny quantities) for wines being made today. The specialty of the house at Story is Zinfandel—in fact, this winery comes close to being all Zinfandel, all the time. Check out the amazing selection of old-vine, single-vineyard Zins to please any red-loving palate. You'll taste these in a charming, casual environment, where you'll be made to feel right at home—even if you're new to high-end wine. Walk outside to admire the estate vineyards ranging down the hills; those gnarled old tree-trunk like things create the special tastes adored by connoisseurs.

### BRAY VINEYARDS

If you want something different in a tasting experience, visit Bray Vineyards (10590 Shenandoah Rd., Plymouth, 209/245-6023, www.brayvineyards.com, Fri.–Mon. 10 A.M.–5 P.M.). With only the barest of nods to California favorite varietals, Bray instead goes its own way, pouring wines made from grapes even savvy wine lovers won't find familiar. Take a taste of a wine made from Verdelho, Tempranillo, Alicante Bouschet, or an intriguing blend of largely unknown-in-America Portuguese grapes. Or if you must, stick with the old faithful varietals, such as Syrah, Zin, and Cabernet Sauvignon. But to really get a feel for what Bray does, go outside of the tasting room and into the vineyards; Bray grows its own grapes, plus olives for estate olive oil, and has a number of native oak trees.

### MONTEVINA

One of the biggest names in the Shenandoah Valley, Montevina (20680 Shenandoah School Rd., Plymouth, 209/245-6942, www.montevina.com, daily 10 A.M.–4:30 P.M.) lives up to its reputation. Montevina prides itself on its Zinfandels, boasting that it makes "the best in the world." That's a bold claim in Amador County, which is the Zinfandel heartland. But Montevina doesn't box itself in—you can taste white wines, light red wines, medium red wines, blends, and more at this fun tasting room. Check out something from each of the three labels: the standard Montevina, reserve Terra d'Ors, and the fun, inexpensive Wild Bunch blends.

### DEAVER VINEYARDS

For a small winery experience, hit the cute small barn at Deaver Vineyards (12455 Steiner Rd., Plymouth, 290/245-4099, www.deavervineyard.com, daily 10:30 A.M.–5 P.M.). Grab a bottle of something fine and some tasty picnic foods and take the whole lot down to the local lake for lunch. Deaver produces a couple white and rosé wines and some flavored sparklers, but reds are unquestionably the mainstay of this winemaker. At the tasting bar, you can sip a range of intense, layered Zins and Syrahs, or get bold with a Carignane or a Barbera. Even if you're not a wine fan, you can't help but be charmed by the farm-style atmosphere, complete with decrepit outbuildings and sweeping green fields (under the vines, of course).

### WILDEROTTER VINEYARD

Wilderotter Vineyard (19890 Shenandoah School Rd., Plymouth, 209/245-6016, www.wilderottervineyard.com) brings great grapes from a loving grower out of the vineyard and into the tasting room. Wilderotter started as a vineyard that sold all its grapes to various winemakers, and only transformed into a winery in its own right in 2002. Even more recently, the charming stone facade of the tasting room was constructed, and the winery got going in earnest. The production is limited both in quantity and in scope. Zinfandel, Grenache, Viognier, and Barbera are what's planted in the vineyards, so that's what's available in the bottles.

## Fair Play

### FITZPATRICK WINERY & LODGE

Fitzpatrick Winery & Lodge (7740 Fairplay Rd., 530/620-6838, www.fitzpatrickwinery.com, Wed.–Mon. 11 A.M.–5 P.M.) was Fair Play's first winery, opened in 1980. Fitzpatrick focuses on "earth-friendly" wines, using organically grown grapes and producing wines in small lots to preserve the essence of the terroir from which the grapes come. Going further, the wine is bottled in recycled glass with untreated cork, then stored in a warehouse running almost entirely on solar energy, on land maintained with tractors running 90 percent vegetable oil. All in all, Fitzpatrick has created an eco-conscious wine-lover's dream winery. The lengthy wine list features some California classics in the way of Zinfandels, Chardonnays, and Merlots. But to get into this winery properly, try some of the less common vintages, which can range from Irish-styled white and red blended wines to a surprisingly complete array of ports in both red and white.

If you love Fitzpatrick so much that you just have to stay, you can. The estate also operates a bed-and-breakfast inn. On weekends between noon and four (or until the food runs out), stay for the Ploughman's Lunch—hearty hot fare that will set you up right for an afternoon of tasting elsewhere in Fair Play and northern Gold Country.

### CHARLES B. MITCHELL VINEYARDS

Charles B. Mitchell Vineyards (8221 Stoney Creek Rd., 530/620-3467, http://charlesbmitchell

.com, Mon.–Fri. 11 A.M.–5 P.M., Sat.–Sun. 10:30 A.M.–5 P.M.) is one of the more recognizable names in the Fair Play appellation. In the tasting room, you'll get a chance to try a wide variety of wines, from sparklers to whites to Amador County–grown reds to lush dessert ports. You can take a tour of the winery as well. But for a special treat, plan ahead to bottle your own wine. Check the website for upcoming bottle-your-own events, which include wine and food during the working day, plus a deep discount on the bottles you create yourself.

### TOOGOOD ESTATE WINE CAVES

A winery with a great name, Toogood Estate Wine Caves (7280 Fairplay Rd., 530/620-1910, www.toogoodwinery.com, Fri.–Sun. 11 A.M.–5:30 P.M.) beckons visitors with its unique winery and its distinctive wines. To get to the tasting room, you must enter the famed Toogood caves. All wines here are aged in the 5,000 square feet of underground space, which maintains a perfect cool temperature year-round. (Bring a coat into the tasting room if you're sensitive to cold.) You'll find almost all red wines in the caves, with a number of intriguing blends, some fun varietals like Barbera and and Cab Franc, plus a couple of unusual dessert wines. (Malbec port—really!) Bottle prices range from a moderate $20 up to $80 for the rarest ports. And finally, with a name like Foreplay (and underpants with matching labels in the gift shop), you know the red table wine has to be good!

### CANTIGA WINEWORKS & DELI

Cantiga Wineworks & Deli (5951 Mt. Aukum Rd., 530/621-1696, www.cantigawine.com, Fri.–Sun. 11 A.M.–5 P.M., tasting free) brings innovation and history to the world of small-batch winemaking. If you're lucky, you'll find one of the owners and winemakers in the tasting room, and learn of the true passion that goes into Cantiga's wines. Many of the whites and several of the reds here are *not* malolactically fermented—highly unusual for California wines. Ask at the unpretentious tasting bar and you'll get the whole story of how each wine gets made and why Cantiga's gone anti-malolactic. Some grapes are grown on the Cantiga estate, but most are lovingly chosen from vineyards around California, especially Lodi (where Cantiga maintains a second tasting room) and Monterey County. During the day, you can grab lunch at the attached deli to help soak up all that fabulous Fair Play wine.

## ENTERTAINMENT AND EVENTS

### Bars and Clubs

Nightlife in northern Gold Country runs to the classic saloons dotted along the main streets of each little town.

In Grass Valley, the saloon that sits on the ground floor of the historic Holbrook Hotel offers some of the best drinks and company in town. The **Golden Gate Saloon** (212 W. Main St., 530/273-1353, http://holbrookehotel.net/saloon) boasts of being the oldest continually operating saloon west of the Mississippi River. Yup, the Golden Gate braved possible Federal raids and kept on serving liquor throughout Prohibition. Today, this old-time saloon has a light lunch and dinner menu, a full bar with beer on tap, high-end wines, and plenty of cocktails. It's also got lots of locals, many of whom stop in to enjoy the live music that entertains patrons on Wednesday–Saturday nights.

If you're looking for something in an old-school biker bar, try **PJ's** (5641 Mother Lode Dr., 530/626-0336) in Old Hangtown. Off the main drag, this place features cheap beer and shots, a small dance floor, and the occasional DJ or live band designed to drag drinkers off their barstools. Expect lots of Harleys out front, precious little light inside, and perhaps a whiff of green emanating from the back porch. Definitely a dive bar!

On the other end of the spectrum, ritzy Nevada City boasts its very own upscale wine bar. The **Citronee Bistro and Wine Bar** (320 Broad St., Nevada City, 530/265-5697, Wed.–Mon. from 5:30 P.M.) offers dozens of California wines, European vintages, wine and champagne cocktails, splits of many types of vino, and more. You can sit at a table and enjoy a glass of wine with a fine California-style meal, belly up to the bar to get your taste on, or peruse bottles in the adjoining wine and cheese shop.

## Theater

Theater is a major aspect of the culture in Gold Country, and local residents devote significant time and energy to keeping their theaters alive and well.

The most prestigious regional theater company in all of Gold Country is the **Foothill Theater Company** (530/265-8587, www.foothilltheatre.org, adults $24–26, children $11–14, students $19–21). This professional company produces big-name works in the century-and-a-half old **Nevada Theater** (401 Broad St.) in Nevada City, with an occasional show in Grass Valley as well. The regular season can include Broadway musical hits like *Urinetown,* classics such as *On Golden Pond,* and unusual newer works including *Doubt, A Parable* (by John Patrick Shanley). In the summertime, the Foothill Theatre Company treks up to Tahoe to put on the annual Lake Tahoe Shakespeare Festival. (See the *Tahoe and the Northern Sierra* chapter for more information.) Check the website for the upcoming season's shows. During the regular season, just visiting the historic Nevada Theater—the oldest operating original-use theater in California—is worth the price of a ticket to a show.

You'll find a mix of live theater and live musical performance at the **Sutter Creek Theatre** (44 Main St., Sutter Creek, 209/296-5495, www.suttercreektheatre.com). Music acts range from folk to flamenco to country-western—smaller-time performers who can really connect with the audience in this intimate venue. Plays go up several times a year, and are generally family-friendly classics such as *A Christmas Carol* and *The Velveteen Rabbit.* Occasionally you might get a chance to see a new work by a local playwright. Check the website for the schedule for the next quarter, and for prices and dates.

Only in Gold Country would a town as tiny as Volcano see a need to maintain its own theater company, complete with both indoor *and* outdoor performance spaces. At the **Volcano Theatre Company** (Main St., Volcano, 209/296-5495, www.volcanotheatre.org, shows Fri.–Sat. 8 P.M., Sun 2 P.M.), the wall of the outdoor amphitheater spans nearly half of one side of Volcano's lone main street, and the indoor space uses a storefront on the other side of that street. Highly regarded throughout the region, the amateur Volcano Theatre Company takes on some serious plays, such as William Nicholson's *Shadowlands* and *Of Mice and Men,* plus unusual comedies like John Cecil Holm's *Gramercy Ghost* and Barbara Pease Weber's *Delval Divas.* You'll see the summer plays in the amphitheater; bring your own chairs, thermoses of warm beverage, and blankets and coats to bundle up as the night cools off. In the spring and fall, shows go up at the 50-seat Cobblestone Theatre, and you'll need to purchase tickets early if you want to get in!

## Festivals and Events

If you crave more serious exercise, plan a trip to the northern Gold Country in late fall for the **Apple Hill Harvest Run** (Camino, www.applehillrun.org). This annual event includes an 8.5-mile loop, a 3.5-mile loop, and 0.25- and 0.5-mile kids' fun runs. Depending on your condition, pick one of the races and get running! The race starts early in the morning and finishes equally early—allowing racers to spend their afternoons perusing the orchards and wineries of Apple Hill. This race, which includes some major hills on the longer loop to challenge runners, benefits local schools.

# SHOPPING

## Antiques

Good retail opportunities abound on Main Street in Old Hangtown. The main shopping blocks run from the 300s through the 500s, and are easily walkable. Placerville is a great place to look for antiques and vintage collectibles. Half a dozen antique shops cluster on Main Street—for straight-ahead antique shops, hit **Empire Antiques** (432 Main St., Placerville, 530/642-1025) or the **Olde**

**Dorado Antique Emporium** (435 Main St., 530/622-4792).

### Art Galleries

Like most Gold Country towns, Placerville has a smattering of art galleries that appeal to a variety of shoppers. The **Bennett Gallery** (440 Main St., Placerville, 530/621-1164) displays art in a variety of media, from modern painting to hand-blown glass pieces. Local artists only show and sell their work at the **Gold Country Artist's Gallery** (379 Main St., Placerville, 530/642-2944). These Foothill artists create everything from painting and sculpture to pottery and gourd art.

At **Chaos Glassworks** (121 A Hanford St., 209/267-9317, Sutter Creek, www.chaosglassworks.com, Wed.–Fri. noon–7 P.M., Sat. 10 A.M.–7 P.M., Sun. 10 A.M.–6 P.M.), you can purchase handmade works of glass art, and watch the glassblower as he creates new pieces before your very eyes.

### Books

Just like the apparel shops, the bookstores of Placerville are unique to the town; get your reading material at either **The Bookery** (326 Main St., Placerville, 530/626-6454) or at **Hidden Passage Books** (352 Main St., Placerville, 530/622-4540).

### Clothing

You won't find any big chain clothing stores in Gold Country. Instead, shop in cute one-off boutiques like **Velvet's Treasures** (434 Main St., Placerville, 530/626-6120), **Empress** (582 Main St., Placerville, 530/642-2555), or **Placerville Clothing Co.** (327 Main St., Placerville, 530/626-3554).

### Gift and Home

To shop Sutter Creek, simply take a stroll down historic Main Street. You'll find cluttered antique shops filled with treasures great and small. For something from the Far East, walk into **Turning East** (205 C Amador Rd., 209/267-1121, Sutter Creek, daily 10 A.M.–5 P.M.). Peruse the lovely Asian furniture imported directly by the owners, plus hundreds of decorative items.

### Gourmet Goodies

Placerville hosts a surprising array of sweet shops. You can take your pick of gooey candies from **Sweet Cravings** (374 Main St., Placerville, 530/295-9144), **CandyStrike - Old Tyme Candy & More** (492 Main St., Placerville, 530/295-1007), or **Copper Kettle Candy** (366 Main St., Placerville, 530/622-6100). For something heartier, get some great cheese and artisan bread from **Dedrick's Main Street Cheese** (312 Main St., Placerville, 530/344-8282).

### Unique

If you prefer your art permanently affixed to your body, check out Placerville's tattoo shops, which include **Moontiger Tattoos** (438 Main St., Placerville, 530/295-3917) and **Hangtown Tattoo and Body Piercing** (537 Main St., Placerville, 530/642-9172).

## SPORTS AND RECREATION

While the museums and mines and quaint scenic towns of northern Gold Country have their appeal, many Californians visit the Sierra Foothills for entirely different reasons. The mixed woods, wilderness, and rivers of the region call to outdoor lovers of all stripes. Whether you fancy a quiet walk through the woods or an ultra-exciting ride down a roaring river, you'll find it here.

### Hiking

In addition to its fabulous historic park and museum, the **Empire Mine State Historic Park** (10791 E. Empire St., Grass Valley, 530/273-8522, www.empiremine.org) doubles as an outdoor hiking park. With 800 acres of former mining lands, this park offers both natural beauty and views of abandoned mines that are being overgrown as nature re-establishes dominance. The Hardrock Trail Area can run 1–3 miles, depending on how far you want to take it. Loop from the visitors center around to see the remains of the Pennsylvania, W.Y.O.D., and Orleans Mines before heading out to the Osborn Loop or back to the parking lot. The Hardrock Trail and its offshoots are reasonably flat and easy to hike, but be aware that you can hit rocky stretches and there are no bathroom facilities on the trails. Along the trail, you'll see, and in some cases climb on, the remains of the major hard-rock mines that once produced gold here. Grab a trail guide from the visitors center to get a better idea of what you're seeing while you're seeing it. A caution: While you're welcome to look and take photos of the mines along the trails, don't leave the trail to attempt to climb on, under, or through abandoned mine structures, and keep an eye on your children. These things can be incredibly dangerous.

Off the Hardrock Trail Area, you can head farther afield on the Osborn Hill Loop Trail Area to check out several more abandoned mines and their detritus. This loop runs about a mile on its own, and is a bit steeper and more challenging than the Hardrock trails.

Finally, if you prefer natural beauty to a manmade landscape, head off in the other direction to the Union Hill Trails. Here you'll find the Pipeline Trail, where the massive pipes that kept water pumping out of the mines still run—for fire protection now. The other Union Hill trails take you out into the Foothills wilderness that was the long-ago home of a Maidu Native American tribe.

For an easy leg-stretching walk, **Gold Bug Park** (see *Sights*) has 61 acres of forested parkland with marked trails. Enjoy the interpretive plaques that describe the local foliage and scenery.

## Biking

If you're looking for a guided bicycle tour through Gold Country, check out **Escape Travel** (916/419-5203, www.escapesactours.com). For about $100 per day, you can take a road bike out into the Amador Wine Country, heading through the Shenandoah Valley and tasting along the way. Or pedal out on a scenic tour of Amador and Sutter Creek, getting a close-up view of the major mining sights. If you prefer a mountain trek, head up into the Sierra Foothills and experience trails at whatever level you feel comfortable with. Advance reservations are required, and all experience levels are welcome.

## Whitewater Rafting and Kayaking

Northern Gold Country doubles as whitewater country from spring through fall. The North, South, and Middle Forks of the vast American River offer great rafting, whether you're an experienced Class V paddler or you've never set foot in a raft. The South Fork also beckons to beginner whitewater rafters, with lots of rapids but none over a Class III. The Middle Fork gets wilder, with some Class III and IV rapids—it's better for intermediate (or adventurous and athletic beginners) paddlers willing to traverse the legendary Tunnel Chute. The season for both Forks usually runs from April to October, but check online for specific dates.

One of the best of outfitters is **All-Outdoors Whitewater Rafting** (925/932-8993, www.aorafting.com, Mon.–Fri. 9 A.M.–5 P.M.). All-Outdoors offers half-day up to three-day trips on the South and Middle Forks of the American River. If all you want to do is float, or you have small children who'll be coming rafting with you, consider the half-day or full-day Tom Sawyer Float Trips down the rapids-free section of the South Fork. All All-Outdoors trips include a life jacket, helmet, safety instruction on dry land, and a certified river guide. On full-day trips, your guides will put together a near-gourmet meal for your party. If budget and time are short, the half-day trips make a great adventure. But if you're interested in exploring the true wilderness of Gold Country, a 2–3 day trip is perfect.

With **Beyond Limits Adventures** (800/234-7238, www.rivertrip.com) you can take half-day up to two-day trips on the South and Middle Forks. Overnight trips include all meals, plus a grassy, shaded campground where you can pitch your own tent or pay extra for tent cabin or yurt accommodations along the river. Shop at the camp store or grab a bite at the on-site snack bar. Beyond Limits loves introducing young people to the fun of the American River—check their website for family trips and special youth rates. But if you're with an up-for-anything rafting party of adults, ask about trips on the North Fork of the Yuba River. Available in spring only, the Yuba offers Class IV and V rapids on the longest stretch of heavy-duty whitewater in the state.

**American Whitewater Expeditions** (800/825-3205, www.americanwhitewater.com) can take you out to the South or Middle Forks, and also to the faster and whiter North Fork of the American River—a Class V adventure run by few companies. Trips run from half a day to three days, and include delicious dinners (with brew for of-age rafters on two- and three-day trips), knowledgeable guides, beautiful scenery, and all kinds of fun.

**O.A.R.S.** (800/346-6277, www.oars.com) also offers trips on the South, Middle, and North Forks of the American River. With almost 40 years' experience in California rafting and the one of highest guide-to-guest ratios in the business, O.A.R.S. will give you a friendly, personal trip to remember. They've got all the standard half- to two-day trips you want, plus a few surprises. Take O.A.R.S.'s South Fork Wine and Raft trip or consider one of the multi-Fork trips.

### Golf

Golf addicts can find plenty to keep themselves busy in northern Gold Country in the summer. One of the best courses in the area is the highly rated public **Castle Oaks Golf Club** (1000 Castle Oaks Dr., Ione, 209/274-0167, www.castleoaksgolf.com, $13–60). This 18-hole, par 71 championship course offers five different levels of tee, making it fun for golfers of any skill level. Lots of water features make the game interesting, and the relatively flat terrain makes for a lovely walk. Located in Ione, west of Jackson and Plymouth, Castle Oaks makes a perfect diversion from the endless museums, mines, and wineries of the area. Even if you're just looking for practice, Castle Oaks has a driving range, chipping green, and putting green for your use. The club recommends that you book your tee time at least one week in advance.

East of Jackson on uncrowded Highway 88, enjoy a game at the **Mace Meadow Golf and Country Club** (26570 Fairway Dr., Pioneer, 209/295-7272, www.macemeadow.com, $10–32, carts extra). This public course offers 18 holes at par 72 for reasonable rates. Three tee levels provide action for beginners, intermediates, and advanced golfers. Check the website for a hole-by-hole description of this course, plus online tee-time reservation and Internet fee specials. Before (or after) your game, kick back and enjoy breakfast or lunch at the Country Club's restaurant, or just grab a quick snack at the Snack Shack.

## ACCOMMODATIONS

The accommodations in northern Gold Country run to quaint bed-and-breakfast inns. Many are reasonably priced for the level of comfort you get, though you can also find some seriously upscale inns if you've got the money to shell out. If B&B decor gives you hives, you can find a few vacation rentals and historic hotels as well. For folks who absolutely must stay in a generic chain, Auburn is a good town to hit for a totally average Travelodge or Comfort Inn.

### Under $100

For a budget hotel adventure deep in northern Gold Country, get off the highway and head for the **St. George Hotel** (16104 Main St., Volcano, 209/296-4458, www.stgeorgehotel.com, $66–140). The only hotel in the tiny town of Volcano, the St. George gives its guests a serious vintage Gold Country hotel experience. The attractively shabby building houses a hodgepodge of all-different second- and third-floor hotel rooms. You can also get an individual bungalow out in the back of the main hotel. As befits a 19th-century mining town hostelry, no rooms in the main building have private baths (though the bungalows do). You must share the hall baths with your fellow guests. Whatever bed configuration you need for your party, you'll find at the St. George—including an ultra-cheap room for solo travelers. In your room, you'll see polished wood floors, antique-styled bedsteads, and floral or quilt-style bedspreads. Take your morning coffee out onto the wraparound verandah each morning to enjoy the cool early hours before the Gold Country heats up in the summertime.

You don't have to go too far for food and entertainment if you're staying at the St. George. Some of the best food in Amador County is served in the restaurant downstairs, The Whiskey Flat Saloon sits right next door, and the Volcano Theatre Company performs in the amphitheater across the street and the small indoor theater down the block.

## $100-150

With the ethos of a classic B&B and the fun touches of a hostel, you'll find the perfect lodging mix at **Hanford House** (61 Hanford St., Sutter Creek, 209/267-0747, www.hanfordhouse.com, $120–275). Unlike the endless Victorians you see in the various Gold Country towns, the Hanford House is a brick manor house. Nine guest rooms grace the interior, each decorated in a floral country style with unique furnishings and textiles. Beds are large and comfy, and bathrooms squeak with cleanliness and feel a little bit like home. When you come to enjoy the hearty breakfast in the morning, don't bother picking up a newspaper. Instead, pass your morning reading the walls and ceiling of the inn. Guests have signed and commented on the plain white walls over the years;they're almost full now, so if you feel a need to add your own John Hancock, you'll have to hunt for a bare spot.

The **Imperial Hotel** (14202 Hwy. 49, Amador City, 209/267-9172, www.imperialamador.com, $115–250) shows off the brick facade and narrow-column architecture of a classic Old West hotel. You'll get a true mining town hotel experience, getting one of six bedrooms on the second floor of the building, or one of three new rooms in the "cottage" out back. These rooms have been updated to include private baths, and are done in simple antique styles that make use of the redbrick interior walls as part of the decor. Your guest room is a haven of peace of quiet, without a TV or even a telephone to bother you. Music and literature make the entertainment at the Imperial. Downstairs, you can take all your meals, including the full hot breakfast that's part of your room rate. Dinner is a special time, featuring gourmet California cuisine made with local organic produce, natural meats, and sustainable seafood.

The **Amador Harvest Inn** (12455 Steiner Rd., Plymouth, 800/217-2304, www.amadorharvestinn.com, $140–160) brings a bit of uptown Napa to the Shenandoah Valley while retaining the down-home feel of Amador County. The outside of the inn feels perfectly unpretentious—a simple farmhouse set on a green lawn surrounded by trees and water. Inside you'll find four guest rooms named for wine grapes, each decorated in a charming country style. Yet the interior feeling is more elegant than the sum of its parts; you could imagine paying half again as much for the same room in Yountville. The dining room continues the farmhouse charm, with kitchen-style tables and chairs waiting for guests to sit and enjoy a home-cooked breakfast each morning. Nearby, you can visit the Deaver Winery and the Amador Flower Farm. The Amador Harvest Inn makes a perfect base from which to explore the whole of the Shenandoah Valley wine country and perhaps beyond.

For a more hippie-California experience in the backwoods of the Foothills, book a cabin at **Rancho Cicada Retreat** (10001 Bell Rd, Plymouth, 209/245-4841, www.ranchocicadaretreat.com, $106–159). The retreat offers both tent cabins and wood-sided cabins, most of which share common single-sex bathrooms. The main attraction of the Rancho runs along outside the tent cabins: the Cosumnes River. Visitors can swim, inner tube, and fish in the river, and your hosts will happily tell you about good spots to bag a trout and peaceful holes to enjoy a relaxing dip. Or you can visit the riverside hot tubs, perhaps after an old-fashioned sweat in the Mi-Wok sweat lodge.

Be aware that Rancho Cicada offers primitive

lodgings. You'll need to bring your own sleeping bags or bedding and pillows, towels, and food to cook, plus ice chests for drinks (refrigerators are provided for perishable foods).

If you're looking for casual accommodations at the right price, consider the **49er Village** (18265 Hwy. 49, Plymouth, 800/339-6981, www.49ervillage.com, $105–150 cabin rentals). Primarily an asphalt-covered RV park, the 49er Village also rents studio and one-bedroom vacation cabins for reasonable rates. Cabins include private bathrooms, full kitchens with utensils, private decks, and full access to park pools and amenities. One-bedroom cabins can sleep five or six people.

### $150-250

For elegance in the land of Gold, you can't beat the **Emma Nevada House** (528 E. Broad St., Nevada City, 800/916-3662, www.emmanevadahouse.com, $190–275). History permeates this large Victorian house, which once belonged to the family of a noted opera singer named Emma Nevada. You'll see real antiquities in the front rooms, and charming collectibles in the guest rooms. The guest rooms all have comfortable beds, attractive appointments, and plush bathrooms, some with clawfoot tubs. Whichever of the six uniquely styled rooms you choose, you're sure to enjoy your stay here. Your hosts can help you with whatever you need, and they have plenty of real opinions about the restaurants and sights in their area. Breakfast is served each morning—come out early to get a seat in the sun room, definitely the best breakfast seat in the house. You'll get a gourmet multi-course treat to fortify yourself for a day out exploring El Dorado and Amador Counties.

For a more up-to-date bed-and-breakfast experience, plus great access to a fabulous wine region, book at room at **Lucinda's Country Inn** (6701 Perry Creek Rd., Fair Play, 888/245-8246, www.lucindascountryinn.com, $190–225). You'll drive up to a thoroughly modern large home, surrounded by green lawns, meadows, and forests. (Keep an eye out for deer!) With the stylings of a luxury hotel, each of the five guest rooms welcomes visitors and convinces them to settle in and stay a while. You'll find classy understated room decor, a fireplace, your own fridge, microwave, and coffee maker, plush robes to relax in, and maybe even a two-person spa tub. Even folks who usually can't take the overwhelming floweriness of most B&Bs will feel comfortable at Lucinda's, with its simple breakfast tables and homelike common rooms. Outside the inn, you've got a great chance to delve into the Fair Play wine region, or to head not too far out to the Shenandoah Valley.

## FOOD

Depending on which town you're in, you'll find everything from one lone hotel restaurant to an array of ethnic eats to a shocking plethora of high-end California cuisine. With relatively easy drives between clusters of towns, you don't need to eat where you're staying. Instead, pick something close to your favorite sights, or choose a restaurant for its own sake.

### California

For some of the best dining in one of the smallest towns in northern Gold Country, have dinner at the **St. George Hotel** (16104 Main St., Volcano, 209/296-4458, www.stgeorgehotel.com, Thurs.–Sun. 5:30–9 P.M., Sun. 9:30 A.M.–2 P.M., $18–27). The white-tablecloth dining room feels fancy yet intimate, with homey touches throughout the violet-colored space. The menu includes an array of upscale entrées, complete with California-style preparations, sauces, and seasonings. Much of the produce comes from local farms, and the herbs are often snipped from the St. George's own backyard garden. The small but interesting wine list focuses heavily on Amador County vintages, though other parts of California and a few European wineries are represented as well. On Sundays, stop by for a hearty brunch.

### Italian

For delicious and inventive Italian food, go to **Cirino's** (309 Broad St., Nevada City, 530/265-2246, lunch Fri.–Sun. 11 A.M.–4 P.M., dinner Sun.–Thurs. 5–9 P.M.,

Fri.–Sat. 5–10 P.M.). This cute, locally favored restaurant offers plenty of tables, a full bar, a relaxed atmosphere, and a large, innovative, and reasonably priced menu. Start with a cocktail from the bar, which doubles as a local watering hole. Enjoy a salad or an appetizer off the antipasti menu, then move on to the main event. The portions, especially of the pasta, are enormous. Despite this, you'll have a hard time resisting the array of delectable pasta dishes, plus the yummy entrées made with seafood, poultry, and meat (even veal). The service is friendly and helpful with menu questions, and the overall feel of the place will encourage you to sit back and enjoy your meal without rushing.

### Mexican

Looking for a good taco or burrito in the northernmost end of Gold Country? Have a meal at **Las Katarinas Mexican Restaurant** (311 Broad St., Nevada City, 530/478-0275, Sun.–Mon. and Wed.–Thurs. 11 A.M.–9 P.M., Fri.–Sat. 11 A.M.–10 P.M.). Right in the middle of the main drag, Las Katarinas doesn't pretend to be anything fancy. You'll find all your favorite items on the menu: enchiladas, tacos, tostadas, and such, plus chile colorado and verde. Dishes are made with whole, fresh ingredients. Vegetarians can get lard-free dishes, while Mexican purists can enjoy the rich taste of traditionally prepared foods. Beware: The salsa's got some kick to it! For children with more sensitive palates, smaller and less spicy entrées populate the kids' menu. The full bar serves Mexican beers, California wines, and strong margaritas. The dining room exudes a casually welcoming feel, and you'll feel perfectly comfortable dining in jeans and a T-shirt.

### Bakeries

Baked goods are the thing to eat in Gold Country. Between the traditional Cornish pastie–makers and the organic patisseries, this is a pastry-lover's heaven. You'll find a good bakery in most every town you visit—just look around and take a chance.

Unpretentious and unassuming, the **Flour Garden Café and Bakery** (999 Sutton Way, Grass Valley, 530/272-2043, Mon.–Sat. 5 A.M.–7 P.M., Sun. 6 A.M.–6 P.M.) serves homemade pastries, soups, sandwiches, cakes, and more to a mostly local crowd who prefer something good to something trendy. Part of what makes this Gold Country mini-chain great is that they use natural, organic ingredients in all their food. If you're looking for an early-morning continental breakfast, purchase an unbelievably flakey and delicious pastry—made with real butter and homemade fruit fillings—plus an espresso drink or a plain old cup of good Fair Trade coffee. For lunch, pick up any number of to-go prepared items, have a sandwich made, grab a baguette to make your own sandwich, or order a bowl of the fresh homemade soup of the day. A menu published monthly describes the hearty hot soups, which make a meal in themselves. Those with dietary restrictions are not left out; ask about vegetarian, vegan, and gluten-free options at the counter. The Flour Garden is beloved by locals, and there's often a line at mealtimes.

Best of all, the Flour Garden has three locations in Gold Country to serve you. Also check out the downtown Grass Valley location at 109 Neal Street and the Auburn store at 340 C Elm Avenue.

If you're in tiny Volcano and you're just longing for a traditional Cornish pastie or a slice of homemade sweet pie, stop in at **Humble Pies** (16154 Main St., Volcano, 209/296-8066, Wed.–Fri. 8 A.M.–5:30 P.M., Sat.–Sun. 8 A.M.–5 P.M., $3–4 single serving). This tiny business has attained more success than even the owners anticipated, so come early for your favorite pie or you may find Humble Pies sold out. The Cornish pasties, whether beef or vegetarian, make a filling lunch. But don't let that stop you from getting a slice of in-season fruit pie or even an old-school, homemade fry pie for dessert. Round out your meal with a latte or a macchiato, and consider adding a "Panic Button" (extra shot of espresso) if you're having trouble getting started.

### Coffee and Tea

Looking for a great cup of coffee from an indie coffee house? If you're in Sutter

## APPLE HILL EATERIES

There's plenty of good, healthy food to be had in the Apple Hill region. But what if you need more than a nice, fresh apple to keep hunger away? Stop at one of the orchard-based restaurant along the meandering trails. A number of these offer a variety of foods, from sandwiches to hot handmade apple pies. The area maps available at almost every orchard point out which establishments offer a restaurant.

Perhaps the best place for lunch in the whole of Apple Hill is the kitschy **Bavarian Hills Orchard** (3100 N. Canyon Rd., Camino, 530/642-2714, Sept.-Dec. daily 11 A.M.-5 P.M., June-Aug. weekends only). Oompah music blares from speakers outside of the white-gingerbread-trimmed brown barn buildings that house the store and the restaurant. Walk into the unprepossessing cafeteria-style restaurant, with its linoleum floor, walk-up counter with refrigerator cases, and tile-lettered menu on the wall. Order a sausage on a roll with some traditional German side dishes, and strap in for one of the best surprises you'll encounter on your trip to Gold Country. Your food will be brought on paper plates to whatever table you can find, inside or outside. The sausages are phenomenal, and the side dishes – from the warm German potato salad to the sauerkraut to the braised red cabbage – are homemade from scratch daily. The owner brought the recipes to Apple Hill from her Bavarian home, and her dedication to creating great authentic German food shows. Finally, your dessert can be any sort of apple pastry, though there's little reason to avoid the homemade strudel from the orchard's own apples.

A "lunch" includes a sausage on a roll, a side dish, and dessert. Portions are eminently reasonable. If you've got a hearty appetite, order an extra side dish or two – they're tasty enough to make it worth it. Or you can get an extra portion of strudel for dessert!

If you're just looking for a fresh slice of pie, some of the best you'll find is sold at the **Apple Pantry Farm** (2310 Hidden Valley Ln., Camino, 530/295-1001, Sept.-Nov. Fri.-Sun. 10 A.M.-4 P.M.). First you'll see the attractive small store, selling apples and an array of frozen uncooked pies ready to be baked in your home oven. Just up and to the right of the main store, a small trailer exudes aromas that draw visitors as if by magic. You can buy just a slice or a whole apple, apple-blackberry, or

---

Creek, get in line at **Sutter Creek Coffee Roasting Company** (20 Eureka St., Sutter Creek, 888/219-4127, www.suttercreekcoffee.com, Mon.–Sat. 6:30 A.M.–5 P.M., Sun. 8 A.M.–2 P.M.). Choose from your favorite regular coffee, espresso drinks, cold blended coffee drinks, chai, and more. On a typically blistering summer day in Sutter Creek, enjoy a snow cone. Or if it's lunchtime, choose from the tasty sandwiches, daily hot dishes, salads, and desserts. For a special treat, stop by on Wednesday, Thursday, or Friday to inhale the intoxicating aroma of coffee beans roasting in-house.

Love your traditional afternoon tea? You can indulge your whims in Sutter Creek at the **Tea Eras Tea Room & Gifts** (34 Main St., Sutter Creek, 209/267-0333, www.teaerastearoom.com, daily 11 A.M.–3 P.M.). A charming alternative to a plain ol' lunch, you can order a full tea service with scones, finger sandwiches, salad, savories, and desserts. Plus tea, of course! Several alternative tea services cater to all appetite sizes, while the è la carte menu offers salads and sandwiches to those who need something more substantial (or less substantial!) for their repast. All this is served in a Victorian atmosphere inside a cute, white wood-framed house in old downtown Sutter Creek.

## INFORMATION AND SERVICES

As a spread-out array of small towns with undeveloped mountainous countryside in between, northern Gold Country doesn't have quite the same plethora of services you'd find in the Bay Area or the Los Angeles Basin. If you need the services of a major city, Sacramento is your

other seasonal fruit pie the likes of which your grandmother wished she could bake. Ask the proprietress if she buys her crusts premade, and she'll look at you as though you'd asked her if she enjoys torturing puppies. Every crumb of every Apple Pantry pie gets made from scratch and slices are sold hot out of the industrial ovens in the trailer. While some say that the apple-blackberry with the crumble crust is the best, everyone has their own take on which pie rules the Pantry. (The frozen ready-bake pies in the shop below are made by the same team; if you've got the means to transport them, pick up as many as you can.)

© LIZ HAMILL SCOTT

closest bet. Out on Highway 49, Auburn is the largest town in this area.

## Tourist Information

Many of the little burgs have their own small visitors centers, usually on or near the local Main Street. The **Nevada City Chamber of Commerce** (132 Main St., 530/265-2692, www.nevadacitychamber.com, Mon.–Fri. 9 A.M.–5 P.M., Sat.–Sun. 11 A.M.–4 P.M.) doubles as the visitors center. Visit while you're in town, or check the website ahead of time for a wealth of information, including a thoughtful and helpful list of public restrooms in town.

## Media and Communications

If you're looking for a major daily paper, pick up the ***Sacramento Bee.*** For a more local take on Nevada City and Grass Valley, read ***The Union*** (www.theunion.com), the Nevada County daily. In Amador, the local twice-weekly paper ***Amador Ledger-Dispatch*** provides information about local entertainment happenings. Several of the little towns have their own weekly or biweekly papers as well, and many of these are free.

A great online visitors guide to the Nevada County area is **Nevada County Gold** (www.ncgold.com). Most of Gold Country is covered in the pages of ***Sierra Heritage Magazine*** (www.sierraheritage.com), a travel magazine dedicated to the Sierra Nevadas and the Foothill region.

Some of the tiny Gold Rush towns did not retain many services when they busted after the gold ran out. In Volcano, for example, you won't find much in the way of bank branches or gas stations. On the other hand, Auburn has all the amenities of a small city, complete with gas stations near the highways, ATMs, and even big-box stores. You'll find ATMs and the occasional bank branch in Nevada City and Grass Valley as well.

Much of Gold Country has cashed in on California's new gold: the Internet. You'll find Internet cafés, hotels with Wi-Fi, and even the occasional war-hackable spot in each of the little towns. Outside of the towns, you won't see much other than trees, grass, and abandoned mines.

**Post offices** sit in Nevada City at 29453 Highway 49 and in Grass Valley at 185 East Main Street. In Auburn, you can mail a letter at 13116 Lincoln Way, and in Placerville, there's a post office at 3045 Sacramento Street.

### Medical Services

For medical assistance, **Sutter Auburn Faith Hospital** (11815 Education St., Auburn, 530/888-4500, http://sutterauburnfaith.org) offers an emergency room and a full range of hospital services. To the north, the major hospital with an emergency room is **Sierra Nevada Memorial Hospital** (155 Glasson Way, Grass Valley, 530/274-6000, www.snmh.org).

## GETTING THERE AND AROUND

When you're in Gold Country, you're out of the big cities and into the California countryside. Your public transit options diminish the farther you get from Sacramento. However, you can still find your way, even with minimal driving. Bicycling in the spring and fall is a great green alternative.

### Air

The closest major airport to the northern Gold Country is the Sacramento International Airport. (See the *Sacramento* section for more information.) General aviation airports abound in the area. You can fly into the **Nevada County Airport** (13083 John Bauer Ave., Grass Valley, 530/273-3347, www.nevadacountyairport.com). Car rentals are available here with Hertz and Enterprise.

### Bus

The **Gold Country Stage** (http://new.mynevadacounty.com/transit, adults $1, children under 6 free, day pass $3) runs buses and minibuses through Nevada City, Grass Valley, down south to Auburn, and up to points north of Gold Country.

### Car

To explore northern Gold Country in depth, your best bet is to rent a car or bring your own. The major thoroughfare, Highway 49, doesn't get city-level crowded even in the high season. Highway 88 delineates the south end of northern Gold Country in this book. To get out to Gold Country from Sacramento (or the Bay Area), you'll take Highway 80, which can get jammed up around the big city.

Parking in the little North Gold Country towns usually isn't too difficult. Most street parking is free or metered, so bring a few quarters on your tours. The historic parks include either complimentary parking or fee parking at the entrance gates.

### Tours

Much of the history of Gold Country isn't found in its museums. To get a real flavor for the Gold Rush era, you need to get out into the little towns that dot the landscape. You can pretty much walk any of the historic downtowns in Northern Gold Country to get a sense of place. Most towns offer a historic tour map to help you pick out the coolest spots.

If you're interested in the mines, take a drive along the **Sutter Creek Gold Mine Trail** (www.suttercreek.org). Highways 49 and 88 are the main thoroughfares through the Amador County gold mining district—a commercial map of the area makes a good companion to the hand-drawn map in the official brochure.

Fall visitors to this area are in for a special treat not usually associated with California: fall colors. Nevada County limns itself in gold and red each October and November, beckoning visitors and locals alike out for walks in the brisk autumn air. For the best colors, take walks in the historic Victorian sections of Grass

Valley and Nevada City. A tour map put out by the Nevada County Chamber of Commerce (www.ncgold.com) points to the best routes for the prettiest trees and shrubs.

If it's agriculture and eco-tourism you're after, take a tour of the **El Dorado County Farm Trails** (530/620-1415, www.edc-farm trails.org). You can get a map from most El Dorado town visitors centers, in the County Visitors Guide, or at the website. Including the famed Apple Hill as well as numerous other agricultural areas stretching all the way up to South Lake Tahoe, the Farm Trails encompass more than 100 farms, ranches, wineries, nurseries, and orchards that make up this diverse growing region. Easily visible signs along the roads can point you to the farms that are part of this association-all of which you can visit. Pet an alpaca, smell the lavender or the Christmas trees, pick your own apples or berries, and sip the latest vintage wines on your Farm Trails tour. If you're really interested in agriculture, you could spend several days exploring the Farm Trails of El Dorado.

# Southern Gold Country

Southern Gold Country runs from the town of Jackson down almost to the Yosemite Valley. You'll find that the Native Sons of the Golden West and other such associations must have gotten two-for-one deals at the Historic Monument store. Every few miles along Highway 49 and the roads through Sonora and Jamestown, you'll see a plaque affixed to a boulder commemorating some historic person or event. History buffs will enjoy a slow journey through the area, stopping to read each one. Some really are worth reading—you'll find bronze commemorations of everything from the local hanging tree to the ladies of the evening who made life more, um, bearable for the rough men working the mines.

You'll also find museums, caverns, mines, parks, wineries, and great restaurants and quirky hotels in this region.

Southern Gold Country includes the towns of Jackson, Murphys, Angels Camp, Columbia, Jamestown, and Sonora. Highway 49 can take you north–south through the region. Highway 4 runs northeast–southwest, intersecting Highway 49 at Angels Camp and running east to Murphys. Highway 4 also runs south from Vallecito to Columbia and then on down to Sonora. You can also drive Highway 49 all the way down to Jamestown, then pick up Highway 108 east to Sonora.

## SIGHTS

From Native American life and times to historic hard-rock mines to natural deep underground caverns, southern Gold Country has something for everyone. Nature lovers can hike in the parks and spelunk in the caves, history buffs can explore the mining era, and everyone can join in the fun.

### Calaveras Big Trees State Park

Can't get enough of the California redwoods? Take some time away from mining history and visit Calaveras Big Trees State Park (three miles east of Arnold on Hwy. 4, 209/795-2334, www.bigtrees.org, summer sunrise–sunset, winter 11 A.M.–3 P.M.). The highlights of the park are the North and South Groves of rare giant sequoia trees; be sure to take a walk in both groves to check out the landmark trees and stumps. Beyond the sequoias, you can hike and bike in the 6,000 acres of pine forest crisscrossed with trails and scattered with campgrounds (call 800/444-7275 for reservations) and pretty groves set up for picnicking. Feel free to take a dip in the cool, refreshing Stanislaus River running through the trees, or cast a line out to try to catch a rainbow trout. In the winter, break out the snowshoes and cross-country skis—the trails are marked for winter sports as well as summer.

Start your day at the visitors center, where

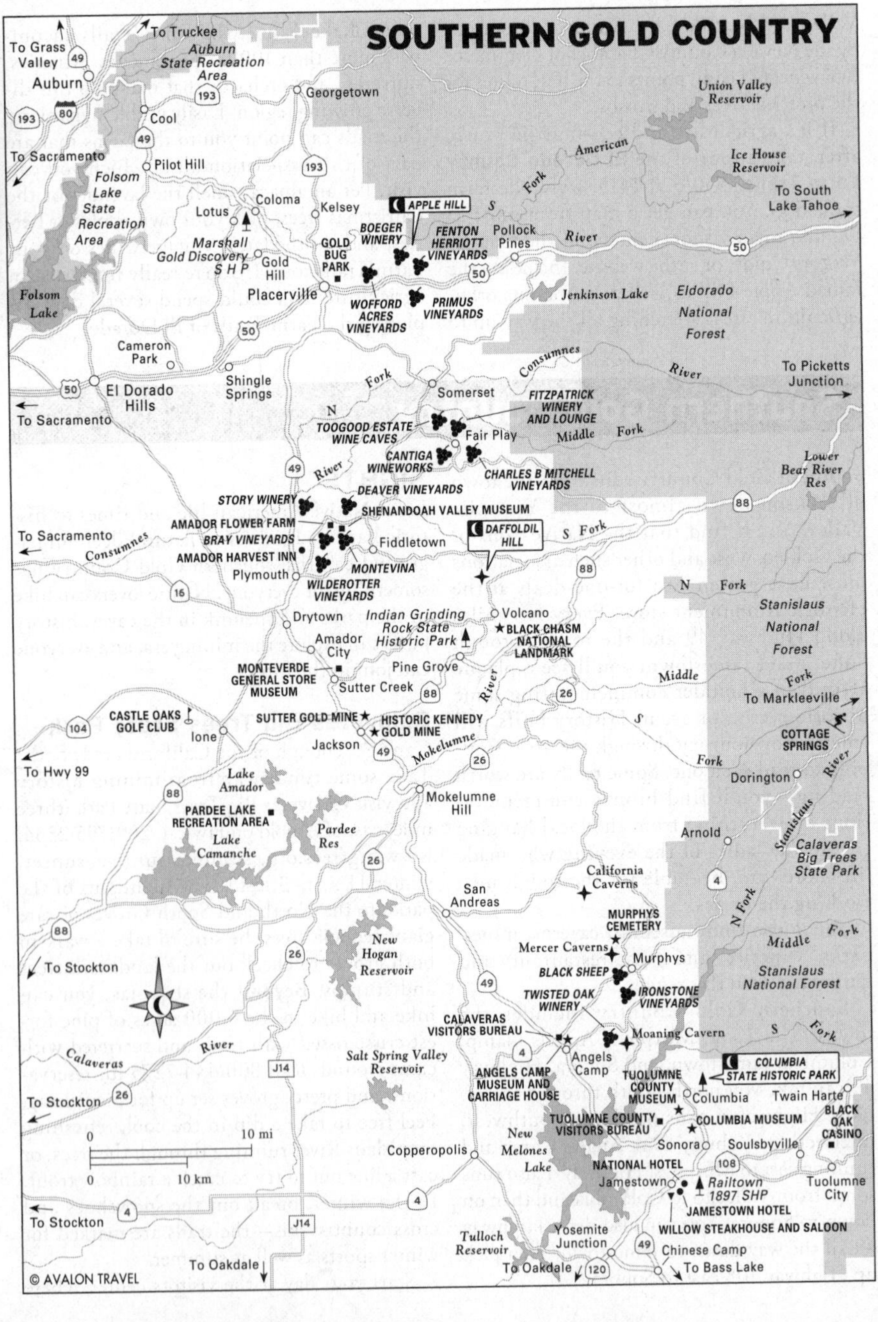

SOUTHERN GOLD COUNTRY
To Grass Valley
To Truckee
Auburn State Recreation Area
Auburn
Georgetown
Cool
Pilot Hill
To Sacramento
Folsom Lake State Recreation Area
Union Valley Reservoir
American
Fork
Ice House Reservoir
To South Lake Tahoe
Coloma
Lotus
Kelsey
APPLE HILL
BOEGER WINERY
FENTON HERRIOTT VINEYARDS
Pollock Pines
River
Marshall Gold Discovery SHP
Gold Hill
GOLD BUG PARK
Placerville
Folsom Lake
WOFFORD ACRES VINEYARDS
PRIMUS VINEYARDS
Jenkinson Lake
Eldorado National Forest
Cameron Park
Consumnes
River
Shingle Springs
Fork
Somerset
To Picketts Junction
El Dorado Hills
To Sacramento
FITZPATRICK WINERY AND LOUNGE
TOOGOOD ESTATE WINE CAVES
Fair Play
Middle Fork
CANTIGA WINEWORKS
CHARLES B MITCHELL VINEYARDS
Lower Bear River Res
River
DEAVER VINEYARDS
STORY WINERY
SHENANDOAH VALLEY MUSEUM
AMADOR FLOWER FARM
DAFFOLDIL HILL
To Sacramento
BRAY VINEYARDS
Consumnes
Fiddletown
S Fork
AMADOR HARVEST INN
MONTEVINA
Plymouth
WILDEROTTER VINEYARDS
N Fork
Stanislaus National Forest
Drytown
Indian Grinding Rock State Historic Park
Volcano
BLACK CHASM NATIONAL LANDMARK
Amador City
MONTEVERDE GENERAL STORE MUSEUM
Pine Grove
Sutter Creek
Middle Fork
River
To Markleeville
CASTLE OAKS GOLF CLUB
SUTTER GOLD MINE
HISTORIC KENNEDY GOLD MINE
Ione
COTTAGE SPRINGS
Jackson
Mokelumne
To Hwy 99
S Fork
Dorington
River
Lake Amador
Mokelumne Hill
PARDEE LAKE RECREATION AREA
Pardee Res
Lake Camanche
Arnold
Stanislaus
Calaveras Big Trees State Park
California Caverns
San Andreas
N Fork
MURPHYS CEMETERY
Middle Fork
Mercer Caverns
Murphys
To Stockton
New Hogan Reservoir
BLACK SHEEP
IRONSTONE VINEYARDS
Stanislaus National Forest
TWISTED OAK WINERY
CALAVERAS VISITORS BUREAU
Moaning Cavern
S Fork
River
Calaveras
Salt Spring Valley Reservoir
Angels Camp
ANGELS CAMP MUSEUM AND CARRIAGE HOUSE
COLUMBIA STATE HISTORIC PARK
To Stockton
TUOLUMNE COUNTY MUSEUM
Columbia
Twain Harte
TUOLUMNE COUNTY VISITORS BUREAU
COLUMBIA MUSEUM
BLACK OAK CASINO
0
10 mi
0
10 km
New Melones Lake
Copperopolis
Sonora
Soulsbyville
NATIONAL HOTEL
Jamestown
Railtown 1897 SHP
Tuolumne City
To Stockton
JAMESTOWN HOTEL
WILLOW STEAKHOUSE AND SALOON
Tulloch Reservoir
Yosemite Junction
Chinese Camp
To Oakdale
To Oakdale
To Bass Lake
© AVALON TRAVEL

you can talk to rangers about the best hikes for you, and pick up trail maps for several of the major hiking areas in the park. In the wintertime, you'll find many of the roads through the park closed, but drive in as far as you can and snowshoe or ski from there.

### Columbia State Historic Park

A stroll down Main Street in Columbia State Historic Park (11255 Jackson St., Columbia, 209/588-9128) is a stroll into California's boomtown past. It's free to wander the streets of the park, which encompasses most of the downtown area. If possible, start with the **Columbia Museum** (corner of Main and State Sts.). Here you'll discover the history of this, one of the early California mining towns. Gold was discovered here in the spring of 1850, and the town sprang up as miners flowed in, growing to become one of California's largest cities for a short time. It inevitably declined as the gold ran out, and in 1945 the state took it over and created the State Historic Park. In the museum, you'll see artifacts of the mining period, from miners' equipment and clothing to the household objects used by women who lived in the bustling city. After the museum, walk the streets, poking your head into the exhibits and shops selling an array of period and modern items. Examine the contents of the Dry Goods Store, imagine multiculturalism of another age in the Chinese Store Exhibit, or grab a bite to eat in the City Hotel Saloon.

This large indoor-outdoor museum experience is an easy flat walk, with plenty of wheelchair-accessible areas. The horses, carriages, and staff in pioneer costume delight children visiting the site. It can get hot in the summer and cold in winter, and you'll be on your feet a lot, so dress accordingly and wear sensible shoes. Docent-led tours happen each Saturday and Sunday at 11 A.M. Check the park schedule for dates of living history events held here.

### Railtown 1897 State Historic Park

Where the State Railroad Museum in Sacramento brings the trains inside to you,

ROBERT HOLMES / CALTOUR

store window in Columbia State Historic Park

Railtown 1897 (Hwy. 108, Jamestown, 209/984-3953, www.railtown1897.org, Apr.–Oct. daily 9:30 A.M.–4:30 P.M., Nov.–Mar. daily 10 A.M.–3 P.M., free, adults $2, children $1) invites you out to the trains. Much of this museum and oft-used film location is scattered on tracks outdoors. But the best plan is to start inside; the old depot waiting room includes artifacts and a video describing the filmography of the Railtown trains. You'll see signs from *Petticoat Junction* (a black-and-white "wild west" sitcom) and locomotives used in all sorts of films and TV shows. Prize locomotives sit in the century-old roundhouse. Some of the locomotives are undergoing active and messy restoration. Tools and parts lie all over the roundhouse and the large machine shop, and can be dangerous to small children and careless adults. Restoration buffs will drool over the work being done and the pieces of historic railroading strewn about the landscape. Train fans, history lovers, film buffs, and children all love this unusual indoor-outdoor museum. Behind the roundhouse you can check out the functioning turntable, then wander out to the rolling stock (some of it in fairly decrepit condition right now) and poke around a little.

Want to ride in the classic cars behind the great old steam locomotives you've seen? You can! From April through October, you can take a six-mile, 40-minute ride out into the woodsy Sierra Foothills. Trains depart on the hour 11 A.M.–3 P.M. If you're in town for the winter, check for holiday-themed rides in November and December.

## Angels Camp Museum & Carriage House

Among the many museums that litter the ground in Gold Country, the Angels Camp Museum & Carriage House (753 S. Main St., Angels Camp, 209/736-2963, www.angelscamp.gov/museum.htm, Mar.–Dec. daily 10 A.M.–3 P.M. and Jan.–Feb. Sat.–Sun. 10 A.M.–3 P.M.) still offers a unique visitor experience. Inside the main museum building, you'll get to see meticulously preserved artifacts of the mining era. Outside, you'll find old, and in some cases decrepit, mining equipment. The huge waterwheel sits in its original position in Angels Camp. A treat for transportation lovers, the Carriage House shelters more than 30 horse-powered vehicles of the 19th and early 20th centuries. Better restored than many similar displays, the carriages and wagons here show off the elegance and function of true horse-powered transportation.

## Historic Kennedy Gold Mine

The Historic Kennedy Gold Mine (Hwy. 49 and Hwy 88, Jackson, 209/223-9542, www.kennedygoldmine.com, guided tours Mar.–Oct. Sat.–Sun. 10 A.M.–3 P.M.) is a great place to bring your family to learn about life in a California gold mine. The Kennedy mine was one of the deepest hard-rock gold mines in the state, extending more than a mile down into the earth. Tour the stately Mine House, marvel at the size of the head frame, and learn how a stamp mill worked to free the gold from the rocks. For the best experience, take a guided tour and learn the true stories of the mine.

## Indian Grinding Rock State Historic Park

Unlike most of the California State Historic Parks, Indian Grinding Rock State Historic Park (14881 Pine Grove-Volcano Rd., 209/296-7488) focuses on the history of the state before the European invasion. This park celebrates the life and culture of the Miwok, specifically the Northern Sierra Miwok who inhabited the Foothills for countless centuries. One of the central aspects of Miwok life was the grinding of acorns, the principal food. Women came to the grinding rock to grind and then soak their acorns for the day's meals. The park's focal point is a huge grinding rock, one used by all the women of the group who lived in the adjacent meadow and forest. The dozens of divots in the rock, plus the fading petroglyphs drawn over generations, attest to the lengthy use this chunk of marble. (The grinding rock's marble is frail; please don't walk on it!)

Follow the pathways past the grinding rock to the reconstructed roundhouse (a sacred space

© LIZ HAMILL SCOTT

Indian Grinding Rock State Historical Park

in current use by local Miwoks, so please be respectful). Then walk farther toward the Miwok village. Here, you can enter the dwellings to see how the Native Californians lived. If you're up for a longer hike, the North Trail winds around most of the total acreage of the park. For a deeper look into Miwok history, spend some time in the visitors center and museum.

### Tuolumne County Museum

If you can hit only one "local" museum in your journey through southern Gold Country, make it the Tuolumne County Museum (158 Bradford St., Sonora, 209/532-1317, www.tchistory.org). The county fathers (and mothers) took entertaining advantage of the museum's location in the old Sonora jailhouse; a number of exhibits sit inside cells, and one cell has been re-created as an exhibit of what incarceration might have been like in 19th-century Tuolumne County. (Unpleasant.) Appropriate homage is paid to a Mr. Tom Horn, a prisoner who died in a jailhouse fire—one he set himself in an ill-conceived escape attempt. Oops!

Throughout the rest of the museum, you'll find plenty of artifacts from the mines, shops, and homes of the county. Interpretive areas describe the process of hard-rock mining, the arduous journey the would-be gold miners took to get from the East to California, and the history of the county.

### Murphys Cemetery

Running up the hill outside downtown Murphys, the Murphys Cemetery (183 Jones St., Murphys) has been in continuous use since the 1860s. It sits adjacent to the old schoolhouse museum up on a small rising hill. You can drive through many parts of the graveyard, which is a good thing unless you've got several hours to spare wandering through the plots. A small fenced area denotes the space where members of the Masonic Order can be buried with their families. Despite its size and the obvious regular maintenance, this cemetery has plenty of ghostly atmosphere. An endless parade of slightly crooked marble and granite markers meander across the acres, and a few elderly oak trees provide light shade for the dead and their visitors. If you enjoy reading headstones, you'll find the graves of war veterans, Masons, miners, immigrants, wives, mothers, and children. You can piece together the Gold Rush history of Murphys by reading the town's collection of tombstones. Locals whose time in Murphys has finished can still be buried here, the modern markers standing in stark contrast to the softened lines of the older stones.

## WINERIES

There's not as much wine in southern Gold Country as you'll find up north. But if you just can't manage without sampling the region's vintages, head for Murphys. A number of tasting rooms cluster in the low buildings downtown, and out in the countryside a few vineyards boast major estates.

The largest of the estates belongs to **Ironstone Vineyards** (1894 Six Mile Rd., Murphys, 209/728-1251, www.ironstonevineyards.com). The huge complex of vineyards, winery buildings, museum, amphitheater, and gardens can draw hundreds of visitors in a single day. If you're into live music, check

## GOLD COUNTRY CAVERNS

Along with the tremendous network of artificial mine shafts, the southern Sierra Foothills are honeycombed through with natural tunnels and caverns. Children and adults love the cavern tours. If you choose to visit a cavern, be aware that you'll need to climb hundreds of stairs and squeeze through tight spots, and that the total walk may be more than half a mile. Check with the tour operators when you buy your tickets to be sure you're up for the trek. Also, the temperature inside the caverns hovers steadily at about 55°F, so bring a coat and hat to keep yourself warm!

Perhaps the most fascinating set of caves in the southern Gold Country is **Mercer Caverns** (1665 Sheep Ranch Rd., Murphys, 209/728-2101, www.mercercaverns.com, daily June–Aug. 9 A.M.–5 P.M., Fri.–Sat. 9 A.M.–6 P.M., Sept.–May 10 A.M.–4:30 P.M.). This network of rooms, tunnels, and river-connected underground lakes was discovered in 1885 by the gentleman who lent them his name. He began leading tours of the caverns almost immediately afterward, and Mercer Caverns have been a tourist draw ever since. The unusual aragonite formations found in several rooms improbably won a Grand Prize at the 1900 Paris World's Fair. Today, the custodians of the caverns require that you do not break off souvenirs, in fact they request that you do your best not to touch any of the numerous and delicate formations. This can be tough; you'll pass through some narrow spots where it's hard not to brush the calcite "angel wings" and stalactites. One of the neatest things about Mercer Caverns is the visible underground lake – a startling cerulean blue pool (lit artificially for your enjoyment) far below the tour pathway. The guides' descriptions of exploring the underground river flowing from lake to lake will make you wish for a reason to join in the research teams!

The popular **Moaning Cavern** (5350 Moaning Cavern Rd., Vallecito, 866/762-2837, www.caverntours.com, May–Sept. daily 9 A.M.–6 P.M., Oct.–Apr. Mon.–Fri. 10 A.M.–5 P.M., weekends and holidays 9 A.M.–5 P.M., adults $14.25, children $7.15) is still fun to visit, despite its sad history as a tourist attraction. Unlike the other caverns you can traverse in California, Moaning Cavern has only one major chamber, and it's a big one! Even folks with claustrophobia can get comfortable in the palatial chamber filled with great formations. You can take the basic 45-minute walking tour, rappel down 165 feet into the cavern (be in good shape), or sign up for a three-hour adventure tour that takes you through narrow passages to see things you'd miss completely from the regular tour (be in great shape and not claustrophobic!). But however you visit the Moaning Cavern, you'll never hear it moan. When it was first discovered and made into a tourist attraction, a big draw was the strange "moaning" sounds of air flowing through the cavern. It became so popular that the operators decided to widen the narrow mouth of the chamber to allow more tourists to enter at once. But when the rock was chiseled away and the mouth nice and wide and group-friendly, the famous "moan" disappeared. The shape of the rock had created the eerie sounds, which have never recurred. So come to Moaning Cavern for what you can see rather than what you can no longer hear.

© LIZ HAMILL SCOTT

Mercer Caverns

out their summer concert series. Buy tickets early, as the concerts tend to be local favorites. Or if you favor ore, visit the Heritage Museum and check out the astonishing 44-pound specimen of natural gold leaf.

Inside the vast tasting room, you'll find three bars and a pleasant surprise. The complimentary regular tasting includes any number of tasty wines, most priced at $10 per bottle. The reserve tasting bar shows off the higher-end vintages, but it's the lovely and shockingly reasonable "low-end" wines that make tasters want to buy their favorites by the case. If you're hungry, grab a bite at the deli inside the tasting room for lunch.

On the other end of the spectrum, the tiny, elegant **Black Sheep** (221 Main St., 209/728-2157, Murphys, www.blacksheepwinery.com, daily 11 A.M.–5 P.M.) tasting room offers higher-end red wines at a bar that can fit six people—if they're friendly. Black Sheep's specialty is Zinfandel made from Calaveras and Amador grapes, but they also make Cabernet Sauvignon, Cab Franc, and more unusual varietals like Cinsault. For a fun kick, be sure to taste the True Frogs Lily Pad blends—named for the celebrated jumping frog so famous in Calaveras.

For a fun third stop in Murphys, check out the **Twisted Oak Winery** (4280 Red Hill Rd. at Hwy. 4, Vallecito, 209/736-9080, www.twistedoak.com, daily 10:30 A.M.–5 P.M.). With a focus on Spanish and Rhone varietals and an unlikely mascot in a rubber chicken, Twisted Oak takes pride in being truly twisted. Their wines, however, are straight-up award-winners. From Viognier to Verdelho to the much-beloved percent@#$! Blend, you'll find a red or a white that's just perfect for you.

## ENTERTAINMENT AND EVENTS

Want to enjoy a night out in southern Gold Country like the locals do? Like they have for the last 150 years? Head down to the local saloon and lift a cold one. You'll find a dearth of fancy lounges, but a wealth of *old*-school bars. Most every town in the area boasts at least one historic saloon that's still open and serving drinks.

Yes, it really does happen. Each May in Angels Camp, the **Calaveras County Fair and Jumping Frog Jubilee** (209/736-2561, www.frogtown.org, adults $7, children $3) comes to town. During the fair each and every year, frogs jump on command in the contest that honors the famous Mark Twain story. You'll also find all sorts of other classic fair activities, such as livestock shows, baking contests, auctions, historic readings and exhibits. During the frog-jumping contest, you'll see literally thousands of frogs leaping toward victory. The top 50 from all heats compete in a final contest; all hope to beat the world record, a feat that carries a $5,000 reward. Practically speaking, visitors to the fair and jubilee will find lots of food at the concessionary, places to camp if they need, and ample restroom facilities.

## SPORTS AND RECREATION

The outdoors beckons to many visitors to Gold Country. Between the land and the water in Calaveras and Tuolumne Counties, the recreation opportunities seem endless. The following lists just a few; talk to the locals and grab fliers and magazines to find the best spots for hiking, biking, kayaking, fishing, golf, and more.

### Rafting and Kayaking

Southern Gold Country is home to a number of wild and turbulent rivers that make for fabulous and exciting river rafting and kayaking. Even if you've gone on float trips in other states, you need to prepare for rafting in California; this isn't a serene, slow paddle that gives you endless time to admire each mile of scenery. Instead, you'll spend a lot of time frantically paddling, screeching, and soaring over huge rapids, shooting through chutes, and hunting for the next restful eddy.

The Outdoor Adventure River Specialist, **O.A.R.S.** (209/736-4677, www.oars.com/california, one-day $147–227/person) operates out of Angels Camp, running rafting trips on the Stanislaus, the Merced, and the Tuolumne. This slick, all-amenities rafting chain offers everything from one-day trips on these popular river to five- and seven-day adventures that include multiple sports (mountain biking, rock climbing, kayaking) and trips into Yosemite proper. Do be aware that many of the rafting trips on these rivers include Class IV and even Class V rapids; be sure to check age minimums before signing up with your family.

**All-Outdoors** (925/932-8993, www.aorafting.com, Mon.–Fri. 9 A.M.–5 P.M.) offers trips on the North Fork Stanislaus, Merced, and Tuolumne, including a serious, adults-only, Class V ride down the Cherry Creek section of the Tuolumne. In addition, A-O Rafting makes regular trips down the Kaweah—a river just outside of Sequoia and Kings Canyon National Parks.

If you prefer to go out on your own with a kayak, check out www.riverfacts.com/rivers/10619.html for information about taking on the local rivers with your friends.

## Boating and Fishing

For a peaceful fishing trip in the Gold Country, go to **Pinecrest Lake** (Hwy. 108 east of Sonora, www.fs.fed.us/r5/stanislaus/fishing/lakes/pinecrest.shtml). The National Forest permits boating, and a launch is available for your convenience. There's also a pier; bring your pole and bait and fish in peace from dry land. The Forest Service stocks the lake with rainbow trout. So long as you have a California fishing license, you're good to go.

A number of other lakes also allow fishing and boating. **New Melones Lake** (6850 Studhorse Flat Rd., Sonora, 209/536-9094) has beautiful hiking and biking trails along its edges. Dive in for a swim, go out on your boat, or cast a line out to catch your dinner. At **Lake Camanche** (2000 Camanche Rd., Iona, 209/763-5121, www.camancherecreation.com), zip around the lake on a personal watercraft, try your skills at waterskiing or wakeboarding, or enjoy a relaxing afternoon or evening of fishing. You can fish at Camanche all year. Beautiful scenery and beautiful fish combine at **Pardee Lake Recreation Area** (4900 Stony Creek Rd., Ione, 209/772-1472).

## Hiking and Biking

If you want more challenging walks than those you'll find in the mine parks, head up into the mountains. At Pinecrest Lake, take a gentle hike on the paved **Pinecrest National Recreation Trail,** or a sedate off-road bike trip on the three-mile **Sugar Pine Railroad Grade** (graded). For a stiffer bike trip, take the **Gooseberry-Crabtree Trail.** You'll ascend 2,000 feet over a difficult seven-mile stretch of gravel and dirt trails and roads.

More than a dozen hiking trails branch out from Pinecrest Lake. Most are easy to moderate and less than four miles long—perfect for day hikes with your family. A 0.25-mile walk takes you to the **Columns of the Giants** to check out the fascinating rock formations. Take a brisk one-mile hike to **Burst Rock** for fabulous views of the Foothills. Go another mile to reach Powell Lake, part of the Emigrant Wilderness. If you're willing to hike for your fish, start at the Kennedy Meadows Trailhead and hike out three miles (moderate) to **Relief Reservoir.**

In the summertime, the **Bear Valley** (Hwy. 4 at Hwy. 207, Bear Valley, 209/753-2301, www.bearvalley.com) ski resort turns its runs into tracks, its slopes into trails. Everyone, from the most sedate walkers and road bikers to the most aggro backpackers and 4x4 riders will find fun at Bear Valley. Check the website for maps and information about the acres of road biking areas, mountain biking tracks, and hiking trails.

## Skiing and Snowboarding

When winter snows come to the southern Gold Country, the skiers and boarders come out to play. Only a few miles past Arnold, **Bear Valley** (Hwy. 4 at Hwy. 207, Bear Valley, 209/753-2301, www.bearvalley.com, daily 9 A.M.–4 P.M.) lures snow-lovers with a big mountain filled with great runs and tracks. Need a lesson? You can get one here on the wide, gentle beginner slopes near the lodge. If you prefer to take your chances, head up the hill to the array of intermediate and advanced trails that make up 75 percent of the skiable terrain at Bear. Ten different lifts make lines short on weekdays. If you're looking for something edgier, take your snowboard out to the "Cub" terrain parks.

Many native Californians cut their first turns in the snow at **Dodge Ridge** (209/965-3474, www.dodgeridge.com, daily 9 A.M.–4 P.M., adults $52, youth $39, children $10). Only a few miles from Sonora, Dodge Ridge is a reasonable drive from the Bay Area, and an easy one from Gold Country towns. A major bowl served by three different chairs has all beginner and advanced-beginner runs. The pee-wee area is reserved for kids learning to ski, while Ego Alley offers a chance for adventurous new skiers to try a slightly steeper slope. The rest of the mountain beckons to intermediate and advanced skiers and boarders. Intermediates love this resort, since you can get all the way down the mountain on blue slopes from almost every lift in the park. For experts, a few double-black diamonds nestle at the top of Chair 3. Freestylers have fun on the five terrain parks scattered throughout the park.

If you prefer cross-country to downhill, head for the trail areas at **Pinecrest Lake** (www.fs.fed.us/r5/stanislaus/summit/nordic.shtml). With a variety of terrain, including unmarked backcountry trails perfect for advanced adventurers, the area offers great fun. **Crabtree** sits only half a mile from the town of Pinecrest. The trails aren't groomed, but you'll find markers leading you in the right direction. Local amenities include restrooms and a small parking lot.

Adjacent to Dodge Ridge, the **Gooseberry** area calls to hardcore cross-country skiers. Trails range from "more difficult" to "most difficult" at this park. The tiny parking lot fits only about eight cars, but there is a restroom for weary skiers needing a break.

### Casino Gambling

It's only fitting that the land where thousands gambled their futures on finding a fortune in gold should play host to a casino or two. If you're already in Sonora or Jamestown, take a detour to the **Black Oak Casino** (19400 Tuolumne Rd. N., 877/747-8777, www.blackoakcasino.com). This full-service, family-friendly casino features games for kids and adults alike. While the under-21 crowd bowl at the Black Oak Lanes or donate their quarters to the Underground Arcade, the grown-ups can play over 1,000 slots and video poker machines, plus a small array of table games. When you're ready for a break, you can eat and drink at any one of Black Oak's seven restaurants and bars, take in some live weekend entertainment at the Willow Creek Lounge, or even spin a few more slots in the smoke-free Manzanita Bar.

## ACCOMMODATIONS

In southern Gold Country, you can stay at any number of charming Victorian B&Bs. Or for a change of pace, get a room in one of the historic downtown hotels in Jamestown or Sonora. These can be the most fun, with unique rooms, in-house restaurants and saloons, and often a great ghost story or two to lend additional atmosphere to the already fascinating inns.

### Under $100

For a charming stay in an upscale Victorian inn, try the **Royal Carriage Inn** (18239 Main St., Jamestown, 209/984-5271, www.royalcarriageinn.com, $75–150). For a reasonable nightly rate, you'll find yourself staying in a uniquely decorated guest room furnished with antiques and collectibles. All rooms have private baths, and several have adjoining doors that make a perfect resting place for families or couples traveling together. You'll love the amenities and special extras in your room. Outside your room, enjoy the hospitality in the parlor by the fireplace or out on one of the two balconies overlooking the town.

If you're looking for history in your hotel room, you can't beat the **Gunn House Hotel** (286 S. Washington St., Sonora, 209/532-3421, gunnhousehotel.com, $75–120). The original home of Dr. Lewis Gunn—a gold prospector and newspaper owner—the building has been a home, hospital, and hotel in its more than 150 year existence. Renovated to create comfortable modern rooms and spaces, the Gunn House Hotel offers affordable luxury. A dozen rooms are done up in elegant jewel tones and rich fabrics, each with a king or queen bed. Upon each bed you'll find your companions for your stay—cute teddy bears that live at the Gunn House and welcome all guests with a whimsical touch of home. Unlike so many B&Bs, the Gunn House offers a TV with cable in every room, plus full heating and air conditioning—a welcome luxury when the summer weather turns scorching. Each morning, head down to the parlor to partake of the sumptuous Innkeeper's Breakfast, which is included with your room rate.

## $100-150

The **Jamestown Hotel** (18153 Main St., Jamestown, 800/205-4901, www.jamestownhotel.com, $100–195) looks just like the perfect Gold Country hostelry. With its brick exterior, long dim hallways trimmed in dark woods, and uniquely funky upstairs guest rooms, this hotel drips Gold Rush history. Each of the eight rooms bears the name of a famous entertainer or figure of the Old West or the Gold Rush—most are women. Whichever room you pick, be sure to read about its namesake during your stay. The hotel itself has been a boarding house, a bordello, a hospital, and the victim of two major fires. Is room 7 really haunted? Book a night in it and decide for yourself.

The rooms themselves have an unusual charm, with a combination of antique furnishings and modern fixtures. You might find a whirlpool bathtub in the same bathroom with a pull-chain toilet. While the appointments and amenities aren't perfect, somehow the little imperfections add to the hotel's character rather than detracting from it. In the mornings, head down the worn wooden staircase to the bar/breakfast room to enjoy a light, pleasant meal. Then go outside, and take a stroll up and down historic Main Street.

If you're looking for a more standard motel room, **Murphys Inn Motel** (76 Main St., Murphys, 888/796-1800, www.centralsierralodging.com, $100–200) has what you need. Centrally located in sophisticated downtown Murphys, this motel makes a perfect base of operations for Gold Country wine tasting, as well as historical tours and outdoor adventures. Check the website for information about special packages that include visits to some of the area's attractions. Most of the 37 rooms have two queen beds, furnished and decorated in traditional motel style. Outside your room, you can take a cooling dunk in the pool or enjoy a hard workout in the small fitness room.

## Over $150

The at-times infamous **National Hotel** (18183 Main St., Jamestown, 800/894-3446, www.national-hotel.com, $155) has been operating as a lodging almost continuously since 1859. Granted, it's also had in its space a brothel, a small casino, and a "back bar" that was repeatedly raided during Prohibition. You'll find the nightlife at the National a bit more sedate than it was back in the 1920s. Today, an upscale gourmet restaurant sits downstairs, complete with an orange cat named Garfield out on the front porch welcoming diners. The Gold Rush Saloon serves up signature cocktails and California wines to a discerning local and visiting crowd each night.

Each of the nine guest rooms tends toward the luxurious, with antique furniture and soft, comfy linens and comforters. All rooms have their own baths with shower, and access to the soaking room, which the hotel describes as its "1800s Jacuzzi." Most rooms have only one queen bed—not the ideal setup or atmosphere for families with children. Indeed, both hotel and restaurant cater primarily to the romantic getaway crowd. Out back, be sure to check out (but do not try to enter!) the old gold mine tunnel, now filled with water most of the time. Or hunt through the hotel building for Flo, the resident friendly ghost.

The **Barretta Gardens Inn** (700 S. Barretta St., Sonora, 800/206-3333, www.barrettagardens.com, $155–425) seems like it ought to be in Sonoma rather than Sonora, with its elegant luxury and its wine-themed guest rooms. The highly polished wood floors of your room will be covered with antique Oriental rugs and an array of high-end antique furniture. Each florally decorated room has its own private bath, and many have two-person whirlpool or deep soaking tubs outfitted with candles and bath salts to create the perfect relaxing or romantic bath. Several multi-room suites are available for couples traveling together or for family groups. Located a few blocks away from downtown Sonora, the Barretta Gardens offers a haven of peace and privacy to Gold Country visitors looking for an upscale B&B experience. Every morning of your stay, you'll take a seat at the long dining table to enjoy a full hot breakfast. And if you're about in the afternoon, you can partake in a drink and a bite to eat downstairs in the common rooms.

From the outside, the blocky square structure of **Dunbar House, 1880** (271 Jones St., Murphys, 800/692-6006, www.dunbarhouse.com, $200–300) evokes a Dickensian air in the unlikely locale that is Murphys. Inside you'll find a plethora of modern comfort and Victorian elegance that calls to mind Dickens' richer characters. Each of the rooms boasts flowers, stripes, wallpaper, fabrics, and furniture reminiscent of the decorative excesses of the Victorian era. In the bathroom you might find an antique clawfoot tub and vintage shower, or the most modern of two-person whirlpool tubs. All rooms have English towel warmers—the very height of luxury on chilly winter mornings. For breakfast, you'll feast on homemade baked goods, a delicious hot entrée, coffee, tea, and specially blended hot chocolate. You can dine in the dining room, the garden, or (if you're in one of the suites) in the privacy of your own room.

If you're traveling with family or a group of friends, or you just want ample space to spread out, consider staying at the **Greenhorn Creek Resort** (711 Mccauley Ranch Rd., Angels Camp, 209/736-9372, www.greenhorncreekvacationcottages.com, $335). Here you can rent a condo or, better yet, a two- or three-bedroom "cottage" that's really your own full-fledged vacation home. Cottages have full kitchens, dining areas, and living rooms decorated in light, bright, homey styles. Each bedroom has its own separate bathroom; most bedrooms have king beds, though some have two twins. These cottages are perfect if you're planning a longer stay in the region and want to really settle in and get comfortable. The Greenhorn Creek Resort property offers every amenity imaginable, from an on-site restaurant to an 18-hole golf course to tennis courts. The pool facilities sparkle on hot summer days, with a shallow "family pool," large main pool, and nice hot whirlpool tub. The only downside to the Greenhorn Creek Resort is the exclusive country club price tag—it's up to you to decide whether it's worth it.

## FOOD

A wealth of great dining awaits you in southern Gold Country.

### American

Just next door to the Jamestown Hotel, you can get a hearty American breakfast or lunch at the **Mother Lode Coffee Shop** (18169 Main St., Jamestown, 209/984-3386). This local's spot offers traditional coffee shop fare: egg and pancake breakfasts, sandwiches, and burgers. The medium-sized dining room can get crowded on weekend mornings, with tourists vying for tables with the local community. Don't expect anything fancy here, but this is a good option if you need a good meal to get started on a long day of touring Gold Country.

One of the top locals' picks in the region, the **Diamondback Grill** (93 S. Washington St., Sonora, 209/532-6661, Mon.–Sat. 11 A.M.–9 P.M., $10) serves good grill food at extremely reasonable prices. Everyone loves the burgers at the Diamondback, but don't ignore the specials. Either the sweet potato fries or the garlic fries are a treat, but expect to feel the effects of the garlic fries for hours after your meal. Fresh salads feed lighter appetites, and everyone can enjoy a glass of California wine with their meal.

A recent move to a larger space increased seating capacity, but expect a wait, especially on weekends. You'll find the old bar present in the new dining room, which retains the great feel of old Sonora.

### Italian

**Carmela's Italian Kitchen** (301 S. Washington St., Sonora, 209/532-8858) brings a tasty bite of Italy to Gold Country. Enjoy home-style food in a casual setting here—just be aware that the portions and full meals can get large.

## Mexican

One of the best Mexican spots in the area is **Morelia** (18148 Main St., Jamestown, 209/984-1432), across the street from the Jamestown Hotel. Locals go to Morelia when they want enchiladas, Mexican grilled meat dishes, good beans and guac, and plenty of other tasty classic fare.

## Steak

In a town thick with Gold Rush atmosphere, Jamestown's **Willow Steakhouse and Saloon** (Willow and Main Sts., Jamestown, 209/984-3998, $20–35) fits right in. The floor creaks as busy wait staff dash across the ancient wooden floor. Or is it the ghost that's reputed to haunt the craggy old building making the funky noises? Whichever it is, you'll hardly care once you dig into an order of the house special cheese fondue. To be honest, the steaks are only good rather than great, but the baked potatoes and the bucket of fixings make up for that. For an after dinner-cocktail, head into the Saloon and have a drink with the locals who frequent the bar area. You might have to wait for a table on weekend evenings; if you do, read the various plaques on the outside of the building to learn its history and the story of its ghost.

## Bakery and Deli

For a truly homemade deli sandwich, go to the **Pickle Barrel** (1225 S. Main St., Angels Camp, 209/736-4704, Tues.–Thurs., Sun. 11 A.M.–4 P.M., Fri.–Sat. 11 A.M.–8 P.M.). The sandwich meats are barbecued out on the back porch of the deli, and the carrot cake is made from the owner's grandmother's recipe. If you're eating on-site, get a hot panini sandwich. If you're looking to carry out food for a picnic, choose from cold sandwiches, prepared salads, and other tasty treats.

## Coffee and Tea

Do you care for a spot of tea? In southern Gold Country, the place to get it is inside **Babcia's Tea Room** (31 S. Washington St., Sonora, 209/532-1306). The Tea Room serves breakfast and lunch, but the best time to come is in the afternoon. You can order a full high tea, with finger sandwiches, scones, sweets, and, of course, a pot of good hot tea. Though you'll be sitting in elegant surroundings, feel free to wear your casual traveling clothes.

Need a cup of Fair Trade in the worst way? You can get it at **T E's Espresso Café** (1227 S. Main St., Angels Camp, 209/736-0927). Scallywag serves espresso drinks, plain ol' coffee, smoothies, baked goods, and more.

# INFORMATION AND SERVICES

## Tourist Information

Check each small town for its own municipal visitors center. For a larger center, head for the **Tuolumne County Visitors Bureau** (542 W. Stockton St., Sonora, 209/533-4420, www.tcvb.com). In Calaveras County, begin your trip at the **Calaveras Visitors Bureau** (1192 S. Main St., 800/225-3764, www.gocalaveras.com).

## Media and Communications

The local southern Gold Country rag is the weekly ***Calaveras Enterprise*** (www.calaverasenterprise.com). This fun, ultra-local paper focuses on current events within the county and is a good place to find information about local nightlife, events, and festivals.

Some of the region's towns are *very* small, so it's sometimes difficult to find ATMs and Internet cafés. Take the opportunities you can to grab cash and check your email. In Angels Camp, hit the **Guaranty Bank** (479 S. Main St., 209/736-4561). They've got a 24-hour external ATM, plus you can cash travelers checks inside during regular business hours. In Murphys, try the **Mother Lode Bank** (150 Big Trees Rd., 209/738-3700) for ATMs and banking services.

For reliable free or inexpensive Internet access, your best bet is probably your lodgings; many inns, B&Bs, and motels offer wireless or high-speed wired connections. Outside your hotel, a local coffee shop (including the ubiquitous Starbucks in many towns) might be able to hook you up.

Each small town in southern Gold Country that has its own ZIP code has its own post office. In Sonora, the main **post office** sits at 781 North Washington Street (800/275-8777), easy to access for downtown visitors.

### Medical Services

Be aware that not all towns in southern Gold Country have hospitals or any form of 24-hour emergency medical service. And if you're out in the backcountry, it might take help awhile to reach you.

One of the few major hospitals in the area is **Sonora Regional Medical Center** (1000 Greenley Rd., Sonora, 209/532-5000, www.sonorahospital.org, which has an emergency room with a helipad for emergency access.

## GETTING THERE AND AROUND

### Air

If you're lucky enough to have your own plane or access to one, you can fly in to the **Calaveras County Airport** (3600 Carol Kennedy Dr., San Andreas, 209/736-2501).

### Train

Railroads in southern Gold Country tend toward tourist excursions rather than viable transportation these days. To access the area via Amtrak (www.amtrak.com), take the San Joaquins line to the Merced station, and make arrangements to catch a bus or get a car from there.

### Car

Your main roads in southern Gold Country are running north—south and Highway 4 running west–east. Most of the towns have a main street (and it's often named Main Street), which can get crowded when a fair or event is happening. You can park on most town streets for free or a nominal meter charge. Unless you're in town for a major event or during a holiday weekend, you shouldn't have too much trouble finding a spot.

# Central Valley

The Central Valley is the garden of California. Garden, not garden spot. Much of the legendary California agricultural industry makes its home out in the Central Valley. A number of ag towns cluster along the major highways (CA-99 and I-5), suffering through the sweltering summers that make the crops grow so well. No ocean breezes make it out here, since the Central Valley sits between the major coastal mountain ranges and the Sierra Nevadas, isolating it and creating a heat bowl each summer. As you drive I-5, you'll see everything from grapefruit trees to rice paddies to cornfields—California grows it all.

Culture and entertainment aren't very plentiful in these parts, though if you need a place to stay for the night on your way someplace else, any of the towns provide you with a motel room, a meal, and maybe even something to do to pass a few hours. If you're into the outdoors, head toward the many lakes and rivers for kayaking, rafting, and boating fun. Hardcore agricultural tourists might enjoy touring some of the massive orchards in the Orange Belt, and Fresno offers some agricultural tours.

Your safest lodging options in the Central Valley are the big chain motels—no quaint Victorian B&Bs or high-end boutique hotels ply their trade out in the great flat expanse.

## STOCKTON

Stockton acts as a way-out commuter town with huge housing tracts that shelter workers who make the long, tortuous drive in to the Bay Area each day. While it's not an inspired tourist haven, Stockton sits at the confluence of several freeways, making it a convenient place to grab a tank of gas, a meal, or a cheap motel room if you find you're too tired to go on.

The **Stockton Asparagus Festival** (www.asparagusfest.com, adults $10, youth $5) takes place in the late spring of each year in downtown Stockton. Enjoy every tasty asparagus dish you can imagine, take in some live entertainment on the performance stage, and taste local vintages and brews at the Wine and Beer Pavilion.

## Accommodations

**Motel 6** (817 Navy Dr., 209/464-3948, www.motel6.com, $57) has some of the cheapest rooms with a good chance of reasonable sanitation. The best of the three Stockton locations is the one at Navy Drive; find another one right off I-5. Rooms have double or queen beds, including some set up for wheelchair accessibility. You can choose between smoking and non-smoking rooms. An outdoor pool completes a round of lower-end amenities, which also include free coffee from the office/lobby.

You can get a somewhat nicer room at the local **Best Western Stockton Inn** (4219 East Waterloo Rd., 209/931-3131, www.bestwesterncalifornia.com, $70), complete with basic amenities. This kid-friendly, low-rise motel has a pool, a wading pool, and a spa outdoors—perfect for getting the kids to relax and enjoy themselves or to cool off after a day in the legendary Central Valley summer heat. In your spacious guest room, you'll find jewel-toned carpets and matching bedspreads, a coffee maker, and high-speed Internet access. For travelers who really need a break, the Sutter Street Bar & Grill sits on the premises, making it easy to grab a drink or a meal.

**La Quinta** (2710 West March Ln., 209/952-7800, www.lq.com, $82) provides comparable lodgings to the Best Western. Grab a sizeable room with a king or two double beds, a coffee maker, and free high-speed Internet access. There's a pool, free continental breakfast, and pets are welcome.

If you want something a bit higher rent with nicer facilities, drop in on the **Residence Inn Stockton** (3240 March Ln., 209/472-9800, www.marriott.com, $140). Here you'll get a suite that includes a full kitchen with all appliances and pots and pans. The Wi-Fi is free, but the premium movies on TV are not. Step outside your room to enjoy the pool and spa or the outdoor sports facility. Enjoy a free continental breakfast daily, do your laundry at the on-site coin-op machines, or take advantage of the valet dry cleaning and grocery shopping services.

## Food

You can get some surprisingly good sushi in Stockton, specifically at **Cocoro Japanese Bistro & Sushi** (2105 Pacific Ave., 209/941-6053, www.cocorobistro.com, Mon.–Sat. 11:30 A.M.–2 P.M., 5:30–9 P.M., $10–30). The neat brick building houses a pretty, post-modern gold and crimson dining room. Take a seat at the table or up at the bar and order some of the fresh, original sushi. In addition to the fabulous rolls and variety of sashimi and sushi entrées, Cocoro offers lots of lovely hot food, including teriyaki, udon, donburi, tempura. Finish off your meal with a mochi ice cream or perhaps an apple tempura á la mode. Folks with lighter appetites can enjoy one of the great salads, many of which include fish.

Just jonesing for a burger? One of the best cheeseburgers in Stockton can be had **Chuck's Burgers** (6034 Pacific Ave., 209/473-9977, www.angelfire.com/biz/chuckshamburgers, Mon.–Sat. 6 A.M.–close, $10). This comfy downtown burger joint has vinyl booths, a counter with classic round stools, and eclectic decor. Chuck's serves more than just its famed gourmet and build-your-own burgers—you can get a down-home breakfast, a tasty sandwich, and even a low-cal dinner plate. Best of all, the owners hate the notion of "no substitutions," so you can create your own version of the perfect hamburger.

## Practicalities

If you find yourself in Stockton, you probably got there on one of the major freeways. Stockon is bordered by I-5 and Highway 99; Highway 4 runs out from the Bay Area, and the 205 connector goes by to the south.

You can get to and from Stockton by **Amtrak** train (www.amtrak.com). The Stockton station services the San Joaquins line, which runs to Oakland, Sacramento, and down to Fresno and Bakersfield.

The ***Stockton Record*** (www.recordnet.com) provides daily local and national news, plus entertainment, food, and information on things to do in Stockton.

For emergency medical care, go to **Dameron Hospital** (525 W. Acacia St., 209/944-5550, www.dameronhospital.org).

## FRESNO

An agricultural town with aspirations, Fresno sprawls in an ungainly fashion across the floor of the Central Valley. It's the "big city" between Sacramento and the passes down to Southern California. Despite recent growth, the culture of Fresno still revolves around the fields that surround it. The Orange Belt starts here, and any number of other warm-weather crops enjoy the hot summer sunshine.

Beyond citrus, there's hockey. Catch a game with the minor league pros of the **Fresno Falcons** (700 M St., 559/485-7825, www.fresnofalcons.com, tickets $12–28). The skating and amenities aren't quite up to NHL standards, but the fun and the energy rise up off the ice like a mist. Join in with the locals for the between-period festivities, which include events like the infamous "Puck Chuck." Groan as the announcer overstates yet another icing call. Have a hot dog and a beer, and become part of the loud cheering section for the Falcons!

### Accommodations

You can get a clean, comfortable room at **EconoLodge Fresno** (6309 N. Blackstone Ave., 559/439-0320, www.fresnoeconolodge.com, $87–154). The modestly decorated rooms have a TV with DVD player, air conditioning, phones, and Internet access. A basic but welcoming outdoor pool can help make a steaming afternoon in Fresno more bearable.

The **Rodeway Inn Fresno** (6730 N. Blackstone Ave., 559/431-3557, www.choicehotels.com, $77–99) has reasonably clean, low-end motel rooms and basic amenities. The free Wi-Fi is a bonus and pets are welcome.

The **Picadilly Shaw Inn** (2305 W. Shaw Ave., 559/226-3850, www.piccadillyinn.com, $132–148) has several locations: the one described here on West Shaw Avenue, another out by the airport, and the third up at 4961

ROBERT HOLMES / CALTOUR

Welcome to Fresno.

North Cedar near the university. These slightly more upscale motels offer rooms with a king or two-queen beds, decorated in fairly standard chain-motel chic. Amenities include free Wi-Fi, small refrigerator, coffee maker, and dual-head shower.

### Food

A true local legend, you'll hear **Grandmarie's Chicken Pie Shop** (861 E. Olive Ave., 559/237-5042, $10) referred to as "Fresno's Chicken Pie Shop." The town feels a sense of ownership of this place, from the avocado green booths and matching giant plastic chickens to the unusually delicious pot pies. The vintage spot looks like it hasn't changed since the 1960s, but the pot pies and other delectable dishes are made fresh daily. You can get a sandwich, a meat dish, or an array of sides, but really the most obvious and best choice are the chicken pot pies. For dessert, grab a slice of homemade fruit pie. If you're looking for takeout for a picnic or a day on the road, Grandmarie's will pack full meals into containers for you. Or if you prefer to cook your own, you can buy unbaked frozen pies to take home with you.

For a great burger and fries, head for the **Dog House Grill** (2789 E. Shaw Ave., 559/294-9920, $10–30), a local favorite. You'll enjoy the classic American grill food in a casual bar and grill atmosphere. Beware that you're likely to run into a rowdier crowd on game days; the Dog House has big TVs and shows popular sporting events.

For something a little different, try the tasty Armenian cuisine at **Nina's Bakery** (2022 W. Shaw Ave., 559/449-9999, $10–20), an unlikely gem tucked in Fresno. If you're a newbie to the wonders of *lahmajoun, choreg,* and other Armenian treats, the staff will help you with suggestions. On the other hand, if you already know that you like your *lahmajoun* spicy, you won't be disappointed.

### Practicalities

Fresno sits on the path of Highway 99. You can also get there on CA-41 (a north–south road) or CA-180, the major east–west thoroughfare.

The San Joaquin **Amtrak** route stops at the Fresno station (2650 Tulare St., www.amtrak.com). You can go north to Sacramento or Oakland, or south to Bakersfield from there.

Get into or out of Fresno by air through the **Fresno Yosemite International Airport** (5175 E. Clinton Ave., 800/244-2359, www.fresno.gov), which has the unenviable international designation FAT. almost every major airline operates in FAT, which is the major Central Valley air hub.

The local daily paper, the ***Fresno Bee*** (www.fresnobee.com), gets respect even from regular readers of the *San Francisco Chronicle* and the *Los Angeles Times.*

For medical services, go to **St. Agnes Medical Center** (1303 E. Hendon, www.samc.com) at the north end of town. In central Fresno, try the **Community Regional Medical Center** (2823 Fresno St., www.communitymedical.org), which has a 24-hour trauma center.

## BAKERSFIELD

Bakersfield acts as a crossroads, separating the Central Valley from Southern California proper. It's the last major town on Highway 99 (also easily accessible from I-5) before you hit the infamous Grapevine and head down into the San Fernando Valley. It's a good place to stop for gas and a meal, and it can also be a necessary overnight stop if the Grapevine closes due to fog or snow.

For local entertainment, your best bet is the **Buck Owens Crystal Palace** (2800 Buck Owens Blvd., 661/328-7560, www.buckowens.com, Tues.–Sat. 5 P.M.–close, Sun. 9:30 A.M.–2 P.M., $10–30, where you can visit a museum, take in a live show, and grab a meal. In the museum, view Buck's favorite guitars and fabulous performance outfits, a collection of album covers, and endless photos and memorabilia chronicling Buck's lengthy music career. Fittingly, live music plays at the Crystal Palace almost every night of the week. Enjoy the lively dancing of the crowd in the dining room, or join in as country musicians play.

The restaurant serves up great American grill

food that matches perfectly with the music. Try the barbecue pizza, have a burger, or enjoy an only-slightly-lighter salad. Just don't expect too much in the Weight Watchers department—even the house salad has cheese and bacon on it. Be sure to save room for dessert, whether you favor the peach crisp or the house mud pie. And of course, you'll need a beer or a shot of Jack from the Buckmobile Bar to wash everything down.

## Accommodations

The **Motel 6 Bakersfield Airport** (5241 Olive Tree Court, 661/392-9700, www.motel6.com, $50) is a good option for an overnight stay. Another reasonable choice is the **Rodeway Inn & Suites** (3400 Chester Ln., 661/328-1100, www.rodewayinn.com, $60).

For a few dollars more, you can get a few more amenities at the **Sleep Inn & Suites** (6257 Knudsen Dr., 661/399-2100, www.sleepinn.com, $90).

In Bakersfield, luxury appears at the **SpringHill Suites** (3801 Marriott Dr., 661/377-4000, www.marriott.com, $150).

## Food

If you'd like to treat yourself to an upscale meal, try the **Valentine Restaurant** (3310 Truxtun Ave., Ste. 160, 661/864-0397, Mon.–Sat. 5–9:30 P.M., lunch Tues.–Sat., $10–30). You'll find treats like quail on the menu, and a great range of California vintages on the wine list. The small, elegant dining room set in an uninspiring strip mall seems almost out of place here—you'd be more likely to find a place like this in Los Angeles or San Francisco. Expect great service, both friendly and well timed, and plan to eat your fill if you order a full three-course meal.

For delectable home-style Mexican in a town that knows its Mexican food, you can't beat **Don Pepito's Restaurant** (1201½ Chester Ave., 661/326-1250, daily 11 A.M.–close, $10). In fact, Don Pepito's serves up both Mexican and Salvadoran dishes. The owner also acts as the chef, and occasionally as the waitress, taking good care of the customers in her tiny dining room. The outside of this restaurant might seem forbidding—a run-down white and blue structure that may once have been Spanish Colonial Revival styled. Inside, there's little in the way of fancy decor, and the star of the show is rightly the food on your plate rather than the cloth on the table or the geegaws on the walls.

If all you need is a quick burger on your way through town, you can get one at **John's Burger** (2637 River Blvd., 661/873-8036, Mon.–Sat. 7 A.M.–11 P.M., Sun. 8 A.M.–11 P.M., $10). You can get a big ol' cheeseburger nearly any way you like it, sautéed mushrooms, fried zucchini, French fries, onion rings, and even a tri-tip sandwich. While it's been voted Best Burger in Bakersfield many times, rumor has it that customer service has gone downhill lately.

## Practicalities

Highway 99 runs north right through the middle of town, and is one of the major corridors from Northern California to Southern California. From I-5, get to Bakersfield on the Stockdale Highway, which becomes CA-58 in the middle of town and heads east.

Bakersfield is also a stop on the **Amtrak** line (601 Truxton Ave., www.amtrak.com), acting as the southern terminus for the San Joaquins line. You can take this train up to Stockton, Oakland, or Sacramento.

**Meadows Field** (3701 Wings Way, 661/391-1800, www.meadowsfield.com) is the local commercial airport. Delta, United, and US Airways all fly into and, more importantly, out of Bakersfield.

For the latest local news in Bakersfield, pick up a copy of the ***Bakersfield Californian*** (www.bakersfield.com), an independent, family-owned daily with plenty of local history.

For medical attention, try **Bakersfield Memorial Hospital** (420 34th St., 661/327-4647, www.bakersfieldmemorial.org), which has a full emergency room. On the other side of town, go to **Mercy Southwest Hospital** (400 Old River Rd., 661/663-6000).

# YOSEMITE

Yosemite National Park might not be one of the seven wonders of the natural world, but its accessibility and beauty make it one of the most visited places in California. Ansel Adams' elegant black-and-white photographs turned Yosemite's stunning natural features—cascading waterfalls, striking granite cliffs, grand vistas—into international icons. Travelers come from all over the world to visit Yosemite, but other parks in the area beckon to those who prefer lighter crowds and a more unusual experience.

Mono Lake greets visitors with a serene stillness that seems almost eerie. No trees grow around this alkaline, salt-filled lake. Surrounded only by tough desert scrub, the still waters of Mono Lake have fallen and risen again amid endless state controversy. Throughout the lake and on the shore, odd calcite formations, called tufa, stand above the waterline, mute testament to the mineral content of the water. The rough High Sierra climate attracts few residents to the small towns nearby, though at one point the historic mining town of Bodie sheltered 10,000 gold-hungry residents.

The quiet, upscale town of Mammoth Lakes acts as the main access to the Mammoth Mountain ski area. Indeed, winter tourism to the mountain plays a big part in sustaining the local economy. But there's much more to do and see in and around Mammoth than just ski and snowboard. Hiking, biking, fishing, backpacking, and sightseeing are great in this part of the Eastern Sierra, and you can find bargains on lodgings in the summertime "off-season."

South of Yosemite, the Sequoia and Kings

© LIZ HAMILL SCOTT

## HIGHLIGHTS

**Yosemite Valley:** Yosemite Valley is the masterpiece of Yosemite National Park. Half Dome, El Capitan, Bridalveil Fall, Yosemite Falls, as well as miles of spectacular hiking trails can all be found here (page 371).

**Mono Lake Tufa Preserve:** Free-standing calcite towers, knobs, and spires dot the alien landscape of Mono Lake. Several interpretive trails provide history and access to these unique formations (page 392).

**Bodie State Historic Park:** A state of "arrested decay" has preserved this 1877 gold mining ghost town. Tours of the abandoned mine provide background on the settlement's sordid history (page 393).

**Devil's Postpile National Monument:** One visit to these strange natural rock formations and you'll understand how they got their name. A mix of volcanic heat and pressure created these near-perfect straight-sided hexagonal posts that have to be seen to be believed (page 398).

**Crystal Cave:** Well-lit tunnels venture into the grand chambers of this marble cavern, filled with dramatic calcite formations and polished marble (page 411).

**Mount Whitney:** With a little bit of advance planning, you can climb or even day-hike California's tallest mountain (page 412).

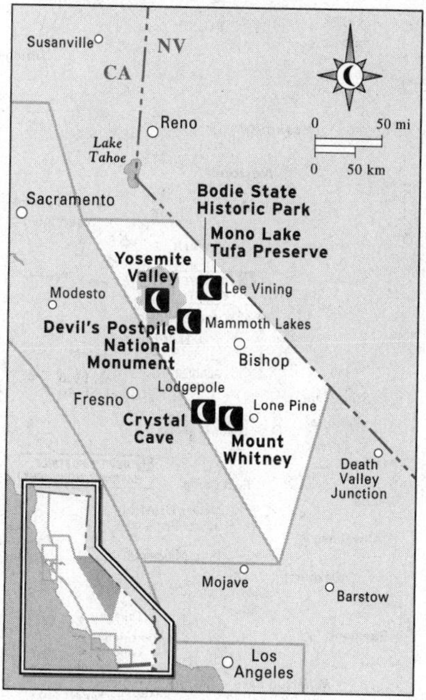


LOOK FOR ☾ TO FIND RECOMMENDED SIGHTS, ACTIVITIES, DINING, AND LODGING.

Canyon National Parks boast gorgeous rugged mountain scenery, immense redwood trees, and far smaller crowds than their more famous neighbor. The traveled part of this area actually encompasses two distinct parks and a forest: Sequoia National Park to the south, Kings Canyon National Park to the north, and Sequoia National Forest between the two in the west.

## PLANNING YOUR TIME

This vast area deserves as much exploration time as you can give it. Both geographically huge and filled with sights and hikes and attractions, this is the perfect region to slow down and take your time.

Though summer is traditionally the high season and spring is best for the waterfalls, Yosemite is gorgeous at any time of year. During the high summer season, however, traffic jams and parking problems plague the park, just as though it were a major city. Seriously consider parking at the visitors center in Yosemite Valley and using the free shuttles to travel to different locations within the park. Tioga Pass is less congested, and parking more available, making it a viable summer option. Try to plan at least two or three days just in

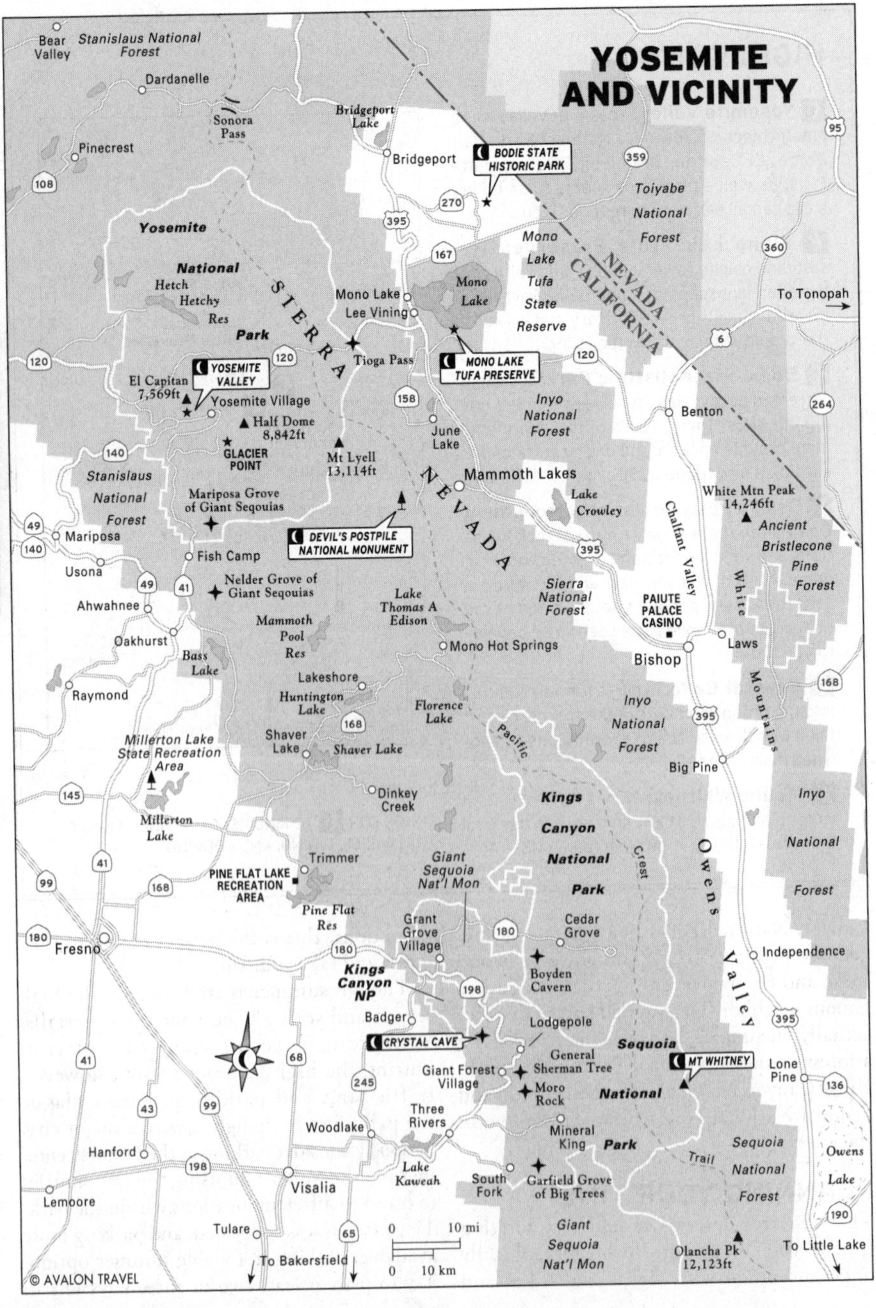
YOSEMITE AND VICINITY
Bear Valley
Stanislaus National Forest
Dardanelle
Sonora Pass
Pinecrest
108
Bridgeport Lake
Bridgeport
BODIE STATE HISTORIC PARK
270
395
359
95
Toiyabe National Forest
360
Yosemite National Park
Hetch Hetchy Res
SIERRA NEVADA
167
Mono Lake Tufa State Reserve
NEVADA
CALIFORNIA
Mono Lake
Lee Vining
Mono Lake
To Tonopah
Tioga Pass
120
YOSEMITE VALLEY
MONO LAKE TUFA PRESERVE
6
El Capitan 7,569ft
Yosemite Village
Half Dome 8,842ft
158
Inyo National Forest
Benton
264
140
GLACIER POINT
Mt Lyell 13,114ft
June Lake
Stanislaus National Forest
Mammoth Lakes
Mariposa Grove of Giant Sequoias
Lake Crowley
White Mtn Peak 14,246ft
Chalfant Valley
Ancient Bristlecone Pine Forest
49
Mariposa
DEVIL'S POSTPILE NATIONAL MONUMENT
Fish Camp
Usona
41
Nelder Grove of Giant Sequoias
Sierra National Forest
White Mountains
Ahwahnee
Lake Thomas A Edison
PAIUTE PALACE CASINO
Oakhurst
Mammoth Pool Res
Mono Hot Springs
Bishop
Laws
Bass Lake
Lakeshore
Raymond
Huntington Lake
Florence Lake
Inyo National Forest
168
Shaver Lake
Shaver Lake
Pacific Crest Trail
Millerton Lake State Recreation Area
Big Pine
145
Dinkey Creek
Kings Canyon National Park
Inyo National Forest
Millerton Lake
Trimmer
Giant Sequoia Nat'l Mon
PINE FLAT LAKE RECREATION AREA
99
Pine Flat Res
Owens Valley
180
Fresno
Grant Grove Village
Cedar Grove
Independence
Kings Canyon NP
Boyden Cavern
198
Badger
Lodgepole
CRYSTAL CAVE
Sequoia National Park
MT WHITNEY
General Sherman Tree
Giant Forest Village
Moro Rock
Lone Pine
136
68
245
43
Three Rivers
Woodlake
Mineral King
Hanford
Lake Kaweah
Sequoia National Forest
Owens Lake
Lemoore
Visalia
South Fork
Garfield Grove of Big Trees
Tulare
65
Giant Sequoia Nat'l Mon
190
To Bakersfield
0 10 mi
0 10 km
Olancha Pk 12,123ft
To Little Lake
© AVALON TRAVEL

YOSEMITE

Yosemite Valley, with an excursion to Glacier Point. Adding Wawona, Tuolumne, or Hetch Hetchy? Plan a week—though it will never be long enough!

Mammoth Lakes makes a great ski weekend getaway, but prepare yourself for a long drive to get there. In winter, take a break from touring and spend your time on the slopes; in summer a week will cover you.

For Mono Lake, plan another full weekend with time to walk around the lake and explore the tufa reserves. Be sure to save a half day for the drive up to Bodie State Historic Park.

When planning a visit to Sequoia and Kings Canyon, you have a couple of options. The parks could almost be done as a day trip if all you want to do is follow the main road and maybe take a couple short hikes. To explore the parks in depth, including longer hikes, plan anywhere from 3–4 days to a week.



# Yosemite National Park

## SIGHTS

### Yosemite Valley

The first place most people go when they reach the park is the floor of Yosemite Valley (Hwy. 140, Arch Rock Entrance). From the Valley floor, you can check out the visitors center, theater, galleries, museum, hotels, and outdoor historic exhibits. Numerous pullouts from the main road invite photographers to capture the beauty of the Valley and its many easily visible natural wonders. It's the most visited place in Yosemite, and many hikes, ranging from easy to difficult, begin in the Valley.

#### VISITORS CENTER

After the scenic turnouts through the park, your first stop in Yosemite Valley should be the visitors center (Yosemite Village off Northside Dr., 209/372-0200, www.nps.gov/yose, daily 9 A.M.–7 P.M., hours vary by season). Here you'll find the ranger station, as well as an intricate interpretive museum describing the geological and human history of Yosemite. Separate from the interpretive museum stands the Yosemite History Museum. Also a part of the big building complex are the theater, the Ansel Adams Gallery, and the all-important public restrooms.

A short flat walk from the visitors center takes you down to the re-created Miwok Native American village. The village includes all different types of structures, including those of the later Miwoks who incorporated European architecture into their building techniques. You can walk right into the homes and public buildings of this nearly lost culture. One of the most fascinating parts of this reconstruction is the evolution of construction techniques—as white settlers infiltrated the area, building cabins and larger structures, the Miwok took note. They examined these buildings and incorporated pieces that they saw as improvements.

#### EL CAPITAN

The first natural stone monument you encounter as you enter the valley is El Capitan (Northside Rd. west of El Capitan Bridge), comprised of Cretaceous granite that's actually named for this formation. This 3,000-foot craggy rock face is accessible in two ways: You can take a long hike west from the Upper Yosemite Fall and up the back side of the formation, or you can grab your climbing gear and scale the face. El Cap boasts a reputation as one of the world's seminal big-face climbs.

#### HALF DOME

At the foot of the valley perhaps the most recognizable feature in Yosemite rests high above the valley floor. Ansel Adams' famed photographs of Half Dome (visible from most of the valley floor) made it known to hikers and photo-lovers the world round. Scientists believe that Half Dome was never a whole dome—in fact, it sits now in its original formation. This

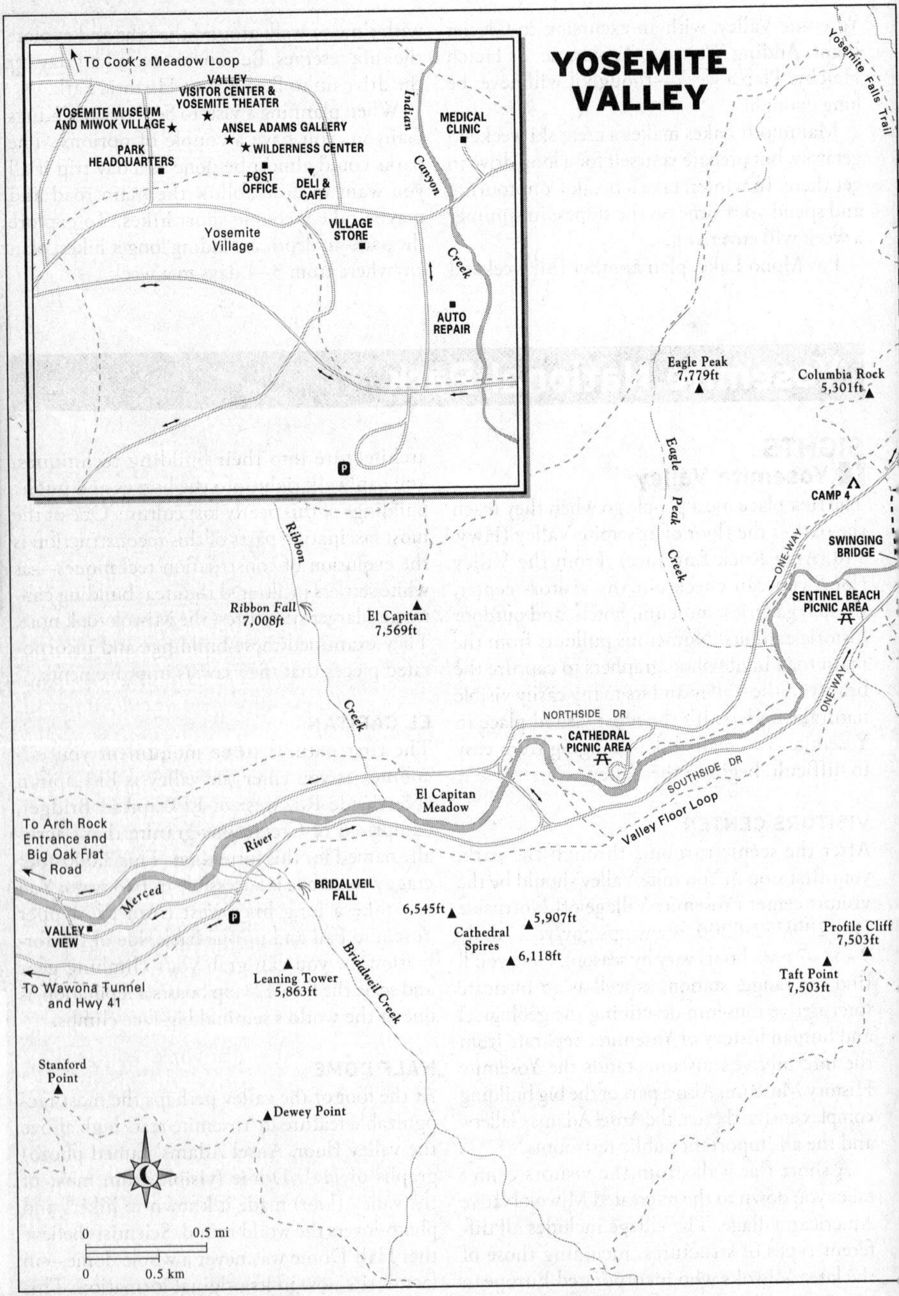
YOSEMITE VALLEY
To Cook's Meadow Loop
VALLEY VISITOR CENTER & YOSEMITE THEATER
YOSEMITE MUSEUM AND MIWOK VILLAGE
ANSEL ADAMS GALLERY
WILDERNESS CENTER
PARK HEADQUARTERS
POST OFFICE
DELI & CAFÉ
VILLAGE STORE
Yosemite Village
Indian Canyon Creek
MEDICAL CLINIC
AUTO REPAIR
P
Yosemite Falls Trail
Eagle Peak 7,779ft
Columbia Rock 5,301ft
Eagle Peak Creek
CAMP 4
SWINGING BRIDGE
ONE-WAY
SENTINEL BEACH PICNIC AREA
Ribbon Creek
Ribbon Fall 7,008ft
El Capitan 7,569ft
NORTHSIDE DR
CATHEDRAL PICNIC AREA
SOUTHSIDE DR
El Capitan Meadow
Valley Floor Loop
To Arch Rock Entrance and Big Oak Flat Road
Merced River
BRIDALVEIL FALL
6,545ft
5,907ft
Cathedral Spires
6,118ft
Profile Cliff 7,503ft
Taft Point 7,503ft
VALLEY VIEW
Leaning Tower 5,863ft
Bridalveil Creek
To Wawona Tunnel and Hwy 41
Stanford Point
Dewey Point
0 0.5 mi
0 0.5 km

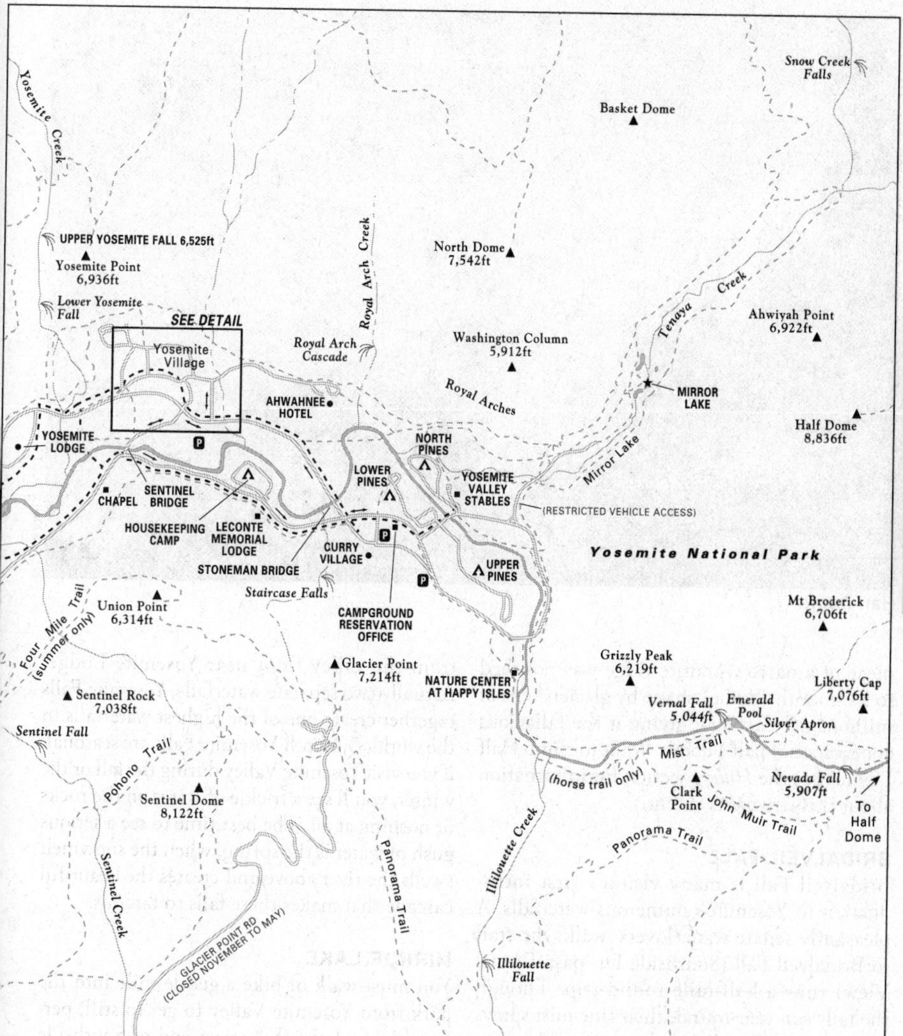
Snow Creek Falls
Basket Dome
Yosemite Creek
UPPER YOSEMITE FALL 6,525ft
Yosemite Point 6,936ft
Lower Yosemite Fall
SEE DETAIL
Yosemite Village
Royal Arch Creek
Royal Arch Cascade
North Dome 7,542ft
Washington Column 5,912ft
Tenaya Creek
Ahwiyah Point 6,922ft
Royal Arches
AHWAHNEE HOTEL
MIRROR LAKE
Half Dome 8,836ft
YOSEMITE LODGE
NORTH PINES
Mirror Lake
CHAPEL
SENTINEL BRIDGE
LOWER PINES
YOSEMITE VALLEY STABLES
(RESTRICTED VEHICLE ACCESS)
HOUSEKEEPING CAMP
LECONTE MEMORIAL LODGE
CURRY VILLAGE
Yosemite National Park
STONEMAN BRIDGE
UPPER PINES
Staircase Falls
Union Point 6,314ft
CAMPGROUND RESERVATION OFFICE
Mt Broderick 6,706ft
Four Mile Trail (summer only)
Glacier Point 7,214ft
Grizzly Peak 6,219ft
NATURE CENTER AT HAPPY ISLES
Liberty Cap 7,076ft
Sentinel Rock 7,038ft
Vernal Fall 5,044ft
Emerald Pool
Silver Apron
Sentinel Fall
Mist Trail
Pohono Trail
(horse trail only)
Nevada Fall 5,907ft
Sentinel Dome 8,122ft
Clark Point
John Muir Trail
To Half Dome
Panorama Trail
Sentinel Creek
Illilouette Creek
GLACIER POINT RD (CLOSED NOVEMBER TO MAY)
Illilouette Fall
Illilouette Ridge
Pothole Meadows
Yosemite Valley Bike Trail
© AVALON TRAVEL

YOSEMITE

Half Dome

piece of a narrow granite ridge was polished to its smooth "dome" shape by glaciers tens of millions of years ago, giving it the fallacious appearance of half a dome. Want to climb Half Dome? See the *Hiking* section for information about this strenuous ascent.

### BRIDALVEIL FALL

Bridalveil Fall is many visitor's first introduction to Yosemite's numerous waterfalls. A pleasantly sedate water-lovers' walk, the trail to Bridalveil Fall (Southside Dr. past Tunnel View) runs a half-mile round-trip. Though the falls run year-round, their fine mist sprays strongest in spring—expect to get wet!

The trailhead comes before the main lodge, parking, and visitors center complex, making it a great first stop as you travel up the valley.

### YOSEMITE FALLS

Springtime and early summer are the best times to view the many waterfalls that cascade down the granite walls of Yosemite. You must hike to most of the falls, but Yosemite Falls are visible from the valley floor near Yosemite Lodge. Actually two separate waterfalls, Yosemite Falls together create one of the highest waterfalls in the world. But both Yosemite Falls are seasonal; if you visit Yosemite Valley during the fall or the winter, you'll see a trickle of water on the rocks or nothing at all. The best time to see a serious gush of water is the spring, when the snowmelt swells the river above and creates the beautiful cascade that makes these falls so famous.

### MIRROR LAKE

You must walk or bike a gentle mile into the park from Yosemite Valley to get to still, perfect Mirror Lake (hike past end of Southside Dr., about 4 miles round-trip). This small lake reflects the already spectacular views of Tenaya Canyon and the ubiquitous Half Dome. But come early in the season—this lake is gradually drying out, losing its water and existing as a meadow in the late summer and fall.

## Glacier Point

The best view of Yosemite Valley may not be

from the valley floor. To get a different look at the familiar formations and falls, drive up Glacier Point Road to Glacier Point. The trail from the road is any easy one—paved and wheelchair accessible—but the vista down into Yosemite Valley is anything but common. Glacier Point Road stays open all year (except when storms make it temporarily impassable) to allow access to the Badger Pass ski area.

## Wawona

The small town-like area of Wawona (Wawona Rd./Hwy. 41, 1.5 hours from Yosemite Valley) sits only a few miles from the south entrance of Yosemite. The historic Wawona Hotel was built in 1917 and also houses a popular restaurant as well as a store. Wawona also plays home to the **Pioneer Yosemite History Center** (trail from Wawona information station, open daily). The first thing you'll see is a big open barn housing an array of vehicles used over a century in Yosemite, from big cushiony carriages for rich tourists to oil wagons once used in an ill-conceived attempt to control mosquitoes on the ponds. Onward, walk under the Vermont-style covered bridge to the main museum area. This rambling, not-overcrowded stretch of land contains many of the original structures built in the park—most over 100 years ago. Most were moved here from various remote locations. Informative placards describe the history of Yosemite National Park through its structures, from the military shacks used by soldiers who comprised the first park rangers, through homes lived in by early settlers in the area presided over by stoic pioneer women. Check your *Yosemite Guide* for living history programs and live demonstrations held at the museum.



### MARIPOSA GROVE OF GIANT SEQUOIAS

One of three groves of rare giant sequoia trees in Yosemite, the Mariposa Grove (Wawona Rd./Hwy. 41) offers a view of these majestic trees even to visitors who aren't up for long walks or strenuous hikes. During high season, a one-hour tram ride meanders through the grove, complete with an audio tour describing the botany of the trees, their history, and more.

carriage at the Pioneer Yosemite History Center

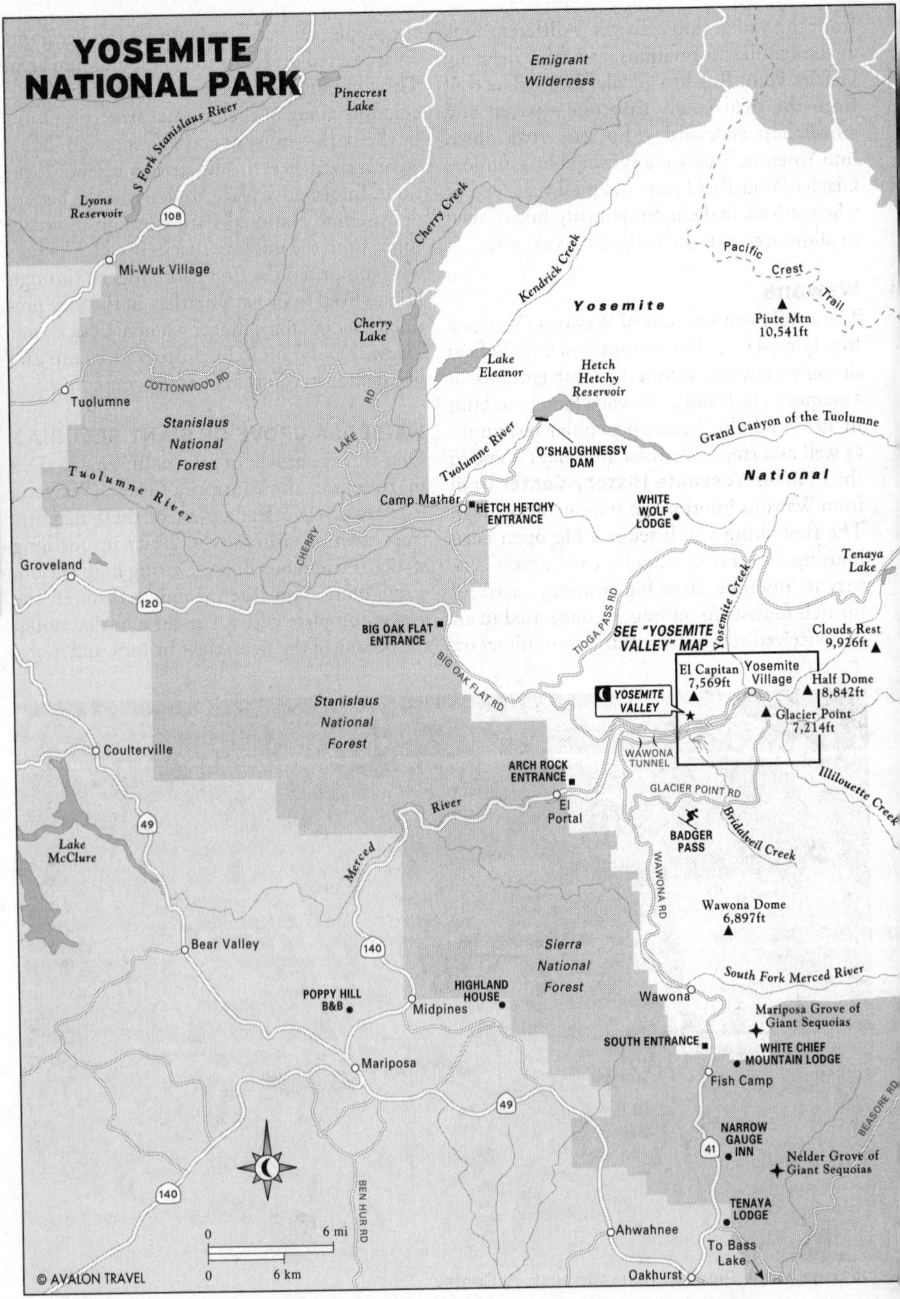
YOSEMITE
NATIONAL PARK
Emigrant
Wilderness
Pinecrest
Lake
S Fork Stanislaus River
Lyons
Reservoir
108
Cherry Creek
Kendrick Creek
Pacific
Crest
Trail
Mi-Wuk Village
Yosemite
Piute Mtn
10,541ft
Cherry
Lake
Lake
Eleanor
Hetch
Hetchy
Reservoir
COTTONWOOD RD
Tuolumne
Stanislaus
National
Forest
LAKE RD
Grand Canyon of the Tuolumne
Tuolumne River
O'SHAUGHNESSY
DAM
National
Tuolumne River
Camp Mather
HETCH HETCHY
ENTRANCE
WHITE
WOLF
LODGE
CHERRY
Groveland
Tenaya
Lake
120
TIOGA PASS RD
Yosemite Creek
BIG OAK FLAT
ENTRANCE
SEE "YOSEMITE
VALLEY" MAP
Clouds Rest
9,926ft
BIG OAK FLAT RD
El Capitan
7,569ft
Yosemite
Village
Half Dome
8,842ft
Stanislaus
National
Forest
YOSEMITE
VALLEY
Glacier Point
7,214ft
Coulterville
WAWONA
TUNNEL
ARCH ROCK
ENTRANCE
Illilouette Creek
GLACIER POINT RD
River
El
Portal
49
Bridalveil Creek
BADGER
PASS
Lake
McClure
Merced
WAWONA RD
Wawona Dome
6,897ft
Sierra
National
Forest
Bear Valley
140
South Fork Merced River
HIGHLAND
HOUSE
POPPY HILL
B&B
Wawona
Midpines
Mariposa Grove of
Giant Sequoias
SOUTH ENTRANCE
WHITE CHIEF
MOUNTAIN LODGE
Mariposa
Fish Camp
49
BEASORE RD
NARROW
GAUGE
INN
41
Nelder Grove of
Giant Sequoias
140
BEN HUR RD
TENAYA
LODGE
0
6 mi
Ahwahnee
To Bass
Lake
0
6 km
© AVALON TRAVEL
Oakhurst

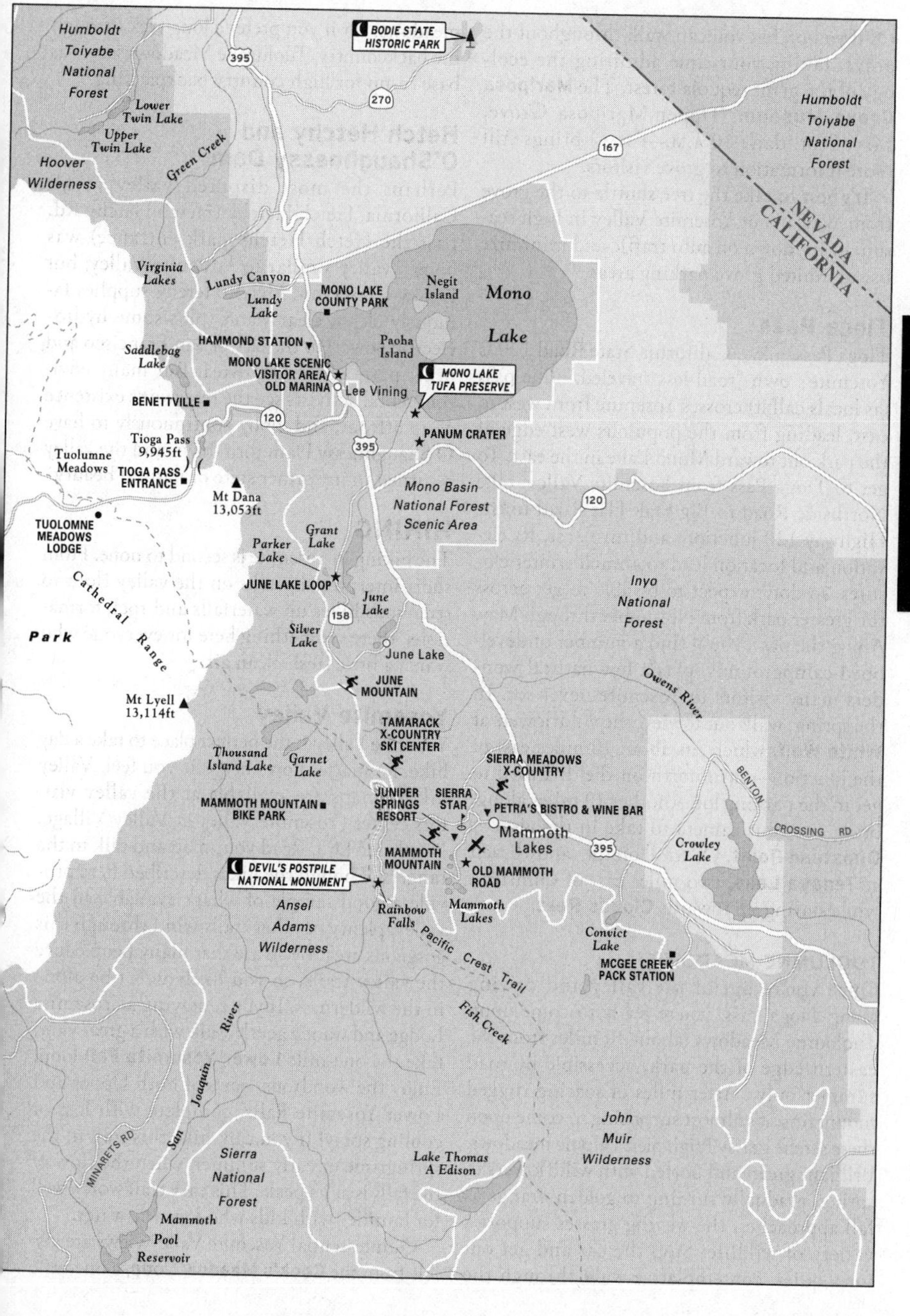

Humboldt Toiyabe National Forest
BODIE STATE HISTORIC PARK
395
270
Lower Twin Lake
Upper Twin Lake
Hoover Wilderness
Green Creek
167
Humboldt Toiyabe National Forest
NEVADA
CALIFORNIA
Virginia Lakes
Lundy Canyon
Lundy Lake
MONO LAKE COUNTY PARK
Negit Island
Mono Lake
Paoha Island
HAMMOND STATION
Saddlebag Lake
MONO LAKE SCENIC VISITOR AREA/ OLD MARINA
Lee Vining
MONO LAKE TUFA PRESERVE
BENETTVILLE
120
PANUM CRATER
Tioga Pass 9,945ft
395
Tuolumne Meadows
TIOGA PASS ENTRANCE
Mt Dana 13,053ft
Mono Basin National Forest Scenic Area
120
TUOLUMNE MEADOWS LODGE
Grant Lake
Parker Lake
JUNE LAKE LOOP
Cathedral Range
June Lake
158
Inyo National Forest
Park
Silver Lake
June Lake
JUNE MOUNTAIN
Owens River
Mt Lyell 13,114ft
TAMARACK X-COUNTRY SKI CENTER
Thousand Island Lake
Garnet Lake
SIERRA MEADOWS X-COUNTRY
BENTON
MAMMOTH MOUNTAIN BIKE PARK
JUNIPER SPRINGS RESORT
SIERRA STAR
PETRA'S BISTRO & WINE BAR
Mammoth Lakes
CROSSING RD
395
Crowley Lake
MAMMOTH MOUNTAIN
OLD MAMMOTH ROAD
DEVIL'S POSTPILE NATIONAL MONUMENT
Ansel Adams Wilderness
Rainbow Falls
Mammoth Lakes
Pacific Crest Trail
Convict Lake
MCGEE CREEK PACK STATION
San Joaquin River
Fish Creek
John Muir Wilderness
MINARETS RD
Sierra National Forest
Lake Thomas A Edison
Mammoth Pool Reservoir

Or if you prefer, you can walk throughout the grove, taking your time admiring the ecology of the giant sequoia forest. The **Mariposa Grove Museum** (Upper Mariposa Grove, May–Sept. daily 10 A.M.–4 P.M.) brings still more information to grove visitors.

It's best to take the free shuttle to the grove from Wawona or Yosemite Valley in high season, to cut down on auto traffic and minimize use of limited grove parking areas.



### Tioga Pass

Tioga Pass, a.k.a. California State Road 120 is Yosemite's own "road less traveled." The pass (as locals call it) crosses Yosemite from west to east, leading from the populous west edge of the park out toward Mono Lake in the east. To get to Tioga Pass from Yosemite Valley, take Northside Road to Big Oak Flat Road to the Highway 120 junction, and turn east. Its elevation and location lead to annual winter closures, so don't expect to be able to get across the greater park from November through May. Along the pass, you'll find a number of developed campgrounds, plus a few natural wonders many visitors to Yosemite never see. In the spring, walk out to view the wildflowers at **White Wolf,** which sits about 10 miles east of the junction—turn north on the dirt road to get to the parking lot. Another 10 miles along, bring out your camera to take in the vista at **Olmstead Point.** Or stroll on the sandy beach at **Tenaya Lake,** two miles east of Olmstead while staring up towards **Clouds Rest.**

#### TUOLUMNE MEADOWS

Once you're out of the valley and driving along Tioga Pass, you're ready to come upon Tuolomne Meadows (about 10 miles from the eastern edge of the park, accessible by road summer only). After miles of soaring rugged mountains, it's almost surprising to come upon these serene grassy High Sierra alpine meadows. Brilliant green and dotted with wildflowers in spring, gradually turning to golden orange as fall approaches, the waving grasses support a variety of wildlife. Stop the car and get out for a quiet, contemplative walk through the meadows. Or if you prefer a long trek through the backcountry, Tuolumne Meadows serves as base camp for high country backpacking.

### Hetch Hetchy and O'Shaughnessy Dam

Perhaps the most disputed valley in all California, Hetch Hetchy (Hetch Hetchy Rd. past the Hetch Hetchy park entrance) was once a valley similar to Yosemite Valley, but is now a reservoir. Hetch Hetchy supplies famously clean, clear water (plus some hydroelectric power) to the city of San Francisco and other parts of the Bay Area. But many environmental activists see the reservoir's existence as an affront, and lobby continuously to have O'Shaughnessy Dam torn down and the valley returned to its former state of natural beauty.

## HIKING

The hiking in Yosemite is second to none. From short interpretive walks on the valley floor to strenuous hikes up waterfalls and rock formations, there's something here for everyone who wants a little fresh clean air.

### Yosemite Valley

Yosemite Valley is the perfect place to take a day hike, no matter how energetic you feel. Valley hiking maps are available at the valley visitors center (Yosemite Valley at Valley Village, Northside Dr.). Read your map and talk to the rangers. Though the hikes described here provide a good sample of what's available in the valley, plenty of other trails wind through this gorgeous area. Be aware that many people love the valley trails, so you likely won't be alone in the wilderness. If you're staying at Yosemite Lodge and want a gentle walk with a great view, take the one-mile **Lower Yosemite Fall** loop. Enjoy the wondrous views of both Upper and Lower Yosemite Falls, complete with lots of cooling spray! If you can, hike this trail in the springtime or early summer, when the flow of the falls is at its peak. This easy trail works well for families with kids who love the water.

Quintessential Yosemite Valley views are visible from the **Cook's Meadow Loop,** a one-mile walk through the heart of the valley. The point of this hike is to observe Ansel Adams' famous view of Half Dome from the Sentinel Bridge, then go on to gaze up at the Royal Arches and Glacier Point.

For walkers with a little more stamina, several trails in the valley are flat, but longer. To see **Mirror Lake** (end of Southside Dr., four miles, moderate), first take the short, wheelchair-accessible paved path. For a longer walk, take the connected loop trail two miles following Tenaya Creek. Read the exhibits around the lake to learn how and why Mirror Lake is transforming from a lake into a meadow (a natural process).

If you've got several hours and a desire to extend your visit to the valley floor, take the **Valley Floor Loop** (Northside Dr. and Southside Dr., paved path alongside road). For visitors who want a mid-length hike, the half loop runs 6.5 miles and takes about three hours to traverse, going over the El Capitan Bridge and following the path of many old wagon roads and historic trails. The full loop is 13 miles long and takes all day (about six hours) to hike. But it's worth it, since you'll see all the most beautiful parts of the valley while escaping the crowds on the roads. If you want to hike the Valley Floor Loop, it's a good idea to talk to the rangers at the visitors center; the route is not entirely clear on the trail map and getting lost in the meadows or forests is a distinct possibility.

Some of the more challenging hikes in Yosemite Valley are also the most rewarding. One of these is the trek up to **Upper Yosemite Fall** (trailhead at Camp 4). You can take the shuttle (Stop #7) to the Upper Yosemite Fall trailhead rather than walking up from Lower Yosemite Fall. From the trailhead, it gets steep—you'll climb 2,700 feet in three miles (seven miles round-trip) to reach the top of America's tallest waterfall. Your reward for the work will be some of the most astonishing aerial views to be had anywhere in the world. You can look down over the fall and out over the valley, with its grassy meadows so tiny far below. Plan all day (6–8 hours) for this hike, and bring plenty of water and snacks to replenish your energy for the tricky climb down.

Perhaps the most famous hardcore climb in Yosemite Valley takes you to the top of the monumental **Half Dome** (Mist Trail to Half Dome Trail, trail parking at the east end of Northside Dr.). This hike can be dangerous! Attempt this climb only in the summer and early fall, when the cables are up (which you hold onto for balance and use to help pull yourself up the steep granite of the last 400 feet to the top of the dome). At a round-trip distance of 17 miles and with a 4,800-foot ascent, this arduous, all-day hike (10–12 hours) is not for small children, the elderly, or the out-of-shape. Take your pack with water, food, and essentials for safety. Once you stagger to the top, you'll find a restful expanse of stone on which to sit and rest and enjoy the scenery.

Starting at the Happy Isles Nature Center, the **Mist Trail** takes you first to Vernal Fall, then on to Nevada Fall over much steep, slick granite—including over 600 stair-steps up to the top of Vernal Fall. The total distance from Happy Isles to Nevada Fall and back is seven miles, with a 2,000-foot elevation rise and fall. Plan 5–6 hours for this hike, and consider taking a lightweight parka since this aptly named trail gets intrepid visitors very wet in the spring and early summer months.

## Glacier Point Road

If you love the thrill of heights, head up Glacier Point Road and take a hike up to or along one of the spectacular (and slightly scary) granite cliffs. Hikes in this area run from quite easy to rigorous, but note that many of the cliffside trails aren't appropriate for hard-to-control children.

The two-mile round-trip hike up **Sentinel Dome** (trailhead just southwest of end of Glacier Point Rd.) makes for a surprisingly easy walk; the only steep part runs right up the dome at the end of the trail. You can do this hike in 2–3 hours, and you'll find views at the top to make the effort and high elevation (more than 8,000 feet at the top) more than worthwhile. On a clear day, you can see from

Yosemite Valley to the High Sierras and all the way out to Mount Diablo in the Bay Area to the west. Be sure to bring a camera! Be aware that there are no guardrails or walls to protect you from the long falls along the side of the trail and at the top of the dome.

Another not-too-long walk to a magnificent vista point is the hike to **Taft Point and the Fissures** (park 1–2 miles southwest of Glacier Point, Glacier Point Rd.). This two-mile round-trip hike takes you along some of Yosemite's unusual rock formations (the Fissures), through the always lovely woods, and on out to Taft Point. This precarious precipice boasts not a single stone wall—only a rickety set of guardrails to keep visitors from plummeting off the point 2,000 feet down to the nearest patch of flat ground. Thrill seekers enjoy challenging themselves to get right up to the edge of the cliff and peer down. Happily for more sedate hikers, the elevation change from the trailhead to the point is only about 200 feet.



If you're looking for a mid-level or challenging hike, plus the most spectacular view of *all* of Yosemite Falls anywhere in the park, take the **Four Mile Trail** (Glacier Point to Southside Dr., eight miles round-trip) that connects Glacier Point to Yosemite Valley. The easiest way to take this hike is to start at the top, from Glacier Point, and hike down to the valley. You can then catch a ride on the Glacier Point Tour Bus (be sure to buy tickets in advance!) back up to your car. The steep climb up the trail from the valley can be much harder on the legs and the lungs, but it affords you an ascending series of views of Yosemite Falls and Yosemite Valley that grow more spectacular with each switchback.

For a longer high-elevation hike, take the 12.5-mile walk to **Ostrander Lake** (trailhead approximately two miles past Bridalveil Creek Rd., Glacier Point Rd.) and back. (You can cross-country ski to the lake in the winter and stay overnight at the local ski hut.) This trek can take all day if you're going at a relaxed pace-especially if you're visiting during June or July and stopping to admire the wildflowers in bloom all along the trail. The lake itself is a lovely patch of shining clear water surrounded by granite boulders and picturesque pine trees. Consider starting up the trail in the morning and packing a picnic lunch to enjoy beside the serene water. And remember to bring bug repellant since the still waters of the lake and nearby streams are mosquito heaven during hiking season.

## Wawona

It's not quite as popular (or populous) as Yosemite Valley, but the hikes near Wawona in southern Yosemite can be just as scenic and lovely. Start with the **Wawona Meadow Loop** (Pioneer Yosemite History Center), a flat and shockingly uncrowded 3.5-mile sweep around the lovely Wawona meadow and somewhat incongruous 9-hole golf course. This wide trail was once fully paved, and is still bikeable, but the pavement has eroded over the years and now you'll find much dirt and tree detritus. Best in late spring because the wildflowers bloom in profusion, this trail takes about two hours to navigate. If you'd like a longer trip, you can extend this walk to five miles (with about 500 feet of climb/descent) by taking the detour at the south end of the meadow.

If you're up for a hardcore hike and a waterfall experience few who visit Yosemite ever see, take the difficult, 8.5-mile trail to **Chilnualna Fall** (trailhead near Pioneer Yosemite History Center). Plan 4–6 hours for this 2,300-foot ascent, and bring water, snacks, and a trail map. On this amazing hike, you'll see a few fellow hikers, and many tantalizing views of the cascades. Sadly, there's no created viewing area, so you'll need to peek through the trees to get the best looks and photos. The trail runs all the way up to the top of the falls, but be careful to avoid the stream during spring and summer high flow—it's dangerous in there, what with the waterfall and everything!

## Tioga Pass and Tuolumne Meadows

For smaller crowds along the trails, take one or more of the many scenic hikes along Tioga Pass. However, be aware that they don't call it "the high country" for nothing; the altitude here *starts* at 8,500 feet and goes up on many trails. If you're not in great shape, or if you have breathing problems, take the altitude into account when deciding which trails to explore.

A great place to start your high country exploration, the loop trail to **Tenaya Lake** (Tioga Pass 20 miles west of the park's east entrance, right along the main road) offers an easy walk, sunny beaches, and possibly the most picturesque views in all of Yosemite. The trail around the lake runs about 2.5 miles, and the only difficult part is fording the outlet stream at the west end of the lake, since the water gets chilly and can be high in the spring and early summer. If the rest of your group is sick of hiking and scenery, you can leave them on the beach while you take this easy one- to two-hour stroll. Just remember the mosquito repellant!

If you're aching to see some giant trees, but you were put off by the parking problems at Mariposa Grove, try the **Tuolumne Grove of Giant Sequoias** (park and find the trailhead at the junction of Tioga Pass Rd. and Old Big Oak Flat Rd.). This 2.5-mile round-trip hike takes you down about 400 feet into the grove, which contains more than 20 mature giant sequoias. (You do have to climb back up the hill to get to your car.) While you'll likely see other visitors, the smaller crowds make this grove an attractive alternative to Mariposa, especially in the high season.

For non-athletes who just want a short walk to an amazing view, **Olmstead Point** (Tioga Pass 1–2 miles west of Tenaya Lake) may be the perfect destination. Only half a mile round-trip from the parking lot to the point, this trail exists to show off Clouds Rest in all its often-underrated grandeur. Half Dome peeks out behind Clouds Rest, and right at the trail parking lot a number of large glacial errata boulders draw almost as many tourists as the point itself.

Hikers willing to tackle somewhat longer, steeper treks will find an amazing array of small scenic lakes within reach of Tioga Pass. **Gaylor Lakes** (trailhead at the Yosemite Park border, Tioga Pass Rd.) starts high (almost 10,000 feet) and climbs a steep 600 feet up the pass to the Gaylor Lakes valley. Once you're in the valley, you can wander at will around the five lovely lakes, stopping to admire the views out to the mountains surrounding Tuolumne Meadows or visiting the abandoned 1870s mine site above Upper Gaylor Lake. The total hike spans about three miles if you don't wander around the valley. Crowd-haters will enjoy this trek, which is one of Yosemite's less crowded scenic hikes.

**May Lake** (one mile southwest of Tenaya Lake, Tioga Pass Rd.) sits peacefully at the base of the sloping granite of Mount Hoffman. While the hike to and from May Lake is only 2.5 miles, there's a steady, steep 500-foot climb from the trailhead up to the lake. One of Yosemite's High Sierra camps perches here, which makes this hike popular with the sorts of visitors who enjoy the much-less-known high-country areas. For truly hardcore hikers, a trail leads from the lake up another 2,000 feet (and six miles round-trip) to the top of Mount Hoffman.

The trail to **Elizabeth Lake** (trailhead at Tuolumne Gas Station and John Muir Trail) begins at Tuolumne Meadows and climbs almost 1,000 feet up to the lake, with most of the climb during the first mile of the 4.5-mile round-trip. Evergreens ring the lake and steep granite Unicorn Peak rises high above it. This stunning little lake makes a perfect photo op that your friends won't necessarily recognize as being Yosemite.

If altitude doesn't bother you and your legs are strong, Tioga Pass offers some stunning hikes good for a full day of hiking (or longer, if that's your thing).

For a different look at a classic Yosemite landmark, take the **North Dome** trail through the woods and out to the dome, which sits right across the valley from Half Dome. You'll hike almost nine miles round-trip, with a few hills thrown in, but getting to stare right at the face of Half Dome (and check out Cloud's Rest just beyond) at what feels like eye-level makes the effort worth it.

If you can't get enough of Yosemite's granite-framed alpine lakes, take the long walk out to one or both of the **Cathedral Lakes** (trailhead at Tuolumne Meadows visitors center, part of the John Muir Trail). Starting at ever-popular Tuolumne Meadows, you'll climb about 800 feet over 3–4 miles (depending on which lake you choose). These picture-perfect lakes show off the dramatic rocky peaks above, surrounding evergreens, and crystalline waters of Yosemite to their best advantage. Be sure to bring your camera, water, and munchies!

The **Glen Aulin Trail** (trailhead at Tuolumne Stables) to Tuolumne Fall and White Cascade is part of the John Muir trail, and several of its forks branch off to pretty little lakes and other nice spots in the area. From Tuolumne Meadows to Tuolumne Fall and back is 13 miles round trip, with some steep and rocky areas in the trail. But if you've got the lungs for it, you'll be rewarded by the fabulous views of the Tuolumne River alternately pooling and cascading right beside the trail. This hike may get a bit crowded in the high season. In the hot summertime, many hikers trade dusty jeans for swimsuits and cool off in the pools at the base of both White Cascade and Tuolumne Fall. A great way to do this hike is to enter the High Sierra Camp lottery and, if you win, arrange to stay the night at the Glen Aulin camp. If you do this, you can take your hike a few miles farther, downstream to California Fall, Le Conte Fall, and finally Waterwheel Fall.



## SPORTS AND RECREATION

The whole point of coming to Yosemite is to get outside and enjoy it. If you're craving more than just endless hiking, the park offers plenty of different outdoor activities suited to all ages and fitness levels.

### Horse and Mule Riding

Miles of trails let visitors of all ability levels take a load off their own feet and explore Yosemite from the back of a horse...or a mule! For some of Yosemite's more rugged terrain, especially in the high country, easygoing, surefooted mules are the best animals for the job of getting both people and gear around.

Three rides begin at the **Yosemite Valley Stable** (end of Southside Dr., 209/372-4386, www.yosemitepark.com/activities_mulehorsebackrides.aspx, half-day $59–119). The sedate two-hour trek to Mirror Lake works well for kids and beginning riders. As part of the ride, your guide explains the geologic forces that are slowly drying out the lake. A half-day ride takes you out to Vernal Fall, where you can admire the views of Nevada Fall and the valley floor. This ride takes about four hours, but isn't terribly difficult. The all-day ride requires a great deal more stamina—going all the way out to Little Yosemite Valley and back.

You'll find more horses than mules at **Wawona Stable** (Wawona Rd. at Pioneer Yosemite History Center, $59–119), and more tourists, too—reservations for the rides out of Wawona are strongly encouraged. From Wawona you can take a sedate two-hour ride around the historic wagon trail running into the area. Or try the five-hour trip out to Chilanualna Falls—you'll get to tell your friends about a waterfall that few Yosemite visitors ever see. Be sure to bring a camera! Both of these rides are fine for less experienced riders, and the wagon trail ride welcomes children with its easy, flat terrain.

Out of **Tuolumne Meadows Stable** (Tioga Pass Rd. past Tuolumne Visitors Center, north side of the road, short dirt road to stables) you can get the perfect overview of the Yosemite high country by taking the introductory-level two-hour ride. For a longer ride deeper into the landscape, do the four-hour trip that passes Twin Bridges and Tuolumne Falls. An all-day ride with a variable route beckons the adventurous traveler, but you need to be both in good shape *and* an experienced rider for this one.

### Bicycling

Biking is a great way to get out of the car and off the crowded roads, and to explore Yosemite at a quicker-than-walking pace. Twelve miles of paved trails are mostly flat. You can bring your own bikes, or rent (www.yosemitepark.com/Activities_Biking_BikeRentals.aspx, daily 8:30 A.M.–8:30 P.M., $9.50/hour, $25/

day) from Yosemite Village. Check at Yosemite Lodge at Yosemite Falls for more information about renting and to get a bike trail map.

### Rock Climbing

The rock climbing at Yosemite is some of the best in the world. **El Capitan,** the face of **Half Dome**, and **Sentinel Dome** in the high country are challenges that draw climbers from all over. If you plan to climb one of these monuments, check with the Yosemite park rangers and the Mountaineering School well in advance of your planned climb for necessary information and permits.

But many of the spectacular ascents are *not* beginners' climbs. Go try to scale El Capitan for your first climb ever, and you'll fail (if you're lucky). The right place to start climbing in Yosemite is the **Yosemite Mountaineering School** (209/372-8344, www.yosemitepark.com/activities_mountaineeringschool.aspx). Here you'll find beginners' "Go Climb a Rock" classes perfect for older kids or adult team-building groups. You'll also find guided climbs out of Yosemite Valley and Tuolumne Meadows, and if you're looking for a one-on-one guided climb experience, you can get it through the school. Also available are guided hikes and backpacking trips, and cross-country skiing lessons and treks in wintertime.

### Skiing

Yosemite prides itself on its 350 miles of cross-country skiing tracks and trails throughout the park. In fact, many places in Yosemite are accessible in winter only by cross-country skis or snowshoes. Check out the **Cross Country Ski School** (www.yosemitepark.com/badgerpass_crosscountryskiing.aspx) for classes, rentals, and guided cross-country ski tours. If you're looking for a fun day out in the snow, the groomed tracks from Badger Pass to Glacier Point run 21 miles and are frequented by day skiers. You'll see fewer other skiers on the backcountry trails, which can also be traversed in a single day by a reasonably strong skier. For the hardcore XCer who wants a serious skiing experience, check out the overnight and multi-day tours—hiring a guide for these trips is recommended for most skiers.

Downhill skiing at **Badger Pass** (Glacier Point Rd., five miles from Wawona, mid-Dec.–Apr., daily 9 A.M.–4 P.M., prices vary) is another favorite wintertime activity at Yosemite. Badger Pass was the first downhill ski area created in California. Today, it's the perfect resort for families and groups who want a relaxed day or three of moderate skiing. With plenty of beginner runs and classes, Yosemite has helped thousands of kids (and adults!) learn to ski and snowboard as friends and family look on from the sun decks at the lodge. There are enough intermediate runs to make it interesting for mid-level skiers, too. Double-black diamond skiers may find Badger Pass too tame for their tastes since there are just a few advanced runs. But everyone agrees that the prices are more reasonable than much of what you'll find at Tahoe's huge resorts, and the focus is on friendliness and learning rather than showing off and extreme skiing.

### Snowshoeing

Even if you're not up for hardcore skiing, you can get out and enjoy the snow-covered landscapes of wintertime Yosemite. Snowshoeing requires no experience and only minimal fitness to get started. "If you can walk, you can snowshoe," claims Yosemite's own website. You can rent snowshoes at several locations in Yosemite and acquire trail maps from the rental centers. The **Cross Country Ski School** (www.yosemitepark.com/badgerpass_snowshoeing.aspx) offers guided hikes and winter camping trips.

## ENTERTAINMENT AND EVENTS

### Photography and Art Classes

The unbelievable scenery of Yosemite inspires visitors young and old to create images to take home with them. Knowing this, Yosemite offers art and photography classes to help people catch hold of their inner Ansel Adams. In the summertime, art classes are offered for free out of the **Yosemite Art and Education Center**

(Yosemite Village, Mon.–Sat. 10 A.M.–2 P.M.). Check the *Yosemite Guide* for a list of classes during your visit. You must bring your own art supplies, chair or cushion to sit on, and walking shoes (you'll take a brief walk out to a good location to see the scenery). If you don't have supplies, you can buy them at the Village Store just before class. Also check the *Guide* for guided tours of the **Ansel Adams Gallery** in the Village.

## Theater and Music

The **Valley Visitors Center Auditorium** (Northside Dr. at Yosemite Village visitors center) in the heart of Yosemite Village acts as home to the Yosemite Theater. For an evening of indoor entertainment, check the copy of *Yosemite Today* you received at the gate for a list of what shows are playing during your visit. Most plays are one- or two-man productions; all center on the theme of the rich history and culture of Yosemite National Park. The John Muir Performances, starring resident actor Lee Stetson, have been running for 25 years.

It's worth making an evening trip out to Wawona one evening to listen to the delightful piano music and singing of legendary Tom Bopp. He plays vintage camp music (and requests, and whatever else strikes his fancy) in the **Piano Lounge at the Wawona Hotel** (209/375-1425) five nights a week. Older visitors especially love his old-style performance



## YOSEMITE AT NIGHT

Yosemite National Park does not roll up its meadows and trails at sunset. In fact, parts of the park come alive at nightfall, showing off another side of Yosemite's natural wonders. Check your *Yosemite Today* guide for more information about these and other activity programs.

If you fancy a nighttime stroll, you can take one regardless of season or weather. In summer, **Night Prowl** (90 minutes, $5) takes you along easy trails near Yosemite Lodge at Yosemite Falls, explaining the nightlife of the inhabitants of the valley floor. This fun guided tour welcomes children and adults. It takes place once or twice a week, starting at different times and places. In winter, take a **Full Moon Snowshoe Walk** ($14.75 rental, $5 without, children over 8). This two-hour trek from the Badger Pass ski lodge takes you out into the sparkling white wonderland that is Yosemite in winter. These walks are offered five days per month – the four days leading up to the full moon, and the day of the full moon itself. Also be aware that the Badger Pass shuttle *does not* run in the evenings, so you must drive yourself to and from the lodge.

If astronomy is your favorite nighttime interest, join experienced guides out in the valley meadows for the **Starry Skies** ($5, summer and fall) program. Well suited for individuals and families, this one-hour program takes groups out to look at the unpolluted lights of stars and moon over the park. You'll learn about constellations, comets, and meteors, and enjoy the myths and legends surrounding the mysteries of the night sky. Starry Skies happens several times each week in Yosemite Valley, and once a week in Wawona.

For families who find themselves tired after a long day running around the park, plenty of non-hiking evening fun can be had at various semi-sedentary evening programs. The **Campfire Program** ($5) does it old-school – groups gather around a nice big campfire (bring blankets and bug repellant!) for stories, singing, and marshmallow toasting. You might need to take a short walk to get to the fire near Camp Curry. If you're out at one of the more primitive lodges or campsites, check with your local rangers or office for campfire programs at your site, since many spring up in the summer and early fall months. **Fireside Storytelling** (fall, winter, and spring, free) focuses on, well, telling stories around the big fire inside the Ahwahnee Great Lounge. Take refuge from the bugs and the cold and listen to great tales in a comfortable indoor environment during the off-season.

and familiar songs, but everyone enjoys the music and entertainment he provides. Even if you're just waiting for a table at the restaurant, stop in to say hello and make a request.

## CAMPING

Many people come to Yosemite specifically to feel the great outdoors all around them all the time. Naturally, that experience includes camping out under the stars. Inside the park, you'll find 13 designated campgrounds and the High Sierra camps. If you prefer less expense and less need for advance reservations, try one of the campgrounds outside the park boundaries.

### Inside the Park

For any Yosemite National Park campground, make reservations early! All the major campgrounds fill up from spring through fall, and reservations can be difficult to come by. Consider making your Yosemite campground reservation *at least six months in advance* to get the campsite you want. To make a reservation, go to www.nps.gov/yose/planyourvisit/camping.htm or call 877/444-6777.

#### YOSEMITE VALLEY

In Yosemite Valley, the campgrounds at **Upper, Middle,** and **Lower Pine** (reservations required, 375 campsites, $20/day) allow trailers and RVs, and you can bring your dog camping here with you. Upper Pine is open through the winter. Camp Curry offers plenty of food options within walking distance, and showers are available nearby. **Camp 4** (near Yosemite Lodge, no reservations required, 35 campsites, $5) stays open year-round. Yes, you can camp in the snow! Bring a tent—no RVs or trailers are allowed at Camp 4—but you'll find showers nearby and lots of food and groceries at Yosemite Lodge.

#### WAWONA

To the south, you can camp at lovely forested **Wawona** (one mile north of Wawona, reservations required Apr.–Oct., 93 sites, $20) year-round. RVs are welcome, though there are no hookups on-site. If you want to camp with your horses, Wawona offers two horse sites. The small grocery store in town can provide a few basics, but most services (including showers) can't be found closer than Yosemite Valley. For a more picturesque southern Yosemite camping experience, check out **Bridalveil Creek** (Glacier Point Rd., no reservations required, 110 campsites, $14/night). You can reserve one of three horse sites if you're traveling with your mount. Mechanical beasts of burdens (RVs) are welcome as well.

#### TIOGA PASS AND TUOLUMNE MEADOWS

Yosemite visitors who favor the high country tend to prefer to camp rather than stay in a lodge. Accordingly, most of Yosemite's campgrounds sit north of the valley, away from the largest tourist crowds (excluding the High Sierra Camps, which are also up north). **Tuolumne Meadows** (Tioga Pass Rd. at Tuolumne Meadows, reservations suggested, $20/night) hosts the largest campsite in the park, with over 300 individual campsites, plus four horse sites. Expect Tuolumne to be crowded for the whole of its season (July–Sept.). Tuolumne is RV-friendly and has most necessary services, including food and showers available at the Tuolumne Meadows Lodge. Other good-sized campgrounds off Tioga Pass include **Crane Flat** (reservations required, 166 campsites, $20/night, RVs ok, open mid-June–mid-Oct.), **White Wolf** (no reservations, 74 campsites, $14/night, open July–mid-Sept.), and **Hodgdon Meadow** (reservations required high season, 105 campsites, $20/night, open year-round) at the west edge of the park.

If you're looking to ditch the RV traffic and crowded central visitor areas, head for **Yosemite Creek** (no reservations, $10/night). This tents-only campground boasts only 40 campsites on a first-come, first-served basis from July through September. The creek flows right through the campground, perfect for cooling off on a hot day, and you can even drink the water if you first treat it properly. Yosemite Creek offers few amenities—no groceries, showers, or on-site potable water. It's just what many outdoorsy visitors want! Another option is **Tamarack Flat** (Tioga Pass Rd., no reservations, 52 campsites, $10/night). Here you'll be closer to Yosemite Valley but still in a more primitive environment.

The **High Sierra Camps** (www.yosemitepark.com/accommodations_highsierra_howtoapply.aspx) at Yosemite offer far more than your average backcountry campground. Rather than carrying heavy packs filled with food, tents, and bedding, multi-day hikers can plan to hit the High Sierra Camps, which provide tent cabins with amenities, breakfast and dinner in camp, and a box lunch to take along during the day. Choose from among the Merced Lake, Vogelsang, Glen Aulin, May Lake, and Sunrise Camp—or hike from one to the next if you get lucky. Why do you need luck? Because you can't just walk up to a High Sierra Camp one weekend at random and expect to find a bed. In the fall, a lottery takes place for spots at High Sierra Camps through the following summer. You'll need to submit an application if you want to join the lottery, and even if you get a spot there's no guarantee you'll get your preferred dates. You can check in at the website during the camping season (June–Sept.) to see if any dates are available.

The bottom line? If you want to take advantage of the Yosemite backcountry, plan for a summer when you can be flexible in your dates, and start making your arrangements a year in advance.

## Outside the Park

Some campers prefer a bit more seclusion, lower campsite prices, or just a different atmosphere. They tend to go for the campgrounds outside Yosemite's boundaries, which abound in the woodsy wilderness surrounding the park.

### GROVELAND

To camp in Big Oak Flat along Hwy. 120 near Groveland, try the Thousand Trails RV campground at **Yosemite Lakes** (31191 Harden Flat Rd., 800/533-1001, ranger station 209/962-0103, www.1000trails.com). This sprawling wooded campground beside the water has more than 250 RV sites with full hookups, 130 tent sites, a few dozen cabins, tent cabins, and yurts, and a 12-bed hostel. It's only five miles from the park entrance, and it's got a full slate of recreational amenities, laundry facilities, and Wi-Fi. You're right on the Tuolumne River, you've got great access to the boating opportunities on Lake Don Pedro, and the Moaning Cavern (see the *Sacramento and Gold Country* chapter) is only a few miles away.

### MARIPOSA

Several campgrounds surround the Arch Rock Entrance to Yosemite on Hwy. 140, near the border town of Mariposa. The **Yosemite Bug Rustic Mountain Resort** (6979 Hwy. 140, 866/826.7108, www.yosemitebug.com, $23/dorm bed, $35–55/tent cabin, $65–135/private cabin rooms) is part hostel, part rustic cabin lodge. This facility includes five hostel dormitories, a number of attractively appointed tent cabins with real beds, and a few cabins with private rooms, some with private baths. Solo travelers and families on tight budget favor Yosemite Bug for its comfortable and cheap accommodations. It's not the Ritz, but the bathrooms are clean and the linens are fresh when you arrive, and the location is great for Yosemite visitors who want to exit the park each night.

RVers aiming for the Arch Rock Entrance flock to the **Indian Flat RV Park** (9988 Hwy. 140, 209/379-2339, www.indianflatrvpark.com, tent sites $20–30, RV sites $35–40, tent cabins $60, cottages $110, pet fee $5). This park is a full-service low-end resort, with everything from minimal-hookup RV sites up through tent cabins and full-fledged cottages. Showers are available here, even for passers-through who aren't staying at Indian Flat. The lodge next door has extended an invitation to all Indian Flat campers to make use of their outdoor pool. Because Indian Flat is relatively small (25 RV sites, 25 tent sites), reservations are strongly recommended. You can make your booking up to a year in advance, and this kind of planning is a really good idea for summertime Yosemite visitors.

### SOUTH ENTRANCE

At the South Entrance down by the spread-out forest town of Fish Camp, book a site at the small, attractive **Summerdale Campground** (northeast of Fish Camp on Hwy. 41, 877/444-6777, www.reserveusa.com, two-night minimum weekends, three-night minimum holiday weekends, $19, June–Nov.). This lovely spot has only 29 campsites and a strict limit on RV size (24 feet), making it a bit quieter and less city-like than the mega-campgrounds. You'll have a fire ring and a grill at your site, plenty of room under mature shade trees for yourself and your friends, and maybe even a running water spigot (on some sites, boiling before drinking recommended).

### INYO NATIONAL FOREST

Out east, near Highway 395 and Tioga Pass, campgrounds tend to cluster in the Inyo National Forest. You can stay at **Ellery Lake** (Hwy. 120 in Upper Lee Vining Canyon, 877/444-6777, www.fs.fed.us/r5/inyo/recreation/campgrounds.shtml, $17, no reservations, pit toilets, garbage cans), which boasts 21 campsites perched at 9,500-feet elevation with available running water. Get there at dawn if you want a site on a weekend!

Another option is **Sawmill Walk-In** (Saddlebag Rd., 1.6 miles from Hwy. 120, 877/444-6777, www.fs.fed.us/r5/inyo/recreation/campgrounds.shtml, $12, June–Oct.). This primitive, no-reservations, hike-in campground (no water) has an astonishing 9,800-foot altitude that will, after a day or two, prepare you for any high-altitude activity you want to engage in.

## ACCOMMODATIONS

### Inside the Park

All the lodges, hotels, and cabin-tent clusters in Yosemite are run by the same booking agency. Contact the Yosemite Park concessionaire (801/559-4884, www.yosemitepark.com) to make reservations. Coming to Yosemite in the summer high season? Make reservations early-6–9 months early, if you have a preference as to where you want to stay. If you wait until the week before your trip, you'll either find the park sold out or end up in a tent cabin at Curry when you wanted a suite at the Ahwahnee.

### YOSEMITE VALLEY

**Curry Village** offers some of the oldest lodgings in the park. Locally called Camp Curry, this sprawling array of wood-sided and tent cabins was originally created in 1899 to provide affordable lodgings so that people of modest means could afford to visit and enjoy the wonders of Yosemite. At Curry Village, you can rent a hard-walled cabin or a tent cabin, with or without heat and with or without a private bath depending on your budget and your needs. The tent cabins ($95), the most affordable option, are small, fitting cot beds and a small dresser on the wood floor. Bear-proof lockers sit outside each tent cabin. Wood cabins ($179) have double beds (one or two) and electricity, but little else. The cabins with private baths are heated and boast daily maid services, but no TVs or phones. A few motel rooms and unique cabins have TVs and more amenities, but still no phones or significant distractions of the modern world. With its perfect location on the valley floor, a swimming pool in the summer and an ice skating rink in the winter, Camp Curry makes an inexpensive vacation at Yosemite a joyful reality.

Want to camp, but don't want to schlep all the gear into the park? Book a tent cabin at **Housekeeping Camp** ($76). Located on the banks of the Merced River, Housekeeping Camp has its own sandy river beach for playing and sunbathing. Cabins have cement walls, white canvas roofs, and a white canvas curtain that separates the bedroom from the covered patio that doubles as a dining room. Every cabin has a double bed plus two bunks (with room for two additional cots), a bear-proof food container, and an outdoor fire ring. You can bring your own linens, or rent a "bed pack" (no towels) for $2.50 per night. No maid service is provided, but you won't miss it as you sit outside watching the sun set over Yosemite Valley.

**Yosemite Lodge at the Falls** ($150–250), situated near Yosemite Village on the Valley floor, has a location perfect for touring all over the park. The motel-style rooms are light and pretty, with polished wood furniture, bright-colored bed linens, and Native American design details. Lodge rooms with king beds offer romantic escapes for couples, complete with balconies overlooking the valley, while the standard rooms can accommodate singles, couples, or families. Enjoy the heated pool in the summertime and the free shuttle transportation up to the Badger Pass ski area in winter. The amphitheater at the middle of the lodge runs nature programs and movies all year. The lodge has a post office, ATM, and plenty of food options, and is central to the Yosemite shuttle system.

If you're looking for luxury amongst the trees and rocks, check in to the **Ahwahnee Hotel** ($379–1,189). Built as a luxury hotel in the early 20th century, the Ahwahnee lives up to its reputation with soaring ceilings in the common rooms, a gorgeous stone facade, and striking stone fireplaces. Guest rooms, whether in the hotel or in the individual cottages, drip sumptuous appointments. The theme is Native American and you'll find intricate, multicolored geometric and zoomorphic designs on linens, furniture, and pillows. Rooms with king beds invite romance for couples, while those with two doubles are perfect for families.

### WAWONA

Consider staying at the charming **Wawona Hotel** ($120–190) near the south entrance of the park. The black-and-white exterior of the hotel complex reminds onlookers of a 19th-century Mississippi riverboat. Indeed the hotel opened in 1879, and has been a Yosemite institution ever since. The interior matches the outside well, complete with Victorian wallpaper, antique furniture, and a noticeable lack of in-room TVs and telephones. The Wawona feels more like a huge European pension than an American motel, complete with shared bathrooms for the more economically minded traveler. (Rooms with private baths are also available.)

### TIOGA PASS AND TUOLUMNE MEADOWS

In the high country, **Tuolumne Meadows Lodge** ($78, June 1–Sept. 16) offers rustic lodgings and good food in a gorgeous sub-alpine meadow setting. Expect no electricity, no private baths, and no other plush amenities. What you will find are small, charming wood-framed tent cabins that sleep up to four, central bath and hot shower facilities, and a dining room. The location is perfect for starting or finishing a backcountry trip through the high-elevation areas of the park.

Another rustic high-country accommodation, the **White Wolf Lodge** ($75–110, July–Sept.) sits back in the trees off Tioga Pass. Here you can rent either the standard wood-platform tent cabin with use of central bath and shower facilities, or a solid-wall cabin with a private bathroom, limited electricity, and daily maid service. All cabins and tent cabins at White Wolf include linens and towels, plus breakfast and dinner served family style in the dining room. You can order box lunches to take with you each day. Amenities are few, but breathtaking scenery is everywhere at White Wolf. Take a day hike to Hardens Lake, or a horseback ride through the backcountry. White Wolf works well for visitors who prefer a smaller crowd, since the lodge boasts only 28 cabins.

## Outside the Park

If you seek a small inn or inexpensive motel for your visit to Yosemite, consider staying outside the park proper and driving in each day. A wealth of inns, lodges, and B&Bs cluster near both the west and south entrances to the park. If you prefer a standard chain motel, Oakhurst (south of Fish Camp on Highway 41) and Mariposa (to the west on Highway 140) have most of the usual suspects.

If you're planning an extended stay at Yosemite with friends or family, it might be more convenient and economical to rent a condo or house with a full kitchen, privacy, and the comforts of home. You can find these at the **Yosemite West Condominiums** (800/669-9300), rented through the Yosemite Four Seasons Vacation Rentals. Modular buildings can be divided into a number of separate units—or not, if you want to rent a large space for a big crowd. The studio and loft condos sleep 2–6 people and have full kitchen and access to all complex amenities. Luxury suites are actually one-bedroom apartments with full kitchens, pool tables, hot tubs, four-poster beds, and all sorts of other amenities. Two- and three-bedroom apartments sleep 6–12 people. And the full houses can fit up to 22 guests, so you can fit an entire family reunion or college ski party into one huge house!

### MARIPOSA

You can't miss the **River Rock Inn and Deli Garden Café** (4993 7th St., Mariposa, 800/627-8493, www.riverrockncafe.com, $100–132) with its vivid orange-and-purple exterior in the heart of Mariposa. What was once a run-down 1940s motor lodge is now a quirky, fun motel with uniquely decorated rooms that make the most of modern Pottery Barn-esque wrought-iron and wood styling and the spaces the decorators had to work with. Never fear: The colors become softer as you step through the door of your reasonably priced guest room. Two suites provide enough space for families, while the other five rooms sleep couples in comfort. The River Rock is a 45-minute drive from the west entrance to Yosemite, and at the southern end of the long chain of Gold Country towns, making it a great base of operations for an outdoorsy, Western-style California vacation.

If you prefer cozy seclusion to large lodge-style hotels, stay at the **Highland House** (3125 Wild Dove Ln., 209/966-3737, www.highlandhousebandb.com, $127–165) outside Mariposa to the west of Yosemite. The house is set deep in the forest far from town, providing endless peace and quiet away from civilization. This tiny B&B has only three guest rooms, each uniquely decorated in soft colors and warm, inviting styles. All rooms have down comforters, sparkling clean bathtubs and showers, and TVs with DVD players.

Another lovely small B&B, **Poppy Hill Bed and Breakfast** (5218 Crystal Aire Dr., Mariposa, 800/587-6779, www.poppyhill.com, $137–165) sits 27 miles from the west entrance to the park. The four airy guest rooms are done in bright white linens, white walls, lacy curtains, and antique furniture. No TVs mar the sounds of the expansive gardens surrounding the old-style farmhouse. But you can take a dip in the totally modern hot tub any time. A full gourmet breakfast served on your schedule puts the right start on a day spent exploring Yosemite or the Mariposa County area. This inn can be hard to find, especially at night. Double-check the directions on the website and consider using a GPS device if you have one.

### SOUTH ENTRANCE

Near the south entrance to Yosemite on Highway 41, the **Narrow Gauge Inn** (48571 Hwy. 41, Fish Camp, 888/644-9050, www.narrowgaugeinn.com, $132–215) recalls the large lodges inside the park, in miniature. This charming 26-room mountain inn offers one- and two-bed guest rooms done in wood paneling, light colors, white linens, or vintage-style quilts. Each room has its own outdoor table and chairs to encourage relaxing outside with a drink on gorgeous summer days and evenings. The restaurant and common rooms feature antique oil lamps, stonework, and crackling fireplaces. Step outside your door and you're in the magnificent High Sierra pine forest. A few more steps takes you to the Yosemite Mountain Sugar Pine Railroad—the narrow-gauge steam train from which the inn takes its name.

For inexpensive lodge-style accommodations in Fish Camp, check in to the **White Chief Mountain Lodge** (east of Fish Camp, 559/683-5444, www.sierratel.com/whitechiefmtnlodge, $112–118). The basic rooms feature light wood paneling, tribal-design textiles, and inoffensive accents and lighting. Small TVs offer in-room entertainment, but the woods outside your door invite you outside to enjoy all that the rich Sierras have to offer. The lodge has its own restaurant and offers packages that show off the best of the Wild West heritage of the area.

The **Tenaya Lodge** (1122 Hwy. 41, 888/514-2167, www.tenayalodge.com, $345–400) sits just outside the south entrance of Yosemite, offering plush lodge-style accommodations at a more reasonable price than comparable rooms inside the park. Guest rooms are styled with rich fabrics in bright oranges and other bold, eye-catching colors. The modern wall art evokes the woods and vistas of Yosemite. The beds are comfortable, the baths attractive, and the views forest-filled. Tenaya Lodge focuses on guest care, offering a three-meal-per-day dining room, a full-service spa that specializes in facials, and daily (and nightly) nature walks complete with costumed guides. Check at the desk for events occurring during your stay.

If you plan to do some fishing during your trip to the Yosemite area, the **Pines Resort** (54432 Road 432, Bass Lake, 800/350-7463, www.basslake.com, $245–375) is perfectly located for your angling convenience right on the shores of Bass Lake; bring your boat! You can choose a suite (a split-level king room with dark floors, light walls, fireplaces, and mountain-y touches, some with spa tub) or rent a chalet (a two-story cabin in a rustic mountain style that sleeps up to six, with a full kitchen and outdoor mini-barbecue). The Pines is a full-service resort, with a restaurant (Ducey's), bar and grill, market, all-weather tennis courts, summer swimming pool, year-round hot tubs, spa services, shaded lakefront chaise lounges, and wedding and meeting facilities.

## FOOD

### Yosemite Valley

There's plenty to eat inside Yosemite National Park, but if you leave the valley floor you'll need to plan for meals. In Yosemite Valley, you have a number of dining options. The **Ahwahnee Dining Room** (Ahwanee Hotel, 209/372-1489, daily 7–10:30 A.M., 11:30 A.M.–3 P.M., 5:30–9 P.M., $20–35) enjoys a reputation for fine cuisine that stretches back to the 1920s. The grand dining room features expansive ceilings, wrought-iron chandeliers, and a stellar valley view. The restaurant serves three meals daily, with dinner the highlight. The California cuisine of an Ahwahnee dinner mirrors that of top-tier San Francisco restaurants (with a price tag to match). Reservations are recommended for all meals, though it's possible to walk in for breakfast and lunch. Dinner requires more formal attire.

At the other side of the valley, you can enjoy a spectacular view of Yosemite Falls at the **Mountain Room Restaurant** (Yosemite Lodge, 209/372-1274, 5:30–9 P.M., year-round, $15–20), part of Yosemite Lodge at the Falls. The glass atrium lets every guest at every table take in the view. The menu runs to American food, and drinks are available from the full bar. A casual bar menu is available at the **Mountain Room Lounge** (noon–11 P.M., inexpensive) immediately across from the restaurant.

For more casual food options, head to Yosemite Village for **Degnan's Loft** (spring–fall) for hot pizza, soups, and appetizers, and **Degnan's Delicatessen** (daily 7 A.M.–5 P.M.) for an array of sandwiches, salads, and other take-away munchies.

Curry Village is where to go for (relatively) cheap, fast food. Hiking clothes are expected! The **Curry Pavilion** (daily Mar.–Nov., $10–15) hosts an all-you-can-eat buffet for breakfast and dinner. There is also a deck, with a full-service bar, a taqueria, pizza, ice cream, and coffee.

### Wawona

If you can, plan a meal at the south end of the park in the **Wawona Dining Room** (Wawona Hotel, 209/375-1425, moderate–expensive). This lesser-known gem of a restaurant serves upscale homey California cuisine for reasonable prices to all comers. No reservations are accepted-all seating is first come, first served. The large, white painted dining room is family friendly, and the menu offers options for vegetarians as well as devout carnivores. Because you'll probably have to wait for a table on high-season weekends, a large common area invites seating, drinks, and live piano music by local legend Tom Bopp. The Wawona Dining room serves breakfast, lunch, dinner, Sunday brunch, and a weekly outdoor barbecue on Saturday evenings during the summer.

## INFORMATION AND SERVICES

With the high density of visitors to Yosemite Valley, the Park Service has thoughtfully put in place any number of guest services, going above and beyond most other venues in the national park system.

### Media and Communications

The print guide you absolutely need as you tour Yosemite is the monthly or biweekly published ***Yosemite Guide.*** This paper provides general information about the park's places and services. More importantly, it's got a detailed schedule of all classes, events, programs, and so on for the coming two weeks (in summer) or month (spring, fall, winter). You'll receive your copy when you enter the park at one of the entrance stations.

Limited Internet access is available in a few spots in Yosemite Valley. The only Wi-Fi to which you can connect your own laptop sits inside Yosemite Lodge. Kiosks are available in Degnan's Café and the Mariposa County Library—the library is free, while the café kiosks are available for a fee.

### Banks and Post Office

A number of ATMs are available throughout Yosemite, making it easy to extract cash with which to pay for souvenirs, food, and more souvenirs. You'll find at least one ATM in Yosemite Village at the Art and Education Center, one in Yosemite Lodge, one at Curry Village, and one at Wawona.

Several post offices provide mailing services in Yosemite. Look for a post office in Yosemite Village (Mon.–Fri. 8:30 A.M.–5 P.M., Sat. 10 A.M.–noon), inside Yosemite Lodge (12:30 P.M.–2:45 P.M.), and in El Portal (Mon.–Fri. 8:30 A.M.–5 P.M., closed 12:30–1:30 P.M.).

### Gas and Automotive Services

No gas is available anywhere inside Yosemite Valley. The nearest gas station sits at **El Portal** (24 hours, pay-at-pump). Limited seasonal gas is also available up at **Tuolumne Meadows** just past the visitors center on Tioga Pass. There's also gas in Mariposa at a **Pioneer Gas/Texaco** (5177 Hwy. 140, Mariposa) that also has a mini-mart.

If your car breaks down, you can take it to the **Village Garage** (Yosemite Village off Northside Dr., 209/372-8320, daily 8 A.M.–5 P.M., towing 24 hours). Because it's the only game in town, expect to pay a high premium for towing and repairs here.

### Laundry and Groceries

There are laundry facilities available to all comers at the Housekeeping Camp inside the Curry Village complex (Apr.–Oct. daily 8 A.M.–10 P.M.). Limited-stock, expensive grocery stores sit in Curry Village at the **Gift and Grocery** (daily 8 A.M.–10 P.M.) and in the **Housekeeping Camp Grocery** (Apr.–Oct. daily 8 A.M.–6 P.M.). For a better selection of goods and much lower prices, you're better off shopping outside the park. You can check out **Bear Valley Grocery** (7313 Hwy. 49 at Road J-16, North Mariposa, 209/377-8424) or the **Pioneer Market** (5034 Coakley Cir. 104, Mariposa, 209/742-5097).

### Medical Services

Yosemite maintains its own **medical center** (209/372-4637) in Yosemite Village at the floor of the valley. It's got a 24-hour emergency room, 8 A.M.–7 P.M. walk-in urgent care center, and a domestic violence crisis center. **Dental services** (209/372-4200) are also available adjacent to the medical center.

## GETTING THERE AND AROUND

### Car

Almost all the most popular sights, attractions, and trailheads are accessible by road. The Arch Rock entrance to the west of the park is accessed via Highway 140. The Big Oak Flat entrance is accessed via Highway 120 from the north; it's about another 45 minutes to Yosemite Valley from there. Both entrances provide access to Tioga Pass Road via Big Oak Flat Road. Tioga Pass reconnects to Highway 120 at the Tioga Pass Entrance on the east side of the park. Tioga Pass closes in November or December each year and reopens in the spring, usually in May. Yosemite's south entrance is accessed via Highway 41 from Oakhurst. Wawona Road leads from the south entrance, through Wawona, and into Yosemite Valley. Glacier Point Road is reached from Wawona Road and allows access to the Badger Pass Ski Area. In winter, chains can be required on any road at any time, so check the website (www.nps.gov/yose) for current road conditions.



### Train and Bus

**Amtrak** (www.amtrak.com) services Merced, an hour away from the park. From Merced, bus service is available on **VIA Bus Lines** (209/384-1314, www.via-adventures.com); call for reservations. The **YARTS** (877/989-2787, www.yarts.com) bus system services Mariposa and Merced.

### Shuttle Services

Yosemite runs an extensive network of shuttles in different areas of the park. One of the most-used travels through **Yosemite Valley** (daily 7 A.M.–10 P.M., year-round, free). The **El Capitan Shuttle** (mid-June to early Sept, daily 9 A.M.–6 P.M., free) also runs around certain parts of Yosemite Valley during the summer season.

# Mono Lake

Mono Lake itself, eerie in its stillness, is the main attraction to this remote area of the Eastern Sierra. It might be enough just to sit on the edge of the lake and enjoy its beauty. Or in the summertime, enjoy an oddly buoyant swim in the heavily salted waters or even a boat trip out to some of the silent uninhabited islands. But if you'd prefer more adventure or exploration, a number of options await.

## SIGHTS

### Mono Lake Scenic Visitor Area

The large building that houses the visitors center for Mono Lake is easy to see from Highway 395, and only a short drive from the highway. The Mono Lake Scenic Visitor Area (Hwy. 395 just north of Lee Vining on the lake side, 760/647-3044, www.monolake.org) is the perfect place to start learning about Mono Lake, to start walking around the lake, and to start taking photos of the unique landscape. The interpretive museum inside the distinctive building describes in detail the natural and human history of the lake, from the way tufa towers form to the endless litigations surrounding the lake like papery ghosts. Walk out the back of the building to take your first closer look at the grassy meadows leading down to the shores of the lake. Talk to the staff to learn about the best hikes and spots to visit, swim, launch a boat, or cross-country ski.

At the visitors center, you can also learn about various guided walks and hikes at Mono Lake, which can give you and your family a more in-depth look at the wonders of the area.

### ☾ Mono Lake Tufa Preserve

The tufa formations—freestanding calcite towers, knobs, and spires—make Mono Lake unique. The Mono Lake Tufa Preserve (Hwy. 395 just north of Lee Vining, 760/647-6331, www.parks.ca.gov, park hours and fees vary) educates and amazes visitors. A one-mile interpretive trail winds through the South Tufa area (southeast of the visitors center, adjacent to Navy Beach, fee for parking) describing the natural history of the area and formations. With some of the most spectacular tufa towers at the lake, this is a good place for newcomers to the lake to start exploring. A boardwalk trail (adjacent to the County Park) provides access to the North Tufa area. Enjoy wandering through the different chunks of this preserve, which appear along the shore all the way around the lake. Be aware that much of the land adjacent to the State Reserve areas is

© LIZ HAMILL SCOTT
Mono Lake



restricted—please care for this delicate terrain and do not venture out of the designated visiting areas. Also, to access some of the reserve at the east side of the lake, you'll need either a boat or a four-wheel-drive vehicle since no paved roads circle Mono Lake.

## Old Marina

Years ago, the stillness of Mono Lake was broken by quite a bit of boat traffic. (Private boats and small tour operators still ply the salt-alkaline lake in the summer, but no major commercial water traffic remains.) The hub of this activity was the Marina a few miles north of Lee Vining. Today, the Old Marina is merely spot off Highway 395 north of town at which you can take a short stroll down to the edge of the lake. From here you can see the two large islands in the middle of the lake, several nearby tufa towers, and much of the lakescape itself. The boardwalk trail here is wheelchair accessible.

## Bodie State Historic Park

Bodie State Historic Park (end of Dirt Road 270, 760/647-6445, www.parks.ca.gov, daily 9 A.M.–4 P.M., weekends Memorial Day–Labor Day 8 A.M.–7 P.M., fees) is the largest ghost town in California. Preservation in a state of "arrested decay" means you get to see each home and public building just as it was when it was abandoned. What you see is not a bright shiny museum display. You get the real thing: dust and broken furniture and trash and all. It would take all day to explore the town on foot, and even then you might not see it all. Tours let you into the abandoned mine and gain a deeper understanding of the history of the buildings and the town.

The town of Bodie sprang up around a gold mine in 1877. It was never a nice place to live—at all. The weather, the work, the scenery, the people...all tended toward the bleak or the foul. By the 1940s, mining had dried up and the remote location and lack of other viable industry in the area led to Bodie's desertion.

A visit to Bodie takes you back in time, to a harsh lifestyle in an extreme climate at least 10 miles from the middle of nowhere. As you stroll down the dusty streets, imagine the whole

Bodie's historic ghost town



town blanketed in 20 feet of snow in winter, then scorched by 100° temperatures in summer with precious few trees anywhere around to provide shade or a hint of green in the unending brown landscape. In a town filled with rough men working the mines hundreds of miles from civilization, you'd hear the funeral bells tolling at the church every single day—the only real honor bestowed upon the many murder victims Bodie saw in its lifetime. Few families came to Bodie (though a few hardy souls did raise children in the hellish town), and most of Bodie's women earned their keep the old-fashioned way. The prostitution business boomed just as mining did.

Today, most of the brothels, stores, and homes of Bodie aren't habitable or even tourable. Structures have been loosely propped up, but it's dangerous to go inside so doors remain locked. However, you can peer in the windows at the remains of the lives lived in Bodie, and get a sense of hard-core California history.

### Panum Crater

Even if you aren't a professional geologist, the volcanic Panum Crater (Hwy. 120 three miles east of Hwy. 395, short dirt road to parking) is worth visiting. This rhyolite crater is only 600 years old—a mere baby in geologic time! Take a hike around the rim of the crater, and if you're feeling up to it climb up the trail to the top of the plug dome. Be sure to slather on the sunscreen since no trees shade these trails and it gets quite warm in the summertime. Check the Mono Lake website for occasional guided tours of Panum Crater.

## SPORTS AND RECREATION

### Hiking

Mono Lake is not like Yosemite, with clusters of trailheads everywhere. But the hiking near Mono Lake affords things the big park can't: unusual scenery and plenty of solitude.

For an easy walk along the lake, go to the **Mono Lake County Park** (Cemetery Road, trailhead 0.5 mile east of the road) and take the boardwalk trail 0.25 mile down to the tufa formations. Wandering through the tufa will add distance to your walk, but the ground is flat and the scenery is diverting.

A lovely interpretive trail, the **Tioga Tarns Nature Walk** (Hwy. 120, east of Tioga Lake) spans about half a mile and includes numerous signs describing the flora, fauna, and geology of the area. Another nature walk is the **Lee Vining Creek Nature Trail** (Best Western Motel, Hwy. 395, moderate). This trail follows the Lee Vining Creek, currently under restoration, returning to its natural state after decades of diversion. The total walk is about three miles and takes an hour or two, depending on how much time you spend admiring the revitalized ecosystem.

You can find any number of moderate hikes in the Mono Lake vicinity. The **Lundy Canyon** (Lundy Lake Rd., dirt lot at trailhead) trail can be anywhere from 0.5 mile of fairly easy walking through Lundy Canyon to a strenuous seven-mile hike all the way out to Saddlebag Lake. Another variable hike takes you out to **Parker Lake** or **Parker Bench** (Parker Lake dirt road off Hwy. 158). This hike is a minimum of four miles round-trip, and can be 10 miles if you take the left trail fork out to Silver Lake and Parker Bench. Steep sections make this trek a bit more demanding, but you'll love the scenic, shady trail that follows Parker Creek out the shorter right fork to Parker Lake. If one or two lakes just aren't enough, take the longish but only moderately tough **20-Lakes Basin Trail** (Saddlebag Lake Rd., parking across from the dam). This six-mile loop trail will take you out past many of the lakes for which the basin is named. Or if you're tired of all that water, take a moderate two-mile round-trip pilgrimage out to the remains of the mining town at **Bennettville** (Junction Campground Rd.). You can prowl around the abandoned mine, but be careful! Old mine shafts and abandoned buildings can be extremely hazardous.

## Boating and Swimming

Go ahead and bring your powered boat, canoe, kayak, or even sailboat out to Mono Lake. A parking lot near the water at Navy Beach makes launching lightweight kayaks and canoes reasonable. If you're putting a heavier boat into the lake, check with the staff at the Mono Lake Scenic Visitor Area for directions to the launch ramp near Lee Vining Creek. Also note that no matter what kind of craft you're piloting, you cannot beach on the islands April 1–August 1.

During the summer, the **Mono Lake Boat Tours** (meet at Tioga Lodge, 760/647-6446, www.monolakeboattours.com, adults $70, children/seniors $65) offers water tours of the lake. You'll get an utterly experienced guide who's been traveling on the lake for ages.

Swimming is allowed (and even encouraged!) in Mono Lake in the summertime. You can swim from your boat, or from any of the unrestricted shore access points. You'll find yourself floating easily since the salt content of Mono Lake is several times that of the ocean. But take care and watch your kids closely, because no lifeguards patrol the area and you're swimming at your own risk.

# ACCOMMODATIONS

You won't see any five-star resorts in the Mono Lake area. The outdoorsy and naturalist types who favor this region find the no-frills motels, lodges, and campgrounds perfectly suitable for their activities.

No camping is allowed on the shores of Mono Lake. Visitors can rent affordable rooms at several motels and lodgings in the lakeside town of Lee Vining.

## Under $100

Rent clean, comfortable, affordable lodgings at **Murphey's Motel** (51493 Hwy. 395, 800/334-6316, www.murpheysyosemite.com, $58–118). Open all year, this motel provides double-queen and king beds with cozy comforters, TVs, tables and chairs, and everything you need for a pleasant stay in the Mono Lake area. Its central location in downtown Lee Vining makes dining, shopping, and trips to the visitors center and Chamber of Commerce convenient. If you plan to make a winter trip to Mono Lake, call to find out about Murphey's discounts for ice climbers.

The **El Mono Motel** (Hwy. 395 at Third St., 707/647-6310, www.elmonomotel.com) offers comfy beds and clean rooms at very reasonable prices. Enjoy the location in downtown Lee Vining, and start each morning with a fresh cup of organic coffee from the attached Latte Da Coffee Café.

### $100–150

Just across the freeway from Mono Lake, the **Tioga Lodge** (54411 Hwy. 395, 760/647-6423, www.tiogalodgeatmonolake.com, $133–165) boasts an astonishing view of the lake from every room. This older lodge at the center of the town of Lee Vining offers the perfect location for sightseeing and outdoor adventures, plus heated rooms and comfortable beds. Guest rooms are simple and uniquely decorated, each with tile floors and a full private bath. Some rooms sleep two, others up to four in two-bedroom suites are perfect for families. Don't expect to find TVs or other digital entertainment here—in keeping with the area, you're encouraged to get outside to find your entertainment. Friendly, helpful staff can assist with everything from room amenities to local restaurants to great places to visit in the area.

At the intersection of Highways 120 and 395, stay at the comfortable and affordable **Lake View Lodge** (51285 Hwy. 395, Lee Vining, 800/990-6614, www.lakeviewlodgeyosemite.com, $138–220). This aptly named lodge offers both motel rooms and cottages. The cottages can be rented in the summer only, but the motel rooms are available all year. Whether you choose a basic room for only a night or two, or a larger accommodation with a kitchen for more than three days, you'll enjoy the simple country-style decor, the outdoor porches, and the views of Mono Lake. All rooms have TVs with cable and Internet access is available. Pick up supplies at the local market for a picnic on the lawns of the lodge, get yourself a latte at the on-site coffee shop, or enjoy one of the nearby restaurants in Lee Vining.

Named for its location only 14 miles from Yosemite's east gate, the **Yosemite Gateway Motel** (51340 Hwy. 395, 760/647-6467, www.yosemitegatewaymotel.com, $143–154) offers a charming rustic experience for travelers to the Eastern Sierra. The red and white exterior echoes in the decoration of the guest rooms, supplemented with gleaming wood, new furnishings, and clean bathrooms. A TV and the Internet provide entertainment on chilly evenings, and of course the wonderful outdoor recreation opportunities of the Eastern Sierra are just outside the door. Enjoy your crystalline views of Mono Lake, or take a day trip to Bodie or indulge in some skiing at Mammoth Lakes or June Lake. Room rates are deeply discounted in the wintertime, making the trek worth the effort.

## FOOD

Your food choices around the Mono Lake area might feel limited if you're coming right from Los Angeles or San Francisco. Nor will you see many of the standard fast-food chains. However, the town of Lee Vining offers a number of respectable eateries, plus adequate groceries for campers and picnickers.

### Restaurants

The ☾ **Hammond Station Restaurant** (54411 Hwy. 395, 760/647-6423, www.tiogalodgeatmonolake.com, $8–20) at the Tioga Lodge serves breakfast, lunch, and dinner. Choose from the health-conscious vegetarian/spa menu (which includes a number of vegan items), the American menu, or the Mexican menu. If you're planning a day out hiking or sightseeing, get a sandwich or a wrap from the "Picnic to Go" menu before you leave for the day. If you're dining in, expect a small dining room with attractive wrought-iron furniture, plus an ample outdoor seating area perfect for warm summer evenings. The food is tasty, and the service makes you feel like a local even if you're from far out of town.

A classic American diner, **Nicely's** (Hwy. 395 and Fourth St., 760/647-6477, summer daily, winter Thurs.–Mon.) offers friendly service and familiar food to locals and visitors alike. Inside, you'll find a large dining room with half-circle booths upholstered in vinyl and many other diner-style touches. The cuisine runs to sandwiches, burgers, and egg breakfasts. Portions are generous, though the service can be slow when the restaurant is busy. Nicely's opens early and stays open through dinnertime, making it a viable dining option year-round—something of a rarity in the area. This is a good place to take the kids for burgers and fries.

If you're looking for a Wild West atmosphere and a good spicy sauce, have dinner at **Bodie Mike's Barbecue** (51357 Hwy. 395, 760/647-6432, summer only). Use your fingers to dig into barbecued ribs, chicken, beef, brisket, and more. A rustic atmosphere with rough-looking wood, red-check tablecloths, and local patrons in cowboy boots completes your dining experience. Just don't expect the fastest service in the world. At the back of the dining room you'll find the entrance to a small, dark bar populated by local characters. The good news is that the bar serves drinks to the dining room.

### Bakeries and Delis

For a unique deli dining experience, stop in for a tank of gas and a meal at the **Whoa Nelly Deli** (Hwys. 120 and 395, 760/647-1088, Apr.–Nov. daily 7 A.M.–9 P.M.) at the Tioga Gas Mart. You'll get a full, hearty meal from the daily offering, be it ribs or meatloaf or something else. Sandwiches and drinks are also available for lighter noshing. Expect to wait in line for a while at the counter to order, then to wait to pick up your own food. Seating, both indoor and out, tends to be limited during high-traffic mealtimes, and heaven help you if you get there in conjunction with a tour bus. But still, compared to the so-called food offered in most gas station mini-marts, you'll find some great stuff at Whoa Nelly, and the rowdy cooks provide something of a show for the dinner crowd.

A great place to get a to-go breakfast or lunch is the **Mono Market** (51303 Hwy. 395, 760/647-1010, daily summer 7 A.M.–10 P.M., winter 7:30 A.M.–8 P.M.). An array of breakfast sandwiches and pastries are made fresh daily, as are the sandwiches, wraps, and messier napkin-requisite entrées you can carry out for lunch or dinner.

### Coffee

Even dedicated outdoor lovers often need their morning coffee to get going on a long day of hiking, climbing, or kayaking. To that end, you'll find some charming independent coffee shops in Lee Vining. The **Latte Da Coffee Café** (1 Third St. at Hwy. 395, 760/647-6310) uses organic coffee and local fresh water to create delicious coffee drinks at the El Mono Motel. Over at the Lakeview Lodge, grab a cup of joe at the **Garden House Coffee Shop** (5185 Hwy. 395, Lee Vining, 760/647-6543, www.lakeviewlodgeyosemite.com, daily 7–11 A.M.). In addition to your favorite espresso drinks, you can pick up a smoothie or a fresh pastry to get a great start to your day.

### Markets

In addition to prepared food, the **Mono Market** (51303 Hwy. 395, 760/647-1010, daily summer 7 A.M.–10 P.M., winter 7:30 A.M.–8 P.M.) offers standard grocery staples and a liquor section.

## INFORMATION AND SERVICES

The **Mono Basic Scenic Area Visitors Center** (Hwy. 395 just north of Lee Vining on the lake side, 760/647-3044, www.monolake.org) includes an interpretive museum that describes the creation of Mono Lake and the strange tufa formations that define it. This visitors center also has a ranger station with knowledgeable staff who can help you with the best seasonal trail and lake advice.

You can use mail services at the **Lee Vining Post Office** (121 Lee Vining Ave., 760/647-6371). Lee Vining boasts few ATMs, but you can find one or two places to grab cash (which you'll need, because many places out here don't take plastic). Try the gas stations, the visitors center, and the local grocery/mini mart.

The nearest medical facilities to Mono Lake lie to the south in Mammoth Lakes at **Mammoth Hospital** (85 Sierra Park Rd., 760/934-3311, mammothhospital.com), which has a 24-hour emergency room.

## GETTING THERE AND AROUND

Getting to Mono Lake from San Francisco or Los Angeles or anyplace else in California with a major airport is, frankly, a royal pain in the you-know-what. Mono Lake sits almost on top of the junction between Tioga Pass Road and Highway 395.

Tioga Pass is closed between November and May each year—check with the Yosemite website to get the exact closing and opening dates for this road. Highway 395 remains open all year (though storms can close it briefly until it is plowed). But accessing Highway 395 from the north or south involves long drives. You might want to consider flying in to Las Vegas or even Reno to get to Mono Lake as directly as possible.

Very little public transit of any kind gets as far as Lee Vining and Mono Lake. To adequately explore this region, you need a vehicle of your own. On the bright side, parking in Lee Vining and around the lake tends to be both easy and free. Few enough others are vying for spots that you won't spend much time looking for your own space.



# Mammoth Lakes

## SIGHTS

### Devil's Postpile National Monument

Compared to the area's other national parks, Devil's Postpile National Monument (Minaret Vista Rd., 760/924-5500, www.nps.gov/depo, summer only, daily 9 A.M.–5 P.M., adults $7, children $4) seems small. But what you'll see is unique to the region. The gem and namesake of the park is the strange, unbelievably natural rock formation called the Devil's Postpile. It's hard to imagine that the near perfect straight-sided hexagonal posts are a natural phenomenon, created by volcanic heat and pressure. You

PHOTO COURTESY OF THE MAMMOTH LAKES VISITORS BUREAU

Devil's Postpile National Monument

June Lake



have to see it to believe it. Less heavily traveled than many other parks, you'll also find hikes to serene meadows, unspoiled streams, and perhaps even see the occasional deer grazing in the woods. If you're lucky, you might get a trail all to yourself for a while.

Also part of the Monument is the crystalline, beautiful **Rainbow Falls.** The thick sheet of water cascades 101 feet down to a pool, throwing up stunning rainbows of mist. For the best rainbows at the falls, hike the three miles (round-trip) from Red Meadow toward the middle of the day when the sun is high in the sky.

In an effort to limit traffic on the narrow road down into the Monument, a shuttle runs from a spot near the gate down to the trailheads. Ample parking is available, and the shuttles run every half-hour, letting you jump on and off as you wish to hike, have a picnic, or just enjoy the fresh smell of the clean woods.

## June Lake Loop

This 15-mile scenic drive takes you out away from the high-traffic tourist areas of the Eastern Sierra. Along the June Lake Loop (Hwy. 158, accessible from Hwy. 395 south of Lee Vining), you get the full-fledged alpine experience. Naturally, the loop's namesake June Lake has the most recreation along its shores. You can take a hike, go fish, or even plan to stay overnight at one of the campgrounds. Next you'll come to Gull Lake, then Silver Lake—two other popular boating and angling waterways. As you drive north on the loop, stop at least once to admire Reversed Peak, a 9,500-foot Sierra peak. Finally, you'll come to Grant Lake. No resorts cluster here, nor will you find any major trailheads. What you will find are a boat launch and some spectacular alpine trout fishing. Finally, take a break at the Mono Craters Monument before heading back out to Highway 395 toward Lee Vining or Mammoth Mountain.

## Mammoth Ski Museum

One of the jewels of Mammoth Lakes, the Mammoth Ski Museum (100 College Pkwy.,

760/934-6592, www.mammothskimuseum.org, Thurs.–Mon. 11 A.M.–6 P.M., $5 adults, $3 children) houses the largest collection of skiing-related art in the world. Here you'll find artistic homage in every medium the human fascination with sliding down snowy mountains on boards. The museum features the permanent Beekley Collection of sculptures, original paintings, vintage posters, and much more. Short films run daily, and each Friday night at 6 P.M. a full-length ski-themed feature film runs in the Pioneer Theater. Visit the gift shop to purchase your own reproduction vintage ski posters, books, and DVDs.



### Old Mammoth Road

Like most of the Eastern Sierra region, Mammoth Lakes became of interest to miners in the 19th century after the Gold Rush began—miners got out this far in 1877. Along Old Mammoth Road (Hwy. 203 to Main St., turn left on Old Mammoth Rd.) you'll find a number of old mining sites. At the height of the short-lived boom in Mammoth, about 20 different small mines operated in the area. You'll see the grave of a miner's wife, a stamp mill's flywheel, and then the meager remains of Mammoth City and the nearby Mammoth Mine. The highlight of this summertime half-day trip is the ruins of the Mammoth Consolidated Mine. You can still see some bits of the camp, housing buildings, the assay office, mill, and mining equipment. The mine shaft also appears, but *do not attempt to get around the security features to head down there!* Old mine shafts are unbelievably dangerous, and should not be explored by anyone for any reason.

## SKIING AND SNOWBOARDING

Mammoth Lakes exists primarily to support the winter sports industry. The downhill skiing, snowboarding, and cross-country skiing here attract sports enthusiasts of all ages and ability levels. If you don't own your own equipment, you can rent skis, snowboards, and all the necessary accessories at a dozen different shops in town.

### Mammoth Mountain

The premier downhill ski and snowboard mountain is, aptly, Mammoth Mountain (800 Mammoth, ski school 760/934-0685, snow report 760/934-6166, http://mammoth

PHOTO COURTESY OF THE MAMMOTH LAKES VISITORS BUREAU

A bronze mammoth stands at the main lodge of Mammoth Mountain.

mountain.com, lift hours daily 8:30 A.M.–4 P.M.). Whether you're completely new to downhill thrills or a seasoned expert looking for different terrain, you'll find something great on Mammoth Mountain. More than two-dozen lifts (including three gondolas and nine express quads) take you up the 3,100-foot vertical rise to the 3,500 acres of skiable and boardable terrain (plus three pipes). If you're staying at Eagle Lodge, Canyone Lodge, Mammoth Mountain Inn, or the Village, enjoy the convenience of a lift or gondola right outside your lodging door. All these, plus the Mill Café and McCoy Station halfway up the mountain offer hot drinks, tasty snacks, and a welcome spot to rest during a long day of skiing.

The easiest runs on the mountain cluster mostly around the ski school and the lower area around the Mammoth Mountain Inn, and are recognizable for their cute nursery-school names. If you're an intermediate skier, runs swing down all over the mountain just for you. Build your confidence by taking the Panorama Gondola up to Panorama Lookout at the top of the mountain, then skiing all the way down the east side of the mountain along the intermediate-to-a-bit-harder ridge runs. Advanced skiers favor the bowls and chutes at the front of the mountain, and hardcore experts go west from Panorama Lookout to chase the dragon.

## June Mountain

South of Mammoth Lakes, the June Mountain ski area (3819 Hwy. 158, 760/648-7733, www.junemountain.com, lifts 7:30 A.M.–4 P.M., adults $60, youth $54, teens $45, children/seniors $30) offers more than 2,500 feet of vertical rise on more than 500 skiable acres. This resort caters to beginners and intermediate skiers, and 80 percent of its trails are green or blue. Beginners can even take a lift up to the top of Rainbow Summit and enjoy a long run down the Silverado Trail. However, a number of black and double-black diamond slopes make a trip to June Mountain fun for more advanced skiers and boarders as well. Thrill-seeking experts and adventurous intermediates head up to the top of June Mountain Summit then plummet down the bowl (hardcore double-blacks) or slide along the ridgeline (blue). Be sure to check your trail map before going up this way unless you're very sure of your abilities. For a cup of hot coffee or chocolate, stop at the June Meadows Chalet at the center of the ski area.

## Sierra Meadows

Go just south of Mammoth Lakes to get to the Sierra Meadows (1 Sherwin Creek Rd., 760/934-6161), a cross-country ski area with 20 miles of groomed trails. Sierra Meadows is perfect for beginner cross-country skiers, offering ski rentals, lessons, and beginner terrain that's easy on the legs—and the mind!

## Tamarack Cross Country Ski Center

Here's your chance to explore the snow-covered Mammoth Lakes Basin in wintertime. Tamarack (Lake Mary Rd. at Twin Lakes, 760/934-2442, www.tamaracklodge.com/xcountry, Nov.–Apr. daily 8:30 A.M.–5 P.M.) offers almost 25 miles of groomed cross-country ski tracks geared for all ability levels. For non-skiers, you'll also fined groomed skating lanes, plus a restaurant in which to enjoy a nice cup of hot chocolate and good book while your more outdoorsy friends and family ply the terrain.

## Blue Diamond Trails

This trail system starts just behind the Mammoth Lakes visitors center and winds through 25 miles of Mammoth forest land, predictably marked by signs bearing a blue diamond on the trees. Blue Diamond Trails (www.mammothdirect.com) are not groomed, so be prepared to deal with varying snow conditions and unbroken trails. However, there's plenty of relatively flat land here for beginners. The Shady Rest Trails (off Hwy. 203 just before visitors center) might sound like a cemetery, but in fact they are beginners' loops with plenty of shade trees that keep skiers cool through their exertions. The Knolls Trail (Mammoth Scenic Loop 1.5 miles north of Hwy. 203) makes a good intermediate day out, passing through lovely stands of Jeffery and Lodgepole pines. If you're up for a serious expert trek, try the Earthquake Fault Trail (Minaret Rd., unlabeled parking lot before Mammoth Mountain Main Lodge). Expect steep descents, unused areas, and narrow paths along this approximately 12-hour trail. Beginners beware of the deceptively named Scenic Loop Trail (Mammoth Scenic Loop across from Knolls Trail); this reasonably short trail (about four miles) includes steep descents and some more difficult terrain.



## SPORTS AND RECREATION

Even beyond skiing and snowboarding, outdoor activities are a central focus of life in and around Mammoth. People come here from all over to hike, bike, fish, and more.

### Hiking

Not surprisingly, hikers find plenty of worthwhile terrain around Mammoth Lakes for both short day walks and longer backpacking adventures. The **Mammoth Mountain Bike Park** (1 Minaret Rd., 800/626-6684, www.mammothmountain.com/bike_ride, daily 8 A.M.–6 P.M.) includes a number of great hiking trails. For an all-downhill walk, take the Scenic Gondola up to the Panorama Overlook and hike back down to town. Just be sure to get a trail map at the **Mammoth Adventure Center** (1 Minaret Rd., 800/626-6684, www.mammothmountain.com/bike_ride/index.cfm, June.–Sept. daily 8 A.M.–6 P.M.) so you can keep to the hiking areas and avoid being flattened by fast-moving mountain bikers.

Mammoth Lakes also acts as a jumping-off point for adventurers who want to take on the **John Muir Wilderness** (south of Mammoth Lakes to Mount Whitney, http://sierranevadawild.gov/wild/john-muir). John Muir pioneered sustainability and preservation in the Sierra Nevadas, and more than half a million acres in the area have been designated national wilderness areas in his honor. Day hikers are welcome and there's plenty to see. Check with the Inyo National Forest service and the Sierra National Forest for trail maps of the area. But the main attractions to the John Muir (as it's called locally) are the John Muir and Pacific Crest Trails—both hundreds of miles long and sought by backpacking enthusiasts around the world. If you're planning an overnight camping trip in the area—on your own or with a tour or guide company—you must obtain a permit. It's also a good idea to plan backcountry trips well in advance, to make sure you've got everything you need and all the proper permits and information ready at hand.

### Biking

Come summertime and melting snow, Mammoth Mountain transforms from a ski resort to a mountain bike mecca. The **Mammoth Mountain Bike Park** (1 Minaret Rd., 800/626-6684, www.mammothmountain.com/bike_ride, daily 8 A.M.–6 P.M., $10–39) spans much of the same terrain as the ski areas, with almost 90 miles of trails that suit all biking ability levels. The park headquarters sits at the **Mammoth Adventure Center** (1 Minaret Rd., 800/626-6684, www.mammothmountain.com/bike_ride/index.cfm, June.–Sept. daily 8 A.M.–6 P.M.). You can take your bike onto the Scenic Gondola and ride all the way to the top of Mammoth Mountain, then ride all the way down (3,000-plus feet) on the single tracks. Be sure to pick the trails that best suit your fitness and experience level! Several other major lodges offer rider services, including the Village at Mammoth, Juniper Springs, the Panorama Lookout, and Outpost 14. If you value scenery as much as extreme adventure, pack your camera and plan to rest at the various scenic overlooks throughout the trail system.

If you need to rent a bike (and to buy park tickets), go to the Adventure Center or to the **Mammoth Mart at the Village** (6201 Minaret Rd., inside The Village, 760/934-2571, ext. 2078). Both locations offer new high-end bikes for adults and kids. These shops can also help with parts and repairs for bikes you've brought up with you, and sell accessories.

## Horseback Riding

Perhaps the most traditional way to explore the Eastern Sierra is on the back of a horse or mule. Early pioneers to the area came on horseback, and you can follow their example from several locations near Mammoth. From the **McGee Creek Pack Station** (760/935-4324, www.mcgeecreekpackstation.com, one hour $30) 10 miles south of Mammoth Lakes on Highway 395, you can ride into McGee Canyon, a wilderness area little visited by tourists. Other one-day destinations include Baldwin Canyon and Hilton Lakes. Standard rides range from one hour to all day. But McGee's specialty is multi-day and pack trips that let you really get out beyond the reach of paved roads to camp for a number of days out by one of the many pristine lakes dotting the mountains. If you love the outdoors and really want a vacation as far "away from it all" as you can get, consider a few days' camping in Convict Basin or near Upper Fish Creek in the John Muir Wilderness. The McGee Creek guides will help you pack your gear and guide you through the incredible backcountry of the Eastern Sierra.

Operating out of Bishop, **Rainbow Pack Outfitters** (760/873-8877, www.rainbowpackoutfit.com) offers day trips to a number of lovely local destinations, plus a full-day fishing trip with all gear carried by mule. Small children will enjoy an at-the-stables led ride on a pony or horse, while the bigger kids and adults can get out for rides to local meadows and lakes. If you're looking for a longer horseback vacation, check into Rainbow's options for full-service guided trips, hunting and fishing trips, photography and birding treks, and more. Rainbow operates from the John Muir Wilderness near Mammoth and Bishop all the way down to Sequoia and Kings Canyon parks. Pick your ideal destination and pack in!

## Snowshoeing

If you prefer walking to all that sliding around on planks, rent or bring your own snowshoes to Mammoth and enjoy a snowy hike through the mountains and meadows. Check the cross-country ski areas first—many have specifically designated snowshoe trails. Or head out to the backcountry and explore Mammoth Lakes Basin or the Sherwin Range. Groomed trails head off from right behind the Mammoth Lakes Welcome Center.

## ATVs and Snowmobiles

ATVs, dirt bikes, and snowmobiles are a big no-no at most national parks. Not so at Mammoth! Here you'll find miles of trails set aside for motorized fun. Eighty miles of groomed trails and 75,000 acres of snow-covered meadows and mountainsides await snowmobilers each winter. Much of the same territory is open to ATV and dirt bike traffic in the summer. Get a copy of the *Mammoth Lakes Winter Recreation Guide* for a complete trail and area map to find the best (and legal) places to play.

If you want to rent a vehicle, you can get single- and double-seat snowmobiles and ATVs at **Arctic Cat/Yamaha of Mammoth** (58 Commerce Dr., Mammoth Lakes, 760/934-0347, www.sierraengine.com). Reservations are recommended! Your rental includes instructions on how to operate your vehicle, local trail maps, and helmets for everyone who's going to ride. At **Bishop Motorsports** (156 E. Pine St., Bishop, 888/872-4717, www.harleyrentalsbishopmammoth.com), in addition to snowmobiles and side-by-side ATVs, you can rent Harleys and dirt bikes to take out on the Eastern Sierra roads and trails. If you're on an extended vacation, check out the weekly rental rates.

## Golf

If you're in the Mammoth area in summertime, you can enjoy a round of golf at a beautiful course with stunning mountain views. The 18-hole, par 70 **Sierra Star Golf Course** (2001 Sierra Star Pkwy., 760/924-4653, http://mammothmountain.com, $125 weekends, $100 weekdays) is open to the public. Walk this wonderful course for the best views of the surrounding Sierras, or concentrate all your efforts on the game. Amenities include a full-service pro shop, PGA golf pro on-site, and a café with full bar.

### Spas

If you want to enjoy some pampering after a hard day of skiing, book a treatment at one of Mammoth Lakes' day spas. The **Bodyworks Mountain Spa** (3399 Main St., 760/924-3161, www.bodyworksmountainspa.com) located upstairs at the Luxury Outlet Mall, offers massage therapy, spa treatments, and facials, plus a wide range of combination packages to maximize your time and money at the spa.

The **InTouch MicroSpa** (3325 Main St., 800/786-4414, www.intouchmicrospa.com) offers a full menu of treatments with a focus on the four elements of earth, air, fire, and water. Using Aveda products exclusively, InTouch caters to spa-goers who care about what's put onto their skin. A number of different styles of facials and aesthetic treatments are available. If you're in town with a group, InTouch offers several spa-party options that get everyone great treatments at discounted rates.



Somewhat incongruously located inside the local Holiday Inn, the **BellaDonna** (3236 Main St., 760/934-3344, www.belladonnamammoth.com) day spa offers a crackling fireplace, serene setting, and massage and aesthetic services. Come for a hot stone massage, a mani-pedi, or a complete makeover with natural mineral-based makeup products. If you're looking for romance, check out the couples side-by-side fireside massage. Yum!

### Casino Gambling

If an hour or three at the slots or the blackjack tables sounds like a good way to unwind, go to the **Paiute Palace Casino** (2742 N. Sierra Hwy., Bishop, 888/372-4883, www.paiutepalace.com). You can play over 300 slots, plus table blackjack and poker. Look for Texas Hold 'Em tournaments every Wednesday and Sunday. The in-house restaurant is open for breakfast, lunch, and dinner.

## ENTERTAINMENT AND EVENTS

### Bars and Clubs

What would a ski resort town be without a selection of aprés-ski activities? Mammoth Lakes has a number of bars that open their doors to chilled and thirsty skiers.

For possibly the best (night) time in Mammoth, try the **Clocktower Cellar Pub** (6080 Minaret Rd. at Alpenhof Lodge, 760/934-2725, www.alpenhof-lodge.com, daily until 2 A.M.). This happening nightspot offers 30 luscious brews on tap and served properly, glasses of fine wine cadged from Petra next door, and a casual atmosphere complete with sports on TV, vintage video games, and a pool table. Instead of an obnoxious yuppie tourist pick-up joint, the Clocktower acts as a refuge for locals looking for some after-work relaxation and a pint or two. Expect informal dress and friendly conversation up at the bar, along with the delicious and unusual variety of beers. The location is perfect—in the basement of the Alpenhof just across the street from the Village.

If you prefer a French-style wine bar experience to a noisy British-ish pub, try the vintages at the **Side Door** (100 Canyon Blvd., #229, 760/934-5200, www.sidedoormammoth.com, daily 6 A.M.–midnight). The bad news: Side Door is only open until midnight. The good news: Not only can you enjoy several glasses of California's top wines, you can order up a delicious dinner or dessert crepe to go with your favorite varietal. Expect to pay ski resort prices here, and to be somewhat disappointed in plain sandwiches. But the crepes rate as excellent and the wine list is sometimes called the best in the Village.

Didn't get enough sports during your day at Mammoth? Spend the evening at **Grumpy's** (361 Old Mammoth Rd., 760/934-8587, http://grumpysmammoth.com, daily 11 A.M.–2 A.M., kitchen closes 10 P.M.). This sports bar has the usual array of TVs showing major sporting events, plus pool tables and an arcade. Grumpy's has a full bar and serves up a full lunch and dinner menu of both Mexican and American specialties. Come for the big-screens, stay for the surprisingly tasty food and drink.

The **Lakanuki Tiki Bar** (6201 Minaret Rd., 760/934-7447, www.lakanuki.com, Mon–Thurs 2 P.M.–2 A.M., Fri–Sun 10 A.M.–2 A.M., kitchen closes 10 P.M.) does serve food, but it's the nightlife in the tacky tiki bar that packs the place, especially on weekends. Just expect the name to hold true—the vast majority of the clientele at the Lakanuki run to the young, male, snowboarding variety. That makes it tough to pick up any cute chicks—they're drinking elsewhere.

### Live Music

For a high-class evening of classical music in the mountains, check out a performance of **Chamber Music Unbound** (760/934-7015, www.chambermusicunbound.org). This nonprofit orchestra performs at several locations in Bishop and Mammoth Lakes, creating unique (often humorous and fun) concerts from familiar and out-of-the-way classical pieces. With titles like Bass-Ic Instinct and Sense and Sensuality, CMU concerts may sound like adult fare, but in fact they are family-oriented shows geared for all ages and genteel musical tastes. At Christmas you might catch a performance of the classic Nutcracker, and in the spring an uplifting vocalist show.

## SHOPPING

While it's not a heavy shopping town, the upscale boutiques and galleries, plus a small outlet mall, allow weary outdoors-lovers to take a day off the slopes and engage in some retail therapy.

If you'd like to take in some art while you're in the Mammoth area, several galleries offer an array of photographic art, some for reasonable prices. The **Mountain Light Gallery** (106 S. Main St., Bishop, 760/873-7700, www.mountainlight.com) showcases the wild scenic photography of Galen and Barbara Rowell, world adventurers who died in an accident in 2002. At the gallery, you can view and purchase prints of their scenic photos as well as calendars, note cards, posters, and books. The guest gallery features the work of other landscape photographers. You can even take classes in nature photography and attend other special events.

Another photo gallery in Bishop, the **Vern Clevenger Gallery** (905 N. Main St., 888/224-8376, www.vernclevenger.com) features only the nature photography of Mr. Clevenger himself. Each of Clevenger's photos is shot on film, then a mixed digital and traditional wet process creates the large-format prints you see in the gallery. What you see is all natural, without digital enhancement to the images or colors. Inexpensive note cards and posters are available for purchase in addition to the lovely framed fine-art prints. Or take a workshop to learn how to create these gorgeous images for yourself.

In downtown Mammoth Lakes, visit the **Mammoth Gallery** (425 Old Mammoth Rd. and Minaret Rd., 888/848-7733, http://mammothgallery.com, daily 10 A.M.–5 P.M.). Here you'll see the work of a number of local photographers and watercolor artists, plus a large collection of vintage ski poster reproductions.



## ACCOMMODATIONS

Accommodations at Mammoth run to luxurious ski condos with full kitchens, perfect for spending a week plying the slopes of the local mountains with family or friends. Motels and inns offer comfort as well, often for a little less money and shorter minimum stays.

### Under $100

Want to ski the slopes of exclusive Mammoth, but can't afford the hoity-toity condo resorts? Stay at the **Innsbruck Lodge** (Forest Trail btwn. Hwy. 203 and Sierra Blvd., 760/934-3035, www.innsbrucklodge.com, $93–240). Economy rooms offer twin beds, table and chairs, and access to the motel whirlpool tub and lobby with stone fireplace at super-reasonable nightly rates. Other rooms can sleep 2–6, and some include kitchenettes. The quiet North Village location sits on the ski area shuttle route for easy access to the local slopes.

If you're planning to ski June Mountain, stay at the **Boulder Lodge** (2282 Hwy. 158, 800/455-6355, $77). This inexpensive lodge provides an array of options, from simple motel rooms for short stays to multi-bedroom

PHOTO COURTESY OF THE MAMMOTH LAKES VISITORS BUREAU

Austria Hof

apartments and even a five-bedroom lake house for longer trips and larger groups. The Boulder Lodge takes guests back a few decades with its decorating style—the browns, wood paneling, and faux leather furniture recall the 1950s. But the views of June Lake, the indoor pool and spa, and the wonderful outdoor recreation area surrounding the lodge are timeless.

## $100-150

The **Sierra Lodge** (3540 Main St., 800/356-5711, www.sierralodge.com, $125–135) boasts reasonably priced all-nonsmoking rooms located right on the ski shuttle line, and only a mile and a half from the Juniper Ridge chair lift. This small motel's rates are rock-bottom in the off-season and on weekdays in wintertime. Rooms have either a king or two double beds, a kitchenette with microwave and dishes, and plenty of space for your snow and ski gear. The decor shows simple motel styling in cool, relaxing blues. Breakfast, cable TV, and Wi-Fi access are included with your room.

## $150-250

From the outside, the ornate, carved-wood, fringed **Austria Hof** (924 Canyon Blvd., 866/662-6668, www.austriahof.com, $170–195) might be a ski hotel tucked into a crevice of the Alps. But on the inside, you'll find the most stylish American appointments. Peaceful sea-green motel rooms—even those with a king bed and a spa bathtub—can be rented for under $200 per night. If you've got a larger party or a desire to cook your own meals, check out the one- and two-bedroom condo options. Austria Hof's location adjacent to the Canyon Lodge and the Village gondola make it a great winter ski or summer mountain bike base camp. In the evenings, head down to the restaurant and bar for some hearty German food and drink. Or if you prefer, slip into a swimsuit and enjoy the views from the large outdoor spa.

## Over $250

It's not cheap, but the **Juniper Springs Resort** (4000 Meridian Blvd., 800/626-6684, www.mammothmountain.com, $290) has absolutely every luxury amenity you could want to make your ski vacation complete. Condos come in studio, one-bedroom, two-bedroom, three-bedroom, and townhouse sizes, sleeping up to eight people. The interiors boast stunning appointments, from snow-white down comforters to granite-topped kitchen counters to 60-inch flat-screen TVs. Bathrooms include deep soaking tubs, perfect to privately relax aching muscles after a long day on the slopes. The resort also features heated pools year-round and three outdoor heated spas—there's nothing like jumping into a steaming hot tub on a snowy evening, then jumping back out to find the cold perfect and refreshing. The Talon restaurant serves breakfast and lunch, and the Daily Grind offers coffee and take-out snacks. Juniper Springs is located next door to the Eagle Lodge, which serves as one of the Mammoth Mountain base lodges complete with a six-person express chair up to the main ski area. You can rent skis right inside the hotel, and ski back down to Juniper after a day on the slopes. In the summertime, Juniper Springs' proximity to local golfing and the Mammoth Mountain bike park make it a perfect retreat.

The company that owns Juniper Springs also owns the luxury condo complex at **The Village at Mammoth** (1111 Forest Trail, 800/626-6684, www.mammothmountain.com, $360). Check them out if you can't get the condo of your dreams at Juniper.

For a unique condo rental, check out **Mountainback** (Lakeview Blvd,. 800/468-6225, www.mountainbackrentals.com, $290–460, two-night minimum). This complex boasts an array of all two-bedroom units, some of which sleep up to six people. Every individual building has its own outdoor spa, and the complex has a heated pool and a sauna. Every condo is decorated differently (and you might be able to buy and redecorate one if you want to and have enough cash). Check the website for photos to find what you like—big stone everywhere, wood paneling, gentle cream walls, or even red-and-green holiday-themed furniture. Walk to the ski lifts, or enjoy a round of golf or day of fishing in the summertime.

## FOOD

Plenty of dining options cluster in Mammoth Lakes. You can get your fast-food cheeseburger and your chain double-latte here, but why would you with so many more interesting independent options just lying around? Fare runs to American food and pizza, with a few ethnic options thrown in for variety.

### American

A favorite with locals and repeat visitors, the **Whiskey Creek** (24 Lake Mary Rd., 760/934-2555, daily 5:30 P.M.–2 A.M., $15–30) combines casually elegant California fare in the downstairs dining room with a homey nighttime bar up above. Only half a block from the Village, you can walk in and enjoy an unusual array of entrées, a surprisingly wide selection of wines, and tasty beers. Whisky Creek maintains its own tiny on-site brewery, so some of the beers they serve really are as local as it gets. The crowd, both for dining and for drinking, feels warm and friendly, as do the hearty dishes served to hungry après-skiers. Be sure to make reservations on weekends as it can get crowded here. If you've just come for a drink and a good time, expect live music to heat up the upstairs starting at about 9 P.M., and to keep on playing long past midnight.

### California

**Petra's Bistro and Wine Bar** (6080 Minaret Rd., 760/934-3500, dinner Tues.–Sun.) brings a bit of the California wine country all the way out to Mammoth Lakes. This eatery offers a seasonally changing menu that's designed to please the palate and complement the wine list. That wine list is worth a visit itself—an eclectic mix of vintages highlights the best of California, while giving a nod to European and South American wines. Winelovers will recognize many names, but still might find something new on the unusual list. The by-the-glass offerings change each night, and your server will happily cork your half-finished bottle to take home for tomorrow. Two dining rooms and a wine bar divide up the seating nicely, and the atmosphere succeeds in feeling romantic without being cave-dark. Petra's stays open all year, so if you're visiting in the off-season you'll get a pleasantly uncrowded treat. Reservations are a good idea during high season.

A popular gourmet establishment, **Skadi** (587 Old Mammoth Rd., Ste. B, 760/934-3902, http://restaurantskadi.com) describes their menu as containing "alpine cuisine." In truth, this chef-owned restaurant boasts a menu filled with California-style innovation using mountain-inspired ingredients to their best advantage. (You'll see a lot of venison!) Everything on the list looks tasty, but if you're not ready for a heavy entrée, consider ordering a couple of items from the long list of appetizers for a "small plates" experience. Oh, and don't skip dessert! Whatever you choose, the European-heavy wine list will have something perfect to pair with it. If you're in town in the ski season, make reservations in advance, especially on weekends.



### Mexican

Even Californians who eat Mexican food on a regular basis tend to agree on the quality of the fare at **Roberto's Mexican Café** (271 Old Mammoth Rd., 760/934-3667). This casual spot serves classic California-Mexican food (*chiles rellenos,* enchiladas, burritos, and so on) in great quantities (check out the huge three-combo platter) perfect for skiers and boarders famished after a long day on the slopes. For a quiet meal, stay downstairs in the main dining room. To join in with a lively younger crowd, head upstairs to the bar, which has tables and serves the full restaurant menu. Wherever you sit, even the stoutest of drinkers should beware Roberto's lethal margaritas.

## INFORMATION AND SERVICES

### Tourist Information

The town of Mammoth Lakes has an awesome **Visitors Bureau** (2520 Main St., 760/934-2712, www.visitmammoth.com) that can help you with everything from condo rentals and restaurant reservations before you arrive, to the latest bar openings and advice about best seasonal recreation options. These folks are well worth a stop early in your visit.

### Media and Communications

Mammoth Lakes does indeed publish its own newspaper, the ***Mammoth Times*** (www.mammothtimes.com). This weekly paper serves the whole of the Eastern Sierra region. Check for local events and good nightspots, and visit the website for up-to-date weather and road conditions.

Despite its tiny size, the town of Mammoth Lakes boasts a cosmopolitan atmosphere that includes plenty of Internet access. Many of the condos and hotel rooms have some species of Internet access, and you're likely to find a Starbucks with Wi-Fi somewhere downtown.

### Banks and Post Offices

Plenty of ATMs crowd into Mammoth Lakes at gas stations, mini-marts, and even bank branches. Check the Village, Main Street, and Minaret Road for the most likely places to find banks and cash machines in town.

The **Mammoth Lakes post office** (760/934-2205) sits at 3330 Main Street, a.k.a. CA-203.

### Gas and Automotive Services

Mammoth Lakes is a great place to gas up before hitting the more wild parts of the Eastern Sierra. Gas stations cluster right at the eastern edge of town, where CA-203 becomes Main Street, and more gas can be found throughout the downtown area. Just be prepared to pay a premium. This is a resort town, and they know how far away the next gas station is!

Many gas stations, plus big-box stores and even pharmacies and supermarkets sell tire chains in the wintertime.

### Medical Services

Need medical service beyond that offered at the ski resorts? You can get it at **Mammoth Hospital** (85 Sierra Park Rd., 760/934-3311, mammothhospital.com), which has a 24-hour emergency room.

## GETTING THERE AND AROUND

### Air

The nearest airport to Mammoth is the **Mammoth Yosemite Airport** (MMH, 437 Old Mammoth Rd., 760/934-8989, www.ci.mammoth-lakes.ca.us/airport/awos.htm). Extensively remodeled in 2008, this airport offers limited, expensive commercial service in and out of the Eastern Sierras, plus a single rental-car outlet. For a less expensive spot to fly into, try the Reno airport and drive in from there.

### Car

California's Highway 395 acts as the main access road to the Mammoth Lakes area. To get to Mammoth Lakes proper, from Highway 395 north or south, turn onto State Highway 203, which will take you right into town.

Mammoth Lakes (and most of the rest of the Eastern Sierra) isn't near any of California's major hot spots. Expect a six-hour drive from Los Angeles and (at best!) a seven-hour drive from San Francisco if the traffic and weather cooperate. If you fly into Reno, the drive out to Mammoth takes about three hours.

In the wintertime, be aware that it snows in Mammoth more than it does in almost any other place in California. Carry chains! Even if the weather is predicted to be clear for your visit, having chains can prevent a world of hurt and turning back in sudden storms. The longer you plan to stay, the better you should stock your car with items such as ice scrapers, blankets, water, food, and a full tank of gas whenever possible. For the latest traffic information, including chain control areas and weather conditions, call CalTrans at 800/427-7623.

Parking in Mammoth Lakes in the off-season is a breeze. In the winter, it can get a bit more complicated, as constant snow removal means that parking on the street is illegal throughout town. Most of the major resorts and hotels offer heated parking structures, and many of the restaurants, bars, and ski resorts have plenty of parking in their outdoor lots. If you're concerned about parking, call ahead to your resort and restaurants to get the lowdown on how best to get there and where to leave your car.

### Shuttles and Buses

Devil's Postpile National Monument (760/924-5500, www.nps.gov/depo, $7) runs a shuttle into the park that's mandatory for all visitors during high season (vehicles with handicap placards excepted). The shuttle runs every 20–30 minutes between Mammoth Mountain Ski Area and Reds Meadow Valley 7 A.M.–7 P.M. mid-June–mid-September.

A daily **Mountain Express Shuttle** (760/924-3184, adults $5.50, reservations recommended) runs from the Mammoth Lakes McDonald's to the June Lake ski area, arriving at 9 A.M. The return shuttle leaves June Lake at 3:30 P.M.



# Sequoia and Kings Canyon National Parks

The trees are the stars of the show at Sequoia and Kings Canyon National Parks (www.nps.gov/seki). Groves of giant sequoias, including the largest known tree on earth, soar out of the fertile Sierra soil. But in these parks you'll also find rugged granite formations (including Kings Canyon—a deeper gulch than the Grand Canyon), marble caverns, rushing rivers, and an astounding variety of ecosystems, from chaparral to alpine meadow.

## SIGHTS

### General Grant Grove

One of the largest of these parks' giant sequoia groves, the General Grant Grove (one mile northwest of the Kings Canyon Visitor Center) is home to dozens of monumental trees. The largest of these is the General Grant Tree, the third-largest tree on earth, an American National Shrine, and "America's Christmas Tree." Another feature of this area, the Fallen Monarch was once

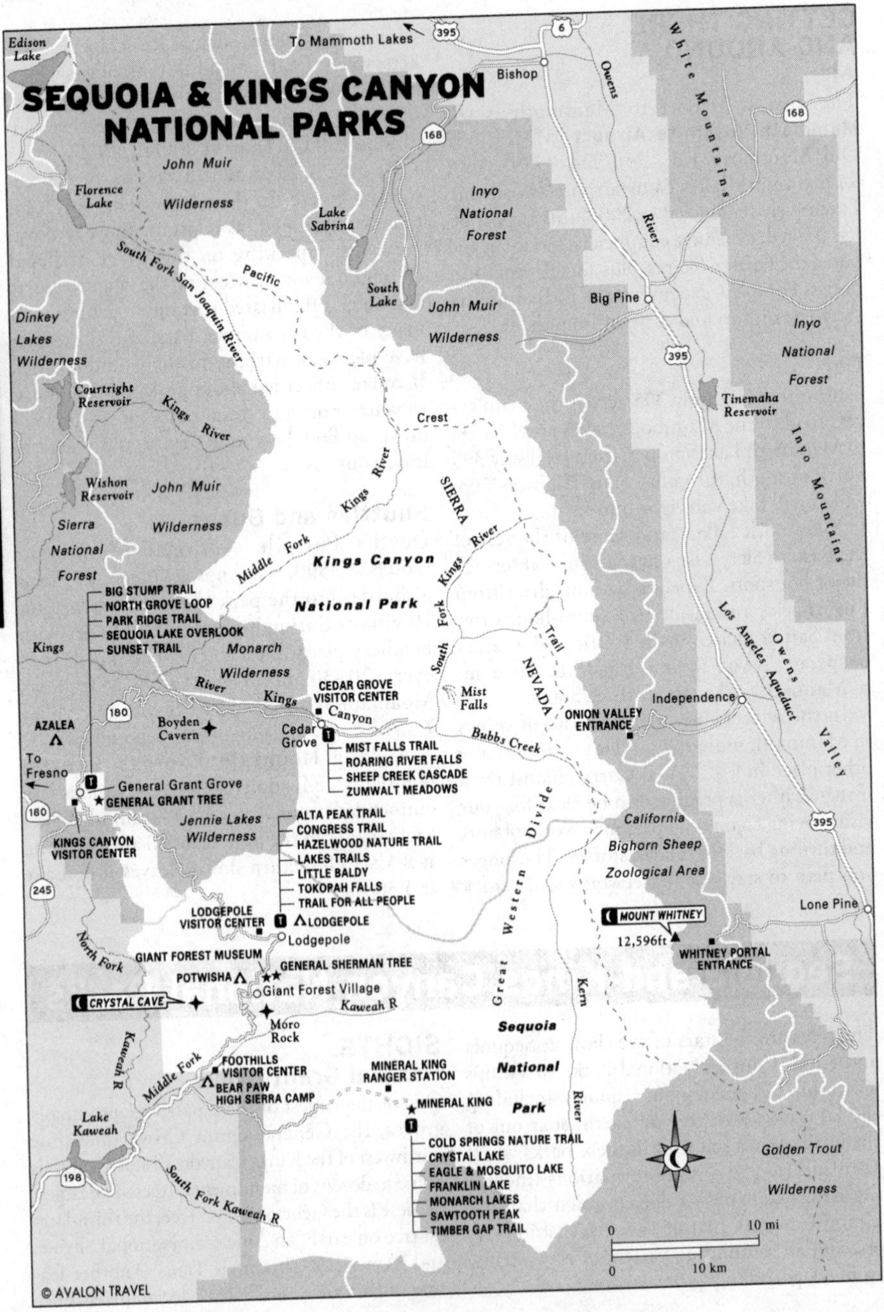
SEQUOIA & KINGS CANYON NATIONAL PARKS
To Mammoth Lakes
395
6
Bishop
168
Edison Lake
Florence Lake
John Muir Wilderness
Lake Sabrina
Inyo National Forest
White Mountains
Owens River
South Fork San Joaquin River
Pacific
South Lake
John Muir Wilderness
Big Pine
Dinkey Lakes Wilderness
Courtright Reservoir
Kings River
Inyo National Forest
Tinemaha Reservoir
Inyo Mountains
Crest
Wishon Reservoir
John Muir Wilderness
Middle Fork Kings River
SIERRA
Sierra National Forest
Kings Canyon National Park
South Fork Kings River
BIG STUMP TRAIL
NORTH GROVE LOOP
PARK RIDGE TRAIL
SEQUOIA LAKE OVERLOOK
SUNSET TRAIL
Kings
Monarch Wilderness
River
Trail
NEVADA
Los Angeles Aqueduct
Owens Valley
CEDAR GROVE VISITOR CENTER
Kings Canyon
Mist Falls
Independence
ONION VALLEY ENTRANCE
180
AZALEA
Boyden Cavern
Cedar Grove
MIST FALLS TRAIL
ROARING RIVER FALLS
SHEEP CREEK CASCADE
ZUMWALT MEADOWS
Bubbs Creek
To Fresno
General Grant Grove
GENERAL GRANT TREE
Jennie Lakes Wilderness
KINGS CANYON VISITOR CENTER
ALTA PEAK TRAIL
CONGRESS TRAIL
HAZELWOOD NATURE TRAIL
LAKES TRAILS
LITTLE BALDY
TOKOPAH FALLS
TRAIL FOR ALL PEOPLE
Divide
California Bighorn Sheep Zoological Area
245
LODGEPOLE VISITOR CENTER
LODGEPOLE
Lodgepole
Great Western
MOUNT WHITNEY
12,596ft
Lone Pine
WHITNEY PORTAL ENTRANCE
North Fork
GIANT FOREST MUSEUM
GENERAL SHERMAN TREE
POTWISHA
Giant Forest Village
CRYSTAL CAVE
Kaweah R
Moro Rock
Kern River
Sequoia National Park
Kaweah R
Middle Fork
FOOTHILLS VISITOR CENTER
BEAR PAW HIGH SIERRA CAMP
MINERAL KING RANGER STATION
MINERAL KING
Lake Kaweah
COLD SPRINGS NATURE TRAIL
CRYSTAL LAKE
EAGLE & MOSQUITO LAKE
FRANKLIN LAKE
MONARCH LAKES
SAWTOOTH PEAK
TIMBER GAP TRAIL
198
South Fork Kaweah R
Golden Trout Wilderness
0
10 mi
0
10 km
© AVALON TRAVEL

© LIZ HAMILL SCOTT

General Grant Tree, "America's Christmas Tree"

an immense tree but now acts as a tunnel along the trail, with enough head room for almost the tallest of visitors to get through without ducking. The walk among the sequoias at all stages of development is easy, with a well-built flat half-mile trail (much of this area is wheelchair accessible). But consider purchasing a trail guide at the nearby visitors center, because the circuitous trail can be difficult to follow and you may find yourself lost in the beautiful forest trying to find its star attraction.

## General Sherman Tree

There can be only one. The General Sherman Tree (Wolverton Rd. off Generals Hwy.) is the largest tree known on the planet. At just under 275 feet, it is not the tallest tree, nor at 2,200 years old is it the oldest, but by sheer volume of wood it is the biggest. If you love statistics, pick up a sheet at any of the visitors centers that lists the worlds' 30 largest giant sequoias. Take the trail down the hill to visit the tree, then past it to the shuttle stop where you can catch a shuttle back up the hill to your car.

## Giant Forest Museum

The Giant Forest Museum (559/565-4480, 16 miles from the Hwy. 198 entrance) perches on the side of the Generals Highway. Inside this fun interactive museum, you'll learn everything you ever wanted or needed to know about giant sequoia trees, which grow only here in the Sierra Nevada range. Kids and adults alike love the touchable, spinnable exhibits that provide context to the stated sizes of the trees. This newer museum goes into great detail about the importance of fire in the life of a giant sequoia (and other plants and trees that grow in the same areas). Ironically, a commitment to stamping out *all* forest fires, even those caused naturally by lightning strikes, severely endangered the giant sequoias, which rely on fire to create the right habitat for their growth and reproduction. You'll also learn about how the park used to look, and why many of the buildings have been removed to make way for more trees. This is a great stop for families whose kids need a rest from hiking and long intervals in the car.

## Crystal Cave

You'll find no trees in the Crystal Cave (Generals Hwy., three miles south of the General Sherman Tree). Instead, you'll find immense underground rooms filled with incredible natural calcite formations and shining polished marble. This is the underside of the parks—perhaps the most impressive (and one of only two publicly accessible) of the over 250 marble caverns within the park and national forest boundaries. The regular tour lasts 45 minutes and takes visitors through walkable, well-lit tunnels and into grand chambers filled with curtains, stalactites, and other weird and beautiful calcite creations. A longer two-hour tour takes you deeper into the caverns, and gives you a much more detailed lesson on the cave's history and geology. Best of all, serious spelunkers can sign up for the Wild Cave Tour, a four- to six-hour crawl off the lit tourist trails in Crystal Cave. With a limit of six people per party, you'll get the most serious caving experience available anywhere in Sequoia and Kings Canyon National Parks.

Sequoia and Kings Canyon

You can't buy a ticket for a tour at the entrance to Crystal Cave. You'll need to stop at either the Foothills or the Lodgepole visitors center to purchase your tickets. Then proceed on to the cave parking lot, which can take over an hour from either visitor center. No trailers or RVs over 22 feet are allowed on the road. Be aware that even in the fall, tours fill up quickly so if possible get tickets early in the morning or even a day in advance.

## Mineral King

Ironically, the onetime boom town of Mineral King (25 miles off Hwy. 198) never had a successful mining industry nearby. Silver was discovered here and mining began in 1873, but not many minerals moved out of the mountain. Instead, the road built in 1879 attracted loggers and the hydroelectric industry, and the town managed to flourish for a while. Today, visitors drive up the long, winding road to enjoy the resurgence of nature in the area at the expense of human construction. Mineral King Valley draws both geology and botany buffs with its unique glacier-carved array of rocks and minerals, some overgrown with a variety of native plants. The Atwell Mill that once cut first-growth sequoia timber has been reduced to a few relics—a steam engine, a wheel, miscellaneous junk—while all around young giant sequoias reclaim their territory. High above the former town, Sawtooth Peak, at more than 12,000 feet, looms large and reminds many visitors and scientists of similar mountains in the Rockies. The peak is perfect for intrepid day hikers, and also allows multi-day treks with a backcountry permit.

Trying to drive your RV or trailer up Mineral King Road is hazardous to you, your vehicle, and other motorists. Also, marmots frequent the Mineral King area, and these furry critters won't seem quite so cute after you discover they've chewed through your radiator hoses! Check with the ranger station for current activity, and notify the rangers if your car has been disabled.

## Mount Whitney

It's not just the tallest mountain in California. At 14,505 feet, Mount Whitney (www.nps

.gov/seki/planyourvisit/whitney.htm) boasts the highest altitude of any peak in the 48 contiguous United States. Yes, it beats out all the mighty Rocky Mountains! You can see and photograph the impressive peak from several points along the Generals Highway in Sequoia and Kings Canyon. However, it's well away from the main part of the parks, sitting near the town of Lone Pine to the southeast. Plan a long drive to get there from either park entrance.

Amazingly, you can climb all the way to the top of Mount Whitney and back in one day, if you're in good shape and prepared properly for the journey. However, you can't just park at the trailhead and head out during high season (May–Nov.). To preserve the natural beauty of the fragile mountain ecosystem, only 100 day-hikers and 60 backpackers are permitted to hit the main trail each day, and you'll find some severe restrictions on how you must behave. Whitney Portal (13 miles west of Lone Pine) provides the most direct access along a 10.7-mile trail.

If you want to make the climb (or even day-hike), apply for a permit in advance and check reservations (Wilderness Permit Office, 760/873-2483, www.fs.fed.us/r5/inyo/recreation/wild/whitneyavail.shtml, daily 8 A.M.–4:30 P.M.). Also check the website for information about how to prepare for a Mount Whitney hike. Mount Whitney also marks the southern end of the John Muir Trail. Whether you begin here or end here, you'll find the mountain a worthwhile marker on this epic foot journey through California.

### Boyden Cavern

Tucked back in the wilds of the Sequoia National Forest, between Sequoia and Kings Canyon Parks, Boyden Cavern (74101 E. Kings Canyon Rd., 559/338-0959, www.caverntours.com/boydenrt.htm, tours daily mid-Apr.–mid-Nov., $20 park fee plus tour cost) gives visitors an up-close and personal cave experience. Inside Boyden, "please try not to touch the formations" takes on a new meaning—that is, turn sideways to avoid the walls and duck to keep from hitting your head on stalactites that are many thousands of yeards old. This modest-sized cavern network contains plenty of draperies, pancakes, stalactites, and other calcite structures. You can stare right at them, up into them, and in some cases walk all the way around them.

## SPORTS AND RECREATION

### Hiking

Sequoia and Kings Canyon attract hikers all year long-especially those looking for a wild Sierra experience without the overcrowding that's so often prevalent at Yosemite. Many areas of the parks offer lovely day hikes, or you can get a backcountry permit for a backpacking trek through this large, gorgeous area, much of which is only accessible on foot.

#### GENERAL GRANT GROVE

This popular stop just north of the northern Kings Canyon park entrance offers a variety of short, flat trails that are perfect for day visitors. After visiting the General Grant Tree, take the **North Grove Loop** half a mile along an old park road through the grove. You might find yourself on the North Grove Loop even if you didn't intend to; it's not particularly well differentiated from the General Grant Tree Trail and it takes in much of the same area.

Outside the grove, take the **Big Stump Trail** (near the Big Stump park entrance) one mile round-trip through a grove that was heavily logged in the late 19th century, but is now reclaiming its true nature as a sequoia grove. Or enjoy the vistas from the **Park Ridge Trail** (Panoramic Point Rd. parking area, closed in winter). If you pick a clear day, you can see all the way out to the Coast Range of mountains in the San Francisco Bay Area from this trail! While there's little elevation change on this almost five-mile walk, consider the altitude of the area before deciding that this trail and the fire-road route back will be an easy trip. For a different view on the life and death of the giant sequoias, and humanity's intervention in this area, hike the **Sequoia Lake Overlook/Dead Giant Loop** (lower end of General Grant Tree parking area). The two-mile trail takes you to the Dead Giant, a first-growth giant sequoia that was mostly likely killed by loggers trying (and failing) to cut it for lumber. Sequoia Lake is actually an old mill pond from the logging days.

For a longer, more demanding day hike, check out the **Sunset Trail** (Grant Grove Visitor Center). You'll climb about 1,400 feet over this six-mile (round-trip) trail, which takes you past Viola Falls and through the magnificent mixed forests.



## MINERAL KING

A good place to start walking in Mineral King is the **Cold Springs Nature Trail.** This easy, one-mile interpretive walk describes and displays the natural wonders and the formation of the valley.

A bit more strenuous, the **Timber Gap Trail** follows an old mining road through a forest of red fir trees. You'll see pretty views out to Alta Peak and the middle fork of the Kaweah River. The short version of this trail runs four miles round-trip. Note the altitude: You'll start at over 7,500 feet. For a longer hike, take the fork to **Monarch Lakes.** This trek runs about 8.5 miles round-trip, but it's mostly flat and easy walking. Consider bringing a picnic to enjoy beside the lakes. For hikers in great shape looking for the most tremendous views of the southern Sierra Nevada range, keep on going past the lakes up to the top of **Sawtooth Peak.** This trail isn't for the faint of breath or shaky of leg. It climbs 1,200 feet in just over a mile of loose, difficult ground. But once you're at the top, you'll get a fine chance to rest as you photograph the majestic peaks all around you.

Many other hikes begin in Mineral King Valley. You can visit a number of charming alpine lakes if you're up for a hike of 7–11 miles. Plan to take food and water and spend all day on hikes out to **Eagle and Mosquito Lakes** or **Crystal Lake.** You can also get to **Franklin Lake** and back in a day, though the pristine beauty of the water and fascinating geology of the area often draw backpackers on their way to Mount Whitney over several days.

## LODGEPOLE

For a charming interpretive walk at the Lodgepole Village area, head down the **Hazelwood Nature Trail** (Giant Forest Lodge). Signs along this flat one-mile stroll tell the history of humans' relationship with the giant sequoia trees—good and bad, beneficial and destructive. This walk works well for families with school-aged kids. In the same vicinity, you can putter along the quarter-mile **Trail For All People.** This interpretive nature walk's pride comes in spring, when the wildflowers bloom. A bit longer but perhaps the most representative of life in Sequoia National Park, the **Congress Trail** starts at the General Sherman Tree. Grab a pamphlet with map at the Sherman Tree to get the best experience on this trail, which includes many of the park's most famous named giant sequoias. This two-mile round-trip trail is paved, making it wheelchair accessible and a non-strenuous walk even for folks who usually aren't big hikers.

How can you resist a hike to a granite formation called **Little Baldy** (11 miles north of General Grant Grove)? This moderate climb takes you up about 700 feet to the top of the cutely named granite dome. Look down from the peak, which tops out at over 8,000 feet, into the Giant Forest and snap a few photos. Or if you prefer water to stone, head for **Tokopah Falls** (Lodgepole Campground). Early summer, when the flow is at its peak, is the best time to trek out the almost two miles along the Marble Fork of the Kaweah River to this fantastic 1,200-foot waterfall.

Hardcore hikers willing to brave steep climbs at high altitudes can either take day hikes or obtain overnight backcountry passes for the region's major trails. The **Lakes Trails** (Wolverton picnic area) vary in length, but you're definitely going to have to climb a ways up to the glacial lake areas. From the trail, you'll be able to visit Heather Lake, Emerald Lake, and Pear Lake. The minimum distance round-trip for a day hike to Heather Lake is eight miles. Heights-lovers choose the **Alta Peak Trail,** which ascends all the way up to the 11,204-foot summit of Alta Peak. Pick a

© LIZ HAMILL SCOTT

Sequoia's namesake stars

clear day for this grueling 14-mile hike and you'll get a view of Mount Whitney across the Great Western Divide.

### CEDAR GROVE

Even if you hate hiking, you'll want to get out of the car and stroll the negligible distance (less than 0.25 mile) from the parking area three miles east of Cedar Grove Village to the **Roaring River Falls.** The whole tiny trail sits under a canopy of trees, making it cool even in the hottest parts of summer, and just looking at the falls feels refreshing after driving the Generals Highway. Another easy meander comes only a mile from Road's End (the northeast terminus of Generals Highway). **Zumwalt Meadows** offers a flat one-mile loop around the meadow of the same name, then a shady walk through a grove of heavenly smelling incense cedar and pine trees along the Kings River.

Moderate hikes abound in this area. A good place to bring a picnic is **Sheep Creek Cascade.** This hike takes about an hour and a half, ascends 600 feet, and runs about two miles total. You end up in a picturesque shaded glen that's perfect for taking a load off your feet and enjoying the serene surroundings. The **Mists Falls Trail** (Road's End) is a popular jumping-off point for backpackers destined for the Kings Canyon backcountry. However, you can go eight miles out and back to Mists Falls in about five hours. Plan for dust and heat on the first couple of miles of the trail, then steep switchbacks that take you up 1,500 feet to the falls. If you're passing through on your way to the John Muir Trail for a longer trek, keep going past the falls, up to Paradise Valley, then to the trail crossing at Upper Woods Creek.



## Climbing

It shouldn't surprise anyone to learn that **Mount Whitney** is a wonderful place to rock climb. You can climb up the steep East Face of the mountain or head up the Needles. These climbs are not beginners' journeys, but the East Face isn't the hardest climb ever either. First climbed by John Muir himself in 1931, most of the East Face rates at a Class 3, with the worst bits rated 5.4. The Needles are famed among big-wall climbers who attack the Sierras each year. See the *Mount Whitney* section for permit information and regulations.

## Horseback Riding

A number of horse-accessible trails meander through Sequoia and Kings Canyon. Rent a horse for a day ride from the pack stations at **Cedar Grove** (559/565-3463 summer, 559/337-2314 off-season) and **Grant Grove** (559/335-9292 summer, 559/337-2314 off-season). If you're new to horses, pick a gentle one-hour ride. For more hardy or experienced riders, both pack stations offer half-day and full-day rides.

If you're looking for a multi-day horseback adventure, you can find that too at Sequoia and Kings Canyon. Call either of the pack stations to arrange a guided backcountry pack trip.

## Fishing

Fishing is allowed in any of the lakes inside Sequoia and Kings Canyon. You can purchase a fishing license and tackle at the markets at the Grant Grove, Cedar Grove, and Lodgepole visitors centers. The visitor centers can also advise about season opening and closing dates. Anglers are permitted up to five trout per day. The lakes and the Kaweah drainage hold rainbows, eastern brook, German brown, and golden trout.

## ACCOMMODATIONS

### Camping



The park offers 13 campgrounds, three of which are open year-round (Lodgepole, Azalea, and Potwisha). Campgrounds are first-come, first-served, except for Lodgepole (summer visits only). A list and map of all campgrounds is available at www.nps.gov/seki/planyourvisit/campgrounds.htm.

**Lodgepole** (summer reservations 877/444-6777, www.recreation.gov, $18–20) is located along the Kaweah River and is 21 miles from the Sequoia entrance. In summer, there are 214 sites for tents and RVs, flush toilets, showers, laundry, and bear-proof containers. Off-season, there are 25 walk-in tent sites (first-come, first-served).

**Azalea** (Grant Grove, 110 sites, $18) is located 3.5 miles from the Kings Canyon park entrance and within a half-mile of the visitor center. **Potwisha** (42 sites, $18) is also on the Kaweah River, about four miles from the Sequoia entrance. Amenities include flush toilets, RV disposal, and bear-proof containers.

More adventurous campers should check out the High Sierra Camps. Start at Crescent Meadow, about 10 miles south of Wuksachi on Generals Highway, to get to the **Bearpaw High Sierra Camp** (866/807-3598, www.visitsequoia.com, June–Sept.), an 11.5-mile hike into the gorgeous Sequoia back country. This camp takes a leaf from Yosemite's book with its accommodations and amenities. This camp offers six tent cabins that sleep two people apiece, and come complete with bedding, towels, and sleeping pads. You can even fit a third person on the floor of your cabin, if that person brings bedding and a towel for herself. A bath house offers flush toilets and hot showers (heaven!), and each stay comes with a full dinner and full breakfast, served family-style. You can even buy a box lunch to take with you on your next day's journey.

### Under $100

Centrally located in the Grant Grove Village, the **Grant Grove Cabins** (866/522-6966, www.sequoia-kingscanyon.com, $65–75/tent cabins) offer a wide array of lodging styles for a variety of prices. Many of these cabins have been around awhile—some since the early days of what was then the General Grant National Park. The economy option here are the tent cabins, which are short on amenities, with no electricity or heat and with shared, central bathrooms. From May through October, a number of Camp, Rustic, and Oversized cabins offer solid walls ($77–140), a small propane heater plus an outdoor wood-burning stove, electricity, and daily maid service. When you make reservations, ask about larger cabins if you've got a bigger group or family. It can start snowing in Sequoia and Kings Canyon as early as mid-September. If you're visiting in the spring or the fall, consider whether you're willing to chance an unheated or minimally heated cabin should a storm come up in the park. Open all year are the historic cabins with private baths. Most are duplexes, one log cabin is a single that sleeps two. These cabins have heating, historic Mission-style decor, and amenities such as coffee makers.

### $150-250

Built in 1999, the **Wuksachi Lodge** (Hwy. 198 just west of Lodgepole, 866/786-3197, www.visitsequoia.com, $215–285, year-round) offers the most luxurious accommodations available inside the parks. With 102 rooms of various sizes, the Wuksachi Lodge offers ample luxury housing for tree-lovers who just can't give up their creature comforts. Guest rooms boast "woodsy-motel" decor, with colorful Native American print bedspreads and slightly more interesting Mission-style wooden furniture. Each room has a private bath, a TV, a phone, a coffee maker, ski racks, and daily maid service.

© LIZ HAMILL SCOTT

Clear water runs through Sequoia National Park.

The Wuksachi's superior rooms offer space and comfort, particularly for families who cannot imagine a vacation without digital entertainment readily available. An on-site restaurant (the best in the parks), a Native American thematic gift shop, and close access to the Lodgepole visitors complex round out the attractions of this popular lodge.

The shining new **John Muir Lodge** (Grant Grove Village, 866/522-6966, www.sequoia-kingscanyon.com, $150–200, year-round) brings together the concepts of a comfortable motel and a classic woodsy lodge. Expect big timber poles combining form and function in the huge common room. This space acts as a living room or lounge, with a fireplace, wireless Internet access, tables, sofas, and a number of board games. Guest rooms are simply decorated in an alpine theme, complete with comfortable beds, clean bathrooms, and charming views out into the forest. Since you're up at the edge of General Grant Village, you'll find plenty of nearby food and services, including the Village restaurant, mini-mart, souvenir shop, and the Grant Grove visitors center. The lodge is convenient to hiking, and to the Generals Highway through the park.

## FOOD

### Restaurants

The national parks have their visitors good and trapped when it comes to dining options. Guests who want a wide range of options should bring in their own food. One option is to bring a cooler and stop at a supermarket before you enter the park.

One of the Sequoia restaurants sits at the Grant Grove complex, servicing both the John Muir Lodge and the surrounding tent cabins. **Grant Grove Restaurant** (Hwy. 180 at Generals Hwy., 559/335-5500, Sun.–Thurs. 8 A.M.–2 P.M., 5–7 P.M., Fri.–Sat. 8 A.M.–2 P.M., 5–8 P.M.) serves three meals each day, and is closed in between. This basic dining room offers standard American fare at pretty high resort prices. Though the food is nothing special at lunch or dinner, you can get a palatable meal and a glass of wine. Breakfast, on the other hand, is a monument to the value of cereal bars, apples, and OJ. Morning service at the Grant Grove

Restaurant is weak to disastrous (expect to wait 20–30 minutes for a table in a half-empty dining room), the coffee has both mediocre taste and strength, and the food is simply appalling. If you have *any* other breakfast option, go with it.

The closest thing to an upscale restaurant in Sequoia and Kings Canyon is the **Wuksachi Lodge Restaurant** (off Generals Hwy. west of Lodgepole, open daily year-round for breakfast, lunch, and dinner, $9–24). The elegant dining room has white cloths on the tables and sweeping forest views outside the picture windows. The Wuksachi Restaurant offers three meals per day to service the lodge's overnight guests. But dinner stars as *the* meal of the day, boasting fancier preparations and California-style ingredients. Make a reservation if you plan to dine at the Wuksachi on a summer weekend.

On the other end of the dining spectrum, but no less fun, you'll find the **Kings Canyon Lodge Restaurant** (Hwy. 180 approx 20 miles east of Grant Grove Village). Warning: If taxidermy puts you off your food, do not eat here! Stuffed heads of deer, elk, and other animals decorate the walls, and every other inch of space in the long narrow dining room/lobby is covered with Western-themed knickknacks, geegaws, and tchotchkes. Some of these might even be antiques. Ancient refrigerators and freezers hold cold soft drinks, beer, and ice cream, and the classic diner food is made to order in the least pretentious open kitchen anywhere in the state of California. The restaurant remains open through the long, hot afternoon, making the Kings Canyon Lodge a welcome rest stop for kids needing ice cream and to run around, and adults who prefer to eat late (or have no other choice).

### Markets

You'll find minimally stocked mini-marts at both the **Grant Grove Village** (Hwy. 180 at Generals Hwy., Sun.–Thurs. 9 A.M.–7 P.M., Fri.–Sat. 9 A.M.–8 P.M.) and the **Lodgepole Market** (Generals Hwy. at Lodgepole, daily late May–fall 8 A.M.–8 P.M., fall–spring 9 A.M.–6 P.M.). These sell a few staples, soda, beer, s'mores makings, and some packaged food suitable for reheating over a campfire.

## INFORMATION AND SERVICES

### Tourist Information

Sequoia and Kings Canyon National Parks boast several visitors centers and rangers stations. When you enter the park, you'll be given both the glossy pamphlet and the up-to-date National Park Guide for Sequoia and Kings Canyon. These will provide you with all the in-park information you need to have a great time and keep up on any activities and events.

In Sequoia, the **Foothills Visitor Center** (559/565-3135, daily) is located on Generals Highway, one mile from the park entrance. Crystal Cave tour tickets are sold here until 3:45 P.M. and wilderness permits are issued here as well. **Lodgepole Visitor Center** (Lodgepole Rd., 559/565-4436, spring–fall), off Generals Highway, is 21 miles from the Sequoia entrance. Crystal Cave tour tickets are sold until 3:30 P.M. and wilderness permits are issued here. The **Mineral King Ranger Station** (Mineral King Rd., 559/565-3768, May–Sept.) is located up a narrow road and offers basic seasonal services.

In Kings Canyon, there is the **Kings Canyon Visitor Center** (Grant Grove, 559/565-4307, Apr.–Oct. daily 8 A.M.–5 P.M., Nov.–Mar. daily 9 A.M.–4:30 P.M.) three miles east of the Highway 180 entrance and **Cedar Grove Visitor Center** (559/565-3793, mid Apr–mid–Nov.) in Cedar Grove Village.

### Media and Communications

You're a long way from civilization when you visit Sequoia and Kings Canyon National Parks. Don't expect flawless coverage from your cell phone. If you're lucky you might find some signal; if you're unlucky, you're stuck with land lines at the visitors centers and lodgings for the duration of your stay. Likewise with Internet service. The more cosmopolitan lodges inside the park offer some Wi-Fi in common areas, but that's about the extent of Internet service here. So consider forgetting the laptop and the PDA and unplugging for a few days so you can get to understand the sights and sounds of the woods all around you.

## Banks and Post Offices

No banks lie inside the park, but you can find ATMs at the major visitors complexes at Grant Grove, Lodgepole, and Cedar Grove (summer only).

Though you can no longer post a letter from the old log cabin post office, you can make use of the **Park Post Office at Lodgepole** (Lodgepole Visitor Center, Mon.–Fri. 8 A.M.–1 P.M., 2–4 P.M.). Address any mail to General Delivery, Sequoia National Park, 93262.

## Medical Services

No medical services beyond the first aid provided by rangers are available in Sequoia and Kings Canyon. In a medical emergency, dial 911 from your cell phone, your lodgings, or a call box if possible. The nearest hospitals sit out in Fresno and Visalia.

# GETTING THERE AND AROUND

## Car

Visitors can enter Sequoia at the Ash Mountain entrance on Highway 198 or at Big Stump in Kings Canyon on Highway 180. There are no road entrances on the east side of either park.

The closest major highway to the park is Highway 99. Turn east onto CA-180 from Fresno to get to the north entrance and onto CA-198 from Visalia in the south. The main road running through the two parks is called **The Generals Highway.** It connects CA-180 (Kings Canyon Highway) in the north to CA-198 in the southwest.

Drive carefully in Sequoia and Kings Canyon. They might call it a "highway," but in truth the Generals Highway is a steep, narrow, twisting mountain road that can be treacherous in bad weather and when driven too fast by unfamiliar and inexperienced motorists. Maximum RV length is 22 feet on Generals Highway and Crystal Cave Road (no trailers permitted on the latter). RVs and trailers are not permitted on Mineral King Road or Moro Rock/Crescent Meadow Road.

Parking lots grace most major attractions, but these can fill up quickly in the summer. Some parking is permitted along the roadsides, but *please* don't park your hot car on dry grass—you can set the park (and your car) on fire this way.

Several of the park's roads close in the winter, though the Generals Highway remains open. The Mineral King Road, Crystal Cave Road, and Panoramic Point Roads close from about the beginning of November to the end of May each year. Check the website or call 559/565-3341 for current road information.

Drive times from either San Francisco or Los Angeles can easily run 5–7 hours, depending on traffic and weather conditions.

When you approach the parks, you'll be told by everybody and their little dog Spot that there's no gas anywhere in Sequoia or Kings Canyon National Parks. And technically, that's true. The Kings Canyon Lodge gas station sits on national forest land rather than inside the park borders proper. And many visitors are dubious when they see the genuine antique gravity gas pumps sitting outside the funky old lodge. But those pumps work, and while you can't fill up your SUV, you can get enough gas here to at least get you out of the park and to one of the border towns.

Two other stations sit in the national forest at Hume Lake (Hwy. 180, 11 miles north of Grant Grove) and Stony Creek (Generals Hwy., btwn. Lodgepole and Grant Grove).

## Shuttles

Sequoia National Park provides free shuttle service (559/565-3341, www.nps.gov/seki/planyourvisit/publictransportation.htm) within the park May 21–September 1. The "green" route connects Giant Forest with the Lodgepole Visitor Center, the General Sherman Tree, and the Giant Forest Museum. The "gray" route connects the Giant Forest Museum to Moro Rock and Crescent Meadow.

The **Sequoia Shuttle** (877/287-4453, www.sequoiashuttle.com, $15) connects Visalia to the Giant Forest Museum.

# CENTRAL COAST

Here begins the California coast that movies and literature have made legendary. Soaring cliffs drop straight down into the sea in some areas, making the white sand beaches that occasionally appear beneath and beyond them all the more inviting. From north to south, the Pacific Ocean changes from slate gray to a gentler blue. Scents of salt and kelp waft up the beaches, and the endless crash of the breakers against the shore is a constant lullaby in the coastal towns.

The seacoast city of Santa Cruz, with its ultra-liberal culture, redwood-clad university, and general sense of funky fun, prides itself on keeping things weird. The beach and Boardwalk are prime attractions for surfing and enjoying the sun.

Gorgeous Monterey Bay is famous for its sealife. Sea otters dive and play at the world-renowned aquarium while sea lions beach themselves for sunning pleasure on offshore rocks. The historic Cannery Row was immortalized by Steinbeck in his novel of the same name, but the now touristy wharf area bears only a superficial resemblance to its fishing past.

One of the most exclusive enclaves of the wealthy in all of California, nearby Carmel rivals Malibu for its charming ocean views, well-traveled beaches and parks, and, most of all, for its unbelievably expensive real estate. (Clint Eastwood was once mayor here.) The legendary Pebble Beach golf course and resort sits just north of downtown.

South of Carmel, Highway 1 begins its scenic tour down Big Sur. The Big Sur coast might be the single most beautiful part of California. The rugged cliffs and protected forests have

© LIZ HAMILL SCOTT

## HIGHLIGHTS

**Santa Cruz Beach Boardwalk:** This is the best traditional beach boardwalk in the state (page 425).

**Monterey Bay Aquarium:** This mammoth aquarium was the first of its kind in the United States and still astonishes with a vast array of sea life and exhibits (page 436).

**17-Mile Drive:** This gorgeous scenic drive is worth the toll for an introduction to the region's coastal beauty (page 444).

**Carmel Mission:** Father Junipero Serra's favorite California mission is still a working parish, with an informative museum and stunning gilded altar (page 446).

**Big Sur Coast Highway:** This twisty, coastal drive is iconic Big Sur, with jutting cliffs, crashing surf, and epics views all the way (page 453).

**Pfeiffer Big Sur State Park:** Whether you're camping at the park or not, it's worth your time to hike through the stunning redwoods of Pfeiffer Big Sur (page 456).

**Hearst Castle:** No visit to the Central Coast is complete without a tour of Hearst Castle, the grand mansion on a hill conceived and built by publishing magnate William Randolph Hearst (page 467).

LOOK FOR TO FIND RECOMMENDED SIGHTS, ACTIVITIES, DINING, AND LODGING.

**Santa Barbara Museum of Natural History:** The museum's large galleries house exhibits highlighting the natural history and inhabitants of the area. Take a stroll along the nature trail or peruse the accompanying planetarium (page 476).

little development to mar their natural charms. Travelers called to the wilderness will feel right at home in Big Sur. It's a sin to remain in your car, however, when an such an embarrassment of natural riches await. Waterfalls and redwoods beckon hikers and campers while cliffside resorts pamper guests.

Seaside Cambria makes a good base from which to visit much of the Central Coast, including Paso Robles and San Simeon, home to the grand Hearst Castle, an homage to excess. The coast becomes less rugged here, though no less beautiful.

Beach lovers will flock to temperate Santa Barbara farther south, where the relaxed yet cultured pace reflects its mission and university influences, as well as its affluence. Wine is a growth industry here as well—look for the Central Coast to become the next great California wine region.

## PLANNING YOUR TIME

The Central Coast is a favorite of many California residents for romantic weekend getaways. If you're coming to this part of the state for a weekend, pick an area and explore it in

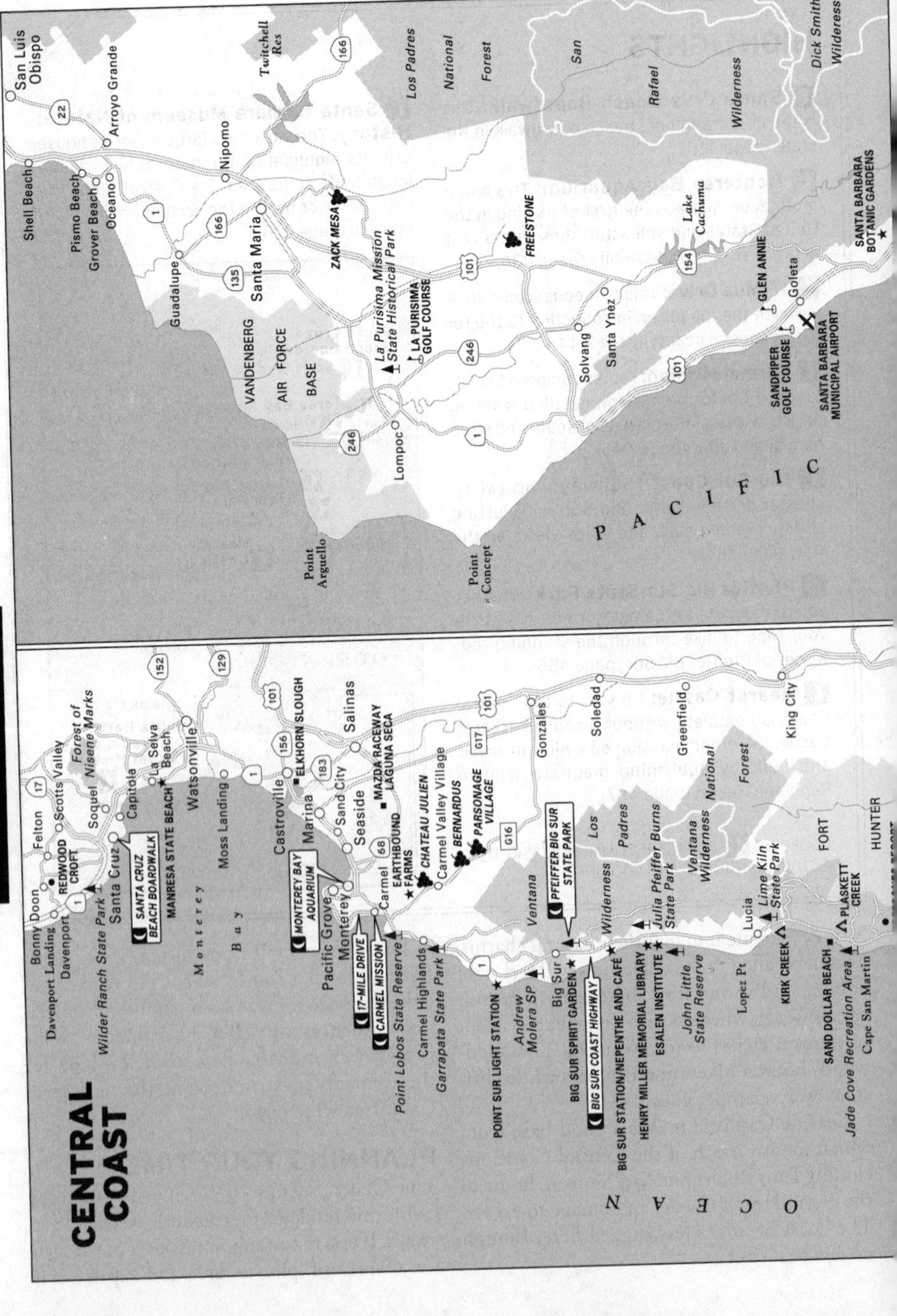

CENTRAL COAST
San Luis Obispo
Shell Beach
Pismo Beach
Grover Beach
Oceano
Arroyo Grande
Nipomo
Twitchell Res
Los Padres National Forest
San Rafael Wilderness
Dick Smith Wilderness
Guadalupe
Santa Maria
ZACK MESA
VANDENBERG AIR FORCE BASE
La Purisima Mission State Historical Park
LA PURISIMA GOLF COURSE
FREESTONE
Lake Cachuma
Solvang
Santa Ynez
GLEN ANNIE
Goleta
SANTA BARBARA BOTANIC GARDENS
SANDPIPER GOLF COURSE
SANTA BARBARA MUNICIPAL AIRPORT
Lompoc
Point Arguello
Point Concept
PACIFIC OCEAN
Bonny Doon
Davenport Landing
Davenport
Felton
Scotts Valley
Forest of Nisene Marks
REDWOOD CROFT
Wilder Ranch State Park
Santa Cruz
SANTA CRUZ BEACH BOARDWALK
Soquel
Capitola
La Selva Beach
MANRESA STATE BEACH
Watsonville
Monterey Bay
Moss Landing
Castroville
ELKHORN SLOUGH
Marina
Sand City
Seaside
Salinas
MAZDA RACEWAY LAGUNA SECA
MONTEREY BAY AQUARIUM
EARTHBOUND FARMS
Pacific Grove
Monterey
Carmel
17-MILE DRIVE
CARMEL MISSION
CHATEAU JULIEN
Carmel Valley Village
BERNARDUS
PARSONAGE VILLAGE
Point Lobos State Reserve
Carmel Highlands
Garrapata State Park
POINT SUR LIGHT STATION
Andrew Molera SP
Big Sur
BIG SUR SPIRIT GARDEN
BIG SUR COAST HIGHWAY
BIG SUR STATION/NEPENTHE AND CAFÉ
PFEIFFER BIG SUR STATE PARK
Ventana Wilderness
HENRY MILLER MEMORIAL LIBRARY
ESALEN INSTITUTE
Julia Pfeiffer Burns State Park
John Little State Reserve
Lopez Pt
Lucia
Lime Kiln State Park
KIRK CREEK
PLASKETT CREEK
SAND DOLLAR BEACH
Jade Cove Recreation Area
Cape San Martin
Los Padres National Forest
Ventana Wilderness
FORT HUNTER
Gonzales
Soledad
Greenfield
King City

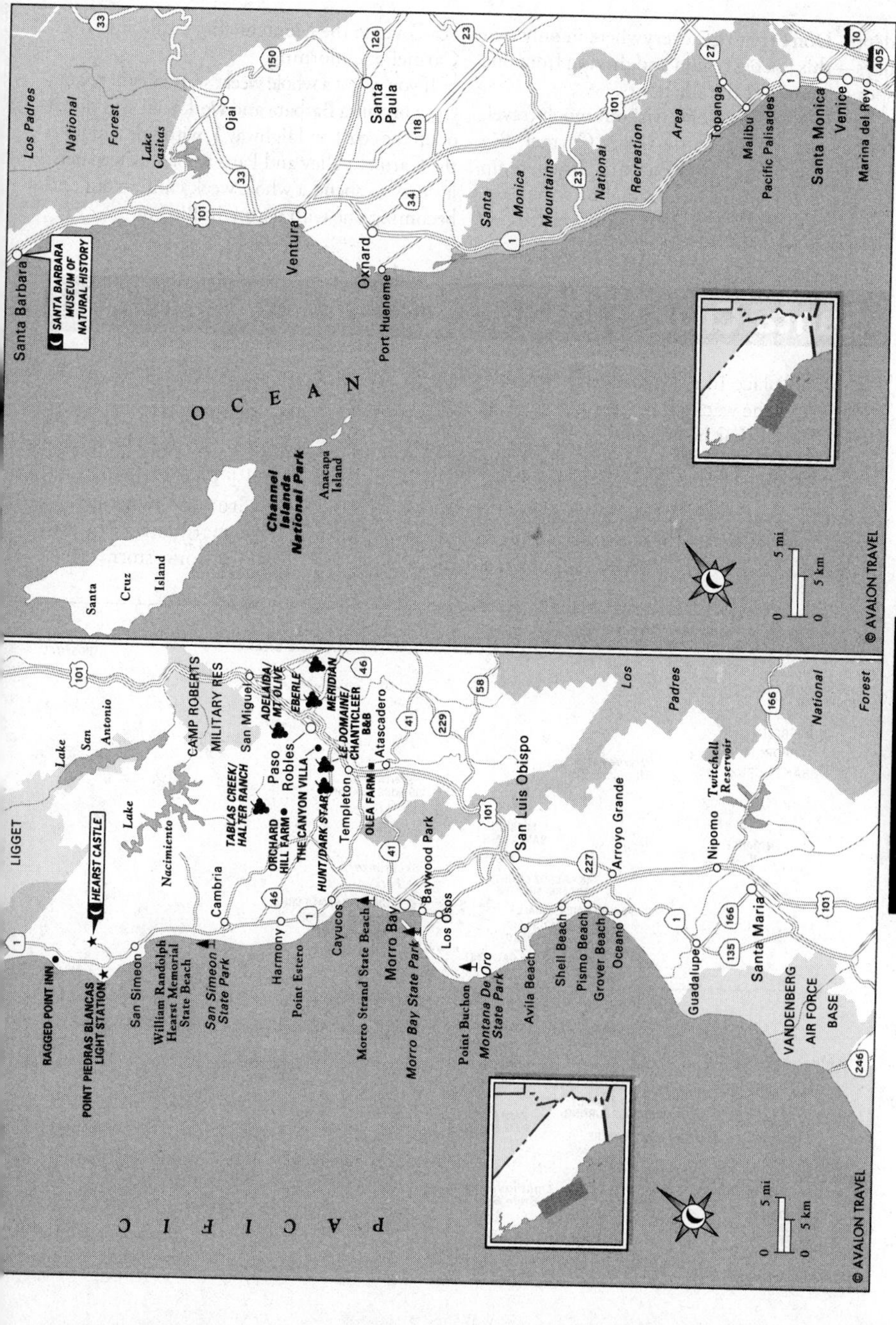
Los Padres
National
Forest
Lake
Casitas
Ojai
Santa
Paula
Santa Barbara
SANTA BARBARA
MUSEUM OF
NATURAL HISTORY
Ventura
Oxnard
Port Hueneme
Santa
Monica
Mountains
National
Recreation
Area
Topanga
Malibu
Pacific Palisades
Santa Monica
Venice
Marina del Rey
O C E A N
Channel
Islands
National Park
Anacapa
Island
Santa
Cruz
Island
0 5 mi
0 5 km
© AVALON TRAVEL
LIGGET
HEARST CASTLE
RAGGED POINT INN
POINT PIEDRAS BLANCAS
LIGHT STATION
San Simeon
William Randolph
Hearst Memorial
State Beach
San Simeon
State Park
Cambria
Nacimiento
Lake
Lake
San
Antonio
CAMP ROBERTS
MILITARY RES
San Miguel
Paso
Robles
TABLAS CREEK/
HALTER RANCH
ORCHARD
HILL FARM
THE CANYON VILLA
HUNT/DARK STAR
ADELAIDA/
MT OLIVE
EBERLE
MERIDIAN
LE DOMAINE/
CHANTICLEER
B&B
OLEA FARM
Templeton
Atascadero
Harmony
Point Estero
Cayucos
Morro Strand State Beach
Morro Bay
Morro Bay State Park
Baywood Park
Los Osos
Point Buchon
Montana De Oro
State Park
San Luis Obispo
Avila Beach
Shell Beach
Pismo Beach
Grover Beach
Oceano
Arroyo Grande
Nipomo
Twitchell
Reservoir
Guadalupe
Santa Maria
VANDENBERG
AIR FORCE
BASE
Los
Padres
National
Forest
P A C I F I C
0 5 mi
0 5 km
© AVALON TRAVEL

depth. Don't try to get everywhere in only two days—this is a big region and driving from one spot to another can take hours.

For a relaxed weekend without much travel, focus your trip on Santa Cruz, Carmel, Big Sur, Cambria, or Santa Barbara. If you're up for more adventure, add a day of wine tasting in Paso Robles to your Cambria trip, or head over to the Monterey Bay Aquarium from Carmel one morning.

If you've got a whole week, start in either Santa Cruz or Santa Barbara and work your way down or up the coast on Highway 1, with side trips into the Carmel Valley and Paso Robles. Alternately, it's easy to spend a whole week chilling out and becoming one with nature in Big Sur.

# Santa Cruz

There's no place like Santa Cruz. Not even elsewhere in the wacky Bay Area can you find another town that has embraced the radical fringe of the nation and made it into a municipal-cultural statement quite like this. In Santa Cruz, you'll find surfers on the waves, nudists on the beaches, tree-huggers in the redwood forests, tattooed and pierced punks on the main drag, and families walking the dog along West Cliff Drive. Oh, and by the way, that purple-haired woman with the tongue stud might well be a dedicated volunteer at her local PTA. With the kind of irony only Santa Cruz (a town that has openly decriminalized marijuana) can produce, a massive illegal fireworks storm erupts



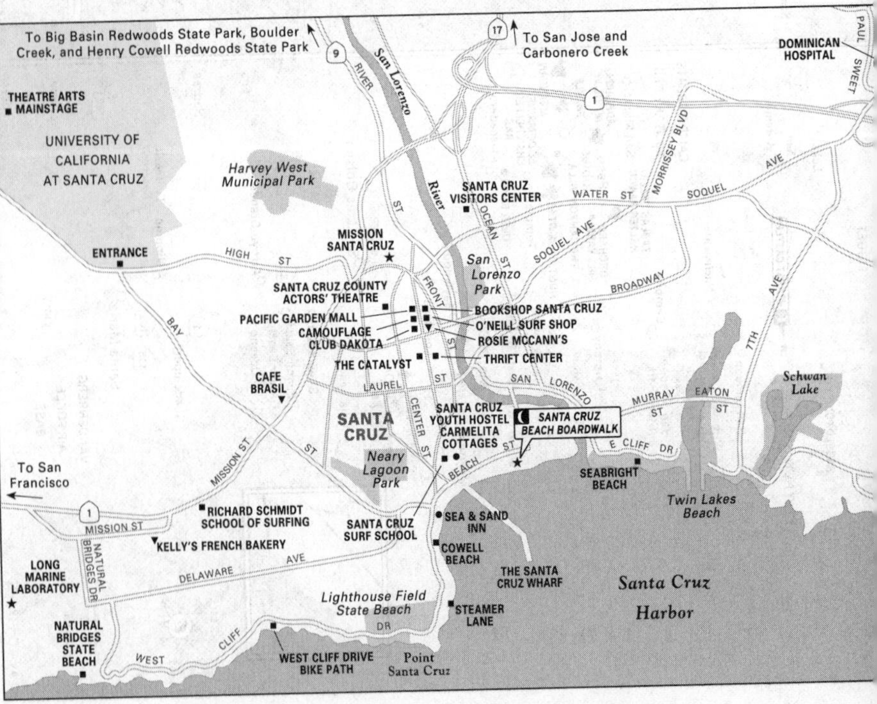

over the beaches in patriotic celebration each Fourth of July.

Most visitors come to Santa Cruz to hit the Boardwalk and the beaches. Locals and UCSC students tend to hang at the Pacific Garden Mall and stroll on West Cliff. The east side of town can get dicey, especially a few blocks from the Boardwalk, while the Westside tends more towards families with children. The food of Santa Cruz qualifies as a hidden treasure, with myriad ethnicities represented.

of the Santa Cruz area includes several tiny towns that aren't inside Santa Cruz proper, but blend into each other with the feeling of beach-town suburbs. Aptos, Capitola, and Soquel all lie to the south of Santa Cruz along the coast. Each has its own small shopping districts, restaurants, and lodgings. They've also got charming beaches all their own, which can be as foggy, as crowded, or as nice to visit as their northern neighbors.

## SIGHTS

### Santa Cruz Beach Boardwalk

The Santa Cruz Beach Boardwalk (400 Beach St., 831/423-5590, www.beachboardwalk.com, daily 11 A.M.–close, parking $10), or just "the Boardwalk" as it's called by the locals, has a rare appeal that beckons to young children, too-cool teenagers, and adults of all ages.

The amusement park rambles along each side of the south end of the Boardwalk; entry is free, but you must buy either per-ride tickets or an unlimited ride wristband. The Great Dipper boasts a history as the oldest wooden roller coaster in the state, still giving riders a thrill after all this time. The spinner and the Zipper tend to be more fun for kids (or at least folks with hardy inner ears). In summertime, a log ride cools down guests hot from hours of tromping around. The Boardwalk also offers several toddler and little-kid rides.

At the other end of the Boardwalk, avid

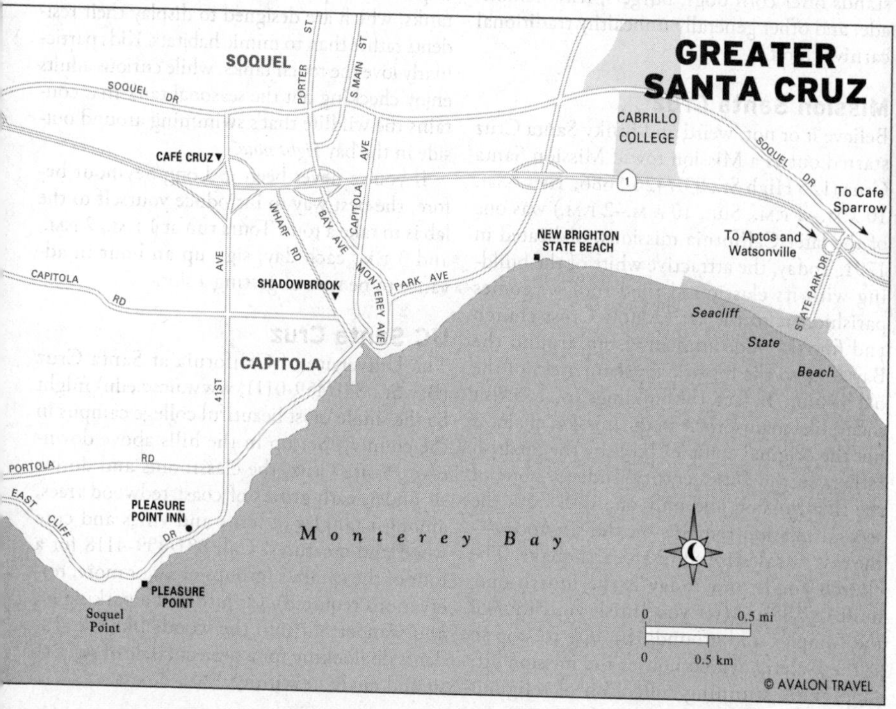

gamesters choose between the lure of prizes from the traditional midway games and the large arcade. Throw baseballs at things, try your arm at skeeball, or take a pass at classic or newer video game. The traditional carousel actually has a brass ring you (or your children) can try to grab.

After you've worn yourself out playing games and riding rides, you can take the stairs down to the broad, sandy beach below the Boardwalk. It's a great place to flop down and sun yourself, or brave a dip in the cool Pacific surf. Granted, it gets a bit crowded in the summertime. But you've got all the services you could ever want right there at the Boardwalk, plus the sand and the water (and the occasional strand of kelp). What could be more perfect?

Looking for something tasty to munch on or a drink to cool you off? You can definitely find it at the Boardwalk. An old-fashioned candy shop sells sweets to the sweet, while the snack stands offer corn dogs, burgers, fries, lemonade, and other generally unhealthy traditional carnival food.



## Mission Santa Cruz

Believe it or not, weird and funky Santa Cruz started out as a Mission town. Mission Santa Cruz (126 High St., 831/426-5686, Tues.–Sat. 10 A.M.–4 P.M., Sun. 10 A.M.–2 P.M.) was one of the later California missions, dedicated in 1791. Today, the attractive white of the building with its classic red-tiled roof welcomes parishioners to the active Holy Cross church and fourth-grade students from around the Bay Area to the historic museum areas of the old mission. In fact, the buildings you can visit today, like many others in the mission chain, is not the original complex built by the Spanish fathers in the 18th century. Indeed, none of the first mission and only one wall from the second mission remains on the site today—the rest was destroyed in an earthquake. The church you'll tour today is the fourth one, built in 1889. After you finish your tour of the complex and grounds, be sure to stop in at the Galeria, which houses the mission gift shop and a stunning collection of religious vestments—something you won't see in many other California missions.

## Long Marine Lab

If you love the sea and all the critters that live in it, be sure to come take a tour of the Long Marine Laboratory (Delaware Ave., 831/459-3800, www2.ucsc.edu/seymourcenter, Tues.–Sat. 10 A.M.–5 P.M., Sun. noon–5 P.M., adults $6, children $4). The large, attractive gray building complex at the end of Delaware Avenue sits right on the edge of the cliff overlooking the ocean—convenient for the research done primarily by students and faculty of UCSC. Your visit will be to the **Seymour Marine Discovery Center**—the part of the lab that's open to the public. You'll be greeted outside the door by a full blue whale skeleton that's lit up at night. Inside, instead of a standard aquarium setup, you'll find a marine laboratory similar to those used by the scientists elsewhere in the complex. Expect to see pipes and machinery around the tanks, which are designed to display their residents rather than to mimic habitats. Kids particularly love the touch tanks, while curious adults enjoy checking out the seasonal tank that contains the wildlife that's swimming around outside in the bay *right now.*

If you've never been to Long/Seymour before, the best way to introduce yourself to the lab is to take a tour. Tours run at 1 P.M., 2 P.M., and 3 P.M. each day; sign up an hour in advance to be sure of getting a slot.

## UC Santa Cruz

The University of California at Santa Cruz (Bay St., 831/459-0111, www.ucsc.edu) might be the single most beautiful college campus in the country. Set up in the hills above downtown Santa Cruz, the classrooms and dorms sit underneath groves of coast redwood trees, amongst tangles of ferns and vines and cute woodland creatures. Call 831/459-4118 for a tour of the campus (groups of six or more, reservations required). Or just find a parking lot and wander out into the woods like the students do, looking for a perfect circle of trees to sit and meditate within.

# ENTERTAINMENT AND EVENTS

## Bars and Clubs

Down on the Mall, you can stroll upstairs to **Rosie McCann's** (1220 Pacific Ave., 831/426-9930, www.rosiemccanns.com) for a pint and a bite. This dark-paneled, Irish-style saloon serves Guinness, Black and Tans, Snake Bites, and several tasty draft beers. You can also get a hefty meal at Rosie's, whose menu runs to sausage, mashed potatoes, and other weighty pub foods. A largely local crowd hangs out here, and you'll find the bar crowded and noisy, but the vibe friendly and entertaining.

For club-goers of the gayer persuasion, there's **Club Dakota** (1209 Pacific Ave., 831/454-9030). This local favorite tends toward the less crowded and more friendly end of the spectrum; the dance club might not be packed, but the bartenders are more likely to be happy when they get you your drinks. The only times the Dakota really gets crowded are on Saturday nights after 11 P.M., and on Pride and Party nights. If you come in before 10 P.M., you won't be charged a cover and you're likely to find plenty of space out on the dance floor. This being Santa Cruz, you might find more straight women than gay men dancing in the Dakota—it's known as a safe haven where few slimy guys hit on women. If you're a guy...well, the bouncers do a good job of keeping things fun rather than creepy here. Thursday nights equal cheap drinks, so come early to imbibe your fill.

## Live Music

**The Catalyst** (1011 Pacific Ave., advance tickets 866/384-3060, door tickets 831/423-1338, www.catalystclub.com, $12–35), right downtown on the Mall, is *the* Santa Cruz nightclub. This live rock venue hosts all sorts of big-name national acts, most of whom now play clubs rather than stadiums. The Catalyst is completely democratic in its booking—you might see Ted Nugent one week, the Indigo Girls the next, and a ska band the week after that. In between, the Catalyst hosts DJ dance nights, teen nights, and other fun events. Be sure to check the calendar when you buy tickets—some shows are 21 and over only. (Mmm... music, dancing, and a full bar!) The main concert hall is a standing-room-only space, while the balconies offer seating. The bar sits downstairs adjacent to the concert space. The vibe at the Catalyst tends to be low-key, but it depends on the night and the event. Some of the more retro acts definitely draw an older crowd, while the techno-DJ dance parties cater to the UCSC set. You can buy tickets online or by phone; purchasing in advance is recommended, especially for national acts.

The **Crow's Nest** (2218 East Cliff Dr., 831/476-4560, www.crowsnest-santacruz.com) functions as a venue for all kinds of live musical acts. You might see a contemporary reggae-rock group one night and a Latin dance band the next. Lots of funk bands play the Nest—it's just appropriate to the Santa Cruz ethos. A few tribute bands, usually to hippie 1960s and '70s legends like Jimi Hendrix and Santana, perform on occasion as well. Most shows are free, but if there's a really popular act you might be charged $5 at the door. Check the website for a performance calendar, but it's a good bet that you'll get live musical entertainment here every night from Wednesday through Saturday.

## Comedy

For a good laugh in Santa Cruz, the **Crow's Nest** (2218 East Cliff Dr., 831/476-4560, www.crowsnest-santacruz.com, comedy Sun. 9 P.M., $7) also hosts a weekly stand-up comedy show. Because the show runs on Sunday nights, the Crow's Nest takes advantage of the opportunity to hire big-name comics who have been in San Francisco or San Jose for weekend engagements. This lets folks see headliners in a more casual setting for a fraction of the cost of the big-city clubs. The Crow's Nest, with its great views out over the Pacific, also has a full bar and restaurant. You can enjoy drinks and dinner while you get your giggle on.

## Theater

Santa Cruz is home to several community theaters and an outdoor summer Shakespeare festival that draws theatergoers from around the Bay Area.

The **Santa Cruz County Actors' Theatre** (1001 Center St., 831/425-7529, www.actorssc.org) acts as Santa Cruz's permanent local theater company. The Actors' Theatre does it all: performs a subscription season, holds theater arts workshops, sponsors playwriting contests for kids and adults, and stages improv shows. All shows at this low-cost theater are contemporary works, including the full production series plays. But the most exciting (though not necessarily the highest quality) shows you can see here are the new works festivals featuring completely new plays, mostly by local authors, which have won Actors' Theatre contests. If one of these, especially the "Eight Tens at Eight," appears during your stay, consider getting tickets so you can see something completely different.

If you prefer historic theater to modern, UCSC puts on an annual summer Shakespeare festival: **Shakespeare Santa Cruz** (831/459-2121, http://shakespearesantacruz.org, adults $32–44, seniors/students $29, children $18). This six-week festival usually runs in the second half of July and through August. Venues both sit on the UCSC campus, one indoor at the Theatre Arts Mainstage (1156 High St.) and the other out in the redwood forests in the Festival Glen (Meyer Dr.). Each year the festival puts up at least two Shakespeare plays—2008 selections included *Romeo and Juliet* and *All's Well That Ends Well*—plus at least one other production (often a more contemporary play). At the outdoor glen, audience members are encouraged to bring their own picnics. This can make for the perfect romantic date, or a fun outing for the whole family.



## SHOPPING

There's no shopping area in California quite like the **Pacific Garden Mall** (Pacific Ave., 831/429-8433). Hanging out "on the Mall," as the locals call it, is a pastime for many teens and adults from Santa Cruz and beyond. The Mall runs on Pacific Avenue and its offshoots, and is usually open to (very slow) auto traffic. Park in one of the structures a block or two off the Mall proper and walk from there. At the north end, shoppers peruse antiques, boutique clothing, and kitchenware. Down at the seedier south end of the mall, visitors can get shining new body jewelry, a great new tattoo, or a silicone sex toy. In the middle (and to a lesser degree throughout the Mall), you can grab a bite to eat, a cappuccino, or a cocktail in one of the many independent eateries. You'll find only a select few chain stores on the Mall, and those are uniformly reviled by the fiercely anti-mega-corporation residents of Santa Cruz. The Borders across the street from the **Book Shop Santa Cruz** (1520 Pacific Ave., 831/423-0900, www.bookshopsantacruz.com, Sun.–Thurs. 9 A.M.–10 P.M., Fri.–Sat. until 11 P.M.) takes shockingly little business away from its local independent rival.

Sure, you will find an **O'Neill Surf Shop** (110 Cooper St., 831/469-4377) on the Mall, but surf shops are a staple of Santa Cruz. This one specializes in surfboards, wetsuits, and brand-name clothing. If your trip to California has gotten you hooked on riding the waves, and you just have to invest in your own equipment, O'Neill can be a good place to start. (If you're an expert who prefers custom work, you already know that pre-fab chain stuff isn't for you.) You can also buy a T-shirt or some sweats here—handy if you didn't pack quite right for Central Coast summer fog.

If you're wanting to buy clothes in Santa Cruz, chances are you're looking for a secondhand store. This town has plenty of 'em. One of the largest of these sits only a block off Pacific Avenue—the aptly if redundantly named **Thrift Center Thrift Store** (504 Front St., 831/429-6975). This big, somewhat dirty retail space offers a wide array of cheap secondhand clothes. You'll need to hunt a bit to find that one perfect vintage item that's just too perfect, but isn't that the fun of thrift shopping?

Down toward the great divide between the "good side" and the "less good side" of the Mall you can price some more adult merchandise. **Camouflage** (1329 Pacific Ave., 888/309-2266, http://experiencethefantasy.com, Mon.–Thurs. 10 A.M.–8 P.M., Fri.–Sat. 10 A.M.–10 P.M., Sun.

11 A.M.–7 P.M.) is an independent, women-operated and women-friendly adult store. The first room contains mostly lingerie and less-shocking items. Dare to walk through the narrow black-curtained passage, and you'll find the *other* room, which is filled with grown-up toys designed to please women of every taste and proclivity. (A few cool gizmos and gadgets can make things fun for the men as well.) As many ladies as men shop here, and can feel comfortable doing so.

## SPORTS AND RECREATION

### Beaches

At the tip of the West Side, **Natural Bridges State Park** (West Cliff Dr., 831/423-4609, www.parks.ca.gov, daily 8 A.M.–sunset) offers nearly every kind of beach recreation possible. The sand strip doesn't stretch wide, but falls back deep, crossed by a creek that feeds out into the sea. An inconsistent break makes surfing at Natural Bridges fun on occasion, while the near-constant winds that sweep the sands bring out windsurfers nearly every weekend. Hardy sun-worshippers brave the breezes, bringing out their beach blankets, umbrellas, and sunscreen on rare sunny days (usually in late spring and fall). Back from the beach, a wooded picnic area has tables and grills for small and larger parties. Even farther back, the visitors center can provide great stories about the various national wonders of this surprisingly diverse state park. Rangers offer guided tours of the tidepools that range out to the west side of the beach. You can access these by a somewhat scrambling short hike (0.25–0.5 mile) on the rocks cliffs. These odd little holes filled with sea life aren't like most tidepools—many are nearly perfect round depressions in the sandstone cliffs worn away by harder stones as the tides move tirelessly back and forth. Just don't touch the residents of these pools, since human hands can hurt delicate tidepool creatures.

At **Cowell Beach** (350 West Cliff Dr.), it's all about the surfing. This West Side beach sits right at a crook in the coastline, which joins with underwater features to create a reliable small break that lures new surfers by the dozens. (See *Surfing* section for more information about surfing Cowell.)

At the south end of Santa Cruz, down by the harbor, beachgoers flock to **Seabright Beach** (East Cliff Dr. at Seabright Ave., 831/685-6500, www.santacruzstateparks.org, daily 6 A.M.–10 P.M., free) all summer long. This miles-long stretch of sand, protected by the cliffs from the worst of the winds, is a favorite retreat for sunbathers and loungers. While there's little in the way of snack bars, permanent volleyball courts, or facilities, you can still have a great time at Seabright. There's lots of soft sand to lie in, plenty of room to play football or set up your own volleyball net, and, of course, easy access to the chilly Pacific Ocean. There's no surfing here—Seabright has a shore break that delights skim-boarders, but makes wave riding impossible.

Each Fourth of July, the Santa Cruz police force cordons off the area surrounding Seabright Beach. No one can park nearby or even walk in after a certain point in the afternoon (which seems to change annually). But if you show up early to cart in yourself and all your stuff down onto the sand, you can participate in the unbelievable fireworks extravaganza that starts almost as soon as the sun goes down. Though it's technically illegal, people still create professional-grade pyrotechnical productions and launch them from Seabright. The effect quickly becomes overwhelming, but for those who can handle, the night is truly magical.

Down in Capitola, one of the favorite sandy spots is **New Brighton State Beach** (1500 Park Ave., Capitola, 831/464-6330, www.parks.ca.gov). This forest-backed beach has everything: a strip of sand that's perfect for lounging and cold-water swimming, a forest-shaded campground for both tent and RV campers, hiking trails, and ranger-led nature programs. If you plan to camp, call in advance to make reservations at this popular state park, or just come for the day and set up your spot out on the sand. New Brighton can get crowded on rare sunny summer days, but it's nothing like the wall-to-wall people of the popular Southern California beaches.

## Surfing

The coastline of Santa Cruz has more than its share of great surf breaks. The water is cold, demanding full wetsuits year-round, and the shoreline is rough and rocky—nothing at all like the flat sandy beaches of SoCal. But that doesn't deter the hordes of locals who ply the waves every day they can. The surfing culture pervades the town—if you walk the cliff, you'll likely pass the *To Honor Surfing* sculpture. Santa Cruz loves this statue, and it's often dressed up and always gets a costume for Halloween.

If you're a beginner, the best place to start surfing Santa Cruz is **Cowell's** (stairs at West Cliff and Cowell Beach). The waves are low and long, making for fun longboard rides perfect for surfers just getting their balance. Because the Cowell's break is acknowledged as the newbie spot, the often sizeable crowd tends to be polite to newcomers and tourists.

For more advanced surfers looking for smaller crowds in the water, **Manresa State Beach** (San Andreas Rd., Aptos, www.parks.ca.gov) offers fun rides under the right conditions. Manresa is several minutes' drive south toward Aptos. You'll usually find a good beach break, and the waves can get big when there's a north swell.

Visitors who know their surfing lore will want to surf the more famous spots along the Santa Cruz shore. **Pleasure Point** (btwn. 32nd Ave. and 41st Ave., Soquel) encompasses a number of different breaks. You may have heard of The Hook (steps at 41st Ave.), a well-known experienced longboarder's paradise. But don't mistake The Hook for a beginner's break; the locals feel protective of the waves here and aren't always friendly towards inexperienced tourists. The break at 36th and East Cliff (steps at 36th Ave.) can be a better place to go on weekdays—on the weekends, the intense crowding makes catching your own wave a challenge. Up at 30th and East Cliff (steps at 36th Ave), you'll find challenging sets and hot-dogging shortboarders.

The most famous break in all of Santa Cruz can also be the most hostile to newcomers. **Steamer Lane** (West Cliff btwn. Cowell's and the Lighthouse) has both a fiercely protective crew of locals and a dangerous break that actually kills someone about every other year. But if you're into adrenaline and there's a swell coming in, you'll be hard pressed to find a more exciting ride on the Central Coast, or indeed in most of California.

Yes, you can learn to surf in Santa Cruz despite the distinct local flavor at some of the breaks. Check out either the **Santa Cruz Surf School** (322 Pacific Ave., 831/426-7072, www.santacruzsurfschool.com) or the **Richard Schmidt School of Surfing** (849 Almar Ave., 831/423-0928, www.richardschmidt.com) to sign up for lessons. Who knows, maybe one day the locals will mistake you for one of their own!

## Windsurfing and Parasurfing

If you prefer to let the wind help you catch the waves, you probably already know that Santa Cruz has some prize windsurfing and parasurfing locales. Beginning windsurfers vie with longboarders for space at **Cowell's,** which sits right next to the City Wharf (stairs at West Cliff and Cowell Beach). For a bigger breeze, head up West Cliff to **Natural Bridges State Park** (West Cliff Dr., www.parks.ca.gov, $6 parking). Natural Bridges offers the best spot to set up, plus restroom facilities and ample parking. Serious sailors head farther north to **Davenport Landing** (Hwy. 1, 20 miles north of Santa Cruz). You'll be able to discern that you've found the right rugged and windswept stretch of coast by the endless crowd of sailors and parasurfers out on the waves. Parking can be a bit haphazard here, but even if you're just stopping by to watch, it can be worth your time since the sight of these athletes using both wind and waves to create ultra-fast rides is nothing short of amazing.

If you want to try your luck at windsurfing for the first time, contact **Club Ed** (831/464-0177, www.club-ed.com) to set up a lesson. They operate in the gentle breezes and small swells at Cowell's, and make it easy for first-timers to gain confidence and have a great time.

### Hiking and Biking

To walk or bike where the locals do, just head out to **West Cliff Drive.** This winding street with a full-fledged sidewalk-trail running its length on the ocean side is the town's favorite walking, dog-walking, jogging, skating, scootering, and biking route. You can start at Natural Bridges (the west end of West Cliff) and go for miles. The *To Honor Surfing* statue lies several miles down the road, as do plenty of fabulous views. Bring your camera if you're strolling West Cliff on a clear day—you won't be able to resist taking photos of the sea, cliffs, and sunset. Just be sure to watch for your fellow path-users. What with the bicyclists and skaters and such, it can get a bit treacherous if you don't watch where you're going.

## ACCOMMODATIONS

### Under $100

Staying at a hostel in Santa Cruz just feels right. And the **Santa Cruz Youth Hostel Carmelita Cottages** (321 Main St., 831/423-8304, www.hi-santacruz.org, $25 dorm, $55 private room, $150 cottage) offers a great local atmosphere. Like most historic Santa Cruz edifices, it doesn't look like much from the outside. And certainly the interior doesn't have the newest furniture and paint. But it's clean, cheap, friendly, and close to the beach. You'll find a spot to store your surfboard or bike for free, and car parking is $1 per day. The big homelike kitchen is open for guest use, and might even be hiding some extra free food in its cupboards. Expect all the usual hostel-style amenities, a nice garden out back, free linens, laundry facilities, and a free Internet kiosk.

### $100-150

The four-room **Adobe on Green Street** (103 Green St., 831/469-9866, www.adobeongreen.com, $132–242) offers lovely bed-and-breakfast accommodations close to the heart of downtown Santa Cruz. The location, within walking distance of the Pacific Garden Mall, lets you soak in the unique local atmosphere to your heart's content. A unifying decorative scheme runs through all four guest rooms—a dark and minimalist Spanish Mission style befitting Santa Cruz's history as a mission town. Each room has a queen bed, a private bathroom (most with tubs), a small TV with DVD player, and lots of other amenities that can make you comfortable even over a long stay. An expanded continental spread is set out in the dining room each morning 8–11 A.M. Expect yummy local pastries, organic and soy yogurts, and multicolored eggs laid by a neighbor's flock of chickens. In keeping with the Santa Cruz ethos, the Adobe runs on solar power.

### $150-250

For a room overlooking the ocean, stay at the **Sea & Sand Inn** (201 West Cliff Dr., 831/427-3400, www.santacruzmotels.com/sea_and_sand.html, $189–229). In an unbeatable location on the ocean side of West Cliff at Bay Street, you'll be close enough to downtown and the Boardwalk to enjoy the action of Santa Cruz. But you'll also have a touch more quiet in a neighborhood that's starting to tend toward the residential. Every room in the house comes with an ocean view (hence the high price for what's really a pretty basic motel room), and suites with hot tubs and private patios make for a wonderful seaside vacation. Rooms and suites do have nicer than average decor with pretty furniture, private baths, and free Internet access.

Some travelers prefer to stay in the woods rather than downtown or out by the busy Boardwalk. **Redwood Croft Bed & Breakfast** (275 Northwest Dr., Bonny Doon, 831/458-1939, www.redwoodcroft.com, $145–230) is a funky two-room B&B, set back in the recently charred ruins of the forest to the northwest of Santa Cruz, formerly a beautiful redwood forest. The inn itself takes the woodsy theme indoors, using natural wood in the walls and furniture to create a serene retreat-house feeling. Each of the two guest rooms bursts with beautiful appointments, lovely stone bathrooms, and views out into the recovering woods.

### Over $250

Despite its bohemian reputation, there's plenty of

money flowing through Santa Cruz. For plush accommodations, consider staying at the **Pleasure Point Inn** (23665 E. Cliff Dr., 831/475-4657, www.pleasurepointinn.com, $275–325). This small, exclusive inn boasts a rooftop deck with a hot tub, an expansive common living room with views out over the ocean, and four luxurious guest rooms. Each room has wood floors, a gas fireplace, a private deck or patio, a private bathroom, and all sorts of posh amenities. Expect to find a TV, phone, and Internet access in your room. A continental breakfast is laid out each morning, giving you just the right start to the day. All rooms also boast views out over the ocean—the inn does indeed sit on *that* Pleasure Point, so you can sit and watch the surfers as you drink your morning coffee. Or if you prefer to be a part of the action, ask about setting up surfing lessons through the inn and Club Ed when you reserve your room.

## FOOD

### American

At **Cafe Cruz** (2621 41st Ave., Soquel, 831/476-3801, www.cafecruz.com, Mon.–Sat. 11:30 A.M.–2:30 P.M., daily 5:30 P.M.–close, $16–30), the menu runs toward homey American favorites done up with a California twist (ribs, rotisserie chicken, bowls of pasta, and crunchy fresh salads). Cafe Cruz purchases the freshest local produce, meats, seafood, and even drinks they can find. You can munch locally caught fish with goat cheese from Half Moon Bay and an organic soda from Monterey. The attractive white-tablecloth dining room welcomes casual and elegant diners alike, and if you choose wisely you can get an upscale meal for medium-scale prices.

### Asian

When locals who love their sushi get that craving for raw fish, they head for **Shogun Sushi** (1123 Pacific Ave., 831/469-4477, Mon.–Wed. 5–9 P.M., Thurs.–Fri. 5–10 P.M., Sat. 3–10 P.M.). Right on the Pacific Garden Mall, Shogun serves big fresh slabs of nigiri and an interesting collection of maki (rolls). The fish served here is some of the freshest you'll find in this seacoast city. Their meats and other dishes also please diners with fresh ingredients and tasty preparations. While service can be spotty, usually it's efficient—you'll get your order quickly and it will be right on. If you're not used to sushi prices, you may find Shogun expensive, but if you're a connoisseur you'll feel that they're quite reasonable. Do be aware that there's often a wait for a table in the evenings, especially on weekends.

### California

The Santa Cruz region boasts one serious upscale eatery. The **Shadowbrook** (1750 Wharf Rd., Capitola, 800/975-1511, www.shadowbrook-capitola.com, Mon.–Fri. 5–8:45 P.M., Sat. 4:30–9:30 P.M., Sun. 4:30–8:45 P.M., $25) has long been worth driving over the hill for. The cliffside location, complete with the namesake brook flowing through the dining room, has perhaps the most impressive views and atmosphere of any restaurant in the area. The Shadowbrook makes for a perfect spot to stage the ultimate romantic date, complete with roses, candlelight, and fine chocolate desserts.

### French

In Aptos, **Cafe Sparrow** (8042 Soquel Dr., Aptos, 831/688-6238, www.cafesparrow.com, Mon.–Sat. 11:30 A.M.–2 P.M., Sun. 9:30 A.M.–2 P.M., daily 5:30 P.M.–close, $20) serves country French cuisine that's consistently tasty. Whatever you order, it will be fantastic. The seafood is noteworthy (especially the Friday night bouillabaisse), as are the steaks. Cafe Sparrow's kitchen prepares all the dishes with fresh ingredients, and the chef (who can sometimes be seen out in the dining room checking on customer satisfaction with the food) thinks up innovative preparations and creates tasty sauces. He's also willing to accommodate special requests and dietary restrictions with good cheer. The best deal for your money is the daily-changing prix-fixe menu. For dessert, treat yourself to the profiteroles, which can be created with either ice cream or pastry cream.

## South American

**Cafe Brasil** (1410 Mission St., 831/429-1855, www.cafebrasil.us, daily 8:00 A.M.–3:00 P.M., $10–20) serves up the Brazilian fare its name promises. Painted jungle green with bright yellow and blue trim, you can't miss this totally Santa Cruz breakfast and lunch joint. In the morning, the fare runs to omelets and ethnic specialties, while lunch includes pressed sandwiches, meat and tofu dishes, and Brazilian house specials. A juice bar provides rich but healthy meal accompaniments that can also act as light meals on their own. To try something different, get an acia bowl—acia is a South American fruit—or an Amazon cherry juice and OJ blend.

## Coffee and Bakeries

For a casual sandwich or pastry, head for **Kelly's French Bakery** (402 Ingalls St., 831/423-9059, www.kellysfrenchbakery.com, Mon.–Thurs. 7–11 A.M. and 11:30 A.M.–7 P.M., Fri. 7–11 A.M. and 11:30 A.M.–8 P.M., Sat.–Sun. 7 A.M.–11:30 A.M. and noon–7 P.M., $10). This popular bakery makes its home in an old industrial warehouse-style space, and its domed shape constructed out of corrugated metal looks like anything but a restaurant. It's got both indoor and outdoor seating, and serves full breakfasts and luncheon sandwiches. You can order to stay in or to go, and pick up a breakfast or sweet pastry, some bread, or a cake while you're there.

# INFORMATION AND SERVICES

## Tourist Information

While it can be fun to explore Santa Cruz just by using your innate sense of direction and the bizarre, those who want a bit more structure on their travels can hit the **Santa Cruz Visitors Center** (1211 Ocean Ave., 800/833-3494, www.santacruzca.org) for maps, advice, and information.

## Media and Communications

Santa Cruz publishes its own daily newspaper, the ***Santa Cruz Sentinel*** (www.santacruzsentinel.com). You'll get your daily dose of national wire service news and current events, local news, plus some good stuff for visitors. The *Sentinel* has a Food section, a Sunday Travel section, and plenty of up-to-date entertainment information.

You can get your mail on at the **post office** near the Mall on 850 Front Street (831/426-0144).

Santa Cruz is like totally wired, man. You'll definitely be able to access the Internet in a variety of cafés and hotels. There are Starbucks locations here, and the many indie cafés often compete with their own (sometimes free) Wi-Fi.

Santa Cruz has plenty of banks and ATMs (including some ATMs on the arcade at the Boardwalk). Bank branches congregate downtown near the Pacific Garden Mall. The West Side is mostly residential, so you'll find a few ATMs in supermarkets and gas stations, but little else.

## Medical Services

Despite its rep as a funky bohemian beach town, Santa Cruz's dense population dictates that it have at least one full-fledged hospital of its own. You can get medical treatment and care at **Dominican Hospital** (1555 Soquel Ave., 831/426-7700, www.dominicanhospital.org).



# GETTING THERE AND AROUND

## Car

If you're driving to Santa Cruz from Silicon Valley, you've got two choices of roads. Most drivers take fast, dangerous Highway 17. This narrow road doesn't have any switchbacks and is the main truck route "over the hill." Most locals take this 50-mile-per hour corridor fast—probably faster than they should. Each year, several people die in accidents on Highway 17, and I once crashed my vehicle into an overturned pickup truck on Big Moody curve. So if you're new to the road, keep to the right and take it slow, no matter what the traffic to the left of you is doing. Check traffic reports before you head out; Highway 17 is known to be one of the worst commuting roads in all of the

Bay Area, and the weekend beach traffic in the summer jams up fastin both directions too.

For a more leisurely drive, you can opt for two-lane Highway 9. The tight curves and endless switchbacks will keep you at a reasonable speed; use the turnouts to let the locals past, please. On Highway 9, your biggest obstacles tend to be groups of bicyclists and motorcyclists, both of whom adore the slopes and curves of this technical driving road. The good news is that you'll get an up-close-and-personal view of the gorgeously forested Santa Cruz Mountains, complete with views of the valley to the north and ocean vistas to the south.

### Parking

Visitors planning to drive or bike around Santa Cruz should get themselves a good map, either before they arrive or at the visitors center in town. Navigating the winding, occasionally broken-up streets of this oddly shaped town isn't for the faint of heart. Highway 1, which becomes Mission Street on the West Side, acts as the main artery through Santa Cruz and down to Capitola, Soquel, Aptos, and coastal points farther south. You'll find that Highway 1 at the interchange to Highway 17, and sometimes several miles to the south, is a parking lot most of the time. No, you probably haven't come upon a major accident or a special event. It's just like that all the time, and will be until the construction widening the highway to deal with the heavy traffic is complete.

Parking in Santa Cruz can be its own special sort of horror. Downtown, head straight for the parking structures one block away from Pacific Avenue on either side. They're much easier to deal with than trying to find street parking. The same goes for the beach and Boardwalk areas. At the Boardwalk, just pay the fee to park in the big parking lot adjacent to the attractions. You'll save an hour and a possible car break-in or theft trying to find street parking in the sketchy neighborhoods that surround the Boardwalk.

### Bus

In town, the buses are run by the **Santa Cruz METRO** (831/425-8600 www.scmtd.com, adults $1.50/single ride, passes available). With 42 routes running in Santa Cruz County, you can probably find a way to get nearly anywhere you'd want to go on the METRO.



# Monterey

Monterey is the "big city" on the well-populated southern tip of the wide-mouthed Monterey Bay. The outlying agricultural towns of Sand City and Marina lie to the northeast (closer to the Bay Area), while sleepy residential Pacific Grove lies to the northeast closer to the big golf courses of Pebble Beach.

Neighboring Carmel-by-the-Sea caters to the wealthy, the artsy, and golf afficianados, while Monterey has a long history as a working class town. Originally inhabited by Native Americans, who fished the bay, Monterey became a fishing hub for the European settlers in the 19th century as well. (Author John Steinbeck immortalized the unglamorous fish-canning industry here in his novel *Cannery Row.*) It wasn't until the 20th century that the city began to lean toward gentrification—the bay just off the shore became a wildlife preserve, the Monterey Bay Aquarium opened, and the tourist trade became a mainstay of the local economy. Today, Cannery Row resembles a giant shopping mall and the Aquarium is constantly packed with visitors.

## SIGHTS

### Cannery Row

Welcome to Monterey's own version of Tourist Hell. Cannery Row (Cannery Row, www.canneryrow.com), sitting right on the water, did once look and feel as John Steinbeck described it in his famed novel of the same name. In days

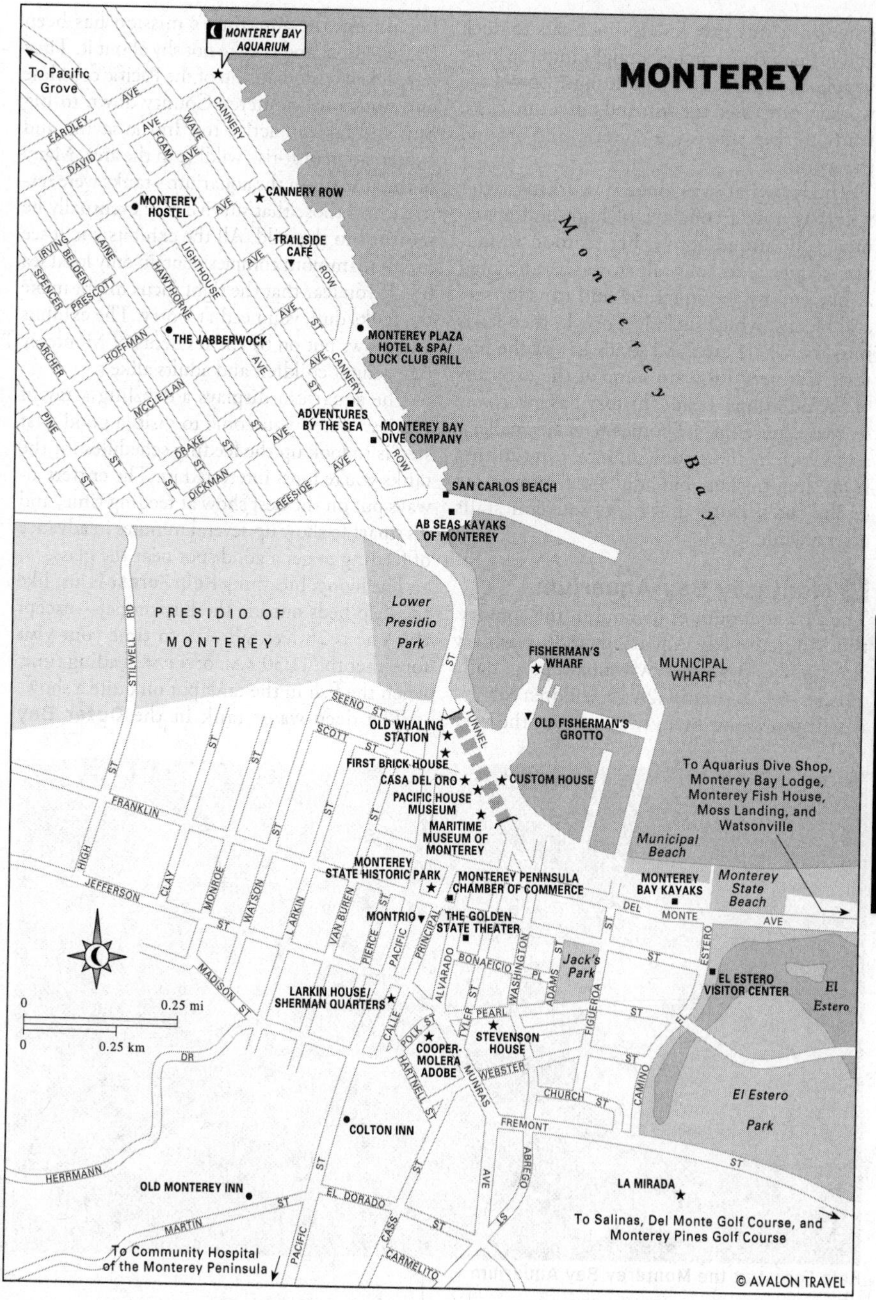
MONTEREY
MONTEREY BAY AQUARIUM
To Pacific Grove
Monterey Bay
CANNERY ROW
MONTEREY HOSTEL
TRAILSIDE CAFÉ
THE JABBERWOCK
MONTEREY PLAZA HOTEL & SPA/ DUCK CLUB GRILL
ADVENTURES BY THE SEA
MONTEREY BAY DIVE COMPANY
SAN CARLOS BEACH
AB SEAS KAYAKS OF MONTEREY
PRESIDIO OF MONTEREY
Lower Presidio Park
FISHERMAN'S WHARF
MUNICIPAL WHARF
OLD FISHERMAN'S GROTTO
OLD WHALING STATION
FIRST BRICK HOUSE
CASA DEL ORO
CUSTOM HOUSE
PACIFIC HOUSE MUSEUM
MARITIME MUSEUM OF MONTEREY
To Aquarius Dive Shop, Monterey Bay Lodge, Monterey Fish House, Moss Landing, and Watsonville
Municipal Beach
MONTEREY STATE HISTORIC PARK
MONTEREY PENINSULA CHAMBER OF COMMERCE
MONTEREY BAY KAYAKS
Monterey State Beach
MONTRIO
THE GOLDEN STATE THEATER
Jack's Park
EL ESTERO VISITOR CENTER
El Estero
LARKIN HOUSE/ SHERMAN QUARTERS
STEVENSON HOUSE
COOPER-MOLERA ADOBE
El Estero Park
COLTON INN
LA MIRADA
OLD MONTEREY INN
To Salinas, Del Monte Golf Course, and Monterey Pines Golf Course
To Community Hospital of the Monterey Peninsula
0 0.25 mi
0 0.25 km
EARDLEY AVE
DAVID AVE
FOAM AVE
WAVE AVE
CANNERY ROW
LIGHTHOUSE AVE
IRVING
BELDEN
LAINE
SPENCER
PRESCOTT AVE
HAWTHORNE ST
HOFFMAN AVE
ARCHER
MCCLELLAN AVE
PINE ST
DRAKE AVE
DICKMAN
REESIDE AVE
STILWELL RD
SEENO ST
SCOTT ST
TUNNEL
FRANKLIN ST
JEFFERSON
HIGH ST
CLAY ST
MONROE ST
WATSON ST
LARKIN ST
VAN BUREN ST
PIERCE ST
PACIFIC ST
PRINCIPAL
ALVARADO ST
WASHINGTON ST
BONAFICIO PL
ADAMS ST
FIGUEROA ST
DEL MONTE AVE
ESTERO
PEARL ST
TYLER ST
POLK ST
CALLE
HARTNELL ST
MUNRAS AVE
WEBSTER
CHURCH ST
CAMINO EL ESTERO
FREMONT ST
ABREGO ST
MADISON ST
HERRMANN DR
EL DORADO
MARTIN ST
CASS ST
CARMELITO
© AVALON TRAVEL

gone by, it was easy for fishing boats to dock and offload their catches straight into the huge warehouse-like cannery buildings. Low-wage workers processed the fish and put it into cans, ready to ship across the country and around the world.

Today, what was once a workingman's wharf is now a conclave of high-end apartments, boutique hotels, big seafood restaurants, and cheesy souvenir stores. It's anchored at one end by the aquarium and runs for several blocks, which include a beach, then leads into the wharf area. All that's left of the historic Cannery Row are some of the exteriors of the buildings. Inside, history has given way to a wax museum, a Thomas Kincaide gallery, and kitsch by the yard. Kids have fun running from shop to shop, but adults may grow tired of the chain stores and tacky souvenir stalls after a while.

### Monterey Bay Aquarium

The first aquarium of its kind in the country, the Monterey Bay Aquarium (886 Cannery Row, 831/648-4800, www.mbayaq.org, daily 10 A.M.–6 P.M., adults $24.95, children $15.95) is still unique in many ways. From the very beginning, the aquarium's mission has been conservation, and they're not shy about it. They have taken custodianship of the Pacific coastline and waters in Monterey County down to Big Sur, and take an active role in the saving and conservation of at-risk wildlife in the area. Many of the animals in the aquarium's tanks were rescued, and those that survive may eventually be returned to the wild. All the exhibits you'll see in this mammoth complex contain only local sea life. If you fear that the tight focus might make the tanks dull, you needn't worry. The exhibits and shows put on by the residents of Monterey Bay delight children and adults alike.

The aquarium displays a dazzling array of species. When you come to visit, a good first step is to look up the feeding schedules for the tanks you're most interested in. The critters always put on the best show at feeding time, and it's smart to show up several minutes in advance of feeding to get a good spot near the glass.

The living, breathing **Kelp Forest** is just like the kelp beds outside the Bay proper—except this one is 28 feet tall. Try to time your visit for either the 11:30 A.M. or 4 P.M. feeding time, when the fish in the tank put on quite a show.

The deep-water tank in the **Outer Bay**

© LIZ HAMILL SCOTT

Kelp Forest at the Monterey Bay Aquarium

## STEINBECK

John Ernst Steinbeck was born in Salinas, California in 1902 and grew up in its tiny, isolated agricultural community. He somehow managed to escape life as a farmer, a sardine fisherman, or a fish canner, and ended up living the glamorous life of a writer for his too-short 66 years.

Steinbeck's experiences in the Salinas Valley farming community and in the fishing town of Monterey informed many of his novels. The best known of these is *Cannery Row*, but *Tortilla Flat* is also set in working-class Monterey (though no one knows exactly where the fictional "Tortilla Flat" neighborhood was supposed to be). The Pulitzer Prize-winning novel *The Grapes of Wrath* takes more of its inspiration from the Salinas Valley. Steinbeck used the Valley as a model for farming in the Dust Bowl – the wretched, impoverished era that was the Great Depression.

In fact, Steinbeck was fascinated by the plight of working men and women; his novels and stories generally depict ordinary folks going through tough and terrible times. Steinbeck lived and worked through the Great Depression – thus it's not surprising that many of his stories do *not* feature happy Hollywood endings. Steinbeck was a realist in almost all of his novels, portraying the good, the bad, and the ugly of human life and society. His work gained almost immediate respect – in addition to his Pulitzer, Steinbeck also won the Nobel Prize for Literature in 1962. Almost every American high school student from the 1950s onward has read at least one of Steinbeck's novels or short stories; his body of work forms part of the enduring American literary canon.

As California's most illustrious literary son in the 20th century, Salinas became equally famous for spawning the author and inspiring his work. You'll find a variety of Steinbeck maps online (www.mtycounty.com/pgs-mty-stnbeck/mty-steinbeck.html) that offer self-guided tours of the regions made famous by his various novels. Poor Steinbeck's name is taken in vain all over now-commercial Cannery Row – even the cheesy Wax Museum tries to draw customers in by claiming kinship with the legendary author. More serious scholars of Steinbeck prefer the **National Steinbeck Center** (1 Main St., 831/796-3833, www.steinbeck.org, Salinas, daily 10 A.M.–5 P.M., $10.95) and the **Steinbeck House** (132 Central Ave., Salinas, 831/424-2735, www.steinbeckhouse.com, summer tours 1–3 P.M.), both in the still-agricultural town of Salinas. And if the museums aren't enough, plan to be in Monterey County in early August for the annual **Steinbeck Festival** (www.steinbeck.org), a big shindig put on by the Steinbeck Center in order to celebrate the great man's life and works in fine style.

exhibit area always draws a crowd. Inside its depths, a monster bluefin tuna that's been an aquarium resident for many years rules the roost. Even the fierce hammerhead sharks and odd-looking enormous sunfish steer clear of the tuna and its brethren.

The **Wild About Otters** exhibit gives visitors an up-close and personal view of rescued otters. The adorable, furry marine mammals come right up to the glass to interact with curious children and enchanted adults. You can watch aquarists feed and train the otters daily at 10:30 A.M., 1:30 P.M., and 3:30 P.M.

In addition to the many exhibits, be sure to check out the life and times of local tidepools, surflines, and even the ecosystems that surround the pillars, cement blocks, chains, and trash of the Monterey piers.

It easy to spend all day at the aquarium. If you get hungry, try for a table at the full-service restaurant and bar, complete with white tablecloths and a view of the bay. A self-service café offers sandwiches, salads, and ethnic dishes. You'll hardly be able to escape the souvenirs as a different gift shop sits in a corner of almost every exhibit hall.

If you possibly can, plan your visit to the Monterey Bay Aquarium on a weekday rather than a weekend. The aquarium is a wildly popular weekend destination. Especially in the summer, the crowds can be forbidding. Weekdays can be less crushing (though you'll run into school groups during much of the year), and the off-season is almost always a better time to visit. The aquarium has facilities for wheelchair access to almost all exhibits.

### Monterey State Historic Park

Monterey State Historic Park (20 Custom House Plaza, 831/649-7118, www.parks.ca.gov, daily 10 A.M.–5 P.M., free), usually called Old Monterey by locals, pays homage to the long and colorful history of the city of Monterey. This busy port town acted as the capital of California when it was under Spanish rule, and then later when the area became part of United States territory. Today, this park provides a peek into Monterey as it was in the middle of the 19th century—a busy place filled with dock workers, fishermen, bureaucrats, and soldiers. And yet it blends into the modern town of Monterey as well, and modern stores, galleries, and restaurants sit next to 150-year-old adobe structures. Free guided tours of several of the museums and adobes are offered most days; a walking tour of Old Monterey takes place at 10:30 A.M. on Monday–Wednesday and on Friday.



It's tough to see everything in just one visit to Old Monterey. If you only get to one spot on your first trip, make it the **Custom House** (Sat.–Thurs. 10 A.M.–4 P.M., Fri. 10:30 A.M.–4 P.M.). It's California State Historic Landmark Number 1, and the oldest bureaucratic building known to still stand in the state. You can spend some time wandering the adobe building, checking out the artifacts on display, or even just looking out the upstairs window towards the sea. Also on the plaza is the **Pacific House Museum** (Fri.–Wed. 10 A.M.–4 P.M., Thurs. 10:30 A.M.–4 P.M.) with exhibits of Native American artifacts.

There are 10 other buildings that comprise the park; most were built with adobe and/or brick between 1834 and 1847. These include: the **Casa del Oro;** the **Cooper-Molera Adobe** (525 Polk St., guided tours Fri.–Wed. 3 P.M.); the **First Brick House;** the **Larkin House** (510 Calle Principal, guided tours Tues.–Wed. 11:30 A.M. and Sat.–Sun. noon); the **Old Whaling Station;** the **Pacific House;** the **Sherman Quarters;** and the **Stevenson House** (530 Houston St., guided tours Mon. and Fri. 2 P.M. and Sat.–Sun. 10:30 A.M.), the former residence of Robert Louis Stevenson.

Famous artists, writers, and military men have stayed in some of these spots, most of which have long histories playing several different roles. Look down as you walk to see if you're stepping on antique whalebone sidewalks. And be sure to take a few minutes to admire the many beautiful gardens surrounding the adobes, which are lovingly maintained by local groups.

### Maritime Museum of Monterey

Part of Old Monterey, the Stanton Center includes the Maritime Museum of Monterey (5 Custom House Plaza, 831/372-2608, www.montereyhistory.org, Tues.–Sun. 10 A.M.–5 P.M.). The large modern facilities provide plenty of space for the art and historical artifacts collected over the decades, most of which pertain directly to the area's history, maritime or otherwise. In the Maritime Museum, explore the history of the native Rumisen and Ohlone people, going through the Spanish exploration and conquistador era, and on in to the American military and fishing presence on the Central Coast. The original Fresnel lens from the Point Sur light station sits in here, as does an array of sardine fishing equipment.

## ENTERTAINMENT AND EVENTS

### Live Music

Classical music aficionados will appreciate the dulcet tones of the musicians who perform for **Chamber Music Monterey Bay** (831/625-2212, www.chambermusicmontereybay.org). This society brings talented ensembles and soloists in from around the world to perform on the lovely Central Coast. One night you might find a local string quartet, and on another night you'll get to see and hear a chamber ensemble. (String quartets definitely rule the small stage and intimate theater.) Far from banning young music fans from the **Sunset Cultural Center** (San Carlos St. btwn. 8th and 10th Sts., Carmel), Chamber Music Monterey Bay reserves up-front seats at all its shows for children and their adult companions.

One of the coolest small-rock venues in California is the **The Golden State Theater** (417 Alvarado St., 831/372-3800, www.goldenstatetheatre.com) in Monterey. This beautiful theater is done up in 1920s era Arabian Nights–style Middle Eastern revival. It's easy to get to, sitting right downtown near the big Hyatt hotel. Get there early so you can spend some time admiring the decor before the lights lower and the show starts. The Golden State hosts acts that often play larger venues, which means that show goers get a reasonably intimate experience in which they can actually *see* their favorite performers. A few performances in 2008 included Los Lonely Boys, the Doobie Brothers, comedienne Paula Poundstone, and a special engagement of the Sally Struthers musical *Nunsense.*

### Festivals and Events

The Monterey region hosts numerous festivals and special events each year. Whether your pleasure is fine food or funky music, you'll probably be able to plan a trip around some sort of multi-day festival with dozens of events and performances scheduled during Monterey's busy year.

In keeping with the Central Coast's obsession with food and wine, the annual **Monterey Wine Festival** (800/422-0251, www.montereywine.com, mid-Oct.) celebrates wine with a generous helping of food on the side. A number of tasting events mark this weekish-long festival, including a major day event at the fairgrounds and possibly a swanky nighttime soiree at the Monterey Bay Aquarium. You can also expect a few private events and parties at participating wineries and restaurants. Check the website for this year's venues, ticket prices, and event dates and times. This festival offers the perfect opportunity to introduce yourself to Monterey and Carmel wineries, many of which have not yet hit the "big time" in major wine magazines. The Wine Festival is just one of many similar events held each year in the region, so if you can't make it you'll have plenty of other opportunities to enjoy all the best edibles and drinkables the Central Coast has to offer.

One of the biggest music festivals in California is the **Monterey Jazz Festival** (2000 Fairground Rd., Monterey, 831/373-3366, www.montereyjazzfestival.org). As the site of the longest-running jazz festival on earth, Monterey attracts the top performers from around the world. Held each September—a month that offers the best chance for beautiful weather on the Monterey Bay—this long weekend of amazing music can leave you happy for the whole year. The event is held at the Monterey County Fairgrounds, which lets visitors enjoy all the different concerts without having to drive from venue to venue. Nine stages put up acts day and night, making it easy to either find your favorite stage and settle in for a long stay and multiple musicians, or wander the length and breadth of the fairgrounds to sample the acts at each unique venue. Camping is not permitted at the fairgrounds, but you can camp nearby, or get a room in one of the Monterey lodgings that partner with the festival to provide reasonably priced lodgings for attendees.

## SPORTS AND RECREATION

The Monterey Bay is the premier Northern California locale for a number of water sports, especially scuba diving.

### Scuba

Any native Northern Californian knows that there's only one really great place in the region to get certified in scuba diving—the Monterey Bay. Even if you go to a dive school up in the Bay Area, they'll take you down to Monterey for your open-water dive. Accordingly, dozens of dive schools cluster in and around the town of Monterey (check Carmel and Santa Cruz as well, if you prefer).

The **Monterey Bay Dive Company** (225 Cannery Row, 831/656-0454, www.mbdcscuba

.com) sits right in the midst of Cannery Row, where all visitors to Monterey eventually end up. You can take dive classes year-round, get certified, rent equipment, fill your own tanks, and even take a quick dive right off San Carlos Beach just behind the dive shop. Monterey Bay Dive Company also maintains its own dive boat, offering both boat and shore guided dive tours of the famous Monterey Bay undersea world.

Another of your many dive shop options is the **Aquarius Dive Shop** (2040 Del Monte Ave., 831/375-1933, www.aquariusdivers.com). Aquarius offers everything you need to go diving out in Monterey Bay, including air and nitrox fills, equipment rental, certification courses, and help booking a trip on a local dive boat. Aquarius works with four boats to create great trips for divers of all interests and ability levels. Call or check the website for current local dive conditions as well.

## Kayaking

With all the focus on sustainable tourism in Monterey, coupled with the lovely recreation area formed by Monterey Bay, it's no wonder that sea kayaking is popular here. Whether you want to try paddling your first kayak, or you're an expert who hasn't brought your own gear out to California, you'll find a local outfit ready and willing to hook you up.

**Adventures by the Sea** (299 Cannery Row, 831/372-1807, www.adventuresbythesea.com, 9 A.M.–sunset, tours $50/person, rentals $30/day) rents kayaks for whole days to let you choose your own route in and around the magnificent Monterey Bay kelp forest. If you're not confident enough to go off on your own, Adventures offers tours from Cannery Row. Your guide can tell you all about the wildlife you're seeing: harbor seals, sea otters, pelicans, seagulls, and maybe even a whale in the wintertime! The tour lasts about 2.5 hours, cost $50 per person, and the available tandem sit-on-top kayaks make it a great experience for school-age children. Adventures by the Sea also runs a tour of Stillwater Cove at Pebble Beach. Reservations are recommended for all tours, but during the summer the Cannery Row tour leaves regularly at 10 A.M. and 2 P.M., so you can stop by on a whim and see if there's a spot available.

**Monterey Bay Kayaks** (693 Del Monte Ave., 831/373-5357, www.montereybaykayaks.com, tours $50–60/person) specializes in tours of both central Monterey and up north in Elkhorn Slough. You can choose between open-deck and closed-deck tour groups, beginning tours perfect for kids, romantic sunset or full moon paddles, or even long paddles designed for more experienced sea kayakers. Most tours cost $50–60 per person; check the website for specific tour prices, times, and reservation information. If you prefer to rent a kayak and explore the bay or slough on your own, Monterey Bay Kayaks can help you out there too. If you really get into it, you can also sign up for closed-deck sea kayaking classes to learn about safety, rescue techniques, tides, currents, and paddling techniques.

A third company, **AB Seas Kayaks of Monterey** (32 Cannery Row, #5, 831/647-0147, www.montereykayak.com, tours $60/person, rentals $30/day), also has plenty of sit-on-top sea kayaks for rent—choose a single or double kayak as you need. Or take a tour of Monterey Bay with an experienced guide.

## Fishing and Whale-Watching

Whales pass quite near the shores of Monterey year-round. While you can sometimes even see them from the beaches, any number of boats can take you out for a closer look at the great beasts as they travel along their own special routes north and south. The area hosts many humpbacks, blue whales, and gray whales, plus the occasional killer whale, Minke whale, fin whale, and pod of dolphins. Bring your own binoculars for a better view, but the experienced boat captains will do all they can to get you as close as possible to the whales and dolphins. Most tours last 2–3 hours and leave from Fisherman's Wharf, which is easy to get to and has ample parking. If you prefer not to rise with the sun, pick a tour that leaves in the afternoon.

**Monterey Bay Whale Watch** (84 Fisherman's Wharf, 831/375-4658, www.montereybaywhalewatch.com) leaves right from an easy-to-find red building on Fisherman's Wharf and runs tours in every season. (Call or check the website for schedules.) You must make a reservation in advance, even for regularly scheduled tours. Afternoon tours are available. **Monterey Whale Watching** (96 Fisherman's Wharf, 800/979-3370, www.baywatchcruises.com) prides itself on its knowledgeable guides/marine biologists and its comfortable, spacious cruising vessels. The *Princess Monterey* offers morning and afternoon tours, and you can buy tickets online or by phone.

If you'd rather catch fish than watch mammals, **Randy's Fishing Trips** (800/979-3370, www.randysfishingtrips.com) can take you out for salmon, halibut, albacore, mackerel, rock cod, flatfish, and even squid and Dungeness crab in season. They can also take you out for a whale-watching trip if that's your preference. Trips begin early in the morning and can last for several hours. You can bring your own food—catering is not provided—including a small cooler for your drinks. If you don't have a California fishing license, you can purchase a one-day license at the shop before your trip. While you can try to walk up to the bright teal-painted shop at Fisherman's Wharf, it's best to get tickets for your trip in advance; either call or buy online from Randy's website.

**Chris's Fishing Trips** (48 Fisherman's Wharf, 831/372-0577, www.chrissfishing.com, $55–90/per person) offers both scheduled trips and boats for charter. If you want to go solo, get on one of the daily salmon or cod trips, which include bait and ice; tackle, a one-day license, and fish cleaning are extras.

## Bird-Watching

Some of the best birding in the state can be had at **Elkhorn Slough** (1700 Elkhorn Rd., Watsonville, 831/728-2822, www.elkhornslough.org, Wed.–Sun. 9 A.M.–5 P.M., free), a few miles north of Monterey proper in Moss Landing. This large waterway/wetland area is incongruously marked by the mammoth smokestacks of the Moss Landing power plant. While you can access the wetlands and bird habitats from Highway 1 in Moss Landing, to get to the visitors center you must drive several miles into the agricultural backcountry. But once you're there, knowledgeable and dedicated rangers can provide you with all the information you need to spot your favorite birds, plus find a few you've never seen before.

## Golf

Yes, you can play golf in middle-class Monterey! And it's often much cheaper to play here than to head for the hallowed courses of Carmel.

The public **Monterey Pines Golf Course** (1250 Garden Rd., 831/656-2167, $25–38, cart $20) offers 18 holes for a comparatively tiny green fee. It's a short par-69 course that's got four levels of tee to make the game fun for players of all levels. Monterey Pines was originally built as a private Navy course for the pleasure of the officers at the major naval installation north of town. Today, it is open to all who want to play. Call ahead for tee times.

A bit more pricy but still not Poppy Hills or Pebble Beach, **Del Monte Golf Course** (1300 Sylvan Rd., 831/373-2700, www.pebblebeach.com, $34–95, cart $20) is part of that legendary set of courses. This historic 18-hole, par-72 course, along with two other courses, still plays host to the Pebble Beach Invitational each year. You won't get the ocean views of Pebble Beach, but you will be treated to lovely green mountains surrounding the course as you play through. The property includes a full-service pro shop and the Del Monte Bar & Grill. You can check available tee times online, then call 800/877-0597 to book your preferred time.

## Motor Sports

If you're feeling the need for speed, you can get lots of it at the **Mazda Raceway Laguna Seca** (1021 Monterey-Salinas Hwy., 831/242-8201, www.laguna-seca.com), one of the country's premier road-racing venues. Here you can see historic auto races, superbikes, speed festivals, and an array of Grand Prix events. The major racing season runs May–October of most years. In addition to the big events, Laguna Seca hosts innumerable auto clubs and small sports car and stock car races. If you've always wanted to learn to drive or ride racecar-style, check the schedule to see if one of the track classes is happening during your visit. These often happen in the middle of the week, and are a near daily event in the off-season.

Be sure to check the website for parking directions specific to the event you plan to attend—this is a big facility. You can camp here, and certainly you'll find plenty of concessions during big races.

## ACCOMMODATIONS

### Under $100

The **Monterey Hostel** (778 Hawthorne St., 831/649-0375, http://montereyhostel.com, $28/bunk, $62/private room) offers inexpensive accommodations within walking distance of the major attractions of Monterey. Frankly, when it comes to rooms and amenities, this isn't the best hostel in California. You must pay extra to rent a locker, there's no laundry facility on-site, and the dorm rooms can be pretty crowded. On the other hand, the hostel puts on a free pancake breakfast every morning, linens are included with your bed, and there are comfy, casual common spaces with couches and musical instruments. And then there's that location.... You can walk to the aquarium and Cannery Row, stroll the Monterey Bay Coastal Trail, or drive over to Carmel to see a different set of sights.

### $100-150

A cute, small, budget motel, the **Monterey Bay Lodge** (55 Camino Aguajito, 831/372-8057, www.montereybaylodge.com, $134) brings a bit of the Côte d'Azur to the equally beautiful coastal town of Monterey. With small rooms decorated in classic yellows and blues, a sparkling pool with a fountain in the shallow end, and an on-site restaurant serving breakfast and lunch, the Lodge makes a perfect base for budget-minded families traveling in the Monterey region.

### $150-250

The **Colton Inn** (707 Pacific St, 831/649-6500, www.coltoninn.com, $165) offers a touch of class above that of a standard beach-town motel. Located in the midst of downtown Monterey, the queen and king bedrooms boast attractive fabrics, designer bathrooms, and pretty appointments. While you'll find restaurants and historic adobe buildings adjacent to the Colton, expect to drive or take public transit to Cannery Row and the Aquarium.

Be sure to call in advance to get a room at **The Jabberwock** (598 Laine St, 831/372-4777, www.jabberwockinn.com, $215), a favorite with frequent visitors to Monterey. This Alice in Wonderland—themed B&B is both whimsical and elegant; expect to find a copy of the namesake novel in your tastefully appointed guest room. Be sure to take the owners up on their daily wine and cheese reception in the afternoon-they are gold mines of information about the area, and will be happy to recommend restaurants and activities for all tastes. Though located up a steep hill, the Jabberwock is within walking distance of Cannery Row and all its adjacent attractions (it's worth the extra exercise to avoid the cost or hassle of parking in the tourist lots).

### Over $250

Monterey visitors looking for elegant accommodations love the **Old Monterey Inn** (500 Martin St., 831/375-8284, www.oldmontereyinn.com, $275–400). The lovely old edifice stands in the midst of mature gardens that blossom all spring and summer, showing their sedate green side in autumn and winter. Inside the inn, the garden motif echoes in the upscale bed linens and window treatments, which compliment the pretty furnishings and cozy fireplaces. Spa bathtubs pamper guests. Additional amenities include a full breakfast (often served in the garden) and a menu of spa treatments that can be enjoyed downstairs in the serene treatment room.

Want to stay right on Cannery Row in a room overlooking the bay? You'll pay handsomely—but it's worth it—at the **Monterey Plaza Hotel & Spa** (400 Cannery Row, 831/646-1700, www.montereyplazahotel.com, $388). This on-the-water luxury hotel has it all: two restaurants, a spa, a private beach, room service, and upscale guest room goodies. Rooms range from "budget" garden and Row-facing accommodations to ocean-view rooms with private balconies and huge suites that mimic a posh private apartment. Bring your credit card and enjoy!

## FOOD

The organic and sustainable food movements have caught hold on the Central Coast. The Monterey Bay Seafood Watch program (www.montereybayaquarium.org) is the definitive resource for sustainable seafood, while the Salinas Valley inland hosts a number of organic farms.

### American

For coffee, espresso, and homebaked beignets, head to the **Trailside Café** (550 Wave St, 831/649-8600, www.trailsidecafe.com, daily 8 A.M.–4 P.M., $10–15). This Cannery Row restaurant offers breakfast, lunch, and dinner on a heated patio overlooking the bay.

For more views and exemplary American cuisine, stop by the **Duck Club Grill** (400 Cannery Row, 831/646-1706, www.montereyplazahotel.com, daily 6:30–11 A.M. and 5:30–9:30 P.M., $30) in the Monterey Plaza Hotel. Steaks, lamb chops, and the namesake duck are what's on order here and the extensive wine list offers many complements. **Montrio** (414 Calle Principal, 831/648-8880, www.montrio.com, $15–20) is another entry in elegantly casual Monterey dining. The crab cakes are legendary.

### Seafood

The **Old Fisherman's Grotto** (39 Fisherman's Wharf, 831/375-4604, daily 11 A.M.–10 P.M., $) is a relaible wharf staple for both seafood and views over Monterey Bay. The menu focuses on fresh seafood and Italian standards and the restaurant includes a full bar. If you're craving fresh seafood but want to esacpe the touristy wharf, head to the **Monterey Fish House** (2114 Del Monte Ave., 831/373-4647, daily 11:30 A.M.–2:30 P.M. and 5–9:30 P.M., $15–25) where the local go for cioppino and grilled oysters. The tiny dining room ensures its social atmosphere.

### Markets

The **Monterey Bay Farmers Market** (980 Fremont St., www.montereybayfarmers.org, Thurs. 2:30–6:30 P.M.) showcases almost 50 farmers and vendors selling fresh produce, flowers, plants every Thursday afternoon.

## INFORMATION AND SERVICES

In Monterey, the **El Estero Visitors Center** (401 Camino El Estero, www.montereyinfo.org) is the local outlet of the Montery Country Convention & Visitors Bureau. The **Monterey Peninsula Chamber of Commerce** (380 Alvarado St., 831/648-5360) can also provide helpful information.

The local newspaper is the ***Monterey County Herald*** (www.montereyherald.com). Monterey has two convenient **post offices:** one at 565 Hartnell St. and another at 686 Lighthouse Ave.

For medical needs, the **Community Hospital of the Monterey Peninsula** (CHOMP, 23625 Holman Hwy., 831/624-5311) provides emergency services to the area.

## GETTING THERE AND AROUND

Most visitors drive into Monterey via the scenic Highway 1. Inland, U.S. 101 allows access into Salinas from the north and south. From Salinas, Highway 68 travels west into Monterey.

For a more leisurely ride, **Amtrak's** Coast Starlight train (Station Pl. and Railroad Ave., Salinas, daily 8 A.M.–10 P.M.) travels through Salinas daily. For Amtrak travelers, there is free bus service to downtown Monterey (30 min.); for everyone else, the **Greyhound** bus station (19 W. Gabilan, Salinas, 831/424-4418, www.greyhound.com, daily 5 A.M.–11:30 P.M.) offers service into Monterey.

Once in Monterey, take advantage of the free **WAVE** bus (9 A.M.–7:30 P.M.) which loops between downtown Monterey and the Aquarium.

# Carmel

Carmel's landscape is divided into two distinct parts. The adorable village of Carmel-by-the-Sea perches on the cliffs above the Pacific, surrounded to the north and the south by golf courses and beach parks. Carmel-by-the-Sea boasts the highest number of art galleries per capita in the United States. When most Californians talk about Carmel, they mean Carmel-by-the-Sea. The streets are perfect for strolling, and if ever there was a town that feels comfortable and safe for a woman traveling alone, it's Carmel.

Inland, the far less-traveled Carmel Valley has its share of huge estates owned by some of the wealthiest folks in the state. The narrow valley, surrounded by verdant hillsides, has recently discovered its footing as a niche wine region. Visitors can also play a few holes at the inevitable golf courses and check out the tiny hamlets that line the lone main road through the valley.

Both Carmel by-the-Sea and Carmel Valley residents love dogs. Your pooch is welcome at many establishments, and a number of stores and restaurants offer doggie treats and keep fresh water outside for the canine set.

## SIGHTS

### 17-Mile Drive

If you're a first-time visitor to the Carmel and Monterey area, 17-Mile Drive ($9/vehicle) can introduce you to some of the most beautiful and representative land and seascapes on the Central Coast. But don't get too excited yet—long ago, the locally all-powerful Pebble Beach Corporation realized what a precious commodity they held in this road, and began charging a toll. The good news is that when you pay your fee at the gatehouse, you'll get a map of the drive that describes the parks and sights that you will pass as you make your way along the winding coastal road. These include the much-photographed Lone Cypress, the beaches of Spanish Bay, and Pebble Beach's golf course,

© LIZ HAMILL SCOTT

the view along 17-Mile Drive

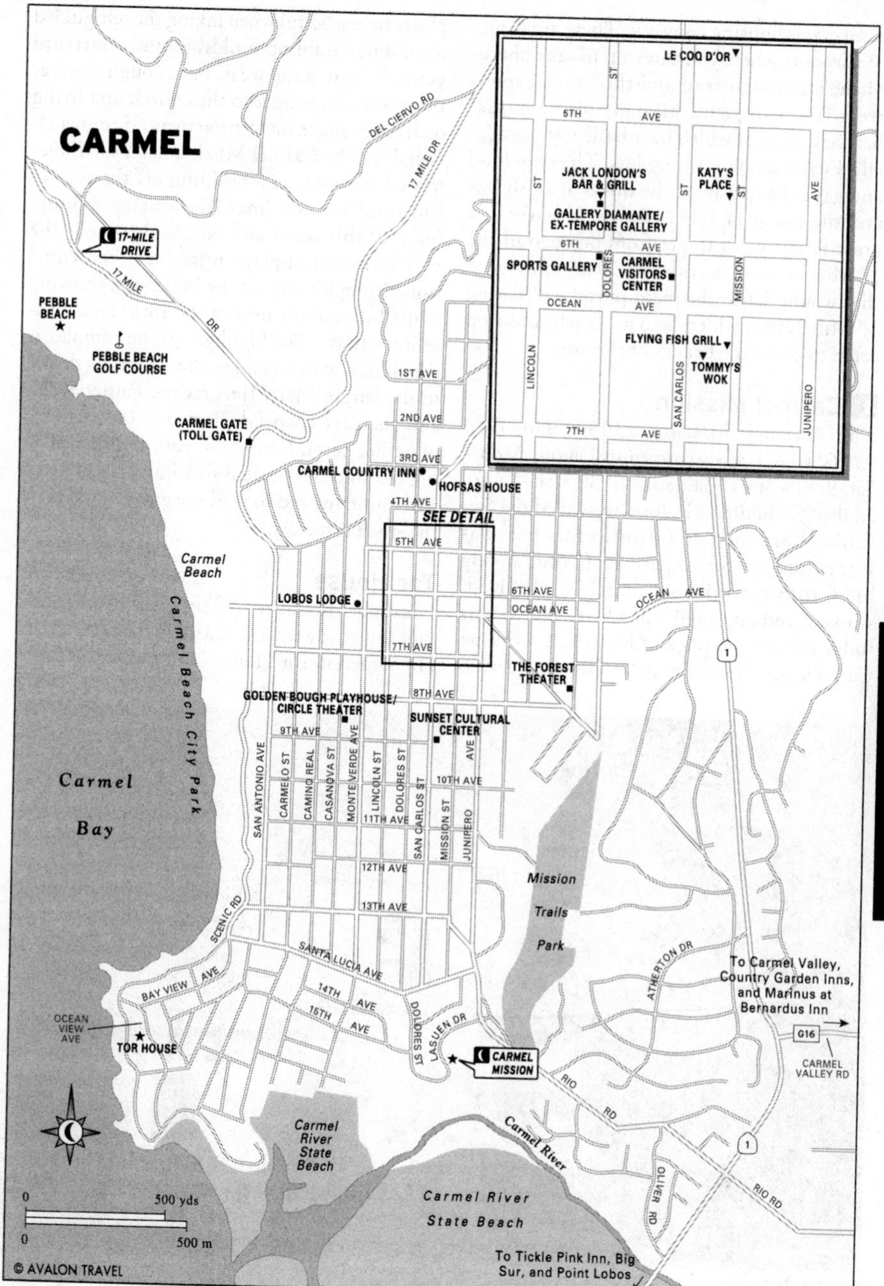
CARMEL
LE COQ D'OR
5TH AVE
JACK LONDON'S BAR & GRILL
KATY'S PLACE
GALLERY DIAMANTE/ EX-TEMPORE GALLERY
6TH AVE
SPORTS GALLERY
CARMEL VISITORS CENTER
OCEAN AVE
FLYING FISH GRILL
TOMMY'S WOK
7TH AVE
LINCOLN ST
DOLORES ST
SAN CARLOS ST
MISSION ST
JUNIPERO AVE
DEL CIERVO RD
17 MILE DR
17-MILE DRIVE
PEBBLE BEACH
PEBBLE BEACH GOLF COURSE
CARMEL GATE (TOLL GATE)
1ST AVE
2ND AVE
3RD AVE
CARMEL COUNTRY INN
HOFSAS HOUSE
4TH AVE
SEE DETAIL
Carmel Beach
LOBOS LODGE
6TH AVE
OCEAN AVE
THE FOREST THEATER
GOLDEN BOUGH PLAYHOUSE/ CIRCLE THEATER
8TH AVE
SUNSET CULTURAL CENTER
9TH AVE
10TH AVE
11TH AVE
12TH AVE
13TH AVE
Carmel Beach City Park
Carmel Bay
SAN ANTONIO AVE
CARMELO ST
CAMINO REAL
CASANOVA ST
MONTE VERDE AVE
Mission Trails Park
SCENIC RD
SANTA LUCIA AVE
BAY VIEW AVE
14TH AVE
15TH AVE
OCEAN VIEW AVE
TOR HOUSE
LASUEN DR
CARMEL MISSION
ATHERTON DR
To Carmel Valley, Country Garden Inns, and Marinus at Bernardus Inn
G16
CARMEL VALLEY RD
RIO RD
Carmel River
Carmel River State Beach
OLIVER RD
0
500 yds
500 m
To Tickle Pink Inn, Big Sur, and Point Lobos
© AVALON TRAVEL

resort, and housing complex. There are plenty of turnouts where you can stop to take photos of the stunning ocean and the iconic cypress trees. You can picnic at many of the formal beaches, most of which have basic restroom facilities and ample parking lots. The only food and gas to be had are at the Inn at Spanish Bay and the Lodge at Pebble Beach. If you're in a great hurry, you can get from one end of the 17-Mile Drive to the other in 20 minutes—but that would defeat the main purpose of taking 17-Mile Drive, which is to go slowly and stop often to enjoy the beauty of the area.

## Carmel Mission

The Carmel Mission (3080 Rio Rd., 831/624-1271, www.carmelmission.org, Mon.–Sat. 9:30 A.M.–5 P.M., Sun. 10:30 A.M.–5 P.M., adults $5, children $1), formally called the San Carlos Borromeo de Carmelo Mission, was Father Junipero Serra's personal favorite among his California mission churches. He lived, worked, and eventually died here, and visitors today can see a replica of his cell. A working Catholic parish remains part of the complex, so please be respectful when taking the self-guided tour. The rambling buildings and courtyard gardens show some wear, but enough restoration work has gone into the church and living quarters to make them attractive and eminently visitable. The Carmel Mission has a small memorial museum in a building off the second courtyard, but don't make the mistake of thinking that this small and outdated space is the only historical display. In fact, the "museum" runs through many of the buildings, showing a small slice of the lives of the 18th- and 19th-century friars. The highlight of the complex is the church with its gilded altar front, its shrine to the Virgin Mary, the grave of Father Serra, and ancillary chapel dedicated to the memory of Father Serra. Round out your visit by walking out into the gardens to admire the flowers and fountains and to read the grave markers in the small cemetery.

## Tor House

Local poet Robinson Jeffers built this rugged-looking castle on the Carmel coast in 1919. He named it Tor House (26304 Ocean View

© LIZ HAMILL SCOTT

Carmel Mission

Ave., 831/624-1813, www.torhouse.org, tours Fri.–Sat. 10 A.M.–3 P.M., $7), after its rocky setting, and added the majestic Hawk Tower a year later. The granite stone structure exists today as an example of the Carmel ethos that Jeffers embodied and as a monument to his work and poetry.

## Earthbound Farms

One of the largest purveyors of organic produce in the United States, Earthbound Farms (7250 Carmel Valley Rd., 831/625-6219, www.ebfarm.com, Mon.–Sat. 8 A.M.–6 P.M., Sun. 10 A.M.–5 P.M.) offers visitors easy access to its smallish facility in the Carmel Valley. Drive up to the farm stand and browse a variety of organic fruits, veggies, and flowers. Outdoors, you can ramble into the fields, checking out the chamomile labyrinth and the kids' garden (yes, your kids can look *and* touch). Select and harvest your own fresh herbs from the cut-your-own garden, or leave the cooking to the experts and purchase delicious prepared organic dishes at the farm stand. If you're interested in a more in-depth guided tour of the farm, check the website for a schedule of walks, which will take you, a group, and an expert guide—perhaps a chef or local famous foodie—out into the fields for a look at what's growing and how to use it.

## Pebble Beach

While the legends of Pebble Beach (Palmero Way, www.pebblebeach.com) surround its championship golf course, there's a lot more to it than just greens and sand traps. A gated community surrounding the course and spreading back towards the trees encompasses some of the most expensive homes in California. From 17-Mile Drive, turn off onto the lengthy driveway to visit the ultra high-end resort. Any visitor can park and walk into the main lobby of the hotel area. Most tourists walk right through and out onto the immense multi-level patio area to take in the priceless and oft-photographed views. Whether you stay on the flagstones and enjoy a drink from the lobby bar or take a walk out onto the wide lawns, your eyes will be caught by the dramatic cliffs plummeting down to the small blue-gray bay. The golf

© LIZ HAMILL SCOTT

Pebble Beach

course draws right up to the lawns, allowing even the poorly heeled to check out a couple of the hallowed greens and fairways dotted with cypress trees. The lodge itself is worth touring, too; you can take footpaths to see the outsides of the posh accommodations, walk in to the lobby of the exclusive spa, and peer at the tables of the gourmet dining room.

## WINERIES

Its tiny size necessarily limits the number of vineyards and wineries that can set up shop in the Carmel Valley. But this small, charming wine region makes for a perfect wine-tasting day trip from Carmel, Monterey, or even Big Sur. Small crowds, light traffic, and meaningful tasting experiences categorize this area, which still has many family-owned wineries. You'll get personal attention and delicious wines, all in a gorgeous green setting.

The **Bernardus Winery** (5 W. Carmel Valley Rd., 800/223-2533, www.bernardus.com/winery, daily 11 A.M.–5 P.M., $5–10) sits on a vineyard estate that also hosts a connected luxurious lodge and gourmet restaurant. Bernardus creates a small list of wines. The grapes growing all around you go into the pride of the winery: the Bordeaux-style blended red Marinus Vineyard wine. Other varietals (Chardonnay, Pinot Noir, and Sauvignon Blanc) come from cool coastal vineyards. If you're interested and lucky, you might also get to sip some small-batch vintages of single-vineyard wines that are available only in the tasting room.

The biggest name in the Carmel Valley is **Chateau Julien** (8940 Carmel Valley Rd., 831/624-2600, www.chateaujulien.com, Mon.–Fri. 8 A.M.–5 P.M., Sat.–Sun. 11 A.M.–5 P.M.). The European-styled white estate building with the round turret is visible from the road. The light, airy tasting room is crowded with barrels, wine cases, souvenirs, and tasting glasses. When you enter, you'll be offered sips from the wide selection of Chardonnays, Cabernets, Syrahs, Merlots, and more. If you're lucky, you might find yourself tasting a rare Reserve blended red or a 10-year-old port. For a treat, call ahead and reserve a spot on the twice-daily complimentary vineyard and winery tours. These tours conclude with a special tasting outside on the flagstone patio when weather permits.

On the other end of the spectrum, tiny **Parsonage Village Vineyard** (19 E. Carmel Valley Rd., 831/659-7322, www.parsonagewine.com, Fri.–Mon. 11 A.M.–5 P.M., $5) often doesn't make it onto Carmel Valley wine maps—which is a shame, because some of the best Syrah coming out of California (arguably) comes from this unpretentious little winery with only a nine-acre estate vineyard to work with. The tasting room sits in a tiny strip of shops, the space glowing with light that bounces off the copper of the bar. On the walls, you'll find an array of quilts made by Mary Ellen Parsons herself. At the bar, you'll taste wonderful Syrahs, hearty Cabernet Sauvignons, and surprisingly deep and complex blends—the Snosrap (that's Parsons spelled backwards) table wine is inexpensive for the region and incredibly tasty. If you find a vintage you love at Parsonage, buy it then and there since they sell out of many of their wines every year.

## ENTERTAINMENT AND EVENTS

The events and entertainment in Carmel tend to center around either art or food. This town loves its haute culture, so you won't find too many sports bars or generic movie theaters here. Instead, enjoy classical music, a wealth of live theater, and a glass of wine in the mild evenings.

### Bars and Clubs

The population of Carmel tends toward wealthy seniors. Hence, the nightlife isn't too hopping here, and live music in bars in Carmel was illegal until 2006—seriously. Most of the drinking tends toward restaurants and the occasional hotel lounge. If you're looking for an evening out within Carmel city limits, try a night at the theater.

If you simply must go out for a drink, try **Jack London's Bar & Grill** (Dolores St. and Fifth Ave., 831/624-2336, www.jacklondons

.com). All dark wood, fancy ceiling, and quiet elegance, it's no surprise that Jack London's has a full menu of fancier-than- average bar food and a wine list that would do a high-end restaurant proud. But it's also got big-screen TVs tuned to the games of the day and live blues each Friday. If you've brought your favorite canine companion, you'll find a welcoming seat outside on the patio, where the full menu is served.

### Theater

Despite its small size, Carmel has nearly a dozen live theater groups. In a town that defines itself by its love of art, theater arts don't get left out. Don't hesitate to ask the locals what's playing where when you're in town.

The **Pacific Repertory Theater** (831/622-0100, www.pacrep.org, adults $16–38, students $10–20, children $7) is the only professional theater company on the Monterey-Carmel Peninsula. Its shows go up all over the region, most often in the **Golden Bough Playhouse** (Monte Verde St. and Eighth Ave.) the company's home theater. Other regular venues include the **The Forest Theater** (Mountain View St. and Santa Rita St.), and the **Circle Theater** (Casanova St. btwn. Eighth and Ninth Aves.) within the Golden Bough complex. Also look for their plays in the Monterey State Historic Park and in Pebble Beach. The company puts up dramas, comedies, and musicals both new and classic. You might see a work of Shakespeare or John Patrick Shanley's *Doubt,* enjoy your favorite songs from *The Fantasticks,* or sing along to the newer tunes of *High School Musical.* Check the website for upcoming shows, and buy tickets online or over the phone to guarantee you'll get seats while you're in town.

Each fall, PacRep puts up the **Carmel Shakespeare Festival** (www.pacrep.org), a short showing of Shakespeare that's good enough to draw the notice of Bay Area theater snobs. Check the website for information on this year's shows and the venues.

### Festivals and Events

In a town famed for art galleries, one of the biggest events of the year is the **Carmel Art Festival** (Mission St., Carmel-by-the-Sea, www.carmelartfestival.org, May). This four-day event celebrates visual arts in all media with shows by internationally acclaimed artists at galleries, parks, and other venues all across town. This wonderful festival also sponsors here-and-now contests, including the prestigious Plein Air (outdoor painting). Visitors get a rare opportunity to witness the artists outdoors, engaging in their creative process as they use the Carmel scenery for inspiration. Round out your festival experience by bidding on paintings at the end-of-event auction. You can get a genuine bargain on original artwork while supporting both the artists and the Festival. Perhaps best of all, the Carmel Art Festival is a great place to bring your family—a wealth of children's activities help even the youngest festival goers become budding artists.

For a more classical experience, one of the most prestigious festivals in Northern California is the **Carmel Bach Festival** (www.bachfestival.org). For three weeks each July and August, Carmel-by-the-Sea and its surrounding towns host dozens of classical concerts. Naturally the works of J. S. Bach are featured, but you can also hear renditions of Mozart, Vivaldi, Handel, and other heavyweights of Bach's era. Choose between big concerts in major venues or intimate performances in smaller spaces with only a small audience between you and the beautiful music. Concerts and recitals take place literally every day of the week—budget-conscious music lovers can just as easily enjoy the Festival in the middle of the week as on the weekends.

## SHOPPING

Downtown Carmel-by-the-Sea is a great place to get out of your car and stroll the streets, peering in the windows of the boutiques and countless galleries.

Carmel boasts more art galleries per capita than any other town in the United States. Accordingly, shopping in the downtown pedestrian area means "checking out the galleries." **Gallery Diamante** (Dolores St. betw. 5th and 6th, 831/624-0852, www.gallerydiamante.com) represents a typical Carmel Gallery, with a large collection of landscape paintings by different artists and interesting sculptures scattered about. The most popular modern styles in painting, sculpture, and even art glass and jewelry are on display. Jewelry here can be reasonably priced, but expect to spend a more for an original painting.

Bucking the current trends in Carmel art is Boban Bursac, sole owner of the tiny **Extempore Gallery** (Dolores St. betw. 5th and 6th, 831/626-1298, bobanart@yahoo.com). Burasac's amazing large-format paintings evoke feelings in even the most casual passerby; lucky visitors might even get to with the artist. Sadly, these works of art do not come cheap, understandable given their size and the skill and devotion with which they are painted.

For something altogether different and perhaps less intimidating, there's the **Sports Gallery** (Dolores St. betw. Ocean and 6th, 831/624-6026, www.sportsgalleryweb.com). In this more casual and down-to-earth space is memorabilia, signed photos, and even paintings of your favorite sports heroes and legends, many at reasonable prices. This is a great spot to look for gifts for that sports fanatic back home.



## SPORTS AND RECREATION

### Beach

At the west end of Ocean Avenue, you'll find the (occasionally) sparkling white sands of **Carmel Beach** (Ocean Ave., 831/624-4909, daily 6 A.M.–10 P.M.). This lovely stretch of south-facing sand offers free running for canine guests, bonfires south of 10th Avenue, and all the surfing, wading, and sunbathing (when there's sun) you can handle. Enjoy the beautiful local cypress trees and consider bringing a kite to fly on this often windy beach.

### Biking

**17-Mile Drive** also makes a great bike route. Cyclists can follow this road and enjoy the smells and sounds of the spectacular scenery in a way that car drivers just can't. Expect fairly flat terrain with lots of twists and turns, and a ride that runs...about 17 miles. Foggy conditions can make this ride a bit slick in the summer, but spring and fall weather are perfect for pedaling here.

### Golf

There's no place for golfing in all of California like Carmel-by-the-Sea. You can play courses trodden by the likes of Tiger Woods and Jack Nicholson, pause a moment before you putt to take in the sight of the stunning Pacific Ocean, and pay $300 or more for a single round of golf. Golf has been a major pastime here since the late 19th century, and today avid golfers come from around the world to tee off in Carmel.

One of the Pebble Beach Resort courses, **Spyglass Hill** (1700 17-Mile Dr., Pebble Beach, 800/654-9300, www.pebblebeach.com, 18-hole Par 72) gets its moniker from the Robert Louis Stevenson Novel *Treasure Island*. But don't be fooled—the holes on this beautiful course may be named for children's characters, but that doesn't mean they're easy. Spyglass Hill boasts some of the most challenging play even in the golf course-laden Carmel region. Expect a few bogeys if you choose to play here, and tee off from the Championship level at your own (ego's) risk.

Another favorite with the Pebble Beach golf crowd is the famed **Poppy Hills Golf Course** (3200 Lopez Rd, Pebble Beach, 831/622-8239, www.poppyhillsgolf.com, 18-hole Par 72). Though it's not managed by the same company, Poppy Hills shares amenities with Pebble Beach golf courses; you can expect the same level of care and devotion to the maintenance of the course and your experience as a player there. If you're looking to improve your game, check out their program that runs two days and gets you out onto both Poppy and Spyglass Hill for a great chance to really pick up some new skills (and a few incidentally gorgeous views).

### Hiking

South of Carmel-by-the-Sea, is **Point Lobos State Reserve** (62 Hwy. 1, 831/624-4909, http://pt-lobos.parks.state.ca.us, daily 8 A.M.–sunset, $10). Known as one of the most beautiful parks in the state park system, Point Lobos offers hiking through forestland and along the beach, scuba diving (831/624-8413) off the shore, picnicking, and nature study. Take a walk through unique ecosystems and observe the indigenous wildlife while strolling through the rugged landscape. Be aware that from July through September fog often dims the summer sun at Point Lobos, even mid-day. Spring and fall are the best times to visit, weather-wise.

## ACCOMMODATIONS

### $100-150

**Lobos Lodge** (Monte Verde and Ocean Aves., 831/624-3874, www.loboslodge.com, $147) sits right in the midst of downtown Carmel-by-the-Sea, making it a perfect spot from which to dine, shop, and admire the endless array of art in the upscale town. Each of the 30 rooms and suites offers a gas fireplace, a sofa and table, a bed in an alcove, and enough space to stroll about and enjoy the quiet romantic setting. Do be aware that Lobos Lodge bills itself as an adult retreat. While families with children can stay here, expect to pay extra for more than two guests in your room, and there is little in the way of child-friendly amenities.

### $150-250

The name and exterior of the **Hofsas House** (San Carlos St. and 3rd Ave., 831/624-2745, www.hofsashouse.com, $150) evokes a quaint inn set in the Netherlands countryside. Yet the Hofsas House actually sits in a quiet semi-residential neighborhood within easy walking distance of downtown Carmel-by-the-Sea. Rooms in the rambling multi-story structure are surprisingly spacious, with nice furniture and linens that show just a touch of wear, and adequate bathrooms. If you can, get an ocean-view room with a patio or balcony, buy a bottle of wine, and spend some time sitting outside looking over the town of Carmel out toward the serene (from a distance) Pacific waters.

For folks who come to Carmel to taste wine, hike in the woods, and enjoy the less expensive golf courses, **Country Garden Inns** (102 W. Carmel Valley Rd., Carmel Valley, 831/659-5361, www.countrygardeninns.com, $170) offers a perfect spot to rest and relax. Actually composed of two inns, the Acacia and the Hidden Valley, Country Garden's small B&Bs offer violet and taupe French Country–style charm in the guest rooms, as well as a pool, a self-serve breakfast bar, and strolling gardens outdoors. Rooms run from romantic king-bed studios up to big family suites and most sleep at least four people (with daybeds in the window nooks).

### Over $250

Travelers with dogs and cats are welcome at the pet-friendly **Carmel Country Inn** (Dolores and 3rd Aves., 831/625-3263, www.carmelcountryinn.com, $245). The Inn does not, however, welcome children under six years old-it's a romantic hideaway, not a family motel. Rooms and suites boast comfortable furnishings that feel more like a friend's home than a generic hotel—you may find a fireplace, a reading nook, or even a Jacuzzi tub inside.

Despite its ghastly name, the cliff top **Tickle Pink Inn** (155 Highland Dr., 831/624-1244, www.ticklepinkinn.com, $314) offers tasteful luxury. Each room has a view of the ocean, an array of high-end furniture and linens, and all the top-end amenities you'd expect from a distinctive Carmel hostelry. For a special treat, shell out for the spa bath suite and watch the ocean while you soak in the tub with your sweetie.

## FOOD

### Breakfast

Need breakfast? Get it at **Katy's Place** (Mission and 6th Aves., 831/624-0199, www.katysplacecarmel.com, daily 7 A.M.–2 P.M., $10–20), a self-described "Carmel Tradition" that can get quite crowded on weekend mornings. You can get your favorite breakfast all day, whether you love heavy eggs Benedict or light Belgian waffles…well, as long as they're open.

### Asian

For a more authentic hole-in-the-wall locals' dining experience, seek out **Tommy's Wok**

(Mission St. and Ocean Ave., 831/624-8518, Tues.–Sun. 11:30 A.M.–2:30 P.M. and 4:30–9:30 P.M., $10–20). All the veggies are fresh and organic, and the dishes taste reliably good whether you dine in or order takeout to enjoy elsewhere.

### California

For a taste of wine country cuisine in the Carmel Valley, reserve a table at **Marinus at Bernardus Lodge** (415 W. Carmel Valley Rd., Carmel Valley, 831/658-3550, www.bernardus.com, daily 6–10 P.M., $40–70). The exquisite California cuisine features the produce, fish, and meat of local producers, and has been served to the likes of Julia Child and Leonardo diCaprio. Choose a three-, four-, or five-course meal, or go for broke and get the chef's tasting menu.

### French

Let go of any prejudices against "fancy French restaurants" and try a country-style meal in the unprepossessing dining room of **Le Coq D'Or** (Mission and 4th Sts., 831/626-9319, www.lecoqdor.com, daily 5–10 P.M., $35). Order a classic French beef stew or a German schnitzel, and perhaps share a juicy morsel with your canine companion, who is always welcome to dine with you out on the heated porch.



### Mediterranean

For cute ambiance, you can't beat the flower gardens and traditional cottage of **PortaBella** (Ocean Ave. and Monte Verde, 831/624-4395, www.carmelsbest.com, daily 11:30 A.M.–11 P.M., $20–40). This upscale-meets-kitsch restaurant serves Mediterranean inspired cuisine with a distinct local flair.

### Seafood

The **Flying Fish Grill** (Mission St. betw. Ocean and 7th Aves., 831/625-1962, Sun.–Thurs. 5–9 P.M., Fri.–Sat. 5–9:30 P.M., $30–40) serves Japanese-style seafood with a California twist in the Carmel Plaza open-air shopping mall. While the food isn't universally revered, the service at the Flying Fish and the presentation of the plates makes a visit worth the time and expense.

## INFORMATION AND SERVICES

You'll find the **Carmel Visitors Center** (San Carlos betw. 5th and 6th, 831/624-2522, www.carmelcalifornia.org, daily 10 A.M.–5 P.M.) right in the midst of downtown Carmel-by-the-Sea.

For more information about the town and current events, pick up a copy of the weekly ***Carmel Pine Cone*** (www.pineconearchive.com), the local newspaper.

The nearest major medical center to Carmel-by-the-Sea and the Carmel Valley is in nearby Monterey. For minor issues, head for the **Community Hospital of Monterey** (23625 Holman Hwy, Monterey, 831/622-2746, www.chomp.org).

## GETTING THERE AND AROUND

If you've made it to Monterey by car, getting to Carmel is a piece of cake. The quick and free way to get to Carmel from the north or the south is via Highway 1. From Highway 1, take Ocean Avenue into the middle of downtown Carmel. A more expensive but more beautiful route is the 17-Mile Drive (see *Sights*).

To get to the Carmel Valley, take Highway 1 to Carmel Valley Road, which is a major intersection with a stop light. Signs point the way to Carmel Valley.

As you read the addresses in Carmel-by-the-Sea and begin to explore the neighborhoods, you'll realize something interesting. There are no street addresses. (Some years ago Carmel residents voted not to enact door-to-door mail delivery, thus there is no need for numeric addresses on buildings.) So you'll need to pay close attention to the street names and the block you're on. Just to make things even more fun, street signs can be difficult to see in the mature foliage and a dearth of streetlights can make them nearly impossible to find at night. If you can, show up during the day to get the lay of the land before trying to navigate after dark.

# Big Sur

Big Sur beckons to many types of visitors. Nature-lovers come to camp and hike the pristine wilderness areas, to don thick wetsuits and surf the oft-deserted beaches, and even to hunt for jade in rocky coves. Some of these folks come to stay and find themselves at the amazing retreats hosted by the Esalen Institute.

On the other hand, some of the wealthiest people from California and beyond visit Big Sur to luxuriate at unbelievably posh hotels and spas with dazzling views of the ocean, flower-strewn meadows, art galleries, and fabulous cuisine.

Whether you prefer a low-cost camping trip or a pampered look into how the other 0.01 percent live, Big Sur offers its beauty and charm to all comers. Part of that charm is Big Sur's determination to remain peacefully apart from the Information Age—yes, this means that your cell phone won't work in many parts of Big Sur. Horrors!

Note: The term "Big Sur" can be confusing to non-locals. It's both a town and the semi-official name of the coastal region that runs south of Carmel and north of San Simeon delineated by Highway 1.

## SIGHTS

### Big Sur Coast Highway

Even if you're not up to tackling the endless hiking trails and deep wilderness backcountry of Big Sur, you can still get a good sense of the glory of this region just by driving through it. The Big Sur Coast Highway, a 90-mile stretch of Highway 1, runs along jagged cliffs and rocky beaches, through dense redwood forest, over historic bridges, and past innumerable parks. Construction on this stretch of road was completed in the 1930s, connecting Cambria to Carmel. You can start out at either of these towns and spend a whole day making your way to the other end of the road. The road has plenty of wide turnouts set into picturesque cliffs to make it easy to stop to admire the glittering ocean and stunning wooded

Big Sur's famous coastline

cliffs running right out to the water. Be sure to bring a camera on your trip along Highway 1-you'll find yourself wanting to take photos every mile for hours on end.

## Bixby Bridge

You'll probably recognize the Bixby Bridge when you come upon it on Highway 1 in Big Sur. The picturesque cement open-spandrel arched bridge is one of the most photographed bridges in the nation, and it's been used in countless car commercials over the years. The bridge was built in the early 1930s as part of the massive Government Works project that completed Highway 1 through the Big Sur area to connect the road from the north end of California to the south. Today, you can pull out either to the north or to the south of the bridge to take photos or just look out at the attractive span and Bixby Creek flowing into the Pacific far below.

Are there two Bixby Bridges? Nope, but the Rocky Creek Bridge (north of Bixby Bridge on Hwy. 1) is similar in design, if not quite as grand and picturesque.



## Big Sur Station

If you haven't yet stopped at one of the larger state parks in the area and hit the visitors center, pull in at Big Sur Station (Hwy. 1 south of Pfeiffer Big Sur, 831/667-2315, daily 8 A.M.–4:30 P.M.). The ranger station offers maps and brochures for all the major parks and trails of Big Sur, plus a minimal bookshop. Frankly, the visitor center and attendant services at Pfeiffer Big Sur State Park have the same or superior information to that available at Big Sur Station, so if you're planning to hit that park, skip this stop. However, several of the lesser parks and beaches (Limekiln, Garrapata, Sand Dollar) have no visitors services, so Big Sur Station serves a good purpose for visitors who plan to go only to those less-traveled spots. You can also get a free backcountry permit for the Ventana Wilderness here.

## Henry Miller Memorial Library

A number of authors have done time in Big Sur, soaking in the remote wilderness and sea air to gather inspiration for their work. Henry Miller lived and wrote in Big Sur for 18 years, and one of his works is titled for the area. Today the Henry Miller Memorial Library (Hwy. 1, 0.25 mile north of Deetjens, 831/667-2574, www.henrymiller.org, Wed.–Mon. 11 A.M.–6 P.M.) celebrates the life and work of Miller and his brethren in this quirky community center/museum/coffee shop/gathering place. The library is easy to find as you drive either north or south on Highway 1—look for the hand-painted sign and funky fence decorations. What you won't find is a typical lending library, bookshop, or slicked-up museum. Instead, you'll wander the lovely sun-dappled meadow soaking in the essence of Miller's life here, come inside and talk to the docents about the racy novels Miller wrote, and maybe sit back with a cup of coffee to meditate on life and art and isolated gorgeous scenery. The library offers a glimpse into the "real" world of Big Sur as a spread-out artists' colony that has inspired countless works by hundreds of people.

## Point Sur Light Station

Sitting lonely and isolated out on its cliff, the Point Sur Light Station (Hwy. 1, 0.25 mile north of Point Sur Naval Facility, 831/625-4419, tours year-round Sat.–Sun. 10 A.M. and 2 P.M., plus Apr.–Oct. Wed. 10 A.M. and 2 P.M., July–Aug. Thurs. 10 A.M., adults $8, children $4) keeps watch over ships navigating near the rocky waters of Big Sur. It's the only complete 19th-century light station in California that you can visit, and even here access is severely limited. First lit in 1889, this now fully automated light station still provides navigational aid to ships off the coast; families stopped living and working in the tiny stone-built compound in 1974. But is the lighthouse truly uninhabited? Take one of the moonlight tours (call for information) to learn about the haunted history of the light station buildings.

You can't make a reservation for a Point Sur tour, so you should just show up and park your car off Highway 1 on the west side by the farm gate. Your guide will meet you there and lead you up the paved road 0.5 mile to the light station. Once there, you'll climb the stairs up to the light, explore the restored keepers' homes and service buildings, and walk out to the cliff edge. Expect to see a great variety of wildlife, from brilliant wildflowers in the spring to gray whales in the winter to flocks of pelicans flying in formation at any time of year. Be sure to dress in layers; it can be sunny and hot or foggy and cold, winter or summertime, and sometimes both on the same tour! Tours last three hours and require more than a mile of walking, with a bit of slope and more than 100 stairs.

The farm gate is locked and there's no access to the light station without a tour group. Tour schedules can vary from year to year and season to season; it's a good idea to call ahead before showing up. If you need special assistance for your tour or have questions about accessibility, call 831/667-0528 as far in advance as possible of your visit to make arrangements. No strollers, food, pets, or smoking are allowed on light station property.

### Big Sur Spirit Garden

A favorite among local art-lovers, the Big Sur Spirit Garden (Hwy. 1, Loma Vista, 831/667-1300, www.bigsurspiritgarden.com, daily 9 A.M.–6 P.M.) changes a little almost every day. The "garden" part includes a variety of exotic plants, while the "spirit" part devotes itself to modern and postmodern Fair Trade art from as nearby as a few miles and as far away as India. The artwork tends toward brightly colored small sculptures done in a childlike, exuberant style. The Spirit Garden offers educational programs, community celebrations, musical events, and more. Call ahead for information on upcoming events.

## HIKING

The main reason to come to Big Sur is to hike its beaches and forests. As you cruise Highway 1, the parks line up for you.

### Garrapata State Park

A narrow two-mile long band of pretty light sand creates the beach at Garrapata State Park (Hwy. 1, gate 18 or 19, 831/624-4909, www.parks.ca.gov), north of the Point Sur Light Station. Stroll along the beach, scramble up the cliffs for a better view of the ocean, or check out the seals, sea otters, and sea lions near Soberanes Point. In the wintertime, grab a pair of binoculars to look for migrating gray whales passing quite close to shore here. The **Soberanes Canyon Trail** to the east of the highway is one of the more challenging and fun hikes to tackle at Garrapata.

Expect little in the way of facilities here—you'll park in a wide spot on Highway 1, and if you're lucky you might find a pit toilet open for use.

### Andrew Molera State Park

The first "Big Sur" park you'll encounter is Andrew Molera State Park (Hwy. 1, 22 miles south of Carmel, 831/667-2315, www.parks.ca.gov, day use $8). Once home to small camps of Esselen Native Americans, then a Spanish land grant, this chunk of Big Sur eventually became the Molera ranch. The land was used to grow crops and ranch animals, and as a hunting and fishing retreat for family and friends. In 1965, Frances sold the land to the Nature Conservancy, and when she died three years later the ranch was sold to the California State Park system as per her will. Today, the **Molera Ranch House Museum** (831/620-0541, bshs@mbay.net, Sat.–Sun. 11 A.M.–3 P.M.) displays stories of the life and times of Big Sur's human pioneers and artists as well as the wildlife and plants of the region. Take the road toward the horse tours to get to the ranch house.

The park has numerous hiking trails that run down to the beach and up into the forest along the river—many are open to biking and horseback riding as well. Most of the park trails lie to the west of the highway. The beach is a one-mile walk down the easy, multi-use **Trail Camp Beach Trail.** From there, climb on out on the **Headlands Trail,** a 0.25-mile loop, for a beautiful view from the headlands. If you prefer to get a better look at the Big Sur River, take the flat, moderate **Bobcat Trail** (5.5 miles round-trip) and perhaps a few of its ancillary loops. You'll walk right along the riverbanks, enjoying the local microhabitats. Just be sure to look out for bicycles and the occasional horse and rider. For an even longer and more difficult trek up the mountains and down to the beach, take the eight-mile **Ridge Bluff Loop.** You'll start at the parking lot on the Creamery Meadow Beach Trail, then make a left onto the long and fairly steep Ridge Trail to get a sense of the local ecosystem. Then turn left again onto the Panorama Trail, which runs down to the coastal scrublands, and finally out to the Bluffs Trail, which takes you back to Creamery Meadow.

At the park entrance, you'll find bathrooms but no drinkable water and no food concessions. If you're camping here, be sure to bring plenty of your own water for washing dishes as well as drinking. If you're hiking for the day, pack in bottled water and snacks.

McWay Falls

© LIZ HAMILL SCOTT

## Pfeiffer Big Sur State Park

The biggest, most developed park in Big Sur is Pfeiffer Big Sur State Park (47225 Hwy. 1, 831/667-2315, www.parks.ca.gov, day use $8). It's got the Big Sur Lodge, a restaurant and café, a shop, an amphitheater, a somewhat incongruous softball field, plenty of hiking-only trails, and lovely redwood-shaded campsites. This park isn't situated by the beach; it's up in the coastal redwoods forest, with a network of roads that can be driven or biked up into the trees and along the Big Sur River.



Pfeiffer Big Sur has the tiny **Ernest Ewoldsen Memorial Nature Center,** which features stuffed examples of local wildlife. It's open seasonally; call the park for days and hours. Another historic exhibit is the **Homestead Cabin,** once the home of part of the Pfeiffer family—the first European immigrants to settle in Big Sur. Day-trippers and overnight visitors can take a stroll through the cabins of the Big Sur Lodge, built by the Civilian Conservation Corps during the Great Depression.

No bikes or horses are allowed on trails in this park, which makes it quite peaceful for hikers. For a starter walk, take the easy, 0.7-mile **Nature Trail** in a loop from Day Use Parking Lot 2. Grab a brochure at the lodge to learn about the park's plant life as you walk the trail. For a longer stroll, head out on the popular **Pfeiffer Falls Trail,** 1.5 miles round-trip. You'll find stairs on the steep sections and footbridges across the creek, then a lovely platform at the base of the 60-foot waterfall where you can rest and relax midway through your hike. For a longer, more difficult, and interesting hike deeper into the Big Sur wilderness, start at the Homestead Cabin and head to the **Mount Manuel Trail** (10 miles round trip, difficult). From the Y-intersection with the Oak Grove Trail, it's four miles of sturdy hiking toMount Manuel, one of the most spectacular peaks in the area.

Need to cool off after hiking? Scramble out to the entirely undeveloped Big Sur River Gorge, where the river slows and creates pools that are great for swimming. Relax and enjoy the water, but don't try to dive here.

This is one of the few Big Sur parks to offer a full array of services. Before you head out into the woods, stop at the Big Sur Lodge restaurant and store complex to get a meal and some water, and to load up on snacks and sweatshirts. Between the towering trees and the summer fogs, it can get quite chilly and somewhat damp on the trails.

### Julia Pfeiffer Burns State Park

One of the best-known and easiest hikes in all of the Big Sur region sits in Julia Pfeiffer Burns State Park (Hwy. 1, 12 miles south of Pfeiffer Big Sur State Park, 831/667-2315, www.parks.ca.gov). The **Overlook Trail** runs only two-thirds of a mile round-trip, along a level wheelchair-friendly boardwalk. Stroll under Highway 1, past the Pelton wheel house, and out to the observation deck and the stunning view of McWay Falls. The medium-sized waterfall cascades year-round off a cliff and onto the beach of a remote cove, where the water wets the sand and trickles out into the sea. The water of the cove gleams bright cerulean blue against the just-off-white sand of the beach—it looks more like the South Pacific than Northern California. Anyone with an ounce of love for the ocean will want to build a hut right there beside the waterfall. But you can't—in fact, the reason you'll look down on a pristine and empty stretch of sand is that there's no way down to the cove that's even remotely safe.

The tiny Pelton wheel exhibit off the Overlook Trail isn't much unless you're a huge fan of hydraulic engineering history. It does have an interpretive exhibit (including the old Pelton wheel itself) describing what a Pelton wheel is and what it does. No other museums make their homes here, though there's a small visitors center adjacent to the parking lot.

If you're up for a longer hike after taking in the falls, go back the other way to pick up the **Ewoldsen Trail** (4.5 miles round-trip, moderate–difficult). This trek takes you through McWay Canyon, and you'll see the creek and surrounding lush greenery as you walk. Then you'll loop away from the water and climb up into the hills. Be sure to bring water, as this hike can take several hours.

If you want to spend all day at Julia Pfeiffer Burns State Park, drive north from the park entrance to the Partington Cove pullout and park along the side of the highway. On the east side of the highway, start out along the **Tanbark Trail** (6.4 miles round-trip, difficult). You'll head through redwood groves and up steep switchbacks to the top of the coastal ridge. Be sure to bring your camera to record the stunning views before you head back down the fire road to your car.

### Jade Cove Recreation Area

Jade Cove Recreation Area (Hwy. 1, two miles south of Sand Dollar Beach) is easy to pass as you barrel down Highway 1 towards San Simeon. A road sign marks the area, but there's not much in the way of a formal parking lot or anything else to denote the treasures of this jagged, rough part of the Big Sur coastline. Park in the dirt/gravel strip off the road and head past the fence and into the park. It's fun to read the unusual signs along the narrow, beaten path that seems to lead to the edge of a cliff. The signs explain that you cannot bring in mining equipment, or take away rocks or minerals obtained from behind the high-tide line. If you're into aerial sports, you can hang-glide off the cliffs here.

Once you get to the edge of the cliff, the short trail gets rough. It's only 0.25 mile, but it's almost straight down a rocky, slippery cliff. Don't try to climb down if you're not in reasonable physical condition, and even if you are, don't be afraid to use your hands to steady yourself. At the bottom, you'll find huge boulders and smaller rocks and very little sand. You may also see a small herd of locals dressed in wetsuits and scuba gear. But most of all, you'll find the most amazing minerals in the boulders and rocks. Reach out and touch a multiton boulder shot through with jade. Search the smaller rocks beneath your feet for chunks of sea-polished jade. If you're a hard-core rock nut, you can join the locals in scuba diving for jewelry-quality jade. As long as you find it in the water or below the high-tide line, it's legal for you to take whatever you find here.

Jade Cove has no water, no restrooms, no visitors center, and no services of any kind.

## SPORTS AND RECREATION

### Horseback Riding

You can take a guided horseback ride into the forests or out onto the beaches of Andrew Molera State Park with **Molera Horseback Tours** (831/625-5486, http://molerahorsebacktours.

com, $25–60). Tours of 1–2.5 hours depart each day starting at 9 A.M.—call ahead to guarantee your spot, or take a chance and just show up at the stables 15 minutes ahead of the ride you want to take. If you prefer, call to book a private guided ride for yourself and your party. Each ride takes you from the modest corral area along multi-use trails through forests or meadows, or along the Big Sur River, and down to Molera Beach. You'll guide your horse along the solid sands as you admire the beauty of the wild Pacific Ocean.

Molera Horseback Tours are suitable for children over six and riders of all ability levels; you'll be matched to the right horse for you. All rides go down to the beach. Tours can be seasonal, so call ahead if you want to ride in the fall or winter. Guides share their knowledge of the Big Sur region and wildlife, and welcome questions about the plants you're seeing as you walk your horse down the trail. Early-morning and sunset rides tend to be the prettiest and most popular.



## Backpacking

If you long for the lonely peace of backcountry camping, the **Ventana Wilderness** (www.ventanawild.org) area is ideal for you. This area comprises the peaks of the Santa Lucia Mountains and the dense growth of the northern reaches of the Los Padres National Forest. You'll find many trails beyond the popular day hikes of the state parks, especially as Big Sur stretches down to the south. Check the website to find reports on the conditions of the trails you've decided to tackle in advance, and stop in at Big Sur Station or the ranger station at Pfeiffer Big Sur State Park to get the latest news on the backcountry areas.

## Fishing

No harbors offer deep-sea charters around Big Sur, but if your idea of the perfect outdoor vacation must include a rod and reel, you can choose between shore and river fishing. Steelhead run up the Big Sur River to spawn each year, and a limited fishing season follows them up the river into **Pfeiffer Big Sur State Park** and other accessible areas. Check with Fernwood Resort (831/667-2422, www.fernwoodbigsur.com) and the other lodges around Highway 1 for the best spots this season.

The numerous creeks that feed into and out of the Big Sur River also play home to their fair share of fish. Cast for trout in the creeks of Pfeiffer Big Sur and other clear-water streams in the area. The California Department of Fish and Game (www.dfg.ca.gov) can give you specific locations for legal fishing, season information, and rules and regulations.

If you prefer the fish from the ocean, you can cast off several of the beaches for the rock fish that scurry about in the near-shore reefs. **Garrapata State Beach** has a good fishing area, as do the beaches at **Sand Dollar.**

## Scuba Diving

There's not much for beginner divers in Big Sur, but if you've got some underwater experience, you'll want to bring your gear when you visit this region. Expect cold water. Temperatures range in the mid 50s in the shallows, dipping into the 40s as you dive deeper down. Visibility is 20–30 feet, though rough conditions can diminish this significantly; the best season for clear water is September through November.

The biggest and most interesting dive locale here is the **Julia Pfeiffer Burns State Park** (Hwy. 1, 12 miles south of Pfeiffer Big Sur, 831/667-2315, www.parks.ca.gov, daily sunrise–sunset). You'll need to acquire a special permit at Big Sur Station and prove your experience to dive at this protected underwater park. The park, along with the rest of the coast of Big Sur, is part of the Monterey Bay National Marine Sanctuary. You enter the water from the shore, which gives you the chance to check out all the ecosystems, beginning with the busy life of the beach sands and heading out to the rocky reefs, then into the lush green kelp forests.

Divers at access-hostile **Jade Cove** (Hwy. 1, two miles south of Sand Dollar Beach) aren't usually interested in cute, colorful nudibranchs or even majestic gray whales. Jade Cove divers come to stalk the wily jade pebbles and rocks that cluster in this special spot. The semiprecious stone striates the coastline right here, and storms tear clumps of jade out of the cliffs and into the sea. Much of it settles just off the shore of the tiny cove, and divers hope to find jewelry-quality stones to sell for a huge profit.

If you're looking for a guided scuba dive of the Big Sur region, contact **Adventure Sports Unlimited** (303 Potrero St., #15, Santa Cruz, 831/458-3648, www.asudoit.com).

## Bird-Watching

Many visitors come to Big Sur just to see the birdies. The Big Sur coast is home to innumerable species, from the tiniest bush tits up to grand pelicans and beyond. The most famous avian residents of this area are no doubt the rare and endangered California condors. Once upon a time, condors were all but extinct, with only a few left alive in captivity and conservationists struggling to help them breed. Today, more than 30 birds soar above the trails and beaches of Big Sur. You might even see one swooping down low over your car as you drive down Highway 1! (You'll know it if one does this—a condor's wingspan can exceed nine feet.) Check with the park rangers for the best times and places to see condors during your visit.

The **Ventana Wilderness Society** (www.ventanaws.org) watches over many of the endangered and protected avian species in Big Sur. As part of their mission to raise awareness of the condors and many other birds, the VWS offers bird-watching expeditions; these can be simple two-hour tours or overnight wilderness camping trips, depending on your level of interest. Check their website for schedules and prices.

One of the hot spots of VWS conservation efforts and tours is Andrew Molera State Park. You can head out on your own to take a look around for some of the most interesting species in the Big Sur area. But wherever you choose to hike, be it beach or forest, you're likely to see a variety of feathered friends fluttering about.

## Spas

The **Allegria Spa at Ventana** (831/667-4222, www.ventanainn.com/spa.asp, daily 9 A.M.–7 P.M., until 8 P.M. in summer, $120/50-minute massage) offers a large menu of spa treatments to both hotel guests and visitors. You'll love the serene atmosphere of the treatment and waiting areas. Greenery and weathered wood create a unique space that help to put you in a tranquil state of mind, ready for your body to follow your mind into a state of relaxation. Indulge in a soothing massage, purifying body treatment, or rejuvenating or beautifying facial. Take your spa experience a step further in true Big Sur fashion with a reiki or craniosacral treatment. Or go for a private New Age reading, a personal yoga or meditation session, or a private guided hike. If you're a hotel guest, you can choose to have your spa treatment in the comfort of your own room or out on your private deck.

© LIZ HAMILL SCOTT

Japanese baths at the Allegria Spa, Ventana

Just across the highway from the Ventana, the **Post Ranch Inn and Spa** (Hwy. 1, 831/667-2200,, $135/hour massage) is another ultra-high-end resort spa. Massage, body, and facial work focuses on organics and gem and crystal therapies. You can also indulge in private sessions, including Shamanic meetings

## ESALEN: AN ADVANCED CALIFORNIA EXPERIENCE

The Esalen Institute is known throughout California as the home of California massage technique, a forerunner and cutting-edge player in ecological living, and a space to retreat from the world and build a new and better sense of self. Visitors journey from all over the state and beyond to sink into the haven that's sometimes called "The New Age Harvard."

One of the biggest draws of the Institute sits down a rocky path right on the edge of the cliffs overlooking the ocean. The bath house includes a motley collection of mineral-fed hot tubs looking out over the ocean – you can choose the Quiet Side or the Silent Side to sink into the water and contemplate the Pacific Ocean's limitless expanse, meditate on a perfect sunset or arrangement of stars, or (on the Quiet Side) get to know your fellow bathers.

Who will be naked. Regardless of gender, marital status, or the presence of others.

Esalen's bath house area is "clothing optional," its philosophy puts the essence of nature above the sovereignty of humanity, and it encourages openness and sharing among its guests – to the point of chatting nude with total strangers in a smallish hot tub. You'll also find a distinct lack of attendants to help you find your way around. Once you've parked and been given directions, it's up to you to find your way down to the cliffs. You'll have to find your own towel, ferret out a cubby for your clothes in the changing rooms, grab a shower, then wander out to find your favorite of the hot tubs. Be sure you go all the way outside past the individual clawfoot tubs to the glorious shallow cement tubs that sit right out on the edge of the cliff with the surf crashing just below.

In addition to the nudity and new-age culture of Esalen, you'll learn that this isn't a day spa. You'll need to make an appointment for a massage (at $150 a pop), which grants you access to the hot tubs for an hour before and an hour after your 75-minute treatment session. If you just want to sit in the mineral water, you'll need to stay up late. Very late. Inexpensive ($20) open access to the Esalen tubs begins on a first-come, first-serve basis at 1 A.M. and ends at 3 A.M. Many locals consider the sleep deprivation well worth it to get the chance to enjoy the healing mineral waters and the stunning astronomical shows.

If you're not comfortable with your own nudity or that of others, you don't approve of meditation or non-Christian spiritual philosophy, or you find it impossible to lower your voice or stop talking for more than 10 minutes, Esalen is not for you. If you've never done anything like this before, think hard about how you'll really feel once you're in the changing area with its open cubbies and naked hippies wandering about.

But if this description of a California experience sounds just fabulous to you, make your reservations now! The Esalen Institute (55000 Hwy. 1, 831/667-3000, fax 831/667-2724, www.esalen.org) accepts reservations by fax, mail, and phone if necessary. Go to the website for more information.



that focus on indigenous techniques that are said to enhance your life.

## ENTERTAIMENT AND EVENTS

The primary entertainment in Big Sur takes place out of doors. Listen to the symphony of the surf against the cliffs, admire the sculpture of 1,000-year-old coast redwoods, and pick up jewelry in the raw right off the beaches. But if you need a bit more, a few events and entertainment options appear in quiet, nature-loving Big Sur.

### Live Music

It probably won't surprise you to learn that Big Sur is not a hotbed of cutting-edge clubs and bars. Most folks who come here spend their days outside, hiking or doing some other vigorous activity. They drop into bed early, exhausted and needing the rest to get back out into the wilderness again the next day. But if you just can't bear to hit the sack before 10 P.M., you can find some fun at the **Fernwood Tavern** (Hwy. 1, 831/667-2422, Sun.–Thurs. noon–midnight, Fri.–Sat. noon–1 A.M.). Live music acts entertain locals and visitors alike, and you might hear country, folk, or even indie rock from the small stage. Most live music happens on weekends, especially Saturday nights, starting at 9 P.M. Even without the music, the tavern can get lively in the evenings (it's good to be the only game in town), with locals drinking from the full bar, eating, and holding parties in the meandering dim rooms.

### Festivals and Events

Each year, the Pacific Valley School hosts the fundraising **Big Sur Jade Festival** (www.bigsurjadeco.com/festival.html, Oct.). Come out to see the artists, craftspeople, jewelry makers, and rock hunters displaying their wares in the early fall. The school is located across Highway 1 from Sand Dollar Beach. Munch snacks as your feet tap to the live music playing as part of the festival. Check the website for the exact dates and information about this year's festival.

## CAMPING

Many visitors to Big Sur want to experience the unspoiled beauty of the landscape daily. To accommodate true outdoors lovers, many of the parks and lodges in the area have overnight campgrounds. You'll find all types of camping here, from full-service, RV-accessible areas to environmental tent campsites to wilderness backpacking. You can camp in a state park, or out behind one of the small resort motels near a restaurant and a store and possibly the cool refreshing Big Sur River. Pick the option that best suits you and your family's needs.

### Andrew Molera State Park

Andrew Molera State Park (Hwy. 1, 22 miles south of Carmel, 831/667-2315, www.parks.ca.gov, $10/night) offers 24 walk-in, tent-only campsites located 0.25–0.5 mile from the parking lot via a level, well-maintained trail. You'll pitch your tent in a pretty meadow near the Big Sur River, in a site that includes a picnic table and a fire ring. No reservations are taken, so come early in summertime to get one of the prime spots under a tree. While you're camping, look out for bobcats, foxes, deer, raccoons (stow your food securely!), and any number of birds.

As of 2007, no potable water was available at Andrew Molera. Toilets sit a short walk from the camping area, but you cannot shower here.

### Fernwood Resort

The Fernwood Resort (Hwy. 1, 831/667-2422, www.fernwoodbigsur.com) maintains a large campground area on both sides of the Big Sur River. You can choose between pitching your own tent, pulling in in an RV, or renting a tent cabin. The resort has easy access to the river, where you can swim, inner tube, and hike. You'll also have access to the restaurant, store, and tavern.

Tent cabins offer small canvas-constructed spaces with room for four in a double and two twins. You can pull your car right up to the back of your cabin. Bring your own linens or sleeping bags, pillows, and towels to make up the inside of your tent cabin. Hot showers and bathrooms are a short walk away. Tent campsites are scattered in great places—tucked in down by the river under vast shady redwood trees. You can even park your RV under a tree, then hook it up to water and electricity.

### Pfeiffer Big Sur State Park

The biggest and most developed campground in Big Sur sits at Pfeiffer Big Sur State Park (Hwy. 1, 800/444-7275, www.parks.ca.gov, $20). With 212 individual sites, each of which can take two vehicles and eight people or an RV (32 feet or shorter, trailers 27 feet max, dump station on-site), there's enough room for almost everybody here. During the summer, a grocery store and laundry facilities operate within the campground for those who don't want to hike down to the lodge, and plenty of flush toilets and hot showers are scattered throughout the campground. In the evenings, walk down to the Campfire Center for entertaining and educational programs. If you prefer a quieter and less asphalt-oriented camping experience, check out the hike-in and bike-in campgrounds that make up part of the Pfeiffer Big Sur complex.

Pfeiffer Big Sur fills up fast in the summertime, especially on weekends. Advance reservations (800/444-7275, www.reserveamerica.com) are highly recommended. Note that some campground sites were scheduled to be under construction until December 2009.

### Limekiln State Park

The small but pretty campground at Limekiln State Park (Hwy. 1 two miles south of Lucia, 831/667-2403, www.parks.ca.gov, summer only, $18) offers 33 campsites with hot showers and flush toilets out along an attractive creek that runs toward the nearby ocean. RVs and trailers can stay here (call for maximum length restrictions), though hookups and dump stations aren't available. In the summertime, the park recommends making reservations early. In the winter, no reservations are available and many sites are closed. Call for more information if you want to camp here in the off-season.

### Treebones Resort

For the ultimate high-end California green lodging-cum-camping experience, book a yurt (a circular structure made with a wood frame covered by cloth) at the Treebones Resort (71895 Hwy. 1, 877/424-4787, www.treebonesresort.com). The resort got its name from the locals' description of this scrap of land, which was once a wood recycling plant with sun-bleached logs lying about—"tree bones." Yurts ($155–280) at Treebones tend to be spacious and charming, with polished wood floors, queen beds, seating areas, and outdoor decks for lounging. There are also five walk-in campsites ($65 for two people). In the central lodge, you'll find nice hot showers and usually clean restroom facilities. Treebones offers a somewhat pricey casual dinner each night, and basic linens. If you like extra pillows and towels, you'll have to bring your own. Check the website for a list of items to bring and the FAQ about the resort facilities to make your stay more fun. While children are allowed in four of the yurts, Treebones recommends leaving behind kids under 12 years old—without any TVs, phones, or digital entertainment, little ones often get bored and unpleasantly loud.

## ACCOMMODATIONS

### Under $100

When locals speak of Deetjens, they could be referring to the inn, the restaurant, or the family that created both. But they all do speak of Deetjens, which operates as a non-profit organization dedicated to offering visitors to the Big Sur region great hospitality for reasonable rates. To stay at **Deetjens Big Sur Inn** (48865 Hwy. 1, 831/667-2377, www.deetjens.com, $80–200) is to become a small part of Big Sur's history and culture. It doesn't look like a spot where legions of famous writers, artists, and Hollywood stars have laid their precious heads, but Deetjens can indeed boast a guest register that many hostelries in Beverly Hills would kill for. And yet, the motley collection of buildings also welcomed transient artists, San Francisco bohemians, and the occasional criminal looking for a spot to sleep as they traversed the coast on bicycles or even on foot.

Your guest room will be unique, still decorated with the art and collectibles chosen and arranged by Grandpa Deetjen many moons ago. The inn prides itself on its rustic historic construction—expect thin weathered walls, funky cabin construction, no outdoor locks on the doors, and an altogether unique experience. Many rooms have shared baths, but you can request a room with private bath when you make reservations. Deetjens prefers to offer a serene environment, and to that end does not permit children under 12 unless you rent both rooms of a two-room building. Deetjens has no TVs or stereos, no phones in guest rooms, and no cell phone service. Two pay phones are available for emergencies, but other than that you're truly cut off from the outside world.

Decide for yourself whether this sounds terrifying or wonderful.

## $100-150

Along Highway 1 in the town of Big Sur, you'll find a couple of small motels. One of the more popular of these is the **Fernwood Resort** (Hwy. 1, 831/667-2422, www.fernwoodbigsur.com, $110). The low sprawl of buildings includes a 12-room motel, a small grocery-cum-convenience store, a restaurant, and a tavern that passes for the local nighttime hot-spot. Farther down the small road, you'll find the campgrounds, which include a number of tent cabins as well as tent and RV sites. If all this a "resort" makes, so be it. Your motel room will be a modest space in a blocky, one-level building off to the side of the main store and restaurant buildings. Not too much sunlight gets into the guest rooms, but the decor is light-colored and reasonably attractive. Rooms have queen beds and attached private bathrooms, but no TVs. If you tend to get chilly in the winter (or the summer fog), ask for a room with a gas stove. One room has a two-person hot tub sitting just outside on the back deck. In the summertime, book in advance to be sure of getting a room, especially on weekends.

Another lodge-style motel set in the redwood forest, the **Big Sur River Inn** (Hwy. 1 at Pheneger Creek, 800/548-3610, www.bigsurriverinn.com, $125–150) sits in one of the "populated" parts of Big Sur. First opened in the 1930s by a member of the legendary Pfeiffer family, the inn has been in continuous operation ever since. Today, it boasts 20 motel rooms, a restaurant, and a gift shop. Guest rooms are small but comfortable, with a juxtaposition of chain-motel comforters and curtains with rustic lodge-style wooden interior paneling. Budget-conscious rooms have one queen bed. Families and small groups can choose between standard rooms with two queen beds and two-room suites with multiple beds and attractive back decks that look out over the Big Sur River. All guests can enjoy the attractively landscaped outdoor pool with its surrounding lawn leading down to the river. The attached restaurant offers three meals a day. Be sure to make reservations in advance for summertime weekends!

## $150-250

If you want to stay inside one of the parks but tents just aren't your style, book a cabin at the **Big Sur Lodge** (47225 Hwy. 1, 800/424-4787, www.bigsurlodge.com, $199–289) in Pfeiffer Big Sur State Park. The lodge was built in the 1930s as a Government Works project to create jobs for people suffering in the Great Depression—by then Big Sur's astounding beauty and peace had been recognized by both federal and state governments, and much of the land was protected as parks for the enjoyment of the populace. Though the amenities have been updated, the cabins of Big Sur Lodge still evoke the classic woodsy vacation cabin. Set in the redwood forest along an array of paths and small roads, the cabins feature patchwork quilts, rustic furniture, understated decor, and simple but clean bathrooms. Many cabins have lots of beds—perfect for larger families or groups of adults traveling together. The largest cabins have fireplaces and kitchens. You can stock your kitchen at the on-site grocery store, or just get a meal at the lodge's restaurant or café.

The lodge has a swimming pool for those rare sunny summer days in the Big Sur forest. But the real attraction is its right-outside-your-door access to the Pfeiffer Big Sur trails. You can just leave your car outside your room and hike the day away inside the park. Or take a short drive to one of the other state parks and enjoy their charms for free with proof of occupancy at Big Sur Lodge.

Despite the forbidding name, **Ragged Point Inn** (19019 Hwy. 1, 805/927-4502, http://raggedpointinn.net, $200–300) takes advantage of its location to create an anything-but-ragged hotel experience for its guests. If you've come to Big Sur to bask in the grandeur of the Pacific Ocean, this is your hotel. The Ragged Point Inn perches on one of Big Sur's famous cliffs, offering stellar views from the purpose-built glass walls and private balconies or patios of almost every room in the house. Budget-friendly rooms still have plenty of space, a comfy king or two double beds, and those unreal ocean views. If you've got a bit more cash to burn, go for a luxury room, with optimal views, soaring interior spaces, plush amenities, and romantic two-person spa bathtubs. Outside your room, enjoy a meal in the full-service restaurant or get picnic supplies from the snack bar or the mini-mart, fill up for a day trip at the on-site gas station, or peruse the works of local artists in the gift shop or jewelry gallery. A special treat is the hotel's own hiking trail, which makes a 400-foot drop past a waterfall to Ragged Point's private beach.

### Over $250

If money is no object, you cannot possibly beat the lodgings at **Ventana** (48123 Hwy. 1, 800/628-6500, www.ventanainn.com, $385), a place where the panoramic ocean views begin in the parking lot. This might well be the best hotel in all of California. Picture home-baked pastries, fresh yogurt, in-season fruit, and organic coffee delivered to your room in the morning, then enjoying that sumptuous breakfast outdoors on your own private patio overlooking a wildflower-strewn meadow that sweeps out toward the blue-gray waters of the ocean. And that's just the beginning of an unbelievable day at the Ventana. Next, don your plush spa robe and rubber slippers (all you are required to wear on the grounds of the hotel and spa) and head for the Japanese bathhouse. Choose from two bath houses, one at each end of the property. Both are clothing-optional and gender segregated, and the upper house has glass and open-air windows that let you look out to the ocean. Two swimming pools offer a cooler hydro-respite from your busy life; the lower pool is clothing-optional, and the upper pool perches on a high spot for enthralling views. Almost every other amenity imaginable, including daily complimentary yoga classes, can be yours for the asking.

The guest rooms range from the "modest" standard rooms with king beds, tasteful exposed cedar walls and ceilings, and attractive green and earth tone appointments, all the way up through generous and gorgeous suites to full-sized multi-bedroom houses. If you have a stupid amount of money available, the Vista Suites boast the most beauteous hotel accommodations imaginable. You'll reach your room by walking along the paved paths crowded by lush landscaping, primarily California native plants that complement the wild lands of the trails behind the main hotel buildings. You can also take an evening stroll down to the Cielo dining room—the only spot on the property where you need to wear more than your robe and flip-flops. If you're headed to the Allegria Spa for a treatment, you can go comfy and casual.

**Post Ranch** (47900 Hwy. 1, 800/527-2200, www.postranchinn.com, $550–2,185) is another exclusive luxury resort perched on the cliffs of Big Sur. Spa, yoga, and a unique yet rustic atmosphere are just a few of its perks.

## FOOD

As you traverse the famed Highway 1 through Big Sur, you'll quickly realize that a ready meal isn't something to take for granted here. You'll see no McDonald's, Starbucks, 7-11s, or Safeways lining the road here. While you can find groceries, they tend to appear in small markets attached to motels. The motels and resorts usually have restaurants attached as well, but they're all-meals all-day or 24-hour kinds of places. Plan in advance to make it to meals during standard hours, and expect to have dinner fairly early. Pick up staple supplies before you enter the area if you don't plan to leave again for a few days to avoid paying premiums at the mini-marts.

### Casual Dining

Serving three meals each day to lodge guests and passersby, the **Big Sur Lodge Café and Restaurant** (47225 Hwy. 1, 800/242-4787, www.bigsurlodge.com, daily 7 A.M.–9 P.M., $23) has a dining room as well as a cute espresso and ice cream bar out front. The dining room dishes up a full menu of American classic for every meal, while you can grab a quick sandwich to go from the espresso bar.

The **Redwood Grill** (Hwy. 1, 831/667-2129,

www.fernwoodbigsur.com, daily 11:30 A.M.–9 P.M., $20) at Fernwood Resort looks and feels like a grill in the woods ought to. Even in the middle of the afternoon, the aging, wood-paneled interior is dimly lit and strewn with slightly saggy couches and casual tables and chairs. Walk up to the counter to order somewhat overpriced burgers and sandwiches, then on to the bar to grab a soda or a beer.

The northernmost restaurant on the Big Sur coast, **Rocky Point Restaurant** (36700 Hwy. 1, 831/624-2933, www.rocky-point.com, daily 9 A.M.–3 P.M. and 5 P.M.–close, $35) offers decent food and great views to Highway 1 travelers. Enjoy the smell of mesquite from the grill as you wait for your steak or fish to bring that scent right to your nose. Though meat-eaters will find all the good solid dishes they want for breakfast, lunch, and dinner, vegetarian options are limited.

The **Big Sur Bakery** (47540 Hwy. 1, 831/667-0520, www.bigsurbakery.com, Tues.–Sat. 5:30 P.M.–close, Sat.–Sun. 10:30 A.M.–2:45 P.M.) might sound like a casual, walk-up eating establishment, and the bakery part of it is. You can stop in from 8 A.M. every day to grab a fresh-baked scone, a homemade jelly donut, or a flaky croissant sandwich for lunch later on. But on the dining room side, an elegant surprise awaits diners who've spent the day hiking the redwoods and strolling the beaches. Be sure to make reservations or you're unlikely to get a table, and you'd miss out on the amazing clam chowder (with whole clams in their shells) and other unique California takes on classic American cuisine.

According to Big Sur locals, the best breakfast in the area can be had at **Deetjens** (48865 Hwy. 1, 831/667-2377, www.deetjens.com, breakfast and dinner daily, $10–28). The funky dining room with its mismatched tables, dark wooden chairs, and cluttered wall decor belies the high quality of the cuisine served here. Enjoy delectable dishes created from the freshest local ingredients for breakfast and then again at dinnertime.

### Fine Dining

You don't need to be a guest at the gorgeous Ventana to enjoy a fine gourmet dinner at **Cielo** (Hwy. 1, 831/667-4242, www.ventanainn.com/dining.asp, daily noon–3:30 P.M., 6–9 P.M., $28–38). The spacious dining room boasts a warm wood fire, an open kitchen, and comfortable banquettes with plenty of throw pillows to lounge against as you peruse the menu. If you're visiting for lunch or an early supper on a sunny day, be sure to request a table outside so you can enjoy the stunning views with your meal. The inside dining room has great views from the bay windows too, along with pristine white tablecloths and pretty light wooden furniture. Even with such a setting as Cielo has, the real star at this restaurant is the cuisine. The chef offers a daily-changing spread of haute California cuisine dishes, many of which feature organic or homegrown produce and local meats. To go with the seascape theme, Cielo's menu is heavy on sustainable seafood offerings. Be sure to tell your server if you're a vegetarian or have other dietary limitations—the chefs can whip up something special just for you. The best value at Cielo is the prix fixe menu, from which you can choose several courses. If you can possibly afford it, get the wine pairing with each course, and be sure to save room for dessert.

When you dine at **Nepenthe** (48510 Hwy. 1, 831/667-2345, www.nepenthebigsur.com, daily 11:30 A.M.–10 P.M., $30), be sure to ask for a table outdoors on even the partly sunny days. That way you get to enjoy both your Ambrosiaburger and the phenomenal cliff-top views. Open for lunch and dinner, the restaurant offers a short but tasty menu of meats, fish, and plenty of vegetarian dishes.

Outside, the seasonal **Café Kevah** at Nepenthe (breakfast and lunch Mar.–Jan., $10–12) patio offers a similar sampling at slightly lower prices. Just remember to keep munching on your Benedict or sandwich as you drape your arms over the wrought-iron railing and stare out into the mesmerizing blue-gray of the Pacific below and beyond you.

The **Sierra Mar** (47900 Hwy. 1, 831/667-2800, www.postranchinn.com, daily 8–10:30 A.M., noon–3 P.M., and 3–9 P.M., $100) restaurant at the Post Ranch Inn offers a decadent four-course prix fixe dinner menu in a stunning ocean-view setting. Lunch and snacks are served all through the afternoon to casual travelers, but expect to put on the ritz for a formal, white-tablecloth dining experience at this over-the-top-of-upscale restaurant.

### Markets

With no supermarkets or chain mini-marts in all of the Big Sur region, the local markets do a booming business. You can stock up on staples such as bread, lunch meat, eggs, milk, marshmallows, and graham crackers at various local stores. In town, the all-encompassing **Fernwood Resort** (Hwy. 1, 831/667-2422, www.fernwoodbigsur.com) has a market. You'll also find a seasonal market in the campground at Pfeiffer Big Sur State Park.

## INFORMATION AND SERVICES

The two most comprehensive visitors centers in Big Sur lie within **Pfeiffer Big Sur State Park** (47225 Hwy. 1, 831/667-2315, www.parks.ca.gov) and **Julia Pfeiffer Burns State Park** (Hwy. 1, 12 miles south of Pfeiffer Big Sur, 831/667-2315, www.parks.ca.gov). At Pfeiffer Big Sur, you'll find the visitors center grouped in with the Big Sur Lodge Restaurant, the hotel check-in, and a small store. A tiny nature museum lies a quarter mile or so up the park's main road. This visitors center is a good spot to get maps and information for hiking here and at other Big Sur parks that don't have manned visitors centers. This large park also offers laundry facilities, some basic staples at the store, and food all day long at the restaurant and attached espresso bar.

Farther south at Julia Pfeiffer Burns, the visitors center is easily accessible from the main parking lot. Again, rangers can advise you about hiking and activities both in their park and at other parks in the region. You'll find fewer services here than at Pfeiffer Big Sur—if you need to shop, do laundry, or gas up, head north.

Be aware that your cell phone may not work in all of Big Sur, especially out in the undeveloped reaches of forest and on Highway 1 away from the town of Big Sur and the Post Ranch. Call boxes are set at regular intervals along the highway.

For health matters, the **Big Sur Health Center** (46896 Hwy. 1, Big Sur, 831/667-2580, Mon.–Fri. 10 A.M.–5 P.M.) can take care of minor medical needs, and provides an ambulance service and limited emergency care. The nearest full-service hospital is the **Community Hospital of the Monterey Peninsula** (23625 Holman Hwy., Monterey, 831/624-5311).

## GETTING THERE AND AROUND

"Highway 1" sounds like a major freeway to many visitors, and down south it does get big and flat and straight. But along Big Sur, Highway 1 is a narrow, twisting, cliff-carved track that's breathtaking both because of its beauty and because of its dangers. Once you get five miles or so south of Carmel, expect to slow down—in some spots north of the town of Big Sur you'll be driving no more than 20 miles per hour around hairpin turns carved into vertical cliffs. If you're coming up from the south, Highway 1 is fairly wide and friendly up from Cambria, only narrowing into its more hazardous form as the cliffs get higher and the woods thicker. Be aware that fog often comes in on the Big Sur coast at sunset, making the drive even more hazardous (and much less attractive). If you must drive at night, take it slow!

Plan to spend several hours driving from Carmel to Cambria, partly to negotiate the difficult road and partly to make use of the many convenient turnouts to take photos of the unending spectacular scenery. Most of the major parks in the Big Sur region spring right off Highway 1, making it easy to spend a couple of days meandering along the road, stopping at Julia Pfeiffer or Andrew Molera to hike for a few hours or have a picnic on the beach.

# Cambria and San Simeon

The small beach town of Cambria becomes surprisingly spacious when you start exploring it. Plenty of visitors come here to ply Moonstone Beach, peruse the charming downtown area, and just drink in the laid-back, art-town feel. But Cambria owes much of its prosperity to the immense tourist trap on the hill that is Hearst Castle. Located about seven miles north in San Simeon, Hearst Castle, quite frankly, *is* San Simeon; the town grew up around it to support the overwhelming needs of its megalomaniacal owner and never-ending construction.

## SIGHTS

When it comes to this area, there is only one true sight. But once you're through with the castle tours, a few attractions in the lower elevations beckon as well. Nearby Cambria began and to a certain extent still is an artists colony; the windswept hills and sparkling ocean provide plenty of inspiration for painters, writers, sculptors, glassblowers, and more.

### Hearst Castle

There's nothing else in California quite like Hearst Castle (Hwy. 1 and Hearst Castle Rd., 800/444-4445, www.hearstcastle.com, tours daily 8:20 A.M.–3:20 P.M., $24). Newspaper magnate William Randolph Hearst conceived of the idea of a grand mansion in the Mediterranean style, on the land his parents bought along the central California coast. His memories of camping on the hills above the Pacific led him to choose the spot on which the castle now stands. He hired Julia Morgan, the first female civil engineering graduate from UC Berkeley, to design and build the house for him. She did a brilliant job with every detail, despite the ever-changing wishes of her employer. By way of decoration, Hearst assisted in the relocation of hundreds of European medieval and Renaissance antiquities, from tiny tchotchkes to whole gilded ceilings. William Randolph also adored exotic animals, and created one of the largest private zoos in the nation on his thousands of Central Coast acres. Though most of the zoo is gone now, you can still see the occasional zebra grazing peacefully along Highway 1 to the south of the castle, acting as heralds to the exotic nature of Hearst Castle ahead.

The visitors center is a lavish affair with a gift shop, restaurant, café, ticket booth, and movie theater. Here you can see the much-touted film *Hearst Castle—Building the Dream,* which will give you an overview of the construction and history of the marvelous edifice, and of William Randolph Hearst's empire. After buying your ticket, board the shuttle that takes you up the hill to your tour. (No private cars are allowed on the roads up to the castle proper.) There are five tours to choose from, each focusing on different spaces and aspects of the castle. Tour 1 is recommended for first-time visitors, and you're welcome to sign up for several tours over the course of one day. Tour 5 is a seasonal evening tour with volunteers

ROBERT HOLMES / CALTOUR

Hearst Castle

dressed in 1930s fashion welcoming guests as if to one of Hearst's legendary parties.

Expect to walk for at least an hour on whichever tour you choose, and to climb up and down many stairs. Even the most jaded traveler can't help but be amazed by the beauty and opulence that drips from every room in the house. Lovers of European art and antiques will want to stay forever. The two swimming pools—one indoor and one outdoor—shine with grandeur, all marble, glass tile, and mixed antique and custom-created statuary and fixtures.

The park recommends that visitors buy tour tickets at least a few days in advance, and even further ahead for Tour 5 and on summer weekends. For visitors with limited mobility, a special wheelchair-accessible tour is available. Strollers are not permitted. The restrooms and food concessions all cluster in the visitors center—but no food, drink, or chewing gum is allowed on any tour.

### Historic San Simeon

The tiny town of San Simeon existed primarily to support the construction efforts up the hill at Hearst Castle. The town dock provided a place for ships to unload tons of marble, piles of antiques, and dozens of workers. The general store and post office acted as a central gathering place for the community, and you can still walk up the weathered wooden steps and make a purchase here. Around the corner at the building's other door, you can buy a book of stamps or mail a letter at the tiny but operational post office.

The **William Randolph Hearst Memorial State Beach** (750 Hearst Castle Rd., San Simeon, 805/927-2020, www.parks.ca.gov, daily dawn–dusk) sits in San Simeon's cute little cove and encompasses the remaining structure of the old pier. You can lie on the beach or have a picnic up on the lawn above the sand.

### Nitt Witt Ridge

While William Randolph Hearst built one of the most expensive homes ever seen in California, local eccentric Arthur Harold Beal (a.k.a. Captain Nit Wit or Der Tinkerpaw) got busy building the cheapest "castle" he could. Nitt Witt Ridge (881 Hillcrest Dr., 805/927-2690, tours free by appointment only) is the result of five decades of scavenging trash and using it as building supplies to create a multi-story home like no other on the coast. Today, you can make an appointment with owners Michael and Stacey O'Malley to take a tour of the property. (Please don't just drop in.) It's weird, it's funky, and it's fun—an oddly iconic experience of the Central Coast.

### Cambria Cemetery

"Artsy" isn't a word that's usually associated with graveyards, but in Cambria it fits. The Cambria Cemetery (6005 Bridge St., 805/927-5158, www.cambriacemetery.com) reflects the artistic bent of the town's residents in its tombstone decor. Unlike many cemeteries, at Cambria the family and friends of the deceased are allowed to place all manner of personal objects at their loved ones' graves. You'll see painted tombstones, beautiful panes of stained glass, unusual wind chimes, and many other unique expressions of love, devotion, and art as you wander the 12 wooded acres.

## ACCOMMODATIONS

### $100-150

A favorite even among the many inns of Cambria, the **Olallieberry Inn** (2476 Main St., Cambria, 888/927-3222, www.olallieberry.com, $145) sits in a charming 19th-century Greek Revival home and adjacent cottage. Each of the nine rooms features its own quaint Victorian-inspired decor with comfortable beds and attractive appointments. A full daily breakfast (complete with olallieberry jam) rounds out the comfortable personal experience.

**Her Castle Homestay Bed and Breakfast Inn** (1978 Londonderry Ln., Cambria, 805/924-1719, www.HerCastle.cc, $127–170) is a bit different from your average B&B, with only two rooms available and lots of personal attention from the owners. When you make your reservations, you can ask about a half-day wine tour, dinner reservations, or even lunch and dinner provided by the inn. The Her Castle can be the perfect hideaway for two couples traveling together who desire the privacy of "their own house."

### $150-250

Many of the accommodations of Cambria sit along the small town's very own Hotel Row, a.k.a. Moonstone Beach Drive. One of these is the **Moonstone Landing** (6240 Moonstone Beach Dr., Cambria, 805/927-0012, www.moonstonelanding.com, $155), which provides inexpensive partial-view rooms with the decor and amenities of a mid-tier chain motel, as well as oceanfront luxury rooms featuring travertine marble bathrooms.

A charming log cabin structure shelters the eight rooms of the **J. Patrick House Bed and Breakfast** (2990 Burton Dr., Cambria, 805/927-3812, www.jpatrickhouse.com, $175). Each room has modern-country kitschy decor, a private bath, and plenty of amenities. They're dedicated to feeding you at the J. Patrick, with a big breakfast in the morning, hor d'oevres in the afternoon, and chocolate chip cookies at bedtime.

**The Burton Inn** (4022 Burton Dr., Cambria, 805/927-5125, www.burtoninn.com, $225) offers modernity in an attractive setting. Even the standard guest rooms offer tons of space, and the family suites have multiple bedrooms that promote both togetherness and privacy.

One of the cuter and more interesting lodgings on Moonstone Beach Drive, **Moonstone Cottages** (6580 Moonstone Beach Dr., Cambria, 805/927-1366, http://moonstone-cottages.com, $234) offers peace and luxury along with proximity to the sea. Expect your cottage to include a fireplace, a marble bathroom with a whirlpol tub, a flat-screen TV with a DVD player, Internet access, and a view of the ocean.

For a great selection of anything from economical standard rooms up to sizeable cabins, pick the **Cambria Pines Lodge** (2905 Burton Dr., 800/445-6868, www.cambriapineslodge.com, $150–400). All rooms have plenty of creature comforts, including TVs, private bathrooms, kitchenettes, and, in some cases, fireplaces.

## FOOD

**The Sow's Ear** (2248 Main St., Cambria, 805/927-4865, www.thesowsear.com, daily 5–9 P.M., $10–30) does its best to create the proverbial "silk purse" dining experience with its upscale comfort foods and romantically dim atmosphere. Some diners feel that the prices for items such as lobster pot-pie and chicken and dumplings can run a bit high, but if you're longing for a taste of old-fashioned Americana, you can get it here.

If the smell of the salt air on Moonstone Beach leaves you longing for a seafood dinner, head for the **Sea Chest Oyster Bar** (6216 Moonstone Beach Dr., Cambria, 805/927-4514, daily 5:30–9 P.M., $20–30, cash only). No reservations are accepted, so expect a long line out the door at opening time, and prepare to get there early (or wait a long while) for one of the window-side tables. The seafood here tends to be fresh, with a good selection of raw oysters, and touristfriendly.

Perhaps the most famous, if slightly overrated, restaurant in Cambria is the **Black Cat Bistro** (1602 Main St., Cambria, 805/927-1600, www.blackcatbistro.com, Thurs.–Mon. 5 P.M.–close, $20–40). An interesting California-French menu contains both small and large plates, each with a suggested wine pairing. Despite its fancy food, the Black Cat prides itself on its casual resort-town atmosphere.

Part of an expansive but still totally local family business, **Linn's Restaurant** (2277 Main St., Cambria, 805/927-0371, www.linnsfruitbin.com/restaurant, daily 8 A.M.–9 P.M., $10) serves tasty, unpretentious American favorites in a casual, family-friendly atmosphere. If you love the olallieberry pie with your meal, you can purchase a ready-to-bake pie, jam, or even vinegar at the Linn's café, gourmet shop, or their original farm stand while you're in Cambria.

In ubiquitously high-priced Cambria, one of the best food bargains in town is **Wild Ginger** (2380 Main St., Cambria, 805/927-1001, www.wildgingercambria.com, Fri.–Wed. 11 A.M.–2:30 P.M., 5–9 P.M., $15). This tiny pan-Asian café serves delicious, fresh food at its few tables, and carries an array of take-out fare displayed in a glass case crammed into the back of the dining room. Come early for the best selection of dishes.

## INFORMATION AND SERVICES

The town of Cambria does not boast a bricks-and-mortar visitors center, but you can do research in advance of your stay at http://cambriavisitorsbureau.com. If your primary interest is Hearst Castle, you'll find a huge visitors center at the parking lot below the castle where all tours start. Inside, you can buy and pick up tour tickets, grab a cup of coffee and a meal, and peruse the extensive bookshop, which includes many books about the Hearst family, the castle, and the town of Cambria.

The nearest hospital to Cambria is the **Twin Cities Hospital** (1100 Las Tablas Rd., Templeton, 805/434-3500), well east of the coast town. It sits near U.S. 101, just south of the junction of state Highway 46 and U.S. 101.

## GETTING THERE AND AROUND

Most Californians making a weekend getaway to Cambria from either Northern California or Southern California drive there. You can drive the Pacific Coast Highway (Highway 1) right into Cambria—this is the prettiest but not the fastest way to get there. For a quicker route, take U.S. 101 to the Paso Robles area and then turn west onto CA-46, which brings you right to the town of Cambria.

If you prefer to travel by rail, you can take **Amtrak's** Coast Starlight (www.amtrak.com) to either the Paso Robles or the San Luis Obispo (SLO) stations, and make arrangements to rent a car (easiest from SLO) or get alternative transportation out to the coast.



# Paso Robles

As an up-and-coming wine-growing region, Paso Robles has become a familiar destination and appellation for state residents and as well as a popular side trip from nearby Cambria. Huge crowds do not descend on Paso every weekend as they do in the more popular wine regions and you can still find room at the tasting bars, engage with knowledgeable tasting room staff, meet the occasional winemaker tending bar, and enjoy a friendly country atmosphere both in town and on the wine roads. For the best tasting experience, visit the Paso region over the weekend—many of the smaller winery tasting rooms are open only Thursday–Monday or even only Friday–Sunday.

## WINERIES

The wine industry is growing by leaps and bounds in and all around Paso. The Paso Robles region now boasts more than 200 wineries, over 100 of which have tasting rooms open to the public. For the purposes of this book, the sprawled landscape is divided into four easily navigable parts: Highway 46 West, Highway 46 East (which does not directly connect to Hwy. 46 West), Downtown Paso Robles, and Remote—the area to the north of town on several roads branching away from U.S.101.

### Highway 46 West

The densest concentration of wineries cluster along Highway 46 West and the little roads that spring off that main thoroughfare. Many intrepid wine tasters never make it past this short and easy-to-travel stretch, which locals refer to as the Westside.

One of the best of wineries in these parts is **Hunt Cellars** (2875 Oakdale Rd., 805/237-1600, www.huntcellars.com, daily 10:30 A.M.–5:30 P.M., tasting fee $5–10). Friendly and intensely knowledgeable staff members pour some of the best wines in Paso at this mid-sized, informal tasting room. You'll enter a building that looks more like a house than a winery, then choose the regular or reserve tasting. Also be sure to check the chalkboard behind the bar for the day's specialty offerings. All the wines at Hunt are grown in the family-owned Destiny Vineyard. The specialty of the house is Cabernet Sauvignon, and Hunt makes some of the best in California. You'll also get to taste a few Chardonnays, other red varietals, some red blends, and the famed (and expensive) port and dessert wines.

If you favor small wineries that only produce tiny runs of wine, **Dark Star Cellars** (2985 Anderson Rd., 805/237-2389, www.darkstarcellars.com, Fri.–Sun. 10:30 A.M.–5 P.M.) is perfect for you. Be sure to ask at the bar about the "synthetic gravity" that's so important to the slow fermentation process used at Dark Star. You'll taste about five vintages here—all red wines of the Bordeaux tribe. Most visitors think that the best of the lot is the much-lauded Ricordati, a Bordeaux blend that wins international awards year after year. Perhaps the nicest surprise of all comes when you've picked your favorites; prices at Dark Star range up to about $35 a bottle, and many are under $30.

## Highway 46 East

It's not as crowded as 46 West, but Highway 46 East has plenty of great wineries. You might even recognize one or two names out in the Eastside.

One of the biggest winemakers to maintain a tasting room in the Paso region is **Meridian** (7000 Hwy. 46 E., 805/226-7133, www.meridianvineyards.com, daily 10 A.M.–5 P.M., tasting fee $5). You've no doubt seen Meridian on many menus and countless supermarket shelves. Meridian makes all the classic California varietal vintages, with bestsellers in Chardonnay and Cabernet Sauvignon. Check out the Limited Release list for, well, a bunch more of the same plus a few slightly less common wines like a Gewurztraminer and a Sangiovese. Meridian's deli and store provide a perfect place to gather up everything you need for the perfect wine picnic.

It might not be the biggest, but **Eberle Winery** (3810 Hwy. 46 E., 3.5 miles east of U.S. 101, 805/238-9607, www.eberlewinery.com, daily 10 A.M.–5 P.M., until 6 P.M. in summer, free) is one of the pioneers of the Paso wine region. Gary Eberle has been making wine here for more than 25 years, and winning a passel of gold medals over that time. Be sure to get a spot on a cave tour while you're visiting, then head to the light-wood tasting room. Despite the fun statuary and the great caves at Eberle, the star attraction here is the wine. The medium-sized list features mostly hearty, bold red wines such as Cabernet Sauvignon, Barbera, Zinfandel, and a few fabulous blends. A few whites find their way to the bar, such as the Paso favorite Viognier and the lesser-known Roussanne. Taste as many as you possibly can—and you'll be surprised at how many bottles you'll want to walk away with. With most vintages selling for $15–25, you might be able to afford a few extras.

## Downtown Paso Robles

Many wineries have set up tasting rooms right in the middle of downtown Paso. It's hard to resist walking into a tasting room that bears the name **Midlife Crisis Winery** (1244 Pine St., Ste. A, 805/237-8730, www.midlifecrisiswinery.com, Thurs.–Mon. 10:30 A.M.–6 P.M.). Midlife Crisis is just that according to its owners, two veterans of the Los Angeles media circus who come up to Paso on the weekends to tend to their new pet winery. They got started in 2004, so you'll find mostly young vintages in the large, eclectic tasting room that's built into an historic Paso building. Heck, you might find one of the owner/winemakers in there, pouring, stocking, or just talking with employees and guests. Though the wines here leave plenty of room for improvement, the chatter and gossip are the best in the area. If you just ask a question or two, you'll learn everything you ever wanted to know about the wines and vineyards of the Paso Robles region.

If you're in town to find the best vintages possible, stop in at **Edward Sellers Vineyards & Wines** (1220 Park St., 805/239-8915, www.edwardsellers.com, Thurs.–Mon. 11 A.M.–6 P.M.). This one's a favorite of California cork dorks, creating a number of Rhone varietals and some fabulous blends that transcend their French roots and California styles to create something new. If you're a varietal lover, try Edward's Grenaches and Viogniers—less common wines that are picking up popularity with serious wine aficionados in California. The small tasting room with distressed white woodwork and a shining black counter makes room for several tasters at once, so belly on up and ask for a glass! And if you don't know your Cinsault from your Counoise, be sure to ask. The pourers are happy to answer any and all questions pertaining to Edward Sellers wines and vineyards.

What matches more perfectly with a glass of small-lot wine than a chunk of artisanal cheese? At **Orchid Hill Vineyard** (1140 Pine St., 805/237-7525, www.orchidhillwine.com, daily 11:30 A.M.–6 P.M.), you can get both. From Friday through Sunday, a tasting at Orchid Hill includes pairings with fine, flavorful cheeses that catch the attention of many a taster. Visitors also spend some time gaping at the walls, which bear original modern artwork by Jean Pierre de Rothschild. The small list of varietals, which includes Viogniers, Syrah, Sangiovese, and Zinfandel, includes some tasty wines (but they aren't the best in the area).



## Remote Wineries

Even if you don't love wine, it's worth the trip up to **Adelaida Cellars** (5805 Adelaida Rd., 800/676-1232, www.adelaida.com, daily 10 A.M.–5 P.M.). You'll get stunning views of Adelaida's mountain vineyards and down to the valley below. Adelaida wines are made with grapes grown on the estate vineyards, and the results can be fabulous. Adelaida takes advantage of its high elevation and difficult soil to raise grapes that produce small lots of top-tier boutique wines. Smoky, rich, angry-tasting Syrahs make up the backbone of Adelaida's list, which also includes Chardonnays, Rousannes, Vin Gris, Zinfandel, Pinot Noir, Cabernet Sauvignon, and a number of different and delicious blends. The winery produces vintages under four labels; the Reserve and Adelaida labels run toward the higher end, while the SLO and Schoolhouse labels provide tasty and affordable table wines suitable for everyday drinking.

A local producer with prestigious founders and backers, **Tablas Creek Vineyard** (9339 Adelaida Rd., 805/237-1231, www.tablascreek.com, daily 10 A.M.–5 P.M.) specializes in Rhone and Chateauneuf-du-Pape varietals and blends. Taste from the longish list of current commercial and winery-only vintages. Tablas Creek takes its winemaking seriously, maintaining its own grapevine nursery, keeping its vineyards organic, and using only its own yeasts created on-site. If such practices interest you, call in advance to get a spot on the daily vineyard and winery tours. End your survey of this showplace with a visit to the dark bar and bright artwork of the tasting room. You'll find many uncommon-for-California blends and varietals here, and the Tablas Creek bar staff can help you expand your palate and your knowledge of wine.

**Halter Ranch Vineyard** (8910 Adelaida Rd., 805/226-9455, www.halterranch.com, daily 11 A.M.–5 P.M.) sits on a 900-acre ranch property once owned by a pioneer of the Paso Robles area. In 2000, the ranch was bought by a Swiss emigrant who planted almost 250 acres to grapes from the Bordeaux and Rhone varietal families. All the vineyards are farmed using organic and sustainable methods, which combine with the limestone-rich soil and unique climate to help create intensely flavorful wines. The ranch is fronted by a charming white Victorian farmhouse, and tours (call in advance) take you around both this house and the other historic buildings on the property, as well as the two winemaking facility structures. This newish winery has a small list from which to taste and purchase; its flagship vintages are Syrah and Cabernet Sauvignon, but the less expensive Ranch Red and Ranch White blends are also good buys.

## Wine Festivals and Events

Consider coming to town during one of the several wine-oriented festivals held in and around Paso Robles each year. The biggest is the **Paso Robles Wine Festival** (www.pasowine.com/events/winefestival.php, $55–125), which happens over the third weekend of May each year. The central event of the festival, the Outdoor Wine Tasting, happens on Saturday in the Paso's downtown city park. More than 80 wineries bring out their wares, making it fabulously easy to find your favorites and learn about some new vintners in the region. In addition to the central tasting, most Paso wineries keep their tasting room doors open, offering tours, special tastings, food pairings, winemakers, and more. A recent addition to the festival, a golf tournament held on the festival weekend brings golfers from all over out for a round in the perfect Central Coast spring weather. Buy your tickets for the wine festival and the golf tournament well in advance; both events always sell out.

At the other side of the year, the **Harvest Wine Tour Weekend** (www.pasowine.com/events/harvest.php) celebrates the changing foliage of the grapevines and the frantic rush to bring in the grapes and start the juices fermenting. Nearly 100 wineries throughout Paso put on events during the third weekend of October. Check with your favorites to learn what's coming this year. You might want to sign up early for a cooking class, or just show up to join in on some messy but fun grape stomping. If you're lucky, you might even get to take a tour of a winemaking facility in full furor, and learn a bit about how your favorite vintages are made. As with the spring Wine Festival, it's a good idea to book your room and make your plans early for the Harvest Tour—the event has become quite popular with wine aficionados across the state and beyond.

### Wine Tours

If you prefer not to do your own driving on your wine-tasting excursions (something to consider if everyone in your party enjoys wine), take one of the many available wine tours. **The Wine Wranglers** (866/238-6400, http://thewinewrangler.com, $90–120 depending on pick-up location) offers daily group tours, plus customized individual tours for a higher fee. Experienced guides will take you to some of the biggest and best wineries in the region. Group tour guests ride in the comfort of a small luxury bus; buses pick up tasters from Cambria, San Luis Obispo, Morro Bay, Pismo Beach, Paso Robles itself, and a number of other towns in the county. A picnic lunch in one of the vineyards is included, as are all tasting fees at the wineries you visit. If you know the region, feel free to request a stop at your favorite winery!

If you prefer to tour the vineyards in the privacy of your own rented limo, book a car with **At Your Service Limousine** (805/239-8785, www.tcsn.net/ays, $200–325). This company offers Paso wine tours up to five hours long, with room for up to eight riders for no additional fee. Tasting fees are included with your car.

## SIGHTS

It's not the biggest or most diverse, but you'll have fun exploring the **Charles Paddock Zoo** (Lago Ave. at Hwy. 41, Atascadero, 805/461-5080, www.charlespaddockzoo.org, daily 10 A.M.–4 P.M., adults $5, children $4). Plan an hour or two to make a leisurely tour of the fierce tigers, funky prehensile-tailed raccoons, and famous slender-tailed meerkats. You can also visit the aviary to enjoy the twitters and squawks of more than a dozen varieties of common and exotic birds. The Zoo makes a fun destination if you've brought your kids to the largely adult playground that is Paso Robles.

A good spot for younger kids is the **Paso Robles Children's Museum at the Volunteer Firehouse** (623 13th St., Paso Robles, 805/238-7432, www.pasokids.org, Mon., Thurs.–Sat. 11 A.M.–5 P.M., adults $7, children $6). As much a playground as a museum, the space offers themed interactive exhibits with a slight educational bent for toddlers and elementary school-aged children. Kids can draw, paint, climb, jump, play, and learn in one of the few spots in Paso Robles dedicated entirely to the younger set.

The **Paso Robles Pioneer Museum** (2010

Riverside Ave., 805/239-4556, www.pasoroblespioneermuseum.org, Thurs.–Sun. 1–4 P.M.) celebrates the settlement of San Luis Obispo County. Exhibits have a distinctly Western Americana flavor and includes some larger displays of carriages, farm equipment, and even an old one-room schoolhouse.

## SPORTS AND RECREATION

**Harris Stage Lines** (5995 N. River Rd., 805/237-1860, www.harrisstagelines.com) doesn't offer the typical sedate trail rides. Instead of climbing up onto the back of a horse, you'll get into a refurbished historic coach or wagon and go for a ride like they did in the 19th century. Harris has a restored stagecoach, a chuck wagon, and even a couple of Hollywood-built Roman-style chariots. Call in advance to arrange the perfect outing for your party. If you're really into the historic vehicle scene, you can even book a private driving lesson. Riding lessons are also available.

The craze for floating above vineyards in a balloon basket has made it as far as Paso Robles. This wine region sits in a pretty valley that's perfect for a romantic ballooning jaunt. **Let's Go Ballooning!** (4295 Union Rd., 805/458-1530, http://sloballoon.com, $189/person) can take you on a one-hour ride up over the Paso wine country any day of the week. You'll meet early at the Rio Seco Winery and spend 2–3 hours with your pilot, preparing and learning about how to ride safely.

Several minutes' drive from downtown Paso, the **River Oaks Hot Springs & Spa** (800 Clubhouse Dr., Paso Robles, 805/238-4600, www.riveroakshotsprings.com, Sun.–Thurs. 9 A.M.–9 P.M., Fri.–Sat. 9 A.M.–10 P.M., $12–16/hour) sits on country club land over one of the local sulfur-heavy mineral springs. You'll smell the sulfur even as you drive up and walk from the parking lot to the spacious lobby. An attendant will show you the facilities and guide you to your room. A popular and reasonably priced option here is an hour of relaxation and healing in one of the outdoor or indoor-open-air hot tubs. You can use the faucets to set your own perfect temperature, and gaze out into the thick gardens that screen the spas from the adjacent golf course. For a more thoroughly relaxing experience, pick a massage or facial treatment to go with your hot tub (or alone, if you don't care for sulfur water). Check the website for package specials (many of which include wine served in the privacy of your hot tub room) and aesthetic treatment options.

## ACCOMMODATIONS

Accommodations around Paso Robles tend toward upscale wine-themed B&Bs. **Le Domaine at Moss Ridge Vineyard** (1855 Twelve Oaks Dr., 805/227-4372, www.ledomainebb.com, $217, no smoking, no children under 16) sits on the Moss Ridge Vineyard, giving guests an up-close and personal view of the vines from each of the three French country style rooms. Serenity, privacy, luscious wine-country food, and luxurious amenities mark your stay at this tiny boutique inn.

The **Orchard Hill Farm Bed & Breakfast** (5415 Fairhills Rd., 805/239-9604, www.orchardhillbb.com, $220) has a more English country feel. The attractive manor house offers luxurious rooms with top-tier amenities, a gourmet breakfast, and attractive grounds for walking and lounging.

Out in the wooded region between Paso and the coast, the **Chanticleer Vineyard Bed and Breakfast** (1250 Paint Horse Pl., 805/226-0600, www.chanticleervineyardbb.com, $217, no smoking, no children) offers relaxed vacationing and fun pets. Each of the three rooms includes an iPod dock, organic spa toiletries, a fresh seasonal breakfast, and access to the house stock of cute fuzzy animals.

Rounding out the B&B offerings, **The Canyon Villa** (1455 Kiler Canyon Rd., 805/238-3362, www.thecanyonvilla.com, $224) is built in the Mediterranean style that suits this area so well. The decor of the four guest rooms continues the Italianate theme, while the oversized spa tubs, posh linens, and gas fireplace create a feeling of lush comfort.

## FOOD

**Gaetanos** (1646 Spring St., 805/239-1070, Mon.–Sat. 11:30 A.M.–2 P.M. and 5:30 P.M.–close, $10–30) serves traditional Italian fare with friendly flare. Order the handmade pizza and a glass of the house wine (the restaurant's own label), all accompanied by above-average service.

Getting back to the heavily Mexican influence of Paso's agricultural roots, grab a taco or two at **Papi's** (840 13th St., 805/239-3720, daily 11 A.M.–9 P.M., $10). Prices may be a bit higher than some taquerias, in honor of Paso's new tourist status, but the casual atmosphere and tasty enchiladas make up for it.

It's not the fanciest place in town, but the food at **Panolivo** (1344 Park St, 805/239-3366, www.panolivo.com, Mon.–Thurs. 8–3 P.M., Fri.–Sat. 8–3:30 P.M., Sun. 9 A.M.–3:30 P.M., dinner Fri.–Sat. nights $17–28) might be the tastiest truly traditional French cuisine in town. Panolivo serves breakfast and lunch on the weekdays, adding dinner on the weekends. The casual dining room makes it easy to linger over a croque monsieur and dark coffee, though visitors just passing through can grab a luscious pastry from the display case up front.

At **Artisan** (1401 Park St., 805/237-8084, www.artisanpasorobles.com, daily 11 A.M.–10 P.M., $10–30) old school American cookery gets a California wine country makeover. The white tablecloths and numerous wine glasses hint at the fancy cuisine to come—unusual

### MORE THAN WINE

The warm Mediterranean valley climate makes a good landscape for growing olives as well as the grape. Several groves of the silvery-green trees produce high-quality fruit that orchard owners press into small batches of artisan olive oil. A number of orchards cluster here, offering fresh local olive oil and an array of cured olives. If you just can't stomach another ounce of wine, clear your palate at one of the open olive tasting rooms.

One of these growers is **Olea Farm** (2985 Templeton Rd., Templeton, 805/610-2258, www.oleafarm.com, Sat.-Sun. 10 A.M.-4:30 P.M.). This orchard and its tasting room are located to the east of downtown Paso Robles. On a visit, you can take a tour of the orchards, then head inside to taste the different types of olive oil made from the Arbequina olive trees grown here. With five or more distinct flavors of oil to choose from, you'll certainly find a favorite to bring home with you. Be sure to say hi to Oak, the orchard dog, when you visit.

**Mt. Olive Organic Farm** (3445 Adelaida Rd, Paso Robles, 805/237-0147, www.mtoliveco.com, Thurs.-Sun. 10 A.M.-5 P.M., Apr.-Oct. until 7 P.M.) grows far more than just olives. The diverse crops at Mt. Olive range from cherries and apricots to sprouts to vegetables, as well as grass-fed beef and free-range chickens. The storefront sells meat, eggs, and the wide variety of produce grown here, plus an array of products made from the produce – such as jams, fruit leathers, dried fruits, and nuts. If you've been trekking through the Far Out wineries and need a meal, you can also get fresh, hot, organic cuisine here. The small menu might include steak and chicken dishes, spaghetti, pizza, and soup. To drink, try the fresh-squeezed seasonal juices and slushies.

Down in Atascadero, call ahead to schedule a visit to the **Green Acres Lavender Farm** (8865 San Gabriel Rd., Atascadero, 805/466-0837, www.greenacreslavenderfarm.com, daily 10 A.M.-6 P.M., by appointment). One thing is certain: You will leave smelling good. This four-plus-acre farm grows 12,000 lavender plants – mostly Grosso and Provencal for their high oil production. At the farm stand or on the website you can purchase an array of natural products made from and with lavender oil. Choose a bottle of pure essential oil to create your own means for scenting your home, soy candles, lavender soaps, lavender sachets, or even a jar of culinary lavender you can use in cooking. The owners and staff will be happy to give you suggestions for using their products, and to expound on the benefits of lavender in your home.

soups and sandwiches at lunch and high-end entrées at dinner.

## PRACTICALITIES

The closest thing to a visitors center is the **Paso Robles Chamber of Commerce** (1225 Park St., 805/238-0506, www.pasorobleschamber.com, Mon.–Fri. 8 A.M.–5 P.M., Sat.–Sun. 10 A.M.–2 P.M.). Pick up a guide to Paso Robles, or specific dining, lodging, and winery information.

For medical attention, the nearest hospital is **Twin Cities Hospital** (see *Cambria* for more information).

The two best ways to get to Paso Robles are by car and by train. Drivers can take Highway 101 from the north or the south to directly to town. Once in Paso Robles, take Highway 46 east for the main wine road.

On the rails, the **Amtrak** Coast Starlight (www.amtrak.com) stops right in Paso. Avoid driving altogether by taking the train into town, then renting a limo or getting on with a wine tour.

# Santa Barbara

It's called the American Riviera, with weather, community, and sun-drenched beaches reminiscent to some of the European coast of the Mediterranean Sea. In truth, Santa Barbara is all California. Culturally, Santa Barbara sits in Southern California but the pace of life slows down just enough to make for a comfortable vacation. Many of the visitors to Santa Barbara do in fact come from elsewhere in California, and the town is known to residents as one of the best "local" beach resorts. In the town proper, you'll find lots of museums, outdoor shopping areas, and great restaurants. Inland a bit, a growing young wine region thrives. Along the soft, flat sandy beaches cluster fabulous four-star beach resorts.



## SIGHTS

### Santa Barbara Maritime Museum

It's only fitting that the Santa Barbara Maritime Museum (113 Harbor Way, 805/962-8404, www.sbmm.org, Thurs.–Tues. 10 A.M.–5 P.M., until 6 P.M. Memorial Day–Labor Day, adults $7, children/seniors $4, free for military personnel in uniform) sits right on the working harbor. It began as a Government Works Project during the Depression. For more than 50 years, the station was used by the U.S. Navy as a training facility. After being sold back to the city of Santa Barbara in 1995, construction began on the museum, which opened in 2000. Over a dozen different exhibits show off the history of the California coast's relationship to the high seas. The Munger Theater screens high- definition educational films each day. The Children's Area features hands-on exhibits that make learning about the sea lots of fun for younger visitors. Many other galleries tell the maritime history of California, beginning with the local Chumash Native Americans, running through the whaling and fur-hunting eras, up through the modern oil drilling and commercial fishing industries. You can also learn a bit about sailing and yachting, safety on the Pacific, and how you can help preserve the ocean's environment.

### Santa Barbara Museum of Natural History

Continuing the outdoors theme that pervades Santa Barbara, the Santa Barbara Museum of Natural History (2559 Puesta del Sol, 805/682-4711, www.sbnature.org, daily 10 A.M.–5 P.M., adults $10, youth $7, children $6) has exhibits to delight visitors of all ages. Inside, visit the large galleries that display stories of the life and times of insects, mammals, birds, and dinosaurs. Learn a little about the human history of the Santa Barbara area at the Chumash exhibit. Head outdoors to circle the immense skeleton of a blue whale, and to hike the Mission Creek Nature Trail. If you're interested in the nature of worlds other than this one, go into the **Gladwin Planetarium** and wander the Astronomy Center exhibits. The Planetarium hosts daily shows portraying the moon and stars, plus monthly Star Parties and special events throughout the year.

If you're more interested in the Earth's array of sea life, head down to Stearns Wharf and visit the **Ty Warner Sea Center** (211 Stearns Wharf, 805/962-2526, www.sbnature.org/seacenter, daily 10 A.M.–5 P.M.), which is operated by the Museum of Natural History (multi-museum passes at either location, adults $8, youth $7, children $5) Check out the tunnel through the 1,500-gallon surge tank, touch a sea cucumber, examine microscopic sea creatures, and get involved in the science of oceanography.

## Santa Barbara Zoo

It's not the biggest zoo in the state, but the Santa Barbara Zoo (500 Ninos Dr., 805/962-5339, www.sbzoo.org, daily 10 A.M.–5 P.M., adults $11, children $8). is a cool little municipal zoo. It shelters its critters in enclosures that resemble those of the San Diego Zoo, including a multi-species habitat that mimics an African savannah with giraffes, tortoises, cranes, and rodents all hanging out together. Granted, the pride of lions next door are corralled away from the giraffes, but you can get close to them and occasionally hear them roar. The Santa Barbara Zoo also takes pride in its local, endangered species—the Channel Island foxes are indigenous to an area only 20 miles from the zoo. The new California condor exhibit shows off one of the rarest birds in the state, still an endangered species. As you slowly stroll along the paths, you'll also see cute lemurs, huge elephants, monkeys, and gibbons. One of the best-named kids' exhibits ever, "Eeeww!" showcases reptiles and wonderful slimy amphibians at children's eye level.

If you need a stroller or wheelchair, you can rent one just inside the zoo. Also close to the gate you'll find the Ridley-Tree House Restaurant, which offers plenty of outside tables and a walk-up arrangement that sells sandwiches and burgers. In season, small carts ply the pathways, selling coffee, popsicles, and more. The gift shop offers cute souvenirs for both kids and adults.

## Santa Barbara Botanic Gardens

The year-round perfect weather makes for a perfect spot to grow the gorgeous Santa Barbara Botanic Gardens (1212 Mission Canyon Rd., 805/682-4726, www.santabarbarabotanicgarden.org, daily 9 A.M.–5 P.M., until 6 P.M. Mar.–Oct., adults $8, youth $6, children $4). The gardens focus solely on the indigenous plants of California, with plantings from the deserts, chaparral, arroyo, and more. The gardens spread out over many acres, and crosses several hiking trails. Check out the coastal redwood forest, the centerpiece of the park, which remains shaded and cool even when the sun beats down in the heat of summertime. Another proud garden shows off the beauty of native California lilacs. The mission of the gardens encompasses conservation of not only the California wilderness areas, but the water and soil in developed areas as well. Visit the Home Demonstration Garden for an example of beautiful landscaping using California natives that are suited to the climate and conditions, and thus need less irrigation and chemical fertilizers.

Guided tours are offered each day with your admission ticket—join the standard tour or call ahead to arrange a private tour. You can take your own self-guided tour with a map and the advice of the docents. The shop offers books and garden-themed gifts, while the nursery sells native Californian plants. The garden does not include a restaurant or snack bar.

## Santa Barbara Mission

Often referred to as "Queen of the Missions," the Santa Barbara Mission (2201 Laguna St., 805/682-4713, http://santabarbaramission.org, daily 9 A.M.–4:30 P.M., tours $5 adults, $4 senior, $1 youth, children 6 and under free) is second to none for its art displays of art and graceful architecture, all of which are complemented by the serene local climate and scenery. Unlike

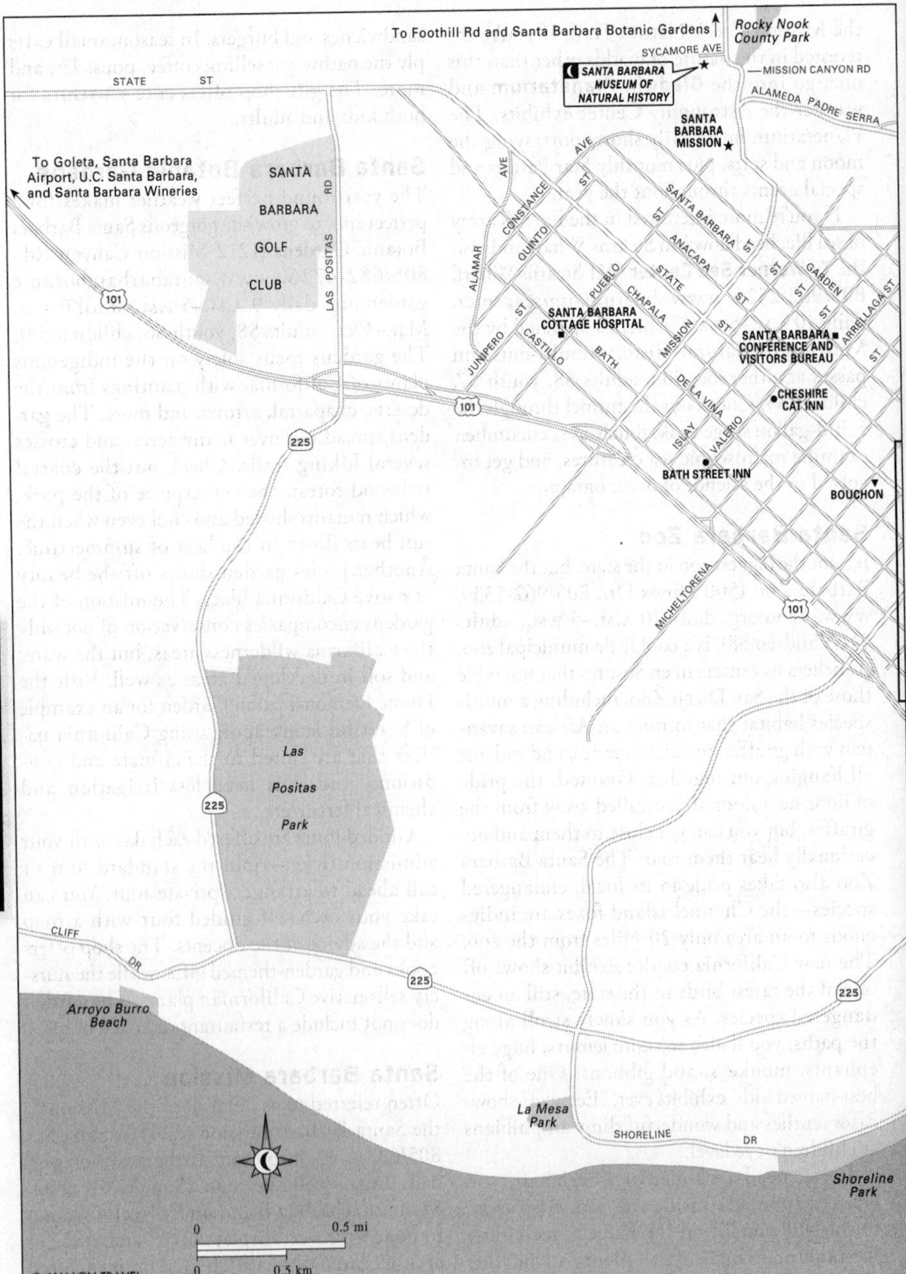
To Foothill Rd and Santa Barbara Botanic Gardens
Rocky Nook County Park
SYCAMORE AVE
SANTA BARBARA MUSEUM OF NATURAL HISTORY
MISSION CANYON RD
ALAMEDA PADRE SERRA
STATE ST
SANTA BARBARA MISSION
To Goleta, Santa Barbara Airport, U.C. Santa Barbara, and Santa Barbara Wineries
SANTA BARBARA GOLF CLUB
LAS POSITAS RD
ALAMAR AVE
CONSTANCE AVE
QUINTO ST
SANTA BARBARA ST
ANACAPA ST
STATE ST
GARDEN ST
ARRELLAGA ST
PUEBLO ST
CHAPALA ST
JUNIPERO ST
CASTILLO ST
BATH ST
MISSION ST
DE LA VINA
SANTA BARBARA COTTAGE HOSPITAL
SANTA BARBARA CONFERENCE AND VISITORS BUREAU
CHESHIRE CAT INN
ISLAY
VALERIO
BATH STREET INN
BOUCHON
MICHELTORENA
101
225
Las Positas Park
CLIFF DR
Arroyo Burro Beach
La Mesa Park
SHORELINE DR
Shoreline Park
0
0.5 mi
0
0.5 km
© AVALON TRAVEL

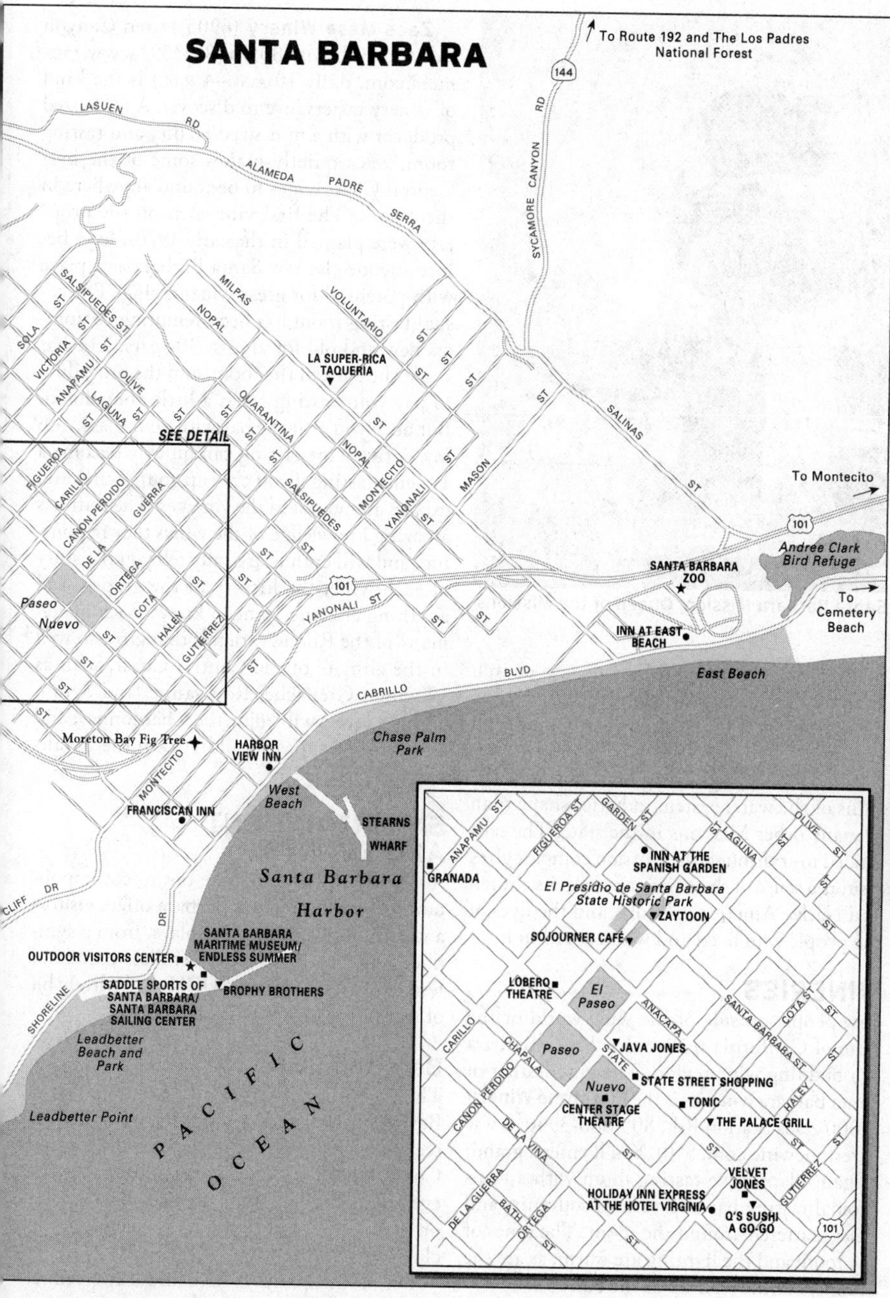


CENTRAL COAST

ROBERT HOLMES / CALTOUR

Santa Barbara Mission, Queen of the Missions



many of the California Missions, the church at Santa Barbara remained in service after the secularization of the Mission chain in the 19th century. When you visit, you'll find the collection of buildings, art work, and even the ruins of the water system in better shape than at many other Missions in the state. The self-guided tour through the Mission complex gives visitors a sense of the Mission's story, its church and Native American history, and the lives of the people who lived and worked within it.

## WINERIES

Few people outside of the wine world or the state of California realize that Santa Barbara is a budding wine region. The grandfather of Santa Barbara wineries is the **Firestone Winery** (5000 Zaca Station Rd., 805/688-3940, www.firestonewine.com, $10). You'll enter a grand, elegant Napa-style tasting room with a trapezoidal tasting bar and various souvenirs and cases scattered around the room. The tones of the room and the lighting are warm, as are the manners of the staff up at the bar.

**Zaca Mesa Winery** (6905 Foxen Canyon Rd., Los Olivios, 805/688-9339, www.zacamesa.com, daily 10 A.M.–4 P.M.) is the kind of winery tasters love to discover. A mid-sized producer with a mid-sized facility and tasting room, Zaca quietly makes some of the best Central Coast wines to be found anywhere in the region. The first vineyards on the property were planted in the early 1970s, long before anyone else saw Santa Barbara as a place with potential for great winemaking. The casual tasting room has been tempting customers new and old for almost 30 years. The bar sits at the back of the room, and the procedure to pay your tasting fee is a little convoluted. But once you're at the bar with your glass...oh my. A five-wine tasting can quickly become a 12-wine tasting if you chat up your pourer and express an interest in the vintages. The staff has amazing knowledge of the wines they're pouring, and will enthusiastically tell you the story of each wine, the history of the grapes, and anything else you want to know. Zaca makes many of the Rhone varietals that grow so well in the climate of the Central Coast, such as Viognier, Grenache, Roussanne, and Syrah. Classics lovers will enjoy the Chardonnay, and adventurous types shouldn't skip the Syrahs and the Z Cuvee.

## ENTERTAINMENT AND EVENTS

A wealthy town with close ties to cosmopolitan Los Angeles, Santa Barbara offers visitors a wealth of live cultural displays, from a symphony and opera to a near-endless parade of festivals. The students of UCSB add a lively bit of zest to the town's after-dark scene.

### Bars and Clubs

The proximity of UCSB to downtown Santa Barbara guarantees a more lively nighttime scene than you'll find elsewhere on the Central Coast. Check with the locals to discover the ever-changing hot spots du jour. Bars cluster on State Street and beyond, and plenty of hip clubs dot the landscape here.

For a uniquely California experience,

head for **Q's Sushi a Go Go** (409 State St., 805/966-9177, www.qsbilliards.com/santa barbara, Mon.–Sat. 4 P.M.–2 A.M.). Shoot a game of pool, get your dance on to local DJs, or sit down to a high-quality sushi dinner. Or do all three in the same night at the same spot! With four bars, a full sushi menu, and a lovely SOS (stands for Sick of Sushi) entrée menu, you can eat and drink the night away at Q's, or fuel up for an energetic session on the dance floor. Q's has three levels to suit a variety of entertainments. At the bar, order any mixed drink you can dream up, or one of the tasty on-tap beers.

Only two blocks up, **Tonic** (634 State St., 805/897-1800, www.tonicsb.com) has a hipster feel, complete with exposed brick walls and a long glass bar. Top-flight DJs spin h a mostly hip hop or house groove, with the occasional mash-up for variety. Check Tonic's Myspace page for a list of upcoming DJs. Two lounges provide a respite from the partiers at the main bar and on the dance floor. To cool down, go outside to the huge outdoor patio, which has its own funky octagonal bar.

If you prefer to dance and drink to live bands, head over to **Velvet Jones** (423 State St., 805/965-8676, www.velvet-jones.com, daily 9 P.M.–2 A.M.). Artists ranging from rapper KRS-One to goth-rock Evanesce to Alien Ant Farm have played Velvet Jones. Thursday through Saturday, bands take the stage for the dancing, yelling crowds. On other nights of the week, you might find karaoke, live comedy, or a DJ spinning. Check the calendar at the website for upcoming events and shows. Even if you're not into the scene, this bar is worth walking into just for the funky giant murals on the walls and the handblown glass ornaments (in a rock club!!) adorning the bar.

## Live Music

The **Lobero Theater** (33 E. Canon Perdido St., 805/966-4946, www.lobero.com) plays host to national and international jazz acts, folk and soft rock groups and singers, an annual percussion festival, and more. Everyone from the SFJazz Collective to Ani DiFranco has performed here. The medium-sized theater has only one level, and it's filled with cushy red velvet seats—perfect for a music-filled night out on the town or a romantic date with your sweetie. Check the website for the shows coming up during your visit. Also be sure to look into the annual film festival. You can buy tickets online, by phone, or at the box office during your stay.

## Classical Music

The **Santa Barbara Symphony** (805/898-9626, www.thesymphony.org) aspires to compete with its brethren in Los Angeles and San Francisco. The symphony orchestra puts up seasons that pay homage to the greatest composers the world has ever seen, plus the works of less-known but equally talented artists. Whether you prefer Mozart or Mahler, you can listen to it at the Granada (1214 State St.) concert hall. Every seat has a great view of the stage, and the acoustics were designed with music in mind, making for an overall great symphony experience.

**Opera Santa Barbara** (www.operasb.com) has put up such classics as *Tosca, Rigoletto,* and *Madama Butterfly.* The festival format OSB has used for the last few years lets you take in two operas in a single weekend, if that's your choice. In fine tradition, OSB enjoys a focus on the classics and little-known works of the Italian masters. Operas are staged at the Lobero Theater (33 E. Canon Perdido St., 805/963-0761, www.lobero.com), a mid-sized space that allows for a more intimate operatic experience than those you find in larger cities.

## Dance

At the **Center Stage Theater** (751 Paseo Nuevo, 805/963-0408, www.centerstage theater.org, $22–50 depending on show), look for everything from Pulitzer Prize–winning dramas to traveling nouveau ballet companies. Center Stage focuses on dance, offering more ballet and modern dance performances than it does plays. But the plays, some of which are staged by the Santa Barbara Theater Company, tend to be some of the newest and best in the country. You won't see much Shakespeare or too many classics—instead you're likely to see *Doubt* or *The Pillowman* or something else that's fresh from Broadway and the Tony Awards.

## SHOPPING

If you're looking for a fairly standard shopping expedition in Santa Barbara, go to **State Street.** From end to end, this busy main drag hosts a near-unbelievable array of mall-style stores, plus a few independent boutiques for variety. You'll find lots of lovely women's apparel, plenty of housewares stores, and all the usual stuff you'd expect to find in a major urban shopping center. In truth, there's little that's truly special on State Street—it's a sprawled-out, mid-to-upper tier mall.

## SPORTS AND RECREATION

With the year-round balmy weather, it's nearly impossible to resist the temptation to get outside and do something energetic and fun in Santa Barbara. From golf to sea kayaking, you've got plenty of options for recreation here.



### Beaches

There's nothing easier than finding a beach in Santa Barbara. Just follow State Street to its end, and you'll be at the coastline. Municipal beaches flank Stearns Wharf on either side—rather uncreatively named **East Beach** (1400 Cabrillo Blvd., www.santabarbaraca.gov, daily sunrise–10 P.M.) and **West Beach** (West Cabrillo Blvd., www.santabarbaraca.gov, daily sunrise–10 P.M.). In fine SoCal tradition, these beaches are broad and flat and sandy, lending themselves to Frisbee and ball games, beach volleyball, and lots of lounging about in the sunshine.

To the north of town, **Arroyo Burro Beach** (Cliff Dr., 805/687-3714, www.sbparks.org, daily 8 A.M.–sunset) is a favorite for dog-owning locals. To the right as you face the water, dogs are allowed off-leash to dash across the packed sand and frolic and fetch out in the gentle surf. Arroyo Burro is rockier than the downtown beaches, making it less friendly to games and sunbathers. But the rocks and shells make for great beachcombing, and you might find a slightly smaller crowd on sunny weekend days. You'll find a snack bar, restrooms, outdoor showers, and a medium-sized pay parking lot for your convenience.

### Surfing

It's not one of the legendary California surfing locales, but there are waves to be caught in Santa Barbara, if you don't mind surfing in the shadow of the ever-present oil derricks.

A great spot for newbies to both surfing and the area is **Leadbetter Point** (Cabrillo past Stearns Wharf). The locals are reasonably welcoming, and the small right break makes for easy and fun rides. Another small-wave spot sits right in front of the east edge of **UC Santa Barbara at Isla Vista** (bordered by El Colegio Rd., Ocean Rd., and Camino Majorca). You'll find a big crowd of college students here (UCSB even has a surf team!), but the point break similar to that at Leadbetter is friendly to longboarders and newer surfers. Do watch out for the naturally occurring tar that mars the water and the beach sands.

For a bit more of a challenge, paddle out to the barrels at **Sand Spit** (Santa Barbara harbor). This break only really works in the wintertime when a big western swell comes in, and the water can be unpleasantly dirty. But its location within sight of the Harbor and Stearns Wharf makes it convenient.

If there's such a thing as One True Break in Santa Barbara, it's **Rincon** (U.S. 101 at Bates Rd. on the Ventura County line). If you start at the right spot, you can catch a ride over a mile long here. The sets are reliable and the waves are bigger than most other Santa Barbara breaks. For obvious reasons, locals flock to Rincon so you'll definitely be part of a crowd when you surf here.

Looking for surfing lessons? Check out the **Santa Barbara Surf School** (www.santabarbarasurfschool.com). The instructors have decades of surfing experience and pride themselves on being able to get beginners up and riding in a single lesson.

surfers paddling



## Kayaking and Sailing

One of the best ways to see the Santa Barbara harbor and bay is under your own power in a kayak. A number of rental and touring companies offer lessons, guided paddles, and good advice for exploring the region. **Paddle Sports of Santa Barbara** (117B Harbor Way, 805/899-4046, www.kayaksb.com, Thurs.–Tues. 10 A.M.–6 P.M., $10–20/hour, tours $50–215) has everything you need to paddle the waters of Santa Barbara and Ventura. You can rent a sit-on-top or closed-deck sea kayak to take your own ride around the harbor or out into the bay. If you want to hit the Channel Islands, you must take a guided tour. Paddle Sports offers all-day trips around Santa Cruz Island, Anacapa Island, and Santa Barbara Island, as well as more sedate two- to four-hour trips around the harbor and down the Santa Barbara waterfront. Most trips are suitable for paddlers of all experience and ability levels, but be sure to tell the staff when you book if you've never been in a kayak before. If that's the case and you prefer to get some experience before you take one of the longer tours, Paddle Sports offers lessons in both sit-on-top and closed-deck kayaking. Whether you choose a lesson or a tour, reservations in advance are recommended, especially for summer weekend days.

The **Santa Barbara Sailing Center** (133 Harbor Way, 805/350-9090, http://sbsail.com, tours $65) offers a full range of kayaking options, from rentals to tours to classes, plus some great trips for more advanced paddlers. The basic excursion takes you to the Mesa Coast via one of the company's yachts, then drops you off onto a single- or double-seat sit-on-top kayak. You might see dolphins, seals, sea lions, or even migrating whales as you paddle along towards your destination: the harbor docks. For something more intense, call the SBSC to arrange a private intermediate or advanced tour.

SBSC also offers sailing excursions aboard the 50-foot *Double Dolphin* sailing catamaran.

## Fishing and Whale-Watching

Santa Barbara's prime location on the coast makes it a great spot for deep-sea fishing and whale-watching. With its proximity to the feeding grounds of the blue and humpback whales, Santa Barbara is one of the best spots to go whale-watching in the state.

If you're looking for a whale-watching expedition or a dinner cruise, check out the **Condor Express** (Harbor Way, 805/882-0088, www.condorcruises.com, adults $50–100, children $30–50). In the summertime, they can take you out to the Channel Islands to see the blue and humpback whales feed; in the winter, the captain sails into the path of migrating gray whales. The boat is a sleek modern speed demon with posh amenities and lots of outdoor deck space that can seat almost 70 people. Whale-watching cruises depart almost daily all year long; call to purchase tickets in advance.

**Captain Don's** (219 Stearns Wharf, Ste. G, 805/969-5217, www.captdon.com) offers whale-watching and pleasure cruises with a fun pirate theme. Pleasure trips include a quick 30-minute ride around the Santa Barbara Harbor that's geared toward fun for the kids or a 90-minute sunset cocktail cruise that includes rum drinks with your ticket. Whale-watching cruises leave several times each day, heading out to the Channel Islands in the summertime and the Channel itself in winter.

If you want to go fishing, give **WaveWalker Charters** (691 Camino Campana, 805/964-2046, www.wavewalker.com) a call. This private six-passenger charter boat rents for $700 for a three-quarter day—expensive unless you bring five friends along to split the cost! Bait and all tackle are included with the charter, but a fishing license is not. Call for more information about what you can fish for when.



## Golf

It might not get the most press of the many golf destinations in California, but with its year-round mild weather and resort atmosphere, Santa Barbara is a great place to play a few holes. There are six public courses within an hour of downtown Santa Barbara—everything from a popular municipal course to championship courses with views of the ocean from the greens.

It's still a golf course, but **Glen Annie** (405 Glen Annie Rd., 805/968-6400, www.glenanniegolf.com, $60–75, carts $6–11) has worked with Audubon International to create wildlife habitats on its land. Who knows what you might see when you're out walking the lush, green, 18-hole, par-72 course? Well, you'll definitely get great views of the town of Santa Barbara, the ocean, and the Channel Islands on this hilly course. The Frog Bar & Grill, the on-site restaurant, draws any number of non-golfers up to Glen Annie for lunch. Set in a castle-like structure, the Frog serves California cuisine dishes that are a far cry from most clubhouse fare. So come for the golf, stay for the unusual and delicious fare.

If you're already interested in exploring Santa Barbara's wine country, consider reserving a tee time at **La Purisima Golf Course** (3455 Hwy. 246, 805/735-8395, $30–80). This golf course, built in 1986, gets high praise for its design and difficulty level—even if you're an expert golfer, "La Piranha" will test your skills. The par 72 course is a 45-minute drive from downtown Santa Barbara, but many locals think it's worth the trip. In addition to the 18 holes, you can access the grass driving range, the short-game practice area, and the pro shop. A number of PGA and LPGA golf pros are on hand to help you improve your game.

The **Sandpiper** (7925 Hollister Ave., 805/968-1541, www.sandpipergolf.com, $60–140, cart $16) boasts some of the most amazing views you'll find in all of Santa Barbara. They're so great because they're right up close, and on several holes your ball is in danger of falling into the world's largest water trap. And hey, there's a great championship rated 74.5, 18-hole, par 72 golf course out there on that picturesque beach too! Take advantage of the pro shop and on-site restaurant, but do be aware of the semi-formal, denim-free dress code Sandpiper enforces. It's not cheap, but a long walk on the beach with a great golf game in the middle of it seems well worth it to an endless stream of golfers who rank Sandpiper as one of their favorite courses.

### Spas

Folks who can afford to live in Santa Barbara tend to be able to afford many of the finer things in life, including massages, facials, and luxe skin treatments. You'll find a wide array of day spas and medical spas in town.

**Beleza Skin Care Center** (219 Gray Ave., 805/966-2373, www.belezaskincare.com) sits in the Studio E Healing Arts center. This high-end spa specializes in the best skin care money can buy, with a focus on anti-aging and acne treatments. Choose from an array of luxurious facials, chemical and herbal peels, microdermabrasion, makeup consultation, and permanent makeup application. You'll walk into the charming spa with its live plants and Eastern decor, check in, and be led back into your treatment room. Most facials and treatments last an hour or more. Beleza also offers a full menu of waxing services.

If you prefer a slightly more natural spa experience, book a treatment at **Le Reve** (21 W. Gutierrez, 805/564-2977, www.le-reve.com). Using biodynamic skin care products and pure essential oils, Le Reve makes good on the advertising billing it as an "aromatherapy spa." Choose from an original array of body treatments, massage, hand and foot pampering, facials, and various aesthetic treatments. If you're up for several hours of relaxation, check out the spa packages that combine facials with massage and body treatments.

**Cielo Spa and Boutique** (1725 State St., Ste. C, 805/687-8979, www.cielospasb.com) prides itself on its warm, nurturing environment. Step inside and admire the scents and the soft lighting and the natural, new agey decor. Contemplate the colorful live orchids, feel soothed by the flickering candlelight, and get lost in the tranquil atmosphere. The menu of services has an almost Northern Californian flare, with signature Champagne treatments and a focus on organics and natural lotions and potions. Check into the luxury packages that combine massages, facials, and more for a full day in the spa.

## ACCOMMODATIONS

If you want a posh beachside room in Santa Barbara, you'd better be prepared to pay for it. All the seaside resorts charge a premium rate. On the other hand, Santa Barbara offers several charming and reasonably priced accommodations near downtown and other attractions.

### $100–150

A lovely little boutique hotel in a quiet residential neighborhood near the beach, the **Franciscan Inn** (109 Bath St., 805/963-8845, www.franciscaninn.com, $125–160) looks just like a Spanish Colonial Revival hacienda, with pale adobe-style walls and a traditional red-tiled roof. Guest rooms offer everything from cute, economical, double-bed rooms to luxurious multiple-room suites. The decor tends toward the flowery, with designer wallpaper and comforters. The largest suite sleeps six comfortably; smaller rooms can sleep four if they're friendly. The amenities add to the charm of the place; you can grab a complimentary fresh croissant and a cup of coffee for breakfast, or a warm cookie in the afternoon. Take a swim in the heated pool, check your email with the free Wi-Fi, or even throw in a load of laundry at the on-site coin-op machines. Stearns Wharf and downtown are a short walk away.

The **Bath Street Inn** (1720 Bath St., 805/682-9680, www.bathstreetinn.com, $140–315) specializes in small-town charm and hospitality. It's large for a B&B, with eight rooms in the Queen Anne main house and another four in the more modern summer house. Each room has its own unique color scheme and style. Certainly you'll find some traditional floral Victorian decor, but many of the rooms are done up with elegant stripes rather that cloying blooms. Some rooms have king beds, others queens, and several have two-person whirlpool tubs. Despite the vintage trappings, the Bath Street Inn features modern amenities such as flat-screen TVs and free Wi-Fi. Early each morning, a sumptuous home-cooked breakfast is served downstairs. Choose between sharing your meal with your fellow guests in the dining room, or escaping to the sunny garden patio for a bit of privacy.

If you're in Santa Barbara to soak up the sun on the sandy beaches, book a room at the **Inn at East Beach** (1029 Orilla Del Mar, 805/965-0546, www.innateastbeach.com, $140–400). Unsurprisingly, it's just across the road from East Beach, and a nice walk along the waterfront boardwalk will take you to Stearns Wharf and to downtown. This smallish motor lodge gained notoriety when President Ronald Regan was in office, and his staff stayed at the inn while he spent time at his Santa Barbara ranch. Today, guests find sizeable rooms done up in blue carpets and comforters with pine furniture and a strange plethora of telephones. The inn prides itself on its attractive swimming pool and courtyard area, and you can feel free to bring down a bottle of wine and enjoy the balmy evenings with fellow guests. If you're planning a longer stay, get a kitchen suite so you can cook your own meals and take advantage of the inn's guest laundry facilities.



## $150-250

If you're willing to pay a premium rate for your room, the **Cheshire Cat Inn** (36 W. Valerio St., 805/569-1610, www.cheshirecat.com) can provide you with true luxury B&B accommodations. Each room has an *Alice in Wonderland* name, but the decor doesn't really match the theme—instead of whimsical and childish, you'll find Victorian floral elegance. Guest rooms are spread out through two Victorian homes ($199–299), the coach house ($279–379), and two private cottages ($369–399). Some rooms have suite-level space and amenities, including spa tubs and private balconies. Relax in the evening in the spacious octagonal outdoor spa, or order a massage in the privacy of your own room. Each morning, come downstairs and enjoy a light breakfast.

It's a chain now, but the **Holiday Inn Express at the Hotel Virginia** (17 W. Haley St., 805/963-9757, www.hotelvirginia.com, $170–275) has lots of history in Santa Barbara. Sitting right on the corner of the main drag, the Hotel Virginia welcomed guests come to take the waters and enjoy the scenery of Santa Barbara starting in 1925. Ten years ago it was renovated to bring it up to code and to spiff up the older guest rooms. Today it is run by the folks at Holiday Inn Express, but they elected not to eradicate the historic charm and atmosphere of the Virginia. When you walk into the lobby, you'll step onto a red-tiled floor and gaze upon a bright, multihued blue fountain. Upstairs, your room will feature antique-looking furnishings, exuberant floral bedspreads and curtains, and swirly green carpets. The smallish bathrooms feature prized showerheads, and the beds have both cotton and feather pillows to choose from. If you choose to stay in your room for a while, you can make yourself coffee to sip while watching your LCD flat-screen. The restaurants and shops of State Street are steps from the lobby, and the beach isn't too much farther.

## Over $250

For a taste of Santa Barbara's posh side, stay at the **Inn at the Spanish Garden** (915 Garden St., 805/564-4700, www.spanishgardeninn.com, $280–575). This small boutique hotel gets it right from the first glimpse; the building in the historic Presidio neighborhood has the characteristic whitewashed adobe exterior with a red-tiled roof, arched doorways, and wooden balconies. Courtyards seem filled with lush greenery and tiled fountains, while the swimming pool promises relief from the heat. Inside, guest rooms and suites whisper luxury with their white linens, earth-toned accents, and rich, dark wooden furniture. Enjoy the benefits of your own gas fireplace, deep soaking bathtub, French press coffee maker, plush bathrobes, and honor bar. The complimentary continental breakfast can be delivered right to your door upon request. Also upon appointment, you can arrange for a massage or facial in the comfort of your room. The Spanish Inn sits only three blocks from State Street, and within walking distance of a number of theaters and historic Santa Barbara attractions.

Are you ready and willing to pay premium prices for a luxury beachfront resort hotel room? If so, check out the **Harbor View Inn** (28 W. Cabrillo Blvd., 805/963-0780, www.harborviewinnsb.com, $352). This stunning Spanish Colonial–style property sits right across the street from the flat white sands of West Beach and steps from Stearns Wharf. Blooming flowers and bright ceramic tiles create beautiful outdoor spaces everywhere on the property. The pool is a focal point of the resort, with long hours and food and beverage service. Inside your lovely guest room, soft lighting and orange-and-red tones create a feeling of warmth. Suites offer palatial spaces and extra amenities. If you want to enjoy a tasty meal without leaving the resort property, choose between room service and the on-site oceanfront restaurant **Eladio's.** Eladio's is best known for its breakfasts, but serves three meals each day and has a good list of wines that's heavy on the local vintages.

## FOOD

### American

Yes, they do mean *that* **The Endless Summer** (113 Harbor Way, 805/564-4666, www.endlesssummerbarcafe.net, daily 11 A.M.–close, $10). When they decided to create a new restaurant out on the pier, the owners went to Bruce Johnson, a Santa Barbara resident and acknowledged creator of the "real" surfing movie genre, and asked him if he would mind having a restaurant named for his most famous film. Bruce thought it was a fine idea, and not only gave the project his blessing, he quickly became a regular in the dining room. Photos of Bruce, other famous surfers, and lots of surfing paraphernalia from the historic to the modern deck the walls of this seaside bar and café. The menu has plenty of salads and sandwiches, includes some intriguing daily specials, and serves from the menu of the Waterfront Grill downstairs. Service is friendly, and the atmosphere tends towards casual local hangout. Many patrons know each other and the staff, and the bar gets crowded as the evening wears on. Live music—sometimes just a talented solo player—provides pleasant background and occasionally a dance track for the more energetic patrons.

### Café

Whether you're a vegetarian or not, you'll find something delicious at the **Sojourner Café** (134 E. Canon Perdido St., 805/965-7922, www.sojournercafe.com, Mon.–Sat. 11 A.M.–11 P.M., Sun. 11 A.M.–10 P.M., $20). In fact, a select few dishes include a bit of lean poultry or fish in amongst the veggies. Sojourner features healthful dishes made with ingredients that showcase local organic and sustainable farms. Lots of the cuisine has ethnic flavors, from familiar Mexico to exotic India. Daily specials use ingredients that are fresh and in-season, including some seafood. Then again, Sojourner also serves a classic root beer float and chocolate milkshakes as well as a big selection of house-baked confections to go along with their health food. Sojourner displays the work of local artists on a rotating schedule. If you fall in love with the wall art over your table, inquire with your server about purchasing it.

### California

Of the many and varied high-end California cuisine restaurants that crowd Santa Barbara, **Bouchon** (9 W. Victoria St., 805/730-1160, www.bouchonsantabarbara.com, daily 5:30 P.M.–close, $30) might be the best. Though it's no relation to the bistro of the same name in Yountville, Bouchon prides itself on both creative cuisine and top-notch service every night. You'll pay a premium to dine here, but it's worth it for a special night out. Your server will be your guide, helping you make selections from the menu, recommending wine pairings with each course, and answering any questions you might have about the restaurant or the food. California-style dishes are prepared with local and organic ingredients whenever possible, and the menu changes often based on what's available. The wine list is a special treat. It consists almost entirely of local wines—really local—from the Santa Barbara and Paso Robles regions. Servers have favorites and they're generally great. The presentation of the food matches its quality. The dining room features romantic low lighting, smallish tables, interesting artwork, and an outdoor patio that's perfect for balmy summer nights.

### Creole

**The Palace Grill** (8 E. Cota St., 805/963-5000, www.palacegrill.com, daily 11 A.M.–3 P.M., 5:30–11 P.M., Fri.–Sat. until midnight, $20–40) boasts of being one of Santa Barbara's most popular restaurants and a little piece of old New Orleans in sunny California. The atmosphere gets lively in the evenings, so this isn't the place to come for a quiet meal. Live entertainers delight the crowds several nights each week, and every once in awhile a restaurant-wide sing-along breaks out. The food is pure Louisiana bayou; look for classically prepared etouffes, jambalaya, and gumbo ya-ya. Most of the seafood is flown in fresh daily, the steaks are aged to perfection, and much of the fresh finned fish and meat is served blackened and spiced in Cajun style. Even the appetizers and desserts drip Creole and Cajun flavors. Start off with a house specialty cocktail or a glass of California wine. While you dine, be sure to take a moment to appreciate the particularly fine service that is a staple of the Palace's reputation.

### Mexican

Have you ever wanted to know what true, authentic Mexican food might taste like? **La Super-Rica Taqueria** (622 N. Milpas St., 805/963-4940, Thurs.–Tues. 11 A.M.–9 P.M., Fri.–Sat. 11 A.M.–9:30 P.M., $10) can hook you up. Of course, you must be prepared to stand in line with dozens of locals and even commuters up from Los Angeles and the occasional Hollywood celeb who think La Super-Rica's got some of the best down-home Mexican cuisine in all of SoCal. This was Julia Child's favorite taco stand, and it's been reviewed by the *New York Times.*

Folks don't come for the ambiance—expect paper plates, plastic chairs, and shorts and sandals on the diners in a genuine shack of a building. You also need to adjust your concept of Mexican food; if you're looking for a fast-food burrito supreme with chips and salsa, you'll definitely be disappointed. But if you're ready for the real deal, you've found it. The corn tortillas are made fresh each day, the meat is slow cooked and seasoned to perfection, and the house special is a grilled pork-stuffed pasilla chile. Vegetarians can choose from a few delicious meat-free dishes, while carnivores will leave satisfied with their pork-, chicken-, or steak-based entrées.

### Middle Eastern

For a Middle Eastern feast, go to **Zaytoon** (209 E. Canon Perdido St., 805/963-1293, www.cafezaytoon.com, Mon.–Sat. 11:30 A.M.–9 P.M., Sun. 4–9 P.M., $10–30). This restaurant and hookah bar appeals to a crowd that wants to enjoy an evening out with a group of friends, to share a hookah around the table, and to ogle talented belly dancers shimmying amongst the tables. While the interior dining room is attractive, with potted palms and gauzy fabric draped from the ceiling, it's not the best place to sit at Zaytoon. Instead, try to get a table out on the garden patio, a large, softly lit space almost completely enveloped by a living green jungle. It is out here that you can order up your own hookah. The menu has most standard Middle Eastern favorites, such as baba ghannouj, hummus, falafel, Greek salad, shawarma, and kebabs of many kinds.

### Seafood

It takes something special to make Santa Barbara residents take notice of a seafood restaurant, and **Brophy Brothers** (119 Harbor Way, 805/966-4418, www.brophybros.com, Sun.–Thurs. 11 A.M.–10 P.M. Fri.–Sat. 11 A.M.–11 P.M., $10–30) has it. Look for a small list of fresh fish done up California style with upscale preparations. The delectable menu goes heavy on locally caught seafood. At the clam bar, you can order some fresh raw clams (duh!) or oysters, a bowl of the house clam chowder, or a tasty seafood salad. With a prime location looking out over the masts of the sailboats in the harbor, it's no surprise that Brophy Brothers gets crowded at both lunch and dinnertime, especially on weekends in the summertime.

### Coffee

Skip the big chains and head for **Java Jones** (728 State St., 805/962-4721, daily 7 A.M.–11 P.M.), conveniently located in the middle of State Street. This local coffee house has brick walls, cushy couches in the upstairs loft seating area, and local art on the walls. It's also got a better-than-average selection of caffeinated go-juice, including Turkish coffee and Vietnamese coffee. In the morning, locals and visitors alike can order from the limited but tasty breakfast menu. Pastries and salads are available all day and late into the night. Go ahead and bring your laptop (yup, they've got Wi-Fi), grab a chair, and settle in.

## INFORMATION AND SERVICES

The **Santa Barbara Conference and Visitors Bureau** (1601 Anacapa St., 805/966-9222, www.santabarbaraca.com) maintains an **Outdoor Visitors Center** (113 Harbor Way, Waterfront Center, 4th Fl., 805/884-1475) for visitors who never want to leave sight of the beach.

As a major metropolitan city, Santa Barbara publishes its own daily newspaper, the ***Santa Barbara News Press*** (www.newspress.com). Look for it in shops, on newsstands, and in your hotel or inn. Check the *Scene and Life* sections for information about entertainment, events, and attractions.

The major hospital in town is **Santa Barbara Cottage Hospital** (320 W. Pueblo St., 805/682-7111, www.sbch.org), which includes a full-service emergency room.

## GETTING THERE AND AROUND

To reach Santa Barbara by air, fly into the **Santa Barbara Municipal Airport** (Moffet Rd., 805/967-7111, www.flysba.com). A number of major commercial airlines fly into Santa Barbara, including United, Alaska/Horizon, Delta, and American Airlines.

A more beautiful and peaceful way to get to Santa Barbara is by train. The **Amtrak** Coast Starlight (www.amtrak.com) runs into town daily. From Los Angeles or San Francisco's east bay, connect to other trains that run into California from points east.

Santa Barbara is located on Highway 101, also known as the Pacific Coast Highway and El Camino Real in this neck of the woods. To head out to the Santa Ynez Valley and other local wine regions, take CA Highway 154 east. If staying in Santa Barbara proper, expect fairly standard city driving, complete with traffic jams during weekday business hours and on beach access roads on the weekends. Parking can be challenging, especial at the beach on sunny summer weekends. Expect to pay a premium for a good-to-mediocre spot, or to walk for several blocks. If possible, take the local public streetcar from the downtown area to the beach and leave your car elsewhere.

Santa Barbara has its own transit authority. The **MTD Santa Barbara** (805/963-336, www.sbmtd.gov) runs both the local bus service ($1.25 regular fare) and the Waterfront Shuttle and Downtown-Waterfront lines ($0.25 regular fare). Have exact change to pay your fare when boarding the bus or shuttle; if transferring buses, ask the driver for a free transfer pass.

# LOS ANGELES AND ORANGE COUNTY

With icons like Hollywood, Disneyland, and Malibu, Los Angeles and Orange County together form the California that rest of the world envisions. It's true that palm trees line sunny boulevards and the Pacific Ocean starts to warm to a swimmable temperature here—and that traffic is always a mess. But celebrities don't crowd every sidewalk signing autographs and movies aren't filming on every corner.

Instead, L.A. combines the glitz, crowds, and speed of the big city with an easier, friendlier feel in its suburbs. A soft haze often envelops the warm beaches, which draw lightly clad crowds vying to see and be seen while children play in the water. Power shoppers pound the sparkling pavement lining the ultra-urban city streets. Tourists can catch a premiere at Grauman's Chinese Theatre, try their feet on a surfboard at Huntington Beach, and ogle the relics of the La Brea Tar Pits.

For visitors who want a deeper look into the Los Angeles Basin, excellent museums dot the landscape, as do theaters, comedy clubs, and live music venues. L.A. boasts the best nightlife in California, with options that appeal to star-watchers, hard-core dancers, and cutting-edge music lovers alike.

Out in the O.C., as Orange County is referred to, lies the single most recognizable tourist attraction in California: Disneyland. Even the most jaded native residents tend to soften at the bright colors, cheerful music, sweet smells, and sense of fun that permeate the House of Mouse. Orange County visitors also find scenic,

ROBERT HOLMES / CALTOUR

# HIGHLIGHTS

**La Brea Tar Pits:** It's worth braving the smell for a glimpse at the fossilized remains of everything from mammoths to mice. The accompanying museums allows visitors a peek at museum's paleontologists at work (page 499).

**LACMA:** LACMA's seven buildings house a diverse and extaordinary array of art in a variety of mediums. Time your visit to coincide with one of their prestigous exhibitions (page 499).

**Hollywood Walk of Fame:** Since 1968, entertainment legends have wished for a star on this three-mile walk of fame (page 500).

**Grauman's Chinese Theatre:** This Hollywood icon opened in 1927 and has played host to hand and footprints of the stars, along with premieres of their movies (page 502).

**Griffith Park:** A welcome expanse of greenery, "L.A.'s Central Park" includes the Griffith Observatory, the L.A. Zoo, and the Hollywood sign, as well as several film locations (page 504).

**Santa Monica Pier:** On a sunny Southern California day, nothing beats a day at the pier. Rides the rides, gorge at the midway-style stands, or simply spread a blanket on the beach (page 505).

**Venice Boardwalk:** From the freaky to the fantastic, the Venice Boardwalk has it all. Park yourself for people-watching of fantastic proportions or even participate a bit yourself (page 506).

**The Gamble House:** Take a tour of the Gamble House, a (potentially haunted!) masterpiece of 20th century Craftsmen architecture (page 509).

**California Adventure:** Disneyland may have the mouse, but it's California Adventure – the Golden State–themed park that acompanies it – that has all the rides (page 543).

**The *Queen Mary*:** This famous former pleasure cruiser is now a famously haunted and historic hotel, musem, and entertainment center. Be sure to book the Paranormal Ship Walk for a highlight of the ship's "most haunted" spots (page 552).

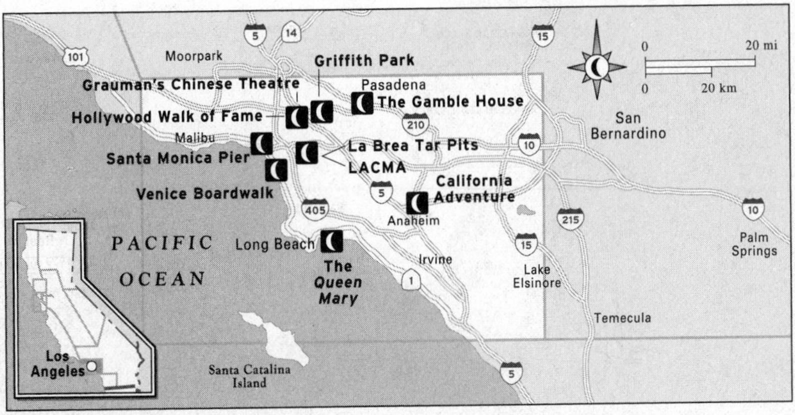


LOOK FOR TO FIND RECOMMENDED SIGHTS, ACTIVITIES, DINING, AND LODGING.

LOS ANGELES

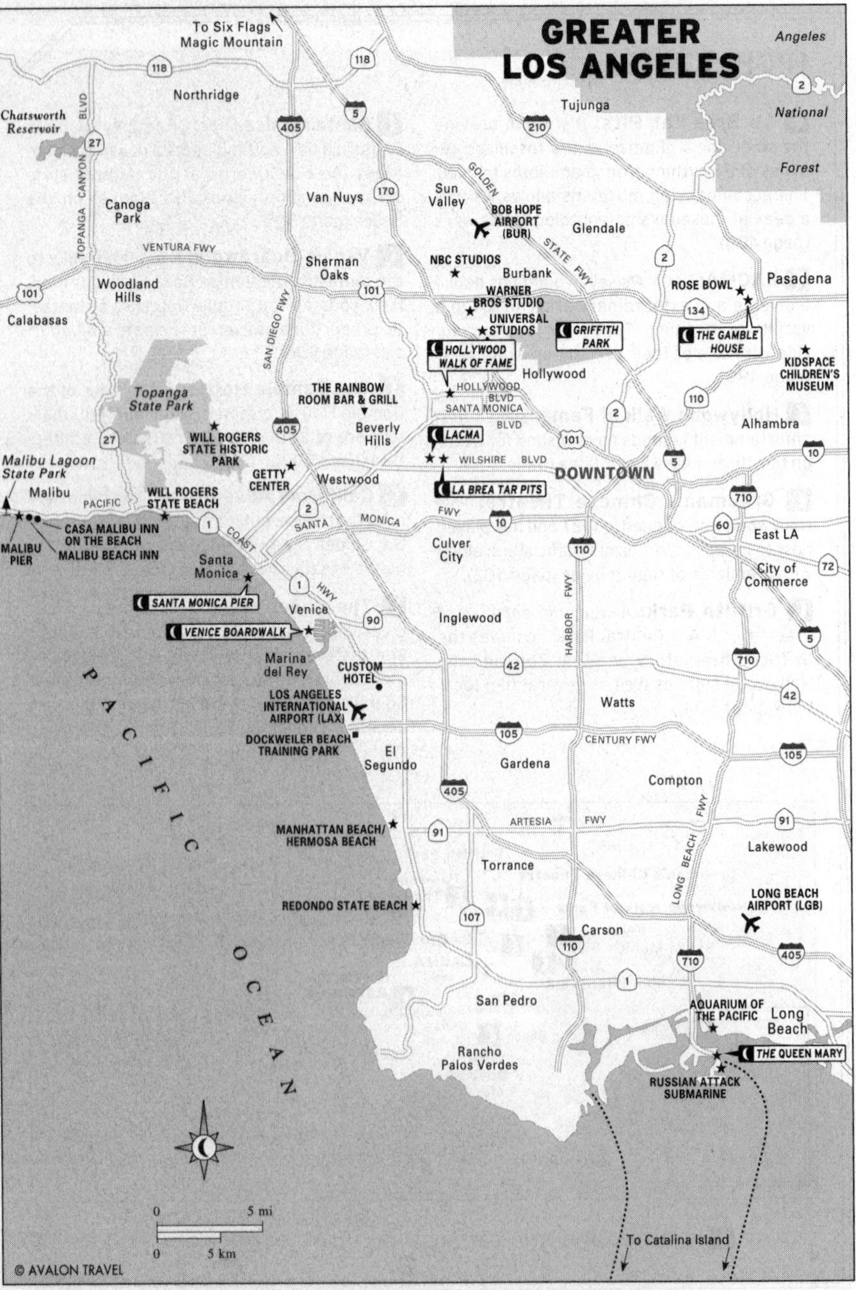
GREATER LOS ANGELES
To Six Flags Magic Mountain
Angeles National Forest
Northridge
Chatsworth Reservoir
Tujunga
TOPANGA CANYON BLVD
Canoga Park
Van Nuys
Sun Valley
GOLDEN STATE FWY
BOB HOPE AIRPORT (BUR)
Glendale
VENTURA FWY
Sherman Oaks
NBC STUDIOS
Burbank
Woodland Hills
WARNER BROS STUDIO
ROSE BOWL
Pasadena
Calabasas
UNIVERSAL STUDIOS
GRIFFITH PARK
THE GAMBLE HOUSE
SAN DIEGO FWY
HOLLYWOOD WALK OF FAME
Hollywood
KIDSPACE CHILDREN'S MUSEUM
Topanga State Park
THE RAINBOW ROOM BAR & GRILL
HOLLYWOOD BLVD
SANTA MONICA BLVD
Beverly Hills
Alhambra
WILL ROGERS STATE HISTORIC PARK
LACMA
Malibu Lagoon State Park
WILSHIRE BLVD
DOWNTOWN
GETTY CENTER
Westwood
Malibu
LA BREA TAR PITS
PACIFIC COAST HWY
WILL ROGERS STATE BEACH
SANTA MONICA FWY
East LA
CASA MALIBU INN ON THE BEACH
MALIBU PIER
MALIBU BEACH INN
Culver City
Santa Monica
City of Commerce
SANTA MONICA PIER
Venice
Inglewood
HARBOR FWY
VENICE BOARDWALK
Marina del Rey
CUSTOM HOTEL
Watts
LOS ANGELES INTERNATIONAL AIRPORT (LAX)
CENTURY FWY
DOCKWEILER BEACH TRAINING PARK
El Segundo
Gardena
Compton
PACIFIC OCEAN
ARTESIA FWY
MANHATTAN BEACH/ HERMOSA BEACH
LONG BEACH FWY
Lakewood
Torrance
REDONDO STATE BEACH
LONG BEACH AIRPORT (LGB)
Carson
San Pedro
AQUARIUM OF THE PACIFIC
Long Beach
Rancho Palos Verdes
THE QUEEN MARY
RUSSIAN ATTACK SUBMARINE
0 5 mi
0 5 km
To Catalina Island
© AVALON TRAVEL

© LANCE SCOTT

Malibu Pier

sun-swept beaches with lots of great activities, state and national parks, and Knott's Berry Farm (the other O.C. amusement park).

## PLANNING YOUR TIME

When you get into Los Angeles, you'll understand quickly that you'll need to pick and choose your itinerary. The vast urban sprawl is just too big to take in unless you've got several weeks in the area. Your best bet is to follow your own heart to whatever types of activities are your favorites. If you're a first-timer to the Los Angeles area, a great initial tour is a drive down Wilshire Boulevard from end to end, stopping to check out all the many and various sights along the 15-mile way.

If you're planning a trip to Disneyland with your family or a group of friends, stick with the Mouse as your main plan. Many people spend several days exploring the parks, never leaving the Anaheim area. Plenty of restaurants and hotels circle the theme park area, making staying and eating a breeze.

Sun-worshippers and surfers will want to stick with the coastline. It's possible to drive from Malibu to San Juan Capistrano over a weekend, stopping at beachside towns for meals and to spend the night.



# Sights

The only problem you'll have with the sights of Los Angeles and its surrounding towns is finding a way to see enough of them to satisfy yourself. You'll find everything from museums to streets, cheese to class, ancient art to modern production studios ready to welcome you throughout the sprawling cityscape.

## DOWNTOWN AND VICINITY

Downtown L.A. has its tall, glass-coated skyscrapers creating an urban skyline, its sports arenas, its rich neighborhoods, its poor neighborhoods, and its endless shopping opportunities. But most of all, it has some of the best and most unique cultural icons in all of L.A. County. Even kids get a kick out of the museums and parkland of Exposition Park, and adults enjoy the kitsch, shopping, and restaurants of Chinatown. Koreatown is thriving in the 21st century. Downtown makes a great start for any trip to Los Angeles.

## Natural History Museum

If you'd like to get your kids some fun with educational purpose, take them to the Natural History Museum (900 Exposition Blvd., 213/763-3466, www.nhm.org, Mon.–Fri. 9:30 A.M.–5 P.M., Sat.–Sun. 10 A.M.–5 P.M., adults $9, teens/seniors $6.50, children $2, parking $6). This huge museum features many amazing galleries; some are transformed into examples of mammal habitats, others display artifacts of various peoples indigenous to the Western Hemisphere. The Discovery Center welcomes children with a wide array of live animals and insects, plus hands-on displays that let kids learn by touching as well as looking. The chapparal exhibit is a favorite, and -it provides a multisensory experience that includes smell as well as sight and sound. Dinosaur lovers can spend a whole day examining the museum's collection of fossils and models, which include a tyrannosaur skull. Be sure to visit the Megamouth as you walk through; it's one of only 17 examples of this species of shark ever discovered by humans. Rock nuts flock to the Natural History Museum to see the fabulous gem and mineral display, complete with gold and a vault filled with rare precious stones. If you're interested in the natural history and culture of California, be sure to spend some time in the Lando Hall of California History.

The Natural History Museum sits within the larger Exposition Park complex. The museum café is open daily 10 A.M.–4 P.M. All exhibits are both wheelchair- and stroller-accessible, but ask at the ticket booths if you need special assistance to tour the museum. Do be aware that the surrounding neighborhood can be dicey, so don't plan to explore the area around the museum on foot.

## California Science Center

Another gem of Exposition Park, the exhibits at

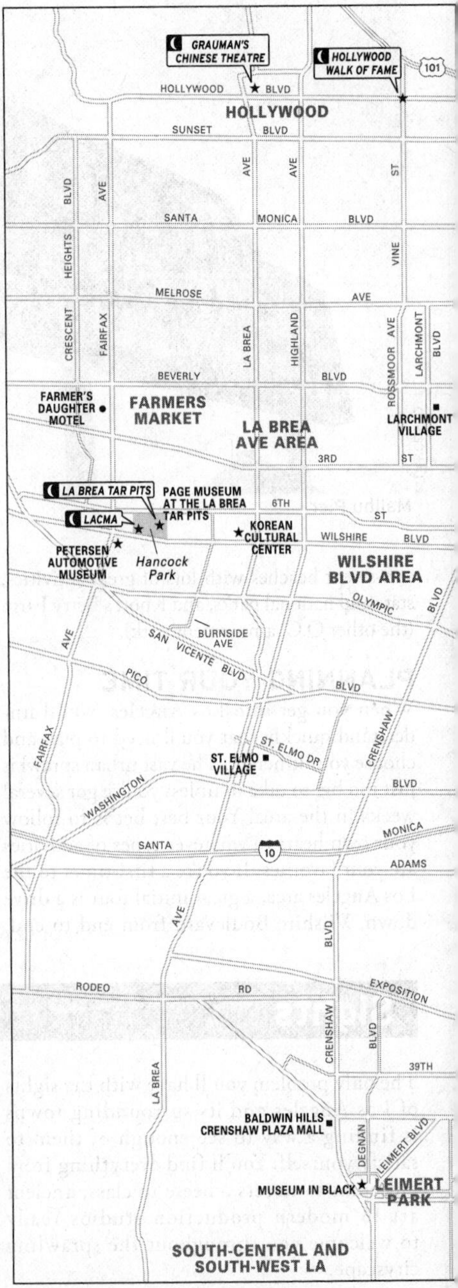

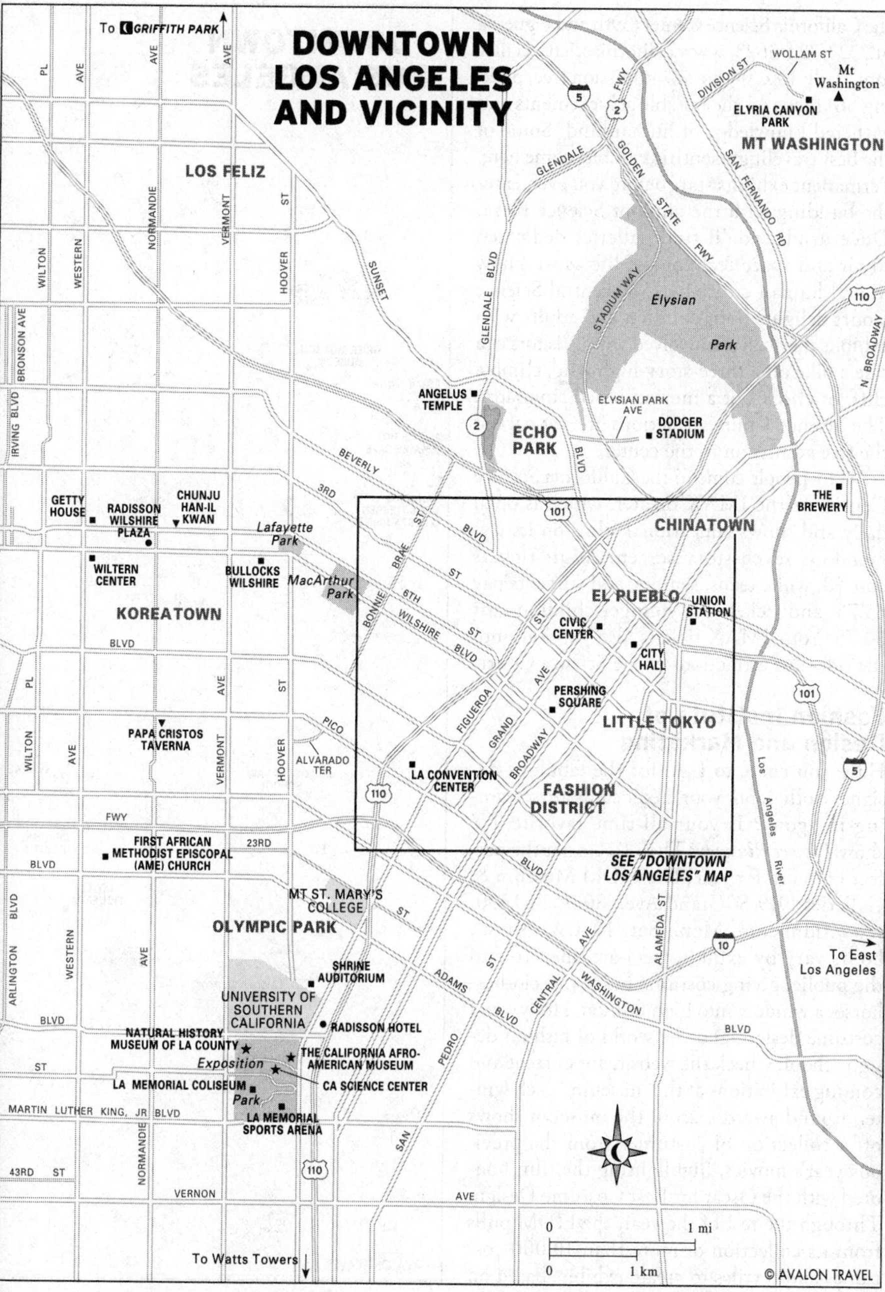
DOWNTOWN LOS ANGELES AND VICINITY
To GRIFFITH PARK
LOS FELIZ
WOLLAM ST
DIVISION ST
Mt Washington
ELYRIA CANYON PARK
MT WASHINGTON
GLENDALE
GOLDEN STATE FWY
SAN FERNANDO RD
GLENDALE BLVD
STADIUM WAY
Elysian Park
N BROADWAY
SUNSET
ANGELUS TEMPLE
ELYSIAN PARK AVE
DODGER STADIUM
ECHO PARK
BLVD
BEVERLY
3RD
THE BREWERY
GETTY HOUSE
RADISSON WILSHIRE PLAZA
CHUNJU HAN-IL KWAN
Lafayette Park
CHINATOWN
WILTERN CENTER
BULLOCKS WILSHIRE
MacArthur Park
KOREATOWN
BONNIE BRAE ST
6TH
WILSHIRE BLVD
EL PUEBLO
UNION STATION
CIVIC CENTER
CITY HALL
PERSHING SQUARE
LITTLE TOKYO
PAPA CRISTOS TAVERNA
PICO
ALVARADO TER
FIGUEROA
GRAND
BROADWAY
LA CONVENTION CENTER
FASHION DISTRICT
Los Angeles River
FWY
23RD
FIRST AFRICAN METHODIST EPISCOPAL (AME) CHURCH
SEE "DOWNTOWN LOS ANGELES" MAP
MT ST. MARY'S COLLEGE
OLYMPIC PARK
ALAMEDA ST
To East Los Angeles
SHRINE AUDITORIUM
ADAMS
CENTRAL AVE
WASHINGTON
UNIVERSITY OF SOUTHERN CALIFORNIA
RADISSON HOTEL
NATURAL HISTORY MUSEUM OF LA COUNTY
THE CALIFORNIA AFRO-AMERICAN MUSEUM
Exposition Park
CA SCIENCE CENTER
LA MEMORIAL COLISEUM
LA MEMORIAL SPORTS ARENA
PEDRO
SAN
MARTIN LUTHER KING, JR BLVD
43RD ST
VERNON AVE
To Watts Towers
WILTON PL
WESTERN AVE
NORMANDIE AVE
VERMONT AVE
HOOVER ST
BRONSON AVE
IRVING BLVD
ARLINGTON BLVD
0 1 mi
0 1 km
© AVALON TRAVEL

the California Science Center (39th and Figueroa St., 323/724-3623, www.californiasciencecenter.org, daily 10 A.M.–5 P.M., admission free, parking $6) focus on the notable achievements and gathered knowledge of humankind. Some of the best traveling scientific exhibits come here. Permanent exhibits start before you even enter the building with the outdoor Science Plaza. Once inside, you'll find galleries dedicated to air and space technology, life as we know it, and human creativity. The central Science Court delights both children and adults with exhibits they can get involved with. Visitors can ride a bike on a three-story-high wire, climb a cliff, or check out a motion-based simulator. The Science Court attractions are *not* part of the free admission to the center.

Many people come to the California Science Center for the IMAX theater, which is open daily and shows educational films on its tremendous seven-story screen. Adult tickets cost $8, while teens, seniors, and students pay $5.75, and tickets for younger children cost $4.75. Your IMAX tickets also get you onto the ride-able attractions of the Science Court.

## Fashion Institute of Design and Marketing

Have you come to L.A. for the fabulous designer clothes, but your credit cards are screaming in agony? Is your all-time favorite TV show *Project Runway?* Then L.A.'s got the perfect museum for you. The FIDM Museum & Galleries (919 S. Grand Ave., 800/624-1200, www.fidm.com, Mon.–Sat. 10 A.M.–5 P.M., hours vary by exhibit, free) are open free to the public, giving costume buffs and clotheshorses a window into high fashion, Hollywood costume design, and the world of fashion design school. Check the website for current and coming exhibitions at the museum. Each winter around award season, the museum shows off a collection of costumes from the previous year's movies, highlighting the film honored with the Oscar for Best Costume Design. Through the rest of the year, the FIDM pulls from its collection of more than 10,000 costumes and textiles to create exhibits based on



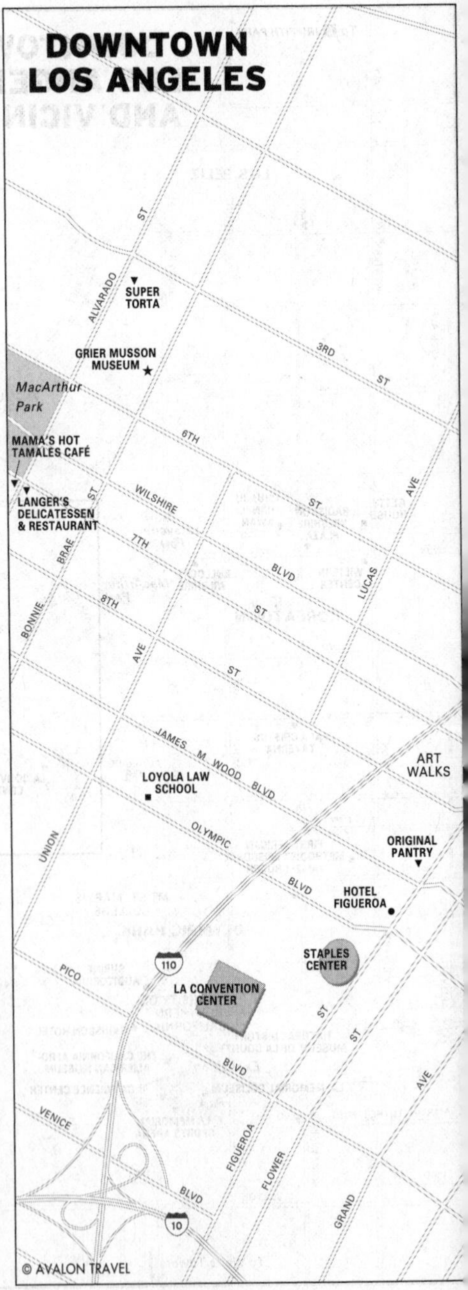

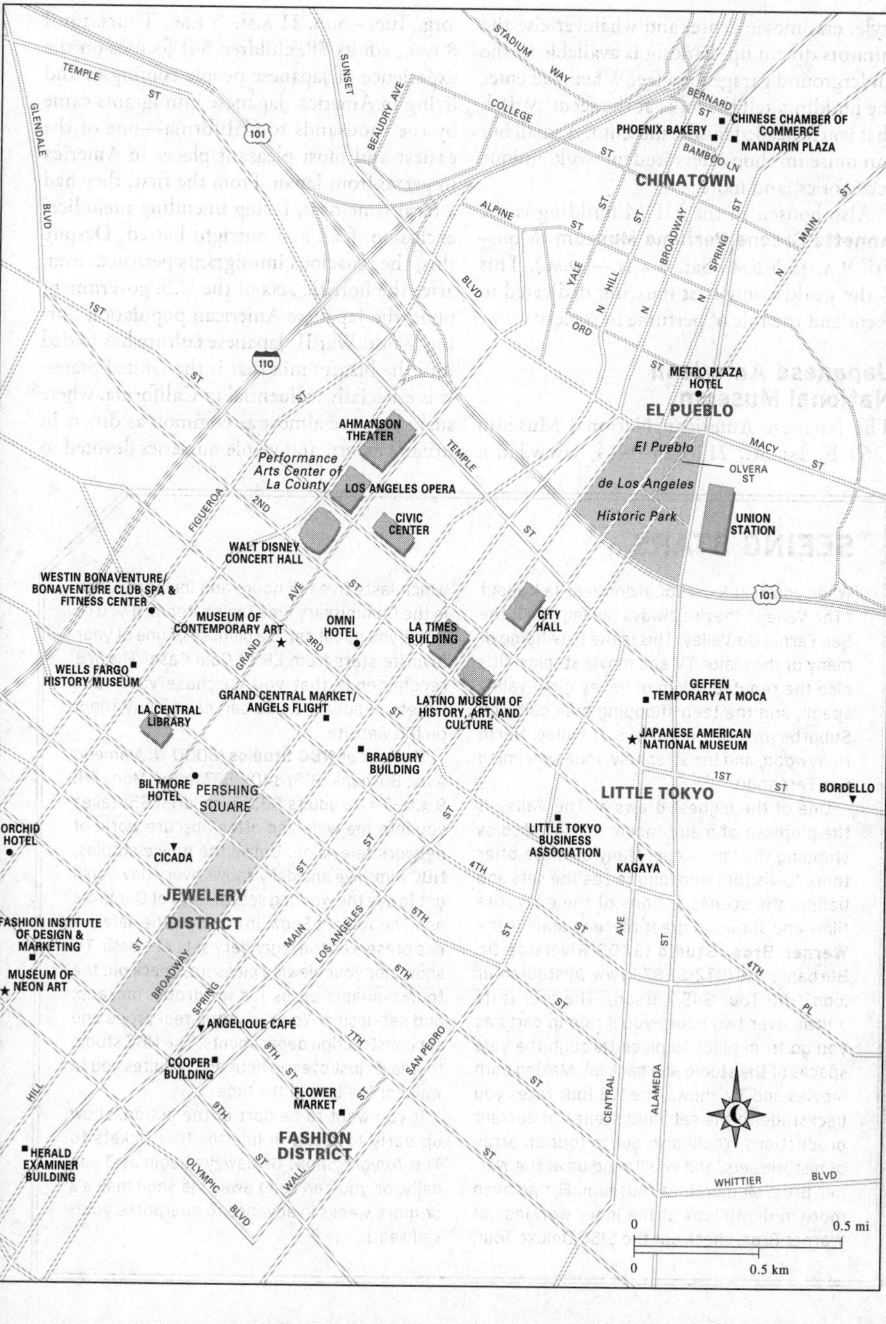

TEMPLE
ST
GLENDALE
BLVD
101
SUNSET
BEAUDRY AVE
STADIUM
WAY
COLLEGE
BERNARD
ST
CHINESE CHAMBER OF COMMERCE
PHOENIX BAKERY
MANDARIN PLAZA
BAMBOO LN
CHINATOWN
ALPINE
YALE
N HILL
BROADWAY
SPRING
N MAIN
BLVD
1ST
ORD
110
METRO PLAZA HOTEL
EL PUEBLO
AHMANSON THEATER
Performance Arts Center of La County
LOS ANGELES OPERA
TEMPLE
MACY
El Pueblo de Los Angeles Historic Park
OLVERA ST
UNION STATION
FIGUEROA
2ND
CIVIC CENTER
WALT DISNEY CONCERT HALL
WESTIN BONAVENTURE/ BONAVENTURE CLUB SPA & FITNESS CENTER
MUSEUM OF CONTEMPORARY ART
GRAND AVE
3RD
OMNI HOTEL
LA TIMES BUILDING
CITY HALL
WELLS FARGO HISTORY MUSEUM
GRAND CENTRAL MARKET/ ANGELS FLIGHT
LATINO MUSEUM OF HISTORY, ART, AND CULTURE
GEFFEN TEMPORARY AT MOCA
LA CENTRAL LIBRARY
JAPANESE AMERICAN NATIONAL MUSEUM
BRADBURY BUILDING
BILTMORE HOTEL
PERSHING SQUARE
LITTLE TOKYO
BORDELLO
ORCHID HOTEL
CICADA
LITTLE TOKYO BUSINESS ASSOCIATION
KAGAYA
4TH
JEWELERY DISTRICT
5TH
LOS ANGELES
MAIN
6TH
FASHION INSTITUTE OF DESIGN & MARKETING
MUSEUM OF NEON ART
BROADWAY
SPRING
ANGELIQUE CAFÉ
7TH
8TH
SAN PEDRO
COOPER BUILDING
CENTRAL AVE
ALAMEDA
4TH PL
HILL
9TH
FLOWER MARKET
FASHION DISTRICT
HERALD EXAMINER BUILDING
OLYMPIC BLVD
WALL
WHITTIER BLVD
0
0.5 mi
0
0.5 km

style, era, movie genre, and whatever else the curators dream up. Parking is available in the underground garage for a fee. When you enter the building, tell the folks at the security desk that you're headed for the museum. A small but fun museum shop offers student work, unique accessories, and more.

Also housed in the FIDM building is the **Annette Greene Perfume Museum** (Mon.–Fri. 9 A.M.–5 P.M., Sat. 9 A.M.–4 P.M.). This is the world's only first museum dedicated to scent and the role of perfume in society.

### Japanese American National Museum

The Japanese American National Museum (369 E. 1st St., 213/625-0414, www.janm.org, Tues.–Sun. 11 A.M.–5 P.M., Thurs. until 8 P.M., adults $8, children $4) focuses on the experience of Japanese people coming to and living in America. Japanese immigrants came by the thousands to California—one of the easiest and most pleasant places in America to get to from Japan. From the first, they had a hard time of it, facing unending prejudice, exclusion, fear, and outright hatred. Despite this, the tenacious immigrants persisted, even after the horrific acts of the U.S. government upon the Japanese American population during World War II. Japanese culture has folded into the bizarre mix that is the United States. It is especially influential in California, where sushi bars are almost as common as diners in urban centers, and whole nurseries devoted to

## SEEING STARS

When you hear local SoCal denizens talk about "The Valley," they're always talking about the San Fernando Valley. This is the true home of many of the major TV and movie studios. (It's also the reputed origin of valley girls, valley speak, and the teen shopping mall culture.) Suburbs include Burbank, Sun Valley, North Hollywood, and the strangely underwhelming San Fernando.

One of the biggest draws of The Valley is the plethora of major movie and TV studios studding the landscape. Many of these offer tours to visitors who long to see the sets and behind-the-scenes actions of their favorite films and shows. A great place to start is the **Warner Bros. Studio** (3400 Riverside Dr, Burbank, 818/972-8687, www.wbstudiotour.com, VIP Tour $45/person). The tour lasts a little over two hours-you'll ride in carts as you go from place to place through the vast spaces of the studio and back lot. Making both movies and TV shows, the WB tour takes you backstage to the sets and scenes of current productions. You'll also get to tour an array of historic sets, and you'll wind up at the Warner Bros. Memorabilia museum. For an even more in-depth look at the inner workings of Warner Bros, check out the $150 Deluxe Tour, which lasts five full hours and includes lunch in the Commissary Fine Dining Room. If you're lucky, you might catch a glimpse of one of your favorite stars from ER or Cold Case! The WB recommends that you purchase your tour tickets in advance-you can call or buy them on the website.

The tour at **NBC Studios** (3000 W. Alameda Ave., Burbank, 818/840-3537, tours Mon.-Fri. 9 A.M.-3 P.M., adults $8.50, children $5) takes you into the wide and often obscure world of network television. Unlike the movie studios, NBC films live and daily shows every day-you'll get to see the working sets of Days of Our Lives and The Tonight Show. In addition, the network has preserved the legendary sets of classic TV shows for your viewing pleasure. Check out the tour-available areas for wardrobe, makeup, and set design. You'll visit the real props and set construction departments. The NBC studio tour lasts just over an hour and requires you to walk for the bulk of the time.

If you want to be part of the action, show up early to stand in line for free tickets to *The Tonight Show*. Giveaways begin at 8 A.M. daily, or you can send away via snail mail six or more weeks in advance to guarantee yourself seats.

bonsai gardening thrive. This museum shows the Japanese American experience in vivid detail, with photos and artifacts telling much of the story. You'll also find galleries sheltering temporary exhibitions, from astonishing displays of ikebana floral art to a show devoted to the *Giant Robot* comic book.

### MOCA

The Museum of Contemporary Art, Los Angeles (250 S. Grand Ave., 213/626-6222, www.moca.org, Mon. and Fri. 11 A.M.–5 P.M., Thurs. 11 A.M.–8 P.M., Sat.–Sun. 11 A.M.–6 P.M., adults $8, students $5, children under 12 free) is better known to its friends as MOCA. Here you'll see an array of artwork created between 1940 and yesterday afternoon. Highlights of the permanent collections include pop art and abstract expressionism from Europe and America.

### La Brea Tar Pits

Even if you've never been within a thousand miles of California before, you've probably heard of the La Brea Tar Pits and the wonders found within them. But where once tour groups made their stinky way around crude fences protecting them from the pits, now paved paths lead around the most accessible pits, and others (mostly those that are in active excavation) are accessible by guided tour only. Nothing can stop the smell of the tar, or the slow bubbling of the shallow miasma of water that covers the tar.

If what interests you most are the fossilized contents of the tar pits, head for the beautiful **Page Museum** (5801 Wilshire Blvd., 323/934-7243, www.tarpits.org, Mon.–Fri. 9 A.M.–5 P.M., Sat.–Sun. 10 A.M.–5 P.M., adults $7, children $4.50, parking $6–8 in lot). The Page contains the bones of many of the untold thousands of animals that became trapped in the sticky tar and met their fate there. The museum's reasonably small size and easy-to-understand interpretive signs make it great for kids, and good for a shorter stop for grown-ups. You'll see some amazing skeletal remains—like sloths the size of Clydesdale horses. Genuine mammoths died and were fossilized in the tar pits, as were the tiniest of mice and about a zillion dire wolves. One of the coolest things for science geeks is the big windowed cage housing the paleontologists at work. You can watch them cleaning, examining, sorting, and cataloging bones from the most recent excavations.

### LACMA

Travelers who desperately need a break from the endless, shiny, and mindless entertainments of L.A. can find respite and solace in the Los Angeles County Museum of Art (5905 Wilshire Blvd., 323/857-6000, www.lacma.org, Mon.–Tues. and Thurs. noon–8 P.M., Fri. noon–9 P.M., Sat.–Sun. 11 A.M.–8 P.M., adults $9, children free). Better known to its friends as LACMA, this large museum complex prides itself on a diverse array of collections and exhibitions of art from around the world, from the ancient to the most ultra-modern. With seven full-sized buildings filled with galleries, don't expect to get through the whole thing in an hour, or even a full day. You'll see all forms of art here, from classic painting and sculpture to all sorts of decorative arts (that is, ceramics, jewels, metalwork, and more). All major cultures are represented, so you can check out Islamic, Southeast Asian, European, and Californian art, plus more. Specialties of LACMA include Japanese art and artifacts in the beautifully designed Pavilion for Japanese Art and the costumes and textiles of the Doris Stein Research Center. Several galleries of LACMA West are dedicated to art and craft for children. Perhaps best of all, some of the world's most prestigious traveling exhibitions come to LACMA; past exhibitions have included the works of Salvador Dali and a new take on Tutankhamen.

You'll do a lot of walking from gallery to gallery and building to building at LACMA. Inquire at one of the two welcome centers for wheelchairs. Not all the buildings are connected; you must walk outside to get to the Japanese Pavilion and LACMA West. The complex is equipped with two full-service museum cafés, an ATM, and a gift and book shop. And finally, if you're in need of some fine rental artwork, LACMA can hook you up.

If you prefer automotive artistry to more conventional forms, head across the street from LACMA to the **Petersen Automotive Museum** (6060 Wilshire Blvd., 323/930-2277, www.petersen.org, Tues.–Sun. 10 A.M.–6 P.M., adults $10, children $3, students $5, parking $8).

ROBERT HOLMES / CALTOUR

Hollywood Walk of Fame

## HOLLYWOOD

You won't find any movie studios in Hollywood, and few stars walk its streets except on premiere evenings. It's an odd irony that what the world perceives to be the epicenter of the film industry has little left of that industry beyond its tourist destinations. The only "real" movie business remaining are the blockbuster premieres at the major movie theaters here. Most of the other destinations range from the oversold to the downright kitschy. But still, if you've ever had a soft spot for Hollywood glamour or American camp, come check out the crowds and bustle of downtown Tinseltown. (And be aware that no local would *ever* call it that.) Hollywood is also famous for its street corners. While the most stuff sits at Hollywood and Highland, the best- known named corner is certainly Hollywood and Vine.

### Hollywood Walk of Fame

One of the most recognizable facets of Hollywood is its star-studded Walk of Fame (Hollywood Blvd. and Vine St.). This area, portrayed in countless movies, contains more than 2,000 five-pointed stars honoring both real people and fictional characters who have contributed significantly to the entertainment industry and the legend that is Hollywood. Each pink star is set into a charcoal square, and has its honoree's name in bronze. The little symbols—movie camera, TV set, record, radio microphone, and tragedy/comedy masks—designate which part of the entertainment industry the honoree is recognized for. The Walk opened in 1968, with its very first star going to Joanne Woodward. Gene Autry has five stars on the walk, one for each industry (film, TV, radio, recording, and live theater) he contributed to. At the corner of Hollywood and Vine, check out the four moons that honor the Apollo XI astronauts. Also look for your favorite cartoon characters; Kermit the Frog, Mickey Mouse, and Bugs Bunny are all honored on the Walk of Fame.

You don't need to pay to get into anything, just get out on the sidewalk and start to stroll; the complete walk is about 3.5 miles. You'll be looking down at the stars, so watch out for other walkers crowding the sidewalks in this tourist-dense area. At the edges of the Walk of Fame, you'll find blank stars waiting to be filled by up-and-comers making their mark on Tinseltown. If you desperately need to find a specific star and want help doing so, you can take a guided tour of the Walk. (But really, it's a waste of money.) Careful reading and an online map (www.gocalifornia.about.com/od/calamenu/a/walkfame.htm) will find you everyone's star you need to see.

### Hollywood Wax Museum

It immortalizes your favorite stars, all right. If

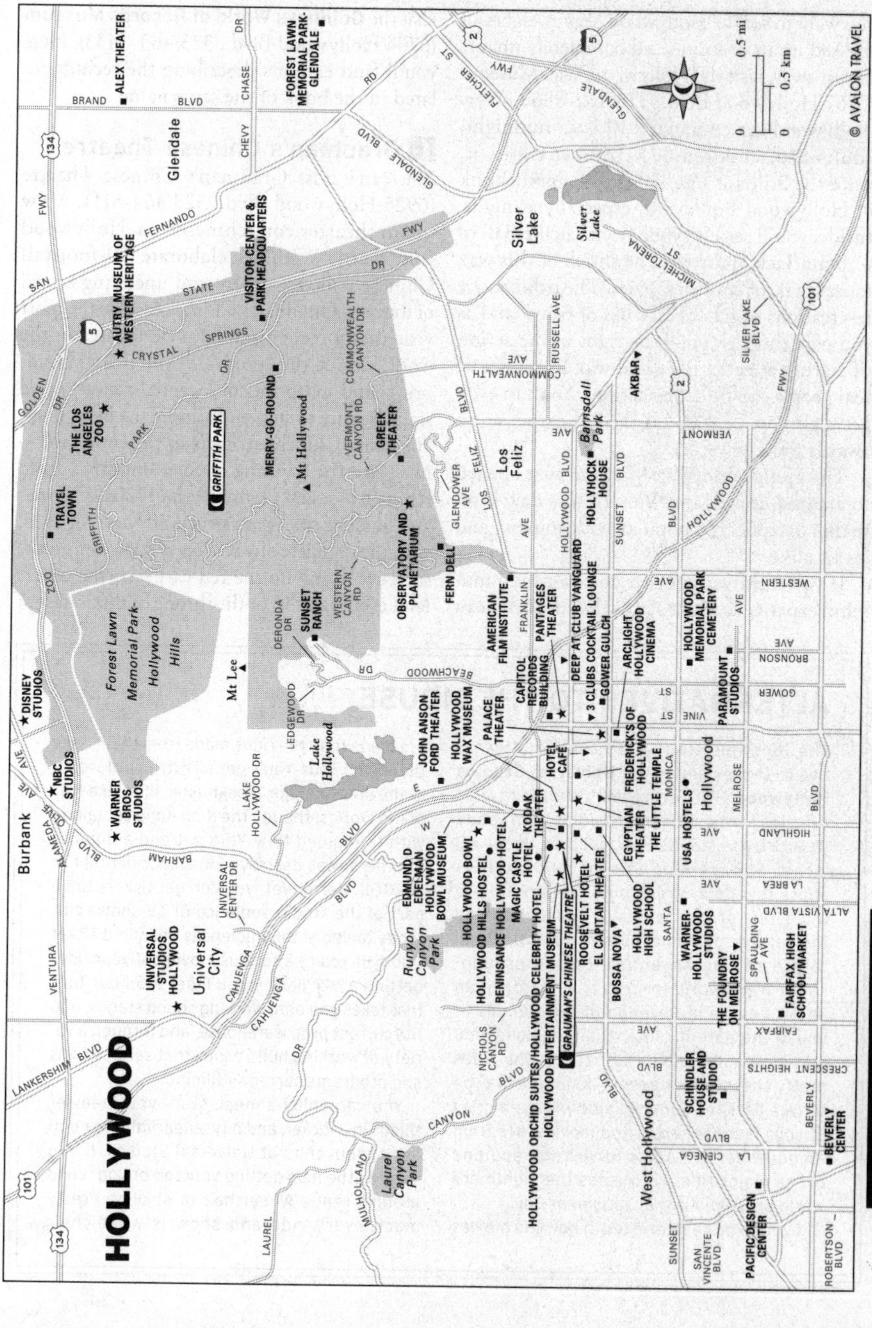
HOLLYWOOD
© AVALON TRAVEL
0 0.5 mi
0 0.5 km
Burbank
Glendale
Universal City
Silver Lake
Los Feliz
Hollywood
West Hollywood
GRIFFITH PARK
Forest Lawn Memorial Park-Hollywood Hills
Runyon Canyon Park
Laurel Canyon Park
Barnsdall Park
Lake Hollywood
Mt Hollywood
Mt Lee
ALEX THEATER
FOREST LAWN MEMORIAL PARK-GLENDALE
AUTRY MUSEUM OF WESTERN HERITAGE
VISITOR CENTER & PARK HEADQUARTERS
THE LOS ANGELES ZOO
MERRY-GO-ROUND
TRAVEL TOWN
GREEK THEATER
OBSERVATORY AND PLANETARIUM
FERN DELL
SUNSET RANCH
DISNEY STUDIOS
NBC STUDIOS
WARNER BROS STUDIOS
UNIVERSAL STUDIOS HOLLYWOOD
JOHN ANSON FORD THEATER
HOLLYWOOD WAX MUSEUM
EDMUND D EDELMAN HOLLYWOOD BOWL MUSEUM
HOLLYWOOD BOWL
HOLLYWOOD HILLS HOSTEL
RENINSANCE HOLLYWOOD HOTEL
MAGIC CASTLE HOTEL
KODAK THEATER
PALACE THEATER
HOTEL CAFÉ
HOLLYWOOD ORCHID SUITES/HOLLYWOOD CELEBRITY HOTEL
HOLLYWOOD ENTERTAINMENT MUSEUM
GRAUMAN'S CHINESE THEATRE
ROOSEVELT HOTEL
EL CAPITAN THEATER
EGYPTIAN THEATER
THE LITTLE TEMPLE
FREDERICK'S OF HOLLYWOOD
HOLLYWOOD HIGH SCHOOL
BOSSA NOVA
USA HOSTELS
AMERICAN FILM INSTITUTE
CAPITOL RECORDS BUILDING
PANTAGES THEATER
DEEP AT CLUB VANGUARD
3 CLUBS COCKTAIL LOUNGE
GOWER GULCH
ARCLIGHT HOLLYWOOD CINEMA
HOLLYWOOD MEMORIAL PARK CEMETERY
PARAMOUNT STUDIOS
HOLLYHOCK HOUSE
AKBAR
WARNER-HOLLYWOOD STUDIOS
THE FOUNDRY ON MELROSE
FAIRFAX HIGH SCHOOL/MARKET
SCHINDLER HOUSE AND STUDIO
PACIFIC DESIGN CENTER
BEVERLY CENTER
VENTURA BLVD
LANKERSHIM BLVD
BARHAM BLVD
CAHUENGA
ALAMEDA AVE
OLIVE AVE
BRAND BLVD
CHEVY CHASE DR
GLENDALE BLVD
SAN FERNANDO RD
GOLDEN STATE FWY
ZOO DR
GRIFFITH PARK DR
CRYSTAL SPRINGS DR
COMMONWEALTH CANYON DR
VERMONT CANYON RD
WESTERN CANYON RD
DERONDA DR
LEDGEWOOD DR
BEACHWOOD DR
LAKE HOLLYWOOD DR
UNIVERSAL CENTER DR
NICHOLS CANYON RD
LAUREL CANYON BLVD
MULHOLLAND DR
LOS FELIZ BLVD
GLENDOWER AVE
FRANKLIN AVE
HOLLYWOOD BLVD
SUNSET BLVD
SANTA MONICA BLVD
MELROSE AVE
BEVERLY BLVD
WESTERN AVE
BRONSON AVE
GOWER ST
VINE ST
HIGHLAND AVE
LA BREA AVE
ALTA VISTA BLVD
SPAULDING AVE
FAIRFAX AVE
CRESCENT HEIGHTS BLVD
LA CIENEGA BLVD
SAN VICENTE BLVD
ROBERTSON BLVD
VERMONT AVE
COMMONWEALTH AVE
RUSSELL AVE
MICHELTORENA ST
SILVER LAKE BLVD
GLENDALE FWY
FLETCHER ST
HOLLYWOOD FWY
101
134
2
5

LOS ANGELES

you want to see the Hollywood heavyweights all dressed up in costume and completely unable to run away, visit the Hollywood Wax Museum (6767 Hollywood Blvd., 323/462-8860, www.hollywoodwax.com, daily 10 A.M.–midnight, adults $16, children $7). You can't miss it, since the brilliant sign lights up a good chunk of Hollywood Boulevard, especially at night. Inside, you'll see everyone from Lucille Ball to Captain Jack Sparrow. The shtick of this wax museum is, of course, movies. The exhibits are re-creations of sets of all sorts of films, and as you pass through you'll be right in the action (if staring at eerie, life-sized wax likenesses of real people can be called action). You can even get a glimpse of stars on the red carpet at an awards show–style set.

The Hollywood Wax Museum first opened to amazed crowds in 1966. To this day, it remains inexplicably popular with tourists and locals alike.

If you need yet another cotton-candy museum experience, right across the street you can visit the **Guinness World of Records Museum** (6764 Hollywood Blvd., 323/463-6433). Here you'll find exhibits describing the records related in the book of the same name.

## Grauman's Chinese Theatre

You can't miss Grauman's Chinese Theatre (6925 Hollywood Blvd., 323/464-8111, www.manntheatres.com/chinese) on Hollywood Boulevard. With its elaborate 90-foot-tall Chinese temple gateway and unending crowd of tourists, Grauman's Chinese may be the most visited and recognizable movie theater in the world. Inside the courtyard, you'll find handprints and footprints of legendary Hollywood stars. Be sure to stop and admire the bells, dogs, and other Chinese artifacts in the courtyard—most are the genuine article, imported from China by special permit in the 1920s. The theater in all its splendor opened on May 18, 1927, with the premiere of *The King of Kings* and all the stars swanning up the red carpet to the cheers (and eventual riot) of the throng of thousands of

## ALTERNATIVES TO THE MOUSE

The longtime Hollywood-centric alternative to Disneyland is the **Universal Studios Hollywood** (100 Universal City Plaza, Los Angeles, www.universalstudios.com, daily 10 A.M.-6 P.M., adults $64, children under 48 inches $54, parking $11) theme park. Kids adore this park, which puts them right into the action of their old favorite movies. Flee the carnivorous dinosaurs of *Jurassic Park*, take a rafting adventure on the pseudo-set of *Waterworld*, or quiver in terror of an ancient curse in *Revenge of the Mummy*. If you're the parent rather than the child, you may find some of the effects on the rides pretty cheesy. On the other hand, you may be thrown back to your childhood with memories of your favorite shows and movies. KIT from *Knight Rider* still talks to visitors, and one of the major rides re-creates the nightmare world of *Terminator 2: Judgment Day*.

If you're more interested in how the movies are made than the rides made from them, take the Studio Tour. You'll get an extreme close-up of the sets of major blockbuster films like *War of the Worlds*, though the *King Kong* set (along with the famed New York set and a number of others) was destroyed in an accidental fire in 2008. Better yet, you can get tickets to be part of the studio audience of TV shows currently taping at the Audiences Unlimited Ticket Booth. If you're a serious movie buff, consider getting a VIP pass – you'll get a 6-hour tour that takes you onto working sound stages, into the current prop warehouse, and through a variety of working build shops that service films and programs currently filming.

You can enjoy a meal, store your heavier things in a locker, and buy a near-infinite number of souvenirs at Universal Studios. If you need a little help getting yourself or your child around, rent a wheelchair or stroller. Pretty much every ride and show is wheelchair fans gathered outside. The next day, the public was allowed into the hallowed theater.

The studios put up premieres at Grauman's all the time. Check the website for showtimes and ticket information. The Chinese Theatre has only one screen, but seats over 1,000 people per showing. While you're welcome to crowd the sidewalk to try to catch a glimpse of the stars at a premiere, be aware that most of these are private events.

## Egyptian Theater

Even before the Grauman's Chinese, Hollywood had the Egyptian Theater (6712 Hollywood Blvd., 323/466-3456, www.americancinematheque.com/egyptian/egypt.htm, tickets $10). Built by the auspices of the legendary Sid Grauman, the Egyptian was the first of the grandiose movie houses build in Hollywood proper and a follower of those in downtown Los Angeles. King Tut's tomb had been discovered in 1922, and the glorified Egyptian stylings of the theater followed the trend for all things Egyptian that followed that discovery. The massive courtyard and the stage both boasted columns, sphinxes, and other Egyptian-esque decor. The first movie to premiere at the Egyptian was *Robin Hood,* soon followed by *The Ten Commandments.* In the 1920s, the showing of a film was preceded by an elaborate live "prologue" featuring real actors in costume on a stage before the screen (the early ancestry of the *Rocky Horror Picture Show*). The Egyptian's stage was second to none, and the prologue of *The Ten Commandments* was billed as the most elaborate to date.

After a haul through the 1950s as a reserved-seat, long-run movie house, the Egyptian fell into disrepair and eventually closed. A massive renovation completed in 1998 restored it to its former glory. Today, you can get tickets to an array of old-time films. Or take a morning tour to get a glimpse at the history of this magnificent old theater. Expect to pay $5–20 for parking in one of the nearby lots.

accessible – ask at the ticket booth for more information about how to get around easily or if you need assisted listening devices and TTD phones.

For yet another amusement park adventure, hit **Six Flags Magic Mountain** (Magic Mountain Parkway, Valencia, www.sixflags.com/magicmountain). This park provides good fun for the *whole* family – even the snarky teenagers who hate almost everything. Magic Mountain has long been the extreme alternative to The Mouse, offering a wide array of thrill rides. You'll need a strong stomach to deal with the G-forces of the major-league roller coasters, the death-defying drops, and the whirling spinners. For the younger set, plenty of "family" style rides offer a less intense but equally fun amusement park experience. Both littler and bigger kids enjoy interacting with the classic Warner Brothers characters, especially in *Bugs Bunny World*, and a kids' show features Bugs, Donald, and others. Other than that, Magic Mountain has little in the way of staged entertainment – this park is all about the rides. The park is divided into areas, just like most other major theme parks – get a map at the entrance to help maneuver around and pick your favorite rides.

You'll find services, souvenirs, and snacks galore throughout the park. The food offerings run to burgers, pizza, and ethnic fast food. The highest concentration of snack shacks sits in the Colossus County Fair area– others are evenly distributed throughout the other areas. You can also by tchochkes in any area, but most of the shopping centers around Cyclone Bay. All major services can be found at the park, including many ATM machines, a First Aid station, ample restrooms, and disability assistance. The Guest Relations office at Six Flags Plaza can help you with just about anything you need.

## Griffith Park

Technically, Griffith Park (Los Feliz Blvd., Zoo Blvd., or Forest Lawn Dr., 213/485-5501, daily 6 A.M.–10 P.M.) is part of the city of Los Angeles, not of Hollywood. This huge park, sometimes called "L.A.'s Central Park" has an endless array of attractions and amenities to suit every style of visitor. If you love the stars, visit the recently renovated **Griffith Observatory** (4730 Crystal Springs Dr.). Golfers can choose between two 18-hole courses and one 9-hole course located on the parklands. A swimming pool cools visitors in the summer. You'll find a baseball field, basketball and tennis courts, and endless miles of hiking and horseback riding trails that thread their way far into the backcountry of the park.

If you prefer a more structured park experience, try the **L.A. Zoo** (5333 Zoo Dr., 323/644-4200, www.lazoo.org, daily 10 A.M.–4 P.M., adults $12, children $7). If the weather is poor (yes, it does rain in L.A.), step inside the **Museum of the American West** (4700 Western Heritage Way, 323/667-2000, www.autry-museum.org, Tues.–Sun. 10 A.M.–5 P.M., adults $9, children $5). Kids love riding the trains of the operating miniature railroad in the **Travel Town Museum** (5200 Zoo Dr., 323/668-0104, http://traveltown.org, Mon.–Fri. 10 A.M.–4 P.M., Sat.–Sun. 10 A.M.–5 P.M.) and taking a spin on the park's carousel.

Griffith Park has played host to many production companies over the years, with its land and buildings providing backdrops for many major films. Scenes from *Rebel Without a Cause* were filmed here, as were parts of the first two *Back to the Future* movies. Its use is appropriate to the park's rich history. The land was donated by miner and Colonel Griffith J. Griffith (really). It has changed much over the years, but remains one of Los Angeles' great prizes.

The **Hollywood Sign** sits on Mount Lee, which is part of the park and indelibly part of the mystique of Hollywood.

## Mulholland Drive

As you drive north out of downtown Hollywood into the residential section of Hollywood Boulevard, you will find folks on street corners hawking maps of stars' homes on Mulholland Drive and its surrounding neighborhoods. Whether you choose to pay up to $10 for a photocopied sheet of dubious information is up to you. What's certain is that you can drive the famed drive yourself. When you reach the ridge, you'll see why so many of the intensely wealthy in the L.A. Basin choose to make their homes here. From the ridgeline, on clear days you can see down to Los Angeles and the coast to the west, and the fertile land of the San Fernando Valley to the east. Whether you care about movie star homes or not, the view by itself is worth the trip, especially if it's rained recently and the smog is down. You won't see the facade of Britney Spears' multimillion-dollar hideaway facing the street, but a few homes do face the drive—most boasting mid-century modern architecture. If you can see them, they probably don't belong to movie stars who guard their privacy from the endless intrusion of paparazzi and fans.

# BEVERLY HILLS AND WEST HOLLYWOOD

Although the truly wealthy live above Hollywood on Mulholland Drive, in Bel-Air, or on the beach at Malibu, there's still plenty of money floating around in Beverly Hills. Some of the world's best and most expensive shops sit on the streets of Beverly Hills. You'll also find more than adequate high-end culture in the area, which bleeds into West L.A. The division seems almost seamless now, compared to the tremendous class gash that used to exist between Beverly Hills and the infamous Sunset Strip.

## Getty Center

Even more famous for art and culture in Los Angeles is The Getty Center (1200 Getty Center Dr., 310/440-7300, www.getty.edu, Tues.–Thurs. and Sun. 10 A.M.–6 P.M., Fri.–Sat. 10 A.M.–9 P.M., admission free, parking $8). Donated by the family of J. Paul Getty to the people of Los Angeles, this museum features European art, sculpture, manuscripts, and European and American photos. The magnificent works are set in a fabulous modern building with soaring architecture and you're guaranteed to find something beautiful to catch your eye and feed your imagination. The spacious galleries have comfy sofas to let you sit back and take in the paintings and drawings on the walls. Be sure to take a stroll outdoors to admire the sculpture collections on the lawns, as well as the exterior architectural itself.

### Wilshire Boulevard

Though the most famous stretch of Wilshire Boulevard runs through Beverly Hills, in truth this major artery reaches from Downtown L.A. all the way out to the coastline (almost) of Santa Monica. If you drive the whole thing, you'll travel 16 slow miles along the densely populated, totally developed strip. Along the way, you'll travel the **Miracle Mile,** pass the **Regent Beverly Wilshire Hotel** and the **La Brea Tar Pits,** see the main drag in **Koreatown,** and whiz past **MacArthur Park.** You can spend more than a day touring L.A. just by making your way from one end of Wilshire to the other, stopping at the dozens of sights and landmarks as you go.

### Sunset Strip

A much shorter but equally famous stretch of road, the Sunset Strip really is part of Sunset Boulevard—specifically the part that runs through West Hollywood from the Hollywood border to the Beverly Hills city limits. The Strip exemplifies all that's grandiose and tacky about the L.A. entertainment industry. Few other places, even in California, boast about the number and glaring overstatement of their billboards. You'll also find many of the Sunset's legendary rock clubs, such as the **Roxy** and the **Whisky** and the infamous after-hours hangout **The Rainbow Bar & Grill.** Decades worth of up-and-coming rock acts first made their names on the Strip, and lived at the "Riot Hyatt."

If you last visited the Strip more than a decade ago, you might fear bringing your children to what was once a distinctly seedy neck of the woods. Then again, old-timers might be horrified *now* by the gentrification of the Strip. Today, a woman alone can stroll the street in comfort in daylight. At night, especially on weekends, no one's alone on the Strip. Don't plan to drive quickly or park on the street after dark; the crowds get big, complete with celebrity hounds hoping for a glimpse of their favorite star out for a night on the town.

## SANTA MONICA, VENICE, AND MALIBU

When many people from around the world think of "L.A.," what they're really picturing are the beach communities skirting the coastline to the west and Los Angeles proper to the east. Some of the most famous (and most expensive) real estate in the world sits on this stretch of sand and earth. Of the communities that call the northern coast of L.A. County home, the focal points are Malibu to the north, Santa Monica, then Venice to the south.

Malibu doesn't look like a town or a city in the conventional sense. If you're searching for the historic downtown or the town center, give up. There isn't one. Instead, the "town" of Malibu stretches for more than 20 miles, hugging the beach the whole way. A few huge homes perch precariously on the mountains rising up over the coastline, also part of Malibu. Many beach-loving superstars make their homes here, and the price of a beach house can easily exceed $20 million.

A few more liberal and social stars prefer to purchase from among the closely packed dwellings of Venice Beach. A bastion of true California liberal-mindedness and the home of several famous landmarks, Venice might be the perfect (if expensive) place to take a movie-style L.A. beach vacation.

Santa Monica comes as close to a community of moderate means as you'll find in this region. With its fun-but-not-fancy pier, its inexpensive off-beach motels, and a huge variety of delicious inexpensive dining options, Santa Monica is a great choice for a family vacation.

### Santa Monica Pier

For the ultimate in SoCal beach kitsch, you can't miss the Santa Monica Pier (Ocean Ave. at Colorado Ave.). As you walk the rather long stretch of concrete out over the water, you'll see an amazing array of carnival-style food stands, an arcade, a small amusement park, the smallest miniature golf course ever paid for by tourists, and restaurants leading out to the fishing area at the tip of the pier. The main attraction is **Pacific Park** (310/260-8744, www.pacpark.com, free). This park features a roller coaster, a scrambler, and the world's first solar-powered Ferris wheel. Several rides are geared for the younger set, and a 20-game midway provides fun for all ages. Beneath the pier lies a sandy beach with a decent surf break—one of the major attractions of the area in the summertime.

You can drive onto the first half of the pier. Parking lots sit both on and beneath it, though your chances aren't great if you're trying for a spot on a summer weekend. Many hotels and restaurants are within walking distance of the pier, as is the Third Street Promenade. Admission to Pacific Park is free, but the rides aren't; you can pay per-ride or buy an all-ride wristband.

## Venice Boardwalk

If the Santa Monica Pier doesn't provide you with enough chaos and kitsch, head on down to the Venice Boardwalk (Ocean Front Walk at Venice Blvd.) for a nearly unlimited supply

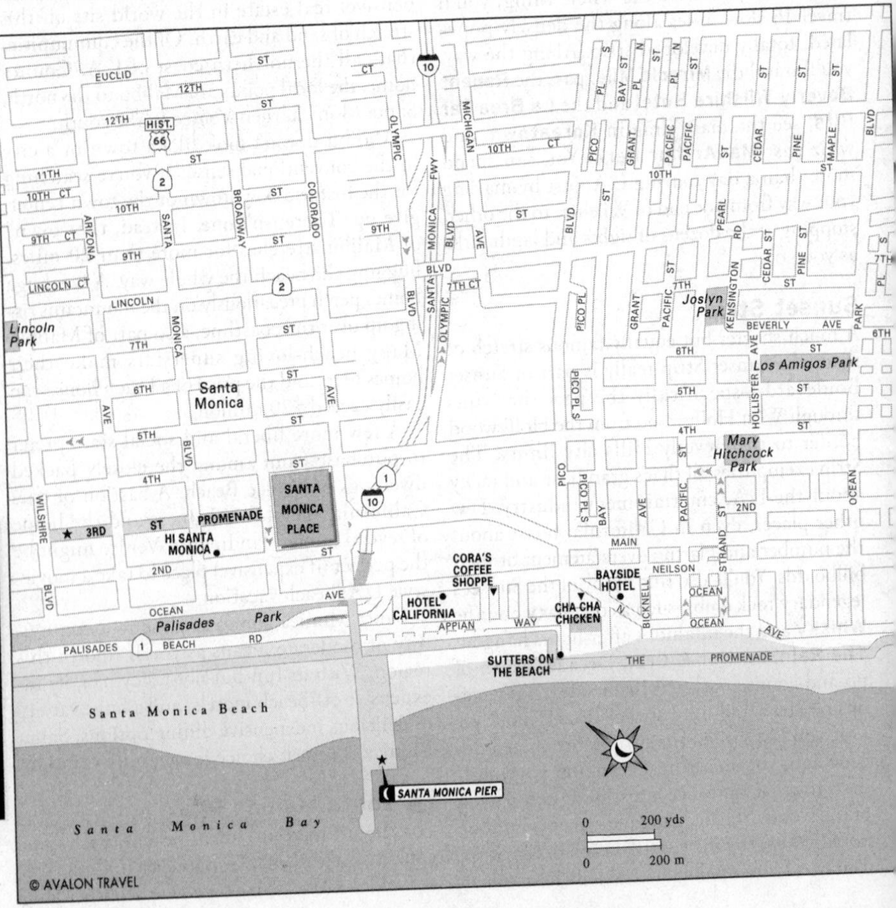

of both all year-round. Locals refer to the Boardwalk as "The Zoo" and tend to shun the area, especially in the frantic summer months. As you shamble down the tourist-laden path, you'll pass an astonishing array of tacky souvenir stores, tattoo and piercing parlors, walk-up food stands, and more. An honest-to-goodness carnival freak show sits near the middle of the Boardwalk, and a surprisingly good bookstore is tucked in beside a large sidewalk café. On the beach side of the path, dozens of artists create sculptures and hawk their wares. You can watch sculptors creating amazing works of art out of sand, or purchase a piece of locally made jewelry. The dude with the roller skates, the turban, and the guitar is pretty much always there—if you talk to him, he may follow you around until you pay him to leave you alone. (He's harmless.) The beach side includes the infamous **Muscle Beach** (two blocks north of Venice Blvd.), an easily distinguished chunk of sand filled with modern workout equipment and encircled by a barrier.

The wide, flat beach adjacent to the Boardwalk gets incredibly crowded in the summer. Parking can be nightmarish in this land of car-free walk streets. Expect to park far from the beach and the Boardwalk and

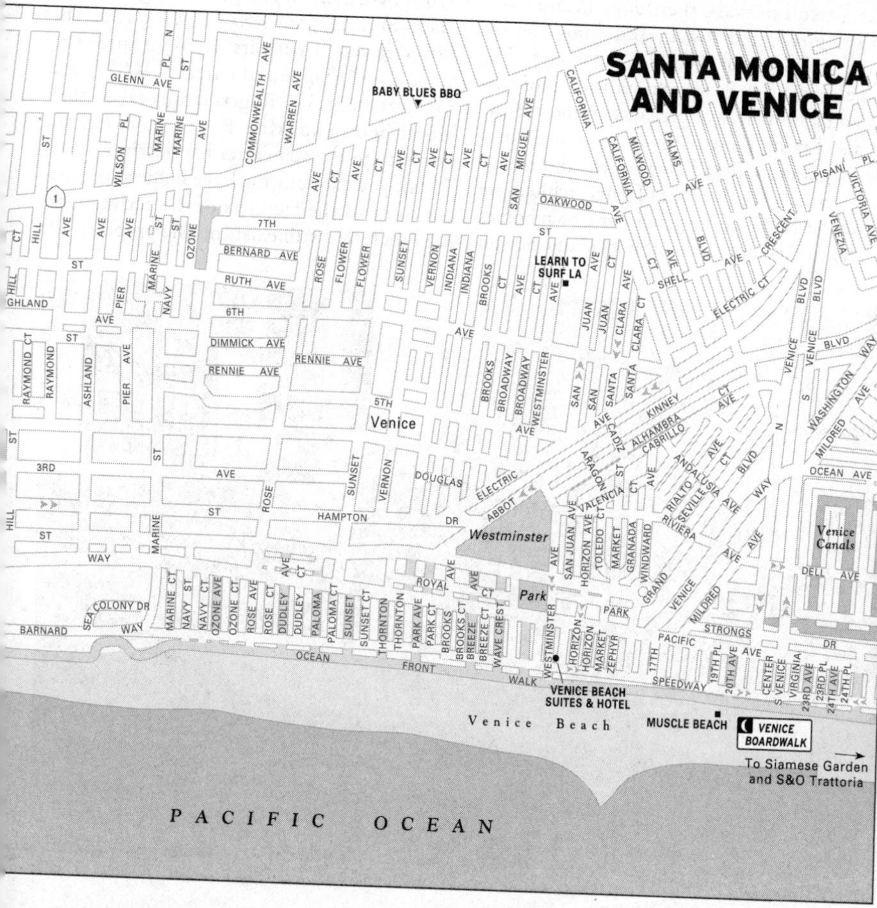

to pay for the privilege. The beach at Venice is lifeguard-protected and has restroom and shower facilities built on the sand. You can get all the junk food you can stomach from the Boardwalk stands.

### Venice Canals

If you've grown tired of the frenzied Boardwalk (or the idea of those crowds just flat make you break out in hives), consider taking a much more sedate walk along the paths of the Venice Canals (btwn. Washington Blvd., Strongs Dr., S. Venice Blvd., and Ocean Ave.). Venice locals seek out the canals when they want to take a stroll or walk their dogs (Venice is a very dog-oriented town), and enjoy the serenity and peace of the quiet waterways. The home gardens and city-maintained landscaping add a lush layer of greenery to the narrow canals. Taking these paths gets you deep into the neighborhood and close to the impressive 20th-century Southern California architecture of Venice. Many of the people who own homes on the canals launch small boats, and put on an annual boat parade for the holidays. As you wander this area, marvel at the history of the canals, modeled after those in this beach town's European namesake city. Also, admire the tenacity with which the city saved these last few from the landfill that removed their brethren from the landscape.

### Will Rogers State Historic Park

Did you grow up loving the films and culture of the early Hollywood western? If so, one of the best sights in Santa Monica for you is the Will Rogers State Historic Park (1501 Will Rogers State Park Rd., Pacific Palisades, 310/454-8212, www.parks.ca.gov, tours Tues.–Sun. 11 A.M., 1 P.M., 2 P.M., free). This 186-acre ranch with its 31-room sprawling home was the home and retreat of Will Rogers and his family. The Rogers family raised their brood here, and Mrs. Rogers donated the property to the state after her death in 1944. Today, you can tour the large home and check out some of the facilities of the active working ranch that still exists on the property. Or

© LANCE SCOTT

Venice Canals

take a walk around the regulation-sized polo field that was Will's joy. If you share Will's love of horses, visit the stables to take a lesson or go out for a ride out on the local range. Travelers who prefer their own two feet can take a three-mile hike to Inspiration Point, or a longer trek on the Backbone Trail out into the Santa Monica Mountains.

### Malibu Pier

There are few true "sights" along the long thin stretch of sand that is Malibu. One of those worth checking out is the Malibu Pier (23000 Pacific Coast Hwy., www.malibupiersportfishing.com). The pier gets busy in the summertime and lonely in the winter, though the die-hard surfers plying the adjacent three-point break stick around year-round. A few pier fishermen also brave the so-called chilly weather of the Malibu off-season, but you'll feel a sense of some solitude when you walk out across the planks. Some attractions out on the pier include interpretive signs describing the history of Malibu, sport-fishing and whale-watching charters, restaurants and food stands. If you'd prefer to ride the waves yourself, you can rent surf and boogie boards as well as other beach toys on the pier.

## PASADENA

If Venice Beach is the liberal haven of L.A., rockers love the Sunset Strip, and the gay community flocks to West Hollywood, Pasadena is the elder statesman of the Los Angeles neighborhoods and towns. Once a resort-like haven for the very wealthy, Pasadena gently decayed, then was re-created as a charming upper-middle-class residential town. Dotted throughout Pasadent, you can still see fabulous examples of the Craftsman architecture that was prevalent throughout Southern California in the early 20th century. This older city also lays claim to one of the best known and most attended parades (and ensuing college football games) in the United States. Finally, Pasadena has the distinction of being the town in which my dad was born and raised.

### Huntington Gardens

Some of the most beautiful botanical gardens in the world grow in Pasadena. The Huntington Gardens (1151 Oxford Ave., San Marino, 626/405-2100, www.huntington.org, Wed.–Mon. noon–4:30 P.M., Sat.–Sun. 10:30 A.M.–close, adults $20, students $10, children $6) also includes an amazing library filled with rare and ancient books and manuscripts. Literary travelers and locals come to the Huntington to view (and worship) the Gutenberg Bible and a manuscript of the *Canterbury Tales*. Art lovers come to view works by van der Weyden, Gainsborough, Hopper, and more. And everyone comes to explore the 120 acres of gardens, the most popular part of the complex.

More than a dozen different gardens beckon, including the Desert Garden, the Japanese Garden, and the Rose Garden. It takes more than one tour to get a real sense of all that grows here; pick your favorite area and enjoy a peaceful respite from the endless chaos of the L.A. Basin. Admission to the center includes a docent-led garden tour. Check the website for a look at what will be in bloom when you're in town.

Some of the best museum café food in the state can be had at the **Rose Garden Tea Room.** You can get a scrumptious buffet-style high tea for as long as the museum is open. For a more traditional snack or light lunch, the walk-up café offers salads, sandwiches, and hot soups.

### ☾ The Gamble House

Where Northern California prides itself on its Victorian architecture, major construction didn't get underway quite as fast in the southern part of the state. Here many of the rich residents, such as the Gambles (of "Procter &" fame), built homes in the early 20th century. The Gamble House (4 Westmoreland Pl., 626/793-3334, www.gamblehouse.org, Thurs.–Sun. noon–3 P.M., adults $10, children under 12 free) was designed and decorated by legendary SoCal architects Greene & Greene in the Craftsman style. The only way to get inside is to take a tour (schedules vary based on

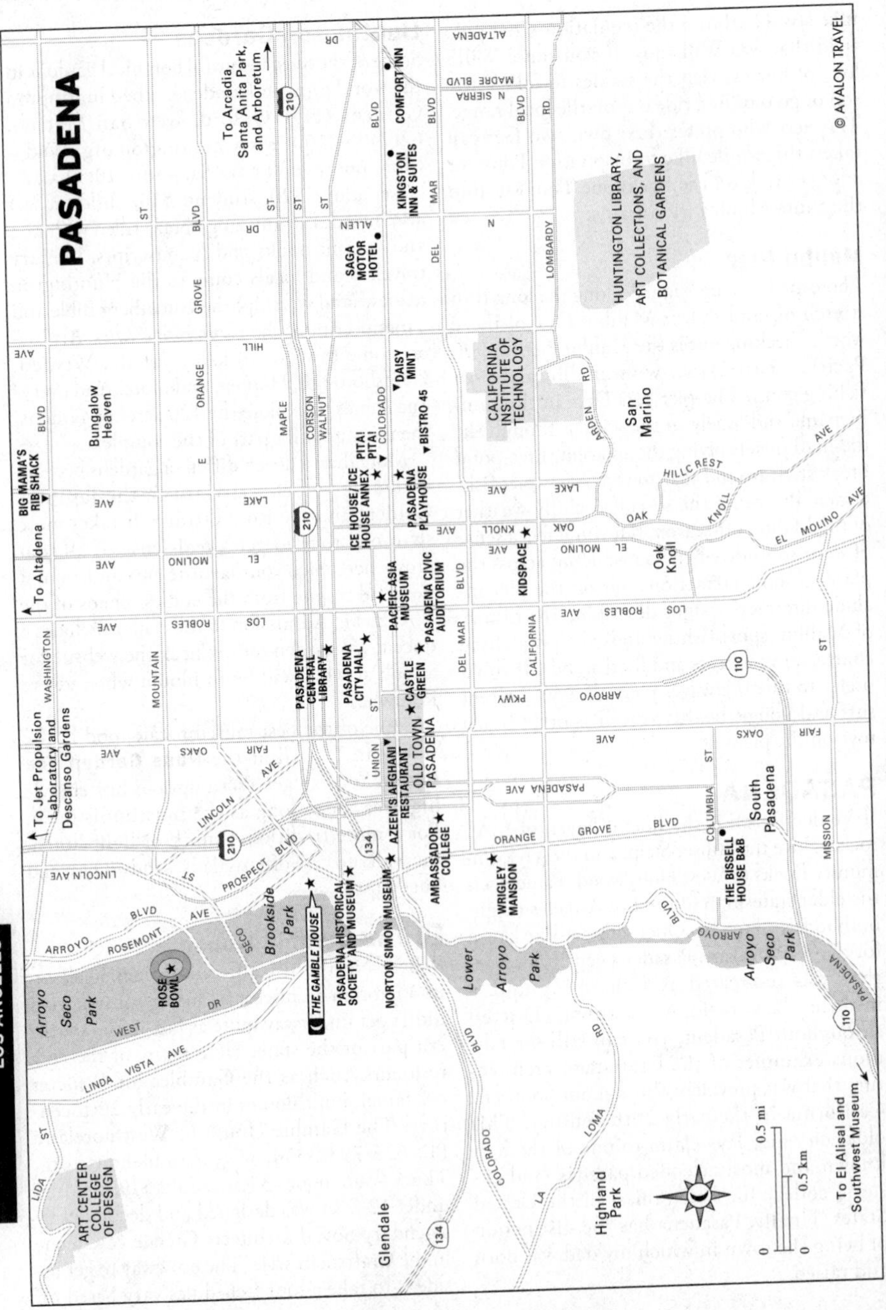
PASADENA
To Arcadia, Santa Anita Park, and Arboretum
To Altadena
To Jet Propulsion Laboratory and Descanso Gardens
Bungalow Heaven
BIG MAMA'S RIB SHACK
SAGA MOTOR HOTEL
KINGSTON INN & SUITES
COMFORT INN
DAISY MINT
BISTRO 45
PITA! PITA!
ICE HOUSE/ICE HOUSE ANNEX
PASADENA PLAYHOUSE
PACIFIC ASIA MUSEUM
PASADENA CIVIC AUDITORIUM
PASADENA CITY HALL
PASADENA CENTRAL LIBRARY
CASTLE GREEN
OLD TOWN PASADENA
AZEEN'S AFGHANI RESTAURANT
AMBASSADOR COLLEGE
NORTON SIMON MUSEUM
PASADENA HISTORICAL SOCIETY AND MUSEUM
THE GAMBLE HOUSE
WRIGLEY MANSION
KIDSPACE
CALIFORNIA INSTITUTE OF TECHNOLOGY
HUNTINGTON LIBRARY, ART COLLECTIONS, AND BOTANICAL GARDENS
San Marino
Oak Knoll
South Pasadena
THE BISSELL HOUSE B&B
ROSE BOWL
Arroyo Seco Park
Brookside Park
Lower Arroyo Park
ART CENTER COLLEGE OF DESIGN
Glendale
Highland Park
To El Alisal and Southwest Museum
0.5 mi
0.5 km
© AVALON TRAVEL

© LANCE SCOTT

The Gamble House

the season). To buy tickets, go to the side of the main mansion and into the garage. The garage, built in the same style as the house, now acts as the house's bookstore and ticket office.

Inside the house, you'll be led from room to room as the docent describes the construction and decor in detail. The Craftsman aesthetic attempted to "answer" the overly ornate and precious Victorian style with long, clean lines and botanical motifs. The Greenes took this philosophy to heart in the construction of the Gamble house-you'll learn how they created this masterpiece as you view each unique room. You'll also see how the Gambles lived inside the house and hear some of their stories, even that of the house's possible haunting by the Gambles' Aunt Julia. The only place in the mansion that you won't see are two upstairs servants' rooms, now the home of two lucky architecture students who live in the house each school year.

## Norton Simon Museum

Believe it or not, the two millennia of art displayed at the Norton Simon Museum (411 W. Colorado Blvd., 626/449-6840, www.nortonsimon.org, Wed.–Mon. noon–6 P.M., Fri. until 9 P.M., adults $8, seniors $4, students free) were once part of a private collection. Wealthy industrialist Norton Simon collected the thousands of works of art over 30 years. He particularly loved the European Renaissance, the works of South and Southeast Asia, and 20th-century sculpture. Several of his most famous Rodins decorate the walkway up to the main entrance to the museum. You can visit the lovely modern building housing large, airy galleries to study the beautiful works of fine art here. Be sure to head outside to walk through the sculpture gardens in the courtyards behind the building. You can purchase books and reproductions in the museum store or grab a bite to eat at the simple, walk-up Garden Café.

## Rose Bowl

The Rose Bowl Stadium (1001 Rose Bowl Dr., 626/577-3101, www.rosebowlstadium.com), true to its name, is the home to the famed "Granddaddy" of the Bowl Games and to the UCLA college football team. Built in 1922, this huge elliptical bowl began with an open side. It was closed only a few years later, and now seats almost (but not quite) 100,000 people—perfect for the Super Bowl, as well as the flea markets and endless parade of college games! In addition to the endless vista of seats, you'll find plenty of restrooms and concessions scattered throughout the stadium—far more than the average college football team's home.

You can visit the Rose Bowl anytime, though you might need a ticket during an event, and you'll definitely need to plan in advance to attend the Rose Bowl game. Check the online calendar to find a fun event to attend for the best sense of this National Historic Landmark.

# Entertainment and Events

## NIGHTLIFE

### Bars and Clubs

Want to know which of the many dance and nightclubs in the L.A. area is the hottest or hippest or most popular with the stars this week? You'll need to ask the locals or read the alt-weeklies when you arrive, since these things change almost weekly. What was hot when this guide was written will no doubt be out by the time it's published. So check out the scene when you arrive, or pick one of these reasonably reliable standards.

Know that clubs in L.A. get crowded (and overcrowded) on weekend nights, and that bouncers take joy in selecting only the most chic hipsters in line to allow into the sacred spaces beyond the doors. Women have a slight edge, but in the top L.A. clubs, this can mean little to nothing. Being young and beautiful helps, of course, as does being dressed in the latest designer fashions and knowing a celebrity or the club's owner. So put on your finest and fanciest clubbing outfit, head out, and go for it!

For a good time dancing into the wee hours on a usually sedate Sunday night, head for **Deep at Club Vanguard** (6021 Hollywood Blvd., Hollywood, 323/463-3331, www.deep-la.com, Sun. only 9:30 P.M.–4 A.M., cover $20). This one-night-only monument to the freshest house music was opened in 1999 and has been growing in popularity ever since. Expect top-shelf house DJs from New York, L.A., and anywhere else the best are spinning these days. In addition to the crowded dance floor, you'll find a full bar and a back patio done up in the finest Asian style.

For the rest of the week, this space is simply **Club Vanguard** (www.vanguardla.com), hosting DJs in various styles, VIP nights, lingerie fashion shows, and other events that draw in the young and hip on the Hollywood scene.

For serious rockers looking for something a little bit heavier, there's the **Key Club** (9039 W. Sunset Blvd., West Hollywood, 310/274-5800, www.keyclub.com, daily 7 P.M.–2 A.M., cover $20). The Key Club caters to the heavy metal-and-dining crowd (yes, there is definitely such a thing in L.A.), with a full stage that hosts live bands and a full-service restaurant. This club feels like a warren, what with the stage and dance room, the casual and (in theory) quieter room down the hall, and the plush VIP suite upstairs. Of course you'll find more than one full bar inside this multi-purpose club.

For an ever-so-slightly more laid-back L.A. clubbing experience, head on down to **The Little Temple** (4519 Santa Monica Blvd., 323/660-4540, www.littletemple.com, Mon. midnight–2 A.M., Tue.–Thurs. 8 P.M.–2 A.M., Fri.–Sat. 9 P.M.–2 A.M., Sun 9 P.M.–midnight, cover $5). This funky, hip space mixes Buddhist Asian decor with deep house, hip-hop, and Latin music for a sometimes dance-heavy, sometimes lounge-centric evening of fun and flirtation. You can get your groove on down on the dance floor, then flop onto the huge communal bed to rest and relax with your oldest and newest friends. Decor mixes the sacred with the profane, and the full bar lubricates an already friendly evening with beer, wine, and cocktails.

Sometimes, a place doesn't need a huge description or build-up to illuminate its atmosphere and theme. **Bordello** (901 E. First St.,

213/687-3766, www.bordellobar.com, daily 7 P.M.–2 A.M., cover $10), with its provocative name and plush red interior, exemplifies such an establishment. Sitting at the former location of Little Pedros, the first bar opened in L.A. with a notorious reputation for its "other" business as a brothel, Bordello strives to be worthy of its historic locale. The interior feels almost cluttered to a modern sensibility; it's crammed with antique glass light fixtures, ornately painted and leafed geegaws, and velvet lounging couches. Musical offerings are deliberately eclectic. You might hear jazz one night, ska the next, and indie rock the night after that. Bordello also hosts regular burlesque shows. The full bar offers beers on tap as well as club-appropriate pink cocktails. Come in and be seduced.

The **3 Clubs Cocktail Lounge** (1123 Vine St., Hollywood, 323/462-6441, www.threeclubs.com, Mon. midnight–2 A.M., Tue.–Sat. 6 P.M.–2 A.M., Sun. 6 P.M.–midnight, no cover) acts at once as a locals' watering hole and a reasonably priced nightclub catering mostly to the collegiate set. Expect to find the dance floor of the rear club crowded and sweaty, with fairly generic modern dance mixes blaring out over the crush of writhing bodies. Two bars serve up drinks to the masses, and drinks are a bit cheaper here than in the "hotter" spots. But if you're a lone female, do be aware that 3 Clubs has no decent parking and you may have to walk several blocks along Hollywood Boulevard long after dark. Consider brining a friend or two along with you to up your safety quotient.

## Gay and Lesbian

An alternative to glammed-up West Hollywood gay bars, **Akbar** (4356 Sunset Blvd., 323/665-6810, www.akbarsilverlake.com, Mon.–Sun. 7 P.M.–2 A.M.) pulls in a gay-friendly crowd with its cozy, Moroccan-themed decor, neighborhood vibe, and friendly, unpretentious bartenders.

Sleek, glamorous, and candlelit, the **Abbey Food and Bar** (692 N. Robertson Blvd., West Hollywood, 310/289-8410, daily 8 A.M.–2 A.M.) is a popular gay bar with a great outdoor patio and pillow-strewn private cabanas—all of which are usually jam-packed. Savvy bartenders mix 40 different specialty martinis.

## Live Music

Los Angeles has long been one of the biggest destinations for struggling young rockers to come out, live cheap, and struggle to grab a spot on stage to take their shot at that all-important record contract. The clubs in the Sunset district, particularly those on the Sunset Strip, incubated some of the biggest rock acts of all time long before anybody knew who they were. The top three clubs drip rock history from their very walls. You might want to hold your nose when you first walk into the **Whisky A Go Go** (8901 Sunset Blvd., West Hollywood, 310/652-4202, www.whiskyagogo.com, cover $10). Despite a stench almost as memorable as its sound, throngs of music fans pack into the Whisky every night of the week. Most nights you'll get a lineup of new bands—sometimes as many as seven in one evening. For those shows, you can pay about $10 in advance or $12 at the door to see groups that might (or might not) be the Next Big Thing. The Whisky also hosts many cover and tribute bands that pay homage to the elder statesmen that once played here, such as Led Zeppelin and The Doors. And once in a great while, the Whisky hosts a major event like The Police reunion tours, or a performance by a current star.

Almost next door to the Whisky you'll find **The Roxy Theatre** (9009 Sunset Blvd., West Hollywood, http://theroxyonsunset.com). A comparative newcomer to the scene, The Roxy opened in 1973 with Neil Young performing. The second(ish) generation of heavy-duty rock acts made their name here (think Guns & Roses, Jane's Addiction, and Pearl Jam). Today you'll find the newest acts gracing the stage. Most shows feature three to five bands. The Roxy also puts up non-musical shows, from standup comedy to full-on theatrical productions to performance art. The big black-box theater has an open dance floor, comfy-ish booths (if you can get one), and bare-bones food service during shows. Nearby parking is nearly non-existent, so think about taking public transit or a cab to the show. You'll find the performance calendar on the website, and tickets available through major ticket agents. For one of the best after-hours parties on the strip, try to get into **On the Rox,** located directly above The Roxy. Or stagger next door to the **Rainbow Bar & Grill** (9015 Sunset Blvd., West Hollywood, 310/278-4232, daily 11 A.M.–2 A.M.).

It's not on the Strip, but its reputation is just as big and bad as its brethren. **The Troubadour** (9081 Santa Monica Blvd., West Hollywood, www.troubadour.com) opened its doors in 1957. Over its more than 50 years, Bob Dylan jammed, total unknown comic Steve Martin sang, Tom Waits was discovered, Billy Joel opened for somebody else, Metallica headlined for the very first time, and countless A-list bands have recorded in and even about The Troubadour (and my husband, also this guidebook's photographer, once played the Troubadour!). Today, you'll find everyone from Coldplay to Fiona Apple to the newest amateur acts at The Troubadour. If you're in town past the weekend, come on down for a fabulous "Free Monday" and save your money for drinks. You can check the events calendar in advance to find your favorite bands, then buy tickets online or via fax. If you've decided on a whim to hit tonight's show, you can buy tickets at the on-site box office on the day of the show only, so long as the show isn't sold out.

If you're looking for something smaller in the way of a semi-underground club, your best bet is to ask around once you're on the ground in L.A. Hot spots turn to cold spots quickly here, and the locals usually know what's up.



## Comedy

Not far behind the live music scene, L.A.'s live comedy scene is second only to Manhattan's as a way to see the brightest current stars and the most impressive young new talent. More than a dozen major live comedy clubs make their home in the smog belt. Pick your favorite, sit back, and laugh (or groan) the night away.

Located in the former Ciro's Nightclub on the Strip, **The Comedy Store** (8433 Sunset Blvd., West Hollywood, 323/656-6225, www.thecomedystore.com, $10, 21 and older) is owned by 1980s comedian Pauly Shore's mother. With three separate rooms, you'll find a show going on at The Store every night of the week; most start at 9 P.M. or later, but you can check the website's calendar for both early and late shows. In all three rooms you'll often find a showcase featuring more than a dozen stand-up comics all performing one after another (and leaving space for possible celebrity drop-ins). Local sketch and improv groups also have regular gigs at The Store. Once upon a time, legendary comics got their starts here, often on Monday Amateur Nights. Imagine being among the first people ever to see Yakov Smirnoff perform, or getting to see Steve Martin or Whoopi Goldberg 10 feet from your table for less than $20. That's the level of talent you'll find performing here on a nightly basis. You can buy tickets online for bigger shows, and at the door for non-sell-outs and The Belly Room. Most shows have a two-drink minimum in addition to the cover; no-cover acts in The Belly Room are your best bet for a bargain.

It seems unlikely that a major comedy club would make its home in peaceful, suburban Pasadena, but that's where the **Ice House** (24 N. Mentor Ave. off Colorado Blvd., 626/577-1894, www.icehousecomedy.com, Tues.–Sun., cover $5–20) sits. With shows running nightly and a double-header most Saturday nights, anyone who wants a laugh will enjoy an evening at the Ice House. Comedians who've performed here recently include Jeff Garcia, Bill Dwyer, and Gabriel Iglesias. You'll also find a focus on female comics and a regular Latino comedy showcase here. The $5 newcomers-heavy showcase on Wednesday nights makes for one of the best bargains in the L.A. entertainment scene, and you never know who you'll see. That bouncing hobbit-shaped guy named Daymon Ferguson or the lanky pseudo-depressive comic songster Phil Johnson might be the next ones to hit it big, and you can say you saw them when! If you actually favor a lower-budget, newer-comic evening, hit the Ice House **Annex,** the smaller ancillary room sitting right next door to the main club.

## THE ARTS

### Theater

Even with all the hoopla over film in L.A., there's still plenty of room for live theatrical entertainment in and around Tinseltown.

The **Kodak Theater** (6801 Hollywood Blvd., 323/308-6300, www.kodaktheatre.com) has as its most notable annual event the Academy Awards, often called The Oscars. But for the rest of the year, the Kodak hosts live shows of various types. Many other awards shows make their homes here, and the stage is often graced by major performers such as Eddie Izzard and Ricky Gervais. Also look for classical music concerts and vocal music performances.

Some theatergoers prefer outdoor entertainment to indoor, and the **Ford Theater** (2580 Cahuenga Blvd. E., 323/461-3673, www.fordamphitheater.org) certainly takes advantage of Hollywood's temperate climate to bring the shows outdoors. Every sort of theatrical event imaginable can find a stage at the Ford, from classical ballet to experimental theater to postmodern circus acts. Lots of musical acts play the Ford—think jazz, folk, world music, and beyond. Children's shows come to the Ford, and the theater even puts up the occasional film-based multimedia production. Check the monthly events calendar to see what's up during your visit.

The **Ahmanson Theater** (135 N. Grand Ave., 213/628-2772, www.centertheatregroup.org, $86–220) specializes in big Broadway-style productions. You might see a grandiose musical, heart-wrenching drama, or gut-busting comedy here. Expect to find the names of many familiar shows on the annual schedule, from *A Chorus Line* to *Death of a Salesman* to *Who's Afraid of Virginia Woolf?* With hundreds of seats (all of them expensive), there's usually enough room to provide entertainment even for the most last-minute of visitors.

### Classical Music

Though L.A. is better known for its rock than its classical music offerings, you can still find plenty of high cultural concerts as well. If you love the grandiose, get a ticket for a show at the **Los Angeles Opera** (135 N. Grand Ave., 213/972-7219, www.losangelesopera.com, $20–238). The L.A. Opera has only existed since 1986, but in that time it has grown to be one of the largest opera companies in the United States, gaining national recognition for the quality of its work. The dazzling performances held at the Dorothy Chandler Pavilion in the Music Center of L.A. County have included such masterworks of the genre as *Don Giovanni, La Bohème,* and *Tristan and Isolde.* If you're in town in 2009, you might catch *The Magic Flute* or *La Traviata.* Each season includes about 10 different operas. The company gets recognition for its amazing production values, which include at least a couple of shows with truly fantastical costumes that in themselves are worth the price of the ticket.

If you prefer your musicians in black and white, take in a show by the **Los Angeles Philharmonic** (323/850-2000, www.laphil.com, $35–150), better known to its friends as the L.A. Phil. The philharmonic performs primarily at the **Walt Disney Concert Hall** (111 S. Grand Ave., 323/850-2000, www.disneyconcerthall.com). Concerts can range from classics by famed composers like Tchaikovsky, Bach, and Beethoven to the world music of Asha Bhosle to jazz by Bobby McFerrin. Guest performers can be the modern virtuosi of classical music—Midori plays here on occasion. Whatever style of music you choose to listen to, conductor Esa-Pekka Salonen or one of his guests will lead you on a wonderful aural journey.

With its art deco band shell set against canyon chaparral, the **Hollywood Bowl** (2301 N. Highland Ave., 323/436-2827 or 323/850-2000, www.hollywoodbowl.com) has long been a romantic setting for outdoor summer concerts by the L.A. Philharmonic and other artists.

If you're interested in supporting the work of amateur musician or just seeing a chamber concert in a more intimate setting, consider getting tickets to the **Los Angeles Doctors Symphony** (www.ladso.org, $10). This lovely community orchestra has been performing regularly since its inception in 1953. Many, though by no means all, of the musicians you'll hear are members of the medical community. They play everything from Mozart and Schubert to traditional music of various cultures, depending on the concert venue and the event. Check the website for the annual schedule, programs, and ticket information. If they're playing when you're in town, it's definitely worth your time to support the musical culture of the Los Angeles community!

### Cinema

Movie premieres are a big deal in L.A. and Hollywood for the obvious reasons. Crowds throng the streets outside of Grauman's Chinese Theatre and the Egyptian, where the stars tromp down the red carpets to enjoy the sight of themselves on the big screen. Even the standard AMC and Century theaters get packed on opening nights, so come early or buy tickets online to assure yourself of seats to your favorite star's latest release.

The current favorite movie house for star sightings is the **ArcLight Hollywood Cinema** (6360 W. Sunset Blvd., Hollywood, 323/464-1478, www.arclightcinemas.com, tickets $12–14). Perhaps this is due to the ArcLight's 21-and-older-only screenings of major blockbuster movies, which allow patrons to purchase beer and wine at the Café and bring their drinks into the theater with them. But most of all, the ArcLight complex offers the best visual and sound technologies, all-reserved seating, and the updated geodesic Cinemarama Dome theater. Do be sure to make reservations in advance (you can buy tickets online or at kiosks at the theater) if you want great seats to the latest films. The ArcLight also shows a few art house flicks and even the occasional "retrospective" (code for old) movie in its hallowed theaters. Ask for parking validation for a discount on the adjacent parking structure. You'll need it, since due to the ArcLight's status as a Hollywood favorite, you'll pay above even the usual high L.A. movie theater rates to see a show here.

# Shopping

In Los Angeles, shopping qualifies as a major source of entertainment for locals and visitors alike. Don't worry about being materialistic or a spendthrift here—that's what you're *supposed* to be. If it exists anywhere on earth, you can probably buy it somewhere in L.A., whether "it" is a Smart Car, a bunch of flowers, an indie CD, or a pair of pants that cost as much as a Smart Car. Different areas and towns have their own unique shopping feel, so decide what kind of retail experience you want and then pick the right spot to find it.

## DOWNTOWN AND VICINITY

### Flower District

If you have even the slightest love of plants and flowers, you can't miss the world-famous Los Angeles Flower District (766 Wall St., 213/622-1966, www.laflowerdistrict.com, Mon.–Sat. mornings). Sometimes called "America's Flower Market," this vast sea of color and beauty is a triumph of American multicultural entrepreneurial spirit. The first flower cultivators in Los Angeles were Japanese Americans, and today many growers are of Hispanic descent—perhaps especially fitting for an industry that creates products in all colors of the rainbow. When you visit this vast sea of beauty, you'll find a fun cacophony of different languages being spoken as floral retailers vie for the best products available on any given day. But never fear: Anyone can come and stroll the narrow aisles of the various markets, and you'll find plenty of pre-made bouquets with which to impress your sweetie. Or better yet, find someone who can create a custom arrangement for you, since just about every kind of cut flower, potted plant, and exotic species can be purchased here. You can take away a bouquet filled with flowers you've never even seen before!

Among other major events, the Flower District supplies the unbelievable needs of the Rose Parade each New Year's. Literally millions of flowers go into the creation of the stunning floats (which *must* incorporate flowers to qualify for most of the awards in the parade). It's hard to image the work necessary to fill the orders for the floats, but the denizens of the flower market do it every year.

One caution: while the flower market itself is safe for visitors, the area to the south is not. Get good directions before you come, and don't plan to wander the neighborhood on foot.

### Jewelry District

If you're looking for the bleeding edge of style when you shop for jewelry, you can't do much better than the Los Angeles Jewelry District (bordered by 5th St., 8th St., Broadway, and Olive St., www.lajd.net). With more than 3,000 wholesalers, even the most avid lover of sparkly stones and glittering gold will get her (or his) fill here. Do be a little bit careful if you're a woman alone, especially at dusk or later, as this isn't the squeakiest clean part of downtown L.A. But you can shop in reasonable peace here, and even in some confidence that you won't get ripped off so long as you do some preliminary research. The district website provides information on vendor ratings and a map to help you get around more easily. From wholesale dealers of unset gems, to professional gem setters who'll create a beautiful piece from the stones you've bought, you can find just about anything you ever dreamed of here.

## BEVERLY HILLS AND WEST HOLLYWOOD

### Rodeo Drive

If you're reading this book, you probably don't have enough money to go on a serious spree in the shops of Rodeo Drive. The hottest stars and other big-spenders come here to purchase the best and most expensive goods the world has to offer.

Have you ever a $1,500 pair of pants? Walk into the **Chanel** (400 N. Rodeo Dr., Beverly Hills, 310/278-5500, www.chanel.com) store and you'll be able to. You'll see original artwork, catalogs, the very edgiest high-end clothes in existence, and salespeople who will look down their noses at you if your outfit cost you less than four figures. Head upstairs for racks of on-sale clothing from last season, though you'll quickly learn that "on sale" is a relative concept. If you're lucky, you might even get dissed by one or more of the überrich women wearing fur hats and carrying little yippy dogs (they're unaware of the irony). Hunt the racks for the classic tweedy Coco Chanel dress—you will find it. Or if you prefer another designer, head outside and find one; all the big leaguers, from Dior to Michael Kors, maintain storefronts on Rodeo.

Though Rodeo Drive is most famous for its designer apparel, many other retailers offer a vast array of expensive things, from sunglasses to jewelry to housewares. If you're looking for (or just want to look at) the perfect diamond ring, walk past the guards into the huge hallowed halls of **Tiffany's** (210 N. Rodeo Dr., Beverly Hills, 310/273-8880, www.tiffany.com, Mon.–Fri. 10 A.M.–7 P.M., Sat.–Sun. 10 A.M.–6 P.M.). The store has three floors of the most exquisite necklaces, bracelets, rings, watches, and accessories you'll ever find anywhere. This storefront compares easily to its sister store in Manhattan. You'll find the sales help here a bit friendlier here than in the clothing stores, since even the middle-class of L.A. come to Tiffany's to purchase special-occasion jewelry.

The wealthy who want to fall asleep with their skin soothed by the softest sheets around go to **Frette** (459 N. Rodeo Dr., Beverly Hills, 310/273-8540, www.frette.com, Mon.–Sat. 10 A.M.–6 P.M., Sun. 12–5 P.M.) to make their purchases. This store doesn't get as crowded as many others on Rodeo and much of Frette's business goes to high-end hotels. But the doors of this open, airy retail store remain defiantly open, beckoning shoppers who love luxury more than life itself. Salespeople encourage you to pet the merchandise, comparing one set of sheets to another and imagining the feel of the plushy bath sheets after your next shower.

### Melrose Avenue

Melrose Avenue (btwn. San Vicente and La Brea Aves.) is really two shopping districts. High-end fashion and design showrooms dominate the western end, near La Cienega Boulevard; head east past Fairfax Avenue for tattoo parlors and used clothing.

If you miss 1960s mod, 1970s grooviness, 1980s power-dressing, or even last year's haute couture, drop by **Decades** (8214½ Melrose Ave., 323/655-0223, www.decadesinc.com, Mon.–Sat. 11:30 A.M.–6 P.M.) and browse among the prime, vintage Courrèges, Hermès, and Pucci castoffs.

If you adore the clothes from *Sex and the City* and *Friends,* stop in at **Fred Segal** (81118 Melrose Ave., 323/651-1935, Mon.–Sat. 10 A.M.–7 P.M., Sun. 12–6 P.M.), a deluxe department store, which has everything from the ridiculously trendy to the severely tasteful.

Futuristic specs from **l.a.Eyeworks** (7407 Melrose Ave., 323/653-8255, www.laeyeworks.com, Mon.–Fri. 10 A.M.–7 P.M., Sat. 10 A.M.–6 P.M.) have appeared in films like *The Matrix* and *Blade Runner,* and celebs like Jennifer Aniston and Wesley Snipes are fans of the store's lightweight, trend-defining frames.

The buyers at **Wasteland** (7428 Melrose Ave., 323/653-3028, www.thewasteland.com) carefully pick out merchandise for their club-hopping clientele, so everything at this secondhand store has style. The selection covers a wide range, from Gucci to Gap.



## SANTA MONICA, VENICE, AND MALIBU

Shopping down by the beaches can be as much fun as anyplace else in the L.A. area. Santa Monica offers your best bet for an entertaining retail experience, since Venice Beach and Malibu tend more toward strip malls.

### Third Street Promenade

Looking for the place where middle-class locals come to shop in the L.A. area? Head for the Third Street Promenade (Third St., Santa Monica, http://thirdstreetpromenade.org). Much of Third Street in Santa Monica is closed to auto traffic to make it easier to walk along the Promenade. This long vertical outdoor mall features all your favorite chain stores for clothing, shoes, jewelry, housewares, computers, and just about anything else you can think of. You'll find people plying the Promenade day and night, seven days a week. If your goal is a serious retail spree, come out to the Promenade on a weekday during daylight hours to avoid the bigger crushes of people that pile into the area on weekends. On the other hand, if you're looking for a fun social outing, the Promenade gets popular with a younger crowd at night. You can hit one of the movie theaters, stop in at a bar, or just stroll the pedestrian walks enjoying the mild night air and the street performers who work the area. The Promenade is within easy walking distance of the Santa Monica Pier and adjacent beach as well.

The Promenade's shops tend toward the classic mall fare. You'll find a tremendous three-story Gap offering classic clothes to the masses. The high-end Anthropologie and Armani Exchange can get you looking fine for the remainder of your L.A. vacation and beyond. If you need a new computer or a shiny iPod or iPhone to get you back home in style and entertained, a huge Apple Store can hook you up. If you're looking to catch the latest flick, choose from three different movie theaters, including a Mann Theater. On weekends, you can get the freshest and tastiest fruits and vegetables from the legendary farmers market at the Promenade.

## PASADENA

### Old Town Pasadena

Old Town Pasadena (Colorado Blvd., www.oldpasadena.com) was once a quaint downtown area serving a small but wealthy resort community. Today, Old Town essentially acts as a street-based shopping mall, with upscale chain stores inhabiting classic deco and mid-century modern buildings.

# Sports and Recreation

You'll find an endless array of ways to get outside and have fun in the L.A. Basin. Among the most popular recreation options are those that get you out onto the beach or into the Pacific Ocean.

## BEACHES

If you're in SoCal for the first time, it's almost a given that one of your destinations is a genuine California beach. You've got plenty to choose from in the L.A. area. From north of Malibu down to Manhattan and Hermosa Beach, you'll find a seemingly endless stretch of public beaches. Most of these have lots of visitor amenities (unlike their Northern California brethren), such as snack bars, boardwalks, showers, beach toy rental shacks, surf schools, and permanent sports courts. Believe it or not, those listed here are just a drop in the bucket; if none of these beaches do it for you, you can choose from dozens of others that stretch in a nearly unbroken line from one end of the county to the other.

Not all L.A. beaches are created equal. With a very few exceptions, you won't find clean, clear water to swim in, since pollution is a major issue on the L.A. coast. Also keep in mind that Los Angeles County is not a tropical zone. The water does warm up in the summer, but not into the 80s like you find in Hawaii. (Happily, it's also not in the icy 50s and 60s, as in the northern reaches of the state.) Expect to cool off significantly when you dive into the surf, and if you plan to be out in the water for an extended period, get yourself a wetsuit to prevent chills that can turn into hypothermia.

### Zuma Beach

If you've ever seen the cult classic film *Earth Girls Are Easy*, you've heard of legendary Zuma Beach (Pacific Coast Highway, 19 miles north of Malibu). This popular surf and boogie-boarding break, complete with a nice, big stretch of clean, white sand, fills up fast on summer weekends but isn't as crowded on weekdays. Grab a spot on the west side of the Pacific Coast Highway for free parking, or pay a little for one of the more than 2,000 spots in the beach parking lot. Zuma has all the amenities you need for a full day out at the beach, from restrooms and showers to a kid-friendly snack bar and a beachside boardwalk.

Water lovers can ride the waves or just take a swim in the cool and (unusual for the L.A. area) crystal-clear Pacific waters. Zuma has lifeguards during daylight hours, and for landlubbers, it's got beach volleyball courts set up and a playground for the kids. Perhaps best of all, this beach doesn't fill up with litter-happy tourists. It's actually a locals' favorite for weekend R&R.

### Malibu Lagoon State Beach

In a sea of private beaches fronting mansions, Malibu Lagoon State Beach (23200 Pacific Coast Hwy., 818/880-0363, www.parks.ca.gov, daily 8 A.M.–sunset) and its ancillary **Malibu Surfriders Beach** offer public access to a great northern L.A. location. Running alongside the Malibu Pier, this pretty stretch of sugar-like sand offers a wealth of activities as well as pure California relaxation. This beach offers a number of unusual attractions, including both the **Adamson House** (310/456-8432, www.adamsonhouse.org) and the **Malibu Lagoon Museum.** You can take a guided tour that goes through the museum and out to the wetlands, butterfly trees, tidepools, and flower gardens. Malibu Creek runs into the ocean here, creating a unique wetlands ecosystem that's well worth exploring. If a beach party is more your style, you can rent beach toys at the pier and stake your spot on the sand. Surfers man the break here year-round; please be careful of your fellow riders.

At the intersection that leads to the museum, you can also drive down to the main parking lot. It's likely to fill up fast in the summer, so get there early for a spot.

### Will Rogers State Beach

If you're a film buff and a beach bum, you must take a day out of your travel schedule to hang out on the Will Rogers State Beach (17700 Pacific Coast Hwy., Pacific Palisades, beaches.co.la.ca.us/bandh/beaches/willrogers.htm). Yet another fabulous full-service L.A. beach, a number of movies have been filmed at Will Rogers. Even if you don't care about that, you'll love the nearly two miles of sandy beach, easy to get to from the parking lot, studded with volleyball courts, playground equipment, restrooms, and picnic tables. The bike path running along the land side of the sand runs for 19 miles all the way down to Redondo State Beach. Out in the water, you can swim, skin dive, and surf. A mild right point break offers a good learning ground for beginners. Lifeguards protect the shores during the day in summer, and the locals think their guards are some of the best-looking in the county. Just be sure to pay attention to the flags and signs, since pollution can be a big problem at Will Rogers due to storm drains emptying out into the ocean.

Bring cash to pay for parking, but be happy that with more than 1,750 spots, you'll probably find one that's legal and reasonably secure.

### Santa Monica State Beach

If you're looking for "The Beach" in Santa Monica, well.it's hard to miss. The waterside edge of town is encompassed by Santa Monica State Beach (Pacific Coast Hwy., www.santamonica.com/index.php/beach.html). For 3.5 miles, the fine sand gets raked daily beneath the sun that shines over the beach more than 300 days each year. Flop down in the sand to enjoy the warm sunshine, take a dip in the endless waves of the Pacific, stroll along the boardwalk, or stand at the edge of the of the water and peer out to see if you can catch sight of a pod of dolphins frolicking in the surf. If you don't mind crowds, hang out on the sand right near the pier. The best people-watching runs south of the pier area and on towards Venice Beach. For a bit more elbow room, head north of the pier to the less populated end of the beach.

Due to its location right "in" town and adjacent to and beneath the Santa Monica Pier, you'll find a near-endless array of services at the beach. On the pier and just across from the beach, you can get snacks and meals, rent surf and boogie boards, hit the arcade, and go shopping. Parking varies, depending on which part of the beach you head for. The north end has spotty parking, the pier area can get really crowded but has more options, and the south probably has the best bet for a good spot.

## SURFING

If you ask anyone the around what the defining sport in California is, they'll tell you it's surfing. And the craze for wave riding began in Los Angeles. The mystical athletic endeavor stars in movies and TV shows, yet it's something lots of folks can learn to do. Whether you've been riding waves for decades or you've never before touched a surfboard, going surfing will add a touch of real California culture to your L.A. visit.

You'll find a fabulous array of surf breaks in the L.A. area, with waves of all sizes beckoning to riders of every ability level. Most folks come out to the beach at Venice to check out the zoolike boardwalk, but you can ride the waves here on the lifeguard-protected beach too. A great break for all levels, the breakwater at Venice Beach is a favorite spot for locals.

### Surf Lessons

If you've never surfed before, your best bet is to sign up for a lesson (or two) with a reputable surf school. Most schools can get you standing up on your longboard on the very first lesson! One of these, **Learn to Surf LA** (641 Westminster Ave., #5, Venice, 310/663-2479, www.learntosurfla.com, $60–120), operates on Venice Beach. You can take a private lesson, a semi-private lesson with friends, or join a regularly scheduled group. Each lesson lasts almost two hours and includes all equipment (you'll get a full wetsuit in addition to a board), shore instruction and practice, and plenty of time in the water. No, the brightly colored foam longboards you'll learn on aren't the coolest or most stylish, but they're perfect for new surfers looking for a stable ride on smaller waves. Learn to

ROBERT HOLMES / CALTOUR

Venice Beach swimmers

Surf LA offers lessons for both kids and adults-, and this can be a great activity for the whole family to tackle together. Intermediate and advanced surfers can also find great fun with this school, which has advanced instructors capable of helping you improve your skills.

## HANG GLIDING

You can pick the kind of ground you want to soar over in L.A.: the ocean or the inland mountains and valleys. If you prefer to see the water slipping past beneath you, head for **Dockweiler Beach Training Park** (12000 Vista del Mar, Playa del Rey, Wed.–Sun. 11 A.M.–sunset). For a higher-altitude adventure, head to the San Fernando Valley and up to **Sylmar Flight Park** (daily 10 A.M.–sunset). For a good school and rental facility, call **Windsports Soaring Center** (818/367-2430, http://windsports.com, prices vary). You can go tandem with an instructor at Sylmar Flight Park (recommended for first-time gliders) or get bold and try a solo ride (which starts at an altitude of five feet out on the beach at Dockweiler). Windsports provides all the equipment and training you need, so all you have to bring are a good pair of athletic shoes, a bottle of water, and, of course, a camera.

## SPAS

Inside the Westin Bonaventure Hotel downtown, enjoy some good pampering at the **Bonaventure Club Spa & Fitness Center** (404 S. Figueroa St., 888/629-0900, http://bonaventureclub.com, daily 11 A.M.–11 P.M., $20–225). With a focus on beauty as well as health and relaxation, the Bonaventure Club features a number of heavy-duty facials, as well as dermabrasion and collagen treatments. You'll also find a full nail and waxing salon, and an array of massages and body scrubs. The Bonaventure isn't the poshest spa around, but you'll get decent service. The locker rooms, sauna, and other facilities are clean, and the spa is open later than most to accommodate busy travelers. Book in advance if you want a specific treatment at a specific time of day, but you're likely to find a same-day appointment if you aren't too picky about exactly which treatment you want.

## SPECTATOR SPORTS

Befitting a major American city, Los Angeles boasts a nearly full complement of professional sports teams. (L.A. no longer has an NFL team in town, but once it had two. Oops!)

The **L.A. Kings** (213/742-7100, http://kings.nhl.com) play lightning-fast NHL hockey downtown at the Staples Center (1111 S. Figueroa St., www.staplescenter.com). Well, they try to play lightning-fast, anyway. The Kings are more famous for their failures than their successes, but going out to the games is still fun, particularly if your home team is playing the Kings while you're in town.

As great legends of the NBA, the individual players and the organization as a whole of the **Los Angeles Lakers** (www.nba.com/lakers) have well and truly earned their places. Though Magic no longer dunks for the Lakers, Kobe Bryant carries on the star torch for the still-winning team.

As for the MLB, baseball takes advantage

of the perfect climate in L.A. to host some of the most beautiful outdoor summer games anywhere in the country. The **Los Angeles Dodgers** (http://losangeles.dodgers.mlb.com) make their home in this hospitable climate, playing often and well throughout the long baseball season. Just one thing: Don't refer to Dodger Stadium (1000 Elysian Park Ave.) as "Chavez Ravine" unless you really mean it. (That old field designation has become a derogatory term used primarily by San Francisco Giants fans.)

# Accommodations

From the cheapest roach-ridden shack motels to the most chi-chi Beverly Hills hotel, Los Angeles has an endless variety of lodgings to suit every taste and budget.

## DOWNTOWN AND VICINITY

If you want to stay overnight in Downtown L.A., plan to pay for the privilege. As expected, most hostelries here run to high-rise towers catering more to the business than the leisure set. Still, if you need a room near the heart of L.A. for less than a month's mortgage, you can find one if you look hard enough. But be aware that once you get into the Jewelry District and farther towards the Flower Market, the neighborhood goes from high-end to sketchy to downright terrifying. If you need a truly cheap room, avoid these areas and head instead for Pasadena or The Valley.

### Under $100

You won't miss the sign for the **Metro Plaza Hotel** (711 N. Main St., 213/680-0200, $88). The low-rise hotel with its white facade and big oddly constructed front marquee sits near Union Station, convenient for train travelers and public transit riders. You can also get transport to and from LAX for about $5, a genuine bargain. Inside, you'll find your room to look like any average, reasonably clean motel room. The bedspreads are floral, the carpets light blue, and the space ample. A complimentary continental breakfast comes with your room, and the Metro Plaza has an on-site fitness center. But the true gems here are the location, central to transportation to all the major L.A. attractions, and the lower-than-average price point for the region.

### $100-150

Can you image staying at a cute B&B only a mile from the towering skyscrapers of downtown Los Angeles? You can, at the **Inn at 657** (657 W. 23rd St., 213/741-2200, www.patsysinn657.com, $145–225). The lovely home has one-bedroom guest accommodations and two-bedroom suites, each individually decorated. You'll find a comfortable antique bed in a room scattered with lovely fabrics and pretty antiques. Each morning, you'll head downstairs to the long, dark table set with fine china for a full breakfast complete with fruit, hot food, great coffee, and fresh juice. The inn has a massage therapist on retainer, a nail salon they love just down the street, Wi-Fi, and a moderate-charge laundry service. You're within easy distance of the Staples Center, the downtown shopping areas, and the rest of the attractions of Los Angeles.

### $150-250

You'd expect plenty of urban, modern hotels in Downtown L.A. What comes as a surprise is the (for what it is) reasonably priced and fantastically fun **Custom Hotel** (8639 Lincoln Blvd., 877/287-8601, www.customhotel.com, $175–300). From the herd of sheep in the lobby to the dog-print bedspreads, a sense of whimsy pervades this otherwise ultra-stylish hotel. Your room might not be the biggest in town, but it will be clean and pristine, with snowy-white linens, comfortable beds, and an attractively appointed bathroom. On the counter you'll find a basket full of fun favors (for a price, of course); we'll leave it to you to figure out why you'd want to purchase a packet of radish seeds from a high-end hotel. The in-room Wi-Fi is free, as are the views of Los Angeles. You'll find the staff incredibly friendly and helpful, ready to help with anything from valet parking to dinner reservations. If you prefer to eat in the hotel, the hip if preciously named Bistrotek can feed you either in the restaurant or in your room. Or if you're in a more casual mood, hit the Hopscotch Pool Bar & Grill, which sits adjacent to the sparkling swimming pool. For a drink in the evening, take the elevators with the slightly scary giant faces down to the Lobby Lounge to enjoy a cocktail and possibly even a local DJ spinning into the evening.

The **Orchid Hotel** (819 S. Flower St., 213/623-9904, www.ohotelgroup.com, $180) is better known as The O to its friends and devoted returning guests. This upscale property takes the modern urban chic hotel concept and does it L.A. style. True to its name, orchids are a major theme of this hotel, and you'll find plants both in the common areas and inside your room. Guest rooms are done in a modern style, with platform beds, sparkling white linens, and black-and-white bathrooms. A boutique establishment, The O has only 68 rooms. You'll find tapas and Mediterranean-inspired cuisine at the on-site restaurant, plus a full bar. The health spa offers both fitness facilities and massage and other spa services. Perhaps best of all for those travelers who come to L.A. for its retail possibilities, you won't need the services of the 24-hour concierge desk to find the Macy's Plaza center just across the street from the hotel.

### Over $250

If you're longing for a taste of true L.A. style, get a room at the **Omni Los Angeles at California Plaza** (251 S. Olive St., 213/617-3300, www.omnihotels.com, $266). From the grand exterior to the elegant lobby and on up to your room, the light colors, live plants, and lovely accents will make you feel rich, even if just for one night. Your room or suite will have plush mattresses and your choice of pillows, stylish decor, plushy towels and robes, and all the right amenities to make your stay perfect. If you're in town for business, you can get a room complete with a fax machine, copier, and office supplies. On the other hand, if you're on vacation with your family you can get a suite decorated especially to delight your children—with a closing door to an adult bedroom to delight you. You can dine at this magnificent hotel, choosing between the Noe Restaurant and the Grand Cafe. Take a swim in the lap pool or a run on the exercise equipment in the large fitness room. Relax with a massage, hot river rock treatment, or facial at the Spa at Omni. Whatever your pleasure, you'll find it at the Omni.

If you're yearning to stay someplace with a movie history, book a room at the **Westin Bonaventure** (404 S. Figueroa, 213/624-1000, www.starwoodhotels.com, $250). The climactic scene of the Clint Eastwood thriller *In the Line of Fire* was filmed in one of the unusual elevators in the glass-enclosed, four-leaf-clover-shaped high-rise building. This hotel complex has every single thing you'd ever need: shops, restaurants, a day spa, a concierge, and plenty of nice guest rooms. You'll find your rooms comfortable and convenient, complete with fancy beds and clean spacious bathrooms. Views range from fairly innocuous streets of L.A. to panoramic cityscapes. The most fun restaurant and lounge to visit at the Bonaventure is without doubt the Bona Vista Lounge, which revolves slowly 360° at the top of the building.

## HOLLYWOOD

If you're star-struck, a serious partier, or a rock music aficionado, you'll want to do more than just visit Hollywood. You'll want to stay the night within staggering distance of the hottest clubs or the hippest music venues. Heck, you might even luck out and find yourself sleeping in the same room where Axl Rose once vomited or David Lee Roth broke all the (hopefully replaced) furniture!

### Under $100

Reputed to be one of the best hostels in the state, the **USA Hostels - Hollywood** (1624

Schrader Blvd., 800/524-6783, www.usahostels.com, $26 dorm bed, $70 private room) still offers the same great prices you'll find at seedier, more bare-bones hostels. Okay, so the exterior doesn't look like much. But in this case, it's what's inside that counts. You can choose between dorm rooms and private rooms, but even the larger dorm rooms have baths attached—a nice convenience that's unusual in the hostel world. (You'll also find several common bathrooms in the hallways, helping to diminish the morning shower rush.) Another great boon is the daily all-you-can-make pancake breakfast, which comes free with your room along with all the coffee or tea you can drink. Add that to the $5 barbecue nights on Monday, Wednesdays, and Fridays, and you've got a great start on seriously diminished food costs for this trip! This smaller hostel also goes a long way to fostering a sense of community among its visitors, offering a standard array of area walking tours and beach shuttle, plus two free comedy nights per week (Wed. and Sun.). If you need to make contact with friends back home, hook up to the free Wi-Fi with your own laptop or use one of the complimentary Internet kiosks.

## $100-150

For a nice modestly priced room in the Hollywood vicinity, stay at the **Hollywood Orchid Suites** (1753 Orchid Ave., 323/874-9678, www.orchidsuites.com, $110–350). The Orchid's location couldn't be better; it's in the Hollywood & Highland Center, right behind Grauman's Chinese Theatre, next door to the Kodak Theater, and around the corner from Hollywood Boulevard and the Walk of Fame. If you're a film lover or star seeker on a moderate budget, it's tough to do better than this—especially with the free parking and proximity to public transit. Guest rooms are actually suites, with plenty of space and an eye toward sleeping your large family or several friends all in the same suite. All suites but the Juniors have full kitchens. Don't expect tons of luxury in the furnishings or the decor; it all looks like last decade's motel stuff, though you'll get a coffee maker, free Wi-Fi, and other better-than-average perks. The rectangular pool offers cooling refreshment in the summertime, perfect after a long day of stalking Brad or Britney!

Only a few steps away, you can get a room at the **Hollywood Celebrity Hotel** (1775 Orchid Ave., 323/850-6464, www.hotelcelebrity.com, $135–200). This nice budget motel aspires to Hollywood's famed luxury. Guest rooms have satin comforters, Hollywood-flavored black-and-white artwork, and a modern aesthetic in the furnishings and accents. Amenities include free, wired high-speed Internet, a valet laundry service, a fitness room, and steam rooms. In the morning, come down to the lobby for a complimentary continental breakfast, and in the evenings take advantage of otherwise hard-to-come-by passes to the **Magic Castle Club** (www.magiccastle.com). Leave your car in the gated, off-street parking lot.

## $150-250

If you've got a little bit more cash, you'll find more lodging options in Hollywood. One good spot is the **Hollywood Hills Hotel** (1999 N. Sycamore Ave., 323/874-5089, www.hollywoodhillshotel.com, $175–275, parking $8/day), not to be confused with the Best Western Hollywood Hills. The Hollywood Hills Hotel offers truth in advertising, set up in the Hollywood Hills offering lovely views of the L.A. skyline on rare smog-free days. The view of the resort itself can be almost as grand, with its Chinese stylings and attractive greenery. All rooms here, even the studios, have fully equipped kitchens for travelers seeking to save money on meals. These suites land somewhere between a standard motel and a more upscale resort in their style. You'll find floral comforters, warm-toned painted walls, and attractive if sparse artistic touches. Best of all, the rooms facing out over the city of Los Angeles have huge windows to help you enjoy the view from the comfort of your bed. On-site, you'll find a cool Chinese pagoda, a prettily landscaped swimming pool, and a grand California-Asian restaurant, Yamashiro.

Named for the world renowned magic club

next door, the **Magic Castle Hotel** (7025 Franklin Ave., 323/851-0800, www.magiccastle hotel.com, $180–350) boasts the best customer service of any L.A. area hostelry. You'll have to make that judgment for yourself, but if one of your goals for your visit to the area is to find a way into the exclusive **Magic Castle Club** (www.magiccastle.com), their ancillary hotel has your ticket waiting at the desk. If you're just looking for a nice place to relax between days filled with touring, you'll definitely get that here. Sparkling light rooms with cushy white comforters and spare, clean decor offer a haven of tranquility. A courtyard pool invites lounging day and night, and you can even enjoy a midnight swim here without breaking the hotel rules (so long as you don't wake the other guests). Many rooms at the Magic Castle have their own kitchens. But be sure to enjoy the little luxurious touches, such as high-end coffee, baked goodies in the free continental breakfast, plushy robes, and nightly turn-down service.

### Over $250

A lovely upscale hotel is the **Renaissance Hollywood Hotel** (1755 N. Highland Ave., 323/856-1200, www.renaissancehollywood.com, $313). Right at the corner of Hollywood and Highland, you'll be in the thick of all the action here. This hotel has taken the SoCal mid-century modern style and given it some new millennium touches to create a colorful, high-end property that appeals to well-heeled travelers of many tastes. With more than 600 rooms, you'll probably find one to suit you. Expect eye-piercingly bright blue, yellow, and red bedspreads and upholstered chairs in sizeable rooms, some with nice city views. Kids are welcome here, and the hotel offers childcare for parents looking a few hours' respite or more adult attractions. If you're not up for the Walk of Fame or the Wax Museum, grab a chaise lounge on the rooftop pool or just order room service. To dine in true style, try **Twist,** the on-site California cuisine restaurant that features small bites to let diners try as many menu items as they can stand. If you're staying at the Renaissance to admire the modern artistic touches, get a brochure from the desk and take a tour of the common spaces, which display more than 70 works of colorful modern art for your admiration (many by local artists).

## BEVERLY HILLS AND WEST HOLLYWOOD

Most travelers don't come to Beverly Hills looking to stay in a youth hostel. In a town whose name equals wealth, the point is to dive headfirst into the lap of luxury. Though you might have to save up to get a room near Rodeo Drive, if you choose wisely you might just get a sense of how the other .001 percent live for just one or two nights.

For budget accommodations in the general vicinity, look to the chain motels in the West Hollywood region. This upscale area, which serves as L.A.'s gay mecca, divides its lodgings between the Ramada and the equal-to-Beverly-Hills upscale unique hotels.

### Over $250

A newcomer to the Beverly Hills luxury hotel scene, **The Mosaic Hotel** (125 Spalding Dr., 800/463-4466, www.mosaichotel.com, $390–710) offers a laid-back, urban vibe in both its chill common areas and its comfortable guest accommodations. Rooms are furnished in contemporary fabrics, with soothing light colors blending into attractive wall art and fluffy white down comforters. Mattresses are topped with feather beds, and the bathrooms sparkle and sooth with Frette towels and BVLGARI bath products. If you've got the cash to spring for a suite, you'll be treated to something that feels like your own elegant apartment, with a living room with 42-inch plasma TV, sofa, and armchair. Downstairs, a hip bar and small dining room offer top-shelf cocktails and tasty California cuisine. Friendly, helpful staff will serve you tidbits in the bar, and can help with any travel or room needs.

The most famous of all the grand hotels of Beverly Hills, the **Beverly Wilshire** (9500 Wilshire Blvd., 310/275-5200, www.fourseasons.com/beverlywilshire, $500) is now a Four Seasons property. But never fear: The recent multimillion-dollar renovation didn't scour away all the classic charm of this historic hotel. Nor did it lower the price of the privilege of sleeping inside these hallowed walls. Even the plainest of guest rooms here feature exquisite appointments such as 42-inch plasma TVs, elegant linens, attractive artwork, and even live plants. Of course, guests with all the money in the world can rent a suite; the Presidential suite resembles nothing so much as a European palace, complete with Corinthian columns. With an in-house spa, a dining room, room service, and every other service you could want, folks who can afford it consider a stay at the Beverly Wilshire well worth the expense.

In West Hollywood, the **Sunset Tower Hotel** (8358 Sunset Blvd., West Hollwyood, 323/654-7100, www.sunsettowerhotel.com, $330) might look familiar to recent visitors of Disney's California Adventure. Indeed, its architecture inspired the "Tower of Terror" ride at the amusement park. But there's no terror in the Sunset Tower today. Instead, you'll find a gorgeous deco exterior paired with a fully renovated modern interior. Guest accommodations range from smallish standard queen guest rooms with smooth linens and attractive appointments up to luxurious suites with panoramic views and limestone bathrooms. All rooms include flat-screen TVs, 24-hour room service, and free Wi-Fi.

The **Le Montrose Suite** (900 Hammond St., West Hollywood, 310/855-1115, www.lemontrose.com, $270) will give you a taste of the kind of luxury celebrities expect in their accommodations, especially in trendy, gay-friendly West Hollywood. The atmosphere and decor are almost desperately modern, from the silver discs behind the front desk to the neo-patchwork bedspreads in the guest rooms. Happily, you'll find lots of plush comfort in amongst the primary colors and plain geometric shapes in your room. A Berber carpet snuggles your feet, a high-end entertainment system sees to your every audio-visual and gaming need, and a gas fireplace provides just the right romantic atmosphere for an evening spent indoors. Outside of your posh suite, you can take a dip in the rooftop saltwater swimming pool and whirlpool, play a set on the lighted tennis courts, or get in a good workout inside the fitness center. Hotel guests alone can enjoy the gourmet delicacies of the private dining room or order from 24-hour room service. If you're dying for some great clubbing or a seat at a show while you're in town, just ask the concierge, who can provide all the assistance you need.

## SANTA MONICA, VENICE, AND MALIBU

Arguably, the best place to stay in Los Angeles is down by the beach. It seems ironic that you can camp in a park for $25 a night in exclusive Malibu, and you can pay over $1,000 for a resort room in so-called "working class" Santa Monica. But whether you choose either of those or a spot in Venice Beach, you'll get some of the best atmosphere

### Under $100

For a bed indoors for cheap, your options near the beach run to youth hostels. The huge **HI-Santa Monica** (1436 2nd St., Santa Monica, 310/393-9913, www.hilosangeles.org, $29) offers 260 beds in a building constructed specifically to house the hostel. You'll be right in the thick of downtown Santa Monica in a good neighborhood, within walking distance of the Santa Monica Pier, the Third Street Promenade, and the beach. Plenty of great, cheap restaurants cluster in the area, or you can make use of the hostel's open kitchen. This ritzy hostel offers tons of amenities for the price, including a computer room, game room, TV room, movie room, excursions, wheelchair access, sheets with the bed price, and even a complimentary continental breakfast every morning. If you prefer to find your own way around L.A., the local public transit system runs right outside the door.

The **Venice Beach Cotel** (25 Windward Ave., Venice Beach, 888/718-8287, www.venicebeachcotel.com, $24–77) claims to be "a hostel with hotel standards." You can make your own judgments on its amenities, which include women's-only and co-ed dorms with and without in-room bath, private rooms, and private rooms with baths. Rooms get maid service daily (a rarity in the hostelling world), and a computer room and kick-back lounge welcome guests and encourage them to socialize. But the best part of the Cotel is undoubtedly its location *on* the Boardwalk right across from Muscle Beach. Fall out of your bunk and into the warm sands of Venice's beach every morning. The fabulous restaurants of Washington Street are reached by an easy walk, and the canals sit just a block or two away. Book well in advance for summer.

## $100-150

If you're looking for a moderate-priced motel near the beach, look to the 1950s-era motor inns of Santa Monica. One of these that manages to be cute and kitschy despite a desperate need for a remodel is the **Bayside Hotel** (2001 Ocean Ave., Santa Monica, 310/396-6000, www.baysidehotel.com, $110–225). The hotel's not right on the beach, but you can walk there in about two minutes. Inside your room, you'll find the 1950s, from the Pepto-pink tile in the bathroom to the odd arrangement of older furniture in the bedroom to the utterly retro kitchens in the suites. If you crave elegance, speedy check-in and check-out, or even spotless cleanliness, the Bayside isn't for you. But if you're seeking a fun stay in a place that looks like it ought to be in a Gidget movie, the Bayside's just right for you.

## $150-250

The **Venice Beach Suites & Hotel** (1305 Ocean Front Walk, 888/877-7602, www.venicebeachsuites.com, $155–250) is a surprisingly lovely and affordable little Venice hotel. It sits right on the beach, but it's far enough from the Boardwalk to acquire a touch of peace and quiet. You can also stroll over to Washington Street to grab a meal or a cup of coffee, or just wander out of the lobby and straight onto the beach. Inside, the rooms and suites all have full kitchens so you can cook for yourself—perfect for budget-conscious travelers and folks staying in Venice for several days. The kitchen's also great for simply coming in from the beach for a quick lunch with ice-cold drinks! The guest room decor is cuter than that of an average motel; you might find exposed brick walls and polished hardwood floors stocked with rattan furniture and cute accessories. Check the website for weeklong rental deals.

For a charming hotel experience only a block from the ever-energetic Boardwalk, stay at the **Inn at Venice Beach** (327 Washington Blvd., 800/828-0688, www.innatvenicebeach.com, $165–275, parking $5/day). The charming yellow-and-blue exterior, complete with a lovely bricked interior courtyard-cum-café, makes all guests feel welcome. Inside, you might be surprised by the brightly colored modern furniture and decor. Common spaces are done in a postmodern, blocky style, while the guest rooms pop with brilliant yellows and vibrant accents. The two-story boutique hotel offers only about 20 rooms, and its location on Washington Street makes it a perfect base from which to enjoy the best restaurants and beaches of Venice. Start each day with a complimentary continental breakfast, either in the dining room or outside in the Courtyard Café. If you need to stay connected while you're in Venice, the inn has complimentary Wi-Fi throughout the hotel.

If you want to bring your family to stay in legendary Malibu, one of the best hotels going is the **Casa Malibu Inn on the Beach** (22752 Pacific Coast Hwy., 800/831-0858, $150–250). This pleasant and kid-friendly property sits right out on the beach. Many of the rooms have ocean views; some also have gas fireplaces for cozy cool winter evenings. White bedsteads match the paint and draperies in the smallish rooms, while colorful bedspreads add visual appeal to the European styling of each unique guest room. Some of the gleaming white bathrooms have oversized bathtubs, perfect for a relaxing soak after a long day out on the beach. Head down to the lobby of this unpretentious 1950s-era building for a genuinely fresh continental breakfast each morning. From there, you can stagger right out onto the sand to pick out a prime spot before the crowds descend. You don't even have to worry about parking!

Yes, you really can stay at the **Hotel California** (1670 Ocean Ave., Santa Monica, 310/393-2363, $197–310). Appropriately decorated with classic longboards and electric guitars, this moderate hotel sits a short block from the beach and next to the Santa Monica Pier. You'll be in the perfect spot to enjoy all the best of Santa Monica without ever having to get into a car or worry about finding parking. Inside the hotel, you'll find hardwood floors and matching bedsteads, calming pale yellow walls, and white comforters and linens. Choose between a classic guest room, a Jacuzzi suite with the obvious amenity, and one- and two-bedroom suites. Outside, enjoy the lush greenery of the oddly named Spanish Courtyard, which looks more like something from the tropics than from Europe. Other perks include free Wi-Fi, a mini-fridge, and a smoke-free hotel experience.

### Over $250

In Malibu, if you've got silly amounts of cash to spare, stay at the **Malibu Beach Inn** (22878 Pacific Coast Hwy., Malibu, 310/456-6444, www.malibubeachinn.com, $350). This oceanside villa offers all the very best furnishings and amenities. Every room has a view of the ocean, and the boutique hotel sits on "Billionaire's Beach," a private and exclusive stretch of sand you can't access unless you're a guest of one of its properties. Your guest room will be done in rare woods, gleaming stone, and the most stylish modern linens and accents. A plasma TV, plush robes, and comfy beds tempt some visitors to stay inside, but equally tempting are the balconies with their own entertainment in the form of endless surf, glorious sunsets, and balmy breezes. The more affordable rooms are a bit small but just as attractively turned out as the over-the-top suites. When lunch and dinnertime come, go downstairs to the airy, elegant, on-site Carbon Beach Club to enjoy delicious cuisine in an upscale beach atmosphere.

One of the best-known resort hotels in the L.A. beach community has long been **Shutters on the Beach** (1 Pico Blvd., Santa Monica, 310/458-0030, www.shuttersonthebeach.com, $475). Make no mistake: You'll pay handsomely for the privilege of laying your head on one of Shutters' hallowed pillows. On the other hand, the gorgeous airy rooms will make you feel like you're home, or at least staying at the home you'd have if you could hire a famous designer to decorate for you. Even the most modest guest rooms have not only the comfortable beds, white linens, plasma TVs, and oversized bathtubs of a luxury hotel, you'll also find a comfortable clutter of pretty ornaments on tables and shelves. If you can pry yourself out of your private space, head down to the famed lobby for a drink and a people-watching session. Get a reservation for the elegant white-tablecloth One Pico or grab a more casual sandwich or salad at beachside Coast.

The impressive multi-level resort edifice sits right on the beach, so there's no need to find a premium parking spot to enjoy a day in the sand. If you long for more formal relaxation, book a massage at the **ONE Spa.** Art lovers can spend hours just wandering the halls of the hotel, examining the works of many famous modern photographers and painters.

## PASADENA

Pasadena lodgings run to the old standard national chains, plus a few funky 1950s-era motor lodges and the occasional upscale B&B. If you're planning to stay in Pasadena over the New Year, book early! The town fills up for the legendary Rose Parade. If your aim is to get yourself a room from which you can watch the Rose Parade, book earlier still; while you can get the perfect view from a room of your own, such places are at a premium during parade season.

### Under $100

The **Kingston Inn & Suites** (2156 E. Colorado Blvd., 626/793-9339, www.kingstonpasadena.com, $80–350) provides good clean rooms right along the Rose Parade route for reasonable nightly rates (which go way up for the Parade). You're also nice and close to Old Town, restaurants, and museums. The guest rooms have standard dark floral bedspreads and matching deep red carpets, enough room to walk around your two queens or king bed, and average motel bathrooms. A sizeable balcony outside each room offers the perfect Parade vantage point, and a sparkling pool with hot tub beckon travelers outside. Modern in-room amenities include Wi-Fi, iPod docking stations, coffee makers, fridges, and more.

### $100-200

The top pick of the quaint motor inns is the **Saga Motor Hotel** (1633 E. Colorado Blvd., 626/795-0431, www.thesagamotorhotel.com, $113). Outside it's all 1950s, from the structure of the low buildings to the Astroturf around the swimming pool. The ambiance extends to the door of your room, which includes a doorknob and an actual metal key to open it with. But inside your room, the decor gets a lot more contemporary. The big space has either a king or two double beds, clean if worn carpeting and linens, and a nice bathroom with a surprisingly good bathtub and nice hot showers. Locationwise, the Saga is right on the Rose Parade route on broad Colorado Boulevard, but it's not right downtown or in Old Town. Sadly, the service is spotty at best, but few people expect concierges at motor hotels.

Of the main chain motels, the best inexpensive one might be the **Comfort Inn** (2462 E. Colorado Blvd., 626/405-0811, www.comfortinn.com, $93). You'll find comfortable amenities in pleasant standard motel rooms here, along with yet another good set of views of the Rose Parade. Expect room prices to skyrocket for the Parade.

### Over $250

Once upon a time, Pasadena was the resort haven of wealthy East Coasters. To revisit this wealthy past, stay at **The Bissell House Bed & Breakfast** (201 Orange Grove Ave. S., 626/441-3535, www.bissellhouse.com, $225–400) on "Millionaire's Row." The tall mint-green Victorian surrounded by the deeper green of lush mature landscaping opens its doors to well-heeled travelers who want a luxurious place to stay while they're in the L.A. area. It is named for one of its residents, Anna Bissell McCay, heiress to the original Bissell vacuum cleaner fortune. Each of the five rooms has a unique decorating scheme, yet each shares a European floral theme that binds the inn together into a coherent whole. Guest rooms have comfy beds, a luxurious bathroom (most have clawfoot tubs), and lots of wonderful amenities, and the property has a swimming pool with a hot tub and lots of lovely plants scattered about. Your room includes a full breakfast each morning, served at the long table in the downstairs dining room.

# Food



You'll find a wide variety of cuisine all over Los Angeles and its surrounding towns. Whatever kind of food you prefer, from fresh sushi to Armenian, you can probably find it in a cool little hole-in-the-wall somewhere in L.A. Local recommendations often make for the best dining experiences, but even just walking down the right street can yield a tasty meal.

## DOWNTOWN AND VICINITY

Sure, you can find plenty of bland, tourist-friendly restaurants serving American and Americanized food in the Downtown area—but why would you, when one of Downtown L.A.'s greatest strengths is its ethnic diversity and the great range of cuisine that goes along with it? An endless array of fabulous holes-in-walls awaits you. Getting local recommendations is the best way to find the current hot spots, or you can choose from among this tiny sampling of what's available.

### American

If you're just looking for a good pastrami sandwich, you can get it at **Langer's Delicatessen and Restaurant** (704 S. Alvarado St.,

213/483-8050, www.langersdeli.com, Mon.–Sat. 8 A.M.–4 P.M., $10–20). Operating continuously since 1947, the house specialty at Langer's is a hot pastrami sandwich that some say is the best in the world (yes, they're including New York). Whether you're willing to go that far or not, Langer's serves both hot and cold dishes in the traditional Jewish deli style to satisfy any appetite level or specific craving. Granted, it's still California, so you can get fresh avocado on your tongue sandwich if you really want to. You'll also find a vast breakfast menu and plenty of desserts (noodle kugel, anyone?). If you don't have time to sit down for lunch, order in advance and pick up your meal curbside. If you can dine in, be sure to take a few minutes to gaze at the photos on the walls; the family you'll see has run this deli since its opening in the post-war era.

## Asian

One of the largest Asian areas in Los Angeles is Koreatown. It's only fitting that a city with such a large Korean population has plenty of good Korean restaurants. One of these is **Chunju Han-il Kwan** (3450 W. Sixth St. 213/480-1799, $10). Beware: This is an authentic Korean restaurant that caters primarily to the expat Korean community. You won't find English menus here, but you will find helpful waitresses who can guide you through the process of ordering. If your server tells you a dish is very spicy, she means it, but that doesn't mean you won't love it anyway. The menu is eclectic to say the least—you can get a hot dog, octopus, fish soup, Korean stew (thickened with American cheese), kimchi, and much more. Many patrons crave the veggie side dishes that come with the entrées here. Don't worry about your standard of dress when you dine here, since this casual restaurant resides in a strip mall and has gas burners on the tables.

For a serious authentic Japanese cuisine experience, visit **Kagaya** (418 E. Second St., 213/617-1016, http://kagaya.dla.menuclub.com, Tues.–Sat. 6–10:30 P.M. Sun. 6–10 P.M., $40–60). Even L.A. denizens who've eaten at shabu shabu places in Japan proper come back to Kagaya again and again. They make reservations in advance, because the dining room is small and the quality of the food makes it popular even on weeknights. The term "shabu shabu" refers to paper-thin slices of beef and vegetable that you dip and swish into a pot of boiling *daishi* (broth), then dunk in *ponzu* or other house-made sauces before eating. The shabu shabu is but one course in the meal you'll get at Kagaya, since all meals include several appetizers (varieties change daily), shabu shabu with beef and seafood, udon, and dessert. You can pay a premium for Wagyu beef if you choose, but the king crab legs in season are part of the regular price of dinner. Even the regular beef here isn't cheap, but the quality makes it worth the price. Sit at the counter if you want to watch all your food being prepared before your very eyes.

## French

A surprisingly cute little brick-fronted café, the **Angelique Café** (840 S. Spring St., 213/623-8698, www.angeliquecafe.com, Mon.–Fri. 8 A.M.–3:30 P.M., Sat.–Sun. 8 A.M.–4 P.M., $7–20) offers a relaxed French atmosphere and good French-styled food. The original chef-owner came from France and brought his recipes and his dining aesthetic with him. The large menu has an array of both French and American dishes, going heavy on the salads and more traditional hot fare. If you come for breakfast, you can choose from a list of omelets and crepes plus a few American egg dishes, or the more traditional continental breakfast of pastry and coffee. Angelique's small green-and-yellow dining room is open for breakfast and lunch only. If it's a nice day, grab a table outside on the wrought-iron fenced patio, which has almost as many tables as the inside dining room does.

## Greek

Originally a Greek import company in the 1960s, the **Papa Cristos Taverna** (2771 W. Pico Blvd., 323/737-2970, www.papacristo.com, Tues.–Sat. 9 A.M.–8 P.M., Sun. 9 A.M.–4 P.M., $10) restaurant opened in the 1990s. The import shop still supplies the local Greek community with hard-to-come-by delicacies, which also become ingredients in the cuisine at the Taverna. Dishes are traditionally Greek, from the salads to the kebabs to the baba ghanouj. After you're finished with your meal, wander the aisles of the store to pick up a few unusual Greek delicacies to take with you.

### Italian

It seems odd to name a high-end restaurant after a decidedly low-end bug, but that's what the owners of **Cicada Restaurant** (617 S. Olive St., 213/488-9488, www.cicadarestaurant.com, Mon.–Sat. 5:30–9 P.M., $40–80) did. Set in the 1920s Oviatt building decorated in high French art deco style, the beautiful restaurant glitters with some of its original Lalique glass panels—be sure to check out the elevator doors on your way in or out. The palatial dining room features huge round tables for large parties, and balcony seating for intimate groups of two. The immense space lets Cicada space its tables farther apart than in most restaurants, giving diners a sense of privacy and romance that can be hard to come by.

As for the food, calling it "Italian" isn't quite right, since the cuisine here fuses Italian concepts with California ingredients, techniques, and presentations. Expect a varied seasonal menu of inventive dishes, including pastas and meats after the Italian style with distinct California flavors. Be sure to save room for Cicada's beloved desserts, which many diners declare to be their favorite part of the meal.

### Mexican

Everyone in L.A. (and most of the rest of California for that matter) knows that the best tamales come from the kitchens of Mexican grandmothers, and get sold on the streets from carts or trucks. If you're not a local and don't feel able to find the best little sidewalk tamale cart, your best option is **Mama's Hot Tamales Café** (2124 W. Seventh St., 213/487-7474, www.iurd.org/mamashottamales, Mon.–Sat. 11 A.M.–3:30 P.M., Sun. 9 A.M.–3:30 P.M., $6–10). You'll even get a little social justice with your lunch, as Mama's operates as a training ground for "informal" food purveyors to develop the skills they need to become higher-paid employees of the formal food service world. Open pretty much for lunch only, Mama's serves salads, appetizers, burritos, tostadas, and other simple Latin American dishes. But if you know what's right, you'll order the house namesake: a homemade tamale.

## HOLLYWOOD

Hollywood's got just as many tasty treats tucked away in strip malls as other areas of Los Angeles. If you want to rub elbows with rock stars, you're likely to find yourself at a big, slightly raunchy bar and grill. For a chance at glimpsing stars of the silver screen, look for upscale California cuisine or perhaps a high-end sushi bar. If all you need is tasty sustenance, you can choose from a range of restaurants.

### American

If you've ever owned a rock album—any rock album—it's worth your time to stop in for a meal at **The Rainbow Bar & Grill** (9015 W. Sunset Blvd., 310/278-4232, www.rainbowbarandgrill.com, lunch Mon.–Fri. 11 A.M.–4 P.M., dinner daily 4 P.M.–2 A.M., $13–30). You'll find a lack of fancy sauces, and an amazing myriad of rock and roll memorabilia in this dark (but no longer smoky) restaurant. To the surprise of some intrepid diners, the hallowed haven, in which countless rockers have been serviced by innumerable groupies, does serve a darn tasty cheeseburger. If you show up for lunch on a weekday, you're likely to have the cavernous space almost to yourself to enjoy your salad and make your slow way along the walls checking out the endless parade of photos, guitars, newspaper snippets, and other cool stuff. In the even dimmer bar area, you can play a for-real game of authentic table Ms. Pac-Man as you sip your favorite cocktail or quaff a beer.

Nighttime is a whole different story. The crowds start trickling into the Rainbow as the sun goes down. By the time the shows let out at the Roxy and the Whisky, your chances of finding a booth diminish significantly. The good news is that the rockers still gather here after playing shows in the neighborhood. You never know who you'll bump into as you weave your way through the main dining room and outdoor patio to get your next drink. The back rooms also open up late, and you'll find dancing, drinking, smoking (shhh!), and fun upstairs in a warren-like space that includes either two or three separate bar-and-club spaces on any given night, depending on whose tales you believe.

As for amenities, expect woefully inadequate and difficult-to-access bathrooms, particularly if you happen to be female. Wait staff runs to cute and buxom young women. You can take your cigarettes just outside of the exits to be legal.

If you prefer to combine your love of live acts and your need for food, head for the **Hotel Café** (1623½ N. Cahuenga Blvd., 323/461-2040, www.hotelcafe.com, daily 7 P.M.–close, $10–30, 21 and over). Food choices run to the casual here—paninis, salads, and desserts, but the restaurant has a beer list, a wine list, and a full bar. The restaurant opens early; it's easiest to secure a table if you show up before the show starts. After 7 P.M., prepare for things to get loud. If you do love yourself some new-to-the-scene music, stick around.

### Brazilian

Need food really, really, *really* late? **Bossa Nova** (7181 W. Sunset Blvd., 323/436-7999, www.bossafood.com, daily 11 A.M.–4 A.M., $10–20) can hook you up. A big menu of inexpensive entrées can satisfy any appetite from lunch to way past dinnertime at Bossa. Some of the dishes bear the spicy flavors of the owners' home country of Brazil, but you'll also find a ton of pastas, plenty of salads, and classic Italian-American build-your-own pizzas. Check out the desserts for some South American specialties if you need sweets after a long night out at the clubs. Not near the Sunset Strip? Bossa Nova has three other L.A. locations: one on Robertson Boulevard, one in Beverly Hills, and one in West L.A. If you've made it back to your hotel room and aren't inclined to leave again, Bossa delivers!



### California

It seems right somehow that the spot in L.A. that combines live music with upscale cuisine sits on Melrose Avenue. At **The Foundry on Melrose** (7463 Melrose Ave., 323/651-0915, www.thefoundryonmelrose.com, Tues.–Wed. 6–10 P.M., Thurs. 6 P.M.–midnight, Fri.–Sat. 6 P.M.–2 A.M., Sun. 2–9 P.M., $25–30), expect to find elegance and art in a style that improbably marries Arts and Crafts, art deco, and modern industrial. The art extends to the plates, where the chef creates elaborate presentations of an array of ingredients. The dinner menu is small, seasonal, and utterly haute California. You might even see an occasional celebrity dining here, though you'll also remark on the refreshing lack of oh-so-trendy 'tude at this restaurant. At the big curving black bar, you can get a lighter (and less pricey) meal from the bar menu. If you prefer an al fresco dining experience, ask for a table out on the patio. (Yes, that's an olive tree dangling its streamers in your soup.) The third room at the Foundry shelters a small piano bar, where a trio called CD3 plays until late into the nights Thursday through Sunday. And for the strong of ear and stomach, a Sunday "Be-Bop Brunch" helps hangovers with a little hair of the dog and some zippy live jazz.

## BEVERLY HILLS AND WEST HOLLYWOOD

Between Beverly Hills and West L.A., you'll find an eclectic choice of restaurants. Unsurprisingly, Beverly Hills tends toward high-end eateries serving European and haute California cuisine. On the other hand, West L.A. boasts a wide array of ethnic restaurants. You'll have to try a few to pick your favorites, since every local has their own take on the area's best eats.

### Asian

For a genuine, locally beloved, and cheap sushi spot, try **Sushi Mac** (2222 Sawtelle, 310/481-9954, daily 11:30 A.M.–9 P.M., $2.50/plate, cash only). Before you order, read the laminated signs on the walls to learn the rules of engagement. Every plate of sushi costs precisely $2.50, whether it's two pieces of nigiri or eight slices of a freshly made roll. The

## A BEGINNER'S GUIDE TO SUSHI

Your first time dining in a sushi restaurant can be an intimidating experience. What to do with the slabs of raw fish, the tentacles, the eggs, the eels, the seaweed – did I mention the raw fish? It's tough to know what's good for a first-timer: The *ebi* or the *unagi?* The *toro* or the *maguro?* Do they cook anything in here??

What follows is a by-no-means-complete beginner's guide to ordering and eating sushi:

***Maki* (Rolls).** When most folks think of sushi, they think of seaweed-wrapped circles of rice with fish and vegetables in the middle. This form is called a roll, or *maki*. Almost every sushi place in California will offer certain common rolls, for example the (duh) California Roll. This newcomer-friendly roll contains no raw fish; instead, it has cooked crab or crab salad, avocado, and cucumber wrapped in sushi rice and *nori* (seaweed). There are also plain cucumber rolls, Philadelphia rolls (smoked salmon, cream cheese, and avocado), shrimp salad rolls, and tempura rolls at most sushi bars. On the other hand, adventurous diners often eat rolls with raw fish or barbecued eel inside and out, perhaps dusted with flying fish eggs for a touch of salty crunch or a raw quail egg for smoothness.

***Nigiri* (Sushi).** *Nigiri*, sometimes called simply "sushi" on restaurant menus, consists of a slice of (usually) raw fish lying on top of a glob of sticky sushi rice, usually with a dab of wasabi paste in between the fish and the rice. *Nigiri* are almost always sold in pairs per order. Order *nigiri* with a rectangle of scrambled egg instead of fish, with a whole cooked shrimp, or with smoked salmon to ease yourself into the fishiness of it all. Hardcore sushi-ites munch on seasonal fish, sweet shrimp, and even octopus.

**Sashimi**. Sashimi refer to slices of raw fish pared to perfection, often arranged in beautiful patterns and designs by the sushi chef. Don't like raw fish? Then don't bother with sashimi. If you want raw fish almost exclusively, then ask for the chef's selection of sashimi.

**Wasabi.** Important safety tip: That little glob of green stuff on the edge of your plate is *not* the avocado! It's wasabi – a hot Japanese horseradish that's been grated or ground then mixed into a paste. (In truth, most California wasabi is actually regular ol' western horseradish mixed with green food coloring.) Take a tiny dab of wasabi and put it into the little empty dish the server brought. Add soy sauce and mix the wasabi in until it dissolves. If you're unaccustomed to spicy foods, use only a tiny fleck of wasabi to start with, and ignore the Japanese diners creating a thick sludge with more wasabi in it than soy sauce. They're professionals.

**Common Raw Fish.** If you've never had raw fish before and are hesitant to start now, ask for smoked salmon. It's not raw (it's like lox) and it's a good stepping stone into a world without fire.

Next, consider ordering a couple of common and easy-to-eat fish. *Maguro* is red tuna. It can be served as *nigiri*, but it's often diced fine and mixed with arcane ingredients to create "spicy tuna," which is often more palatable for sushi newcomers who don't mind spicy food. *Sake* is raw salmon. It's often served as *nigiri*, and used to decorate the outside of rolls. If you prefer a delicate flavored white fish, try some *hamachi* (yellowtail, a firm white fish) or *tai* (red snapper). To take the next step, order some *unagi*. Hey, it's cooked! In fact, it's barbecued eel.

**How to Order Sushi.** While you can order your own plate of rolls and *nigiri*, most sushi fans will tell you that sushi tastes best when shared family-style. Each diner orders a few of their favorite items, all the food comes out on platters, and you and your friends dig in with fingers or chopsticks to try at least one piece of everything.

**How to Eat Sushi.** Contrary to popular American belief, it is acceptable to pick up both *nigiri* and roll slices with your fingers. You can then dip your sushi into your dish of wasabi and soy sauce. Be gentle – don't soak your *nigiri* rice in the sauce, or you'll completely cover up the taste of the fish. Next, eat! Chase with hot green tea, sake, or Japanese beer. Repeat until plate or wooden serving tray empties.

decor is nothing to write home about, but the ever-frantic chefs will slice and dice their way right in front of you. It might not be the biggest or most creative sushi, but you can get your fill for about half the cost of most other sushi spots. Be aware that Sushi Mac can get crowded with locals on weekdays at lunchtime. However, they've got another location at 8474 West Third Street.

## Italian

If you're looking for upscale Italian cuisine in a classy environment, enjoy lunch or dinner at **Il Pastaio Restaurant** (400 N. Canon Dr., Beverly Hills, 310/205-5444, www.giacominodrago.com/pastaio.htm, Mon.–Sat. 11:30 A.M.–11 P.M., Sun. 5–10 P.M., $15–30). The bright dining room offers a sunny luncheon experience, and the white tablecloths and shiny glassware lend an elegance to dinner, which is served reasonably late into the evening even on weekdays. Boasting a large menu for a high-end restaurant, Il Pastaio offers a wide variety of salads, risotto, and pasta dishes, as well as some overpriced antipasti and a smaller list of entrées. Preparations and dishes evoke authentic Italy, so you might see osso bucco or fettuccine Bolognese on the menu. The blue-painted bar offers a tasteful selection of California and Italian vintages, and serious wine lovers will be pleased to see the Italian selections broken out by region.

Happily located right on the Strip, the **Vivoli Cafe & Trattoria** (7994 Sunset Blvd., West Hollywood, 323/656-5050, www.vivolicafe.com, Mon.–Thurs. and Sun. 11:30 A.M.–10 P.M., Fri.–Sat. 11:30 A.M.–11 P.M., $15–30) offers a copious menu of Italian cuisine. Expect white tablecloths, wooden chairs, and friendly service at this locals' favorite. The broad menu focuses on seafood and a surprising variety of salads. But you can also get your favorite cheese-heavy pasta dishes or hearty, meaty entrées. Don't forget dessert—leave the guns, take the cannolli!



## Steak

There's nothing like a good steak dinner, Brazilian style. At **Fogo de Chao** (133 N. La Cienega Blvd., Beverly Hills, 310/289-7755, http://fogodechao.com, Mon.–Fri. 11 A.M.–2 P.M. and 5–10 P.M., Fri. until 10:30 P.M., Sat. 4:30–10:30 P.M., Sun. 4–9:30 P.M., $40–80), be prepared for an interactive dining experience. The meat is slow roasted, then skewered and cut right onto your plate by ever-moving servers. Be sure to use the red-and-green token on your table; if you don't turn it over to the red side occasionally, you will be continuously bombarded with the 15 different kinds of meat the restaurant offers. The fixed-price meal includes endless trips to the salad bar, fresh-cut veggies, and traditional Brazilian side dishes (fried bananas are a starch here, not a dessert). The extensive wine list includes plenty of both California and European vintages, plus a wider-than-average selection of ports and dessert wines. While the food is fabulous, you'll get the most out a meal here with a lively group that will enjoy the service as much as the spicy flavors.

## Coffee and Tea

A grand afternoon tea in stately Beverly Hills just seems like the right thing to do at least once. You can get some of the best tea in L.A. at **The Living Room in The Peninsula Hotel** (9882 Santa Monica Blvd., Beverly Hills, 310/975-2736, www.peninsula.com, seatings at 2:30 P.M. and 5 P.M., $18–45). The Peninsula has three restaurants, but for tea head to the elegant Living Room and grab a comfy chair near the fireplace. Sit back and enjoy the delicate harp music while admiring the elegant and tasteful furnishings in this posh space. If you skipped lunch or plan to miss dinner, go with the heartier Royal Tea or Imperial Tea. Lighter eaters prefer the Full Tea or the Light Tea. All come with tea sandwiches, scones, pastries, and, of course, a pot of tea. The loose-leaf teas are Peninsula originals; many are flavored. For an extra fee, you can add a glass of champagne to complete your high tea experience.

Dress properly for the occasion: Jackets are required even for tea. Ladies have more latitude, but shouldn't show up in jeans and a T-shirt.

## SANTA MONICA, VENICE, AND MALIBU

Yes, there's lots of junky beach food to be found in Santa Monica and Venice Beach. But there are also an amazing number of gems hiding in these towns.

### American

**Cora's Coffee Shoppe** (1802 Ocean Ave., Santa Monica, 310/451-9562, Tues.–Fri. 6:30 A.M.–3 P.M., Sat.–Sun. 7 A.M.–3 P.M., $10) doesn't look like much; it's a tiny building with a smallish sign. But don't be fooled by the unpretentious exterior. The small, exquisite restaurant inside is something of a locals' secret hiding in plain sight, serving breakfast and lunch to diners who are more than willing to pack into the tiny spaces that Cora's calls dining rooms. In addition to the two tiny, marble-topped tables and miniature marble counter inside, a small patio area off to one side, screened by latticework and venerable bougainvillea vines, offers a warm and pleasant atmosphere.

What's best about Cora's is simply the food. The chefs crammed into the eensie kitchen use high-end and sometimes organic ingredients to create breakfast and lunch dishes that don't seem like anything fancy on the menu, but will make you rethink your opinion of humble scrambled eggs or lowly oatmeal when they get to your table. The espresso drinks are reminiscent of European coffees—dark, bitter, and served in cups the size of bowls. Perhaps it's the coffee that keeps the staff moving so fast, endlessly serving and busing and serving some more to keep up with the steady flow of diners, many of whom the waiters seem to know quite well.

### Asian

If your tastes run to the exotically spicy and romantic, walk across Pacific Avenue from Venice Beach into Marina Del Ray and to the **Siamese Garden** (301 Washington Blvd., Marina Del Rey, 310/821-0098, www.siamesegarden.com, Mon.–Thurs. 11 A.M.–10 P.M., Fri. 11 A.M.–11 P.M., Sat. 5–11 P.M., Sun. 5–10 P.M., $10–30). A favorite of local couples both straight and otherwise looking for a romantic evening out, Siamese Garden boasts outdoor tables set in an overhanging lantern-lit garden, complete

Cora's Coffee Shoppe

with glimpses of the Venice Canals through the foliage and fencing. In the kitchen, Siamese Garden prides itself on creating delightful dishes created with only the freshest and best produce and ingredients available. The wide menu offers all of your favorite Thai classics, such as coconut soup, pad thai, and a rainbow of curries. Mint, lemongrass, peanut sauce, basil, and hot chiles crowd the menu with their strong and distinct flavors. Vegetarians have a great selection of tasty dishes, while carnivores can enjoy plenty of good beef, poultry, and seafood. For dessert, try one of the fun sticky rice and fruit dishes. To accompany your meal, you can get a rich Thai iced tea (ask to see one before you order if you've never had it before) or a light Thai beer.

## Barbecue

As is right and proper in California, you have to go to the seedier part of town to get the best authentic Southern barbecue. **Baby Blues BBQ** (444 Lincoln Blvd., Venice, 310/396-7675, www.babybluesbarbq.com, Mon.–Thurs. 11:30 A.M.–10 P.M., Sat. 11:30 A.M.–11 P.M., Sun. noon–10 P.M., $10–30) disobeys the haute Venice rule of AWOL (Always West of Lincoln), sitting right on Lincoln Boulevard with its grubby sidewalks and elderly strip malls. This disreputable street corner location (really, it's not that bad) does not dissuade locals, who line up at lunchtime to grab a plate of ribs or chicken. The menu pays little attention to cholesterol or carb counters. Choose from sausages, pulled pork, beer-braised brisket, barbecued chicken, and pork or beef ribs, all covered in homemade sauces and spice rubs. The cooks know their business, and regional specialties from different parts of the South are created with specific intent and understanding of the cuisine. Fixin's (side dishes) include Baby Blues' famed hot cornbread, baked beans, slaw, mac and cheese, and other appropriate stuff.

## Caribbean

How can you not love a restaurant called **Cha Cha Chicken** (1906 Ocean Ave., Santa Monica, 310/581-1684, www.chachachicken.com, Mon.–Fri. 11 A.M.–10 P.M. Sat.–Sun. 10 A.M.–10 P.M., $10)? It looks just like it sounds—a slightly decrepit but brightly painted shack only a short walk from the Santa Monica Pier and the Third Street Promenade. You can't miss it even if you're driving quickly down Ocean Avenue. The best place to get a table is definitely the palm tree–strewn patio area outdoors. It's the perfect atmosphere to enjoy the wonderful and inexpensive Caribbean dishes that come from the fragrant kitchen. The jerk dishes bring a tangy sweetness to the table, while the *ropa vieja* heats up the plate, and the funky enchiladas put a whole new spin on a Mexican classic. Salads, sandwiches, and wraps are popular with lighter eaters and the lunch crowd. Quaff an imported Jamaican soda or a seasonal *agua fresca* with your meal, since Cha Cha Chicken doesn't have a liquor license.

## Italian

A Venice institution, the **C&O Trattoria** (31 Washington Blvd., Venice Beach, 310/823-9491, www.cotrattoria.com, Mon.–Thurs. 11:30 A.M.–10 P.M., Fri. 11:30 A.M.–11 P.M., Sat. 8 A.M.–11 P.M., Sun. 8 A.M.–10 P.M., $13–18) manages to live up to its hype, and then some. Pick a seat in the dimly lit indoor dining room with rustic wood furniture and red-checked tablecloths, or sit outside in the big outdoor dining room, enjoying the mild weather and the soft pastel frescoes on the exterior walls surrounding the courtyard. C&O is known for its self-described gargantuan portions, which are best shared family-style among a group of diners. Be sure to start off with the addictive little garlic rolls. Next, seriously consider the pasta list, which includes some truly creative and delectable preparations. If you need help deciding on dishes, be sure to ask your friendly, knowledgeable server, who will be attentive but not overzealous. While C&O has a nice wine list, it's worth trying a jug of the surprisingly tasty house Chianti.

## Mexican

Looking for good cheap tacos in an unfamiliar town can be a scary proposition, but you have no need to fear **El Tarasco** (109 Washington

© LANCE SCOTT

El Tarasco

Blvd., Marina Del Rey, 310/306-8552, www.eltarascoburritos.com, daily 9 A.M.–11 P.M., $5–10). This walk-up dive taqueria has the locals' stamp of approval, and boasts of the freshness of its food. Specialties of the house are the burritos and tostadas, which are big and cheap and yummy. Even the full-fledged dinners that come with rice and beans and a combination of items please budget diners, since nothing on the menu costs more than $10. You can eat at El Tarasco in the decidedly down-rent but charming dining room, or get your food to go, perhaps for a quick walk down Washington to chow down on your burritos at the beach.

### Seafood

**Neptune's Net** (42505 Pacific Coast Hwy., Malibu, 310/457-3095, www.neptunesnet.com, Mon.–Thurs. 10:30 A.M.–7 P.M., Fri. 10:30 A.M.–8 P.M., Sat.–Sun. 10 A.M.–7:30 P.M., $10–20) in Malibu catches all kinds of seafood to serve to hungry diners. Locals call it The Net and usually order the fish and chips. Situated on the Malibu coastline adjacent to the County Line surf break, you'll often find sandy and salt-encrusted local surfers satisfying their enormous appetites after hours out on the waves. Even Midwestern visitors who are put off by the endless raw and rare fish eaten in California will feel comfortable dining in this casual palace of fried seafood. The large menu includes a seemingly endless variety of combinations, à la carte options, and side dishes.

## PASADENA

### Afghan

For a delicious and upscale dining experience, have lunch or dinner at **Azeen's Afghani Restaurant** (110 E. Union St., 626/683-3310, www.azeensafghanirestaurant.com, Mon.–Fri. 11:30 A.M.–2 P.M., 5:30–9:30 P.M., $20–30). Inside, you'll find white tablecloths, black furniture, and unusual paintings. On the menu, the offerings take you into another world—one largely mysterious to denizens of the West. Trade routes, invasions, religion, tribal culture, and lots and lots of sand all contribute to the way Afghanistan and its cuisine have evolved. Vegetarians, be aware that while you will find some limited options, Afghani food tends heavily toward meat. Kabobs of all kinds are a regional specialty, and the country's proximity to India brings with it a love for truly spicy (and incredibly flavorful) dishes. At Azeen's, you can get kabobs, spicy lamb dishes, dumplings, and traditional desserts.

### Asian

If you're just dying for Thai or Vietnamese food, one of the better spots in Pasadena is **Daisy Mint** (1218 E. Colorado Blvd. 626/792-2999, www.daisymint.com, Mon.–Fri. 11 A.M.–9 P.M., Sat.–Sun. noon–9 P.M., $10–30). The tiny green dining room's exposed brick and original artwork speak of SoCal, while the menu items tend to come from Southeast Asia and beyond. You'll find the aforementioned Thai and Vietnamese, plus Korean and uniquely Californian Asian-fusion dishes here. Some of the fun special touches of the house include a variety of steamed rice that you can choose to accompany your meal, and a large selection of unusual and fragrant teas. Pick whatever you think will go best with your satay, curry, seafood, or soup. Reservations are recommened on weekend evenings.

### Barbecue

If you're looking for some down-home Southern food, head straight for **Big Mama's Rib Shack** (1453 N. Lake Ave., 626/797-1792, www.bigmamas-ribshack.com, Tues.–Thurs. 11:30 A.M.–9 P.M., Fri.–Sat. 11:30 A.M.–10 P.M., Sun. noon–8 P.M., $10–30). While Big Mama never brewed up the sauce at this Pasadena kitchen, she was a Southern restaurateur who made her way from Georgia across the country to California over her long life. Today, her legacy lives on in the big ol' menu at Big Mama's, which boasts traditional Southern cuisine plus a number of Creole and Cajun dishes that speak to a strong New Orleans influence. Whether your poison is a po' boy or good gumbo, you can get it (in good hearty portions) at Big Mama's. Fish lovers will find oysters and catfish, but strict vegetarians will find their dining options limited here. And Big Mama's isn't adiet-friendly establishment since few salads balance out the weight of the fried chicken, smothered ribs, and velvet cake.

### California

For an upscale meal without having to fight the crowds in Westside or Downtown, check out **Bistro 45** (45 S. Mentor Ave., 626/795-2478, www.bistro45.com, lunch Tues.–Fri. 11:30 A.M.–2 P.M., dinner Tues.–Thurs. 6–9 P.M., Fri.–Sat. 6–9:30 P.M., Sun. 5–9 P.M., $40–80). This nationally lauded restaurant has beautiful dining rooms: one light and bright with hardwood floors and peach walls with beautiful glass lantern fixtures, and one semi-outdoor space done in gray-blues with distinctive woven chairs and classic French prints. The cuisine is grounded in the French tradition, but includes a hearty twist of California in the preparation. Menus change seasonally (or more often), and offer lots of fresh seafood as well as high-end meat and veggie-based dishes. For lunch, lighter appetites can be satisfied with fancy salads, but don't expect much of a midday price break on the bigger entrées. The wine list shifts seasonally to complement the food, and Bistro 45 boasts a full bar with a list of signature martini-esque cocktails.

### Greek

For a quick and reasonably healthy lunch in downtown Pasadena, try **Pita! Pita!** (927 E. Colorado Blvd., #101, 626/356-3099, $8–10). This walk-up Greek place offers tasty meals with lots of fresh veggies that fill you up without emptying your wallet in the process. If you eat in, you can find your own seat on the uncovered tables in the narrow dining room with its worn tile floor. Fill up your own cup with soda or water while you wait for your pita wrap or falafel and hummus plate to be made up. If you're in a hurry, order your food to-go; the pita wrap sandwiches are big and a bit juicy, but properly wrapped they can be reasonably sidewalk-friendly.



# Information and Services

## INFORMATION

### Tourist Information

New to L.A.? Make one of your first stops one of the two visitors centers. The Los Angeles Convention and Visitors Bureau (www.discoverlosangeles.com) maintains Visitor Information Centers adjacent to two METRO stations. One of these sits up in Hollywood at **Hollywood and Highland Visitors Center** (6801 Hollywood Blvd., 323/467-6412) and the other **Downtown Visitors Center** (685 S. Figueroa St., 213/689-8822). L.A. has also created a Mobile Visitors Center, so just look to the streets for the brightly decorated Honda Element. The denizens of this van can give you maps, brochures, information, and advice about visiting the greater Los Angeles area.

If you're an advance planner, you can take

advantage of the Visitors Bureau website to grab half-price tickets to all sorts of shows all around L.A. Just visit the website on Tuesday, about a week in advance of the date you want to see a show. You'll see all available tickets posted here. These tickets are also offered at the bricks-and-mortar Visitor Information Centers in town.

### Media and Communications

Los Angeles publishes one of the country's major daily newspapers, the ***Los Angeles Times*** (www.latimes.com). Pick one up at any newsstand anywhere in the L.A. Basin for a healthy dose of national news, regional current events, and even some good up-to-the-minute restaurant and nightlife information. The Food section comes out once per week, and the Travel section and glossy magazine are included with the Sunday edition.

You'll find Wi-Fi at nearly every hotel, an Internet café on nearly every corner, and a need to pay a fee for that access in most places. Expect to pay $10–20 per day to hook your laptop to the Internet.

All those Hollywood agents would probably spontaneously combust if they ever lost signal on their cell phones. You'll get coverage pretty much everywhere in L.A., regardless of your provider, with the possible exception of a few minutes going over a mountain pass.

## SERVICES

### Post Offices

Each separate municipality in the L.A. Basin has at least one post office. You can find them at: 750 West Seventh Street, at 1122 East Seventh Street, and 8383 Wilshire Boulevard, #106.

### Medical Services

The greater L.A. area offers some of the best medical care in the world. People come from all over to get novel treatments and plastic surgery in the hospitals frequented by the stars. If you need immediate assistance, **L.A. County General Hospital** (1200 N. State St., 323/226-2622, www.ladhs.org/wps/porta) can fix you up, no matter what's wrong with you.

# Getting There and Around

## GETTING THERE

### Air

L.A. is one of the most commercial airport–dense metropolitan areas in the country. Wherever you're coming from and whichever part of L.A. you're headed for, you can get there by air. **Los Angeles International Airport** (1 World Way, Los Angeles, www.airport-la.com), known as LAX, has the most flights to and from the most destinations of any area airport. LAX is also the most crowded of the L.A. airports, with the worst security and check-in lines. If you can find a way around flying into LAX, do so. One option is to fly into Other airports in the area include the **Bob Hope Airport** (2627 N. Hollywod Way, Burbank, 818/840-8840, www.burbankairport.com). It may provide a slightly longer drive to your final destination but can be well worth the hassle. If you must use LAX, be sure to arrive a *minimum* of two hours in advance of your domestic flight time for your flight out, and consider three hours on busy holidays.

### Train

**Amtrak** (800/872-7245, www.amtrak.com) has an active rail hub in Los Angeles. Most trains come in to **Union Station** (800 N. Alameda St., 213/683-6875, www.westworld.com). From Union Station, you can get to the Bay Area, Redding, and eventually Seattle on the Coast Starlight train, or you can take the Surfliner down the coast to San Diego. The San Joaquin runs out to Sacramento via the Bay Area. To get to and from L.A. from the east, the Southwest Chief comes in from Chicago, Kansas City, and Albuquerque. The famed Sunset Limited runs from Jacksonville, Florida, out to New Orleans, on to El Paso, and then into California.

From Union Station, which also acts as a Metro hub, you can take the Metro Rail to various spots in Los Angeles.

### Car

Los Angeles is crisscrossed with freeways, providing numerous yet congested access points into the city. From the north and south, I-5 provides the most direct access to downtown L.A. From I-5, Highway 101 south leads directly into Hollywood; from here, Santa Monica Boulevard can take you west to Beverly Hills. Connecting from I-5 to I-210 will take you east to Pasadena. The best way to reach Santa Monica, Venice, and Malibu is via Highway 1, also known as the Pacific Coast Highway. I-10 can get you there from the east, but it will be a long, tedious, and trafficked drive.

## GETTING AROUND

### Car

Think you're up to the challenge of driving the world-infamous L.A. freeway system? Consider carefully. It's not as much fun as you might think. Traffic can be awful all the time. (If you believe you'll miss the jam on I-405 just because it's 8 P.M., you're flat wrong. I-405 often stays jammed up.) Local drivers accustomed to the conditions don't bother being polite, so expect to be cut off constantly and to deal with drivers paying attention to everything in the world but the road. And finally, if you're planning to use the traffic reports or local advice, there's a catch. Most road signs use numbers. But locals, including the radio traffic reporters, use names. There's no visible name-to-number translation on most maps, and just to make things even more fun, the names change (sometimes into one another) depending on where you are. Public transit is an increasingly viable and definitely preferable alternative.

Parking in Los Angeles can be as much of a bear as driving. And it can cost you quite a lot of money. You will find parking lots and structures included with many hotel rooms—L.A. is actually better than San Francisco about that. But parking on the street can be difficult or impossible, parking lots in sketchy areas (like the Flower and Jewelry Districts) can be dangerous, and parking structures at popular attractions can be expensive.

### Metro

Against fairly significant odds in the region that invented car culture, Los Angeles has created a functional and useful public transit system. The **Metro** (www.metro.net, cash fare $1.25, day pass $5) runs both the subway Metro Rail system and a network of buses throughout the L.A. metropolitan area. You can pay on board a bus if you have exact change. Otherwise, purchase a ticket or a day pass from the ticket vending machines present in all Metro Rail Stations.

Some buses run for 24 hours. The Metro Rail lines can start running as early at 4:30 A.M. and don't stop until as late as 1:30 A.M. See the website for route maps, timetables, and fare details.

### Taxis

Taxis aren't cheap, but they're quick, easy, and numerous. And in some cases, when you add up gas and parking fees, you'll find that the cab ride isn't that much more expensive than driving yourself.

To call a cab, try: **Yellow Cab** (800/200-1085, L.A., LAX, Beverly Hills, Hollywood) and **City Cab** (800/750-4400, San Fernando Valley, Hollywood, and LAX). Or check out www.taxicabsla.org for a complete list of providers and phone numbers.

### Tours

If you don't feel up to driving around Los Angeles on your own (and no one will blame you if you don't), dozens of tour operators would love to do the driving for you and let you sit back and enjoy the sights and sounds of Southern California. You can choose between driving tours, walking tours, and even helicopter tours that take you up to get a bird's-eye view of the city, beaches, and the wide Pacific Ocean.

### WALKING TOURS

In amongst the dozens of cheesy "walking tour" operators who will charge you to walk you over the stars on Hollywood Boulevard (which you can do yourself for free), one organization can give you a better, more in-depth look into the true history of the Los Angeles area. The **Los Angeles Conservancy** (www.laconservancy.org, tours Sat. 10 A.M., adults $10, children $5) offers more than a dozen different walking tours that explore the architectural history of different parts of Los Angeles in depth. You can pick a style-themed tour, such as Art Deco or Evolving Skyline or a specific street, area, or major structure such as Union Station, the Broadway Theaters, or the Biltmore Hotel. Check the website for tour schedules, and for a few self-guided tours you can take on your own if you can't make your chosen guided tour. While children are welcome on Conservancy tours, the nature of the entertainment focuses much more on adult visitors; consider leaving the kids elsewhere so they are not bored to bits by all the talk of moldings and archways.

### BUS TOURS

For bus tours, you can't beat the weight of history provided by **Starline Tours** (800/959-3131, www.starlinetours.com, adults $40–65, children $20–45), which has been in the business of showing L.A. and Hollywood to the tourists since 1935. Take a tour of Movie Stars Homes (which actually covers many famous star-studded spots around the region), Hollywood, or try the Grand Tour of Los Angeles (can be narrated in many languages) for a start. Starline can pick you up at almost any hotel in the L.A. Basin. Your tour vehicle will be either an air-conditioned mini-bus, full-sized bus, or topless "Fun Bus" with a second open-air deck that lets visitors breathe the native smog of L.A. unhindered. Fun Tours also allow passengers to jump on and off at various sights and attractions as they please. Expect your tour to last 2–6 hours, depending on which route you choose. Once you're on board, sit back, relax, and enjoy the sights and stories of Los Angeles.

# Disneyland

The "Happiest Place on Earth" lures millions of visitors of all ages each year with promises of fun and fantasy. During high seasons, waves of humanity flow through Disneyland (1313 S. Disneyland Dr., Anaheim, 714/781-4565, http://disneyland.disney.go.com, daily 8 A.M.–midnight), moving slowly from Land to Land and ride to ride. The park is well set up to handle the often-immense crowds. Everything from foot-traffic control to ample restrooms make even a Christmastime trip to Disneyland a happy time for the whole family. Despite the undeniable cheese factor, even the most cynical and jaded resident Californians can't quite keep their cantankerous scowls set once they're ensconced inside Uncle Walt's dream. It really *is* a happy place.

Disney's rides, put together by the park's "Imagineers," are better than those at any other amusement park in the state—perhaps better than any in the world. The technology of the rides isn't more advanced than other parks, but it's the attention to detail that makes a Disneyland ride experience so enthralling. Even the spaces where you stand in line match the theme of the ride you're waiting for, from the archaeological relics of Indiana Jones to the tombstones of the Haunted Mansion. If you've got several days in the park, try them all! But if you don't, pick from the best of the best in each Land.

## SIGHTS

Your first stop inside the park should be one of the information kiosks near the front entrance gates. Here you can get a map, a schedule of the day's events, and the inside scoop on what's going on in the park during your visit.

In California Adventure, you'll find two information booths just inside the main park entrance, one off to the left as you walk through the turnstile and one at the opening to Sunshine Plaza. Here's where you'll get your park guide, Time Guide, and more information about what's going on in the park that day.

## Downtown Disney

You don't need an admission ticket to take a stroll through the shops of Downtown Disney. In addition to the mammoth World of Disney Store, you'll find an Anne Geddes gallery, a Build-a-Bear workshop, and a LEGO Imagination Center. For a more adult audience, the Illuminations candle shop, Sephora, and the Sunglass Icon boutique beckon. If you need reading material, the small but adequate Compass Books & Café has the most recent bestsellers, travel books, and a few more interesting tomes and titles. You can also have a bite to eat or take in some jazz or a new release movie at Downtown Disney.

## New Orleans Square

In New Orleans Square, the unquestioned favorite ride for the 21st century is the newly revamped **Pirates of the Caribbean.** If you haven't visited Disneyland in a few years, you'll notice some major changes to this old favorite. Beginning in the dim swamp overlooked by the Blue Bayou restaurant, inside the ride's classic scenes have been revamped to more closely tie to the movies. Look for Jack Sparrow to pop up among your other favorite disreputable characters engaged in all sorts of debauchery. Lines for Pirates can get long, so consider grabbing a FastPass for this one if you don't want to wait. Even if you don't FastPass, the line for Pirates moves fast. Pirates is suitable for younger children as well as teens and adults.

For a taste of truly classic Disney, line up in the graveyard for a tour of the **Haunted Mansion.** Next to Pirates, this ride hasn't changed much in the last 40 years. It hasn't needed to. The sedate motion makes the Haunted Mansion suitable for younger children, but beware! The ghosties and ghoulies that amuse adults can be intense for little kids.

## Adventureland

Adventureland sits next to the New Orleans Square area. **Indiana Jones** is arguably one of the best rides in all of Disneyland, and the details make it stunning. As you stand in the queue, check out the signs, equipment, and artifacts in mock-dusty tunnels winding toward the ride. The ride itself, in a roller-coaster style variant of an all-terrain vehicle, jostles and jolts you through a landscape that Indy himself might dash through, pursued by booby-traps and villains. Hang on to your hat—literally! Use the pouches provided in your seat to secure your unattached things or they will get jostled out of this exciting ride. This one isn't the best for tiny tots, but the big kids love it and everyone might want a FastPass for the endlessly popular attraction.

On the other end of the spectrum, you'll either love the **Tiki Room** or you'll hate it. Up a tree, literally, you'll take a seat and enjoy some classic pseudo-Polynesian tiki entertainment. Even the smallest children love the bright colors and cheerful songs in the Tiki Room, though some adults can't quite hack the cheesiness here.

## Frontierland

Take a ride on a Wild West train on the **Big Thunder Mountain Railroad.** This older roller coaster whisks away passengers on a brief but fun thrill-ride through a "dangerous, decrepit" mountain's mine shafts. As you stand in line, be sure to read the names of the locomotives as the trains come rushing by.

## Fantasyland

The favorite of many Disneyland visitors, Fantasyland rides tend to cater to the younger set. And for many Disneyphiles, the ultimate expression of Uncle Walt's dream is the **Small World.** Toddlers adore this ride, which introduces their favorite Disney characters and the famous (some would say infamous) song. You can almost feel the fairy dust sprinkling down on you as you tour this magical miniature kingdom. (Warning: If ultra-cutesiness makes you gag, you might want to skip this one.)

Kids who are just a little bit older might prefer the crazy fun of **Mr. Toad's Wild Ride.** Even though it's not really a roller coaster, this ride makes for big fun for children and adults alike. What's cool about Mr. Toad's is the wacky scenery you'll get to see along the ride, from a sedate library to the gates of hell.

If it's a faster thrill you're seeking, head for one of the most recognizable landmarks at Disneyland. The **Matterhorn** roller coaster looks like a miniature version from its namesake in the Swiss Alps. Inside it, you'll board a sled-style coaster car and plunge down the mountain on a twisted track that takes you past rivers, glaciers, and the Abominable Snowman.

### Tomorrowland

In order to keep up with the realities of the future, many of the rides in this section of the 50-year-old park have been updated or even replaced over the years. Completely revamped after being down for years, the microscope-style ride is now named **"Honey, I Shrunk the Audience."** Now associated with the Disney movie with a similar title, this ride shrinks the audience down to a miniscule size. You'll be surrounded by immense shapes—familiar objects blown up to help make you feel little.

Another classic that's been given a makeover to connect it to a recent Disney blockbuster movie is the **Finding Nemo Submarine.** On this ride, you and fellow guests board a submarine and descend into a manmade pool. Under water, you'll find yourself in the brightly colored world of Nemo and his frantic father, filled with an astonishing array of sea life. Help your kids count the number of familiar fish!

Finally, for the bigger visitors, the best thrill ride of the main park sits inside a space-aged building. **Space Mountain** is a fast roller coaster that whizzes through an almost entirely darkened world. All you'll see are the stars overhead. You will hear your screams, and those of your fellow passengers, as your "spaceship" swerves and plunges along tracks you cannot see. Despite its age, Space Mountain remains one of the more popular rides in the park. Consider getting a FastPass to keep out of sometimes-long lines.

## ☾ CALIFORNIA ADVENTURE

Disney's California Adventure (daily 10 A.M.–9 P.M.) celebrates much of what makes California special. If Disney is your only stop on this trip but you'd like to get a sense of the state as a whole, California Adventure can give you a little taste. (Though for my money, you'll do better to extend your vacation and spend some time exploring California in all its real non-Disneyfied glory.)

Like Disneyland proper, California Adventure is divided into themed areas. Rides in California Adventure tend toward the thrills of other major amusement parks, but include the great Disney touches that make the Mouse special.

### Hollywood Pictures Backlot

Celebrating SoCal's famed film industry, the Backlot holds the ultimate thrill ride inside: **The Twilight Zone Tower of Terror.** Enter the creepy "old hotel," go through the "service area," and take your place inside an elevator straight out of your worst nightmares. This ride aims for teens and adults rather than little kids, and it's not a good one for folks who fear heights or don't do well with free-fall rides.

Less extreme but also fun, **Monsters, Inc. Mike & Sully to the Rescue!** invites guests into the action of the movie of the same name. You'll help the heroes as they chase the intrepid Boo. This ride jostles you around a bit, but can be suitable for smaller kids as well as bigger ones.

### a bug's land

Wanna live like a bug? Get a sample of the world of tiny insects on **It's Tough to Be a Bug!** This big-group, 3-D, multi-sensory ride offers fun for little kids and adults alike. You'll fly through the air, scuttle through the grass, and get a good idea of what life is like on six little legs. But beware:When they say this ride engages *all your senses,* they mean it.

For the littlest California Adventurers, **Flik's Fun Fair** offers almost half a dozen rides geared toward toddlers and little children. They can ride pint-sized hot-air balloons, climb aboard a bug-themed train, or run around under a gigantic faucet to cool down after hours of hot fun.

### Paradise Pier

Paradise Pier mimics the Santa Monica Pier and other waterfront attractions like it, with thrill rides and an old-fashioned midway. Most of the extreme rides cluster in the Paradise Pier area. It seems reasonable that along with everything else, Disney does the best roller coasters in the business. They prove it with **California Screamin',** a high-tech roller coaster designed after the classic wooden coasters of carnivals past. This extra-long ride includes drops, twists, a full loop, and plenty of time and screaming fun. California Screamin' has a four-foot height requirement and is just as popular with nostalgic adults as with kids. Get a ride on a big-kid swing inside an improbable gigantic orange on the **Orange Stinger.** The Stinger requires riders to be at least four feet tall and in good health, and it's probably a good idea to have a strong stomach as well.

### Golden State

For a glimpse into other parts of the state, with attractions styled after the Bay Area, Wine Country, and Cannery Row, head to the aptly named Golden State. Want a bird's-eye view of California? Get on board **Soarin' Over California.** This combination ride and show puts you and dozens of other guests on the world's biggest "glider" and sets you off over the hills and valleys of California. You'll feel the wind in your hair as you see the vineyards, mountains, and beaches of this diverse state. If you prefer water to wind, take a ride down the **Grizzly River Run,** a Disney version of one of the many wild California rivers that rafters love to run.



Smaller visitors can get some exercise and fun in the **Redwood Creek Challenge Trail.** This adventure course mimics the ropes courses adults love, but it's sized small enough for kids. Parents can join in on some of the course, but must wait and watch for their charges to swing on the ropes.

### Parades and Shows

Do you remember the brilliant, colorful **Electric Light Parade** of years past? While bright lights are no longer the biggest or most advanced thing, thousands of people still love the kitsch and fun of this classic parade. So it moved from the main Disney parade route, where newer shows run, to California Adventure where you can relive your childhood joys most evenings. Check the park's Times Guide for the schedule during your visit.

Other regular shows in California Adventure are **High School Musical 2: School's Out!** and **Disney's Aladdin – A Musical Spectacular.** Both of these shows hearken back to favorite children's movies. Your kids can sing along with favorite songs and characters while you take a load off your feet and relax for a while. Check your park guide and Time Guide for more information about these and other live shows throughout California Adventure.

## ACCOMMODATIONS

The best way to get fully Disneyfied is to stay at one of the park's hotels. Several sit just beside or across the street from the park.

### Disney Hotels

For the most iconic Disney resort experience, you must stay at the **Disneyland Hotel** (1150 Magic Way, 714/956-6425 or 714/778-6600, http://disneyland.disney.go.com, $350). This nearly 1,000-room high-rise monument to brand-specific family entertainment has everything a vacationing Brady-esque bunch could want: themed swimming pools, themed play areas, and even character-themed guest rooms that allow the kids to fully immerse themselves in the Mouse experience. Adults and families on a budget can also get rooms with either a king or two queen beds and more traditional motel fabrics and appointments. The monorail stops inside the hotel, offering guests the easiest way into the park proper without having to deal with parking or even walking.

It's easy to find the **Paradise Pier Hotel** (1717 S. Disneyland Dr., 714/956-6425 or 714/999-0990, http://disneyland.disney.go.com, $450); it's that high-rise thing just outside of the parks on the California Adventure side. This hotel boasts what passes for affordable lodgings within walking distance of California Adventure, Downtown Disney, and Disnelyand's main gate. Rooms are cute, colorful, and clean; many have two double or queen beds to accommodate families or couples traveling together on a tighter budget. You'll find a (possibly refreshing) lack of Mickeys in the standard guest accommodations at the Paradise, which has the feel of a beach resort motel.

The **Grand Californian** (1600 S. Disneyland Dr., 714/956-6425 or 714/635-2300, http://disneyland.disney.go.com, $200–450) lies inside California Adventure, attempting to mimic the famous Ahwahnee Lodge in Yosemite. While it doesn't quite succeed (much of what makes the Ahwahnee so great is its views), the big-beam construction and soaring common spaces do feel reminiscent of a great luxury lodge. The hotel is surrounded by gardens and has restaurants, a day spa, and shops attached on the ground floors; it can also get you right out into Downtown Disney and thence to the parks proper. Guest rooms at the Californian offer more luxury than the other Disney resorts, with dark woods and faux-Craftsman detailing creating an attractive atmosphere. You can get anything from a standard room that sleeps two up to spacious family suites with bunk beds that can easily handle six people. As with all Disney resorts, you can purchase tickets and a meal plan along with your hotel room (in fact, if you book via the website they'll try to force you to do it that way).

### Outside the Parks

The massive park complex is ringed with motels, both popular chains and more interesting independents. **The Anabella** (1030 W. Katella Ave., Anaheim, 714/905-1050, www.anabellahotel.com, $94–119) offers a touch of class along with a three-block walk to the parks. The elegant marble-clad lobby seems like it belongs closer to Downtown L.A. than Downtown Disney. Guest rooms are furnished with an eye toward modern, stylish decor (occasionally at the expense of practicality). Adults looking for an overnight escape from the endless parade of kid-oriented entertainment and attractions will find a welcome respite at the Anabella. A decent restaurant, nail salon, and mini-mart sit on the hotel property, and a fairly lousy diner is right next door. You can get limited room service at the Anabella, and you can leave your car in their parking lot to avoid the expense of parking at Disneyland.

Another nice out-of-park hotel, in walking distance of Disneyland, is the **Desert Palms Hotel & Suites** (631 W. Katella Ave., 714/535-1133, www.desertpalmshotel.com, $180–550). Its spacious and elegant lobby welcomes visitors, the pool and spa provide fun for children and adults alike, and the many amenities make travelers comfortable. Regular rooms have one king or two queen beds, a TV, a phone, Internet access, and not a ton of room to walk around after all your luggage is crowded in with the furniture. Bedspreads catch the eye with their bright, multicolored palm design; the rest of the decor is neutral by comparison. Guests with more discretionary income can choose from a number of suites, some designed to delight children and others aimed at couples on a romantic getaway.

## FOOD

### Disneyland

One of the few things the Mouse doesn't do too well is haute cuisine. For a truly good or healthy meal, get a hand stamp and go outside the park. But if you're stuck inside and you absolutely need sustenance, you can get it. The best areas of the park to grab a bite are Main Street, New Orleans, and Frontierland—they offer the most variety in concessions—but you can find at least a snack almost anywhere in the park.

For a sit-down restaurant meal inside the park, make reservations in advance for a table at the **Blue Bayou Restaurant** (New Orleans Square, 714/781-3463, $20–30). The best part about this restaurant is its setting in the dimly lit swamp overlooking the Pirates of the Caribbean ride. Appropriately, the Bayou has a reputation for being haunted. The Cajun-ish cuisine matches the jungle-like setting, though if you're looking for authenticity you'd do better looking elsewhere. You will get large portions, and tasty sweet desserts make a fine finish to your meal. Watch your silverware, though—the alleged ghosts in this restaurant like to mess around with diners' tableware.

If you need to grab a quicker bite, *don't* do it at the French Market restaurant in the New Orleans area. It sells what appears to be day-old (or more) food from the Bayou that's been sitting under heat lamps for a good long time. You're better off finding one of the McDonalds Fries carts and getting some greasy food that at least tastes good.

### California Adventure

If you need a snack break in California Adventure, you'll find most of the food clustered in the Golden State area. Take a tour of the **Mission Tortilla Factory** or the **Boudin Bakery,** then taste the delectable products of these places in the nearby restaurants. For a Mexican feast, try **Cocina Cucamonga Mexican Grill,** which uses the products of the tortilla factory. For more traditional American fare, enjoy the food at the **Pacific Wharf Cafe** or the **Taste Pilots' Grill.**

Unlike Disneyland proper, in California Adventure responsible adults can quaff their thirst with a variety of alcoholic beverages. If you're just dying for a cold beer, get one at the **Pacific Wharf Distribution Co.** Or if your love is for the endless variety of high-quality wines produced in the Golden State, head for the **Golden Vine Winery,** where you can learn the basics of wine creation and production. Have a glass and a pseudo-Italian meal at the sit-down **Wine Country Trattoria at the Golden Vine Winery.**

## PRACTICALITIES

### Tickets

There are as many varying ticket prices and plans as there are themes in the park. A single-day theme park ticket will run you $66 ($56 for children age 3–9). A variety of other combinations and passes are available online (http://disneyland.disney.go.com).

To buy tickets, go to one of the many kiosks

### HERE AT DISNEY, WE HAVE A FEW RULES

Think that anything goes at the Happiest Place on Earth? Think again. Uncle Walt had distinct ideas about what his dream theme park would look like, and that vision extended to the dress and manner of his guests. When the park opened in 1955, among the many other restrictions, no man sporting facial hair was allowed into Disneyland. The rules on dress and coiffure have relaxed a bit since the opening, but you still need to mind your manners when you enter the Magic Kingdom.

- Adults may not wear costumes of any kind except on Halloween.
- No shirt, no shoes, no Disneyland.
- If you must use the "F-word," do it quietly. If staff catches you cussing or cursing in a way that disturbs others, you can be asked to desist. Or leave.
- The happiest of happiness is strictly prohibited inside the Magic Kingdom. If you're caught having sex on park grounds, not only will you be thrown out, you'll be banned from Disneyland for life. (At least that's the rumor.)
- Ditto for any illicit substances.

in the central gathering spot that serves as the main entrance to both Disneyland proper and California Adventure. Bring your credit card, since a day at Disney is not cheap. After you've got tickets in hand (or if you've bought them online ahead of time), proceed to the turnstiles for the main park. You'll see the Disneyland Railroad terminal and the large grassy hill with the flowers planted to resemble Mickey's famous face. Pass through, and head under the railroad trestle to get to Main Street and the park center.

Horrifyingly, the already expensive regular one-day Disneyland ticket doesn't include California Adventure. If you're interested in checking out California Adventure as well as Disneyland proper, your best bet is to buy a **Park Hopper** pass ($81–91 single day, $112–132 two days), which lets you move back and forth between the two parks at will for a slight discount. If you're planning to spend several days touring the Houses of Mouse, buy multi-day passes in advance online to save a few more bucks per day. It'll help you feel a little bit better about the wads of cash you'll undoubtedly drop on junk food, giant silly hats, stuffed animals, and an endless array of Disney apparel.

The magical **FastPasses** are free with park admission and might seem like magic after awhile. The newest and most popular rides offer FastPass kiosks near the entrances. Feed your ticket into one of the machines, and it will spit out both your ticket and a FastPass with your specified time to take the ride. Come back during your window and enter the always-much-shorter FastPass line, designated by a sign at the entrance. If you're with a crowd, be sure you all get your FastPasses at the same time, so you all get the same time window to ride the ride.

## Services

Check your park map or look for signs to the restrooms available in each Land of the park. Restrooms have ample space, so you'll rarely find lines even on the most crowded days.

If mobility is a problem for you or for a small child in your family, consider renting (no, they're not free) a stroller, wheelchair, or scooter. Ask for directions to the rental counter when you enter the park.

Cell phones work inside Disneyland, which is actually a fabulous thing. It's already loud and raucous in the parks, and the ability to use cell phones to connect up with lost family or party members at Disneyland is one of *the* finest advances in modern technology in a long, long time.

Disneyland offers its own minor medical facilities, which can dispense first aid for scrapes, cuts, and mild heat exhaustion. They can also call an ambulance if something nastier has occurred.

If you need to stow your bags or hit the restroom before plunging into the fray, banks of lockers and restrooms sit in the main entrance area.

## Getting There

Disneyland is located on Disneyland Drive in Anaheim and is most accessible from I-5 south where it crosses Ball Rd. (stay in the left three lanes for parking). The parking lot is located at 1313 S. Disneyland Drive and costs $12.

If you're coming to the park from elsewhere in the O.C., consider bailing on the car (avoiding the parking fees) and taking public transit instead. Shuttles from LAX and John Wayne airport take you directly to the park or the hotels. **Anaheim Resort Transit** (ART, www.rideart.org) can take you to and from the Amtrak station and all around central Anaheim for $3 per ride.

## Getting Around

Disney's California Adventure sits across the main Disney entry plaza from Disneyland. You can enter from the main parking lots, from Downtown Disney, or you can hop over from Disneyland. Need a tram for the long-distance walk in or out of the park? The **Lion King Tram Route** can get you to and from the main parking areas. The **Mickey & Friends Tram Route** takes you toward Downtown Disney and the resort hotels.

## INLAND ORANGE COUNTY

The lure of the inland O.C., a primarily residential area, tends to be dominated by the Mouse. But if you just have to get away from the overwhelming cutesy happiness for a while, a few other entertaining attractions lurk in the shadows.

### Knott's Berry Farm

Believe it or not, other amusement parks make their home in Orange County. For a taste of history along with some ultra-modern thrill rides and plenty of cooling waterslides, head for Knott's Berry Farm (8039 Beach Blvd., Buena Park, 714/220-5200, http://knotts.com, Mon.–Fri. 10 A.M.–6 P.M., Sat. 10 A.M.–10 P.M., Sun. 10 A.M.–7 P.M., adults $43, seniors and children $20). This park's unusual name stems from its agricultural past. The fertile land beneath the roller coasters really was a berry farm decades ago. The Knott family grew strawberries, raspberries, boysenberries, and more here, then made the fruits of their labors into preserves. Knott's jams retain

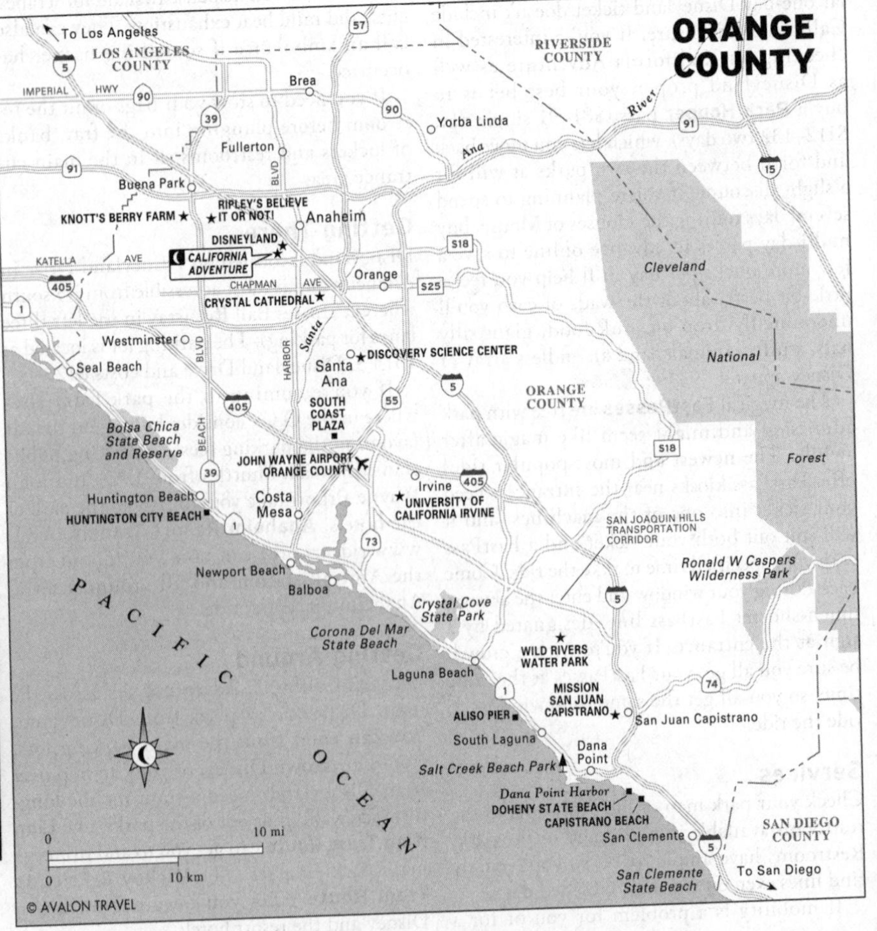

their popularity in supermarkets across the country to this day.

Today, instead of berry vines you'll find twisting tracks at this thrill-oriented park. From the tall landmark GhostRider wooden coaster to the 30-story vertical drop ride to the screaming Silver Bullet suspended coaster, even the most hard-core ride lover will get excited by Knott's. For the younger crowd, Camp Snoopy offers an array of pint-sized rides and attractions, plus Snoopy and all the characters they love from the Peanuts comics and TV shows.

In the heat of the summer, many park visitors adjourn from the coasters to **Knott's Soak City** (daily Memorial Day–Labor Day, weekends May–Sept., adults $24, seniors and children $18). The full-sized water park has 22 rides, a kid pool and water playground, and plenty of space to spread out and enjoy the O.C. sunshine after cooling off on the waterslides.

### Wild Rivers Water Park

If you've been to the O.C. in July, you know why the county can support two large water parks. Out in Irvine, head for Wild Rivers Water Park (8770 Irvine Center Dr., 949/788-0808, www.wildrivers.com, adults $32, children $20). One of the biggest parks of its kind in the state, Wild Rivers has not one but two wave pools, more than 40 slides and rides, and areas geared for both kids and adults. You can't bring your own food into the park, but two restaurants, a coffee kiosk, and a sweet shop serve all comers all day long.

### Discovery Science Center

If you'd like your kids to spend at least one day in the O.C. doing something educational, take them to the Discovery Science Center (2500 N. Main St., Santa Ana, 714/542-2823, www.discoverycube.org, daily 10 A.M.–5 P.M., adults $13, children $10). The star attraction, the interactive DinoQuest, lets kids get inside the lost world of dinosaurs. Way inside! You can also take a quick nap on a bed of nails, create your own clouds and tornadoes, and experience the buffeting of a hurricane inside a wind tunnel. The Discovery Science Center combines interactive play with scientific learning to create a fun day that's not wasted.

### Ripley's Believe It or Not

For a totally education and enlightenment-free trip to a sort of museum, walk one block up from Knott's to Ripley's Believe It or Not (7850 Beach Blvd., 714/522-7045, www.ripleysbp.com, Mon.–Fri. 10 A.M.–6 P.M., Sat.–Sun. 9 A.M.–7 P.M.). Here you'll see the wild and wacky artifacts said to be "collected" by Robert Ripley on his travels around the globe. In fine old sideshow style, see exhibits such as the eight-legged pig, the world's tallest man, the bearded lady, and the human unicorn. Wild tattoos and body modifications figure large into this "museum's" cache of oddities, so be prepared for small children to get a little bit freaked out by some of the weirdness here.

### Crystal Cathedral

Looking to see a modern cathedral, O.C. style? Visit the shiny and immense Crystal Cathedral (12141 Lewis St., Garden Grove, 714/971-4000, www.crystalcathedral.org). You may already have seen it from the road or the air during your travels around the O.C.! This modern-day megachurch offers free tours daily; stop by the Welcome Center for information and tour times. On a tour or wandering by yourself, you'll see the 2,800-seat auditorium that acts as both congregational seating and a TV studio, beautiful religious sculptures, and the magnificent glass walls of the interior. The Crystal Cathedral hosts the taping of the *Hour of Power* each Sunday, and you can be a part of this national and international inspirational telecast. Or just show up on Sunday morning or evening for the regular services, which include music from the outstanding organ, the 20-piece church orchestra, and the 80-member choir.

ROBERT HOLMES / CALTOUR

Crystal Cathedral

## Accommodations

Away from the Disney resorts, the accommodations in inland Orange County run to chain motels. The good news is that you can find a decent room for a reasonable price almost everywhere you go in the O.C. The less-good news is that you won't find much of anything in the way of character or distinction in any of them.

The **Red Roof Inn Buena Park** (7121 Beach Blvd., Buena Park, 714/522-7280, www.redroof.com, $74) offers a clean bed and bathroom near Knott's and Disney. Amenities include a heated pool and a spa, free Wi-Fi, and a fitness center. Medium-sized motel rooms feature a standard motel setup with a variety of bed configurations, dark carpets, and floral bedspreads.

At the **Best Western Orange County Airport** (2700 Hotel Terrace, Santa Ana, 714/432-8888, www.bestwestern-oc.com, $110) you'll find everything you expect of the popular national chain, including floral and wine-colored édecor in your comfortable guest room, a pool and hot tub, and a free shuttle to and from John Wayne Airport. Down in the lobby, you'll find a complimentary "cook-to-serve" breakfast each morning (that is, prepackaged heat-and-eat items plus cold cereals, bagels, and coffee).

In Garden Grove, stay at the **Hyatt Regency Orange County** (11999 Harbor Boulevard Garden Grove, 714/750-1234, http://orangecounty.hyatt.com/hyatt/hotels/index.jsp, $165). The attractive rooms are decorated in the latest style inside a tall glass-fronted tower. White linens emphasize the cleanliness of beds and bathrooms, while bright yellows and deep blues provide classy artistic touches. In the sun-drenched atrium, enjoy a cocktail or sit back and read a good book in the attractive atmosphere. Grab a chaise lounge by the pool or take a refreshing dip. If you're bringing your family, consider renting one of the "family-friendly suites" that have separate bedrooms with bunk beds and fun édecor geared toward younger guests.

If your major destination is Knott's Berry

Farm, consider staying at the **Knott's Berry Farm Resort Hotel** (7675 Crescent Ave., Buena Park, 714/995-1111, $175–250). This high-rise resort includes all the extras and amenities you'd expect from a corporate hotel. You can lounge by the pool and spa, work out at the fitness center, and have dinner in one of the onsite restaurants, the **Amber Waves** dining room or the **Citrus Café.** Get a drink at the **Sports Bar** after a long day out at the park or seeing the sights of O.C. Your comfortable room will greet you each night; choose one queen, two queens, or a king bed. Check the Internet for a variety of specials and discount rates.

## Food

Want to keep the kids—and yourself—entertained during dinner? Check out one of the dinner-and-a-show restaurants, both near Disney and Knott's Berry Farm at Buena Park. At the famous **Medieval Times** (7662 Beach Blvd., Buena Park, 888/935-6878, http://medievaltimes.com, adults $52, children 12 and under $35), you'll enter a castle-shaped building, take your seat, and watch as gallant knights battle for the title of First Knight. You'll see live jousts (there's a big courtyard in this restaurant!), swordfights, and ladies in gowns parading for your pleasure. Your meal, served on a pewter-styled plate, provides hearty if not particularly healthy or high-quality sustenance. Vegetarian and kids' meal options are available upon request.

If you prefer pirates to knights, the O.C. can hook you up. Practically next door to the castle, buckle your swash at the **Pirate's Dinner Adventure** (7600 Beach Blvd., 714/690-1497, www.piratesdinneradventure.com, adults $55, children 3–11 $36). Combining dinner theater, the current pirate craze, and a touch of Cirque du Soleil, everyone in your family will find something to watch at dinner with the Pirates. Even if the cheesy acting and the swordfights don't do it for you, the aerobatics that form an integral part of this show can be great fun to marvel at. A four-course meal includes both chicken and meat (or fish), plus salad and dessert. It's not the best food, but hopefully you'll be too busy enjoying the show to care. Check for special holiday shows in season.

If you're looking for a bite to eat sans pirates and knights **Casa De Soto Restaurant** (8562 Garden Grove Blvd., Garden Grove, 714/530-4200, www.casadesoto.com, Sun.–Thurs. 11:30 A.M.–9 P.M., Fri.–Sat. 11:30 A.M.–10 P.M., $10) offers standard Mexican fare in three festive rooms. **Whole Pita Greek Island Grill** (3940 S. Bristol St., Santa Ana, 714/708-3000, www.greekislandgrille.com, Sun.–Thurs. 11 A.M.–9 P.M., Fri.–Sat. 11 A.M.–9:30 P.M., $10) serves Mediterranean specialties including soulvlaki. gyros, and moussaka.

## Information and Services

For information, visit the **Anaheim Visitor and Postal Center** (640 W. Katella Ave., 714/991-4636, www.anaheim411.com, daily 8 A.M.–7 P.M.). As the name implies, not only does this facility have the 411 on the O.C., you can also mail a letter or a package here. The office lies inside the Jolly Roger Hotel at the corner of Katella and Harbor.

Need a dose of hard news? Get in a copy of the ***Los Angeles Times*** (www.latimes.com), Orange County Edition.

The O.C. has plenty of Internet access, though you'll find few people crouched over laptops inside Disneyland. Look to your hotel, or find a Starbucks outside the park to hook up to the world. The **West Anaheim Medical Center** (3033 W. Orange Ave., Anaheim, 714/827-3000, wamc.phcs.us) is a full-service hospital with an emergency room.

## Getting There and Around

The nearest airport to Disneyland, serving all of Orange County is **John Wayne Airport** (18601 Airport Way, Santa Ana, 949/252-5200, www.ocair.com). It's much easier to fly into and out of John Wayne than LAX, though it can be more expensive. John Wayne's terminal has plenty of rental car agencies, and many shuttle services that can get you where you need to go—especially to the House of Mouse.

If you have to fly into LAX for scheduling or

budget reasons, you can catch a shuttle straight from the airport to your Disneyland hotel. Among the many companies offering and arranging such transportation, the one with the best name is **MouseSavers** (www.mousesavers.com). Working with various shuttle and van companies, MouseSavers can get you a ride in a van or a bus from LAX or John Wayne to your destination at or near Disneyland.

To get around the O.C., your major freeway will be I-5. See the *Getting Around* section for Los Angeles for information about driving here.

If you prefer to use public transit rather than drive, see the the *L.A. and O.C. Coasts* section of this chapter for information about OCTA bus services.

# The L.A. and O.C. Coasts

If you're looking for the famed surf beaches of SoCal, look no further than the coast of Orange County. Sadly, when you look out over the pretty white sands of Huntington and Laguna, you're likely to see the lighted towers of the local oil rigs. Echoing rigs dot the shoreline of Newport and Huntington as well, and as you drive up the legendary Pacific Coast Highway you'll see honest-to-goodness oil fields that will make you wonder if you took a wrong turn into Texas somehow. In truth, the Southern California oil industry has been thriving for many a decade now.

And so you'll surf, sun yourself, bike, inline skate, eat, drink, and be merry in the sight of the rigs. Despite their unsightliness, the beaches of the O.C. and their surrounding resort-oriented towns offer great vacationing potential to all comers.



## LONG BEACH AND THE L.A. COAST

The L.A. coast passes the Palos Verde Penninsula, stretching further south to Redondo Beach and Long Beach, where haunted ships and sunny coasts await.

### The *Queen Mary*

The major tourist attraction of Long Beach is the *Queen Mary* (1126 Queens Highway, Long Beach, 562/435-3511, www.queenmary.com, daily 10 A.M.–6 P.M.), one of the most famous ships ever to ply the high seas. This great ship, once a magnificent pleasure cruise liner, now sits at permanent anchor (it's been gutted and is no longer seaworthy) in Long Beach Harbor. The *Queen Mary* acts as a hotel, a museum, an entertainment center with several restaurants and bars, and a gathering place for both locals and visitors. You can book a stateroom and stay aboard, come for dinner, or just buy a regular ticket and take a self-guided tour. The museum exhibits describe the history of the ship, with special emphasis on its tour of duty as a troop transport during World War II. You can explore many of the decks at the bow, including the engine room that still boasts much of its massive machinery, the art gallery, and the various upper exterior decks where vacationers once relaxed on their way to Europe.

But it's not just the extensive museum and the attractive hotel that make the *Queen Mary* famous today. The ship is also one of the most famously haunted places in California. Over its decades of service, a number of unfortunate souls lost their lives aboard the *Queen Mary,* and it is rumored that several of them have stuck with the ship ever since their tragic deaths. If you're most interested in the ghost stories of the *Queen Mary,* book a spot on one of the "Attractions at Night," which include the Paranormal Ship Walk (562/499-1666, Thurs.–Sat. 8 P.M.) that takes you to the hottest haunted spots and Dining With the Spirits (Sat. 7 P.M.), a combination of dinner and haunted tour. For more serious ghost hunters, Paranormal Investigation tours happen on the first and third Fridays of each month.

Appropriately, the investigations begin at midnight.

The *Queen Mary* offers a large pay parking lot near the ship's berth. You'll walk from the parking area up to a square with a ticket booth and several shops and a snack bar. Purchase your general admission ticket to get on board the ship. It's also a good idea to buy any guided tour tickets now. Night tours can fill up in advance, so consider calling ahead to reserve a spot.

## Russian Attack Submarine

Berthed right next to the luxurious *Queen Mary* you'll find a much smaller and more lethal little boat, The Russian Attack Submarine (562/432-0424, daily 10 A.M.–6 P.M., adults $11, children $10), code-named the Scorpion, helped the Soviet Union spy on the United States for more than 20 years during the Cold War. Your admission includes a brief history film and the opportunity to explore the innards of the submarine. Squeeze through the tiny spaces and learn how members of the Soviet Navy lived and worked aboard this attack submarine, which has a history that's still shrouded in secrecy.

## Aquarium of the Pacific

Even the locals enjoy the exhibits at Aquarium of the Pacific (100 Aquarium Way, 562/590-3100, www.aquariumofpacific.org, daily 9 A.M.–6 P.M., adults $21, children $12). The large aquarium hosts animal and plant life native to the Pacific Ocean, from the local residents of SoCal's sea up to the North Pacific and down to the tropics. While the big modern building isn't much to look at from the outside, it's what's inside that's beautiful. Aquarium of the Pacific has far more than the average number of touch-friendly tanks. Kids and adults all love the unusual feel of sea stars, urchins, and rays. More exciting, you can dip your fingers into the Shark Lagoon and "pet" a few of the more than 150 sharks the Aquarium cares for. If you prefer tamer and more colorful denizens of the air, spend time in the loud Lorikeet Forest. For visitors who are just too cool for fish, there's the Catch a Wave exhibit, which displays the history and culture of surfing, the science of waves, and the species that inhabit this turbulent small part of the ocean.

## Redondo State Beach

At the other end of the 20-mile bike and pedestrian path from Will Rogers State Beach, you'll find Redondo State Beach (400–1700 Esplanade, http://beaches.co.la.ca.us). Sitting next to the Redondo Beach Pier, this sand stretch gets really crowded in the summertime, so if rubbing elbows with your fellow sun worshippers doesn't work for you, Redondo isn't your best bet. On the other hand, the lack of surfers makes swimming a prime activity here, complete with lifeguards during the daytime. You'll also find the usual volleyball and other beach games, the bike path (which is lit at night), and the restaurants of the pier. The beach features restrooms and showers, and a large multilevel pay parking structure at the pier offers ample space to stow your car for the day.

# Entertainment and Events

For a low-key good time, grab a table and a drink at the **Starboard Attitude** (202 The Pier, Redondo Beach, 310/379-5144, www.starboardattitude.com, no cover) on the Redondo Beach Pier. This cool little local's joint features live music four nights a week and karaoke on the off nights. Pro acts tend towards talented classic rock cover bands and soulful blues groups. Expect folks to get up and dance to their favorite songs, and be prepared to be asked to dance if you're a woman on your own. However, the atmosphere here is more friendly than scary, with a mix of younger to middle-aged patrons who all seem to know each other and the servers. Talk up your bartender, and you'll get the whole scoop on the local scene as well as any drink you can imagine and probably one or two you've never heard of. The staff takes good care of the patrons too, so you'll find yourself drinking as much water as liquor as the evening wears on. There's no cover, but you will get hit with a two-drink minimum that's easy to meet, because it's easy to sit down, enjoy the mellow vibe, and stay a good long while at the Attitude.

## Accommodations

Rooms down in this stretch of beach towns don't come cheap, but you'll find some attractive independent inns and B&Bs in this area.

### $100-150

For a quiet, private inn experience in the midst of the big city, try the **The Turret House** (556 Chestnut, Long Beach, 562/624-1991, www.turrethouse.com, $130–160). This cute late-Victorian home sits on a street corner in the densely packed residential section of Long Beach. Each of the five guest rooms has its own decorative theme, an antique bedstead, a clawfoot tub, plenty of knick-knacks, and a few pieces of high-end original art—all for a surprisingly reasonable rate. After your breakfast, stroll out into town for more coffee or perhaps a brief downtown shopping spree.

For a cute near-the-sand motel in Manhattan Beach, stay at the **Sea View Inn at the Beach** (3400 Highland Ave., Manhattan Beach, 310/545-1504, www.seaview-inn.com, $143–250). With only a block to the sands of the beach, this is a great place to hole up if you're in town for some surfing, volleyball, or sunbathing along the shore. (You'll avoid the traditional summer beach parking nightmare by leaving your car at the motel.) Just grab a boogie board and some beach chairs from the lobby and head on out. Inside, the guest room appointments are prettier and more coordinated than those of most moderate motels. Rooms are done in light blues and whites, with matching prints on the walls and possibly even a live plant to add a homelike touch. The complex of blocky, mid-century modern buildings has its own small swimming pool as well, set in a small, plant-strewn courtyard. Just around the corner, you'll find an array of restaurants, shops, bars, and clubs.



Of the three Best Westerns that comprise much of Redondo Beach's hospitality, the **Best Western Sunrise** (400 North Harbor Dr., Redondo Beach, www.bestwestern-sunrise.com, $148) is the best of the lot, with rooms overlooking Redondo's King Harbor and the location within walking distance of the pier and its restaurants and bars. Rooms are clean and comfortable, and the decor is cute and modern, with plaid bedspreads and light wood furniture. You'll get all the standard amenities you'd expect at a Best Western, plus a nice pool and spa, a gym, free Wi-Fi, and a complimentary breakfast.

### $150-250

Looking for something completely different? Check in to the **Dockside Boat and Bed** (316 East Shoreline Dr., Dock 5A, Rainbow Harbor, Long Beach, 562/436-3111, www.boatandbed.com, $235–330). You won't get a regular old hotel room—instead, you'll get one of four yachts. The yachts run 38–54 feet and can sleep four or more people apiece. The amenities include TVs with DVD players, stereos, kitchen facilities, wet bars, and ample seating. No, you can't actually take your floating accommodations out for a spin; these yachts are permanent residents of Rainbow Harbor.

### OVER $250

For a fabulous high-end hotel stay on the beach, go to the **Beach House at Hermosa Beach** (1300 The Strand, Hermosa Beach, 310/374-3001, www.beach-house.com, $275–400). It might be the tiniest bit pretentious, but it's hard not to love this larger boutique hotel that looks right out over the water. The "loft suite" has a cushy king bed with Frette sheets, a big bathroom with separate tub and shower, two TVs and a stereo, and a real wood-burning fireplace. The casual, upscale decor makes visitors feel at home, but you'll probably want to spend more time out on the porch or balcony on sunny days. Guests get a free continental breakfast, the use of the outdoor spa, and access to the on-site gym. If you prefer an outdoor workout, enjoy The Strand for a walk, run, or bike ride. Head downstairs to The Strand Café for a bite and a tasty view from the outside tables, or to the spa for a delightful massage or facial.

## Food

Combining elegance, fine Continental-

California cuisine, and great ghost stories, **Sir Winston's** (1126 Queens Hwy., Long Beach, 562/499-1657, www.queenmary.com, Mon.–Thurs. and Sat.–Sun. 11 A.M.–11 P.M., $30) floats gently onboard the *Queen Mary*. For the most beautiful dining experience, request a window table and make reservations for sunset. And dress in your finest; Sir Winston's requests that diners adhere to their semi-formal dress code.

Have you come to Los Angeles to seek genuine homestyle Mexican food? You can find it at **Sion's Mexican Restaurant** (235 N. Sepulveda Blvd., Manhattan Beach, 310/372-4504, Sun.–Mon. 8 A.M.–2 P.M., Tues.–Sat. 8 A.M.–9 P.M., $10). Expect nothing fancy, but everything fresh—from tacos to salsa—in this utterly casual and family owned hole in the wall.

A local's favorite down where the shops and cafes cluster, **Natraj Cuisine of India** (5262 E. 2nd St., Long Beach, 562/930-0930, Mon.–Thurs. 11 A.M.–2:30 P.M. and 5–10 P.M., Fri. 11 A.M.–2:30 P.M. and 5–11 P.M., Sat.–Sun. 11 A.M.–11 P.M., $10–30) offers good food for reasonable (by L.A. standards) prices. Come by for the all-you-can-eat lunch buffet to sample a variety of properly spiced meat and vegetarian dishes created in classic Indian tradition.

The **Green Temple Vegetarian Restaurant** (1700 S. Catalina Ave., Redondo Beach, 310/944-4525, www.greentemple.net, Mon. 12–4 P.M., Tues.–Thurs. 11 A.M.–4 P.M. and 5–9 P.M., Fri.–Sat. 11 A.M.–4 P.M. and 5–10 P.M., Sun. 9 A.M.–12 P.M., $10–20) strives for a Southern California zen in both its cuisine and its dining room. All the vegetarian cuisine comes from sustainable and (whenever possible) organic sources, including Trader Joes and Whole Foods stores.

### Practicalities

For information, maps, brochures, and advice about Long Beach and the surrounding areas, visit the **Long Beach Convention and Visitors Bureau** (1 World Trade Center, 3rd Fl., 562/436-3645, www.visitlongbeach.com).

There is a **post office** in Long Beach (300 Long Beach Blvd., 562/628-1303).

For medical attention, visit the emergency room at the **Long Beach Memorial Medical Center** (2801 Atlantic Ave., Long Beach, 562/933-2000, www.memorialcare.org).

While you can get to the coast easily enough from LAX, the **Long Beach International Airport** (4100 Donald Douglas Dr., 562/570-2600, www.longbeach.gov/airport) is both closer to the beach and less crowded than the LAX.

I-710, which runs north–south, is known as the Long Beach Freeway. Along the coast, the Pacific Coast Highway can get you from one beach town to the next.

Parking in Long Beach and the other beach towns is just bad as parking anywhere else in L.A. Prepare to pay for the privilege of stuffing your car someplace for the day. Beach parking on summer weekends is the worst, but on weekdays and in the off-season you can occasionally find a decent space down near the beach for reasonable rates.

## ORANGE COUNTY COAST

The Orange County coast begins at Huntington Beach and stretches south across a collection of sunny scenic beaches until ending at San Juan Capistrano. Along the way, Newport Beach, Huntington Beach, Laguna Beach, and Dana Point provide surf, sun, and sand galore.

### Newport Beach

Most of the activity in Newport Beach (www.visitnewportbeach.com) centers around Newport Pier (McFadden Pl.) and Main Street on the Balboa Peninsula. Some folks like to hearken back to the old days of individual beach houses and long, lazy summer vacations. The **Crystal Cove Beach Cottages** (35 Crystal Cove, Newport Beach, 949/497-0900, www.crystalcovebeachcottages.org, dorm rooms $30, cabins $180) can help recreate the feeling of another time. Right out on the sands of historic Crystal Cove south of downtown Newport Beach, this collection of 14 cabins offer a delightful and serene beach vacation experience to all who stay here. Eleven of the cabins are individual rentals where you get the whole house to yourself. The other three "dorm cottages" offer by-the-room accommodations (linens included, room doors lock) that let even solo budget travelers the opportunity to experience life on a Southern California beach. Cottages include a common refrigerator and microwave, but no full kitchen so you'll need to make plans to eat out—perhaps at the adjacent **Beachcomber Restaurant** or concession-style **Shake Shack.** Maid service is minimal, with towels changed every four days and trash taken out daily. None of the cottages have TVs or any type of digital entertainment.

**The Island Hotel Newport Beach** (690 Newport Center Dr., Newport Beach, 949/759-0808, www.theislandhotel.com, $400) offers perhaps the ultimate O.C. experience. It's a luxury, high-rise hotel situated in a giant shopping mall, within a few minutes' drive of the beach. No, really. On the bright side, the tropical-themed rooms really do have both luxury and comfort in abundance. Expect cushy beds with white linens, attractive private bathrooms, big TVs, views over the mall (and if you're lucky, out to the ocean beyond the city), and all the best amenities. Perhaps the most innovative of these goodies rests within the room service menu; it's called the "In-Flight Menu" and it's a selection of gourmet box lunches. The idea is to allow airline travelers to carry on their own food.

The hotel's **Palm Terrace** (690 Newport Center Dr., Newport Beach, 949/760-4920, www.theislandhotel.com, daily 6:30 A.M.–10:30 P.M., $10–35) offers stylish small bites and sophisticated entrées in a picturesque setting. For something French, colorful **Pescadou Bistro** (3325 Newport Blvd., Newport Beach, 949/675-6990, www.pescadoubistro.com, Tues.–Sun. 5:30–close, $20–35) will fill the bill.



## Huntington Beach

The main reason to come to the west edge of Orange County is to hit the beach. The good news is that the coast of the O.C. is rife with wide, flat, sandy beaches. The bad news is that the beaches still get crowded in the summer. If you want a prime spot, come early in the morning and try to avoid having to park a car if you possibly can.

**Huntington City Beach** (Pacific Coast Hwy. from Beach Blvd. to Seapoint St., daily 5 A.M.–10 P.M.) runs the length of the south end of town, petering out as the oil industry gets going at the north end. This famous beach hosts major sporting events such as the X Games and the U.S. Open of Surfing & Beach Games. But even the average beachgoer can enjoy all sorts of activities on a daily basis, since Huntington City Beach includes a cement walkway for biking, inline skating, jogging, and walking. On the sand, get up a game of Frisbee or take advantage of the beach volleyball courts. Out in the water, catch a wave at the famous Huntington surf break or make use of prevailing winds for a thrilling kite-surfing run. Non-riders can boogie-board, bodysurf, and skim board closer to the shore. Anglers and lovers prefer the Huntington Beach Pier, which leads out over the water. While dogs aren't allowed on the main portion of Huntington City Beach, the beach offers a dog-friendly section at the north end where dogs can be let off-leash, and you'll even see the occasional surfer riding tandem with a four-legged friend.

This beach offers plenty of services and amenities. In high season, lifeguards keep watch over surfers and swimmers. A number of concessions stands make their homes along Huntington City Beach, so you can buy drinks and snacks, or rent a wetsuit and surfboard. Buildings with restrooms and outdoor showers also rise from the sand at regular intervals, though lines do form during the most crowded summer weekends and holidays.

Most visitors to the O.C. coast want to stay as close to the beaches as they can. You can have your beachfront room at the **Sun 'N Sands Motel** (1102 Pacific Coast Hwy., Huntington Beach, 714/536-2543, www.sunnsands.com, $143–300). At this tiny place (17 rooms total) you can expect standard motel room decor in your king or double-queen guest room, plus an adequate private bathroom, a TV with movie channels, and Wi-Fi access. But the main attraction lies across the treacherous Pacific Coast Highway: long, sweet Huntington Beach. Please *be careful* crossing the highway to get to the sand. Find a traffic light and a crosswalk rather than risking life and limb for the minor convenience of jaywalking.

For a quick bite to eat, stop off at the **Bodhi Tree Café** (501 Main St., Huntington Beach, 714/969-9500, daily 10 A.M.–9 P.M., $5–15) for vegetarian soups, salads, and sandwiches. **Sugar Shack Café** (213 Main St., Huntington Beach, 714/536-0355, Thurs.–Tues. 6 A.M.–4 P.M., Wed. 6 A.M.–8 P.M., $20) is a great place for breakfast.

## Laguna Beach

Farther south, the town of Laguna Beach has some of the nicest sands in the county. You'll find more than a dozen separate beaches here, though many connect to one another—you'll just have to choose your favorite. **Heisler Park** and the **Main Beach Park** (Pacific Coast Hwy.) offer protected waterways, with tidepools and plenty of water-based playground equipment. The two parks are connected, so you can walk from one to the other. Both display works of local art in the form of benches and sculptures. Hang out on a bench, pick a spot on the sand to lounge about, or take a swim in the cool Pacific. If you're into scuba diving, you can dive several reefs right off the beach.

You'll find all the facilities and amenities you need at Heisler and Main Beach Parks, from picnic tables to lawns to restrooms. Please use the provided charcoal grills rather than bringing your own. You can park on the street if you find a spot, but be aware that the meters get checked all the time, so feed them well!

## Dana Point

At the southern tip of the O.C., Dana Point (www.danapoint.org) has a harbor-turned-recreation-marina that draws visitors and locals from all around. It also has several beaches nearby. One of the prettiest of these is **Capistrano Beach** (35005 Beach Blvd., www.capistranobeach.com, daily 6 A.M.–10 P.M.). You can relax on the soft sand or paddle out and catch a wave here. Paths make biking, inline skating, and walking popular pastimes here, while others prefer a rousing game of volleyball out on the sand. You'll find a metered parking lot adjacent to the beach, plus showers and restrooms available.

For travelers looking to escape the endless crowds of the Newport/Huntington Beach scene, options beckon from farther south on the O.C. coast. The **Blue Lantern Inn** (34343 Blue Lantern St., Dana Point, 949/661-1304, www.bluelanterninn.com, $190–550) sits south of San Juan Capistrano, making access to the small mission town easy. This attractive contemporary inn offers beachfront elegance, from the exterior to the downstairs restaurant to the guest rooms. Each of the 29 rooms boasts soothing colors, charming appointments, and lush amenities, including a spa tub in every bathroom and honest-to-goodness free drinks in the mini-fridge. All beds come with their own teddy bear, and many of the rooms have private patios facing the sea and sunsets.

## Mission San Juan Capistrano

One of the most famous and beloved of all the California missions is Mission San Juan Capistrano (26801 Oretga Hwy., 949/234-1300, http://missionsjc.com, daily 8:30 A.M.–5 P.M., adults $9, children $8). The lovely little town of San Juan Capistrano hosts flocks of swallows, which return every year at about the same time in the spring to fanfare and celebration by the whole town. These celebrations began during the mission's heyday in the 18th century, and may have been started by Native Americans centuries before that. (Swallows are really, really loyal to their nesting grounds!)

Today, thanks in part to the famous birds, this mission has a beautiful new Catholic church on-site, extensive gardens and land, and an audio tour of the museum, which was created from the old mission church and buildings. In late fall and early spring, monarch butterflies flutter about in the flower gardens and out by the fountain in the courtyard.

ROBERT HOLMES / CALTOUR

Mission San Juan Capistrano

Inside the original church, artifacts from the early time of the mission tell the story of its rise and fall. This was the only mission church where Father Serra presided over Sunday services. The graveyard outside continues that narrative, as do the bells and other buildings of the compound. If you love stories of times past, you could spend hours wandering Mission San Juan Capistrano, with or without the audio tour. The complex includes adequate restrooms for visitors, plus plenty of garden and courtyard benches for rest, relaxation, and quiet meditation and reflection.

Regrettably, when you exit the mission into the charming town of San Juan Capistrano and stroll back to look at the historic buildings, you'll be standing next to a Starbucks. But if you turn the corner, you'll find yourself on the town's main street, which positively drips Spanish Colonial history. Each old adobe building boasts a brass plaque describing its history and use over the years. In names and decor, the swallow is a major theme in San Juan Capistrano, which nestles in a tiny valley only minutes from the sea.

## Information and Services

Need assistance upon arriving on the O.C. coast? A good place to get it is the **Huntington Beach Convention and Visitors Bureau** (301 Main St., Ste 208, 800/729-6232, www.surfcityusa.com, Mon.–Fri. 9 A.M.–5 P.M.).

The major newspaper on the O.C. coast is the Orange County edition of the *Los Angeles Times,* which you can pick up at any newsstand.

Each town on the coast has at least one **post office.** In Huntington Beach, head for the post office at 6671 Warner Avenue (714/843-4200). In Newport Beach, choose between the post office on the inland tip of the bay at 1133 Camelback Street, or pick the one down by the ocean at 204 Main Street, Newport Beach.

If you need medical care while you're visiting the beach, **Hoag Hospital** (1 Hoag Dr., Newport Beach, 949/764-4624, www.hoaghospital.org) can probably fix whatever's broken.

## Getting There and Around

Two airports serve the O.C. coast region. On the coast side, the **Long Beach Airport** (4100 Donald Douglas Dr., 562/570-2600, www.longbeach.gov/airport) serves as one of L.A.'s metropolitan satellite airports. Lots of commercial flights go in and out of Long Beach, making it a good alternative to LAX for the coast-bound. The other regional airport is John Wayne International; see the *Disneyland* section of this chapter for more information.

The Orange County Transportation Authority, **OCTA** (www.octa.net) runs buses along the O.C. coast. The appropriately numbered Route 1 Bus runs right along the Pacific Coast Highway from Long Beach down to San Clemente and back. Other routes can get you to and from inland O.C. destinations, including Anaheim. Regular bus fares run $1.25 per ride, payable in cash on the bus with exact change. You can also buy a day pass from the bus driver for $3.

The one true highway on the O.C. coast is the Pacific Coast Highway, often called the PCH for short and officially designated as Highway 1. You can get to the PCH from I-405 near Seal Beach, or catch I-710 to Long Beach and then drive south from there. From Disneyland, you'll take I-5 to Route 55, which takes you into Newport Beach. If you stay on I-5 going south, you'll eventually find yourself in San Juan Capistrano.

Parking along the beaches of the O.C. on a sunny summer day has been compared to one of Dante's circles of Hell. You're far better off staying near the beach and walking out to your perfect spot in the sand. Other options include public transit and pay parking, which means "up to $40 per day and still six blocks to the beach."

# Catalina Island

For a slice of Greece in Southern California, take a ferry or a helicopter out to Catalina Island (www.catalina.com). You can see Catalina from the shore of Long Beach on a clear day, but for a better view you've got to get out onto the island. The port town of Avalon welcomes visitors with plenty of European-inspired hotels, restaurants, and shops. But the main draw of Catalina lies outside the walls of its buildings. With its Mediterranean summer climate, Catalina draws hikers, horseback riders, and ecotourists. Most of all, it beckons to water-lovers of all kinds, from scuba divers and snorkelers to kayakers and anglers.

The climate on Catalina tends toward the temperate, with beautiful, warm, sunny summer days that make getting out into the ocean a pleasure. Even in the winter, you'll find pleasantly warmish days and cool nights. But every once in a while, when the Santa Ana winds come billowing down from the mainland, life in Avalon harbor gets exciting. Storms and winds can whip up the seas, which then come crashing up onto and over the beaches and walkways of Avalon. When you see the yellow sandbags, be aware that the locals are serious. Even on a non-flooding morning, the Pacific can completely engulf the harborside beaches, hit the retaining walls, and spray dozens of feet into the air. If you're lucky enough to be around, take a walk down toward the waterside and enjoy the show!

## SIGHTS

### The Casino

No, it's not that kind of casino. The Casino Building at Avalon harkens back to the older Italian meaning of the word ("place of entertainment"). The round, white, Art Deco building acts as a community gathering place and

© LANCE SCOTT

the Via Casino arch

©LANCE SCOTT

the Casino door

home for all sorts of different activities. The Avalon Theatre, home to a Page organ, is located on the main level. Be sure to check out the murals by John Gabriel Beckman, he of Grauman's Chinese Theatre fame, inside.

## Wrigley Memorial and Botanical Garden

Upcountry, the coolest place to visit may be the Wrigley Memorial and Botanical Garden (Avalon Canyon Rd., 1.5 miles west of town, 310/510-2595, daily 8 A.M.–5 P.M., adults $5, children free). Stroll through serene gardens planted with flowers, trees, and shrubs that are native to the California or even to Catalina specifically. You'll see a number of endangered species among the unique plants that grow nowhere else in the world. The temperate climate on Catalina lends itself to hardy, drought-tolerant species that still manage to produce beautiful colors and fragrances. Just don't eat (or let your kids eat) the wild tomatoes—they're incredibly poisonous! Also don't bother with the Catalina cherries. They're not deadly, but they don't taste too good.

At the center of the garden you can't miss the Wrigley Memorial, an edifice dedicated to the memory of chewing-gum magnate William Wrigley, Jr. Wrigley adored Santa Catalina Island, and used his sticky fortune to make many improvements to it; most notably, he funded the building of the Avalon Casino. The monument is made and decorated with mostly local materials; the crushed stone on the facade comes from the island, as do the blue flagstones, the red roof tiles, and the brightly colored decorative ceramic tiles. All the local-centric construction makes a perfect centerpiece to the gardens.

For a more thorough look at the history, culture, and diverse natural abundance of Catalina, visit the **Interpretive Center** (Avalon Canyon Rd.) just down the road from the botanical garden. Here you can learn more about the native plants, indigenous people, and the ocean channel and its islands (of which Catalina is the most visited).

## Catalina Island Museum

Another take on the history of Catalina is displayed at the Catalina Island Museum (The Casino, Avalon, 310/510-2414, www.catalinamuseum.org, daily 10 A.M.–4 P.M., closed Thurs. Jan.–Mar., adults $4, children $1). Located on the top floor of the landmark Casino, this small museum makes for a great 15–30 minute culture stop in the midst of a beach vacation. Learn about the history of the Chicago Cubs' spring training camp on the island, the short but famed production of Catalina tile and ceramics, the World War II history of Catalina, and more. You'll find a good-sized collection of Native American artifacts from the island's original inhabitants, plus a huge collection of historic photos. Look for Hollywood stars enjoying Catalina's natural beauty and luxurious resort amenities among the photographic history of the island. Purchase reproductions of tiles, photos, and more in the museum store, and check the website for museum activities geared to kids and adults.

## SPORTS AND RECREATION

Outdoor recreation is the main reason most people venture across the channel to Catalina. On land or in the water, you'll find the activities that are right for you.

### Scuba and Snorkeling

If you want to get out into the water on your own, you'll find plenty of places to kick off from shore. The most popular spot is the **Avalon Underwater Park** (Casino Point). This protected area at the north end of town has buoys and markers to help you find your way around the reefs and keep safe. Not only will you see the famous bright-orange garibaldi fish, you'll get the opportunity to meet jellyfish, anemones, spiny lobsters, and plenty of other sealife. Out at the deeper edge of the park, nearly half a dozen wrecked ships await your examination. Snorkeling and scuba tours groups come here, as do locals and visitors who rent equipment from local shops and shacks or bring their own. Expect big crowds on summer weekends.

If you prefer to take a guided tour, a number of companies offer snorkeling, scuba, kayaking, and combinations all around the island. **Catalina Snorkel & Scuba** (877/766-7535, www.divecatalina.com) offers guided snorkel tours of the Lover's Cove Marine Reserve that include all equipment with the fees. This clear-water preserve sits just southeast of the boat terminal, and includes a life-filled kelp forest. If you're a certified scuba diver, you can book a two-hour guided tour of Avalon Underwater Park. If you want to become a scuba diver, Catalina Snorkel & Scuba offers certification classes as well as intro tours that give you a taste of the world underwater. Catalina Snorkel & Scuba also offers equipment rental for snorkelers and divers who want to take off on their own.

Another company to try is **Snorkel Catalina** (877/218-9156, www.snorkelingcatalina.com). This company specializes in deeper water excursions farther away from shore, taking guests out on a custom pontoon boat all year long. If your purpose in coming to Catalina is to swim with the dolphins, Snorkel Catalina can make it happen for you. Standard tours run 2–4 hours, and let you check out the prettiest fish, sleekest seals, and friendliest dolphins around the island.

If it's hardcore scuba you're interested in, take a walk out onto the Avalon pier to **Catalina Divers Supply** (800/353-0330, www.catalinadiverssupply.com). The little blue shack out toward the end of the pier offers everything from certification and referral classes to guided shore dives at the Avalon Marine Preserves to charter trips on the 46-foot *Scuba Cat*. You'll see things that just aren't visible from the surface with a snorkel. The company highly recommends making reservations for any of their tours and trips.

### Kayaking

Kayaking is one of the most popular ways to see otherwise unreachable parts of Catalina. Rent a kayak, or if you're not confident in your own navigation abilities, take a tour with a reputable company. **Descanso Beach Ocean Sports/Catalina Island Kayak & Snorkel** (310/510-1226, www.kayakcatalinaisland.com, $40–80) offers several kayak tours to different parts of the island. You don't need previous river or sea kayaking experience to take these tours, since double-sized, sit-on-top kayaks make the trip easy and safe even for total beginners and small kids. But if you are a rescue-certified sea kayaker, the folks at Descanso Beach also have an array of lean, sleek, enclosed ocean kayaks for advanced paddlers. This company offers regular, year-round trips to Frog Rock (2 hours), Fox Canyon (3 hours, includes a nature walk), and Willow Cove (half-day excursion with snorkeling and hiking). All trips start north of Avalon and the Casino at Descanso Beach Club.

Another kayak tour provider, **Wet Spot Rentals** (310/510-2229, www.catalinakayaks.com, $40–150) specializes in a full-day land and sea tour that includes both kayaking and an auto tour into the Catalina backcountry. After a van trip and nature tour at the airport on top of the hill, you'll travel down to the less-traveled windward side of the island. You'll get a rare opportunity to kayak on the other side of the island from Avalon, exploring the coves and cliffs around Little Harbor. A brief portage and hike takes you to a waterfall. This fabulous, nearly whole-island tour takes all day, and lunch, water, and all equipment (including sit-on-top beginner kayaks) are provided. Wet Spot also offers several shorter kayak expeditions; they're a great operator if you want to combine kayaking with snorkeling the reefs of the leeward (Avalon) side of the island.

These operators also rent kayaks to individuals (you'll have to prove yourself capable to rent an enclosed sea kayak). They also have an array of snorkel equipment, and you can take a kayak out for some fabulous fish-watching and even skin-diving.

## Rafting

For an adventurous ocean tour, head out with **Catalina Ocean Rafting** (103 Pebbly Beach Rd., 800/990-7238, www.catalinaoceanrafting.com, $41). From the Avalon harbor, you'll head out on a two-hour, half-day, or full-day trip on a small, powered, inflatable raft. The small maneuverable craft can take you right up to cliffs and into sea caves, around Eagle Rock and Ribbon Rock, and into reef areas perfect for snorkeling (equipment is provided with your tour). You'll get to harbors beyond Avalon, and enjoy lunch, drinks, and snacks as part of your trip. A raft tour is a great way for adventurous newcomers to get the lay of the land and sea before striking off on their own.

## Swimming

In the summertime, the waters of Catalina can reach the more than 70°F—perfect for taking a long, lazy swim in the salty waters of the Pacific! Bring your family out to any one of the charming beaches in the sunny coves for a lazy day on the beach and in the water. The most crowded spots will be at the Avalon Underwater Park, the harbor, and other coves near Avalon. For a more deserted beach, try the windward side of the island; just be aware that it may be, well, windy. Keep a close eye on your children and even adult friends wherever you swim. Catalina's beaches, like most of the California coastline, are subject to dangerous rip currents.

## Wildlife-Watching

If you're not keen on swimming in the ocean, but you want a peek at the famous Catalina garibaldi (a bright-orange fish), take a semi-submersible or glass-bottom boat tour. The **Undersea Tour** (310/510-8687, www.visitcatalinaisland.com, adults $28–35.50, children $14–17.75) takes you a few feet underwater in a comfy cabin to watch the abundant array of aquatic life around Avalon. For a special (and budget-conscious) treat, book a nighttime Undersea Tour to check out a whole different variety of sea species. Every seat on the boat has a great view of the water, and kids love the colorful fish and mysterious bat rays that glide gracefully by.

In the summertime, take another boat trip out to see one of the legends of Catalina. A **Flying Fish Boat Trip** (800/626-1496, www.visitcatalinaisland.com, adults $19.50, children $9.75) lights up the air just over the waterline, making visible the famous Catalina flying fish as they leap out, putting on a unique show.

## Horseback Riding

Perhaps the best and most ecologically sound way to explore the backcountry of inland Catalina, with all its diverse wildlife, is on a horseback ride. **Catalina Stables** (600 Avalon Canyon Rd., Avalon, 310/510-0478, catalinasstables@catalinaisp.com, $42–82 for standard rides, more for custom tours) offers guided rides up into the hills above Avalon. Walk a sedate, well-behaved horse along trails used by Native Americans for thousands of years, viewing buffalo, bald eagles, and other wildlife. Enjoy knowing that the likes of John Wayne and Tom Mixx have ridden the trails on this island, taking in the immediate wildlife and distant glorious views of the ocean surrounding the island (plus the regrettable but usual smog-smear that is the L.A. coastline). Choose from half-hour, one-hour, or two-hour rides that go out every day (weather permitting). If you're a serious equestrian, call in advance to arrange a half-day, full-day, or even overnight horseback riding adventure. Catalina Stables can arrange exactly the trip you've always wanted to take. Even if you only want a 30-minute standard trail ride, call in advance for a reservation to guarantee yourself a horse, especially in high season.

## Biking

Even most of the locals on Catalina eschew cars in favor of smaller, lighter forms of transportation. A great way to get around and beyond Avalon is on a bicycle. You can bring your own aboard the ferries that travel to and from the airport. If you don't have one, you can rent a bicycle right on the island at **Brown's Bikes** (underneath Holly Hill House, 100 yards from the ferry dock, 310/510-0986, www.catalinabiking.com, $5–15/hour, $12–40/day). If you're looking for a simple, one-speed cruiser to putter around downtown Avalon and down to the beach, you can get one for $5 per hour or $12 per day. With no gas to buy, it's the ultimate in affordable transportation! Brown's also has six- and 21-speeds, tandems, and an array of mountain bikes. You'll also get a map of the bikeable roads and trails in Avalon and around the island.

Mountain bikers, this island's for you! An array of trails from easy to steep and difficult take you up into the hills, providing views and thrills galore. Street bikers will find that Avalon is bike-friendly; the road that runs along the shore on either side of the town is paved, mostly level, and zoned for bicycles. If you've got the legs for it, you can obtain a permit from the Catalina Conservancy to ride farther afield. Call or email Brown's Bikes for more information on biking outside of Avalon.

## Golf

As most of Catalina Island is devoted to wildlife preservation, you won't find a wealth of golf courses here. But if just can't abide the notion of going for a trip without exercising your clubs, get yourself a tee time at the nine-hole **Catalina Island Golf Course** (1 Country Club Rd., Avalon, 310/510-0530, www.visitcatalinaisland.com, $30–85). You'll be walking on greens built in 1892, used for the Bobby Jones Tournament from the 1930s through the 1950s, and more recently played on by up-and-coming SoCal junior players like Craig Stadler and Tiger Woods as they built their skills. Heck, even if you don't play, it's worth walking the course on a sunny day just to enjoy the unbelievable views out to the Casino, the town of Avalon, and the clutch of sailboats bobbing in the harbor. The full-service pro shop provides rental equipment and golf carts, as well as a set of **tennis courts** you can rent by the hour.

If your taste in golf runs a little less serious, head for **Golf Gardens** (Sumner Ave., 1 block inland from the fountain, 310/510-1200), a miniature golf course. This is a great break for kids tired of sightseeing and eco-touring. This cute, 18-hole course has a tropical feel, complete with palm trees, and good putting challenges.

## Yoga

After hours or days of recreating outdoors on Catalina, you might really appreciate a good massage or a nice relaxing hour of yoga.

For yoga, go to **Pisces Yoga** (310/510-1803 or 310/510-1666) takes place at the Seaport Village Inn (119 Maiden Ln., Avalon) on Mondays and Wednesdays at 8 A.M. and Tuesdays and Thursdays at 6 P.M.

## Spas

You've got a surprising number of massage and spa options right in and around Avalon. If you prefer your massage in the privacy of your hotel room or condo, call **In-Room Massage by Michelle** (310/510-8920, www.catalinamassagebymichelle.net, $85–95 massage, $120–300 spa treatments). Michelle loves to work with couples looking for a relaxing day or evening of romance, and she is trained in a variety of massage techniques and spa therapies, including heated stones and Thai massage. Book a simple Swedish massage or a full spa package with facials, body scrubs, and massages for one or two people. Check the website for a full list of available treatments. Be sure to book in advance to get the date and time you want. Studio sessions are also available.

Whether you're looking for a divine romantic

experience with your sweetie or a solo day of spa-induced respite from your busy life, you'll find it at **The Spa at Catalina** (888 Country Club Rd., Avalon, 310/510-9255, www.catalinaspa.com, $60–325). This full-service day spa offers all sorts of massage and treatment packages, from a simple half-hour of bodywork up to nearly three hours of head-to-toe bliss. The spa has dual rooms (many complete with private baths for two) to serve couples or pairs of friends who want to enjoy their treatments together. Choose from the many packages that focus on facials and scalp treatments using lavender, peppermint, and other delicious essential oils. You can also breathe deep and detox with a body wrap or heated stone massage. The spa sits in Falls Canyon outside of downtown Avalon; ask about getting a free shuttle from your hotel to the spa at the Best Western Canyon Hotel when you book your treatments. It's best to make reservations at least a couple of days in advance; even in wintertime, same-day appointment availability is rare.

Decide for yourself whether the treatments you receive in downtown Avalon live up to the name **A Touch of Heaven** (205 Crescent Ave., 310/510-1633, daily 9 A.M.–5 P.M., $45–200). This day spa echoes the European flavor of the town surrounding it; you'll find an extensive menu of Euro-styled facials, from the intense relaxation of a LaStone Facial to the aesthetically focused glycolic/lactic acid peel and facial. Also look for a few unusual treatments including raindrop therapy and ear candling, as well as practitioners of both Eastern and Western massage modalities. The spa also offers massage for children, and well-behaved young people are welcome to enjoy the the treatments here.



## ACCOMMODATIONS

You'll find plenty of charming inns and hotels on Catalina; most sit in or near Avalon. You can also camp on Catalina, and eco-tourists often prefer to immerse themselves in the natural world of the island by sleeping and eating outdoors.

### Camping

Camping is the best way to get away from Avalon and stay on other parts of the island. It's also a great way to get to know the precious Catalina wilderness in an up close and personal way. Check the island's visitor website (www.visitcatalinaisland.com) for a list and descriptions of all the major campgrounds around the island. Also be sure to read the regulations, which are more stringent than at some other camping areas and are strictly enforced. Permits are required for all campsites. Also check out the equipment rentals; if you don't want to bring your own tent and gear, you can rent it at the Two Harbors ranger station.

You have a choice of more than half a dozen campgrounds, some on the coast and some up the mountains in the interior. One of the largest and most developed campgrounds sits just outside the tiny town of **Two Harbors** (adults $12, children $6). You can bring your own tent and equipment, rent it, or book one of the tent cabins at this site. The tent cabins come with cots and mattresses, sunshades, and a camp stove and lantern in addition to the usual barbecue grill, fire ring, and picnic table. All campers have access to showers, restroom facilities, and lockers to keep valuables safe while you're out exploring the area.

If you're looking to camp on the beach, check out the **Little Harbor** (adults $12, children $6) campground. Located seven miles away from the town of Little Harbor, the sandy campsites make a perfect place to sleep if your aim is snorkeling, kayaking, and playing out away from all the casual tourists. You'll find potable water, showers, and toilets here. The best way to get to the Little Harbor campground is to take the Safari Bus, so be sure to book seats and space for your gear when you book your campsite.

Perhaps the coolest way to stay on Catalina is to bring or rent a kayak and paddle into one of the **boat-in campsites** (adults $12, children $6). These nine primitive campsites can't be accessed by land at all—you must bring and moor your own boat. You'll get a wholly natural experience at any of these beautiful remote locations, with no running water, shower or toilet facilities, or shade structures. Whatever you want and need, you must pack into your boat with you. A ranger checks each campsite daily, so you're not completely cut off from the outside world. However, take precautions such as bringing a two-way radio and an above-average first-aid kit just in case an emergency crops up.

## $100-150

For inexpensive indoor accommodations, your best bet is the **Hermosa Hotel & Cottages** (131 Metropole St., 877/453-1313, www.hermosahotel.com, $75–155). This simple budget hotel has rooms with shared bathrooms in the main building—in the way-off season, some of these clean rooms are dirt cheap if you're willing to walk down the hall to the shower. Even in the summer, you can get a decent room for under $100. (Be aware of a two-night minimum for stays involving a Saturday night in the high season.) The cottages have private baths, and some have kitchens and TVs. "Family units" can sleep up to six people in the main building and have kitchens—perfect for larger families or groups of friends traveling together on a budget. The 100-plus-year-old building sits only about a block from the harbor beaches and a short walk from the Casino, shops, and restaurants.

The **Hotel Atwater** (125 Sumner Ave., 800/626-1496, www.visitcatalinaisland.com, $107–219) also has bright cheerful rooms for reasonable rates. Take in the history of a budget hotel that's been hosting guests since the 1920s. Clean, light-colored economy rooms provide the best value for your buck, while the more posh suites cost more and offer prettier decor and better amenities. Whichever type of room you book, you'll have a TV, coffee maker, air conditioning, and more. You'll find storage for your diving gear and bikes, and a rinse-off area outside for divers, snorkelers, and swimmers. The Atwater closes each winter; call ahead to confirm their availability.

## $150-250

Want to stay right on the waterfront? Book a room at the bright yellow **Hotel Mac Rae** (409 Crescent Ave., 800/698-2266, www.hotelmacrae.com, $239–259). This bit of Catalina history has been in the Mac Rae family for four generations, and they've been running the hostelry since 1920. The Mediterranean flavor of Avalon follows you into the rooms and common spaces of the Mac Rae. Relax with a drink in the bright brick courtyard. You can choose one of the premium rooms that looks right out into the harbor, or a more economical courtyard-view room. Grab a complimentary continental breakfast downstairs, and either eat in the courtyard or take your coffee and your pastries back to your pretty Côte d'Azur–styled room for more privacy. Catching the afternoon ferry but want to enjoy one last morning in the warm Catalina water? The Mac Rae has luggage storage and even a public shower for use after you check out.

For a European hotel experience in Avalon, stay at the **Hotel Metropole** (205 Crescent Ave., 310/510-1884, www.hotel-metropole.com, $175–550). The comfortably cluttered and warmly decorated rooms feel like home almost immediately. You'll find gas fireplaces in some rooms and oversized two-person whirlpool bathtubs in a few pretty, tiled bathrooms. The beds feel great after a long day of ocean swimming or the ferry ride over from Long Beach. The little extras are nice too from the nightly turn-down service to the L'Occitane toiletries. You can also use the Wi-Fi service in your room and grab a snack from the honor bar. The Metropole is built in a modern style with a pretty gray paint job. On the roof you'll find a whirlpool tub with glass walls enclosing its deck, letting you look out over the rooftops into the harbor. The lower-end rooms don't have much in the way of ocean views, so for a window on the water you'll need to pay premium rates for an oceanfront suites. You can walk half a block down the street to the oceanside. For extra pampering, make an appointment at the day spa located on the bottom floor of the hotel. Just outside by the back elevator, start a shopping jaunt in the little Metropole center, where you can grab a cup of coffee, or walk down Crescent Avenue for a meal.

The **Villa Portofino** (111 Crescent Ave.,

888/510-0555, www.hotelvillaportofino.com, $215) offers Mediterranean elegance on the Avalon waterfront. The bright-white exterior with red tile roofs invites you inside this 34-room boutique hotel. Guest rooms range from small standard rooms up through immense, lush, individually named suites with fireplaces, soaking tubs, and richly colored furnishings. Amenities include a complimentary continental breakfast, free Wi-Fi, free beach chairs and towels, and an on-site restaurant. The Portofino's location is perfect—right on the main drag running along the harborside beach.

## FOOD

To be honest, the culinary presence on Catalina isn't much to write home about. While there's certainly no lack of restaurants in Avalon, the trend toward delicious cuisine at both the high and low ends hasn't made it across the island to the channel yet. You might consider getting a room or a condo with a kitchen and cooking a few of your own meals to save a bit of cash while you're here. Still, a tourist's gotta go out to eat sometimes! Here are a few places to try.

### American

So where do the locals go? Many of them crowd into **El Galleon** (411 Crescent Ave., 310/510-1188, daily 11 A.M.–9 P.M., $10–30). It's easy to get to since it's part of the walk-only area on Crescent Avenue, and the porch has a fabulous view out to the harbor. The large menu speaks to hearty American diners with lots of aged steaks, chicken dishes, and fresh fish. Lighter eaters can peruse the selection of salads, soups, and seafood appetizers. For a major feast, take a look at the prix-fixe menu, which offers a hearty four-course dinner for about $70 per person. The dessert menu offers a few unusual treats, plus a wide array of sweet and strong coffee drinks to round off your evening. El Galleon boasts a full bar and a fun vibe, and live karaoke runs into the night. If you prefer an earlier evening, happy hour is 3–6 P.M. each evening.

For a more serious upscale dining experience, get a table in the dining room at the **Catalina Country Club** (310/510-7404, www.visitcatalinaisland.com, $30). You don't need to be a member to enjoy a refined dinner here, or at one of the Country Club's two more casual dining venues. Unlike most of the rest of the island's restaurants, here you'll be served some high-end California cuisine, complete with a focus on organic and sustainable ingredients.

### Italian

The **Ristorante Villa Portofino** (101 Crescent Ave., 310/510-2009, www.ristorantevillaportofino.com, $15–35), attached to the Villa Portofino hotel, serves tasty pasta and protein dishes with a distinct Italian flare—and you'll get a fabulous harbor view with your cannelloni or calamari. In homage to the locale, the menu here runs to seafood, with some classic and a few inventive preparations. The pastas bring homey comfort food to Catalina, and the hot appetizer menu is well worth a look. For dessert, the Ristorante offers a goodly selection of Italian favorites such as cannoli and panna cotta. In the summertime, see if you can get a table out on the patio to enjoy the balmy island breezes—you'll feel almost as though you're really on the Mediterranean coast of Italy.

### Mexican

Looking for an unpretentious taco? You can get one at the **Catalina Cantina** (313 Crescent Ave., 310/510-0100, $7–15) or its fast-food walk-up neighbor, the **Topless Taco.** Serving a mix of American diner (think burgers and fries, wings, and fish and chips) and Americanized Mexican staples (burritos, fajitas, combo plates), the Catalina Cantina offers tasty food for decent prices. Better still, if you come in the evening, cool off with one of the Cantina's buckets o' liquor. Rum punch, margaritas, something called the Blue Shark, and more come in either normal human-sized glasses or in a 28-ounce bowl that they really hope you'll share with friends!

### Seafood

If all you want is a slab of really fresh fish, you can get it down on the Pleasure Pier at **Avalon**

© LANCE SCOTT

Avalon Seafood

**Seafood** (Pleasure Pier, 310/510-0197). That's the cute blue building at the end of the pier bearing a sign that says "Fish and Chips." It's part fish-and-chips stand, part fresh seafood market, and you can get a casual eat-at-the-picnic-table lunch or barbecued fish dinner here. Or if you've got kitchen or barbecue access, pick up the catch of the day and make a fresh fish dinner for yourself and your family or friends.

### Steak

All the locals recommend that tourists try **Steve's Steakhouse** (417 Crescent Ave., 310/510-0333, www.stevessteakhouse.com, daily lunch 11:30 A.M.–2 P.M., dinner from 5 P.M., $10–33). It's possible that the locals are trying to keep the tourists away from their favorite spots by sending them here. Sure, Steve's offers a wide array of classic steakhouse fare with plenty of seafood options thrown in as a nod to the water lapping the harbor beach just outside. Generous portions of meat or fish are accompanied by traditional steakhouse sides, and the desserts up the ante with some tasty sweetness. (The mud pie's not half bad.) But compared to the lush cuisine you can get on the mainland, the quality of the ingredients and the preparations seem a bit lackluster at Steve's, and the tourist-high prices can be a bit painful.

### Coffee

Looking for a cup of coffee and maybe a quick pastry down by the Casino? Stop by **El Encanto Courtyard Coffee** ($1.50–5). In the wintertime, the hot lattes and chais offer steamy warmth, while the summertime sees customers ordering refreshingly icy smoothies and frappes. Courtyard Coffee sits in the El Encanto marketplace, across from the Via Casino Arch.

## INFORMATION AND SERVICES

If you are camping in a remote location, talk to the rangers at the Two Harbors station before leaving to learn how best to contact them or the police in an emergency. Bring a two-way radio, since cell signal may be unreliable or nonexistent.

For medical assistance, go to the **Avalon Municipal Hospital** (100 Falls Canyon Rd., 310/510-0700).

Your major local daily newspaper on Catalina is the ***Los Angeles Times.*** Your hotel might have copies. A good website for visitors is www.visitcatalinaisland.com.

Catalina isn't one of Orange County's major shopping destinations; if you're hoping to put a serious dent in your credit cards, you'll want to head back to the mainland. But if you're looking for kitschy souvenirs and reproduction ceramic tiles, you can find them in downtown Avalon in the area sometimes called the **South Coast Plaza.**

## GETTING THERE AND AROUND

There are two ways to get to Catalina: by boat and by air.

### Boat

Most folks take the ferry over from the mainland coast. The **Catalina Express** (310/519-1212, www.catalinaexpress.com, adults $60–62/round-trip, children $46–48)

© LANCE SCOTT

Catalina seaside

serves as the major carrier, with multiple departures every day, even in the off-season. During high season, you can choose to leave from two docks in Long Beach, one dock in San Pedro, and another in Dana Point. Most ferries dock at Avalon, but you can arrange to travel directly to Two Harbors if you prefer. You can bring your bike, your luggage, and your camping gear aboard for a comfortable hour-long ride on one of eight ferries. Bars on both levels offer snacks and drinks, and TVs help make the cruise go by a little bit faster. Though on the way it's worth looking out the window—you might spot seals or sea lions, different varieties of pelicans, or even a pod of dolphins playing in the swells. Catalina Express also offers plenty of return cruises to the mainland each day.

An alternate ferry service, the **Catalina Flyer** (400 Main St., Newport Beach, 949/673-5245, www.catalinainfo.com, adults $61/round-trip, children $46) offers one trip out and one trip back each day. The Flyer operates primarily from March through November.

## Air

You can also get to Catalina by air. A helicopter pad sits just northwest of Avalon harbor. **Island Express Helicopter Service** (1175 Queens Highway S., Long Beach, 310/510-2525, www.islandexpress.com, $160/round trip) can fly you from Long Beach or San Pedro to Catalina in about 15 minutes. You can get a cab into town from the helipad. Island Express also offers aerial tours of the island and various travel packages. Or if you prefer to fly your own small plane into Catalina, the **Airport-in-the-Sky** (310/510-2196, Apr.–Oct. daily 8 A.M.–7 P.M., Nov.–Mar. daily 8 A.M.–5 P.M.) offers general aviators a 3,000-plus-foot runway and $5 tie-downs—no gas, though, so fuel up for a round-trip before you head out.

## Car

On Catalina, cars just aren't the fashionable way to get around. Even the locals tend to eschew full cars since they aren't practical in the tiny town of Avalon. Instead, locals and visitors in the know prefer to drive golf carts. Walk from the ferry dock down toward town, and you'll see any number of rental services, complete with herds of carts out and ready for use. The cost runs about $40 per hour for a 4–6 passenger cart. A couple of easy-to-find companies include **Island Rentals** (125 Pebbly Beach

Rd., 310/510-1456) underneath the Holly Hill House near the ferry dock and **Cartopia** (615 Crescent Ave., 310/510-2493).

You can also grab a taxi if you need to get somewhere in a hurry, especially with your luggage. Taxis hover near the ferry dock when the ferries are due in each day, and it's customary to share your ride with as many people as can fit into the car (which is often a minivan). To get a cab back to the ferry or the helipad when it's time to leave, call 310/510-0025. It only takes about 10 minutes for a taxi to get to just about anywhere in town.

## Bus

Public transit on Catalina includes the **Safari Bus** (310/510-2800, adults $4–26 depending on distance, children $2.75–20), which runs from Avalon to Two Harbors each day. The bus stops at the southeast corner of Island Plaza in Avalon. You can buy tickets at visitors services and the Discovery Tours booth on the Pleasure Pier. Alternately, the **Avalon Trolley** (310/510-0342, June 15–Sept. 15 Fri.–Sat. 9 A.M.–10 P.M., Sun.–Thurs. 9 A.M.–6 P.M., Sept. 16–June 14 daily 9 A.M.–5 P.M., $2–6) runs in and around Avalon, hitting most of the major sightseeing and outdoor adventuring spots near town. With two lines that converge inland, you can get where you need to go for a reasonable fare without having to hoof it. The trolley runs approximately every 30–40 minutes.

## Tours

One of the main forms of entertainment on the island is touring. You can take a bus tour, Jeep tour, glass-bottom boat tour, and more. The Catalina Island Conservancy offers **Jeep Eco-Tours** (310/510-2595, www.catalinaconservancy.org, $495/half-day, $795/full day, up to 6 people) for either a half-day or a full day out in the wilds of Catalina. You can go much farther on these tours than you can by yourself—out into the wilderness to see the bison, the wild horses, plant species unique to this one island, and more. Be sure to bring your camera, both for close-ups and for views out toward the sea. On the full-day trips, you'll get lunch, drinks, and snacks, while on the half-day trip you'll get snacks and drinks.

For a sedate view of Catalina's more settled areas as well as it's road-viewable wilderness, try a **Classic Inland Motor Tour** (310/510-8687, www.visitcatalinaisland.com, adults $69, children $34.50). This four-hour tour aboard a restored 1950s cruising bus takes you away from the coastline and into the island's interior via old stagecoach routes. Along the way you'll see Middle Ranch, the magnificent Arabian horses and Old West mementos of El Rancho Escondido, and the Airport-in-the-Sky Nature Center. A shorter version of this tour is the **Skyline Drive** (adults $34, children $17), a two-hour trip that takes you up from Avalon to the Airport-in-the-Sky Nature Center along a route cluttered with spectacular vistas of island and ocean.

If you want a guided walking tour of Avalon, consider taking an **Avalon Walk-About Tour with Chuck Liddell** (310/510-1356 or 310/510-8401, avalonwalkabout@yahoo.com, adults $10/hour, children $7/hour). Pick a one-hour tour of downtown Avalon ending at the Casino for an easy walk. The two-hour tour can include a variety of routes, most of which require that you climb some moderately steep hills. Or try an evening tour that takes you past the nighttime hot spots of Avalon. Wear comfy shoes for any tour you take, bring a camera, and be prepared to enjoy the narration. Chuck Liddell can tell you all about the places you're passing as you stroll along.

Another company that offers both land and sea tours of Catalina is **Catalina Adventure Tours** (877/510-2888, www.catalinaadventuretours.com). Whether you want to board the semi-submersible Nautilus, take a 1–2 hour adventure drive around the island, or get a guided walking view of the botanical garden or the Casino, Catalina Adventure Tours can hook you up.

# THE DESERTS

Cosmopolitan Palm Springs and its many outlying towns are havens for wealthy residents of northern climates who come down each winter to escape the cold. Great golf and wonderful day spas are hallmarks of Palm Springs proper, Rancho Mirage, Palm Desert, and Indian Wells.

But beauty can be harsh, and nowhere is this more true than in the California deserts. Only a few miles away from Palm Springs, Joshua Tree National Monument sprawls across the desert landscape, connecting two major California desert climates—the Mojave Desert and the lower Colorado Desert. Joshua Tree is easier to access from the Los Angeles area, featuring the strange shapes of the plant that is its namesake. North, the seemingly endless Mojave stretches across the state, offering hiking trails, preserve areas, ghost towns, and even camping for the hardy traveler.

Death Valley hugs the Nevada border at the east side of the state and its barrenness is legendary. In truth, Death Valley is misnamed. This vast forbidding landscape encompasses a wealth of life; a vast variety of plants, animals, birds, and even fish call the Valley home. Spring is the best time to experience this contradiction, when an astonishing bloom of wildflowers brightens the desert landscape.

The southernmost desert park of California is Anza-Borrego State Park. The biggest of all California's state parks, Anza-Borrego is part of the Colorado Desert region and home to its diverse array of wildlife. From ocotillo fields to palm oases to profuse spring wildflower blooms, the beauty of this desert's gardens

© LANCE SCOTT

## HIGHLIGHTS

**Palm Springs Aerial Tramway:** For a stunning view of Palm Springs and the San Jacinto Mountains, nothing beats an exhilarating ride up the Aerial Tramway, which zips up 2.5 miles in about 10 minutes and provides a 360° view of the valley below (page 573).

**Oasis of Mara:** No, it's not a mirage! The lush Oasis of Mara, accessible via a 0.5-mile nature loop, provides an up-close glimpse into the history and ecology of Joshua Tree National Park (page 590).

**Keys View:** This panoramic view is one of the best in Joshua Tree. Pick a clear day to take in the vista from Palm Springs all the way out to the Salton Sea (page 593).

**Scotty's Castle:** Don't miss touring the only private mansion built in Death Valley. This grand home, albeit unfinished, provides an entertaining Gold Rush–era history to the region (page 602).

**Badwater Basin:** Take a walk along the esoteric landscape of this dried-out lakebed, situated at the lowest elevation in the Western Hemisphere (page 604).

**Artist's Palette:** Nature is the ultimate artist here, where a combination of minerals paints the badlands in brilliant colors. Time your visit at sunset, when the fading light washes the already colorful mountains in glistening gold (page 604).

**Borrego Palm Canyon:** This canyon provides the best overview of Anza Borrego flora and fauna. An easy three-mile loop takes visitors from sandy desert to shady palm groves with interpretive stops along the way (page 617).

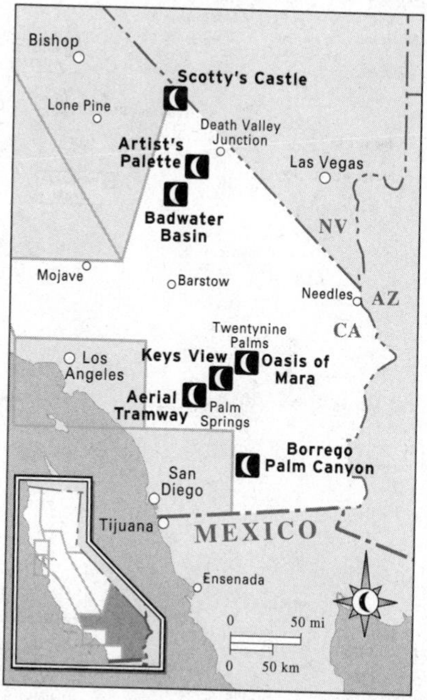


LOOK FOR ☾ TO FIND RECOMMENDED SIGHTS, ACTIVITIES, DINING, AND LODGING.

rivals any in the world. Nearby, the former mining town of Julian offers a taste of Southern California gold rush history.

## PLANNING YOUR TIME

Palm Springs makes a great weekend getaway or a relaxing spot to kick back for a whole season—just ask the thousands of Californians who maintain vacation condos here or are regulars at the coolest hotels. In the summertime, many Los Angelenos who want to escape the summer fog at the coast come out to the desert for some serious heat and swimming pool time. In the winter, mild temperatures lure Palm Springs visitors out for easy day trips to Joshua Tree.

Death Valley makes another great weekend destination, as does Anza-Borrego. You can pick lodgings right in the center of these deserts, then spend your time on Saturday and

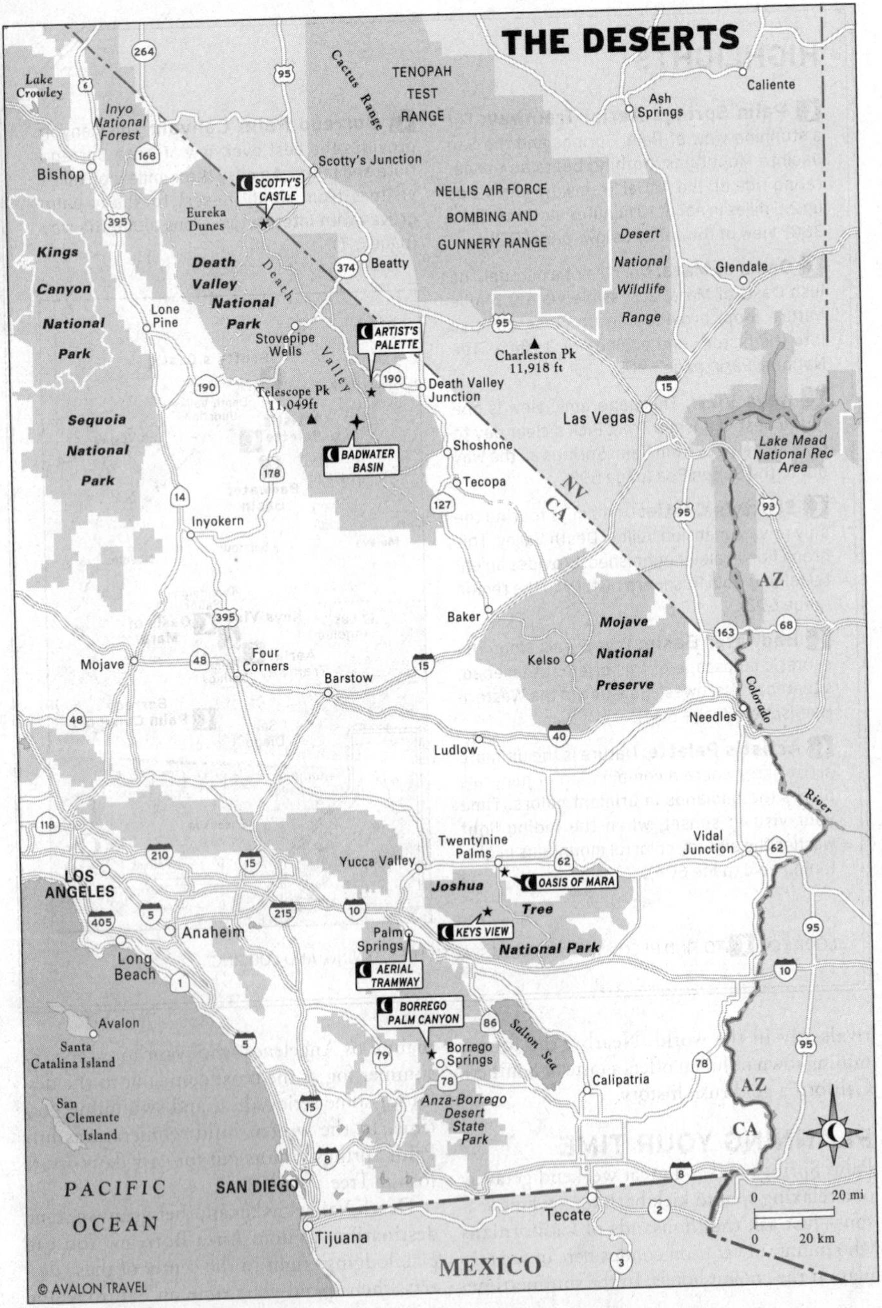
THE DESERTS
Lake Crowley
Inyo National Forest
Bishop
Kings Canyon National Park
Sequoia National Park
Lone Pine
Eureka Dunes
SCOTTY'S CASTLE
Scotty's Junction
Cactus Range
TENOPAH TEST RANGE
NELLIS AIR FORCE BOMBING AND GUNNERY RANGE
Death Valley National Park
Death Valley
Beatty
Stovepipe Wells
ARTIST'S PALETTE
Telescope Pk 11,049ft
BADWATER BASIN
Death Valley Junction
Charleston Pk 11,918 ft
Desert National Wildlife Range
Caliente
Ash Springs
Glendale
Las Vegas
Lake Mead National Rec Area
Shoshone
Tecopa
NV
CA
AZ
Inyokern
Baker
Mojave National Preserve
Kelso
Mojave
Four Corners
Barstow
Needles
Colorado River
Ludlow
Twentynine Palms
Vidal Junction
Yucca Valley
LOS ANGELES
Anaheim
Long Beach
Joshua Tree National Park
OASIS OF MARA
KEYS VIEW
Palm Springs
AERIAL TRAMWAY
BORREGO PALM CANYON
Borrego Springs
Salton Sea
Anza-Borrego Desert State Park
Calipatria
Avalon
Santa Catalina Island
San Clemente Island
PACIFIC OCEAN
SAN DIEGO
Tijuana
Tecate
MEXICO
0 20 mi
0 20 km
© AVALON TRAVEL

Sunday driving to the major sights and picking a few spectacular hikes before heading out on Sunday afternoon.

If you're a true desert rat and want to do a tour of all California's major deserts, plan at least a week to 10 days. The parks cover broad swaths of California's southern regions, and the distances between them can take hours to drive, especially along some of the more interesting back roads. Then you'll want to spend at least a day or two exploring within each desert. Leaving yourself enough time to enjoy the diverse ecosystems and unique sights will make the trip worthwhile.

## HISTORY

The history of the deserts of California is actually the geological history of the American continent. Two major deserts collide in California: the high-altitude Mojave to the north and the lower-lying Colorado in the southeast.

The most famous desert park in California, Death Valley, has its own story. Death Valley's formation began at least two billion years ago, and its landscape has been evolving ever since. Lakes have formed and dried up in its famous below-sea-level basin to the south, and recent volcanic activity is evident at the north end of the valley. Even as you wander around, the desert is changing all around you. Wind, gravity, and even water erode the valley's walls, shift its dunes, and create a new and different place every single day.

At heart, Palm Springs is a Hollywood town. As the movie industry heated up in the Los Angeles Basin, the industry had to find someplace to shoot desert and "Old West" locations. And the stars started seeking someplace to escape Hollywood and enjoy themselves on their own time. In the Golden Age of Hollywood (the 1930s, '40s, and '50s), film crews crowded into Palm Springs and stars built weekend homes with sparkling swimming pools. Today, many of the original 1940s and '50s inns that once housed producers and film crews now open their doors to guests of the area, and architecture buffs come to tour the original mid-century modern mansions and villas.

# Palm Springs

Palm Springs is a desert town with many faces. Some folks think of it as a wintertime snowbird retreat—that is, the spot where thousands of retired folks come to escape the harsh winter weather of their hometowns. To Hollywood star-followers, it's both a vacation haven for actors and a major on-location shooting site for many classic films of the 1940s and '50s. And for the young and vivacious gay crowd, it's a thriving and accepting town that's been known for its tolerance for more than five decades, complete with plenty of hot nightspots.

The Palm Springs area actually encompasses several medium-sized towns that have grown enough to bleed together into one sprawling urban area. Palm Springs proper maintains its status as the poshest and most happening place to be. As you drive south through Ranch Mirage, Palm Desert, Indian Wells, and down to Indio, you'll find more residential communities and country clubs with clusters of mall-style shopping but no real historic downtown areas. By the time you get to Indio, the industrial part of the area begins to take over, and the only real tourist sights are the date farms.

## SIGHTS

### Palm Springs Aerial Tramway

At first glance, Palm Springs doesn't seem like a spot where a gondola ride would be a big attraction. And yet, the Palm Springs Aerial Tramway (1 Tramway Rd., 760/325-1391, www.pstramway.com, Mon.–Fri. 10 A.M.–9:45 P.M., Sat.–Sun. 8 A.M.–9:45 P.M., adults $21.95, children 3–12 $14.95, seniors $19.95 ) draws both visitors and a surprising number of locals nearly every day of the year. The idea for the tramway was conceived by prominent and sweaty resident Francis Crocker in 1935. Crocker longed to visit the cool, snow-capped peak of Mount San Jacinto when the sun beat down mercilessly on the valley floor. It took nearly 30 years of wartime delays and political missteps to realize the dream, but in 1963 the structure was complete and the first visitors took a ride up to the peak of the 10,834-foot mountain. In 2000, the tramway was renovated, and now runs the biggest revolving cars operating in the world.

To take a ride on the tramway, you first drive up a winding road to the parking lots of the Valley Station. Purchase or pick up your tickets, then wait for your tram to depart. (Schedules vary based on season and weather conditions.) You'll board the tram car and find a good place to stand on the circular metal platform, which can get fairly crowded. As the tram begins to climb, the platform revolves, letting passengers take in all the different views up and down the valley. The whole trip takes only 10 minutes as the tram ascends about 8,000 feet. When you get off the tram, you'll be in the Mountain Station, which includes a bar, a restaurant, a souvenir shop, and a visitors center for the surrounding Mount San Jacinto State Park (see *Sports and Recreation*).

But most folks head straight out the back door and into the park. In the wintertime, the park is usually covered by several feet of snow.

Locals bring their snowshoes, cross-country skis, sleds, and snow toys up on the tram (all of these are allowed in the car) for a fun few hours in the snow. The park creates a **Winter Adventure Center** (Thurs.–Fri. and Mon., 10 A.M.–4 P.M., Sat.–Sun. 8 A.M.–4 P.M., Nov.–Apr., ski package $21/day), a snow park with sled tracks, each winter. In the summertime when the snow is gone, those same locals take picnic supplies and walking sticks up to the mountain for a cool day's hiking and nature-loving.

## Palm Springs Art Museum

Just a couple of blocks from the main drag, the Palm Springs Art Museum (101 Museum Dr., 760/322-4800, http://psmuseum.org, Tues.–Sun. 10 A.M.–5 P.M., Thurs. until 8 P.M., adults $12.50, children $5) shows off the finest modern art in a variety of media. From your first steps up to the museum entrance, which is flanked by a pair of large sculptures, you'll be ensconced in the forms and shapes of modern art. The museum's central permanent collection is a mix of Western and Native American fine art and crafts. From local artists and craftspeople as well as those from around the Western states, these pieces evoke the sense of space and beauty found in Palm Springs and beyond. Other permanent exhibits include an ever-changing array of modern glass sculpture and an almost-new installation by Patrick Dougherty. The Palm Springs Art Museum also hosts an endless parade of traveling shows and special exhibitions, from video installations to sculpture collections to photography.

## Moorten Botanical Garden

Visitors who've come to the desert to learn and view the variety of desert wildlife will love the Moorten Botanical Garden (1701 S. Palm Canyon Dr., 760/327-6555, Mon.–Sat. 9 A.M.–4:30 P.M., Sun. 10 A.M.–4 P.M., adults $3, children $1.50). Set right near downtown, this charming garden specializes in cacti and succulents, growing over 3,000 varieties. The desert plants originate from all over the world, from South Africa and Madagascar to South America and much more locally in the Mojave and Sonora deserts of California. You can wander the outdoor gardens, then head inside to the "Cacterium," a greenhouse in which the more delicate (and less adapted to the Palm Springs locale) specimens thrive.

The Moorten gardens were created and expanded by Patricia and "Slim" Moorten; Slim was one of the original Keystone Cops. Today, their son Clark owns and operates the gardens. Be sure to say hi if you see him out working on his pride and joy.

## The Living Desert

Do you prefer animal life to an endless parade of plants? Then head for The Living Desert (47900 Portola Ave., Palm Desert/Indian Wells, 760/346-5694, www.livingdesert.org, daily 9 A.M.–5 P.M., summer 8 A.M.–1 P.M., adults $12.50, children $7.50). The truth is you can visit a bunch more botanical gardens at The Living Desert. But you can also visit the animals—furry, scaly, feathered, and bald—that inhabit the world's great deserts. The Living Desert focuses primarily on the desert habitats of Africa and the Western United States. Some

ROBERT HOLMES / CALTOUR

desert bighorn sheep at The Living Desert

of the African natives, such as the gazelles and sand cats, are endangered species; others, like the meerkats, are stars of the small screen. The Discovery Center welcomes children of all ages, offering basic educational opportunities and interactive exhibits. The WaTuTu Village focuses on the lives of human natives of desert regions, and a somewhat incongruous but nonetheless impressive model train setup round out The Living Desert offerings.

Visitors can expect plenty of amenities at The Living Desert, including two café-style restaurants, two gift shops, and plenty of restrooms with baby-changing stations. The paved paths are wheelchair- and stroller-accessible. In addition, a number of shaded spots have water misters that cool off guests during the heat of summer.

## Date Farms

In the south part of the urban region, groves of dates provide most of the United States' crop of the sweet Middle Eastern staple fruit. The **Oasis Date Farm** (59–111 Hwy. 111, Thermal, 800/827-8017, http://oasisdategardens.com, Mon.–Sat. 8 A.M.–5 P.M.) in the thriving metropolis of Thermal has a good-sized storefront and a demonstration "arbor" of date palms that visitors can walk around in. In the store, you can learn about the many different varieties of dates (interestingly, most dates originally come from Iraq) and taste almost all of them. You can buy whole dates, mixed boxes, and date candies. Over at the ice cream counter, the one thing you simply must try is the date shake—a super-sweet regional specialty that's perfect on both hot summer and mild winter days. Out in the orchard, you'll see how dates cluster and grow as you enjoy a few minutes in the shade of the thickly fronded palm trees.

© LANCE SCOTT

Oasis Date Farm

Another famous date orchard that's open to the public is the **Shields Date Farm** (80–225 Hwy. 111, Indio, 800/414-2555, www.shieldsdates.com, daily 9 A.M.–5 P.M.) in Indio. If you can't make it as far as Oasis, check it out!

## Desert Memorial Park

It's not on most tourist destination lists for Palm Springs, but visiting star seekers and locals alike make pilgrimages to Desert Memorial Park (31750 Da Vall Dr., Cathedral City). Unlike the craggy old cemeteries in more historically oriented parts of California, you won't find slightly sunken marble tombstones, illegible wooden board memorials, or dried up weeds. Here all the grave markers are flat and uniform, the deep green lawn is meticulously maintained, and the shade trees are trimmed to perfection. Stop by the office to pick up a map and listing of the graves, some of which are inhabited by the remains of famous Hollywood celebrities. The best known of these are Frank Sinatra and Sonny Bono. Several members of Sinatra's family rest beside him. You might also see the markers for members of the Gabor family and actor William Powell.

# ENTERTAINMENT AND EVENTS

Unlike most of the rest of California's desert towns, Palm Springs is a thriving entertainment center. If you love to see shows, go out dancing, and stay up till 3 A.M. partying, this is the town for you! The nightlife has a friendly vibe, the shows appeal to all ages (for real), and the festivals can fill the whole town with fun-loving visitors from around California and beyond.

## Bars and Clubs

**Red 74** (72–990 El Paseo, Palm Desert, 760/568-6774, Tues.–Sat. 6 P.M.–2 A.M., cover $5–15) in the suburb of Palm Desert offers truth in advertising; red fabric adorns the walls, and red decorative elements create a womblike monochromatic atmosphere. You'll find a younger crowd here enjoying the original signature cocktails, the dancing, and the eye candy. Beware: You might find yourself trying to grab a drink during a six-minute speed-dating session. But if you're lucky, you'll make it on a night with world music or a particularly good local DJ.

Two other suburban bar/clubs you can try out are the **Village Lounge** (73196 Hwy. 111, Palm Desert, 760/568-1200) and the **Club Rio** (68449 Perez Rd., Cathedral City, 760/321-5526).

## Gay and Lesbian

To be frank, most of the good nightlife in Palm Springs sits squarely within the gay community. The liveliest bars, the best dance clubs, the smoothest lounges—all gay.

But then again, "gay bar" doesn't mean quite the same thing in Palm Springs as it does in San Francisco or even Los Angeles. Here in the desert, there's a very casual, relaxed vibe to almost all of these spots. There's far less regimentation of straight vs. gay vs. lesbian here than elsewhere in California. It's not at all unusual to hit a gay bar at 11 P.M. on a Saturday night and find pretty shirtless boys, crew-cut lesbians, gorgeous drag queens, threesomes of indeterminate relationship, and straight married senior citizens all grooving on the same dance floor. Most "gay" bars and clubs welcome straights of all ages—just be aware that you'll see open same-sex affection, and if you freak out over it, *you'll* be the one who's asked to leave. Same goes the other way; if you're gay, you're expected to tolerate straight folks smooching on your turf. But if you're open minded about your fun, you'll love the scene here in Palm Springs.

One of the premier gay clubs in Palm Springs offers you a respite from the desert heat at the **Oasis Nightclub & Lounge** (611 S. Palm Canyon Dr., 760/416-0950, www.cluboasisps.com, Wed.–Thurs. 3 P.M.–midnight, Fri. until 2 A.M., Sat. until 4 A.M.). The regrettable strip-mall exterior belies the big industrial interior, which includes tons of room for dancing as well as drinking and meeting people. The unfinished ceiling and ductwork make the dance floor feel bigger, anyway. The crowd tends towards the boys, but women are welcome too. The club hosts many parties and special events each year, plus a regular calendar of nightly fun. Go to the website for more information before you come, or just show up and be surprised. Looking for a slightly mellower evening? Order your favorite fruity cocktail at the **O Lounge,** a quieter spot within the Oasis.

If your tastes run to leather, the one club in Palm Springs you must visit is **The Tool Shed** (600 E. Sunny Dunes Rd., 760/320-3299, www.toolshed-ps.com, daily 7 A.M.–2 A.M., Fri.–Sat. until 3 A.M.). Wear your leather and your Levi's when you come to shoot a game of pool or enjoy the rugged scenery. Inside, you'll find mostly men drinking and having fun in the appropriately industrial-styled bar, complete with chain-link fence. Check the website for a list of upcoming events.

For the ladies, **Delilah's** (67855 Hwy. 111, Cathedral City, 760/770-1210) offers a more estrogen-oriented atmosphere.

A newcomer on the proverbial block, **Mixie's Boy Bar** (120 S. Palm Canyon Dr., 760/203-0147) offers a big, meandering, multi-level dance floor, two bars, and a patio where you can hang out and smoke. The video system provides nonstop visual entertainment (as if the dance floor wasn't enough!) and DJ Mixtress rocks the house with a totally danceable blend of hip-hop, house, pop, and the occasional '80s classic thrown in to keep things lively. The art prints on the wall definitely have a theme, and there's actually a fair amount of seating for patrons who aren't quite up to dancing the whole night away. Is that totally shapely cocktail waitress male or female? Does it matter? This club and bar is one of the all-sexualities-welcome establishments, so feel free to climb the stairs for a fun late-night party no matter what your proclivities.

Even in gala Palm Springs, **Toucan's Tiki Lounge** (2100 N. Palm Canyon Dr., 760/416-7584, www.toucanstikilounge.com) draws notice. It's also a locals' favorite, almost a bar-around-the-corner, despite the wild tiki decor. This fun nightspot has pretty boy go-go dancers, a tiny dance floor that gets crowded on weekends, and a drag show every Sunday night. Bring a friend or four to make the most of a night out at Toucan's.

Can you picture a gay sports bar? **Score** (301 E. Arenas Rd., 760/866-1905) brings these two usually mutually exclusive concepts together to create a unique queer-jock experience on Arena Road, the longtime gay main drag. Imagine big-screen TVs, beer on tap, and dozens of beautiful men to stare at. Sounds like heaven!

## Live Shows

One of the staples of the Palm Springs entertainment scene is its exuberant Vegas-style shows. With singing, dancing, amazing costumes, and wonderful comedy, these shows delight audiences all year long.

Perhaps the most popular of the big shows is the **Palm Springs Follies** (128 S. Palm Canyon Dr., 760/327-0225, www.psfollies.com, shows Wed.–Sun. most weeks, see current schedule, $48–90). This vaudeville-meets-Vegas-style show draws national guest acts (Oct.–May). So what's the twist? Those lovely bejeweled showgirls wearing the glitter and the giant feather headdresses are old. Really, really old. The youngest performer in the Palm Springs Follies is 54 years old, and the oldest showgirl is well past her 80th birthday. You'll be surprised and delighted by a cast that's old enough to remember when this kind of live singing and dancing entertainment was more than just a curiosity. Heck, a few of these performers remember Prohibition! Perhaps best of all, the dancers and singers come out to meet their audience after each show. Get autographs on your program and express your appreciation of the sexy seniors.

Advance reservations are highly recommended, as the Palm Springs Follies often sells out. You can purchase tickets for this three-hour show online or by phone, or at the box office. This long show can get boring quickly for small children, so it might be better to leave them at home, especially for evening shows.

Visitors who want to blend the various cultures of Palm Springs can't help but love **Copy Katz** (Casino Morongo Resort and Spa, 49500 Seminole Dr., Cabazon, 800/252-4499, www.morongocasinoresort.com or www.copykatzps.com). This celebrity impersonator and drag show features talented performers who'll make you believe you're watching Barbra Streisand or Michael Jackson. You can check online for the shows coming up in the following week, and you can buy tickets at the website. Cabazon is 20 minutes west of Palm Springs.

## Festivals and Events

With tourism and glamour as its major industries, it's no surprise that the Palm Springs area hosts an immense array of festivals each year to bring even more visitors into town.

One of the biggest festivals each year celebrates the area's signature crop: dates. The **Riverside County Fair and Date Festival** (82–503 Hwy. 111, Indio, 760/863-8247, www.datefest.org, Mon.–Fri. 10 A.M.–10 P.M., Sat.–Sun. 10 A.M.–midnight, adults $8, youth 5–12 $6) takes place in mild and lovely February of each year at the County Fairground in Indio. The Fairgrounds were created with a fun and funky Arabian Nights theme, which decorates the big space from the entrance gates inward. Be sure to get a place to view the Queen Scheherazade parade, check out the ostrich and camel races, and definitely grab a date shake from one of the many vendors. Kids and teens flock to the carnival area to ride the tilting, whirling, zipping rides (unlimited rides $23) that light up at night. You can't help but be entertained as you ramble through the rows of vendors, view the county fair contest entrants, and taste every dish that can possibly be made with dates. In the evenings, musical acts draw fairgoers to the stage to watch everything from local jazz to headlining national classic rock acts.

A perennial favorite of serious rock lovers from all over the state is the **Coachella Valley Music Festival** (www.coachella.com, single-day pass $95, three-day pass $275). Literally dozens of bands crowd onto the roster each year. In 2008, the lineup featured Roger Waters as the headliner, with such bands as The Verve, Death Cab for Cutie, and Fatboy Slim adding spice. For three days, concertgoers can immerse themselves in music from sunup to sundown and beyond. (Well, not quite from sunup...your hangover will appreciate the restraint.)

The Festival runs over a long weekend each spring, usually toward the end of April. Attendees can choose from the endless array of local motels and inns, or they can bring tents to pitch on-site so as to stick as close as possible to the action. The festival is held at the Empire Polo Field. Car access isn't too difficult, but the festival organizers encourage the use of public transit and carpooling to minimize auto traffic and crowding in the parking lots. Check the website for gate-opening hours and current prices. You can buy tickets online through the festival site, or call one of the major ticket handlers.

To no one's surprise, the Palm Springs region holds not one but many gay-themed events each year. While the annual **Greater Palm Springs Pride Parade** (www.pspride.org, Nov.) and festival are plenty of fun and well-attended, and the **Dinah Shore Weekend** (www.dinahshoreweekend.com, Apr.) is held especially for the girls, these are not *the* events of the season. Instead, break out your best croquet whites and take yourself and your friends to the annual **White Party** (277 Avenida Caballeros, www.jeffreysanker.com). Although the signature party takes place on the third Saturday night of April each year, the whole week beforehand sees pool parties, after-hours club events, and plenty of other themed social entertainments livening up the nights. The Saturday night White Party hosts up to 20,000 white-clad men intent on bumping and grinding and dancing the night away to fabulous, top-end DJs. Drag and dance shows light up the stage throughout the evening, and side lounges offer spots to sit down, kick back, and relax...or whatever...in a quieter space. The White Party typically runs 9 P.M.–5 A.M., with an after-party for seriously dedicated partiers. Other festival-sponsored parties include the fabulous and very popular Underwear Party and Pool Party. Check the website to buy tickets for your favorite events and get a look at this year's theme.

## SHOPPING

Shopping is a major pastime for the wealthy golfers and condo owners who frequent the Palm Springs area. The whole of Palm Canyon Drive from La Quinta up to Palm Springs seems to be one long strip mall, with everything from auto parts shops to Targets and on up through high-end chain clothing stores. On the other hand, for unique boutiques, your best bet is downtown Palm Springs or El Paseo.

### El Paseo

El Paseo is actually a mile-long avenue in the town of Palm Desert. Literally hundreds of shops, galleries, salons, restaurants, and more cluster on both sides of this legendary shopping street. El Paseo hosts a number of festivals each year, and weekly Art Walks during the wintertime high season. Whether you've come for the culture or for some simple retail therapy, El Paseo can hook you up.

The largest block of shops, an outdoor mall of sorts, is called **The Gardens** (El Paseo and San Pablo). The Gardens is anchored by Saks Fifth Avenue (73–555 El Paseo, 760/837-2900, www.saksfifthavenue.com, Mon.–Thurs. 10 A.M.–6 P.M., Fri.–Sat. 10 A.M.–7 P.M., Sun. 11 A.M.–6 P.M.) on one side and Tiffany & Co. (73–585 El Paseo, 760/341-3444, www.tiffany.com, Mon.–Sat. 10 A.M.–6 P.M., Sun.

11 A.M.–5 P.M.) on the other. But you can walk, or take one of the bright-yellow Courtesy Carts from end to end of the long street to make carrying your accumulation of shopping bags a bit easier.

At the south end, between Ocotillo and Sage Streets, shoppers interested in Native Americana and New Age merchandise can find an array of lovely things at shops such as **Earth Spirits** (73–130 El Paseo #N., 760/779-8766). Apparel for men and women can be purchased all up and down El Paseo—choose from chain shops or unique boutiques such as **She She** (73–061 El Paseo, Ste. 2, 760/779-0417) and **Mister Marcus** (73–540 El Paseo, Ste. B, 776-8454). Art lovers enjoy wandering in the **Edenhurst Gallery** (73–655 El Paseo, 760/346-7900) and **Gallery 1000** (73–400 El Paseo, #1, 760/346-2230), among others. The street also hosts an endless selection of interior designers and home stores for those looking to pick up just the right Southwestern item to add to their home's decor.

### Outlets

Outside of Palm Springs, you can load up on discount designer merchandise at the **Desert Hills Premium Outlets** (48400 Seminole Dr., Cabazon, 951/849-6641, http://premiumoutlets.com/deserthills, Sun.–Thurs. 10 A.M.–8 P.M., Fri. 10 A.M.–9 P.M., Sat. 9 A.M.–9 P.M.). From Palm Springs, drive west on Highway 11 to I-10 and into Cabazon. Highlights of this huge sprawl of high-end outlet stores include Dolce & Gabbana, Ralph Lauren, Gucci, Cole Haan, Waterford Wedgewood, and Bose. If all that bargain-hunting makes you hungry or you need a hit of energy, the mall has an array of coffee shops and quickie restaurants at each end to satisfy your cravings.

## SPORTS AND RECREATION

The Palm Springs and Coachella Valley area hosts a staggering 100-plus golf courses. If you're not a golf lover, beautiful desert and mountain parks beckon hikers and even cross-country skiers and showshoers. Water parks cool children and adults alike during the long, hot desert summers.

### Parks

The closest gorgeous scenery and good hiking to downtown Palm Springs is found at the **Indian Canyons** (1097 E. Murray Canyon Rd., 760/327-6550, www.palmsprings.com/points/canyon, daily 8 A.M.–5 P.M., adults $8, children $4). These canyons were once home to the ancestors of the Agua Caliente Cahuilla Native Americans. The abundant streams and diverse plant and animal species made the series of canyons a wonderful place to live—plenty of fresh drinking water, food, and materials to build shelter sit all around. The progressive tribes even diverted water from the streams to irrigate planted crops. Today, all the canyons bear trace evidence of these long-gone communities, and it's fun for kids (and grown-ups) to search for housing foundations, dam remnants, and food-processing areas.

The most stunning (and most-visited) of the canyons is **Palm Canyon,** an aptly named 15-mile-long oasis of color, water, and beauty improbably set in the midst of a dry and barren patch of desert. You'll bask in the shade of the lush and naturally growing palm trees, admire the colorful spring wildflowers, and dip your fingers in the creek that feeds the abundant life in the canyon. The paved footpath makes it easy to explore. For an extra $3, you can take a ranger-guided one-mile walk to learn more about the history and nature of the canyon. Or if you prefer to let a strong equine do the walking, horseback riding is permitted through Palm Canyon. And in the grand tradition of popular outdoor sights in Southern California, the **Trading Post** offers souvenirs, maps, and refreshments to all comers.

Another beautiful and well-traveled spot is **Tahquitz Canyon** (500 W. Mesquite Rd., 760/416-7044, adults $12.50, children $6). The highlight of Tahquitz Canyon is a waterfall that cascades down 60 feet down and splashes into a pool. The fall is seasonal, and you'll want to come in the springtime to see the best show. Tahquitz Canyon has its own

© LIZ HAMILL SCOTT

Snow in Palm Springs!

visitors center, complete with an interpretive exhibit, short educational film, and observation deck.

Other canyons include **Murray Canyon** and **Andreas Canyon.** If you prefer seclusion and a wilder version of natural beauty, these canyons might be more appealing to you than the well-developed Tahquitz and Palm Canyons.

At the top of the Aerial Tramway, **Mount San Jacinto State Park** (25905 Hwy. 243, 951/659-2607, www.parks.ca.gov, daily dawn–dusk) offers fabulous hiking, camping, and winter snow play only 10 minutes from Palm Springs by gondola ride. You can also access the park from the other side by driving in from CA-243 or CA-74. The south end of the Pacific Crest Trail runs through this beautiful high-elevation park. Many day-hike trails crisscross the mountain peak, letting visitors enjoy cool, shaded forests and fabulous valley views as they walk. A number of campgrounds throughout the park, some hike-in and some car-campsites, offer outdoorsy travelers the opportunity to acclimate to the altitude and explore the area in depth. But no matter how fit you are, take care when you first arrive and begin to hike here—you'll be well over a mile and possibly as much as two miles above sea level, and altitude sickness can be a real danger.

Nature lovers can look for lots of wildlife as they ply the trails of the park. Sniff the wildflowers and admire the butterflies drinking from them, touch the bark of a Jeffrey Pine tree, or bring your birding list and look out for winged friends. While bears aren't a problem at San Jacinto, do keep an eye out for mountain lions. If you see one, get as big as you can and don't run; face the cat down.

## Golf

*The* major form of outdoor exercise in and around Palm Springs and the Coachella Valley is golf. The region boasts more than 100 courses, about half of which are public or semi-public. The rest belong to a variety of private country clubs. Among the publicly accessible courses, players can try anything from low-fee municipal courses up to swanky PGA championship country clubs. If you're a serious golfer, pick up a guide to all the courses or look on the web to find those that will fit your game best.

**Indian Springs Golf and Country Club** (79-940 Westward Ho Dr., Indio, 760/200-8988, www.indianspringsgc.com) boasts some of the best golfing in all the region for under $100 (most of the time). Naturally, the best rates going are in the blistering summertime, but you can find bargains in the moderate months of September, October, and March as well. Whatever your skill level, this 6,770-yard, par 72 course will offer fun in the desert sunshine. You can also make good use of the driving range and pro shop, and grab breakfast, lunch, or dinner before or after your game.

Looking for hardcore championship golf the likes of which you've only seen before on TV? Book a tee time at **Trilogy La Quinta** (60–151 Trilogy Pkwy., La Quinta, 760/771-0707, www.trilogygolfclub.com/laquinta, $30–120). The likes of Tiger Woods and Annika Sorenstam have walked the greens here at the oftentimes home of the PGA Skins Game. Six tee positions provide a challenge for new, mid-level, and experienced players. As at most courses, afternoon golfers get the best price breaks, as do those willing to brave the torturous summer heat. The attached Azul Restaurant has gone modern in its decor, serving upscale California cuisine for breakfast, lunch, and dinner to golfers and non-players alike.

The **Cimarron Golf Resort** (67–603 30th Ave., Cathedral City, 760/777-6060, www.cimarrongolf.com) prides itself on offering a different experience from the plethora of country club courses. In truth it has two separate courses: Pebble and Boulder. Boulder is the par-71 championship course that draws the best golfers out on weekend morning, while Pebble's par-58 provides fun for even the newest of golfers and good practice for more advanced players who only have a couple of hours to enjoy a game. You can book your tee time up to 120 days in advance. Call for rates during your stay.

## SAFETY IN THE DESERT

People who've never spent time in a desert before often underestimate the very real dangers of trekking in a harsh, dry climate, while experienced desert rats can become overconfident and complacent about their safety precautions, to their detriment.

No matter who you are, or how many times you've gone hiking or camping or backpacking or driving out into the desert, you *must* plan for problems and practice for safety. Here are a few recommendations from the various desert state and national parks:

- **Carry water.** This is possibly *the* most important desert safety tip of them all. You're not likely to find much water if you're out hiking in the desert. In Death Valley, 1-2 gallon per person per day is recommended, and they mean it. Even if you're driving around the park on mostly paved roads, carry water in your car. Water is a big concern in all the big desert parks – you won't find much, even at the major sights with big parking lots. No matter which desert you're visiting or for how long, bring twice as much water as you think you'll need. Better to have too much than too little!
- **Wear a hat.** In the desert, wear a hat with a wide brim to shade your face and your neck. Do it even if you hate hats; if you don't have one, buy one at the gift shop. Hats are the single best way to keep the punishing desert sun off your head, a must if you get into any trouble in the desert.
- **Wear sunglasses.** Again, don shades even if they're not your usual style. The harsh sunlight bouncing off the light-colored landscape can cause real damage to unprotected eyes. Many of the visitors centers sell sunglasses.
- **Use sunscreen.** You've never experienced sun like it pounds down in the desert, so be good to your skin and go for a high-SPF sun-

Looking for something else? A few more of seemingly infinite options include **Eagle Falls Golf Course** (84–245 Indio Springs Parkway, Indio, 760/238-5633, www.eaglefallsgolf.com, $50), **Mesquite** (2700 E. Mesquite Ave., Palm Springs, 800/727-8331, www.palmsprings.com/golf/mesquite.html), where Bob Hope used to bring his cronies, and the ritzy **Indian Wells Golf Resort** (44-500 Indian Wells Ln., Indian Wells, 760/346-4653, www.indianwellsgolfresort.com, $75–200).

## Biking

Bicycling opportunities abound in Palm Springs. Wintertime, when the weather is mild to cool, is the best time to take a bike out on the desert roads and bike trails. In the city of Palm Springs, an interconnected maze of bike trails help folks get around with ease and relative safety. Check www.palmsprings.com/city/palmsprings/bikemap.html for a map of the in-town loops.

## Water Parks

Summer visitors and locals looking to both cool off and enjoy active outdoor fun head for **Knott's Soak City USA** (1500 S. Gene Autry Tr., 760/327-0499, www.knotts.com/soakcity/ps/index.shtml, adults $18–30, children $18). As with most major California water parks, Soak City has fast and furious slides, as well as the funky new Pacific Spin, a slow-moving river for inner tubers, a wave pool, and a children's splash area. Soak City also offers plenty of dry land, complete with some chairs and chaises. Amenities include coin-op lockers, food concessions, restrooms and changing rooms, and rentable shaded cabanas.

## Winter Sports

With the well-known scorching desert climate of the valley floor, Palm Springs doesn't seem like much of a winter sports destination. And yet, visitors and locals (especially locals) can take advantage of nearby mountains to ski,

screen. (It'll also help with the unbelievably dry skin most folks get when hanging out in ultra-dry climates.)

- **Stay away from old mines and other man-made hazards.** You'll find cool old abandoned mines in Death Valley, Joshua Tree, Mojave, and possibly even Anza-Borrego. Such places have zillions of hidden dangers, from invisible vertical shafts to collapsing timbers to piles of old explosives. Don't wander into old mine shafts or touch explosives, and tell park rangers about the latter.
- **Be aware of potential flash floods.** All the desert parks in California are rife with washes – spots where water rushes across the landscape during rare but often intense desert storms. And if you're in a wash during one of those storms, you can get fatally swept away. If the weather looks stormy, take care in washes: don't park your car in one, don't use one for a hiking trail, and don't pitch your tent in or beside a wash.
- **Tell someone where you're going.** Tell a friend or a family member back home where you're going and when you plan to be home. That way, somebody will miss you if you don't come back and can alert the park or the police to your potential location and predicament. If you're planning to go backcountry camping in a park that allows it, register with the rangers as required for the same reason.
- **If something happens, stick with your vehicle or your companions.** It's easier to find several people than one alone, and it's easier to find a bright shiny car than it is a person. So if the worst happens and you find yourself stranded, stay with your group and with your car for the best chance of being found.

sled, snowboard, or just play in the snow for a day.

For a nearby day of snow play, cross-country skiing, or snowshoeing, grab your gear and take the Palm Springs Aerial Tramway up to **Mount San Jacinto State Park** (25905 Hwy. 243, 951/659-2607, www.parks.ca.gov, daily dawn–dusk). If you've got sleds and kids, head out of the Mountain Station and down the main trail to the Adventure Center. Here you'll find groomed sledding tracks and even the occasional sled-racing event. For the adventurous and fit crowd, many of the summer hiking trails turn into cross-country ski and snowshoe tracks when the snow covers them. Check with the rangers at the Mountain Station for current conditions and a trail map.

SoCal downhill skiers and snowboarders think of the ski resorts at **Big Bear** (880 Summit Blvd., 800/424-4232, http://bigbear.com) as their home mountains. Choose between **Snow Summit** (909/866-5766, www.snowsummit.com, adult lift tickets $20–65, children $8–53) and **Bear Mountain** (909/866-5766, www.bearmountain.com). At Snow Summit, 14 lifts service more than 30 trails. This resort caters primarily to beginning and intermediate skiers, complete with a ski school and fun beginner terrain parks. On the other hand, Bear Mountain appeals more to the intermediate and advanced crowd. With dozens of jumps, jibs, and a Superpipe, Bear Mountain beckons to boarders and freestylers from SoCal and beyond.

Big Bear also offers cross-country ski and snowshoeing trails and tours, plus a snow park.

## Spas

With all that money running around Palm Springs, it's understandable that plenty of it gets spent on relaxing massages and rejuvenating facials. You'll find many day spas and spa resorts clustered north of Palm Springs proper in the town of Desert Hot Springs, taking advantage of the smallish locale's namesake waters. For example, **Living Waters Spa** (13340 Mountain View Rd., Desert Hot Springs, 866/329-9988, www.livingwatersspa.com, day use $45/couple or single) features multiple pools filled with the local mineral water, massage services, and comfortable European-style hotel accommodations (most with full kitchens). The other European aspect of Living Waters its clothing-optional and, in fact, somewhat clothing-discouraged facilities. Expect to see day-use and overnight guests strolling, bathing, and lounging in the nude all around the resort. The emphasis of this spa is on freedom (especially freedom from binding clothing) and relaxation for all visitors.

On the other hand, **Desert Mystique Spa** (4721 E. Palm Canyon Dr., Ste. F, Palm Springs, 760/960-4597, www.desertmystiquespa.com, Mon.–Sat. 10 A.M.–7 P.M., Sun. by appt, $80–90/hour massage) in the midst of downtown Palm Springs gives more modest spa-goers a traditional day spa experience. Desert Mystique has a full menu of spa treatments, including half a dozen different massage styles and an array of facial and body treatments. The facials tend toward SoCal aesthetic and post-surgical treatments, while the massages have an almost Northern California flair.

If you're serious about pampering your face, book an appointment at **European Experience Luxury Facials** (2225 Tahquitz Canyon Rd., Ste. 6, Palm Springs, 760/902-2751, www.palmspringsfacials.com). Whether you're a man or a woman, this day spa can concoct the perfect treatment. Men also seek out the specialized back treatment, and everyone loves a relaxing Swedish massage. Ear candling and waxing services are also available.

## Casino Gambling

The **Fantasy Springs Casino** (84–245 Indian Springs Pkwy, Indio, 800/827-2946, www.fantasyspringsresort.com) has all sorts of entertainment options, from bowling to live shows. You can stay at the high-rise hotel and pass all day and half the night down on the casino floor. This isn't a full-fledged Vegas-style casino, but you'll find plenty of slot machines, table games, bingo, and even horse-race betting. Enjoy a game of easy-rules blackjack or mini-baccarat, or try your luck at one of the newer progressive slot machines. When you need a break, head for one of several restaurants or the nearby attached cocktail bar.

At the **Spa Resort Casino** (401 E. Amado Rd., Palm Springs, 760/883-1000, www.sparesortcasino.com) you can try your luck at one of 1,000 slot machines or 30 tables. Got lots of cash to bet? Head for the high-limit room. Poker lovers tend to stick close to the card room, while casual gamers take a break from the endless noises and flashing lights of the casino floor to get a soothing massage or facial at the resort's in-house spa.

## ACCOMMODATIONS

The range of accommodations in Palm Springs is both broad and deep. As a town with nearly 100 years' history as a tourist mecca, it's hard not to find a room here, even on the spur of the moment (as long as it's not a festival weekend). You can go for a cheap motel, a historic mid-century modern hotel with Hollywood history, or even a plush high-end casino style hotel. Sure, you can stay at one of the standard national chain motels, but why would you when so many lovely boutique hotels dot the landscape?

If you're gay, you've got even more choices. Palm Springs has an array of gay-only and gay-friendly lodgings. Most of these cater to men only, except during the woman-oriented Dinah Shore Weekend.

### Under $100

**Chase Hotel Palm Springs** (200 W. Arenas Rd., 760/320-8866, www.chasehotelpalmsprings.com, $90–235) offers classic Palm Springs–style accommodations at reasonable nightly or weekly rates. The charming mid-century modern motel sits only a block from Palm Canyon Drive. Outdoors, it boasts a charming garden area complete with palm trees and a saline swimming pool. Inside, while the style of the guest room furnishings evokes the 1950s, the beds and chair are in fact comfortable and totally modern. Choose between a king or two-bed room, or a larger suite with a kitchenette and perhaps even a mosaic-tiled fireplace. Each morning, grab a bite to eat from the tasty continental breakfast spread, and don't forget to indulge in a freshly baked chocolate chip cookie in the evening!

### $100-150

Only a few minutes from the center of town, **A Place in the Sun** (754 E. San Lorenzo Rd., 760/325-0254, www.aplaceinthesunhotel.com, $112–340) was first built in the early 1950s to shelter the cast and crew working on the film of the same name. Then and now, a meandering set of 16 semi-individual bungalows offer spacious quarters for visitors. All guest bungalows include full kitchens, living rooms with modern TVs, and tropical-resort-style decor with old-school movie prints decorating the rather thin walls. Bedrooms have cushy mattresses and older wall heaters—you might even see a radiator unit original to the property in your vintage pink-tiled bathroom. You'll also have your own small private patio (on which you can relax with a cigarette),

© LANCE SCOTT

A Place in the Sun

plus access to the central courtyard with its ill-kept miniature putting green and its lovely modern gentle-salt pool and spa. A continental breakfast is served in the office each day, or out in the gazebo by the pool with more variety of food and drink on the weekends in wintertime. Friendly owners will help you out with all aspects of your stay (the office is open 9 A.M.–5 P.M. six days per week). Pets are welcome.

If you want to stay in a real William F. Cody original building, check in to the **Del Marcos Hotel** (225 W. Baristo Rd., 760/325-6902, www.delmarcoshotel.com, $110–200). This small boutique hotel has won awards for its dedication to preserving its mid-century modern design. Indeed, even the guest room decor screams late 1940s and early '50s, complete with prints of Hollywood idols of the time, period artwork, and brightly colored chairs of funky design. You'll be greeted at the front entrance by the hallmark diagonally sloping roofs and faux-stonework, and muted colors of the period. The interior courtyard boasts a saline pool surrounded by chaise lounges with umbrellas and an expanse of concrete. With only 16 rooms, the Del Marcos Hotel feels more like an inn than an impersonal hotel, and it's convenient to the shops and restaurants of Palm Canyon Drive.

### $150–250

The **Movie Colony Hotel** (726 N. Indian Canyon Dr., 888/953-5700, www.moviecolonyhotel.com, $180–400) takes the famed mid-century modern style and kicks it into an upper scale. While you'll still see the clean diagonal lines and blocky structural details, the amenities inside and out of the rooms and townhouses here breathe with a vintage-meets-modern luxury. You'll find high thread-count linens, light-colored designer furnishings, plenty of space, and designer accents. All rooms have California king beds and pristine bathrooms. Townhouses include large living areas with great 1950s style sofas, fireplaces, and travertine bars with refrigerators. Pay a little extra for a room with a door out to the attractive pool area. It's the focal point of the hotel, and includes a large spa and a fire pit where complimentary wine is served in the evenings. With your room rate, you'll also receive a daily continental breakfast, concierge service, and loaner bicycles on which you can explore downtown Palm Springs.

### Over $250

If you can afford serious luxury in the desert, stay at the **Villa Royale Inn** (1620 S. Indian Trail, 760/327-2314, www.villaroyale.com, $200–350). This lovely boutique hotel seeks to evoke the feel of Europe—a Tuscan villa, perhaps. Guest rooms range from small "hideaways" to spacious two-bedroom villas that feel more like home than a hotel room. Each of the 30 rooms has its own unique antique furnishings, down duvet, fluffy bathrobes, and charming bathroom stocked with herbal toiletries. Though the rooms are fabulous, it's the amenities at Villa Royale that make you feel like royalty. Choose between two pools and one large Jacuzzi, book an in-room massage, or ask the concierge to help you get a tee time or a tennis court at one of the famed local golf courses or country clubs. Every morning you'll awaken to a full, hot, cooked-to-order breakfast, which can be served in your room. For lunch and dinner, enjoy the Continental cuisine served by the attached restaurant Europa, or have them bring the food to you in your room or out at poolside.

## Gay and Lesbian Resorts

Among the dozens of resort hotels and inns catering to gay men, **The Triangle Inn** (555 E. San Lorenzo Rd., 760/322-7993, www.pridenation.com/triangle, $135–560) stands out for a number of reasons. The Triangle was the first commercial design of one Hugh Kaptur, the architect who went on to do much important mid-century modern work in and around Palm Springs, including William Holden's home. The unique structures and interesting lines have been preserved, making the lushly landscaped buildings fun to look at for passersby outside the compound. Inside, each of the nine guest suites has a unique decorative scheme.

You can rent anything from a studio suite up to a fully furnished four-bedroom house. Out at the pool, in the hot tub, under the cooling misters, and in the other common areas of the Triangle, clothing is optional. Hosts Michael and Stephen live at the resort and their talent as hosts helps make the Triangle what it is today. Oh, and be sure to pet Duncan, the orange tabby cat who runs the place, when you see him prowling the grounds.

A larger oasis for gay men, the **Vista Grande Resorts** (574 S. Warm Sands Dr., 760/322-2404, www.mirage4men.com, $100–325) sits in the popular Warm Sands area. This hedonistic clothing-optional resort offers 30-some guest rooms, three pools, three spas, and a steam room. The pool-and-spa complex in the Mirage section of the three-resort complex has two waterfalls, curved naturalistic pools, and lots of foliage and rocks surrounding the swimmable waters. Rooms range from an economical studio room to a luxurious suite by the waterfall with a living room and a full kitchen. All amenities are taken care of, so kick back, relax by (or in) the pool, and concentrate on making new friends.

For the ladies, the **Queen of Hearts** (435 E. Avenida Olancha, 760/322-5793, www.queenofheartsps.com, $120–180) provides laid-back elegance for reasonable nightly rates. This recently renovated nine-room inn was the first lesbian-oriented hotel to be opened in Palm Springs nearly 40 years ago (then called the Desert Knight). Today, each room includes lovely light designer appointments, a queen bed, a full kitchen, and a comfortable bathroom. Unlike the men's resorts, guests of the Queen of Hearts wear clothes in the common areas, including while swimming in the sparkling courtyard pool or soaking in the outdoor, above-ground whirlpool tub. While you don't need to be a gay woman or couple to stay at the Queen, this inn does cater to that crowd and you should expect to see happy female couples engaging in public displays of affection here. If you're among those couples, be sure to let management know if you're celebrating a birthday or anniversary!

## FOOD

The dining in Palm Springs exemplifies the best of California. You'll find high-end California and French cuisine, fun ethnic eateries, and tasty snack foods all through the area, though the greatest concentration of serious independent restaurants collects downtown, on and around Palm Canyon Drive.

### American

A favorite local downtown breakfast spot is **Billy Reed's** (1800 N. Palm Canyon Dr., 760/325-1946, daily 7 A.M.–9 P.M., $7–22). The interior dining room and bar have low lights and air conditioning, while the out-front patio offers plenty of seating and great people-watching. The casual atmosphere welcomes everyone all day long, though shoes and shirts are required. Expect the quality of service to depend a bit on the level of crowding. The extensive menu includes everything from classic omelets and giant cinnamon rolls for breakfast to every kind of salad and sandwich for lunch and on up to prime rib and salmon for dinner. Whatever you order, you'll get hearty portions of classic American food, perhaps with a tiny Mexican twist here and there. In all honesty, the food isn't the best you'll ever taste, but it's good enough, it's hot, and it's plentiful.

### Asian

Looking for a little Eastern flair with your dinner in the desert? Try **Wang's in the Desert** (424 S. Indian Canyon Dr., 760/325-9264, www.wangsinthedesert.com, $12–20). Friday evening happy hour tends to draw a big and mostly gay crowd, and likewise a group more interested in socializing than chowing down shows up to "Chill" on Sunday afternoons with a DJ spinning to help add to the atmosphere. But if you're looking for great Chinese food, you can find it here too. Take a seat on a banquette in the attractive gold and cream dining room and order from the distinctive menu. The dishes ring familiar, but Wang's puts its own stamp on the cuisine. You'll find unique appetizers and entrées that you won't taste anyplace else. Just be sure to get reservations at least a couple of days in advance, since Wang's gets crowded with locals at dinnertime, especially on weekends.

### French

When you turn sideways to thread your way into **Pomme Frite** (256 S. Palm Canyon Dr., 760/778-3727, www.pomme-frite.com, lunch Sat.–Sun. 11:30 A.M.–2:30 P.M., dinner Wed.–Mon. 4:30–10:30 P.M., $18–28), you might believe you've somehow been transported to France or even Belgium. This hole-in-the-wall does not pretend to serve haute cuisine; instead, Pomme Frite offers casual bistro dishes cooked to perfection. The food fits in perfectly with the atmosphere—sunny yellow walls, black-and-white prints, real wooden wine boxes, and other tchotchkes. Tables are scrunched so close together in the tiny front dining room that even the wait staff has trouble getting through. Though the back dining room's setup is a tiny bit more spacious, it's still loud and has a friendly, crowded feeling. On weekends, reservations are highly recommended, though they fit in as many walk-ins as they can.

The menu provides a look at both Paris brasserie favorites such as mussels and steak and fries, plus a few fun Belgian dishes. The fresh, delicate salads are delicious too, but as you eat, try to save just a little bit of room for the delectable desserts.

### Italian

Do you just want an ultra-casual pizza meal? Walk up to the counter at **Lotza Mozza Pizza & Pasta** (119 S. Indian Canyon Dr., 760/325-5571, $10) and order a handmade pizza, a tasty pasta dish, or a big crisp salad. Grab a seat at any of the red-checker-covered tables and the cute young wait staff will bring your food out to you. Pizzas have New York–style thin crusts, tasty tomato sauce, and gooey mozzarella cheese. While the service isn't always stellar, the price is right and the food does come out piping hot and tasty.

### Mexican

Among the best of the many Mexican restaurants throughout the Palm Springs region, the **Las Casuela** (368 N. Palm Canyon Dr., 760/325-3213, www.lascasuelas.com, Sun.–Thurs. 11 A.M.–9 P.M., Fri.–Sat. 11 A.M.–9:30 P.M., $10–12) group offers some of the best and most authentic Mexican cuisine. Las Casuela Original was the first of them, opened by the Delgado family in 1958 with the recipes Maria brought up from her home. The small dining room looks bigger because of the wall-length mirror along one side, which reflects the wonderful hand-painted mural on the opposite walls that depicts pastoral life in Mexico, complete with cows. The service feels as friendly as the restaurant sounds—if you have any food allergies or special requests, they'll be happy to accommodate you. The family opened Las Casuela Nuevas and **Las Casuela Terraza** (222 S. Palm Canyon Dr.), two bigger and slightly fancier versions of the original, still using Grandma's old recipes as the basis for their menus. Terraza boasts a beautiful outdoor patio seating area and some fabulous margaritas made with top-shelf tequilas.

### Steak

The restaurateurs of Palm Springs have opened a near-countless array of steakhouses. It's hard to go more than a mile or two without running into one. The king of the local chains is undoubtedly **LG's Prime Steakhouse** (255 S. Palm Canyon Dr., Ste. B, 760/416-1779, www.lgsprimesteakhouse.com, daily 5 P.M.–close, $25–55). All three of their restaurants (one in Palm Springs, one in Palm Desert, and one in La Quinta) offer the best beef available, much of it dry aged in specially designed meat lockers on the premises. The sides are steakhouse classics that complement the huge cuts of meat, but some of the appetizers are LG's originals. While the atmosphere at LG's has a splash of upscale elegance, you'll still see plenty of exposed brick and feel a touch of casual friendliness.

### Vegetarian

Desperately looking for a meat-free meal in steak-loving Palm Springs? Head downtown to **Native Foods** (1775 E. Palm Canyon Dr., Ste. F, 760/416-0070, www.nativefoods.com, Mon.–Sat. 11 A.M.–9:30 P.M., $8–15). This vegan restaurant offers a large menu of salads, sandwiches, soups, and hot food of all kinds, plus delicious desserts. You'll find some tasty seitan (a grain protein) faux meats and tempeh, as well as lots of bean dishes, veggie pizzas, and Middle Eastern–inspired cuisine. Native Foods even has a small kids' menu. This small SoCal chain also has a restaurant in Palm Desert (at 73–890 El Paseo Dr.) to satisfy the appetites of hungry vegan shoppers.

### Coffee and Tea

Okay, so it's a chain. At least it's a Southern California regional chain. Still, the **Coffee Bean and Tea Leaf** (100 N. Palm Canyon Dr., 760/325-9402, $5) at the corner of Palm Canyon Drive serves up tasty coffee in a pleasant local atmosphere. You can get your favorite espresso drink and a pastry, and sit either inside or out to enjoy a quick breakfast.

## INFORMATION AND SERVICES

Though it's the only one in the stark desert region, Palm Springs and its suburbs create a major urban center, and an affluent one at that. Expect to find all the goods and services you need and want someplace in or around Palm Springs.

### Tourist Information

For newcomers to Palm Springs, a good first stop is the **Palm Springs Visitors Center** (777 N. Palm Canyon Dr., 760/778-8415, www.palm-springs.org). Here you'll get everything you need to enjoy your visit to the area, including real opinions on local attractions and restaurants. The website can help you even before you arrive—use it to select an inn, print up maps, and get the low-down on the best events and parties while you're in town.

### Media and Communications

The local Palm Springs newspaper is ***The Desert Sun*** (www.mydesert.com). It's published daily and available at many local motels and restaurants, plus it's for sale at public newsstands and shops in all the various towns.

Cell phones work fine in Palm Springs, as do laptops with wireless Internet capability (though you'll often have to pay for the privilege to connect up).

All major American banks do business in Palm Springs, and you'll find a plethora of ATMs ready to help you access (and ultimately spend) your cash. Palm Springs and its satellite towns also have full-service **post offices**—at least one per town. The Palm Springs branch sits at 333 East Amado Road.

### Medical Services

In a town full of retirees, medical care is easy to come by. If you need an emergency room, you'll definitely find one. Right in downtown Palm Springs, you can head for the **Desert Regional Medical Center** (1150 N. Indian Canyon Dr., 760/323-6511, www.desertmedctr.com), which provides both emergency and trauma care services. On the other hand, if you're looking for a plastic surgeon, the phone book can hook you up. I can't.

## GETTING THERE AND AROUND

### Air

The **Palm Springs International Airport** (3400 E. Tahquitz Canyon Way, 760/318-3800, www.palmspringsairport.com) offers flights with most major carriers and a few minor airlines. It is the only commercial airport in the region—if you can't fly into or out of here, you'll be driving in from the Los Angeles Basin. While the weather in Palm Springs is usually fabulous, when it gets bad it can shut down the whole airport, so keep that in the back of your mind when you plan your wintertime flights.

### Bus

The **SunLine Transit Agency** (800/347-8628, www.sunline.org, adults $1, seniors $0.50) runs a number of bus lines throughout the Palm Springs region, running from Desert Hot Springs down through Palm Springs proper, into Indio and all the way down to Coachella and Thermal. Check out the route map online.

### Car

Palm Canyon Drive is the main drag through downtown Palm Springs. Then it takes off and connects the back sides of all the other towns, from Palm Desert down to Indio. While it might sound like it, this drive isn't all that attractive unless you're really into strip malls and chain stores. There's little scenery otherwise.

If you're driving in from Los Angeles, I-10 is the most direct route east. I-10 runs through Palm Springs and down through Indio, out east past the south entrance of Joshua Tree.

### Tours

If you love to go touring, you can find a variety of different styles and modes of transit in Palm Springs tours, self-guided or prepackaged. **Celebrity Tours** (760/770-2700, www.celebrity-tours.com, adults $35, children $14) offers two short city tours that focus on the (surprise) celebrity residents and their homes in the town of Palm Springs and in the connecting cities beyond. A luxury bus brings visitors to the homes of Bob Hope and Celine Dion, to the date farms at the edge of the urban center, then back to the Old Movie Colony of Palm Springs proper. You can also check out Celebrity's day trip tours into Los Angeles, Las Vegas, and other spots in the region.

The discerning boonie-crasher can check into **Adventure Hummer Tours** (760/285-0876, www.adventurehummer.com, adults $110–160, children $70–90). You'll board a militaristic H-1 Hummer for your open-air adventure out into the desert canyons beyond the city. Whether you want to see the remote off-road regions of Joshua Tree or check out the legendary earthquake-producing San Andreas Fault or both, Adventure Hummer can take you there.

If you prefer wait till after dark to head outside, check out **Sky Watcher Tours** (73–091 Country Club Dr., Ste. A42, Palm Desert, 760/831-0231, www.sky-watcher.com). You'll get an educational and entertaining tour of the night sky over the deserts surrounding Palm Springs that's perfect for kids and adults, plus fun takeaway sheets to help you identify constellations wherever (in the Northern Hemisphere) you are.

# Joshua Tree

Joshua Tree National Monument and its namesake "trees" lies just east of Palm Springs and offers easy access from the Los Angeles area. The northern half of the park sits in the high-altitude Mojave Desert. But as the park's lands stretch south, they also dip down into the lower-set Colorado Desert. It's actually not too hard to see where the landscape starts to change; Joshua trees become fewer and fewer, while ocotillos and teddy bear cacti start to pop up in their place. Even the dust-dry ground changes in color and character, with the characteristic light tan boulders of the north country giving way to a darker gray ground in the south. While many visitors stick exclusively to the north end of the park, it's worth the time to drive the main park road south to check out a really different desert region.

## SIGHTS

### Oasis of Mara

The best known and best visited oasis in Joshua Tree is undoubtedly the well-developed Oasis of Mara (Hwy. 62 and Utah Trail). A number of small springs well out of the ground along the Pinto Mountain fault here, providing the life-giving water that supports a large and lush (well, lush for the Mojave Desert) ecosystem. The earliest known residents of the Oasis were the Serrano people, who planted a new palm tree each time a boy was born, then used the products of those palm trees for tools,

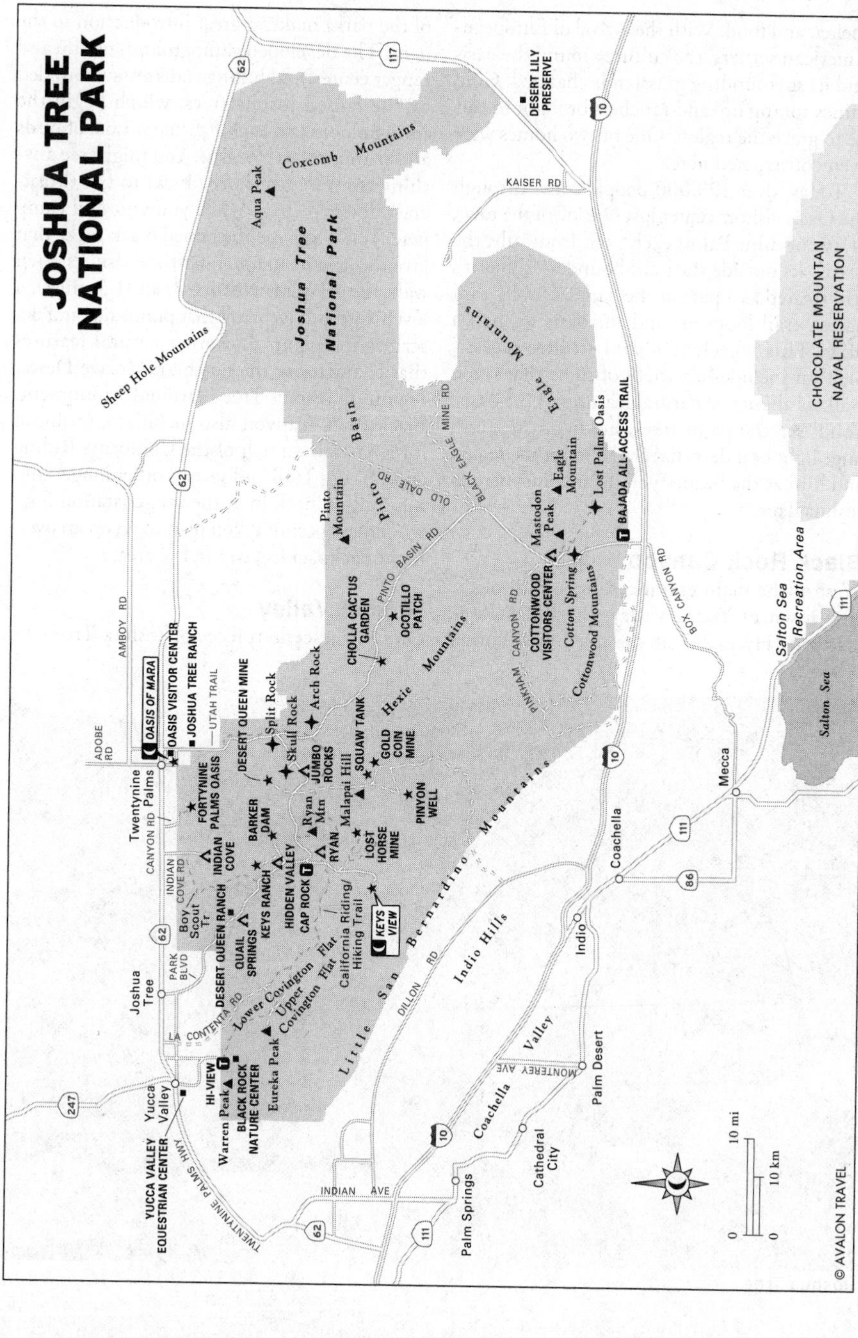
JOSHUA TREE NATIONAL PARK
Joshua Tree National Park
Sheep Hole Mountains
Coxcomb Mountains
Aqua Peak
DESERT LILY PRESERVE
KAISER RD
Eagle Mountains
CHOCOLATE MOUNTAIN NAVAL RESERVATION
BLACK EAGLE MINE RD
OLD DALE RD
Pinto Basin
Pinto Mountain
PINTO BASIN RD
BAJADA ALL-ACCESS TRAIL
Lost Palms Oasis
Eagle Mountain
Mastodon Peak
COTTONWOOD VISITORS CENTER
Cotton Spring
Cottonwood Mountains
PINKHAM CANYON RD
BOX CANYON RD
Salton Sea Recreation Area
Salton Sea
Mecca
Coachella
Indio
AMBOY RD
OASIS OF MARA
OASIS VISITOR CENTER
JOSHUA TREE RANCH
UTAH TRAIL
ADOBE RD
Twentynine Palms
CANYON RD
DESERT QUEEN MINE
Split Rock
Skull Rock
Arch Rock
CHOLLA CACTUS GARDEN
OCOTILLO PATCH
Hexie Mountains
SQUAW TANK
GOLD COIN MINE
JUMBO ROCKS
Ryan Mtn
Malapai Hill
PINYON WELL
FORTYNINE PALMS OASIS
BARKER DAM
INDIAN COVE
INDIAN COVE RD
RYAN
LOST HORSE MINE
KEYS RANCH
HIDDEN VALLEY
CAP ROCK
KEYS VIEW
California Riding/Hiking Trail
Boy Scout Tr
DESERT QUEEN RANCH
QUAIL SPRINGS
PARK BLVD
Joshua Tree
LA CONTENTA RD
Lower Covington Flat
Upper Covington Flat
Eureka Peak
Little San Bernardino Mountains
DILLON RD
Indio Hills
HI-VIEW
Warren Peak
BLACK ROCK NATURE CENTER
Yucca Valley
YUCCA VALLEY EQUESTRIAN CENTER
TWENTYNINE PALMS HWY
Coachella Valley
MONTEREY AVE
Palm Desert
Cathedral City
Palm Springs
INDIAN AVE
0 10 mi
0 10 km
© AVALON TRAVEL

shelter, and food. With the arrival of European-American settlers, the culture around the oasis and its surrounding grasslands changed. Gold mines sprang up, and ranchers brought in cattle to graze the region. One or two homes were even constructed here.

Today, over 100,000 people come through the Oasis visitors center just outside of the town of Twentynine Palms each year. Ironically, the Oasis sits outside the park boundaries, but it's still treated as a part of the park. A lovely easy nature trail loops around the oasis for half a mile. This wheelchair- and stroller-accessible trail includes a variety of signs that teach walkers about the natural features of the oasis. You'll see the palm trees, hardy grasses, and huge light boulders that characterize the region and hint at the beauty you'll find elsewhere in Joshua Tree.

## Black Rock Canyon

West of the main entrances, just south of the tiny town of Yucca Valley, the Black Rock Canyon (Hwy. 247 at the northwest corner of the park) makes a great introduction to the park. The developed campground, nature and ranger center, and hiking trails are surrounded by the famed Joshua trees, which begin the spring bloom late each February. Lots of birds and mammals live nearby. You might see anything from a great horned owl to the threatened desert tortoise while you visit and camp here. You'll also see the famed black rocks that give the area its name. First-time visitors often walk the **Hi-View Nature Trail** (1.3 miles), a lovely interpretive stroll that points out and describes the plants and other natural features that characterize the northern Mojave Desert region of Joshua Tree National Monument. Black Rock Canyon also includes a trailhead for a 35-mile stretch of the California Riding and Hiking Trail and several other longer hiking trails. Check in at the ranger station for a wilderness permit if you plan to go on an overnight backpacking trip in the area.

## Hidden Valley

One of the centerpieces of Joshua Tree, the

© LANCE SCOTT

Joshua Tree

Hidden Valley (Park Blvd., 10 miles south of West Entrance) offers hikes, a nature trail, a campground, and a rare view of a tiny desert valley. If you're day-tripping in Joshua Tree, park in the day lot and follow the tourists off to the right to the sort-of trail onto and through the big tan boulders. You'll scramble up, getting a great up-close view of the surprising granite mineral content of the pale boulders on either side of you. Emerge from the rocky trail into a small rocky meadowlike area, which includes small signs describing the natural features. Keep walking across the clearing and on to the next miniature pass.

### Cap Rock and Skull Rock

Among the wonders of Joshua Tree are the fabulous boulder formations scattered about the landscape. As you drive or hike, especially in the northern reaches, you'll have a hard time missing at least a few of these great light orangeish-tan rocks. Sit and stare at them, thinking up different common animals and other things that the boulders and clusters resemble—kind of like cloud gazing, but without the movement.

Two rocks that are fairly close together by the road so resemble other objects that they're named and marked on park maps. If you take the east–west connecting road from Pinto Basin Road (the main north–south corridor) to the road to Keys View and Hidden Valley, you'll first pass Skull Rock (Park Blvd., seven miles east of Hidden Valley), one of the many giant stones that provide shade at the aptly named Jumbo Rocks campground. Guess what this rock is shaped like? Just past the intersection towards Hidden Valley, Cap Rock and its buddies offer interesting geology, a small picnic area, and a good spot for rock climbers to dig in and start scrambling.

### Keys Ranch

The only way to get a real look at Keys Ranch (Keys Ranch Rd., Oct.–May Sat.–Sun. 10 A.M. and 1 P.M., adults $5, children $2.50) is to take a docent-guided tour of the buildings and land. William and Frances Keys were among the rugged settlers of the Mojave Desert. They ranched on the sparse desert grasses and raised five children on this patch that would become part of Joshua Tree. Today, visitors see the weathered pine buildings that housed the original ranch house, the schoolhouse that educated the few local children, the local general store, and a workshop. The orchard and landscaping have been replanted and revived. A collection of mining and farm equipment sits in the dry desert air, and relics like the old well dot the property here.

To get to Keys Ranch, drive half a mile north of the Hidden Valley campground, then turn off onto a bumpy one-lane dirt road (passenger cars okay) that runs for about a mile. Park near the gate and meet your tour guide just inside the property. Buying tickets in advance (you can call ahead and use a credit card) is recommended, especially on holiday weekends. If you're feeling lucky, you can just head up to the gate and ask the ranger if any spots are available on the next tour. Check the ranger schedule for weekday tours throughout the year.

### Keys View

One of the best views in all of Joshua Tree is the Keys View (end of Keys View Rd., bear right off Park Blvd. past Cap Rock). On a clear day, the view from here redefines the concept of "panoramic," letting travelers see the whole of the Palm Springs urban sprawl, the Coachella Valley farmland, the notorious San Andreas fault, and even the Salton Sea many miles to the southeast. You'll drive all the way to the end of the road out of the West Ranger Station, up to about 5,000 feet elevation and the sizeable parking lot. Get out of your car and climb a brief paved trail to the vantage point at the top of the ridge.

Sadly, crystal clear days are hard to come by. Not only is the ever-expanding Palm Springs cityscape polluting its valley, a pass to the west and prevailing winds often blow smog into the region from the Los Angeles Basin. The best time to catch a good view at Keys is the early morning, and the best way to help make the views better is to read the signs up on the path and do what you can to decrease your own emissions. Sure, you're only one person, but imagine what the mid-afternoon would look like at Keys View if even two out of three people did *only one person's* worth of responsible pollution reduction?

### Cottonwood Spring Oasis

The Cottonwood Spring Oasis (Box Canyon Rd., turn onto spur road at visitors center) gets fewer visitors than many of the northern park sights, but it's one of the most beautiful oases in Joshua Tree. The catch? No Joshua trees, because Cottonwood sits at the transitional area between the Mojave and Colorado Deserts. Instead, at the oasis you'll see a fabulous grove of desert fan palms, which are native to California. The thick growth of flora and fauna at this oasis is fed by Cottonwood Spring, a naturally occurring spring caused by the seismic activity in the region. (Caution: Do not drink the spring water! It's not potable.) The Cahuilla Native Americans used the spring water for washing, cooking, and more. They also hunted and gathered from the abundant natural resources here. You can still see

## WHAT IS A JOSHUA TREE?

You'll see them everywhere in the north end of Joshua Tree National Park, and indeed they're common throughout much of the Mojave Desert. They do look almost like deciduous trees from a distance, and up close their foliage and "bark" looks like nothing else most folks have ever seen – spiky and scaly, green and brown and odd, with funky creamy greenish flowers every once in a while. It's definitely not a "regular" tree, but it doesn't look much like a cactus species either.

So what is a Joshua tree?

Desert botanists will probably figure out on their own that Joshua trees are members of the yucca family. Specifically, Joshua trees are *Yucca brevifolia* – a type of yucca that grows almost exclusively in the high-altitude (2,000-6,000 feet) Mojave Desert ecosystem. Though the trees can be delicate – they've got a shallow root system and all those branches get heavy – Joshua trees can live up to a thousand years.

If you get to see the Joshua trees bloom, you're lucky! They don't bloom every spring; it happens only when enough rain falls at the right time, and after the tree has experienced at least one hard freeze. Once they bloom, specially adapted yucca moths fertilize the flowers by laying eggs in them. This spreads pollen, and the blossoms turn into a greenish-brown fruit filled with seeds. The fruit drops, the seeds spread out on the ground and sprout, and new Joshua trees begin to grow.

You'll see other types of yucca plants throughout California, even in unlikely spots such as the Big Sur coast. Most of the common yuccas grow wider and closer to the ground than Joshua trees, and have much longer dagger-like leaves. Once you study their shape and the way the leaves grow, then the family resemblance becomes clear.

© LANCE SCOTT

evidence of their presence in left-behind artifacts. You'll also find the remains of more recent use of the spring: primitive, hand-built gold milling equipment left over from several 19th- and early 20th-century gold mills.

In the early springtime, the Cottonwood area leads the park's beautiful wildflower bloom with colorful desert dandelions, lupine, and others. Check in February for the first flowers. Any number of hiking trails encircle the area, perfect for day trips, and a campground offers rare shady spots with the sound of trickling water to lull you to sleep at night.

## SPORTS AND RECREATION

Even more than the other California deserts, Joshua Tree invites outdoor sports enthusiast of all kinds into its wilderness to take advantage of the beauty and challenge of the diverse region. Whether you're a leave-no-trace backcountry backpacker, a hardcore climber, or a Jeep-driving boonie-crasher, you'll find your bliss here.

### Hiking

Dozens of great hikes crisscross the length and breadth of Joshua Tree. Though many of these start in or near the visitors centers and developed campgrounds, don't neglect the trails that begin off the paved and unpaved roads of the park.

Before you begin a hike here—even a short two or three mile jaunt—be sure you're properly prepared. It's not as dry as Death Valley, but Joshua Tree National Monument is still a harsh and unforgiving desert. Bring lots of water (up to a gallon per person). For longer hikes, pack more water, food, and a first-aid kit. Talk to the rangers about safety, climate, and what to bring on a long day or multi-day backcountry adventure.

A number of trails start at the Black Rock Canyon campground. In addition to the **Hi-View Nature Trail,** many longer hikes begin here. To get to the summit of **Eureka Peak** (approx. 12 miles round-trip, difficult), first take the Burnt Hill Trail south to connect to the Eureka Peak Trail. You'll ascend 1,500 feet on this all-day trek up to some of the most beautiful views in the whole park. Another option is the **Panorama Loop** (approx. 12 miles round-trip, difficult). Be sure to bring your camera!

Down south, the Cottonwood Spring area offers everything from quarter-mile nature walks to multi-mile intense hikes. If you're more into cactus than quadriceps strain, try the **Cholla Cactus Garden** (0.25 mile, easy). It's definitely worth it to spend the $0.50 on the descriptive pamphlet that will give you a greater understanding of the "jumping" cholla catci and the rest of the surrounding ecosystem. Look for the desert wood rats and cactus wrens that feed here, but be sure not to touch the pretty but vicious teddy bear cholla—the nasty little needles seem to jump off the cactus to bury themselves in unsuspecting hands.

Farther south, only half a mile from the park gate, the **Bajada All-Access Trail** (0.25 mile, easy) offers great views of the myriad plants that populate the Colorado Desert climate. As implied by the name, this nature trail is wheelchair-accessible.

For a longer and tougher hike, climb **Mastodon Peak** (3 miles round-trip, difficult). This steep hike takes you back up above 3,000 feet, where you'll take in views of Eagle Mountain and out to the Salton Sea. Check out the Mastodon Mind and the Winona Mill on your way. One of the longest and most rewarding hikes in this region takes you out to the **Lost Palms Oasis** (8 miles round-trip, difficult). Here grows the largest grove of fan palms in Joshua Tree, fed by natural year-round pools of fresh water.

### Rock Climbing

Joshua Tree is one of the finest rock climbing parks in the United States, indeed in the world. Whether you're into bouldering or climbing, you'll find a plethora of climbing areas and routes here. The good climbing regions are almost all found in the northern reaches—the Mojave area, which is filled with granite canyons and fantastical boulder formations. Even the most dedicated of climbers can't chip the surface of Joshua Tree in just

© LIZ HAMILL SCOTT

climbing Cap Rock

one trip, which is why many come back to the park year after year.

If you need equipment and supplies, the small towns along the north border of Joshua Tree support a number of climbing outfitters. Curious newcomers can even arrange guided climbs and climbing lessons through these companies. Obviously, **Joshua Tree Rock Climbing School** (760/366-4745, www.joshuatreerockclimbing.com, $120/one-day session) is prominent among these outfits. From one-day beginning seminars that teach the fundamentals of rock climbing up through four-day intensive sessions and lead climbing classes that take newbies up to the intermediate level in only half a week, this school offers a wonderful opportunity for aspiring climbers to start building their skills.

More than a dozen climbing spots surround the Indian Cove Campground. A tangle of paved roads service the area, and a large parking lot provides easy access to the boulders and cliff faces. Test your skills against Dos Equis Wall or Apparition Rock to the west, or Upper and Lower Dodge City to the south of the central camping area.

The climbing areas associated with the Hidden Valley are more spread out, but there are more of them and several of these range out into the wilderness area of the park. Near the parking area and campground you'll find The Real Hidden Valley Area, Cyclops, Echo Cove, and a number of others. Out to the northeast, you can hike or drive a dirt road out to Willow Hole to climb the Fortress, Super Dome, or Valley of Kings.

Between the Sheep Pass and Ryan campgrounds, several parking lots make it easy to stage climbs at Cap Rock, Hall of Horrors, and Love Nest. Other good places to stage climbs include the rough roads of the Geology Tour, the Queens Valley, and Split Rock.

Do be aware that strict rules govern climbing at Joshua Tree, and climbers are responsible for knowing those rules before they start up any boulders or steep faces. Be sure to check the park website or stop in at the ranger station to pick up a copy of those rules and the Fixed

Anchor Checklist. The website also offers topographical maps of the major climbing areas.

## Horseback Riding

Several trails at Joshua Tree are open to equestrians as well as hikers. You can bring your own horse and ride the trails solo, or arrange with one of the local ranches to take a guided ride of the park and the area that surrounds it.

**Joshua Tree Ranch** (Park Blvd. Mile 2.9, 760/366-2788, www.joshuatreeranch.com, $65–125) offers easy rides on its own land just north of Joshua Tree, and moderately challenging rides into the park. You can also work with the ranch to create your own private ride for a higher fee. This ranch takes its horses and its riding quite seriously, so consider your real riding ability level and that of your companions and family before booking a ride with them. Reservations for all rides are required, but rides are available most days with enough advance warning.

A full-service equestrian center, the **Yucca Valley Equestrian Center** (7429 Avalon Ave., Yucca Valley, 760/365-4433, www.yuccavalleyequestriancenter.com, $35/hour) leads easy rides across flat desert lands of Joshua Tree as well as more challenging rides through narrow canyons and up steep hills. While the standard trail tack is Western, you can request an English saddle when you reserve your ride.

If you'd rather strike out on your own, the most popular riding trail in Joshua Tree is the **California Riding and Hiking Trail.** This 35-mile section of what is actually a statewide trail has many access points throughout the north end of the park. Its park boundaries are the Black Rock Canyon campground (which includes a horse camp) in the west and the North Entrance Station to the east. You can see many of the most beautiful areas of Joshua Tree while riding this trail, many of which are not directly accessible by road. Ride through forests of Joshua trees and past amazing and rarely seen rock formations. You can do a two-day ride on this trail, stopping at the Ryan campground, which includes horse facilities, near the middle of the trail's length.

The 16-mile **Boy Scout Trail** also permits equestrian traffic. Running roughly from Indian Cove to Hidden Valley, it offers another scenic view of northern Joshua Tree for hikers and riders alike.

## Off-Roading

Unlike many of California's wilderness parks, Joshua Tree welcomes off-road vehicles and provides more than half a dozen backcountry roads for four-wheel drives to bump out to explore otherwise inaccessible parts of the park. (Mountain bikes are also allowed on these roads, so keep a lookout while driving out there.)

One of the most popular backcountry roads is **Geology Tour Road** (Geology Tour Rd. and Park Blvd.). Pick up a printed road guide at the start of the road so you'll know about each of the 16 major geological (and other landscape) features you're looking at when you stop at them. In truth, during good years regular passenger cars (but not trailers and motor homes) can make part of this tour, from the turn off the main road to the Squaw Tank.

**Queen Valley Roads** are a network of smallish roads running for a total of about 13 miles. You'll get to see plenty of big granite boulders and Joshua trees as you bump along out here on the other side of the paved road from Hidden Valley. This makes a great mountain biking trek if you prefer to travel under your own steam.

In the south, several great roads offer a fun crash through the boonies of the Colorado Desert region of the park. The **Black Eagle Mine Road** (six miles north of Cottonwood visitors center) offers nine miles of scenic canyon vistas within the park boundaries, and BLM road and driveable side trails beyond. Outside of the park on the side roads, you'll come upon abandoned mines and old homesteads—beware of the dangerous and unstable mine shafts and equipment if you find them. Leading from the same cutoff, the **Old Dale Road** runs 23 miles through the Pinto Basin dry lakebed and up a steep mountain, then out of the park. More unstable mines and abandoned homes greet you once you cross the park boundary.

## MOJAVE DESERT NATIONAL PRESERVE

California's Mojave Desert stretches for endless miles across the state. For the best views of the unique climate, formations, and ecosystem of this famous desert, visit the Mojave National Preserve (located btwn. I-15 and I-40, www.nps.gov, free). The Mojave is vast so don't expect to see all of the desert in one trip, even if you've got a whole week to spend. Pick your drives, hikes, and attractions carefully in order to see the Joshua Trees, caverns, cinder cones, and abandoned mines that most appeal to your interests.

The **Mojave Scenic Drive** is an easy day trip from Twentynine Palms or even Palm Springs. If you've only got one day, the best (and easiest) introduction to the Preserve is at the northern edge of the park along the smooth, well-kept pavement of I-15. From the town of Baker, turn south off I-15 onto Kelbaker Road for the 35-mile drive to Kelso. You'll traverse an alien landscape composed of volcanic activity, part of the Cinder Cones National Natural Landmark. Stop in Kelso to explore the fabulous visitors center. The Spanish Revival facade of the **Kelso Depot Visitor Center** (Kelbaker Rd., Kelso, 760/252-6108, daily 9 A.M.–5 P.M.) welcomes travelers from all over the world. The visitor center once held the all-important Kelso Depot, which served the railroad that supported the many desert mining camps. The original structure has been renovated to include exhibits on the desert landscape and natural history, historically furnished dorm rooms, and a restored lunch counter. An abundance of park rangers are on hand with advice on yearly road conditions. (Not all roads are passable in standard cars each year. Be sure to ask here or at one of the other visitors centers about passable roads before striking out on your own.)

Snap a few photos of the Kelso Dunes along the horizon before climbing back into your car to turn onto Kelso-Cima Road. The road follows the Union Pacific rail line along the edge

If you're looking for a more serious adventure, the **Pinkham Canyon-Thermal Canyon Roads** is advised only for hardcore booniecrashers who know what they're doing and carry proper emergency supplies.

### Mountain Biking

As of this book's publication, the only mountain biking allowed in Joshua Tree is along the backcountry roads shared with off-road vehicles. Check with the rangers at any of the visitors centers to learn whether 29 miles of designated mountain biking trails have opened by the time of your visit.

## CAMPING

Many of the outdoors-loving visitors to Joshua Tree prefer to sleep out under the brilliantly glittering stars. If that's you, you've got your choice of mostly first-come campgrounds with tent and RV sites and at least basic facilities, and backcountry rough camping.

If you plan to backpack out into the wilderness, you must register on one of the backcountry boards or get a permit at one of the ranger stations. Most of the major drive-in campsites have backcountry boards (bulletin boards where you can sign up and indicate your general planned route and destination.

At all the developed campgrounds, you must observe quiet hours, generator use restrictions, and deal with the lack of showers. In fact, only a few campgrounds offer any water at all. If you bring a solar shower, take care! The sun in this area can quickly give you a near-boiling shower experience.

The **Black Rock** (Black Rock Canyon, reservations Sept.–May 877/444-6777, $15) campground is one of the biggest and most developed in Joshua Tree. With 100 sites, running potable water, and full bathroom facilities, Black Rock offers a semblance of comfort in the harsh desert. Some spots take RVs, and the site has a dump station. Black Rock is one of the two park facilities where equestrians can camp with their horses.

of the Providence Mountains to the town of Cima, where you'll find snacks and drinks (but no gas). Cima also serves as a convenient fork; if you're in a hurry to get back to I-15, staying left on Cima Road will get you there the quickest. The right fork, **Morning Star Mine Road,** offers a more interesting route, including a turnoff to the abandoned mine that gives the road its name. From the mine, turn left onto Ivanpah Road and continue to Nipton Road to return to the freeway.

This drive takes about 90 minutes without stops, but feel free to hike the many great desert trails, photograph the Joshua Trees or the blossoming spring wildflowers, and explore (safely) an abandoned mine.

Planning to spend a weekend or longer exploring Mojave? For a total immersion into the desert world, spend your nights in one of the park's many campgrounds. **Hole-in-the Wall** campground is accessible from the Kelso-Cima Road and has toilet facilities, potable water, and an RV dump station. If your primary goal is to explore Mitchell Caverns, Hole-in-the-Wall's 37 campsites are closest to this major attraction.

Not too far from Hole-in-the-Wall, **Mid Hills** campground also has bathrooms, water, picnic tables, and fire rings for its 26 available sites. Like Hole-in-the-Wall, no reservations are accepted – all sites are first-come, first-served, so get there early during spring wildflower season. If you've come to Mojave to ride your horse through the beautiful and varied desert, make a reservation at the **Black Canyon** equestrian and group campground ($12, reservations 760/928-2572).

Want to camp all on your own, with no other campers nearby? Mojave has a number of existing roadside campsites that have sheltered independent desert-lovers for years. Just be sure to use an already existing site; look for stone fire rings and pre-disturbed earth to avoid further disturbing the fragile desert ecosystem.

The other horse-friendly campground is **Ryan** (Park Blvd. south of Hidden Valley, first-come, first-served, $10), which has more primitive facilities and fewer sites. Expect pit toilets and no available drinking or washing water here. Each site has a grate for cooking and campfires, and a picnic table.

Two other popular campgrounds, **Hidden Valley** (Park Blvd. south of West Entrance, first-come, first-served, $10) and **Jumbo Rocks** (Park Blvd. east of Geology Tour Rd., first-come, first-served, $10), sit near the center of the most traveled areas of the park. Both are primitive, with pit toilets and no water, but Jumbo Rocks has over 100 sites in great locations. Many of these sites sit beneath the shelter of boulders, a natural and historic way to camp. Both of these campgrounds are first-come, first-served. At Hidden Valley, RVs must be 25 feet or less.

**Indian Cove** (Indian Cove Rd. south of Entrance Station, reservations Sept.–May 877/444-6777, $15) offers over 100 campsites along the north park boundary in a location convenient to the small towns just north of Joshua Tree. While there's no water on-site, it's easy to come by at Joshua Tree and Twentynine Palms—and you can even get a hot meal in the evenings with only a short drive back to your tent! The Indian Cove area offers a half-mile nature trail for tourists who want to check out the local wildlife and traces of seasonal Native American settlements.

In the south of the park, **Cottonwood** (CA-195 at the Cottonwood Visitors Center, first-come, first-served, $15) offers water and flush toilets, as well as a dump station for RVs. The nearby visitors center offers a few basic supplies, and some of the loveliest hikes and wildflower viewings start in this region.

## ACCOMMODATIONS

If you're looking for luxury in your accommodations, you'll need to stay in Palm Springs and day-trip in to Joshua Tree. A few town motels offer plain but clean and comfortable indoor beds just outside of the northern park boundary. Inside the park, your choices are campgrounds with flush toilets, campgrounds without flush toilets, and backcountry hike-to-it and do-it-yourself camping.

Most of the motel rooms adjacent to Joshua Tree lie in the town of Twentynine Palms. You'll find the usual array of national chains, plus a few independents vying for your business.

## Under $100

Any U2 fans who've come to Joshua Tree to pay homage simply must stay at the **Harmony Hotel** (71161 29 Palms Hwy., 760/367-3351, www.harmonymotel.com, $77–95). This is where the band stayed when they were hard at work on the album named for the National Monument. It's a small, casual motel with only eight rooms total. The guest rooms have been recently remodeled, and you'll find white and light-patterned linens, cute sitting and dining areas in the larger rooms, and original artwork in each room. Pick a room with a king or two double beds, request one of the rooms with a kitchenette, or make yourself a pot of coffee in the guests' kitchenette/break room. Be sure to take a break in either the piping-hot outdoor spa in the evening or the deliberately unheated pool in the heat of the summer's day. For a quick break from the natural wonders, take in the artwork that surrounds the inn.

## $100–150

**Sunnyvale Garden Suites Hotel** (73843 Sunnyvale Dr., Twentynine Palms, 760/361-3939, www.sunnyvalesuites.com, $100–190) is perfectly located downtown, but off the noisy highway, in Twentynine Palms. Don't let the rugged exterior with its Western-style weathered pine boards fool you—the interiors feature comfortable modern amenities. All rooms have vintage tubular brass-style or wooden bedsteads, simple and soothingly colored linens and curtains, and plenty of space. Rooms sleep 2–6 people, and some have full kitchens. Outside of the guest room, enjoy the fitness center and the large outdoor spa, or take a walk in the climate-appropriate desert garden that surrounds the property. Bring the kids out to the playground in the cool mornings and evenings to burn off some energy, or just take a family stroll around the residential neighborhood of Twentynine Palms.

A favorite with repeat visitors, the **Circle C Lodge** (6340 El Ray Ave., Twentynine Palms, 760/367-7615, www.circleclodge.com, $135–150) offers lovely accommodations away from the noisy center of town and out in the desert. Choose from a guest room with a king bed or two queens; each room has its own well-equipped kitchenette (all the kitchen lacks is an oven). Light, floral decor with colorful blue and red accents and TVs with VCRs (but no DVD players just yet) make the oversized rooms pleasant and homey. Each morning head down to the courtyard for a complimentary bagel with fresh fruit, juice, and coffee. The sparkling pool and cute circular shaded spa invite visitors to relax after a dusty day of hiking at Joshua Tree.

## $150–250

**Roughley Manor** (74744 Joe Davis Dr., Twentynine Palms, 760/367-3238, www.roughleymanor.com, $150–185) seems to be poorly named; this lovely B&B is anything but rough, inside or out. Once the homestead of a young couple named Campbell who dreamed of ranching in the desert, the inn now welcomes guests all year long. With a dozen rooms, two in the lovely stone-clad main house and the rest in a handful of other buildings scattered throughout the large garden property, Roughley offers more space and better privacy than most similar inns. Each individually decorated guest room uses floral themes as they should be used—sparingly—to create the sense of a guest suite in a private elegant farmhouse. Many of the suites have kitchenettes and dining areas to create an additional sense of staying at home rather than at an impersonal motel. The prices are amazingly cheap if you're accustomed to the B&Bs of the big cities and Wine Country, and the location is perfect for sojourns out into Joshua Tree.

# FOOD

There's no food inside Joshua Tree National Park. Picnickers and campers must pack in every bite of food they intend to eat. The only visitors centers that maintain snack bars reside just outside the park boundaries.

Multi-night campers sometimes long for a hot meal served by someone else at a clean table. If that's what you need, you can drive into Twentynine Palms or even Palm Springs for a tasty meal.

### Restaurants

The most talked-about eatery adjacent to Joshua Tree is the **Crossroads Cafe & Tavern** (61715 29 Palms Hwy., Joshua Tree, 760/366-5414, www.crossroadscafeandtavern.com, Sun.–Tues. 6:30 A.M.–8 P.M. Thurs.–Sat. 6:30 A.M.–9 P.M., $5–10). It sure doesn't look like much from the outside, with its rusted aluminum siding and bright blue painted trim. But it's what's inside that counts, and inside the Crossroads you'll find friendly owners running their own place with the assistance of a tiny tribe of well-trained employees. The food is as unpretentious and tasty as the owners. At breakfast you can get an array of egg dishes, while lunch and dinner run to salads and sandwiches. The price is right at the Crossroads, so you won't break the bank for a reasonably health conscious meal here. Plenty of vegetarian options dot the menu, though carnivores aren't left out either.

Longing for a gooey slice of pizza or a big ol' hearty sub? Try **Sam's Pizza** (61380 29 Palms Hwy., Joshua Tree, 760/366-9511, www.samspizza.com, Mon.–Thurs. 11 A.M.–8 P.M., Fri.–Sat. 11 A.M.–7 P.M., Sun. 3–8 P.M., $5–20). The big menu features an array of reasonably priced Italian and American dishes that are perfect after a long day of hiking or climbing. Create your own pizza, or go for a classic hot meatball sub. If you're planning a late afternoon in the park, order cold subs and have them wrapped up to go. Specialties include calzones, paninis, and even a few Greek dishes beckon, while full-sized dinners appeal to seriously hungry diners.

Decent and inexpensive Mexican cuisine in the Joshua Tree desert region is served at **Santana's Mexican Food** (73680 Sun Valley Dr., Twentynine Palms, 760/361-0202, open daily, $5–10). Grab a burrito, a couple of tacos, or even a combo plate here, and top it off with an offering from the open salsa bar. Yum!

### Cafés

The **Park Rock Café** (6554 Park Blvd., Joshua Tree, 760/366-3622, Mon.–Sat. 9 A.M.–6 P.M., Sun. 9 A.M.–4 P.M., $10–20) serves casual café food and espresso drinks next door to the Joshua Tree Visitors Center near the West Entrance to the park. Park Rock is a good place to grab a quick bite before entering the park or just after leaving.

### Markets

Need to stock up on groceries before hitting the park? Two local markets can supply hungry hikers and campers in need of supplies. **Stater Bros** (58060 29 Palms Hwy., Yucca Valley, 760/365-2415) sits near the western entrances. Near the Oasis entrance, check out the **Plaza Market** (5668 Historic Plz., Twentynine Palms, 760/367-3464).

## INFORMATION AND SERVICES

### Tourist Information

It's hard to drive more than a dozen miles in Joshua Tree without tripping over a ranger station or a nature center. Most of these are tiny, but they're prolific and you'll get the information you need wherever you stop. If you're camping at any of the larger campgrounds, you'll probably find a nature center somewhere in it.

The **Oasis Visitors Center** (760/367-5500, year-round daily 8 A.M.–5 P.M.) sits at the Oasis of Mara. It's got all you need in terms of rangers, a bookshop, special exhibits including videos, and more.

West of the Oasis, you can enter the park at the **Joshua Tree Visitors Center** (760/366-1855, year-round daily 8 A.M.–5 P.M.). A fun little interpretive museum explains the origins and current fun available in Joshua Tree, and knowledgeable rangers can inundate you with maps and advice. Day-trippers often grab a quick bite and some extra water from the adjoining café before heading into the foodless desert park.

If you're entering the park from I-10 in the

south, your first stop will be the **Cottonwood Visitors Center** (no phone, year-round daily 9 A.M.–3 P.M.). This tiny center has maps and rangers, a picnic ground, and flush toilets and running water, but very little else.

### Media and Communications

The National Park publishes several pamphlets and papers for visitors. Ask for these at any of the visitors centers.

In an emergency, call **San Bernardino dispatch** (909/383-5651). Cell phone coverage is unreliable in the park, especially in the backcountry. Don't depend on your cell phone in cases of emergency. You can find public phones at the Joshua Tree and Oasis visitors centers.

You won't find Internet access inside the park. You might find a Wi-Fi connection at your motel in Twentynine Palms, and there's certainly plenty of Internet in Palm Springs.

The Twentynine Palms **post office** is located at 73839 Gorgonio Drive.

### Medical Services

For non-emergency medical needs, the nearest place to find a wide variety of clinics open at all hours is Palm Springs. In an emergency, dial 911 or 909/383-5651 (San Bernardino dispatch).

## GETTING THERE AND GETTING AROUND

### Air

The nearest major airport to Joshua Tree is at **Palm Springs** (3400 E. Tahquitz Canyon Way, 760/318-3800, www.palmspringsairport.com). It only takes about an hour to drive from the airport out to the park.

### Car

You can drive from Palm Springs or even Los Angeles to the south entrance of Joshua Tree on I-10. From I-10 heading east, turn north (left) onto Box Canyon Road, which takes you right up to the Cottonwood Springs Visitors Center.

To enter at the north side of the park, find your way to Twentynine Palms Highway, also known as State Highway 62. Highway 62 originates at I-10 northwest of Palm Springs, or to avoid the freeway take Indian Avenue up through Desert Hot Springs and around to the north side of the park. From Highway 62, you can turn in to Black Rock Canyon, the Joshua Tree Visitors Center, or the Oasis of Mara.

Parking inside Joshua Tree usually isn't too difficult, as ample parking lots are provided for the major attractions. On holiday weekends, come early for the best spots and least crowded hikes.

# Death Valley

For a valley famed for its uncompromising climate, Death Valley teems with life. Desert plants, including funky pickleweed and more common creosote, wildflowers, and even desert-dwelling fish and snails live here in profusion. Even the rocks, cliffs, salt flats, and mountains seem to live and breathe here. The best way to experience the amazing world that is Death Valley is to visit for at least a weekend, driving from sight to sight and then getting out of the car to walk out into the desert.

## SIGHTS

### ☾ Scotty's Castle

If you ask the locals around Death Valley if there's one single thing not to miss, almost to a person they will tell you to see Scotty's Castle (Hwy. 267 in Grapevine Canyon, 3 miles northeast of Grapevine intersection, adults $11). The unfinished grand Spanish-styled home is the only private mansion ever built in Death Valley. Contrary to popular legend, it never was the home of infamous huckster Death Valley Scotty—he actually lived in a rough cabin on the property, only hanging out in the castle with his friend Albert Johnson. In truth, the mansion was built and furnished by Johnson and his wife, a wealthy couple from Chicago who initially invested in Scotty's oft-lauded but never seen gold mine but became

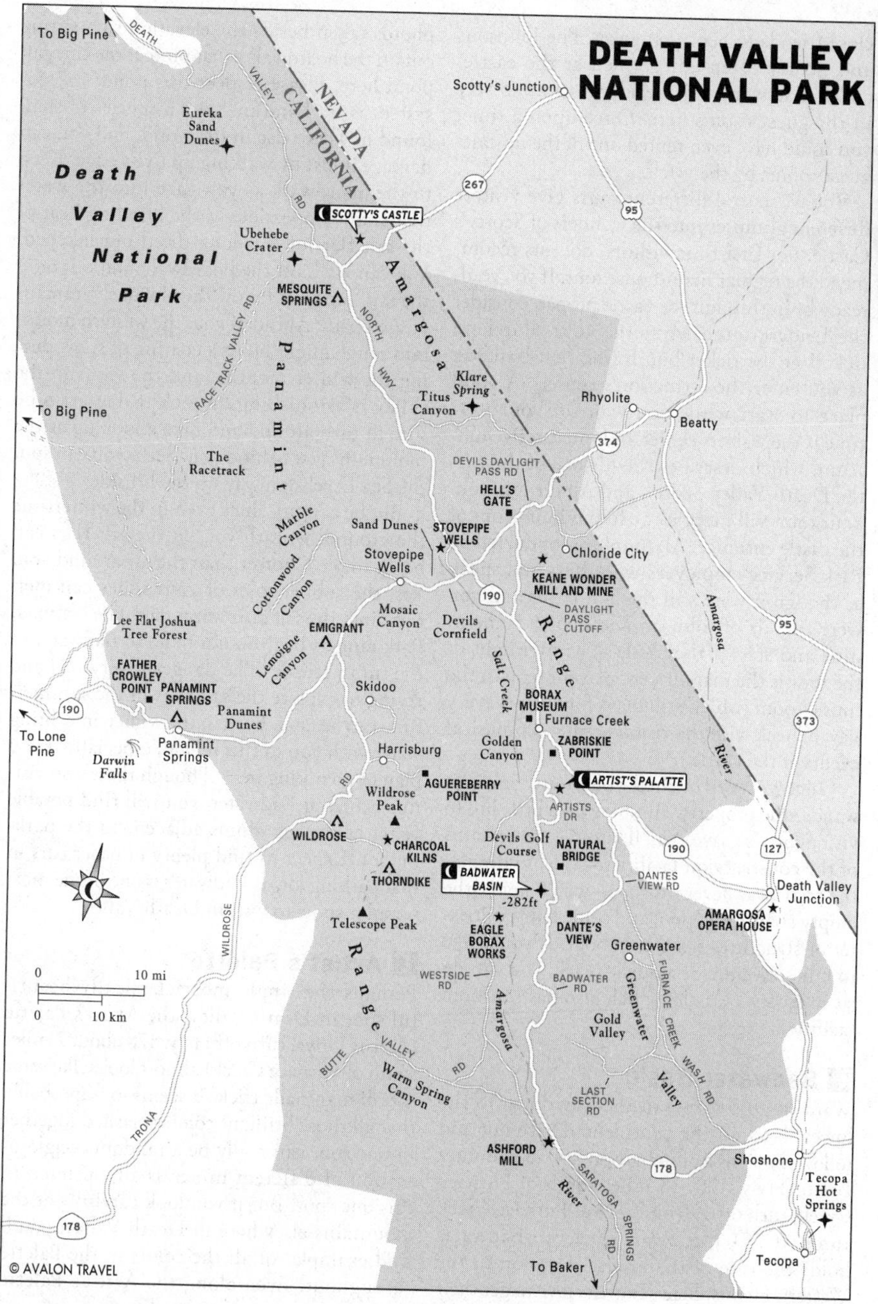
DEATH VALLEY NATIONAL PARK
Death Valley National Park
To Big Pine
DEATH VALLEY RD
NEVADA
CALIFORNIA
Scotty's Junction
Eureka Sand Dunes
267
95
SCOTTY'S CASTLE
Ubehebe Crater
MESQUITE SPRINGS
Amargosa
NORTH HWY
RACE TRACK VALLEY RD
Panamint
Klare Spring
Titus Canyon
Rhyolite
Beatty
To Big Pine
374
The Racetrack
DEVILS DAYLIGHT PASS RD
HELL'S GATE
Marble Canyon
Sand Dunes
STOVEPIPE WELLS
Chloride City
Stovepipe Wells
Cottonwood Canyon
KEANE WONDER MILL AND MINE
190
DAYLIGHT PASS CUTOFF
Mosaic Canyon
Devils Cornfield
Lee Flat Joshua Tree Forest
EMIGRANT
Range
Amargosa
95
Lemoigne Canyon
Salt Creek
FATHER CROWLEY POINT
PANAMINT SPRINGS
Skidoo
BORAX MUSEUM
190
Panamint Dunes
Furnace Creek
373
To Lone Pine
Panamint Springs
Golden Canyon
ZABRISKIE POINT
Darwin Falls
Harrisburg
RD
AGUEREBERRY POINT
ARTIST'S PALATTE
River
Wildrose Peak
ARTISTS DR
WILDROSE
CHARCOAL KILNS
Devils Golf Course
NATURAL BRIDGE
190
127
THORNDIKE
BADWATER BASIN
DANTES VIEW RD
Death Valley Junction
-282ft
Telescope Peak
EAGLE BORAX WORKS
DANTE'S VIEW
AMARGOSA OPERA HOUSE
WILDROSE
Greenwater
0
10 mi
0
10 km
Range
WESTSIDE RD
BADWATER RD
FURNACE CREEK WASH RD
Amargosa
Greenwater
Gold Valley
BUTTE VALLEY RD
Warm Spring Canyon
LAST SECTION RD
Valley
TRONA
ASHFORD MILL
Shoshone
178
SARATOGA SPRINGS RD
River
Tecopa Hot Springs
178
To Baker
Tecopa
© AVALON TRAVEL

close friends to Scotty anyway. The Johnsons and Scotty often entertained at the castle, and movie stars and presidents came to stay in the guest rooms here. Once upon a time, you could have even rented one of the upstairs guest rooms by the week.

Today, several different tours give visitors different glimpses into the wonders of Scotty's Castle. For first-time visitors, docents recommend the regular main-house tour. If you've already been through the castle proper, consider the Underground Mysteries tour. Purchase tickets at the ticket booth (the first building as you enter the attraction's center). A good place to start while you wait for your tour time is the visitors center and interpretive museum, which describes the history of the castle, Death Valley Scotty, and Albert Johnson. Your tour will meet at the fountain in front of the castle entrance. All tours are conducted by Park Service employees who dress and speak as though it were still the late 1930s and you were friends of Johnson and Scotty come to dine and stay at the castle. The highlight of the tour is the magnificent player organ in the music room, which still plays for visitors every day. (Check with the visitors center for musical events at the castle.)

Once you've finished your tour, you can wander the property, climbing up a little hill to visit Scotty's grave. You'll also see the remains of the construction facilities—the building of the castle was never finished—you'll notice the empty swimming pool and some half-built exterior structures scattered about. If you'd like to buy souvenirs or a quick snack, you can do so at Scotty's Castle, which also has restroom facilities.

### Badwater Basin

Want to go down—all the way down to the lowest land on the continent? Drive out and follow the signs from Highway 190 to Badwater Basin (Hwy. 178, 18 miles south of Furnace Creek, turn off 190 onto 178 at Furnace Creek Inn). At 281 feet *below* sea level, Badwater holds the title of the lowest elevation in the Western Hemisphere. Tourists love to get their photos taken beside the elevation sign sitting out on the boardwalks that protect the tiny salt pond here. Please respect this pond; its ecosystem is frail and includes a species of snail found nowhere else in the world, and you can damage it just by walking up to its edge. Keep to the boardwalk as you gaze into the water that seems impossible in the blinding heat of the salt flats of this long-dried-out lakebed. You can walk off the boardwalk and out onto the salt flats; just follow the obviously human-created path. Ahead of you, the western mountain range might boast a coating of snow during the winter months, and the view up the valley is astonishing on a clear day. Also be sure to turn around and take a look up at the mountains just behind you. See if you can spot the Sea Level sign way up the hillside.

But be careful, since even in the wintertime the ground beneath you on the salt flats can be up to 80°F hotter than the air around you. Yes, the rubber soles of your shoes can melt right into the salt on a warm day! The National Park rangers beg you not to go to Badwater in the summertime. The danger is very real and trying to explore the salt flats in the summertime can be fatal. Even in the wintertime, bring water with you to this region, especially if you plan to go hiking here. Though there's no visitors center at Badwater, you will find potable water at the restrooms adjacent to the parking lot. Expect to find plenty of other cars in that parking lot, as Badwater is one of the most popular spots to visit in Death Valley.

### Artist's Palette

Perhaps the single most classically beautiful spot in Death Valley, the Artist's Palette (Artists Drive, turn off Hwy. 178 about 7 miles south of Furnace Creek) almost looks like some sort of manmade trick. It seems so improbably that all those brilliant colors splashed together in one spot can really be a random conglomeration of different minerals all clustered in this one spot. But if you look carefully at the mountains elsewhere in Death Valley, you'll find examples of all the colors in the Palette throughout. Even along the Artist's Palette

© LANCE SCOTT

Artist's Palette

cutoff, swaths of color spill down the mountains for miles through the narrow canyon. It's worth your time to slow down on the road, even to stop and photograph some of the "secret" painted spots.

The one-way road through Artist's Palette splits off from Highway 178 and runs for about five miles (entrance at the south side), and the road is paved and driveable by regular cars. The best time to hit the Palette is just before sunset, when the falling sun limns the already amazing colors with gold. You'll see bunches of people pulled off the road and walking up and down a rise to take photos of a colorful cliff, but this is *not* the Palette proper. Stop to look, but then keep driving until you see the Artist's Palette sign and turn right into the drive for the parking lot. Walk a few steps up a tiny rise and you'll see the Palette right in front of you in all its pastel glory. You'll also see a number of other tourists at all times of day. No restrooms or water are available at Artist's Palette.

## Devil's Golf Course

One of the eeriest formations in Death Valley is the ground at Devil's Golf Course (Hwy. 178 about 11 miles south of Furnace Creek). This part of the low salt flat that was the bottom of a long-vanished lake got stirred up somehow. The results are spectacular, with acre upon acre of chewed-up ground covered with delicate crystalline salt formations. It's a good idea to wear long pants and sturdy shoes and to be very careful if you plan to walk out onto the Golf Course. The ruts, holes, and crevices can be knee-deep, rocks and crystals are razor-sharp, and to call the walking "uneven" is the understatement of the year. If you're a photographer, be sure to bring your camera to capture the fragile salt crystal growths proliferating here.

Yes, every step you take out onto Devil's Golf Course destroys countless beautiful crystals. So why does the park let you walk out there? Because these crystals aren't a permanent feature of the region. Every time it rains, the crystals melt down to a salty liquid, then as the Golf Course dries out, the crystals start growing anew.

The road in to Devil's Golf Course is dirt and can get rough, but it's passable by passenger car. The slower you drive, the better condition the road will stay in. There's a parking lot in the Golf Course and a couple of plaques describing the formation and geology of the area. However, there are no restrooms or water here.

## Dante's View

One of the many glorious views of Death Valley can be accessed by car at Dante's View (end of Dante's View Rd., turn off Hwy. 190 about 10 miles southeast of Furnace Creek). From more than a mile high, you can look out over what feels like the whole valley—right down into the salt flats of Badwater, up to Furnace Creek, and beyond. Right next door you can wave at the thematically named Coffin Peak to the south of Dante's. As the main views spread out to the west, Dante's Peak is a great place to watch the sun set over Death Valley.

## Salt Creek

You may have heard of the famous Death Valley pupfish, a species of fish that lives in only one spot on the globe—here at Salt Creek (Hwy. 190, about 15 miles north of Furnace Creek, turnoff on west side of the highway). It's a strange contradiction, with a shining creek flowing through some of the most dry and desolate landscape on Earth. Toward the center of the valley off Highway 190, Salt Creek runs all year, its source a small spring, its terminus the hard ground where a miniature delta spreads out then dries up. To protect the delicate ecosystem in and around the heavily salinated creek, the Park Service has built a boardwalk that lets visitors see the plants, algae, and pupfish without treading on and in the delicate landscape here. The boardwalk runs from the parking lot up to the area where the pupfish spawn early in the wintertime. As spring comes, the pupfish swim downstream, making viewing easy even for visitors who don't want to take a hike. All around the boardwalk you'll see plants that thrive on salty water, including the funky pickleweed. That's the big bushy plant with the succulent-like tentacles divided into small greenish-orange droplets. This plant is so salty that early pioneers in the area used it to make pickles instead of adding salt—hence its name.

The drive from the highway is about two miles on a dirt road that's passable in a passenger car. Pit toilets sit in the parking lot area. The boardwalk trail is wheelchair accessible.

## Ubehebe Crater

Just about every type of major geological feature was once a part of the Death Valley landscape. In the north end of the valley, a recent (in geologic time) volcano left behind Ubehebe Crater (8 miles west of Scotty's Castle, from Hwy. 190 take left fork at the Grapevine). A quick walk up from the parking lot takes you right to the edge of the crater, which consists of razor-sharp black volcanic rock that is on the opposite inner face of the crater fading into a bright salmon pink and even a stark white. The view over the edge of the crater back down the valley is worth coming up here, and when you turn around you see the less visited but also lovely north end of the valley. Ubehebe is a great place to go hiking if you're in good shape—among other things, you can climb up from the parking area along the crater's rim to Little Hebe crater, a smaller crater created by the same volcano about 2,000 years ago.

Get to Ubehebe Crater by taking the other fork at the intersection that takes you to Scotty's Castle. The road is easily traversable by passenger cars; there's a parking lot but no restroom or water here.

## Museums

In the town of Furnace Creek, out by the Ranch, you'll find two tiny museums that give guests a deeper understanding of both the natural and human history of Death Valley. The **Borax Museum** (admission free) at Furnace Creek Ranch focuses on the mining history of the area, with a tiny interior gallery/bookshop filled with mineral samples, books and documents, and smaller mining tools. The bulk of the museum sits outdoors, displaying an array of desiccated large mining and support equipment. Get a map indoors for $1 that

© LANCE SCOTT

Borax Museum

describes each numbered exhibit outside. You'll see hand-built mining machines, carriages and wagons, a steam locomotive, and more.

Just a few yards north of the Ranch sits the **Furnace Creek Visitors Center and Museum** (Hwy. 190 at the gas station, 760/786-3200, year-round daily 9 A.M.–5 P.M.). The interpretive museum here tells the story of Death Valley's long, slow formation and erosion. Even if you're not a rock nut, it's worth your time to stop in here to learn more about the natural wonders you'll witness when you get out on the road to explore. This is also a good spot to talk to rangers about the relative passability of the various rugged roads in the park, and to learn about the very real dangers of exploring Death Valley and how to keep yourself as safe as possible during your journey.

## ENTERTAINMENT AND EVENTS

The main entertainment in Death Valley are the sights and (lack of) sounds of the valley itself. If you're an energetic night owl, plan to enjoy full-moon hikes rather than dance clubs, since you can count the number of saloons in the whole of the valley on one hand.

### Bars and Clubs

For a drink or two to cap off a long day out in the desert, head on down to the **Corkscrew Saloon** at Furnace Creek Ranch (Hwy. 190 at Furnace Creek, 760/786-2345, daily noon–midnight). Go ahead and wear your boots and hat into the cowboy-styled bar with its wood floor and dim lighting. Drink a mug of beer on tap, grab a glass of wine, or sip your favorite cocktail from the full bar. They've got a TV with the game on for sports fans, and a pool table for desert sharks. The crowd mixes the ubiquitous tourists and a few die-hard locals who serve as the Corkscrew's regulars.

The other local watering hole sits a little north of Furnace Creek: the **Badwater Saloon at Stovepipe Wells** (Hwy. 190 past the big bend, 760/786-2387, daily 5:30 P.M.–9 P.M.). Attached to the Toll Road Restaurant, this saloon has beer, wine, cocktails, and a small snack menu to satisfy evening munchers over 21. It's not open too late, so you'll need to get your quaffing in early in the evening.

## Live Music

Outside the park proper in the town of Amargosa Valley, Nevada, you'll find one of the most original entertainments available anywhere at the **Amargosa Opera House** (Death Valley Junction, 760/852-4441, www.amargosa-opera-house.com, adults $15, children $12). This lovely small theater is the pride and joy of Marta Beckett, a dancer from New York City who found her "home" in an abandoned theater in Death Valley Junction, where her car was getting a flat tire fixed. She and her husband repaired and renovated the theater, creating an intimate space where Marta could perform for an appreciative, if small, audience. That was in 1968. In the early 1970, Marta was inspired to paint murals on the walls and ceiling of her Opera House—a permanent audience for her ballets.

It's been 40 years, and Marta still dances at the Opera House each Saturday night from November through the middle of May. Reservations are required, as the seating is limited and Marta's shows often sell out. The show you see was created and choreographed by Marta, incorporating music, ballet, and comedy. The best way to learn about these unique entertainments is to see one for yourself.

You can also stay at the Amargosa if you like, since the old adobe hotel building has been renovated and is open to guests all year long. You can even ask for one of the rooms in which Marta has painted some of her lovely murals.

## Festivals and Events

The Death Valley mythos—a place where intrepid miners and hardy pioneers couldn't find water and sought to leave ASAP—wouldn't be complete without an annual tribute to those first white visitors. The **49er Encampment** (www.deathvalley49ers.org) takes place throughout the first week of November each year. Thousands of history buffs flock to the valley to camp, tell stories, sing songs, dance, and take tours of the park. Participants and guests alike enjoy the parade, which is one of the highlights of the many activities put on by the Encampment.

# SPORTS AND RECREATION

The outdoor recreation comprises much of Death Valley's attraction to the million visitors the park sees each year. Whether you're an extreme sandboarder, an aggro four-wheeler, or a slow walker, you'll find something worth doing out-of-doors in Death Valley.

## Off-Roading

If you've got a 4x4, or you know how to drive one and can rent one, it's well worth it to bring a hardy off-road vehicle into Death Valley. Many of the off-the-beaten-track sights and trails can only be accessed by high-clearance and four-wheel-drive vehicles.

The drive out to the **Natural Bridge** (about 1 mile off Hwy. 190, 1–2 miles south of Devil's Golf Course) isn't long or aggressive, but the road condition makes high-clearance or 4WD a good idea in most seasons. Check with the rangers for current conditions. Once you park, you've got a half-mile walk in to see the magnificent stone arch stretching across yet another beautiful desert canyon.

One of the most out-of-the-way sights in the park is **The Racetrack** (27 miles from Ubehebe Crater). You'll take a 27-mile drive on an incredibly rough road out to a patch of desert where a mysterious (but explicable) phenomenon draws hardy visitors out beyond the crowded main valley sights. You don't really need to hike anywhere—just get out of your car and stare out across the plateau at the deep grooves in the barren lakebed. The tracks are made by rocks sliding across the lakebed. See a track with no rock at the end of it? Sadly, uncaring tourists often pick up the rocks and take them home. Please leave the rocks where nature put them to allow future visitors to enjoy the unusual sight.

Also in the north end of the valley, the **Eureka Dunes** (10 miles south of Big Pine

Rd.) are some of the most unusual dunes you'll ever see, no matter how far you travel. The sand composing the dunes is the only sand nearby, and it rises 700 feet off the valley floor. You can walk up the Eureka Dunes, but no horseback riding and sandboarding aren't allowed here. This is a measure to protect the delicate ecosystem that evolved right here at the dunes and exists nowhere else on Earth. The drive runs about 40 miles or so, first on a long unpaved road running north from the Y-intersection to Scotty's Castle, then on a 4WD track about 10 miles to the dunes. Out towards the dunes, sand can get deep, so rangers recommend that *experienced 4WD drivers only* attempt this road.

The lovely **Titus Canyon** (Hwy. 190 about 20 miles north of Stovepipe Wells intersection) can be traversed on foot or by a 26-mile one-way 4WD track that connects directly to the ghost town of Rhyolite. Along the many miles of canyon, you'll see some of the most diverse and arguably most beautiful desert canyon scenery anywhere in Death Valley. It's got Native American petroglyphs, bighorn sheep, colorful mineral deposits, and skinny "narrows" where the walls soar overhead and almost black out the sun. Because the 4WD road runs only one way, you must come back into Death Valley by making a long loop into Nevada. Take Highway 374 past Rhyolite to Highway 95. Head either north to Highway 267, which will take you back to Scotty's Castle, or south to Highway 373 through Amargosa Valley, which becomes 127, then turn onto 190 which takes you back to Furnace Creek. Consider making your viewing of Titus Canyon an all-day adventure.

Out west in the Panamint Springs area, take your truck on a drive up to **Aguereberry Point** (Emigrant Canyon Rd. about 13 miles south of Emigrant intersection). This drive includes passing the ghost town of Harrisburg—an early 20th-century gold mining town that once had a population of 300 living in tents. You can actually walk right into this mine, which has been stabilized and made safe for visitors to spelunk in. Just be sure that the mine isn't closed to protect hibernating bats. All the way up the road, park and climb up to the point, which provides more beautiful valley vistas to enjoy. If you're staying in Panamint Springs, Aguereberry Point makes a good sunset or sunrise destination.

## Hiking

Though you can reach most of the major sights of Death Valley by driving and perhaps a short walk, to get off the beaten track you'll need to take a hike. In fact, that's why many visitors come here. The best time to hike in the floor of Death Valley is the wintertime, when temperatures are cool to moderate. On the other hand, if you're interested in hiking the high country, the best time to explore the ridges is in the summer when the snow has melted.

For a fun easy or moderate walk where you can control both the distance and the elevation change, park on the side of the road and wander on out to the **Sand Dunes** (2–4 miles round-trip, easy) near Stovepipe Wells. The dunes are constantly shifting, and regular visitors love them because they're never the same two years in a row. They're beautiful at sunset when the golden light hits them, and if you're visiting during a full moon you'll find few more romantic spots to share an outdoor stroll with your sweetie.

From the roadside parking area, just walk out toward the cluster of dunes. They look like they're only a few yards away, but the desert air creates false senses of distance and it's about a mile to the edge of the dunes. There's no trail. You can walk right up the sides of the dunes. The hundreds of pockmark-like footprints bear witness to other visitors' climbs. If you climb as far as you can up the tallest dune, the round-trip is four miles.

**Mosaic Canyon** (1–4 miles round-trip, moderate) offers a variable length and difficulty hike with beautiful rock formations that resemble mosaics. Check out the canyon walls on the first half-mile of the walk for the best mosaics. If you want to, you can continue a couple of miles farther into the canyon. This hike starts at the Mosaic Canyon parking lot, a couple of miles past Stovepipe Wells Village.

If you don't have a 4x4 vehicle but you want to see the charming **Titus Canyon Narrows** (3–13 miles round-trip, easy), you can leave your car at the Titus Canyon parking lot and walk down the unpaved road. The Narrows go on for about a mile and a half of level road—if you're up for a much longer walk, you can get all the way to Klare Springs and the local petroglyphs.

For a scenic summer walk, **Dante's Ridge** (1–8 miles, moderate) offers soaring vistas and cool temperatures even in July. If you want a short hike, climb 0.5 mile from the Dante's View parking lot to the first peak in the chain. If you're done, feel free to walk back down; if you're feeling energetic, keep descending and climbing the ridge to the top of Mount Perry. You'll need to be an adventurous sort, as there's no trail past the first peak, though hiking is allowed.

Bring a detailed map if you plan to take on the hike through **Fall Canyon** (6 miles round-trip, difficult). Start at the Titus Canyon parking lot and from there, head north along a trampled path, and from there you're on your own as you descend a wash into the canyon and to a "dryfall." If you're up to it, you can skirt around the dryfall and head down to the most spectacular narrows area of the canyon.

If you're into the mining history of Death Valley, the **Keane Wonder Mine Trail** (2 miles, difficult) is a must-hike. It's a rough go—steep and rocky the whole mile up from the ruins of the mill to the ruins of the mines. Ruin crawlers will love the whole area. When the Keane Wonder Mine ceased production, it was abandoned and has been slowly desiccating ever since. At the top of the trail, you'll find the abandoned and incredibly dangerous mine entrances. The Park Services begs you not to enter these unstable structures. Be sure to take a break from the mines to look out over the whole of Death Valley from your perch.

If you're an aggro hiker visiting Death Valley in the summertime, check out **Telescope Peak Trail** (14 miles round-trip, difficult). The trail begins at the Mahogany Flat Campground and climbs 3,000 feet to the peak of the tallest mountain in Death Valley. The sweeping views will take what's left of your breath away after your climb. The snow usually melts by the beginning of June; if you want to try this trail in the winter you'll need an ice axe, crampons, and lots of previous winter climbing experience.

### Biking

You've got to be pretty tough to bring your bike to a place called Death Valley. But plenty of folks do. The main biking road is Highway 190, which runs north–south along the east side of the valley. You can cut off the highway onto any paved road if you want to take in some sights. However, no bikes are allowed off the pavement in Death Valley.

### Horseback Riding

At Furnace Creek Ranch (Hwy. 190, 760/786-2345, www.furnacecreekresort.com), you can take a horseback ride out into the desert from October through May. Horse-and-carriage rides are also available on occasion. Call the ranch or ask at the front desk for more information and to make reservations.

### Golf

It's not a golfing destination, but if you're just burning to play a round in the hottest valley on earth, book a tee time at the **Furnace Creek Ranch Golf Course** (Hwy. 190, 760/786-2345, www.furnacecreekresort.com/golf-1203.htm, green fee $30–55, cart rental $12.50). Nope, it's not the shining green you'll find at most golf courses, for obvious reasons. Even in winter, limited water can be spared to irrigate greens and fairways. This 18-hole, par 70 course is part of the Furnace Creek Ranch complex near the center of Death Valley. You'll find restaurants and a general store at the Ranch. Check the website for golf and lodging packages.

## CAMPING

Folks who want to explore Death Valley on the cheap quickly the fill the campsites that dot the park. Whether you're in an RV or just have a tent to pitch, you'll find someplace that suits your fancy. Just be aware that during high season (winter), the popular central campgrounds fill up fast. You can make reservations for a spot at many of the popular campgrounds by calling 877/444-6777 or online at www.recreation.gov. During the summer, camping in Death Valley can be extremely unpleasant, since few campgrounds here offer shade of any kind to take the edge off the extreme heat. Camping from June to September is not recommended in the lowland areas, and many campgrounds are closed from May to September.

## RV and Tent Campgrounds

RV campers love to hang out in Death Valley. Accordingly, several full hook-up RV campgrounds offer space to settle in for a stay.

Both on the same side as the ranch and across the road, **Furnace Creek** (Hwy. 190 at Furnace Creek, 800/365-2267, www.furnacecreekresort.com, open year-round, $12–18) offers both RV spaces and tent camping. Campers gain access to the facilities at the Ranch, including the swimming pool, golf course, restaurants, and store. The RV camping sits mostly on the opposite side of Highway 190 from the Ranch, and the "campground" is in fact a stretch of barren asphalt with no shade whatsoever. This campground fills up fast during the busy winter months and you must make a reservation to get a spot here. Expect to find running water, flushies, and fireplaces at or near your site.

If you want to camp near, but not in, Furnace Creek Ranch, you can choose between **Texas Springs** (east of Furnace Creek, $12) and **Sunset** (east of Furnace Creek, north of Texas Springs, $10). Both are open from October through April, and feature running water, flush toilets, and RV dump stations. Of the two, Texas Springs has the nicest amenities, with picnic tables and fire rings. Both campgrounds are wheelchair accessible.

Another popular RV park sits at the tiny villagelet of **Stovepipe Wells** (Hwy. 190 at Stovepipe Wells, 760/786-2387, open Oct.–Apr., $12). Again, you get access to the small general store and the tavern if you park on the wide patch of asphalt here. There are also several fun sights nearby, and Stovepipe Wells is close enough to Furnace Creek to make a good spot from which to base your trip. Stovepipe Wells spots are first-come, first-served only.

**Mesquite Springs** (spur road left off Hwy. 190, south of Scotty's Castle, open year-round, $10) offers both tent and RV spots on the west side of Death Valley. It's the only campground in the high north country, near Scotty's Castle. It's a long drive to either Stovepipe Wells or Furnace Creek, the nearest spots that offer major services such as food and gasoline. But if you're specifically looking for isolation and a more rugged experience, Mesquite Springs might be just the place for you. It is first-come, first-served, with self registration, and the campground has potable water, flush toilets, and an RV dump station.

If you're willing to camp on the far west side of the park, **Panamint Springs** (Hwy. 190 past Western Entrance, west of Panamint Valley Rd., $15–30) offers a camping experience unique to all of Death Valley—that is, campsites along a river shaded by mature trees. No, really! One of the few year-round rivers in Death Valley runs and even cascades down a 20-foot fall about five miles back from the Panamint Springs Resort. With 40 RV spaces and 26 tent sites, call to make a reservation or arrive early in the morning if you want a spot in the winter months. You'll also find water and toilets throughout the campground, and 15 of the RV spots have full hookups with 50-amp electricity.

## Tent-Only Campgrounds

If you want to camp Death Valley in the summertime, head up into the Panamint mountain range to the tent-only **Thorndike** (Mar.–Nov., free) campground. Be aware that you may need a four-wheel-drive vehicle to access this campground. Thorndike is a primitive campground, so you must bring all your own water for drinking and washing (bring lots more than you think you need to be safe). You will find pit toilets, and your site will include a picnic table and a fireplace. The nearby **Wildrose** (year-round, free) campground has a lower elevation and a wintertime crowd. It offers a few more in-season amenities, including potable water from November through April and a road you can drive in a passenger car. The nearest major services, such as food and gas, are a goodly drive to either Panamint Springs or Furnace Creek.

If you're into the western side of the park, consider camping at **Emigrant** (year-round, free), which sits about halfway between Panamint Springs and Stovepipe Wells. You'll get a spot to pitch your tent, access to potable water and flush toilets, but no fire rings here.

## ACCOMMODATIONS

### Under $100

If you prefer to stay on the west side of Death Valley (a good idea for at least one night if you're driving in from the California side), book a room or a camping spot at the tiny **Panamint Springs Resort** (Hwy. 190, 775/482-7680, www.deathvalley.com/psr, $89–170). This rustic lodge-style motel is the only independently owned lodging in Death Valley, and also has a temperature that's generally 10–15°F lower than the other motels in the park. Your amenities will not include a TV or much in the way of good phone service, but the resort does offer free Wi-Fi. You will have access to the resort's restaurant, which serves three meals a day year-round. If you're visiting in the wintertime and the weather is mild, get a seat out on the patio so you can enjoy a view of the valley with your food.

### $100-250

The biggest resort complex in the park, **Furnace Creek Ranch** (Hwy. 190, 800/236-7916, www.furnacecreekresort.com, $135–225) acts as the human center of eastern Death Valley. It's in close proximity to many of the major attractions people come to see. If you stay here, you're on the same property as two restaurants, a tavern, a general store, a museum, a gas station, a golf course, an airstrip, and the main park visitors center. With a wide lawn, a playground, and a mineral spring–fed swimming pool, this is a great place to bring your kids for

© LANCE SCOTT

Furnace Creek Ranch

a desert vacation. The guest accommodations at Furnace Ranch were deliberately created to be casual and, well, ranch-like. You can choose from standard, deluxe, or cabin-style accommodations. Rooms have one or two double or queen beds, chain-motel styling, and adequate bathroom facilities. Some rooms have tiny patios or balconies overlooking the lawns and pools. No smoking is permitted in any room.

The motel at **Stovepipe Wells** (Hwy. 190 past the big bend, 760/786-2387, www.stovepipewells.com, $135) offers basic rooms and amenities at reasonable prices. Choose between king or two-bed rooms, all ground floor rooms only a few steps from the restaurant and saloon, the swimming pool, and across the street from the general store. Your room will have a TV but no phone, beds with motel-style bedspreads and wall art, and a bathroom with a shower or tub combo—everything you'd expect (well, except the phone) from an inexpensive motel. From the motel, you'll have easy access to Mosaic Canyon, the local dunes, and Salt Creek.

## Over $250

The lone high-end resort in all of Death Valley is the **Furnace Creek Inn** (Hwy 190. at Hwy. 178, 800/236-7916, www.furnacecreekresort.com, $310–475, mid-Oct.–mid-May only). This beautiful property was constructed early in the 20th century by the Pacific Borax Company. It's a lovely place to come upon as you drive up Highway 190, with its palm oasis and multi-level adobe buildings rising up onto the hillside. As you pull up to the front of the hotel, you'll see the ingenious tunnels that perforate the complex, and the wonderful views out over the salt flats of southern Death Valley.

Inside, you might find your guest room a bit small given the price you're paying for it. The bathrooms are tiled and sparking clean, though the fixtures can be on the old side unless you're in a spa room. And not all rooms look out over the valley, so you might get a fabulous view of the Dumpsters in the back parking area. But the interior design is mellow and pleasant, with colors and patterns that

the pool at Furnace Creek Inn

echo the desert outside. You've got a TV and a phone, room service, and access to all the lovely amenities the resort has to offer. Most rooms have king-sized beds and a couple of unique suites are available.

It's really those amenities you're paying so much for: the bathtub-warm mineral pool that's fed by a local hot spring and open late into the night, the poolside food service, the gazebo in the palm oasis, the fine dining room, spa services, and more. While you're visiting, be sure to take a leisurely tour of the property. The architecture and artwork are more than worth your time and attention. The staff, who take pains to provide every service a guest could ever want, will be happy to assist you in planning your park exploration as well.

## FOOD

You'll need to plan your meals each day during your trip to Death Valley, since there are no fast food joints or 24-hour supermarkets where you can grab a quick bite at 4 P.M. or 4 A.M. In fact, Death Valley has no supermarkets or fast food, period. Either bring a cooler stocked with picnic supplies to carry with you each day as you explore the valley, or plan to be near one of the three resort areas at mealtimes. If you do plan to feed yourself, stock up on staples (particularly the nonperishable stuff like soda and water) outside the park to save money.

### Casual Dining

If you're looking for a good, casual, diner-style meal, you won't do better in Death Valley than the **49er Café** (Hwy. 190 at Furnace Creek, 760/786-2345, daily until 9 P.M., $8–15) at the Furnace Creek Ranch. One of two restaurants on the property, the 49er Café is open the longest, serving a traditional American breakfast, filling lunches, and hearty dinners. While big eaters can get huge portions if they want them, it's a relief for the lighter eaters to find smaller items such as single eggs and half-grapefruits on the menu. The rustic dining room has some fun touches, including an original wood plank floor and plastic-covered maps of the valley on each table. You can plan out your day's travels as you sit sipping your coffee and waiting for your eggs to arrive. The service staff gets the job done, and can be quite friendly especially if you choose a seat at the counter. Feel free to wear jeans and a T-shirt.

If you've burned untold hundreds of calories hiking around the valley during the day, you'll find the perfect replenishment at the **Wrangler Steakhouse** (Hwy. 190 at Furnace Creek, 760/786-2345, 6–9 A.M., 11 A.M.–2 P.M., 5–9 P.M., $23–35). The Wrangler offers a menu loaded with steaks, plus ribs and chicken smothered with tangy barbecue sauce. In the same weathered wooden structure with the 49er Café, you'll be treated to a casual atmosphere where you'll feel at home in jeans and boots. The short wine list includes a few California favorites. You can also grab a beer or a cocktail, and finish off your meal with a cappuccino or a latte. For breakfast and lunch, the Wrangler puts up a casual buffet with both hot and cold dishes.

If you're in the northern reaches of Death Valley around dinnertime, your option for a restaurant meal is the **Toll Road Restaurant** (Hwy. 190, Stovepipe Wells, 760/786-2387, www.stovepipewells.com, daily 7–10 A.M., 11:30 A.M.–2 P.M., and 5:30–9 P.M.). The Toll Road serves biscuits and gravy for breakfast, a burger for lunch, and some chicken or pasta for dinner. The small dining room manages to accommodate both the residents in the motel and the campground, plus the occasional tourist stopping in for lunch from another part of the park. But do be prepared to wait for a table on weekends in the high season.

The small size and lower traffic out west mean that the **Panamint Springs Resort Restaurant** (Hwy. 190 at west side of park, 775/482-7680, www.deathvalley.com/psr, $10–30) can serve home-cooked food to its diners all year long. Take a seat out on the large patio and enjoy a glass of beer before lunch or dinner—the restaurant offers more than 100 varieties from around the world.

### Fine Dining

The few restaurants in Death Valley tend

toward solid American food with little frill or pretense. The only high-end dining establishment in the park is the **Furnace Creek Inn Dining Room** (Hwy. 190 at Hwy. 178, 760/786-3385, www.furnacecreekresort.com, Oct.–May, $18–30). Serving three meals per day to accommodate inn guests, the Dining Room offers large portions of delectable if sometimes a little bit overwrought California cuisine. Reservations are recommended for dinner, especially on weekend evenings. The servers make sure everything you need is taken care of in a timely fashion. Bring your appetite. The appetizers can be too tempting to resist, which might make the entrée and the luscious desserts seem a bit overwhelming. The lunch menu includes lighter but no less elegant fare, and breakfast is a reasonably standard California list of egg dishes and waffle-like things. The Dining Room bleeds elegance, with its white tablecloths and designer china. If you eat here in the daytime, you'll get a lovely view out towards the mountains from the picture windows. The Dining Room has a dress code, so be sure to bring at least one non-hiking outfit if you plan to dine here.

### Markets

If you need groceries, you can buy them in two spots in Death Valley. The widest selection of food, drink, and goods is sold at the **Furnace Creek Ranch General Store** (Hwy. 190 at Furnace Creek Ranch). The exterior is quaint, but the interior is stuffed with shiny modern souvenirs. You can find clothes if you need them—even swimsuits! The food clusters at the back of the store, and you can get staples, drinks, milk, produce, and other perishables. The market also has ice cream and plenty of junk food.

Much smaller, but adequate in an emergency, is the **Stovepipe Wells General Store** (Hwy. 190 past the big bend at Stovepipe Wells). This store is more like an understocked mini-mart than a real general store, and more than half of the merchandise sold is souvenirs. You can buy water, soft drinks, and a few limited food items here, but don't plan to stock up since for that you must go to Furnace Creek or outside the park.

## INFORMATION AND SERVICES

People can be lulled into a false sense of security because Death Valley is a national park. Yes, there are rangers here, and this is a geographically large park. But you are leaving civilization for real when you go to Death Valley. You can drive for miles without seeing another living soul, a telephone, or any means of assistance. Take some time to plan your trip to this enchanted but desolate region, making sure you've got lots of water (one full gallon per person, per day), a first-aid kit, a spare tire, and a good pair of walking shoes.

That said, most of the 1.2 million visitors who come to Death Valley each year have a fabulous time and no need to worry about the lack of nearby civilization.

### Tourist Information

The main **Furnace Creek Visitors Center** (Hwy. 190, 760/786-3200, daily 9 A.M.–5 P.M.) sits just north of Furnace Creek Ranch. The rangers at this center tend to be experienced with the park and can give you good advice about the best spots to go at the best times. They'll also tell you where *not* to go. This visitors center also has a book and souvenir store, and an interpretive museum.

The other major in-park visitors center sits at **Scotty's Castle Visitor Center and Museum** (SR 267, 760/786-2392, summer daily 9 A.M.–4:30 P.M., winter daily 8:30 A.M.–5 P.M.). Here again you'll find an interpretive museum and rangers to help you with your itinerary. The bookshop is smaller, but an attached snack shop sells munchies and plenty of bottled water.

### Media and Communications

Expect your cell phone to be out of commission for the whole of your stay in Death Valley. You might get lucky if you've got the right carrier, but most folks get no bars. Even many of the motels offer no in-room telephones, and most have little or no Internet access either. To come to Death Valley is to "disconnect" from modern communication gadgets almost completely. Some adults come here specifically for that reason, but be prepared for whining from older kids and teenagers when they discover they won't be able to text their friends for days at a time.

All the major resort areas have phones that can be used in an emergency, but you won't find any call boxes along the highway. Highway 190 has plenty of traffic traversing it every day—if you need to, you'll probably see plenty of cars and ranger trucks you can flag down for assistance. If you're serious about heading into Death Valley's back country, consider bringing a long-range, two-way radio just in case.

You can pick up a wealth of literature about the park from either visitors center. The major resort motels may offer the *LA Times*.

### Medical Services

No significant medical services are available inside Death Valley. The closest hospital is **Barstow Community Hospital** (555 S. Seventh Ave., Barstow, 760/256-1761). On the Nevada side, contact the **Beatty Clinic** (775/553-2208) or the **Pahrump Urgent Care Facility** (775/727-6060).

## GETTING THERE AND AROUND

A trip to Death Valley isn't like a trip to Los Angeles. The remote, harsh valley is surrounded by treacherous mountain ranges with few paved roads

### Air

The closest major airport to Death Valley is the **Las Vegas International Airport** (5757 Wayne Newton Blvd., Las Vegas, 702/261-5211, www.mccarran.com). From Vegas, it's a two- to three-hour drive to Furnace Creek.

If you're lucky enough to have access to a light plane, you can fly right into the **Furnace Creek Ranch** (Hwy. 190, 760/786-2345, www.furnacecreekresort.com). The Ranch has an uncontrolled 3,000-foot runway with tie-down space for general aviators.

### Car

The main north–south corridor through Death Valley is CA-190. CA-190 makes a hard turn to the west just before it passes through Stovepipe Wells and on out through Panamint Springs. Numerous paved, unpaved, and four-wheel-drive-only roads branch off from CA-190 throughout the park, letting visitors access the park's main attractions and trailheads.

## THE HIGH PRICE OF GETTING STUCK

Before you visit Death Valley, check in with the rangers at the main visitors center (Furnace Creek, Hwy. 190, 760/786-3200, daily 9 A.M.–5 P.M.) to get up-to-the-minute information about the state of the four-wheel-drive roads in the park. Particularly at the north end of the park, razor-sharp volcanic rock can scatter across roads, not just cutting but actually shredding all but the heaviest duty all-terrain tires. The road to The Racetrack is the worst; it's not unusual for Hummers to lose more than one tire and end up stranded more than a dozen miles from the nearest paved road or source of help. Add to that the fact that most cell phones receive no signal anywhere in Death Valley, and you have a recipe for disaster.

So how do you extricate yourself from such a mess? You stay put, or walk out to the road until a park ranger comes to find you. The ranger will call the one and only tow company that makes runs out into Death Valley's backcountry. As the only game in town, this company happily charges whatever they want to help you. If they've got a spare tire or two in your size, the service might only cost you $800–1,000. But if you need a tow back to civilization, expect to shell out upwards of $2,000 for the privilege.

What's the moral of this story? Listen to the rangers if they tell you that a certain road is treacherous this season and consider carefully how much money you're willing to spend for your off-road adventure before you bump out beyond the reach of civilization.

To drive in to the park, you'll come either from NV-95 or CA-395, then turn off onto smaller roads that lead into the park. Get a map before you leave for the best navigation; GPS units also work in the park.

The nearest major California town to Death Valley is Bakersfield. (Baker is closer, but it has fewer services.) See the *Yosemite* chapter for information about this useful waypoint city.

You'll need to keep an eye on your gas gauge and plan well when exploring Death Valley by car. Gas is available *only* at the resort areas of Panamint Springs, Stovepipe Wells, and Furnace Creek. In spring of 2008, the gas station at Scotty's Castle was not functional or open for business; check with the Park Service for an update before or during your visit.

### Tours

It doesn't happen every year, but most years Death Valley receives just a very little bit of winter rainfall. When these miniscule rains bunch up, especially in January and February, the water is absorbed by the seeds of countless wildflowers. Come late February and March, these newly sprouted seeds grow up and then bloom, creating a stunning profusion of color spreading across the normally bleak and barren desert floor. The most prominent color you'll see is yellow, since the Desert Gold grows a foot or more tall and produces a brilliant golden daisy-like flower with an orange center. In amongst the gold you'll see streaks of purple, dots of pink, and puffs of white. In fact, flowers of every color in the rainbow grow in Death Valley when conditions are right.

The best way to see the flowers is to get out of your car and take a stroll out into the desert where they grow. Ironically, often the water vapor and carbon dioxide cars emit make the strips of land right beside the road the most colorful and prolific flowered areas. If you haven't studied botany recently and you'd like to know more about the beauty surrounding you, take a Wildflower Walk led by one of the park rangers during the season. Check with the Furnace Creek Visitors Center for a schedule of Walks.

# Anza-Borrego Desert State Park

Anza-Borrego has a rich human history. Native Americans hunted bighorn sheep (still found here today) and gathered from the diverse plant life here, occasionally taking the time to draw and paint on the rocks. Later, European and Colonial explorers crisscrossed the desert with trails that you can still see traces of today.

The civilized center of the region is the town of Borrego Springs, a tiny patch of land that's not part of the state park. Most folks who come to enjoy the Borrego Desert's charms spend their nights here.

Many of the 600,000 acres of Anza-Borrego Desert State Park are pristine wilderness, yet camping is allowed anywhere in the park. Two of the best times to view the park as a whole are at sunrise and sunset. When the light is low and golden, the multicolored desert spreads out from the mountains to the south.

## SIGHTS

### Visitors Center

For first-time desert park visitors, a great place to start is the Visitors Center (200 Palm Canyon Dr., 760/767-4205, www.abdsp.org, Oct.–May daily 9 A.M.–5 P.M., June–Sept. weekends only). The Visitor Centers offers information, maps, trail updates, and interactive displays. An interpretive desert garden surrounds the center and provides the names and stories of many common plants and animals in the park. The stroll is easy and mostly flat, and includes a pupfish pond.

### Borrego Palm Canyon

If there's one natural feature you must see when you visit Anza-Borrego, it should be the Borrego Palm Canyon (spur road, just north of visitors center). An easy drive or walk from

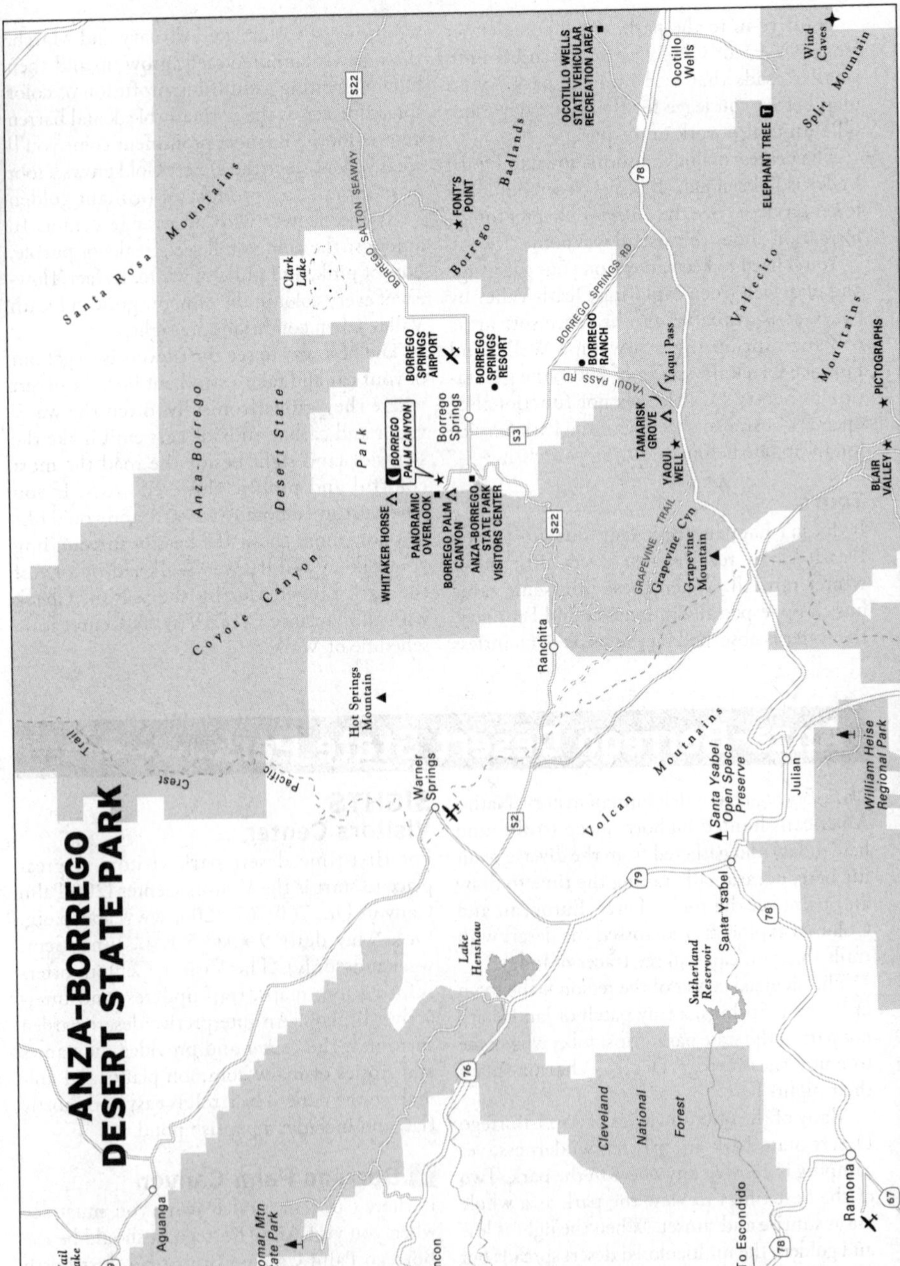
ANZA-BORREGO
DESERT STATE PARK
Santa Rosa Mountains
Anza-Borrego
Desert State
Park
Coyote Canyon
Clark Lake
BORREGO SALTON SEAWAY
S22
Borrego Badlands
FONT'S POINT
OCOTILLO WELLS STATE VEHICULAR RECREATION AREA
Ocotillo Wells
Wind Caves
Split Mountain
ELEPHANT TREE
78
BORREGO SPRINGS RD
Vallecito
Mountains
PICTOGRAPHS
BLAIR VALLEY
BORREGO SPRINGS AIRPORT
BORREGO SPRINGS RESORT
BORREGO RANCH
Borrego Springs
BORREGO PALM CANYON
YAQUI PASS RD
Yaqui Pass
TAMARISK GROVE
YAQUI WELL
S3
WHITAKER HORSE
PANORAMIC OVERLOOK
BORREGO PALM CANYON
ANZA-BORREGO STATE PARK VISITORS CENTER
S22
GRAPEVINE TRAIL
Grapevine Cyn
Grapevine Mountain
Ranchita
Hot Springs Mountain
Pacific Crest Trail
Warner Springs
S2
Volcan Moutnains
Santa Ysabel Open Space Preserve
Julian
William Heise Regional Park
Santa Ysabel
79
78
Lake Henshaw
Sutherland Reservoir
76
Cleveland National Forest
Aguanga
Palomar Mtn State Park
Vail Lake
79
Rincon
To Escondido
Ramona
67
78

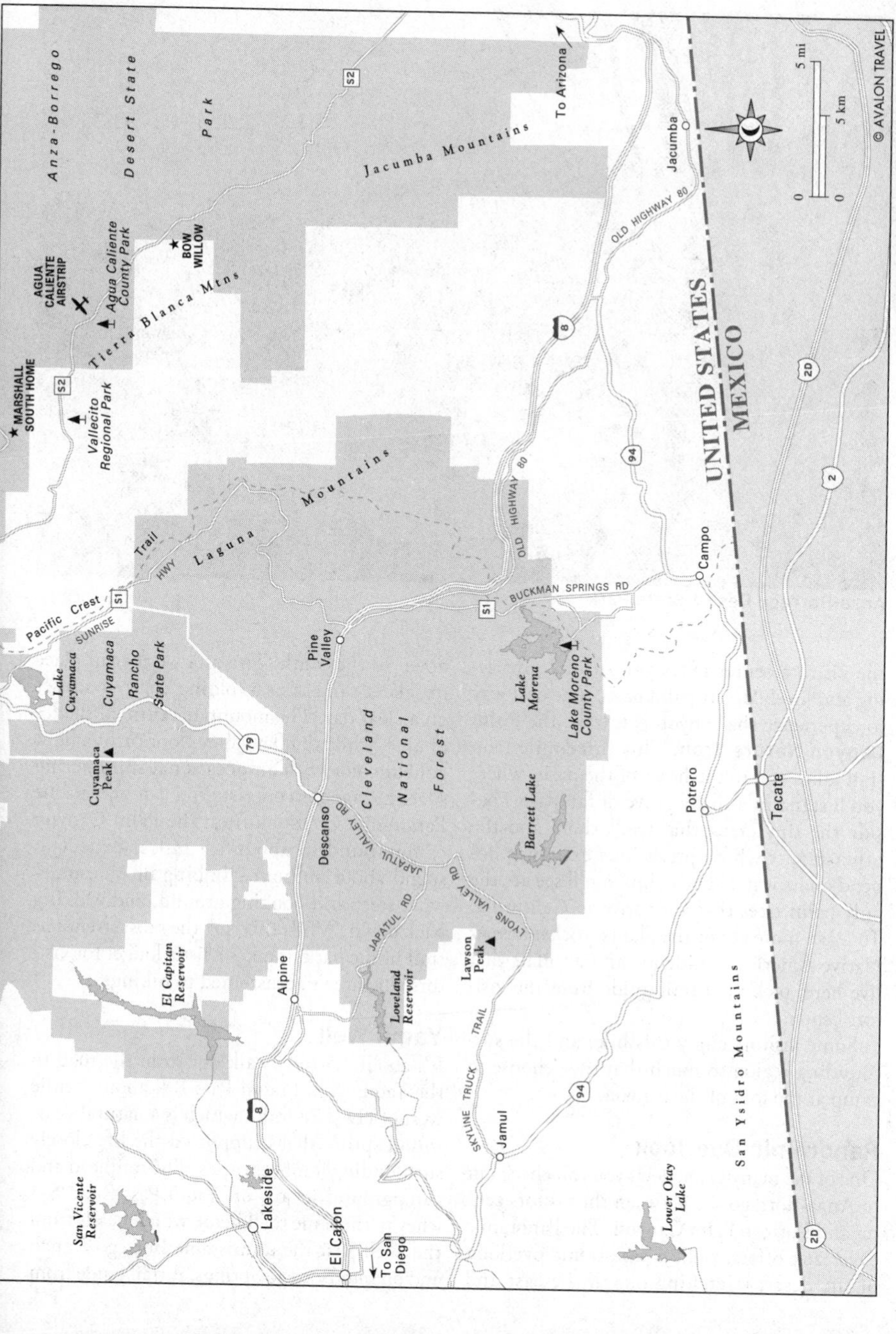
Anza-Borrego Desert State Park
To Arizona
Jacumba Mountains
Jacumba
OLD HIGHWAY 80
AGUA CALIENTE AIRSTRIP
Agua Caliente County Park
BOW WILLOW
Tierra Blanca Mtns
MARSHALL SOUTH HOME
Vallecito Regional Park
S2
8
UNITED STATES
MEXICO
2D
2
94
Laguna Mountains
Trail
HWY
Pacific Crest
SUNRISE
S1
Campo
BUCKMAN SPRINGS RD
Pine Valley
Lake Cuyamaca
Cuyamaca Rancho State Park
Cuyamaca Peak
79
Lake Morena
Lake Moreno County Park
Cleveland National Forest
Descanso
JAPATUL VALLEY RD
Potrero
Tecate
Barrett Lake
LYONS VALLEY RD
JAPATUL RD
Lawson Peak
Alpine
Loveland Reservoir
El Capitan Reservoir
SKYLINE TRUCK TRAIL
San Ysidro Mountains
Jamul
Lakeside
San Vicente Reservoir
El Cajon
To San Diego
Lower Otay Lake
0 5 mi
0 5 km
© AVALON TRAVEL

© LIZ HAMILL SCOTT

Anza-Borrego Desert State Park

the visitors center takes you to this surprising and lovely desert palm oasis. The best way to experience the canyon is to take the **Palm Canyon Nature Trail.** This three-mile loop trail takes you to the heart of the oasis, where you'll stand in a shady grove of fan palms beside the tiny creek that feeds them and the other plants whose precarious existence depend on its water. The palms you'll see are the only palm trees that are native to California. To learn more about the plants, rocks, former Native American residents, and animals that live here, pick up a trail guide from the visitors center.

Some visitors enjoy this hike and the surrounding region so much that they choose to camp at the foot of the canyon.

## Panoramic Overlook

One of the many great views you can check out in Anza-Borrego sits between the visitors center and Borrego Palm Canyon. The Panoramic Overlook offers, well, a panoramic overlook of the desert stretching out to the east and down to the south. This is a wonderful place to take a camera or a folding chair at sunset on a clear day. The mountains turn all shades of blue, while the flat valley floor turns a light golden color with an occasional shimmering silver mirage for contrast. You can hike to the Panoramic Overlook from the Palm Canyon campground in about 1.5 miles. Expect to spend about an hour climbing up the somewhat steep hill, looking around, and walking back down. While this isn't the most strenuous trail in the park, it takes a little longer for visitors who aren't accustomed to hiking.

## Yaqui Well

It's about 1.5-mile walk out from the road to the Yaqui Well (Yaqui Pass Rd. about 1 mile west of Hwy. 78 fork), which is a natural year-round spring that's supported the life closely surrounding it for centuries. The trailhead and campground sit just off Yaqui Pass Road/S-3 (they're the same road here), which heads from the Well past the unmissable Borrego Ranch and on into Borrego Springs. A trail guide from the visitors center to the north of town points out the interesting and in some cases unique features of the trail out to the spring, and of the spring itself. Because of the water, visitors get to see more abundant foliage and wildlife at Yaqui Well. Once upon a time, before conservation and state parks came along, ranchers actually grazed and watered cattle here. Before that, the Kumeyaay Native Americans camped here seasonally. Do be aware that any Kumeyaay artifacts you see lying on the ground are protected as part of the park—picking them up and taking them home is not only rude, it's actually illegal.

From the Yaqui Well trailhead you can also access the Cactus Loop Trail and the Tamarisk Campground, which has water and restroom facilities.

## Font's Point

When you stand atop the visitors center or up on the Panoramic Overlook and gaze out east to see the funky rock formation that is Font's Point (Font's Wash, off the Borrego-Salton Seaway), it looks like it's only a mile or two away. Looks can be deceiving—especially in the desert where the clear, dry air distorts distances. It's actually about 10 miles from the visitors center in the Borrego Badlands. After you negotiate the four miles of dirt road (usually passable by passenger cars) and park in the dirt lot, you'll take a short walk up to Font's Point proper. From here, you'll get arguably the best look at the formation of the desert, from its time as lakes and marshes, ancient to current fault activity, uplift and drying, all the way to current washes and canyons created by flash floods and gradual erosion. Paleontologists come here to excavate fossils from the Pliocene and Pleistocene epochs—believe it or not, woolly mammoths once lived here! Font's Point makes for another great sunrise or sunset vantage point, and there's no sight in the world quite like that of the sun hitting the badlands.

## Coyote Canyon

Coyote Canyon (entrances at the end of Horse Camp Rd. and DiGiorgio Rd.) encompasses the northernmost reaches of Anza-Borrego. Many seasonal creeks flow through this region during the flash-flood season, and the whole area is closed to human traffic from June through September to allow wildlife—especially the rare Borrego Bighorn Sheep—easy and fear-free access to the water here. Winter visitors can traverse the canyon's rough dirt roads in four-wheel-drive vehicles. Passenger cars can make it from the Borrego Springs Road cutoff up to Desert Gardens, but probably shouldn't try to go too far past due to deepening sand and rougher ruts.

**Desert Gardens** and the adjoining **Ocotillo Flats** offer some of the best cactus and ocotillo viewing in the whole of Anza-Borrego. Just park your car off to the side of the road (but not too far off—the sandy ground gets treacherously soft quickly!) and walk out into the desert to check out the variety of native plants that manage to thrive in this arid and inhospitable environment. The star of Ocotillo Flats gave the area its name and if you're there just after a rainstorm, you'll get to see the strangely beautiful ocotillos sprouting leaves and blooming. Ocotillos aren't cacti; they're a deciduous shrub that goes through a full cycle of leafing and dropping leaves each time it rains on the desert. It takes about a month for the new leaves to turn pretty colors and fall off, then the plant just sits and waits for the next rain. Out in the gardens, you'll find the misleadingly named teddy bear cactus (do not let your children hug them), the ubiquitous creosote bushes, wildflowers in the springtime, and all sorts of other desert cacti and plants.

One of the few leftovers of Anza-Borrego's years as ranchland is **Bailey's Cabin.** You can't reach the cabin from the 4WD road in Coyote Canyon. You'll have to park and hike several miles through desert sand out to the small but intact stone edifice. Originally used by the Bailey and Larner families as a line cabin on their ranch, today the state owns and maintains the cabin as part of the park. You can even camp inside it if you get there before anybody else claims it.

### Blair Valley

Off the S-2 paved road you'll find the campground and attractions in and around Blair Valley (S-2 about 7 miles south of Hwy. 78). This central western region of the park offers any number of hiking trails, plus a high density of sights worth walking out to. If you're a big fan of Native American cultural archaeology, hike on out to the **pictographs,** figures painted by early residents of the desert. One big boulder contains all the artwork—mostly Kumeyaay girls' puberty drawings that formed part of the ritual that girls went through upon becoming adult women. Though the pictographs have faded severely in the harsh sunlight over the centuries, you can still see distinctive diamond chain patterns, intricate designs, shining suns, and other symbols.

For something different and yet rather similar, take the steep three-mile hike up to the remains of the **Marshall South Home** at the top of Ghost Mountain. Marshal and Tanya South were a couple ahead of their time, heading for the middle of the desert to live an anti-commercial, totally natural, and intensely difficult existence on a lonely desert peak. They raised three children in a small hilltop cabin without electricity, running water, or access to the modern world. Today, only the skeleton of the cabin remains for visitors to poke around in.

### Split Mountain

At the eastern edge of the park, Split Mountain Road splits off from CA-78 and heads south toward the Fish Creek Mountains. It passes through the Ocotillo Wells recreation area to the north, then heads back into the park and terminates at the remains of an old **Gypsum Mine** (end of Split Mountain Rd.). From there, you can take the 4WD road out to the Split Mountain campground, or past it to the **Wind Caves** (about 5 miles south of Gypsum Mine). These are a cluster of sandstone boulders out of which the wind has carved holes, caves, and even arches over the centuries. While the formations aren't huge, they make a great place to enjoy lunch in the meager shade as the weather gets hot in the late spring and summertime. If you're visiting in the winter and looking for a walk, check out the **Elephant Tree Trail** (Split Mountain Rd., about 9 miles south of Hwy. 78) about midway down the paved road.

### Bow Willow

Down at the south end of the park, the Bow Willow (S-2, about 20 miles north of I-8) region has both water and totally dry badlands topography.

If you take a fairly stout hike, you'll find the **Mountain Palm Springs.** Several springs feed palm oases and in one case a grove of the rare elephant trees. The moderate three-mile round-trip hike seems worth it when you get the chance to rest and relax in the natural shade of the tiny groves. Sit still enough and you might get to see some of the abundant wildlife coming out to drink from the year-round water sources.

Visitors more fascinated with the harsh side of the desert head for the **Carrizo Badlands Overlook.** From here you'll get to see old washes and ridges of rock that were originally deposited by a Colorado River that ran a very different course than the modern version does.

One attraction of this region that's changed recently is the **San Diego Imperial Railway.** The tracks, some of which run across amazing trestles, cross the southern tip of the park. *But,* unlike in previous years, walking the tracks and checking the tunnels is *not* a safe activity! The railroad, which lay dormant and essentially abandoned for years, now has trains running over it on a regular basis. The tunnels and trestles are especially dangerous for explorers, because there's no safe haven. The rails and their access are now private property of the railroad, and you can be ticketed (or worse) if you're found walking the tracks.

## ENTERTAINMENT AND EVENTS

Anza-Borrego, similar to most desert parks, doesn't have too much in the way of happening nightlife. You can get a drink, though, if you're willing to do it fairly early in the evening. The **Krazy Coyote Saloon & Grille** (2220 Hoberg

Rd., Borrego Springs, 760/767-7788, www.thepalmsatindianhead.com, daily 5 P.M.–close, closed summer), despite its Western name, feels more like a cocktail bar than a classic saloon. Sure, they've got beer, but most guests at the Krazy Coyote sip a nice California wine or quaff a top-shelf margarita or a high-end vodka martini. Call ahead to get the variable closing time by season.

Another hotel bar worth looking into is the **Hog Trough Cafe & Saloon** (221 Palm Canyon Dr., Borrego Springs, 760/767-5341, www.palmcanyonresort.com/saloon.htm, daily 5–10 P.M.). This saloon, with its oak bar and eclectic decor, has more of the feel of a true Western watering hole. The Hog Trough prides itself on its Super Bowl party and its welcome for two-wheeled desert travelers. So, bikers, you've a friendly spot to show up, complete with dedicated motorcycle parking.

## SPORTS AND RECREATION

The outdoors calls to many visitors of Anza-Borrego. Countless acres of unspoiled desert are just waiting to be discovered by hikers, bikers, and riders. The Borrego Springs resorts have a few golf courses and plenty of tennis courts and swimming pools.

As always, it's important to remember that when you go outside, you're entering a real desert. It's hot, dry, dangerous, and remote. People really can, and do, die out here every year. Before you venture on even a moderate hike or a flat-ish 4WD road, be sure you've got plenty of water (up to one gallon per person per day), some snacks, sunscreen, a hat, a map, and good walking shoes (even if you're not walking right now, you never know when you might have to). A first-aid kit, extra gas, a spare tire, and a vehicle emergency kit might also be a good idea.

The best time for outdoor recreation at Anza-Borrego is from the fall through the spring; temperatures are moderate and in the spring the wildflowers bloom, adding to the beauty of a hike or off-road trek. In the summertime, the dangerously high temperatures make serious outdoor adventuring a bad idea.

### Hiking

You can hike just about anywhere in the bounds of Anza-Borrego State Park. If you want to, you can just start at the visitors center and wander straight off into the desert. On the other hand, dozens of trails interlace the more visited and accessible areas. Many hikes center around the major sights in the park. Some of these trails are more heavily maintained than others, but don't expect pavement or boardwalks here. All trails are primitive, and many get steep, rocky, rough, sandy, or all of the above.

The **Bill Kenyon Overlook Trail** (Yaqui Pass primitive camp, 1 mile round-trip, easy) offers an easy walk in the **Tamarisk Grove Area.** Shamble along, checking out the different kinds of cactus, before getting out to the payoff-the view. You'll get a chance to look out over the Pinyon Mountains, San Felipe Wash, and other gorgeous features of the Anza-Borrego desert.

A fascinating hike that shows off the best of the Fish Creek Wash runs from **Mud Hills Wash to Elephant Knees** (4.5 miles up Fish Creek Rd. unpaved, off Split Mountain Rd., 4 miles round-trip, moderate). Before you and your ample supply of water set out, take a moment to read up on oyster shell reefs described in the sign at the trail fork. The Fish Creek Wash region was once a part of the long-gone and dried up Gulf of California. You'll be seeing such reefs as you come upon the Mud Hills Wash, and you'll even encounter loose shells from more recent flooding. Once you've thoroughly explored the wash, it's time to climb up the funky Elephant Knees Mesa. You'll be tromping right up the oyster shell reef; in fact, it's a good idea to watch your step here, because the loose shells can be hazardous. At the top, hikers can look down and see the "knee" formation of the bottom of the mesa. For the best views on this hike, go at sunrise or towards sunset, when the lower sun limns the layers of shells and ancient sediment in beautiful colors.

In the south of the park, the **Bow Willow** region offers lots of great hiking, including the network of trails in and around the oases of the **Mountain Palm Springs.** The **North Fork** (2.5 miles, moderate) takes you on a good leg-stretching walk out to the Palm Bowl and Mary's Bowl Grove—a good place to see an elephant tree if you missed them to the north. The **South Fork** (3 miles, moderate) gets you to Pygmy Grove and the Totore Bowl. You can also walk the South Carrizo Creek road across S-2 and all the way out to the Carrizo Creek Wash if you're feeling energetic enough for a 20-mile round-trip trek!

For an easy and educational hike in the **Blair Valley** region, check out the **Trail to the Morteros** (unpaved Blair Valley Rd., 0.5 mile, easy). In less than an hour of easy walking, you'll get to see ancient grinding rocks used by local Native Americans to grind grains. The characteristic mortar-holes are all that remain of a once-industrious community here.

## Horseback Riding

At Anza-Borrego, all the primitive roads open to 4WD vehicles and mountain bikes are also open to equestrian traffic. That makes more than 500 miles of trails to check out within the park boundaries. In addition, part of the **California Riding and Hiking Trail** (near the visitors center) runs through the park. You can also ride on the portion of the **Pacific Crest Trail** that passes through Anza-Borrego briefly at Granite Mountain. The PCT actually runs mostly parallel to and outside the western edge of the park.

Inside Anza-Borrego, one of the best-used trails is at **Coyote Canyon** in the northern reaches. Take care, and please don't let your horse trample the delicate landscape where the road tapers off. This is where you'll find the Vern Whitaker Horse Camp, with its corrals making a desert trip with your horse both possible and comfortable. Another stand-out riding road is the **Jasper Trail** (15 miles) that runs through Grapevine Canyon in the middle western section of the park.

Didn't bring your own horse to Anza-Borrego? You can take a two-hour ride on one of the few and extremely well-tended Arabians of the **Smoketree Arabian Ranch** (302 Palm Canyon Dr., 866/408-1812, www.smoketreearabianranch.com, $95/person). This isn't your typical meat-grinding rental ranch. Yu'll find no sad, tired old nags wearing their saddles all day here. Instead, your ride will include grooming and preparing your mount as you get to know him or her before you ever climb into the saddle. You and your horse will enjoy learning about one another as you take a ride out into the beautiful desert landscape. Serious equestrians will love the way the folks at Smoketree take care of their beloved horses. But because there are few of them available for "guest" rides, be sure to call in advance to make reservations. The spring wildflower season is the busiest for Smoketree.

## Golf

Yes, there is golfing even out here in this wild desert country. The "premier" local courses sit on the land of the **Borrego Springs Resort** (1112 Tilting T Dr., 760/767-3330, www.borregospringsresort.com, greens fees $40–65, cart included). You'll find three separate nine-hole courses: The Palms, Desert Willow, and Mesquite. Pick any two to create an 18-hole day. Or take advantage of the short, cool mornings for a quick nine holes before the desert really heats up. Borrego Springs also has practice facilities, a pro shop, and regularly scheduled tournaments. Check the website for hotel-and-golf packages, as well as year-round lessons and clinics to improve your game.

Another great nine-hole course in the Borrego Springs region is **The Springs at Borrego** (2255 DiGiorgio Rd., 866/330-0003, www.springsatborrego.com/golf.htm). The Springs is adjacent to the RV park that goes by the same name. At a par-36 with a practice range, this small but technical course is perfect for golfers who want a challenging but not too-long day on a desert course. For golfers who've come to the desert specifically to play the game, there's also the **RoadRunner Golf Course** (1010 Palm Canyon Dr., 760/767-5374, www.roadrunnerclub.com/golf). This short 18-hole, par-3 course is great for newer golfers while helping more experienced players improve their short game.

### Off-Roading

Anza-Borrego State Park offers over 500 miles of dirt and sand roads accessible by highway-legal four-wheel-drive vehicles. These run around almost all areas of the park, letting you explore many places that are inaccessible otherwise. So bring your favorite tagged boonie-crasher and have a blast!

The **Jasper Trail & Grapevine Canyon** (access via Jasper Trail of S22, 13.5 miles, easy to moderate) offers a graded trail for most of the ride. You can stop and see some rare desert water welling up from Stuart Spring. Take a left here to remain on the trail and go toward the Yaqui Well primitive campground, or a right to head back out to Highway 78. If you pass Yaqui Well and head out onto the *bajada,* you'll get to see some lovely cactus varieties alongside the trail.

Want to feel like a serious boonie-crasher? Take the **Fish Creek Trail** (easy to moderate). You'll first find yourself bumping along a fault on a fairly wide track. Extremely primitive camping (no restrooms) is available at Fish Creek. From here, the trail narrows into Fish Creek Canyon, where you'll get to see the famous oyster reef cliffs. *Don't* take the Arroyo Seco del Diablo cutoff, since it's got a nasty drop that makes it dangerous to drive from this direction. Instead, keep going toward the **Sandstone Canyon Trail** (moderate to difficult). Here you'll get a great experience: tight maneuvering through narrow canyons of wind-eroded soft sandstone.

**Pinyon Mountain Road** (end of Big Rock Creek Rd., 7 miles plus 4-mile spur, easy to moderate) crosses in and out of the state park and starts close to Camp Fenner State Prison—so don't pick up any hitchhikers here! You'll get a good mix of open trail driving and creek fording, and on the spur road you can head up for a view of Devil's Punchbowl and Big Rock Creek and even on into a pine forest. Lots of out-of-the-car activities stem from this road, including access to the Pacific Crest Trail for hikers and deer hunting on the U.S. Forest Service land.

Longing for a glimpse of another country? Take the **Calcite Mine Trail** (S22 18.5 miles east of Borrego Springs, difficult). You'll bump up a difficult and slick trail (take care and use a spotter) that will take you up to a ridge that lets you look south toward Mexico. From there, the road gets even bumpier and more boulder-filled, so consider hoofing it the rest of the way to the abandoned calcite mine. When you get there, look but don't take; it's illegal to remove calcite crystals from the State Park.

While Anza-Borrego has many primitive roads worth checking out in your (mandated by the park) street-legal, possibly four-wheel-drive vehicle, the park might not make for your idea of great four-wheeling fun. Right next door, so to speak, sits the immense **Ocotillo Wells State Vehicular Recreation Area** (760/767-5391, ohv.parks.ca.gov, year-round, free). Countless (well, 80,000) acres of desert have been set aside specifically for boonie-crashers to test the mettle of their baddest trucks and best dirt bikes. Bring your rock-crawling 4WDs, open dune buggies, and other toys. Tags aren't required here. You can camp for up to 30 days, but you must bring your own water, as *no water is available inside the park.*

Be aware that Ocotillo Wells is immensely popular, and 4WD lovers come from all over California to drive here. If you're planning to visit on a holiday weekend, expect severe traffic congestion (especially when leaving) and crowding on the trails and in the camping areas.

### Biking

You're welcome to break out your mountain bike and bump along any of the primitive roads in Anza-Borrego, some of which are sandy, rough, and steep. However, no bikes are permitted on hiking trails or overland off the roads. Check out adjoining Ocotillo Wells for more extreme mountain biking opportunities.

## CAMPING

Anza-Borrego is the only state park in the California system to allow camping anywhere within its boundaries. For real. Just pull your car off the road and tromp off into the desert with your tent, find a big rock, and pitch your tent in its shadow. The catch? You'll need to take care of yourself out in the unrelenting desert. No bathrooms, no water, no nothing—just you and a shovel. If you want a more civilized desert camping experience, pick one of the RV-friendly campgrounds or even the minimally developed backcountry campgrounds.

## Developed Campgrounds

Few well-developed campgrounds grace the parched lands of Anza-Borrego. But if you really want an RV slot or a tent site with access to flush toilets and showers, you can find one. For the developed campgrounds, be sure to make a reservation in advance at 800/444-7275. Nearest to the visitors center you can stay at the **Borrego Palm Canyon Campground.** This large and somewhat desolate campground has over 100 campsites, 55 with RV hookups. (Call ahead to see if the dump station is functioning before your visit.) In addition to the showers and restrooms, working phones are available here. Some campsites have fire rings.

The **Tamarisk Grove Campground** (Road S-3 and Hwy. 78, $10–15) has 27 RV sites with access to showers, toilets, and phones. It is the southernmost fully developed campground in Anza-Borrego.

For equestrians, Anza-Borrego maintains the **Vern Whitaker Horse Camp** (Horse Camp Rd., $16). Forty corrals lie adjacent to 10 campsites, making it possible for campers to sleep near their horses. Though running water and full bathrooms grace the campground, the showers are solar heated so you may be taking a chance by using them.

## Primitive Campgrounds

Plenty of primitive campgrounds dot the land of Anza-Borrego. Also, you're permitted to camp anywhere in the park. Just be sure you've got the equipment and supplies you'll need before you pull off at your favorite cactus garden and pitch your tent. (Remember: There are no bathrooms out in the middle of the desert!) Most of the primitive campgrounds have pit or chemical toilet facilities and very little else in the way of amenities. Camping at either the primitive campgrounds or off in the rocks and sands is usually free.

The campgrounds at **Culp Valley, Yaqui Pass,** and **Arroyo** have reasonable access to paved roads. From dirt roads (most accessible via passenger cars), you can get to the sites at **Fish Creek, Yaqui Well, Blair Valley,** and **Bow Willow.** Bow Willow has more sites than most, takes reservations, and has a $7–9 per night fee. If you're interested in solitude and silence, and you're up for a hike in to your campsite, you might consider the sites at **Marshall South Home** and **Sheep Canyon.**

# ACCOMMODATIONS

Many visitors to the desert prefer not to experience its harsh beauty 24 hours a day. For them, the town of Borrego Springs, which sits right in the middle of the park, offers a wide range of motels and resorts to suit every taste and budget range.

## Under $100

The **Stanlunds Resort Inn and Suites** (2771 Borrego Springs Rd., 760/767-5501, www.stanlunds.com, $62–175) offers a convenient motel room at the right price for desert rats on a budget. Nope, it's not much to look at, but the guest rooms are reasonably clean, the beds are comfortable, and the bathroom plumbing works most of the time. You'll find the rooms rather small and decorated in standard motel florals and dark carpets, many with at least one white-painted brick wall. Larger rooms have dining areas and some have kitchens and patios as well. An outdoor pool beckons to guests who need to cool off after a long day exploring the desert, and the location downtown makes it great for dining and shopping in Borrego Springs.

## $100–150

For affordable luxury on your desert vacation, get a room at the **Borrego Springs Resort** (1121 Tilting T Dr., 760/767-5700, www.borregospringsresort.com, $115–200). Spacious rooms include comfortable modern wood-framed beds, fine cotton bedding, big bathrooms, and pretty views of mountains or the pool areas. For multiple rooms and a kitchenette, choose one of the suites. Decor tends toward the simple motel style, with quiet soothing colors. Outside of your room, take a dip in one of the two pools or lounge beside them in a covered cabana to keep the sun off. One of the biggest attractions of the resort is the attached country club golf course; check the website for packages. You can also play tennis, or ask at the desk about guided tours of Anza-Borrego State Park. Plenty of dining is available on-site, from the fancy white tablecloths at The Arches dining room to the casual Roadrunner Café. If you just want a nice before or after dinner drink, take a seat beside the column-shaped fireplace and order a classic cocktail.

## $150-250

For some travelers, it's important that their motel match with the nature and culture of its surroundings. The **Borrego Valley Inn** (405 Palm Canyon Dr., 800/333-5810, www.borregovalleyinn.com, $195–300) does just that, with low, blocky, orange adobe-style buildings with red tile roofs, and desert garden landscaping throughout. Wander the grounds, or just sit on a wooden bench and watch the birds hop about enjoying the flowers and bugs. If you're serious about your nature loving, you can take a skinny-dip in the clothing-optional swimming pool and spa (privacy fenced for everyone's comfort, and directly accessible from rooms 1–7).

Even the smallest rooms are characteristic of its charm. All guest rooms have red-tiled floors, desert floral or Native American–inspired bedspreads and decor, matching accent decorations, cable TV, patios, and nice bathrooms. Bigger rooms might have gas fireplaces, walk-in showers, or soaking tubs, while all rooms have fridges, microwaves, and coffee makers. The largest suite offers a full homey kitchen, one bedroom, and stunning tile work.

## Over $250

For the big spenders who want the beauty of the desert without any of its discomforts, there's **Borrego Ranch Resort & Spa** (3845 Yaqui Pass Rd., Borrego Springs, 800/824-1884, www.borregoranch.com, $400–1,700). This

© LANCE SCOTT

Borrego Ranch Resort & Spa

great sprawling resort has everything a luxury vacationer could ever need or want for a night, a week, or a month in Anza-Borrego. The recreation facilities include tennis courts, a state-of-the-art fitness center, an archery range, a tournament croquet field, and no fewer than five swimming pools. Families can enjoy pools designated just for them, complete with complimentary toys, while adults can relax or exercise in peace at the adults-only pools and spas. If you're renting one of the casitas, you may have your own private large spa or small swimming pool.

Nineteen such casitas grace the property, and they're more the size and shape of comfortable small homes than hotel rooms. You can bring your family and friends to share the comfy multiple bedrooms, beautiful desert-themed decor, and top-shelf amenities of these detached houses. Even the regular poolside rooms (yup, they're all poolside) offer tremendous space, cushy furniture, spacious bathrooms, and all the wonderful extras Borrego Ranch lavishes upon its guests to justify the lavish prices. Each room includes a full breakfast in the dining room each day.

Another reason to spend all that money on your lodgings here is the service—from the dining room to the desk staff to the fitness attendants, most everyone at Borrego Ranch will go out of their way to help you. If you need advice on activities either inside or outside the resort, they can definitely hook you up.

## FOOD

### Casual Dining

Looking for a tasty breakfast or lunch? Try locals' favorite ☾ **Red Ocotillo** (2220 Hoberg Rd., Borrego Springs, 760/767-7400, daily 7 A.M.–9 P.M., $10–20). Despite the exotic desert name, this friendly and welcoming restaurant serves up classic diner food. Just look for the Palms at Indian Head. The interior dining room is done in retro-American kitsch, while the small outdoor dining area lets diners with dogs eat in the company of their canine friends. You'll find the service good even when there's a crowd, but the real reason to come to Red Ocotillo is the food. Diners rave about the simple but delectable fresh biscuits and gravy, served all day along with the rest of the breakfast menu. Lunch and dinner items run to classic American staple entrées, sandwiches, and so on. For a great inexpensive meal in the desert, Red Ocotillo is your best bet.

After hours out in the southwestern desert scenery of Anza-Borrego, a Mexican dinner seems like the perfect way to end the day. **Pablito's of The Desert** (590 Palm Canyon Drive, Borrego Springs, 760/767-5753, daily 11 A.M.–2:30 P.M., 5–9 P.M., $5–15) offers good solid Mexican staples with a little bit of a desert twist—such as cactus in a breakfast egg dish. Yes, they serve breakfast even though Pablito's doesn't open until later in the morning. You'll also find extremely tasty lunch and dinner options.

### Fine Dining

For an upscale meal in the low desert, you can't beat the **Cimarrón Room** at Borrego Ranch (3845 Yaqui Pass Rd., Borrego Springs, 800/824-1884, www.borregoranch.com, daily 7–11 A.M. and 11:30 A.M.–3:30 P.M., dinner nightly, $25). True, it has the advantage of being pretty much the top game in a small town, but you'll still find a low-lit, rambling dining room with a charming romantic atmosphere. Or ask for a table out on the patio on the endless warm desert evenings. The service can be variable, but the quality of the innovative dishes remains constant here. Look for high-end California stylings, including organic and sustainable produce and meat. The wine list is a star, and you'll find a long, long list of California and European wines. For a special treat, try a different glass with each course, including dessert.

The **Krazy Coyote Saloon & Grille** (2220 Hoberg Rd., Borrego Springs, 760/767-7788, www.thepalmsatindianhead.com, opens daily at 5:30 P.M., closed during summer, $20–40) is a Borrego Springs favorite. The the entrées are interesting and the homemade complimentary breads and "nibbles" make diners feel pampered. Visitors enjoy the casual-elegant atmosphere with windows overlooking the resort pool. Do expect to pay handsomely for the privilege of eating here, but most diners feel that the experience (and the martinis) are worth it.

### Markets

Need to stock up on groceries before a camping stint out in the park? Head for the **Center Market** (590 Palm Canyon Dr., # 304, Borrego Springs, 760/767-3311, Mon.–Sat 8:30 A.M.–6:30 P.M., Sun. 8:30 A.M.–5 P.M.) for the basics. For good fresh produce, join the locals at the **Borrego Springs Farmers' Market** (Christmas Circle and Palm Canyon Dr., Borrego Springs, Fri. 7 A.M.–noon) on Friday mornings. Grapefruit are the specialty of the region, so be sure to pick up some of the local Borrego breed if you can. They're sweet and pink and juicy.

## INFORMATION AND SERVICES

The only town within an easy distance of the park is Borrego Springs. It's not a one-streeter, but Borrego Springs is definitely a small town, so don't expect all the services and conveniences of a major city here.

### Tourist Infomation

The **Anza-Borrego State Park Visitors Center** (200 Palm Canyon Dr., 760/767-4205, www.abdsp.org, Oct.–May daily 9 A.M.–5 P.M., June–Sept. weekends only) sits right outside of town, beyond an odd little turnoff near the end of Palm Canyon Road. It includes a ranger station, an interpretive display area, and a demonstration desert garden outside and on its roof. Rangers here can help you plan drives and hikes, and give you advice on the best places for views, wildflowers, and wildlife.

### Media and Communications

The Internet and cell phone towers have come to Borrego Springs. Many of the resorts and motels offer Wi-Fi (sometimes free, sometimes not). Cell service is easy to come by in town, but can get spotty as you get farther out into the park. Don't expect your cell phone to save you if you get trapped in the badlands—have plenty of supplies on hand in case of emergency.

The ***Borrego Sun*** is the local paper, available in newspaper stands outside the Center Market.

### Medical Services

The nearest major hospital to Anza-Borrego with an emergency room is the **John F. Kennedy Memorial Hospital** (47111 Monroe St., Indio, 760/347-6191, www.jfkmemorialhosp.com), 34 miles away in Indio. The **Borrego Medical Clinic** (4343 Yaqui Pass Rd., 760/767-5051) is open 8:30 A.M.–5 P.M. on weekdays only. They do have a 24-hour answering service that can get you in touch with a doctor if you need to ask a medical question.

## GETTING THERE AND AROUND

### Air

The closest commercial airports to Anza-Borrego are the **San Diego International Airport** (3665 N. Harbor Drive, San Diego, 619/400-2400 www.san.org) and the **Palm Springs International Airport** (3400 E. Tahquitz Canyon Way, Palm Springs, 760/318-3800, www.palmspringsairport.com). There is a private airport three miles east of **Borrego Springs** (1820 Palm Canyon Dr., 760/767-7415).

### Car

Anza-Borrego State Park sits about an hour from Palm Springs to the north and from San Diego to the west. The major east–west road through the park is CA-78. County roads S-2 and S-3 run north and south through the desert, and S-22 heads east out of Borrego Springs toward CA-86.

On holiday weekends and popular spring Sundays, traffic can get very heavy on Highway 78 to the adjoining Highway 79 leaving the park to the west. Expect to creep along, possibly for hours, and plan extra time and maybe a food stop on the way out.

While you can get around the park in a passenger car, if you want to explore the dirt roads of the back country in-depth, you'll need a four-wheel-drive vehicle. Check with park rangers about current road conditions.

## Tours

Anza-Borrego has a long wildflower season, which can run from January all the way through April in moister years. Check with the state park headquarters (760/767-4684, www.parks.ca.gov) for annual wildflower predictions and status reports. You can also either call or check in at the ranger station for information on guided wildflower tours during your stay.

# JULIAN

Between San Diego and Anza-Borrego State Park sits the tiny mining town of Julian. When gold fever struck California, it quickly spread throughout the whole huge territory—even this far south. But if you've been exploring the small towns of Gold Country proper, you're in for a shock when you enter the town limits of Julian. This is a Gold Town, complete with endless crowds and parking nightmares. Residents of both San Diego and Los Angeles escape to the small-town atmosphere of Julian, with its cute shops and many public events, almost every weekend of the year.

## Sights

Most folks who come to Julian spend their time walking up and down the sidewalks of **Historic Downtown Julian.** With its many shops and restaurants, pretty old-style buildings, and attractive woodsy setting, Downtown Julian makes a nice change from the arid valleys all around it. Expect a crowd, but you'll still enjoy a stroll downtown.

Believe it or not, you can actually go wine-tasting in Julian. **Orfila Vineyards** (4470 Hwy. 78, Julian, 760/765-0102, www.orfilawines.com, Wed.–Mon. 10 A.M.–5 P.M.) has a notable reputation throughout the state. They're famous for their Rhone wines, including Viognier, Marsanne, and perhaps most of all Syrah. Their cooler weather varietals come from vineyards in coastal California. Orfila's other tasting room sits in the San Pasqual Valley north of San Diego.

The **Witch Creek Winery** (2000 Main St., Julian, 760/765-2023, www.witchcreekwinery.com, daily 11 A.M.–5 P.M.) has a fabulous long list of red wines, a few whites, and a fun cat theme running through their labels. You'll find some fascinating and unusual wines here. Ever tasted a Montepulciano before? How about an Aglianico? Witch Creek also offers a delicious array of red blends, and even a hard apple cider. Whatever your tastes, you'll find something to love at this fabulous small winery. Check out Carlsbad for the winery's other tasting room.

## Accommodations

If the heat of the desert in Anza-Borrego gets to you after a while, Julian can make a nice cool base of operations to escape back to after a day of desert explorations. Lodgings in Julian run to rustic B&Bs and vacation cabin rentals in the woods outside of town.

For a reasonably priced, rustic room in Julian, stay at the **Angels Landing Country Inn and Resort** (2323 Farmer Rd., Julian, 760/765-2578, www.angelresort.com, $90–160). Angels Landing offers quite a few family- friendly rooms and suites with multiple beds per room. Rooms fairly small with cute decor. The Lilac Building can sleep up to 10 people. The best part about this lodging is the setting—outside of town in the meadows and forested mountainside.

The **Butterfield Bed & Breakfast** (2284 Sunset Dr., Julian, 760/765-2179, www.butterfieldbandb.com, $135–185) is just as cute and country-kitsch as Julian itself. Each of the five rooms has unique decor, from elegant antique European to patchwork-quilted country Americana. All rooms have private bathrooms and cable TV, and the large private cottage can sleep up to four for an additional fee (all other rooms sleep two). Guest rooms come with a full breakfast each morning, served outdoors in the gazebo in summer and inside by the fire in winter.

A nod to luxury in Julian, **Orchard Hill Country Inn** (2502 Washington St., Julian, 760/765-1700, www.orchardhill.com, $210–500) offers 22 elegant guest rooms in a serene garden setting. Expect elegant updated decor and appointments, complete with lovely tiles, restored antique furniture, and a homelike clutter of linens and pillows. Some cottage rooms have whirlpool tubs, and all cottages have patios or porches for summer lounging and fireplaces for winter snuggling. All guests receive a full breakfast, afternoon nibbles and wine (or beer), and upscale amenities.

For a more independent lodging experience, Julian's many vacation cabin rentals are a great choice. The **Artists' Loft, Big Cat Cabin,** and **Strawberry Hill Cabin** (4811 Pine Ridge Ave., Julian, 760/765-0765, www.artistsloft.com, $195) are all managed by the same folks. Each cabin is unique, but all share a combination of rustic construction and decoration juxtaposed with comfortable amenities. Expect to find a large sitting room with fireplace, a full kitchen with a few basic staples provided, a separate comfortable bedroom with season-appropriate bedding, and a porch or window-seat area. You're welcome to bring a full supply of groceries and cook for yourself throughout your stay at any of the cabins.

## Food

The acknowledged favorite pie shop in town is **Mom's Pie House** (2119 Main St., Julian, 760/765-2472, www.momspiesjulian.com, Mon.–Fri. 8 A.M.–5 P.M., Sat.–Sun. 8 A.M.–6 P.M., $10). Naturally, the specialty of the house is old-fashioned apple pie. You'll also find crumb-crust pies, apple-boysenberry, apple-cherry, strawberry rhubarb, and more pie flavors. If you can't take a whole pie, just stop in for a slice of your favorite flavor, maybe topped with ice cream or real whipped cream. You can also grab a sandwich and a cup of coffee while you're here. Expect crowds and lines on holiday and event weekends.

For a full meal, check out the **Julian Grille** (2224 Main St., Julian, 760/765-0173, daily 11 A.M.–3 P.M., Tues.–Sun. 5–9 P.M., $10–20), which serves higher-than-expected quality seafood and steaks in a quaint cottage. Another American diner-style eatery is the **Cowgirl Café** (2116 Main St., Julian, 760/765-2167, $10–20). The kitsch factor gets high in this tiny eatery—check out the cowgirl memorabilia on the walls. But the main reason to brave the lines at this eight-table restaurant is the quality of the food. Expect salads to be fresh, sandwiches balanced and tasty, and desserts to be made with local apples (of course). Despite the oft-crowded dining room and small staff, service is both friendly and fast, prompting locals to give their names and wait up to 30 minutes for a table on weekends. Call for the current operating hours.

**Romano's Dodge House** (2718 B St., Julian, 760/765-1003, www.romanosjulian.com, Wed.–Mon. 11:30 A.M.–8:30 P.M., $18) is billed as the most romantic restaurant in Julian. Certainly it's cute, with its red-checked tablecloths and soft mood lighting. But what's really delightful here is the food. Sure, you can get a good bowl of pasta or a pizza but even better are the specialty entrées—unique dishes made with local ingredients (yes, apples and cider) that combine an Italian aesthetic with California creativity. The wine list features local Julian vintages as well as wines from around California and imported from Italy. Reservations are recommended for dinner, especially on weekends in fall and winter. Oh, and bring cash, as Romano's does not accept credit cards.

## Practicalities

The **Julian Chamber of Commerce** (2129 Main St., 760/765-1857, www.julianca.com, daily 10 A.M.–4 P.M.) consists of a tiny office and a big rack of brochures. You'll find almost everything you need in the brochures, including over a dozen possible places to stay overnight.

Julian lies at the junction of CA-78 and CA-79. You can drive there from Anza-Borrego in the east or San Diego to the west. Because Julian is incredibly popular as a weekend getaway destination, parking on Main Street can be challenging. You'll probably need to find parking on a side street two or three blocks from the action. During events, signs and townsfolk can help guide you to dirt lots (which you'll have to pay to use) near but not in of the center of town.

# SAN DIEGO

San Diego is the ideal destination for anyone whose idea of the perfect California vacation is a day (or a week, or a month) lying on a white sand beach, sipping cocktails, and looking out over the Pacific Ocean. Resort hotels and restaurants perch along the seaside, beckoning visitors to what is often thought to be the friendliest big city in California.

Even though San Diego's physical area seems small compared to other parts of California, it can't be beat for density of things to see. From a world-famous zoo to dozens of museums to the thick layer of military and mission history, San Diego offers education, enlightenment, and fun to visitors with all different interests.

Animal lovers flock to the San Diego Zoo and Sea World, while water spirits dive into the Pacific Ocean to catch a wave or examine a variety of sea life in their natural habitat. Travelers who want a little more of the trappings of city life will enjoy the bar and club scene, as well as a thriving theater community.

Across the bay, the long, blue Coronodo Bridge connects San Diegans to Coronado, an island-like encalve that beckons beach bums and film aficionados alike to the grandly historic (and reputedly haunted) Hotel del Coronado, where the Marilyn Monroe film *Some Like It Hot* was filmed.

North of San Diego proper, the towns of La Jolla, Del Mar, and North County offer a more relaxed pace for exploring. Snorkel the azure water of La Jolla Cove or vye for a piece of that pristine sand with the beach crowd. Splurge

© SAN DIEGO CVB

## HIGHLIGHTS

**Gaslamp Quarter:** This former red-light district is now the re-imagined epicenter of downtown San Diego's restaurants, shops, and nightlife (page 636).

**San Diego Zoo:** The San Diego Zoo is world renowned for a reason. The 80-acre park and botanical garden is home to a vast array of plants and animals both exotic and ordinary, from elephants and tigers to meerkats and pythons (page 638).

**Whaley House:** The most haunted house in the United States can be found in Old Town San Diego. Built in 1857, this historic Greek Revival mansion housed members of the Whaley family – and is reputed to house their ghosts as well (page 641).

**Mission San Diego del Alcala:** California's first mission is still a working Catholic church, as well as a museum, with insights into mission life for both the Franciscan monks and native Kumeyaay people (page 642).

**California Surf Museum:** Southern California is synonymous with surfing, and this museum explores the sport's California origins with a wealth of exhibits and events (page 649).

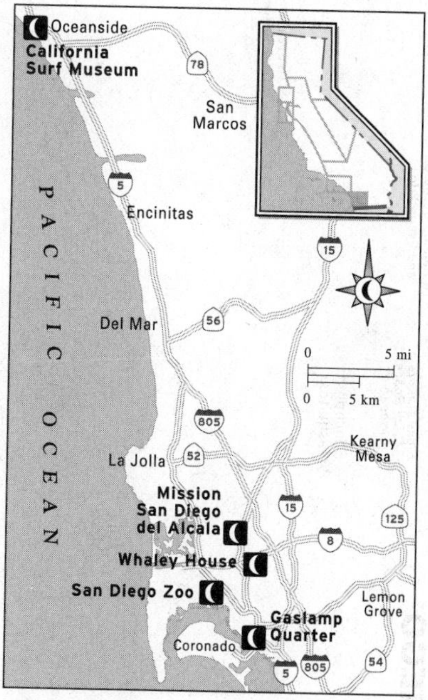


LOOK FOR TO FIND RECOMMENDED SIGHTS, ACTIVITIES, DINING, AND LODGING.



some of that vacation cash on a horse race at the Del Mar Racetrack, or get up-close and personal interaction with the exotic animals at the Wild Animal Park.

## PLANNING YOUR TIME

Compared to other parts of California, San Diego's major attractions sit relatively close together, and it's easy to get from one place to another in a reasonable amount of time. San Diego County has arguably the best beaches in the state. If your travel goals are focused on sand and surf, consider staying in Mission Bay or Point Loma, or farther afield in the North County coastal area. On the other hand, if you're in town to see the zoo or take in some museums, you'll be spending time in Balboa Park, which abuts the Old Town and downtown areas. If you're starting a tour of California Missions, head for Old Town first. Military history and Navy buffs will be content to spend their whole trip within the city limits of San Diego, dividing their time between the Harbor and Point Loma. If you've got an extra couple of hours and you haven't been out there yet, take the bridge over to Coronado to gawk at the ridiculous exuberance of the Hotel del Coronado.

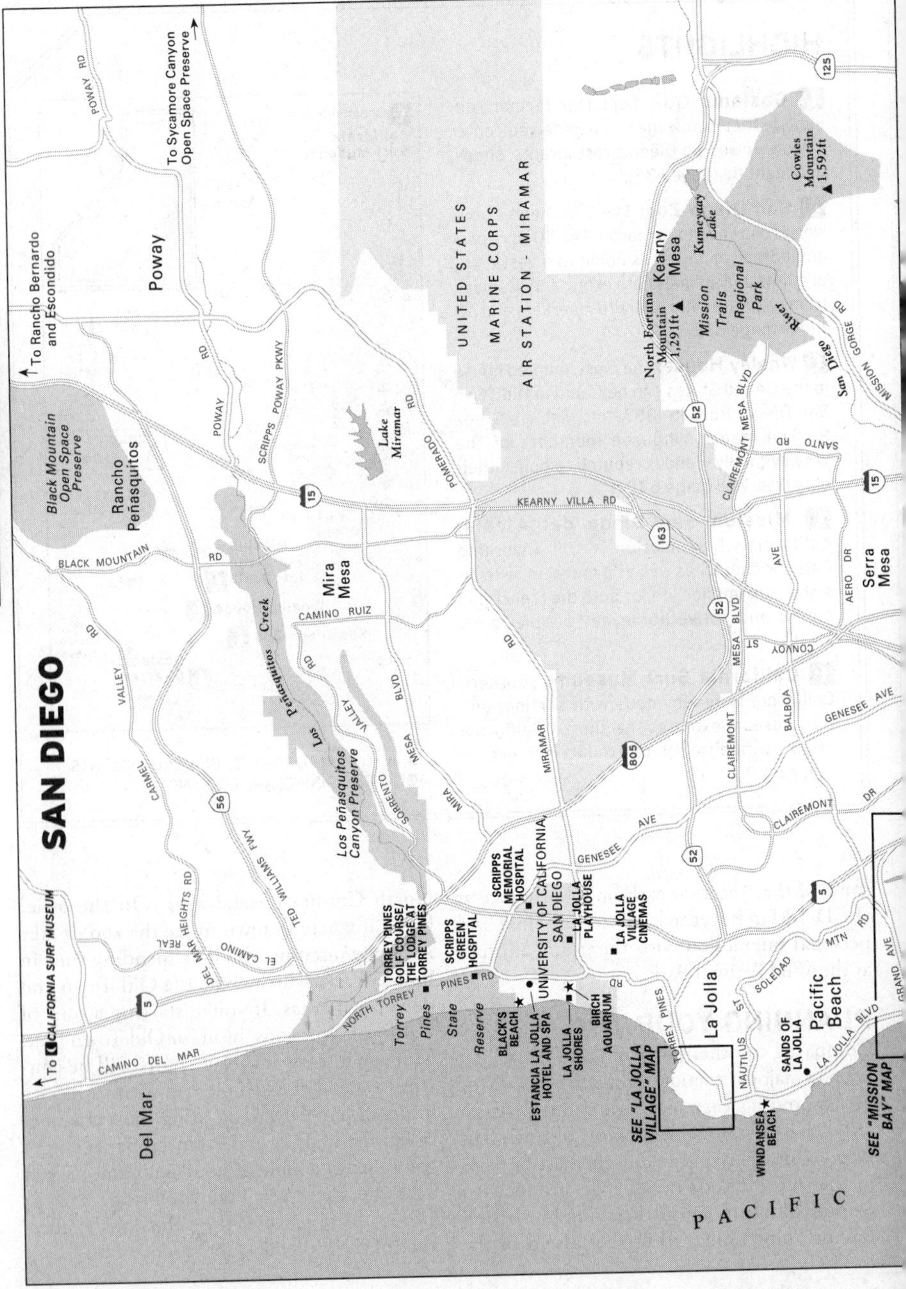
SAN DIEGO
Del Mar
To Rancho Bernardo and Escondido
To Sycamore Canyon Open Space Preserve
Poway
Black Mountain Open Space Preserve
Rancho Peñasquitos
Mira Mesa
Los Peñasquitos Canyon Preserve
Los Peñasquitos Creek
UNITED STATES MARINE CORPS AIR STATION - MIRAMAR
Lake Miramar
North Fortuna Mountain 1,291ft
Kearny Mesa
Mission Trails Regional Park
Kumeyaay Lake
Cowles Mountain 1,592ft
San Diego River
Serra Mesa
Torrey Pines State Reserve
TORREY PINES GOLF COURSE/ THE LODGE AT TORREY PINES
SCRIPPS GREEN HOSPITAL
SCRIPPS MEMORIAL HOSPITAL
UNIVERSITY OF CALIFORNIA SAN DIEGO
LA JOLLA PLAYHOUSE
LA JOLLA VILLAGE CINEMAS
BLACK'S BEACH
ESTANCIA LA JOLLA HOTEL AND SPA
LA JOLLA SHORES
BIRCH AQUARIUM
To CALIFORNIA SURF MUSEUM
SEE "LA JOLLA VILLAGE" MAP
La Jolla
SANDS OF LA JOLLA
WINDANSEA BEACH
Pacific Beach
SEE "MISSION BAY" MAP
PACIFIC
CAMINO DEL MAR
EL CAMINO REAL
DEL MAR HEIGHTS RD
CARMEL VALLEY RD
TED WILLIAMS FWY
BLACK MOUNTAIN RD
POWAY RD
SCRIPPS POWAY PKWY
POMERADO RD
CAMINO RUIZ
SORRENTO VALLEY RD
MIRA MESA BLVD
MIRAMAR RD
KEARNY VILLA RD
NORTH TORREY PINES RD
TORREY PINES RD
GENESEE AVE
CLAIREMONT MESA BLVD
CLAIREMONT DR
BALBOA AVE
CONVOY ST
AERO DR
SANTO RD
MISSION GORGE RD
SOLEDAD MTN RD
NAUTILUS ST
LA JOLLA BLVD
GRAND AVE
5
15
52
56
125
163
805

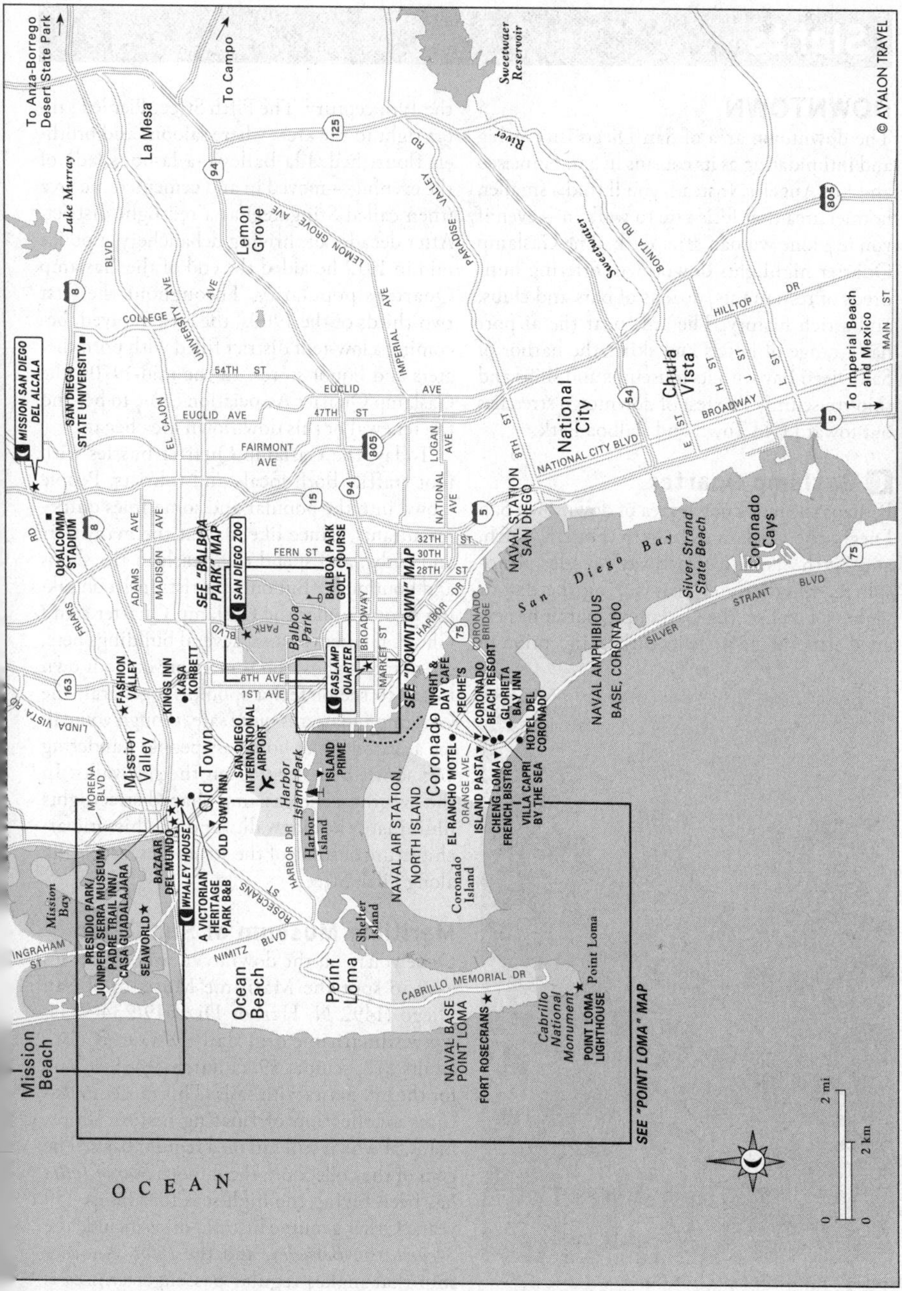
To Anza-Borrego Desert State Park
To Campo
La Mesa
Lake Murray
Lemon Grove
Sweetwater Reservoir
Sweetwater River
National City
Chula Vista
To Imperial Beach and Mexico
© AVALON TRAVEL
MISSION SAN DIEGO DEL ALCALA
SAN DIEGO STATE UNIVERSITY
QUALCOMM STADIUM
COLLEGE AVE
EUCLID AVE
FAIRMONT AVE
54TH ST
47TH ST
EL CAJON BLVD
UNIVERSITY AVE
IMPERIAL AVE
LEMON GROVE AVE
VALLEY RD
PARADISE
BONITA RD
HILLTOP DR
BROADWAY
NATIONAL CITY BLVD
MAIN ST
8TH ST
LOGAN AVE
NATIONAL AVE
FERN ST
32TH ST
30TH ST
28TH ST
ADAMS AVE
MADISON AVE
FRIARS RD
LINDA VISTA RD
MORENA BLVD
SEE "BALBOA PARK" MAP
SAN DIEGO ZOO
BALBOA PARK GOLF COURSE
Balboa Park
PARK BLVD
6TH AVE
1ST AVE
GASLAMP QUARTER
BROADWAY
MARKET ST
SEE "DOWNTOWN" MAP
HARBOR DR
CORONADO BRIDGE
NAVAL STATION SAN DIEGO
San Diego Bay
Silver Strand State Beach
Coronado Cays
SILVER STRANT BLVD
NAVAL AMPHIBIOUS BASE, CORONADO
FASHION VALLEY
Mission Valley
KINGS INN
KASA
KORBETT
Old Town
SAN DIEGO INTERNATIONAL AIRPORT
Harbor Island Park
ISLAND PRIME
Harbor Island
OLD TOWN INN
WHALEY HOUSE
BAZAAR DEL MUNDO
A VICTORIAN HERITAGE PARK B&B
PRESIDIO PARK/ JUNIPERO SERRA MUSEUM/ PADRE TRAIL INN/ CASA GUADALAJARA
SEAWORLD
Mission Bay
Mission Beach
INGRAHAM ST
NIMITZ BLVD
ROSECRANS ST
Ocean Beach
Point Loma
Shelter Island
NAVAL AIR STATION, NORTH ISLAND
Coronado Island
Coronado
ORANGE AVE
NIGHT & DAY CAFÉ
PEOHE'S
CORONADO BEACH RESORT
GLORIETA BAY INN
HOTEL DEL CORONADO
EL RANCHO MOTEL
ISLAND PASTA
CHENG LOMA FRENCH BISTRO
VILLA CAPRI BY THE SEA
CABRILLO MEMORIAL DR
NAVAL BASE POINT LOMA
FORT ROSECRANS
Cabrillo National Monument
POINT LOMA LIGHTHOUSE
SEE "POINT LOMA" MAP
OCEAN
0
2 mi
2 km

# Sights

## DOWNTOWN

The downtown area of San Diego isn't as big and intimidating as its cousins in San Francisco and Los Angeles. Instead, you'll find a smaller, homier area that feels safe to walk in—even if you're a lone woman after dark. The Gaslamp Quarter highlights downtown, offering hundreds of restaurants, dozens of bars and clubs, and a rich history. The area near the airport has a range of hotels and skirts the harbor of San Diego Bay with its museums and ships and ship-museums. The rest of downtown stretches out toward Old Town and Balboa Park.

### Gaslamp Quarter

Perhaps the best known area of downtown San Diego, the Gaslamp Quarter (Fourth, Fifth, and Sixth Sts. and Broadway) exudes atmosphere, whether you visit during the day or night. Of course, the Gaslamp Quarter has exuded atmosphere since its earliest inception in the 19th century. The Fifth Street Pier led sailors right to the area, where saloons and brothels flourished. Ida Bailey—a famous lady of the evening—moved in and cemented the area (then called Stingaree) as a red-light district. After decades of thriving debauchery, a police raid in 1912 heralded the end of the Gaslamp Quarter's popularity. Throughout the first two-thirds of the 1900s, the area decayed, becoming a low-rent district filled with porn theaters and liquor stores. In the mid-1970s, the Gaslamp Quarter Association came to be, and the renewal of this downtown area began.

© SAN DIEGO CVB

Gaslamp Quarter architecture

Today, the Gaslamp Quarter bustles with foot traffic, both locals and tourists. People crowd into the popular and sometimes quirky restaurants, dance like mad at the many bars and clubs, and spend their cash in the shops and boutiques. (But only tourists insist on taking photos under the Gaslamp Quarter sign.) Ghosts reputedly haunt several buildings here; check into a ghost tour or explore on your own to try to see or feel a spook. In general, the Gaslamp Quarter is quite safe, though you will see a scattering of homeless people wandering and sometimes sleeping on the sidewalks. In the evenings, the gaslamp-shaped streetlights illuminate the sidewalks and the historic architecture of some of the structures, especially along Fifth Street.

### Maritime Museum of San Diego

Once you're on the downtown waterfront, it's easy to spot the Maritime Museum of San Diego (1492 N. Harbor Dr., 619/234-9153, www.sdmaritime.org, daily 9 A.M.–8 P.M., adults $12, seniors $9, children $8): Just look for the tall masts with sails. This museum features a collection of floating historic ships, many of which still sail on a regular basis. The gem of the collection, the famous *Star of India* has been plying the high seas for almost 150 years. Other genuine historic ships include the *Medea,* the *Berkeley,* and the *Pilot.* Another ship that makes regular passenger cruises is

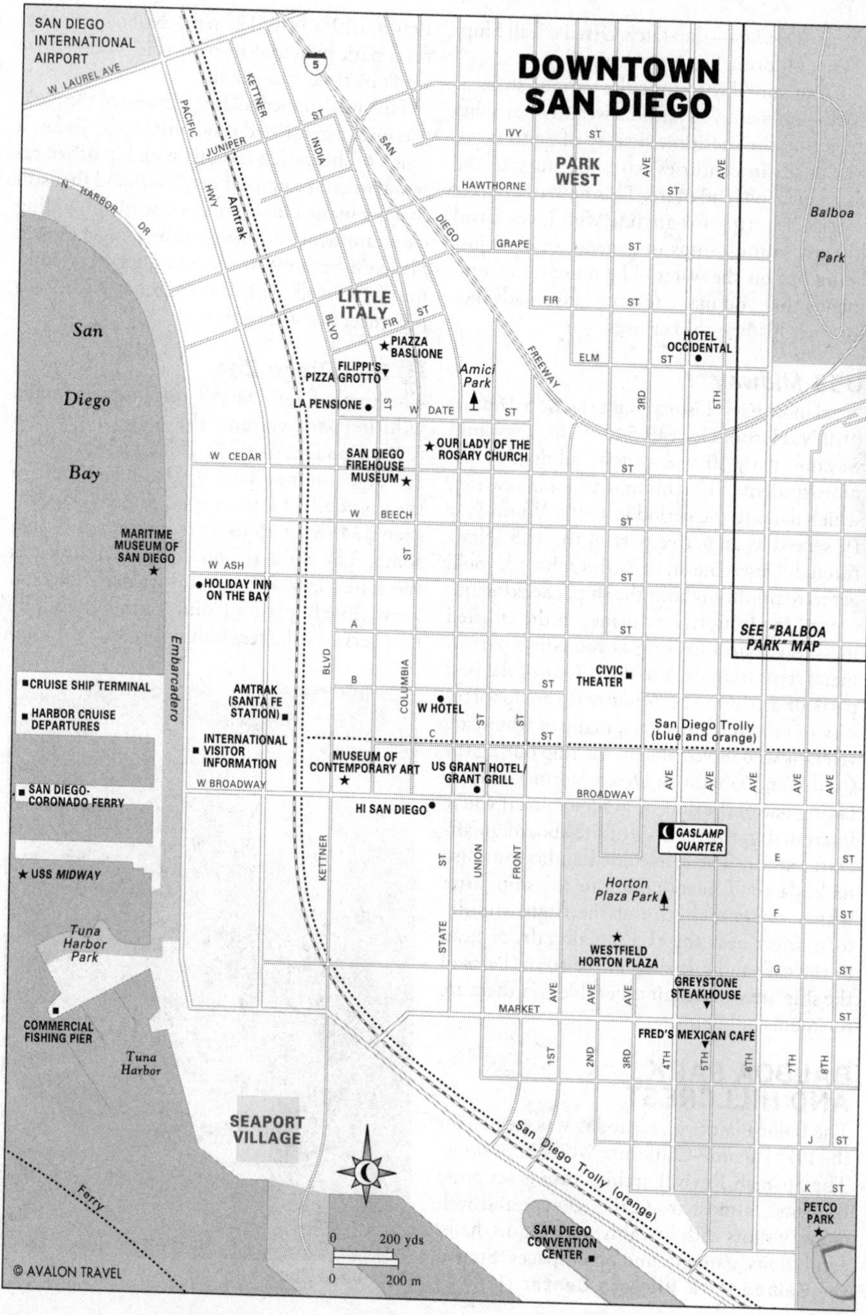
DOWNTOWN
SAN DIEGO
SAN DIEGO
INTERNATIONAL
AIRPORT
W LAUREL AVE
5
PACIFIC
HWY
KETTNER
BLVD
JUNIPER
ST
INDIA
ST
SAN DIEGO FREEWAY
Amtrak
N HARBOR DR
IVY ST
PARK
WEST
HAWTHORNE ST
GRAPE ST
FIR ST
ELM ST
Balboa
Park
HOTEL
OCCIDENTAL
LITTLE
ITALY
PIAZZA
BASLIONE
FILIPPI'S
PIZZA GROTTO
Amici
Park
LA PENSIONE
W DATE ST
OUR LADY OF THE
ROSARY CHURCH
W CEDAR
SAN DIEGO
FIREHOUSE
MUSEUM
W BEECH
San
Diego
Bay
MARITIME
MUSEUM OF
SAN DIEGO
W ASH
HOLIDAY INN
ON THE BAY
Embarcadero
A
SEE "BALBOA
PARK" MAP
CRUISE SHIP TERMINAL
HARBOR CRUISE
DEPARTURES
AMTRAK
(SANTA FE
STATION)
B
COLUMBIA
CIVIC
THEATER
W HOTEL
San Diego Trolly
(blue and orange)
C ST
INTERNATIONAL
VISITOR
INFORMATION
MUSEUM OF
CONTEMPORARY ART
US GRANT HOTEL/
GRANT GRILL
W BROADWAY
BROADWAY
SAN DIEGO-
CORONADO FERRY
HI SAN DIEGO
GASLAMP
QUARTER
E ST
USS MIDWAY
KETTNER
STATE ST
UNION
FRONT
Horton
Plaza Park
F ST
Tuna
Harbor
Park
WESTFIELD
HORTON PLAZA
G ST
GREYSTONE
STEAKHOUSE
MARKET
ST
COMMERCIAL
FISHING PIER
FRED'S MEXICAN CAFÉ
1ST
2ND
3RD
4TH
5TH
6TH
7TH
8TH
AVE
Tuna
Harbor
SEAPORT
VILLAGE
San Diego Trolly (orange)
J ST
K ST
Ferry
PETCO
PARK
0 200 yds
0 200 m
SAN DIEGO
CONVENTION
CENTER
© AVALON TRAVEL

the *Californian*—the state's Official Tall Ship. (Yes, California has such a thing!)

Come any day to tour the various ships at dock—onboard you'll find a wealth of exhibits depicting the maritime history of San Diego, war at sea in centuries past, the story of the ship you're on, and more. This museum makes a perfect outing for anyone who loves naval history, sailing, ships in general, or even just being out on the water. The museum recommends that you make reservations in advance for their historic ship cruises.



### USS *Midway*

Need more naval history? Visit the USS *Midway* (910 N. Harbor Dr., 619/544-9600, www.midway.org, daily 10 A.M.–4 P.M., adults $15, seniors/students $10, children $8). This carrier, which dates to the period just after World War II, served as an active part of the U.S. Navy through Desert Storm in 1991. Onboard, you'll get to roam throughout the ship, checking out everything from fighter planes to the enlisted mess to the dreaded brig as you climb narrow metal steps from deck to deck. One of the best parts of a trip to the *Midway* is the opportunity to talk to the docents, many of whom are veterans who served aboard the ship during the Cold War, Vietnam, or Desert Storm. Consider taking one of the docent-guided tours if you're interested in the realities of life aboard an aircraft carrier. The self-guided audio tour also makes a good introduction to the ship, after which you can check out the flight simulators, linger near the exciting aircraft, or head to the café and gift shop at the stern. Parts of the ship are wheelchair accessible and there are restrooms onboard.

## BALBOA PARK AND HILLCREST

The Balboa Park you see today was created for the 1915 Panama-California World Exposition. The Spanish Revival architecture is set amid immense, almost tropical, greenery and welcomes visitors with a wealth of museums, halls, exhibitions, gardens, and open spaces. Stop at the **Balboa Park Visitors Center** (1549 El Prado, 619/239-0512, www.balboapark.org) for a park map and to plan your visit—there won't be time to see it all!

Hillcrest, immediately northwest of the park, was once a gentrified residential area. Today, a touch of shabbiness has met with hip urban renewal to create a mixed neighborhood that still shelters many older residents, while providing entertainment and energy to a younger crowd. Hillcrest beckons to the San Diego gay community as well, with clubs and bars creating a hip queer nightlife scene.

### San Diego Zoo

The jewel of San Diego's vast interconnected wildlife park system, the San Diego Zoo (2920 Zoo Dr., 619/234-1515, www.sandiegozoo.org, summer daily 9 A.M.–8 P.M., rest of the year daily 9 A.M.–4 P.M., adults $34, children $24) lives up to its reputation and then some. The 80-acre zoo actually doubles as the state's largest botanical garden. The zoo grows lovely plants from around the globe that serve as shelter, hiding places, and food

San Diego Zoo

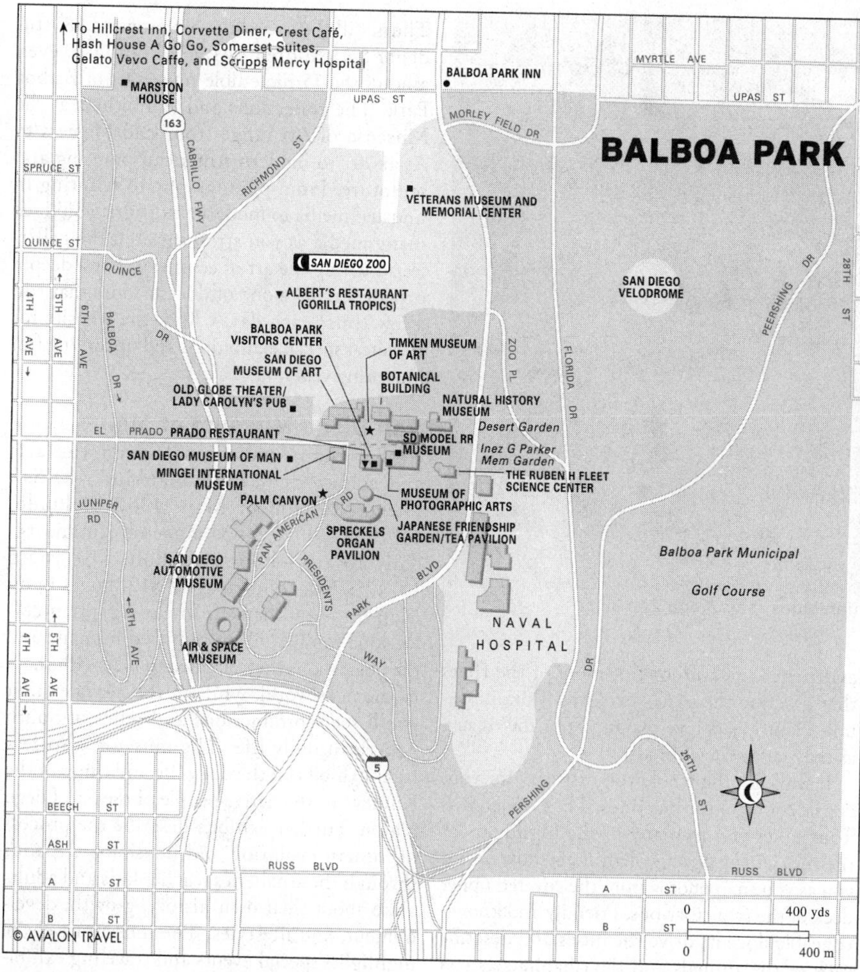


for the hundreds of exotic animals that inhabit state-of-the-art enclosures. You'll see perennial zoo favorites including elephants, lions, polar bears, and you'll also meet a host of other famous and exotic species, such as meerkats, one-foot-tall deer, pythons, and parrots. For the comfort of the human visitors, ample restrooms, benches, concessions, and gift shops scatter through the zoo.

To get the best zoo experience possible, stroll its meandering paved walkways, stopping whenever and wherever you feel a need to watch the birds and beasts as they sleep, eat, and play. Some of the paths can be steep—if you're visiting with kids or folks who have trouble walking, keep that in mind when you plan. The map provided by the zoo can help with good walking routes for your party's endurance levels. If you can't do it all, pick the paths that take you to your primary points of interest—be those pandas, birds, or big kitty-cats. For another great way to enhance your

© LIZ HAMILL SCOTT

flamingos, San Diego Zoo



experience, pick up one or more of the fliers that describe the park's extensive flora in detail. Plant lovers love playing Spot the Acacia as they enjoy the animals.

If walking the whole zoo just isn't for you, consider one of the bus rides. The Guided Bus Tour takes you to many of the highlights of the zoo, letting dozens of animals show off for you as you snap photos from the coveted upper deck of the two-story bus. Friendly and knowledgeable docents drive the buses and describe each of the animals and their habitats as you pass. If you just want to get from one section of the zoo to another, jump on an Express Bus. For a special treat, take the Skyfari from the front of the park to the rear, where the polar bears play in their pond. You'll get a lovely view of the whole of Balboa Park out to the sea as you traverse the length of the zoo in less than 10 minutes.

## San Diego Museum of Art

The San Diego Museum of Art (1450 El Prado, www.sdmart.org, Tues.–Sun. 10 A.M.–6 P.M., Thurs. till 9 P.M., adults $10, seniors $8, students $7, children $4) is a highlight, even among the 15 incredible museums of Balboa Park. The collections and exhibitions at the Museum of Art range from Old Masters to Asian art to modern American painting and sculpture. From photography to painting in unusual media to modern sculpture, you'll see many media as you stroll through the galleries admiring the art of centuries. For a deeper experience, take one of docent tours that run a few times each day. Check the website for the latest special exhibitions and upcoming fun museum events.

## San Diego Museum of Man

Rather than focusing solely on the arts and achievements of humankind, the San Diego Museum of Man (1350 El Prado, 619/239-2001, www.museumofman.org, daily 10 A.M.–4:30 P.M., adults $10, youth 13–17 $7.50, children 3–12 $12) hones in on Man him- and herself. In the Egyptian collection, you'll find mummified humans and the possessions they planned to take with them to the next world, while in the Maya exhibit you'll see reproductions and relics of South American daily life. The museum also features exhibits on the daily life and times of the Kumeyaay, the native people of the San Diego region. Further exhibits describe the process of human evolution and physiology. A tour through these galleries teaches kids and adults alike about their own history, growth, development, and lifestyles. The museum website highlights special events and traveling exhibitions. (In 2007, the Museum of Man hosted the Dead Sea Scrolls!)

## Palm Canyon

For a peaceful break from the endless educational opportunities of Balboa Park, take a walk through Palm Canyon (location 34 on the Balboa Park map, daily). The canyon offers visitors an intense look at various varieties of that ubiquitous California icon: the palm tree. With 58 species of palms creating a cool, shady space, the Canyon is a perfect place to slow down and enjoy a break on a hot summer day. The Mexican fan palms at the center of the garden have lived here almost 100 years. The groomed paths connect the canyon to the Old Cactus Garden; the Alcazar Garden also sits adjacent to the palms, and a tram stop nearby makes access a breeze.

### Japanese Friendship Garden

Cultural centers form an important element of Balboa Park. The Japanese Friendship Garden (2125 Park Blvd., 619/232-2721, www.niwa.org, Tues.–Sun. 10 A.M.–4 P.M.) began as a teahouse during the 1915–1916 Exposition, and grew over the years to include many elements of a traditional Japanese formal garden. You can enjoy the tranquility of the Zen garden, koi pond, and wisteria arbor, or take tea and sushi at the Tea Pavilion. This is the perfect place to enjoy a quiet walk hand-in-hand with your sweetie. For variety, the garden displays temporary exhibitions that mesh with the Japanese cultural traditions exemplified here. Check the website for one-day classes in Japanese arts, usually held on weekends.

### Other Museums and Gardens

Balboa Park is filled with a number of other worthy museums, and meandering paths lead to even more botanical areas and gardens. It's impossible to see everything in one day, but a repeat visit could include the **Air and Space Museum** (2001 Pan American Plaza, 619/234-8291, www.aerospacemuseum.org, $15) for a history through human flight; the **Reuben H. Fleet Science Center** (1875 El Prado, 619/238-1233, www.rhfleet.org, Mon.–Thurs. 9:30 A.M.–5 P.M., Fri. 9:30 A.M.–9 P.M., Sat. 9:30 A.M.–8 P.M., Sun. 9:30 A.M.–6 P.M., $8), where young ones can explore the interactive science exhibits; and the **Natural History Museum** (1788 El Prado, 619/232-3821, www.sdnhm.org, Mon.–Thurs. 10 A.M.–6:30 P.M., Fri. 10 A.M.–7:30 P.M., Sat.–Sun. 9 A.M.–8:30 P.M., $9), which houses a vast collection of fossils and other artifacts presenting San Diego's geologic history.

The **Botanical Building** (El Prado, Fri.–Wed. 10 A.M.–4 P.M., free) is a lovely centerpiece to the Prado and a perfect way to relax in the Zen-like atmosphere its thousands of exotic plants provide.

## OLD TOWN

San Diego is the oldest European-settled "town" in California. The Old Town area encompasses the first Spanish settlements of what would eventually become California, 19th-century homes and businesses, parks, and modern shops and restaurants. Old Town is the perfect place to get started on a historic tour of California, a ghost-hunting visit to San Diego, or a good sightseeing trip.

### Whaley House

Billed as the most haunted house in all of the United States, the Whaley House (2476 San Diego Ave., 619/297-7511, www.whaleyhouse.org, Mon.–Tues. 10 A.M.–5 P.M., Thurs.–Sun. 10 A.M.–10 P.M., summer daily 10 A.M.–10 P.M., adults $6, seniors $5, children $4) was built by Thomas Whaley in 1857—and over the century it was inhabited, many members of the Whaley family lived and died inside the brick-constructed Greek Revival mansion. The house was also leased out as a home, and used as a courthouse, general store, and billiards hall, among other things. Before Whaley built the house on the corner of San Diego Avenue and Harney Street, the spot was used for at least one public hanging on record.

Reportedly, the haunting of the Whaley House began almost as soon as the Whaleys first moved in. Thomas Whaley believed that the specter of a criminal hanged on the land was the source of loud, ominous footfalls that rattled the floorboards of his new home late at night. More recently, visitors have spotted many different ghosts inside the house, which has been featured on *America's Most Haunted*. Children and adults have seen male shades, female spirits, and even the vision of a spaniel dog that matches the description of Thomas Whaley's family pet. If you love a good ghost story and long to see the spirits of the Whaley House yourself, consider coming to visit at night, or even calling ahead and booking a private tour (two people minimum) after 10 P.M.

Even if you don't believe all the ghost stories, the Whaley House Museum contains enough concrete lore pertaining to the house and its various incarnations to entertain history buffs for hours. Self-guided tours are enhanced by the wandering docents, who can answer questions about the artifacts inside the house as well as the house itself. And should you feel an unexpected chill or see an inexplicable shadow as you wander through a room, well, the staff is used to that sort of thing and will be happy to help you out with the experience!



### Old Town State Historic Park

The Old Town San Diego State Historic Park (corner of San Diego Ave. and Twigg St., 619/291-4903, www.parks.ca.gov, daily 10 A.M.–5 P.M., free) makes a great place to start exploring the history of California's first town. The visitors center sits in a house first built in 1853 as a family home and set of local offices by attorney James Robinson. Another major home, the McCoy House, was built in 1869, excavated and reconstructed over the years 1995–2000. Move on to the early 19th-century Mexican pueblos, including La Casa de Machado y Stewart; this adobe structure contains many artifacts that would have been part of the daily life of San Diego citizens in 1821–1872. Out and about in the park, you can enjoy period music, pet the burros, and observe the park staff engaging in activities folks might have done 150 years ago. Wednesdays are living history days, and the park hosts many events over the course of each year. If you're more into the afterlife of the residents of Old San Diego, you can visit the El Campo Santo Cemetery—the oldest cemetery in the city. The park also includes a number of known haunted sites, including the Robinson-Rose House, Casa de Bandini, and La Casa de Estudillo.

### Presidio Park

One of the early Mexican settlements in San Diego was a military installation, now Presidio Park (2811 Jackson St., 619/692-4918). The **Junípero Serra Museum** (2727 Presidio Dr., 619/297-3258, daily 10 A.M.–4:30 P.M., adults $5, seniors $4, children $2) sits inside the park, on the spot where Father Junipero Serra and Captain Gaspar de Portola established the Presidio fort. Its collections include housewares, artifacts, and a cannon from the Mexican occupation through the early California period of San Diego through 1929. If you prefer nature with your history, take a stroll along the more than two miles of trails winding through the acres of gardens and wild areas of the park. Palm Canyon features lawns surrounded by stately old palm trees. The Arbor has a more formal garden feel, complete with pillars and flowers. It's hard to believe as you wander the charming parkland that you're on the site of a former military base.

### Mission San Diego del Alcala

The first mission erected in California was Mission San Diego del Alcala (10818 San Diego Mission Rd., www.missionsandiego.com, daily 9 A.M.–4:45 P.M.). It was blessed by Father Junipero Serra in 1769, making it the first Christian church in California. Ironically, it was also the poorest Mission for most of its hey-dey. Native Americans raided and burned it, the harsh soil resisted cultivation, and eventually the Mexican independence from Spain rendered the church a secular building. Time and renovation came to the Mission, and it was re-established as a sacred space. It still operates as an active Catholic church today; if you visit, please respect the Mission as a house of worship even as you appreciate its significance as a museum. The church you see is actually the fifth church built on this site, erected and fortified against California's infamous earthquakes. One of the bells in the tower is original (dating to 1801). Inside, you'll see evidence of the life of the Franciscan monks who operated the Mission until 1834, and of the native Kumeyaay people who lived here before the Europeans came and whose lives were changed forever by their arrival.

ROBERT HOLMES / CALTOUR

Mission San Diego del Alcala



## POINT LOMA

Point Loma is at once one of the most beautiful and one of the most important pieces of land in the San Diego region. From the tip of the point, you can see everywhere, from the Cuyamaca Mountains to the land and seas of Mexico, and down into the safe harbor of the San Diego Bay. This fabulous view also meant a perfect place to build a defense for the harbor and the settlements beyond. Accordingly, Point Loma has served more than 200 years as a military installation. From owl limpets to soldiers' graves, there are innumerable unique items to see in the area.

### Fort Rosecrans Military Reserve

San Diego has historically maintained an extensive military presence, regardless of whose rule the land fell under. Even today, a large U.S. Navy installation remains here, guarding the Pacific shores. Fort Rosecrans began as a Spanish Presidio that was fortified against imminent British threat in the late 1700s. Then called Fort Guijarro, it lasted as an active Spanish military base only 40 years, after which it began to decay. After the creation of California as a state, the U.S. government refurbished the fort to protect the San Diego harbor once more. It was rechristened Fort Rosencrans, and parts of it are still used to this day for Army Reserve activities.

Today, when you visit the parklands of Cabrillo National Monument, you can see remnants of old buildings belonging to the fort, many used during the two World Wars. But the highlight of any visit to the fort is the **Fort Rosecrans National Cemetery** (1880 Cabrillo Memorial Dr., 619/553-2084). In addition to the haunting rows of stark white tombstones marching in dressed line across green lawns, you'll find graves here from combatants who fought wars of the California Republic. Wander the grounds to view graves old and recent, as well as monuments to fallen soldiers from little-known battles long past.

### Cabrillo National Monument

Cabrillo National Monument (1800 Cabrillo

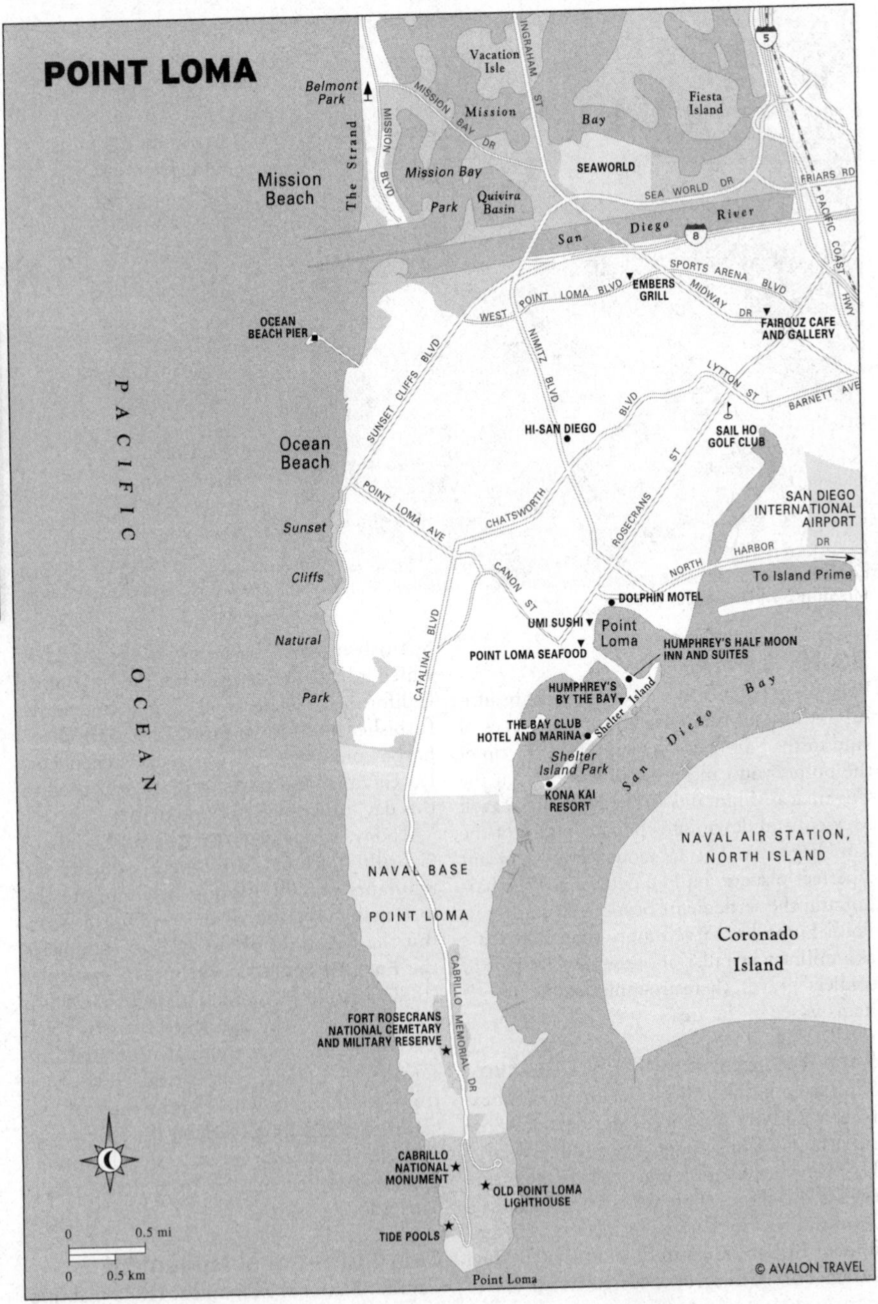
POINT LOMA
Vacation Isle
Belmont Park
Mission Bay
Fiesta Island
The Strand
MISSION BAY DR
MISSION BLVD
INGRAHAM ST
SEAWORLD
Mission Beach
Mission Bay Park
Quivira Basin
SEA WORLD DR
FRIARS RD
PACIFIC COAST HWY
San Diego River
SPORTS ARENA BLVD
WEST POINT LOMA BLVD
EMBERS GRILL
MIDWAY DR
FAIROUZ CAFE AND GALLERY
OCEAN BEACH PIER
SUNSET CLIFFS BLVD
NIMITZ BLVD
LYTTON ST
BARNETT AVE
PACIFIC OCEAN
HI-SAN DIEGO
SAIL HO GOLF CLUB
Ocean Beach
ROSECRANS ST
CHATSWORTH BLVD
POINT LOMA AVE
SAN DIEGO INTERNATIONAL AIRPORT
Sunset Cliffs Natural Park
NORTH HARBOR DR
To Island Prime
CANON ST
DOLPHIN MOTEL
UMI SUSHI
Point Loma
POINT LOMA SEAFOOD
HUMPHREY'S HALF MOON INN AND SUITES
CATALINA BLVD
HUMPHREY'S BY THE BAY
Shelter Island
San Diego Bay
THE BAY CLUB HOTEL AND MARINA
Shelter Island Park
KONA KAI RESORT
NAVAL AIR STATION, NORTH ISLAND
NAVAL BASE POINT LOMA
Coronado Island
CABRILLO MEMORIAL DR
FORT ROSECRANS NATIONAL CEMETARY AND MILITARY RESERVE
CABRILLO NATIONAL MONUMENT
OLD POINT LOMA LIGHTHOUSE
TIDE POOLS
0 0.5 mi
0 0.5 km
Point Loma
© AVALON TRAVEL

Memorial Dr., 619/557-5450, www.nps.gov/cabr) celebrates the initial discovery of San Diego Bay by Spanish Explorer Juan Rodriguez Cabrillo in the mid-16th century. This was the first landing of the Spanish—indeed of any Europeans—on the West Coast of North America. Today, a large statue of Cabrillo stands within the monument lands, overlooking the San Diego Bay. At the visitors center, you can learn more about the history of Cabrillo's life and explorations.

The wildlife and the scenery are other great reasons to visit the national monument. Views from the high places here are second to none. Turning around, you can see the harbor, the San Diego cityscape, the Pacific Ocean, and all the way south to Mexico. Be sure to bring your camera! For a micro-view of San Diego's seas, check the tide tables and head down to the tide pools on the west side of Point Loma. Here you'll find a myriad of sea life waiting for discovery. Just be sure that you and your children look with your eyes, not your fingers—many tide pool creatures can be injured or even killed by a mere touch from a human.

The parkland of Cabrillo offers hiking trails through the southern coastal scrub ecosystem so precious and unique to this part of the state. Enjoy the wildlife and lovely plants, and come in spring for the best profusion of wildflowers.

### Old Point Loma Lighthouse

Among the oldest lighthouses in California, the Old Point Loma Lighthouse (1800 Cabrillo Memorial Dr., daily 9 A.M.–5 P.M.) began its watch over the San Diego Bay in 1855. Unfortunately, the light was often dimmed by pernicious fog, and a new lighthouse went into operation in a better location in 1891. Luckily for visitors today, the old lighthouse remained unmolested. Come in to peruse the exhibits, or sign up for a ranger-led tour and talk that goes into detail about the history of the lighthouse. You'll see the restoration of the lighthouse by the National Park Service to its original mid-19th-century glory. Perhaps the most interesting stories you'll hear during your visit are of the lighthouse-keepers and their families. Several descendents of the original keepers have provided family stories to round out the human history of the lighthouse. Old Point Loma Lighthouse is part of the Cabrillo National Monument, perfectly located for a day out exploring the early history of California's statehood.

## MISSION BAY

Mission Bay offers serene waters untroubled by the sometimes pounding Pacific surf. It's a perfect place to center your family vacation, take in the natural wonders of Mission Bay Park, or head for the colorful fun of Sea World.

### Mission Bay Park

The acres of Mission Bay Park (Mission Blvd.) are not a natural wonder. In fact, the land and sea of the popular recreation area were once a tidal marsh—the primary outlet of the San Diego River. In the 1940s, the marsh was dredged and the beaches and land formations you see today were created. Among them are 19 miles of charming sandy beach perfect for sunbathing, sandcastle-making, beach volleyball, and more—and 14 miles of bike paths. Half of the designated parkland is actually off the shore, in the abundant calm waterways. Swim in one of the eight designated, lifeguard-protected areas throughout the park, or take a deeper dive out into the channel to windsurf or water-ski. In the non-swimming, non-skiing areas, you can string out a line and go fishing. Despite the manmade nature of this park, it has several areas that have become significant wildlife preserves. You can go birding at Perez Cove, Telecote Creek, Fiesta Island, or a number of other spots throughout the park.

### SeaWorld San Diego

With a charming mix of rides and sea-life attraction, SeaWorld San Diego (500 SeaWorld Dr., 800/257-4268, www.seaworld.com, hours vary, adults $60, children $50) makes a fun destination for families. SeaWorld is

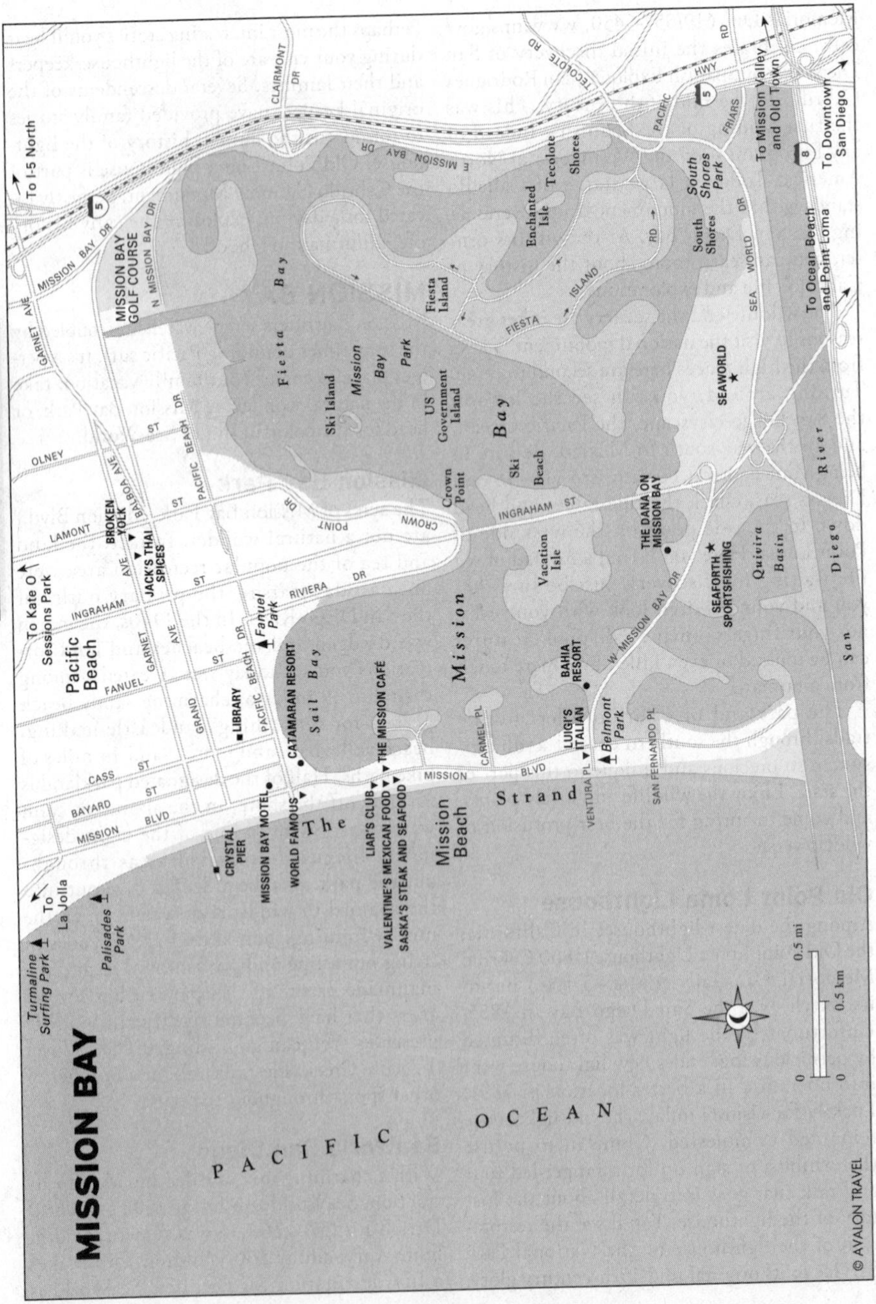
MISSION BAY
PACIFIC OCEAN
Mission Bay
Fiesta Bay
Sail Bay
Mission Bay Park
Mission Beach
The Strand
Pacific Beach
Fiesta Island
Ski Island
US Government Island
Crown Point
Ski Beach
Vacation Isle
Enchanted Isle
Tecolote Shores
South Shores
South Shores Park
Quivira Basin
San Diego River
MISSION BAY GOLF COURSE
SEAWORLD
SEAFORTH SPORTSFISHING
THE DANA ON MISSION BAY
BAHIA RESORT
LUIGI'S ITALIAN
Belmont Park
CATAMARAN RESORT
THE MISSION CAFÉ
LIAR'S CLUB
VALENTINE'S MEXICAN FOOD
SASKA'S STEAK AND SEAFOOD
WORLD FAMOUS
MISSION BAY MOTEL
CRYSTAL PIER
LIBRARY
JACK'S THAI SPICES
BROKEN YOLK
Fanuel Park
Palisades Park
Turmaline Surfing Park
To La Jolla
To Kate O Sessions Park
To I-5 North
To Mission Valley and Old Town
To Downtown San Diego
To Ocean Beach and Point Loma
MISSION BLVD
BAYARD ST
CASS ST
GRAND AVE
GARNET AVE
FANUEL ST
INGRAHAM ST
LAMONT ST
BALBOA AVE
OLNEY ST
PACIFIC BEACH DR
RIVIERA DR
CROWN POINT DR
CARMEL PL
VENTURA PL
SAN FERNANDO PL
W. MISSION BAY DR
SEA WORLD DR
FIESTA ISLAND RD
E MISSION BAY DR
N MISSION BAY DR
MISSION BAY DR
CLAIRMONT DR
TECOLOTE RD
PACIFIC HWY
FRIARS RD
5
8
0
0.5 mi
0.5 km
© AVALON TRAVEL

navigable in half a day, even when taking the time to include some rides and shows. Kids love meeting Shamu and his brothers and sisters in the killer whale pool just inside the park entrance. Also in SeaWorld you'll meet sea lions, endangered sea turtles, dolphins, and other denizens of the deep. On hot days, the river ride and splash-down roller coaster cool off overheated park visitors. Plenty of food concessions (including a coffee stand) revive weary families, getting them ready for more animal shows and action-packed rides. If you want to have breakfast or dinner with Shamu at the restaurant looking out into the killer whale tank, advance reservations are recommended.

While SeaWorld offers great fun for small children, the laboriously cute decor, roller-coaster-style rides, and trained animal acts can get a bit tiresome for more sophisticated or outdoor-oriented adult travelers. The food in the park also caters to the younger set, and tends to be higher on fat content than quality. Frankly, better adult-oriented wild animal experiences are available in the San Diego area at both the zoo and the Wild Animal Park.

## LA JOLLA

North of San Diego, La Jolla (which means "The Jewel") is a well-to-do neighborhood filled with high-end boutiques, exemplary restaurants, and a coastline awash in scenic beauty.

### Sunny Jim's Cave

Of the seven sea caves in the La Jolla cliffs, Sunny Jim's Cave (1325 Cave St., daily 9 A.M.–5 P.M., adults $4, children $3) is unique. You don't need a kayak or scuba gear to get down into this cave; a manmade tunnel created 100 years ago lets visitors into the cavern via a reliable land route. You'll purchase admission at the weathered, shingle-fronted Cave Store, then climb carefully down the 145 steps to the cavern proper. You'll see a sizeable sea cave of sandstone, carved over the millennia by the Pacific into the cliffside. You can look from inside the cave out towards the ocean—an interesting and perhaps just a little bit eerie view.

But how did the tunnel get built? Gustav Schultz, a retiree and painter, hired laborers to hand-dig the tunnel in 1903 as a tourist attraction. The cave was later named "Sunny Jim's" after a cartoon breakfast cereal mascot by the author of *The Wizard of Oz.* (No, I am not making this up.) Schultz painted local landscapes in the Cave Store until his death in 1912.

### La Jolla Cove and Scripps Park

One of the most photographed beaches in the state, La Jolla Cove (1100 Coast Rd.) differs from other San Diego beaches. The small cove sits sandwiched between two sandstone cliffs, and the coarse sand feels more like the rough pebbles of the northern part of the state than the silky-soft stretches of the south. Visitors snap pictures of the picturesque scenery, swim in the warm water, and trek up to Ellen Browning Scripps Park (Coast Blvd., 4–8 P.M.) for a picnic or a game of soccer on the manicured lawn. La Jolla Cove is famous for its sparkling clear water, and at low tide scuba divers and snorkelers enjoy the local marine life. Lifeguards stay on duty year-round from 9 A.M. until sunset during the high season and from 10 A.M. in wintertime. Up at Scripps Park, land-lovers enjoy walking on the boardwalk along the cliffs overlooking the vast Pacific, playing on the lawns, and admiring the oddly grown trees scattered around providing shade. The park has restrooms and showers. Parking for either the beach or the park can be tough, especially in the summer. Consider parking in a pay lot downtown and hoofing it down to the beach.

### Birch Aquarium

The Birch Aquarium at Scripps (2300 Expedition Way, 858/534-3474, http://aquarium.ucsd.edu, daily 9 A.M.–5 P.M., adults $11, seniors $9, youth 3–17 $7.50) is run by the University of California at San Diego. Both children and adults love the Scripps Institute's research and displays in this state-of-the-art

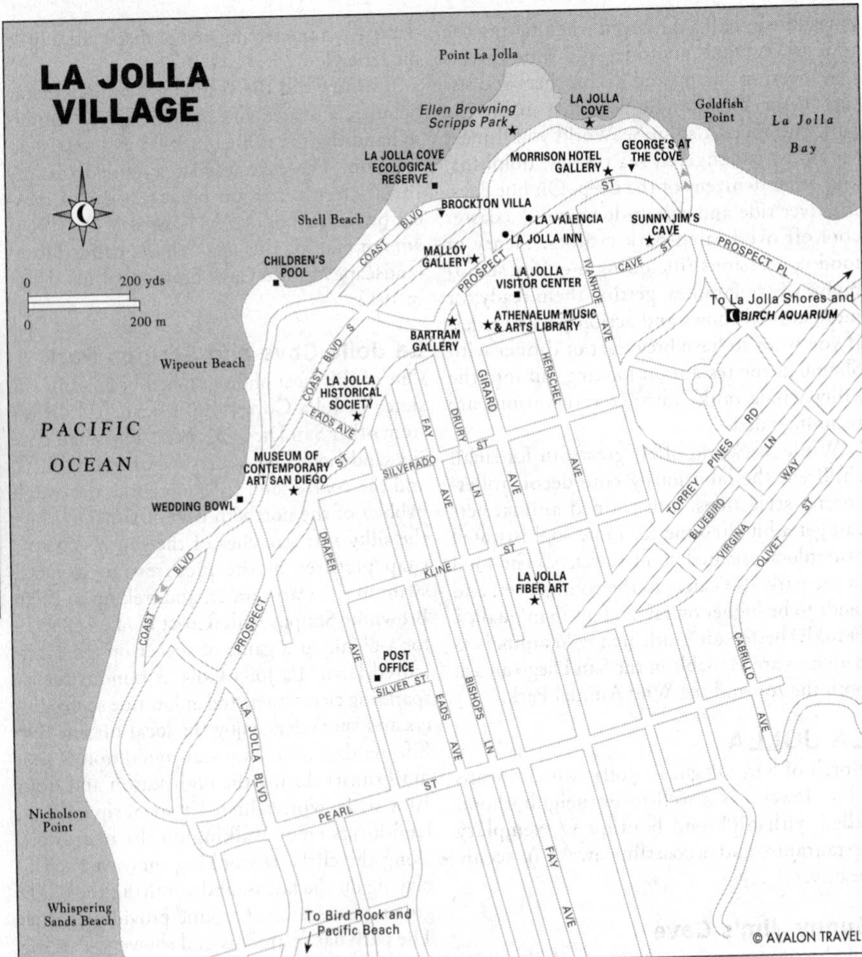


aquarium complex. For a classic beginning, view sea life from oceans the world over along the Hall of Fishes. This area includes coral reef displays from Mexico and the Caribbean, a kelp forest similar to the ones right off the La Jolla coast, and the fabulous and fascinating Shark Reef. The Art of Deception display allows visitors to see the amazing camouflaging defenses of sea creatures from various marine environments. Kids love to splash in the Wonders of Water exhibit, and playing here is not only allowed, it's encouraged!

## Museum of Contemporary Art San Diego–La Jolla

The MCASD La Jolla (700 Prospect St., 858/454-3541, www.mcasd.org, Fri.–Tues. 11 A.M.–5 P.M., Thurs. 11 A.M.–7 P.M., general admission $10, free for those 25 and under) is one of two MCASD campuses in the area.

(The other is in downtown San Diego.) At the La Jolla site, perfectly located on Prospect Street for easy access, you'll see works of art in all media created from 1950 to the present. MCASD takes particular pride in its collections of Pop and Minimalist art from the 1960s and '70s, as well as a selection of pieces from artists working in the San Diego and Tijuana areas. If you love the new, unique, and misunderstood arts of the modern era, the MCASD La Jolla is a must-see. And if all that art makes you hungry, be sure to stop at the museum café for a quick bite.

## NORTH COUNTY

As you drive north up the Pacific Coast Highway from downtown San Diego, you begin to see where all the legends about California beaches and surfing came from. The sun shines down over desert plants, pale sands, cute little towns, the mountains to the east, and the glittering blue sea to the west. If you want a movie-style California beach vacation, you can't do better than a weekend (or a whole week or two!) in Encinitas, Del Mar, or Solano Beach. At the same time, the north end of San Diego County offers some great sights and activities, from the Wild Animal Park to Mission San Luis Rey.

### California Surf Museum

Nothing says "California" quite like the image of a lithe young man (or woman) standing tall on an impossibly small slab of wood (or fiberglass), riding a wild wave in to shore. And at the legendary California Surf Museum (223 N. Coast Hwy., Oceanside, 760/721-6876, www.surfmuseum.org, daily 10 A.M.–4 P.M., free), you can admire, appreciate, and learn about the ancient sport and art of surfing. While surfing's origins may be in the South Pacific islands, the unusual sport began to catch on at the warm beaches of Southern California, catching on big once surf movies began to appear in theaters. From the silly Frankie Avalon and bongo drum fluff pieces to the semi-documentary *Endless Summer,* surf movies inspired thousands of boys and young men to get out and try to catch a wave. With the novel *Gidget* and subsequent movies, what had been an almost all-male endeavor caught on with girls, too. Surfing became a part of the California version of the 1960s and '70s hippie movement—earning the respect of the young and the animosity of the older generation. Today, there's no such thing as an "average" surfer. You might find a 10-year-old out tearing it up and a 70-year-old hanging ten, both at the same break.

At the Surf Museum, you'll see and pay homage to all that has gone into the California surf scene over its many decades. From exhibits on board-shaping to photo essays by and about legendary surfers, you'll see all there is to see about the history and current events of the unique world of surfing. Check the website for current exhibitions and events at the museum. (And yes, if you're in town especially to ride the waves, ask around at the museum for the latest "secret" local breaks.)

### San Diego Wild Animal Park

The San Diego Zoo doesn't keep too many large animals in the confines of its limited site. To see and experience the life and times of giraffes, lions, elephants, and other natives of spacious grasslands in Africa and Asia, visit the wildly popular San Diego Wild Animal Park (15500 San Pasqual Valley Rd., Escondido, www.sandiegozoo.org/wap, daily 9 A.M.–4 P.M. or later, $28.50 adults, $17.50 children, parking $8). Deliberately set well away from the center of urban San Diego, this huge park gives a variety of animals the space they crave to live more naturally. You could spend days in the Wild Animal Park and not see all the diverse species that live here. Walking trails offer miles of adventure through different areas of the park, such as Condor Ridge, Lion Camp, Lorikeet Landing, and the Heart of Africa. If you're not up for a day of hardcore hiking, consider paying extra for one of the "Safari" tours that take guests out into different areas of the park in colorful vehicles. On Safaris, docents tell

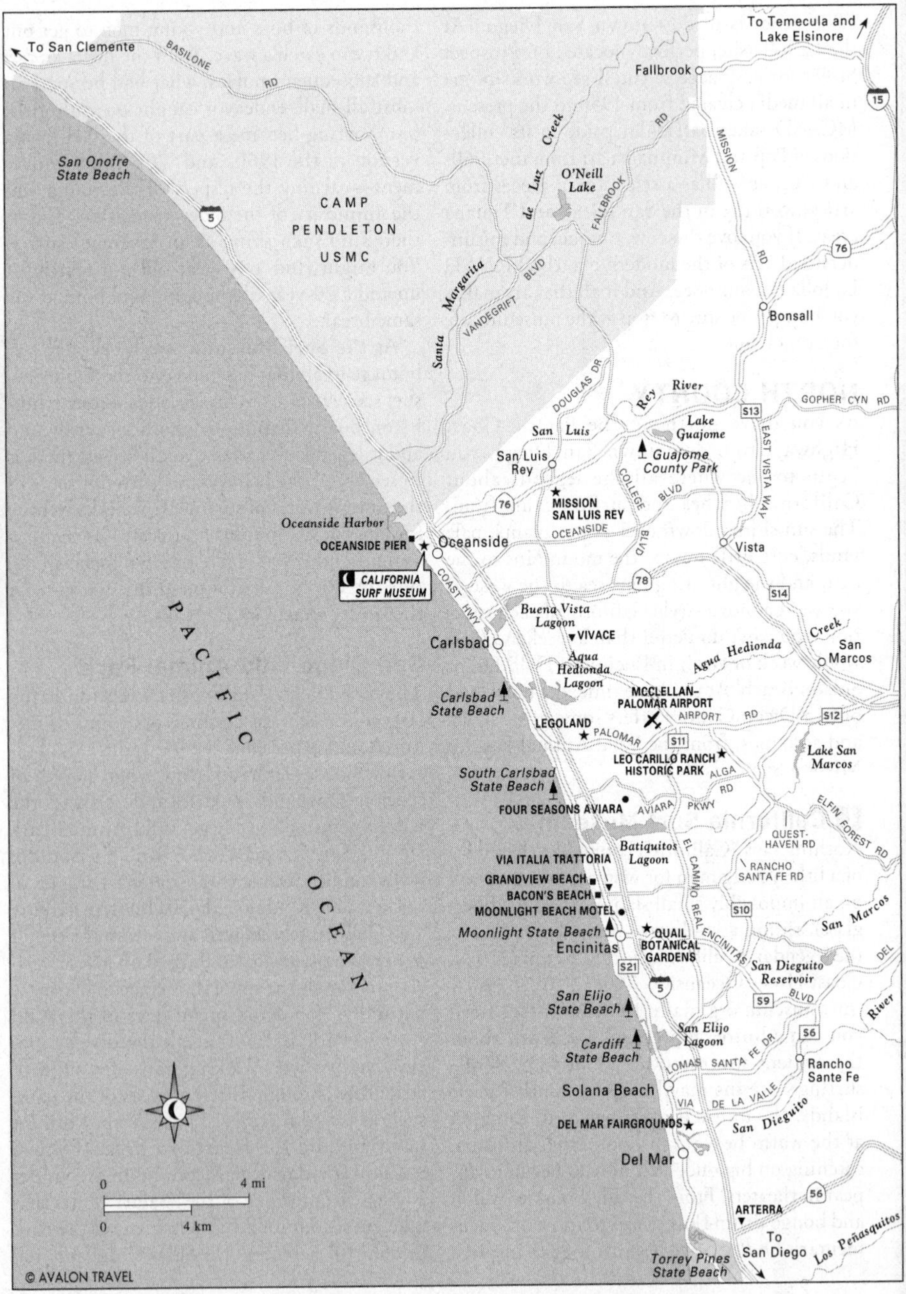
To San Clemente
BASILONE RD
To Temecula and Lake Elsinore
Fallbrook
15
San Onofre State Beach
5
CAMP PENDLETON USMC
Santa Margarita
de Luz Creek
O'Neill Lake
FALLBROOK
RD
MISSION RD
VANDEGRIFT BLVD
76
Bonsall
DOUGLAS DR
Rey River
San Luis
GOPHER CYN RD
S13
EAST VISTA WAY
Lake Guajome
Guajome County Park
San Luis Rey
MISSION SAN LUIS REY
COLLEGE BLVD
OCEANSIDE
Oceanside Harbor
OCEANSIDE PIER
Oceanside
Vista
CALIFORNIA SURF MUSEUM
COAST HWY
78
S14
PACIFIC
OCEAN
Buena Vista Lagoon
VIVACE
Carlsbad
Creek
Agua Hedionda
San Marcos
Aqua Hedionda Lagoon
Carlsbad State Beach
MCCLELLAN-PALOMAR AIRPORT
AIRPORT RD
S12
LEGOLAND
PALOMAR
S11
Lake San Marcos
LEO CARILLO RANCH HISTORIC PARK
ALGA RD
South Carlsbad State Beach
FOUR SEASONS AVIARA
AVIARA PKWY
ELFIN FOREST RD
QUEST-HAVEN RD
Batiquitos Lagoon
VIA ITALIA TRATTORIA
EL CAMINO REAL
RANCHO SANTA FE RD
GRANDVIEW BEACH
BACON'S BEACH
MOONLIGHT BEACH MOTEL
S10
San Marcos
Moonlight State Beach
QUAIL BOTANICAL GARDENS
Encinitas
ENCINITAS
DEL
S21
San Dieguito Reservoir
5
S9
BLVD
River
San Elijo State Beach
S6
San Elijo Lagoon
Cardiff State Beach
LOMAS SANTA FE DR
Rancho Sante Fe
Solana Beach
VIA DE LA VALLE
DEL MAR FAIRGROUNDS
San Dieguito
Del Mar
0
4 mi
0
4 km
56
ARTERRA
To San Diego
Los Peñasquitos
Torrey Pines State Beach
© AVALON TRAVEL

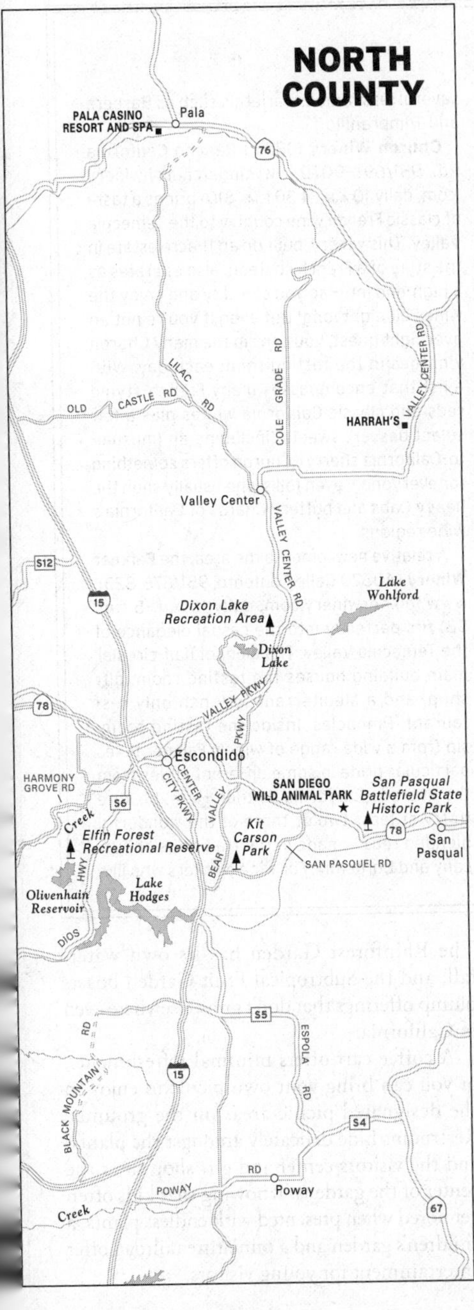


their groups about the wildlife (both animal and vegetable) as they come upon it. You can experience the thrill of seeing a cheetah run full-speed, the simple pleasure of the grazers enjoying an afternoon munching grasses and leaves, or the vista of the full park from the air on the Balloon Safari.

The Wild Animal Park caters both to families and to adults without children seeking a more grown-up experience. Check your map for the location of playgrounds and family-themed attractions. On the website, you can find out which tours and dates are best for an adults-only day at the park. Ample food, restrooms, and concessions cluster around the entrance area, but services get thinner as you get farther out into the park.

## Mission San Luis Rey

Sometimes referred to as the "King of the Missions," Mission San Luis Rey (4050 Mission Ave., Oceanside, 760/757-3651, www.sanluisrey.org, tours daily 10 A.M.–4 P.M., adults $6, children $4) certainly is the biggest of the California missions. It is also one of the most lavishly restored. You can visit the stately formal gardens, complete with manicured lawns, roses, antique sculptures, and ruins of structural elements of the mission buildings. Or take a tour of the museum and church, both of which contain the history of Mission San Luis Rey through interpretive panels and many artifacts. Out in front of the mission, a unique experience awaits as you explore the ruins of the Lavanderia. This large open space contains the remains of the area where Native Americans washed their clothes and themselves outside of the mission grounds. Take the stairs down to seek out the remains of the gargoyles that once sprayed water for laundry. The cemetery is one of the largest and best maintained in the mission system, with memorials dating from the earliest days of this 1798-founded Franciscan church.

## Quail Botanical Gardens

Plant and garden lovers come from around the world to visit the Quail Botanical Gardens (230

SAN DIEGO

## TEMECULA WINERIES

Wine? In San Diego? Yes, indeed! It's not Napa or Sonoma, but if you're in California to sample all the best wine the state has to offer, don't miss out on the terrific SoCal vintages available in the San Diego region.

The major wine-producing region of San Diego is the Temecula Valley. An hour north of San Diego proper, off I-15, this small, hot valley plays home to well over a dozen wineries. Most of the tasting rooms cluster along the main wine drag, Rancho California Road, but it's also worth your time to explore farther into the valley for hidden gems off the beaten path. The Temecula Valley Winegrowers Association (www.temeculawines.org) offers a tasting map and brochure highlighting the wineries and other attractions of the area.

To check out an early example of a quality-heavy boutique winery, visit the **Hart Family Winery** (41300 Avenida Biona, 951/676-6300, www.thehartfamilywinery.com, daily 9 A.M.–4:30 P.M., $5). With vineyards first planted by the Hart family in 1974, this small vintner produces only 5,000 cases of wine, total, each year. This low production allows for intense attention to detail and quality of every single bottle of wine. And despite the small total case number, you can try a number of varietals suited perfectly to the hot climate of the high-altitude Temecula Valley. The grapes used and wines released vary from year to year, but if you can, be sure to try the fruity white Viognier, the stunning Syrah, and several less famous varietals such as Barbera and Tempranillo.

**Churon Winery** (33233 Rancho California Rd., 951/694-9070, www.innatchuronwinery.com, daily 10 A.M.–4:30 P.M., $10) brings a taste of classic French wine country to the Temecula Valley. This winery, built on an 11-acre estate in the style of a French chateau, also operates as a high-end inn – so you can stay and enjoy the wines all night long! But even if you're not an overnight guest, you can sip the many Churon vintages in the tasting room each day. With a list that encompasses many French-styled reds and classic California whites plus a few select dessert sweets (including an unusual-to-California sherry), Churon offers something for everyone – even folks who usually shun the heavy Cabs and buttery Chards of California's wine regions.

A relative newcomer to the area, the **Falkner Winery** (40620 Calle Contento, 951/676-8231, www.falknerwinery.com, daily 10 A.M.–5 P.M., $8) fits perfectly into the casual elegance of the Temecula Valley. The elegant half-circular main building houses the tasting room, gift shop, and a Mediterranean lunch-only restaurant, Pinnacles. Inside the tasting room, sip from a wide range of wines; Falkner takes particular pride in some different styles from the average California vintner. Here, be sure to try at least two or three of the wonderful blended reds – made in the traditions of Tuscany and Bordeaux. For wine drinkers who like

Quail Gardens Dr., Encinitas, 760/436-3036, www.qbgardens.org, 9 A.M.–5 P.M. daily, adults $10, seniors $7, children $5). The plants in this 30-plus-acre spread come from around the world too, as Quail plays home to sub-gardens highlighting rare plant species from almost every continent. Paths meander through the dozens of sub-gardens, inviting visitors to take their time and enjoy the multihued beauty surrounding them on all sides. No visit to the Quail Gardens is complete without viewing the famous Bamboo Garden and the new Undersea Garden filled with rare succulents. The Rainforest Garden has its own waterfall, and the Subtropical Fruit Garden boasts plump offerings that don't grow elsewhere even in California.

A coffee cart offers minimal refreshments, or you can bring your own picnic to enjoy in the designated picnic areas on the grounds. Restrooms hide delicately amongst the plants, and the visitors center and gift shop sit at the center of the gardens. Knowing that kids often get bored when presented with endless plants, a children's garden and a miniature railroad offer entertainment for young visitors.

a little sweet with their savory, Falkner offers a number of not-quite-dry wines that are *not* as syrupy as a standard dessert wine. For added fun, take a tour of the winery any day of the week 11 A.M.–2 P.M. for $3 per person.

Even if you're not into wine, the **South Coast Winery & Resort** (34843 Rancho California Rd., 951/587-9463, www.wineresort.com, daily 10 A.M.–6 P.M., $10) will make a stop worth your while. From the colorful frescoes decorating the tasting room to the posh GrapeSeed Spa, South Coast caters to the most luxury-loving travelers. For the full South Coast experience, book one of their private villas for your stay and reserve a table at the Tuscan-style Vineyard Rose restaurant. Back in the beautiful tasting room, you can try wines under the four different South Coast labels. From the splashy and moderately priced Elevation wines to the elegant Wild Horse Peak Mountain vintages, you'll find a wine for every taste and every budget level. For a special experience, take the inclusive $20 estate tour, which includes the vineyards as well as the production facilities and barrel rooms, and concludes with a private wine-and-cheese tasting.

A large extended family owns and runs most every aspect of the **Wilson Creek Winery & Vineyards** (35960 Rancho California Rd., 951/699-9463, www.wilsoncreekwinery.com, daily 10 A.M.–5 P.M., $10). You might even catch a Wilson when you visit the light, bright tasting room. You'll find some different wines here – one of the Wilson mainstays is Almond Champagne, a truly special occasion beverage. Other sweet wines might include Muscat Canelli, Angelica cream sherry, chocolate port, and luscious late-harvest red wines. (You might want to avoid the "white" wines made from red grave varietals, though. They can be a little bit strange.) More traditional wine lovers will enjoy the hefty Cabernet, Zinfandel, and Petit Sirah. On the other hand, if jazz is your favorite vice, check the website for the annual calendar of concerts held on the purpose-built stage.

At **Palumbo Family Vineyards & Winery** (40150 Barksdale Circle, 951/676-7900, www.palumbofamilyvineyards.com, Fri. noon–5 P.M., Sat.–Sun. 10 A.M.–5 P.M.), you won't find the immense tasting room complex and thousands of cases of wines available at other local wineries. A tiny family operation, Palumbo takes pride in growing every grape that goes into each bottle of wine. With 12 acres of vineyards, the winery produces 1,500 cases of wine each year. A season's release might include five wines – mostly reds with a token Viognier or other hot-weather white for variety. Though they're only open regularly on the weekends, you can call the winery for a private tasting appointment during the week. Or better yet, offer to bring 7–15 of your friends down to the winery for a private winemaker's dinner! Nicholas Palumbo is a chef as well as viticulturalist and winemaker, and has been known to entertain private parties who express an interest in his fabulous food and wine.



# Entertainment and Events

## NIGHTLIFE

### Bars and Clubs

The Gaslamp Quarter is the hottest part of downtown San Diego for the young and energetic nighttime crowd. Consider just walking around Fourth Street and picking a club at random, or try one of the ones mentioned here.

**Belo** (919 Fourth St., 619/231-9200, www.belosandiego.com, Fri.–Sat. 7 P.M.–2 A.M.) is a favorite hotspot with young club-hoppers. They're drawn by the regular appearances of big-name DJs, the size of dance floors, and the big, strong drinks that aren't *too* expensive, especially compared to those sold in competing Gaslamp clubs. Women, be aware: Lots of men at Belo are on the prowl, but security is tight and you'll still have fun, especially if you're part of a group. Dressy attire is encouraged, and cover charge run $15 and up, depending on the night.

After a fashion, you'll find truth in advertising at the **On Broadway Event Center** (615 Broadway, 619/231-0011, www.obec.tv). It is on Broadway—in the Gaslamp, not Manhattan. But it might feel like Manhattan, with the major-league weekend crowds and the overpriced drinks and the hot-stuff VIP room. (If you can get a VIP table, you'll have a blast. Otherwise, the service On Broadway is nothing to write home about.) With five dance floors with different DJs, dancers who love house, trance, '80s, and even salsa can find a place on the floor. Just beware of the lines at the door, especially if you've grabbed a spot on the VIP list, and the size of the cover charge if you're *not* on the list.

You can have it all if you get into **Aubergine** (500 Fourth St. at Island St., 619/232-8100, www.aubergineon4th.com, Fri.–Sat. 6 P.M.–2 A.M., 21 and over). This complex offers three rooms for dancing, a restaurant and sushi bar, and a comedy club all in the same (big) place. If you're coming to dance, get yourself on the guest list in advance to avoid the $20 cover. Expect a significant singles scene, good DJs spinning a mix of classics and new top hits, and crowds seeking sushi at happy hour (6–8 P.M.). The dress code tends toward the upscale, so leave the jeans behind and break out the slacks and cocktail dresses.

How can you not finish out your night at a club called **The Bitter End** (770 Fifth St., 619/338-9300, www.thebitterend.com, daily 3 P.M.–2 A.M., $10)? A step more mellow than most Gaslamp clubs, Bitter End has a distinct lounge feel with a dance club downstairs. The middle level is the main bar, which serves up pool, conversation, and the house special Black Martini. Upstairs is filled with soft couches and armchairs to recline on, plus Victorian architectural details and a historic atmosphere to please even a picky Goth. With a $10 cover, Bitter End offers one of the less expensive club experiences in the Gaslamp, but mind your dress. After happy hour, the dress code gets strictly enforced, and that means no tennis shoes.

## Gay and Lesbian

With a young, hip scene and a significant gay presence, nightlife in Hillcrest is happening most every night of the week.

**The Brass Rail** (3796 Fifth Ave., 619/298-2233, www.thebrassrailsd.com, Mon., Thurs.–Sat. hours vary) is one of San Diego's oldest gay venues. The lounge features theme nights, DJs, and live music in a historic Hillcrest location. Ladies should head to **The Flame** (3780 Park Blvd., 619/295-4163, www.flamesd.com, daily 1 P.M.–1 A.M.) on Saturdays for dancing, drinks, or just people-watching from the raised, circular couches.

## Live Music

San Diego enjoys its music, and you'll find plenty of opportunities to hear live classical, jazz, rock, and more throughout town. You'll have no trouble finding everything from tiny dive bars with mini-stages up to huge multi-day music festivals. Whether you prefer mellow jazz, danceable blues, or hard-hitting rock, odds are it's playing live. Check web guides to the Gaslamp (www.gaslamp.org) and Hillcrest (http://gothere.com/sandiego/Hillcrest) for listings of who's hosting what when you're in town.

If you're in Point Loma for the evening, head to Humphrey's for live music any time of year. **Humphrey's Backstage Music** (2241 Shelter Island Blvd., www.humphreysbythebay.com/backstagemusicclub.cfm) offers a lounge-style venue with live music or DJs spinning danceable tunes or playing charming smooth jazz to drink and converse by. Check the website for this month's schedule. If you're around in the summer season, buy tickets in advance for the local favorite concert series, **Humphreys Concerts by the Bay** (www.humphreysconcerts.com). National acts come out to play against the backdrop of the marinas of Shelter Island as the sun sets over San Diego Bay. The outdoor venue takes advantage of the evening climate, so you can bask in the warm air under the stars as you listen to the tunes of your favorite rock band or folk singer.

## Comedy

Laugh it up in the Gaslamp Quarter! The

# FESTIVALS AND EVENTS

Summer is event season in San Diego. If you're visiting between June and October, you can hardly help tripping over some fun congregation of folks. Check the web or with the tourist bureau for tickets to your favorite events, or information about what's going on in the area during your visit.

## SAN DIEGO COUNTY FAIR

The San Diego County Fair (2260 Jimmy Durant Blvd, Del Mar, 858/755-1161, www.sdfair.com, June–July) runs for several weeks every summer and boasts being one of the very best in the state. Naturally it's held at the famed Del Mar County Fairgrounds, which were purposely built for this celebration of San Diego agriculture.

## LGBT PRIDE PARADE AND FESTIVAL

There's nothing sexier than loving yourself. To celebrate being yourself, each year San Diego hosts its own LGBT Pride Parade and Festival (sandiegopride.org, June). Smaller than the mammoth festival in San Francisco each year, San Diego Pride beckons to those who want the fun of Pride without the mega-crowds. (But still, with all that bikini weather, expect plenty of people to be in attendance at all events and on both days of the festival.) The weekend is packed with events and attractions, from a 5K run to a Ferris wheel. No matter who you are or what you're into, there's something for you here. You'll find almost a dozen stages, each offering a different style of music from hip-hop to acoustic to Latino to lavender. Just about every possible lifestyle choice is represented with its own fun area; you can get hardcore in the leather space, explore your sexuality in the bisexual area, or bring your children to the family place. If you love baseball and queer life, plan ahead and purchase tickets to the Padres Pride event.

The parade and festival take place in Balboa Park, spilling out to the Hillcrest neighborhood especially in the evening, and out to Petco Park for the Padres baseball event. Check the website for information about park-and-ride services, parking, bicycle parking, public transit, and more. You can purchase tickets in advance, or at the festival. There's no smoking at the festival, but if you need wheelchair assistance, contact the festival organizers in advance.

## STREET SCENE

For a rockin' good time, check out Street Scene (Coors Amphitheater, Chula Vista, www.streetscene.com, Sept.) if you're in the San Diego area in September. This major rock-and-more festival draws name-brand pop and rock acts from around the world for a two-day show. Once you're inside the amphitheater, you'll have your choice of several stages featuring up-and-comers, experimental music, and of course the big-leaguers. Check the website for this year's lineup of musicians and a look into the stage setup and facilities for the concert. You'll find plenty of food and drink available at the indoor concessions, though it's always a good idea to eat well before venturing into a major music festival. Also, be sure to bring your sunscreen; September weekends in San Diego are often blazing hot with fiery sunshine.

## THUNDERBOAT REGATTA

For an event that's unique to San Diego and totally noisy, you can't beat the Thunderboat Regatta (www.thunderboatregatta.com, Sept.). For one weekend each September, Mission Bay revs up and gets loud, hosting a supercharged powerboat-racing event. You can see drag boat racing, Formula One, cracker box inboards, and much more. Stands are set up on beaches around the bay to allow the most people the best views of the races – be sure to buy your tickets in advance to get a good seat. The excitement at this event is contagious, and the tension is real. Be sure to bring earplugs, and extra money for parking if you want a space anywhere near the bay. (Alternately, check the website and the local resorts for deals on hotel rooms within walking distance of race-viewing areas.) Kids of all ages are welcome – check the schedule for this year's family-oriented events.

**John Lovitz Comedy Club** (Fourth and Island Sts., 866/468-3399, www.jonlovitzcomedyclub.com) has comics making with the funny most every night of the week. Come out to see major stars you'll recognize from TV and film, or up-and-coming comics from the showcase specials on Comedy Central. As a part of the Aubergine complex, the John Lovitz Comedy Club offers far better dining options than the average comedy venue. (Think sushi rather than nachos.) This makes getting yourself to the two-item (food or drink) minimum an easy prospect.



## THE ARTS

Live theater lives well in San Diego. Most every area and district has at least a theater or two, and several big houses garner national acclaim for world-class productions. If you're in San Diego for more than one night, it will be worth your while to take in a show at the Old Globe, the La Jolla Playhouse, or one of the innumerable repertory theaters.

### Theater

The **Old Globe** (Copley Plaza, Balboa Park, 619/234-5623, www.oldglobe.org, box office daily noon–6 P.M. or end of show), one of the most famous theater complexes in California, sits in the middle of Balboa Park. Originally constructed to produce abbreviated Shakespeare plays for the 1935 California Pacific International Exposition, the magnificent Old Globe was remodeled to permanence in 1937. It has been producing a full season ever since, growing to add two auxiliary theaters: the Cassius Carter Centre Stage and the Lowell Davis Festival Stage. The Old Globe, restored to its original magnificence after a fire in 1978, seats almost 600 people, and has produced world premieres of plays such as *Into the Woods* and *The Full Monty* that go on to become Broadway spectaculars and worldwide hits. If you can get a ticket to something new at the Old Globe, you may find yourself seeing history being made.

The Old Globe theaters are reminiscent of the complex at the legendary Ashland Shakespeare festival. The huge outdoor Lowell Davis facility can seat almost 700 spectators and puts up shows during the summer and fall festival season. The smaller Cassius Carter Stage presents theater in the round, in an intimate black-box-style setting. See the website for a list of the shows playing at each theater, as well as for ticket sales and seating charts. At the Copley Theater complex, enjoy a snack and a drink at Lady Carolyn's Pub or browse for souvenirs at the gift shop.

For a night of high budget, fabulous Broadway theater or an adventurous off-center world premiere, check out a show at the **La Jolla Playhouse** (La Jolla Village Dr. and Gilman Dr., 858/550-1010, www.lajollaplayhouse.com, box office Sun.–Mon. noon–7 P.M., Tues.–Wed. noon–7:30 P.M., Thurs.–Sat. noon–8 P.M., shows Tues.–Sun.). This top-tier theater company produces big musicals, small experimental plays, historical dramas, and everything in between. Check the website for this year's main season schedule as well as the off-season "The Edge" plays. The Playhouse actually encompasses a building complex with three separate theater. Originally created by an ensemble of Hollywood actors, the Playhouse delights in showing off both well-known popular shows and great world premieres. Look for originality in sets and costuming, as well as top-notch acting.

For a charming night out on the North Coast, grab a seat at the **North Coast Repertory Theater** (987 Lomas Santa Fe Dr., Solano Beach, 858/481-1055, http://northcoastrep.org, shows Wed.–Sun.). The North Coast Rep produces about eight shows each year, including musicals, dramas, comedies, and family favorites. With ticket prices at around $20 per show, a laid-back evening of good repertory theater isn't hard to obtain. The theater at Lomas Santa Fe Plaza is located conveniently near I-5 and the Del Mar Racetrack, for easy access after a day's sightseeing.

### Classical Music

The **Organ Concerts in Balboa Park** (www.sosorgan.com) provide a unique, free live music experience that all visitors and locals can enjoy. Every week of the year for almost a century, the

Spreckels Organ has serenaded the park with beautiful music. Concerts happen on Sundays 2–3 P.M., and on Monday nights at 7:30 P.M. in the summertime. Come out, take a seat on a park bench, and relax as the music washes over you.

If you love opera, be sure to get tickets to the **San Diego Opera** (box office 619/533-7000, www.sdopera.com, Mon.–Fri. 8:30 A.M.–4:30 P.M.) during your visit. Originally created to produce San Francisco Opera productions in the 1950s, the San Diego Opera quickly grew into an independent production company to rival even its famed neighbor to the north. In addition to the regular season filled with original productions of famous operas, you'll find the San Diego Opera hosting international stars at special concerts, and presenting a variety of musicales to the San Diego community.

All regular Opera performances take place at the Civic Theatre (Third Ave. and B St.). You'll find several parking structures and surface lots nearby—parking usually starts at $10 and goes up on concert nights. The MTS trolley stops right behind the Theatre entrance, and is a great option if you're staying anywhere near the trolley line or are taking the train into the Santa Fe station. If you're coming from the North County for a night of culture, check the Opera's website for information about the San Diego Opera Caravan, a pay bus service to and from Carlsbad to the Civic Theatre.

### Cinema

You'll find plenty of first-run multi-screen cineplexes scattered throughout the San Diego area. But if you're looking for a fun vintage moviegoing experience, try the **Ken Cinema** (4061 Adams Ave., 619/819-0236). Built in 1946, this single-screen theater now specializes in running independent and foreign films. You can also attend the Gay and Lesbian Film Festival at the Ken each year. Happily, the seats are not the same vintage as the rest of the theater—new, comfortable theater chairs were installed in 2004. There's no parking lot, so you'll have to try your luck on the street with the locals who come to the Ken regularly to see something other than the standard new Hollywood fare.

If you're in La Jolla and looking for fun and unusual film entertainment, head up to the **La Jolla Village Cinemas** (8879 Villa La Jolla Dr., 619/819-0236). This four-screener shows a variety of different styles of movie, from independent to foreign to popular. Enjoy better-than-average concessions, plus an array of good food and drink centered right around the theater. If you're looking for a midnight movie experience, call and see if they're running something while you're in town.

# Shopping

Shopping in San Diego runs primarily to malls and shopping centers that offer a good, if selective, experience. Downtown, wander the Gaslamp Quarter for San Diego—grown clothing or hit the immense Horton Plaza for stores you know. Old Town is fun for unique, Mexican souvenirs and is a short jump from Mission Valley where the mall is king. Farther north, La Jolla provides a more relaxed, upscale experience.

## DOWNTOWN

### Gaslamp Quarter

As you stroll the streets of the Gaslamp Quarter you'll find many stores are local chains, like the **San Diego Trading Company** (534 Fifth Ave., 619/237-0062, www.sandiegotrading company.com) or surfing/resort wear purveyors such as **Hilo Hattie's** (301 Fifth Ave., 619/546-7289, www.hilohattie.com) and **Quiksilver Boardriders Club** (402 Fifth Ave., 619/234-3125, www.quiksilver.com).

For the ladies, trendy clothes are sold at **Mango Clothing** (230 Fifth Ave., 619/237-1344). Men looking for serious suits go to **Boutique Voss** (946 Fifth Ave., 619/235-8999), a purveyor of fine Italian designer fashions.

In casual California, it makes sense to find several stores devoted to the sale of jeans. **G-Star** (470 Fifth Ave., 619/283-7088, www.g-star.com) offers fun, eclectic men's and women's wear made mostly from denim. You'll find familiar jeans, jackets, and accessories inside the chain **Lucky Brand Jeans** (621 Fifth Ave., 619/230-9260, www.luckybrandjeans.com).

While the district's gaslamps don't glow red anymore, you can find some risqué items here, most a couple of blocks off the main drag. The large **Hustler** (929 Sixth Ave., 619/696-9007, www.hustlerhollywood.com) chain has a presence here. This huge, two-floor emporium is astonishingly well-lit and woman friendly. The downstairs area is devoted to lingerie and novelty items—things that can be displayed in the big plate-glass windows. Upstairs, you'll find the good stuff, including young, friendly employees who will be happy to help you with any product needs you might have. A huge toy wall has something for every woman's needs, and the DVD collection makes men swoon with… er…joy. Be sure to check out the fun foam sex chairs and couches while you're up there!



A small but sweet selection of home stores hang out in the Gaslamp. You can check out the latest styles at the familiar **Z Gallerie** (611 Fifth Ave., 619/696-8137, www.zgallerie.com) or the funky **Avitatt** (232 Fifth Ave., 619/338-8245, www.avitatt.com). Specialty items of obvious types are available at **Kita Ceramics + Glassware** (517 Fourth Ave. #101, 619/239-2600, www.kitaceramicsglass.com), **Urban Lighting** (301 Fourth Ave., 619/232-6064, www.urbanlighting.net), and **Fourth Avenue Rug Gallery** (827 Fourth Ave., 619/234-8700).

### Horton Plaza

Looking for a big mall to gather all your favorite shops together into one place? Visit Westfield Horton Plaza (324 Horton Plaza, San Diego, 619/239-8180, www.westfield.com/hortonplaza, Mon.–Fri. 10 A.M.–9 P.M., Sat. 10 A.M.–8 P.M., Sun. 11 A.M.–7 P.M.). With all the standard Westfield mall amenities, including day spas, salons, and plenty of food options, you'll feel right at home here.

Many of your favorite midrange to upscale chain boutiques make a home at Horton Plaza. Shop at Baby Gap, Bebe, Guess, and Victoria's Secret, among others. Horton Plaza also offers an immense array of jewelry shops, accessory stores, and leather boutiques, from Coach and Louis Vuitton for the stylish adult looking for handbags to Metal Zone and Stone Waterfall for younger shoppers looking for hot new jewelry. For shoes, you'll find everything from Crocs to Foot Locker.

## OLD TOWN

### Bazaar Del Mundo

A perfect way to experience shopping in Mexico without making the trek down to Tijuana is to visit Old Town's famed Bazaar del Mundo (4133 Taylor St., 619/296-3161, Sun.–Mon. 10 A.M.–5:30 P.M., Tues.–Sat. 10 A.M.–9 P.M.). Easily accessed from I-5 and I-8, this cheerful and colorful shopping center brings the best of Mexico across the border. From the familiar figures in the **Laurel Burch Gallerita** to the unusual and often elegant imports of **Artes,** you'll find perfect gifts for everyone on your list (and for yourself, of course). When you come down to the Bazaar, come hungry! Some of the best and most visitor-friendly Mexican food is served here (see *Food*).

### Fashion Valley

Another big urban mall, Fashion Valley (7007 Friars Rd., 619/688-9113, www.simon.com/mall, Mon.–Sat. 10 A.M.–7 P.M., Sun. 11 A.M.–7 P.M.) has plenty of the shopping experience you desire. A bit higher end than Horton Plaza, Fashion Valley focuses more on the home and offers some designer boutiques.

Appropriately, fashions for men, women, and children of all ages abound at Fashion Valley. Kids can grow up here, going from Gymboree to GapKids and on up to The Limited Too. Gentlemen have a number of options for all parts of life, from the casual times at J. Crew and Old Navy to more formal situations in Bernini, Gucci, and After Hours Formal Wear.

Not surprisingly, women have the most clothing options here at the mall. The mature crowd prefers Ann Taylor and Talbots, while the teens and twenties shoppers flock to Abercrombie & Fitch and Forever 21. For inexpensive and sporting shoes, run to Footlocker or Shiek Shoes. Fancy sunglasses peek out the windows at Occhiala da Sole and thousands of watches keep the time inside Tourneau.

### LA JOLLA

Shopping in La Jolla feels a little like a spending spree in the sophisticated areas of Los Angeles. This upscale suburb prides itself on its walking-and-shopping, much of which is centered around Prospect Street. Be sure to veer off onto the side streets, which hide some true gems!

#### Prospect La Jolla

Big name and upscale chain stores rent space on Prospect, as do locally owned one-of-a-kind boutiques. You can go lingerie shopping at **Victoria's Secret** (1111 Prospect St., 858/459-0688, www.victoriassecret.com) or the unique **Neroli** (7944 Girard Ave., 858/456-9618). Look for monochromatic women's wear at **White House/Black Market** (7927 Girard Ave., 858/459-2565, www.whitehouseblackmarket.com), or a matching man's tuxedo at **Imperial Taylor and Formal Wear** (7744 Fay Ave., 858/459-8891). Dozens more apparel stores, from the casual to the highest of high-end cluster in La Jolla.

Naturally, only the funkiest or fanciest jewels will do to complement the lovely clothing sold in La Jolla (a town whose name translates as "The Jewel"). You can browse in dozens of jewelry stores, from reasonably priced costume jewelry all the way up to designer diamonds. For something fun and unique, head for **The Artful Soul** (7660 Fay Ave., 858/459-2009, www.artfulsoul.com) to check out everything from earrings and bracelets to purses and belts, all sparkling and creatively designed. For local fine jewelry, visit **Jewels by the Sea** (1237 Prospect St. B, 858/459-5166) and **Jewel of La Jolla** (1250 Prospect St., Ste B20, 858/729-1849).

Elegant antique stores cluster in La Jolla, beckoning wealthy patrons to furnish and decorate their homes with the beautiful artifacts of the past. Pick up a great new piece for your collection at shops such as **AJA Antiques & Art** (955 Prospect St. E, 858/459-0333), **Renaissance Art and Antiques** (7715 Fay Ave., 858/454-3887), or the **Girard Avenue Collection** (7505 Girard Ave., 858/459-7765).



## Sports and Recreation

San Diego has more than its share of sunny days year-round, so get outside! With dozens of miles of beaches, zoos, parks, trails, and endless opportunities for recreation, even the most dedicated couch potatoes can find something great to do under the famed California sun.

### BEACHES

If you come to San Diego, you must go to the beach. It's an imperative. From Encinitas and Del Mar down almost to the Mexican border, the California coast shows off its best. The San Diego beaches all seem to be 100 yards wide, perfectly flat, 100 percent pale, soft, sugar sand, and run as far in either direction as the eye can see. A few rocks appear in spots, but they're few and far between (especially in comparison to the rugged northern coastline). Bring your towel, umbrella, sunscreen, swimsuit, and surfboard. And if it's a weekend in the summertime, come early in the morning to stake a prime spot in the sand.

For a list of beaches maintained by the City of San Diego, check out this website: www.sandiego.gov/lifeguards/beaches.

#### Ocean Beach

Yes, the Ocean Beach (1950 Abbot St., Ocean Beach, 24 hours/day) sandy spot is part of the community of Ocean Beach townlet. Small for a San Diego beach, this one-mile stretch of sand beckons locals and visitors alike with its lifeguard-protected waters, multi-use areas, and famous Dog Beach. On Dog Beach, at the north end of Ocean Beach, dogs are allowed off-leash all day, every day. (Please clean up after your dog!) Farther south, you'll find designated areas for fishing, surfing, and swimming. Check with the lifeguards to figure out which is which. Be aware that rip currents can be strong at Ocean Beach, and take care when you're out in the water. At the south end of the beach, you can take a walk out on the Ocean Beach pier; some people even bring a pole to spend some quiet time fishing out on the pier.

If you need a restroom or showers, head for the main lifeguard station at Abbot Street, which has both. Lifeguards stay on duty from 9 A.M. to dusk daily. Amazingly ample parking can be found at three lots that range from the south to the north end of the beach. (The smallest lot is the one by the lifeguard station; go north or south for better parking opportunities.)



### Black's Beach

Black's Beach (south of Torrey Pines State Beach) sits north of downtown La Jolla, and this local's favorite finds fame as a surf break; head for the south end of the two-mile beachfront to find the best surfing. But pause a second before grabbing your board and clambering down the cliffs: Black's doubles as a well-known nude beach.

The main difficulty with Black's Beach is getting there. As an unofficial beach without a permanent lifeguard station, you won't find any parking lots; you'll have to do the best you can on the street. No well-built or easily climbed stairways lead down to Black's, so you can either scramble down the cliff paths, or take your chances with the tides and enter from an adjacent beach to the north or south. Finally, lifeguards are stationed here in the summer months only and the waters are unregulated, so be extremely careful of your fellow surfers and swimmers!

### Coronado Main Beach

The can't-miss Hotel del Coronado marks the Coronado Main Beach (Ocean Blvd.). Anyone can walk through the outdoor common areas of the Del to get out to this charming sandy beach. Yet another fabulous sun-drenched chunk of coastline, the Coronado Main Beach gets ultra-crowded in the summertime, so come early if you want a prime spot of your own. Do pay attention to the signs and flags—a nasty breakwater of large boulders hides under the water just in front of the Del at high tide. Also take a look at the odd-shaped dunes; from the air, they spell out "Del Coronado."

### Del Mar City Beach

Running along the length of downtown Del Mar, without tons of easy parking, Del Mar City Beach (15th St. and Coast Blvd. to the Rivermouth, Del Mar) is touted as one of the best beaches in an area famous for its welcoming sands. This huge strip of coastline has it all. The soft sand invites sunbathers, who can spend all day soaking up rays. The ocean beckons, the cool Pacific making a perfect counterpoint to hot San Diego summer days. A decent surf break near the center of City Beach beckons to new and experienced wave riders alike. (You can even take surf lessons here.) Lifeguards protect the shores, complete with the *Baywatch*-esque pale blue towers that mark all guarded San Diego county beaches. Be sure to pay attention to the colored flags on the beach. Blue means swimming is okay, and a yellow flag with a black ball means *no surfing* in the surrounding area.

Once you find a place on the street to park (bring quarters for the meters) getting onto the beach is easy. The area is flat and simple to access, and in some places boardwalks and paths make beach access even simpler. Just off the beach, the Powerhouse community center offers restrooms, a restaurant, and a community theater.

## SURFING

With its endless sunshine, temperate water, and magnificent breaks, San Diego offers some of the best surfing in California. You can surf year-round down here, though San Diego is not the South Pacific and wet suits can be a good idea in winter.

The average water temperature of the Pacific Ocean in summer stands at 65–70°F—perfect for surfing, snorkeling, diving, kayaking, or just plain old swimming.

## Surf Breaks

San Diego boasts plenty of classic southern California surfing. For the coolest local breaks, you'll have to consult the coolest locals. But even the more popular spots offer reliable breaks. In La Jolla, **Black's Beach** is both a local's favorite and visitor's joy. Modest surfers beware: Black's also operates as a nude beach. **Del Mar City Beach** (15th St. and Coast Blvd. to the Rivermouth, Del Mar), in addition to being a great sandy spot to hang out, offers fine beginning and intermediate waves. **Mission Beach** has a good break as well as lifeguards, restroom facilities, and about a zillion tourists and sun worshippers in the summertime. If you're serious about surfing, check out **Windansea Beach** (6800 Neptune Pl.), which has a heavy shore break and a rockier coastline than most of San Diego—and therefore fewer sunbathers and swimmers hanging out here. You will find dense crowds of fellow surfers, so this isn't the best spot for beginners to try out their boards. On the other hand, the small, consistent waves at **La Jolla Shores** (8200 Camino del Oro, La Jolla) bore the hardcore masters, but are perfect for novice surfers. Just stick within the lifeguard-designated surfing areas to avoid the swimmers and scuba divers sharing the water here.

## Surf Schools

Never ridden a wave before? Always wanted to? Check out one of San Diego's many surf schools. You'll go to a small-wave beach, learn the basics of the sport on dry land, then paddle out for the first time. Most schools promise to get you up and riding (if only for a few seconds) the very first time! Or if you've come to Southern California specifically to surf, check with the schools about multi-day, all-inclusive (lodging too!) "surf camps" that get you surfing all day, every day for a few days or a whole week.

**Surfari** (3740 Mission Blvd., 858/337-3287, www.surfarisurf.com, $50/day group lesson, $75/day private lesson, start times 9 A.M., 11 A.M., 1 P.M., 3 P.M.) was started by competitive surfer Rick Gehris and operates close to downtown San Diego at Mission Beach. Each 2.5-hour lesson includes land instruction, interactive in-the-water instruction, and an hour afterward on your own to play. Regular group lessons happen almost every day of the year. For a more intense learning experience, book a discounted three-day lesson series.

The **San Diego Surfing Academy** (800/447-7873, www.surfingacademy.com, $60/group lesson, $55/hour private) runs year-round at the north end of South Carlsbad State Beach Campgrounds. You must make an appointment to take lessons with the SDSA, but the quality of instruction makes it worth the bother. All equipment is included in the fee—perfect for hours of fun surfing the waves of the North Coast. With two-hour group classes and by-the-hour private lessons, this safety-oriented school makes certain you'll know what you're doing out there in the surf. If you want to take your surfing to the next level, look into SDSA's surf camps, which include meals, tent cabin lodgings, and photos of you out on your board.

If you're female, and you want to learn to surf but you find the male-dominated sport intimidating, come out to **Surf Diva** (2160 Avenida de la Playa, La Jolla, 858/454-8273, www.surfdiva.com, $65/hour private lessons, $135/two-day clinic). The first all-women's surf school in the world, Surf Diva creates an estrogen-friendly, supportive atmosphere for girls ages five and up to learn the ins and outs of the waves at La Jolla Shores. (The "Guys on the Side" semi-private and group lessons include men too!) Book a private lesson, or take a two- to five-day clinic to get serious about the sport. Lessons at Surf Diva can make a fun and creative start to your best friend's bachelorette party!

## Board and Equipment Rental

Most of the surf schools, including **Surfari** and **Surf Diva,** rent and sell boards, leashes, wetsuits, and board care equipment—everything you need for your first surf set-up, and repair and replacement equipment if you're an expert.

## BOATING

In Mission Bay and San Diego Bay, the calm waters make great fun of all forms of boating, from paddle-boating to waterskiing to sailing. Kayaking is a special local favorite pastime, especially for would-be explorers of the famous La Jolla Caves. If you plan to exit the bays for the open ocean, be sure you're either competent to navigate a watercraft on the open sea, or have somebody with you who can do it. Watch the weather reports, and pay attention to local experts.

### Power Boating and Waterskiing

On the calm waters of the two bays, you can water-ski and wakeboard, dash around on a Jet-Ski, or just cruise offshore in a speedboat. **Seaforth Boat Rentals** (888/834-2628, www.seaforthboatrentals.com, $35–145) has three locations: in Mission Bay, downtown San Diego, and Coronado. If you're planning to cruise, rent one of the large (up to 240 horsepower) speedboats, which has plenty of room for passengers, coolers, and snacks. If you've got an athletic crew with you, reserve a ski boat. They come with wakeboards, ski tubes, skis. For a more motorcycle-like on-the-water experience, pick up a modern, powerful Jet-Ski that rides 2–3 people.

Another multi-boat rental outfit with several locations in and around San Diego is **Action Sport Rentals** (858/581-5939, www.actionsportrentals.com, $95–150). Rent yourself a three-seater Jet-Ski or a six- or seven-passenger speedboat and tool around the bays. For a bigger party, Action offers 13-passenger power pontoon boats. If you want to water-ski or wakeboard but don't have anyone to drive the boat, reserve some time with Action's professional driver. You'll get rides on whatever type of toy (wakeboard, skis, kneeboard, tube) you want behind their competitive-class ski boat.

### Sailing

Whether you want a quiet putter around the bay or an exhilarating adventure on the open ocean, you can get just the sailing experience you want in San Diego. **Seaforth Boat Rentals** (888/834-2628, www.seaforthboatrentals.com) offers rental sailboats from 14 to 36 feet. You can also book a sailing lesson, or even hire a captain to take care of the practicalities while you and your party enjoy a glass of wine and a meal or snack on the water.

### Kayaking

With so many calm, protected bays, plus an array of exciting sea caves, it's no wonder that San Diego boasts some of the best sea kayaking in the state. Whether you've got your own boat or you plan to rent or take a tour, the most popular spot to paddle are the La Jolla Caves, part of the larger **La Jolla Cove Ecological Reserve** (1100 Coast Blvd., www.sandiego.gov). **Scuba San Diego** (619/260-1880, www.scubasandiego.com) offers guided paddles of this well-traveled area. You don't need any previous sea kayaking experience to take this easy two-hour tour; the sit-on-top kayaks are easy to get into and out of, and safe if you happen to fall off. On the tour, you'll visit soaring sea cliffs and a vast kelp forest, and paddle through the famed local sea caves.

## SNORKELING AND SCUBA

The reefs and wrecks off San Diego offer amazing sights, clear waters, and brightly colored sea life—whether you want a guided tour or go off on your own.

A great place to enjoy a calm snorkel with your family is the **La Jolla Cove.** Make a reservation with a professional outfit such as **Scuba San Diego, Inc** (619/260-1880, www.scubasandiego.com) to take a guided tour of the La Jolla Cove Ecological Reserve. They also offer an exciting night dive, and a Scuba Adventure trip for new divers who are not yet certified. Or bring your own (or rent some) equipment and kick off the shore on your own (with at least one friend, of course).

Looking for a deeper dive experience? Take a scuba trip to one of the San Diego area's many fabulous dive locations. Depending on your interests, you can view the abundance of life in the La Jolla Outer Reef, human history and mechanical failure at Wreck Alley, or the undersea forest at the Giant Kelp Beds.

## FISHING

Any number of charter companies offer half- to full-day deep sea fishing trips for everything from rock cod to yellowfin tuna and mahimahi, depending on the season. Most companies include both Mexican and California fishing licenses with your charter as needed, as well as rental or included tackle and fish cleaning and filleting services. The tuna season (for fishing well offshore for large tuna) runs from early summer through the fall most years.

Leaving right out of the San Diego harbor, **H&M Landing** (2803 Emerson St., 619/222-1144, www.hmlanding.com, half-day adults $40, tackle $9.50) offers half-, three-quarter-, full-day, and evening trips year-round. Shorter trips ply the Point Loma kelp beds, while longer trips can head out to the Coronado Islands or farther into the open water.

**Seaforth Sportfishing** (1717 Quivira Rd., 619/224-3383, www.seaforthlanding.com, tackle extra) offers half-day through multiday trips to fish for most of the major species fishable in the San Diego area. You can even catch a barracuda! Seaforth's year-round half-day trips last five hours (morning or afternoon), allow the catching of more than half a dozen types of fish, and are perfect for families with children or new anglers. Three-quarter day trips really last all day (eight hours) and can range down as far as the Coronado Islands in Mexico. The Overnight Mexico and Multi-Day Tuna trips are best for more experienced fishers who don't suffer from too much seasickness, and are looking to reel in a bigger catch. On any Seaforth trip, expect a full galley with snacks, meals, and beverage service. You can get a bay skiff for $40 per half-day, plus rent tackle and buy live bait.

**Point Loma Sportfishing** (1403 Scott St., 619/223-1627, www.pointlomasportfishing.com, adults half-day from $40, multi-day from $250, tackle extra) offers more than six boats and an extensive list of fishing options. With Point Loma, hardcore anglers can book a two-week cruise that ranges more than 1,000 miles from San Diego, going after enormous deep-water tuna and other major-league sport fish. On the other hand, several of Point Loma's boats offer sedate, family- and beginner-friendly half-day (six hours) and three-quarter-day (8–10 hours) trips for rockfish, sea bass, barracuda, and yellowtail near the San Diego and northern Mexico coastlines. Private charter boats are available for parties of 5–25.

For small groups looking to fish together, **Action Sport Rentals** (2580 Ingraham St., 619/226-2929, www.danalanding.com) at Dana Landing maintains a fleet of six-passenger fishing boats that can handle half-day to two-day fishing trips. Action Sport Rentals offers bay-safe skiffs, tackle, and bait year-round. You'll also find a launch there if you've brought your own boat.



## WHALE-WATCHING

If you prefer to catch marine life with your camera rather than a hook and line, consider taking a whale-watching cruise out from the San Diego coastline. Most of the sportfishing outfits also offer whale-watching trips and charters in season (winter through mid-spring). **Hornblower Cruises** (1066 N. Harbor Dr., 619/686-8700, www.hornblower.com) offers daily nature cruises at 9:30 A.M. and 1:30 P.M. year-round. This nearly four-hour adventure is great for families, and includes a kid-friendly marine habitat video; seal, sea lion, and dolphin viewing; and guaranteed whale spotting. Hornblower offers one of the most comfortable, tourist-friendly sea experiences, with a snack bar, indoor decks with panel windows for good viewing, and a yacht highly rated for its stability.

## AIR SPORTS

With a strong military history and endlessly fabulous weather, it's no wonder that aviation-based sports are a big deal in San Diego.

### Flying and Skydiving

Yes, you really can go to "war" during your otherwise tranquil vacation in San Diego. **Biplane Air Combat & Warbird Flights** (800/759-5667, www.barnstorming.com, $200–450 per person, depending on type of flight) offers the rare opportunity to fly an air combat mission in a light plane designed for dogfighting. Or take a ride in an SNJ-4 Texan, a real World War II aircraft. For a more peaceful aviation experience, book a scenic flight for one or two people in an old-fashioned biplane.

If you prefer jumping out of planes to riding in them, head up north to **Skydive Elsinore** (20701 Cereal St., Lake Elsinore, 951/245-9939, www.skydiveelsinore.com). This full-service skydiving school and outfitter can take you on a great jump, regardless of your experience level. Beginners can take a tandem jump after a brief introductory lesson, or go more intensive with a full-fledged skydiving course culminating with a solo jump. If you're a more experienced jumper, take a look at the website for your diving options.

### Gliding

For perhaps the most unusual views of northern San Diego County you can get, go **Sky Sailing** (31930 Hwy. 79, Warner Springs, 760/782-0404, www.skysailing.com, daily, scenic trips from $70/person, lessons from $110). In a silent glider or "sail plane," you'll catch thermal updrafts, see Palomar Mountain and Warner Springs Ranch, and feel the wonder of birdlike flight. If you're interested in sightseeing, make a weekday reservation or just drop by on the weekend for a flight flown by an FAA-certified pilot. If it's actually flying a glider yourself that lights your fire, book a lesson or rent a glider of your own. (Hand-controlled gliders are available for pilots with special needs.) And if you've got a strong stomach and great faith in your ability to survive, ask about the Sensational Aerobatic Rides.

If you prefer the notion of gliding off a sea cliff into the air above the Pacific Ocean, your destination is the **Torrey Pines Glider Port** (2800 Torrey Pines Scenic Dr., 858/452-9858, La Jolla, $150–175 for a 20-minute tandem flight). Here you can book a tandem flight on either a hang glider or a paraglider with only 20 minutes of pre-flight instruction. The specialty of the house is paragliding, and you can sign up for lessons and get certified to paraglide all on your own.

## GOLF

With fabulous sunny weather year-round, San Diego and its surrounding countryside are a golfer's dream. Wherever you go, you'll find a course or two awaiting you, from easy nine-holers up to U.S. Open hosts. If you're new to the area, consider calling **Showtime Golf** (888/661-2334, www.showtimegolf.com). This golf service provider can get you advance or last-minute tee times, book you into local tournaments, and answer all your questions about the vast range of golfing options in the San Diego area.

If you know anything about golf in San Diego and La Jolla, you know that the One True Golf Course here is **Torrey Pines** (11480 N. Torrey Pines Rd., La Jolla, 858/452-3226, www.torreypinesgolfcourse.com). Home of the 2008 U.S. Open, the Torrey Pines Golf Course has two championship 18-hole courses. Plan to book well in advance for a tee time at this gorgeous course.

## HIKING

In addition to walks on the beach, the **Torrey Pines State Reserve** (North Torrey Pines Rd., 858/755-2063, www.torreypine.org, daily sunrise–sunset) offers some unusually beautiful wilderness trails. Be sure to look for *Pinus torreyana*—the rarest species of pine tree in the United States. The shortest walk is the High Point Trail, only 100 yards up to views of the whole reserve, from the ocean to the lagoon to the forest and back. For an easy, under one-hour walk, take the Guy Fleming Trail for a level two-thirds of a mile through forest, wildflower patches, and views of the ocean. For a longer walk, leave the visitors center by the road, then take the North Fork Trail west to the Broken Hill Trail, which will bring you right down to the beach stairway and a great view of Flat Rock.

## CASINO GAMBLING

If your first love is a night donating money to the local Native American tribe, a number of casinos outside the city proper can hook you up.

A few miles east of San Diego, two casinos offer a good time. **Club Sycuan** (5469 Casino Way, El Cajon, 619/445-6002, www.sycuan.com) sits in the suburb of El Cajon. This casino and resort offers fun for all comers, with a hotel, several restaurants (including a buffet), a golf course, tennis courts, and gaming floors. At Club Sycuan, you'll find thousands of slot machines, plus an array of table games including blackjack, pai gow poker, mini-baccarat, roulette, and craps. You can also enjoy the tension of the Bingo Palace and the smoke-free atmosphere of the Poker Room. Vegas-style stage acts entertain weary gamers and golfers in the evening.

Nope, that's not a Back East boarding school. That big, classically styled building east of La Jolla is actually the **Barona Valley Ranch Resort and Casino** (1932 Wildcat Canyon Rd., San Diego, 619/443-2300, www.barona.com). This upscale resort brings a touch of class to the Las Vegas–style casino. Stay in the large, posh hotel (that's the big building), eat dinner at the Steakhouse or the Buffet and grab lunch at the noodle house, pamper yourself in the day spa or out at the pool, or play around at the Barona Creek Golf Club. Finally, hit the casino for plenty of up-to-date loose slots plus 70 table games, including craps, roulette, cash baccarat, and much more. You can also hang out in the poker room, or play the ponies at the off-track betting parlor.

While no casinos grace the North County coastline, if you're vacationing in Del Mar or Encinitas, gaming possibilities lurk only a few miles east. You'll find part of the ever-popular **Harrah's** (777 Harrah's Rincon Way, Valley Center, 877/777-2457, www.harrahsrincon.com) chain off Highway 76 northeast of Oceanside. The typical Harrah's tower rises high over the tiny town of Valley Center, offering over 600 hotel rooms, nine different eateries (including an oyster bar, a buffet, and a coffee house), and a full-service spa. The gaming rooms offer hundreds of slots, a World Series of Poker room, and plenty of table games, including craps, roulette bingo, and blackjack. To cool off in the heat of summer, rent a cabana or pull up a chaise lounge at the gorgeous two-tiered pool.

Yet another large, blocky, luxurious casino, the **Pala Casino Resort and Spa** (11154 Hwy. 76, Pala, 877/946-7252, www.palacasino.com) dominates the landscape on hot, dry Highway 76 east of Oceanside. The dining options are especially fine here; you can get entertainment with your meal at Mama's Cucina Italia, a casual Asian meal at Noodles, all you can eat at the Terrace Buffet, or elegance at The Oak Room. Entertainment also comes big at the Pala, with two large theaters (one indoor, one outdoor), a lounge, and an event center. In the casino proper, you'll find the largest array of new slot machines in the area, plus more than 80 table games. A high-limit room offers fun for high rollers, and a smoke-free room provides relief for sensitive noses who still want to play.

## SPECTATOR SPORTS

### San Diego Chargers

Are you ready for some football, without snow, sleet, or freezing rain of the back east outdoor stadiums? Then grab tickets to **Qualcomm Stadium** (entrance on Friars Rd., www.sandiego.gov/qualcomm) in the Mission Valley neighborhood. The San Diego Chargers (www.chargers.com) are a good team in the AFC West, and they tend to make the playoffs most years (albeit as a wildcard in 2007–2008). If you're driving in, plan to arrive at the parking lot at least two hours early since the lot often fills up and even closes an hour before kickoff. Also, try to avoid going in or out via Highway 15, which is the most congested route to the stadium. A better way to get there might be the Mission Trolley System (MTS), which has special event bus service to the stadium, as well as regular stops at Qualcomm on the Blue and Green trolley lines. The NTCD system also provides express bus service to all home games.

Once you've made it into the stadium, you'll find ample food, drink, restrooms, souvenirs, ID bracelets for your kids, and first aid and other services throughout. Alcohol sales are limited and end at the close of the third quarter. For a more posh NFL experience, check whether tickets are available at the club level, which has squishier seats and a wait staff.

### San Diego Padres

While you're in San Diego, why not take yourself and your family out to a baseball game? The San Diego Padres (http://sandiego.padres.mlb.com) play throughout the regular season (and hopefully into the World Series) at **Petco Park** (100 Park Blvd., 619/795-5000) in downtown San Diego. Few rain-outs mar the Padres' home season, and in addition to the game, you can view Balboa Park, the cityscape, and San Diego Bay from the lovely and spacious modern stadium. Sit back with a brew or a soda, enjoy the extra leg room, and bask in the perfect spring baseball weather of San Diego.

Petco Park is well situated for fans who prefer to avoid the inevitable parking nightmares and take public transit in to the game. The MTS trolleys and buses have multiple stops within a block or two of the ballpark, and the Coaster rail line offers extra trains on game nights for fans coming in from the North County towns. If you're staying in the Gaslamp Quarter, consider just walking over to the stadium from your lodgings. If you must drive, prepare to pay $8–15 for downtown lot parking and $20 for a slot right by the park.

### Del Mar Racetrack and Fairgrounds

In horseracing season, you'll find significant crowds descending on the tiny town of Del Mar and its coastside neighbors. All these folks are intent on the famous **Del Mar Fairgrounds** (2260 Jimmy Durante Blvd., Del Mar, 858/755-1141, www.sdfair.com), where some of the finest thoroughbreds ever to grace a track have raced to victory. The track was built in the late 1930s, with Bing Crosby supplying both funds and fame to create the glorious equestrian facilities that continue to delight race and horse fans to this day. The various structures at the Fairgrounds are built in the style of various California missions, and careful attention to detail has created possibly the most beautiful permanent indoor-outdoor exhibition facilities in the state.

Races usually run from July through early September. Wagering rules can be found at the track or on the Fairgrounds website, as can information about the off-season telecast racing series. Come out and join in the excitement of live thoroughbred racing in one of the most hospitable climates in the world! Show up on Friday afternoons to enjoy a concert by a big-name band in addition to the races.

If you prefer a different style of equestrian event, come to Del Mar a little bit earlier in the year for the **Del Mar National Horse Show** (www.sdfair.com/horseshow). This event lasts three weeks each spring, with a full week each devoted to Western events, dressage, and hunter/jumper activities. Be sure to book your room and buy tickets in advance, as this is one of the most popular horse shows in the western United States each year.

Any number of other events take place at the Fairgrounds every month of the year. Check the website for a calendar of upcoming events, plus ticket information. Ample pay parking surrounds the Fairgrounds, or if you're taking the train, grab a free shuttle from the Coaster straight to the racetrack.

## Accommodations

### DOWNTOWN

Acres of hotels cluster throughout downtown San Diego. Whether you need a budget hostel or want a high-end luxury resort, you'll find it. Many mid-tier and upscale chains offer bed and board downtown—all you have to do is walk around to find the Sheraton, Hilton, or Holiday Inn. For a more interesting lodging experience, look to the smaller chains and the independents.

#### Under $100

Looking for budget accommodations in the heart of San Diego? For a start, call the **HI-San Diego** (521 Market St., 800/909-4776, www.sandiegohostels.org, $20–30). Located perfectly right in the middle of the Gaslamp Quarter, you can get just about anywhere from this almost-elegant youth hostel. (Bring your HI card for lower rates!) Inside, you'll find private and double rooms, as well as dorm rooms that sleep 4–10 people in single beds. The amenities include all standard hostel fare: coin-op laundry, an open kitchen, common rooms with and without TVs, and a garden area. Plan to bring or buy a lock for the lockers provided in the dorm rooms. The hostel's packed events calendar includes free walking tours of Balboa Park and the downtown area, and regular free trips down to Tijuana. Between the food and nightlife of the Gaslamp and the endless stream of interesting people and activities, the HI-San Diego is the perfect resting place for young people visiting San Diego.

Looking for a Mediterranean-style student hotel? Try the **Hotel Occidental** (410 Elm St., 619/232-1336, www.hoteloccidental-sandiego.com, $80–150). Located only a block and a half from the entrance to Balboa Park, you can visit the zoo and museums, or head downtown to the Gaslamp Quarter. Don't expect tons of in-room luxury here—smaller rooms share baths, and even some of the larger rooms have only a half-bath, with shower facilities down the hall. Decor feels European (in the Ikea sense when it comes to furniture), with lots of clean lines and plain linens and small, ingeniously used spaces. Hotel-wide amenities include free Wi-Fi, complimentary continental breakfast, and private kitchenettes that let you keep some of your own food rather than depending on restaurants for every meal.

## $100-150

With enough rooms for a medium-sized motel, but the feel of a small inn, **La Pensione Hotel** (606 W. Date St., 800/232-4683, www.lapensionehotel.com, $100–110) prides itself on offering the best value in the best location in downtown San Diego. The exterior blends the look of a Mediterranean home with the Spanish Colonial Revival style of Southern California. Inside, each room has one queen-sized bed, unusual photographic wall art, and a clean bathroom. It's not posh or plush, but you'll find comfort. The hotel is located in Little Italy, within easy walking distance of great restaurants and cafés, and only blocks from the Gaslamp Quarter. The staff can help you with taxis and public transit, making it possible to avoid driving.

La Pensione does not have as many off-street parking spots as they do rooms, so parking is limited during the high season. And if you're bringing your kids, be aware that trundle beds and such are not available, and the hotel requests that only two people stay in any one room.

## Over $250

For a fun hotel stay downtown, hit the exclusive **W Hotel San Diego** (421 W. B St., 619/398-3100, www.starwoodhotels.com, $250–300). This swanky, ultra-modern hotel has the perfect location—convenient to the airport, walking distance to the harbor, and a short jaunt to the fabulous restaurants in the Gaslamp Quarter. Upper-level guest rooms offer views of city and the bay. Rooms feature cushy beds with featherbeds and down comforters, and are done in an almost-industrial, urban-chic style that echoes the grander decor of the entrance, lobby, and bars. Despite the hard lines and cool blue-and-silver color scheme, touches of whimsy abound. (Be sure to take a moment to read the labels on your toiletries—it's worth the time.) But best of all, the service here is exceptional, even in this tourist-friendly region. Just call down, and anything you want will be at your doorstep, probably in about 15 minutes. You'll find every amenity you could dream of, from 24-hour room service to first-aid kits to Wi-Fi to condoms—but beware, none of these are complimentary.

For a fun night out without the hassle of a car or a cab, head up to The Beach, the W's bar created with real sand and fruity umbrella drinks to mimic an actual SoCal beach scene.

If you want to stay in *the* classic San Diego hotel and you've got the money to do it, book a room at the **US Grant Hotel** (326 Broadway, 619/232-3121, www.starwoodhotels

.com, $350). Built in 1910, the US Grant has anchored the Gaslamp Quarter for almost 100 years. Inside, you'll be showered with luxury, from the elegant lobby to the in-house spa to the gorgeous guest rooms (which include luxurious showers). Even the standard guest rooms have plush linens, original artwork, and the many amenities that mark the US Grant as worth the cost of admission.

For additional pampering, make an appointment for an in-room or in-spa massage with Spa Velia. You've got all the restaurant options of the Gaslamp within staggering distance, or you can stay in the hotel and dine at the upscale California-style Grant Grill. Whether your interests are surfing or golfing, the concierges can help you with arrangements for activities around the city.



## BALBOA PARK AND HILLCREST

Lodgings right by the park aren't plentiful. For a better selection, check out downtown and Old Town, which are within easy public transit and driving distance to the wonders of Balboa Park and the fun of Hillcrest.

### $100-150

Looking to stay at an inn that evokes the true spirit of San Diego? Try the Spanish-Colonial Revival-style **Balboa Park Inn** (3402 Park Blvd., 619/298-0823, www.balboaparkinn.com, $100–250). This funky boutique hotel offers 26 unique rooms and suites with names like Harlequin and Emma's Diary, each beautiful in its own decorative style. Smaller rooms just offer a simple bed-and-bath setup, while the more numerous suites offer multiple rooms, kitchens, decks, and often more than one bed. Balboa Park Inn is the perfect place for families looking for moderate prices and the attractions of Balboa Park. Situated just north of the park, you can walk from the inn to the San Diego Zoo. The quiet neighborhood isn't much for nightlife, but offers peace for visitors who long for a good night's sleep.

Another small, stylish charmer is the **Hillcrest Inn** (3754 5th Ave., 800/258-2280, www.hillcrestinn.net, $120–150). Situated in the up-and-coming Hillcrest neighborhood within a few minutes' drive of Balboa Park, this small hotel offers entirely acceptable rooms at reasonable prices. While amenities aren't luxe, you will get a TV, refrigerator, microwave, and clean private bathroom, as well as access to the hotel's outdoor spa. Around the Hillcrest area, you'll find the center of San Diego's gay culture, plus easy access to Downtown and the Gaslamp Quarter. If you can snag an unmetered on-street parking spot, take it, since parking at the inn costs extra. Luckily, lots of restaurants, shops, parks, bars, and clubs are within easy walking distance of the inn, so you may only need to park once.

Only a few blocks' walk from the center of the Hillcrest neighborhood, **Kasa Korbett - Hillcrest Bed and Breakfast** (4050 Front St., 800/757-5272, www.kasakorbett.com, $110–130) expresses a gentle residential charm that's hard to find in the bustling downtown. Pick from one of four charming little rooms, each done with a distinct theme and color palate. (The Gulf Coast Room is *pink*—you'll love it or you'll hate it.) Rooms here sleep one or two people; all have private baths and charming amenities. In the classic B&B tradition, no TVs or DVD players can be found in the guest rooms, and the setup is generally better for couples enjoying a romantic vacation than for families on a beach trip. Enjoy the hospitality of your host, Bob, who can provide you with the best recommendations for what to do, where to eat, and what to see in Hillcrest and beyond. Parking off-street is free, and weekly rates are available.

## OLD TOWN

You'll find a massive cluster of national chain motels in Old Town, so this is a great place to land if you need a place to stay on short notice. However, if you want something a little less generic but still reasonably priced, Old Town can hook you up with that too.

### Under $100

For thrift, exterior charm, and location, location, location, you can't beat the **Old Town Inn**

(4444 Pacific Hwy., 800/643-3025, www.oldtown-inn.com, $60–140). Built to resemble a rancho with a low profile and narrow columns, this motel sits across the street from the Old Town Transit Center, so you can catch a bus or trolley and get virtually anywhere in San Diego County from here. The white-painted, red-tile-roofed exterior of the motel gives way to plain motel rooms inside, with muted pastels, dark carpets, and floral bedspreads. If you plan to cook your own meals, go for an efficiency room, which includes a two-burner stove, refrigerator, and microwave. This family-friendly motel allows kids 12 and under to stay free, has a heated pool, and offers a free daily continental breakfast.

### $100-150

For a cheerful modern stay in San Diego that feels almost like home, stay in the **Sommerset Suites Hotel** (606 Washington St., 800/962-9665, www.sommersetsuites.com, $125–225). Light, bright bedrooms offer a touch of class in this 80-unit, all-suite, non-smoking motel, and each room offers a full kitchen. Enjoy free Wi-Fi in your room or down by the pool, where you can take a refreshing dip on a hot day or a hot spa soak on a cool evening. Technically the Sommerset is in the Uptown neighborhood adjacent to Old Town, but it's easy to reach shopping and dining in Old Town, or all the major attractions in San Diego.

The **Kings Inn** (1333 Hotel Circle S., 619/297-2231, www.kingsinnsandiego.com, $140) offers spacious, nonsmoking motel rooms at affordable prices. Guest rooms are done in florals with jewel-colored carpets and light walls, with either one king or two queen beds. Outside, take a dip in the cute apostrophe-shaped pool or accompanying spa. The location is convenient to sightseeing and transportation, and attached are two family restaurants that provide room service to the motel. The Amigo Spot serves authentic Mexican cuisine, and the Waffle Spot has (surprise) waffles, as well as Mexican and American egg breakfast dishes and a kids' menu.

### $150-250

Though Craftsman architecture holds sway in much of Southern California, the Victorians had their say too. To immerse yourself in the Victorian era in San Diego, stay at **A Victorian Heritage Park Bed & Breakfast Inn** (2470 Heritage Park Row, 800/995-2470, www.heritageparkinn.com, $140–350). This B&B has a dozen amazing guest rooms, each with a unique decorative scheme that complements the classic Queen Anne lines of the mansion itself. Expect to be pampered with featherbeds, private baths (many with clawfoot or whirlpool tubs), antique canopy and poster beds, and glorious views out the windows. A traditional afternoon tea is served downstairs each day, complete with finger sandwiches. Surrounding the inn you'll find the Victorian Heritage Park of San Diego, a small cluster of immaculately restored 19th-century homes and gardens set in almost eight acres of space, complete with cobble-stoned streets and views of downtown and the ocean to the west.

The **Padre Trail Inn** (4200 Taylor St., 619/756-7800, www.padretrailinn.com, $165–175) has upscale furniture and brand-name toiletries, so you'll feel just a little bit pampered in your pleasant room here. Spend a few hours lounging by the side of the pool, or dive right into sightseeing in Old Town. The exterior matches the locale—a Spanish Revival hacienda was the inspiration for the Padre Trail Inn.

## POINT LOMA

While your kids will love the proximity to SeaWorld, you'll love the almost European stylings of the classic ocean-side resorts on Point Loma and Shelter Island. You're still within easy driving range of all major San Diego attractions, without the crowds and the downtown feel. If you own your own boat and plan to bring it to San Diego, consider one of the resorts on Shelter Island—most have private marinas that rent slips.

### Under $100

For the cheapest accommodations near the

beach, book a bed or a family room in the **HI-San Diego, Point Loma Hostel** (3790 Udall St., 800/909-4776, www.sandiegohostels.org, $18–22). A short drive or a longish walk from famous Ocean Beach, this charming bright-red hostel sits in the midst of a residential area of Point Loma. The proprietors encourage bicycling exploration of San Diego by providing ample bike racks for secure storage. Or if you prefer, the bus stop is only a block away from the hostel, making it easy to get to the zoo, Old Town, the beaches, or wherever else you want to go. Inside, you'll find four- to eight-bed dorms and private or family rooms include linens, Internet access, and storage lockers. Cook in the common kitchen and eat in the living room or out in the cute courtyard. The owners love to see families, as well as budget-minded singles here at the hostel, and this is a great place to stay for a truly inexpensive family beach vacation.

For folks who want a budget bed with more privacy than a hostel can afford, the **Dolphin Motel** (2912 Garrison St., 619/758-1404, www.dolphin-motel.com, $66–100) offers comfortable rooms at reasonable rates. The white walls match the pristine white bedspreads, daring you to find fault with the cleanliness at this budget motel. Pick a queen-bed room or a slightly larger room that has a twin bed as well. While the rooms aren't huge, you'll get a comfortable bed for the duration of your stay. One building has smoking rooms. Best of all, you're only a short walk from the sea, and the fishing, kayaking, and other water sports of San Diego are easily accessible (some only across the street). Enjoy a pastry and a morning cup of coffee on the house out in the attractive little courtyard. Or get your own and sit out on the balcony, enjoying the calm air of Point Loma.

## $150–250

Consider staying across the bay from downtown San Diego, on Shelter Island at **Humphrey's Half Moon Inn & Suites** (2303 Shelter Island Dr., 800/542-7400, www.halfmooninn.com, $175–575, parking $10). This resort property looks out over the bay towards the city skyline. It has its own private marina and a lush tropical garden (heavy on the palm trees, of course). Your large, homey-styled room might look out into the greenery or over the great blue bay. If you're in the mood for luxury, add an "enhancement," such as champagne and strawberries or an in-room massage, to your room reservation. If you're feeling lazy, spend a day by the pool, enjoying fruity rum drinks from the poolside bar. On the other hand, energetic travelers can take a boat out onto the water, head into town to check out the attractions, or take a bike ride around Shelter Island. Come evening, you can dine at the on-site gourmet restaurant, then dance the night away to live music at the hotel's own club. In the summertime, get tickets to one of the famed outdoor concerts held on the resort property.

Another Shelter Island charmer, **The Bay Club Hotel and Marina** (2131 Shelter Island Dr., 619/224-8888 or 800/672-0800, www.bayclubhotel.com, $139–189) provides bay and harbor views, comfortable rooms, and charming amenities. Guest rooms have tasteful decorative touches in earth tones and soft pink florals—perfect for a restful vacation. Outside your room, you'll find a funky geometric swimming pool with matching spa, a fitness center, and a brown-and-white bar and grill with a 1950s-style tropical resort feel. Be sure to stop at the desk before heading out into town to grab discount passes to various attractions. Bringing your boat to San Diego? Call the Bay Club to make arrangements to rent a slip in the private marina, which is convenient to the bay, the open ocean, and an on-water fuel station.

The exterior of the **Kona Kai Resort** (1551 Shelter Island Dr., 619/221-8000 or 800/566-2524, www.resortkonakai.com, $189) evokes the legendary Hotel del Coronado. But on the property, you'll find a sense of peace and tranquility that feels more like a Hawaiian resort out away from the city. With a fitness center, a pool, and a full-service spa, you won't lack for pampering and amenities as you bask in the Shelter Island sunshine. Inside, your room will fulfill all your oceanside vacation ideals with soft neutral tones on the walls, and cute colorful and green accents creating a tropical paradise. If you plan to take a seagoing adventure, you can moor your personal or rental boat at the private marina (slips up to 200 feet), or you can head over to SeaWorld or downtown for land-lubbing activities. Even if you get seasick, it might be worth a stroll down to the marina to check out the mega-yacht docking area and get a glimpse at how the other 1 percent live.

## CORONADO

While the Del dominates the Coronado scenery and certainly makes for a fun place to stay, the island town also offers an array of other accommodations. You can find a good place to lay your head for a reasonable rate here, or go over the top at the Del or one of the other big beach resorts.

### Under $150

For an inexpensive stay on Coronado Island, visit the **El Rancho Motel** (370 Orange Ave., 619/435-2251, www.elranchocoronado.com). A few blocks from the Del, the beaches, and the downtown area of Coronado, the El Rancho lets you enjoy the high life without the high prices. Each unit of the El Rancho has its own air conditioning, TV, fridge, and microwave, plus a comfortable bed and a pleasant tiled bathroom. You'll feel right at home in the small lodge-like motel with its white exterior and mostly matching interior. Be sure to ask the innkeeper (who lives on-site at the motel) about the best food, shopping, and good beach spots on the island.

### $150-250

If you can't quite afford a stay at the Del this time, the next best thing might be the **Glorietta Bay Inn** (1630 Glorietta Blvd., 619/435-3101, www.gloriettabayinn.com, $185–360). Literally across the street from the Del, the stately white mansion was the dream home of John D. Spreckels, who in the latter half of the 19th century owned the Del and most of the rest of San Diego in the bargain. Today, the lovely structure oozes charm, even as the less-glamorous motel buildings behind it offer spacious budget accommodations. For a premium, you can book a room inside the mansion proper; each of these is uniquely decorated and includes upscale services and amenities. The "Inn Rooms" behind the mansion are spacious, with adequate amenities and cheerful tropical-resort decor. If you're bringing your family for several days of beach time, the Inn Suites offer a full kitchen and a living room as well as one or two bedrooms, making them an ideal base of operations. No matter which building you stay in, a free continental breakfast is served each morning in the mansion's breakfast room. Grab a pastry and your coffee and enjoy exploring the downtown common rooms boasting photos commemorating the history of the house and the Spreckels family. Then jog across the street to gape at the Del or just pass through onto Coronado Beach.

At **Villa Capri By the Sea** (1417 Orange Ave., 800/231-3954, www.villacapribythesea.com, $150) you get all the benefits of staying right at the hot center of Coronado (that is, near the Del), without the costs or the ghosts. Bring your whole family or several friends—the suites sleep up to six people, and include a full kitchen with all pots and pans necessary for cooking great meals. Yet you can still walk across the street to enjoy the restaurants and shops of the Del, and to get out onto Coronado Beach. Inside, the living rooms are dimly lit but comfortable, the kitchens are light and homey, and the bright bedrooms look perfect for a sunny beach vacation. On the hottest days, you'll appreciate your own oasis of air conditioning, cable TV, and Wi-Fi after hours out on the sand playing with on-loan beach toys. Check the website for special Internet rates.

### Over $250

**Hotel del Coronado** (1500 Orange Ave., 800/468-3533, www.hoteldel.com, $500) dominates the landscape of Coronado Island. Even in Southern California, the Del, as it's called by its friends and neighbors, wins a prize for grandiosity. The white-painted, red-roofed mammoth sprawls for acres from the beach to the

the Del from the beach side



road, taking up a couple of blocks all its own. Inside, the Del is at once a historical museum, shopping mall, food court, and, oh yeah, it's a hotel too! Famously haunted, the Del offers almost 700 rooms, plus another 70-plus individual cottages at Beach Village. Your best bet to catch a ghost in action is to book a room in the Victorian Building. For a more modern hotel experience, stay in the Ocean Towers or California Cabanas. Room sizes and decor vary, from smaller Victorian-decorated guest rooms to expansive resort-themed suites. Pick what you (and your budget) like best! If you want a view, be aware that ocean-facing rooms cost extra.

The best thing about staying at the Del is that you almost never have to leave. You can fall out of the hotel onto Coronado Beach, grabbing a spot early on this oft-crowded strip of sand in the summertime. In the winter, the hotel puts up an improbable ice rink out on the "back porch." You can pick from among several restaurant (or room service) for meals, and even shop for a new bikini in the downstairs of the main building.

For a luxury-oriented longer stay on Coronado Island, rent a true condo at the **Coronado Beach Resort** (1415 Ocean Ave., 877/477-7368, www.coronadobeachresort.com, $250–475). Studio, one-bedroom, and two-bedroom units all have full kitchens (most with dishwashers) with plenty of pots and pans to help you cook your own meals as you gaze out over the beach and ocean below you. You'll eat, live, and sleep in subdued tropical-themed decor, with high-class amenities surrounding you. Head up to the roof to enjoy the spa-with-a-view, or over to Loew's to take a dip in one of their three pools or many sports facilities. If you fancy a day at the beach with your family, just call down to the desk to gather up an array of beach chairs and toys, plus the all-important boogie boards. Also nearby you can access all of downtown Coronado, with its restaurants and boutiques.

## MISSION BAY

The perfect location to find a room if you're traveling with your family to SeaWorld, or planning a wild-water vacation off the shore,

Mission Bay offers plenty of inexpensive chain and independent motels. If you're looking for luxury, you can also check in to one of the upscale resorts along the beach.

## Under $150

**Mission Bay Motel** (4221 Mission Blvd., 866/649-5828, www.missionbaymotel.com, $70–150) offers clean, comfortable accommodations at the right price near the beach and Mission Bay Aquatic Park. This cheerful, white-and-blue-painted, low-built motor hotel has small, white-painted and pastel-decorated rooms, and makes a perfect base from which to enjoy the many sights and sun-drenched beaches of San Diego. You can choose from rock-bottom priced singles (which actually sleep two people) up to multi-bed rooms with kitchenettes that can accommodate the whole family. The residential Pacific Beach neighborhood offers affordable local restaurants, a beach a block a way, and car or public transit access to the rest of the San Diego area.

## $150-250

Almost affordable rates seem a surprise at oceanside **The Dana on Mission Bay** (1710 W. Mission Bay Dr., 800/445-3339, www.thedana.com, $180–300). It's so close to SeaWorld that you can walk to the park, and it has its own private marina for serious sea-lovers. Pick from two blocks of rooms—the Marina Cove section offers less expense without views of the ocean—you might look over the garden or the pool. Inside, Marina Cove rooms are fairly small, with brightly colored, tropical-themed decor. The Waters Edge premium rooms have wonderful views out over the Pacific and a more subtle, elegant design scheme. When it's time to get out of the room and enjoy San Diego, take advantage of the many free shuttles to attractions such as the San Diego Zoo and the Gaslamp Quarter. Rent a personal watercraft or a boat directly from The Dana and take a spin on Mission Bay. Or stay on the 10-acre resort property and splash in one of the two large swimming pools.

If your reason for coming to San Diego is to loll about on the beach sipping fruity cocktails, the **Bahia Resort** (998 W. Mission Bay Dr., 800/576-4229, www.bahiahotel.com, $185–310) is the perfect place to drop your suitcase and change into your swimsuit. Set right on the beach in Mission Bay, you can stumble out of your hotel room onto a strip of sun-warmed sugar sand. If you prefer your water a bit more contained, the charming Moroccan decor surrounding the large pool and tremendous (30-person) spa is for you. For the ultimate in splendid relaxation, order from the café and waiters will deliver right to you at poolside. Inside, the understated guest rooms are done in a variety of styles. Enjoy the comfort of the plush beds, the overstuffed furniture, and the homey touches prevalent especially in the larger apartment-like suites. The hotel restaurant, Café Bahia, offers tasty traditional breakfast, lunch, and dinner with just a touch of Middle Eastern flavor. For a treat, eat outdoors!

## Over $250

San Diego seems littered with gorgeous high-end resort hotels, and the Mission Bay area is no exception. One of the nicest of these is the **Catamaran Resort** (3999 Mission Blvd., 800/422-8386, www.catamaranresort.com, $355). Garden rooms and studios, which have one or two beds, stylish decor, and top-tier amenities (plus full kitchens in the studios), can have surprisingly reasonable rates. The premier rooms—bayfront rooms and suites—have grand views of the ocean, some with direct access right down to the Catamaran's own private beach. A great reason to stay at the Catamaran, the private beach runs to a private pier with a water-sports rental facility that can hook you up whether you prefer high-powered, wind-powered, or human-powered watercraft. (Windsurfing is a favored activity on Mission Bay.) For younger guests, the Mad Scientist Kid's Camp and Catamaran Kids Club keep children occupied and happy while their parents enjoy the sea, the spa, or the private comforts of their hotel room. Also on-site you'll find the Atoll Restaurant, which serves three meals a day and a sumptuous champagne brunch on Sunday mornings and early afternoons.

## LA JOLLA

If you want to stay in ritzy La Jolla, be prepared to bust out your credit card. This uptown burg doesn't come cheap. While a few motels offer decent rooms for under $200, you'll find the best locations and rooms well over that price point. If you simply must stay in La Jolla on a budget, a few major chain motels lurk around near downtown.



### $100-150

One of the few pleasant lower-budget La Jolla accommodations is the **Sands of La Jolla** (5417 La Jolla Blvd., 800/643-0530, www.sandsoflajolla.com). It's not located in the center of the action, which helps the price point stay a little bit lower, but you can still use a car to reach the beaches, the La Jolla Cove, and the top attractions in San Diego proper. Inside, you'll find pleasant motel rooms furnished with light woods and sunny yellow wall and window treatments. Deluxe rooms and suites offer full kitchenettes, and all rooms have refrigerators, microwaves, and toaster ovens to help you save money by buying some of your own food from the store rather than a pricey restaurant. This nice little motel also offers family-friendly, multi-bed rooms and suites for great beach vacations.

### $150-250

Perfectly located and reasonably priced (for La Jolla), the **La Jolla Inn** (1110 Prospect St., 888/855-7829, www.lajollainn.com, $159–189) sits comfortably between the main shopping drag and the sloping sidewalk down to the beach. The brick facade with dark blue awnings stands out in an area of wood and adobe-style construction. Inside, you'll think you've found a boutique hotel on the Mediterranean, with small bright rooms that feature natural wood furniture and colorful homemade quilts. Upper rooms also offer the best art ever: a view out over the Pacific. All guests get to take advantage of the free continental breakfast and the afternoon snack (served at 2 P.M.—perfect for a quick break from the beach). Be sure to take advantage of the free underground parking as this area gets crowded in high season.

### Over $250

In La Jolla, upscale accommodations abound. One of the most charming is the **Estancia La Jolla Hotel and Spa** (9700 Torrey Pines Rd., 858/550-1000, www.estancialajolla.com, $350–400). Built on an historic Mexican rancho, the traditional arrangement of buildings and courtyards gleam with restoration and vitality. (When driving in, look for the resort name on a standard cross-street sign.) Palm trees and succulents grace the landscape. Inside, spacious guest rooms in neutral tones are accented with bright oranges, yellows, and greens. Beds offer an extra-comfy night's sleep, made even better by a visit to the spa or a day spent lounging under a cabana by the vast swimming pool, sipping drinks from the poolside bar. The hotel offers many of the amenities of a full-scale resort, including a restaurant, wine bar, and casual sports bar. As you stroll the groomed paths through the endless gardens dotted with native plants, you'll also find a small store, the main lobby, and the main sitting room complete with huge stone fireplace and all the help you need from friendly concierges at the desk.

The candy-colored **La Valencia Hotel** (1132 Prospect St., 858/454-0771, www.lavalencia.com, $275) has it all: ocean views, high-end restaurants, sumptuous guest rooms, and a great downtown location. Guest rooms, suites, and villas are decorated tastefully in earth tones with splashes of bright color. Living plants provide both oxygen and a homey sense of elegance both in the rooms and throughout the resort. Downstairs, take advantage of the state-of-the-art workout room, then cool off in the large sparkling blue pool. You can walk to the cliffside boardwalk or down to the beach from the La Valencia, and enjoy the shopping and restaurants of Prospect Street.

**The Lodge at Torrey Pines** (11480 N.

Torrey Pines Rd., 858/453-4420, www.lodgetorreypines.com, $450) offers luxury, service, amenities, and access to the amazing Torrey Pines Golf Course. You'll be struck by the classic Southern California Craftsman architecture—the exterior of the lodge is a work of art in itself. The Craftsman elegance continues into the rooms, with designer fabrics, tasteful appointments, gorgeous marble bathrooms, and views of the golf course and ocean. If you plan to play golf, check the golf packages and arrange your tee time through the hotel. Non-golfers have a number of great recreation options too. Book an appointment at the full-service spa, rent one of the charming cabanas down at the beach, or take a guided hike at the state reserve. If traveling with family, their are numerous kids' activities and amenities available at the resort.

## NORTH COUNTY

If your one major purpose in coming to the San Diego area is to lounge on a white-sand beach, consider booking a stay north of the city proper. Some of the best beaches cluster in the North County area. Accordingly, you'll find everything from modest motels to chi-chi resorts available in the area.

### Under $150

For a good, modest motel that's clean and reasonably close to the beach and everything else, stay at the **Moonlight Beach Motel** (233 Second St., Encinitas, 800/323-1259, www.moonlightbeachmotel.com). Cheerful budget motel rooms greet guests with floral bedspreads and light-painted walls. Most rooms have a kitchenette, complete with refrigerator and microwave, making it easy to store and chill beach drinks and snacks in your room. Rooms are clean enough to feel comfortable sleeping in, but not so fancy that you'll be horrified if a little bit of sand makes it onto the carpet. The motel sits near both U.S. 101 and I-5, making it a perfect base from which to get anywhere in the San Diego area. If you prefer to stay close by, you're only a few blocks from Moonlight Beach. Go surfing, play a game of volleyball, or just relax into the sand for a day. (From the motel on a busy summer weekend day, walk to the beach if you can to avoid the parking nightmare down closer to the sand.)

Built in the charming Spanish Colonial Revival style, **Les Artistes** (944 Camino Del Mar, Del Mar, 858/755-4646, www.lesartistesinn.com, $85–200) offers something different from the standard chain motel experience. Each room is named for and decorated in the style of a particular artist or style, from the French countryside of Monet to the peace of Zen. Despite its unique and fun style, this is a budget motel; the rooms are small and you won't be able to trip over your doorsill and fall into the ocean. But the beach and downtown Del Mar with its restaurants and shops are only a few blocks away. And you can bring your family (several rooms have multiple beds), including your beloved pet, to Les Artistes and receive a warm welcome. Don't bring your cigarettes, however, as Les Artistes is entirely non-smoking.

### $150-250

If you want a beach house of your own rather than a motel room that's part of a huge block, book a daily or weekly bungalow or suite at the **Wave Crest Resort** (1400 Ocean St., Del Mar, 858/755-0100, www.wavecrestresort.com, $200–500). Here you'll get a studio, one-bedroom, or two-bedroom private unit. These are condo-style accommodations, so you'll get nice furnishings but no daily maid service. Even if you go for a more economical garden-facing unit, you'll enjoy the view of the meticulously landscaping that makes the whole complex lovely. For a modest extra fee, your unit will face the near-enough-to-touch Pacific Ocean. Take a quick walk to Seagrove Park and down to the beach beyond. Perhaps the only downside, which can also be an upside, is its proximity to the rail line and the highways. They provide both easy transportation and noise.

### Over $250

For a classic luxury resort experience, complete with a golf course, multiple swimming pools, ocean views, and almost every service you can dream up, stay at the **Four Seasons Aviara** (7100 Four Seasons Point, Aviara, 760/603-6800, www.fourseasons.com, $395). You'll find everything in your guest room exactly as you'd expect from a Four Seasons hotel, from the L'Occitane toiletries to the specially made comfy beds to the tasteful tropical decor. Downstairs, the lobby and common areas shine with marble floors and columns. You can indulge at the various independently owned shops, including a wonderful little jewelry store that specializes in unique colored gems, many of which are mined in San Diego County. The concierge and desk staff are as friendly and helpful as possible at all times—you can get whatever you want whenever you want, pretty much.

On the Four Seasons property you can play 18 holes of golf, a set of tennis, splash with the kids in the family swimming pool, or get serious in the adults-only lap pool. Round out your day with a treatment from the hotel spa. In the evening, dine at one of the three on-site restaurants. If you've come with your family, you can get the kids involved in a number of activities tailored for the younger set, and escape and enjoy some of the more adult aspects of the resort.

For another tip-top resort experience, book a room at the newly reopened **L'Auberge Del Mar** (1540 Camino Del Mar, Del Mar, 800/245-9757, www.laubergedelmar.com, $425). Enjoy the elegant guest rooms, posh spa, upscale dining, and superior amenities, all with glorious views overlooking the ocean. For guaranteed access to the tennis courts, book a court and a time in advance.



# Food

San Diego doesn't have the celebrated culinary culture of San Francisco or the Wine Country, but you can still get a good meal in this town. Due to San Diego's proximity to the border and the ocean, you'll easily find delicious Mexican food and fresh seafood. In places like the Gaslamp Quarter, Hillcrest, and La Jolla, you can find great food just by wandering down the main drag and reading menus as you go.

## DOWNTOWN

Downtown San Diego offers an astonishing array of dining choices, from comfortable American fare to understandably fabulous Mexican food and surprisingly diverse Italian option, on to upscale California cuisine.

### California

A local legend, the **Grant Grill** (326 Broadway, 619/744-2077, www.grantgrill.com, breakfast, lunch, and dinner, $22–38) has been serving upscale cuisine since 1951. The wonderful ambiance of the posh dining room makes even the most casual of diners feel wealthy and "part of the crowd." The Grant Grill, part of the US Grant hotel, serves breakfast, lunch, and dinner every day, and offers a full-service lounge with live music and a lobby where you can enjoy top-end aperitifs and digestifs. At lunch and dinner, you'll find the fanciest of California-style cuisine on the menu. For dinner, choose from the á la carte menu, or enjoy a full five-course tasting menu that's something of a bargain. For an extra fee, you can add wine pairings to each course of the tasting menu. The wine list is short compared to many high-end restaurants, which makes it happily manageable, and it focuses almost exclusively on California wines. On Sundays, come in late in the morning or early in the afternoon to enjoy a wonderful brunch.

If you're female, coming into the Grant Grill makes you a part of history. In the 1950s and '60s, the Grill was an exclusive and exclusionary men's club. In 1969, a group of local businesswomen staged a sit-in, and the Grant Grill was forced to move into the modern era.

## DINNER CRUISES

An unforgettable way to dine in this coastside community is to take a dinner cruise in the calm waters of San Diego Bay. While you shouldn't expect the food on these cruises to be the best for the price, the atmosphere and scenery make up for any culinary deficiencies. Be forewarned that the drinks tend to be a bit weak as well; if you love a strong cocktail, plan to hit one of the many downtown bars before or after your cruise.

The juggernaut of the dinner and event cruise industry in California, **Hornblower** (1066 N. Harbor Dr., 619/686-8715, boarding 6:30 P.M., $65) offers a popular three-hour dinner cruise every night. Pick up a glass of complimentary champagne as you walk down the gangplank onto the yacht. Enjoy your three-course dinner (or more, if you pay extra) as the sun drops below the horizon. Take a constitutional stroll on the deck and return for dessert, or make for the entertainment deck and dance the evening away as the yacht slowly makes its way around the bay. If you prefer a daytime cruise, book passage for a Sunday champagne brunch.

**San Diego Harbor Excursion** (1050 N. Harbor Dr., 619/234-4111, www.sdhe.com, $60 for no-host bar and dinner, $80 for hosted bar and dinner) also offers nightly dinner cruises and Sunday champagne brunches out on the bay. With an array of options, including vegetarian entrées and a children's dinner package at a reduced rate, San Diego Harbor Excursion offers a fun cruise and a tasty meal. Be sure to reserve your place at the table a few days in advance for Friday and Saturday nights and for Sunday brunches in summertime.

### Italian

Looking for some comfortable, warm Italian food without high prices or pretenses? Go where the locals go: **Filippi's Pizza Grotto** (1747 India St., 619/232-5094, www.realcheesepizza.com, Mon.–Thurs. 11 A.M.–10:30 P.M., Fri.–Sat. 11 A.M.–11:30 P.M., Sun. 11 A.M.–10 P.M., $10–15). Walk through the tempting Italian market at the front into the dimly lit restaurant at the rear of the building. Enjoy the classic atmosphere, complete with red-and-white-check tablecloths. Order a pizza, some lasagna, or a giant meatball sandwich. Pastas come with classic and uncomplicated marinara and the pizza might be the best in all of San Diego. Best of all, Filippi's serves late into the evening—until almost midnight on weekends. You'll definitely have to jostle with the local crowd for a seat on Friday and Saturday nights.

You can find Filippi's locations in other parts of San Diego County, but the original is this Little Italy location.

### Mexican

For some heavily hyped California-ized Mexican food in the Gaslamp, you can't beat **Fred's Mexican Café** (527 Fifth Ave., San Diego Ave., 619/232-8226, www.fredsmexicancafe.com). Blending San Diego seafood, the California fresh-ingredient craze, and tradition Mexican dishes, Fred's has earned top honors from local restaurant polls. The extensive menu offers up creative takes on burritos, tacos, enchiladas, and much more. Fred's prides itself on its margaritas as well—amazing concoctions that take the margarita concept to the next level, served in faux martini glasses or thick-stemmed bowls. The casual atmosphere features trestle tables and cluttered walls, appealing to a young crowd preparing for a night out on the town.

### Steak

Looking for a rich slab of beef after a long day playing outside? Head for the **Greystone Steakhouse** (658 Fifth Ave., 619/232-0225, www.greystonesteakhouse.com, dinner only $30–48) in the heart of the Gaslamp. This upscale eatery makes a great start to a night out on the town with your sweetie. The white tablecloths light up the dim interior, where the dining area surrounds a staircase leading down into the belly of the restaurant. Or if you prefer, get a table on the small patio out front so you can people-watch as the Gaslamp heats up with the evening crowd. The menu includes all your favorite steakhouse standards—great cuts of beef, lobster and prawns, and an array of yummy sides. You'll also find some interesting California-style entrées and appetizers. Portions are big, so consider splitting an entrée with your dinner partner so you can both enjoy an appetizer and some dessert. The wine list focuses on California wines and includes a good selection of local vintages, and the full bar offers pre-dinner cosmos and martinis. The service can be a bit slow during the dinner hours, but it's friendly and helpful.

## BALBOA PARK AND HILLCREST

The fun and funky Hillcrest neighborhood offers an array of dining options, from ethnic to upscale to down-home. To pick your own favorite, wander up and down India Street and read the menus in the windows. Most every restaurant on India wins local approval.

### American

If you're looking for dinner and nightlife all in one spot, come out to the **Corvette Diner** (3946 Fifth Ave., 619/542-1476, www.cohnrestaurants.com, Sun.–Thurs. 11 A.M.–10 P.M., Fri.–Sat. 11 A.M.–11 P.M., $8–14). This crazy, crowded diner is all about the atmosphere, from the outlandish 1950s decor to the rock-and-roll to the bouffant-topped waitresses. The food runs to standard American diner fare, though you'll find any number of Corvette original dishes. And don't skip the soda fountain—the fountain and dessert menu includes classics and originals galore.

If you're looking for a quiet meal, the Corvette is *not* your place. A DJ spins nightly, and on weekdays you can find child-oriented entertainers performing for an appreciative audience. Kids love the wild, loud fun of the family-friendly Corvette.

If it *is* a quiet American dinner you want, try the **Crest Café** (425 Robinson Ave., 619/295-2510, www.crestcafe.net, daily 7 A.M.–midnight, $8–16). This colorful, cheerful diner welcomes a more sedate crowd with a bright dining room and three wonderful meals per day. In amongst the traditional diner fare, you'll find a few upscale dishes, such as lemon-ricotta pancakes and orange marmalade–stuffed French toast. You'll also see a wide array of Mexican-inspired entrées, alongside diner dishes that have been made over with an eye towards modern health consciousness. Open till midnight, the Crest is the perfect place to stop and grab a late-night snack after (or during) a night out in Hillcrest.

If you're looking for a hearty breakfast or a unique American dinner, the local Hillcrest favorite hangout is **Hash House A Go Go** (3628 5th Ave., 619/298-4646, www.hashhouseagogo.com, Mon.–Fri. 7:30 A.M.–2 P.M. and 5:30–9 P.M., Sat.–Sun. 7:30 A.M.–2:30 P.M. and 5:30–10 P.M.). The Hash House puts its own spin on casual American food, including an array of fresh local ingredients that take the dishes up a notch. You'll dine in a modern atmosphere with an industrial-urban decorative scheme, complete with brushed-metal tabletops. For breakfast, the obvious choice is of course hash, though you've got dozens of other options as well. Lunch and dinner feature especially wonderful salads, plus plenty of great entrées in a variety of styles. Look for fresh veggies and fruit, lean meats, and preparations that start to transcend American diner food and lean into the world of haute California cuisine.

If you're in Balboa Park, chances are you're visiting the museums or the zoo. At the zoo, grab a bite at **Albert's Restaurant** (Gorilla Tropics at the San Diego Zoo, 619/685-3200). This sit-down eatery serves lunch year-round and dinner during the summer nights when the zoo stays open late. Sit indoors to escape the heat, or out on the patio to enjoy the view of the gardens surrounding the animal enclosures. Relax with a drink at the bar, order a simple salad or sandwich, or enjoy a hearty steak dinner.

### Cafés

If you need a quick bite before a show at one of the Old Globe Theaters, the closest eats can be had at **Lady Carolyn's Pub** (619/231-1941, ext. 2751, Tues.–Fri. from 7 P.M., Sat.–Sun. from

1 P.M.). This walk-up snack bar offers soups in sourdough bowls, salads, wine, and Irish coffees. Open every day a show goes up (until the theater shuts its doors), Lady Carolyn's can get crowded on weekends. Dine early if you can.

### Coffee and Tea

Round out your Balboa Park experience with a cup of tea and a meal at the **Tea Pavilion** (619/231-0048, daily 10 A.M.–5 P.M., later in the summer). As advertised, the specialty of the house is tea. You'll find a great cuppa, whether you favor herbal, green, or black teas. You can also get a bowl of noodles, some sushi, or a quick snack. To take some of the Japanese experience home with you, wander into the market section to peruse the unusual imported food and drink.

If all that tromping around through the park has tired you out, perk up with a drink from **Daniel's Coffee Cart** (House of Hospitality Courtyard, Tues.–Sun. 8 A.M.–5:30 P.M., Mon. 8 A.M.–4:30 P.M.). You'll find all your favorite espresso drinks, plain ol' coffee, tea, and pastries.

A favorite Hillcrest coffee shop is **Gelato Vero Caffe** (3753 India St., 619/295-9269, Mon.–Thurs. 6 A.M.–midnight, Fri. 6 A.M.–1 A.M., Sat. 7 A.M.–1 A.M., Sun. 7 A.M.–midnight, $10), which serves the workday-morning caffeine-jonesing crowd *and* the late-night dessert and coffee hounds. The gelato is all made in-house, and the owners and fans assert that you won't find any better this side of Italy. The small café has little seating in the main room; if you want to sit down and enjoy your coffee or gelato and there doesn't seem to be room, hit the stairway off to the side out the door of the café to find the upper deck and inside cottage seating.

## OLD TOWN

Old Town is more about the history, shopping, and sights than it is about dining. Most locals head downtown for a meal. But if you really want to eat here, Mexican food is your best bet.

In Old Town's little corner of Mexico, Bazaar del Mundo, you can find some great South-of-the-Border eats in a variety of styles and price ranges. Join the party at **Casa Guadalajara** (4105 Taylor St., 619/295-5111, http://bazaardelmundo.com/guad2006.shtml, Mon.–Thurs. 11 A.M.–10 P.M., Fri. 11 A.M.–11 P.M., Sat. 7 A.M.–11 P.M., Sun. 7 A.M.–10 P.M., happy hour Mon.–Fri. 4–7 P.M.). From the moment you see the low, whitewashed, adobe-style building with the red-tiled roof, you'll start to feel the Mexican atmosphere. Inside, enjoy the music of strolling mariachis as you sip a margarita and dine on excellent regional Mexican cuisine. The seafood-heavy menu features Mexican classics as well as the chef's unique creations. Be sure to check out the daily specials!

## POINT LOMA

Out on Point Loma, the food is all about the fish—not a surprise, considering that this spit of land sits out in the water, surrounded on three sides by bay and ocean. Whatever style you like your fish cooked (or uncooked) in, Point Loma can serve it to you.

### California

The **Embers Grill** (3924 W. Point Loma Blvd., 619/222-6877, Sun.–Tues. and Thurs. 11:30 A.M.–9 P.M., Fri.–Sat. 11:30 A.M.–10 P.M., $25–50) offers casual dining to the masses with plenty of patio room for outdoor dining. Expect sometimes-huge portions of fairly common American dishes with a California twist. If you're looking for a lighter meal, order a sandwich, salad, or personal-sized pizza. Embers is also a great place for a full-sized tasty lunch.

### Japanese

In the world of high-end seafood, the Japanese are famed for creating some of the best dishes on Earth. For some amazing sushi, go to **Umi Sushi** (2806 Shelter Island Blvd., 619/226-1135, www.umisushisandiego.com, Mon.–Sat. 11:30 A.M.–2:30 P.M., 5–10 P.M., $4–11). If you love your rolls, choose from three-dozen on the menu, plus plenty of nigiri, sashimi, specialty platters, and "sushi boats." For folks who love Japanese food but quail at the thought of raw fish, Umi offers hot entrées, noodle dishes, salads, and more. Sit up at the sushi bar to see your food put together, or pick a table out in the classically Japanese-styled dining room.

## Mediterranean

Weary of fish and looking for a respite from the endless seafood of Point Loma? Grab a bite of something completely different at the **Fairouz Cafe and Gallery** (3166 Midway Dr., 619/225-0308, www.alnashashibi.com, $14–19). The bright, cheerful dining room features the original artwork of Al Nashashibi, a painter with roots in Jerusalem. (Yes, you can purchase works you see while dining; inquire with your server.) As for the food, you'll find meat and vegetarian entrées in the Middle Eastern tradition, with lots of lamb and chicken, plus several Greek specialties, such as stuffed grape leaves. At lunchtime, look to the appetizers and salads for lighter fare.



## Steak and Seafood

For the best of the land out by the sea, visit **Island Prime** (880 Harbor Island Dr., 619/295-6801, www.cohnrestaurants.com, lunch from 11:30 A.M., dinner 5–10 P.M., $30–50). This huge house of steak and fish seats more than 600 on a top evening. Ask in advance for a window seat or a table out on the deck overlooking the harbor and the San Diego skyline. On the deck, you might find yourself by one of the fires, feeling as though you were dining at your own private beach house (well, except for the crowd, of course). The simple decor makes use of the wooden architectural features of the building. If you're boating on the San Diego waters, dock-and-dine at the neighboring Sunroad Marina. The menu boasts shellfish, finned fish, and plenty of hearty meats in a classic steakhouse-meets-California style. Start (or finish) your meal with a martini or another fabulous cocktail.

For a lighter meal, head for the C-Level cocktail lounge. In addition to the high-octane libations, the lounge serves a light dinner menu—that really isn't all that light. Whichever you choose, you'll find a pleasant trend towards local and organic ingredients in Prime's dishes.

One of the best things about dining in San Diego is the opportunity to enjoy a fabulous meal while looking out over the harbor or the ocean. That's just what you'll get at **Humphreys by the Bay** (2241 Shelter Island Blvd., 619/224-3577, www.humphreysbythebay.com, daily 7 A.M.–2 P.M., Sun.–Thurs. 5:30–9 P.M., Fri.–Sat. 5:30–11 P.M., $22–50). The white tablecloths on the candlelit tables look right out over the Humphreys Marina and off towards the San Diego city skyline. This hotel-based restaurant serves three meals a day, plus brunch on Sundays. On the dinner menu, seafood reigns, though various land-based entrées get their due as well. Or combine the two for an extravagant meal that makes for the best of everything. At lunchtime, upscale sandwiches and salads make the most of lighter midday standards. Whichever you choose, lunch or dinner, don't miss the awesome seafood soups! The breakfast menu includes all the egg-based standards, fresh fruits and pastries, and a few scrumptious surprises. Sunday brunches are buffet-style, with plenty of made and carved-to-order specialties.

If what you really want is the freshest slab of fish to be found on Point Loma, eat at the aptly named **Point Loma Seafoods** (2805 Emerson St., 619/223-1109, Mon.–Sat. 9 A.M.–6:30 P.M., Sun. 11 A.M.–6:30 P.M., $5–14). Much of the fish sold here, either as a hot meal to eat right there or chilled in paper ready to cook, comes straight off the fishing boats in the harbor. Shellfish, including local spiny lobster, is fresh, top quality, and sold only in season—making Point Loma Seafood the perfect place for a seafood lunch. Hot food and sandwiches come with slaw and fries—perfect accompaniments for fish. The cold foods include seafood salads plus a small array of sushi and sashimi. The atmosphere is the antithesis of upscale, which make it perfect for many visitors looking for reasonable prices and truly great fish.

# CORONADO

To find your own food in Coronado, stroll down Orange Avenue. While you'll definitely find your fellow tourists there, you'll also find a large number of restaurants in a bunch of different styles and ethnicities that are worth trying out.

## American

If you're a night owl and find yourself looking for nourishment after hours, you can find it at the **Night & Day Café** (847 Orange Ave., 619/522-2912, open 24 hours daily, $10). This small hole-in-the-wall diner will make you feel right at home. You'll find all your old standard American favorite foods in an atmosphere that's unique to Coronado.

## French

With the opulence of the Del overseeing the town, a night out for French cuisine seems appropriate here. You'll do well at **Chez Loma French Bistro** (1132 Loma Ave., 619/435-0661, www.chezloma.com, Tues.–Sun. 5 P.M.–close, $23–36). You can walk to this charming restaurant that's located in the historic Carez Hizar House—a white-frame house that leads into warm, red dining rooms. The cuisine tends toward the classic French brasserie style, with the occasional hint of California color in some of the dishes. The wine list is worth a visit all on its own; it's not immense, but it shows off the best of California and France, including a large selection of flights (samples of three different wines all in one type). The food and the ambiance have caught the attention of local foodies, and Chez Loma has been highly reviewed and presented with a number of regional restaurant awards.

## Italian

Looking for a good plate of spaghetti on the island? Go to **Island Pasta** (1202 Orange Ave., 619/435-4545, www.islandpastacoronado.com, Sun.–Thurs. 11 A.M.–9 P.M., Fri.–Sat. 11 A.M.–9:30 P.M.). Island Pasta brings out the best in the Italian staples, serving up thin-crust pizzas and handmade pastas, as well as seafood and sandwiches.

## Steak and Seafood

For good food in a fanciful atmosphere, get a table at **Peohe's** (1201 First St., 619/437-4474, www.peohes.com, lunch daily 11:30 A.M.–2:30 P.M., dinner Mon.–Sat. 5:30 P.M.–close, Sun. 4:30 P.M.–close, $22–80). It offers a cute tropical atmosphere, great views of San Diego Bay, and tasty offerings from land and sea. The menu is friendly to tourists new to the fresh California fish concept, while still offering pros at the game some interesting new preparations. If you prefer to keep your fish off the grill, order from the sushi bar. To go with your meal, enjoy a festive cocktail. The Volcano is the house special, and it serves two with near-lethal potency. Finally, Peohe's prides itself on its huge and tasty homemade desserts. If you possibly can, round out your meal with a Hot Chocolate Lava cake.

## Thai

If your preference is hot and casual, eat at **Swaddee Thai Restaurant** (1001 C St., 619/435-8110, daily 11 A.M.–3 P.M., 5–10 P.M.). Off the main tourist drag, Swadee's tasty Thai cuisine appeals to locals, and is something of a hidden gem.



# MISSION BAY

Locals and visitors alike flock to Mission Bay for a day's entertainment. As the sun sets, the need for food kicks in. Along Mission Bay, you'll find an array of ethnic eats to please any palate.

## Italian

**Luigi's Italian** (3210 Mission Blvd., 858/488-2818, Sun.–Thurs. 11:30 A.M.–10 P.M., Fri.–Sat. 11:30 A.M.–11:30 P.M., $11–30) is the place to go for Italian food at Mission Bay. Sit outside for the best people-watching, or inside for a loud, bright, tasty meal. The house red wine accompanies the inexpensive cuisine perfectly—including the pizza. Speaking of Luigi's pizza, you'll want to order a single slice unless you're part of a large crowd. A whole Luigi's pie barely fits on a four-top. Luigi's can get loud and rowdy, especially on game day, as many locals bring their posse for pizza and the game on the big-screen.

## Mexican

For great, cheap Mexican food right on the main drag, you can't beat **Valentine's Mexican**

**Food** (3852 Mission Blvd., 858/539-0939, daily 10 A.M.–10 P.M., $4–7). You can order tacos to go or enjoy an enchilada plate inside the restaurant, taking advantage of the free serve-yourself chips and salsa. There's nothing fancy about Valentine's food, but it's high quality and plentiful, with the proper toppings and sides, such as guacamole, sour cream, and house-made salsa. Lunching here during a day on the beach or the water will fill you up and get you back out for a long afternoon of playing in the sunshine.



### Seafood

At the boastfully named **World Famous** (711 Pacific Beach Dr., 858/272-3100, daily 7 A.M.–11 P.M., $11–30), enjoy breakfast, lunch, or dinner with a view. Fish, purchased fresh daily, is the specialty of the house here, and preparations range from classic American to a variety of ethnic stylings that might be called "fusion" if this were San Francisco. Grab a drink at the bar and take a seat either indoors in the Vegas-inspired dining room or outdoors on the seaside patio. The wine list features some of the best-known California vintners.

### Thai

Not enough heat out on the beach? Have a meal at **Jack's Thai Spices** (1768 Garnet Dr., 858/483-9830, www.jackthaispices.com, daily 11 A.M.–10 P.M., $13–20). Bright yellow walls and palm trees make this a welcoming and exotic place to dine. With Thai-style spare ribs, curries, peanut sauce dishes, noodles, rice, and a wide array of vegetarian options, Jack's has something for everyone. Jack himself might be on-site. (Look for an older Thai gentleman with a noticeably big grin.) He acts as both owner and chef, and created many of the specialty dishes himself. If you know in advance that you plan to eat at Jack's, check the website for a chance to win a free lunch in a weekly drawing. Also, check out the "Speak Thai" section to learn a few restaurant-friendly phrases.

## LA JOLLA

For a good selection of food in La Jolla, stroll or drive down Prospect Street. You'll find an array of high-class California cuisine, plus coffee shops and more casual dining options.

### California

**Georges at the Cove** (1250 Prospect St., 858/454-4244, www.georgesatthecove.com) is a La Jolla institution. The complex actually includes three separate restaurants. The favorite, **Ocean Terrace** (lunch and dinner, $15–20) offers casual outdoor seating on the roof of the building year-round, with unpretentious and delicious cuisine. Enjoy seafood as you look out over La Jolla Cove, or choose a simple salad or sandwich for a lighter meal. Downstairs, you'll find the ultra-urban **Georges California Modern** (dinner, $35–40). The industrial design of the dining room precedes the chic, if sometimes a bit overwrought, dishes you'll find on the menu here. Windows offer views of the Cove, while cushioned banquetess make diners along the wall comfortable as they settle in for a multi-course dinner. Finally, if you're really looking for a cocktail out on the balcony, **Georges Bar** (lunch and dinner, $15–20) has just what you're looking for. You can order from the Ocean Terrace menu, or just sip your drinks as you enjoy the warm evening air.

### Seafood

Looking for good seafood and a fabulous view to go with it? Have a meal at **Brockton Villa** (1235 Coast Blvd., 858/454-7393, http://brocktonvilla.com, Mon. 8 A.M.–3 P.M., Tues.–Sun. 8 A.M.–9 P.M., $30), which is open for breakfast, lunch, and dinner. Here you can enjoy classic American dishes with a California twist, plus plenty of fish, of course. The casual atmosphere of this beach bungalow blends perfectly with the sugar sand beaches of the San Diego area. Wooden tables, funky mismatched chairs, and the bright white paint inside evoke a sense of the casual resort atmosphere of historic La Jolla. For fun, read the menu for information on the quirky history of the bungalow, which dates from the late 1800s.

## NORTH COUNTY

Each town ranging up the Pacific Coast Highway to Del Mar and Carlsbad has a main drag filled with restaurants. You'll find ethnic enclaves, homey diners, and more.

### California

Looking for elegant yet casual beach town dining? Try the famed **Arterra** (11966 El Camino Real, Del Mar, 858/369-6032, www.arterrarestaurant.com, Mon.–Fri. 6:30–10:30 A.M., 11:30 A.M.–2 P.M., 4–9:30 P.M., Sat. 7–11:30 A.M., 4–9:30 P.M., Sun. 7–11:30 A.M., $35). Improbably located inside the San Diego Marriott Del Mar, Arterra offers anything but standard chain hotel fare. Start with a drink and perhaps a seafood appetizer in the modern, comfortable outdoor lounge. Once you're seated for dinner inside the plush, red-splashed dining room, you'll find great service and top cuisine created from the freshest local and organic ingredients around. The tasting menus (with or without wine pairing) are a popular option, letting you sample the greatest variety of dishes. Get adventurous and try something new, since there's plenty of cutting-edge cuisine on the menu. And don't forget the wine; the list includes many boutique California charmers that pair wonderfully with the cuisine. If your preference is for uncooked fish, go for something from the surprisingly good sushi bar.

### Italian

On the almost Mediterranean-feeling north coast of San Diego County, sunny Italian food somehow seems appropriate. Some of the best just off the beach is served in Encinitas at **Via Italia Trattoria** (569 S. Pacific Coast Hwy., Encinitas, 760/479-9757, Mon.–Thurs. and Sun. noon–9 P.M., Fri.–Sat. noon–10:30 P.M., $10–25). This Italian-owned and -operated casual restaurant feels like a real trattoria on the coast of Italy. You can get a budget-friendly yet fabulously delicious thin-crust pizza, a dish of steaming pasta with your choice of traditional sauce, or an upscale seafood entrée. The food is fresh, cooked just right, and delectable. Whatever you order from the large menu, you'll enjoy eating it in the casual dining room with classic red-and-white-checked tablecloths. Or if you just want a quick drink and an appetizer, take a seat at the bar.

For haute cuisine with an Italian flair, make the drive out to the Four Seasons Aviara and have dinner at **Vivace** (7100 Four Seasons Pt., Carlsbad, 760/603-3773, Sun.–Thurs. 6–9:30 P.M., Fri.–Sat. 6–10 P.M., $35–50). A perfect restaurant for a romantic night out, Vivace offers California-Italian cuisine in several courses, with a menu that changes nightly and seasonally to take advantage of the freshest local ingredients. Attentive, knowledgeable servers can help you with both the menu and the wine list, which provides great menu-matching selections from California, Italy, and other wine regions of Europe. As you sip your wine, you can admire the elegant tropical-themed decor throughout the several interconnected dining spaces. (Be sure to look down; the floor is gorgeous!) Be sure to plan at least an hour and a half so that you can enjoy the whole dining experience, right through dessert and coffee.



# Information and Services

## INFORMATION

### Tourist Information

The San Diego Convention and Visitor's Bureau operates two visitors centers, each of which can help you with everything from flight information to restaurant coupons to hotel reservations. Downtown, head for the **International Visitor Information Center** (1040⅓ W. Broadway at Harbor Dr., 619/236-1212, Oct.–May daily 9 A.M.–4 P.M., June–Sept. daily 9 A.M.–5 P.M.). In La Jolla, make use of the **La Jolla Visitor Center** (7966 Herschel Ave., 619/236-1212, daily 11 A.M.–4 P.M.). To get a feel for the town before you arrive, check out the SDCVB website at www.sandiego.org. Friendly folks can answer emails and phone calls about most anything pertaining to San Diego County.

## Media and Communications

As a well-traveled tourism destination, San Diego has a wide range of publications you can pick up to help you plan the details of your visit. The daily newspaper is the ***San Diego Union-Tribune*** (www.signonsandiego.com).

Some stores and hotels carry ***San Diego Magazine,*** a glossy monthly publication focused on the culture and lifestyle of the region. While this isn't a tourist-centered magazine, you can still find good information about what's hot *right now,* especially in the dining and shopping scenes.

It's pretty easy to get online in San Diego. Most hotels have either wireless or cabled high-speed Internet access in rooms, though it isn't always free. Business-oriented accommodations also often maintain several public-access computers for guests. You can also find Wi-Fi in many coffee houses, both chain and independent, plus public libraries and some bookshops. As of this writing, San Diego does not have free municipal wireless service.

# SERVICES

## Banks and Post Offices

Banking in San Diego is easy—like most big cities, ATM machines abound not only at bank branches, but in restaurants, bars, and mini-marts as well. You'll find branches of most of the major American banks here, including Wells Fargo, Bank of America, Washington Mutual, and many more.

You'll find plenty of U.S. Post Office branches scattered throughout San Diego. If you need to ship your shopping home, you'll find a **post office** at 51 Horton Plaza, convenient to the mall and much of downtown. South of Balboa Park, the post office sits at 815 E Street. In La Jolla, there's a branch only a few blocks from Prospect downtown at 720 Silver Street. Each town in the North County has its own post office, of course. In Encinitas, it's at 1130 Second Street.

## Medical Services

With UC San Diego in town, the number of major medical centers in and around San Diego is higher than the average. If you must get sick on vacation, San Diego isn't the worst place to do it. In town, the **UCSD Medical Center - Hillcrest** (200 West Arbor Dr., 619/543-6222) offers emergency and clinic services, as does **Scripps Mercy Hospital** (4077 Fifth Ave., 619/294-8111). The **Kaiser Permanente Medical Center** (4647 Zion Ave., 619/528-5000) includes a full-service, 24-hour emergency room. La Jolla also has a heavy load of hospitals, with **Scripps Green Hospital** (10666 N. Torrey Pines Rd., 858/554-9100) and **Scripps Memorial Hospital** (9888 Genesee Ave., 858/626-4123).

In the North County area, the only trauma center is within the **Palomar Medical Center** (555 East Valley Parkway, 760/739-3000) in Escondido. You can get regular hospital services at the **Scripps Memorial Hospital** (354 Santa Fe Dr., 760/633-6501) in Encinitas.

Most of the beaches in San Diego County maintain a lifeguard presence in the summertime, and many have lifeguards patrolling in the winter as well. Look for the light blue towers on the beach to find the nearest available lifeguards, or for permanent buildings bearing a large red cross.

# Getting There and Around

If you're coming to San Diego from Los Angeles, you'll be relieved by the easing of traffic. If you're coming from anyplace else, you may be horrified by the packed highways. In the grand scheme of California transit, San Diego isn't the worst place to try to get around. The highway network makes some sense, there's almost adequate in-town public transit, and the rail and air travel centers bustle with activity.

If you prefer human-powered transportation, San Diego's fabulous weather, generally safe streets, and miles of mostly along-the-coast paths make bicycling and walking eminently possible as your major mode of transportation.

## GETTING THERE

### Air

The major-league **San Diego International Airport** (3665 N. Harbor Dr., www.san.org), a.k.a. Lindbergh Field, is stuffed right along San Diego Bay, convenient to downtown, Coronado, and almost every major San Diego attraction. Short-term parking sits adjacent to the terminals and costs $1 per hour on average. Long-term lots surround the airport; check the airport website for specifics. A 60-minute maximum, free "cell phone lot" lets drivers wait for incoming passengers without having to drive endlessly around the airport.

If you're flying a light plane in, the most convenient general aviation airports to downtown San Diego are Brown Field (8,000-foot runway) and Montgomery Field (4,600-foot runway). Eight additional general aviation airports are scattered throughout the county. For information, check www.miramarairshow.com/airports.html.

### Train

To get to San Diego by train from the north or the east, find your way aboard the **Amtrak Pacific Surfliner** (www.amtrak.com), a train that runs a dozen times a day from Paso Robles along the Pacific Coast down to San Diego.

SAN DIEGO

ROBERT HOLMES / CALTOUR

Amtrak's Santa Fe station

Boarding is easy from most major California destinations in the area, including San Luis Obispo, Santa Barbara, Los Angeles, and Anaheim. Check into transfers from the Coast Starlight and the Capitol Corridor routes as well. Amtrak services the Santa Fe station (1050 Kettner Blvd.) and the Old Town Transit Center (4005 Taylor St.).

For a reliable local commuter train, jump on board **The Coaster** (www.sdcommute.com). The Coaster runs from Oceanside into downtown San Diego and back a dozen times a day Monday–Friday, with five trains running Saturdays, plus special event and holiday service. Fares run $4–5.50 for adults one-way ($2–2.75 for seniors/disabled, children under 6 ride free). Purchase tickets from the vending machines in every train station. In the North County, NCTD Coaster Connecter bus routes can connect to the train station. In San Diego proper, catch the trolley or the bus from either the Old Town Transit Center or the Santa Fe station.



### Car

Most visitors drive into San Diego via the heavily traveled I-5 from the north or south. I-805 runs parallel to I-5 at La Jolla and leads south into Mission Valley. To drive between the North County and San Diego, take I-15, which runs north–south farther inland. Be sure to avoid rush hour, as the back-up on I-15 can become extensive after Poway. Both I-805 and I-15 cross I-8, which runs east–west through Mission Valley. The smaller yet surprisingly pretty Route 163 runs north–south from I-5 in Balboa Park north to I-15 in Miramar.

## GETTING AROUND

### Car

This is Southern California. Most people drive here whether they need to or not. Happily, this is *not* the Los Angeles Basin, so traffic sometimes relaxes into a bearable state and the people who named the freeways weren't actually insane.

Parking is the hardest at the beaches in the summertime. Everyone else in the state seems to be trying to find a parking spot close to the sand between June and September. If you possibly can, find another way to get from your accommodations to the beach, be it bicycle, public transit, or your own two feet. If you must drive, check out the parking situation ahead of time (most beaches' websites offer parking information) and plan ahead. Bring cash for pay parking, come early in the morning, and be prepared to walk up to a mile from your parking spot down to the beach itself.

In the various downtown areas, you'll find fairly average city parking issues. Happily, San Diego's major attractions and event venues tend to be accompanied by large parking structures. Just be prepared to pay a premium if you're doing something popular.

### Bus and Trolley

In downtown San Diego, Coronado, and La Jolla, the **MTS** (www.sdcommute.com) operates both an extensive bus system and trolley routes. The North County is served by the North County Transit District, or NCTD. Trolley tickets cost $1.25–6. Bus fares range $1–5, depending on where you're headed. If you plan to make serious use of the trolleys and buses, use the vending machines at trolley stations to get a day pass—a regular day pass is a bargain at $5, and two-, three-, and four-day passes can save you even more money. Day passes work on NCTD Breeze buses as well as most MTS routes.

See the website for more information about schedules, routes, and fares for both the MTS and NCTD services. If you plan to pay your fare for buses or trolleys on-board, have exact change available. The vending machines are more forgiving, as many take $1 and $5 bills and make change.

If you don't have a car with you, or just want to avoid driving for a while, hop onto the **Old Town Trolley** (www.trolleytours.com/san-diego, adults $30, children $15) for a great look at the highlights of San Diego without the headaches of parking and traffic. The trolley can take you in a loop through downtown (including the Gaslamp Quarter), Old Town, out over the bridge to the Del on Coronado, and around the San Diego Bay Harbor. You can get on and off the trolley at any time to visit a museum, go shopping, or grab a bite to eat. Another trolley will appear to take you on your way. As long as you stay onboard, the driver will narrate, pointing out the sights as you pass them and make stops at the biggest and most important. While the Old Town Trolley is way too expensive to use in place of public transportation, it's a great way to get out and see the highlights of the city in a day.

## Tours

If you've only got a limited time in the San Diego area and want to see as much as possible, consider taking a tour. Several fun, unique tours show off different sides of the city, some you may not have explored before. For instance, to see the city from the bay, consider a harbor tour. **San Diego Harbor Excursion** (619/234-4111, www.sdhe.com, adults $18, seniors $16, children $9) offers one-hour tours of the north and south ends of the bay, and a two-hour tour that covers the bay in full. You'll see some of the most famous San Diego sights from a new perspective: the Maritime Museum ships, the USS *Midway,* the Coronado Bay Bridge, and Fort Rosencrans. This excursion company also provides regular dinner and brunch cruises; reservations in advance are recommended!

For a unique look at the San Diego Bay, add a **Seal Tour** (www.trolleytours.com/san-diego, seal tour $30 or less) to your Old Town Trolley ticket. You'll get a ride on a strange-looking amphibious contraption that will take you from the road around the harbor out into the harbor to look at the city from the water.

To take your own tour of San Diego with just a little bit of help, book a cute talking **Go Car** (639 Kettner Blvd. or 2415 San Diego Ave., 619/696-9002, www.gocartours.com, daily 9 A.M.sunset). In your Go Car, you'll be directed through town by a talking GPS navigation unit that also knows stories about the sights of San Diego. With a Go Car, you can either take a standard tour, or program your own routes through the area.

Looking for something fun and a little spooky to fill the after-dark hours? Take the **Haunted San Diego Ghost Tour** (877/642-8683, www.hauntedsandiegotours.com, $30, June–mid-Sept. nightly, mid-Sept.–May Thurs.–Sun.). This combination bus and walking tour takes about two hours, and includes stops at haunted sites in the Gaslamp District, downtown, and Old Town. Visit the haunted houses and hotels and hear the ghost stories that make each one famous. Highlights of the tour include a historic cemetery and the notorious Whaley House. For the best haunted experience, take the 8:30 P.M. tour so you'll be sure to experience the haunted places of San Diego in darkness.

# BACKGROUND

## The Land

### GEOGRAPHY

California includes just about every geographical feature imaginable, from alpine lakes to parched and delicate deserts to active volcanoes and sun-swept Pacific beaches. The state is trisected vertically by mountain ranges, with valleys in between, and terminates west at the coast of the Pacific Ocean. Many rivers flow west as the ocean wears away at the land, creating coves, waterfalls, and immense bays.

To the east, the Sierra Nevada mountain range looms above all other geography, with craggy snowcapped peaks, alpine lakes and meadows, and gold-producing foothills. The northern mountains—Shasta and Lassen—are the southern tip of the Cascade Range that stretches far into the Pacific Northwest, all the way through Oregon and into Washington. This youthful volcanic chain is part of the Pacific Ring of Fire, contributing recent eruptions by Mount Lassen and Mount St. Helens. Though it's been a while since Shasta's fires last burbled to the surface, the mountain is classed as dormant, not extinct; if she ever blows again, the effects on the whole of the American West will be staggering.

© LIZ HAMILL SCOTT

At the foot of the Sierras sits a giant fertile valley that is the produce capital of the state, and much of the West. Maps and books refer to it as the San Joaquin Valley, but Californians usually call it the Central Valley, and much of the state's massive agriculture industry resides here.

To the south, deserts rule the landscape. California boasts two distinct desert regions: the northern and higher-elevation Mojave Desert, and the southern and low-elevation Colorado Desert (which encompasses Anza-Borrego State Park and the southern half of Joshua Tree National Monument).

The coastal region is bounded by a mountain range, famed in the north for forests filled with enormous coast redwood trees. The northern coastline winds along soaring craggy cliffs overlooking rocky beaches and coves, while the southern coastline tends toward the broad, sandy beaches that California is famous for.

## CLIMATE

Though California is known for the mild climate along its southern shores, the state can claim a number of distinct climate zones.

Mark Twain's famous 19th-century quote—"The coldest winter I ever spent was a summer in San Francisco!"—still stands. If you're visiting "the City" in July or August, don't bother bringing shorts—the weather is generally foggy and cool, with temperatures in the 50s and 60s. These cool temperatures persist along the Bay Area coastline as well. But if you head south to Silicon Valley or to the East Bay, expect temperatures to get up to 20–30° warmer and to see sun instead of fog.

Up along the North Coast, the weather stays about the same year-round: chilly, windy, and foggy. Temperatures can get up into the sunny 80s on rare hot summer days, and winter storms can pound the area with rain. These weather patterns turn milder toward coastal Sonoma in the southern Wine Country. Napa's scorching hot valley summers and mild-to-cool winters are perfect for the grapes growing everywhere—and the tourists who come to drink them.

Lake Tahoe, Mount Shasta, Mount Lassen, Yosemite, and the Eastern Sierras all experience harsh, snow-filled winters that can close roads and wreak havoc with travel plans, but present ideal conditions for a multitude of winter sports. The short, hot summers also draw tourists out in droves.

Sacramento and the Central Valley boast high heat in the summers—often over 100°F—and cool but usually clear winters. The surrounding Gold Country, however, often receives snow in winter and can make roads here impassible.

The Central Coast has somewhat warmer temperatures than the Bay Area beaches, but you can still expect average cool temperatures and plenty of fog in the summer, with chill winds and some rain in the winter. The inland Central Coast wine regions mimic the climate patterns of the Wine Country and are more mild.

From the Los Angeles Basin down to San Diego and up the coast to Santa Barbara, temperatures are mild all year long. Expect fog on the beaches during the summer, cool days in the wintertime, and hotter temperatures in the inland valleys and Disneyland. For the best summertime beach weather in the state, head for San Diego.

The central and eastern deserts in the southern end of the state experience typical desert climates. That means mild, comfortable winters perfect for hiking and outdoor sports, but with nighttime temperatures in the 30s and 40s. The deserts' dangerously hot summers can easily reach 110–120°F.

## ENVIRONMENTAL ISSUES

Environmental issues are California's political bread-and-butter. Los Angeles is rightly famous for its smog, though the San Francisco Bay Area is rapidly catching up in this unattractive race. If you're sensitive to airborne pollution, take special precautions on days that local air quality officials designate "Spare the Air." These are days, mostly in the summer, when pollution levels are especially high. Stay indoors or, when going out, use public transportation.

Water pollution is also an issue in California;

plenty of sensational news stories crucify the state's drinking water, while others laud it. Most tap water is safe to drink, but swimming in California's plentiful rivers and ocean requires more caution. Sadly, water pollution from dumping into the ocean affects beach goers. Dirt and pollution are common in the waters and on the beaches of Los Angeles and Orange Counties, while fishing is no longer permitted in the San Francisco Bay due to the long-standing pollution problems and high mercury levels in the bay's fish.

There are major restrictions on the types of power boats you can launch at Lake Tahoe, due to protections instituted to keep the azure-blue waters of this huge alpine lake pristine. Similar restrictions can also be found for waterways across the state; check the regulations for any lake or river before planning a boating trip.

The good news is that environmental conservation and protection are taken very seriously in California. Recycling, public transit growth, and water cleanup programs proliferate throughout the state. Even as a short-time visitor, you can help California's efforts to get and stay clean: Use any recycling bins you see on the street; minimize your use of plastic bags; and don't leave litter on the beach or out in wilderness areas—either throw it away or pack it out with you.

## FLORA AND FAUNA

California's diverse geography gives rise to dozens of different ecosystems, each of which has its own unique native plants and animals. Botanical gardens, zoos, and wildlife preserves abound throughout the state, giving visitors ample opportunities to smell the flowers, pet the animals, and learn about the complex and varied life that abounds all through the Golden State.

### Redwoods

The most famous trees native to California are undoubtedly the redwoods. The **coast redwood** *(Sequoia sempervirens)* grows on the North Coast and down through the Bay Area all the way to Big Sur. Coast redwood trees perch on cliffs overlooking the sea, but most of the best groves are inland, in the mountains. The Redwood National and State Parks do

redwoods in the sky

the best job of showcasing these grand trees, though any hiker in the Santa Cruz Mountains can reach out and touch soft redwood bark.

The truly immense redwood trees don't grow along the coast—they're much farther inland. The **giant sequoia** *(Sequoiadendron giganteum)* grow in the Sierra Nevada mountains. These redwoods can live for thousands of years and grow to unimaginable heights. The museum at Sequoia-Kings Canyon National Park includes a wonderful interpretive display describing the life cycle of the giant sequoia, including information about the importance of fire to the health and propagation of these trees. Sequoia groves grow aplenty in Yosemite National Park, Calaveras Big Trees, and a few other select spots in the Sierras.

## Joshua Trees

One famous California tree isn't a tree at all. The desert-dwelling **Joshua tree** *(Yucca brevifolia)* is actually a member of the yucca family. You can't miss a Joshua tree—from a distance, it almost resembles an honest-to-goodness deciduous tree. But when you get up close, the scaly "bark" starts to look strange and the "leaves" even odder—spiky and big. Larger Joshua trees can get up to 15 feet tall with dozens of leafy "branches" at their tops. While the best place to see forests of Joshua trees is, of course, in Joshua Tree National Monument, Joshua trees thrive in the Mojave Desert ecosystem—they're all over the Mojave Preserve and can even be found alongside the desert's highways.

## Wildflowers

California's state flower is the **California poppy** *(Eschscholzia californica).* The pretty little orange blossom grows just about everywhere, even on the sides of the busiest highways. Though most California poppies are bright orange, they also appear occasionally in white, cream, and even deeper red-orange.

## Reptiles

If you spot California's most infamous native reptile, keep your distance. Several varieties of **rattlesnakes** are indigenous to the state. The Pacific Northwest rattler makes its home in Northern California, while more than half

© LANCE SCOTT

a funky Joshua tree

a dozen different rattlesnake varieties live in Southern California, including the Western diamondback and the Mojave rattlesnake.

All rattlesnakes are venomous, though death by snakebite is extremely rare in California. Most parks with known rattlesnakes in residence post signs alerting hikers; your best bet to keep safe is to stay on trails and avoid tromping off into meadows or brush. Pay attention when hiking, especially when negotiating rocks and woodpiles, and never put a foot or a hand down in a spot you can't see first. Wear long pants and heavy hiking boots for protection (from snakes, plus insects, other critters, and unfriendly plants you might encounter).

### Butterflies

California isn't the tropics, but its vast population of wildflowers attract an array of gorgeous butterflies. The **Monarch butterfly** has become an emblem of the state. These large orange-and-black butterflies have a migratory pattern that's reminiscent of birds. Each winter, the butterflies fly south from their summertime wanderings to cluster in several groves of eucalyptus trees throughout the temperate coastal zone. As they close up their wings to hibernate for the winter, their crowding and dull outer wing color makes them resemble clumps of dried leaves, thus protecting them from predators. In spring, the butterflies begin to wake up, fluttering lazily in the groves a bit before flying north to seek out milkweed on which to lay their eggs. Santa Cruz and Cambria are two great places to visit the California "butterfly trees."

# History and Economy

California boasts a rich history, filled with great stories and fascinating characters. The state's timeline flows from the Native Americans through the first European explorations to the building of the Spanish missions, then the Gold Rush, and on into the millennium.

Today, California takes an active role in the economy and culture of the United States and indeed the world. The Internet began, took off, boomed, busted, and settled into its current iteration as a worldwide communication and commerce web in the Bay Area. Central Valley agriculture remains the state's economic mainstay, while the motion picture industry continues to dominate the Los Angeles landscape. Movie stars keep getting into politics; actors Ronald Regan and Arnold Schwarzenegger have claimed residence in the Governor's Mansion and Clint Eastwood's credits include a stint as mayor of Carmel-by-the-Sea.

California has had good times and bad, triumphs and shame, but one thing has remained constant—the story of California is never, ever boring.

## THE MISSION PERIOD

California's earliest explorers and European colonists were mostly from Spain—hence the proliferation of Spanish-named streets, towns, and even colleges that persist to this day. Monuments to many of these men can be found in various parts of the state.

No single man is credited with as much influence on the early development of California than Father Junipero Serra. The Franciscan monk took an active role in bringing Christianity (and, unfortunately, the corollary syphilis, measles, and smallpox) to native peoples from San Diego all the way up to Sonoma. To that end, the Franciscan order built a string of missions, each of which was meant to be a self-sufficient parish that grew its own food, kept up its own buildings, and took care of its own people. The monks also created a road between the missions—El Camino Real—with the idea that a pilgrim could travel the length of El Camino Real and find a bed at the next mission after only one day's journey. Today, El Camino Real remains a vital part of the state and much of the original path still exists; just look for the mission bells mounted on curved poles posted along the sides of the road. In the Bay Area, El Camino Real isn't a highway—it's a business street running the length of the Peninsula. To the south, El Camino Real and U.S. 101 sometimes merge into one; at other points El Camino rambles away from any main roads.

The missions prospered in the early 1800s, then gradually deteriorated until they were ordered to secularize in the middle of the 19th century. Some took on new uses; others fell into disrepair and outright abandonment. It was only in the 20th century that interest in the history of the missions was rekindled and money was invested into restoring many of the churches and complexes. Today, many (but not all) of the missions have been restored as Catholic parishes, with visitors centers and museum displays of various levels of quality and polish.

## THE GOLD RUSH

In 1849, a worker discovered nuggets of gold in the machinery at Sutter's Mill. The news that chunks of gold were just sitting there on the riverbeds for the taking spread like wildfire. The Gold Rush was on. People from the East Coast and all over the world streamed into California by land and by sea, seeking a fortune in gold—or a fortune in serving or selling to the gold-seekers. Thousands of men panned every available stream for nuggets, then water-blasted hillsides away seeking the elusive precious metal. Even then, the wanton destruction caused by the blasting was quickly seen to be a problem. And so the famous hard-rock mines of California began construction. Though panning continued (hope springs eternal, after all), by the 1860s most of the rough men had taken jobs working in the deep, dangerous mines.

Sutter's Mill, the birthplace of California's Gold Rush

With the influx of gold seekers, new cities sprang up almost overnight. The previously small town of San Francisco became the major port of entry for immigrants. Sacramento's river location made it a perfect transportation hub and waypoint between San Francisco and the gold fields. Mining towns like Sonora, Volcano, Placerville, Sutter's Creek, and Nevada City swelled to huge proportions, only to shrink back into obscurity as the mines closed one by one in the 20th century.

As American and European men came to California to seek their fortunes in gold, a few wives and children joined them, but the number of families in the average mining town was small. Yet a few lone women did join in the rush to the gold fields. These ladies took up "the oldest profession," servicing the population of single male miners and laborers in desperate need of (ahem) female companionship.

The other major group of immigrants at this time came to California from a land distant in both distance and culture: China. Thousands of Chinese men came, not to mine, but to labor and serve the white miners. Most were forced to pass through the wretched immigration facilities on Angel Island in the middle of San Francisco Bay—sometimes being essentially imprisoned for months before either being allowed onto the mainland or summarily shipped back to China. San Francisco's Chinatown became a hub for the immigrants,

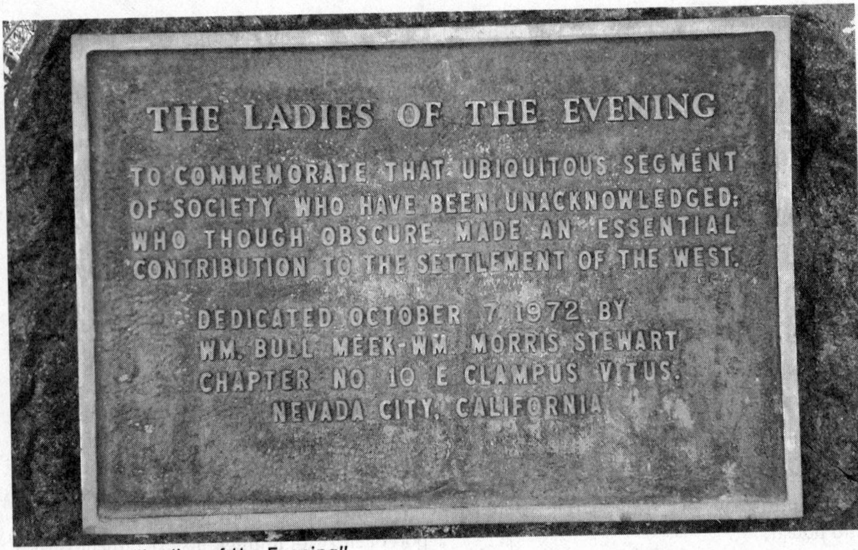

© LIZ HAMILL SCOTT

to honor the "Ladies of the Evening"

a place where their language was spoken and their culture comprehended. But thousands headed east, becoming low-level laborers in the industry surrounding the mines, or workers on the railroads endlessly spooling out to connect Gold Country to the rest of the state and eventually to the East Coast by way of the Transcontinental Railroad.

## THE 1960S

Few places in the country felt the impact of the radical 1960s more than California. In fact, it's arguable that the peace and free love movements began right here, probably on the campus of the infamous and indomitable University of California at Berkeley. Certainly Berkeley helped to shape and grow the culture of hippies, peaceniks, and radical politics. The college campus was the home of the Black Panthers, anti-Vietnam War sit-ins, and numerous protests for all sorts of liberal causes.

If Berkeley was the de facto home of 1960s political movements, then San Francisco was the base of its social and cultural phenomena. Free concerts in Golden Gate Park and the growing fame of the hippie community taking over an area called Haight-Ashbury drew teenagers from across the country. Many found themselves living on Haight Street for months, experiementing with the most popular mind-altering chemicals of the era. The music scene became the stuff of legend and song (sorry). The Grateful Dead—one of the most famous and longest lasting of the 1960s rock bands—hailed from the Bay Area.

## ECONOMY

The state of California boasts the eighth-largest economy in the *world.* California's contribution to the United States outpaces even its immense size and population.

### Agriculture

Many people guess incorrectly when asked what California's number one economic sector is. It's not high tech. It's not films. It's farming! California's agricultural juggernaut supplies much of the world with crops of almost all kinds, from grapefruit to grass-fed beef.

In warm Southern California, citrus trees rule much of the landscape; you can even find grapefruit groves in the harsh climate of the

Anza-Borrego Desert. The Central Valley's flat, fertile fields produce everything from rice to corn to tomatoes. In the summertime, tomato trucks drive routes all around Sacramento to processing plants that create that all-important American staple food: ketchup. The cooler Central Coast region grows sweet strawberries and spiky artichokes in abundance. As the fog gets colder and drippier in Marin, ranchers take advantage of the naturally growing grasses to ranch herds of cattle destined for the growing sustainable-food market. In truth, cattle are ranched all over the state, from the far-north reaches down to the southern deserts.

Today, as awareness grows about the harmful affects of pesticides and petrochemical fertilizers on both the land and consumers, organic farms and ranches are proliferating across California. In addition to the giant factory farms so prevalent in the Central Valley, you'll also see an increasing number of small farms and ranches growing a variety of crops using organic, sustainable, and even biodynamic practices. Most of these farmers sell directly to consumers by way of farmers markets and farm stands—almost every town or county in the state has a weekly farmer's market in the summertime, and many last year-round.

And then there's the wine. It seems like every square inch of free agricultural land in the state now has a grapevine growing on it. The vineyards that were once primarily seen in Napa and Sonoma Counties can now be found on the slopes of the Sierra Foothills, down south in Santa Barbara, and even close to coastside in Mendocino and Carmel. Surprising to some, it's actually the wine industry that's leading the charge beyond mere organic and into biodynamic growing practices, such as using sheep to keep the weeds down in the vineyards and provide natural fertilizer, or harvesting grapes and pruning vines according the moon's cycles to promote optimum wine quality. (In truth, it makes sense, and serious wine drinkers are willing to pay premium prices for top-quality vintages.)

## Industry

The motion picture industry draws the most publicity to California. Though little filming takes place in and around Hollywood today, it's still the home of the major studios and their prominent executives.

© LIZ HAMILL SCOTT

Agriculture is California's major economic sector.

In Northern California, Silicon Valley has made a name for itself as the epicenter of the technology industry. Despite the expense of property in the Bay Area, nearly every major high-tech company maintains a presence somewhere near Silicon Valley, as many were founded and are still headquartered there. Major tech legends include Hewlett-Packard in Palo Alto, Apple Computer in Cupertino, and Intel on the border of Santa Clara and San Jose. Google remains loyal to its hometown of Mountain View, and Microsoft has opened offices throughout Silicon Valley. During the "dot-com boom" of the early 1990s, nearly everyone in the region seemed to somehow be employed by the tech industry, and when the bust came it hit the region like a ton of outdated CRT monitors.

Today, the tech industry still provides hundreds of thousands of top-paying jobs in Silicon Valley and throughout the greater Bay Area and most residents of the region tend towards the tech-savvy.

# People and Culture

## RELIGION

A wide variety of religions and belief systems have come to characterize California. The state is home to large populations of Catholics, Protestants, Jews, Muslims, Buddhists, and even Wiccan religions and Scientologists. Many urban centers, especially San Francisco and Los Angeles, provide houses of worship or religious centers for practitioners of these and many other faiths.

Many Californians cherish the religious tolerance found here, and the right and ability of all to practice their desired form of worship is widely protected. So expect to see everything from rigorous observance of Lent to traditional Chinese New Year to pagan solstice rituals in the park.

## LANGUAGE

As in the rest of the United States, English is the official language in California. However, the state's large immigrant population has resulted in equally large non-English speaking communities. Due to the state's proximity to Mexico, Spanish is the most widely spoken foreign language. Other major spoken and written languages include Chinese, Cantonese, Korean, Vietnamese, Japanese, and various East Indian dialects. Throughout the state, this multilingualism often results in a colorful blend of cultures, creating a multiethnic tapestry of California residents. However, in both Los Angeles and the Bay Area, tightly knit Asian and Hispanic communities sometimes feature little-to-no signs or menus in English, and few proprietors speak standard English. Exploring the culture of California means exploring the backgrounds of those who live here, so be prepared to learn more about the world even as you learn more about the state.

© BOB ECKER / SFCVB

Signs in Chinatown reflect a mix of languages.

# ESSENTIALS

## Getting There

### BY AIR

It's easy to fly in to California, particularly if you're heading for one of the major metropolitan areas. Reaching the more rural or outlying regions of the state is a bit trickier and you'll probably find yourself driving—possibly for hours—from one of the major airports.

### Los Angeles

The greater Los Angeles area is thick with airports. **Los Angeles International Airport** (LAX, www.lawa.org) serves the greater Los Angeles area, and is located about 10 miles south of the city of Santa Monica. If you're coming in from another country or from across the continent, you're likely to find your flight coming into this endlessly crowded hub. If you're flying home from LAX, plan plenty of time to get through security and the check-in lines—up to three hours for a domestic flight on a holiday weekend.

To miss the major crowds, consider flying into one of the many suburban airports. **John Wayne International** (www.ocair.com) services Disneyland perfectly, and the **Long Beach** airport (www.longbeach.gov/airport)

PHOTO COURTESY OF THE MAMMOTH LAKES VISITORS BUREAU

is convenient to the beaches. Ontario Airport is farther out but a good option for travelers planning to divide their time between Los Angeles, Palm Springs, and the deserts.

In Los Angeles, free shuttle buses provide service to the Los Angeles County **Metropolitan Transportation Authority Metro Rail** (800/266-6883), accessible at the Green Line Aviation Station. Metro Rail trains connect into Long Beach, Hollywood, North Hollywood, downtown Los Angeles, and Pasadena. Passengers should wait under the "LAX Shuttle Airline Connection" signs outside the lower-level terminals and board the "G" shuttle. Passengers may also take the "C" shuttle to the **Metro Bus Center** (800/266-6883), which connects to buses that serve the entire L.A. area. Information about bus service is provided via telephones on the Information Display Board inside each terminal.

Shuttle services are also available if you wish to share a ride. **Prime Time Shuttle** (800/733-8267, www.primetimeshuttle.com) and SuperShuttle (800/258-3826, www.supershuttle.com) are authorized to serve the entire Los Angeles area out of LAX. These vans can be found on the lower/arrivals deck in front of each terminal, under the orange "Shared Ride Vans" signs. Average fares for two people are about $32 into downtown Los Angeles, $34 into West Hollywood, and $30 into Santa Monica.

**Taxis** can be found on the lower/arrivals level islands in front of each terminal, below the yellow "Taxi" signs. Only licensed taxis are allowed into the airport; they have standard rates of about $40 to downtown and $30 to West Los Angeles.

## San Francisco Bay Area

San Francisco has one major airport surrounded by a few ancillary and less-crowded airports. **San Francisco International Airport** (SFO, www.flysfo.com) isn't in San Francisco proper—it's actually located approximately 13 miles south of the City.

Several public and private transportation options can get you into the City: rental car, taxi, BART, or even CalTrain. As in Los Angeles, if your flight is out of SFO, plan to arrive at the airport up to three hours before your flight leaves. Airport lines, especially on weekends and holidays, are notoriously long.

To avoid the SFO crowds, consider booking a flight into **Oakland International Airport** (1 Airport Dr., Oakland, 510/563-3300, www.flyoakland.com), which services the East Bay with access to San Francisco across the Bay Bridge, or **San Jose International Airport** (Airport Blvd., San Jose, www.sjc.org), south of San Francisco in the heart of Silicon Valley. These airports are quite a bit smaller than SFO, but service is brisk from many U.S. destinations.

**Bay Area Rapid Transit** (BART, www.bart.gov) connects directly with SFO's international terminal, providing a simple and relatively fast trip to downtown San Francisco (under an hour). The BART station is an easy walk or free shuttle ride from any point in the airport, and a one-way ticket to any downtown station costs $5.35.

**Shuttle vans** are also a cost-effective option for door-to-door service, though these include several stops along the way. From the airport to downtown, the average one-way fare is $15–20 per passenger. Shuttle vans congregate on the second level of SFO above the baggage claim area for domestic flights, and on the third level for international flights. Advance reservations guarantee a seat, but they aren't required and don't necessarily speed the process. Some companies to try: Bay Shuttle (415/564-3400, www.bayshuttle.com), Quake City Shuttle (415/255-4899, www.quakecityshuttle.com), and SuperShuttle (800/258-3826, www.supershuttle.com).

For **taxis,** the average fare to downtown is around $40.

## San Diego

Three terminals at **San Diego International Airport** (N. Harbor Dr., San Diego, www.san.org) provide easy access to Southern California. (They somehow managed to squeeze the runways in right downtown by the ocean, making it incredibly convenient for visitors to the seaside city.) Long- and short-term parking is available by the hour or day. The airport is serviced daily by **Amtrak** (800/872-7245, www.amtrak.com) and by **Coaster** (www.gonctd.com, 800/262-7837, Mon.–Sat., $4) trains via the Santa Fe Deport train station downtown. The Flyer Route No. 992 metro **bus** (http://transit.511sd.com, 5 A.M.–12:50 A.M., $2.25) stops downtown and connects with the San Diego Trolley, Coaster, and Amtrak. Note that the Trolley does not connect directly to the airport.

## BY TRAIN

Several cross-country **Amtrak** (www.amtrak.com) trains rumble into California each day. If you're arriving from another part of the country, the train can be a relaxing way to make the journey to the Golden State; long-distance train routes usually include dining and lounge cars. There are eight train routes that service California: The California Zephyr travels to Chicago, Denver, and Emervyille; the Capitol Corridor services Auburn, Sacramento, Emeryville, Oakland, and San Jose, and a popular route with local communters; the Coast Starlight travel down the west coast, from Seattle to Portland and ending in Los Angeles; the Pacific Surfliner will get you to the Central Coast and southern California, while the San Joaquins services the Central Valley; the Southwest Chief, Sunset Limited, and Texas Eagle brings travelers from the south and midwest into California.

## BY CAR

Many Americans get to visit California by driving here. A number of interstate highways run into the state from points east and north. From the Pacific Northwest, I-5 runs north and south through the state and will get you here quickly. The coastal routes along Highway 1 and Highway 101 are longer, but prettier. I-10 and I-15 allow access from the southeastern regions.

### Car Rental

Most major car rental companies are located in one central area at the major airports. To reserve a car in advance, contact **Budget Rent A Car** (800/527-0700), **Dollar Rent A Car** (866/434-2226), **Enterprise** (www.enterprise.com), or **Hertz** (www.hertz.com).

# Getting Around

## BY AIR

When traversing major cities within the state, flying can be an economical (and faster) option. The **San Francisco International Airport** (SFO, www.flysfo.com), located south of the City provides convenient access to the northern part of the state. Across the bay, the **Oakland Airport** (Hegenberger Rd., Oakland, www.oaklandairport.com) often avoids the fog and inclement weather that socks in SFO.

**Los Angeles International Airport** (LAX,www.lawa.org) serves the greater Los Angeles, offers a wealth of airline options, and can connect with flights both to San Francisco and Los Angeles. But it can be a hectic and time-consuming maze to navigate. Other options in the area include the **Bob Hope Airport** (2627 N. Hollywod Way, Burbank, 818/840-8840, www.burbankairport.com) and the **Long Beach Airport** (4100 Donald Douglas Dr., 562/570-2600, www.longbeach.gov/airport).

The **San Diego International Airport** (N. Harbor Dr., San Diego, www.san.org) provides easy access to southern California and Mexico, if your travelers take you further south.

## BY TRAIN

**Amtrak** (www.amtrak.com) trains run several corridors through the state. The California Zephyr, Capitol Corridor, Coast Starlight, and San Joaquins routes offer services to Auburn,

Sacramento, Emeryville, Oakland, San Jose, Los Angeles, the Central Coast, and the Central Valley. Train are roomy, comfortable, and offer a dining car for affordable snacks and meals.

### BY CAR

California is great for road-tripping. Scenic coastal routes such as Highway 1 and Highway 101 are often destinations in themselves, while inland I-5 is the most direct route north and south through the state. However, traffic jams, accidents, mudslides, fires, and snow can affect highways and interstates at any time. Before heading out on your adventure, check road conditions online at the Calfiornia Department of Transportation (Caltrans, www.dot.ca.gov). Note that mountain passes such as I-80 into Tahoe, I-5 at the Grapevine, and the Shasta and Lassen regions may require snow tires and/or chains. In rural areas and in the deserts, gas stations may be few and far between.

## Visas and Officialdom

### PASSPORTS AND VISAS

If you're visiting California from another country, you must present a valid passport upon entry into the United States. You must also hold a return plane or cruise ticket to your country of origin dated less than 90 days from your date of entry (Canada excepted).

If you hold a passport from one of the following countries, you do not need a visa to enter California: Andorra, Australia, Austria, Belgium, Brunei, Denmark, Finland, France, Germany, Iceland, Ireland, Italy, Japan, Liechtenstein, Luxembourg, Monaco, the Netherlands, New Zealand, Norway, Portugal, San Marino, Singapore, Slovenia, Spain, Sweden, Switzerland, and the United Kingdom.

In most other countries, the local U.S. embassy should be able to provide a free tourist visa, often within 24 hours of request. Do plan more time for visa processing if you're requesting travel in the high summer season (June–Aug.).

### EMBASSIES

San Francisco and Los Angeles both shelter embassies and consulates from many countries around the globe. If you should lose your passport or find yourself in some other trouble while visiting California, contact your country's offices for assistance. To find an embassy, check www.travel.state.gov for a list of embassies within the state.

### CUSTOMS

Before you enter California from another country by sea or by air, you'll be required to fill out a customs form. Check with the U.S. embassy in your country or the Customs Bureau website (www.cbp.gov) for an updated list of items you must declare.

If you require medication administered by injection, you must pack your syringes in a checked bag; syringes are not permitted in carry-ons coming into the United States.

Also pack documentation describing your need for any narcotic medications you've brought with you. Failure to produce documentation for narcotics upon request can result in severe penalties in the United States.

If you're driving into California along I-5 or another major freeway, prepare to stop at Agricultural Inspection stations few miles inside the state line. You don't need to present a passport, a visa, or even a driver's license. Instead, you must be prepared to present all your fruits and vegetables.

California's largest economic segment lies in agriculture, and a number of the major crops grown here are sensitive to pests and diseases. In an effort to prevent known pests from entering the state and endangering the crops, travelers are asked to identify all produce they're carrying in from other states or from Mexico. If you've got produce, especially homegrown or from a farm stand, that might be infected by a known problem pest or disease, expect it to be confiscated on the spot.

You'll also be asked about fruits and veggies on your customs form, which you'll be asked to fill out on the airplane or ship before you reach the United States.

# Tips for Travelers

## CONDUCT AND CUSTOMS

The legal drinking age in California is 21. Expect to have your ID checked if you look under 30, especially in bars and clubs, but also in restaurants and wineries.

Most California bars and clubs close at 2 A.M.; you'll find the occasional after-hours nightspot in Los Angeles, San Francisco, and Palm Springs.

Cigarette smoking has been all but criminalized throughout the state of California. Don't expect to find a smoking section in any restaurant or an ashtray in the bars. Smoking is illegal in all bars and clubs, but your new favorite watering hole might have an outdoor patio where smokers can huddle. Taking the ban one step further, many hotels, motels, and inns throughout the state are strictly nonsmoking, and you'll be subject to fees of several hundred dollars if your room smells of smoke when you leave.

There's no smoking in any public building, and even some of the state parks don't allow cigarettes. There's often good reason for this; fire danger in California is extreme in the summertime, and one carelessly thrown lit butt can cause a genuine catastrophe.

## TRAVELING WITH CHILDREN

Many spots in California are ideal destinations for families with children of all ages. In both the San Francisco Bay Area and the Los Angeles region, amusement parks, interactive museums, zoos, parks, beaches, and playgrounds all make for family-friendly fun. Even some of the upscale hotels offer great programs for young people, and many Southern California resorts designate at least one swimming pool as "family" or "loud" to accommodate rambunctious fun and outside voices.

You know your children best, so you can plan a great trip they'll love based on their special interests. Would they prefer Disneyland or the San Diego Zoo? Surf lessons at Huntington Beach or rock climbing school at Joshua Tree? Redwood trees or youth nightclubs?

On the other hand, there are a few spots in the Golden State that beckon more to adults than to children. Frankly, there aren't many family activities in Wine Country. This adult playground is all about alcoholic beverages and high-end dining. Similarly, the North Coast's focus on original art and romantic B&Bs brings out couples looking for weekend getaways rather than families. In fact, before you book a room at a B&B that you expect to share with your kids, check to be sure that the inn can accommodate extra people in their guest rooms and allows guests under 16 years old.

## WOMEN TRAVELERS

California's a pretty friendly place for women traveling alone. Most of the major outdoor attractions are incredibly safe, and even many of the urban areas boast pleasant neighborhoods that welcome lone female travelers.

But you'll need to take some basic precautions and pay attention to your surroundings just as you would in any unfamiliar place. Carry your car keys in your hand when walking out to your car. Don't sit in your parked car in a lonely parking lot at night; just get in, turn on the engine, and drive away. When you're walking down a city street, be alert and keep an eye on your surroundings and on anyone who might be following you. In rural areas, don't go tromping into unlit wooded areas or out into grassy fields alone at night without a flashlight; many of California's critters are nocturnal. (Actually, this caution applies to men traveling alone as well. Mountain lions and rattlesnakes don't tend to discriminate.)

Some neighborhoods in the big cities are best avoided by lone women, especially at night. Besides the obvious—the Tenderloin in San Francisco and the Compton, Watts, and Inglewood neighborhoods of Los Angeles—some other streets and neighborhoods can turn distinctly hostile after dark.

## SENIOR TRAVELERS

California makes an ideal destination for retired folks looking to relax and have a great time. You'll find senior discounts nearly every place you go, from restaurants to golf courses to major attractions, and even at some hotels, though the minimum age can vary from 50–65. Just ask, and be prepared to produce ID if you look young or are requesting an AARP discount.

For landlubbers, RV parks abound throughout the state, and even many of the state and national parks can accommodate RVs and trailers. The Southern California deserts are particularly popular with snowbirds. Check with the parks you want to visit for size and location restrictions, hookup and dump station information, and RV slot prices.

## GAY AND LESBIAN TRAVELERS

California is known for its thriving gay and lesbian communities. In fact, the Golden State is a golden place for gay travel—especially in the bigger cities, and even some of the smaller towns both in the north and the south parts of the state. As with much of the country, the further you venture into more rural and agricultural regions, the less likely you're to experience the liberal acceptance the state is known for.

In Northern California, San Francisco has the biggest and arguably best Gay Pride Festival (www.sfpride.org) in the nation, usually held down Market Street the last weekend in June. All year-round, the Castro District offers fun of all kinds, from theater to clubs to shopping, mostly targeted for gay men but with a few places sprinkled in for lesbians. If the Castro is your primary destination, you can even find a place to stay right in the midst of the action (see *Accommodations* in the *San Francisco Bay Area* chapter).

Both gay men and women flock to Santa Cruz on the coastline, though the quirky town is specially known for its lesbian-friendly culture. A relaxed vibe informs everything from underground clubs to unofficial nude beaches to live-action role playing games in the middle of downtown. Even the lingerie and adult toy shops tend to be female-owned and -operated.

So where do gay and lesbian San Francisco residents go to get away for the weekend? Many flock to Guerneville—an outdoorsy town on the Russian River. Rustic lodges offer cabins down by the river, rafting and kayaking companies offer summertime adventures, and nearby wineries offer and relaxation. The short but colorful Main Street is home to queer-friendly bars and festivals.

Down south, the most gay-friendly town has to be Palm Springs. Gay bars and clubs proliferate here in a relaxed and friendly atmosphere that welcomes men, women, and even straight senior citizens. The White Party and Gay Pride (www.pspride.org, first weekend in November) are huge events that draw tens of thousands of visitors to the desert city. Perhaps best of all, more than a dozen gay resorts cluster in the sun-drenched town, offering swimming pools, hot tubs, and clothing-optional common spaces.

West Hollywood in the Los Angeles Basin has its own upscale gay culture. Just like the rest of L.A.'s clubs, the gay clubs are havens of the see-and-be-seen crowd. The famous Barney's Beanery offers beans and boys, and now has a second location on the Promenade in Santa Monica.

The oh-so-fabulous California vibe has even made it to the interior of the state—Sacramento's newly revitalized Midtown neighborhood offers a more low-key but visible gay evening scene.

# Information and Services

When visiting California, you might be tempted to stop in at one of several Golden State Welcome Centers scattered throughout the state. In all honesty, these visitors centers aren't that great. If you're in an area that doesn't have its own visitors venter or tourist bureau, the State Welcome Center might be a useful place to pick up maps and brochures. Check www.visitcwc.com to find a local Welcome Center wherever you're visiting. Otherwise, stick with local, regional, state, and national park visitors centers (see *Internet Resources*), which tend to be staffed by volunteers or rangers who feel a real passion for their locale.

## MAPS AND TOURIST INFORMATION

Almost all gas stations and drugstores sell maps both of the locale you're traversing and of the whole state. California State Automobile Association (CSAA, www.csaa.com) offices offer maps to members for free.

Many local and regional visitors centers also offer maps, but you'll need to pay a few dollars for the bigger and better ones. But if all you need is a wine-tasting map in a known wine region, you can probably get one for free (plus a few tasting coupons) at the nearest regional visitors center. Basic national park maps come with your admission fee. State park maps can be free, or can cost a few dollars at the visitors centers.

## HEALTH AND SAFETY

Have an emergency anywhere in California? Dial 911. Inside hotels and resorts, check your emergency number as soon as you get into your room. In urban and suburban areas, full-service hospitals and medical centers abound. But in the more remote regions, help can be more than an hour away.

If you're planning a backcountry expedition, follow all rules and guidelines for obtaining wilderness permits and for self-registration at trailheads. These are for your safety, letting the rangers know roughly where you plan to be and when to expect you back. National and state park visitors centers can advise in more detail as to any health or wilderness alerts in the area.

### Poison Oak

There is only one major variety of plant in California that can cause an adverse reaction in humans merely upon touching the leaves or stems. That is poison oak, a common shrub that inhabits forests up and down the state. Poison oak has a characteristic three-leaf configuration, with scalloped leaves that are shiny green in the spring and then turn yellow, orange, and red in late summer and fall. In fall the leaves drop, leaving a cluster of innocuous-looking branches. The oil in poison oak is present all year long in both the leaves and branches. Your best protection is to wear long sleeves and long pants when hiking, no matter how hot it is. A product called Tecnu is available at most California drugstores—slather it on *before* you go hiking to protect yourself from poison oak. If your skin comes in contact with poison oak, expect a nasty rash well known for its itchiness and irritation. Poison oak is also extremely contagious, so avoid touching your eyes, face, or other parts of your body to prevent spreading the rash. Calamine lotion can help, and in extreme cases a doctor can administer cortisone to help decrease the inflammation.

## MONEY

California businesses accept the U.S. dollar ($). Most businesses also accept major credit cards: Visa, MasterCard, Discover, Diner's Club, and American Express. ATM and check-cards work at many stores and restaurants, and you're likely to find ATMs in most every town of any size.

You can change currency in any international airport in the state. Currency exchange points also crop up in downtown San Francisco and Los Angeles and at some of the major business hotels in the urban areas.

# RESOURCES

## Internet Resources

It should come as no surprise that California travel leads the way in use of the Internet as a marketing, communications, and sales tool. The overwhelming majority of destinations have their own websites—even tiny towns in the middle of nowhere proudly tout their attractions on the Web.

### CALIFORNIA

**California Department of Transportation**
**www.dot.ca.gov/hq/roadinfo/statemap.htm**
This website contains state map and highway information.

**Visit California**
**www.visitcalifornia.com**
The official tourism site of the state of California.

### REGIONAL SITES

**Central Coast Regional Tourism**
**www.centralcoast-tourism.com**
A guide to the Central Coast region, including Santa Cruz, Monterey, and Santa Barbara.

**LATourist.com**
**www.latourist.com**
An informative Los Angeles tourist website.

**Los Angeles County Visitors Bureau**
**www.lacvb.com**
The official website of the Los Angeles Convention and Visitors Bureau.

**NapaValley.com**
**www.napavalley.com**
A Napa Valley tourist website from WineCountry.com.

**Sacramento Convention and Visitors Bureau**
**www.sacramentocvb.org**
The official website of the Sacramento Convention and Visitors Bureau.

**San Diego Visitors Bureau**
**www.sandiego.org/nav/visitors**
The official website of the San Diego Visitors Bureau.

**Shasta and Lassen Regional Tourism**
**www.shastacascade.org**
The California Travel and Tourism Information Network includes information and a downloadable visitors guide to Mt. Shasta, Shasta Lake, Redding, and Lassen.

**Visit California Gold Country**
**www.calgold.org**
The website from the Gold Country Visitors Association, with information about Grass Valley, Navada City, Placer Country, Sacramento, and Amador Country.

## PARKS AND OUTDOORS

### California Outdoor and Recreational Information
### www.caoutdoors.com

This recreation-focused website includes links to maps, local newspapers, festivals and events, as well as a wide variety of recreational activities throughout the state.

### California State Parks
### www.parks.ca.gov

The official website lists hours, accessibility, activities, camping areas, fees, and more information for all parks in the state system.

### Death Valley National Park
### www.nps.gov/deva

The official website for Death Valley National Park.

### Disneyland
### http:/disneyland.disney.go.com

The official website for Disneyland and all Disney attractions.

### Joshua Tree National Park
### www.nps.gov/jotr

The official website for Joshua Tree National Park.

### Lassen Volcanic National Park
### www.nps.gov/lavo

The official website for Lassen Volcanic National Park.

### Redwood National Park
### www.nps.gov/redw

The official website for all Redwood National and State Parks.

### Sequoia and Kings Canyon National Parks
### www.nps.gov/seki

The official website for Sequoia and Kings Canyon.

### State of California
### www.ca.gov/tourism/greatoutdoors.html

Outdoor resources for California state and government organizations. Check for information about fishing and hunting licenses, backcountry permits, boating regulations, and more.

### Yosemite National Park
### www.nps.gov/yose

The National Park Service website for Yosemite National Park.

### Yosemite National Park Vacation and Lodging Information
### www.yosemitepark.com

The concessionaire website for Yosemite National Park lodging, dining, and reservations.

# Index

## A



## B

## T

## UVW



## XYZ

# Map Index

# MAP SYMBOLS

| | | | |
|---|---|---|---|
| Expressway | Highlight | Airfield | Golf Course |
| Primary Road | City/Town | Airport | Parking Area |
| Secondary Road | State Capital | Mountain | Archaeological Site |
| Unpaved Road | National Capital | Unique Natural Feature | Church |
| Trail | Point of Interest | Waterfall | Gas Station |
| Ferry | Accommodation | Park | Glacier |
| Railroad | Restaurant/Bar | Trailhead | Mangrove |
| Pedestrian Walkway | Other Location | Skiing Area | Reef |
| Stairs | Campground | | Swamp |

# CONVERSION TABLES

°C = (°F - 32) / 1.8
°F = (°C x 1.8) + 32
1 inch = 2.54 centimeters (cm)
1 foot = 0.304 meters (m)
1 yard = 0.914 meters
1 mile = 1.6093 kilometers (km)
1 km = 0.6214 miles
1 fathom = 1.8288 m
1 chain = 20.1168 m
1 furlong = 201.168 m
1 acre = 0.4047 hectares
1 sq km = 100 hectares
1 sq mile = 2.59 square km
1 ounce = 28.35 grams
1 pound = 0.4536 kilograms
1 short ton = 0.90718 metric ton
1 short ton = 2,000 pounds
1 long ton = 1.016 metric tons
1 long ton = 2,240 pounds
1 metric ton = 1,000 kilograms
1 quart = 0.94635 liters
1 US gallon = 3.7854 liters
1 Imperial gallon = 4.5459 liters
1 nautical mile = 1.852 km

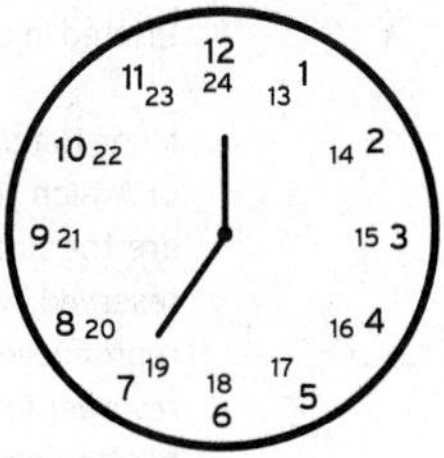


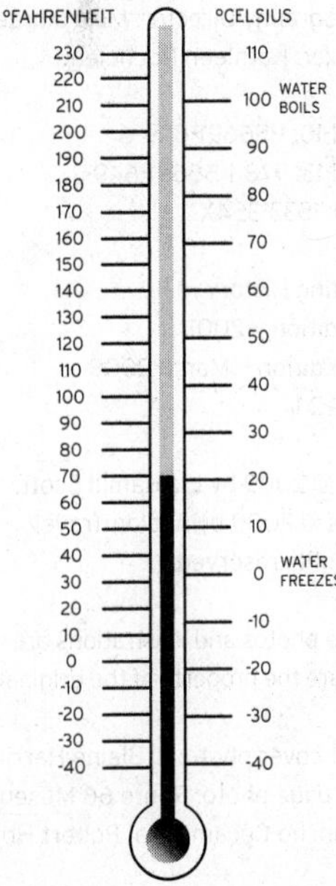


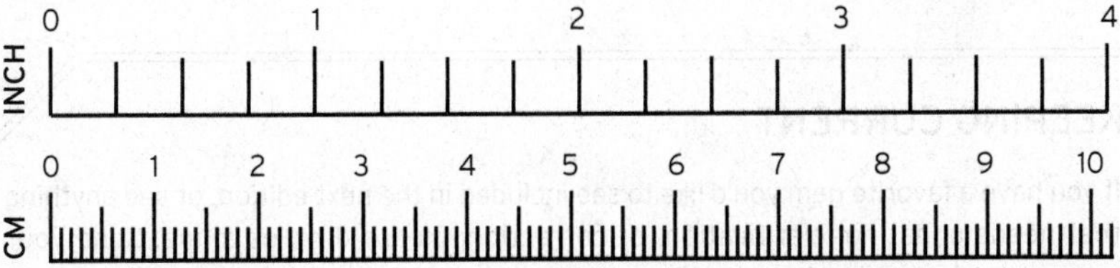

**MOON CALIFORNIA**

Avalon Travel
a member of the Perseus Books Group
1700 Fourth Street
Berkeley, CA 94710, USA
www.moon.com

Editor: Sabrina Young
Series Manager: Kathryn Ettinger
Copy Editor: Ellie Behrstock
Graphics Coordinator: Elizabeth Jang
Production Coordinator: Elizabeth Jang
Cover Designer: Stefano Boni
Map Editor: Albert Angulo
Cartographers: Chris Markiewicz, Kat Bennett, Jon Niemczyk, Brice Ticen
Cartography Director: Mike Morgenfeld
Indexer: Kathleen Rocheleau

ISBN-10: 1-56691-649-6
ISBN-13: 978-1-56691-649-3
ISSN: 1533-354X

Printing History
1st Edition – 2001
2nd Edition – March 2009
5 4 3 2 1



Front cover photo: © Blaine Harrington III
Title page photo: Route 66 Museum, Rancho Cucamonga: Robert Holmes/CalTour

Interior photos: pg. 6 © Liz Hamill Scott; pg. 7 (left) courtesy of Laguna Beach Visitor Bureau; (middle) © San Francisco Convention & Visitors Bureau; (right) © Lance Scott; pg. 8 (bottom left) © Lance Scott; (bottom middle spread) © Liz Hamill Scott; pg. 9 (top right) © The Pasadena Convention and Visitors Bureau; (bottom right) © Liz Hamill Scott; pg. 10 © Lance Scott; pg. 11 (top left) © Liz Hamill Scott; (top middle) © Robert Holmes/CalTour; (top right) © Lance Scott; (in boxed callout) © Robert Holmes/CalTour; pg. 12 (top left) © Lance Scott; (top right) © Lance Scott; pg. 13 © Lance Scott; pg. 14 © Tom Zikas / Pettit Gilwee; pg. 15 (top left) © Lance Scott; (top right) © Liz Hamill Scott; pg. 16 © Liz Hamill Scott; pg. 17 (top left) © Robert Holmes/CalTour; (top right) © Lance Scott; pg. 18 © Lance Scott; pg. 19 © Lance Scott; pg. 20 © Robert Holmes/CalTour; pg. 21 (top left) © Lance Scott; (top right) © Liz Hamill Scott; pg. 22 © Lance Scott; pg. 23 © Lance Scott; pg. 24 © Mammoth Lakes Tourism

Printed in United States by RR Donnelley.



## KEEPING CURRENT

If you have a favorite gem you'd like to see included in the next edition, or see anything that needs updating, clarification, or correction, please drop us a line. Send your comments via email to feedback@moon.com, or use the address above.